American Casebook Series
Hornbook Series and Basic Legal Texts
Black Letter Series and Nutshell Series

of

WEST PUBLISHING COMPANY
P.O. Box 64526
St. Paul, Minnesota 55164–0526

Accounting

FARIS' ACCOUNTING AND LAW IN A NUTSHELL, 377 pages, 1984. Softcover. (Text)

FIFLIS, KRIPKE AND FOSTER'S TEACHING MATERIALS ON ACCOUNTING FOR BUSINESS LAWYERS, Third Edition, 838 pages, 1984. (Casebook)

SIEGEL AND SIEGEL'S ACCOUNTING AND FINANCIAL DISCLOSURE: A GUIDE TO BASIC CONCEPTS, 259 pages, 1983. Softcover. (Text)

Administrative Law

BONFIELD AND ASIMOW'S STATE AND FEDERAL ADMINISTRATIVE LAW, 826 pages, 1989. Teacher's Manual available. (Casebook)

GELLHORN AND LEVIN'S ADMINISTRATIVE LAW AND PROCESS IN A NUTSHELL, Third Edition, approximately 420 pages, 1990. Softcover. (Text)

MASHAW AND MERRILL'S CASES AND MATERIALS ON ADMINISTRATIVE LAW—THE AMERICAN PUBLIC LAW SYSTEM, Second Edition, 976 pages, 1985. (Casebook) 1989 Supplement.

ROBINSON, GELLHORN AND BRUFF'S THE ADMINISTRATIVE PROCESS, Third Edition, 978 pages, 1986. (Casebook)

Admiralty

HEALY AND SHARPE'S CASES AND MATERIALS ON ADMIRALTY, Second Edition, 876 pages, 1986. (Casebook)

MARAIST'S ADMIRALTY IN A NUTSHELL, Second Edition, 379 pages, 1988. Softcover. (Text)

SCHOENBAUM'S HORNBOOK ON ADMIRALTY AND MARITIME LAW, Student Edition, 692 pages, 1987 with 1989 pocket part. (Text)

Agency—Partnership

FESSLER'S ALTERNATIVES TO INCORPORATION FOR PERSONS IN QUEST OF PROFIT, Second Edition, 326 pages, 1986. Softcover. Teacher's Manual available. (Casebook)

HENN'S CASES AND MATERIALS ON AGENCY, PARTNERSHIP AND OTHER UNINCORPORATED BUSINESS ENTERPRISES, Second Edition, 733 pages, 1985. Teacher's Manual available. (Casebook)

REUSCHLEIN AND GREGORY'S HORNBOOK ON THE LAW OF AGENCY AND PARTNERSHIP, Second Edition, 683 pages, 1990. (Text)

SELECTED CORPORATION AND PARTNERSHIP STATUTES, RULES AND FORMS. Softcover. 727 pages, 1989.

STEFFEN AND KERR'S CASES ON AGENCY-PARTNERSHIP, Fourth Edition, 859 pages, 1980. (Casebook)

STEFFEN'S AGENCY-PARTNERSHIP IN A NUTSHELL, 364 pages, 1977. Softcover. (Text)

Agricultural Law

MEYER, PEDERSEN, THORSON AND DAVIDSON'S AGRICULTURAL LAW: CASES AND MATERIALS, 931 pages, 1985. Teacher's Manual available. (Casebook)

Alternative Dispute Resolution

KANOWITZ' CASES AND MATERIALS ON ALTERNATIVE DISPUTE RESOLUTION, 1024 pages,

List current as of July, 1990

Alternative Dispute Resolution—Cont'd

1986. Teacher's Manual available. (Casebook) 1990 Supplement.

RISKIN AND WESTBROOK'S DISPUTE RESOLUTION AND LAWYERS, 468 pages, 1987. Teacher's Manual available. (Casebook)

RISKIN AND WESTBROOK'S DISPUTE RESOLUTION AND LAWYERS, Abridged Edition, 223 pages, 1987. Softcover. Teacher's Manual available. (Casebook)

American Indian Law

CANBY'S AMERICAN INDIAN LAW IN A NUTSHELL, Second Edition, 336 pages, 1988. Softcover. (Text)

GETCHES AND WILKINSON'S CASES AND MATERIALS ON FEDERAL INDIAN LAW, Second Edition, 880 pages, 1986. (Casebook)

Antitrust—see also Regulated Industries, Trade Regulation

FOX AND SULLIVAN'S CASES AND MATERIALS ON ANTITRUST, 935 pages, 1989. Teacher's Manual available. (Casebook)

GELLHORN'S ANTITRUST LAW AND ECONOMICS IN A NUTSHELL, Third Edition, 472 pages, 1986. Softcover. (Text)

HOVENKAMP'S BLACK LETTER ON ANTITRUST, 323 pages, 1986. Softcover. (Review)

HOVENKAMP'S HORNBOOK ON ECONOMICS AND FEDERAL ANTITRUST LAW, Student Edition, 414 pages, 1985. (Text)

OPPENHEIM, WESTON AND MCCARTHY'S CASES AND COMMENTS ON FEDERAL ANTITRUST LAWS, Fourth Edition, 1168 pages, 1981. (Casebook) 1985 Supplement.

POSNER AND EASTERBROOK'S CASES AND ECONOMIC NOTES ON ANTITRUST, Second Edition, 1077 pages, 1981. (Casebook) 1984–85 Supplement.

SULLIVAN'S HORNBOOK OF THE LAW OF ANTITRUST, 886 pages, 1977. (Text)

Appellate Advocacy—see Trial and Appellate Advocacy

Architecture and Engineering Law

SWEET'S LEGAL ASPECTS OF ARCHITECTURE, ENGINEERING AND THE CONSTRUCTION PROCESS, Fourth Edition, 889 pages, 1989. Teacher's Manual available. (Casebook)

Art Law

DUBOFF'S ART LAW IN A NUTSHELL, 335 pages, 1984. Softcover. (Text)

Banking Law

LOVETT'S BANKING AND FINANCIAL INSTITUTIONS LAW IN A NUTSHELL, Second Edition, 464 pages, 1988. Softcover. (Text)

SYMONS AND WHITE'S TEACHING MATERIALS ON BANKING LAW, Second Edition, 993 pages, 1984. Teacher's Manual available. (Casebook) 1987 Supplement.

Business Planning—see also Corporate Finance

PAINTER'S PROBLEMS AND MATERIALS IN BUSINESS PLANNING, Second Edition, 1008 pages, 1984. (Casebook) 1990 Supplement.

Statutory Supplement. *See Selected Corporation and Partnership*

SELECTED CORPORATION AND PARTNERSHIP STATUTES, RULES AND FORMS. 727 pages, 1989. Softcover.

Civil Procedure—see also Federal Jurisdiction and Procedure

AMERICAN BAR ASSOCIATION SECTION OF LITIGATION—READINGS ON ADVERSARIAL JUSTICE: THE AMERICAN APPROACH TO ADJUDICATION, 217 pages, 1988. Softcover. (Coursebook)

CLERMONT'S BLACK LETTER ON CIVIL PROCEDURE, Second Edition, 332 pages, 1988. Softcover. (Review)

COUND, FRIEDENTHAL, MILLER AND SEXTON'S CASES AND MATERIALS ON CIVIL PROCEDURE, Fifth Edition, 1284 pages, 1989. Teacher's Manual available. (Casebook)

COUND, FRIEDENTHAL, MILLER AND SEXTON'S CIVIL PROCEDURE SUPPLEMENT. Approximately 450 pages, 1990. Softcover. (Casebook Supplement)

FEDERAL RULES OF CIVIL PROCEDURE—EDUCATIONAL EDITION. Softcover. Approximately 635 pages, 1990.

FRIEDENTHAL, KANE AND MILLER'S HORNBOOK ON CIVIL PROCEDURE, 876 pages, 1985. (Text)

KANE AND LEVINE'S CIVIL PROCEDURE IN CALIFORNIA: STATE AND FEDERAL 498 pages, 1989. Softcover. (Casebook Supplement)

Civil Procedure—Cont'd

KANE'S CIVIL PROCEDURE IN A NUTSHELL, Second Edition, 306 pages, 1986. Softcover. (Text)

KOFFLER AND REPPY'S HORNBOOK ON COMMON LAW PLEADING, 663 pages, 1969. (Text)

MARCUS, REDISH AND SHERMAN'S CIVIL PROCEDURE: A MODERN APPROACH, 1027 pages, 1989. Teacher's Manual available. (Casebook)

MARCUS AND SHERMAN'S COMPLEX LITIGATION–CASES AND MATERIALS ON ADVANCED CIVIL PROCEDURE, 846 pages, 1985. Teacher's Manual available. (Casebook) 1989 Supplement.

PARK'S COMPUTER-AIDED EXERCISES ON CIVIL PROCEDURE, Second Edition, 167 pages, 1983. Softcover. (Coursebook)

SIEGEL'S HORNBOOK ON NEW YORK PRACTICE, 1011 pages, 1978, with 1987 pocket part. (Text)

Commercial Law

BAILEY AND HAGEDORN'S SECURED TRANSACTIONS IN A NUTSHELL, Third Edition, 390 pages, 1988. Softcover. (Text)

EPSTEIN, MARTIN, HENNING AND NICKLES' BASIC UNIFORM COMMERCIAL CODE TEACHING MATERIALS, Third Edition, 704 pages, 1988. Teacher's Manual available. (Casebook)

HENSON'S HORNBOOK ON SECURED TRANSACTIONS UNDER THE U.C.C., Second Edition, 504 pages, 1979, with 1979 pocket part. (Text)

MURRAY'S COMMERCIAL LAW, PROBLEMS AND MATERIALS, 366 pages, 1975. Teacher's Manual available. Softcover. (Coursebook)

NICKLES' BLACK LETTER ON COMMERCIAL PAPER, 450 pages, 1988. Softcover. (Review)

NICKLES, MATHESON AND DOLAN'S MATERIALS FOR UNDERSTANDING CREDIT AND PAYMENT SYSTEMS, 923 pages, 1987. Teacher's Manual available. (Casebook)

NORDSTROM, MURRAY AND CLOVIS' PROBLEMS AND MATERIALS ON SALES, 515 pages, 1982. (Casebook)

NORDSTROM, MURRAY AND CLOVIS' PROBLEMS AND MATERIALS ON SECURED TRANSACTIONS, 594 pages, 1987. (Casebook)

RUBIN AND COOTER'S THE PAYMENT SYSTEM: CASES, MATERIALS AND ISSUES, 885 pages, 1989. (Casebook)

SELECTED COMMERCIAL STATUTES. Softcover. Approximately 1650 pages, 1990.

SPEIDEL'S BLACK LETTER ON SALES AND SALES FINANCING, 363 pages, 1984. Softcover. (Review)

SPEIDEL, SUMMERS AND WHITE'S COMMERCIAL LAW: TEACHING MATERIALS, Fourth Edition, 1448 pages, 1987. Teacher's Manual available. (Casebook)

SPEIDEL, SUMMERS AND WHITE'S COMMERCIAL PAPER: TEACHING MATERIALS, Fourth Edition, 578 pages, 1987. Reprint from Speidel et al., Commercial Law, Fourth Edition. Teacher's Manual available. (Casebook)

SPEIDEL, SUMMERS AND WHITE'S SALES: TEACHING MATERIALS, Fourth Edition, 804 pages, 1987. Reprint from Speidel et al., Commercial Law, Fourth Edition. Teacher's Manual available. (Casebook)

SPEIDEL, SUMMERS AND WHITE'S SECURED TRANSACTIONS: TEACHING MATERIALS, Fourth Edition, 485 pages, 1987. Reprint from Speidel et al., Commercial Law, Fourth Edition. Teacher's Manual available. (Casebook)

STOCKTON'S SALES IN A NUTSHELL, Second Edition, 370 pages, 1981. Softcover. (Text)

STONE'S UNIFORM COMMERCIAL CODE IN A NUTSHELL, Third Edition, 580 pages, 1989. Softcover. (Text)

WEBER AND SPEIDEL'S COMMERCIAL PAPER IN A NUTSHELL, Third Edition, 404 pages, 1982. Softcover. (Text)

WHITE AND SUMMERS' HORNBOOK ON THE UNIFORM COMMERCIAL CODE, Third Edition, Student Edition, 1386 pages, 1988. (Text)

Community Property

MENNELL AND BOYKOFF'S COMMUNITY PROPERTY IN A NUTSHELL, Second Edition, 432 pages, 1988. Softcover. (Text)

VERRALL AND BIRD'S CASES AND MATERIALS

Community Property—Cont'd

ON CALIFORNIA COMMUNITY PROPERTY, Fifth Edition, 604 pages, 1988. (Casebook)

Comparative Law

BARTON, GIBBS, LI AND MERRYMAN'S LAW IN RADICALLY DIFFERENT CULTURES, 960 pages, 1983. (Casebook)

GLENDON, GORDON AND OSAKWE'S COMPARATIVE LEGAL TRADITIONS: TEXT, MATERIALS AND CASES ON THE CIVIL LAW, COMMON LAW AND SOCIALIST LAW TRADITIONS, 1091 pages, 1985. (Casebook)

GLENDON, GORDON AND OSAKWE'S COMPARATIVE LEGAL TRADITIONS IN A NUTSHELL. 402 pages, 1982. Softcover. (Text)

LANGBEIN'S COMPARATIVE CRIMINAL PROCEDURE: GERMANY, 172 pages, 1977. Softcover. (Casebook)

Computers and Law

MAGGS AND SPROWL'S COMPUTER APPLICATIONS IN THE LAW, 316 pages, 1987. (Coursebook)

MASON'S USING COMPUTERS IN THE LAW: AN INTRODUCTION AND PRACTICAL GUIDE, Second Edition, 288 pages, 1988. Softcover. (Coursebook)

Conflict of Laws

CRAMTON, CURRIE AND KAY'S CASES–COMMENTS–QUESTIONS ON CONFLICT OF LAWS, Fourth Edition, 876 pages, 1987. (Casebook)

HAY'S BLACK LETTER ON CONFLICT OF LAWS, 330 pages, 1989. Softcover. (Review)

SCOLES AND HAY'S HORNBOOK ON CONFLICT OF LAWS, Student Edition, 1085 pages, 1982, with 1988–89 pocket part. (Text)

SEIGEL'S CONFLICTS IN A NUTSHELL, 470 pages, 1982. Softcover. (Text)

Constitutional Law—Civil Rights—see also Foreign Relations and National Security Law

ABERNATHY'S CASES AND MATERIALS ON CIVIL RIGHTS, 660 pages, 1980. (Casebook)

BARRON AND DIENES' BLACK LETTER ON CONSTITUTIONAL LAW, Second Edition, 310 pages, 1987. Softcover. (Review)

BARRON AND DIENES' CONSTITUTIONAL LAW IN A NUTSHELL, 389 pages, 1986. Softcover. (Text)

ENGDAHL'S CONSTITUTIONAL FEDERALISM IN A NUTSHELL, Second Edition, 411 pages, 1987. Softcover. (Text)

FARBER AND SHERRY'S HISTORY OF THE AMERICAN CONSTITUTION, 458 pages, 1990. Softcover. Teacher's Manual available. (Text)

GARVEY AND ALEINIKOFF'S MODERN CONSTITUTIONAL THEORY: A READER, 494 pages, 1989. Softcover. (Reader)

LOCKHART, KAMISAR, CHOPER AND SHIFFRIN'S CONSTITUTIONAL LAW: CASES–COMMENTS–QUESTIONS, Sixth Edition, 1601 pages, 1986. (Casebook) 1990 Supplement.

LOCKHART, KAMISAR, CHOPER AND SHIFFRIN'S THE AMERICAN CONSTITUTION: CASES AND MATERIALS, Sixth Edition, 1260 pages, 1986. Abridged version of Lockhart, et al., Constitutional Law: Cases–Comments–Questions, Sixth Edition. (Casebook) 1990 Supplement.

LOCKHART, KAMISAR, CHOPER AND SHIFFRIN'S CONSTITUTIONAL RIGHTS AND LIBERTIES: CASES AND MATERIALS, Sixth Edition, 1266 pages, 1986. Reprint from Lockhart, et al., Constitutional Law: Cases–Comments–Questions, Sixth Edition. (Casebook) 1990 Supplement.

MARKS AND COOPER'S STATE CONSTITUTIONAL LAW IN A NUTSHELL, 329 pages, 1988. Softcover. (Text)

NOWAK, ROTUNDA AND YOUNG'S HORNBOOK ON CONSTITUTIONAL LAW, Third Edition, 1191 pages, 1986 with 1988 pocket part. (Text)

ROTUNDA'S MODERN CONSTITUTIONAL LAW: CASES AND NOTES, Third Edition, 1085 pages, 1989. (Casebook) 1990 Supplement.

VIEIRA'S CONSTITUTIONAL CIVIL RIGHTS IN A NUTSHELL, Second Edition, 322 pages, 1990. Softcover. (Text)

WILLIAMS' CONSTITUTIONAL ANALYSIS IN A NUTSHELL, 388 pages, 1979. Softcover. (Text)

Consumer Law—see also Commercial Law

EPSTEIN AND NICKLES' CONSUMER LAW IN A NUTSHELL, Second Edition, 418 pages,

Consumer Law—Cont'd

1981. Softcover. (Text)

SELECTED COMMERCIAL STATUTES. Softcover. Approximately 1650 pages, 1990.

SPANOGLE AND ROHNER'S CASES AND MATERIALS ON CONSUMER LAW, 693 pages, 1979. Teacher's Manual available. (Casebook) 1982 Supplement.

Contracts

CALAMARI AND PERILLO'S BLACK LETTER ON CONTRACTS, Second Edition, approximately 450 pages, 1990. Softcover. (Review)

CALAMARI AND PERILLO'S HORNBOOK ON CONTRACTS, Third Edition, 1049 pages, 1987. (Text)

CALAMARI, PERILLO AND BENDER'S CASES AND PROBLEMS ON CONTRACTS, Second Edition, 905 pages, 1989. Teacher's Manual Available. (Casebook)

CORBIN'S TEXT ON CONTRACTS, One Volume Student Edition, 1224 pages, 1952. (Text)

FESSLER AND LOISEAUX'S CASES AND MATERIALS ON CONTRACTS—MORALITY, ECONOMICS AND THE MARKET PLACE, 837 pages, 1982. Teacher's Manual available. (Casebook)

FRIEDMAN'S CONTRACT REMEDIES IN A NUTSHELL, 323 pages, 1981. Softcover. (Text)

FULLER AND EISENBERG'S CASES ON BASIC CONTRACT LAW, Fifth Edition, approximately 1100 pages, 1990. (Casebook)

HAMILTON, RAU AND WEINTRAUB'S CASES AND MATERIALS ON CONTRACTS, 830 pages, 1984. (Casebook)

JACKSON AND BOLLINGER'S CASES ON CONTRACT LAW IN MODERN SOCIETY, Second Edition, 1329 pages, 1980. Teacher's Manual available. (Casebook)

KEYES' GOVERNMENT CONTRACTS IN A NUTSHELL, Second Edition, approximately 530 pages, 1990. Softcover. (Text)

SCHABER AND ROHWER'S CONTRACTS IN A NUTSHELL, Third Edition, approximately 438 pages, 1990. Softcover. (Text)

SUMMERS AND HILLMAN'S CONTRACT AND RELATED OBLIGATION: THEORY, DOCTRINE AND PRACTICE, 1074 pages, 1987. Teacher's Manual available. (Casebook)

Copyright—see Patent and Copyright Law

Corporate Finance

HAMILTON'S CASES AND MATERIALS ON CORPORATION FINANCE, Second Edition, 1221 pages, 1989. (Casebook)

Corporations

HAMILTON'S BLACK LETTER ON CORPORATIONS, Second Edition, 513 pages, 1986. Softcover. (Review)

HAMILTON'S CASES AND MATERIALS ON CORPORATIONS—INCLUDING PARTNERSHIPS AND LIMITED PARTNERSHIPS, Fourth Edition, approximately 1250 pages, 1990. (Casebook) 1990 Statutory Supplement.

HAMILTON'S THE LAW OF CORPORATIONS IN A NUTSHELL, Second Edition, 515 pages, 1987. Softcover. (Text)

HENN'S TEACHING MATERIALS ON THE LAW OF CORPORATIONS, Second Edition, 1204 pages, 1986. Teacher's Manual available. (Casebook)

Statutory Supplement. *See Selected Corporation and Partnership*

HENN AND ALEXANDER'S HORNBOOK ON LAWS OF CORPORATIONS, Third Edition, Student Edition, 1371 pages, 1983, with 1986 pocket part. (Text)

SELECTED CORPORATION AND PARTNERSHIP STATUTES, RULES AND FORMS. Softcover. 727 pages, 1989.

SOLOMON, SCHWARTZ AND BAUMAN'S MATERIALS AND PROBLEMS ON CORPORATIONS: LAW AND POLICY, Second Edition, 1391 pages, 1988. Teacher's Manual available. (Casebook) 1990 Supplement.

Statutory Supplement. *See Selected Corporation and Partnership*

Corrections

KRANTZ' CASES AND MATERIALS ON THE LAW OF CORRECTIONS AND PRISONERS' RIGHTS, Third Edition, 855 pages, 1986. (Casebook) 1988 Supplement.

KRANTZ' THE LAW OF CORRECTIONS AND PRISONERS' RIGHTS IN A NUTSHELL, Third Edition, 407 pages, 1988. Softcover. (Text)

ROBBINS' CASES AND MATERIALS ON POST-CONVICTION REMEDIES, 506 pages, 1982. (Casebook)

Creditors' Rights

BANKRUPTCY CODE, RULES AND OFFICIAL FORMS, LAW SCHOOL EDITION. Approximately 875 pages, 1990. Softcover.

EPSTEIN'S DEBTOR-CREDITOR RELATIONS IN A NUTSHELL, Third Edition, 383 pages, 1986. Softcover. (Text)

EPSTEIN, LANDERS AND NICKLES' CASES AND MATERIALS ON DEBTORS AND CREDITORS, Third Edition, 1059 pages, 1987. Teacher's Manual available. (Casebook)

LOPUCKI'S PLAYER'S MANUAL FOR THE DEBTOR-CREDITOR GAME, 123 pages, 1985. Softcover. (Coursebook)

NICKLES AND EPSTEIN'S BLACK LETTER ON CREDITORS' RIGHTS AND BANKRUPTCY, 576 pages, 1989. (Review)

RIESENFELD'S CASES AND MATERIALS ON CREDITORS' REMEDIES AND DEBTORS' PROTECTION, Fourth Edition, 914 pages, 1987. (Casebook) 1990 Supplement.

WHITE'S CASES AND MATERIALS ON BANKRUPTCY AND CREDITORS' RIGHTS, 812 pages, 1985. Teacher's Manual available. (Casebook) 1987 Supplement.

Criminal Law and Criminal Procedure—see also Corrections, Juvenile Justice

ABRAMS' FEDERAL CRIMINAL LAW AND ITS ENFORCEMENT, 866 pages, 1986. (Casebook) 1988 Supplement.

AMERICAN CRIMINAL JUSTICE PROCESS: SELECTED RULES, STATUTES AND GUIDELINES. 723 pages, 1989. Softcover.

CARLSON'S ADJUDICATION OF CRIMINAL JUSTICE: PROBLEMS AND REFERENCES, 130 pages, 1986. Softcover. (Casebook)

DIX AND SHARLOT'S CASES AND MATERIALS ON CRIMINAL LAW, Third Edition, 846 pages, 1987. (Casebook)

GRANO'S PROBLEMS IN CRIMINAL PROCEDURE, Second Edition, 176 pages, 1981. Teacher's Manual available. Softcover. (Coursebook)

HEYMANN AND KENETY'S THE MURDER TRIAL OF WILBUR JACKSON: A HOMICIDE IN THE FAMILY, Second Edition, 347 pages, 1985. (Coursebook)

ISRAEL, KAMISAR AND LAFAVE'S CRIMINAL PROCEDURE AND THE CONSTITUTION: LEADING SUPREME COURT CASES AND INTRODUCTORY TEXT. Approximately 725 pages, 1990 Edition. Softcover. (Casebook)

ISRAEL AND LAFAVE'S CRIMINAL PROCEDURE—CONSTITUTIONAL LIMITATIONS IN A NUTSHELL, Fourth Edition, 461 pages, 1988. Softcover. (Text)

JOHNSON'S CASES, MATERIALS AND TEXT ON CRIMINAL LAW, Fourth Edition, approximately 790 pages, 1990. Teacher's Manual available. (Casebook)

JOHNSON'S CASES AND MATERIALS ON CRIMINAL PROCEDURE, 859 pages, 1988. (Casebook) 1990 Supplement.

KAMISAR, LAFAVE AND ISRAEL'S MODERN CRIMINAL PROCEDURE: CASES, COMMENTS AND QUESTIONS, Seventh Edition, 1593 pages, 1990. (Casebook) 1990 Supplement.

KAMISAR, LAFAVE AND ISRAEL'S BASIC CRIMINAL PROCEDURE: CASES, COMMENTS AND QUESTIONS, Seventh Edition, 792 pages, 1990. Softcover reprint from Kamisar, et al., Modern Criminal Procedure: Cases, Comments and Questions, Seventh Edition. (Casebook) 1990 Supplement.

LAFAVE'S MODERN CRIMINAL LAW: CASES, COMMENTS AND QUESTIONS, Second Edition, 903 pages, 1988. (Casebook)

LAFAVE AND ISRAEL'S HORNBOOK ON CRIMINAL PROCEDURE, Student Edition, 1142 pages, 1985, with 1989 pocket part. (Text)

LAFAVE AND SCOTT'S HORNBOOK ON CRIMINAL LAW, Second Edition, 918 pages, 1986. (Text)

LANGBEIN'S COMPARATIVE CRIMINAL PROCEDURE: GERMANY, 172 pages, 1977. Softcover. (Casebook)

LOEWY'S CRIMINAL LAW IN A NUTSHELL, Second Edition, 321 pages, 1987. Softcover. (Text)

LOW'S BLACK LETTER ON CRIMINAL LAW, Revised First Edition, approximately 430 pages, 1990. Softcover. (Review)

SALTZBURG'S CASES AND COMMENTARY ON AMERICAN CRIMINAL PROCEDURE, Third Edition, 1302 pages, 1988. Teacher's Manual available. (Casebook) 1990 Supplement.

Criminal Law and Criminal Procedure—Cont'd

UVILLER'S THE PROCESSES OF CRIMINAL JUSTICE: INVESTIGATION AND ADJUDICATION, Second Edition, 1384 pages, 1979. (Casebook) 1979 Statutory Supplement. 1986 Update.

VORENBERG'S CASES ON CRIMINAL LAW AND PROCEDURE, Second Edition, 1088 pages, 1981. Teacher's Manual available. (Casebook) 1990 Supplement.

Decedents' Estates—see Trusts and Estates

Domestic Relations

CLARK'S HORNBOOK ON DOMESTIC RELATIONS, Second Edition, Student Edition, 1050 pages, 1988. (Text)

CLARK AND GLOWINSKY'S CASES AND PROBLEMS ON DOMESTIC RELATIONS, Fourth Edition. Approximately 1125 pages, 1990. Teacher's Manual available. (Casebook)

KRAUSE'S BLACK LETTER ON FAMILY LAW, 314 pages, 1988. Softcover. (Review)

KRAUSE'S CASES, COMMENTS AND QUESTIONS ON FAMILY LAW, Third Edition, 1433 pages, 1990. (Casebook)

KRAUSE'S FAMILY LAW IN A NUTSHELL, Second Edition, 444 pages, 1986. Softcover. (Text)

KRAUSKOPF'S CASES ON PROPERTY DIVISION AT MARRIAGE DISSOLUTION, 250 pages, 1984. Softcover. (Casebook)

Economics, Law and—see also Antitrust, Regulated Industries

GOETZ' CASES AND MATERIALS ON LAW AND ECONOMICS, 547 pages, 1984. (Casebook)

MALLOY'S LAW AND ECONOMICS: A COMPARATIVE APPROACH TO THEORY AND PRACTICE, Approximately 152 pages, 1990. Softcover. (Text)

Education Law

ALEXANDER AND ALEXANDER'S THE LAW OF SCHOOLS, STUDENTS AND TEACHERS IN A NUTSHELL, 409 pages, 1984. Softcover. (Text)

Employment Discrimination—see also Women and the Law

ESTREICHER AND HARPER'S CASES AND MATERIALS ON THE LAW GOVERNING THE EMPLOYMENT RELATIONSHIP, 962 pages, 1990. Teacher's Manual available. (Casebook) Statutory Supplement.

JONES, MURPHY AND BELTON'S CASES AND MATERIALS ON DISCRIMINATION IN EMPLOYMENT, (The Labor Law Group). Fifth Edition, 1116 pages, 1987. (Casebook) 1990 Supplement.

PLAYER'S FEDERAL LAW OF EMPLOYMENT DISCRIMINATION IN A NUTSHELL, Second Edition, 402 pages, 1981. Softcover. (Text)

PLAYER'S HORNBOOK ON EMPLOYMENT DISCRIMINATION LAW, Student Edition, 708 pages, 1988. (Text)

PLAYER, SHOBEN AND LIEBERWITZ' CASES AND MATERIALS ON EMPLOYMENT DISCRIMINATION LAW, Approximately 810 pages, 1990. (Casebook)

Energy and Natural Resources Law—see also Oil and Gas

LAITOS' CASES AND MATERIALS ON NATURAL RESOURCES LAW, 938 pages, 1985. Teacher's Manual available. (Casebook)

SELECTED ENVIRONMENTAL LAW STATUTES—EDUCATIONAL EDITION. Softcover. Approximately 1040 pages, 1990.

Environmental Law—see also Energy and Natural Resources Law; Sea, Law of

BONINE AND MCGARITY'S THE LAW OF ENVIRONMENTAL PROTECTION: CASES—LEGISLATION—POLICIES, 1076 pages, 1984. Teacher's Manual available. (Casebook)

FINDLEY AND FARBER'S CASES AND MATERIALS ON ENVIRONMENTAL LAW, Second Edition, 813 pages, 1985. (Casebook) 1988 Supplement.

FINDLEY AND FARBER'S ENVIRONMENTAL LAW IN A NUTSHELL, Second Edition, 367 pages, 1988. Softcover. (Text)

RODGERS' HORNBOOK ON ENVIRONMENTAL LAW, 956 pages, 1977, with 1984 pocket part. (Text)

SELECTED ENVIRONMENTAL LAW STATUTES—EDUCATIONAL EDITION. Softcover. Approximately 1040 pages, 1990.

Equity—see Remedies

Estate Planning—see also Trusts and Estates; Taxation—Estate and Gift

LYNN'S AN INTRODUCTION TO ESTATE PLANNING IN A NUTSHELL, Third Edition, 370 pages, 1983. Softcover. (Text)

Evidence

BROUN AND BLAKEY'S BLACK LETTER ON EVIDENCE, 269 pages, 1984. Softcover. (Review)

BROUN, MEISENHOLDER, STRONG AND MOSTELLER'S PROBLEMS IN EVIDENCE, Third Edition, 238 pages, 1988. Teacher's Manual available. Softcover. (Coursebook)

CLEARY, STRONG, BROUN AND MOSTELLER'S CASES AND MATERIALS ON EVIDENCE, Fourth Edition, 1060 pages, 1988. (Casebook)

FEDERAL RULES OF EVIDENCE FOR UNITED STATES COURTS AND MAGISTRATES. Softcover. Approximately 380 pages, 1990.

GRAHAM'S FEDERAL RULES OF EVIDENCE IN A NUTSHELL, Second Edition, 473 pages, 1987. Softcover. (Text)

LEMPERT AND SALTZBURG'S A MODERN APPROACH TO EVIDENCE: TEXT, PROBLEMS, TRANSCRIPTS AND CASES, Second Edition, 1232 pages, 1983. Teacher's Manual available. (Casebook)

LILLY'S AN INTRODUCTION TO THE LAW OF EVIDENCE, Second Edition, 585 pages, 1987. (Text)

MCCORMICK, SUTTON AND WELLBORN'S CASES AND MATERIALS ON EVIDENCE, Sixth Edition, 1067 pages, 1987. (Casebook)

MCCORMICK'S HORNBOOK ON EVIDENCE, Third Edition, Student Edition, 1156 pages, 1984, with 1987 pocket part. (Text)

ROTHSTEIN'S EVIDENCE IN A NUTSHELL: STATE AND FEDERAL RULES, Second Edition, 514 pages, 1981. Softcover. (Text)

Federal Jurisdiction and Procedure

CURRIE'S CASES AND MATERIALS ON FEDERAL COURTS, Fourth Edition, approximately 1125 pages, 1990. (Casebook)

CURRIE'S FEDERAL JURISDICTION IN A NUTSHELL, Third Edition, approximately 260 pages, 1990. Softcover. (Text)

FEDERAL RULES OF CIVIL PROCEDURE—EDUCATIONAL EDITION. Softcover. Approximately 635 pages, 1990.

REDISH'S BLACK LETTER ON FEDERAL JURISDICTION, 219 pages, 1985. Softcover. (Review)

REDISH'S CASES, COMMENTS AND QUESTIONS ON FEDERAL COURTS, Second Edition, 1122 pages, 1989. (Casebook) 1990 Supplement.

VETRI AND MERRILL'S FEDERAL COURTS PROBLEMS AND MATERIALS, Second Edition, 232 pages, 1984. Softcover. (Coursebook)

WRIGHT'S HORNBOOK ON FEDERAL COURTS, Fourth Edition, Student Edition, 870 pages, 1983. (Text)

Foreign Relations and National Security Law

FRANCK AND GLENNON'S FOREIGN RELATIONS AND NATIONAL SECURITY LAW, 941 pages, 1987. (Casebook)

Future Interests—see Trusts and Estates

Health Law—see Medicine, Law and

Human Rights—see International Law

Immigration Law

ALEINIKOFF AND MARTIN'S IMMIGRATION PROCESS AND POLICY, Second Edition, approximately 1100 pages, October, 1990 (Casebook)

Statutory Supplement. *See Immigration and Nationality Laws*

IMMIGRATION AND NATIONALITY LAWS OF THE UNITED STATES: SELECTED STATUTES, REGULATIONS AND FORMS. Softcover. Approximately 400 pages, 1990.

WEISSBRODT'S IMMIGRATION LAW AND PROCEDURE IN A NUTSHELL, Second Edition, 438 pages, 1989, Softcover. (Text)

Indian Law—see American Indian Law

Insurance Law

DEVINE AND TERRY'S PROBLEMS IN INSURANCE LAW, 240 pages, 1989. Softcover. Teacher's Manual available. (Course book)

DOBBYN'S INSURANCE LAW IN A NUTSHELL, Second Edition, 316 pages, 1989. Softcover. (Text)

KEETON'S CASES ON BASIC INSURANCE LAW,

Insurance Law—Cont'd

Second Edition, 1086 pages, 1977. Teacher's Manual available. (Casebook)

KEETON'S COMPUTER-AIDED AND WORKBOOK EXERCISES ON INSURANCE LAW, 255 pages, 1990. Softcover. (Coursebook)

KEETON AND WIDISS' INSURANCE LAW, Student Edition, 1359 pages, 1988. (Text)

WIDISS AND KEETON'S COURSE SUPPLEMENT TO KEETON AND WIDISS' INSURANCE LAW, 502 pages, 1988. Softcover. (Casebook)

WIDISS' INSURANCE: MATERIALS ON FUNDAMENTAL PRINCIPLES, LEGAL DOCTRINES AND REGULATORY ACTS, 1186 pages, 1989. (Casebook)

YORK AND WHELAN'S CASES, MATERIALS AND PROBLEMS ON GENERAL PRACTICE INSURANCE LAW, Second Edition, 787 pages, 1988. Teacher's Manual available. (Casebook)

International Law—see also Sea, Law of

BUERGENTHAL'S INTERNATIONAL HUMAN RIGHTS IN A NUTSHELL, 283 pages, 1988. Softcover. (Text)

BUERGENTHAL AND MAIER'S PUBLIC INTERNATIONAL LAW IN A NUTSHELL, Second Edition, 275 pages, 1990. Softcover. (Text)

FOLSOM, GORDON AND SPANOGLE'S INTERNATIONAL BUSINESS TRANSACTIONS—A PROBLEM-ORIENTED COURSEBOOK, 1160 pages, 1986. Teacher's Manual available. (Casebook) 1989 Documents Supplement.

FOLSOM, GORDON AND SPANOGLE'S INTERNATIONAL BUSINESS TRANSACTIONS IN A NUTSHELL, Third Edition, 509 pages, 1988. Softcover. (Text)

HENKIN, PUGH, SCHACHTER AND SMIT'S CASES AND MATERIALS ON INTERNATIONAL LAW, Second Edition, 1517 pages, 1987. (Casebook) Documents Supplement.

JACKSON AND DAVEY'S CASES, MATERIALS AND TEXT ON LEGAL PROBLEMS OF INTERNATIONAL ECONOMIC RELATIONS, Second Edition, 1269 pages, 1986. (Casebook) 1989 Documents Supplement.

KIRGIS' INTERNATIONAL ORGANIZATIONS IN THEIR LEGAL SETTING, 1016 pages, 1977. Teacher's Manual available. (Casebook) 1981 Supplement.

WESTON, FALK AND D'AMATO'S INTERNATIONAL LAW AND WORLD ORDER—A PROBLEM-ORIENTED COURSEBOOK, Second Edition, approximately 1305 pages, 1990. Teacher's Manual available. (Casebook) Documents Supplement.

Interviewing and Counseling

BINDER AND PRICE'S LEGAL INTERVIEWING AND COUNSELING, 232 pages, 1977. Teacher's Manual available. Softcover. (Coursebook)

BINDER, BERGMAN AND PRICE'S LAWYERS AS COUNSELORS: A CLIENT CENTERED APPROACH, Approximately 400 pages, October, 1990 Pub. Softcover. (Coursebook)

SHAFFER AND ELKINS' LEGAL INTERVIEWING AND COUNSELING IN A NUTSHELL, Second Edition, 487 pages, 1987. Softcover. (Text)

Introduction to Law—see Legal Method and Legal System

Introduction to Law Study

HEGLAND'S INTRODUCTION TO THE STUDY AND PRACTICE OF LAW IN A NUTSHELL, 418 pages, 1983. Softcover. (Text)

KINYON'S INTRODUCTION TO LAW STUDY AND LAW EXAMINATIONS IN A NUTSHELL, 389 pages, 1971. Softcover. (Text)

Judicial Process—see Legal Method and Legal System

Jurisprudence

CHRISTIE'S JURISPRUDENCE—TEXT AND READINGS ON THE PHILOSOPHY OF LAW, 1056 pages, 1973. (Casebook)

Juvenile Justice

FOX'S CASES AND MATERIALS ON MODERN JUVENILE JUSTICE, Second Edition, 960 pages, 1981. (Casebook)

FOX'S JUVENILE COURTS IN A NUTSHELL, Third Edition, 291 pages, 1984. Softcover. (Text)

Labor and Employment Law—see also Employment Discrimination, Social Legislation

FINKIN, GOLDMAN AND SUMMERS' LEGAL PROTECTION OF INDIVIDUAL EMPLOYEES, (The La-

Labor and Employment Law—Cont'd

bor Law Group). 1164 pages, 1989. (Casebook)

GORMAN'S BASIC TEXT ON LABOR LAW—UNIONIZATION AND COLLECTIVE BARGAINING, 914 pages, 1976. (Text)

LESLIE'S LABOR LAW IN A NUTSHELL, Second Edition, 397 pages, 1986. Softcover. (Text)

NOLAN'S LABOR ARBITRATION LAW AND PRACTICE IN A NUTSHELL, 358 pages, 1979. Softcover. (Text)

OBERER, HANSLOWE, ANDERSEN AND HEINSZ' CASES AND MATERIALS ON LABOR LAW—COLLECTIVE BARGAINING IN A FREE SOCIETY, Third Edition, 1163 pages, 1986. (Casebook) Statutory Supplement.

RABIN, SILVERSTEIN AND SCHATZKI'S LABOR AND EMPLOYMENT LAW: PROBLEMS, CASES AND MATERIALS IN THE LAW OF WORK, (The Labor Law Group). 1014 pages, 1988. Teacher's Manual available. (Casebook) 1988 Statutory Supplement.

Land Finance—Property Security—see Real Estate Transactions

Land Use

CALLIES AND FREILICH'S CASES AND MATERIALS ON LAND USE, 1233 pages, 1986. (Casebook) 1988 Supplement.

HAGMAN AND JUERGENSMEYER'S HORNBOOK ON URBAN PLANNING AND LAND DEVELOPMENT CONTROL LAW, Second Edition, Student Edition, 680 pages, 1986. (Text)

WRIGHT AND GITELMAN'S CASES AND MATERIALS ON LAND USE, Third Edition, 1300 pages, 1982. Teacher's Manual available. (Casebook) 1987 Supplement.

WRIGHT AND WRIGHT'S LAND USE IN A NUTSHELL, Second Edition, 356 pages, 1985. Softcover. (Text)

Legal History—see also Legal Method and Legal System

PRESSER AND ZAINALDIN'S CASES AND MATERIALS ON LAW AND JURISPRUDENCE IN AMERICAN HISTORY, Second Edition, 1092 pages, 1989. Teacher's Manual available. (Casebook)

Legal Method and Legal System—see also Legal Research, Legal Writing

ALDISERT'S READINGS, MATERIALS AND CASES IN THE JUDICIAL PROCESS, 948 pages, 1976. (Casebook)

BERCH AND BERCH'S INTRODUCTION TO LEGAL METHOD AND PROCESS, 550 pages, 1985. Teacher's Manual available. (Casebook)

BODENHEIMER, OAKLEY AND LOVE'S READINGS AND CASES ON AN INTRODUCTION TO THE ANGLO-AMERICAN LEGAL SYSTEM, Second Edition, 166 pages, 1988. Softcover. (Casebook)

DAVIES AND LAWRY'S INSTITUTIONS AND METHODS OF THE LAW—INTRODUCTORY TEACHING MATERIALS, 547 pages, 1982. Teacher's Manual available. (Casebook)

DVORKIN, HIMMELSTEIN AND LESNICK'S BECOMING A LAWYER: A HUMANISTIC PERSPECTIVE ON LEGAL EDUCATION AND PROFESSIONALISM, 211 pages, 1981. Softcover. (Text)

KEETON'S JUDGING, 842 pages, 1990. Softcover. (Coursebook)

KELSO AND KELSO'S STUDYING LAW: AN INTRODUCTION, 587 pages, 1984. (Coursebook)

KEMPIN'S HISTORICAL INTRODUCTION TO ANGLO-AMERICAN LAW IN A NUTSHELL, Third Edition, approximately 302 pages, 1990. Softcover. (Text)

REYNOLDS' JUDICIAL PROCESS IN A NUTSHELL, 292 pages, 1980. Softcover. (Text)

Legal Research

COHEN'S LEGAL RESEARCH IN A NUTSHELL, Fourth Edition, 452 pages, 1985. Softcover. (Text)

COHEN, BERRING AND OLSON'S HOW TO FIND THE LAW, Ninth Edition, 716 pages, 1989. (Text)

COHEN, BERRING AND OLSON'S FINDING THE LAW, 570 pages, 1989. Softcover reprint from Cohen, Berring and Olson's How to Find the Law, Ninth Edition. (Coursebook)

Legal Research Exercises, 3rd Ed., for use with Cohen, Berring and Olson, 229 pages, 1989. Teacher's Manual available.

ROMBAUER'S LEGAL PROBLEM SOLVING—

Legal Research—Cont'd

ANALYSIS, RESEARCH AND WRITING, Fourth Edition, 424 pages, 1983. Teacher's Manual with problems available. (Coursebook)

STATSKY'S LEGAL RESEARCH AND WRITING, Third Edition, 257 pages, 1986. Softcover. (Coursebook)

TEPLY'S LEGAL RESEARCH AND CITATION, Third Edition, 472 pages, 1989. Softcover. (Coursebook)

Student Library Exercises, 3rd ed., 391 pages, 1989. Answer Key available.

Legal Writing

CHILD'S DRAFTING LEGAL DOCUMENTS: MATERIALS AND PROBLEMS, 286 pages, 1988. Softcover. Teacher's Manual available. (Coursebook)

DICKERSON'S MATERIALS ON LEGAL DRAFTING, 425 pages, 1981. Teacher's Manual available. (Coursebook)

FELSENFELD AND SIEGEL'S WRITING CONTRACTS IN PLAIN ENGLISH, 290 pages, 1981. Softcover. (Text)

GOPEN'S WRITING FROM A LEGAL PERSPECTIVE, 225 pages, 1981. (Text)

MELLINKOFF'S LEGAL WRITING—SENSE AND NONSENSE, 242 pages, 1982. Softcover. Teacher's Manual available. (Text)

PRATT'S LEGAL WRITING: A SYSTEMATIC APPROACH, 422 pages, 1989. Teacher's Manual available. (Coursebook)

RAY AND RAMSFIELD'S LEGAL WRITING: GETTING IT RIGHT AND GETTING IT WRITTEN, 250 pages, 1987. Softcover. (Text)

SQUIRES AND ROMBAUER'S LEGAL WRITING IN A NUTSHELL, 294 pages, 1982. Softcover. (Text)

STATSKY AND WERNET'S CASE ANALYSIS AND FUNDAMENTALS OF LEGAL WRITING, Third Edition, 424 pages, 1989. Teacher's Manual available. (Text)

TEPLY'S LEGAL WRITING, ANALYSIS AND ORAL ARGUMENT, 576 pages, 1990. Softcover. Teacher's Manual available. (Coursebook)

WEIHOFEN'S LEGAL WRITING STYLE, Second Edition, 332 pages, 1980. (Text)

Legislation

DAVIES' LEGISLATIVE LAW AND PROCESS IN A NUTSHELL, Second Edition, 346 pages, 1986. Softcover. (Text)

ESKRIDGE AND FRICKEY'S CASES AND MATERIALS ON LEGISLATION: STATUTES AND THE CREATION OF PUBLIC POLICY, 937 pages, 1988. Teacher's Manual available. (Casebook) 1990 Supplement.

NUTTING AND DICKERSON'S CASES AND MATERIALS ON LEGISLATION, Fifth Edition, 744 pages, 1978. (Casebook)

STATSKY'S LEGISLATIVE ANALYSIS AND DRAFTING, Second Edition, 217 pages, 1984. Teacher's Manual available. (Text)

Local Government

FRUG'S CASES AND MATERIALS ON LOCAL GOVERNMENT LAW, 1005 pages, 1988. (Casebook)

MCCARTHY'S LOCAL GOVERNMENT LAW IN A NUTSHELL, Third Edition, approximately 400 pages, 1990. Softcover. (Text)

REYNOLDS' HORNBOOK ON LOCAL GOVERNMENT LAW, 860 pages, 1982, with 1990 pocket part. (Text)

VALENTE'S CASES AND MATERIALS ON LOCAL GOVERNMENT LAW, Third Edition, 1010 pages, 1987. Teacher's Manual available. (Casebook) 1989 Supplement.

Mass Communication Law

GILLMOR, BARRON, SIMON AND TERRY'S CASES AND COMMENT ON MASS COMMUNICATION LAW, Fifth Edition, 947 pages, 1990. (Casebook)

GINSBURG'S REGULATION OF BROADCASTING: LAW AND POLICY TOWARDS RADIO, TELEVISION AND CABLE COMMUNICATIONS, 741 pages, 1979 (Casebook) 1983 Supplement.

ZUCKMAN, GAYNES, CARTER AND DEE'S MASS COMMUNICATIONS LAW IN A NUTSHELL, Third Edition, 538 pages, 1988. Softcover. (Text)

Medicine, Law and

FURROW, JOHNSON, JOST AND SCHWARTZ' HEALTH LAW: CASES, MATERIALS AND PROBLEMS, 1005 pages, 1987. Teacher's Manual available. (Casebook) 1989 Supplement.

HALL AND ELLMAN'S HEALTH CARE LAW AND

Medicine, Law and—Cont'd

ETHICS IN A NUTSHELL, 401 pages, 1990. Softcover (Text)

KING'S THE LAW OF MEDICAL MALPRACTICE IN A NUTSHELL, Second Edition, 342 pages, 1986. Softcover. (Text)

SHAPIRO AND SPECE'S CASES, MATERIALS AND PROBLEMS ON BIOETHICS AND LAW, 892 pages, 1981. (Casebook)

SHARPE, BOUMIL, FISCINA AND HEAD'S CASES AND MATERIALS ON MEDICAL LIABILITY, Approximately 500 pages, September, 1990 Pub. (Casebook)

Military Law

SHANOR AND TERRELL'S MILITARY LAW IN A NUTSHELL, 378 pages, 1980. Softcover. (Text)

Mortgages—see Real Estate Transactions

Natural Resources Law—see Energy and Natural Resources Law, Environmental Law

Negotiation

GIFFORD'S LEGAL NEGOTIATION: THEORY AND APPLICATIONS, 225 pages, 1989. Softcover. (Text)

WILLIAMS' LEGAL NEGOTIATION AND SETTLEMENT, 207 pages, 1983. Softcover. Teacher's Manual available. (Coursebook)

Office Practice—see also Computers and Law, Interviewing and Counseling, Negotiation

HEGLAND'S TRIAL AND PRACTICE SKILLS IN A NUTSHELL, 346 pages, 1978. Softcover (Text)

STRONG AND CLARK'S LAW OFFICE MANAGEMENT, 424 pages, 1974. (Casebook)

Oil and Gas—see also Energy and Natural Resources Law

HEMINGWAY'S HORNBOOK ON OIL AND GAS, Second Edition, Student Edition, 543 pages, 1983, with 1989 pocket part. (Text)

KUNTZ, LOWE, ANDERSON AND SMITH'S CASES AND MATERIALS ON OIL AND GAS LAW, 857 pages, 1986. Teacher's Manual available. (Casebook) Forms Manual. Revised.

LOWE'S OIL AND GAS LAW IN A NUTSHELL, Second Edition, 465 pages, 1988. Softcover. (Text)

Partnership—see Agency—Partnership

Patent and Copyright Law

CHOATE, FRANCIS AND COLLINS' CASES AND MATERIALS ON PATENT LAW, INCLUDING TRADE SECRETS, COPYRIGHTS, TRADEMARKS, Third Edition, 1009 pages, 1987. (Casebook)

MILLER AND DAVIS' INTELLECTUAL PROPERTY—PATENTS, TRADEMARKS AND COPYRIGHT IN A NUTSHELL, Second Edition, approximately 440 pages, 1990. Softcover. (Text)

NIMMER'S CASES AND MATERIALS ON COPYRIGHT AND OTHER ASPECTS OF ENTERTAINMENT LITIGATION ILLUSTRATED—INCLUDING UNFAIR COMPETITION, DEFAMATION AND PRIVACY, Third Edition, 1025 pages, 1985. (Casebook) 1989 Supplement.

Products Liability

FISCHER AND POWERS' CASES AND MATERIALS ON PRODUCTS LIABILITY, 685 pages, 1988. Teacher's Manual available. (Casebook)

NOEL AND PHILLIPS' CASES ON PRODUCTS LIABILITY, Second Edition, 821 pages, 1982. (Casebook)

PHILLIPS' PRODUCTS LIABILITY IN A NUTSHELL, Third Edition, 307 pages, 1988. Softcover. (Text)

Professional Responsibility

ARONSON, DEVINE AND FISCH'S PROBLEMS, CASES AND MATERIALS IN PROFESSIONAL RESPONSIBILITY, 745 pages, 1985. Teacher's Manual available. (Casebook)

ARONSON AND WECKSTEIN'S PROFESSIONAL RESPONSIBILITY IN A NUTSHELL, 399 pages, 1980. Softcover. (Text)

MELLINKOFF'S THE CONSCIENCE OF A LAWYER, 304 pages, 1973. (Text)

PIRSIG AND KIRWIN'S CASES AND MATERIALS ON PROFESSIONAL RESPONSIBILITY, Fourth Edition, 603 pages, 1984. Teacher's Manual available. (Casebook)

ROTUNDA'S BLACK LETTER ON PROFESSIONAL RESPONSIBILITY, Second Edition, 414 pages, 1988. Softcover. (Review)

SCHWARTZ AND WYDICK'S PROBLEMS IN LE-

Professional Responsibility—Cont'd

GAL ETHICS, Second Edition, 341 pages, 1988. (Coursebook)

SELECTED STATUTES, RULES AND STANDARDS ON THE LEGAL PROFESSION. Softcover. Approximately 600 pages, 1990.

SMITH AND MALLEN'S PREVENTING LEGAL MALPRACTICE, 264 pages, 1989. Reprint from Mallen and Smith's Legal Malpractice, Third Edition. (Text)

SUTTON AND DZIENKOWSKI'S CASES AND MATERIALS ON THE PROFESSIONAL RESPONSIBILITY FOR LAWYERS, 839 pages, 1989. Teacher's Manual available. (Casebook)

WOLFRAM'S HORNBOOK ON MODERN LEGAL ETHICS, Student Edition, 1120 pages, 1986. (Text)

Property—see also Real Estate Transactions, Land Use, Trusts and Estates

BERNHARDT'S BLACK LETTER ON PROPERTY, 318 pages, 1983. Softcover. (Review)

BERNHARDT'S REAL PROPERTY IN A NUTSHELL, Second Edition, 448 pages, 1981. Softcover. (Text)

BOYER'S SURVEY OF THE LAW OF PROPERTY, Third Edition, 766 pages, 1981. (Text)

BROWDER, CUNNINGHAM, NELSON, STOEBUCK AND WHITMAN'S CASES ON BASIC PROPERTY LAW, Fifth Edition, 1386 pages, 1989. Teacher's Manual available. (Casebook)

BRUCE, ELY AND BOSTICK'S CASES AND MATERIALS ON MODERN PROPERTY LAW, Second Edition, 953 pages, 1989. Teacher's Manual available. (Casebook)

BURKE'S PERSONAL PROPERTY IN A NUTSHELL, 322 pages, 1983. Softcover. (Text)

CUNNINGHAM, STOEBUCK AND WHITMAN'S HORNBOOK ON THE LAW OF PROPERTY, Student Edition, 916 pages, 1984, with 1987 pocket part. (Text)

DONAHUE, KAUPER AND MARTIN'S CASES ON PROPERTY, Second Edition, 1362 pages, 1983. Teacher's Manual available. (Casebook)

HILL'S LANDLORD AND TENANT LAW IN A NUTSHELL, Second Edition, 311 pages, 1986. Softcover. (Text)

KURTZ AND HOVENKAMP'S CASES AND MATERIALS ON AMERICAN PROPERTY LAW, 1296 pages, 1987. Teacher's Manual available. (Casebook) 1988 Supplement.

MOYNIHAN'S INTRODUCTION TO REAL PROPERTY, Second Edition, 239 pages, 1988. (Text)

Psychiatry, Law and

REISNER AND SLOBOGIN'S LAW AND THE MENTAL HEALTH SYSTEM, CIVIL AND CRIMINAL ASPECTS, Second Edition, approximately 1127 pages, 1990. (Casebook)

Real Estate Transactions

BRUCE'S REAL ESTATE FINANCE IN A NUTSHELL, Second Edition, 262 pages, 1985. Softcover. (Text)

MAXWELL, RIESENFELD, HETLAND AND WARREN'S CASES ON CALIFORNIA SECURITY TRANSACTIONS IN LAND, Third Edition, 728 pages, 1984. (Casebook)

NELSON AND WHITMAN'S BLACK LETTER ON LAND TRANSACTIONS AND FINANCE, Second Edition, 466 pages, 1988. Softcover. (Review)

NELSON AND WHITMAN'S CASES ON REAL ESTATE TRANSFER, FINANCE AND DEVELOPMENT, Third Edition, 1184 pages, 1987. (Casebook)

NELSON AND WHITMAN'S HORNBOOK ON REAL ESTATE FINANCE LAW, Second Edition, 941 pages, 1985 with 1989 pocket part. (Text)

Regulated Industries—see also Mass Communication Law, Banking Law

GELLHORN AND PIERCE'S REGULATED INDUSTRIES IN A NUTSHELL, Second Edition, 389 pages, 1987. Softcover. (Text)

MORGAN, HARRISON AND VERKUIL'S CASES AND MATERIALS ON ECONOMIC REGULATION OF BUSINESS, Second Edition, 666 pages, 1985. (Casebook)

Remedies

DOBBS' HORNBOOK ON REMEDIES, 1067 pages, 1973. (Text)

DOBBS' PROBLEMS IN REMEDIES. 137 pages, 1974. Teacher's Manual available. Softcover. (Coursebook)

DOBBYN'S INJUNCTIONS IN A NUTSHELL, 264 pages, 1974. Softcover. (Text)

Remedies—Cont'd

FRIEDMAN'S CONTRACT REMEDIES IN A NUTSHELL, 323 pages, 1981. Softcover. (Text)

LEAVELL, LOVE AND NELSON'S CASES AND MATERIALS ON EQUITABLE REMEDIES, RESTITUTION AND DAMAGES, Fourth Edition, 1111 pages, 1986. Teacher's Manual available. (Casebook)

MCCORMICK'S HORNBOOK ON DAMAGES, 811 pages, 1935. (Text)

O'CONNELL'S REMEDIES IN A NUTSHELL, Second Edition, 320 pages, 1985. Softcover. (Text)

SCHOENBROD, MACBETH, LEVINE AND JUNG'S CASES AND MATERIALS ON REMEDIES: PUBLIC AND PRIVATE, Approximately 807 pages, 1990. Teacher's Manual available. (Casebook)

YORK, BAUMAN AND RENDLEMAN'S CASES AND MATERIALS ON REMEDIES, Fourth Edition, 1029 pages, 1985. Teacher's Manual available. (Casebook)

Sea, Law of

SOHN AND GUSTAFSON'S THE LAW OF THE SEA IN A NUTSHELL, 264 pages, 1984. Softcover. (Text)

Securities Regulation

HAZEN'S HORNBOOK ON THE LAW OF SECURITIES REGULATION, Second Edition, Student Edition, approximately 1000 pages, 1990. (Text)

RATNER'S MATERIALS ON SECURITIES REGULATION, Third Edition, 1000 pages, 1986. Teacher's Manual available. (Casebook) 1989 Supplement.

Statutory Supplement. *See Selected Securities Regulation*

RATNER'S SECURITIES REGULATION IN A NUTSHELL, Third Edition, 316 pages, 1988. Softcover. (Text)

SELECTED STATUTES, REGULATIONS, RULES, DOCUMENTS AND FORMS ON SECURITIES REGULATION. Softcover. 1272 pages, 1990.

Social Legislation

HOOD, HARDY AND LEWIS' WORKERS' COMPENSATION AND EMPLOYEE PROTECTION LAWS IN A NUTSHELL, Second Edition, 361 pages, 1990. Softcover. (Text)

LAFRANCE'S WELFARE LAW: STRUCTURE AND ENTITLEMENT IN A NUTSHELL, 455 pages, 1979. Softcover. (Text)

MALONE, PLANT AND LITTLE'S CASES ON WORKERS' COMPENSATION AND EMPLOYMENT RIGHTS, Second Edition, 951 pages, 1980. Teacher's Manual available. (Casebook)

Sports Law

SCHUBERT, SMITH AND TRENTADUE'S SPORTS LAW, 395 pages, 1986. (Text)

Tax Practice and Procedure

GARBIS, STRUNTZ AND RUBIN'S CASES AND MATERIALS ON TAX PROCEDURE AND TAX FRAUD, Second Edition, 687 pages, 1987. (Casebook)

MORGAN'S TAX PROCEDURE AND TAX FRAUD IN A NUTSHELL, Approximately 382 pages, 1990. Softcover. (Text)

Taxation—Corporate

KAHN AND GANN'S CORPORATE TAXATION, Third Edition, 980 pages, 1989. Teacher's Manual available. (Casebook)

WEIDENBRUCH AND BURKE'S FEDERAL INCOME TAXATION OF CORPORATIONS AND STOCKHOLDERS IN A NUTSHELL, Third Edition, 309 pages, 1989. Softcover. (Text)

Taxation—Estate & Gift—see also Estate Planning, Trusts and Estates

MCNULTY'S FEDERAL ESTATE AND GIFT TAXATION IN A NUTSHELL, Fourth Edition, 496 pages, 1989. Softcover. (Text)

PENNELL'S CASES AND MATERIALS ON INCOME TAXATION OF TRUSTS, ESTATES, GRANTORS AND BENEFICIARIES, 460 pages, 1987. Teacher's Manual available. (Casebook)

Taxation—Individual

DODGE'S THE LOGIC OF TAX, 343 pages, 1989. Softcover. (Text)

GUNN AND WARD'S CASES, TEXT AND PROBLEMS ON FEDERAL INCOME TAXATION, Second Edition, 835 pages, 1988. Teacher's Manual available. (Casebook) 1990 Supplement.

HUDSON AND LIND'S BLACK LETTER ON FEDERAL INCOME TAXATION, Third Edition, approximately 390 pages, 1990. Softcover. (Review)

Taxation—Individual—Cont'd

KRAGEN AND MCNULTY'S CASES AND MATERIALS ON FEDERAL INCOME TAXATION—INDIVIDUALS, CORPORATIONS, PARTNERSHIPS, Fourth Edition, 1287 pages, 1985. (Casebook)

MCNULTY'S FEDERAL INCOME TAXATION OF INDIVIDUALS IN A NUTSHELL, Fourth Edition, 503 pages, 1988. Softcover. (Text)

POSIN'S HORNBOOK ON FEDERAL INCOME TAXATION, Student Edition, 491 pages, 1983, with 1989 pocket part. (Text)

ROSE AND CHOMMIE'S HORNBOOK ON FEDERAL INCOME TAXATION, Third Edition, 923 pages, 1988, with 1989 pocket part. (Text)

SELECTED FEDERAL TAXATION STATUTES AND REGULATIONS. Softcover. Approximately 1650 pages, 1991.

SOLOMON AND HESCH'S PROBLEMS, CASES AND MATERIALS ON FEDERAL INCOME TAXATION OF INDIVIDUALS, 1068 pages, 1987. Teacher's Manual available. (Casebook)

Taxation—International

DOERNBERG'S INTERNATIONAL TAXATION IN A NUTSHELL, 325 pages, 1989. Softcover. (Text)

KAPLAN'S FEDERAL TAXATION OF INTERNATIONAL TRANSACTIONS: PRINCIPLES, PLANNING AND POLICY, 635 pages, 1988. (Casebook)

Taxation—Partnership

BERGER AND WIEDENBECK'S CASES AND MATERIALS ON PARTNERSHIP TAXATION, 788 pages, 1989. Teacher's Manual available. (Casebook)

Taxation—State & Local

GELFAND AND SALSICH'S STATE AND LOCAL TAXATION AND FINANCE IN A NUTSHELL, 309 pages, 1986. Softcover. (Text)

HELLERSTEIN AND HELLERSTEIN'S CASES AND MATERIALS ON STATE AND LOCAL TAXATION, Fifth Edition, 1071 pages, 1988. (Casebook)

Torts—see also Products Liability

CHRISTIE AND MEEKS' CASES AND MATERIALS ON THE LAW OF TORTS, Second Edition, 1264 pages, 1990. (Casebook)

DOBBS' TORTS AND COMPENSATION—PERSONAL ACCOUNTABILITY AND SOCIAL RESPONSIBILITY FOR INJURY, 955 pages, 1985. Teacher's Manual available. (Casebook) 1990 Supplement.

KEETON, KEETON, SARGENTICH AND STEINER'S CASES AND MATERIALS ON TORT AND ACCIDENT LAW, Second Edition, 1318 pages, 1989. (Casebook)

KIONKA'S BLACK LETTER ON TORTS, 339 pages, 1988. Softcover. (Review)

KIONKA'S TORTS IN A NUTSHELL: INJURIES TO PERSONS AND PROPERTY, 434 pages, 1977. Softcover. (Text)

MALONE'S TORTS IN A NUTSHELL: INJURIES TO FAMILY, SOCIAL AND TRADE RELATIONS, 358 pages, 1979. Softcover. (Text)

PROSSER AND KEETON'S HORNBOOK ON TORTS, Fifth Edition, Student Edition, 1286 pages, 1984 with 1988 pocket part. (Text)

ROBERTSON, POWERS AND ANDERSON'S CASES AND MATERIALS ON TORTS, 932 pages, 1989. Teacher's Manual available. (Casebook)

Trade Regulation—see also Antitrust, Regulated Industries

MCMANIS' UNFAIR TRADE PRACTICES IN A NUTSHELL, Second Edition, 464 pages, 1988. Softcover. (Text)

OPPENHEIM, WESTON, MAGGS AND SCHECHTER'S CASES AND MATERIALS ON UNFAIR TRADE PRACTICES AND CONSUMER PROTECTION, Fourth Edition, 1038 pages, 1983. Teacher's Manual available. (Casebook) 1986 Supplement.

SCHECHTER'S BLACK LETTER ON UNFAIR TRADE PRACTICES, 272 pages, 1986. Softcover. (Review)

Trial and Appellate Advocacy—see also Civil Procedure

APPELLATE ADVOCACY, HANDBOOK OF, Second Edition, 182 pages, 1986. Softcover. (Text)

BERGMAN'S TRIAL ADVOCACY IN A NUTSHELL, Second Edition, 354 pages, 1989. Softcover. (Text)

BINDER AND BERGMAN'S FACT INVESTIGATION: FROM HYPOTHESIS TO PROOF, 354 pages, 1984. Teacher's Manual available. (Coursebook)

Trial and Appellate Advocacy—Cont'd

CARLSON AND IMWINKELRIED'S DYNAMICS OF TRIAL PRACTICE: PROBLEMS AND MATERIALS, 414 pages, 1989. Teacher's Manual available. (Coursebook)

GOLDBERG'S THE FIRST TRIAL (WHERE DO I SIT? WHAT DO I SAY?) IN A NUTSHELL, 396 pages, 1982. Softcover. (Text)

HAYDOCK, HERR, AND STEMPEL'S FUNDAMENTALS OF PRE-TRIAL LITIGATION, 768 pages, 1985. Softcover. Teacher's Manual available. (Coursebook)

HEGLAND'S TRIAL AND PRACTICE SKILLS IN A NUTSHELL, 346 pages, 1978. Softcover. (Text)

HORNSTEIN'S APPELLATE ADVOCACY IN A NUTSHELL, 325 pages, 1984. Softcover. (Text)

JEANS' HANDBOOK ON TRIAL ADVOCACY, Student Edition, 473 pages, 1975. Softcover. (Text)

LISNEK AND KAUFMAN'S DEPOSITIONS: PROCEDURE, STRATEGY AND TECHNIQUE, Law School and CLE Edition. 250 pages, 1990. Softcover. (Text)

MARTINEAU'S CASES AND MATERIALS ON APPELLATE PRACTICE AND PROCEDURE, 565 pages, 1987. (Casebook)

NOLAN'S CASES AND MATERIALS ON TRIAL PRACTICE, 518 pages, 1981. (Casebook)

SONSTENG AND HAYDOCK'S TRIAL: THEORIES, TACTICS, TECHNIQUE, Approximately 650 pages, 1990. Softcover. (Text)

SONSTENG, HAYDOCK AND BOYD'S THE TRIALBOOK: A TOTAL SYSTEM FOR PREPARATION AND PRESENTATION OF A CASE, 404 pages, 1984. Softcover. (Coursebook)

WHARTON, HAYDOCK AND SONSTENG'S CALIFORNIA CIVIL TRIALBOOK, Law School and CLE Edition. Approximately 300 pages, 1990. Softcover. (Text)

Trusts and Estates

ATKINSON'S HORNBOOK ON WILLS, Second Edition, 975 pages, 1953. (Text)

AVERILL'S UNIFORM PROBATE CODE IN A NUTSHELL, Second Edition, 454 pages, 1987. Softcover. (Text)

BOGERT'S HORNBOOK ON TRUSTS, Sixth Edition, Student Edition, 794 pages, 1987. (Text)

CLARK, LUSKY AND MURPHY'S CASES AND MATERIALS ON GRATUITOUS TRANSFERS, Third Edition, 970 pages, 1985. (Casebook)

DODGE'S WILLS, TRUSTS AND ESTATE PLANNING–LAW AND TAXATION, CASES AND MATERIALS, 665 pages, 1988. (Casebook)

KURTZ' PROBLEMS, CASES AND OTHER MATERIALS ON FAMILY ESTATE PLANNING, 853 pages, 1983. Teacher's Manual available. (Casebook)

MCGOVERN'S CASES AND MATERIALS ON WILLS, TRUSTS AND FUTURE INTERESTS: AN INTRODUCTION TO ESTATE PLANNING, 750 pages, 1983. (Casebook)

MCGOVERN, KURTZ AND REIN'S HORNBOOK ON WILLS, TRUSTS AND ESTATES–INCLUDING TAXATION AND FUTURE INTERESTS, 996 pages, 1988. (Text)

MENNELL'S WILLS AND TRUSTS IN A NUTSHELL, 392 pages, 1979. Softcover. (Text)

SIMES' HORNBOOK ON FUTURE INTERESTS, Second Edition, 355 pages, 1966. (Text)

TURANO AND RADIGAN'S HORNBOOK ON NEW YORK ESTATE ADMINISTRATION, 676 pages, 1986. (Text)

UNIFORM PROBATE CODE, OFFICIAL TEXT WITH COMMENTS. 615 pages, 1989. Softcover.

WAGGONER'S FUTURE INTERESTS IN A NUTSHELL, 361 pages, 1981. Softcover. (Text)

WATERBURY'S MATERIALS ON TRUSTS AND ESTATES, 1039 pages, 1986. Teacher's Manual available. (Casebook)

Water Law—see also Energy and Natural Resources Law, Environmental Law

GETCHES' WATER LAW IN A NUTSHELL, Second Edition, approximately 441 pages, 1990. Softcover. (Text)

SAX AND ABRAMS' LEGAL CONTROL OF WATER RESOURCES: CASES AND MATERIALS, 941 pages, 1986. (Casebook)

TRELEASE AND GOULD'S CASES AND MATERIALS ON WATER LAW, Fourth Edition, 816 pages, 1986. (Casebook)

Wills—see Trusts and Estates

Women and the Law—see also Employment Discrimination

KAY'S TEXT, CASES AND MATERIALS ON SEX–BASED DISCRIMINATION, Third Edition, 1001 pages, 1988. (Casebook) 1990 Supplement.

THOMAS' SEX DISCRIMINATION IN A NUTSHELL, 399 pages, 1982. Softcover. (Text)

Workers' Compensation—see Social Legislation

WEST'S LAW SCHOOL ADVISORY BOARD

FEDERAL COURTS

CASES AND MATERIALS

Fourth Edition

By

David P. Currie

Harry N. Wyatt Professor of Law, University of Chicago

AMERICAN CASEBOOK SERIES®

WEST PUBLISHING CO.

ST. PAUL, MINN., 1990

50 West Kellogg Boulevard
P.O. Box 64526
St. Paul, MN 55164–0526

Printed in the United States of America

Library of Congress Cataloging-in-Publication Data

Currie, David P.
Federal courts : cases and materials / by David P. Currie. — 4th ed.
p. cm. — (American casebook series)
Includes bibliographical references and index.
ISBN 0–314–74485–1
1. Jurisdiction—United States—Cases. 2. Courts—United States—Cases. I. Title. II. Series.
KF8858.A7C8 1990
347.73'2—dc20
[347.3071] 90–37924
CIP

ISBN 0–314–74485–1

Currie—Fed'l Courts, 4th Ed. ACB

Preface

The jurisdiction and powers of the federal courts present the student with some of the most intricate and challenging problems in the law-school curriculum. On the one hand, the subject is full of highly technical problems of statutory interpretation that sharpen the lawyer's indispensable analytical skills. At the same time, these problems confront the student with fundamental issues both of federalism and of the separation of powers.

The basic plan of this casebook is first to introduce students to (or to remind them of) the nature of the judicial power itself, which they may already have studied in constitutional law, and to basic issues of Congress's power over the jurisdiction, and then to follow the litigant's path more or less in order through the federal courts. Chapters 2 and 3 spell out the basic contours of district-court jurisdiction in federal-question, admiralty, and diversity cases, with notes on venue and on the Supreme Court's original jurisdiction. Chapter 4 tells the student something about the applicable law governing federal proceedings, including remedies against government officers. Chapters 5 and 6 deal with limitations on the exercise of jurisdiction that cut across the various jurisdictional categories: sovereign and official immunities and a variety of statutory and judicial abstention doctrines. Chapter 7 follows the litigant into situations in which a federal court is asked to pass upon what another tribunal has already done.

Plainly there are a number of alternative organizing principles for which equally plausible arguments can be made, and I have tried to write the materials in such a way as to allow maximum freedom to rearrange the pieces of the puzzle. For example, I often find it desirable to use the materials on congressional power over the jurisdiction (sections 4 and 5 of Chapter 1) at the very end of the course. Plainly, too, there is more to be said about each of the topics than I have chosen to put in the book. My aim was to produce a manageable package of material that a student could reasonably be expected to master in a single course.

The present revision has two principal goals: to bring the book up to date and to make it a more effective tool for classroom use.

Federal jurisdiction is a fast-moving field. New principal cases in this edition include *Merrell Dow Pharmaceuticals v. Thompson* on state incorporation of federal law, *Finley v. United States* on pendent jurisdiction, *Carden v. Arkoma Associates* on limited partnerships and diversity, *Harlow v. Fitzgerald* on official immunity, *Northern Pipeline* on bankruptcy judges. All other significant Supreme Court developments as well as statutory changes and a number of lower-court decisions are also noted, so that the student will get a complete picture of the current law as well as an insight into its historical development.

My second aim has been to make the book as manageable as possible for students and teachers. Major cases have been carefully pruned to a readable length—without, it is hoped, leaving out anything of significance. Wherever possible I have chosen only one principal case for each topic, supplementing each with notes—themselves significantly reduced in length and complexity from prior editions—designed to provide the essence of additional important decisions as well as other materials necessary for thorough understanding of the subject. The goal is to enable the student to prepare satisfactorily for a single class without having to read more than ten or fifteen pages.

I should like to thank Larry Kramer and William Marshall for valuable advice, David Lyle for ensuring the accuracy of the new material, and Tom Dimond for help with the index.

DAVID P. CURRIE

Chicago, Ill.
May, 1990

Summary of Contents

Appendices

Table of Contents

*

Table of Cases

The principal cases are in bold type. Cases cited or discussed in the text are roman type. References are to pages. Cases cited in principal cases and within other quoted materials are not included.

*

FEDERAL COURTS

CASES AND MATERIALS

*

INTRODUCTORY NOTE ON THE FEDERAL JUDICIAL SYSTEM

The place to begin, as the King said to the White Rabbit, is at the beginning. Article III of the Constitution lays down the fundamental principles of federal judicial power; its text appears in Appendix A at p. 655 and should be read carefully.

One of the basic functions of Article III is to help define the contours of federal as contrasted with state authority: The "judicial Power of the United States" (§ 1) "shall extend to" enumerated classes of "Cases" and "Controversies" (§ 2). The most familiar of these are "Cases . . . arising under this Constitution, the Laws of the United States, and Treaties made . . . under their Authority" (federal-question cases) and "Controversies . . . between Citizens of different States" (diversity cases). Other categories of significance include "Cases of admiralty, and maritime Jurisdiction;" "Controversies between two or more States;" and "Controversies to which the United States shall be a Party." The Constitution does not say whether state courts may also exercise jurisdiction over the listed cases.

The second essential function of Article III relates to the separation of powers within the Federal Government. The "judicial Power" is defined to extend to "Cases" and "Controversies" (§ 2), and it is to be vested in "Courts" (§ 1). One is tempted to infer that the courts may decide *only* "Cases" and "Controversies," and that *only* the courts may decide them; but the text does not expressly say so.

The character of the courts that are to exercise this judicial power is the third central concern of Article III. Congress appears to have considerable latitude in determining what tribunals to create, for the power is to be vested in "one supreme Court, and in such inferior Courts as the Congress may from time to time ordain and establish" (§ 1). The independence of the judges, on the other hand, is not left to the mercy of Congress: Though judges, like many other "Officers of the United States," are appointed by the President "by and with the Advice and Consent of the Senate" (Art. II, § 2), they "shall hold their Offices during good Behavior," and their "Compensation . . . shall not be diminished during their Continuance in Office" (Art. III, § 1). "Good Behavior" is not defined in Article III; Article II, § 4 provides for removal of "all civil Officers of the United States . . . on Impeachment[1] for, and Conviction[2] of, Treason, Bribery, or other high Crimes and Misdemeanors."

1. By the House of Representatives, Art. I, § 2.

2. By a ⅔ vote of the Senate, Art. I, § 3.

For present purposes, the final significant provision of Article III is that respecting the division of authority between the Supreme Court and other tribunals: In certain cases, most notably "those in which a State shall be Party, the Supreme Court shall have original Jurisdiction. In all the other Cases before mentioned, the Supreme Court shall have appellate Jurisdiction, both as to Law and Fact, with such Exceptions, and under such Regulations as the Congress shall make."

The First Congress lost no time in implementing the judiciary article, adopting an "Act to establish the Judicial Courts of the United States" on September 24, 1789, 1 Stat. 73. This statute, which Justice Brown termed "probably the most important and the most satisfactory Act ever passed by Congress," [3] is reprinted in full in Appendix B and will repay reading. The Act provided that the Supreme Court should consist of a Chief Justice and five Associate Justices; it divided the country, essentially along state lines, into thirteen districts, establishing in each a District Court manned by a single District Judge; it lumped the districts (excluding those of Kentucky and Maine) into three circuits, directing that a Circuit Court composed of two Supreme Court Justices and the local District Judge sit twice yearly in each district within its circuit.

The jurisdiction of the district courts, defined in section 9, was partly exclusive and partly concurrent with that of the state courts. It extended to maritime cases, to prosecution for petty federal crimes, to suits for $100 or more brought by the United States, and to a few other cases of little current importance. Sections 21 and 22 gave the circuit courts power to review final decisions of the district courts in civil and maritime cases when a specified amount was in controversy; section 11 conferred upon the circuit courts original jurisdiction to try serious federal crimes and diversity, government, and alienage cases involving over $500; section 12 made these diversity and alien cases removable from state to circuit court by defendants from outside the forum State. Significantly, no provision was made for jurisdiction in the federal trial courts of civil cases arising under federal law. The Supreme Court was declared in section 13 to have trial-court jurisdiction of a small category of cases; its power to review circuit-court decisions was spelled out in section 22 and its authority over state-court judgments denying certain federal rights in the famous section 25. Section 34 provided that state laws should be "regarded as rules of decision in trials at common law in the courts of the United States in cases where they apply," unless the constitution, treaty, or federal statute otherwise required.

Bits of subsequent history of the federal courts are recounted throughout this book; detailed accounts can be found in Charles Warren's two entertaining and informative volumes on The Supreme Court

3. Quoted in 1 C. Warren, The Supreme Court in United States History 12 n. 1 (Rev. ed. 1926).

in United States History (rev. ed. 1926) and in F. Frankfurter & J. Landis, The Business of the Supreme Court (1928).

The circuit courts, Warren relates, were expected "to be of great value in keeping the Federal Judiciary in touch with the local communities." But the burden of riding circuit twice a year through several States in days of poor transportation induced Chief Justice Jay to urge the abolition of circuit duty as early as September, 1790; Justice Iredell was moved to describe his life as that of a "travelling postboy;" and Justice Thomas Johnson "resigned rather than take the labor." 1 Warren, supra, at 58, 85–86. Congress permitted the circuit courts to be held after 1793 by one Justice and a district judge, 1 Stat. 333, and after 1802 by the district judge alone, 2 Stat. 156, 158. Attendance by Supreme Court Justices became less frequent, and the circuit courts were abolished in 1911, 36 Stat. 1087, 1167.

The number of federal districts, the volume of cases, and the areas of federal jurisdiction grew enormously during the nineteenth century; the most important single change was the provision for general federal-question jurisdiction in 1875, 18 Stat. 470. In 1891 the Congress relieved the burden on the Supreme Court by creating new Circuit Courts of Appeals to review most district-court decisions and by introducing the discretionary writ of certiorari in many cases within the Supreme Court's jurisdiction, 26 Stat. 826.

Many changes have been made in the judicial code since 1891, including thorough revisions in 1911 and 1948, 36 Stat. 1087; 62 Stat. 869, and the "Judges' Bill" of 1925, 43 Stat. 936, which further narrowed the Supreme Court's mandatory jurisdiction. Today the federal judicial establishment consists of the district courts, at least one in each State and in the District of Columbia, which are the principal federal trial courts; twelve Courts of Appeals, which are the primary forums for initial review of district-court decisions and of many types of federal administrative orders; the Supreme Court, whose jurisdiction is for the most part both appellate and discretionary, and which alone has authority to review directly the decisions of state courts, if only (as a rule) on federal questions; and assorted specialized and local tribunals such as the Court of Appeals for the Federal Circuit. At the same time there are a number of federal administrative agencies—such as the National Labor Relations Board and the Federal Trade Commission—that exercise powers suspiciously similar to those of the federal courts; and the existence of such agencies raises interesting constitutional problems.

In 1969 the American Law Institute completed a comprehensive proposal for revision of the Judicial Code; although bills were promptly introduced to enact the ALI proposals, nothing ever came of them.[4] More recently, radical increases in federal caseloads have elicited vigorous pleas for contraction of the jurisdiction (e.g., H. Friendly,

4. ALI, Study of the Division of Jurisdiction Between State and Federal Courts (1969); S. 1876, 92d Cong., 1st Sess. (1971); S. 1876, 93d Cong., 1st Sess. (1973).

Federal Jurisdiction: A General View (1973); R. Posner, The Federal Courts (1985)) and for the creation of a separate court to sift petitions seeking Supreme Court review (Federal Judicial Center, Report of the Study Group on the Case Load of the Supreme Court (1972)), or to resolve conflicts among the circuits (Commission on Revision of the Federal Court Appellate System, Structure and Internal Procedures: Recommendations for Change (1975)). As early as 1973 Judge Friendly concluded that the federal courts were "faced with the prospect of a breakdown" from overwork (supra at 3–4, 16, 27, 31–32); and the workload of the courts of appeals tripled between 1970 and 1986. See P. Bator, D. Meltzer, P. Mishkin, D. Shapiro, Hart & Wechsler's The Federal Courts and the Federal System 56 (3d ed. 1988) [hereinafter cited as Hart & Wechsler]. In 1988, concerned with these problems, Congress set up a committee to "develop a long-range plan for the future of the Federal judiciary." P.L. 100–702, 102 Stat. 4642, 4644.[5]

The first chapter of this book deals with the definition of the judicial function and the relationship between the federal courts and Congress. The second and third consider in detail three of the most important heads of district-court jurisdiction: federal-question, admiralty, and diversity cases. Chapter four is concerned with the relations between state and federal law, with a separate section on the important problem of remedies against governments and their officers. Chapter five is about sovereign and official immunities limiting judicial authority and chapter six about a variety of other limiting doctrines, both statutory and judge-made, that can be loosely described under the heading of abstention. The last chapter deals essentially with appellate and collateral review of judicial decisions.

A considerable time must plainly be invested in order to sort out the current jurisdictional and choice-of-law principles. But a recurring question throughout these materials, emphasized by the comprehensive efforts of the ALI, of Judges Posner and Friendly, and of others to reexamine the subject, is to determine the optimal functions of the federal courts. Is there still justification, for example, for the existing system of both federal and state courts, with its inevitable frictions and its enormous costs in terms of litigating the boundaries of jurisdiction? What can be done to ameliorate those frictions and others arising from the clash of substantive federal and state policies? What can be done to simplify the task of determining whether or not there is federal jurisdiction? What is the proper scope of jurisdiction for federal courts today?

Because the principal focus of this book is upon the relation of the federal courts to the States and to the other federal branches, such procedural questions as discovery, pleading, and other subjects often taught in connection with jurisdiction are generally excluded. They are considered in detail in J. W. Moore's Federal Practice and in C.

5. The Study Committee filed its report in April, 1990.

Wright, A. Miller & E. Cooper, Federal Practice and Procedure. The most concise treatment of procedural matters in the Supreme Court, and a helpful supplement to these materials insofar as Supreme Court jurisdiction is concerned, is R. Stern, E. Gressman, & S. Shapiro, Supreme Court Practice (6th ed. 1986). Current statistics on the work of the federal courts are found in the annual reports of the Administrative Office of the United States Courts and summarized every autumn in the Harvard Law Review. Relevant articles are cited extensively in these materials; those who desire the comforts of a hornbook may see Charles Wright, Federal Courts (4th ed. 1983), or Erwin Chemerinsky, Federal Jurisdiction (1989); Hart and Wechsler's monumental casebook The Federal Courts and the Federal System (3d ed. 1988) is a valuable source of historical and intellectual material; the ALI Study, the Study Group Report on Supreme Court Caseload, and the thoughtful books of Judges Friendly and Posner are recommended reading.[6]

Judicial review of federal administrative agencies is obviously a critical part of any study of the functions of the federal courts, and references to that subject are included at several points in the book. In deference to the tradition that such matters are covered in detail in courses on administrative law, however, they are not given here the treatment they otherwise would demand.

6. My own views on many of the issues considered in this course are spelled out in D. Currie, The Federal Courts and the American Law Institute, 36 U.Chi.L.Rev. 1 and 268 (1968–69), and in Federal Jurisdiction in a Nutshell (3d ed. 1990).

Chapter I

CONGRESS, THE COURTS, AND THE CONSTITUTION

SECTION 1. INTRODUCTION

1. MARBURY v. MADISON

William Marbury was one of the Midnight Judges. Signed on the run by outgoing President Adams and sealed, his commission as a District of Columbia Justice of the Peace reposed in the Department of State, for the new Anti-Federalist Secretary refused to deliver it. Marbury sought mandamus from the Supreme Court of the United States.

The Court denied the writ. First, and of no current importance, it held the commission complete when signed and sealed; Marbury had a right to the office. Second, and important in establishing a measure of judicial control over the Executive, the Court held that mandamus could be issued to compel even a Cabinet officer to perform a "ministerial" duty. Third, the Court found in the Judiciary Act of 1789 authority for the Supreme Court to issue writs of mandamus as a court of first instance. People have criticized the Court for failing to construe the statute more narrowly, but the provision is now obsolete and its construction of no present significance. Fourth, the Court held this grant of jurisdiction unconstitutional: Article III provides that the Supreme Court shall have original jurisdiction in certain enumerated cases, not including Marbury's, and appellate jurisdiction "in all other cases;" if Congress could expand the original jurisdiction, the specification would be "mere surplusage." This construction is not obvious, and its converse is not true: The Court has often accepted appellate jurisdiction where the Constitution provides that it shall have original. See, e.g., Börs v. Preston, 111 U.S. 252, 260 (1884). Finally, the Court held that it need not obey an unconstitutional act of Congress. 5 U.S. (1 Cranch) 137 (1803).

Many things have been said about *Marbury v. Madison*. Some people have rather snidely suggested that, because the Court held it had no jurisdiction, its remarks on the merits constituted an unconstitutional advisory opinion. Others have described the opinion as a stroke of political genius: Chief Justice Marshall contrived to annoy the Administration by declaring that Madison was violating the law, by asserting judicial power to issue orders to Cabinet members, and by establishing judicial review of legislation; yet he managed to avoid the very real danger of impeachment by ultimately deciding in Madison's favor.

The words of the Constitution are unclear with respect to judicial review, and the scholars are in disagreement over the intentions of the Framers. See pp. 26–28, infra. As Mark Twain once said, "The researches of many antiquarians have already thrown much darkness on the subject, and it is probable, if they continue, that we shall soon know nothing at all." But for our purposes it is less important to determine whether judicial review was correctly found in the Constitution, or where it was found, than to determine *why* it was found. For several important and timely issues of judicial power depend in large part upon one's conception of the policy or the philosophy of government that gives rise to judicial review.

The opinion in *Marbury v. Madison* is ambiguous on this score. Sometimes Marshall appears to treat judicial review as something of an accident, an incidental consequence of the courts' basic job of deciding particular cases, a sort of clean-hands doctrine for judges:

> It is emphatically the province and duty of the judicial department to say what the law is. Those who apply the rule to particular cases, must of necessity expound and interpret that rule. If two laws conflict with each other, the courts must decide on the operation of each.
>
> So, if a law be in opposition to the constitution; if both the law and the constitution apply to a particular case, so that the court must either decide that case conformably to the law, disregarding the constitution; or conformably to the constitution, disregarding the law; the court must determine which of these conflicting rules governs the case. This is the very essence of judicial duty.
>
> If, then, the courts are to regard the constitution, and the constitution is superior to any ordinary act of the legislature, the constitution, and not such ordinary act, must govern the case to which they both apply.

Other passages in the opinion, however, suggest that Marshall viewed judicial review as an instrument for keeping the Congress within constitutional bounds, a vital element in a system of checks and balances:

> Those, then, who controvert the principle that the constitution is to be considered, in court, as a paramount law, are reduced to the necessity of maintaining that courts must close their eyes on the constitution, and see only the law.
>
> This doctrine would subvert the very foundation of all written constitutions. It would declare that an act which, according to the

> principles and theory of our government, is entirely void, is yet, in practice, completely obligatory. It would declare that if the legislature shall do what is expressly forbidden, such act, notwithstanding the express prohibition, is in reality effectual. It would be giving to the legislature a practical and real omnipotence, with the same breath which professes to restrict their powers within narrow limits. It is prescribing limits and declaring that those limits may be passed at pleasure.

The implications of these two justifications for judicial review will be considered in connection with the assigned cases.

2. "CASES" AND OTHER LIMITATIONS

Article III provides that the Judicial Power shall extend to specified classes of "Cases" and of "Controversies," and the Supreme Court has repeatedly held that matters which are not "Cases" or "Controversies" cannot be entrusted to courts established under Article III. Moreover, the Court has supplemented this constitutional limitation with "prudential" doctrines further restricting judicial review, and it is not always easy to distinguish the constitutional from the prudential. See, for example, the split-level standing doctrine explained in *Warth v. Seldin*, infra p. 32, the element of "discretion" in declaratory-judgment litigation, *Abbott Laboratories v. Gardner*, infra p. 57; and Justice Brandeis's famous list of devices developed by the Supreme Court for avoiding constitutional issues in cases within its "jurisdiction," Ashwander v. TVA, 297 U.S. 288, 345–48 (1936) (concurring opinion).

It should be obvious that both constitutional and prudential limits upon justiciability may affect ordinary private lawsuits as well as constitutional litigation. Should the strictures applicable to ordinary cases be tightened in constitutional litigation because of the danger of conflict with other departments, or should they be relaxed because of the importance of enforcing constitutional limitations? And should there be a difference, as suggested by the Justices' letter to President Washington, infra p. 10, between the limitations upon the Supreme Court and those upon the lower courts?

A. *Hayburn's Case*

An act of Congress adopted in 1792 authorized Revolutionary veterans to file pension claims in the United States Circuit Courts, directed the judges to certify to the "Secretary at War" the degree of a claimant's disability and their opinion as to the proper percentage of monthly pay to be awarded, and empowered the Secretary to withhold judicially certified claimants from the pension list if he suspected "imposition or mistake."

The Supreme Court as such never passed on the validity of this statute. But five of the six Justices, sitting on circuit, found it unconstitutional, 2 U.S. (2 Dall.) 408 (1792)—eleven years before *Marbury v.*

Madison. The problem, clearly enough, was one of the separation of powers: "By the Constitution of the United States, the government thereof is divided into *three* distinct and independent branches, and . . . it is the duty of each to abstain from, and to oppose, encroachments on either." But the Justices were not altogether lucid as to who was encroaching upon whom. Each of the three opinions declared that the authority assigned to the courts was "not of a judicial nature," suggesting that the courts, if they complied, would invade executive or legislative domains. But the reason given for holding the authority non-judicial was that the courts' decisions were subject to review by the Secretary of War, and the Justices also suggested that this review allowed the executive to exercise judicial power at the expense of the judiciary.

The doctrine that the courts cannot be given nonjudicial duties was to crop up again the following year in pure form, but *Hayburn's Case* is most easily understood in terms of the independence of the courts. The Constitution protects the judges from indirect pressures on their decisions by guaranteeing them tenure during good behavior at an irreducible salary; to subject their decisions to executive review is a much more direct interference. If, as Hamilton maintained, one reason for judges' tenure was to enable the courts to function as a safeguard against legislative and executive oppression (The Federalist No. 78), then executive power to set aside court decisions is intolerable.[1]

Two further aspects of *Hayburn's Case* deserve mention. First, several of the judges, while refusing to comply with the statute, expressed willingness to perform exactly the same function "as Commissioners." Whatever the vice of the pension statute, it is difficult to

1. For similar situations in which the Court refused jurisdiction over cases in which its judgment would have been subject to executive or legislative revision see United States v. Ferreira, 54 U.S. (13 How.) 40 (1852) (claims under Florida cession treaty to be paid if Secretary of Treasury finds them "just and equitable"); Gordon v. United States, 69 U.S. (2 Wall.) 561 (1865) (Court of Claims judgment payable only if certified by Treasury and approved by appropriation act); Chicago & Southern Air Lines v. Waterman S. S. Corp., 333 U.S. 103, 113–14 (1948) (CAB denial of overseas license subject to President's approval).

How far should this principle be carried? Congress, after all, can defeat any money judgment against the United States by failing to vote money to pay it; should the courts therefore refuse to entertain money actions against the Government? Since the President might refuse to enforce judgments against state officers or private litigants, should the courts decline to act at all? Is it material whether Congress passes separate appropriations for each Government judgment, as it did for a time during the late nineteenth century, or enacts a lump sum to satisfy a large block of judgments, as it has done since 1890? Is it material that the United States has in fact been more reliable than most private parties in satisfying judgments against it? See Hart & Wechsler, The Federal Courts and the Federal System 102–06 (3d ed. 1988); Note, 46 Harv.L.Rev. 677 (1933). The Court has not been troubled; it upheld its jurisdiction to review Court of Claims judgments against the Government after the offensive provision for Treasury review was eliminated. United States v. Jones, 119 U.S. 477 (1886). Perhaps it was the difficulty of drawing the line that led Professor Bickel to the surprising conclusion that *Hayburn's* finality principle was "the least important" element of the "Case" requirement: "The finality or lack of it in judicial judgments is rather a matter of degree." A. Bickel, The Least Dangerous Branch 117 (1962).

believe the trouble was eliminated by the use of a pseudonym. Second, the judges in the North Carolina court had no pension application before them; their opinion was rendered in the form of a letter to the President, despite their confessed doubts as to the propriety of giving an advisory opinion.

B. Advisory Opinions

In 1793 President Washington, through his Secretary of State, asked the advice of the Supreme Court Justices on a long list of legal questions such as the following, respecting American neutrality in the war between England and France:

> Do the treaties between the United States and France give to France or her citizens a *right*, when at war with a power with whom the United States are at peace, to fit out originally in and from the ports of the United States vessels armed for war, with or without commission?

The Justices refused to answer, and this time there was no nonsense about making it all right to act nonjudicially by removing the robe:

> We have considered the previous question . . . [respecting] the lines of separation drawn by the Constitution between the three departments of the government. These being in certain respects checks upon each other, and our being judges of a court in the last resort, are considerations which afford strong arguments against the propriety of our extra-judicially deciding the questions alluded to, especially as the power given by the Constitution to the President, of calling on the heads of departments for opinions, seems to have been *purposely* as well as expressly united to the executive departments.[2]

In the main the Court has adhered to the position that neither it nor the general inferior federal courts may render advisory opinions. In several States, however,—notably Massachusetts—, and in Canada, the courts have been empowered to give advice on "important questions of law" when requested to do so by other departments. See Hart & Wechsler, supra, at 70. This procedure has the advantage of avoiding

2. 3 H. Johnston, Correspondence and Public Papers of John Jay 486–89 (1891); 10 Sparks, Writings of Washington 542–45 (1847), as reprinted in F. Frankfurter & H. Shulman, Cases on Federal Jurisdiction and Procedure 36–38 (1937), and later in Hart & Wechsler, The Federal Courts and the Federal System 65–67 (3d ed.1988).

As *Hayburn's Case* shows, the Justices have not always been so chary of extrajudicial advice. Additional examples may be found in Hart & Wechsler, supra, at 69–70. Compare also the question of judges' assignment to nonjudicial tasks, id. at 102–05 (1st ed.1953), as vividly illustrated by Justice Jackson's service as prosecutor at the Nürnberg trials and by Chief Justice Warren's chairmanship of the commission investigating President Kennedy's assassination. In August 1800, with one of the six Justices ill, Chief Justice Ellsworth was off serving as Envoy to France and Justice Chase busy electioneering for President Adams. 1 C. Warren, The Supreme Court in United States History 156 (Rev.ed.1926). See also Westin, Out-of-Court Commentary by United States Supreme Court Justices, 1790–1962: Of Free Speech and Judicial Lockjaw, 62 Colum.L.Rev. 633 (1962); Mistretta v. United States, 488 U.S. 361 (1989), permitting federal judges to sit on a commission to draft guidelines for criminal sentencing: "[T]he Constitution . . . does not forbid judges from wearing two hats; it merely forbids them from wearing both hats at the same time."

the delay, uncertainty, and disruption incident to determining the constitutionality of statutes by the process of ordinary litigation, and it makes a judicial check upon other branches of government more freely available. What is objectionable about it?

The policy arguments against advisory opinions fall into several distinct groups. The first group consists of reasons relating to the optimal conditions for reaching correct decisions: Concrete facts enable the judges to understand the practical impact of their holdings; adverse presentation is some assurance that arguments on both sides will be considered; and, as argued by the then Professor Frankfurter, "the advisory opinion deprives constitutional interpretation of the judgment of the legislature upon facts." Note on Advisory Opinions, 37 Harv.L. Rev. 1002, 1005 (1924). The second group of reasons points toward fortifying the court's institutional position: Lawmaking by appointed judges is least difficult to reconcile with democratic principles when it is the inevitable byproduct of the stock business of judging; the courts should not squander their power of moral suasion or multiply conflicts with other branches by deciding unnecessary constitutional questions; the "case" requirement, as Professor Bickel wrote, "creates a time lag between legislation and adjudication" that "cushions the clash . . . and strengthens the Court's hand in gaining acceptance for its principles." A. Bickel, The Least Dangerous Branch 116 (1962). Third, acceptance of nonjudicial duties leaves the courts less time to devote to their essential functions. Fourth, as argued by Frankfurter, reliance on judges for advice may cause a "weakening of legislative and popular responsibility," 37 Harv.L.Rev. at 1007. A fifth type of objection, of less obvious applicability in advisory-opinion situations, is that the ability to accept nonjudicial assignments might compromise the judges' independence by making them expect rewards—either judicial advancement in return for outside work, or extracurricular plums in return for favorable decisions. See generally Hart & Wechsler, supra, at 66–71; id. at 102–05 (1st ed.1953). Finally, since an advisory opinion may be disregarded, it may be possible to describe it, like the objectionable proceeding in *Hayburn's Case*, as a judicial decision subject to executive or legislative revision.[3]

Professor Bickel, in addition to subscribing in principle to the advisory-opinion ban and many of its emanations, found them "not so much limitations of the power of judicial review as necessary supports for Marshall's arguments in establishing it:"

> If, as Marshall argued, the judiciary's power to construe and enforce the Constitution against the other departments is to be deduced from the obligation of the courts to decide cases conformably to law, which may sometimes be the Constitution, then it must follow that the power may be exercised only in a case.

3. For a recent reformulation of the reasons for objecting to advisory opinions see Brilmayer, The Jurisprudence of Article III: Perspectives on the "Case or Controversy" Requirement, 93 Harv.L.Rev. 297 (1979).

The Least Dangerous Branch 114–15 (1962). If this syllogism does not tell us exactly what a "case" is, it is not far from doing so. For *this part* of Marshall's argument suggests that judicial review is not an end in itself but a mere side effect of the Court's ordinary function—which seems, on this hypothesis, to mean the determination of garden-variety lawsuits. To Marshall's other argument, however, Mr. Bickel's statement has no application; no logical corollary, the restrictions he approved represent an often uneasy accommodation of the Judicial Guardian theory with policies such as those enumerated just above.

President Washington's request for advice was an extreme instance that did not begin to resemble the ordinary lawsuit, and the Justices did not clearly base their refusal to answer on a negative inference from Article III. But the principle that federal courts may decide only judicial cases or controversies has often been invoked to exclude consideration of matters far less remote. Five variants to this theme, not necessarily always of constitutional origin, are here discussed: The controversy must be between adverse parties; it must be ripe and concrete; the issue must not be "administrative" or "political."

C. *Adverseness and Standing*

It is often said to be a fundamental element of the case-or-controversy requirement that issues be presented in adversary litigation. The absence of opposing positions does not always require dismissal: Professor Davis points to antitrust consent decrees, criminal guilty pleas, and the powers of bankruptcy and naturalization courts when all parties agree, 3 K. Davis, Administrative Law Treatise 118–19 (1958); Hart and Wechsler, supra, at 104–05 (2d ed.1973), note the Solicitor General's practice of confessing error below and the Supreme Court's occasional propensity to ignore his confession, see Young v. United States, 315 U.S. 257, 258–59 (1942). However, the lack of adverseness is at least one factor behind the refusal of the courts to entertain suits that are moot, California v. San Pablo & Tulare R. R., 149 U.S. 308 (1893), or collusive, United States v. Johnson, 319 U.S. 302 (1943), or in which one of the parties lacks "standing" because he is insufficiently affected by the conduct of which he complains, Doremus v. Board of Education, 342 U.S. 429 (1952).

The difficult and controversial application of these principles is considered in greater detail at pp. 32–57 below. For introductory or review purposes the questions of the extent to which adverseness requirements serve the policies adumbrated in the preceding note, and of the price of heeding these policies, are raised in sharpest form by the well-known case of Massachusetts (Frothingham) v. Mellon, 262 U.S. 447 (1923).

Ms. Frothingham picked an opponent with an unfair advantage: a federal statute making grants, with strings, to the States for the health of Mothers. She claimed the statute invaded States' rights, and she said she was injured because she was a federal taxpayer whose money was being taken for improper uses. Although municipal taxpayers had been permitted to enjoin illegal use of city funds, the Supreme Court held Ms. Frothingham lacked standing:

> The interest of a taxpayer of a municipality in the application of its moneys is direct and immediate. . . . The reasons which support the extension of the equitable remedy to a single taxpayer in such cases are based upon the peculiar relation of the corporate taxpayer to the corporation, which is not without some resemblance to that subsisting between stockholder and private corporation. . . . But the relation of a taxpayer of the United States to the federal government is very different. His interest in the moneys of the treasury—partly realized from taxation and partly from other sources—is shared with millions of others, is comparatively minute and indeterminable, and the effect upon future taxation, of any payment out of the funds, so remote, fluctuating and uncertain, that no basis is afforded for an appeal to the preventive powers of a court of equity. . . . The party who invokes the power must be able to show, not only that the statute is invalid but that he has sustained or is in immediate danger of sustaining some direct injury as the result of its enforcement, and not merely that he suffers in some indefinite way in common with people generally.

To Professor Bickel this case was nothing but a request for an advisory opinion: To entertain such a suit would "materially alter the function of judicial review and seriously undermine any acceptable justification for it." Ms. Frothingham in his opinion was a meddler, because she could not show that a victory would reduce her tax bill. The Least Dangerous Branch 119–22 (1962). Others have disagreed with the conclusion that a taxpayer is not injured by illegal expenditures and with the Court's distinction between national and local taxes; Professor Davis has argued that the drastic increase in federal taxation has drained the decision of any force it may originally have had, 3 Administrative Law Treatise 243–48 (1958); and the holding has been modified by Flast v. Cohen, 392 U.S. 83 (1968), infra p. 53, allowing taxpayers to challenge federal aid to church schools.

As this dispute shows, application of the principle limiting standing to persons injured by the contested action (reaffirmed as a constitutional matter in *Warth v. Seldin*, p. 32 below) is not automatic, but the extent to which abandonment of the principle itself would implicate the policies against advisory opinions deserves serious consideration. Not least, it should be borne in mind that this basic component of standing is no artificial limitation designed simply to avoid constitutional questions: In ordinary as well as constitutional litigation people are not generally allowed to sue when they have nothing at stake.

Yet the benefits of the injury requirement, like most good things, are not costless; for the consequence of *Frothingham* was to make it unlikely that anybody could challenge unconstitutional federal expenditures. On one view of *Marbury v. Madison* this is no cause for concern: Judicial review is "little more," the Court said in *Frothingham*, "than the negative power to disregard an unconstitutional enactment, which otherwise would stand in the way of the enforcement of a legal right"— a clean-hands principle that the judges themselves shall not violate the Constitution. But there was another face to *Marbury:* the high-school-civics principle of a system of checks and balances, firmly advocated by Hamilton in his defense of the Constitution:

> The courts were designed to be an intermediate body between the people and the legislature, in order, among other things, to keep the latter within the limits assigned to their authority. . . . Limitations . . . [such as the prohibition of ex post facto laws and of bills of attainder] can be preserved in practice no other way than through the medium of the courts of justice; whose duty it must be to declare all acts contrary to the manifest tenor of the constitution void.

The Federalist, No. 78.

On this view of the function of judicial review, what is to be said for *Frothingham?* Was the decision, as the Court thought, compelled by the separation of powers? Or did it violate the correlative principle of checks and balances by making it possible for Congress to spend money unconstitutionally whenever it chose?

To the extent that Congress has the power to grant or to withhold standing, what is its responsibility? Is it appropriate for a Congressman to vote against a provision allowing a federal taxpayer to challenge a spending program on the ground that judicial review might interfere with the program?[4]

D. "Ripeness" and "Concreteness"

In United Public Workers v. Mitchell, 330 U.S. 75 (1947), Government employees challenged the validity of the Hatch Act, which forbade them to "take any active part in political management or in political campaigns." The complaint alleged "that the individual plaintiffs desire to engage in the following acts" among others:

> write for publication letters and articles in support of candidates for office; . . . solicit votes, aid in getting out voters, act as accredited checker, watcher, or challenger; transport voters to and from the polls . . .; participate in and help in organizing political parades; initiate petitions . . .; serve as party ward committeeman or other party official. . . .

The Supreme Court held that these allegations presented not a case or controversy but a request for an "advisory opinion":

> The power of courts, and ultimately of this Court to pass upon the constitutionality of acts of Congress arises only when the interests of litigants require the use of this judicial authority for their protection against actual interference. A hypothetical threat is not enough. We can only speculate as to the kinds of political activity the appellants desire to engage in or as to the contents of their proposed public statements or the circumstances of their publication. . . . No threat

4. For consideration of the complicated nonconstitutional dimensions of standing see pp. 46–57 infra.

> of interference by the Commission with rights of these appellants appears beyond that implied by the existence of the law and the regulations. . . .

To use Hart and Wechsler's formulation, the situation was "doubly contingent:" It was not certain that the plaintiffs would be politically active, and it was not certain that they would be prosecuted if they were. The Federal Courts and the Federal System 132 (2d ed.1973). The case could be explained as holding that, because the plaintiffs had not yet been injured, they lacked standing; and their contingent situation suggested, as in the typical standing cases, uncertainty over both the plaintiffs' concern and the unavoidability of litigation. But the *Mitchell* plaintiffs, unlike Ms. Frothingham, alleged their desire to do things that would give them an undoubted interest in the issue. Consequently the Court spoke in terms of prematurity rather than of standing, expressly invoking a factor not always present in standing cases: The controversy must be concrete, in order to avoid overstatement, to focus attention on a narrow problem, and to bring home to the judges the actual impact of their decision. In *Mitchell*, indeed, knowledge of the content of a proposed speech or article might have been relevant to whether it was constitutionally protected.

In contrast to *Frothingham*, a decision that suit is premature does not make judicial review of the challenged statutes impossible; the Court in *Mitchell* upheld the Hatch Act on the merits because one of the plaintiffs had already broken the law. Nevertheless, stringent application of ripeness principles can be quite harsh, as the Senate Committee argued in urging adoption of the Declaratory Judgment Act:

> The procedure has been especially useful in avoiding the necessity, now so often present, of having to act at one's peril or to act on one's own interpretation of his rights, or abandon one's rights because of a fear of incurring damages. So now it is often necessary, in the absence of the declaratory judgment procedure, to violate or purport to violate a statute in order to obtain a judicial determination of its meaning or validity. . . . In jurisdictions having the declaratory judgment procedure, it is not necessary to bring about such social and economic waste and destruction in order to obtain a determination of one's rights. . . .

S.Rep.No.1005, 73d Cong., 2d Sess. 2–3 (1934), quoted by Justice Douglas, dissenting, in *United Public Workers v. Mitchell.*

Was the Senate Committee's goal unconstitutional? If not, has the Court discretion to reject it as improper? Consider the position of a government employee if the statutory penalty for violating the Hatch Act had been death. As James Thurber once wrote, "The chances of being eaten by a leopard on Main Street aren't one in a million, but once is enough."[5]

5. For more recent decisions indicating the Court has receded considerably from the extreme hostility toward anticipatory litigation illustrated by the *Mitchell* case see pp. 57–69 infra.

E. Administrative Questions

In Federal Radio Commission v. General Electric Co., 281 U.S. 464 (1930), the Commission ordered renewal of a broadcasting license on terms unfavorable to the licensee. The statute provided an appeal to the Court of Appeals of the District of Columbia, empowering the court to take additional evidence and to "alter or revise the decision appealed from and enter such judgment as to it may seem just." The Supreme Court refused to review the decision of the Court of Appeals:

> The powers confided to the commission respecting the granting and renewal of station licenses are purely administrative, and . . . the provision for appeals to the Court of Appeals does no more than make that court a superior and revising agency in the same field. . . . This court . . . was brought into being by the judiciary article of the Constitution, is invested with judicial power only and can have no jurisdiction other than of cases and controversies falling within the classes enumerated in that article. . . . It cannot . . . exercise or participate in the exercise of functions which are essentially legislative or administrative.

What was wrong? There was plainly no lack of adverse parties, and the Court did not suggest that the record was lacking in concrete facts needed for an informed decision. When Congress amended the Radio Act to limit review to "questions of law," providing that the Commission's findings of fact should be conclusive unless arbitrary, capricious, or not supported by substantial evidence, the Supreme Court took jurisdiction: "The limitation manifestly demands judicial, as distinguished from administrative review." Federal Radio Comm. v. Nelson Bros. Co., 289 U.S. 266 (1933). Is the finding of facts not a judicial task? Hart and Wechsler suggest that the difficulty in this type of case may be the "range of discretion" given by the statute. The Federal Courts and the Federal System 214 (1953). Is the standard of "public convenience and necessity" under the Radio Act appreciably less suited to judicial application than the concepts of unreasonable searches or unreasonable restraints of trade, or than the law of nuisance?

See United Steelworkers v. United States, 361 U.S. 39 (1959), upholding the national-emergency injunctive provision of the Taft-Hartley Act against a challenge that the statute conferred nonjudicial power on the courts because it failed to set up "any standard of lawful or unlawful conduct on the part of labor or management." The Court said it was enough that the statute recognized the right of the public to unimpeded production in vital industries, that the United States was made guardian of this right in litigation, and that relief was made to depend upon findings of fact judicially made. A concurring opinion stressed that the jurisdiction conferred was much like that traditionally exercised over public nuisances.

The Bank Merger Act of 1966, 12 U.S.C. § 1828(c)(5)(B), authorizes the Comptroller of the Currency to approve an anti-competitive bank merger if he finds it justified by "the probable effect of the transaction in meeting the convenience and needs of the community to be served." In an antitrust proceeding the federal courts are instructed to apply the same standard and in so doing to "review de novo the issues presented." Without mentioning the *Federal Radio* case the Supreme Court held the statute did not impose nonjudicial tasks on judges: "The courts are not left at large as planning agencies. The effect on competition is the standard; and it is a familiar one. If the anti-competitive effect is adverse, then it is to be excused only if 'the convenience and needs of the community to be served' *clearly* outweigh it." The issues were no more nonjudicial, the Court concluded, than those commonly considered in antitrust cases under the "rule of reason." United States v. First City Nat. Bank, 386 U.S. 361, 369–70 (1967).

Why didn't the Court just overrule *Federal Radio?*

F. Political Questions

In Luther v. Borden, 48 U.S. (7 How.) 1 (1849), the Court refused to determine which of two competing bodies was the legitimate government of Rhode Island. In Pacific States Tel. Co. v. Oregon, 223 U.S. 118 (1912), it refused to decide whether a State might constitutionally adopt legislation by initiative or referendum. In Colegrove v. Green, 328 U.S. 549 (1946), it refused to determine the constitutionality of an unequal apportionment of congressional seats. A reason given by the Court in the first two cases, and by the famous opinion of Justice Frankfurter for three of the seven participating Justices in *Colegrove*, was that the issues were "political," not judicial.

The all-important decision in this area is Baker v. Carr, 369 U.S. 186 (1962), in which the Court upheld a federal court's authority to determine the constitutionality of electoral districts for state legislators. The political-question doctrine, wrote Justice Brennan for the Court, is based upon "the relationship between the judiciary and coordinate branches of the Federal Government, and not the federal judiciary's relationship to the States."

> Prominent on the surface of any case held to involve a political question is found a textually demonstrable constitutional commitment of the issue to a coordinate political department; or a lack of judicially discoverable and manageable standards for resolving it; or the impossibility of deciding without an initial policy determination of a kind clearly for nonjudicial discretion; or the impossibility of a court's undertaking independent resolution without expressing lack of the respect due coordinate branches of government; or an unusual need for unquestioning adherence to a political decision already made; or the potentiality of embarrassment from multifarious pronouncements by various departments on one question. . . .

None of these characteristics, the Court said, was present in *Baker v. Carr*. In particular, "judicial standards under the Equal Protection Clause are well developed and familiar, and it has been open to courts since the enactment of the Fourteenth Amendment to determine, if on the particular facts they must, that a discrimination reflects *no* policy, but simply arbitrary and capricious action."

Justice Frankfurter, in dissent, argued that there were no adequate standards for judicial decision; that there would be difficulty in devising an effective remedy; that invalidation of the existing apportionment might leave the State without a legislature; that intervention would "add a virulent source of friction and tension in federal-state relations"; and that by injecting itself into "the clash of political forces in political settlements" the Court might impair "public confidence in its moral sanction," on which confidence its authority as interpreter of the Constitution ultimately rests.

The political question is an elusive and difficult animal. Professor Bickel deemed it another device for avoiding decision of issues the Court wishes to bypass. The Least Dangerous Branch 183 (1962). But Professor Scharpf points out an important distinction: While a dismissal for lack of ripeness or standing often leaves open the possibility that the issue will be considered in a better case or at a more propitious time, the political-question device purports to foreclose consideration of the issue altogether. Judicial Review and the Political Question: A Functional Analysis, 75 Yale L.J. at 537–38. The tension between the political-question theory and the notion of the courts as guardians of the Constitution is obvious: Except where the designation reflects a decision that the Constitution commits the matter to discretion, to characterize an issue as political means that the executive or the legislature may violate the Constitution and get away with it. Indeed, the argument that judicial review is indispensable to enforcement of the Constitution was made with special force in regard to legislative apportionment, an area believed "political" before *Baker v. Carr*: The political processes for correcting intolerable legislation were not fully open, because in States lacking machinery to bypass the legislature in amending their Constitutions political reform would have required people to vote to surrender their own political power.

When, if ever, does the risk of disobedience or reprisal justify the courts in refusing to decide a case? By running away today, as Justice Frankfurter argued in *Baker v. Carr*, the Court may preserve its power to fight another day. Is it fair to say the Court was pushing its moral authority pretty close to the limit by deciding, in close succession, to outlaw school segregation, school prayers, and legislative malapportionment? Yet, if the courts are too cautious to enter the lists when they are most needed, what is to become of the Constitution? Compare the eloquent words of Chief Justice Taney after a military officer had refused to honor his writ of habeas corpus:

> I have exercised all the power which the constitution and laws confer upon me, but that power has been resisted by a force too strong for me to overcome. It is possible that the officer who has incurred this grave responsibility may have misunderstood his instructions, and exceeded the authority intended to be given him; I shall, therefore,

order all the proceedings in this case, with my opinion, to be filed and recorded in the circuit court of the United States for the district of Maryland, and direct the clerk to transmit a copy, under seal, to the president of the United States. It will then remain for that high officer, in fulfillment of his constitutional obligation to "take care that the laws be faithfully executed" to determine what measures he will take to cause the civil process of the United States to be respected and enforced.

Ex parte Merryman, 17 F.Cas. 144, 153 (D.Md.1861) (No. 9,487).

SECTION 2. JUDICIAL REVIEW

MARBURY v. MADISON

5 U.S. (1 Cranch) 137 (1803).

MARSHALL, C. J. At the last term on the affidavits then read and filed with the clerk, a rule was granted in this case, requiring the secretary of state to show cause why a *mandamus* should not issue, directing him to deliver to William Marbury his commission as a justice of the peace for the county of Washington, in the District of Columbia.

No cause has been shown, and the present motion is for a *mandamus*. . . .

1st. Has the applicant a right to the commission he demands? . . .

Some point of time must be taken when the power of the executive over an officer, not removable at his will, must cease. That point of time must be when the constitutional power of appointment has been exercised. And this power has been exercised when the last act, required from the person possessing the power, has been performed. This last act is the signature of the commission. . . .

Mr. Marbury, then, since his commission was signed by the president, and sealed by the secretary of state, was appointed; and as the law creating the office, gave the officer a right to hold for five years, independent of the executive, the appointment was not revocable, but vested in the officer legal rights, which are protected by the laws of his country. . . .

2dly. If he has a right, and that right has been violated, do the laws of his country afford him a remedy?

The very essence of civil liberty certainly consists in the right of every individual to claim the protection of the laws, whenever he receives an injury. . . . Where the heads of departments are the political or confidential agents of the executive, merely to execute the will of the president, or rather to act in cases in which the executive possesses a constitutional or legal discretion, nothing can be more perfectly clear than that their acts are only politically examinable. But where a specific duty is assigned by law, and individual rights depend upon the performance of that duty, it seems equally clear that the individual who considers himself injured, has a right to resort to the laws of his country for a remedy. . . .

It remains to be inquired whether,

3dly. He is entitled to the remedy for which he applies. . . .

This writ, if awarded, would be directed to an officer of government, and its mandate to him would be, to use the words of Blackstone, "to do a particular thing therein specified, which appertains to his office and duty, and which the court has previously determined, or at least supposes, to be consonant to right and justice." Or, in the words of Lord Mansfield, the applicant, in this case, has a right to execute an office of public concern, and is kept out of possession of that right. . . .

Still, to render the *mandamus* a proper remedy, the officer to whom it is to be directed, must be one to whom, on legal principles, such writ may be directed; and the person applying for it must be without any other specific and legal remedy.

1st. With respect to the officer to whom it would be directed. The intimate political relation subsisting between the President of the United States and the heads of departments, necessarily renders any legal investigation of the acts of one of those high officers peculiarly irksome, as well as delicate; and excites some hesitation with respect to the propriety of entering into such investigation. Impressions are often received without much reflection or examination, and it is not wonderful that in such a case as this the assertion, by an individual, of his legal claims in a court of justice, to which claims it is the duty of that court to attend, should at first view be considered by some, as an attempt to intrude into the cabinet, and to intermeddle with the prerogatives of the executive.

It is scarcely necessary for the court to disclaim all pretentions to such a jurisdiction. An extravagance, so absurd and excessive, could not have been entertained for a moment. The province of the court is, solely, to decide on the rights of individuals, not to inquire how the executive, or executive officers, perform duties in which they have a discretion. Questions in their nature political, or which are, by the constitution and laws, submitted to the executive, can never be made in this court.

But, if this be not such a question; if, so far from being an intrusion into the secrets of the cabinet, it respects a paper which, according to law, is upon record, and to a copy of which the law gives a right, on the payment of ten cents; if it be no intermeddling with a subject over which the executive can be considered as having exercised any control; what is there in the exalted station of the officer, which shall bar a citizen from asserting, in a court of justice, his legal rights, or shall forbid a court to listen to the claim, or to issue a *mandamus*, directing the performance of a duty, not depending on executive discretion, but on particular acts of congress, and the general principles of law? . . . It is not by the office of the person to whom the writ is directed, but the nature of the thing to be done, that the propriety or impropriety of issuing a *mandamus* is to be determined. . . .

This, then, is a plain case for a *mandamus*, either to deliver the commission, or a copy of it from the record; and it only remains to be inquired,

Whether it can issue from this court.

The act to establish the judicial courts of the United States authorizes the supreme court "to issue writs of *mandamus*, in cases warranted by the principles and usages of law, to any courts appointed, or persons holding office, under the authority of the United States." . . .

The constitution vests the whole judicial power of the United States in one supreme court, and such inferior courts as congress shall, from time to time, ordain and establish. This power is expressly extended to all cases arising under the laws of the United States; and, consequently, in some form, may be exercised over the present case; because the right claimed is given by a law of the United States.

In the distribution of this power it is declared that "the supreme court shall have original jurisdiction in all cases affecting ambassadors, other public ministers and consuls, and those in which a state shall be a party. In all other cases, the supreme court shall have appellate jurisdiction." . . .

If it had been intended to leave it in the discretion of the legislature to apportion the judicial power between the supreme and inferior courts according to the will of that body, it would certainly have been useless to have proceeded further than to have defined the judicial power, and the tribunals in which it should be vested. The subsequent part of the section is mere surplusage, is entirely without meaning, if such is to be the construction. If congress remains at liberty to give this court appellate jurisdiction, where the constitution has declared their jurisdiction shall be original; and original jurisdiction where the constitution has declared it shall be appellate; the distribution of jurisdiction, made in the constitution, is form without substance. . . .

To enable this court, then, to issue a *mandamus*, it must be shown to be an exercise of appellate jurisdiction, or to be necessary to enable them to exercise appellate jurisdiction. . . .

It is the essential criterion of appellate jurisdiction, that it revises and corrects the proceedings in a cause already instituted, and does not create that cause. Although, therefore, a *mandamus* may be directed to courts, yet to issue such a writ to an officer for the delivery of a paper, is in effect the same as to sustain an original action for that paper, and, therefore, seems not to belong to appellate, but to original jurisdiction. Neither is it necessary in such a case as this, to enable the court to exercise its appellate jurisdiction.

The authority, therefore, given to the supreme court, by the act establishing the judicial courts of the United States, to issue writs of *mandamus* to public officers, appears not to be warranted by the constitution; and it becomes necessary to inquire whether a jurisdiction so conferred can be exercised.

The question, whether an act, repugnant to the constitution, can become the law of the land, is a question deeply interesting to the United States; but, happily, not of an intricacy proportioned to its interest. It seems only necessary to recognize certain principles, supposed to have been long and well established, to decide it.

That the people have an original right to establish, for their future government, such principles as, in their opinion, shall most conduce to their own happiness is the basis on which the whole American fabric has been erected. The exercise of this original right is a very great exertion; nor can it, nor ought it, to be frequently repeated. The principles, therefore, so established, are deemed fundamental. And as the authority from which they proceed is supreme, and can seldom act, they are designed to be permanent.

This original and supreme will organizes the government, and assigns to different departments their respective powers. It may either stop here, or establish certain limits not to be transcended by those departments.

The government of the United States is of the latter description. The powers of the legislature are defined and limited; and that those limits may not be mistaken, or forgotten, the constitution is written. To what purpose are powers limited, and to what purpose is that limitation committed to writing, if these limits may, at any time, be passed by those intended to be restrained? The distinction between a government with limited and unlimited powers is abolished, if those limits do not confine the persons on whom they are imposed, and if acts prohibited and acts allowed, are of equal obligation. . . .

Certainly all those who have framed written constitutions contemplate them as forming the fundamental and paramount law of the nation, and, consequently, the theory of every such government must be, that an act of the legislature, repugnant to the constitution, is void.

This theory is essentially attached to a written constitution, and, is consequently, to be considered, by this court, as one of the fundamental principles of our society. It is not therefore to be lost sight of in the further consideration of this subject.

If an act of the legislature, repugnant to the constitution, is void, does it, notwithstanding its invalidity, bind the courts, and oblige them to give it effect? Or, in other words, though it be not law, does it constitute a rule as operative as if it was a law? This would be to overthrow in fact what was established in theory; and would seem, at first view, an absurdity too gross to be insisted on. It shall, however, receive a more attentive consideration.

It is emphatically the province and duty of the judicial department to say what the law is. Those who apply the rule to particular cases, must of necessity expound and interpret that rule. If two laws conflict with each other, the courts must decide on the operation of each.

So if a law be in opposition to the constitution; if both the law and the constitution apply to a particular case, so that the court must either decide that case conformably to the law, disregarding the constitution; or conformably to the constitution, disregarding the law; the court must determine which of these conflicting rules governs the case. This is of the very essence of judicial duty.

If, then, the courts are to regard the constitution, and the constitution is superior to any ordinary act of the legislature, the constitution, and not such ordinary act, must govern the case to which they both apply.

Those, then, who controvert the principle that the constitution is to be considered, in court, as a paramount law, are reduced to the necessity of maintaining that courts must close their eyes on the constitution, and see only the law.

This doctrine would subvert the very foundation of all written constitutions. It would declare that an act which, according to the principles and theory of our government, is entirely void, is yet, in practice, completely obligatory. It would declare that if the legislature shall do what is expressly forbidden, such act, notwithstanding the express prohibition, is in reality effectual. It would be giving to the legislature a practical and real omnipotence, with the same breath which professes to restrict their powers within narrow limits. It is prescribing limits, and declaring that those limits may be passed at pleasure.

That it thus reduces to nothing what we have deemed the greatest improvement on political institutions, a written constitution, would of itself be sufficient, in America, where written constitutions have been viewed with so much reverence, for rejecting the construction. But the peculiar expressions of the constitution of the United States furnish additional arguments in favour of its rejection.

The judicial power of the United States is extended to all cases arising under the constitution.

Could it be the intention of those who gave this power, to say that in using it the constitution should not be looked into? That a case arising under the constitution should be decided without examining the instrument under which it arises?

This is too extravagant to be maintained.

In some cases, then, the constitution must be looked into by the judges. And if they can open it at all, what part of it are they forbidden to read or to obey?

There are many other parts of the constitution which serve to illustrate this subject.

It is declared that "no tax or duty shall be laid on articles exported from any state." Suppose a duty on the export of cotton, of tobacco, or of flour; and a suit instituted to recover it. Ought judgment to be rendered in such a case? Ought the judges to close their eyes on the constitution, and only see the law?

The constitution declares "that no bill of attainder or *ex post facto* law shall be passed."

If, however, such a bill should be passed, and a person should be prosecuted under it; must the court condemn to death those victims whom the constitution endeavours to preserve?

"No person," says the constitution, "shall be convicted of treason unless on the testimony of two witnesses to the same overt act, or on confession in open court."

Here the language of the constitution is addressed especially to the courts. It prescribes, directly for them, a rule of evidence not to be departed from. If the legislature should change that rule, and declare *one* witness, or a confession *out* of court, sufficient for conviction, must the constitutional principle yield to the legislative act?

From these, and many other selections which might be made, it is apparent, that the framers of the constitution contemplated that instrument as a rule for the government of *courts*, as well as of the legislature.

Why otherwise does it direct the judges to take an oath to support it? This oath certainly applies in an especial manner, to their conduct in their official character. How immoral to impose it on them, if they were to be used as the instruments, and the knowing instruments, for violating what they swear to support!

The oath of office, too, imposed by the legislature, is completely demonstrative of the legislative opinion on this subject. It is in these words: "I do solemnly swear that I will administer justice without respect to persons, and do equal right to the poor and to the rich; and that I will faithfully and impartially discharge all the duties incumbent on me as ______, according to the best of my abilities and understanding, agreeably to *the constitution* and laws of the United States."

Why does a judge swear to discharge his duties agreeably to the constitution of the United States, if that constitution forms no rule for his government? If it is closed upon him, and cannot be inspected by him?

If such be the real state of things, this is worse than solemn mockery. To prescribe, or to take this oath, becomes equally a crime.

It is also not entirely unworthy of observation, that in declaring what shall be the *supreme* law of the land, the *constitution* itself is first mentioned; and not the laws of the United States generally, but those only which shall be made in *pursuance* of the constitution, have that rank.

Thus, the particular phraseology of the constitution of the United States confirms and strengthens the principle, supposed to be essential to all written constitutions, that a law repugnant to the constitution is void; and that *courts*, as well as other departments, are bound by that instrument.

The rule must be discharged.

Notes on Judicial Review

(1) *Marbury v. Madison* was not the first exercise of federal-court power to disregard unconstitutional statutes. Charles Warren recounted, among other early examples, newspaper reports of a circuit-court decision as early as May, 1791, holding a Connecticut statute invalid because it conflicted with the treaty of peace, and of another in 1792 holding a Maryland law to impair the obligation of contract. 1 The Supreme Court in United States History 65–69 (Rev.ed.1926). In Ware v. Hylton, 3 U.S. (3 Dall.) 199 (1796), the Supreme Court itself, in a case coming from a federal trial court, held state statutes impairing debts owed to Englishmen ineffective because in conflict with the treaty.

The foregoing cases all concerned state laws, but there were also early indications of judicial authority to disregard unconstitutional acts of Congress. The most noteworthy example was Hayburn's Case, 2 U.S. (2 Dall.) 408, 410 n. (a) (1792), p. 8 supra, in which five Justices on circuit refused on constitutional grounds to act under a statute subjecting their decisions to executive review. In the Supreme Court itself there were several obiter references to the existence of such a power,[1] and in Hylton v. United States, 3 U.S. (3 Dall.) 171 (1796), the Court considered on the merits and rejected a claim that a federal tax on carriages was a direct tax and therefore unconstitutional because not apportioned according to population. Of the seriatim opinions, only Justice Chase's mentioned the issue of the Court's power, and he left it open:

> As I do not think the tax on carriages is a direct tax, it is unnecessary at this time for me to determine, whether this court, constitutionally possesses the power to declare an act of congress void, on the ground of its being made contrary to, and in violation of, the constitution; but if the court have such power, I am free to declare, that I will never exercise it, but in a very clear case.

3 U.S. (3 Dall.) at 175.

Nor was judicial review wholly unknown in other jurisdictions at the time *Marbury* was decided. In England itself, where there were no written limitations on the power of Parliament, Coke's famous dictum that a court might declare void an act of Parliament "against common right and reason" (Bonham's Case, 8 Co.Rep. 114a, 118a, 77 Eng.Rep. 646, 652 (1610)), had fallen on infertile soil. Municipal corporations and colonial assemblies, however, were limited by their charters; Professor Goebel reports that British courts customarily exercised judicial review of the enactments

1. See D. Currie, The Constitution in the Supreme Court: The First Hundred Years, chs. 1–2 (1985).

of such inferior legislative bodies under the familiar doctrine of ultra vires. J. Goebel, Antecedents and Beginnings to 1801 (vol. 1 of the History of the Supreme Court of the United States), ch. 2. There were also a few pre-1789 state-court precedents, which Professor Crosskey dismissed as establishing "no more, at most, than a right in the courts, in two or, possibly three of the thirteen states," to disregard statutes affecting the courts' own constitutional functions. 2 W. Crosskey, Politics and the Constitution in the History of the United States 941–75 (1953).

Do you find it striking that Marshall in *Marbury* made no use of any of this precedential material? How compelling is it?

(2) Where is judicial review found in the Constitution? Later observers have found plausible alternative readings for each of the three clauses on which Marshall relied: Reliance on the oath requirement may beg the question, since a judge does not offend the Constitution by enforcing a law he has no right to strike down; jurisdiction over cases "arising under this Constitution" need not mean the Constitution is supreme over federal laws as well as over executive or state action; that only those federal statutes made "in Pursuance" of "*this* Constitution" are supreme may serve to distinguish those passed under the Articles of Confederation. Indeed, if the last interpretation is correct, the Supremacy Clause furnishes a powerful argument *against* judicial review of federal as opposed to state laws. For while that clause plainly subordinates state laws to the Constitution, it equates Acts of Congress with the Constitution itself as "the supreme Law of the Land." See, e.g., A. Bickel, The Least Dangerous Branch 2–12 (1962); 2 Crosskey, supra note 1, at 982–1002 (1953).

(3) One of the most fascinating aspects of the *Marbury* opinion is that Marshall appears to have turned to the text of the Constitution only as an afterthought: "[T]he peculiar expressions of the constitution of the United States furnish *additional* arguments" for judicial review. His principal reliance was on "fundamental principles:" "Certainly all those who have framed written constitutions contemplate them as forming the fundamental and paramount law of the nation, and, consequently, the theory of every such government must be, that an act of the legislature, repugnant to the constitution, is void." Is this persuasive as a matter of theory? Can you conceive of a written constitution that limits legislative power and explicitly forbids judicial review? On the empirical level, there have been nations with written constitutions in which judicial review was unknown. See, e.g., Cappelletti and Adams, Judicial Review of Legislation: European Antecedents and Adaptations, 79 Harv.L.Rev. 1207 (1966). Why do you suppose Marshall relied on overgeneralization rather than on the Supremacy Clause for the conclusion that our Constitution is "the fundamental and paramount law of the nation?"

(4) Marshall's hyperbole aside, to what extent does the existence of written limitations on legislative and executive power support, in the absence of contrary evidence, an inference of judicial review? If the Framers wanted to preserve cabbages, Marshall argued, they would hardly have entrusted them to rabbits for safe-keeping. Hamilton had made the same point in The Federalist (p. 14 supra); Marshall closely echoed his ideas without citing him.

Professor Bickel thought this argument proved too much:

> To leave the decision with the legislature, [Marshall] said, is to allow those whose power is supposed to be limited themselves to set the limits—an absurd invitation to consistent abuse. Perhaps so, but the Constitution does not limit the power of the legislature alone. It limits that of the courts as well, and it may be equally absurd, therefore, to allow courts to set the limits. It is, indeed, more absurd, because courts are not subject to electoral control.

Bickel, supra note 2, at 3–4. Is it an answer to Professor Bickel to point out that the courts are subject to significant checks too? E.g., impeachment, constitutional amendment, the appointing power, the power to regulate jurisdiction, the power to withhold funds other than judges' salaries? Or are all these checks limited by the argument in *Marbury* too?

Professor Crosskey, on the other hand, found the present scheme of judicial review so unfit for its asserted purpose that it could not have been intended: Because of the case-or-controversy limitation a "very considerable range of constitutional questions" could never be brought to the courts at all, and the protection of the "profoundly important" rights of the States was usually left to the vagaries of private litigants. Finally, if the Court was meant to protect the States and the people against other branches, it was "highly irrational" to give the President and Congress the power to reverse the Court's decisions by adding new Justices. 2 Crosskey, supra note 1, at 976–82.

Can *both* Bickel and Crosskey have been right?

(5) The records of the Constitutional Convention, not surprisingly, have been interpreted variously in respect to judicial review. Professor Beard, observing that no explicit proposal to grant courts the power of passing upon acts of Congress was submitted to the Convention, found that seventeen of the twenty-five most influential members of the Convention "declared, directly or indirectly, for judicial control," and that only three members of the entire Convention were on record to the contrary. Among many other statements he quoted Rufus King's opinion, recorded in the notes of William Pierce, that the judges ought not to sit on the proposed Council of Revision "because the judges will have the expounding of those [congressional] laws when they come before them; and they will no doubt stop the operation of such as shall appear repugnant to the constitution." C. Beard, The Supreme Court and the Constitution 15–67 (1938 ed.). Many of the statements upon which Beard relied were made outside the Convention itself, and many are not inconsistent with Professor Crosskey's view that the courts were meant to have power to strike down only those acts of Congress respecting the operations of the courts themselves.

Professors Hart and Wechsler found Beard's demonstration "conclusive:"

> The grant of judicial power was to include the power, where necessary in the decision of cases, to disregard state or federal statutes found to be unconstitutional. Despite the curiously persisting myth of usurpation, the Convention's understanding on this point emerges from its records with singular clarity. . . .

> The crux of the long controversy over the proposed Congressional negative of state laws was whether the check of judicial invalidation of unconstitutional state laws was a sufficient safeguard or whether an additional one was needed. The existence of this power in the federal courts was common ground, unquestioned throughout the debate. And the issue in the end was settled by acceptance of Luther Martin's proposal of the supremacy clause, strengthening the judicial check by express statement of the parallel power and responsibility of state judges.

The Federal Courts and the Federal System 9 (3d ed.1988).

Professor Crosskey's view of the Convention record was based largely upon his opinion, spelled out at length in his book, that Madison's notes had been altered for partisan purposes:

> With the exception of a single inconclusive sentence from the notes of William Pierce . . ., our *entire* record of what was said on the subject of judicial review, in the Federal Convention, consists of parts of James Madison's famous notes. . . . Since the man in question was not, for several reasons, a very credible witness on this particular subject, the possibility that his testimony may have been, not inadvertently, but deliberately, false and misleading, as to what the various members had said, is one that cannot lightly be passed over.

Statements such as those in the Federalist Crosskey viewed with great skepticism: "Advocates for the Constitution, in the ratification campaign, were apt to say about it, not what they actually thought, but what they thought would help it to be adopted." 2 Crosskey, supra note 1, at 1008–28.

(6) Judge Learned Hand, unable to find textual support for judicial review in the Constitution, accepted the practice because of the canon permitting courts to interpolate in documents "such provisions, though not expressed, as are essential to prevent the defeat of the venture at hand," The Bill of Rights 14–15 (1958), but he insisted that the power of review must be exercised sparingly, and he was not convinced it was an effective safeguard:

> I often wonder whether we do not rest our hopes too much upon constitutions, upon laws and upon courts. These are false hopes; believe me, these are false hopes. Liberty lies in the hearts of men and women; when it dies there, no constitution, no law, no court can save it; no constitution, no law, no court can even do much to help it. While it lies there it needs no constitution, no law, no court to save it.

The Spirit of Liberty 189–90 (3d ed.1960). See also id. at 164.

(7) A common argument against judicial review as a matter of policy is that it is undemocratic (see, e.g., 2 Crosskey, supra note 1, at 1006), or, as Bickel less emotively put it (supra note 2, at 16–19): "counter-majoritarian:"

> Judicial review is a deviant institution in the American democracy. . . . The policy-making power of representative institutions, born of the electoral process, is the distinguishing characteristic of the system.

However, as Bickel also pointed out, our concept of democracy is "much more sophisticated and complex than the making of decisions in town meeting by a show of hands." There is much in our Constitution that protects against what Mill called the "tyranny of the majority;" perhaps judicial review is undemocratic in the complimentary sense, as is the Bill of Rights. See The Federalist, No. 10; C. Beard, The Supreme Court and the Constitution 90, 94–96 (1938 ed.).

Professor Bickel's defense of judicial review was based upon a sophisticated assessment of the comparative fitness of judges and of other officials to establish and to adhere to general principles:

> It is a premise we deduce not merely from the fact of a written constitution but from the history of the race, and ultimately as a moral judgment of the good society, that government should serve not only what we conceive from time to time to be our immediate material needs but also certain enduring values. . . . Courts have certain capacities for dealing with matters of principle that legislatures and executives do not possess. Judges have, or should have, the leisure, the training, and the insulation to follow the ways of the scholar in pursuing the ends of government. This is crucial in sorting out the enduring values of a society, and it is not something that institutions can do well occasionally, while operating for the most part with a different set of gears. It calls for a habit of mind, and for undeviating institutional customs. Another advantage that courts have is that questions of principle never carry the same aspect for them as they did for the legislature or the executive. Statutes, after all, deal typically with abstract or dimly foreseen problems. The courts are concerned with the flesh and blood of an actual case. This tends to modify, perhaps to lengthen, everyone's view. It also provides an extremely salutary proving ground for all abstractions. . . . Their insulation and the marvelous mystery of time give courts the capacity to appeal to men's better natures, to call forth their aspirations, which may have been forgotten in the moment's hue and cry.

A. Bickel, The Least Dangerous Branch 23–28 (1962).

Whatever may have been said of the desirability of judicial review as an original matter, is it irrelevant that the *Marbury* doctrine has been established in this country for so many years? "Settled expectations," Professor Bickel said, have formed around judicial review of federal and state legislation; "the life of a nation" has come to depend upon it "in a hundred different aspects of its organization and coherence." Bickel, supra, at 14. Thayer's famous argument that judicial review should be very limited because it induces legislators to pass the buck in disregard of their own constitutional obligations (J. Thayer, John Marshall 103–07 (1901)) cuts both ways: Judicial review may have unfortunate consequences, but might its abolition today leave us with no institution alert to the preservation of constitutional rights? [2]

2. Consider President Roosevelt's 1935 letter urging enactment of a regulatory bill:

Manifestly, no one is in a position to give assurance that the proposed act will withstand constitutional tests, for the

(8) 1 C. Warren, The Supreme Court in United States History, 232, 243, 266–67 (rev.ed.1926):

> Contemporary writings make it very clear that the Republicans attacked the [*Marbury*] decision, not so much because it sustained the power of the Court to determine the validity of Congressional legislation, as because it enounced the doctrine that the Court might issue mandamus to a Cabinet official who was acting by direction of the President. . . .
>
> The opposition to the Judiciary during the early years of the nineteenth century, found in both the Republican and the Federalist parties, was directed not so much at the *possession of the power* of the Court to pass upon the validity of Acts of Congress, as at the *effect of its exercise* in supporting or invalidating some particular measure in which the particular political party was interested. So far from denying the existence of the power to pass upon the constitutionality of the detested Sedition Act or of the obnoxious United States Bank Charter, the Republicans in 1800 and in 1819 complained of the Federal Court for its failure to declare these Acts to be unconstitutional; and prior to 1800 . . . it was the Republicans (or Anti-Federalists) who had especially championed the right of the Court to protect the people and the States against the passage of unconstitutional laws by the Legislatures. So, in the same manner, the Federalists in 1808 assailed the Federal Courts for failing to hold the hated Embargo Act unconstitutional. . . . The history of the years succeeding 1800 clearly shows that, with regard to this judicial function, the political parties divided not on lines of general theory of government, or of constitutional law, or of Nationalism against Localism, but on lines of political, social or economic interest.

Is it desirable, as the foregoing notes assume, to judge judicial review as an abstract institution, without regard to the merits of a particular controversy? Or were the politicians of the early 1800's right to argue for review of bad but not of good legislation? The question of neutrality in constitutional matters, Professor Wechsler reminds us, is but one aspect of the pervasive question of the rule of law in general—a matter of tolerating inequitable results in the short run in order to preserve an institution capable of avoiding injustice in other cases. See Wechsler, Toward Neutral Principles of Constitutional Law, 73 Harv.L.Rev. 1, 12 (1959). But the long-run risks are always conjectural and the immediate goal often tempting; can we be certain that the Court would not have got away with integration

simple fact that you can get not ten but a thousand differing legal opinions on the subject. But the situation is so urgent and the benefits of the legislation so evident that all doubts should be resolved in favor of the bill, leaving to the courts, in an orderly fashion, the ultimate question of constitutionality. A decision by the Supreme Court relative to this measure would be helpful as indicating, with increasing clarity, the constitutional limits within which this Government must operate. The proposed bill has been carefully drafted by employers and employees working cooperatively. An opportunity should be given to the industry to attempt to work out some of its major problems. I hope your committee will not permit doubts as to constitutionality, however reasonable, to block the suggested legislation.

4 Public Papers and Addresses of Franklin D. Roosevelt 297–98 (1938).

or reapportionment in the 1950's and '60's if Roosevelt had packed it in 1937?

(9) Are other branches of the Government required to accept the constitutional views of the judiciary? In Cooper v. Aaron, 358 U.S. 1, 18 (1958), the Court in ordering desegregation of the Little Rock schools relied on *Marbury* as establishing that "the federal judiciary is supreme in the exposition of the law of the Constitution" and that "the interpretation of the Fourteenth Amendment enunciated by this Court in the Brown case is the supreme law of the land. . . ." On the other hand, after the Supreme Court had upheld the constitutionality of the Bank of the United States, President Jackson vetoed a bill to continue the Bank because he thought it unconstitutional: "The Congress, the Executive, and the Court must each for itself be guided by its own opinion of the Constitution." 3 Richardson, Messages and Papers of the Presidents 1145 (1897).

Would Jackson have felt equally free to sign a bill that he knew the Court would hold unconstitutional? Lincoln once promised to vote to reenact the Missouri Compromise in disregard of the *Dred Scott* decision. Lincoln-Douglas Debates 36 (Angle ed.1958). In Ex parte Merryman, 17 F.Cas. 144 (D.Md.1861) (No. 9,487), Lincoln went still further, allowing his subordinate to disobey a writ of habeas corpus. See C. Swisher, Roger B. Taney 550–56 (1936). This position is the ultimate denial of the principle that courts exist to keep the other branches within their powers; is it consistent with the judicial clean-hands doctrine also embraced in *Marbury*?

Should it be held that each branch is entitled to follow its own *negative* views of the Constitution—i.e., the President may veto a bill the Court would uphold, but he may not enforce one the Court would strike down? Apart from other difficulties with this theory, is there not a difference between vetoing an act on constitutional grounds and refusing, on the same grounds, to enforce a statute passed over the President's veto? See H. Hart & A. Sacks, The Legal Process 1078–89 (Tent.ed.1958), recounting among other things Senator Millard Tydings's argument that prosecutorial discretion to refuse ever to enforce a statute was contrary to the constitutional provision allowing Congress to override the veto.

(10) Efforts to modify or abolish judicial review have not been wanting. Such attacks on the Court as impeachment, packing, and deprivation of jurisdiction are considered in detail below, pp. 98–113. Suggestions for permanent alteration of the institution itself have included outright abolition of judicial review, requirement of an extraordinary majority, and the recall of judges or of their constitutional decisions. See generally C. Haines, The American Doctrine of Judicial Supremacy 467–91 (2d ed.1959); Nagel, Court-Curbing Periods in American History, 18 Vand.L.Rev. 925 (1965); p. 580 infra.

SECTION 3. JUSTICIABILITY AND STANDING

WARTH v. SELDIN

422 U.S. 490 (1975).

MR. JUSTICE POWELL delivered the opinion of the Court.

Petitioners, various organizations and individuals resident in the Rochester, N.Y., metropolitan area, brought this action in the District Court for the Western District of New York against the town of Penfield, an incorporated municipality adjacent to Rochester, and against members of Penfield's Zoning, Planning and Town Boards. Petitioners claimed that the town's zoning ordinance, by its terms and as enforced by the defendant board members, respondents here, effectively excluded persons of low and moderate income from living in the town, in contravention of petitioners' First, Ninth, and Fourteenth Amendment rights and in violation of 42 U.S.C. §§ 1981, 1982, and 1983. The District Court dismissed the complaint and denied a motion to add petitioner Housing Council in the Monroe County Area, Inc., as party-plaintiff and also a motion by petitioner Rochester Home Builders Association, Inc., for leave to intervene as party-plaintiff. The Court of Appeals for the Second Circuit affirmed, holding that none of the plaintiffs, and neither Housing Council nor Home Builders Association, had standing to prosecute the action. 495 F.2d 1187 (1974). We . . . affirm.

. . . In essence the question of standing is whether the litigant is entitled to have the court decide the merits of the dispute or of particular issues. This inquiry involves both constitutional limitations on federal-court jurisdiction and prudential limitations on its exercise. E.g., Barrows v. Jackson, 346 U.S. 249, 255–256 (1953). In both dimensions it is founded in concern about the proper—and properly limited—role of the courts in a democratic society. . . .

In its constitutional dimension, standing imports justiciability: whether the plaintiff has made out a "case or controversy" between himself and the defendant within the meaning of Art. III. This is the threshold question in every federal case, determining the power of the court to entertain the suit. As an aspect of justiciability, the standing question is whether the plaintiff has "alleged such a personal stake in the outcome of the controversy" as to warrant *his* invocation of federal-court jurisdiction and to justify exercise of the court's remedial powers on his behalf. Baker v. Carr, 369 U.S. 186, 204 (1962). The Art. III judicial power exists only to redress or otherwise to protect against injury to the complaining party, even though the court's judgment may benefit others collaterally. A federal court's jurisdiction therefore can be invoked only when the plaintiff himself has suffered "some threatened or actual injury resulting from the putatively illegal action. . . ."
. . .

Apart from this minimum constitutional mandate, this Court has recognized other limits on the class of persons who may invoke the courts' decisional and remedial powers. First, the Court has held that when the asserted harm is a "generalized grievance" shared in a substantially equal measure by all or a large class of citizens, that harm alone normally does not warrant exercise of jurisdiction. E.g., Schlesinger v. Reservists to Stop the War, . . . [418 U.S. 208 (1974)]; United States v. Richardson, . . . [418 U.S. 166 (1974)]; Ex parte Lévitt, 302 U.S. 633, 634 (1937). Second, even when the plaintiff has alleged injury sufficient to meet the "case or controversy" requirement, this Court has held that the plaintiff generally must assert his own legal rights and interests, and cannot rest his claim to relief on the legal rights or interests of third parties. E.g., Tileston v. Ullman, 318 U.S. 44 (1943). See United States v. Raines, 362 U.S. 17 (1960); Barrows v. Jackson, supra. Without such limitations—closely related to Art. III concerns but essentially matters of judicial self-governance—the courts would be called upon to decide abstract questions of wide public significance even though other governmental institutions may be more competent to address the questions and even though judicial intervention may be unnecessary to protect individual rights. . . .

. . . Moreover, the source of the plaintiff's claim to relief assumes critical importance with respect to the prudential rules of standing that, apart from Art. III's minimum requirements, serve to limit the role of the courts in resolving public disputes. Essentially, the standing question in such cases is whether the constitutional or statutory provision on which the claim rests properly can be understood as granting persons in the plaintiff's position a right to judicial relief.[12] In some circumstances, countervailing considerations may outweigh the concerns underlying the usual reluctance to exert judicial power when the plaintiff's claim to relief rests on the legal rights of third parties. See United States v. Raines, 362 U.S., at 22–23. In such instances, the Court has found, in effect, that the constitutional or statutory provision in question implies a right of action in the plaintiff. . . . Moreover, Congress may grant an express right of action to persons who otherwise would be barred by prudential standing rules. Of course, Art. III's requirement remains: the plaintiff still must allege a distinct and palpable injury to himself, even if it is an injury shared by a large class of other possible litigants. . . . But so long as this requirement is satisfied, persons to whom Congress has granted a right of action, either expressly or by clear implication, may have standing to seek relief on the basis of the legal rights and interests of others, and, indeed, may invoke the general public interest in support of their

12. A similar standing issue arises when the litigant asserts the rights of third parties defensively, as a bar to judgment against him. E.g., Barrows v. Jackson, 346 U.S. 249 (1953); McGowan v. Maryland, 366 U.S. 420, 429–430 (1961). In such circumstances, there is no Art. III standing problem; but the prudential question is governed by considerations closely related to the question whether a person in the litigant's position would have a right of action on the claim. . . .

claim. E.g., . . . FCC v. Sanders Radio Station, 309 U.S. 470, 477 (1940). . . .

III

With these general considerations in mind, we turn first to the claims of petitioners Ortiz, Reyes, Sinkler, and Broadnax, each of whom asserts standing as a person of low or moderate income and, coincidentally, as a member of a minority racial or ethnic group. We must assume, taking the allegations of the complaint as true, that Penfield's zoning ordinance and the pattern of enforcement by respondent officials have had the purpose and effect of excluding persons of low and moderate income, many of whom are members of racial or ethnic minority groups. We also assume, for purposes here, that such intentional exclusionary practices, if proved in a proper case, would be adjudged violative of the constitutional and statutory rights of the persons excluded.

But the fact that these petitioners share attributes common to persons who may have been excluded from residence in the town is an insufficient predicate for the conclusion that petitioners themselves have been excluded, or that the respondents' assertedly illegal actions have violated their rights. . . .

In their complaint, petitioners Ortiz, Reyes, Sinkler, and Broadnax alleged in conclusory terms that they are among the persons excluded by respondents' actions. None of them has ever resided in Penfield; each claims at least implicitly that he desires, or has desired, to do so. Each asserts, moreover, that he made some effort, at some time, to locate housing in Penfield that was at once within his means and adequate for his family's needs. Each claims that his efforts proved fruitless. We may assume, as petitioners allege, that respondents' actions have contributed, perhaps substantially, to the cost of housing in Penfield. But there remains the question whether petitioners' inability to locate suitable housing in Penfield reasonably can be said to have resulted, in any concretely demonstrable way, from respondents' alleged constitutional and statutory infractions. Petitioners must allege facts from which it reasonably could be inferred that, absent the respondents' restrictive zoning practices, there is a substantial probability that they would have been able to purchase or lease in Penfield and that, if the court affords the relief requested, the asserted inability of petitioners will be removed. . . .

We find the record devoid of the necessary allegations. As the Court of Appeals noted, none of these petitioners has a present interest in any Penfield property; none is himself subject to the ordinance's strictures; and none has ever been denied a variance or permit by respondent officials. . . . Instead, petitioners claim that respondents' enforcement of the ordinance against third parties—developers, builders, and the like—has had the consequence of precluding the construction of housing suitable to their needs at prices they might be able to afford. The fact that the harm to petitioners may have resulted indirectly does not in itself preclude standing. When a governmental prohibition or restriction imposed on one party causes specific harm to a third party, harm that a constitutional provision or statute was intended to prevent, the indirectness of the injury does not necessarily deprive the person harmed of standing to vindicate his rights. E.g., Roe v. Wade, 410 U.S. 113, 124 (1973). But it may make it substantially more difficult to meet the minimum requirement of Art. III: to establish that, in fact, the asserted injury was the consequence of the defendants' actions, or that prospective relief will remove the harm.

Here, by their own admission, realization of petitioners' desire to live in Penfield always has depended on the efforts and willingness of third parties to build low- and moderate-cost housing. The record specifically refers to only two such efforts: that of Penfield Better Homes Corp., in late 1969, to obtain the rezoning of certain land in Penfield to allow the construction of subsidized cooperative townhouses that could be purchased by persons of moderate income; and a similar effort by O'Brien Homes, Inc., in late 1971. But the record is devoid of any indication that these projects, or other like projects, would have satisfied petitioners' needs at prices they could afford, or that, were the court to remove the obstructions attributable to respondents, such relief would benefit petitioners. Indeed, petitioners' descriptions of their individual financial situations and housing needs suggest precisely the contrary—that their inability to reside in Penfield is the consequence of the economics of the area housing market, rather than of respondents' assertedly illegal acts. In short, the facts alleged fail to support an actionable causal relationship between Penfield's zoning practices and petitioners' asserted injury. . . .

IV

The petitioners who assert standing on the basis of their status as taxpayers of the city of Rochester . . . claim that . . . Penfield's persistent refusal to allow or to facilitate construction of low- and moderate-cost housing forces the city of Rochester to provide more such housing than it otherwise would do; that to provide such housing, Rochester must allow certain tax abatements; and that as the amount of tax-abated property increases, Rochester taxpayers are forced to assume an increased tax burden in order to finance essential public services. . . .

. . . Apart from the conjectural nature of the asserted injury, the line of causation between Penfield's actions and such injury is not apparent from the complaint. Whatever may occur in Penfield, the injury complained of—increases in taxation—results only from decisions made by the appropriate Rochester authorities, who are not parties to this case.

But even if we assume that the taxpayer-petitioners could establish that Penfield's zoning practices harm them, their complaint nonetheless was properly dismissed. Petitioners do not, even if they could, assert any personal right under the Constitution or any statute to be free of action by a neighboring municipality that may have some incidental adverse effect on Rochester. On the contrary, the only basis of the taxpayer-petitioners' claim is that Penfield's zoning ordinance and practices violate the constitutional and statutory rights of third parties, namely, persons of low and moderate income who are said to be excluded from Penfield. In short the claim of these petitioners falls squarely within the prudential standing rule that normally bars litigants from asserting the rights or legal interests of others in order to obtain relief from injury to themselves. As we have observed above, this rule of judicial self-governance is subject to exceptions, the most prominent of which is that Congress may remove it by statute. Here, however, no statute expressly or by clear implication grants a right of action, and thus standing to seek relief, to persons in petitioners' position. In several cases, this Court has allowed standing to litigate the rights of third parties when enforcement of the challenged restriction against the litigant would result indirectly in the violation of third parties' rights. See, e.g., Doe v. Bolton, 410 U.S. 179, 188 (1973); Griswold v. Connecticut, 381 U.S. 479, 481 (1965); Barrows v. Jackson, 346 U.S. 249 (1953). But the taxpayer-petitioners are not themselves subject to Penfield's zoning practices. Nor do they allege that the challenged zoning ordinance and practices preclude or otherwise adversely affect a relationship existing between them and the persons whose rights assertedly are violated. . . . No relationship, other than an incidental congruity of interest, is alleged to exist between the Rochester taxpayers and persons who have been precluded from living in Penfield. Nor do the taxpayer-petitioners show that their prosecution of the suit is necessary to insure protection of the rights asserted, as there is no indication that persons who in fact have been excluded from Penfield are disabled from asserting their own right in a proper case. In sum, we discern no justification for recognizing in the Rochester taxpayers a right of action on the asserted claim.

V

We turn next to the standing problems presented by the petitioner associations—Metro-Act of Rochester, Inc., one of the original plaintiffs; Housing Council in the Monroe County Area, Inc., which the original plaintiffs sought to join as a party-plaintiff; and Rochester Home Builders Association, Inc., which moved in the District Court for leave to intervene as plaintiff. . . . Even in the absence of injury to itself, an association may have standing solely as the representative of its members. E.g., National Motor Freight Assn. v. United States, 372 U.S. 246 (1963). The possibility of such representational standing, however, does not eliminate or attenuate the constitutional requirement of a case or controversy. . . . The association must allege that its members, or any one of them, are suffering immediate or threatened injury as a result of the challenged action of the sort that would make out a justiciable case had the members themselves brought suit. . . .

A

. . . Metro-Act . . . alleges . . . that 9% of its membership is composed of present residents of Penfield. It claims that, as a result of the persistent pattern of exclusionary zoning practiced by respondents and the consequent exclusion of persons of low and moderate income, those of its members who are Penfield residents are deprived of the benefits of living in a racially and ethnically integrated community. Referring to our decision in Trafficante v. Metropolitan Life Ins. Co., 409 U.S. 205 (1972), Metro-Act argues that such deprivation is a sufficiently palpable injury to satisfy the Art. III case-or-controversy requirement, and that it has standing as the representative of its members to seek redress.

We agree with the Court of Appeals that *Trafficante* is not controlling here. In that case, two residents of an apartment complex alleged that the owner had discriminated against rental applicants on the basis of race, in violation of § 804 of the Civil Rights Act of 1968, 82 Stat. 83, 42 U.S.C. § 3604. They claimed that, as a result of such discrimination, "they had been injured in that (1) they had lost the social benefits of living in an integrated community; (2) they had missed business and professional advantages which would have accrued if they had lived with members of minority groups; (3) they had suffered embarrassment and economic damage in social, business, and professional activities from being 'stigmatized' as residents of a 'white ghetto.' ". . . In light of the clear congressional purpose in enacting the 1968 Act, and the broad definition of "person aggrieved" in § 810(a), 42 U.S.C. § 3610(a), we held that petitioners, as "person[s] who claim[ed] to have been injured by a discriminatory housing practice," had standing to litigate violations of the Act. We concluded that Congress had given residents of housing facilities covered by the statute an actionable right to be free from the adverse consequences to them of racially discriminatory practices directed at and immediately harmful to others. . . .

Metro-Act does not assert on behalf of its members any right of action under the 1968 Civil Rights Act, nor can the complaint fairly be read to make out any such claim. In this, we think, lies the critical distinction between *Trafficante* and the situation here. As we have observed above, Congress may create a statutory right or entitlement the alleged deprivation of which can confer standing to sue even where the plaintiff would have suffered no judicially cognizable injury in the absence of statute. . . . No such statute is applicable here.

Even if we assume, *arguendo*, that apart from any statutorily created right the asserted harm to Metro-Act's Penfield members is sufficiently direct and personal to satisfy the case-or-controversy requirement of Art. III, prudential considerations strongly counsel against according them or Metro-Act standing to prosecute this action. We do not understand Metro-Act to argue that Penfield residents themselves have been denied any constitutional rights, affording them a cause of action under 42 U.S.C. § 1983. Instead, their complaint is that they have been harmed indirectly by the exclusion of others. This is an attempt to raise putative rights of third parties, and none of the exceptions that allow such claims is present here. In these circumstances, we conclude that it is inappropriate to allow Metro-Act to invoke the judicial process.

B

Petitioner Home Builders, in its intervenor-complaint, asserted standing to represent its member firms engaged in the development and construction of residential housing in the Rochester area, including Penfield. Home Builders alleged that the Penfield zoning restrictions, together with refusals by the town officials to grant variances and permits for the construction of low- and moderate-cost housing, had deprived some of its members of "substantial business opportunities and profits." . . .

[W]hether an association has standing to invoke the court's remedial powers on behalf of its members depends in substantial measure on the nature of the relief sought. If in a proper case the association seeks a declaration, injunction, or some other form of prospective relief, it can reasonably be supposed that the remedy, if granted, will inure to the benefit of those members of the association actually injured. Indeed, in all cases in which we have expressly recognized standing in associations to represent their members, the relief sought has been of this kind. . . .

The present case, however, differs significantly as here an association seeks relief in damages for alleged injuries to its members. . . . Moreover, in the circumstances of this case, the damages claims are not common to the entire membership, nor shared by all in equal degree. To the contrary, whatever injury may have been suffered is peculiar to the individual member concerned, and both the fact and extent of injury would require individualized proof. Thus, to obtain relief in damages, each member of Home Builders who claims injury as a result of respondents' practices must be a party to the suit, and Home Builders has no standing to claim damages on his behalf.

Home Builders' prayer for prospective relief fails for a different reason. It can have standing as the representative of its members only if it has alleged facts sufficient to make out a case or controversy had the members themselves brought suit. No such allegations were made. The complaint refers to no specific project of any of its members that is currently precluded either by the ordinance or by respondents' action in enforcing it. There is no averment that any member has applied to respondents for a building permit or a variance with respect to any current project. Indeed, there is no indication that respondents have delayed or thwarted any project currently proposed by Home Builders' members, or that any of its members has taken advantage of the remedial processes available under the ordinance. In short, insofar as the complaint seeks prospective relief, Home Builders has failed to show the existence of any injury to its members of sufficient immediacy and ripeness to warrant judicial intervention. See, e.g., United Public Workers v. Mitchell, 330 U.S. 75, 86–91 (1947). . . .

A like problem is presented with respect to petitioner Housing Council. The affidavit accompanying the motion to join it as plaintiff states that the Council includes in its membership "at least seventeen" groups that have been, are, or will be involved in the development of low- and moderate-cost housing. But, with one exception, the complaint does not suggest that any of these groups has focused its efforts on Penfield or has any specific plan to do so. Again with the same exception, neither the complaint nor any materials of record indicate that any member of Housing Council has taken any step toward building housing in Penfield, or has had dealings of any nature with respondents. The exception is the Penfield Better Homes Corp. As we have observed above, it applied to respondents in late 1969 for a zoning variance to allow construction of a housing project designed for persons of moderate income. . . . It is therefore possible that in 1969, or within a reasonable time thereafter, Better Homes itself and possibly Housing Council as its representative would have had standing to seek review of respondents' action. The complaint, however, does not allege that the Penfield Better Homes project remained viable in 1972 when this complaint was filed, or that respondents' actions continued to block a then-current construction project. . . .

Affirmed.

MR. JUSTICE BRENNAN, with whom MR. JUSTICE WHITE and MR. JUSTICE MARSHALL, join, dissenting. . . .

[The Court's] opinion, which tosses out of court almost every conceivable kind of plaintiff who could be injured by the activity claimed to be unconstitutional, can be explained only by an indefensible hostility to the claim on the merits. I can appreciate the Court's reluctance to adjudicate the complex and difficult legal questions involved. . . . But courts cannot refuse to hear a case on the merits merely because they would prefer not to, and it is quite clear, when the record is viewed with dispassion, that at least three of the groups of plaintiffs have made allegations, and supported them with affidavits and documentary evidence, sufficient to survive a motion to dismiss for lack of standing. . . .

II

Low-income and Minority Plaintiffs

. . . [P]laintiffs Ortiz, Broadnax, Reyes, and Sinkler alleged that "as a result" of respondents' exclusionary practices, they were unable, despite attempts, to find the housing they desired in Penfield, and consequently have incurred high commuting expenses, received poorer municipal services, and, in some instances, have been relegated to live in substandard housing. The Court . . . insists that these petitioners' allegations are insufficient to show that the harms suffered were *caused* by respondents' allegedly unconstitutional practices, because "their inability to reside in Penfield [may be] the consequence of the economics of the area housing market, rather than of respondents' assertedly illegal acts." . . . But, as the allegations recited above show, these petitioners have alleged precisely what our cases require—that *because* of the exclusionary practices of respondents, they cannot live in Penfield and have suffered harm.

Thus, the Court's real holding is not that these petitioners have not *alleged* an injury resulting from respondents' action, but that they are not to be allowed to prove one, because "realization of petitioners' desire to live in Penfield always has depended on the efforts and willingness of third parties to build low- and moderate-cost housing," . . . and "the record is devoid of any indication that . . . [any] projects, would have satisfied petitioners' needs at prices they could afford." . . .

Certainly, this is not the sort of demonstration that can or should be required of petitioners at this preliminary stage. In [United States v. SCRAP, 412 U.S. 669 (1973)], . . . a similar challenge was made: it was claimed that the allegations were vague, . . . and that the causation theory asserted was untrue. . . . We said: "If . . . these allegations were in fact untrue, then the appellants should have moved for summary judgment on the standing issue and demonstrated to the District Court that the allegations were sham and raised no genuine issue of fact. We cannot say . . . that the appellees could not prove their allegations which, if proved, would place them squarely among those persons injured in fact." . . .[6]

Here, the very fact that, as the Court stresses, these petitioners' claim rests in part upon proving the intentions and capabilities of third parties to build in Penfield suitable housing which they can afford, coupled with the exclusionary character of the claim on the merits, makes it particularly inappropriate to assume that these petitioners' lack of specificity reflects a fatal weakness in their theory of causation. Obviously they cannot be expected, prior to discovery and trial, to know the future plans of building companies, the precise details of the housing market in Penfield, or everything which has transpired in 15 years of application of the Penfield zoning ordinance, including every housing plan suggested and refused. To require them to allege such facts is to require them to prove their case on paper in order to get into court at all, reverting to the form of fact pleading long abjured in the federal courts. . . .

6. There is some suggestion made in the briefs that, by virtue of the inclusion in the record of affidavits and documents, the motion to dismiss was, under Fed.Rule Civ. Proc. 12(b), converted into a Rule 56 motion for summary judgment. In terms, the portion of Rule 12(b) concerning conversion to a Rule 56 motion applies only to a motion to dismiss for failure to state a cause of action, and not to a motion to dismiss for other reasons. At any rate, respondents filed no counter-affidavits proper under Rule 56(e), so, that even if Rule 56 were applied, respondents have not at this stage disproved the allegations.

III

Associations Including Building Concerns

Two of the petitioners are organizations among whose members are building concerns. Both of these organizations, Home Builders and Housing Council, alleged that these concerns have attempted to build in Penfield low- and moderate-income housing, but have been stymied by the zoning ordinance and refusal to grant individual relief therefrom. . . .

The Court finds that these two organizations lack standing to seek prospective relief for basically the same reasons: none of their members is, as far as the allegations show, *currently* involved in developing a *particular* project. . . .

Again, the Court ignores the thrust of the complaints and asks petitioners to allege the impossible. According to the allegations, the building concerns' experience in the past with Penfield officials has shown any plans for low- and moderate-income housing to be futile for, again according to the allegations, the respondents are engaged in a purposeful, conscious scheme to exclude such housing. Particularly with regard to a low- or moderate-income project, the cost of litigating, with respect to any particular project, the legality of a refusal to approve it may well be prohibitive. And the merits of the exclusion of this or that project is not at the heart of the complaint; the claim is that respondents will not approve *any* project which will provide residences for low- and moderate-income people.

When this sort of pattern-and-practice claim is at the heart of the controversy, allegations of past injury, which members of both of these organizations have clearly made, and of a future intent, if the barriers are cleared, again to develop suitable housing for Penfield, should be more than sufficient. The past experiences, if proved at trial, will give credibility and substance to the claim of interest in future building activity in Penfield. . . .

I would reverse the judgment of the Court of Appeals.

[The separate dissent of Justice Douglas is omitted.]

Notes on the Injury Requirement

(1) *Warth v. Seldin* squarely bases the requirement that a party be injured by the action of which he complains on Article III's limitation to "Cases" and "Controversies." Numerous statutes also authorize suits to be brought by persons "adversely affected or aggrieved" by the action they challenge; the Supreme Court has construed § 10 of the Administrative Procedure Act (5 U.S.C. § 702), which contains this formulation, to require an "injury in fact" to the plaintiff. Sierra Club v. Morton, 405 U.S. 727 (1972).

(2) What constitutes a sufficient "injury" to satisfy either Article III or statutes such as the APA? In Sierra Club v. Morton, supra note 1, the

Sierra Club sought declaratory and injunctive relief against the issuance of a permit to construct a ski resort in the Mineral King Valley in California. Alleging among other things that the proposed development "would destroy or otherwise adversely affect the scenery, natural and historic objects and wildlife" of an adjacent National Park and asserting "a special interest in the conservation and the sound maintenance of the national parks, game refuges, and forests of the country," the Club claimed to be "adversely affected or aggrieved" under the Administrative Procedure Act. The Court held it was not:

> The alleged injury will be felt directly only by those who use Mineral King and Sequoia National Park, and for whom the aesthetic and recreational values of the area will be lessened by the highway and ski resort. The Sierra Club failed to allege that it or its members would be affected in any of their activities or pastimes by the . . . development. Nowhere in the pleadings or affidavits did the Club state that its members use Mineral King for any purpose, much less that they use it in any way that would be significantly affected by the proposed actions of the respondents. . . . [A] mere "interest in a problem," no matter how longstanding the interest and no matter how qualified the organization is in evaluating the problem, is not sufficient by itself to render the organization "adversely affected" or "aggrieved" within the meaning of the APA. . . . [The plaintiffs] seek to do no more than vindicate their own value preferences through the judicial process.[1]

Was the crux of the problem that the Club had failed to allege that its members were offended at the prospect of a ski resort at Mineral King? Or did the Court mean to limit standing to those who actually set foot on the premises? Would that be consistent with the test of "injury in fact?" Cannot people be deeply hurt by things that happen to people they do not know? How can anyone but the plaintiff know whether he is injured by the destruction of the last grizzly bear, or by the mistreatment of blacks in South Africa?[2] Is it an answer that to allow suit on the basis of such harm would effectively allow everybody to sue under the APA, although Congress must have thought the words "affected" and "aggrieved" imposed some limit? Has this argument any force at the constitutional level?[3]

1. Cf. Valley Forge Christian College v. Americans United for Separation of Church & State, Inc., 454 U.S. 464 (1982). The lower court had held that every citizen had standing to attack the transfer of Government property to a religious organization, because the Establishment Clause arguably created "a 'personal constitutional right' to a government that does not establish religion." The Supreme Court reversed: The complaint "fail[s] to identify any personal injury suffered by the plaintiffs *as a consequence* of the alleged constitutional error, other than the psychological consequence presumably produced by the observation of conduct with which one disagrees."

2. Justice Blackmun's dissent in *Sierra* invoked John Donne: "No man is an Iland, intire of itselfe; every man is a peece of the Continent, a part of the maine; if a Clod bee washed away by the Sea, Europe is the lesse, as well as if a Promontorie were, as well as if a Mannor of thy friends or of thine owne were; any man's death diminishes me, because I am involved in Mankinde; And therefore never send to know for whom the bell tolls; it tolls for thee." Devotions XVII.

3. See Allen v. Wright, 468 U.S. 737 (1984), denying standing to blacks alleging they had been stigmatized by tax exemptions for segregated private schools to

(3) A second significant decision interpreting the injury requirement of the APA was United States v. Students Challenging Regulatory Agency Procedures (SCRAP), 412 U.S. 669 (1973). The plaintiffs argued that the National Environmental Policy Act required the Interstate Commerce Commission to prepare an environmental impact statement before allowing railroads to increase their rates for transporting scrap materials. Increased rates, the plaintiffs contended, would discourage recycling, "resulting in the need to use more natural resources to produce . . . goods, some of which . . . might be taken from the Washington area, and resulting in more refuse that might be discarded in national parks" there. Educated by *Sierra Club*, the plaintiffs in *SCRAP* alleged specifically that their members "[u]se[d] the forests, rivers, streams, mountains, and other natural resources surrounding the Washington Metropolitan Area . . . for camping, hiking, fishing, [and] sightseeing. . . ." The Court upheld standing:

> In [*Sierra Club*] . . . we made it clear that standing was not confined to those who could show "economic harm". . . . Nor, we said, could the fact that many persons shared the same injury be sufficient reason to disqualify from seeking review of an agency's action any person who had in fact suffered injury. Rather, we explained: "Aesthetic and environmental well-being, like economic well-being, are important ingredients of the quality of life in our society, and the fact that particular environmental interests are shared by the many rather than the few does not make them less deserving of legal protection through the judicial process." . . . Consequently, neither the fact that the appellees here claimed only a harm to their use and enjoyment of the natural resources of the Washington area, nor the fact that all those who use those resources suffered the same harm, deprives them of standing. . . . To deny standing to persons who are in fact injured simply because many others are also injured, would mean that the most injurious and widespread Government actions could be questioned by nobody. . . .
>
> [T]he injury alleged here is . . . very different from that at issue in *Sierra Club* because . . . [h]ere, the Court was asked to follow a far more attenuated line of causation to the eventual injury. . . . But we deal here simply with the pleadings. . . . If, as the railroads now assert, these allegations were in fact untrue, then the appellants should have moved for summary judgment . . . and demonstrated . . . that the allegations . . . raised no genuine issue of fact. . . . The railroads object to the fact that the allegations were not more precise. . . . But . . . the railroads could have moved for a more definite statement, see Fed.Rule Civ.Proc. 12(e), and certainly normal civil discovery devices were available. . . .
>
> The Government urges us to limit standing to those who have been "significantly" affected by agency action. But, even if we could begin to define what such a test would mean, we think it fundamentally misconceived. "Injury in fact" reflects the statutory requirement that

which they had not sought admission: "Recognition of standing in such circumstances would transform the federal courts into 'no more than a vehicle for the vindication of the value interests of concerned bystanders.' "

a person be "adversely affected" or "aggrieved," and it serves to distinguish a person with a direct stake in the outcome of a litigation—even though small—from a person with a mere interest in the problem. We have allowed important interests to be vindicated by plaintiffs with no more at stake in the outcome of an action than a fraction of a vote, . . . a $5 fine and costs, . . . and a $1.50 poll tax. . . . As Professor Davis has put it: ". . . an identifiable trifle is enough for standing. . . ."

Notice that this opinion resolved no fewer than five separate issues with respect to the test of injury under the APA. How does the "aesthetic" harm recognized by *SCRAP* differ from the "value preferences" rejected in *Sierra Club*? Have I standing to object to the shape of a government building on "aesthetic" grounds if I walk past without using it?

(4) The low-income plaintiffs in *Warth v. Seldin*, who alleged they were unable "as a result" of the town's practices to find housing in Penfield, were denied standing because they failed to state "facts from which" their "conclusory" allegation "reasonably could be inferred." Is this disposition consistent with *United States v. SCRAP*? Does it sit well with your recollection of the pleading requirements of the Federal Rules of Civil Procedure? Cf. the following sample complaint (Form 9) appended to these Rules and described in Rule 84 as "intended to indicate the simplicity and brevity of statement which the rules contemplate:" "On June 1, 1936, in a public highway called Boylston Street in Boston, Massachusetts, defendant negligently drove a motor vehicle against plaintiff who was then crossing said highway." See also Glus v. Brooklyn Eastern District Terminal, 359 U.S. 231 (1959): "It may well be that petitioner's complaint as now drawn is too vague, but that is no ground for dismissing his action. . . ."[4]

(5) One of the issues in the *SCRAP* case was the speculative nature of the plaintiffs' prediction of harm. Cases raising this kind of question are legion, and as often as not the Court discusses the issue as one of ripeness rather than standing. Note, for example, the treatment of the builders' standing in *Warth*; and see pp. 57–69 infra.[5] Is there any principled reason to assign this problem to one category rather than the other? Is there any need to do so?

(6) In the *SCRAP* case it was uncertain whether the plaintiffs would ever be harmed at all; what was uncertain in Linda R. S. v. Richard D., 410 U.S. 614 (1973), was whether an undoubted injury was fairly traceable to

4. Village of Arlington Heights v. Metropolitan Housing Development Corp., 429 U.S. 252 (1977), upheld the standing of a builder and a prospective tenant to challenge the refusal to rezone to allow a specific low-rent housing development. "If a court grants the relief [the latter] . . . seeks, there is at least a 'substantial probability' . . . that the Lincoln Green project will materialize, affording . . . the housing opportunity he desires in Arlington Heights. . . . [His complaint] focuses on a particular project and is not dependent on speculation about the possible actions of third parties. . . ."

5. See also City of Los Angeles v. Lyons, 461 U.S. 95 (1983), holding a plaintiff who had been subjected by police to a chokehold had no standing to seek an injunction against similar conduct in the future: "That Lyons may have been illegally choked by police on October 6, 1976, . . . does nothing to establish a real and immediate threat that he would again be stopped for a traffic violation, or for any other offense, by an officer or officers who would illegally choke him. . . ."

the challenged government action. The plaintiff was an unwed mother seeking to compel enforcement of criminal penalties for nonsupport of illegitimate children. Standing was denied: "[I]f appellant were granted the requested relief, it would result only in the jailing of the child's father. The prospect that prosecution will . . . result in payment of support can, at best, be termed only speculative." Justices White and Douglas dissented:

> I had always thought our civilization has assumed that the threat of penal sanctions had something more than a "speculative" effect on a person's conduct. . . . Texas . . . assumes that criminal sanctions are useful in coercing fathers to fulfill their support obligations to their legitimate children. . . .[6]

(7) Was the Court in *Warth* right to find the injury requirement compelled by Article III? Consider the assortment of policy reasons suggested at p. 11 supra as underlying the limitation to "Cases" and "Controversies." Is the problem the lack of assurance that an unaffected litigant will pursue his claim vigorously? Can anyone honestly entertain fears of inadequate presentation when the Sierra Club sues to protect the environment? But can the courts afford to ask in every case whether the plaintiff is comparably qualified? Or is the whole problem imaginary? "If [the] plaintiff did not have the minimal personal involvement and adverseness which Article III requires, he would not be engaging in the costly pursuit of litigation." Scott, Standing in the Supreme Court: A Functional Analysis, 86 Harv.L.Rev. 645, 674 (1973). If the fear is that suits by disinterested plaintiffs may be collusive, have we no means of preventing collusion short of an absolute bar that excludes non-collusive suits as well?

Is the problem essentially that there is insufficient public interest to justify the expenditure of scarce judicial resources and the risk of conflict with other organs of government when the plaintiff has not been hurt by the action of which he complains? Would that be true of a suit to prevent government action that injures nobody in the *Sierra Club* sense, such as destruction of the last specimen of a deep-sea organism of no commercial value? See Sax, Standing to Sue: A Critical Review of the Mineral King Decision, 13 Nat.Resources J. 76, 78–79, 81 (1973), arguing that *Sierra Club* means some issues worthy of judicial attention may never be decided. But see Schlesinger v. Reservists Committee to Stop the War, 418 U.S. 208, 227 (1974): "The assumption that if respondents have no standing . . ., no one would . . ., is not a reason to find standing."

Justice Frankfurter's famous concurring opinion in Joint Anti-Fascist Refugee Committee v. McGrath, 341 U.S. 123, 149 (1951), viewed the "Case"

6. See also Simon v. Eastern Ky. Welfare Rights Org., 426 U.S. 26 (1976), denying indigent plaintiffs standing to attack a revenue ruling allowing charitable tax status to hospitals in their area that offered only limited service to indigents: It was "purely speculative" that the Revenue Ruling was responsible for the limitation of services, and "the complaint suggests no substantial likelihood that victory in this suit would result in respondents' receiving the hospital treatment they desire." Accord Allen v. Wright, 468 U.S. 737 (1984), terming it "speculative" whether invalidation of tax exemptions for segregated private institutions would promote integration of public schools.

or "Controversy" requirement in historical terms, limiting the courts to those determinations "consonant with what was, generally speaking, the business of the Colonial courts and the courts of Westminster when the Constitution was framed." Is this the correct approach? If so, is the injury requirement at all surprising? Can I sue at common law because my neighbor has been swallowed by a garbage compactor? Yet Professor Berger, in Standing to Sue in Public Actions: Is it a Constitutional Requirement? 78 Yale L.J. 816, 827 (1969), argues that historical practice does not support any constitutional requirement of injury in challenges to governmental action: "At the adoption of the Constitution . . . the English practice in prohibition, certiorari, quo warranto, and informers' and relators' actions encouraged strangers to attack unauthorized action."

(8) In the *Sierra Club* case, supra note 1, the Court declared in dictum: "[W]here a dispute is otherwise justiciable, the question whether a litigant is a 'proper party to request an adjudication of a particular issue' . . . is one within the power of Congress to determine." And see the explicit dictum of Mr. Justice Harlan, of all people, dissenting from the upholding of jurisdiction in Flast v. Cohen, 392 U.S. 83, 116 (1968), that "public actions" (i.e., those in which a citizen sues as representative of the public interest) are "within the jurisdiction conferred . . . by Article III. . . . Any hazards to the proper allocation of authority among the three branches of the Government would be substantially diminished if public actions had been pertinently authorized by Congress and the President." Do these observations retain any validity after *Warth*? [7]

Notes on Standing Requirements Beyond Injury

(1) The preceding notes dealt with the question whether injury was necessary for standing. The remaining question is whether injury is sufficient.

Warth v. Seldin denied standing to two groups of plaintiffs the Court assumed to have been injured: Penfield residents wishing to live in a diversified community and Rochester residents paying extra taxes. Earlier decisions had often refused to allow attacks by persons clearly suffering injury, but the applicable criteria have varied over the years.

Illustrative of the Court's early approach are Alabama Power Co. v. Ickes, 302 U.S. 464 (1938), and Tennessee Electric Power Co. v. TVA, 306 U.S. 118 (1939), in which electric companies were denied standing to argue that States' rights were infringed and the plaintiffs deprived of property without due process by federal loans to their municipal competitors and by direct TVA competition. Any injury to the plaintiffs, the Court said in *Tennessee Power*, was "damnum absque injuria," for the plaintiffs had no

7. See also United States ex rel. Marcus v. Hess, 317 U.S. 537, 541 n. 4 (1943), where without adverting to any constitutional problem the Court upheld a judgment in favor of an apparently unconcerned plaintiff who had sued as authorized by statute to recover damages, half for himself and half for the government, from a contractor for defrauding the United States: "'Statutes providing for actions by a common informer, who himself has no interest whatever in the controversy other than that given by the statute, have been in existence for hundreds of years in England, and in this country ever since the foundation of our government.' . . ."

"legal right" to be free from competition; in a private suit a corporation could not argue that its competitor was acting ultra vires, and that was the essence of the complaint.

(2) The "legal right" limitation was much criticized, e.g., 3 K. Davis, Administrative Law Treatise 217–18 (1958), and in an important 1970 decision it was abandoned, at least for purposes of the Administrative Procedure Act. Association of Data Processing Service Organizations, Inc. v. Camp, 397 U.S. 150 (1970). The plaintiffs were in the data processing business; they challenged a ruling by the Comptroller of the Currency allowing national banks to provide similar services. Injury in the Article III sense was clear: "The petitioners not only allege that competition by national banks . . . might entail some future loss of profits . . ., they also allege that respondent American National Bank . . . was performing or preparing to perform such services for two customers for whom petitioner Data Systems, Inc., had previously agreed or negotiated to perform such services." This was precisely the sort of injury the Court had held insufficient in the *TVA* cases, but the Court in *Data Processing* upheld standing:

> The "legal interest" test goes to the merits. The question of standing is different. It concerns, apart from the "case" or "controversy" test, the question whether the interest sought to be protected by the complainant is arguably within the zone of interests to be protected or regulated by the statute or constitutional guarantee in question. Thus the Administrative Procedure Act grants standing to a person "aggrieved by agency action within the meaning of a relevant statute." 5 U.S.C. § 702. . . .

Section 4 of the Bank Service Corporation Act, Justice Douglas continued, expressly limited bank service corporations to "the performance of bank services . . .," and a lower court had held the purpose of the statute was to protect competitors. "We do not put the issue in those words," said the Court, "for they implicate the merits. We do think, however, that § 4 arguably brings a competitor within the zone of interests protected by it. . . ." Do you read this opinion as announcing a new test for standing in general or only an interpretation of the APA?

(3) *Warth* did not mention the "zone of interests" test; the opinion seems to say that "prudential" standing limitations bar only those parties who seek to litigate "generalized grievances" or the rights of third parties. But the zone test was restored to the list of general prudential considerations in Valley Forge Christian College v. Americans United for Separation of Church & State, Inc., 454 U.S. 464 (1982) (dictum), and applied to uphold standing in Clarke v. Securities Industry Ass'n, 479 U.S. 388 (1987), with the admonition that it was "not a test of universal application" but a "gloss" on the " 'generous review provisions' " of the APA.

(4) Cited by *Warth* in support of the "generalized grievance" exception was Schlesinger v. Reservists Committee to Stop the War, 418 U.S. 208 (1974), an action alleging that Article I's provision forbidding persons "holding any Office under the United States" to serve in Congress excluded legislators from the military reserves: Any violation of this clause "would adversely affect only the generalized interest of all citizens in constitution-

al governance, and that is an abstract injury" to an interest "too abstract to constitute a 'case or controversy' . . ." Notice that *Warth* purports to shift this exception out of the constitutional category into the prudential.

Is the "generalized grievance" theory compatible with the *SCRAP* case, summarized at p. 43 above? Is there any answer to the policy argument made against such an exception in that case?

(5) Why shouldn't parties be allowed to assert the rights of others? Sometimes the answer is easy. In McGowan v. Maryland, 366 U.S. 420 (1961), defendants on trial for selling goods on Sunday were denied standing to argue that the blue laws violated the religious freedom of unidentified Sabbatarians. Given the prevalent severability principle, had a non-Sabbatarian anything to gain in the Article III sense by proving that the statute could not be applied to somebody else?

Did the claims of third-party rights in *Warth v. Seldin* fit this pattern? Could the constitutional rights of persons excluded from Penfield have been vindicated without removing the asserted obstacle to the diversified community the plaintiffs desired? Why should standing to raise a third party's rights be denied to one who, as in the latter case, stands to gain by raising them?

Prominent among decisions allowing a party to assert the rights of others is Barrows v. Jackson, 346 U.S. 249 (1953), in which a "Caucasian," sued for damages for selling a home to "non-Caucasians" in breach of a restrictive covenant, was permitted to argue that enforcement of the covenant would deny equal protection to "unidentified but identifiable" non-Caucasians: "[I]t would be difficult if not impossible for the persons whose rights are asserted to present their grievance before any court." [1]

1. See also NAACP v. Alabama, 357 U.S. 449 (1958), allowing the association to resist a demand for its membership lists by invoking the constitutional rights of its members to keep their affiliation secret: "To require that it be claimed by the members themselves would result in nullification of the right at the very moment of its assertion."

Should it matter, in determining standing to raise the rights of others, whether the party seeking to do so is a plaintiff or a defendant? Professor Davis thinks so:

> When the judicial machinery is already in motion and the question before the court is the direction of the action to be taken, the court on its own motion, whether or not any party urges it, may reject a course of action which would involve unconstitutionality . . ., for the court has the affirmative obligation of avoiding any judicial action that would be unconstitutional. . . .

3 Administrative Law Treatise 234 (1958). Notice how this argument builds upon the clean-hands idea of *Marbury v. Madison.*

The Davis theory received some support in Griswold v. Connecticut, 381 U.S. 479 (1965), a criminal prosecution in which a doctor was allowed to argue the rights of his patients to use contraceptives. An earlier case refusing to hear a similar contention was distinguished because it had been a suit for declaratory relief: "Certainly the accessory should have standing to assert that the offense which he is charged with assisting is not, or cannot constitutionally be, a crime." But the Court added, citing *Barrows v. Jackson*, that the patients' rights might be diluted if the doctor were not allowed to assert them. Moreover, in Craig v. Boren, 429 U.S. 190, 196 n. 5 (1976), a suit to enjoin enforcement of a statute, the Court relied on a precedent involving a criminal defendant to sustain standing:

> The fact that Baird [in the earlier case] chose to disobey the legal duty imposed upon him by the Massachusetts anticontraception statute, resulting in his criminal conviction, . . . does not distinguish the standing inquiry. . . . The exis-

When the issue is phrased in terms of standing to assert the rights of others, the answer may seem easy. Why was it so clear in *Warth* that the constitutional provisions invoked did not also give the residents of Penfield the right to live in an integrated community?

(6) "[A]part from Art. III's minimum requirements," said the Court in *Warth*, the essence of the standing question "is whether the constitutional or statutory provision on which the claim rests properly can be understood as granting persons in the plaintiff's position a right to judicial relief."

Many statutes expressly authorize suits by specified classes of litigants: Witness the provision in the *Trafficante* case, discussed in *Warth*, permitting actions by "any person who claims to have been injured by a discriminatory housing practice." [2]

Another historically significant example is the Communications Act, 47 U.S.C. § 402(b)(6), which authorizes challenges to the grant of broadcast licenses by any "person who is aggrieved or whose interests are adversely affected." In FCC v. Sanders Bros. Radio Station, 309 U.S. 470 (1940), the Court on the basis of this section allowed a broadcaster not only to attack the issuance of a license to a competitor (despite the *TVA* cases discussed in note 1 supra), but to assert the interests of the public as well as his own:

> Congress . . . may have been of opinion that one likely to be financially injured by the issue of a license would be the only person having a sufficient interest to bring to the attention of the appellate court errors of law in the action of the Commission. . . . It is within the power of Congress to confer such standing. . . .

(7) Section 10(a) of the Administrative Procedure Act, 5 U.S.C. § 702, contains an important standing provision:

> A person suffering legal wrong because of agency action, or adversely affected or aggrieved by agency action within the meaning of a relevant statute, is entitled to judicial review thereof.

Professor Davis has long argued that this provision subjects governmental action, otherwise reviewable, to challenge by any person "in fact adversely affected," 3 K. Davis, Administrative Law Treatise 291 (1958), and his view received some judicial support. See Scanwell Laboratories, Inc. v. Shaffer, 424 F.2d 859 (D.C.Cir. 1970). The committee reports had explained that the provision "confers a right of review upon any person adversely affected in fact by agency action or aggrieved within the meaning of any statute." See S.Doc.No. 248, 79th Cong., 2d Sess. 212, 276 (1946). This purported paraphrase of the statutory language, argues Professor Davis, "tends to show that the words 'within the meaning of any statute' do not modify 'adversely affected in fact,' " and thus that any person adversely affected in fact by agency action is entitled to review. See Davis, The Liberalized Law

tence of Art. III "injury in fact" and the structure of the claimant's relationship to the third parties are not altered by the litigative posture of the suit.

2. In support of its broad construction of this provision the Court observed that proponents of the bill had recognized that "[t]he person on the landlord's blacklist is not the only victim of discriminatory housing practices; it is, as Senator Javits said . . ., 'the whole community.' " Trafficante v. Metropolitan Life Insurance Co., 409 U.S. 205 (1972).

of Standing, 37 U.Chi.L.Rev. 450, 466–67 (1970); Administrative Law Text 436–37 (3d ed. 1972).

The initial judicial interpretation, however, was otherwise. The Attorney General's Manual on the Administrative Procedure Act, an influential contemporaneous explanation of the statute for the guidance of affected agencies, had described the standing provision as follows:

> "[L]egal wrong" means such wrong as particular statutes and the courts have recognized as constituting grounds for judicial review. "Adversely affected or aggrieved" has frequently been used in statutes to designate the persons who can obtain judicial review of administrative action [citing, among others, the Communications Act provision referred to in note 6, supra]. . . . The determination of who is "adversely affected or aggrieved . . . within the meaning of any relevant statute" has "been marked out largely by the gradual judicial process of inclusion and exclusion, aided at times by the courts' judgment as to the probable legislative intent derived from the spirit of the statutory scheme." . . . The Attorney General advised the Senate Committee . . . of his understanding that section 10(a) was a restatement of existing law. More specifically he indicated . . . that section 10(a) preserved the rules developed by the courts in such cases as Alabama Power Co. v. Ickes [supra note 1] . . . and Federal Communications Commission v. Sanders Bros. Radio Station [supra note 6]. . . . This construction of section 10(a) was not questioned or contradicted in the legislative history.

Relying on the Manual, the District of Columbia Circuit in Kansas City Power and Light Co. v. McKay, 225 F.2d 924, 931–32 (D.C.Cir. 1955), refused standing of an APA suit to enjoin the Secretary of Interior from allegedly unlawful assistance to competitors of the plaintiffs. As in the *TVA* cases described in note 1 supra, the plaintiffs had no "legal right" to be free from competition; "[n]or are we confronted with any relevant statute within the meaning of which the plaintiffs are 'adversely affected or aggrieved.'" In short § 10(a), like many other provisions of the APA, created no new rights of its own; it merely recognized standing created by other statutes for persons "adversely affected or aggrieved. . . ."

The Supreme Court in the *Data Processing* case (supra note 2), however, adopted yet a third construction of the APA provision. As paraphrased in Sierra Club v. Morton, 405 U.S. 727 (1972), *Data Processing* held "that persons had standing to obtain judicial review of federal agency action under § 10 of the APA where they had alleged that the challenged action had caused them 'injury in fact,' and where the alleged injury was to an interest 'arguably within the zone of interests to be protected or regulated' by the statutes that the agencies were claimed to have violated."

How does one fit the zone test into the language of the APA?

(8) The Court in *Data Processing* relied on decisions finding standing on the basis of substantive statutory provisions that were silent on the subject. Especially noteworthy was Hardin v. Kentucky Utilities Co., 390 U.S. 1 (1968), which allowed a competing public utility to enforce a geographical limitation on TVA operations. It was true, wrote Justice

Black, that cases such as *Tennessee Power Co. v. TVA* (supra note 1) had often held mere competitive injury insufficient; but

> competitive injury provided no basis for standing in the above cases simply because the statutory and constitutional requirements that the plaintiff sought to enforce were in no way concerned with protecting against competitive injury. In contrast, it has been the rule, at least since the Chicago Junction Case, 264 U.S. 258 (1924), that when the particular statutory provision invoked does reflect a legislative purpose to protect a competitive interest, the injured competitor has standing to require compliance with that provision. . . .
>
> [I]t is clear and undisputed that protection of private utilities from TVA competition was almost universally regarded as the primary objective of the limitation. Since the respondent is thus in the class which § 15d is designed to protect, it has standing under familiar judicial principles to bring this suit, . . . and no explicit statutory provision is necessary to confer standing.

Doesn't *Hardin* equate the test of whether a statute implicitly creates standing with the question whether a statute implicitly creates a right of action on behalf of those injured by its violation? See *J. I. Case Co. v. Borak*, infra p. 376, upholding a private damage action by a shareholder for violation of SEC proxy rules: Among the "chief purposes" of the statutory provision in question, wrote Justice Clark, "is 'the protection of investors,' which certainly implies the availability of judicial relief where necessary to achieve that result."

Does *Data Processing* mean that a person is "adversely affected or aggrieved within the meaning of a relevant statute" whenever the statute is construed, as in *Hardin*, to provide an implicit remedy to members of the protected class? If so, *Data Processing* does not reject the basic principle of the *Kansas City Power* case (supra note 7) at all: The APA still is not an independent grant of standing.[3]

(9) The doctrine of implicit remedies applied in the *Hardin* and *Borak* cases just noted has an impressive common-law-pedigree. Section 286 of the first Restatement of Torts, for example, announced in 1934:

> The violation of a legislative enactment . . . makes the actor liable for an invasion of an interest of another if:
>
> (a) the intent of the enactment is exclusively or in part to protect an interest of the other as an individual; and
>
> (b) the interest invaded is one which the enactment is intended to protect. . . .

The lawmaking powers of the federal courts, however, are severely limited. 28 U.S.C. § 1652 provides that "[t]he laws of the several states, except where the Constitution or treaties of the United States . . . otherwise

3. See, however, Clarke v. Securities Industry Ass'n, 479 U.S. 388 (1987), contrasting a later decision in the *Borak* line that had required plaintiffs to show they were within " 'the class for whose *especial* benefit the statute was enacted' ": "Clearly, the Court was requiring more from the would-be plaintiffs in [that case] than a showing that their interests were arguably within the zone protected or regulated by" the statute.

require or provide, shall be regarded as rules of decision in civil actions in the courts of the United States, in cases where they apply." After Erie Railroad Co. v. Tompkins, 304 U.S. 64 (1938), the term "laws" includes judge-made law: "There is no federal general common law." Can it really be said in a case like *Hardin* or *Borak* that *Congress* has implicitly created a right of action?

Recent Supreme Court decisions, responsive to these concerns, have cut back sharply on the *Borak* doctrine that statutory beneficiaries enjoy implicit rights to sue for damages. See pp. 370–79 below. Shouldn't these decisions have implications for implicit "standing" cases like *Hardin* and *Data Processing*?

(10) The Court in *Warth* described the nonconstitutional standing question as one of implied remedies; yet it dismissed the resident and taxpayer claims on the unrelated "prudential" ground that they sought to litigate the rights of third parties, without inquiring whether any statute or constitutional provision gave the plaintiffs a right to sue. Shouldn't that have been the threshold question?

Warth, the opinion tells us, was an action under (inter alia) 42 U.S.C. § 1983, whose language the Court never considered:

> Every person who, under color of any statute, ordinance, regulation, custom, or usage, of any State or Territory, subjects . . . any . . . person . . . to the deprivation of any rights, privileges, or immunities secured by the Constitution and laws, shall be liable to the party injured in an action at law, suit in equity, or other proper proceeding for redress.

Did any of the *Warth* plaintiffs have standing under § 1983?

A second relevant statute in *Warth* was the Declaratory Judgment Act, 28 U.S.C. § 2201, for the plaintiffs asked the court to "declare" the ordinance unconstitutional:

> In a case of actual controversy within its jurisdiction, . . . any court of the United States . . . may declare the rights and other legal relations of any interested party seeking such declaration. . . .

Did this Act confer standing on the plaintiffs in *Warth*? Or does it merely affect the timing and party alignment of controversies otherwise litigable in federal court? See Skelly Oil Co. v. Phillips Petroleum Co., p. 151 infra.

If no statute gives the plaintiffs a right to sue, has the Court any right to entertain the action after the *Erie* decision? If on the other hand a statute *did* give the plaintiffs in *Warth* a right to sue, what business had the Court in invoking its own "prudential" notions to refuse to hear them?[4]

Notes on Special Standing Problems: Taxpayers, Governments, and Officers

(1) In Massachusetts (Frothingham) v. Mellon, 262 U.S. 447 (1923), the Supreme Court held a federal taxpayer had no standing to challenge the

4. See generally Currie, Misunderstanding Standing, 1981 Sup.Ct.Rev. 41.

constitutionality of conditional federal grants to the States to promote maternal health: The interest of a taxpayer in federal funds "is shared with millions of others; is comparatively minute and indeterminable; and the effect upon future taxation, of any payment out of the funds, so remote, fluctuating and uncertain, that no basis is afforded for an appeal to the preventive powers of a court of equity." To resolve the case, the Court added, "would be not to decide a judicial controversy. . . ."

The grants in *Frothingham* were paid out of general revenues; when a special tax was levied solely to finance the challenged expenditure, the Court upheld taxpayer standing, United States v. Butler, 297 U.S. 1, 57–61 (1936). What is the basis for distinction?

Did Ms. Frothingham suffer no constitutionally sufficient injury? Or was the decision based on what the Court now calls "prudential" considerations?

(2) Flast v. Cohen, 392 U.S. 83 (1968), upheld the standing of federal taxpayers to enjoin expenditures from general revenues that they argued were used to support religious instruction in violation of the Establishment Clause of the First Amendment. Chief Justice Warren's opinion established a two-stage test for taxpayer standing:

> First, the taxpayer must establish a logical link between that status and the type of legislative enactment attacked. Thus, a taxpayer will be a proper party to allege the unconstitutionality only of exercises of congressional power under the taxing and spending clause of Art. I, § 8, of the Constitution. It will not be sufficient to allege an incidental expenditure of tax funds in the administration of an essentially regulatory statute. . . . Secondly, the taxpayer must establish a nexus between that status and the precise nature of the constitutional infringement alleged. Under this requirement the taxpayer must show that the challenged enactment exceeds specific constitutional limitations imposed upon the exercise of the congressional taxing and spending power and not simply that the enactment is generally beyond the powers delegated to Congress by Art. I, § 8. . . .
>
> The taxpayer-appellants in this case have satisfied both nexuses to support their claim of standing under the test we announce today. Their constitutional challenge is made to an exercise by Congress of its power under Art. I, § 8, to spend for the general welfare, and the challenged program involves a substantial expenditure of federal tax funds. In addition, appellants have alleged that the challenged expenditures violate the Establishment and Free Exercise Clauses of the First Amendment. Our history vividly illustrates that one of the specific evils feared by those who drafted the Establishment Clause and fought for its adoption was that the taxing and spending power would be used to favor one religion over another or to support religion in general. . . . The Establishment Clause was designed as a specific bulwark against such potential abuses of governmental power, and that clause of the First Amendment operates as a specific constitutional limitation upon the exercise by Congress of the taxing and spending power conferred by Art. I, § 8.

> The allegations of the taxpayer in *Frothingham v. Mellon* . . . were quite different from those made in this case, and the result in *Frothingham* is consistent with the test of taxpayer standing announced today. The taxpayer in *Frothingham* attacked a federal spending program and she, therefore, established the first nexus required. However, she lacked standing because her constitutional attack was not based on an allegation that Congress, in enacting the Maternity Act of 1921, had breached a specific limitation upon its taxing and spending power. The taxpayer in *Frothingham* alleged essentially that Congress, by enacting the challenged statute, had exceeded the general powers delegated to it by Art. I, § 8, and that Congress had thereby invaded the legislative province reserved to the States by the Tenth Amendment. . . . In essence, Mrs. Frothingham was attempting to assert the States' interest in their legislative prerogatives and not a federal taxpayer's interest in being free of taxing and spending in contravention of specific constitutional limitations imposed upon Congress' taxing and spending power. . . .

Justice Douglas concurred on the ground that *Frothingham* should be overruled, and Justice Harlan dissented.

Was the test of injury in fact satisfied in *Flast*? Or did *Flast*, by its inattention to the question, hold that injury was not required? If there was a constitutionally sufficient injury, was it any less a "generalized grievance" than the alleged injury in *Frothingham*? What law supplied the plaintiff's right of action in *Flast*? Is there any reason why the Court should have set up totally different criteria for determining taxpayer standing from those governing all other cases?

(3) In United States v. Richardson, 418 U.S. 166 (1974), a taxpayer sought a statement of CIA expenditures on the basis of Article I's requirement that "a regular Statement . . . of the . . . Expenditures of all public Money shall be published from time to time." Standing was denied:

> Although the status [Richardson] . . . rests on is that he is a taxpayer, his challenge is not addressed to the taxing or spending power. . . . Respondent makes no claim that appropriated funds are being spent in violation of a "specific constitutional limitation upon the . . . taxing and spending power. . . . Thus there is no "logical nexus" between the asserted status of taxpayer and the claimed failure of the Congress to require the Executive to supply a more detailed report of the expenditures of that agency.

The Court went on, quite unnecessarily, to add that Richardson was asserting a "generalized grievance . . . 'common to all members of the public.'" Wouldn't it have sufficed to point out that Richardson's tax bill would not have been reduced if he had won?

(4) Valley Forge Christian College v. Americans United for Separation of Church & State, Inc., 454 U.S. 464 (1982). Taxpayers challenged the transfer of Government property to a religious institution on Establishment Clause grounds. Over four dissents, *Flast* was distinguished and standing denied:

> First, the source of [the plaintiffs'] . . . complaint is not a congressional action, but a decision by HEW. . . . Second, and perhaps

> redundantly, the property transfer was not an exercise of authority conferred by the taxing and spending clause [but] . . . the authorizing legislation . . . was an evident exercise of Congress' power under the Property Clause, Art. IV, § 3, cl. 2.

Why these distinctions ought to make a difference the Court did not say.[1]

(5) The *Flast* opinion explains *Frothingham* on the ground that the wrong party sued: The taxpayer was asserting the rights of the State. But the same opinion that held Ms. Frothingham could not attack the Maternity Act because the issue was of "public" rather than "individual" concern held that Massachusetts could not attack it either:

> In the last analysis, the complaint of the plaintiff State is brought to the naked contention that Congress has usurped the reserved powers of the several States by the mere enactment of the statute, though nothing has been done and nothing is to be done without their consent; and it is plain that that question, as it is thus presented, is political, and not judicial in character, and therefore is not a matter which admits of the exercise of the judicial power. . . . [W]e are called upon to adjudicate, not rights of person or property, not rights of dominion over physican domain, not quasi-sovereign rights actually invaded or threatened, but abstract questions of political power, of sovereignty, or government. . . .

If the constitutionality of the Maternity Act was a political question in the sense in which that term is used in such cases as *Baker v. Carr*, infra p. 80, then why was it necessary to go on and discuss the standing of Ms. Frothingham? Isn't it true that no one may raise a political question? Perhaps the Court meant that the only interest of the State allegedly injured was a governmental rather than a proprietary one, and that only the latter would suffice for standing.[2] Why should that be? How would that square with the general principle that a government officer has standing to defend the constitutionality of a statute he is charged with enforcing?

(6) The State also attempted to achieve standing in *Massachusetts v. Mellon*, supra, as the representative of its citizens. The Court again said no:

> The citizens of Massachusetts are also citizens of the United States. It cannot be conceded that a State, as *parens patriae*, may institute judicial proceedings to protect citizens of the United States from the operation of the statutes thereof. While the State, under some circumstances, may sue in that capacity for the protection of its citizens (Missouri v. Illinois, 180 U.S. 208, 241), it is no part of its duty or power to enforce their rights in respect of their relations with the Federal Government. In that field it is the United States, and not the State,

1. See also Bowen v. Kendrick, 487 U.S. 589 (1988), reaffirming *Flast* and permitting a taxpayer to attack a spending law on establishment grounds both on its face and as applied.

2. See Gladstone, Realtors v. Village of Bellwood, 441 U.S. 91, 110–111 (1979), upholding the constitutional standing of a municipality to attack allegedly discriminatory practices tending to replace "an integrated neighborhood with a segregated one": The resultant "reduction in property values directly injures a municipality by diminishing its tax base . . . ."

> which represents them as *parens patriae*, when such representation becomes appropriate. . . .

Just why it was appropriate to look to the federal government to protect the citizen from the federal government, the Court did not say. Cf. New Hampshire v. Louisiana, 108 U.S. 76 (1883), holding a State's suit as assignee for collection of its citizens' bonds barred by the Eleventh Amendment; Oklahoma v. Atchison, T. & S. F. Ry., 220 U.S. 277, 289 (1911), holding that a State could not invoke the Supreme Court's original jurisdiction to restrain the carrier from charging unreasonable rates in Oklahoma:

> The words, in the Constitution, conferring original jurisdiction on this court, in a suit "in which a State shall be a party" are not to be interpreted as conferring such jurisdiction in every cause in which the State elects to make itself strictly a party plaintiff of record and seeks not to protect its own property, but only to vindicate the wrongs of some of its people. . . .

In view of the particular policies limiting suits against States and the Supreme Court's original jurisdiction, should these decisions be authority for precluding comparable suits by States against individual defendants in the federal district courts for lack of standing?

In *Missouri v. Illinois*, which the Court distinguished in *Massachusetts*, the Court entertained an original suit by a State objecting to the dumping of sewage into an interstate channel to the detriment of its citizens: "If the health and comfort of the inhabitants of a State are threatened, the State is the proper party to represent and defend them." In Georgia v. Pennsylvania R. R., 324 U.S. 439, 446–52 (1945), the Court allowed a State to sue in the original jurisdiction "as *parens patriae* acting in behalf of her citizens" under the federal antitrust laws. Unlike *Massachusetts v. Mellon*, the Court said, the case was not one "where the United States rather than Georgia stands as *parens patriae* to the citizens of Georgia" nor "where a State sought to protect her citizens from the operation of federal statutes." Will these distinctions hold water?

(7) Coleman v. Miller, 307 U.S. 433, 438 (1939), upheld the standing of members of a state legislature to challenge the efficacy of the State's purported ratification of a proposed constitutional statement against which they had voted: "[T]he plaintiffs include twenty senators, whose votes against ratification have been overridden and virtually held for naught although if they are right in their contentions their votes would have been sufficient to defeat ratification." Board of Education v. Allen, 392 U.S. 236, 241 n. 5 (1968), allowed local school board members to attack the constitutionality of a state statute they were charged with enforcing:

> Appellants have taken an oath to support the United States Constitution. Believing § 701 to be unconstitutional, they are in the position of having to choose between violating their oath and taking a step—refusal to comply with § 701—that would be likely to bring their expulsion from office and also a reduction in state funds for their school districts. There can be no doubt that appellants thus have a "personal stake in the outcome" of this litigation.[3]

3. The Ninth Circuit, believing *Allen* no longer law because of *Warth* and other decisions "which significantly tightened standing requirements," has refused to fol-

In Mitchell v. Laird, 488 F.2d 611, 614 (1973), the District of Columbia Circuit upheld the standing of members of Congress to attack the Vietnam war because a declaration that the war was unconstitutional "would bear upon the duties of plaintiffs to consider whether to impeach defendants, and upon plaintiffs' quite distinct and different duties to make appropriations to support the hostilities, or to take other legislative actions related to such hostilities, such as raising an army or enacting other civil or criminal legislation." Is this any more than to say they had reason to request an advisory opinion? Another panel of the same court held in Harrington v. Bush, 553 F.2d 190, 198, 209 (D.C.Cir. 1977), that *Mitchell* was no longer law.[4] Has Congress itself standing to protect its own prerogatives?

ABBOTT LABORATORIES v. GARDNER

387 U.S. 136 (1967).

MR. JUSTICE HARLAN delivered the opinion of the Court.

In 1962 Congress amended the Federal Food, Drug, and Cosmetic Act (. . . 21 U.S.C. § 301 *et seq.*), to require manufacturers of prescription drugs to print the "established name" of the drug "prominently and in type at least half as large as that used thereon for any proprietary name or designation for such drug," on labels and other printed material. . . . The underlying purpose of the 1962 amendment was to bring to the attention of doctors and patients the fact that many of the drugs sold under familiar trade names are actually identical to drugs sold under their "established" or less familiar trade names at significantly lower prices. The Commissioner of Food and Drugs . . . promulgated the following regulation for the "efficient enforcement" of the Act, § 701(a), 21 U.S.C. § 371(a):

> "If the label or labeling of a prescription drug bears a proprietary name or designation for the drug or any ingredient thereof, the established name, if such there be, corresponding to such proprietary name or designation, shall accompany each appearance of such proprietary name or designation." 21 CFR § 1.104(g)(1).

A similar rule was made applicable to advertisements for prescription drugs, 21 CFR § 1.105(b)(1).

low it: The prospect of liability for enforcing the challenged provision was "wholly speculative," and "no consequences, save those of conscience . . ., flow from the violation of the oath. . . ." City of South Lake Tahoe v. California Tahoe Regional Planning Agency, 625 F.2d 231, 236–39 (9th Cir. 1980).

4 "[The Congressman] does not allege that he as a litigant would profit or lose, depending upon our determination of legality. . . . Appellant's real interest is in having the question of . . . legality . . . decided *one way or the other*. . . . *[E]ither* result would serve his asserted need for information bearing upon legislative action relating to the CIA."

See also the en banc decision in Goldwater v. Carter, 617 F.2d 697, 702 (D.C.Cir. 1979), reversed on other grounds, 444 U.S. 996, p. 97 infra, reviewing the cases and upholding the standing of Senators to challenge the President's unilateral termination of a treaty: "By excluding the Senate from the treaty termination process, the President has deprived each individual Senator of his alleged right to cast a vote that will have binding effect on whether the Treaty can be terminated."

The present action was brought by a group of 37 individual drug manufacturers and by the Pharmaceutical Manufacturers Association, of which all the petitioner companies are members, and which includes manufacturers of more than 90% of the Nation's supply of prescription drugs. They challenged the regulations on the ground that the Commissioner exceeded his authority under the statute by promulgating an order requiring labels, advertisements, and other printed matter relating to prescription drugs to designate the established name of the particular drug involved every time its trade name is used anywhere in such material. . . . [The District Court held the challenged regulations invalid; the Court of Appeals reversed for want of jurisdiction.

[The Administrative Procedure Act provides for judicial review of "final agency action for which there is no other adequate remedy in a court," unless some statute precludes relief or commits the action to agency discretion, 5 U.S.C. §§ 704, 701(a). The Court first held that "nothing in the Food, Drug, and Cosmetic Act itself precludes this action."]

The injunctive and declaratory judgment remedies are discretionary, and courts traditionally have been reluctant to apply them to administrative determinations unless these arise in the context of a controversy "ripe" for judicial resolution. Without undertaking to survey the intricacies of the ripeness doctrine it is fair to say that its basic rationale is to prevent the courts, through avoidance of premature adjudication, from entangling themselves in abstract disagreements over administrative policies, and also to protect the agencies from judicial interference until an administrative decision has been formalized and its effects felt in a concrete way by the challenging parties. The problem is best seen in a twofold aspect, requiring us to evaluate both the fitness of the issues for judicial decision and the hardship to the parties of withholding court consideration.

As to the former factor, we believe the issues presented are appropriate for judicial resolution at this time. First, all parties agree that the issue tendered is a purely legal one: whether the statute was properly construed by the Commissioner to require the established name of the drug to be used *every time* the proprietary name is employed. Both sides moved for summary judgment in the District Court, and no claim is made here that further administrative proceedings are contemplated. It is suggested that the justification for this rule might vary with different circumstances, and that the expertise of the Commissioner is relevant to passing upon the validity of the regulation. This of course is true, but the suggestion overlooks the fact that both sides have approached this case as one purely of congressional intent, and that the Government made no effort to justify the regulation in factual terms.

Second, the regulations in issue we find to be "final agency action" within the meaning of § 10 of the Administrative Procedure Act, 5 U.S.C. § 704, as construed in judicial decisions. An "agency action" includes any "rule," defined by the Act as "an agency statement of general or particular applicability and future effect designed to implement, interpret, or prescribe law or policy," §§ 2(c), 2(g), 5 U.S.C. §§ 551(4), 551(13). The cases dealing with judicial review of administrative actions have interpreted the "finality" element in a pragmatic way. Thus in Columbia Broadcasting System v. United States, 316 U.S. 407, . . . this Court held reviewable a regulation of the Federal Communications Commission setting forth certain proscribed contractual arrangements between chain broadcasters and local stations. The FCC did not have direct authority to regulate these contracts, and its rule asserted only that it would not license stations which maintained such contracts with the networks. Although no license had in fact been denied or revoked, and the FCC regulation could properly be characterized as a statement only of its intentions, the Court held that "Such regulations have the force of law before their sanctions are invoked as well as after. When as here they are promulgated by order of the Commission and the expected conformity to them causes injury cognizable by a court of equity, they are appropriately the subject of attack. . . ." . . .

We find decision in the present case following *a fortiori*. . . . The regulation challenged here, promulgated in a formal manner after announcement in the Federal Register and consideration of comments by interested parties is quite clearly definitive. There is no hint that this regulation is informal, . . . or only the ruling of a subordinate official, . . . or tentative. It was made effective upon publication, and the Assistant General Counsel for Food and Drugs stated in the District Court that compliance was expected.

The Government argues, however, that the present case can be distinguished from [the precedents] . . . on the ground that in those instances the agency involved could implement its policy directly, while here the Attorney General must authorize criminal and seizure actions for violations of the statute. In the context of this case, we do not find this argument persuasive. These regulations are not meant to advise the Attorney General, but purport to be directly authorized by the statute. Thus, if within the Commissioner's authority, they have the status of law and violations of them carry heavy criminal and civil sanctions. Also, there is no representation that the Attorney General and the Commissioner disagree in this area; the Justice Department is defending this very suit. It would be adherence to a mere technicality to give any credence to this contention. Moreover, the agency does have direct authority to enforce this regulation in the context of passing upon applications for clearance of new drugs, § 505, 21 U.S.C. § 355, or certification of certain antibiotics, § 507, 21 U.S.C. § 357.

This is also a case in which the impact of the regulations upon the petitioners is sufficiently direct and immediate as to render the issue appropriate for judicial review at this stage. These regulations purport to give an authoritative interpretation of a statutory provision that has a direct effect on the day-to-day business of all prescription drug companies; its promulgation puts petitioners in a dilemma that it was the very purpose of the Declaratory Judgment Act to ameliorate. As the District Court found on the basis of uncontested allegations, "Either they must comply with the every time requirement and incur the costs of changing over their promotional material and labeling or they must follow their present course and risk prosecution." . . . The regulations are clear-cut, and were made effective immediately upon publication; as noted earlier the agency's counsel represented to the District Court that immediate compliance with their terms was expected. If petitioners wish to comply they must change all their labels, advertisements, and promotional materials; they must destroy stocks of printed matter; and they must invest heavily in new printing type and new supplies. The alternative to compliance—continued use of material which they believe in good faith meets the statutory requirements, but which clearly does not meet the regulation of the Commissioner—may be even more costly. That course would risk serious criminal and civil penalties for the unlawful distribution of "misbranded" drugs.

It is relevant at this juncture to recognize that petitioners deal in a sensitive industry, in which public confidence in their drug products is especially important. To require them to challenge these regulations only as a defense to an action brought by the Government might harm them severely and unnecessarily. Where the legal issue presented is fit for judicial resolution, and where a regulation requires an immediate and significant change in the plaintiffs' conduct of their affairs with serious penalties attached to noncompliance, access to the courts under the Administrative Procedure Act and the Declaratory Judgment Act must be permitted, absent a statutory bar or some other unusual circumstance, neither of which appears here. . . .

The Government further contends that the threat of criminal sanctions for noncompliance with a judicially untested regulation is unrealistic; the Solicitor General has represented that if court enforcement becomes necessary, "the Department of Justice will proceed only civilly for an injunction . . . or by condemnation." We cannot accept this argument as a sufficient answer to petitioners' petition. This action at its inception was properly brought and this subsequent representation of the Department of Justice should not suffice to defeat it.

Finally, the Government urges that to permit resort to the courts in this type of case may delay or impede effective enforcement of the Act. We fully recognize the important public interest served by assuring prompt and unimpeded administration of the Pure Food, Drug, and Cosmetic Act, but we do not find the Government's argument convincing. First, in this particular case, a pre-enforcement challenge by nearly all prescription drug manufacturers is calculated to speed enforcement. If the Government prevails, a large part of the industry is bound by the decree; if the Government loses, it can more quickly revise its regulation.

The Government contends, however, that if the Court allows this consolidated suit, then nothing will prevent a multiplicity of suits in various jurisdictions challenging other regulations. The short answer to this contention is that the courts are well equipped to deal with such eventualities. The venue transfer provision, 28 U.S.C. § 1404(a), may be invoked by the Government to consolidate separate actions. Or, actions in all but one jurisdiction might be stayed pending the conclusion of one proceeding. . . . Further, the declaratory judgment and injunctive remedies are equitable in nature, and other equitable defenses may be interposed. If a multiplicity of suits are undertaken in order to harass the Government or to delay enforcement, relief can be denied on this ground alone. . . . In addition to all these safeguards against what the Government fears, it is important to note that the institution of this type of action does not by itself stay the effectiveness of the challenged regulation. . . . It is scarcely to be doubted that a court would refuse to postpone the effective date of an agency action if the Government could show, as it made no effort to do here, that delay would be detrimental to the public health or safety. . . .

[Justice Brennan did not participate. Justice Fortas, joined by the Chief Justice and by Justice Clark, dissented:]

In evaluating the destructive force and effect of the Court's action in these cases, it is necessary to realize that it is arming each of the federal district judges in this Nation with power to enjoin enforcement of regulations and actions under the federal law designed to protect the people of this Nation against dangerous drugs and cosmetics. Restraining orders and temporary injunctions will suspend application of these public safety laws pending years of litigation. . . . Where personal status or liberties are involved, the courts may well insist upon a considerable ease of challenging administrative orders or regulations. . . . Where a regulatory scheme designed to protect the public is involved, this Court has held that postponement of the opportunity to obtain judicial relief in the interest of avoiding disruption of the regulatory plan is entirely justifiable. . . .

Notes on Premature Litigation

(1) The cases in the preceding section were concerned with the question *who* is a proper party to litigate; the issue here to be considered is *when* a proper party may litigate.

The typical lawsuit comes after the relevant events have occurred: I am sued because I copied your invention; you are prosecuted for having shown dirty movies. The policies against advisory opinions (see p. 11 supra) have made courts understandably cautious about entertaining actions seeking to determine the legal effect of hypothetical future actions: If the predicted occurrences never come to pass, judicial intervention will have been unnecessary; and the want of concrete facts may be an invitation to error. When the challenge is to anticipated administrative action, at least two further policies may be implicated: The advisability of obtaining the views of an expert agency on questions within its special knowledge, and the undesirability of interrupting ongoing proceedings.[1]

A variety of related doctrines have been developed to avoid premature litigation. Prominent among them are ripeness, finality, and the exhaustion of administrative remedies.[2]

(2) The ripeness problem was described in *Abbott* as one of "discretion [ ]," but other opinions make clear that ripeness, like standing, has a constitutional component as well. E.g., Steffel v. Thompson, 415 U.S. 452, 458 (1974), infra p. 540: "At the threshold we must consider whether petitioner presents an 'actual controversy,' a requirement imposed by Art. III of the Constitution. . . ."

Finality, on the other hand, is often prescribed by statute as a condition for reviewing administrative action. E.g., 42 U.S.C. § 7607(b)(1) ("any other final action of the Administrator" under the Clean Air Act reviewable in the courts of appeals). The Administrative Procedure Act, as noted in *Abbott*, generalizes this principle: While all "final agency action" is reviewable under the APA unless some other statute otherwise provides, nonfinal action is reviewable only if "made reviewable by statute." 5 U.S.C. §§ 701(a), 704.

The exhaustion doctrine is best exemplified by Myers v. Bethlehem Shipbuilding Corp., 303 U.S. 41 (1938). The company sued to enjoin the NLRB from entertaining an unfair-labor-practice charge, arguing that its activities were outside interstate commerce and thus beyond the Board's jurisdiction. The Court held the complaint improper, invoking the "long settled rule of judicial administration that no one is entitled to judicial relief for a supposed or threatened injury until the prescribed administrative remedy has been exhausted."

What is the legal basis for the Court's exhaustion requirement? Was the controversy in *Myers* so unripe that there was no Article III controversy? Can exhaustion be defended as an application of traditional equitable discretion? See footnote 9 of the *Myers* opinion: "The rule has been most frequently applied in equity where relief by injunction was sought. . . . But because the rule is one of judicial administration—not merely a rule governing the exercise of discretion—it is applicable to proceedings at law as well as suits in equity." Elsewhere in the opinion the Court observed that Congress had vested authority over unfair-labor-practice cases exclusively in the Board and in the courts of appeals and argued that to entertain the complaint would "substitute the District Court for the Board as the tribunal to hear and determine what Congress declared the Board exclusively should hear and determine in the first instance." Does a

1. Cf. the general federal rule against interlocutory appeals from trial courts, 28 U.S.C. § 1291, considered at pp. 592–94 infra.

2. The boundaries among these doctrines are indistinct. While the *Abbott* opinion spoke of finality as a necessary but insufficient dimension of ripeness, the Court has since described all of *Abbott's* ripeness factors as elements of finality itself. FTC v. Standard Oil Co. of California, 449 U.S. 232, 239–40 (1980). Similarly, the *Standard Oil* case threw out for want of final administrative action a complaint essentially indistinguishable from one the Court had dismissed on exhaustion grounds in the famous case of Myers v. Bethlehem Shipbuilding Corp., 303 U.S. 41 (1938), without so much as a citation.

provision for review of "final" administrative decisions implicitly preclude review of matters that are not final?

(3) Thus there is a formidable array of legal tools available to preclude premature litigation. As *Abbott* recognizes, however, a strict requirement that lawsuits await the occurrence of all relevant events could impose severe hardship:

> It often happens that courts are unwilling to grant injunctions to restrain the enforcement of penal statutes or ordinances, and relegate the plaintiff to his option, either to violate the statute and take his chances in testing constitutionality on a criminal prosecution, or else to forego, in the fear of prosecution, the exercise of his claimed rights. . . . The court, in effect, . . . informs the prospective victim that the only way to determine whether the suspect is a mushroom or a toadstool, is to eat it.

Hearings on H.R. 5623 before a Subcomm. of the Senate Comm. on the Judiciary, 70th Cong., 1st Sess. 75 (1928) (Professor Borchard). In fact there have long been instances of injunctions against threatened future harm, when necesssary to prevent irreparable injury, e.g., Pierce v. Society of Sisters, 268 U.S. 510 (1925); and the Declaratory Judgment Act, for which Professor Borchard was testifying, was enacted in 1934 precisely to deal with this problem. See S.Rep. No. 1005, 73d Cong., 2d Sess. 2–3 (1934), quoted at p. 15 supra.

The Act itself, 28 U.S.C. § 2201, provides that a court "may declare the rights and other legal relations of any interested party" in any "case of actual controversy within its jurisdiction . . . whether or not further relief is or could be sought." [3] Is it plain that this statute authorizes the court to act whenever there is a constitutionally ripe controversy? [4] In any event, as *Abbott* suggests, the statute's use of the word "may" has led the Court to conclude that it allows the invocation of discretionary or prudential notions of ripeness that further limit the availability of the remedy. See, e.g., Public Affairs Associates v. Rickover, 369 U.S. 111 (1962).

(4) There have been occasions when the Court's stringent application of prematurity doctrines has appeared to place parties in the dilemma it was the stated purpose of the Declaratory Judgment Act to avoid. One

3. In the light of the legislative history, what do you think of Justice Frankfurter's statement that "the test for determining whether a federal court has authority to make a declaration . . . is whether the controversy 'would be justiciable in this Court if presented in a suit for injunction' "? Colegrove v. Green, 328 U.S. 549 (1946) (speaking for three Justices).

4. At one time it was doubtful that a suit seeking only declaratory relief could ever present a "Case" or "Controversy." One of the grounds for the notorious decision of non-justiciability in Muskrat v. United States, 219 U.S. 346 (1911), was that the judgment sought—a declaration of the validity of a statute argued to impair vested rights—was nonjudicial because it "could not be executed." See also the undelivered draft opinion of Chief Justice Taney in Gordon v. United States, recorded at 117 U.S. 697: "The award of execution is a part, and an essential part of every judgment passed by a court exercising judicial power." This objection made little sense in light of the established jurisdiction to remove clouds from and to quiet titles to land and to resolve interstate boundary disputes, and the matter was settled by Nashville, C. & St. L. Ry. v. Wallace, 288 U.S. 249 (1933), and Aetna Life Ins. Co. v. Haworth, 300 U.S. 227 (1937), in which the Court first held it had jurisdiction to review a state declaratory judgment on the merits and then upheld the federal Declaratory Judgment Act.

example was United Public Workers v. Mitchell, p. 14 above; a second was International Longshoremen's and Warehousemen's Union v. Boyd, 347 U.S. 222 (1954), in which aliens residing legally in the States and intending to continue a past practice of working summers in Alaska sued to enjoin an immigration officer from treating them upon return as if they were entering the United States for the first time. Dissenting Justices Black and Douglas said it was admitted the official "intended to enforce" a new statute "as . . . these workers feared" and thought irreparable harm shown, since "aliens generally can be excluded from this country for many reasons which would not justify deporting aliens lawfully residing here." The Court (Frankfurter, J.) held the case not ripe:

> Appellants in effect asked the District Court to rule that a statute the sanctions of which had not been set in motion against individuals on whose behalf relief was sought, because an occasion for doing so had not arisen, would not be applied to them if in the future such a contingency should arise. That is not a lawsuit to enforce a right; it is an endeavor to obtain a court's assurance that a statute does not govern hypothetical situations that may or may not make the challenged statute applicable. Determination of the scope and constitutionality of legislation in advance of its immediate adverse effect in the context of a concrete case involves too remote and abstract an inquiry for the proper exercise of the judicial function. United Public Workers v. Mitchell. . . .

In Poe v. Ullman, 367 U.S. 497 (1961), married women with histories of abnormal pregnancies and their doctor unsuccessfully attacked a Connecticut statute prohibiting the use of contraceptives and medical advice about them. Justice Frankfurter wrote for four Justices:

> Appellants' complaints in these declaratory judgment proceedings do not clearly . . . allege that appellee Ullman threatens to prosecute them for use of, or for giving advice concerning, contraceptive devices. The allegations are merely that, in the course of his public duty, he intends to prosecute any offenses against Connecticut law, and that he claims that use of and advice concerning contraceptives would constitute offenses. The lack of immediacy of the threat described by these allegations might alone raise serious questions of non-justiciability of appellants' claims. . . . But, even were we to read the allegations to convey a clear threat of imminent prosecutions, we are not bound to accept as true all that is alleged on the face of the complaint and admitted, technically, by demurrer. . . .
>
> The Connecticut law prohibiting the use of contraceptives has been on the State's books since 1879. . . . During the more than three-quarters of a century since its enactment, a prosecution for its violation seems never to have been initiated, save in State v. Nelson, . . . a test case. . . . We were advised by counsel for appellants that contraceptives are commonly and notoriously sold in Connecticut drug stores. . . . The undeviating policy of nullification by Connecticut of its anti-contraceptive laws throughout all the long years they have been on the statute books bespeaks more than prosecutorial paralysis. . . . The fact that Connecticut has not chosen to press the

> enforcement of this statute deprives these controversies of the immediacy which is an indispensable condition of constitutional adjudication. . . .

Justice Brennan concurred in the judgment; there were four dissents. Is it conceivable that *Mitchell, Boyd,* or *Poe* would have been decided the same way by the Justices who decided *Abbott*? [5]

(5) *Abbott* firmly established that there are instances in which pre-enforcement challenges to the validity of generally applicable prohibitions will be entertained. There remain cases, however, in which the risk of harm to the plaintiffs from the challenged action is too speculative to justify review. Sometimes, as in the cases noted at pp. 32–45 above, this question is phrased as one of standing; in others it is dealt with under the rubric of ripeness. How speculative is too speculative is of course the difficult question. Consider the following examples from the field of constitutional litigation:

(a) Lake Carriers' Ass'n v. MacMullan, 406 U.S. 498, 507–08 (1972), unanimously declared ripe a challenge by shipowners to a statute allegedly forbidding the discharge of sewage from vessels, even though state officials had "indicated that they will not prosecute . . . until adequate land-based pumpout facilities are available":

> If appellants are to avoid prosecution, they must be prepared, according to Michigan authorities, to retain all sewage on board as soon as pumpout facilities are available, which, in turn, means that they must promptly install sewage storage devices. In this circumstance, compliance is coerced by the threat of enforcement, and the controversy is both immediate and real.

(b) Roe v. Wade, 410 U.S. 113 (1973). While entertaining the claim of another plaintiff, see p. 77 infra, the Court refused to hear a challenge to the validity of an abortion law brought by a married couple wishing to avoid future pregnancies and unwilling to use birth-control pills:

> We thus have as plaintiffs a married couple who have, as their asserted immediate and present injury, only an alleged "detrimental effect upon [their] marital happiness" because they are forced to "the choice of refraining from normal sexual relations or of endangering Mary Doe's health through a possible pregnancy." Their claim is that sometime, in the future, Mrs. Doe might become pregnant because of possible failure of contraceptive measures, and at that time in the future, she might want an abortion that might then be illegal under the Texas statutes.
>
> This very phrasing of the Does' position reveals its speculative character. . . . [W]e are not prepared to say that the bare allegation of so indirect an injury is sufficient to present an actual case or controversy.

5. For later decisions finding ripe pre-enforcement controversies in each of the fields represented by *Poe, Mitchell,* and *Boyd* see Doe v. Bolton, 410 U.S. 179 (1973); United States Civil Service Commission v. National Association of Letter Carriers, 413 U.S. 548 (1973); Itzcovitz v. Selective Service Local Board, 447 F.2d 888, 891 n. 7 (2d Cir. 1971).

Was the Court fair in characterizing the Does' allegations as attacking the hypothetical possibility of future prosecution rather than the present inhibiting effect of the statute upon their sexual behavior? See Epstein, The Abortion Cases, 1973 Sup.Ct.Rev. 159, 165–66.

(c) O'Shea v. Littleton, 414 U.S. 488, 497 (1974). The Court threw out a complaint by blacks and other persons engaged in civil-rights activities in Cairo, Illinois, seeking to enjoin state-court judges from discriminating on racial and other grounds in imposing sentences and setting bail. There was no allegation, wrote Justice White, "that any relevant criminal statute . . . is unconstitutional . . . or that plaintiffs have been or will be improperly charged with violating criminal law . . ." or that any plaintiff "expects to violate valid criminal laws";

> Apparently, the proposition is that *if* respondents proceed to violate an unchallenged law and *if* they are charged, held to answer, and tried in any proceedings before petitioners, they will be subjected to the discriminatory practices that petitioners are alleged to have followed.

Justice Douglas, dissenting for himself and two others, contradicted an essential prop of this argument, quoting from the complaint the allegation that another defendant, the State's Attorney, "has made or caused to be made . . . arrests and . . . charges against plaintiffs . . . where such charges are not warranted and are merely for the purpose of harassment and to discourage and prevent plaintiffs and their class from exercising their constitutional rights."

(d) In Steffel v. Thompson, 415 U.S. 452 (1974), infra p. 540, a challenge to the threatened application of a trespass statute was unanimously held ripe:

> [P]etitioner has alleged threats of prosecution that cannot be characterized as "imaginary or speculative". . . . He has been twice warned to stop handbilling that he claims is constitutionally protected and has been told by the police that if he again handbills at the shopping center and disobeys a warning to stop he will likely be prosecuted. The prosecution of petitioner's handbilling companion is ample demonstration that petitioner's concern with arrest has not been "chimerical," Poe v. Ullman. . . . In these circumstances, it is not necessary that petitioner first expose himself to actual arrest or prosecution to be entitled to challenge a statute that he claims deters the exercise of his constitutional rights.

(6) *Abbott* has not put an end to controversies over the ripeness of administrative action for review in non-constitutional cases either. In Toilet Goods Association v. Gardner, 387 U.S. 158 (1967), decided the same day as *Abbott*, the challenged regulation provided as follows:

> (a) When it appears to the Commissioner that a person has: . . .
>
> (4) Refused to permit duly authorized employees of the Food and Drug Administration free access to all manufacturing facilities, processes, and formulae involved in the manufacture of color additives and intermediates from which such color additives are derived;

he may immediately suspend certification service to such a person and may continue such suspension until adequate corrective action has been taken.

The manufacturers' attack upon this regulation was held premature, despite the Court's concessions that the agency's action was "final" under the Administrative Procedure Act and that the question was a purely legal one—"whether the regulation is totally beyond the agency's power under the statute":

> The regulation serves notice only that the Commissioner *may* under certain circumstances order inspection of certain facilities and data, and that further certification of additives *may* be refused to those who decline to permit a duly authorized inspection until they have complied in that regard. At this juncture we have no idea whether or when such an inspection will be ordered and what reasons the Commissioner will give to justify his order. . . . Whether the regulation is justified . . . will depend not merely on an inquiry into statutory purpose but concurrently on an understanding of what types of enforcement problems are encountered by the FDA, the need for various sorts of supervision in order to effectuate the goals of the Act, and the safeguards devised to protect legitimate trade secrets. . . . We believe that judicial appraisal of these factors is likely to stand on a much surer footing in the context of a specific application of this regulation than could be the case in the framework of the generalized challenge made here. . . . Moreover, no irremediable adverse consequences flow from requiring a later challenge to this regulation by a manufacturer who refuses to allow this type of inspection. Unlike the other regulations challenged in this action, in which seizure of goods, heavy fines, adverse publicity for distributing "adulterated" goods, and possible criminal liability might penalize failure to comply, . . . a refusal to admit an inspector here would at most lead only to a suspension of certification services to the particular party, a determination that can then be promptly challenged through an administrative procedure, which in turn is reviewable by a court. . . .

See also Lever Brothers Co. v. FTC, 325 F.Supp. 371 (D.Me.1971), rejecting a rare attempt to challenge a regulation that had merely been proposed and not adopted; National Automatic Laundry & Cleaning Council v. Shultz, 443 F.2d 689 (D.C.Cir. 1971), allowing a challenge to a letter of the Secretary of Labor declaring that a statutory exemption of laundries from the Fair Labor Standards Act was inapplicable to the plaintiffs; FTC v. Standard Oil Co. of California, 449 U.S. 232 (1980), refusing for want of "final agency action" to allow a judicial attack on the issuance of a complaint by the Commission. This last decision seems obvious, doesn't it? Then do you understand why the Court in *Abbott* and in *Steffel* (supra note 5(d)) permitted challenges to mere threats of enforcement when no complaint had ever been issued? Cf. pp. 540–51 infra.

(7) The contours of the finality and exhaustion requirements are explored in detail in courses on administrative law and cannot be fully covered here. Suffice it to say that interpretation of the former has proved by no means as simple as it appears (see, e.g., Pepsico, Inc. v. FTC, 472 F.2d

179 (2d Cir. 1972)), and that the latter is by no means absolute. See, e.g., Public Utilities Commission v. United Fuel Gas Co., 317 U.S. 456 (1943); Allen v. Grand Central Aircraft Co., 347 U.S. 535 (1954); and the discussion in Lone Star Cement Corp. v. FTC, 339 F.2d 505 (9th Cir. 1964), quoting from 3 K. Davis, Administrative Law Treatise 69 (1958), with respect to what the court called considerations relevant to whether "one may seek court relief against anticipated agency action:"

> The key factors are three: extent of injury from pursuit of administrative remedy, degree of apparent clarity or doubt about administrative jurisdiction, and involvement of specialized administrative understanding in the question of jurisdiction.

See also the discussion of exhausting state administrative remedies in civil-rights cases, pp. 505–06 infra.[6]

(8) Some commentators, perceiving inconsistency in the decisions, have concluded that the Court manipulates such doctrines as ripeness and standing to avoid reaching questions it does not wish to decide. To Professor Bickel this was not sin but virtue: By these and other devices the Court could avoid not only the usual hazards of premature litigation but also the evil of "legitimating" laws that were constitutional but undesirable. A. Bickel, The Least Dangerous Branch 71, 111–98 (1962).

Professor Scharpf, on the other hand, believes many apparent inconsistencies can be reconciled if one recognizes that the necessary degree of concreteness is often dependent upon the judge's view of the merits. His example is Adler v. Board of Education, 342 U.S. 485 (1952), in which, without discussing jurisdiction, the Court upheld on the merits a New York law requiring dismissal of teachers advocating violent overthrow of the government. Justice Frankfurter dissented, saying there was no case or controversy:

> The allegations in the present action fall short of those found insufficient in the *Mitchell* case. These teachers do not allege that they have engaged in proscribed conduct or that they have any intention to do so. They do not suggest that they have been, or are, deterred from supporting causes or from joining organizations for fear of the Feinberg Law's interdict, except to say generally that the system complained of will have this effect on teachers as a group. They do not assert that they are threatened with action under the law, or that steps are imminent whereby they would incur the hazard of punishment. . . .

6. When there is no attempt to review or to forestall administrative action, federal courts have at times invoked the doctrine of primary jurisdiction to stay decision of a case pending resort to an administrative agency for resolution of a question within its competence. The seminal case is Texas & Pac. Ry. v. Abilene Cotton Oil Co., 204 U.S. 426 (1907), in which, in the teeth of a statute specifically allowing court suits for damages for unreasonable railroad rates, the Court held the plaintiff must first obtain an ICC ruling as to the reasonableness of the rate, because otherwise divergent judicial determinations would render rates disuniform. Later cases have also stressed the degree of need for agency expertise in resolving the disputed issue, e.g., United States v. Western Pac. R. R., 352 U.S. 59 (1956). What is the statutory warrant for this doctrine? Compare the doctrine of abstention pending resolution of state-law questions by a state court, infra pp. 485–97.

Neither the majority nor the other dissenters in *Adler*, Scharpf argues, had any need of concrete facts, for the former were convinced the State was free to condition the privilege of public employment upon a sacrifice of speech or association, and the latter thought the State powerless to punish teachers for exercising First Amendment freedoms:

> Justice Frankfurter alone advocated avoidance because he alone defined the substantive issues in terms of a close balance between the equally legitimate interests of society in its self-preservation and of the teachers in their freedom of thought, inquiry and expression. Thus, in order to strike this balance in the particular case, Frankfurter would have had to know much more about the actual practices of enforcement and the degree of surveillance to which the teachers would be subjected than the bare text of an unenforced statute permitted him to know.

In short, he concludes, the Court employs the case-or-controversy requirement and other devices of avoidance "to screen the cases in order to select those which provide an adequate basis for the responsible performance of the reviewing function." Scharpf, Judicial Review and the Political Question: A Functional Analysis, 75 Yale L.J. 518, 529–33 (1966).

UNITED STATES PAROLE COMMISSION v. GERAGHTY

445 U.S. 388 (1980).

MR. JUSTICE BLACKMUN delivered the opinion of the Court. . . .

In 1973, the United States Parole Board adopted explicit Parole Release Guidelines for adult prisoners. These guidelines establish a "customary range" of confinement for various classes of offenders. The guidelines utilize a matrix, which combines a "parole prognosis" score (based on the prisoner's age at first conviction, employment background, and other personal factors) and an "offense severity" rating, to yield the "customary" time to be served in prison. . . .

[Geraghty, who was serving sentences for conspiracy and for false statements to a grand jury, was denied parole on the basis of these guidelines. He then filed a class action attacking the guidelines and the procedures by which they had been applied to his case, claiming to represent "all federal prisoners who are or who will become eligible for . . . parole." The district court denied the request for class certification and ruled against Geraghty on the merits. He appealed, "individually 'and on behalf of a class.' " While the appeal was pending, he was released from prison. The parole board argued that the case was moot, but the court of appeals disagreed.]

Article III of the Constitution limits federal "Judicial Power," that is, federal court jurisdiction, to "Cases" and "Controversies." This case or controversy limitation serves "two complementary" purposes. Flast v. Cohen, 392 U.S. 83, 95 (1968). It limits the business of federal courts to "questions presented in an adversary context and in a form historically viewed as capable of resolution through the judicial process," and it defines the "role assigned to the judiciary in a tripartite allocation of power to assure that the federal courts will not intrude into areas committed to the other branches of government." Ibid. Likewise, mootness has two aspects: "when the issues presented are no longer 'live' or the parties lack a legally cognizable interest in the outcome." Powell v. McCormack, 395 U.S. 486, 496 (1969).

It is clear that the controversy over the validity of the Parole Release Guidelines is still a "live" one between petitioners and at least some members of the class respondent seeks to represent. . . . We therefore are concerned here with the second aspect of mootness, that is, the parties' interest in the litigation. The Court has referred to this concept as the "personal stake" requirement. E.g., Franks v. Bowman Transportation Co., 424 U.S. 747, 755 (1976); Baker v. Carr, 369 U.S. 186, 204 (1962). . . .

The "personal stake" aspect of mootness doctrine . . . serves primarily the purpose of assuring that federal courts are presented with disputes they are capable of resolving. One commentator has defined mootness as "the doctrine of standing set in a time frame: The requisite personal interest that must exist at the commencement of the litigation (standing) must continue throughout its existence (mootness)." Monaghan, Constitutional Adjudication: The Who and When, 82 Yale L.J. 1363, 1384 (1973).

On several occasions the Court has considered the application of the "personal stake" requirement in the class action context. In Sosna v. Iowa, 419 U.S. 393 (1975), it held that mootness of the named plaintiff's individual claim *after* a class has been duly certified does not render the action moot. It reasoned that "even though appellees . . . might not again enforce the Iowa durational residency requirement against [the class representative], it is clear that they will enforce it against those persons in the class that appellant sought to represent and that the District Court certified." . . . The Court stated specifically that an Art. III case or controversy "may exist . . . between a named defendant and a member of the class represented by the named plaintiff, even though the claim of the named plaintiff has become moot." . . .[6]

Although one might argue that *Sosna* contains at least an implication that the critical factor for Art. III purposes is the timing of class certification, other cases, applying a "relation back" approach, clearly demonstrate that timing is not crucial. When the claim on the merits is "capable of repetition, yet evading review," the named plaintiff may litigate the class certification issue despite loss of his personal stake in

6. The claim in *Sosna* also fit the traditional category of actions that are deemed not moot despite the litigant's loss of personal stake, that is, those "capable of repetition, yet evading review." See Southern Pacific Terminal Co. v. ICC, 219 U.S. 498, 515 (1911). In Franks v. Bowman Transportation Co., 424 U.S., at 753–755, however, the Court held that the class action aspect of mootness doctrine does not depend on the class claim's being so inherently transitory that it meets the "capable of repetition, yet evading review" standard.

the outcome of the litigation. E.g., Gerstein v. Pugh, 420 U.S. 103, 110, n. 11 (1975). The "capable of repetition, yet evading review" doctrine, to be sure, was developed outside the class action context. . . . But it has been applied where the named plaintiff does have a personal stake at the outset of the lawsuit, and where the claim may arise again with respect to that plaintiff; the litigation then may continue notwithstanding the named plaintiff's current lack of a personal stake. See, e.g., Weinstein v. Bradford, 423 U.S. 147, 149 (1975); Roe v. Wade, 410 U.S. 113, 123–125 (1973). Since the litigant faces some likelihood of becoming involved in the same controversy in the future, vigorous advocacy can be expected to continue.

When, however, there is no chance that the named plaintiff's expired claim will reoccur, mootness still can be avoided through certification of a class prior to expiration of the named plaintiff's personal claim. E.g., Franks v. Bowman Transportation Co., 424 U.S., at 752–757. . . . Some claims are so inherently transitory that the trial court will not have even enough time to rule on a motion for class certification before the proposed representative's individual interest expires. The Court considered this possibility in Gerstein v. Pugh, 420 U.S., at 110, n. 11. *Gerstein* was an action challenging pretrial detention conditions. The Court assumed that the named plaintiffs were no longer in custody awaiting trial at the time the trial court certified a class of pretrial detainees. There was no indication that the particular named plaintiffs might again be subject to pretrial detention. Nonetheless, the case was held not to be moot because:

> "The length of pretrial custody cannot be ascertained at the outset, and it may be ended at any time by release on recognizance, dismissal of the charges, or a guilty plea, as well as by acquittal or conviction after trial. It is by no means certain that any given individual, named as plaintiff, would be in pretrial custody long enough for a district judge to certify the class. Moreover, in this case the constant existence of a class of persons suffering the deprivation is certain. The attorney representing the named respondents is a public defender, and we can safely assume that he has other clients with a continuing live interest in the case." Ibid.

See also Sosna v. Iowa, 419 U.S., at 402, n. 11.

In two different contexts the Court has stated that the proposed class representative who proceeds to a judgment on the merits may appeal *denial* of class certification. First, this assumption was "an important ingredient," . . . in the rejection of interlocutory appeals, "as of right," of class certification denials. Coopers & Lybrand v. Livesay, 437 U.S. 463, 469, 470, n. 15 (1978). The Court reasoned that denial of class status will not necessarily be the "death knell" of a small claimant action, since there still remains "the prospect of prevailing on the merits and reversing an order denying class certification." . . .

Second, in United Airlines, Inc. v. McDonald, 432 U.S. 385, 393–395 (1977), the Court held that a putative class member may intervene, for the purpose of appealing the denial of a class certification motion, after the named plaintiffs' claims have been satisfied and judgment entered in their favor. Underlying that decision was the view that "refusal to certify was subject to appellate review after final judgment at the behest of the named plaintiffs." . . . And today, the Court holds that named plaintiffs whose claims are satisfied through entry of judgment over their objections may appeal the denial of a class certification ruling. Deposit Guaranty Nat. Bank v. Roper, 445 U.S. 326.

Gerstein, *McDonald*, and *Roper* are all examples of cases found not to be moot, despite the loss of a "personal stake" in the merits of the litigation by the proposed class representative. The interest of the named plaintiffs in *Gerstein* was precisely the same as that of Geraghty here. Similarly, after judgment had been entered in their favor, the named plaintiffs in *McDonald* had no continuing narrow personal stake in the outcome of the class claims. And in *Roper* the Court points out that an individual controversy is rendered moot, in the strict Art. III sense, by payment and satisfaction of a final judgment. . . .

These cases demonstrate the flexible character of the Art. III mootness doctrine[7]. . . .

[T]he fact that a named plaintiff's substantive claims are mooted due to an occurrence other than a judgment on the merits does not mean that all the other issues in the case are mooted. A plaintiff who brings a class action presents two separate issues for judicial resolution. One is the claim on the merits; the other is the claim that he is entitled to represent a class. . . . The imperatives of a dispute capable of judicial resolution are sharply presented issues in a concrete factual setting and self-interested parties vigorously advocating opposing positions. . . . We conclude that these elements can exist with respect to the class certification issue notwithstanding the fact that the named plaintiff's claim on the merits has expired. The question whether class certification is apppropriate remains as a concrete, sharply presented issue. In *Sosna v. Iowa* it was recognized that a named plaintiff whose

7. Three of the Court's cases might be described as adopting a less flexible approach. In Indianapolis School Comm'rs v. Jacobs, 420 U.S. 128 (1975), and in Weinstein v. Bradford, 423 U.S. 147 (1975), dismissal of putative class suits, as moot, was ordered after the named plaintiffs' claims became moot. And in Pasadena City Bd. of Education v. Spangler, 427 U.S. 424, 430 (1976), it was indicated that the action would have been moot, upon expiration of the named plaintiffs' claims, had not the United States intervened as a party plaintiff. Each of these, however, was a case in which there was an attempt to appeal the merits without first having obtained proper certification of a class. In each case it was the defendant who petitioned this Court for review. As is observed subsequently in the text, appeal from denial of class classification is permitted in some circumstances where appeal on the merits is not. In the situation where the proposed class representative has lost a "personal stake," the merits cannot be reached until a class properly is certified. Although the Court perhaps could have remanded *Jacobs* and *Weinstein* for reconsideration of the class certification issue, as the Court of Appeals did here, the parties in those cases did not suggest "relation back" of class certification. Thus we do not find this line of cases dispositive of the question now before us.

claim on the merits expires *after* class certification may still adequately represent the class. Implicit in that decision was the determination that vigorous advocacy can be assured through means other than the traditional requirement of a "personal stake in the outcome." Respondent here continues vigorously to advocate his right to have a class certified.

We therefore hold that an action brought on behalf of a class does not become moot upon expiration of the named plaintiff's substantive claim, even though class certification has been denied.[10] The proposed representative retains a "personal stake" in obtaining class certification sufficient to assure that Art. III values are not undermined. If the appeal results in reversal of the class certification denial, and a class subsequently is properly certified, the merits of the class claim then may be adjudicated pursuant to the holding in *Sosna*.

Our holding is limited to the appeal of the denial of the class certification motion. . . . If, on appeal, it is determined that class certification properly was denied, the claim on the merits must be dismissed as moot. . . .

We need not decide here whether Geraghty is a proper representative for the purpose of representing the class on the merits. . . .

MR. JUSTICE POWELL, with whom THE CHIEF JUSTICE, MR. JUSTICE STEWART and MR. JUSTICE REHNQUIST join, dissenting. . . .

"In order to satisfy Art. III, the plaintiff must show that he personally has suffered some actual or threatened injury as a result of the putatively illegal conduct of the defendant." . . . As the Court notes today, the same threshold requirement must be satisfied throughout the action. . . .

. . . Art. III contains no exception for class actions. Thus, we have held that a putative class representative who alleges no individual injury "may seek relief on behalf of himself or any other member of the class." O'Shea v. Littleton, 414 U.S. 488, 494 (1974). Only after a class has been certified in accordance with Rule 23 can it "acquir[e] a legal status separate from the interest asserted by [the named plaintiff]." Sosna v. Iowa, supra, 419 U.S. at 399 (1975). "Given a properly certified class," the live interests of unnamed but identifiable class members may supply the personal stake required by Art. III when the named plaintiff's individual claim becomes moot. . . .

This case presents a fundamentally different situation. No class has been certified, and the lone plaintiff no longer has any personal stake in the litigation. In the words of his own lawyer, respondent "can obtain absolutely no additional personal relief" in this case. . . . In these circumstances, Art. III and the precedents of this Court require

10. We intimate no view as to whether a named plaintiff who settles the individual claim after denial of class certification may, consistent with Art. III, appeal from the adverse ruling on class certification. See United Airlines, Inc. v. McDonald, 432 U.S. 385, 393–394, and n. 14 (1977).

dismissal. . . . The Court . . . relies on . . . Gerstein v. Pugh, 420 U.S. 103, 110–111, n. 11 (1975), United Airlines, Inc. v. McDonald, 432 U.S. 385 (1977), and today's decision in Deposit Guaranty Nat. Bank v. Roper, 445 U.S. 326. Each case is said to show that a class action is not mooted by the loss of the class representative's personal stake in the outcome of the lawsuit, even though no class has been certified. . . . *Sosna* itself is cited for the proposition that the requirements of Art. III may be met "through means other than the traditional requirement of a 'personal stake in the outcome.'" . . . In my view, the Court misreads these precedents.

A

In *Sosna*, the Court simply acknowledged that actual class certification gives legal recognition to additional adverse parties. . . .[8] And in *Gerstein*, the Court applied a rule long established, outside the class action context, by cases that never have been thought to erode the requirement of a personal stake in the outcome. . . . The action continued only because of the transitory nature of pretrial detention, which placed the claim within "that narrow class of cases" that are "distinctly 'capable of repetition, yet evading review.'" . . .

McDonald and *Roper* sanction some appeals from the denial of class certification notwithstanding satisfaction of the class representative's claim on the merits. But neither case holds that Art. III may be satisfied in the absence of a personal stake in the outcome. In *McDonald*, a putative class member intervened within the statutory time limit to appeal the certification ruling. . . .[10] Because the Court found that her claim was not time-barred, the intervenor in *McDonald* possessed the stake necessary to pursue the action. Indeed, the Court devoted its entire opinion to showing that the intervenor's claim for relief had not expired. At most, *McDonald* holds only that an action which is kept alive by interested parties within prescribed periods of limitations does not "die" in an Art. III sense.

There is dictum in *McDonald* that the "refusal to certify was subject to appellate review after final judgment at the behest of the named plaintiffs. . . ." . . . That gratuitous sentence, repeated in Coopers & Lybrand v. Livesay, 437 U.S. 463, 469, 470, n. 15 (1978), apparently is elevated by the Court's opinion in this case to the status of new doctrine. There is serious tension between this new doctrine

8. Certification is no mere formality. It represents a judicial finding that injured parties other than the named plaintiff exist. It also provides a definition by which they can be identified. Certification identifies and sharpens the interests of unnamed class members in the outcome; only thereafter will they be bound by the outcome. . . . Vigorous advocacy is assured by the authoritative imposition on the named plaintiffs of a duty adequately to represent the entire class. . . . After certification, the case is no different in principle from more traditional representative actions involving, for example, a single party who cannot participate himself because of his incompetence but is permitted to litigate through an appointed fiduciary.

10. The individual claims of the original named plaintiffs had been settled after judgment on the question of liability. . . .

and the much narrower reasoning adopted today in *Roper*. In *Roper* the Court holds that the named plaintiffs, who have refused to accept proffered individual settlements, retain a personal stake in sharing anticipated litigation costs with the class. . . .

. . . Here, there is not even a speculative interest in sharing costs, and respondent affirmatively denies that he retains any stake or personal interest in the outcome of his appeal. . . .

B

The cases cited by the Court as "less flexible"—and therefore less authoritative—apply established Art. III doctrine in cases closely analogous to this one. Indianapolis School Comm'rs v. Jacobs, 420 U.S. 128 (1975) (per curiam); Weinstein v. Bradford, 423 U.S. 147 (1975) (per curiam); Pasadena City Board of Education v. Spangler, 427 U.S. 424, 430 (1976). As they are about to become second class precedents, these cases are relegated to a footnote. . . .

In *Jacobs*, six named plaintiffs brought a class action to challenge certain high school regulations. The District Court stated on the record that class treatment was appropriate and that the plaintiffs were proper representatives, but the court failed to comply with Rule 23. After this Court granted review, we were informed that the named plaintiffs had graduated. We held that the action was entirely moot because the "class action was never properly certified nor the class properly identified by the District Court." . . . We reached precisely the same conclusion in *Spangler*, an action saved from mootness only by the timely intervention of a third party. . . . And in *Bradford*, where the District Court had denied certification outright, the Court held that the named plaintiff's release from prison required the dismissal of his complaint about parole release procedures. . . .

The Court suggests that *Jacobs* and *Spangler* may be distinguished because the plaintiffs there were not appealing the denial of class certification. The Court overlooks the fact that in each case the class representatives were defending a judgment on the merits from which the defendants had appealed. The plaintiff/respondents continued vigorously to assert the claims of the class. They did not take the procedural route of appealing a denial of certification only because the District Court had granted—albeit defectively—class status. We chose not to remand for correction of the oral certification order in *Jacobs* because we recognized that the putative class representative had suffered no injury that could be redressed by adequate certification. Underlying *Jacobs*, and *Bradford* as well, is the elementary principle that no one has a personal stake in obtaining relief for third parties, through the mechanism of class certification or otherwise. . . .

In short, this is a case in which the putative class representative—respondent here—no longer has the slightest interest in the injuries alleged in his complaint. No member of the class is before the Court; indeed, none has been identified. The case therefore lacks a plaintiff with the minimal personal stake that is a constitutional prerequisite to the jurisdiction of an Art. III court. In any realistic sense, the only persons before this Court who appear to have an interest are the defendants and a lawyer who no longer has a client.

I would vacate the decision of the Court of Appeals and remand with instructions to dismiss the action as moot.

Notes on Mootness

(1) The argument in the cases considered in the preceding section was that they had been brought too soon. The present focus is upon cases that are arguably sought to be litigated too late.

Not so long ago it was understood that, if the controversy giving rise to the litigation disappeared, the case became moot and had to be dismissed. For example, in Golden v. Zwickler, 394 U.S. 103 (1969), the plaintiff attacked a statute forbidding the distribution of anonymous handbills. But the complaint alleged an intention to distribute such literature only in connection with the campaign of a particular congressman who had subsequently left the House to become a judge. The test, the Court said, was whether there was a controversy at the time of the hearing, not at the time the complaint was filed. Because it was "wholly conjectural that another occasion might arise when Zwickler might be prosecuted for distributing the handbills referred to in the complaint," he had not established the existence of "the elements governing the issuance of a declaratory judgment."

Notice how the question of mootness in *Golden* blends into the issue of ripeness of a future controversy. Contrast the square holding that mootness is to be reexamined at the time of the hearing with the doctrine, infra p. 241, that a change of citizenship after the complaint is filed does not destroy diversity jurisdiction. Why this difference?

To what extent do the objections to advisory opinions apply to cases that are moot when filed? To cases that have become moot after argument?

(2) Of course it is not always obvious whether a controversy has truly disappeared. Release from prison, for example, does not always moot an attack on a criminal conviction; collateral effects of the conviction, such as voting disqualification or the possible enhancement of sentences for future crimes, may keep the controversy alive. See, e.g., Sibron v. New York, 392 U.S. 40 (1968). Cases in which the defendant has interrupted a challenged course of conduct have presented special problems. For example, in United States v. W. T. Grant Co., 345 U.S. 629 (1953), the Court upheld jurisdiction in an antitrust proceeding after the defendant had resigned from the interlocking directorates that were the basis of the complaint, although there was no showing that the illegality had been or was about to be resumed:

> Both sides agree to the abstract proposition that voluntary cessation of allegedly illegal conduct does not deprive the tribunal of power to hear and determine the case. . . . The defendant is free to return to his old ways. This, together with a public interest in having the

> legality of the practices settled, militates against a mootness conclusion. . . . The courts have rightly refused to grant defendants such a powerful weapon against public law enforcement.
>
> The case may nevertheless be moot if the defendant can demonstrate that "there is no reasonable expectation that the wrong will be repeated." The burden is a heavy one. Here the defendants told the court that the interlocks no longer existed and disclaimed any intention to revive them. Such a profession does not suffice to make a case moot although it is one of the factors to be considered in determining the appropriateness of getting an injunction. . . .[1]

(3) *Geraghty* is one in a series of steps away from the traditional mootness doctrine that essentially began with Moore v. Ogilvie, 394 U.S. 814 (1969), in which independent candidates seeking places on the 1968 Presidential and Vice-Presidential ballot sought injunctive and declaratory relief against a state law requiring petition signatures from each of 50 counties. Declaring the law unconstitutional after the 1968 election had passed, the Court in an opinion by Justice Douglas observed that the "burden" of the signature law

> remains and controls future elections, as long as Illinois maintains her present system. . . . The problem is therefore "capable of repetition, yet evading review" . . . . The need for its resolution thus reflects a continuing controversy in the federal-state area where our "one man, one vote" decisions have thrust.[2]

Citing *Golden*, Justices Stewart and Harlan dissented: "In the absence of any assertion that the appellants intend to participate as candidates in any future Illinois election, . . . there simply remains no judicially cognizable dispute . . . ."

There is a resemblance between this case and *Golden*, isn't there? Was the court confusing the existence of a continuing unresolved legal issue with the presence of a concrete controversy between adverse parties? Was the Court saying the importance of deciding the constitutional question justified doing so in a moot case?[3]

1. However, the Court held over two dissents that the trial judge did not abuse his discretion in denying equitable relief despite the argument that the director had committed three distinct (but apparently concurrent) violations, had failed to terminate them until after suit was filed "despite five years of administrative attempts to persuade him of their illegality," and had refused to concede he had violated the law or to promise not to commit similar violations in the future.

2. *Moore* invoked the authority of Southern Pacific Terminal Co. v. ICC, 219 U.S. 498, 515 (1911), from which the quoted language was taken. The ICC had ordered the company not to give unlawful preferences for two years, and the two years had elapsed; the Court, citing a case in which "there was an attempt to defeat the purposes of the suit by a voluntary dissolution of the [challenged] agreement," rejected the mootness argument: "The questions involved in the orders of the Interstate Commerce Commission are usually continuing (as are manifestly those in the case at bar) and their consideration ought not to be, as they might be, defeated, by short term orders, capable of repetition, yet evading review. . . ."

3. See also Roe v. Wade, 410 U.S. 113 (1973), entertaining in 1973 an abortion-law challenge by a woman who had alleged she was pregnant when she filed suit in 1970:

> The usual rule in federal cases is that an actual controversy must exist at stages of appellate or certiorari review, and not simply at the date the action is

(4) *Moore* was applied in the class-action context in Sosna v. Iowa, 419 U.S. 393, 398–403 (1975). Mrs. Sosna challenged an Iowa law imposing a one-year residency requirement as a condition for seeking an Iowa divorce. By the time the case reached the Supreme Court, she had both satisfied the requirement and obtained a divorce elsewhere. If she "had sued only on her own behalf," wrote Justice Rehnquist for the Court, these facts would have mooted the case. But *Sosna* was a class action; and "[w]hen the District Court certified the propriety of the class action, the class of unnamed persons described in the certification acquired a legal status separate from the interest asserted by appellant."

In contrast to *Moore*, the Court acknowledged, there was no likelihood that the law would ever be applied to Mrs. Sosna again. Nevertheless it was clear that the State would continue to enforce it against other persons in the certified class; "yet, because of the passage of time, no single challenger will remain subject to its restrictions for the period necessary to see such a lawsuit to its conclusion. . . ."

> We believe that a case such as this, in which . . . the issue sought to be litigated escapes full appellate review at the behest of any single challenger, does not inexorably become moot by the intervening resolution of the controversy as to the named plaintiffs. . . . We note, however, that the same exigency that justifies this doctrine serves to identify its limits. In cases in which the alleged harm would not dissipate during the normal time required for resolution of the controversy, the general principles of Art. III jurisdiction require that the plaintiff's personal stake in the litigation continue throughout the entirety of the litigation.

initiated. United States v. Munsingwear, Inc., 340 U.S. 36 (1950). . . .

> But when, as here, pregnancy is a significant fact in the litigation, the normal 266-day human gestation period is so short that the pregnancy will come to term before the usual appellate process is complete. If that termination makes a case moot, pregnancy litigation seldom will survive much beyond the trial stage, and appellate review will be effectively denied. Our law should not be that rigid. Pregnancy often comes more than once to the same woman, and in the general population, if man is to survive, it will always be with us. Pregnancy provides a classic justification for a conclusion of nonmootness. It truly could be "capable of repetition, yet evading review." . . . See Moore v. Ogilvie. . . .

Given the fact that an additional plaintiff in *Roe* was the subject of a criminal prosecution in which the constitutionality of the statute would be tested, was this a fair conclusion? See Epstein, The Abortion Cases, 1973 Sup.Ct.Rev. 159, 164.

Roe was distinguished in the notorious case of DeFunis v. Odegaard, 416 U.S. 312 (1974), where a bare majority held moot a white law-school applicant's argument that he had been unconstitutionally excluded on racial grounds. By the time the case was ready for Supreme Court decision, the plaintiff was in his last quarter of law school pursuant to a stay, and the school had agreed not to bounce him during the quarter.

> Just because this particular case did not reach the Court until the eve of the petitioner's graduation from law school, it hardly follows that the issue he raises will in the future evade review. If the admissions procedures of the Law School remain unchanged, there is no reason to suppose that a subsequent case attacking those procedures will not come with relative speed to this Court, now that the Supreme Court of Washington has spoken.

DeFunis, one federal official was heard to say, announced a new principle: "Difficult cases are moot."

(5) The next step came in Franks v. Bowman Transportation Co., 424 U.S. 747 (1976), a class action seeking relief for racial discrimination in employment. By the time the case reached the Supreme Court the sole issue related to the appropriate remedy for victims of discrimination, and the sole representative of the complaining class who was in court had been determined ineligible for any relief since he had been discharged for cause. Yet the Court refused to hold the case moot: Other members of the class still had an interest in the outcome, and *Sosna* had held it immaterial that "the named representative no longer had a personal stake." It was also irrelevant, wrote Justice Brennan, that the issue was not one "capable of repetition, yet evading review;" "nothing in our *Sosna* . . . opinion [ ] holds or even intimates" to the contrary.[4]

Geraghty may not seem a giant step beyond these precedents; was Justice Powell protesting too late?

(6) The Court purported to recognize Geraghty as a proper party to litigate only the question of class certification, leaving open the question whether he could represent the class on the merits if it was later certified. Is there any sense in that distinction?

(7) Also relied on in *Geraghty* was its companion case of Deposit Guaranty National Bank v. Roper, 445 U.S. 326 (1980), which held that class members who had been offered in settlement all they individually requested could nevertheless appeal the denial of class certification. The *Roper* opinion was written by Chief Justice Burger, who dissented in *Geraghty*.

Despite the entry of a judgment in their favor, said the Court, the named plaintiffs have asserted "a continuing individual interest in the resolution of the class certification question in their desire to shift part of the costs of litigation to those who will share in its benefits if the class is certified and ultimately prevails." This cost-sharing principle, the Court continued, was a "central concept" of Federal Rule 23, which authorizes class actions: "Here the damages claimed by the two named plaintiffs totaled $1,006.00. Such plaintiffs would be unlikely to obtain legal redress at an acceptable cost, unless counsel were motivated by the fee-spreading incentive and proceeded on a contingent-fee basis. . . . To deny the right to appeal simply because the defendant has sought to 'buy off' the individual private claims of the named plaintiffs . . . would frustrate the objectives of class actions. . . ."

The last statement is true enough, isn't it? But is it relevant to the question of what Article III allows? Could a person who is not a member of the affected class *commence* an action on its behalf on the basis of his expectation of sharing the expenses of suit? Then why can he continue an action on that basis after he has ceased to be a member of the class?[5]

4. For an anguished scream directed at each step in this line of authority, see Currie, The Supreme Court and Federal Jurisdiction: 1975 Term, 1976 Sup.Ct.Rev. 183, 187–90.

5. See Justice Powell's dissenting opinion, which Justice Stewart joined:

[N]either the Court nor the respondents have suggested that the *petitioner* [defendant] is or ever will be liable for the fees or expenses relied upon. . . . Whatever may be the basis for the respondents' asserted desire to share fees and expenses with unnamed members of a

(8) Do you deny that a plaintiff would be entitled, so far as Article III is concerned, to take an interlocutory appeal from the denial of class certification? Are *Geraghty* and *Roper* really different?

(9) Does it surprise you that a Court that could be so pernickety about standing in *Warth v. Seldin* (p. 32 supra) would be so tolerant of mootness problems in *Geraghty* and *Roper*?

BAKER v. CARR

369 U.S. 186 (1962).

MR. JUSTICE BRENNAN delivered the opinion of the Court.

This civil action was brought under 42 U.S.C. §§ 1983 and 1988 to redress the alleged deprivation of federal constitutional rights. The complaint, alleging that by means of a 1901 Statute of Tennessee apportioning the members of the General Assembly among the State's 95 counties, "these plaintiffs and others similarly situated, are denied the equal protection of the laws accorded them by the Fourteenth Amendment to the Constitution of the United States by virtue of the debasement of their votes," was dismissed by a three-judge court convened under 28 U.S.C. § 2281 in the middle district of Tennessee. The court held that it lacked jurisdiction of the subject matter and also that no claim was stated upon which relief could be granted. 179 F.Supp. 824. We noted probable jurisdiction of the appeal. . . . We hold that the dismissal was error, and remand the cause to the District Court for trial and further proceedings consistent with this opinion. . . .

Tennessee's standard for allocating legislative representation among her counties is the total number of qualified voters resident in the respective counties, subject only to minor qualifications. . . . The complaint alleges that the 1901 statute, even as of the time of its passage, "made no apportionment of Representatives and Senators in accordance with the constitutional formula . . ., but instead arbitrarily and capriciously apportioned representatives in the Senate and House without reference . . . to any logical or reasonable formula whatever." It is further alleged that "because of the population changes since 1900, and the failure of the Legislature to reapportion itself since 1901," the 1901 statute became "unconstitutional and obsolete." Appellants also argue that, because of the composition of the legislature effected by the 1901 Apportionment Act, redress in the form of a state constitutional amendment to change the entire mechanism for reapportioning, or any other change short of that, is difficult or impossible.[14] The complaint concludes that "these plaintiffs and others

class, the petitioner is merely a bystander. . . . I know of no decision by any court that holds that a lawyer's interest in a larger fee, to be paid by third persons not present in court, creates the personal stake in the outcome required by Art. III.

14. The appellants claim that no General Assembly constituted according to the 1901 Act will submit reapportionment proposals either to the people or to a Constitutional Convention. There is no provision for popular initiative in Tennessee. . . .

similarly situated, are denied the equal protection of the laws accorded them by the Fourteenth Amendment to the Constitution of the United States by virtue of the debasement of their votes." They seek a declaration that the 1901 statute is unconstitutional and an injunction restraining the appellees from acting to conduct any further elections under it. . . .

In light of the District Court's treatment of the case, we hold today only (a) that the court possessed jurisdiction of the subject matter; (b) that a justiciable cause of action is stated upon which appellants would be entitled to appropriate relief; and (c) because appellees raise the issue before this Court, that the appellants have standing to challenge the Tennessee apportionment statutes. Beyond noting that we have no cause at this stage to doubt the District Court will be able to fashion relief if violations of constitutional rights are found, it is improper now to consider what remedy would be most appropriate if appellants prevail at the trial. . . .

In holding that the subject matter of this suit was not justiciable, the District Court relied on Colegrove v. Green [328 U.S. 549 (1946)] . . . and subsequent *per curiam* cases. . . . We understand the District Court to have read the cited cases as compelling the conclusion that since the appellants sought to have a legislative apportionment held unconstitutional, their suit presented a "political question". . . . We hold that this challenge to an apportionment presents no nonjusticiable "political question." The cited cases do not hold the contrary.

Of course the mere fact that the suit seeks protection of a political right does not mean it presents a political question. Such an objection "is little more than a play upon words". . . . Rather, it is argued that apportionment cases, whatever the actual wording of the complaint, can involve no federal constitutional right except one resting on the guaranty of a republican form of government,[30] and that complaints based on that clause have been held to present political questions which are nonjusticiable. . . .

It is the relationship between the judiciary and the coordinate branches of the Federal Government, and not the federal judiciary's relationship to the States, which gives rise to the "political question." . . . The nonjusticiability of a political question is primarily a function of the separation of powers. . . .

Foreign relations: There are sweeping statements to the effect that all questions touching foreign relations are political questions. Not only does resolution of such issues frequently turn on standards that defy judicial application, or involve the exercise of a discretion demonstrably committed to the executive or legislature; but many such questions uniquely demand single-voiced statement of the Govern-

30. "The United States shall guarantee to every State in this Union a Republican Form of Government, and shall protect each of them against Invasion; and on the Application of the Legislature or of the Executive (when the Legislature cannot be convened) against domestic Violence." U.S.Const., Art. IV, § 4.

ment's views. Yet it is error to suppose that every case or controversy which touches foreign relations lies beyond judicial cognizance. Our cases in this field seem invariably to show a discriminating analysis of the particular question posed, in terms of the history of its management by the political branches, of its susceptibility to judicial handling in the light of its nature and posture in the specific case, and of the possible consequences of judicial action. For example, though a court will not ordinarily inquire whether a treaty has been terminated, since on that question "governmental action . . . must be regarded as of controlling importance," if there has been no conclusive "government action" then a court can construe a treaty and may find it provides the answer. . . .

While recognition of foreign governments so strongly defies judicial treatment that without executive recognition a foreign state has been called "a republic of whose existence we know nothing," and the judiciary ordinarily follows the executive as to which nation has sovereignty over disputed territory, once sovereignty over an area is politically determined and declared, courts may examine the resulting status and decide independently whether a statute applies to that area. Similarly, recognition of belligerency abroad is an executive responsibility, but if the executive proclamations fall short of an explicit answer, a court may construe them seeking, for example, to determine whether the situation is such that statutes designed to assure American neutrality have become operative. . . . Similar judicial action in the absence of a recognizedly authoritative executive declaration occurs in cases involving the immunity from seizure of vessels owned by friendly foreign governments. . . .

Dates of duration of hostilities: Though it has been stated broadly that "the power which declared the necessity is the power to declare its cessation, and what the cessation requires," Commercial Trust Co. v. Miller, 262 U.S. 51, 57, here too analysis reveals isolable reasons for the presence of political questions, underlying this Court's refusal to review the political departments' determination of when or whether a war has ended. Dominant is the need for finality in the political determination, for emergency's nature demands "A prompt and unhesitating obedience," Martin v. Mott, 12 Wheat. [25 U.S.] 19, 30 (calling up of militia). Moreover, "the cessation of hostilities does not necessarily end the war power. . . ." But deference rests on reason, not habit. The question in a particular case may not seriously implicate considerations of finality—e.g., a public program of importance (rent control) yet not central to the emergency effort. Further, clearly definable criteria for decision may be available. In such case the political question barrier falls away: "[A] Court is not at liberty to shut its eyes to an obvious mistake, when the validity of the law depends upon the truth of what is declared. . . . [It can] inquire whether the exigency still existed upon which the continued operation of the law depended." . . .

Validity of enactments: In Coleman v. Miller [307 U.S. 433] . . . this Court held that the questions of how long a proposed amendment to the Federal Constitution remained open to ratification, and what effect a prior rejection had on a subsequent ratification, were committed to congressional resolution and involved criteria of decision that necessarily escaped the judicial grasp. Similar considerations apply to the enacting process:

"The respect due to coequal and independent departments," and the need for finality and certainty about the status of a statute contribute to judicial reluctance to inquire whether, as passed, it complied with all requisite formalities. . . . But it is not true that courts will never delve into a legislature's records upon such a quest: If the enrolled statute lacks an effective date, a court will not hesitate to seek it in the legislative journals in order to preserve the enactment. Gardner v. Collector, 6 Wall. [73 U.S.] 499. The political question doctrine, a tool for maintenance of governmental order, will not be so applied as to promote only disorder.

The status of Indian tribes: . . .

While " 'It is for [Congress] . . ., and not for the courts, to determine when the true interests of the Indian require his release from [the condition of tutelage' . . ., it is not meant by this that Congress may bring a community or body of people within the range of this power by arbitrarily calling them an Indian tribe . . . ." United States v. Sandoval, 231 U.S. 28, 46. . . .

It is apparent that several formulations which vary slightly according to the settings in which the questions arise may describe a political question, although each has one or more elements which identify it as essentially a function of the separation of powers. Prominent on the surface of any case held to involve a political question is found a textually demonstrable constitutional commitment of the issue to a coordinate political department; or a lack of judicially discoverable and manageable standards for resolving it; or the impossibility of deciding without an initial policy determination of a kind clearly for nonjudicial discretion; or the impossibility of a court's undertaking independent resolution without expressing lack of the respect due coordinate branches of government; or an unusual need for unquestioning adherence to a political decision already made; or the potentiality of embarrassment from multifarious pronouncements by various departments on one question. . . .

Republican form of government: Luther v. Borden, 7 How. [48 U.S.] 1, though in form simply an action for damages for trespass was, as Daniel Webster said in opening the argument for the defense, "an unusual case." The defendants, admitting an otherwise tortious breaking and entering, sought to justify their action on the ground that they were agents of the established lawful government of Rhode Island, which State was then under martial law to defend itself from active insurrection; that the plaintiff was engaged in that insurrection; and that they entered under orders to arrest the plaintiff. The case arose "out of the unfortunate political differences which agitated the people of Rhode Island in 1841 and 1842," 7 How., at 34, and which had resulted in a situation wherein two groups laid competing claims to recognition as the lawful government. The plaintiff's right to recover depended upon which of the two groups was entitled to such recognition; but the lower court's refusal to receive evidence or hear argument on that issue, its charge to the jury that the earlier established or "charter" government was lawful, and the verdict for the defendants, were affirmed upon appeal to this Court.

Chief Justice Taney's opinion for the Court reasoned as follows: (1) If a court were to hold the defendants' acts unjustified because the charter government had no legal existence during the period in question, it would follow that all of that government's actions—laws enacted, taxes collected, salaries paid, accounts settled, sentences passed—were of no effect; and that "the officers who carried their decisions into operation [were] answerable as trespassers, if not in some cases as criminals." There was, of course, no room for application of any doctrine of *de facto* status to uphold prior acts of an officer not authorized *de jure*, for such would have defeated the plaintiff's very action. A decision for the plaintiff would inevitably have produced some significant measure of chaos, a consequence to be avoided if it could be done without abnegation of the judicial duty to uphold the Constitution. . . .

Clearly, several factors were thought by the Court in *Luther* to make the question there "political": the commitment to the other branches of the decision as to which is the lawful state government; the unambiguous action by the President, in recognizing the charter government as the lawful authority; the need for finality in the executive's decision; and the lack of criteria by which a court could determine which form of government was republican.

But the only significance that *Luther* could have for our immediate purposes is in its holding that the Guaranty Clause is not a repository of judicially manageable standards which a court could utilize independently in order to identify a State's lawful government. The Court has since refused to resort to the Guaranty Clause—which alone had been invoked for the purpose—as the source of a constitutional standard for invalidating state action. See Taylor & Marshall v. Beckham (No. 1), 178 U.S. 548 (claim that Kentucky's resolution of contested gubernatorial election deprived voters of republican government held nonjusticiable); Pacific States Tel. Co. v. Oregon, 223 U.S. 118 (claim that initiative and referendum negated republican government held nonjusticiable). . . .

Just as the Court has consistently held that a challenge to state action based on the Guaranty Clause presents no justiciable question so has it held, and for the same reasons, that challenges to congressional action on the ground of inconsistency with that clause present no justiciable question. In Georgia v. Stanton, 6 Wall. [73 U.S.] 50, the State sought by an original bill to enjoin execution of the Reconstruction Acts, claiming . . . that enforcement of the new Acts "Instead of keeping the guaranty against a forcible overthrow of its government by foreign invaders or domestic insurgents, . . . is destroying that very government by force." Congress had clearly refused to recognize the republican character of the government of the suing State. It seemed to the Court that the only constitutional claim that could be presented was under the Guaranty Clause, and Congress having determined that the effects of the recent hostilities required extraordinary measures to restore governments of a republican form, this Court refused to interfere with Congress' action at the behest of a claimant relying on that very guaranty. . . .

We come, finally, to the ultimate inquiry whether our precedents as to what constitutes a nonjusticiable "political question" bring the case before us under the umbrella of that doctrine. A natural beginning is to note whether any of the common characteristics which we have been able to identify and label descriptively are present. We find none: The question here is the consistency of state action with the Federal Constitution. We have no question decided, or to be decided, by a political branch of government coequal with this Court. Nor do we risk embarrassment of our government abroad, or grave disturbance at home if we take issue with Tennessee as to the constitutionality of her action here challenged. Nor need the appellants, in order to succeed in this action, ask the Court to enter upon policy determinations for which judicially manageable standards are lacking. Judicial standards under the Equal Protection Clause are well developed and familiar, and it has been open to courts since the enactment of the Fourteenth Amendment to determine, if on the particular facts they must, that a discrimination reflects *no* policy, but simply arbitrary and capricious action. . . .

We conclude then that the nonjusticiability of claims resting on the Guaranty Clause which arises from their embodiment of questions that were thought "political," can have no bearing upon the justiciability of the equal protection claim presented in this case. Finally, we emphasize that it is the involvement in Guaranty Clause claims of the elements thought to define "political questions," and no other feature, which could render them nonjusticiable. Specifically, we have said that such claims are not held nonjusticiable because they touch matters of state governmental organization. Brief examination of a few cases demonstrates this.

When challenges to state action respecting matters of "the administration of the affairs of the State and the officers through whom they are conducted" have rested on claims of constitutional deprivation which are amenable to judicial correction, this Court has acted upon its view of the merits of the claim. For example, in Boyd v. Nebraska ex rel. Thayer, 143 U.S. 135, we reversed the Nebraska Supreme Court's decision that Nebraska's Governor was not a citizen of the United States or of the State and therefore could not continue in office. In

Kennard v. Louisiana ex rel. Morgan, 92 U.S. 480, and Foster v. Kansas ex rel. Johnston, 112 U.S. 201, we considered whether persons had been removed from public office by procedures consistent with the Fourteenth Amendment's due process guaranty, and held on the merits that they had. And only last Term, in Gomillion v. Lightfoot, 364 U.S. 339, we applied the Fifteenth Amendment to strike down a re-drafting of municipal boundaries which effected a discriminatory impairment of voting rights, in the face of what a majority of the Court of Appeals thought to be a sweeping commitment to state legislatures of the power to draw and redraw such boundaries. . . .

We have already noted that the District Court's holding that the subject matter of this complaint was nonjusticiable relied upon Colegrove v. Green, supra, and later cases. Some of those concerned the choice of members of a state legislature, as in this case; others, like *Colegrove* itself and earlier precedents, . . . settled the issue in favor of justiciability of questions of congressional redistricting. . . .

Mr. Justice Rutledge [whose vote for dismissal in *Colegrove* was decisive] joined in the conclusion that the case was justiciable, although he held that the dismissal of the complaint should be affirmed. His view was that "The shortness of the time remaining [before forthcoming elections] makes it doubtful whether action could, or would, be taken in time to secure for petitioners the effective relief they seek. . . . I think, therefore, the case is one in which the Court may properly, and should, decline to exercise its jurisdiction. . . ."

The refusal to award relief in *Colegrove* resulted only from the controlling view of a want of equity. Nor is anything contrary to be found in those *per curiams* that came after *Colgrove.* This Court dismissed the appeals in Cook v. Fortson and Turman v. Duckworth, 329 U.S. 675, as moot. MacDougall v. Green, 335 U.S. 281, held only that in that case equity would not act to void the State's requirement that there be at least a minimum of support for nominees for the statewide office, over at least a minimal area of the State. . . . In Kidd v. McCanless, . . . the Supreme Court of Tennessee held that it could not invalidate the very statute at issue in the case at bar, but its holding rested on its state law of remedies, i.e., the state view of *de facto* officers. . . . Of course this Court was there precluded by the adequate state ground, . . . 352 U.S. 920. . . .

We conclude that the complaint's allegations of a denial of equal protection present a justiciable constitutional cause of action upon which appellants are entitled to a trial and a decision. The right asserted is within the reach of a judicial protection under the Fourteenth Amendment.

The judgment of the District Court is reversed and the cause is remanded for further proceedings consistent with this opinion. . . .

MR. JUSTICE CLARK, concurring. . . .

I believe . . . that a patent violation of the Equal Protection Clause . . . has been shown. . . . No one—except the dissenters advocating the Harlan "adjusted 'total representation'" formula—contends that mathematical equality among voters is required by the Equal Protection Clause. But certainly there must be some rational design to a State's districting. The discrimination here does not fit any pattern—as I have said, it is but a crazy quilt. . . .

Although I find the Tennessee apportionment statute offends the Equal Protection Clause, I would not consider intervention by this Court into so delicate a field if there were any other relief available to the people of Tennessee. But the majority of people of Tennessee have no "practical opportunities for exerting their political weight at the polls" to correct the existing "invidious discrimination." Tennessee has no initiative and referendum. . . . The people have been rebuffed at the hands of the Assembly; they have tried the constitutional convention route, but since the call must originate in the Assembly it, too, has been fruitless. They have tried Tennessee courts with the same result, and Governors have fought the tide only to flounder. It is said that there is recourse in Congress and perhaps that may be, but from a practical standpoint this is without substance. To date Congress has never undertaken such a task in any State. . . .

MR. JUSTICE FRANKFURTER, whom MR. JUSTICE HARLAN joins, dissenting.

The Court today reverses a uniform course of decision established by a dozen cases, including one by which the very claim now sustained was unanimously rejected only five years ago. . . . Disregard of inherent limits in the effective exercise of the Court's "judicial Power" not only presages the futility of judicial intervention in the essentially political conflict of forces by which the relation between population and representation has time out of mind been and is now determined. It may well impair the Court's position as the ultimate organ of "the supreme Law of the Land" in that vast range of legal problems, often strongly entangled in popular feeling, on which this Court must pronounce. The Court's authority—possessed of neither the purse nor the sword—ultimately rests on sustained public confidence in its moral sanction. Such feeling must be nourished by the Court's complete detachment, in fact and in appearance, from political entanglements and by abstention from injecting itself into the clash of political forces in political settlements. . . .

We were soothingly told at the bar of this Court that we need not worry about the kind of remedy a court could effectively fashion once the abstract constitutional right to have courts pass on a state-wide system of electoral districting is recognized as a matter of judicial rhetoric, because legislatures would heed the Court's admonition. This is not only a euphoric hope. It implies a sorry confession of judicial impotence in place of a frank acknowledgement that there is not under our Constitution a judicial remedy for every political mischief, for every undesirable exercise of legislative power. The Framers carefully and with deliberate forethought refused so to enthrone the judiciary. In this situation, as in others of like nature, appeal for relief does not belong here. Appeal must be to an informed civically militant electorate. In a democratic society like ours, relief must come through an aroused popular conscience that sears the conscience of the people's representatives. In any event there is nothing judicially more unseemly nor more self-defeating than for this Court to make *in terrorem* pronouncements, to indulge in merely empty rhetoric, sounding a word of promise to the ear, sure to be disappointing to the hope. . . .

The present case involves all of the elements that have made the Guarantee Clause cases non-justiciable. It is, in effect, a Guarantee Clause claim masquerading under a different label. But it cannot make the case more fit for judicial action that appellants invoke the Fourteenth Amendment rather than Art. IV, § 4, where, in fact, the gist of their complaint is the same—unless it can be found that the Fourteenth Amendment speaks with greater particularity to their situation. . . . Art. IV, § 4, is not committed by express constitutional terms to Congress. It is the nature of the controversies arising under it, nothing else, which has made it judicially unenforceable. . . .

Here appellants attack "the State as a State," precisely as it was perceived to be attacked in the *Pacific States* case . . . . They assert that "a minority now rules in Tennessee," that the apportionment statute results in a "distortion of the constitutional system," that the General Assembly is no longer "a body representative of the people of the State of Tennessee," all "contrary to the basic principle of representative government. . . ." . . . Such a claim would be non-justiciable not merely under Art. IV, § 4, but under any clause of the Constitution, by virtue of the very fact that a federal court is not a forum for political debate. Massachusetts v. Mellon, supra. . . . What is actually asked of the Court in this case is to choose among competing bases of representation—ultimately, really, among competing theories of political philosophy—in order to establish an appropriate frame of government for the State of Tennessee and thereby for all the States of the Union. . . .

The notion that representation proportioned to the geographic spread of population is so universally accepted as a necessary element of equality between man and man that it must be taken to be the standard of a political equality preserved by the Fourteenth Amendment—that it is, in appellants' words "the basic principle of representative government"—is, to put it bluntly, not true. However desirable and however desired by some among the great political thinkers and framers of our government, it has never been generally practiced, today or in the past. It was not the Englisn system, it was not the colonial system, it was not the system chosen for the national government by the Constitution, it was not the system exclusively or even predominantly practiced by the States at the time of adoption of the Fourteenth

Amendment, it is not predominantly practiced by the States today. . . .

Apportionment, by its character, is a subject of extraordinary complexity, involving—even after the fundamental theoretical issues concerning what is to be represented in a representative legislature have been fought out or compromised—considerations of geography, demography, electoral convenience, economic and social cohesions or divergencies among particular local groups, communications, the practical effects of political institutions like the lobby and the city machine, ancient traditions and ties of settled usage, respect for proven incumbents of long experience and senior status, mathematical mechanics, censuses compiling relevant data, and a host of others. Legislative responses throughout the country to the reapportionment demands of the 1960 Census have glaringly confirmed that these are not factors that lend themselves to evaluations of a nature that are the staple of judicial determinations or for which judges are equipped to adjudicate by legal training or experience or native wit. And this is the more so true because in every strand of this complicated, intricate web of values meet the contending forces of partisan politics. The practical significance of apportionment is that the next election results may differ because of it. Apportionment battles are overwhelmingly party or intra-party contests. It will add a virulent source of friction and tension in federal-state relations to embroil the federal judiciary in them. . . .

In all of the apportionment cases which have come before the Court, a consideration which has been weighty in determining their non-justiciability has been the difficulty or impossibility of devising effective judicial remedies in this class of case. An injunction restraining a general election unless the legislature reapportions would paralyze the critical centers of a State's political system and threaten political dislocation whose consequences are not foreseeable. A declaration devoid of implied compulsion of injunctive or other relief would be an idle threat. Surely a Federal District Court could not itself remap the State: the same complexities which impede effective judicial review of apportionment *a fortiori* make impossible a court's consideration of these imponderables as an original matter. And the choice of elections at large as opposed to elections by district, however unequal the districts, is a matter of sweeping political judgment having enormous political implications, the nature and reach of which are certainly beyond the informed understanding of, and capacity for appraisal by, courts. . . .

Although the District Court had jurisdiction in the very restricted sense of power to determine whether it could adjudicate the claim, the case is of that class of political controversy which, by the nature of its subject, is unfit for federal judicial action. The judgment of the District Court, in dismissing the complaint for failure to state a claim on which relief can be granted, should therefore be affirmed.

[Separate opinions by Justices Douglas, Stewart, and Harlan are omitted. Justice Whittaker did not participate.]

Notes on Political Questions

(1) The issue in *Baker v. Carr* was neither hypothetical nor moot; the plaintiffs were alleging, in the terms of 42 U.S.C. § 1983, that they had been deprived of constitutional rights under color of state law; as the Court held in a portion of the opinion not here reproduced, there was jurisdiction under 28 U.S.C. § 1343(3). Was there any legal basis for Justice Frankfurter's position? Or was he just arguing that he would rather not take jurisdiction? Cf. Brennan, J., dissenting, in *Warth v. Seldin*, at p. 39 supra: "[C]ourts cannot refuse to hear a case on the merits merely because they would prefer not to. . . ." [1]

(2) Can one derive a general political-question principle from Article III? Was that what Justices Brennan and Frankfurter were suggesting when they spoke in *Baker* of "justiciability" and of "inherent limits in the effective exercise of the Court's 'judicial power'?" Or were they invoking what the Court has elsewhere termed "prudential" considerations? As a pure matter of policy, were Frankfurter's arguments persuasive?

Notice that the availability of judicially manageable standards for decision, which both Brennan and Frankfurter stressed in *Baker*, has a great deal to do with one's opinion on the merits. Justice Frankfurter viewed apportionment as a complex process involving numerous elusive factors; for anyone convinced that the one-person-one-vote rule is required by the Constitution there is no difficulty with standards. Didn't Justice Frankfurter pick a tough case in which to make his point? Or was Justice Clark imposing a doubtful rule in requiring a state to apportion according to some rational plan? Even accepting the Frankfurter position on the merits, is the apportionment decision so much more subjective than the limits of free speech or the reasonableness of a search?

If Frankfurter believed that the Equal Protection Clause did not guarantee equal voting power, why didn't he just say the complaint failed to state a claim on the merits?

(3) Some have attempted to trace the political-question doctrine to *Marbury v. Madison*, where Marshall protested in dictum that "[q]uestions in their nature political, or which are, by the constitution and laws,

1. By the time *Baker* was decided, the reapportionment issue was not new, and Frankfurter had an impressive argument from precedent at his disposal. See Kurland, Foreword: "Equal in Origin and Equal in Title to the [Legislative] and Executive Branches of the Government," 78 Harv.L.Rev. 143, 149 (1964), finding it "difficult to believe that the Court thought it could find an audience ingenuous enough" to think *Baker* consistent with prior apportionment decisions.

On the other hand, it was Justice Frankfurter who had written for the Court, one year earlier, in striking down (under the Fifteenth Amendment) boundaries drawn to exclude black voters from the city of Tuskegee, Alabama. *Colegrove* and the other apportionment cases were distinguished: "In no case involving unequal weight in voting distribution that has come before the court did the decision sanction a differentiation on racial lines. . . ." Gomillion v. Lightfoot, 364 U.S. 339, 346 (1960). Why was this not also a "Guarantee Clause" case for Justice Frankfurter?

submitted to the executive, can never be made in this court." See p. 19 supra. Take another look at the context of that remark; do you think Marshall meant that there were violations of the Constitution that the courts could not redress when presented in a concrete controversy? Can Frankfurter's doctrine be reconciled with *Marbury's* principle that written limitations on legislative power imply judicial review, or with its insistence that the "essence of civil liberty . . . consists in the right of every individual to claim the protection of the laws, whenever he receives an injury?"

(4) The granddaddy of cases cited as illustrating the political-question doctrine was Luther v. Borden, 48 U.S. (7 How.) 1 (1849), which Justice Brennan distinguished in *Baker*. Rhode Island officials had broken into Luther's house in an effort to suppress what they viewed as an insurrection; suing for trespass, Luther contended that the charter government in whose name the defendants had acted had been displaced by his own contending faction. The circuit court refused to entertain this argument and decided for the defendant; the Supreme Court, in an opinion by Chief Justice Taney, affirmed.

The question of which faction constituted the legitimate government of Rhode Island, the Court said, was one of state law; the state Supreme Court, in holding that the inquiry "belonged to the political power and not to the judicial," had already held "that the charter government was the lawful and established government;" and the circuit court was bound to "follow the decisions of the State courts in questions which concern merely the constitution and laws of the State."

Taney went on to suggest practical considerations that made it undesirable to undertake the inquiry: Evidentiary difficulties would surround the investigation whether the new state constitution under which Luther claimed had received the support of a majority of eligible voters; the issue would depend upon witness credibility and might produce conflicting jury verdicts in various cases; a decision against the charter government would mean that "the laws passed by its legislature . . . were nullities; its taxes wrongfully collected; its salaries and compensation to its officers illegally paid; its public accounts improperly settled; and the judgments and sentences of its courts . . . null and void. . . . When the decision of this court might lead to such results, it becomes its duty to examine very carefully its own powers before it undertakes to exercise jurisdiction."

Finally,

> [T]he Constitution of the United States, as far as it has provided for an emergency of this kind, and authorized the general government to interfere in the domestic concerns of a state, has treated the subject as political in nature, and placed the power in the hands of that department. . . .
>
> Under this article of the Constitution it rests with Congress to decide what government is the established one in a State. For as the United States guarantee to each State a republican government, Congress must necessarily decide what government is established in the State before it can determine whether it is republican or not. And when the senators and representatives of a State are admitted into the

> councils of the Union, the authority of the government under which they are appointed, as well as its republican character, is recognized by the proper constitutional authority. And its decision is binding on every other department of the government. . . .

In addition, Congress had authorized the President, pursuant to the clause of Article IV respecting domestic violence, to call out the militia when necessary upon application of state authorities; "he must determine what body of men constitute the legislature, and who is the governor, before he can act." Indeed the charter governor had asked the President to exercise this power in the present controversy; and in response "the President recognized him as the executive power of the state. . . . In the case of foreign nations, the government acknowledged by the President is always recognized in the courts of justice. And this principle has been applied by act of Congress to the sovereign States of the Union."

Did this decision establish a general principle that federal courts may not decide "political" questions? Was it persuasive in its interpretation of the Guarantee Clause?

(5) Outside the ambit of the Guarantee Clause, one of the leading political-question discussions before *Baker* was found in Coleman v. Miller, 307 U.S. 433 (1939). Congress had proposed a Child Labor Amendment to the Constitution in 1924; Kansas had rejected it in 1925 but ratified it in 1937. The suit challenged this ratification on three grounds: that Kansas's original rejection was final; that the proposed amendment had expired because not ratified within a "reasonable time;" and that the Lieutenant Governor could not cast the tie-breaking vote in the state legislature. All these arguments were based upon Article V, which provides only that Congress "shall propose Amendments" and that they become effective "when ratified by the Legislatures of three fourths of the several States. . . ."

The Supreme Court, over two dissents, affirmed the denial of relief. Chief Justice Hughes wrote the "Opinion of the Court," but four of the seven majority Justices concurred separately "in the result" in an opinion by Justice Black, "for somewhat different reasons."

Hughes noted that "Article V, speaking solely of ratification, contains no provision as to rejection;" that no statute spoke to the issue; that Congress and the Secretary of State had proclaimed the Fourteenth Amendment effective on the basis of ratification by States that had previously rejected the Amendment; and that "[t]his decision . . . has been accepted."

> We think that in accordance with this historic precedent the question of the efficacy of ratifications by state legislatures, in the light of previous rejection or attempted withdrawal, should be regarded as a political question pertaining to the political departments, with the ultimate authority in the Congress in the exercise of its control over the promulgation of the adoption of the amendment.

The Court had held in Dillon v. Gloss, 256 U.S. 368 (1921), that Congress had power to limit the time in which a proposed amendment could be ratified. That did not mean, said the Chief Justice, that the Court should determine a "reasonable time" when Congress had not done so:

> [T]he question of a reasonable time in many cases would involve, as in this case it does involve, an appraisal of a great variety of relevant conditions, political, social and economic, which can hardly be said to be within the appropriate range of evidence receivable in a court of justice and as to which it would be an extravagant extension of judicial authority to assert judicial notice. . . . The questions they involve are essentially political and not justiciable. . . .
>
> Our decision that the Congress has the power under Article V to fix a reasonable limit of time for ratification in proposing an amendment proceeds upon the assumption that the question, what is a reasonable time, lies within the congressional province. If it be deemed that such a question is an open one when the limit has not been fixed in advance, we think that it should also be regarded as an open one for the consideration of the Congress when, in the presence of certified ratifications by three-fourths of the States, the time arrives for the promulgation of the adoption of the amendment.

Citing the early Guarantee Clause cases and noting "many illustrations in the field of our conduct of foreign relations," Hughes noted that "the appropriateness . . . of attributing finality to the action of the political departments" and "the lack of satisfactory criteria for a judicial determination" were "dominant considerations" in deciding which questions were political and concluded that "Congress in controlling the promulgation of the adoption of a constitutional amendment has the final determination of the question whether by lapse of time its proposal of the amendment had lost its vitality. . . ."[2]

Justice Black and those joining him thought the Hughes opinion asserted too much judicial authority over the amending process:

> [W]hether submission, intervening procedure or Congressional determination of ratification conforms to the commands of the Constitution, calls for decisions by a "political department" of questions of a type which this Court has frequently designated "political." And decision of a "political question" by the "political department" to which the Constitution has committed it "conclusively binds the judges. . . ." . . . Article V . . . grants power over the amending of the Constitution to Congress alone. . . . The process itself is "political" in its entirety, from submission until an amendment becomes part of the Constitution, and is not subject to judicial guidance, control or interference at any point. . . .

Did *Coleman* hold that there was no judicial remedy if Kansas's ratification offended the Constitution, or that Article V did not forbid congressional acceptance of Kansas's ratification on the merits? Does *Coleman* establish a general principle that "political" issues are nonjusticiable? Does *Coleman* survive *Baker*?[3]

2. On the question whether the contention regarding the Lieutenant Governor was "justiciable" or "political," said Hughes, the Court was equally divided.

3. In Hollingsworth v. Virginia, 3 U.S. (3 Dall.) 378, 382 (1798), the Court held on the merits that the Presidential-veto clause of Article I was inapplicable to constitu-

(6) *Baker* was generally understood to have weakened the political-question doctrine, and this process was carried further in Powell v. McCormack, 395 U.S. 486 (1969), which cast cold water on categories of questions left political by the famous exposition in *Baker*. Congressman Adam Clayton Powell had been excluded from the House of Representatives for such alleged misbehavior as the diversion of House funds for private purposes. Over a single dissent arguing only that the case was moot, the Court in an opinion by Chief Justice Warren held his request for declaratory relief justiciable and rejected a claim of congressional immunity (see p. 480 infra).

The only political-question argument the Court took seriously was that Art. I, § 5, which makes the House "the Judge of the Elections, Returns and Qualifications of its own Members," constituted a "textually demonstrable constitutional commitment" of the exclusion issue to the House. But the Court set a significant role for itself in determining the scope of the alleged commitment:

> In order to determine whether there has been a textual commitment to a coordinate department of the Government, we must interpret the Constitution. In other words, we must first determine what power the Constitution confers upon the House through Art. I, § 5, before we can determine to what extent, if any, the exercise of that power is subject to judicial review. . . .

The Court thereupon undertook an intensive examination of the Qualifications Clause, concluding on the merits, because of history embracing Hamilton's policy "that the people should choose whom they please to govern them," that the House may exclude an elected member only for failure to meet the three qualifications (age, citizenship, and residence) specified in Art. I, § 2: "The Constitution does not vest in the Congress a discretionary power to deny membership by a majority vote." Because, therefore, "Art. I, § 5 is at most a 'textually demonstrable commitment' to Congress to judge only the qualifications expressly set forth in the Constitution," Powell's claim was not barred by the "textual commitment" formulation of the political-question doctrine.

Other political-question contentions were given short shrift:

> Respondents' alternate contention is that the case presents a political question because judicial resolution of petitioners' claim would produce a "potentially embarrassing confrontation between coordinate branches" of the Federal Government. But, as our interpretation of Art. I, § 5, discloses, a determination of petitioner Powell's right to sit would require no more than an interpretation of the Constitution. Such a determination falls within the traditional role accorded courts to interpret the law, and does not involve a "lack of the respect due [a] coordinate [branch] of government," nor does it involve an "initial

tional amendments, with no suggestion that the issue was "political" rather than justiciable. In Dyer v. Blair, 390 F.Supp. 1291 (N.D.Ill.1975), a three-judge court held justiciable the question whether Article V permitted a State to require a three-fifths majority for the ratification of federal amendments, holding that the reference in the Article to the state "Legislature[ ]" meant that body itself, but not the state Constitution, could impose such a requirement. Was the decision consistent with *Coleman*?

policy determination of a kind clearly for nonjudicial discretion." . . . Our system of government requires that federal courts on occasion interpret the Constitution in a manner at variance with the construction given the document by another branch. The alleged conflict that such an adjudication may cause cannot justify the courts' avoiding their constitutional responsibility. . . .

Nor are any of the other formulations of a political question "inextricable from the case at bar." . . . Petitioners seek a determination that the House was without power to exclude Powell from the 90th Congress, which, we have seen, requires an interpretation of the Constitution—a determination for which clearly there are "judicially . . . manageable standards." Finally, a judicial resolution of petitioners' claim will not result in "multifarious pronouncements by various departments on one question." For, as we noted in Baker v. Carr, . . . it is the responsibility of this Court to act as the ultimate interpreter of the Constitution. Marbury v. Madison, 5 U.S. (1 Cranch) 137 (1803).[4, 5]

(7) Nevertheless political-question noises continue to be made.

Gilligan v. Morgan, 413 U.S. 1 (1973), was an action by students at Kent State University in the wake of campus violence during which several persons had been shot to death by members of the Ohio National Guard. The Court of Appeals thought the complaint stated a justiciable claim for declaratory and injunctive relief on the ground that the Guard had been so poorly trained, equipped and commanded as to make "inevitable" the unnecessary use of lethal force. The Supreme Court reversed.

4. Not surprisingly, suits attacking the constitutionality of the Vietnam war engendered a spate of political-question decisions. Early opinions tended to hold the issue political without much discussion, e.g., Eminente v. Johnson, 361 F.2d 73 (D.C.Cir. 1966) (alternative holding). After *Powell*, however, the Second Circuit held that the claim that orders to fight in Vietnam must be authorized by "joint executive-legislative action" was both justiciable and meritorious, and that such authorization had been given by repeated congressional actions in support of the undeclared war. The "constitutional propriety of the means by which Congress has chosen to ratify and approve" military operations, however, was a political question because of the lack of any "intelligible and objectively manageable standards by which to judge such actions" short of requiring an explicit declaration of war, which would "destroy the flexibility of action which the executive and legislative branches must have in dealing with other sovereigns." Orlando v. Laird, 443 F.2d 1039 (2d Cir. 1971). See also DaCosta v. Laird, 471 F.2d 1146 (2d Cir. 1973), refusing on similar grounds to determine the constitutionality of the President's decision to mine Haiphong harbor and to bomb North Vietnam.

5. In United States v. Nixon, 418 U.S. 683 (1974), the President sought to quash a judicial subpoena on the ground of executive privilege and argued, among other things, that "the separation of powers doctrine precludes judicial review of a President's claim of privilege." The court rejected this contention, quoting *Marbury* and *Baker*: " 'It is emphatically the province and duty of the judicial department to say what the law is.' . . . 'Deciding whether a matter has in any measure been committed by the Constitution to another branch of government . . . is itself a delicate exercise in constitutional interpretation, and is a responsibility of this Court as ultimate interpreter of the Constitution.' "

Would any of this have precluded holding that the Constitution made the President's decision unreviewable? See Gunther, Judicial Hegemony and Legislative Autonomy: The *Nixon* Case and the Impeachment Process, 22 U.C.L.A.L.Rev. 30, 34 (1974).

The action was not, Chief Justice Burger said, one for damages for past harm or one seeking to restrain "some specified and imminently threatened unlawful action" but rather "a broad call on judicial power to assume continuing regulatory jurisdiction over the activities of the Ohio National Guard," involving "continued judicial surveillance to assure compliance with the changed standards." The Court stressed that Art. I, § 8 of the Constitution vested in Congress the power "to provide for organizing, arming and disciplining, the Militia, . . . reserving to the States . . . the Authority of training the Militia according to the discipline prescribed by Congress." Congress, the Court noted, had enacted statutes pursuant to this authority and delegated further powers to the President as Commander-in-Chief to prescribe regulations governing organization and discipline of the Guard, which was "an essential reserve component of the Armed Forces." "The relief sought . . . would therefore embrace critical areas of responsibility vested by the Constitution in the Legislative and Executive Branches of the Government."

Moreover, said the Court, the decision below "would plainly and explicitly require a judicial evaluation of a wide range of possible dissimilar procedures and policies approved by different law enforcement agencies or other authorities . . . . It would be inappropriate for a district judge to undertake this responsibility, even if in the unlikely event that he possessed requisite technical competence to do so."

The Court then said the dissenting judge below had "correctly read *Baker v. Carr*" in stating that the relief sought would offend every one of the *Baker* criteria and quoted extensively from his opinion:

> "The congressional and executive authority to prescribe and regulate the training and weaponry of the National Guard . . . clearly precludes any form of judicial regulation of the same matters. . . . Any such relief . . . would necessarily draw the courts into a nonjusticiable political question."

But the Court did not stop there; it went on to quote from *Flast v. Cohen*, supra p. 53, which it said suggested there was no controversy when the parties sought an advisory opinion, when the question had been mooted, or when there was no standing; and the Court found "serious deficiencies" with respect to each of these factors in the case before it.[6]

6. Four Justices argued that the case was moot. Justices Blackmun and Powell joined the Court's opinion "on the understanding" that it held (a) that "a complaint based on a single past incident, containing allegations of unspecified, speculative threats of uncertain harm that might occur at some indefinite time in the future, cannot support respondents' standing;" and (b) that because the case "relates to prospective relief in the form of judicial surveillance of highly subjective and technical matters" it requires the court " 'to enter upon policy determinations for which judicially manageable standards are lacking.' " The same questions "in the context of a particular factual setting as a predicate to relief in the form of an injunction against continuing activity or for damages would present wholly different issues." In Scheuer v. Rhodes, 416 U.S. 232, 249 (1974), the Court despite *Gilligan* held that damage actions lay on the basis of the same incident.

See also Roudebush v. Hartke, 405 U.S. 15 (1972), holding that Article I's provision making the Senate "Judge of the Elections . . . of its own Members" did not forbid a State to order a recount after a disputed election but adding in dictum that "[w]hich candidate is entitled to be seated in the Senate" was "a nonjusticiable political question"; O'Brien v. Brown, 409 U.S. 1

(8) In Goldwater v. Carter, 444 U.S. 996 (1979), the Court refused to entertain a challenge to the President's power to terminate a treaty, over three dissents. Justice Marshall concurred only in the result, and Justice Powell based his concurrence on lack of ripeness; but Justice Rehnquist, writing for four Justices, argued that the question was political. As with the rejection of proposed amendments in *Coleman v. Miller*, supra note 5, the Constitution contained no "provision governing the termination of a treaty"; "different termination procedures may be appropriate for different treaties"; and "the justifications for concluding that the question here is political . . . are even more compelling than in *Coleman* because it involves foreign relations. . . . [W]e are asked to settle a dispute between coequal branches of our Government, each of which has resources available to protect and assert its interests. . . ."

Justice Powell disagreed: The question was not committed to anyone else; there was no lack of standards, for the Court had only "to apply normal principles of interpretation to the constitutional provisions at issue;" there were no countervailing prudential considerations, for if the President and Congress reached conflicting conclusions, a judicial decision "would eliminate, rather than create, multiple constitutional interpretations."

(9) "All the [political-question] doctrine can defensibly imply is that the courts are called upon to judge whether the Constitution has committed to another agency of government the autonomous determination of the issue raised. . . ." Wechsler, Toward Neutral Principles of Constitutional Law, 73 Harv.L.Rev. 1, 7–8 (1959), finding such a commitment explicit with respect to impeachments and to the seating and expulsion of members of Congress, and implicit with respect to congressional elections and to the guarantee of a republican form of government.

A. Bickel, The Least Dangerous Branch 191 (1962):

> To be sure, the Constitution specifically empowers Congress to make or alter regulations about the times, places, and manner of holding elections for Senators and Representatives, and it confers upon Congress the duty to apportion Representatives among the states "according to their respective Numbers," and to "be the Judge of the Elections, Returns, and Qualifications of its own Members." But there is no textual reason that these duties and functions of Congress should be deemed proof against judicial intervention, any more than the language of the Commerce Clause, which provides that "Congress shall have Power . . . to regulate Commerce with foreign Nations, and among the several States, and with the Indian Tribes," is read to foreclose judicial review.

Scharpf, Judicial Review and the Political Question: A Functional Analysis, 75 Yale L.J. 517, 539–40 (1966):

> The trial of impeachment, and the decision whether a member of Congress was validly elected, or whether he should be punished or expelled for misconduct, all seem to involve the determination of a

(1972), making strong suggestions along the political-question line in granting an interlocutory stay of a decision requiring the seating of elected delegates to the Democratic National Convention.

concrete dispute in the light of pre-existing constitutional, statutory or conventional standards. They concern disputes which might well be regarded as "cases or controversies" in the sense of Article III of the Constitution, and which under some constitutions are, indeed, decided by the judiciary. It may therefore be reasonable to construe the express constitutional authorization of Congress to decide these disputes as an equally explicit exception to the general grant of judicial power to the courts in Article III. But this rationale is unavailable, even as the basis of a valid analogy, where the Court, as is normal in political question cases, is presented with a challenge to the validity of a *legislative* or *executive* decision of one of the co-ordinate branches of the federal government.

(10) Professor Henkin has argued that the cases do not establish any general political-question doctrine. *Luther v. Borden*, for example, he says held "that the actions of Congress and the President were within their constitutional authority," *Coleman v. Miller* that the Constitution imposed no relevant restrictions on the amending process; only the Guarantee Clause cases held a constitutional provision not judicially enforceable. While conceding that traditional equitable considerations may induce a court on occasion to deny a remedy for a constitutional violation, he sees "no place . . . for an exemption [from judicial review] for uncertain 'political questions.'" Henkin, Is There a "Political Question" Doctrine?, 85 Yale L.J. 597 (1976).

SECTION 4. CONGRESSIONAL POWER TO CURTAIL JURISDICTION

SHELDON v. SILL

49 U.S. (8 How.) 441 (1850).

MR. JUSTICE GRIER delivered the opinion of the Court.

The only question which it will be necessary to notice in this case is, whether the Circuit Court had jurisdiction.

Sill, the complainant below, a citizen of New York, filed his bill in the Circuit Court of the United States for Michigan, against Sheldon, claiming to recover the amount of a bond and mortgage, which had been assigned to him by Hastings, the President of the Bank of Michigan.

Sheldon, in his answer, among other things, pleaded that "the bond and mortgage in controversy, having been originally given by a citizen of Michigan to another citizen of the same state, and the complainant being assignee of them, the Circuit Court had no jurisdiction."

The eleventh section of the Judiciary Act, which defines the jurisdiction of the Circuit Courts, restrains them from taking "cognizance of any suit to recover the contents of any promissory note or other chose in action, in favor of an assignee, unless a suit might have been prosecuted in such court to recover the contents, if no assignment had been made, except in cases of foreign bills of exchange."

The third article of the Constitution declares that "the judicial power of the United States shall be vested in one Supreme Court, and such inferior courts as the Congress may, from time to time, ordain and establish." The second section of the same article enumerates the cases and controversies of which the judicial power shall have cognizance, and, among others, it specifies "controversies between citizens of different states."

It has been alleged, that this restriction of the Judiciary Act, with regard to assignees of choses in action, is in conflict with this provision of the Constitution, and therefore void.

It must be admitted, that if the Constitution had ordained and established the inferior courts, and distributed to them their respective powers, they could not be restricted or divested by Congress. But as it has made no such distribution, one of two consequences must result,—either that each inferior court created by Congress must exercise all the judicial powers not given to the Supreme Court, or that Congress, having the power to establish the courts must define their respective jurisdictions. The first of these inferences has never been asserted, and could not be defended with any show of reason, and if not, the latter would seem to follow as a necessary consequence. And it would seem to follow, also, that, having a right to prescribe, Congress may withhold from any court of its creation jurisdiction of any of the enumerated controversies. Courts created by statute can have no jurisdiction but such as the statute confers. No one of them can assert a just claim to jurisdiction exclusively conferred on another or withheld from all.

The Constitution has defined the limits of the judicial power of the United States, but has not prescribed how much of it shall be exercised by the Circuit Court; consequently, the statute which does prescribe the limits of their jurisdiction, cannot be in conflict with the Constitution, unless it confers powers not enumerated therein.

Such has been the doctrine held by this court since its first establishment. To enumerate all the cases in which it has been either directly advanced or tacitly assumed would be tedious and unnecessary.

In the case of Turner v. Bank of North America, 4 Dall. [4 U.S.], 10, it was contended, as in this case, that, as it was a controversy between citizens of different states, the Constitution gave the plaintiff a right to sue in the Circuit Court, notwithstanding he was an assignee within the restriction of the eleventh section of the Judiciary Act. But the court said,—"The political truth is, that the disposal of the judicial power (except in a few specified instances) belongs to Congress; and Congress is not bound to enlarge the jurisdiction of the Federal courts to every subject, in every form which the Constitution might warrant." This decision was made in 1799; since that time, the same doctrine has been frequently asserted by this court, as may be seen in McIntire v. Wood, 7

Cranch [11 U.S.], 506; Kendall v. United States, 12 Pet. [37 U.S.], 616; Cary v. Curtiss, 3 How. [44 U.S.], 245.

The only remaining inquiry is, whether the complainant in this case is the assignee of a "chose in action," within the meaning of the statute. . . .

The complainant in this case is the purchaser and assignee of a sum of money, a debt, a chose in action, not of a tract of land. He seeks to recover by this action, a debt assigned to him. He is therefore the "assignee of a chose in action," within the letter and spirit of the act of Congress under consideration, and cannot support this action in the Circuit Court of the United States, where his assignor could not.

The judgment of the Circuit Court must therefore be reversed, for want of jurisdiction.

EX PARTE McCARDLE

74 U.S. (7 Wall.) 506 (1869).

[The act of February 5, 1867, authorized the federal courts to grant habeas corpus "in all cases where any person may be restrained of his or her liberty in violation of the Constitution, or any treaty or law of the United States" and provided an appeal from the circuit courts to the Supreme Court. McCardle, held in military custody, petitioned for habeas and appealed the denial of his petition to the Supreme Court. After the Court had upheld its jurisdiction, 73 U.S. (6 Wall.) 318, Congress enacted "that so much of the Act approved February 5, 1867 . . . as authorized an appeal from the judgment of the Circuit Court to the Supreme Court of the United States, or the exercise of any such jurisdiction by said Supreme Court, on appeals which have been, or may hereafter be taken, be, and the same is hereby repealed."]

THE CHIEF JUSTICE delivered the opinion of the Court.

The first question necessarily is that of jurisdiction; for, if the act of March, 1868, takes away the jurisdiction defined by the act of February, 1867, it is useless, if not improper, to enter into any discussion of other questions.

It is quite true, as was argued by the counsel for the petitioner, that the appellate jurisdiction of this court is not derived from acts of Congress. It is, strictly speaking, conferred by the Constitution. But it is conferred "with such exceptions and under such regulations as Congress shall make."

It is unnecessary to consider whether, if Congress had made no exceptions and no regulations, this court might not have exercised general appellate jurisdiction under rules prescribed by itself. For among the earliest acts of the first Congress, at its first session, was the act of September 24th, 1789, to establish the judicial courts of the United States. That act provided for the organization of this court, and prescribed regulations for the exercise of its jurisdiction.

The source of that jurisdiction, and the limitations of it by the Constitution and by statute, have been on several occasions subjects of consideration here. In the case of Durousseau v. The United States,* particularly, the whole matter was carefully examined, and the court held, that while "the appellate powers of this court are not given by the judicial act, but are given by the Constitution," they are, nevertheless, "limited and regulated by that act, and by such other acts as have been passed on the subject." The court said, further, that the judicial act was an exercise of the power given by the Constitution to Congress "of making exceptions to the appellate jurisdiction of the Supreme Court." "They have described affirmatively," said the court, "its jurisdiction, and this affirmative description has been understood to imply a negation of the exercise of such appellate power as is not comprehended within it."

The principle that the affirmation of appellate jurisdiction implies the negation of all such jurisdiction not affirmed having been thus established, it was an almost necessary consequence that acts of Congress, providing for the exercise of jurisdiction, should come to be spoken of as acts granting jurisdiction, and not as acts making exceptions to the constitutional grant of it.

The exception to appellate jurisdiction in the case before us, however, is not an inference from the affirmation of other appellate jurisdiction. It is made in terms. The provision of the act of 1867, affirming the appellate jurisdiction of this court in cases of *habeas corpus* is expressly repealed. It is hardly possible to imagine a plainer instance of positive exception.

We are not at liberty to inquire into the motives of the legislature. We can only examine into its power under the Constitution; and the power to make exceptions to the appellate jurisdiction of this court is given by express words.

What, then, is the effect of the repealing act upon the case before us? We cannot doubt as to this. Without jurisdiction the court cannot proceed at all in any cause. Jurisdiction is power to declare the law, and when it ceases to exist, the only function remaining to the court is that of announcing the fact and dismissing the cause. And this is not less clear upon authority than upon principle.

Several cases were cited by the counsel for the petitioner in support of the position that jurisdiction of this case is not affected by the repealing act. But none of them, in our judgment, afford any support to it. They are all cases of the exercise of judicial power by the legislature, or of legislative interference with courts in the exercising of continuing jurisdiction.

On the other hand, the general rule, supported by the best elementary writers, is, that "when an act of the legislature is repealed, it must

* 6 Cranch [10 U.S.], 312; Wiscart v. Dauchy, 3 Dallas [3 U.S.], 321.

be considered, except as to transactions past and closed, as if it never existed." And the effect of repealing acts upon suits under acts repealed, has been determined by the adjudications of this court. The subject was fully considered in Norris v. Crocker,† and more recently in Insurance Company v. Ritchie.* In both of these cases it was held that no judgment could be rendered in a suit after the repeal of the act under which it was brought and prosecuted.

It is quite clear, therefore, that this court cannot proceed to pronounce judgment in this case, for it has no longer jurisdiction of the appeal; and judicial duty is not less fitly performed by declining ungranted jurisdiction than in exercising firmly that which the Constitution and the laws confer.

Counsel seem to have supposed, if effect be given to the repealing act in question, that the whole appellate power of the court, in cases of habeas corpus, is denied. But this is an error. The act of 1868 does not except from that jurisdiction any cases but appeals from Circuit Courts under the act of 1867. It does not affect the jurisdiction which was previously exercised.**

The appeal of the petitioner in this case must be dismissed for want of jurisdiction.

Notes on the Power of Congress to Limit the Jurisdiction of the Federal Courts

(1) Judicial opinions do not always tell the whole story. What was at stake in McCardle's case was the entire program of post-Civil War Reconstruction, in which Congress had substituted military for civil government in ten of the former Confederate States. McCardle had been imprisoned by the military government of Mississippi on charges of having published "incendiary and libellous" articles, and his ground for habeas corpus was that the Reconstruction Acts were unconstitutional. The basic statute had been enacted March 2, 1867, 14 Stat. 428:

> Whereas no legal State governments or adequate protection for life or property now exists in [ten named States] . . ., Said rebel States shall be divided into military districts and made subject to the military authority of the United States. . . . It shall be the duty of each officer [commanding one of these district] . . . to protect all persons in their rights of person and property, to suppress insurrection, disorder, and violence, and to punish, or cause to be punished, all disturbers of the public peace and criminals; and to this end he may allow local civil tribunals to take jurisdiction of and to try offenders, or, when in his judgment it may be necessary for the trial of offenders, he shall have power to organize military commissions or tribunals for that purpose. . . . Until the people of said rebel States shall be by law admitted to representation in the Congress of the United States, any civil governments which may exist therein shall be deemed provisional

† 13 Howard [54 U.S.], 429.

* 5 Wallace [72 U.S.], 541.

** Ex parte McCardle, 6 Wallace [73 U.S.], 324.

only, and in all respects subject to the paramount authority of the United States at any time to abolish, modify, control, or supersede the same. . . .

This statute had been passed over President Johnson's veto, and it was immediately challenged on constitutional grounds. In Mississippi v. Johnson, 71 U.S. (4 Wall.) 475 (1867), the Supreme Court held it was without power to enjoin the President from carrying out non-ministerial duties under the Reconstruction Acts; in Georgia v. Stanton, 73 U.S. (6 Wall.) 50 (1868), it refused to enjoin the Secretary of War from enforcing the Acts because the State had no standing to assert merely "political" rights. Then, to everyone's surprise, the Court upheld its jurisdiction of McCardle's case, 73 U.S. (6 Wall.) 318 (1868). The House had just passed a bill purporting to forbid the Supreme Court to invalidate acts of Congress except by a two-thirds vote; Thaddeus Stevens introduced a bill to deny the Supreme Court jurisdiction in any case arising out of the Reconstruction Acts; and the provision repealing the Supreme Court's 1867 appellate habeas corpus jurisdiction was slipped through as a rider to an unrelated bill in order, according to one Congressman, "to clip the wings of that Court." President Johnson had the courage to veto the jurisdiction bill during his own impeachment trial, but it was passed again over his veto. Although McCardle's case had been argued before final passage of the bill, the Court, over strenuous protest by Justice Grier, declined to decide the case while the bill was being considered. See 2 C. Warren, The Supreme Court in United States History, ch. 30 (Rev.ed. 1926).

See Glidden Co. v. Zdanok, 370 U.S. 530, 605, n. 11 (1962) (Douglas and Black, JJ., dissenting): "There is a serious question whether the *McCardle* case could command a majority view today."

(2) During the same term in which it dismissed McCardle's appeal the Supreme Court was faced again with a challenge to the validity of the Reconstruction Acts, in Ex parte Yerger, 75 U.S. (8 Wall.) 85 (1869). Yerger, like McCardle, had been imprisoned by the military authorities in Mississippi and had been denied habeas corpus. But Yerger, educated by McCardle's failure, did not file an appeal in the Supreme Court; he petitioned the Court for a writ of certiorari to review the Circuit Court judgment and for a writ of habeas corpus. The Supreme Court upheld its jurisdiction under § 14 of the Judiciary Act of 1789, which after defining the jurisdiction of the Supreme Court and the District and Circuit Courts in other cases provided that "all the beforementioned courts of the United States shall have power to issue writs of *scire facias, habeas corpus*, and all other writs, not specially provided for by statute, which may be necessary for the exercise of their respective jurisdictions, and agreeable to the principles and usages of law." 1 Stat. 81. The Court agreed that appellate jurisdiction was "subject to exception and regulation by Congress; but it is too plain for argument that the denial to this court of appellate jurisdiction in this class of cases must greatly weaken the efficacy of the writ, deprive the citizen in many cases of its benefits, and seriously hinder the establishment of that uniformity in deciding upon questions of personal rights which can only be attained through appellate jurisdiction. . . . These considerations forbid any construction giving to doubtful words [in the

statute] the effect of withholding or abridging the jurisdiction." Moreover, as suggested in the *McCardle* opinion, this jurisdiction had not been taken away by the 1868 statute considered in that case: The words of that statute "repeal only so much of the act of 1867 as authorized appeals, or the exercise of appellate jurisdiction by this court. They affected only appeals and appellate jurisdiction authorized by that act. They do not purport to touch the appellate jurisdiction conferred by the Constitution, or to except from it any cases not excepted by the act of 1789. They reach no act except the act of 1867."

After this decision bills were again introduced in Congress to deny the Court jurisdiction in Reconstruction Act cases, and one proposal would have denied all federal courts power to invalidate Acts of Congress. But Yerger was released, the case became moot, the bills were not enacted, and the Supreme Court never passed on the validity of the Reconstruction Acts. See Warren, supra note 1, ch. 30.

(3) United States v. Klein, 80 U.S. (13 Wall.) 128 (1872), was a suit to recover the proceeds of cotton that had fallen into Government hands during the Civil War. The statute allowed the owner of such property to recover its proceeds by proving that he had never given aid or comfort to the "rebellion," and the Supreme Court had held in an earlier case that a Presidential pardon, by purging the owner of his offense, satisfied this burden of proof. Klein, armed with a pardon, recovered judgment from the Court of Claims, and the Government appealed to the Supreme Court. While the appeal was pending, Congress enacted a statute providing that a pardon was to be taken, instead, as proof that the claimant had given aid to the rebellion. It went on to provide that in cases in which the Court of Claims had found for the plaintiff on the basis of a pardon "the Supreme Court shall, on appeal, have no further jurisdiction of the cause, and shall dismiss the same for want of jurisdiction," and that "on proof of such pardon" the jurisdiction of either the Court of Claims or the Supreme Court "shall cease, and the court shall forthwith dismiss the suit. . . ." The Court affirmed the award, holding this provision unconstitutional:

> Undoubtedly the legislature has complete control over the organization and existence of [the Court of Claims] . . . and may confer or withhold the right of appeal from its decisions. And if this act did nothing more, it would be our duty to give it effect. If it simply denied the right of appeal in a particular class of cases, there could be no doubt that it must be regarded as an exercise of the power of Congress to make "such exceptions from the appellate jurisdiction" as should seem to it expedient.
>
> But the language of the proviso shows plainly that it does not intend to withhold appellate jurisdiction except as a means to an end. Its great and controlling purpose is to deny to pardons granted by the President the effect which this court had adjudged them to have. . . . The court has jurisdiction of the cause to a given point; but when it ascertains that a certain state of things exists, its jurisdiction is to cease and it is required to dismiss the cause for want of jurisdiction.

It seems to us that this is not an exercise of the acknowledged power of Congress to make exceptions and prescribe regulations to the appellate power. . . . We are directed to dismiss the appeal, if we find that the judgment must be affirmed, because of a pardon granted to the intestate of the claimants. Can we do so without allowing one party to the controversy to decide it in its own favor? Can we do so without allowing that the legislature may prescribe rules of decision to the Judicial Department of the government in cases pending before it? We think not. . . . We must think that Congress has inadvertently passed the limit which separates the legislative from the judicial power. . . .

The rule prescribed is also liable to just exception as impairing the effect of a pardon, and thus infringing the constitutional power of the Executive. . . .

Why was Klein's case different from McCardle's? Was *Klein* related to *Hayburn's Case*, supra p. 8?

(4) Lauf v. E. G. Shinner & Co., 303 U.S. 323, 330 (1938). The Norris-LaGuardia Act, 29 U.S.C. §§ 101–15, narrowly restricts the authority of federal courts to grant injunctions in labor disputes and makes unenforceable in those courts the so-called "yellow dog" contract, in which an employee promises not to join a union. But earlier Supreme Court decisions had suggested there might be due-process objections to these provisions as a matter of substantive law, see Truax v. Corrigan, 257 U.S. 312 (1921); Coppage v. Kansas, 208 U.S. 161 (1908). Consequently the Norris-LaGuardia Act throughout was phrased as a limitation on the jurisdiction of the federal courts, in an attempt to avoid the constitutional issue. See H.R.Rep.No.670, 72d Cong., 1st Sess. 10. The Supreme Court upheld the statute, saying only that "there can be no question of the power of Congress thus to define and limit the jurisdiction of the inferior courts of the United States."

(5) Yakus v. United States, 321 U.S. 414 (1944). Petitioners were convicted by a federal district court of selling beef at prices in excess of the maximum prescribed by regulations promulgated by the Price Administrator under the Emergency Price Control Act, 56 Stat. 23 (1942). They argued that the regulations deprived them of property without due process of law and did not conform to the standards prescribed by the Act, but the Supreme Court held that these objections could not be raised in defense of a criminal prosecution. The statute provided for attack on the regulations by filing a protest with the Administrator and for review of his adverse decision in the Emergency Court of Appeals, which was composed of federal District and Circuit Judges. Although other federal and state courts were given jurisdiction to enforce the Act in civil and criminal proceedings, the jurisdiction of the Emergency Court to determine the validity of the regulations was declared to be exclusive. The Court held that this provision deprived the district court of power to determine the validity of the regulations, and that it was constitutional.

In Lockerty v. Phillips [319 U.S. 182 (1943)], we held that these provisions conferred on the Emergency Court of Appeals, subject to review by this Court, exclusive equity jurisdiction to restrain enforcement of price regulations of the Administrator and that they withdrew such jurisdiction from all other courts. This was accomplished by the exercise of the constitutional power of Congress to prescribe the jurisdiction of inferior federal courts, and the jurisdiction of all state courts to determine federal questions, and to vest that jurisdiction in a single court, the Emergency Court of Appeals.

The considerations which led us to that conclusion with respect to the equity jurisdiction of the district court, lead to the like conclusion as to its power to consider the validity of a price regulation as a defense to a criminal prosecution for its violation. . . .

The present statute provides a mode of testing the validity of a regulation by an independent administrative proceeding. There is no constitutional requirement that that test be made in one tribunal rather than in another, so long as there is an opportunity to be heard and for judicial review which satisfies the demands of due process, as is the case here. . . . No procedural principle is more familiar to this Court than that a constitutional right may be forfeited in criminal as well as civil cases by the failure to make timely assertion of the right before a tribunal having jurisdiction to determine it. . . .[1]

Justices Rutledge and Murphy dissented:

I have no difficulty with the provision which confers jurisdiction upon the Emergency Court of Appeals to determine the validity of price regulations or, if that had been all, with the mandate which makes its jurisdiction in that respect exclusive. . . .

Congress however was not content to create a single national tribunal, give it exclusive jurisdiction to determine all cases arising under the statute, and deny jurisdiction over them to all other courts. It provided for enforcement by civil and criminal proceedings in the federal district courts and in the state courts throughout the country. . . .

It is one thing for Congress to withhold jurisdiction. It is entirely another to confer it and direct that it be exercised in a manner inconsistent with constitutional requirements or, what in some instances may be the same thing, without regard to them. Once it is held that Congress can require the courts criminally to enforce unconstitutional laws or statutes, including regulations, or to do so without regard for their validity, the way will have been found to circumvent the supreme law and, what is more, to make the courts parties to doing so. This Congress cannot do. . . . Whenever the judicial power is called into play, it is responsible directly to the fundamental law and no other authority can intervene to force or authorize the judicial body to disregard it. The problem is therefore not solely one of individual

1. The Court also upheld a provision forbidding even the Emergency Court to issue interlocutory injunctions against enforcement of the regulations, citing a case upholding summary destruction of contaminated food against a due-process challenge: "[W]hen justified by compelling public interest the legislature may authorize summary action subject to later judicial review of its validity." What would the Court hold if Congress, purporting not to disturb a constitutional right, denied the courts power on the merits to grant either damages or an injunction for its violation?

right or due process of law. It is equally one of the separation and independence of the powers of the government and of the constitutional integrity of the judicial process. . . .[2]

(6) The Reconstruction Congress was not the only one in which there has been sentiment in favor of limiting the jurisdiction of the courts in constitutional cases. Consider, for example, H.R. 867, 97th Cong., 1st Sess. (1981), proposing to add the following sections to Title 28:

> § 1259. . . . Notwithstanding the provisions of sections 1253, 1254, and 1257 of this chapter the Supreme Court shall not have jurisdiction to review, by appeal, writ of certiorari, or otherwise, any case arising out of any State statute . . . which relates to abortion. . . .
>
> § 1363. . . . Notwithstanding any other provision of law, the district courts shall not have jurisdiction of any case or question which the Supreme Court does not have jurisdiction to review under section 1259 of this title. . . .[3]

After *Sheldon, McCardle,* and the Norris-LaGuardia and Price Control cases, can it be argued that this bill would have been unconstitutional?

(7) Justice Story was of the opinion that Congress was obliged by the Constitution to allow the federal courts jurisdiction over all cases or controversies within Article III:

> The language of the article throughout is manifestly designed to be mandatory upon the legislature. . . . The judicial power of the United States *shall be vested* (not may be vested) in one supreme court, and in such inferior courts as congress may, from time to time, ordain and establish. . . .
>
> If, then, it is the duty of congress to vest the judicial power of the United States, it is a duty to vest the *whole judicial power.* The language, if imperative as to one part, is imperative as to all. If it were otherwise, this anomaly would exist, that congress might successively refuse to vest the jurisdiction in any one class of cases enumerated in the constitution, and thereby defeat the jurisdiction as to all; for the constitution has not singled out any class on which congress are bound to act in preference to others.
>
> The next consideration is as to the courts in which the judicial power shall be vested. It is manifest that a supreme court must be established; but whether it be equally obligatory to establish inferior courts is a question of some difficulty. If congress may lawfully omit to establish inferior courts, it might follow, that in some of the enumerated cases the judicial power could nowhere exist. The supreme court can have original jurisdiction in two classes of cases only,

2. Did the Court reject Justice Rutledge's distinction? Henry Hart thought not: "Yakus . . . dealt directly with the scope of constitutional rights, with no nonsense about any question being foreclosed by the power to regulate jurisdiction." Hart & Wechsler's The Federal Courts and the Federal System 404 (3d ed. 1988).

3. If these bills passed, would state courts be legally bound to follow existing Supreme Court precedents in abortion cases? See also S. 528, 97th Cong., 1st Sess. (1981), which would have limited the remedial power of federal courts to order busing in school-segregation cases.

> viz. in cases affecting ambassadors, other public ministers and consuls, and in cases in which a state is a party. Congress cannot vest any portion of the judicial power of the United States, except in courts ordained and established by itself; and if in any of the cases enumerated in the constitution, the state courts did not then possess jurisdiction, the appellate jurisdiction of the supreme court (admitting that it could act on state courts) could not reach those cases, and, consequently, the injunction of the constitution, that the judicial power "*shall be vested*," would be disobeyed. It would seem, therefore, to follow, that congress are bound to create some inferior courts, in which to vest all that jurisdiction which, under the constitution, is *exclusively* vested in the United States, and of which the supreme court cannot take original cognizance. They might establish one or more inferior courts; they might parcel out the jurisdiction among such courts, from time to time, at their own pleasure. But the whole judicial power of the United States should be, at all times, vested either in an original or appellate form, in some courts created under its authority. . . .

Martin v. Hunter's Lessee, 14 U.S. (1 Wheat.) 304, 328–31 (1816) (dictum).[4]

Professors Hart and Wechsler suggest that Story's position is not "consistent with the deliberate compromises of the Constitutional Convention." The delegates, they report, rejected a proposal that would have required Congress to establish inferior federal courts. Madison and Wilson then moved " 'that the National Legislature be empowered to institute inferior tribunals,' saying that 'there was a distinction between establishing such tribunals absolutely, and giving a discretion to the Legislature to establish or not establish them.' The compromise was agreed to. . . ." Moreover, they point out, Story's view was rejected in the first Judiciary Act, which did not extend federal jurisdiction to every case within Article III. The Federal Courts and the Federal System 10–11, 368 (3d ed. 1988). See also the dictum in Palmore v. United States, 411 U.S. 389, 401 n. 9 (1973), that Story's position "did not survive later cases." Are there objections to a constitutional doctrine that would forbid the Congress to impose a minimum jurisdictional amount, or to exclude cases in which diversity of citizenship had been created by assignment?

(8) Eisentrager v. Forrestal, 174 F.2d 961 (D.C.Cir. 1949). Imprisoned in Germany following a trial by United States Military Commission, Eisentrager petitioned for habeas corpus. The court first held that he had a "substantive right" to habeas corpus if he could establish that he was deprived of liberty by United States officials in violation of the Constitution. Then it upheld its jurisdiction to grant the writ, though the statute authorized judges to grant habeas only "within their respective jurisdictions," and though the Supreme Court had suggested this required that the

4. See also 1 W. Crosskey, Politics and the Constitution in the History of the United States 610–18 (1953); Amar, A Neo-Federalist View of Article III: Separating the Two Tiers of Federal Jurisdiction, 65 B.U.L.Rev. 205 (1985). But in White v. Fenner, 29 F.Cas. 1015 (C.C.D.R.I.1818) (No. 17,547), Justice Story dismissed a diversity suit that was excluded from the statutory grant of jurisdiction: Although it was "singular the jurisdiction actually conferred on the courts of the United States should have stopped so far short of the constitutional extent," the court had "no jurisdiction which is not given by statute."

petitioner be restrained in the district where the court sat, Ahrens v. Clark, 335 U.S. 188 (1948). Reasoning that "if a person has a right to a writ of habeas corpus, he cannot be deprived of the privilege by an omission in a federal jurisdictional statute," the court construed the statute to give jurisdiction to a court with power over the jailer's superior—here the Secretary of Defense—in order to avoid holding it unconstitutional. In part the argument was based on Story's position that Article III required Congress "to confer the whole of the federal judicial power upon some federal court." But the court made the further argument that a denial of jurisdiction would violate the constitutional limitation on suspension of the the writ of habeas corpus:

> The Federal Government cannot suspend the privilege, except when, in cases of rebellion or invasion, the public safety may so require. . . . Congress could not effectuate by omission that which it could not accomplish by affirmative action. . . . A state court cannot inquire, upon petition for habeas corpus, into the validity of the confinement of a person held under the authority of the United States. Therefore, unless the federal jurisdiction statute be construed as co-extensive with governmental action by United States officials, such action outside the specifications of the statute would be wholly immune from judicial power; in other words, outside the necessity for compliance with the Constitution. To state the proposition would seem to refute it. [174 F.2d at 965–66]

(9) Is the latter argument one that can be made only in habeas corpus cases, because Article I specifically ensures the jurisdiction of the courts in habeas corpus? See Battaglia v. General Motors Corp., 169 F.2d 254 (2d Cir. 1948), which concerned an action for overtime pay under the Fair Labor Standards Act, 29 U.S.C. §§ 201–19. The plaintiffs claimed that time spent in walking to their work stations, in changing clothes, and in washing up after their work was done was part of the compensable "work week." The Supreme Court had held similar incidental activities compensable in Tennessee Coal, Iron & R. Co. v. Muscoda Local, 321 U.S. 590 (1944). Congress had responded by enacting the Portal-to-Portal Act, 61 Stat. 84 (1947), 29 U.S.C. § 251 et seq., which in effect overruled this decision retroactively, because the Court had construed the statute "in disregard of long-established customs, practices and contracts between employers and employees, thereby creating wholly unexpected liabilities, immense in amount and retroactive in operation." Section 2(d) of this statute provided that "No court of the United States, of any State, Territory or possession of the United States, or of the District of Columbia, shall have jurisdiction of any action or proceeding, whether instituted prior to or on or after May 14, 1947, to enforce liability or impose punishment for or on account of the failure of the employer to pay minimum wages or overtime compensation" contrary to the substantive provisions of the new statute.

The plaintiffs in *Battaglia* argued that the Portal-to-Portal Act destroyed vested rights in violation of the Due Process Clause of the Fifth Amendment. The court rejected this argument on the merits, but it did not think the jurisdictional provision determinative:

A few of the district court decisions sustaining section 2 of the Portal-to-Portal Act have done so on the ground that since jurisdiction of federal courts other than the Supreme Court is conferred by Congress, it may at the will of Congress be taken away in whole or in part. . . . We think, however, that the exercise by Congress of its control over jurisdiction is subject to compliance with at least the requirements of the Fifth Amendment. That is to say, while Congress has the undoubted power to give, withhold, and restrict the jurisdiction of courts other than the Supreme Court, it must not so exercise that power as to deprive any person of life, liberty, or property without due process of law or to take private property without just compensation. . . . [169 F.2d at 257]

Why does the court conclude that to oust all courts of jurisdiction would violate the Due Process Clause? Due process has on occasion been held to require a hearing as a condition of governmental action against the individual, e.g., Fuentes v. Shevin, 407 U.S. 67 (1972) (attachment). *Battaglia* goes further, suggesting that the individual must be afforded the opportunity to file suit to effectuate his constitutional rights.[5]

To what extent does this position derive support from *Marbury v. Madison*, supra p. 19? Notice that even the narrow clean-hands argument in *Marbury* sustains the distinction drawn by Justice Rutledge in his dissent in *Yakus v. United States*, supra note 5: "Name me a single Supreme Court case that has squarely held that, in a civil enforcement proceeding, questions of law can be validly withdrawn from the consideration of the enforcement court where no adequate opportunity to have them determined by a court has been previously accorded. When you do, I'm going back to re-think Marbury v. Madison." Hart & Wechsler's The Federal Courts and the Federal System 404 (3d ed. 1988). Consider, however, the significance for *Battaglia* of Marshall's argument that judicial review is an indispensable means of keeping the legislature within constitutional limitations.

Does *Battaglia* help in arguing against the constitutionality of the abortion bill quoted in note 6? Does *Marbury v. Madison*?[6]

5. The *Battaglia* theory that due process sometimes entitles a plaintiff to a judicial remedy derives support from Mr. Justice Harlan's concurring opinion in Oestereich v. Selective Service System, 393 U.S. 233, 243 n. 6 (1968), construing an apparently absolute ban on pre-induction review of draft classification orders narrowly in order to avoid a "serious" constitutional question. Indeed the Harlan suggestion goes far beyond *Battaglia*, for, in contrast to the Portal-to-Portal Act, the draft statute did not forbid all judicial review of such orders; classifications could be challenged either by way of defense to a prosecution for disobeying the draft or by habeas corpus after submitting to induction. Neither of these remedies, the opinion argued, seemed constitutionally adequate: "It is doubtful whether a person may be deprived of his personal liberty without the prior opportunity to be heard by some tribunal competent fully to adjudicate his claims."

6. See Bartlett v. Bowen, 816 F.2d 695 (D.C.Cir.1987), concluding both that Congress had not meant to preclude all judicial review of the constitutionality of a limitation on Medicare benefits and that it could not constitutionally do so: "The delicate balance implicit in the doctrine of separation of powers would be destroyed if Congress were allowed not only to legislate, but also to judge the constitutionality of its own actions." Judge Bork dissented: "No Supreme Court decision has ever denied sovereign immunity, in a case where it otherwise would apply, because a constitutional challenge to a statute was ad-

(10) Professor Hart argued in his dialogue, Hart & Wechsler's The Federal Courts and the Federal System 394 (3d ed. 1988), that Congress's authority to make "exceptions" to the appellate jurisdiction of the Supreme Court ought not to be construed to permit Congress to "destroy the essential role of the Supreme Court in the constitutional plan." See also Ratner, Congressional Power Over the Appellate Jurisdiction of the Supreme Court, 109 U.Pa.L.Rev. 157 (1960), arguing that Professor Hart's thesis is supported by the Constitutional Convention's rejection of a proposal that apart from the original jurisdiction "the judicial power shall be exercised in such manner as the legislature shall direct;" by contemporaneous decisions holding invalid an "exception" in a deed or lease withholding an essential part of the property conveyed; and by the Supreme Court's opinions in Martin v. Hunter's Lessee, 14 U.S. (1 Wheat.) 304 (1816); Cohens v. Virginia, 19 U.S. (6 Wheat.) 264 (1821), and Ableman v. Booth, 62 U.S. (21 How.) 506 (1859), which he argues "upheld the Court's jurisdiction to review state court decisions under section 25 of the Judiciary Act not only because that jurisdiction was authorized by the Constitution, but also because it was required by the Constitution." Is the Hart-Ratner thesis precluded by *Sheldon* and *McCardle*? By any of the decisions discussed in these notes? See also Merry, Scope of the Supreme Court's Appellate Jurisdiction: Historic Basis, 47 Minn.L.Rev. 53 (1962), suggesting that the power to make "exceptions" and "regulations" to the Court's appellate jurisdiction may well have been intended by the Constitutional Convention to apply only to "the treatment of fact issues;"[7] Van Alstyne, A Critical Guide to Ex Parte McCardle, 15 Ariz.L.Rev. 229, 263–65 (1973), arguing that Congress may offend the equal-protection component of the Due Process Clause if it exercises its power over jurisdiction so as to discriminate arbitrarily against litigants with certain constitutional contentions; Sager, Foreword: Constitutional Limitations on Congress' Authority to Regulate the Jurisdiction of the Federal Courts, 95 Harv.L.Rev. 17 (1981); Gunther, Congressional Power to Curtail Federal Court Jurisdiction, 36 Stan.L.Rev. 895 (1984). Could Congress limit the jurisdiction to cases brought by white persons? Can it really be said that a statute barring *everyone* from litigating reapportionment claims treats some people less favorably than others?

(11) Consider also the relevance of *Marbury's* watchdog argument in connection with other methods of congressional control over the Court. See for example, 1 C. Warren, The Supreme Court in United States History, ch. 6 (rev. ed. 1926), describing the nearly successful attempt to remove Justice Chase from office in 1805:

vanced." See also Marozsan v. United States, 852 F.2d 1469 (7th Cir.1988) (Easterbrook, J., dissenting, agreeing with Bork).

7. See the Federalist, No. 81, arguing that Article III would not require Supreme Court re-examination of facts found by a jury: "The legislature of the United States would certainly have full power to provide, that in appeals to the Supreme Court there should be no reexamination of facts where they had been tried in the original causes by juries. This would certainly be an authorized exception. . . ." From the beginning the Court respected the statutory jurisdictional-amount restriction on its power to review circuit-court decisions, and in United States v. More, 7 U.S. (3 Cranch) 159, 172–74 (1805), it dismissed a writ of error in a federal criminal case from the District of Columbia on the ground that Congress had implicitly excepted such cases from the Supreme Court review.

> It is an undoubted fact, that had the effort been successful, it was the intention of the Republicians to institute impeachment proceedings against all the Judges of the Court. . . . The Republican leaders in the House . . . contended that impeachment must be considered a means of keeping the Courts in reasonable harmony with the will of the Nation, as expressed through Congress and the Executive, and that a judicial decision declaring an Act of Congress unconstitutional would support an impeachment and the removal of a Judge, who thus constituted himself an instrument of opposition to the course of government.

Compare President Roosevelt's proposal, S. 1392, 75th Cong., 1st Sess. (1937), for "Reorganization of the Federal Judiciary:"

> (a) When any judge of a court of the United States, appointed to hold his office during good behavior, has heretofore or hereafter attained the age of seventy years and has held a commission or commissions as judge of any such court or courts at least ten years, continuously or otherwise, and within six months thereafter has neither resigned nor retired, the President, for each such judge who has not so resigned or retired, shall nominate, and by and with the advice and consent of the Senate, shall appoint one additional judge to the court to which the former is commissioned: *Provided*, that no additional judge shall be appointed hereunder if the judge who is of retirement age dies, resigns, or retires prior to the nomination of such additional judge. . . .

The unfavorable report of the Senate Judiciary Committee is a classic defense of judicial review:

> The President tells us in his address to the Nation of March 9 (appendix D), Congressional Record, March 10, page 2650:
>
> > "When the Congress has sought to stabilize national agriculture, to improve the conditions of labor, to safeguard business against unfair competition, to protect our national resources, and in many other ways to serve our clearly national needs, the majority of the Court has been assuming the power to pass on the wisdom of these acts of the Congress and to approve or disapprove the public policy written into these laws. . . .
> >
> > "We have, therefore, reached the point as a Nation where we must take action to save the Constitution from the Court and the Court from itself. We must find a way to take an appeal from the Supreme Court to the Constitution itself. We want a Supreme Court which will do justice under the Constitution—not over it. In our courts we want a government of laws and not of men." . . .
>
> Here is the frank acknowledgment that neither speed nor "new blood" in the judiciary is the object of this legislation, but a change in the decisions of the Court—a subordination of the views of the judges to the views of the executive and legislative, a change to be brought about by forcing certain judges off the bench or increasing their number. . . .

> If this bill be supported by the toilers of this country upon the ground that they want a Court which will sustain legislation limiting hours and providing minimum wages, they must remember that the procedure employed in the bill could be used in another administration to lengthen hours and to decrease wages. If farmers want agricultural relief and favor this bill upon the ground that it gives them a Court which will sustain legislation in their favor, they must remember that the procedure employed might some day be used to deprive them of every vestige of a farm relief.
>
> When members of the Court usurp legislative powers or attempt to exercise political power, they lay themselves open to the charge of having lapsed from that "good behavior" which determines the period of their official life. But, if you say, the process of impeachment is difficult and uncertain, the answer is, the people made it so when they framed the Constitution. It is not for us, the servants of the people, the instruments of the Constitution, to find a more easy way to do that which our masters made difficult. [S.Rep.No.711, 75th Cong., 1st Sess. (1937) [8]]

Was Roosevelt's bill unconstitutional?

Finally, consider the action of the Jefferson party in Congress after repealing the Midnight Judges Act in 1802, as described in 1 C. Warren, The Supreme Court in United States History 222–24 (Rev. ed. 1926):

> Realizing that the question of [the repeal statute's] . . . constitutionality would be at once questioned in the Courts and presented to the Supreme Court for final decision, they resolved to prevent, or at least postpone, any such decision until at least after lapse of time sufficient to strengthen the political power of the Administration. Accordingly, immediately after the enactment of the Repeal Law, a further bill was introduced, and after a short debate passed, abolishing the new June and December Terms of the Supreme Court (created by the Act of 1801), and restoring the old February Term but *not* the August Term. By this extraordinary Legislative maneuver, an adjournment of the Court was enforced for fourteen months (from December, 1801, to February, 1803). "Could a more dangerous precedent than this be established?" Bayard asked in his debate in the House: "May it not lead to the virtual abolition of a Court, the existence of which is required by the Constitution? If the functions of the Court can be extended by law for fourteen months, what time will arrest us before we arrive at ten or twenty years?" . . .

Was this statute unconstitutional? [9]

8. The President's message proposing reorganization was delivered February 5, 1937, and hearings on the bill began March 10. On March 29 the Supreme Court, by a vote of five to four, overruled its recent decision invalidating minimum-wage legislation. West Coast Hotel Co. v. Parrish, 300 U.S. 379 (1937). "Mr. Justice Roberts," said Robert H. Jackson, "had shifted from the reactionary to the liberal side of the Court." The Struggle for Judicial Supremacy 191, 207–35 (1941). Describing the outcome of the Court Fight, Professor Powell invoked Fielding: "He . . . would have ravished her, if she had not, by a timely compliance, prevented him." Jonathan Wilde, Book iii, ch. vii, as quoted in Vagaries and Varieties of Constitutional Litigation 19–20 (1956).

9. See also Atkins v. United States, 556 F.2d 1028, 1040–57 (Ct.Cl.1977), holding

SECTION 5. JUDICIAL POWER OUTSIDE ARTICLE III

NORTHERN PIPELINE CONSTRUCTION CO. v. MARATHON PIPE LINE CO.

458 U.S. 50 (1982).

JUSTICE BRENNAN announced the judgment of the Court and delivered an opinion in which JUSTICE MARSHALL, JUSTICE BLACKMUN, and JUSTICE STEVENS joined.

The question presented is whether the assignment by Congress to bankruptcy judges of the jurisdiction granted in § 241(a) of the Bankruptcy Act of 1978, 28 U.S.C. § 1471 (1976 ed., Supp. III), violates Art. III of the Constitution.

I

A

In 1978, after almost ten years of study and investigation, Congress enacted a comprehensive revision of the bankruptcy laws. The Bankruptcy Act of 1978 (Act) [1] made significant changes in both the substantive and procedural law of bankruptcy. It is the changes in the latter that are at issue in this case.

Before the Act, federal district courts served as bankruptcy courts and employed a "referee" system. Bankruptcy proceedings were generally conducted before referees, except in those instances in which the district court elected to withdraw a case from a referee. See Bkrptcy. Rule 102. The referee's final order was appealable to the district court. Bkrptcy.Rule 801. The bankruptcy courts were vested with "summary jurisdiction"—that is, with jurisdiction over controversies involving property in the actual or constructive possession of the court. And, with consent, the bankruptcy court also had jurisdiction over some "plenary" matters—such as disputes involving property in the possession of a third person.

The Act eliminates the referee system and establishes "in each judicial district, as an adjunct to the district court for such district, a bankruptcy court which shall be a court of record known as the United States Bankruptcy Court for the district." 28 U.S.C. § 151(a) (1976 ed., Supp. III). The judges of these courts are appointed to office for 14-year terms by the President, with the advice and consent of the Senate. §§ 152, 153(a). They are subject to removal by the "judicial council of

the constitutional provision that judges' salaries may not be "diminished" did not require that they be increased to keep pace with inflation: "Indirect, nondiscriminatory diminishments of judicial compensation, those which do not amount to an assault upon the independence of the third branch or any of its members, fall outside the protection of the Compensation Clause. . . ."

1. Pub.L. 95–598, 92 Stat. 2549, U.S. Code Cong. & Admin.News 1978, p. 5787. The Act became effective October 1, 1979.

the circuit" on account of "incompetence, misconduct, neglect of duty or physical or mental disability." § 153(b). In addition, the salaries of the bankruptcy judges are set by statute and are subject to adjustment under the Federal Salary Act, 2 U.S.C. §§ 351–361. 28 U.S.C. § 154 (1976 ed., Supp. III).

The jurisdiction of the bankruptcy courts created by the Act is much broader than that exercised under the former referee system. Eliminating the distinction between "summary" and "plenary" jurisdiction, the Act grants the new courts jurisdiction over all "civil proceedings arising under title 11 [the Bankruptcy title] or arising in or *related to* cases under title 11." 28 U.S.C. § 1471(b) (1976 ed., Supp. III) (emphasis added).[3] This jurisdictional grant empowers bankruptcy courts to entertain a wide variety of cases involving claims that may affect the property of the estate once a petition has been filed under title 11 of the Act. Included within the bankruptcy courts' jurisdiction are suits to recover accounts, controversies involving exempt property, actions to avoid transfers and payments as preferences or fraudulent conveyances, and causes of action owned by the debtor at the time of the petition for bankruptcy. The bankruptcy courts can hear claims based on state law as well as those based on federal law. See 1 Collier on Bankruptcy, ¶ 3.01, at 3–47 to 3–48 (15th ed. 1981).

The judges of the bankruptcy courts are vested with all of the "powers of a court of equity, law and admiralty," except that they "may not enjoin another court or punish a criminal contempt not committed in the presence of the judge of the court or warranting a punishment of imprisonment." 28 U.S.C. § 1481 (1976 ed., Supp. III). In addition to this broad grant of power, Congress has allowed bankruptcy judges the power to hold jury trials, § 1480; to issue declaratory judgments, § 2201; to issue writs of habeas corpus under certain circumstances, § 2256; to issue all writs necessary in aid of the bankruptcy court's expanded jurisdiction, § 451; see 28 U.S.C. § 1651 (1976 ed.); and to issue any order, process or judgment that is necessary or appropriate to carry out the provisions of title 11, 11 U.S.C. § 105(a) (1976 ed., Supp. III).

The Act also establishes a special procedure for appeals from orders of bankruptcy courts. The circuit council is empowered to direct the Chief Judge of the circuit to designate panels of three bankruptcy judges to hear appeals. 28 U.S.C. § 160 (1976 ed., Supp. III). These panels have jurisdiction of all appeals from final judgments, orders, and decrees of bankruptcy courts, and, with leave of the panel, of interlocutory appeals. § 1482. If no such appeals panel is designated, the

3. Although the Act initially vests this jurisdiction in district courts, 28 U.S.C. § 1471(a) (1976 ed., Supp. III), it subsequently provides that "[t]he bankruptcy court for the district in which a case under title 11 is commenced shall exercise *all* of the jurisdiction conferred by this section on the district courts," § 1471(c) (emphasis added). Thus the ultimate repository of the Act's broad jurisdictional grant is the bankruptcy courts. See 1 Collier on Bankruptcy ¶ 3.01, at 3–37, 3–44 to 3–49 (15th ed. 1981).

district court is empowered to exercise appellate jurisdiction. § 1334. The court of appeals is given jurisdiction over appeals from the appellate panels or from the district court. § 1293. If the parties agree, a direct appeal to the court of appeals may be taken from a final judgment of a bankruptcy court. § 1293(b).[5] . . .

B

This case arises out of proceedings initiated in the United States Bankruptcy Court for the District of Minnesota after appellant Northern Pipeline Construction Co. (Northern) filed a petition for reorganization in January 1980. In March 1980 Northern, pursuant to the Act, filed in that court a suit against appellee Marathon Pipe Line Co. (Marathon). Appellant sought damages for alleged breaches of contract and warranty, as well as for alleged misrepresentation, coercion, and duress. Marathon sought dismissal of the suit, on the ground that the Act unconstitutionally conferred Art. III judicial power upon judges who lacked life tenure and protection against salary diminution. The United States intervened to defend the validity of the statute.

The bankruptcy judge denied the motion to dismiss. . . . But on appeal the District Court entered an order granting the motion, on the ground that "the delegation of authority in 28 U.S.C. § 1471 to the Bankruptcy Judges to try cases otherwise relegated under the Constitution to Article III judges" was unconstitutional. Id., at 1a. Both the United States and Northern filed notices of appeal in this Court. . . .

II

A

Basic to the constitutional structure established by the Framers was their recognition that "The accumulation of all powers, legislative, executive, and judiciary, in the same hands, whether of one, a few, or many, and whether hereditary, self-appointed, or elective, may justly be pronounced the very definition of tyranny." The Federalist No. 47 (J. Madison), p. 300 (H. Lodge ed. 1888). To ensure against such tyranny, the Framers provided that the Federal Government would consist of three distinct Branches, each to exercise one of the governmental powers recognized by the Framers as inherently distinct. . . .

The Federal Judiciary was therefore designed by the Framers to stand independent of the Executive and Legislature—to maintain the checks and balances of the constitutional structure, and also to guarantee that the process of adjudication itself remained impartial. Hamilton explained the importance of an independent Judiciary:

> Periodical appointments, however regulated, or by whomsoever made, would, in some way or other, be fatal to [the courts'] necessary independence. If the power of making them was committed either to

5. Although no particular standard of review is specified in the Act, the parties in the present case seem to agree that the appropriate one is the clearly erroneous standard, employed in the old Bankruptcy Rule 801 for review of findings of fact made by a referee. . . .

> the Executive or legislature, there would be danger of an improper complaisance to the branch which possessed it; if to both, there would be an unwillingness to hazard the displeasure of either; if to the people, or to persons chosen by them for the special purpose, there would be too great a disposition to consult popularity, to justify a reliance that nothing would be consulted but the Constitution and the laws. The Federalist No. 78, p. 489 (H. Lodge ed. 1888).

The Court has only recently reaffirmed the significance of this feature of the Framers' design: "A Judiciary free from control by the Executive and Legislature is essential if there is a right to have claims decided by judges who are free from potential domination by other branches of government." United States v. Will, 449 U.S. 200, 217–218 (1980).

As an inseparable element of the constitutional system of checks and balances, and as a guarantee of judicial impartiality, Art. III both defines the power and protects the independence of the Judicial Branch. It provides that "The judicial Power of the United States, shall be vested in one supreme Court, and in such inferior Courts as the Congress may from time to time ordain and establish." Art. III, § 1. The inexorable command of this provision is clear and definite: The judicial power of the United States must be exercised by courts having the attributes prescribed in Art. III. Those attributes are also clearly set forth:

> The Judges, both of the supreme and inferior Courts, shall hold their Offices during good Behaviour, and shall, at stated Times, receive for their Services, a Compensation, which shall not be diminished during their Continuance in Office. Art. III, § 1.

The "good Behaviour" Clause guarantees that Art. III judges shall enjoy life tenure, subject only to removal by impeachment. Toth v. Quarles, 350 U.S. 11, 16 (1955). The Compensation Clause guarantees Art. III judges a fixed and irreducible compensation for their services. United States v. Will, supra, 449 U.S. at 218–221. Both of these provisions were incorporated into the Constitution to ensure the independence of the judiciary from the control of the executive and legislative branches of government. . . .

B

It is undisputed that the bankruptcy judges whose offices were created by the Bankruptcy Act of 1978 do not enjoy the protections constitutionally afforded to Art. III judges. The bankruptcy judges do not serve for life subject to their continued "good Behaviour." Rather, they are appointed for 14–year terms, and can be removed by the judicial council of the circuit in which they serve on grounds of "incompetence, misconduct, neglect of duty or physical or mental disability." Second, the salaries of the bankruptcy judges are not immune from diminution by Congress. . . . In short, there is no doubt that the bankruptcy judges created by the Act are not Art. III judges. . . .

III . . .[15]

Appellants first rely upon a series of cases in which this Court has upheld the creation by Congress of non-Art. III "territorial courts." This exception from the general prescription of Art. III dates from the earliest days of the Republic, when it was perceived that the Framers intended that as to certain geographical areas, in which no State operated as sovereign, Congress was to exercise the general powers of government. For example, in American Ins. Co. v. Canter, 1 Pet. 511 (1828), the Court observed that Art. IV bestowed upon Congress alone a complete power of government over territories not within the States that comprised the United States. The Court then acknowledged Congress' authority to create courts for those territories that were not in conformity with Art. III. Such courts were

> created in virtue of the general right of sovereignty which exists in the government, or in virtue of that clause which enables Congress to make all needful rules and regulations, respecting the territory belonging to the United States. The jurisdiction with which they are invested . . . is conferred by Congress, in the execution of those general powers which that body possesses over the territories of the United States. Although admiralty jurisdiction can be exercised in the states in those Courts, only, which are established in pursuance of the 3d article of the Constitution; the same limitation does not extend to the territories. In legislating for them, Congress exercises the combined powers of the general, and of a state government. 1 Pet., at 546.

The Court followed the same reasoning when it reviewed Congress' creation of non-Art. III courts in the District of Columbia [Palmore v. United States, 411 U.S. 389 (1973)]. . . .

Appellants next advert to a second class of cases—those in which this Court has sustained the exercise by Congress and the Executive of the power to establish and administer courts martial. The situation in these cases strongly resembles the situation with respect to territorial courts: It too involves a constitutional grant of power that has been historically understood as giving the political branches of Government extraordinary control over the precise subject matter at issue. Art. I, § 8, cls. 13, 14, confer upon Congress the power "to provide and maintain a Navy," and "to make Rules for the Government and

15. Justice White's dissent finds particular significance in the fact that Congress could have assigned all bankruptcy matters to the state courts. But, of course, virtually all matters that might be heard in Art. III courts could also be left by Congress to state courts. This fact is simply irrelevant to the question before us. Congress has no control over state court judges; accordingly the principle of separation of powers is not threatened by leaving the adjudication of federal disputes to such judges. See Krattenmaker, Article III and Judicial Independence: Why the New Bankruptcy Courts are Unconstitutional, 70 Geo.L.J. 297, 304–305 (1981). The Framers chose to leave to Congress the precise role to be played by the lower federal courts in the administration of justice. See Hart and Wechsler's The Federal Courts and the Federal System, supra, at 11. But the Framers did not leave it to Congress to define the character of those courts—they were to be independent of the political branches and presided over by judges with guaranteed salary and life tenure.

Regulation of the land and naval Forces." The Fifth Amendment, which requires a presentment or indictment of a grand jury before a person may be held to answer for a capital or otherwise infamous crime, contains an express exception for "cases arising in the land or naval forces." And Art. II, § 2, cl. 1, provides that "The President shall be Commander in Chief of the Army and Navy of the United States, and of the Militia of the several States, when called into the actual Service of the United States." Noting these constitutional directives, the Court in Dynes v. Hoover, 20 How. 65 (1858), explained:

> These provisions show that Congress has the power to provide for the trial and punishment of military and naval offences in the manner then and now practiced by civilized nations; and that the power to do so is given without any connection between it and the 3d article of the Constitution defining the judicial power of the United States; indeed, that the two powers are entirely independent of each other. . . .

Finally, appellants rely on a third group of cases, in which this Court has upheld the constitutionality of legislative courts and administrative agencies created by Congress to adjudicate cases involving "public rights." The "public rights" doctrine was first set forth in Murray's Lessee v. Hoboken Land & Improvement Co., 18 How. 272 (1855):

> [W]e do not consider congress can either withdraw from judicial cognizance any matter which, from its nature, is the subject of a suit at the common law, or in equity, or admiralty; nor, on the other hand, can it bring under the judicial power a matter which, from its nature, is not a subject for judicial determination. At the same time there are matters, *involving public rights,* which may be presented in such form that the judicial power is capable of acting on them, and which are susceptible of judicial determination, but which congress may or may not bring within the cognizance of the courts of the United States, as it may deem proper. . . .

This doctrine may be explained in part by reference to the traditional principle of sovereign immunity, which recognizes that the Government may attach conditions to its consent to be sued. . . . But the public-rights doctrine also draws upon the principle of separation of powers, and an historical understanding that certain prerogatives were reserved to the political branches of government. The doctrine extends only to matters arising "between the Government and persons subject to its authority in connection with the performance of the constitutional functions of the executive or legislative departments," Crowell v. Benson, 285 U.S. 22, 50 (1932), and only to matters that historically could have been determined exclusively by those departments, see Ex parte Bakelite Corp., 279 U.S. 438, 458 (1929). The understanding of these cases is that the Framers expected that Congress would be free to commit such matters completely to non-judicial executive determination, and that as a result there can be no constitutional objection to Congress' employing the less drastic expedient of committing their determination to a legislative court or an administrative agency. . . .

The public-rights doctrine is grounded in a historically recognized distinction between matters that could be conclusively determined by the Executive and Legislative Branches and matters that are "inherently . . . judicial." . . . For example, the Court in *Murray's Lessee* looked to the law of England and the States at the time the Constitution was adopted, in order to determine whether the issue presented was customarily cognizable in the courts. . . . Concluding that the matter had not traditionally been one for judicial determination, the Court perceived no bar to Congress' establishment of summary procedures, outside of Art. III courts, to collect a debt due to the Government from one of its customs agents.[20] On the same premise, the Court in Ex parte Bakelite Corp., supra, held that the Court of Customs Appeals had been properly constituted by Congress as a legislative court:

> The *full* province of the court under the act creating it is that of determining matters arising between the Government and others in the executive administration and application of the customs laws. . . . The appeals include nothing which inherently or necessarily requires judicial determination, but only matters the determination of *which may be, and at times has been, committed exclusively to executive officers.* 279 U.S., at 458 (emphasis added).[21]

The distinction between public rights and private rights has not been definitively explained in our precedents. Nor is it necessary to do so in the present case, for it suffices to observe that a matter of public rights must at a minimum arise "between the government and others." Ex parte Bakelite Corp., supra, at 451.[23] In contrast, "the liability of one individual to another under the law as defined," Crowell v. Benson, 285 U.S., at 51, is a matter of private rights. Our precedents clearly establish that *only* controversies in the former category may be removed from Art. III courts and delegated to legislative courts or administrative agencies for their determination. See Atlas Roofing Co. v. Occupational Safety Comm'n, 430 U.S., at 450, n. 7; Crowell v. Benson, supra, 285 U.S., at 50–51. See also Katz, Federal Legislative Courts, 43 Harv.L.Rev. 894, 917–918 (1930). Private-rights disputes, on the other hand, lie at the core of the historically recognized judicial power.

20. Doubtless it could be argued that the need for independent judicial determination is greatest in cases arising between the government and an individual. But the rationale for the public-rights line of cases lies not in political theory, but rather in Congress' and this Court's understanding of what power was reserved to the Judiciary by the Constitution as a matter of historical fact.

21. See also Williams v. United States, 289 U.S. 553 (1933) (holding that Court of Claims was a legislative court and that salary of a judge of that court could therefore be reduced by Congress).

23. Congress cannot "withdraw from [Art. III] judicial cognizance *any* matter which, *from its nature,* is the subject of a suit at common law, or in equity or admiralty." Murray's Lessee v. Hoboken Land & Improvement Co., 18 How., at 284 (emphasis added). It is thus clear that the presence of the United States as a proper party to the proceeding is a necessary but not sufficient means of distinguishing "private rights" from "public rights." . . .

In sum, this Court has identified three situations in which Art. III does not bar the creation of legislative courts. In each of these situations, the Court has recognized certain exceptional powers bestowed upon Congress by the Constitution or by historical consensus. Only in the face of such an exceptional grant of power has the Court declined to hold the authority of Congress subject to the general prescriptions of Art. III.[25]

We discern no such exceptional grant of power applicable in the case before us. The courts created by the Bankruptcy Act of 1978 do not lie exclusively outside the States of the Federal Union, like those in the District of Columbia and the territories. Nor do the bankruptcy courts bear any resemblance to courts martial, which are founded upon the Constitution's grant of plenary authority over the Nation's military forces to the Legislative and Executive Branches. Finally, the substantive legal rights at issue in the present action cannot be deemed "public rights." Appellants argue that a discharge in bankruptcy is indeed a "public right," similar to such congressionally created benefits as "radio station licenses, pilot licenses, and certificates for common carriers" granted by administrative agencies. . . . But the restructuring of debtor-creditor relations, which is at the core of the federal bankruptcy power, must be distinguished from the adjudication of state-created private rights, such as the right to recover contract damages that is at issue in this case. The former may well be a "public right," but the latter obviously is not. . . .

IV

Appellants advance a second argument for upholding the constitutionality of the Act: that "viewed within the entire judicial framework set up by Congress," the bankruptcy court is merely an "adjunct" to the district court, and that the delegation of certain adjudicative functions to the bankruptcy court is accordingly consistent with the principle that the judicial power of the United States must be vested in Art. III courts. . . . As support for their argument, appellants rely principally upon Crowell v. Benson, supra, and United States v. Raddatz, 447 U.S. 667 (1980). . . .

The congressional scheme challenged in *Crowell* empowered an administrative agency, the United States Employees' Compensation Commission, to make initial factual determinations pursuant to a federal statute requiring employers to compensate their employees for work-related injuries occurring upon the navigable waters of the United States. . . . The agency was thus left with the limited role of determining "questions of fact as to the circumstances, nature, extent and consequences of the injuries sustained by the employee for which

25. . . . What clearly remains subject to Art. III are all private adjudications in federal courts within the States—matters from their nature subject to "a suit at common law or in equity or admiralty"—and all criminal matters, with the narrow exception of military crimes. There is no doubt that when the Framers assigned the "judicial Power" to an independent Art. III branch, these matters lay at what they perceived to be the protected core of that power. . . .

compensation is to be made." . . . The agency did not possess the power to enforce any of its compensation orders: On the contrary, every compensation order was appealable to the appropriate federal district court, which had the sole power to enforce it or set it aside, depending upon whether the court determined it to be "in accordance with law" and supported by evidence in the record. . . . The Court found that in view of these limitations upon the Compensation Commission's functions and powers, its determinations were "closely analogous to findings of the amount of damages that are made, according to familiar practice, by commissioners or assessors." . . . Observing that "there is no requirement that, in order to maintain the essential attributes of the judicial power, all determinations of fact in constitutional courts shall be made by judges," . . . the Court held that Art. III imposed no bar to the scheme enacted by Congress. . . .

Crowell involved the adjudication of congressionally created rights. But this Court has sustained the use of adjunct fact-finders even in the adjudication of constitutional rights—so long as those adjuncts were subject to sufficient control by an Art. III district court. In United States v. Raddatz, supra, the Court upheld the 1978 Federal Magistrates Act, which permitted district court judges to refer certain pretrial motions, including suppression motions based on alleged violations of constitutional rights, to a magistrate for initial determination. The Court observed that the magistrate's proposed findings and recommendations were subject to *de novo* review by the district court, which was free to rehear the evidence or to call for additional evidence. . . . Moreover, it was noted that the magistrate considered motions only upon reference from the district court, and that the magistrates were appointed, and subject to removal, by the district court. . . .[30] In short, the ultimate decisionmaking authority respecting all pretrial motions clearly remained with the district court. . . .[31]

30. Thus in *Raddatz* there was no serious threat that the exercise of the judicial power would be subject to incursion by other branches. "The only conceivable danger of a 'threat' to the 'independence' of the magistrate comes from within, rather than without the judicial department." . . .

31. Appellants and JUSTICE WHITE's dissent also rely on the broad powers exercised by the bankruptcy referees immediately before the Bankruptcy Act of 1978. . . . But those particular adjunct functions, which represent the culmination of years of gradual expansion of the power and authority of the bankruptcy referee, see 1 Collier on Bankruptcy ¶ 1.02 (15th ed. 1981), have never been explicitly endorsed by this Court. In Katchen v. Landy, 382 U.S. 323 (1966), on which the dissent relies, there was no discussion of the Art. III issue. Moreover, when *Katchen* was decided the 1973 Bankruptcy Rules had not yet been adopted, and the District Judge, after hearing the report of the magistrate, was free to "modify it or . . . reject it in whole or in part or . . . receive further evidence or . . . recommit it with instructions." Gen.Order in Bankruptcy No. 47, 305 U.S. 679 (1935).

We note, moreover, that the 1978 Act made at least three significant changes from the bankruptcy practice that immediately preceded it. First, of course, the jurisdiction of the bankruptcy courts was "substantially expanded by the Act." H.R. Rep No. 95–595, supra, p. 13 (1977). Before the Act the referee had no jurisdiction, except with consent, over controversies beyond those involving property in the actual or constructive possession of the court. . . . Second, the bankruptcy judges have broader powers than those exercised by the referees.

Together these cases establish two principles that aid us in determining the extent to which Congress may constitutionally vest traditionally judicial functions in non-Art. III officers. First, it is clear that when Congress creates a substantive federal right, it possesses substantial discretion to prescribe the manner in which that right may be adjudicated—including the assignment to an adjunct of some functions historically performed by judges. . . . Second, the functions of the adjunct must be limited in such a way that "the essential attributes" of judicial power are retained in the Art. III court. . . .

Appellants assume that Congress' power to create "adjuncts" to consider all cases related to those arising under title 11 is as great as it was in the circumstances of *Crowell.* But while *Crowell* certainly endorsed the proposition that Congress possesses broad discretion to assign factfinding functions to an adjunct created to aid in the adjudication of congressionally created statutory rights, *Crowell* does not support the further proposition necessary to appellants' argument—that Congress possesses the same degree of discretion in assigning traditionally judicial power to adjuncts engaged in the adjudication of rights *not* created by Congress. Indeed, the validity of this proposition was expressly denied in *Crowell,* when the Court rejected "the untenable assumption that the constitutional courts may be deprived in all cases of the determination of facts upon evidence even though a *constitutional* right may be involved," . . . and stated that

> the essential independence of the exercise of judicial power of the United States in the enforcement of *constitutional* rights requires that the Federal court should determine . . . an issue [of agency jurisdiction] upon its own record and the facts elicited before it. . . .[34]

Appellants' proposition was also implicitly rejected in *Raddatz.* Congress' assignment of adjunct functions under the Federal Magistrates Act was substantially narrower than under the statute challenged in *Crowell.* Yet the Court's scrutiny of the adjunct scheme in *Raddatz*—which played a role in the adjudication of *constitutional* rights—was far stricter than it had been in *Crowell.* Critical to the Court's decision to uphold the Magistrates Act was the fact that the ultimate decision was made by the district court. . . .

. . . Finally, and perhaps most significantly, the relationship between the district court and the bankruptcy court was changed under the 1978 Act. Before the Act, bankruptcy referees were "subordinate adjuncts of the district courts." . . . In contrast, the new bankruptcy courts are "independent of the United States district courts." . . . Before the Act, bankruptcy referees were appointed and removable only by the district court. . . . And the district court retained control over the reference by his power to withdraw the case from the referee. . . .

34. *Crowell's* precise holding, with respect to the review of "jurisdictional" and "constitutional" facts that arise within ordinary administrative proceedings, has been undermined by later cases. See St. Joseph Stock Yards Co. v. United States, 298 U.S. 38, 53 (1936). . . . But the general principle of *Crowell*—distinguishing between congressionally created rights and constitutionally recognized rights—remains valid. . . . See Agosto v. INS, 436 U.S. 748, 753 (1978) (*de novo* judicial determination required for claims of American citizenship in deportation proceedings).

The case before us, which centers upon appellant Northern's claim for damages for breach of contract and misrepresentation, involves a right created by *state* law, a right independent of and antecedent to the reorganization petition that conferred jurisdiction upon the bankruptcy court. Accordingly, Congress' authority to control the manner in which that right is adjudicated, through assignment of historically judicial functions to a non-Art. III "adjunct," plainly must be deemed at a minimum. Yet it is equally plain that Congress has vested the "adjunct" bankruptcy judges with powers over appellant's state-created right that far exceed the powers that it has vested in administrative agencies that adjudicate only rights of Congress' own creation.

Unlike the administrative scheme that we reviewed in *Crowell,* the Act vests all "essential attributes" of the judicial power of the United States in the "adjunct" bankruptcy court. First, the agency in *Crowell* made only specialized, narrowly confined factual determinations regarding a particularized area of law. In contrast, the subject matter jurisdiction of the bankruptcy courts encompasses not only traditional matters of bankruptcy, but also "all civil proceedings arising under title 11 or arising in or *related to* cases arising under title 11." . . .

Second, while the agency in *Crowell* engaged in statutorily channeled factfinding functions, the bankruptcy courts exercise "*all* of the jurisdiction" conferred by the Act on the district courts. . . . Third, the agency in *Crowell* possessed only a limited power to issue compensation orders pursuant to specialized procedures, and its orders could be enforced only by order of the district court. By contrast, the bankruptcy courts exercise all ordinary powers of district courts, including the power to preside over jury trials, . . . the power to issue declaratory judgments, . . ., the power to issue writs of habeas corpus, . . . and the power to issue any order, process or judgment appropriate for the enforcement of the provisions of title 11. . . . Fourth, while orders issued by the agency in *Crowell* were to be set aside if "not supported by the evidence," the judgments of the bankruptcy courts are apparently subject to review only under the more deferential "clearly erroneous" standard. See n. 5, supra. Finally, the agency in *Crowell* was required by law to seek enforcement of its compensation orders in the district court. In contrast, the bankruptcy courts issue final judgments, which are binding and enforceable even in the absence of an appeal. In short, the "adjunct" bankruptcy courts created by the Act exercise jurisdiction behind the facade of a grant to the district courts, and are exercising powers far greater than those lodged in the adjuncts approved in either *Crowell* or *Raddatz.*[39]

We conclude that § 241(a) of the Bankruptcy Act of 1978 has impermissibly removed most, if not all, of "the essential attributes of

39. Appellants suggest that *Crowell* and *Raddatz* stand for the proposition that Art. III is satisfied so long as some degree of appellate review is provided. But that suggestion is directly contrary to the text of our Constitution: "The Judges, *both* of the supreme and inferior Courts, shall hold their Offices during good Behaviour, and shall . . . receive [undiminished] Compensation." . . .

the judicial power" from the Art. III district court, and has vested those attributes in a non-Art. III adjunct. Such a grant of jurisdiction cannot be sustained as an exercise of Congress' power to create adjuncts to Art. III courts. . . .

JUSTICE REHNQUIST, with whom JUSTICE O'CONNOR joins, concurring in the judgment. . . .

None of the cases has gone so far as to sanction the type of adjudication to which Marathon will be subjected against its will under the provisions of the 1978 Act. To whatever extent different powers granted under that Act might be sustained under the "public rights" doctrine of Murray's Lessee v. Hoboken Land & Improvement Co., 18 How. 272 (1855), and succeeding cases, I am satisfied that the adjudication of Northern's lawsuit cannot be so sustained.

I am likewise of the opinion that the extent of review by Art. III courts provided on appeal from a decision of the Bankruptcy Court in a case such as Northern's does not save the grant of authority to the latter under the rule espoused in Crowell v. Benson, 285 U.S. 22 (1932). All matters of fact and law in whatever domains of the law to which the parties' dispute may lead are to be resolved by the Bankruptcy Court in the first instance, with only traditional appellate review apparently contemplated by Art. III courts. Acting in this manner the Bankruptcy Court is not an "adjunct" of either the District Court or the Court of Appeals. . . .

[Justice White, joined by Chief Justice Burger and Justice Powell, wrote a long dissent concluding, in light of the decisions discussed by Justice Brennan, that it was "too late to return to the simplicity of the principle pronounced in Article III and defended so vigorously and persuasively by Hamilton in the Federalist." Consequently "Article III . . . should be read as expressing one value that must be balanced against competing constitutional values and legislative responsibilities." On this test, he argued, the jurisdiction given the bankruptcy courts was constitutional. "[T]he presence of appellate review by an Article III court" went "a long way toward insuring a proper separation of powers"; because bankruptcy litigation presented "issues likely to be of little interest to the political branches, there [was] less reason to fear . . . a dangerous accumulation of power in one of the political branches"; the need for specialization was patent; and "the existence of several hundred bankruptcy judges with life tenure would have severely limited Congress' future options."]

Notes on Legislative Courts

(1) On occasion the Court has been firm in enforcing the tenure and salary provisions of Article III. In ordering the release of a civilian who had been sentenced to death by a military commission during the Civil War, for example, the Court invoked Article III as well as the right to jury trial: "One of the plainest constitutional provisions was . . . infringed when Milligan was tried by a court not ordained by Congress, and not

composed of judges appointed during good behavior." Ex parte Milligan, 71 U.S. (4 Wall.) 2 (1867).[1] Three quarters of a century later the Justices confirmed that the Great Depression did not justify reducing judicial salaries in the face of Article III. O'Donoghue v. United States, 289 U.S. 516 (1933).

On other occasions, as detailed by Justice Brennan in *Northern Pipeline,* the Court has permitted matters falling within Article III to be entrusted to decisionmakers who did not satisfy the guarantees of judicial independence. Can any of these decisions be justified? Were they all distinguishable from *Northern Pipeline?* See generally Currie, Bankruptcy Judges and the Independent Judiciary, 16 Creighton L.Rev. 441 (1983).

(2) In response to *Northern Pipeline,* Congress limited the jurisdiction of nontenured bankruptcy judges essentially to a laundry list of "core proceedings" including "the administration of the estate," "claims against the estate," "counterclaims . . . against persons filing claims against the estate," and "proceedings to determine, avoid, or recover preferences [or] . . . fraudulent conveyances." "Personal injury tort and wrongful death claims" are expressly excluded. Other matters related to a bankruptcy case may be referred to a bankruptcy judge for hearing and recommendation, but he may decide them only "with the consent of all the parties to the proceeding." 28 U.S.C. § 157(b), (c). Are these provisions constitutional?

(3) Thomas v. Union Carbide Agricultural Products Co., 473 U.S. 568 (1985). The Federal Insecticide, Fungicide, and Rodenticide Act (FIFRA), provides for the sharing of costs of registering pesticides among various manufacturers. If the parties fail to agree on the amount of compensation due to the applicant who provided the original information, either party may submit the matter to an arbitrator whose decision is subject to judicial review for "fraud, misrepresentation, or other misconduct."

Stressing that the claim arose under federal law and that Article III was not offended simply because the controversy was between private parties, the Court upheld the arbitration provision. The right to compensation for the use of data, wrote Justice O'Connor for the majority, "bears many of the characteristics of a 'public' right." "Use of a registrant's data to support a follow-on registration serves a public purpose as an integral part of a program safeguarding the public health." Congress could have authorized the Environmental Protection Agency to charge fees to cover information costs and to compensate data suppliers out of the proceeds; the arbitration procedure merely "collapses these two steps into one." Moreover, the arbitrator's order could be enforced, if at all, only against an applicant "who explicitly consents to have his rights determined by arbitration," as everyone seeking to register a pesticide was required to do. Finally, the statutory judicial review provision permitted Article III judges to protect against "constitutional error" as well as "against arbitrators who abuse or exceed their powers or willfully misconstrue their mandate under the governing law." In short, "Congress, acting for a valid legislative

1. See also United States ex rel. Toth v. Quarles, 350 U.S. 11 (1955), and Reid v. Covert, 354 U.S. 1 (1957), holding respectively that neither ex-servicemen nor servicemen's spouses could be tried by military tribunals for crimes committed abroad.

purpose pursuant to its constitutional powers under Article I, may create a seemingly 'private' right that is so closely integrated into a public regulatory scheme as to be a matter for agency resolution with limited involvement by the Article III judiciary."

Justice Brennan, joined by Marshall and Blackmun, concurred: "[I]n my judgment the FIFRA compensation scheme . . . should be viewed as involving a matter of public rights as that term is understood in the line of cases culminating in *Northern Pipeline,*" and the review provision "preserves the judicial authority over questions of law. . . ."

(4) Commodity Futures Trading Commission v. Schor, 478 U.S. 833 (1986). The Commodity Exchange Act outlaws fraudulent and manipulative conduct in connection with commodity futures transactions and authorizes an administrative commission to grant reparations to persons injured by violations of the Act. Schor filed a complaint against its broker seeking reparations under these provisions, but objected when the Commission ruled against it on a counterclaim for sums owing on Schor's account with the broker. The Court held the Commission could constitutionally pass upon the counterclaim.

Insofar as the tenure and salary provisions of Article III gave the litigant a "personal right" to "an independent federal adjudication," wrote Justice O'Connor, their protection (like other personal rights such as jury trial) was "subject to waiver"; by filing a reparations claim Schor had "effectively agreed to an adjudication by the [Commission] of the entire controversy." Insofar as Article III reflected institutional concerns beyond the interests of the parties, she continued, those concerns were not offended. Although the counterclaim involved a "private" right created by state law, *Thomas* had "rejected any attempt to make determinative for Article III purposes" the distinction between public and private rights, and "there is no reason inherent in separation of powers principles to accord the state law character of a claim talismanic power." The Commission dealt "only with a 'particularized area of law' "; it had no power "to preside over jury trials or issue writs of habeas corpus"; its orders were "enforceable only by order of the district court" and "reviewed under the same 'weight of the evidence' standards sustained in *Crowell.*" The "reparations scheme itself" was "of unquestioned constitutional validity," and "[i]t was only to ensure the effectiveness of this scheme that Congress authorized the [Commission] to assert jurisdiction over common law counterclaims." Finally, "the decision to invoke this forum is left entirely to the parties and the power of the federal judiciary to take jurisdiction of these matters is unaffected. In such circumstances, separation of powers concerns are diminished. . . ." [2]

Justices Brennan and Marshall dissented. What is left of *Northern Pipeline?* Of Article III?

2. See also Geldermann, Inc. v. Commodity Futures Trading Commission, 836 F.2d 310 (7th Cir.1987), concluding that a commodities broker had consented to arbitration of a dispute with one of his clients by remaining a member of the exchange after the Commission required it to adopt a rule making arbitration compulsory. Is this holding consistent with your understanding of the doctrine of unconstitutional conditions?

(5) In United States v. Woodley, 726 F.2d 1328 (9th Cir.1983), a panel of the Ninth Circuit held that, despite a long history of legislative and executive acceptance, Article III forbade application of Article II's provision for recess appointments to federal judges: "[I]f the recess appointment clause applies to judicial vacancies, a person may exercise the judicial power without the institutional protections of Article III that the Framers considered essential to judicial independence. A judge receiving his commission under the recess appointment clause may be called upon to make politically charged decisions while his nomination awaits approval by popularly elected officials. Professor Freund aptly summarized the problem when he referred to the recess appointee as a judge sitting 'with one eye over his shoulder on Congress.'" The panel decision was set aside en banc, over four dissents, 751 F.2d 1008 (9th Cir.1985). Was there anything to the panel's argument?

(6) For a relaxed view of what Article III requires see Bator, The Constitution as Architecture: Legislative and Administrative Courts Under Article III, 65 Ind.L.J. 233 (1990), summarized in Hart & Wechsler at 471–72 (3d ed. 1988):

> [T]he essence of the federal judicial power—and a sufficient guarantee of its independence—lies not in any question of trial jurisdiction, but in a power of judicial review that assures that an Article III court will have the final say in determining whether the law was correctly applied and the findings of fact had reasonable support in the evidence.

Is this any different from saying that Article III requires tenure only for appellate judges? Would that be consistent with its text or purpose? Cf. Osborn v. Bank of the United States, p. 140 below.

NATIONAL MUTUAL INSURANCE CO. v. TIDEWATER TRANSFER CO.

337 U.S. 582 (1949).

MR. JUSTICE JACKSON announced the judgment of the Court and an opinion in which MR. JUSTICE BLACK and MR. JUSTICE BURTON join.

This case calls up for review a holding that it is unconstitutional for Congress to open federal courts in the several states to action by a citizen of the District of Columbia against a citizen of one of the states. The petitioner, as plaintiff, commenced in the United States District Court for Maryland an action for a money judgment on a claim arising out of an insurance contract. No cause of action under the laws or Constitution of the United States was pleaded, jurisdiction being predicated only upon an allegation of diverse citizenship. The diversity set forth was that plaintiff is a corporation created by District of Columbia law, while the defendant is a corporation chartered by Virginia. . . .

In the Judiciary Act of 1789, Congress created a system of federal courts of first instance and gave them jurisdiction of suits "between a citizen of the State where the suit is brought, and a citizen of another State." In 1804, the Supreme Court, through Chief Justice Marshall, held that a citizen of the District of Columbia was not a citizen of a State within the meaning and intendment of this Act. This decision closed federal courts in the states to citizens of the District of Columbia in diversity cases, and for 136 years they remained closed. In 1940 Congress enacted the statute challenged here. It confers on such courts jurisdiction if the action "Is between citizens of different States, or citizens of the District of Columbia, the Territory of Hawaii, or Alaska, and any State or Territory." The issue here depends upon the validity of this Act. . . . [see 28 U.S.C. § 1332(d)].

Our first inquiry is whether, under the third, or Judiciary, Article of the Constitution, extending the judicial power of the United States to cases or controversies "between Citizens of different States," a citizen of the District of Columbia has the standing of a citizen of one of the states of the Union. This is the question which the opinion of Chief Justice Marshall answered in the negative, by way of dicta if not of actual decision. Hepburn & Dundas v. Ellzey, 2 Cranch [6 U.S.] 445. To be sure, nothing was before that Court except interpretation of a statute which conferred jurisdiction substantially in the words of the Constitution with nothing in the text or context to show that Congress intended to regard the District as a state. But Marshall resolved the statutory question by invoking the analogy of the constitutional provisions of the same tenor and reasoned that the District was not a state for purposes of the Constitution and, hence, was not for purposes of the Act. . . .

To now overrule this early decision of the Court on this point and hold that the District of Columbia is a state would, as that opinion pointed out, give to the word "state" a meaning in the Article which sets up the judicial establishment quite different from that which it carries in those Articles which set up the political departments and in other Articles of the instrument. While the word is one which can contain many meanings, such inconsistency in a single instrument is to be implied only where the context clearly requires it. There is no evidence that the Founders, pressed by more general and immediate anxieties, thought of the special problems of the District of Columbia in connection with the judiciary. This is not strange, for the District was then only a contemplated entity. But had they thought of it, there is nothing to indicate that it would have been referred to as a state and much to indicate that it would have required special provisions to fit its anomalous relationship into the new judicial system, just as it did to fit it into the new political system. . . .

We therefore decline to overrule the opinion of Chief Justice Marshall, and we hold that the District of Columbia is not a state within Article III of the Constitution. In other words, cases between citizens of the District and those of the states were not included in the catalogue of controversies over which the Congress could give jurisdiction to the federal courts by virtue of Article III.

This conclusion does not, however, determine that Congress lacks power under other provisions of the Constitution to enact this legislation. . . .

The judiciary Committee of the House of Representatives recommended the Act of April 20, 1940, as "a reasonable exercise of the constitutional power of Congress to legislate for the District of Columbia and for the Territories." This power the Constitution confers in broad terms. By Art. I, Congress is empowered "to exercise exclusive Legislation in all Cases whatsoever, over such District." And of course it was also authorized "to make all Laws which shall be necessary and proper for carrying into Execution" such powers. . . .

It is elementary that the exclusive responsibility of Congress for the welfare of the District includes both power and duty to provide its inhabitants and citizens with courts adequate to adjudge not only controversies among themselves but also their claims against, as well as suits brought by, citizens of the various states. It long has been held that Congress may clothe District of Columbia courts not only with the jurisdiction and powers of federal courts in the several states but with such authority as a state may confer on her courts. Kendall v. United States, 12 Pet. [37 U.S.] 524, 619; Capital Traction Co. v. Hof, 174 U.S. 1; O'Donoghue v. United States, 289 U.S. 516. The defendant here does not challenge the power of Congress to assure justice to the citizens of the District by means of federal instrumentalities, or to empower a federal court within the District to run its process to summon defendants here from any part of the country. And no reason has been advanced why a special statutory court for cases of District citizens could not be authorized to proceed elsewhere in the United States to sit, where necessary or proper, to discharge the duties of Congress toward District citizens.

However, it is contended that Congress may not combine this function, under Art. I, with those under Art. III, in district courts of the United States. Two objections are urged to this. One is that no jurisdiction other than specified in Art. III can be imposed on courts that exercise the judicial power of the United States thereunder. The other is that Art. I powers over the District of Columbia must be exercised solely within that geographic area.

Of course there are limits to the nature of duties which Congress may impose on the constitutional courts vested with the federal judicial power. The doctrine of separation of powers is fundamental in our system. . . . And this statute reflects that doctrine. It does not authorize or require either the district courts or this Court to participate in any legislative, administrative, political or other nonjudicial function or to render any advisory opinion. The jurisdiction conferred is limited to controversies of a justiciable nature, the sole feature distinguishing them from countless other controversies handled by the same courts being the fact that one party is a District citizen. Nor has the Congress by this statute attempted to usurp any judicial power. It has deliberately chosen the district courts as the appropriate instrumentality through which to exercise part of the judicial functions incidental to exertion of sovereignty over the District and its citizens. . . .

It is too late to hold that judicial functions incidental to Art. I powers of Congress cannot be conferred on courts existing under Art. III for it has been done with this Court's approval. O'Donoghue v. United States, 289 U.S. 516. In that case it was held that, although District of Columbia courts are Art. III courts, they can also exercise judicial power conferred by Congress pursuant to Art. I. The fact that District of Columbia courts, as local courts, can also be given administrative or legislative functions which other Art. III courts cannot exercise, does but emphasize the fact that, although the latter are limited to the exercise of judicial power, it may constitutionally be received from either Art. III or Art. I, and that congressional power over the District, flowing from Art. I, is plenary in every respect. . . .

[In] Schumacher v. Beeler, 293 U.S. 367 . . ., Chief Justice Hughes for a unanimous court wrote that by virtue of its Art. I authority over bankruptcies the Congress could confer on the regular district courts jurisdiction of "all controversies at law and in equity, as distinguished from proceedings in bankruptcy, between trustees as such and adverse claimants" to the extent specified in § 23(b) of the Bankruptcy Act as amended. Such jurisdiction was there upheld in a plenary suit, in a district court, by which the trustee sought equitable relief relying on allegations raising only questions of Ohio law concerning the validity under that law of a sheriff's levy and execution. . . . [To the same effect, said Mr. Justice Jackson, was Williams v. Austrian, 331 U.S. 642, 657.]

Nevertheless, it is now asserted, in retrospect, that those cases did arise under the laws of the United States. . . . This would indeed be difficult if we still adhere to the doctrine of Mr. Justice Holmes that "a suit arises under the law that creates the cause of action," American Well Works Co. v. Layne Co., 241 U.S. 257, 260, for the cause of action in each case rested solely on state law. . . .

The only way in which any law of the United States contributed to the case was in opening the district courts to the trustee, under Art. I powers of Congress, just as the present statute, under the same Article, opens those courts to residents of the District of Columbia. In each case, in the words of Chief Justice Stone, the federal law provided, not the right sought to be established, but only the authority of the trustee to establish it. The fact that the congressional power over bankruptcy granted by Art. I could open the court to the trustee does not mean that such suits arise under the laws of the United States; but it does mean that Art. I can supply a source of judicial power for their adjudication. . . .

We conclude that where Congress in the exercise of its powers under Art. I finds it necessary to provide those on whom its power is exerted with access to some kind of court or tribunal for determination of controversies that are within the traditional concept of the justiciable, it may open the regular federal courts to them regardless of lack of diversity of citizenship. . . .

The argument that congressional powers over the District are not to be exercised outside of its territorial limits also is pressed upon us. But this same contention has long been held by this Court to be untenable. . . .

We could not of course countenance any exercise of this plenary power either within or without the District if it were such as to draw into congressional control subjects over which there has been no delegation of power to the Federal Government. But, as we have pointed out, the power to make this defendant suable by a District citizen is not claimed to be outside of federal competence. If Congress has power to bring the defendant from his home all the way to a forum within the District, there seems little basis for denying it power to require him to meet the plaintiff part way in another forum. . . . We see no justification for holding that Congress in accomplishing an end admittedly within its power is restricted to those means which are most cumbersome and burdensome to a defendant. . . .

The judgment is reversed.

MR. JUSTICE RUTLEDGE, with whom MR. JUSTICE MURPHY agrees, concurring.

I join in the Court's judgment. But I strongly dissent from the reasons assigned to support it in the opinion of Mr. Justice Jackson. . . .

The Sixth Amendment's guarantee of "an impartial jury of the State . . . wherein the crime shall have been committed" extends to criminal prosecutions in the Nation's capital. Similarly, the word "Citizens" has a broader meaning in Article III, § 2, where it now includes corporations, than it has in the privileges and immunities clause of Article IV, § 2, or in the like clause of the Fourteenth Amendment. . . .

Since the District was not in existence when the Constitution was drafted, it seems in no way surprising that the Framers, after conferring on Congress plenary power over the future federal capital, made no express provision for litigating outside the boundaries of a hypothetical city conjectured controversies between unborn citizens and their unknown neighbors. Under these circumstances I cannot accept the proposition that absence of affirmative inclusion is, here, tantamount to deliberate exclusion. . . .

Whatever the need for federal jurisdiction over suits between litigant citizens of the several states, the same need equally compels the safeguards of federal trial for suits brought by citizens of the District of Columbia against citizens of the several states. . . .

Although I agree with the Court's judgment, I think it overrules the *Hepburn* decision in all practical effect. With that I am in accord. But I am not in accord with the proposed extension of "legislative" jurisdiction under Article I for the first time to the federal district courts outside the District of Columbia organized pursuant to Article III, and the consequent impairment of the latter Article's limitations upon judicial power. . . .

MR. CHIEF JUSTICE VINSON, with whom MR. JUSTICE DOUGLAS joins, dissenting.

While I agree with the views expressed by Mr. Justice Frankfurter and Mr. Justice Rutledge which relate to the power of Congress under Art. I of the Constitution to vest federal district courts with jurisdiction over suits between citizens of States and the District of Columbia, and with the views of Mr. Justice Frankfurter and Mr. Justice Jackson as to the proper interpretation of the word "States" in the diversity clause of Art. III, I am constrained to state my views individually because of the importance of these questions to the administration of the federal court system. . . .

That the federal judicial power was restricted to those classes of cases set forth in Art. III was clearly the opinion of those who had most to do with its drafting and acceptance. In the 80th Number of the Federalist, Hamilton listed the types of cases to which it was thought necessary that the judiciary authority of the nation should extend. All are found represented in Art. III. In the 81st Number, he wrote:

> "The amount of the observations hitherto made on the authority of the judicial department is this: *That it has been carefully restricted to those causes which are manifestly proper* for the cognizance of the national judicature. . . ." P. 511. (Emphasis added.)

while in No. 82, the following appears:

> "The only outlines described [for inferior courts] are that they shall be 'inferior to the Supreme Court,' and that *they shall not exceed the specified limits of the federal judiciary*." P. 516. . . .

In a series of three cases decided between 1800 and 1809, the Court refused to give literal effect to § 11 of the Judiciary Act of 1789, which had extended the jurisdiction of Circuit Courts to suits where "an alien is a party," because of the limitations imposed by Art. III. In Mossman v. Higginson, 4 Dall. [4 U.S.] 1314 (1800), it was decided that "as the legislative power of conferring jurisdiction on the federal Courts, is, in this respect, confined to suits *between citizens and foreigners*, we must so expound the terms of the law, as to meet the case, 'where, indeed, an alien is one party,' but a citizen is the other." This construction of the statute was adhered to in Montalet v. Murray, 4 Cranch [8 U.S.] 46 (1807); and in Hodgson v. Bowerbank, 5 Cranch [9 U.S.] 303 (1809), where Chief Justice Marshall dismissed the contention that "The judiciary act gives jurisdiction to the circuit courts in all suits in which *an alien is a party*" with this admonition: "Turn to the article of the constitution of the United States, for the statute cannot extend the jurisdiction beyond the limits of the constitution." . . .

Two separate but related points concerning the *O'Donoghue* case [relied on by Mr. Justice Jackson at p. 131, supra] should be emphasized. The first is that since District of Columbia courts may be given nonjudicial duties, . . . Keller v. Potomac Electric Power Co., [261 U.S. 428] . . . reliance upon that case to support the Act now under consideration is incompatible with the position that constitutional courts may only decide "cases" and "controversies" of a judicial nature. The second is that the rationale of the *O'Donoghue* case is, by its terms, limited to courts of the District. For the Court said (at p. 546): "If, in creating and defining the jurisdiction of the courts of the District, Congress were limited to Art. III, as it is in dealing with the other federal courts, the administrative and other jurisdiction spoken of could not be conferred upon the former." . . .

Except in the District of Columbia, therefore, American Ins. Co. v. Canter . . . and a long line of cases in the same vein prohibit the intermixture or combination of the personnel, powers, or duties of constitutional and legislative courts. . . .

The framers unquestionably intended that the jurisdiction of inferior federal courts be limited to those cases and controversies enumerated in Art. III. I would not sacrifice that principle on the altar of expediency. . . .

MR. JUSTICE FRANKFURTER, with whom MR. JUSTICE REED concurs, dissenting. . . .

There was a deep distrust of a federal judicial system, as against the State judiciaries, in the Constitutional Convention. This distrust was reflected in the evolution of Article III. Moreover, when they dealt with the distribution of judicial power as between the courts of the States and the courts of the United States, the Framers were dealing with a technical subject in a professional way. More than that, since the judges of the courts for which Article III made provision not only had the last word (apart from amending the Constitution) but also enjoyed life tenure, it was an essential safeguard against control by the judiciary of its own jurisdiction, to define the jurisdiction of those courts with particularity. The Framers guarded against the self-will of the courts as well as against the will of Congress by marking with exactitude the outer limits of federal judicial power.

According to Article III only "judicial power" can be "vested" in the courts established under it. At least this limitation, which has been the law of the land since 1792, Hayburn's Case, 2 Dall. [2 U.S.] 409, is not yet called into question. And so the President could not today elicit this Court's views on ticklish problems of international law any more than Washington was able to do in 1793. . . .

But if courts established under Article III can exercise wider jurisdiction than that defined and confined by Article III, and if they are available to effectuate the various substantive powers of Congress, such as the power to legislate for the District of Columbia, what justification is there for interpreting Article III as imposing one restriction in the exercise of those other powers of the Congress—the restriction to the exercise of "judicial power"—yet not interpreting it as imposing the restrictions that are most explicit, namely, the particularization of the "cases" to which "the judicial Power shall extend"? . . .

If Congress, in its law-making power over the District of Columbia, created some right for the inhabitants of the District, it could choose to provide for the enforcement of that right in any court of the United States, because the case would be one arising under "the Laws of the United States." But here the controversy is one arising not under the laws of the United States but under the laws of Maryland. By the command of the Constitution, this Maryland-created right can be enforced in a federal court only if the controversy is between "Citizens of different States" in relation to the State in which the federal court is sitting. . . .[3]

[T]o expand "the judicial Power" of Article III to include a controversy between a citizen of the District of Columbia and a citizen of one of the States by virtue of the provision extending "the judicial Power" to controversies "between Citizens of different States" would disregard an explicit limitation of Article III. For a hundred and fifty years "States" as there used meant "States"—the political organizations that form the Union and alone have power to amend the Constitution. The word did not cover the district which was to become "the Seat of the Government of the United States," nor the "Territory" belonging to the United States, both of which the Constitution dealt with in differentiation from the States. A decent respect for unbroken history since the country's foundation, for contemporaneous interpretation by those best qualified to make it, for the capacity of the distinguished lawyers among the Framers to express themselves with precision when dealing with technical matters, unite to admonish against disregarding the explicit language of Article III extending the diversity jurisdiction of the federal courts "to Controversies . . . between Citizens of different States," not to controversies between "Citizens of different States, including the District and the Territory of the United States." . . .

It is suggested that other provisions of the Constitution relating to "States" apply to the District. If the mere repetition of an inaccuracy begets truth, then that statement is true, not otherwise. Decisions concerned with the District involving trial by jury in criminal and civil

3. Reliance on Williams v. Austrian, 331 U.S. 642, 657, seems singularly inapposite. . . . That a particular claim dissociated from the fact of bankruptcy would have to be brought in a State court for want of any ground of federal jurisdiction is irrelevant. This is so because in the exercise of its power to "pass uniform laws on the subject of bankruptcies" Congress may deem it desirable that the federal courts be utilized for all the claims that pertain to the bankrupt estate whether in the federal court in which the bankruptcy proceeding is pending or in a more convenient federal court. The congeries of controversies thus brought into being by reason of bankruptcy may be lodged in the federal courts because they arise under "the Laws of the United States," to wit, laws concerning the "subject of bankruptcies." . . .

cases, full faith and credit for its proceedings, and the power to tax residents, rest on provisions in the Constitution not limited to "States." . . .

Notes on Tidewater

(1) Complete the following sentence: "The Supreme Court held in *Tidewater* that Congress has power to grant the courts jurisdiction over controversies between District of Columbia citizens and citizens of States under Article . . . of the Constitution."

(2) Was the controversy in *Tidewater* one between "Citizens of Different States" within Article III? Would Justice Rutledge permit a diversity action between citizens of two foreign countries in the face of Article III's language distinguishing between foreign states and States of the Union? Would Justice Jackson?

Notice that both parties in *Tidewater* were corporations. Section 1332(c) of the Judicial Code, added since that decision, provides that for diversity purposes a corporation "shall be deemed a citizen of any State by which it has been incorporated and of the State where it has its principal place of business." Is this statute unconstitutional? Cf. Paul v. Virginia, 75 U.S. (8 Wall.) 168 (1869), holding that a corporation was not a citizen within the Privileges and Immunities Clause. The prior diversity statute was silent as to corporations, but the Supreme Court found ways of including them. See infra pp. 267–87.

(3) Was *Tidewater* a case "arising under the Constitution, the Laws of the United States, and Treaties made . . . under their authority" within Article III? Were the bankruptcy cases that Justice Jackson cited? Would it be appropriate to hold that a case arises under federal law whenever federal law gives a federal court jurisdiction to hear the case?

(4) Could Congress enact laws governing the validity and interpretation of contracts made by District of Columbia residents? Could it provide a federal forum to enforce such laws? If so, why should Congress be forbidden to make a lesser encroachment upon state authority by giving the federal courts jurisdiction to administer state law? See Textile Workers Union v. Lincoln Mills, infra, p. 147. Professors Hart and Wechsler would go still further: Even if Congress cannot enact such a substantive law (consider the bankruptcy cases), "may not Congress have power to protect citizens of the District of Columbia from discrimination, or the possibility of it, by means falling short of declaring a substantive law to govern their legal relations?" The Federal Courts and the Federal System 416 (2d ed. 1973).

(5) Decisions forbidding Congress to exceed the limits of Article III in giving jurisdiction to constitutional courts are of two distinct kinds. The first (see pp. 8–19, supra) consists of instances in which Congress has attempted to give the courts non-judicial powers, that is, authority to deal with matters outside the Article III limitation to "Cases" and "Controversies." Within this category are such decisions as Muskrat v. United States, 219 U.S. 346 (1911), dealing with the requirement of adverse parties and what the Court considered a request for an "advisory opinion"; Federal

Radio Commission v. General Electric Co., 281 U.S. 464 (1930), dealing with the exercise of administrative discretion; and Hayburn's Case, 2 U.S. (2 Dall.) 409 (1792), in which court decisions were subjected to executive review. What policies underlie the refusal of the courts to take on nonjudicial functions at the request of Congress? Are these policies relevant to *Tidewater*?

The second class of cases in which Congress has been held without power to confer jurisdiction outside Article III is exemplified by Hodgson v. Bowerbank, 9 U.S. (5 Cranch) 303 (1809), in which Congress had tried to give jurisdiction in all cases to which an alien was a party. Such decisions, according to Chief Justice Vinson, are based on the principle that "any powers not specifically granted to the national judiciary by Art. III were reserved to the states or the people." To Justice Frankfurter the enumeration of the cases to which the judicial power extends reflected "a deep distrust of a federal judicial system, as against the State judiciaries, in the Constitutional Convention." It is this principle that the Chief Justice believed infringed by Justice Jackson's position. Is it reasonable to fear for States' Rights in the face of Congress's "exclusive" legislative power over the District of Columbia? Moreover, the defendant conceded, and the Chief Justice did not deny, that Congress had power to create a legislative court to hear cases such as *Tidewater*. Doesn't this concession put an end to any argument about States' Rights?

(6) The rejection of Mr. Justice Jackson's view in *Tidewater* is an extreme example of the zeal of the Supreme Court in refusing to permit Congress to give the courts more jurisdiction than the Constitution allows. Contrast with this the relative willingness of the Court, in such cases as *McCardle, Thomas*, and *Schor*, supra pp. 100, 126, 127, to permit Congress to withdraw Article III jurisdiction and even to transfer the courts' jurisdiction to administrative agencies. Which presents a greater threat to judicial independence: expansion or contraction of jurisdiction? Doesn't the *O'Donoghue* case, which permitted Article III courts in the District of Columbia to exercise administrative and advisory functions, demonstrate that the Supreme Court's fears of non-judicial functions are chimerical? Do not overlook the glaring non sequitur by which the Court reached its decision in that case: What has the absence of States-rights considerations in the District of Columbia to do with the necessity for a separation of judicial from legislative or executive powers?

(7) Can a federal district court entertain an action, not based on federal law, between a citizen of a State and a citizen of the Commonwealth of Puerto Rico? The statute says so, 28 U.S.C. § 1332(d), and the Third Circuit has upheld the statute. Americana of Puerto Rico, Inc. v. Kaplus, 368 F.2d 431, 435–36 (3d Cir.1966). But see Mora v. Torres, 113 F.Supp. 309 (D.P.R.1953), concluding that by approving the grant of considerable autonomy in the Commonwealth Constitution Congress relinquished its power over the island's local affairs. Does this mean Puerto Rico has become a "State" within Article III or ceased to be a "Territory" under Article IV? The Third Circuit in *Kaplus*, assuming the Commonwealth was not a "State," held it still a "Territory", partly because its people lack "control of their external relations with other nations" and partly because

legislative history indicated that the creation of the Commonwealth "would not change Puerto Rico's fundamental political, social, and economic relationship to the United States."

(8) Does Justice Jackson's argument sustain the jurisdiction of District of Columbia courts over state-law actions between Maryland residents? If so, was it so frivolous to suggest that jurisdiction conferred under the District clause could be exercised only in courts within the District?

Chapter II

FEDERAL–QUESTION AND ADMIRALTY CASES

SECTION 1. IDENTIFYING FEDERAL–QUESTION CASES

Introductory Note on Federal–Question Jurisdiction

That federal-question jurisdiction—though not permanently conferred until 1875—should be retained at the core of district-court business does not seem to be a matter of much controversy today. The ALI Study accurately marshalled the arguments: Federal judges have relative expertise in dealing with federal law; uniform interpretation is promoted by federal jurisdiction; state courts may be hostile to federal rights. Supreme Court review of state courts, limited by docket pressures, narrow review of the facts, the debilitating possibilities of delay, and the necessity of deferring to adequate state grounds of decision, cannot do the whole job. The Institute endorsed the general federal-question jurisdiction of the district courts in order "to protect litigants relying on federal law from the danger that state courts will not properly apply that law, either through misunderstanding or lack of sympathy." ALI Study 164–68. Even such a dedicated pruner of the federal caseload as Judge Friendly agreed that federal-question cases were appropriate grist for federal tribunals. Federal Jurisdiction: A General View 55, 62, 109 (1973).

But state courts are not the sole alternatives to federal district courts as forums of initial resort. Mindful of the burden of fact-finding in complex cases, the advantages of expert decision on technical matters, and the much-discussed shortcomings of negligence litigation, Judge Friendly suggested that federal workers' compensation be provided for railroad workers and seamen, that greater use be made of quasi-judicial administrative agencies in federal regulatory programs such as antitrust, securities, and pollution, that a specialized court be given exclusive patent jurisdiction, and that the Tax Court be reconstituted under Article III and given exclusive jurisdiction of tax cases, with appeals to a special Court of Tax Appeals whose decisions, except on constitutional questions, would be immune from Supreme Court review. Id. at 62–68, 129–33, 153–71. What considerations should determine such questions? See Judge Friendly's lament, id. at 65:

> Perhaps I would not feel so strongly that determinations under regulatory statutes normally should be lodged in the first instance in the administrative process if I could discern some meaningful standard which has guided Congress in making jurisdictional allocations between the courts and the agencies. But I cannot. . . . Certainly the statutes of the late 1960's and early 1970's reveal a pronounced tendency to bypass administrative agencies, born, no doubt, of legislative dissatisfaction with their performance.

Recall also the one-time issue whether conferring quasi-judicial powers on administrators lacking life tenure was consistent with Article III, pp. 114–28, supra.

The relative merits of courts and administrative agencies are explored in the courses on administrative law and cannot be here. The following cases deal with the intricate problems that have arisen in determining whether or not particular cases fall within the deceptively simple category of cases "arising under" federal law.

OSBORN v. BANK OF THE UNITED STATES

22 U.S. (9 Wheat.) 738 (1824).

[In McCulloch v. Maryland, 17 U.S. (4 Wheat.) 316 (1819), the Supreme Court affirmed the power of Congress to establish a national bank and denied the power of the States to tax it. Annoyed but undaunted, Ohio made clear its intention to enforce a tax of $50,000 on each branch of the Bank. The Bank went to federal court and obtained a temporary injunction restraining the state auditor from collecting the tax. Before the battle was over, the auditor's men had invaded the vaults and spirited away $120,475 of the Bank's money; federal commissioners had taken the state treasurer's keys and recaptured $98,000 from the state treasury; the Ohio legislature had reaffirmed the Kentucky and Virginia Resolutions and outlawed the Bank entirely; and the state treasurer was in federal prison. The federal court ordered the defendants to return all the money taken from the Bank, and they appealed. See 1 C. Warren, The Supreme Court in United States History, ch. 12 (Rev. ed. 1926).]

MR. CHIEF JUSTICE MARSHALL delivered the opinion of the Court. . . .

The appellants contest the jurisdiction of the Court on two grounds:

1st. That the act of Congress has not given it.

2d. That, under the constitution, Congress cannot give it.

1. The first part of the objection depends entirely on the language of the act. The words are, that the Bank shall be "made able and capable in law," "to sue and be sued, plead and be impleaded, answer

and be answered, defend and be defended, in all State Courts having competent jurisdiction, and in any Circuit Court of the United States."

These words seem to the Court to admit of but one interpretation. They cannot be made plainer by explanation. They give, expressly, the right "to sue and be sued," "in every Circuit Court of the United States," and it would be difficult to substitute other terms which would be more direct and appropriate for the purpose. . . .

The act of incorporation, then, confers jurisdiction on the Circuit Courts of the United States, if Congress can confer it.

2. We will now consider the constitutionality of the clause in the act of incorporation, which authorizes the Bank to sue in the federal Courts.

In support of this clause, it is said, that the legislative, executive, and judicial powers, of every well constructed government, are co-extensive with each other; that is, they are potentially co-extensive. The executive department may constitutionally execute every law which the Legislature may constitutionally make, and the judicial department may receive from the Legislature the power of construing every such law. . . .

[T]he constitution declares, that the judicial power shall extend to all cases arising under the constitution, laws, and treaties, of the United States.

The suit of The Bank of the United States v. Osborn and others, is a case, and the question is, whether it arises under a law of the United States?

The appellants contend, that it does not, because several questions may arise in it, which depend on the general principles of the law, not on any act of Congress.

If this were sufficient to withdraw a case from the jurisdiction of the federal Courts, almost every case, although involving the construction of a law, would be withdrawn; and a clause in the constitution, relating to a subject of vital importance to the government, and expressed in the most comprehensive terms, would be construed to mean almost nothing. There is scarcely any case, every part of which depends on the constitution, laws, or treaties of the United States. The questions, whether the fact alleged as the foundation of the action, be real or fictitious; whether the conduct of the plaintiff had been such as to entitle him to maintain his action; whether his right is barred; whether he has received satisfaction, or has in any manner released his claims, are questions, some or all of which may occur in almost every case. . . .

The constitution establishes the Supreme Court, and defines its jurisdiction. It enumerates cases in which its jurisdiction is original and exclusive; and then defines that which is appellate, but does not insinuate, that in any such case, the power cannot be exercised in its original form . . . in the Courts of the Union, but must first be exercised in the tribunals of the State; tribunals over which the government of the Union has no adequate control, and which may be closed to any claim asserted under a law of the United States.

We perceive, then, no ground on which the proposition can be maintained, that Congress is incapable of giving the Circuit Courts original jurisdiction, in any case to which the appellate jurisdiction extends.

We ask, then, if it can be sufficient to exclude this jurisdiction, that the case involves questions depending on general principles? A cause may depend on several questions of fact and law. Some of these may depend on the construction of a law of the United States; others on principles unconnected with that law. If it be a sufficient foundation for jurisdiction, that the title or right set up by the party, may be defeated by one construction of the constitution or law of the United States, and sustained by the opposite construction, provided the facts necessary to support the action be made out, then all the other questions must be decided as incidental to this, which gives that jurisdiction. . . . On the opposite construction, the judicial power never can be extended to a whole case, as expressed by the constitution, but to those parts of cases only which present the particular question involving the construction of the constitution or the law. We say it never can be extended to the whole case, because, if the circumstance that other points are involved in it, shall disable Congress from authorizing the Courts of the Union to take jurisdiction of the original cause, it equally disables Congress from authorizing those Courts to take jurisdiction of the whole cause, on an appeal, and thus will be restricted to a single question in that cause; and words obviously intended to secure to those who claim rights under the constitution, laws, or treaties of the United States, a trial in the federal Courts, will be restricted to the insecure remedy of an appeal upon an insulated point, after it has received that shape which may be given to it by another tribunal, into which he is forced against his will.

We think, then, that when a question to which the judicial power of the Union is extended by the constitution, forms an ingredient of the original cause, it is in the power of Congress to give the Circuit Courts jurisdiction of that cause, although other questions of fact or of law may be involved in it.

The case of the Bank is, we think, a very strong case of this description. The charter of incorporation not only creates it, but gives it every faculty which it possesses. The power to acquire rights of any description, to transact business of any description, to make contracts of any description, to sue on those contracts, is given and measured by its charter, and that charter is a law of the United States. This being can acquire no right, make no contract, bring no suit, which is not authorized by a law of the United States. It is not only itself the mere creature of a law, but all its actions and all its rights are dependent on the same law. Can a being, thus constituted, have a case which does not arise literally, as well as substantially, under the law?

Take the case of a contract, which is put as the strongest against the Bank.

When a Bank sues, the first question which presents itself, and which lies at the foundation of the cause, is, has this legal entity a right to sue? Has it a right to come, not into this Court particularly, but into any Court? This depends on a law of the United States. The next question is, has this being a right to make this particular contract? If this question be decided in the negative, the cause is determined against the plaintiff; and this question, too, depends entirely on a law of the United States. These are important questions, and they exist in every possible case. The right to sue, if decided once, is decided for ever; but the power of Congress was exercised antecedently to the first decision on that right, and if it was constitutional then, it cannot cease to be so, because the particular question is decided. It may be revived at the will of the party, and most probably would be renewed, were the tribunal to be changed. But the question respecting the right to make a particular contract, or to acquire a particular property, or to sue on account of a particular injury, belongs to every particular case, and may be renewed in every case. The question forms an original ingredient in every cause. Whether it be in fact relied on or not, in the defence, it is still a part of the cause, and may be relied on. The right of the plaintiff to sue, cannot depend on the defence which the defendant may choose to set up. His right to sue is anterior to that defence, and must depend on the state of things when the action is brought. The questions which the case involves, then, must determine its character, whether those questions be made in the cause or not.

The appellants say, that the case arises on the contract; but the validity of the contract depends on a law of the United States, and the plaintiff is compelled, in every case, to show its validity. The case arises emphatically under the law. The act of Congress is its foundation. The contract could never have been made, but under the authority of that act. The act itself is the first ingredient in the case, is its origin, is that from which every other part arises. That other questions may also arise, as the execution of the contract, or its performance, cannot change the case, or give it any other origin than the charter of incorporation. The action still originates in, and is sustained by, that charter.

The clause giving the Bank a right to sue in the Circuit Courts of the United States stands on the same principle with the acts authorizing officers of the United States who sue in their own names, to sue in the Courts of the United States. The Postmaster General, for example, cannot sue under that part of the constitution which gives jurisdiction to the federal Courts, in consequence of the character of the party, nor is he authorized to sue by the Judiciary Act. He comes into the Courts of the Union under the authority of an act of Congress, the constitutionality of which can only be sustained by the admission that his suit is a case arising under a law of the United States. If it be said, that it is such a case, because a law of the United States authorizes the contract, and authorizes the suit, the same reasons exist with respect to a suit brought by the Bank. . . .

It is said, that a clear distinction exists between the party and the cause; that the party may originate under a law with which the cause has no connexion; and that Congress may, with the same propriety, give a naturalized citizen, who is the mere creature of a law, a right to sue in the Courts of the United States, as give that right to the Bank.

This distinction is not denied; and, if the act of Congress was a simple act of incorporation, and contained nothing more, it might be entitled to great consideration. But the act does not stop with incorporating the Bank. It proceeds to bestow upon the being it has made, all the faculties and capacities which that being possesses. . . .

A naturalized citizen is indeed made a citizen under an act of Congress, but the act does not proceed to give, to regulate, or to prescribe his capacities. He becomes a member of the society, possessing all the rights of a native citizen, and standing, in view of the constitution, on the footing of a native. . . . The constitution then takes him up, and, among other rights, extends to him the capacity of suing in the Courts of the United States, precisely under the same circumstances under which a native might sue. . . .

Upon the best consideration we have been able to bestow on this subject, we are of opinion, that the clause in the act of incorporation, enabling the Bank to sue in the Courts of the United States, is consistent with the constitution, and to be obeyed in all Courts. . . .

[The judgment in the Bank's favor was affirmed except as to the award of interest.]

MR. JUSTICE JOHNSON [dissenting]. . . .

I have very little doubt that the public mind will be easily reconciled to the decision of the Court here rendered; for, whether necessary or unnecessary originally, a state of things has now grown up, in some of the States, which renders all the protection necessary, that the general government can give to this Bank. The policy of the decision is obvious, that is, if the Bank is to be sustained; and few will bestow upon its legal correctness, the reflection, that it is necessary to test it by the constitution and laws, under which it is rendered. . . .

In the present instance, I cannot persuade myself, that the constitution sanctions the vesting of the right of action in this Bank, in cases in which the privilege is exclusively personal, or in any case, merely on the ground that a question might *possibly* be raised in it, involving the constitution, or constitutionality of a law, of the United States.

When laws were heretofore passed for raising a revenue by a duty on stamped paper, the tax was quietly acquiesced in, notwithstanding it entrenched so closely on the unquestionable power of the States over the law of contracts; but had the same law which declared void contracts not written upon stamped paper, declared, that every person holding such paper should be entitled to bring his action "in any Circuit Court" of the United States, it is confidently believed that there could have been but one opinion on the constitutionality of such a provision. The whole jurisdiction over contracts, might thus have been taken from the State Courts, and conferred upon those of the United States. Nor would the evil have rested there; by a similar exercise of power, imposing a stamp on deeds generally, jurisdiction over the territory of the State, whoever might be parties, even between citizens of the same State—jurisdiction of suits instituted for the recovery of legacies or distributive portions of intestates' estates—jurisdiction, in fact, over almost every possible case, might be transferred to the Courts of the United States. . . . But still farther, as was justly insisted in argument, there is not a tract of land in the United States, acquired under laws of the United States, whatever be the number of mesne transfers that it may have undergone, over which the jurisdiction of the Courts of the United States might not be extended by Congress, upon the very principle on which the right of suit in this Bank is here maintained. Nor is the case of the alien, put in argument, at all inapplicable. The one acquires its character of individual property, as the other does his political existence, under a law of the United States; and there is not a suit which may be instituted to recover the one, nor an action of ejectment to be brought by the other, in which a right acquired under a law of the United States, does not lie as essentially at the basis of the right of action, as in the suits brought by this Bank. . . .

And here I must observe, that I altogether misunderstood the counsel, who argued the cause for the plaintiff in error, if any of them contended against the jurisdiction, on the ground that the cause involved questions depending on general principles. No one can question, that the Court which has jurisdiction of the principal question, must exercise jurisdiction over every question. Neither did I understand them as denying, that if Congress could confer on the Circuit Courts appellate, they could confer original jurisdiction. The argument went to deny the right to assume jurisdiction on a mere hypothesis. It was one of description, identity, definition; they contended, that until a question involving the construction or administration of the laws of the United States did actually arise, the *casus federis* was not presented, on which the constitution authorized the government to take to itself the jurisdiction of the cause. . . .

And this doctrine has my hearty concurrence in its general application. A very simple case may be stated, to illustrate its bearing on the question of jurisdiction between the two governments. By virtue of treaties with Great Britain, aliens holding lands were exempted from alien disabilities, and made capable of holding, aliening, and transmitting their estates, in common with natives. But why should the claimants of such lands, to all eternity, be vested with the privilege of bringing an original suit in the Courts of the United States? It is true, a question might be made, upon the effect of the treaty, on the rights claimed by or through the alien; but until that question does arise, nay, until a decision against the right takes place, what end has the United States to subserve in claiming jurisdiction of the cause? . . .

By possibility, a constitutional question may be raised in any conceivable suit that may be instituted; but that would be a very insufficient ground for assuming universal jurisdiction; and yet, that a question has been made, as that, for instance, on the Bank charter, and may again be made, seems still worse, as a ground for extending jurisdiction. . . . Indeed, I cannot perceive how, with ordinary correctness, a question can be said to be involved in a cause, which only may possibly be made, but which, in fact, is the very last question that there is any probability will be made; or rather, how that can any longer be denominated a question, which has been put out of existence by a solemn decision. . . .

Efforts have been made to fix the precise sense of the constitution, when it vests jurisdiction in the general government, in "cases arising under the laws of the United States." To me, the question appears susceptible of a very simple solution; that all depends upon the identity of the case supposed; according to which idea, a case may be such in its very existence, or it may become such in its progress. An action may "live, move, and have its being," in a law of the United States; such is that given for the violation of a patent-right, and four or five different actions given by this act of incorporation; particularly that against the President and Directors for over-issuing; in all of which cases the plaintiff must count upon the law itself as the ground of his action. And of the other description, would have been an action of trespass, in this case, had remedy been sought for an actual levy of the tax imposed. Such was the case of the former Bank against Deveaux, and many others that have occurred in this Court, in which the suit, in its form, was such as occur in ordinary cases, but in which the pleadings or evidence raised the question on the law or constitution of the United States. In this class of cases, the occurrence of a question makes the case, and transfers it, as provided for under the twenty-fifth section of the Judiciary Act, to the jurisdiction of the United States. . . .

But until the plaintiff can control the defendant in his pleadings, I see no practical mode of determining when the case does occur, otherwise than by permitting the cause to advance until the case for which the constitution provides shall actually arise. If it never occurs, there can be nothing to complain of; and such are the provisions of the twenty-fifth section. The cause might be transferred to the Circuit Court before an adjudication takes place; but I can perceive no earlier stage at which it can possibly be predicated of such a case, that it is one within the constitution; nor any possible necessity for transferring it then, or until the Court has acted upon it to the prejudice of the claims of the United States. It is not, therefore, because congress may not vest an *original* jurisdiction, where they can constitutionally vest in the circuit courts *appellate* jurisdiction, that I object to this general grant of the right to sue; but, because that the peculiar nature of this jurisdiction is such, as to render it impossible to exercise it in a strictly original form. . . .

Notes on the Constitutional Definition of Cases Arising Under Federal Law

(1) Was there any doubt that the Bank's suit to enjoin the enforcement of an unconstitutional tax was a case arising under the Constitution? But the more difficult question resolved in the opinions was presented by a companion case, Bank of United States v. Planters' Bank, 22 U.S. (9 Wheat.) 904 (1824), in which the National Bank sued to recover on negotiable notes made by a state bank; jurisdiction was upheld on the authority of *Osborn*.

Aren't there potential federal questions in every litigation—if nothing else, questions as to the constitutionality of the governing state law? Was Justice Johnson therefore right in protesting that the result of *Osborn* was to make every case one arising under federal law?

(2) The philosophy of *Osborn* was applied (was it extended?) in the Pacific Railroad Removal Cases (Texas & P. Ry. v. Kirk), 115 U.S. 1 (1885), which permitted federally incorporated railroads to remove to the federal courts actions brought against them for personal injuries and an action respecting payment for railroad property taken by eminent domain. The statute then in force allowed removal of cases "arising under the laws of the United States." There was no suggestion that issues such as negligence or damages were governed by federal law; but *Osborn*, the Supreme Court said, had "substantially decided" that "a suit by or against a corporation of the United States is a suit arising under the laws of the United States." These corporations, created by acts of Congress, "not only derive their existence, but their powers, their functions, their duties, and a large portion of their resources, from those acts, and, by virtue thereof sustain important relations to the Government of the United States." Two dissenters, conceding the power of Congress to grant jurisdiction in these cases, denied that Congress had done so.

(3) Schumacher v. Beeler, 293 U.S. 367 (1934), upheld federal jurisdiction over a state-law action brought by a bankruptcy trustee although there was no allegation of diverse citizenship: "The Congress, by virtue of its constitutional authority over bankruptcies, could confer or withhold jurisdiction to entertain such suits and could prescribe the conditions upon which the federal courts should have jurisdiction." Does this mean that a case arises under federal law whenever a federal statute purports to place it within the jurisdiction of a federal court?

(4) Textile Workers Union v. Lincoln Mills, 353 U.S. 448 (1957), was a suit by the union in federal court to compel arbitration of grievances under a collective bargaining agreement affecting interstate commerce. Section 301(a) of the Labor Management Relations Act, 29 U.S.C. § 185, grants the district courts jurisdiction over such actions without regard to the citizenship of the parties. The majority, finding in the statute "a federal policy

that federal courts should enforce these agreements," held that "the substantive law to apply in suits under § 301 is federal law" and upheld the jurisdictional provision as an implementation of the federal-question clause of Article III.

Justice Frankfurter, who disagreed with the Court's conclusion that federal law determined the meaning and enforceability of labor contracts, thought § 301 unconstitutional. "Almost without exception," he argued, "decisions under the general statutory grants have tested jurisdiction in terms of the presence, as an integral part of the plaintiff's cause of action, of an issue calling for interpretation or application of federal law." It was not enough that, as Professor Wechsler had suggested (Federal Jurisdiction and the Revision of the Judicial Code, 13 Law & Contemp.Probs. 216, 224–25), Congress could have provided for federal jurisdiction if it had gone further by prescribing federal rules of decision as well:

> Surely the truly technical restrictions of Article III are not met or respected by a beguiling phrase that the greater power here must necessarily include the lesser. . . . [U]nder th[is] theory of "protective jurisdiction," . . . every contract or tort arising out of a contract affecting commerce might be a potential cause of action in the federal courts, even though only state law was involved in the decision of the case. At least in *Osborn* and the bankruptcy cases [see note 3 supra], a substantive federal law was present somewhere in the background.

Nor would it be enough, Frankfurter argued, if § 301 were construed to give unions a federal right to enter into binding agreements and to sue to enforce them. Although "[t]his was all that was immediately and expressly involved in the *Osborn* case," *Osborn*'s "premise . . . that every case in which a federal question might arise must be capable of being commenced in the federal courts" was "subject to criticism." Moreover, "the historical setting" of *Osborn* "was vastly different" and the Bank a "creature of federal law . . . engaged in carrying out essential governmental functions," while the *Pacific Railroad Removal Cases* (note 2 supra) were a " 'sport' " entitled to little respect. The bankruptcy cases, he added, had not been based simply on the fact that federal law transferred the bankrupt's claims to the trustee:

> [T]he bankruptcy power . . . may be deemed to sweep within its scope interests analytically outside the "federal question" category, but sufficiently related to the main purpose of bankruptcy to call for comprehensive treatment. . . . [Moreover,] if all the suits by the trustee, even though in many federal courts, are regarded as one litigation for the collection and apportionment of the bankrupt's property, a particular suit by the trustee . . . might be analogized to the ancillary or pendent jurisdiction cases in which, in the disposition of a cause of action, federal courts may pass on state grounds for recovery that are joined to federal grounds [see pp. 188–200 below].

Did Justice Frankfurter adequately distinguish the precedents? How much of the case must be federal in order to satisfy his criteria?

(5) Verlinden B.V. v. Central Bank of Nigeria, 461 U.S. 480 (1983). The Foreign Sovereign Immunities Act, enacted in 1976, confirms the immunity of foreign states from suit in either federal or state court but

makes a number of exceptions, which include cases involving commercial activities or specified torts or in which the defendant has consented to be sued. 28 U.S.C. §§ 1604–07. Section 1330(a) gives the district courts jurisdiction of "any nonjury civil action against a foreign state . . . as to any claim for relief in personam with respect to which the foreign state is not entitled to immunity under sections 1605–1607 of this title or under any applicable international agreement." Invoking these provisions, Verlinden (a Dutch corporation) sued the Bank of Nigeria (a state instrumentality) in federal court for breach of a contract involving the sale of cement. The Supreme Court construed § 1330(a) to apply to an action brought by a foreign corporation against a foreign state and upheld its constitutionality under the federal-question clause of Article III.

No foreign state could be sued, said Chief Justice Burger, unless the action fell within one of the exceptions enumerated in the statute. "At the threshold of every action . . . against a foreign state, therefore, the court . . . must apply the detailed federal law standards set forth in the Act." It was immaterial for constitutional purposes that sovereign immunity was a defense and its exceptions a matter for reply rather than an ingredient of the plaintiff's initial complaint; decisions drawing such a distinction (see pp. 149–60 infra) had been interpreting the statutory federal-question provision, and Congress's power was broader. Nor, the opinion continued, was this an instance in which Congress had attempted to bootstrap cases into federal court by enacting a statute that did "nothing more than grant jurisdiction": "The Act codifies the standards governing foreign sovereign immunity as an aspect of substantive federal law." Thus "every action against a foreign sovereign necessarily involves application of a body of substantive federal law, and accordingly 'arises under' federal law, within the meaning of Article III."

LOUISVILLE & NASHVILLE RAILROAD CO. v. MOTTLEY

211 U.S. 149 (1908).

The appellees (husband and wife), being residents and citizens of Kentucky, brought this suit in equity in the Circuit Court of the United States for the Western District of Kentucky against the appellant, a railroad company and a citizen of the same state. The object of the suit was to compel the specific performance of the following contract:

> "Louisville, Ky., Oct. 2nd, 1871.
>
> "The Louisville & Nashville Railroad Company, in consideration that E. L. Mottley and wife, Annie E. Mottley, have this day released Company from all damages or claims for damages for injuries received by them on the 17th of September, 1871, in consequence of a collision of trains on the railroad of said Company at Randolph's Station, Jefferson County, Ky., hereby agrees to issue free passes on said Railroad and branches now existing or to exist, to said E. L. & Annie E. Mottley for the remainder of the present year, and thereafter, to renew said passes annually during the lives of said Mottley and wife or either of them."

The bill alleged that in September, 1871, plaintiffs, while passengers upon the defendant railroad, were injured by the defendant's negligence and released their respective claims for damages in consideration of the agreement for transportation during their lives, expressed in the contract. It is alleged that the contract was performed by the defendant up to January 1, 1907, when the defendant declined to renew the passes. The bill then alleges that the refusal to comply with the contract was based solely upon that part of the act of Congress of June 29, 1906, 34 Stat. 584, which forbids the giving of free passes or free transportation. The bill further alleges: First, that the act of Congress referred to does not prohibit the giving of passes under the circumstances of this case; and, second, that, if the law is to be construed as prohibiting such passes, it is in conflict with the Fifth Amendment of the Constitution, because it deprives the plaintiffs of their property without due process of law. The defendant demurred to the bill. The judge of the circuit court overruled the demurrer, entered a decree for the relief prayed for, and the defendant appealed directly to this court.

MR. JUSTICE MOODY, after making the foregoing statement, delivered the opinion of the court:

Two questions of law were raised by the demurrer to the bill, were brought here by appeal, and have been argued before us. They are, first, whether that part of the act of Congress of June 29, 1906, . . . which forbids the giving of free passes or the collection of any different compensation of passengers than that specified in the tariff filed, makes it unlawful to perform a contract for transportation of persons who in good faith, before the passage of the act, had accepted such contract in satisfaction of a valid cause of action against the railroad; and, second, whether the statute, if it should be construed to render such a contract unlawful, is in violation of the Fifth Amendment of the Constitution of the United States. We do not deem it necessary, however, to consider either of these questions, because, in our opinion, the court below was without jurisdiction of the cause. Neither party has questioned that jurisdiction, but it is the duty of this court to see to it that the jurisdiction of the Circuit Court, which is defined and limited by statute, is not exceeded. This duty we have frequently performed of our own motion. Mansfield & C. Railway Co. v. Swan, 111 U.S. 379, 382. . . .

There was no diversity of citizenship, and it is not and cannot be suggested that there was any ground of jurisdiction, except that the case was a "suit . . . arising under the Constitution or laws of the United States." . . . It is the settled interpretation of these words, as used in this statute, conferring jurisdiction, that a suit arises under the Constitution and laws of the United States only when the plaintiff's statement of his own cause of action shows that it is based upon those laws or that Constitution. It is not enough that the plaintiff alleges some anticipated defense to his cause of action and asserts that the defense is invalidated by some provision of the Constitution of the

United States. Although such allegations show that very likely, in the course of the litigation, a question under the Constitution would arise, they do not show that the suit, that is, the plaintiff's original cause of action, arises under the Constitution. In Tennessee v. Union & Planters' Bank, 152 U.S. 454, the plaintiff, the State of Tennessee, brought suit in the circuit court of the United States to recover from the defendant certain taxes alleged to be due under the laws of the state. The plaintiff alleged that the defendant claimed an immunity from the taxation by virtue of its charter, and that therefore the tax was void, because in violation of the provision of the Constitution of the United States, which forbids any state from passing a law impairing the obligation of contracts. The cause was held to be beyond the jurisdiction of the Circuit Court, the court saying, by Mr. Justice Gray (p. 464), "A suggestion of one party, that the other will or may set up a claim under the Constitution or laws of the United States, does not make the suit one arising under that Constitution or those laws." . . .

SKELLY OIL CO. v. PHILLIPS PETROLEUM CO.

339 U.S. 667 (1950).

MR. JUSTICE FRANKFURTER delivered the opinion of the Court. . . .

[Phillips had contracted to buy gas from Skelly and other defendants for resale to Michigan-Wisconsin Pipe Line Company. Each contract gave the seller the right to terminate the arrangement "in the event Michigan-Wisconsin . . . shall fail to secure from the Federal Power Commission on or before [October 1, 1946] a certificate of public convenience and necessity for the construction and operation of its pipe line." Notice of termination was to be delivered "after December 1, 1946, but before the issuance of such certificate."

[On November 30, 1946, the Commission ordered that "A certificate of public convenience and necessity be and it is hereby issued" to Michigan-Wisconsin, but the order was hedged with several conditions, and for computing the time allowed for seeking rehearing the date of the order was postponed. On December 2 Skelly and the other defendants gave notice of termination. Phillips sued for a declaratory judgment, arguing that the contracts were still in effect because a certificate had been obtained before the attempted termination. The District Court and the Court of Appeals agreed with this contention, and certiorari was granted to consider whether the case was one arising under federal law.]

"[T]he operation of the Declaratory Judgment Act is procedural only," Aetna Life Ins. Co. v. Haworth, 300 U.S. 227, 240. Congress enlarged the range of remedies available in the federal courts but did not extend their jurisdiction. When concerned as we are with the power of the inferior federal courts to entertain litigation within the restricted area to which the Constitution and Acts of Congress confine them, "jurisdiction" means the kinds of issues which give right of entrance to federal courts. Jurisdiction in this sense was not altered by the Declaratory Judgment Act. Prior to that Act, a federal court would entertain a suit on a contract only if the plaintiff asked for an immediately enforceable remedy like money damages or an injunction, but such relief could only be given if the requisites of jurisdiction, in the sense of a federal right or diversity, provided foundation for resort to the federal courts. The Declaratory Judgment Act allowed relief to be given by way of recognizing the plaintiff's right even though no immediate enforcement of it was asked. But the requirements of jurisdiction—the limited subject matters which alone Congress had authorized the District Courts to adjudicate—were not impliedly repealed or modified. See Great Lakes Dredge & Dock Co. v. Huffman, 319 U.S. 293, 300; Colegrove v. Green, 328 U.S. 549, 551–552.

If Phillips sought damages from petitioners or specific performance of their contracts, it could not bring suit in a United States District Court on the theory that it was asserting a federal right. And for the simple reason that such a suit would "arise" under the State law governing the contracts. Whatever federal claim Phillips may be able to urge would in any event be injected into the case only in anticipation of a defense to be asserted by petitioners. "Not every question of federal law emerging in a suit is proof that a federal law is the basis of the suit." Gully v. First National Bank, 299 U.S. 109, 115; compare 28 U.S.C. § 1257, with 28 U.S.C. § 1331. Ever since Metcalf v. Watertown, 128 U.S. 586, 589, it has been settled doctrine that where a suit is brought in the federal courts "upon the sole ground that the determination of the suit depends upon some question of a Federal nature, it must appear, at the outset, from the declaration or the bill of the party suing, that the suit is of that character." But "a suggestion of one party, that the other will or may set up a claim under the Constitution or laws of the United States, does not make the suit one arising under that Constitution or those laws." Tennessee v. Union & Planters' Bank, 152 U.S. 454, 464. The plaintiff's claim itself must present a federal question "unaided by anything alleged in anticipation of [*sic*] avoidance of defenses which it is thought the defendant may interpose." Taylor v. Anderson, 234 U.S. 74, 75–76; Louisville & Nashville R. Co. v. Mottley, 211 U.S. 149, 152. . . .

To be observant of these restrictions is not to indulge in formalism or sterile technicality. It would turn into the federal courts a vast current of litigation indubitably arising under State law, in the sense that the right to be vindicated was State-created, if a suit for a declaration of rights could be brought into the federal courts merely because an anticipated defense derived from federal law. Not only would this unduly swell the volume of litigation in the District Courts but it would also embarrass those courts—and this Court on potential review—in that matters of local law may often be involved, and the District Courts may either have to decide doubtful questions of State law or hold cases pending disposition of such State issues by State courts. To sanction suits for declaratory relief as within the jurisdiction of the District Courts merely because, as in this case, artful pleading anticipates a defense based on federal law would contravene the whole trend of jurisdictional legislation by Congress, disregard the effective functioning of the federal judicial system and distort the limited procedural purpose of the Declaratory Judgment Act. See Developments in the Law—Declaratory Judgments—1941–1949, 62 Harv.L.Rev. 787, 802–803 (1949). Since the matter in controversy as to which Phillips asked for a declaratory judgment is not one that "arises under the laws . . . of the United States" and since as to Skelly and Stanolind jurisdiction cannot be sustained on the score of diversity of citizenship, the proceedings against them should have been dismissed. . . .

MR. CHIEF JUSTICE VINSON, with whom MR. JUSTICE BURTON joins, dissenting in part.

I concur in that part of the Court's judgment that directs dismissal of the cause as to Skelly and Stanolind. I have real doubts as to whether there is a federal question here at all, even though interpretation of the contract between private parties requires an interpretation of a federal statute and the action of a federal regulatory body. But the Court finds it unnecessary to reach that question because it holds that the federal question, if any, is not a part of the plaintiff's claim and that jurisdiction does not, therefore, attach. While this result is not a necessary one, I am not prepared to dissent from it at this time. . . .

Notes on the Raising and Foreclosure of Jurisdictional Issues

(1) After their federal case had been thrown out, the Mottleys brought suit in a state court. The railroad raised the expected federal defense, and the Mottleys made their expected federal reply. The state courts gave judgment for the plaintiffs, and the Supreme Court of the United States reversed, deciding the federal questions in favor of the railroad. Louisville & N. R. R. v. Mottley, 219 U.S. 467 (1911).

Whatever may be said for the rule directing trial courts to dismiss cases such as *Mottley*, isn't it preposterous for the Supreme Court to require dismissal, for want of a federal question, of a case in which two federal questions have been argued and decided below?

(2) The Supreme Court has often held that the absence of subject-matter jurisdiction can be raised at any time in the trial court or on appeal, even by the party who invoked federal jurisdiction, Capron v. Van Noorden, 6 U.S. (2 Cr.) 126 (1804), or by the court on its own motion, Mansfield, Coldwater & L. M. Ry. v. Swan, 111 U.S. 379 (1884), because "the judicial power of the United States must not be exerted in a case to which it does not extend, even if both parties desire to have it exerted." Section 80 of the earlier Title 28, which required federal courts to dismiss or remand an action in which it appeared "at any time . . . that such suit does not really and substantially involve a dispute or controversy properly within the [court's] jurisdiction," was omitted as unnecessary in 1948 because "any court will dismiss a case not within its jurisdiction when its attention is

drawn to the fact, or even on its own motion." See Rule 12(b) & (h) of the Federal Rules of Civil Procedure, permitting a motion to dismiss for lack of subject-matter jurisdiction, but not for lack of jurisdiction over the person, to be made "at any time." Why the difference? Cf. Neirbo Co. v. Bethlehem Shipbuilding Corp., 308 U.S. 165, 167–68 (1939), stating that an objection to venue may be "lost by failure to assert it seasonably" because venue, unlike subject-matter jurisdiction, "relates to the convenience of litigants." [1]

(3) See, however, McCormick v. Sullivant, 23 U.S. (10 Wheat.) 192 (1825), refusing to permit collateral attack in a suit to enforce a federal judgment on the ground that diversity had been lacking in the original suit. Is this decision reconcilable with those in note 2, supra? Cf. Durfee v. Duke, 375 U.S. 106 (1963), holding the jurisdiction of one state court over land to be immune from collateral attack in a later proceeding in another State, when the issue had been litigated in the first proceeding; Chicot County Drainage Dist. v. Baxter State Bank, 308 U.S. 371 (1940), refusing to investigate collaterally a jurisdictional issue that had not been litigated in the original proceedings.

(4) In the *Mansfield* case, supra note 2, there was incomplete diversity of citizenship at the time the suit was filed, and the allegations were insufficient to show the defect had been cured by a later change of residence; presumably there was still no diversity at the time the Supreme Court ordered dismissal. Even if that decision was correct, what sense does it make to extend it to cases like *Mottley*, in which the original defect has been remedied by subsequent events?

(5) The American Law Institute, condemning the present law as a "fetish . . . wholly inconsistent with sound judicial administration," proposed the following new statute (ALI Study 64–65, 366–69):

§ 1386. Raising of jurisdictional issues . . .

(a) After the commencement of trial on the merits in the district court, or following any prior decision of a district court that is dispositive of the merits, no court of the United States shall consider, either on its own motion or at the instance of any party, a question of jurisdiction over the subject matter of the case, unless:

(1) The court is acting pursuant to a prior judicial determination deferring the resolution of such question of jurisdiction; or

(2) The question is raised by a party on the basis of facts of which he had no knowledge, and that he could not be expected to have discovered in the exercise of reasonable diligence, at an

1. The Court has not invariably adhered to the rule that jurisdictional questions unrelated to party convenience must always be investigated. See, e.g., Louisiana Power & Light Co. v. City of Thibodaux, 360 U.S. 25, 26 n. 1 (1959), in which the question of appellate jurisdiction was eliminated by a limited grant of certiorari. But an attempt of a court of appeals to create a doctrine estopping a party to attack jurisdiction after participating in extensive pretrial procedures, Di Frischia v. New York Central Railroad Co., 279 F.2d 141 (3d Cir. 1960), seems to have been rebuffed: Because "the District Court lacked power to entertain the respondent's lawsuit against the petitioner, . . . the asserted inequity in the respondent's alleged concealment of its citizenship is irrelevant." Owen Equipment & Erection Co. v. Kroger, 437 U.S. 365, 377 n. 21 (1978).

earlier stage in the proceedings, or on the basis of change in the applicable law; or

(3) The question was not raised at an earlier stage in the proceedings as a result of an attempt, by collusion or connivance (including conscious concealment of a known jurisdictional defect by two or more opposing parties, whether or not accompanied by an agreement between or among such parties), to confer jurisdiction on the court; or

(4) The question arises on appeal or other review or reconsideration on the record already made, of a decision with respect to such question not rendered contrary to the provisions of this section, and is raised by a party who has previously challenged the jurisdiction; or

(5) Consideration of a jurisdictional defect at that stage of the proceedings is required by the Constitution. . . .

See Dobbs, Beyond Bootstrap: Foreclosing the Issue of Subject-Matter Jurisdiction Before Final Judgment, 51 Minn.L.Rev. 491, 527 (1967), arguing that the ALI's proposal is at once "too broad and too narrow. Once trial has commenced the proposed section leaves no place for a belated consideration of jurisdictional objections that may be truly important; on the other hand, it makes possible the most unjust sort of tardy attacks on jurisdiction, so long as they are made before trial is commenced." When, if ever, is tardy consideration of a jurisdictional defect "required by the Constitution?"

Notes of the Well-Pleaded Complaint Rule

(1) In Hopkins v. Walker, 244 U.S. 486 (1917), holders of a federal patent to a mining claim sued to *remove a cloud* on their title, alleging, among other things, that the defendants' claim did not comply with federal law. Federal jurisdiction was upheld: "The facts showing the plaintiff's title and the existence and invalidity of the instrument on record sought to be eliminated as a cloud upon the title are essential parts of the plaintiffs' cause of action." But in Marshall v. Desert Properties Co., 103 F.2d 551 (9th Cir. 1939), the court held that a bill to *quiet* title in a similar situation did not arise under federal law: "In an action to quiet title . . . it is not necessary for the plaintiff to do more than allege his own title and that the defendant claims adversely to him. The nature of the adverse claim, and source and manner from and in which it originated, are immaterial."

In White v. Sparkhill Realty Corp., 280 U.S. 500 (1930), a landowner sued to enjoin state officials from turning his property into a state park, alleging that the statutes under which they acted were unconstitutional. There was jurisdiction under *Mottley*, but ejectment was an adequate legal remedy, so the injunction was denied. The bill was dismissed instead of being transferred to the "law side" because an ejectment complaint, "without anticipating possible defenses, would not present a case arising under the Constitution or a treaty or law of the United States."

Does this make any kind of sense? Professor Mishkin is overly polite, isn't he, when he says that "some of these distinctions resulting from the implicit adoption of pleading rules seem ill-suited as jurisdictional determinants?" The Federal "Question" in the District Courts, 53 Colum.L.Rev. 157, 177 (1963). But would you recommend that the federal courts take jurisdiction in every case in which there is a potential federal question, and dismiss if no federal dispute materializes?

Is the *Mottley* rule compelled by the language of § 1331? Was *Verlinden* (p. 148 supra) right in concluding that it was not compelled by Article III?

(2) Ordinarily the contention that a state-law claim is preempted by federal law is a defense, and under *Mottley* the case does not arise under federal law. Franchise Tax Board v. Construction Laborers Vacation Trust, 463 U.S. 1 (1983). But in Avco Corp. v. Aero Lodge, 390 U.S. 557 (1968), the Court upheld federal jurisdiction over a complaint seeking to enforce a no-strike clause in a collective bargaining agreement even though the plaintiff had not invoked federal law in its complaint. Under *Lincoln Mills* (p. 147 supra), wrote Justice Douglas, the governing substantive law was federal, and thus the case arose under federal law. Justice Brennan attempted to explain this decision in preemption terms in *Franchise Tax Board:*

> The necessary ground of decision was that the preemptive force of § 301 [of the Labor–Management Relations Act, on which the federal substantive law was based] is so powerful as to displace entirely any state cause of action "for violation of contracts between an employer and a labor organization." Any such suit is purely a creature of federal law, notwithstanding the fact that state law would provide a cause of action in the absence of § 301. *Avco* stands for the proposition that if a federal cause of action completely preempts a state cause of action any complaint that comes within the scope of the federal cause of action necessarily "arises under" federal law.

Does it help to speak of "preemption" in concluding that the plaintiff's cause of action is federal? And why wasn't the answer to *Avco* itself that the plaintiff has no federal claim unless he pleads it? See The Fair v. Kohler Die & Specialty Co., 228 U.S. 22, 25 (1913): "[T]he party who brings a suit is master to decide what law he will rely upon."

(3) What is to be said for the *Skelly* Court's disposition of the *Mottley* problem? If, as Professors Hart and Wechsler seemed to believe, The Federal Courts and the Federal System 895 (2d ed. 1973), Phillips was required to plead the issuance of a certificate of convenience as a part of its claim for declaratory relief, was not the purpose of the *Mottley* rule satisfied? Isn't it bad enough that federal jurisdiction turns on the technicalities of pleading, without compounding the problem by requiring an analysis of hypothetical cases? Or did the Court in *Skelly* hold only that the declaratory plaintiff was not required to plead the federal question?[1]

1. See also Public Service Commission v. Wycoff Co., 344 U.S. 237, 248–49 (1952), finding it unnecessary to decide the question but noting: "If the cause of action, which the declaratory defendant threatens to assert, does not itself involve a claim under federal law, it is doubtful if a federal court may entertain an action for a declaratory judgment establishing a defense to that claim." For a more recent application of *Skelly* see Arizona v. Atchison, Topeka and Santa Fe Railroad Co., 656 F.2d 398 (9th Cir. 1981).

(4) The Court returned to the declaratory judgment problem in *Franchise Tax Board,* supra note 2. The action was brought by the Board to enforce tax levies against a pension fund, and one of the claims was for a declaration that the levies were not forbidden by ERISA, the federal pension statute. After holding that the *Skelly* rule could not be circumvented by invoking a *state* declaratory judgment provision, Justice Brennan predictably concluded it was not enough that federal preemption was a necessary element of the declaratory judgment claim.

More challenging was the argument that there was jurisdiction because an action by the pension fund to enjoin the levies would have arisen under the federal statute.

> Federal courts have regularly taken jurisdiction over declaratory suits in which, if the declaratory defendant brought a coercive action to enforce its rights, that suit would necessarily present a federal question. . . . For instance, federal courts have consistently adjudicated suits by alleged patent infringers to declare a patent invalid, on the theory that an infringement suit by the declaratory judgment defendant would raise a federal question over which the federal courts have exclusive jurisdiction.

Nevertheless there was no jurisdiction in *Franchise Tax Board:*

> There are good reasons why the federal courts should not entertain suits by the States to declare the validity of their regulations despite possibly conflicting federal law. States are not significantly prejudiced by an inability to come to federal court for a declaratory judgment in advance of a possible injunctive suit by a person subject to federal regulation. They have a variety of means by which they can enforce their own laws in their own courts, and they do not suffer if the preemption questions such enforcement may raise are tested there. The express grant of federal jurisdiction in ERISA is limited to suits brought by certain parties, . . . as to whom Congress presumably determined that a right to enter federal court was necessary to further the statute's purposes. It did not go so far as to provide that any suit *against* such parties must also be brought in federal court. . . .

What has all of this to do with the question whether the case arose under federal law? Are those patent cases still law?

(5) Suppose Ms. Mottley had sued in a state court, and the railroad had raised the anticipated federal defense in its answer. Could the railroad have removed to the federal court? The statute in force at the time was substantially the same as the present § 1441(a).

Note Professor Wechsler's criticism of § 1441(a):

> Though the plaintiff who puts forth the federal claim is content to seek its vindication in the state tribunals, the defendant may insist upon an initial federal forum. When, on the other hand, the plaintiff's reliance is on state law and the defendant claims a federal defense, neither party may remove. . . . It would, it seems to me, be far more logical to shape the rule precisely in reverse, granting removal to defendants when they claim a federal defense against the plaintiff's state-created claim and to the plaintiff when, as the issues have

> developed, he relies by way of replication on assertion of a federal right. . . . The reason for providing the initial federal forum is the fear that state courts will view the federal right ungenerously. That reason is quite plainly absent in the only situation where, apart from federal officers, removal now obtains: the case where the *defendant* may remove because the *plaintiff's* case is federal.

Federal Jurisdiction and the Revision of the Judicial Code, 13 Law & Contemp.Probs. 216, 233–34 (1948). Yet Professor Wechsler concludes there should never be removal in federal-question cases: "There is no need for the original jurisdiction when litigants rely on federal rights to furnish them a shield but not a sword." Ibid. Why not?

(6) If the defendant in a state-court action involving only state law files a counterclaim arising under federal law, is the suit removable by the plaintiff? By the defendant? See Shamrock Oil & Gas Corp. v. Sheets, 313 U.S. 100 (1941). Plaintiff sued in the state court but sought to remove on diversity grounds when the defendant filed a counterclaim against him. Removal was disallowed. From 1875 to 1889 the statute had permitted removal by "either party," but at all other times, including the present, removal has been limited to a "defendant." Though the original plaintiff was in a defensive position respecting the counterclaim, the Supreme Court had held before 1875 that this did not give him the right to remove as a "defendant;" Congress had restored the language limiting removal to defendants in 1889 because it was "just and proper to require the plaintiff to abide his selection of a forum." Some lower-court decisions had suggested that a plaintiff who sued in state court for less than the jurisdictional amount had not waived his right to remove; but in the present case the plaintiff's claim could have been brought initially in the federal court, and in any case "the amount of the plaintiff's demand in the state court is immaterial, for one does not acquire an asserted right by not waiving it." Finally, statutes conferring federal jurisdiction ought to be narrowly construed out of regard for the independence of the States.

(7) The ALI proposed to retain the *Mottley* rule insofar as original jurisdiction is concerned and to clarify the *Skelly* problem: "The district courts shall have original jurisdiction . . . of all civil actions, including those for declaratory judgment, in which the initial pleading sets forth a substantial claim arising under the Constitution, laws, or treaties of the United States." ALI Study, proposed § 1311, p. 24. The Reporters supported this proposal by urging, id. at 190, that jurisdiction should be determined at the outset of the proceeding:

> A litigant who invokes the jurisdiction of the federal court ought to be able to do so with some fair assurance that the case will be determined in that court. He cannot do so if his jurisdictional allegation is, of necessity, no more than a guess as to the strategy his opponent will follow. The time of the court and the lawyers, and the money of the litigants, would be wasted needlessly on the preliminary stages in federal court of a case which is ultimately dismissed. Some protection would have to be given the plaintiff, in a case which is so dismissed, against being barred from a subsequent state action by a state statute of limitations.

However, the Institute proposed to permit removal in certain cases in which a federal question is actually raised by a later pleading (id. at pp. 25–27, 187–203):

> **§ 1312. General federal question jurisdiction; removal of actions brought in State courts**
>
> (a) Except as otherwise provided by Act of Congress, a civil action brought in a State court may be removed to the district court of the United States for the district embracing the place where such action is pending:
>
> (1) Without regard to amount in controversy, by any defendant against whom a claim is asserted on which an action might have been brought in a district court under section 1311 of this title;
>
> (2) If the amount in controversy exceeds the sum or value of $10,000, exclusive of interest and costs, by any defendant, or any plaintiff, by or against whom, subsequent to the initial pleading, a substantial defense arising under the Constitution, laws, or treaties of the United States is properly asserted that, if sustained, would be dispositive of the action or of all counterclaims therein;
>
> (3) Without regard to amount in controversy, by any defendant properly asserting a counterclaim compulsory under State law or by any party against whom a counterclaim is asserted, if the counterclaim sets forth a substantial claim arising under the Constitution, laws, or treaties of the United States. . . .[2]

The Commentary pointed out that the requirement that the federal defense be "dispositive of the action" or of the counterclaims would forbid removal "where defendant claims that damages are limited by the Warsaw Convention . . . or that plaintiff's claim is supported by illegally obtained evidence:" "Since the action will ultimately be resolved by state law, the need for a federal forum is less pressing." Removal based on a federal reply would be disallowed because "if both the complaint and the answer rest entirely on state law, the state issues are likely to dominate the case even though some federal issue emerges in a reply," unless the reply contained a defense to a counterclaim. (Tent. Draft No. 5, pp. 98–99 (1967)).[3]

2. The right to remove was to be given to both parties, not only to the party asserting the federal right, because

> federal law may be misapplied through misunderstanding as well as through lack of sympathy. . . . Defendant should be permitted to remove to guard against the danger that the state court, through lack of familiarity with the federal law or otherwise, will give an unduly expansive construction to the plaintiff's claim. By similar reasoning, plaintiff should be allowed to remove if the defendant has relied on a federal defense which the state court might read too broadly.

3. Several additional explicit exceptions were made by the proposed § 1312(b). Removal was to be barred when the sole federal defense was the preclusive effect of a prior adjudication or a constitutional objection to service of process or to choice of law (why?); and a federal defense or claim, without more, would not allow removal in condemnation suits or in actions to enforce or to require the enforcement of most state or local laws. "Proper respect for the states," said the commentary (p. 201), "suggests that they should be allowed to use their own courts for routine matters of law enforcement."

Since the ALI said it believed federal questions raised after the answer deserved to be litigated in federal courts, why was it so chary about allowing removal? See Bator, The State Courts and Federal Constitutional Litigation, 22 Wm. & Mary L.Rev. 605, 611 (1981).

Were there constitutional objections to the ALI proposal? Cf. 28 U.S.C. §§ 1442, 1443; see Tennessee v. Davis, 100 U.S. 257 (1880), upholding a provision authorizing federal officers to remove proceedings filed against them in state court on the ground that the officer had raised an immunity defense under federal law.

T. B. HARMS CO. v. ELISCU

339 F.2d 823 (2d Cir. 1964).

FRIENDLY, CIRCUIT JUDGE. A layman would doubtless be surprised to learn that an action wherein the purported sole owner of a copyright alleged that persons claiming partial ownership had recorded their claim in the Copyright Office and had warned his licensees against disregarding their interests was not one "arising under any Act of Congress relating to . . . copyrights" over which 28 U.S.C. § 1338 gives the federal courts exclusive jurisdiction. Yet precedents going back for more than a century teach that lesson and lead us to affirm Judge Weinfeld's dismissal of the complaint. . . .

[Eliscu, who had written lyrics for copyrighted songs, had allegedly assigned his interest in the copyrights to the principal stockholder of Harms. Later, however, he assigned the same rights to Jungnickel subject to a judicial determination of ownership and sued in state courts to establish his continuing interest.]

Harms then began the instant action in the District Court for the Southern District of New York for equitable and declaratory relief against Eliscu and Jungnickel. Jurisdiction was predicated on 28 U.S.C. § 1338; plaintiff alleged its own New York incorporation and did not allege the citizenship of the defendants, which concededly is in New York. . . . The district court dismissed the complaint for want of federal jurisdiction, 226 F.Supp. 337 (1964).

In line with what apparently were the arguments of the parties, Judge Weinfeld treated the jurisdictional issue as turning solely on whether the complaint alleged any act or threat of copyright infringement. He was right in concluding it did not. Infringement, as used in copyright law, does not include everything that may impair the value of the copyright; it is doing one or more of those things which § 1 of the Act, 17 U.S.C. § 1, reserves exclusively to the copyright owner. See Nimmer, Copyright §§ 100, 141 (1963). The case did not even raise what has been the problem presented when a defendant licensed to use a copyright or a patent on certain terms is alleged to have forfeited the grant; in such cases federal jurisdiction is held to exist if the plaintiff has directed his pleading against the offending use, referring to the license only by way of anticipatory replication, but not if he has sued to set the license aside, seeking recovery for unauthorized use only incidentally or not at all. See Chief Justice Taft's review of the cases in Luckett v. Delpark, 270 U.S. 496 (1926); and Hart & Wechsler, The Federal Courts and the Federal System, 754–58 (1953). Here neither Eliscu nor Jungnickel has used or threatened to use the copyrighted material; their various acts, as the district judge noted, sought to establish their ownership of the copyrights by judicial and administrative action, including notice to the parties concerned.

However, the jurisdictional statute does not speak in terms of infringement, and the undoubted truth that a claim for infringement "arises under" the Copyright Act does not establish that nothing else can. Simply as a matter of language, the statutory phrasing would not compel the conclusion that an action to determine who owns a copyright does not arise under the Copyright Act, which creates the federal copyright with an implied right to license and an explicit right to assign. But the gloss afforded by history and good sense leads to that conclusion as to the complaint in this case.

Although Chief Justice Marshall, construing the "arising under" language in the context of Article III of the Constitution, indicated in Osborn v. Bank of the United States, 9 Wheat. 738, 22 U.S. 738, 822–827 (1824), that the grant extended to every case in which federal law furnished a necessary ingredient of the claim even though this was antecedent and uncontested, the Supreme Court has long given a narrower meaning to the "arising under" language in statutes defining the jurisdiction of the lower federal courts. Romero v. International Terminal Operating Co., 358 U.S. 354, 379, n. 51 (1959); Mishkin, The Federal "Question" in the District Courts, 53 Colum.L.Rev. 157, 160–63 (1953). If the ingredient theory of Article III had been carried over to the general grant of federal question jurisdiction now contained in 28 U.S.C. § 1331, there would have been no basis—to take a well-known example—why federal courts should not have jurisdiction as to all disputes over the many western land titles originating in a federal patent, even though the controverted questions normally are of fact or of local land law. Quite sensibly, such extensive jurisdiction has been denied. Shoshone Mining Co. v. Rutter, 177 U.S. 505 (1900).

The cases dealing with statutory jurisdiction over patents and copyrights have taken the same conservative line. The problem apparently first reached the Supreme Court in Wilson v. Sanford, 10 How. 99, 51 U.S. 99 (1850), under the Act of July 4, 1836, § 17, 5 Stat. 17, which allowed appeal to the Court, irrespective of the amount, in actions "arising under" the patent laws. The suit aimed to prevent use of a patented invention by a licensee who allegedly had failed to comply with the terms of the license and thus had forfeited its rights. Chief Justice Taney, dismissing the appeal, held the statute inapplicable to a dispute as to license or contract rights which "depended altogether upon the rules and principles of equity, and in no degree whatever upon any act of Congress concerning patent rights." The same principle was applied, and sometimes stated less cautiously, in decisions construing later legislation granting the federal courts exclusive jurisdiction of all suits "arising under" the patent or copyright laws of the United States. . . . To take one of many examples, the Court said in New Marshall Engine Co. v. Marshall Engine Co., 223 U.S. 473, 478 (1912):

> "The Federal courts have exclusive jurisdiction of all cases arising under the patent laws, but not of all questions in which a patent may be the subject-matter of the controversy. For courts of a state may try questions of title, and may construe and enforce contracts relating to patents. Wade v. Lawder, 165 U.S. 624, 627."

Just as with western land titles, the federal grant of a patent or copyright has not been thought to infuse with any national interest a dispute as to ownership or contractual enforcement turning on the facts or on ordinary principles of contract law. Indeed, the case for an unexpansive reading of the provision conferring exclusive jurisdiction with respect to patents and copyrights has been especially strong since expansion would entail depriving the state courts of any jurisdiction over matters having so little federal significance.

In an endeavor to explain precisely what suits arose under the patent and copyright laws, Mr. Justice Holmes stated that "[a] suit arises under the law that creates the cause of action"; in the case *sub judice*, injury to a business involving slander of a patent, he said, "whether it is a wrong or not depends upon the law of the State where the act is done" so that the suit did not arise under the patent laws. American Well Works Co. v. Layne & Bowler Co., 241 U.S. 257, 260 (1916). The Holmes "creation" test explains the taking of federal jurisdiction in a great many cases, notably copyright and patent infringement actions, both clearly authorized by the respective federal acts, 17 U.S.C. § 101; 35 U.S.C. § 281, and thus unquestionably within the scope of 28 U.S.C. § 1338; indeed, in the many infringement suits that depend only on some point of fact and require no construction of federal law, no other explanation may exist.

Harms' claim is not within Holmes' definition. The relevant statutes create no explicit right of action to enforce or rescind assignments of copyrights, nor does any copyright statute specify a cause of action to fix the locus of ownership. To be sure, not every federal cause of action springs from an express mandate of Congress; federal civil claims have been "inferred" from federal statutes making behavior criminal or otherwise regulating it. See, e.g., Tunstall v. Brotherhood of Locomotive Firemen, 323 U.S. 210 (1944); Reitmeister v. Reitmeister, 162 F.2d 691 (2 Cir. 1947); Note, Implying Civil Remedies From Federal Regulatory Statutes, 77 Harv.L.Rev. 285 (1963). Such statutes invariably impose a federal duty and usually create some express remedy as well, while the relevant copyright provision merely authorizes an assignment by written instrument, 17 U.S.C. § 28. It is true that although this difference carries the present case outside the classic doctrine of implied remedies, see Restatement, Torts § 286 (1934), expansion may not be foreclosed where appropriate, cf. Wheeldin v.

Wheeler, 373 U.S. 647, 661–663 (1963) (Brennan, J., dissenting); we would not be understood, for example, as necessarily agreeing with the implication of Republic Pictures Corp. v. Security-First National Bank, 197 F.2d 767, 770 (9 Cir. 1952), that federal jurisdiction would not exist if a complaint alleged that a state declined to enforce assignments of copyright valid under federal law. But no such case is here presented.

It has come to be realized that Mr. Justice Holmes' formula is more useful for inclusion than for the exclusion for which it was intended. Even though the claim is created by state law, a case may "arise under" a law of the United States if the complaint discloses a need for determining the meaning or application of such a law. The path-breaking opinion to this effect was Smith v. Kansas City Title & Trust Co., 255 U.S. 180 (1921), pointedly rendered over a dissent by Mr. Justice Holmes, 255 U.S. at 213–215. A recent application of this principle to 28 U.S.C. § 1338 is De Sylva v. Ballentine, 351 U.S. 570 (1956), where the Supreme Court decided on the merits a claim to partial ownership of copyright renewal terms. Since there was no diversity of citizenship and no infringement, the only, and a sufficient, explanation for the taking of jurisdiction was the existence of two major questions of construction of the Copyright Act. But Harms likewise does not meet this test. The crucial issue is whether or not Eliscu executed the assignment to Dreyfus; possibly the interpretation of the initial May, 1933, contract is also relevant, but if any aspect of the suit requires an interpretation of the Copyright Act, the complaint does not reveal it.

Having thus found that appropriate pleading of a pivotal question of federal law may suffice to give federal jurisdiction even for a "state-created" claim, we cannot halt at questions hinging only on the language of the Copyright Act. For a new and dynamic doctrine, taking its name from Clearfield Trust Co. v. United States, 318 U.S. 363 (1943), instructs us that even in the absence of express statute, federal law may govern what might seem an issue of local law because the federal interest is dominant. . . . If this "federal common law" governed some disputed aspect of a claim to ownership of a copyright or for the enforcement of a license, federal jurisdiction might follow—though one would wish to consider whether this might be founded on 28 U.S.C. § 1331 rather than on § 1338 and thus be concurrent and require a jurisdictional amount. But there is not the slightest reason to think that any legal question presented by Harms' complaint falls in the shadow of a federal interest suggested by the Copyright Act or any other source.

Mindful of the hazards of formulation in this treacherous area, we think that an action "arises under" the Copyright Act if and only if the complaint is for a remedy expressly granted by the Act, e.g., a suit for infringement or for the statutory royalties for record reproduction, 17 U.S.C. § 101, cf. Joy Music, Inc. v. Seeco Records, Inc., 166 F.Supp. 549 (S.D.N.Y.1958), or asserts a claim requiring construction of the Act, as in De Sylva, or, at the very least and perhaps more doubtfully, presents a case where a distinctive policy of the Act requires that federal principles control the disposition of the claim. The general interest that copyrights, like all other forms of property, should be enjoyed by their true owner is not enough to meet this last test. . . .

Affirmed.

Further Notes on Cases "Arising Under" Federal Law

(1) At the time *Harms* was decided, 17 U.S.C. § 28 provided that "copyright secured under this title or previous copyright laws of the United States may be assigned, granted or mortgaged by an instrument in writing signed by the proprietor of the copyright, or may be bequeathed by will." Why, then, was not the question whether an assignment had been made a matter of federal law? If it had been a federal question, would there have been jurisdiction in *Harms*? [1]

(2) Is the *Harms* decision an application of the *Mottley* rule that the federal question must appear as a part of the plaintiff's cause of action, or does it represent a distinct requirement? If so, what is it? Is it clear that the plaintiff in *Harms* was not required to plead the existence of a valid copyright?

(3) Although the *Harms* case concerned 28 U.S.C. § 1338, the cases dealing with rights to land derived from the federal government present analogous problems under § 1331. Joy v. St. Louis, 201 U.S. 332 (1906), was an action for ejectment from land allegedly acquired from the United States; the Court held there was no jurisdiction on the *Mottley* basis that the plaintiff was not required to allege the source of his title. But in Shulthis v. McDougal, 225 U.S. 561 (1912), which concerned a dispute over Indian lands derived from the Government, federal-question jurisdiction was denied without discussion of pleading requirements:

> A suit to enforce a right which takes its origin in the laws of the United States is not necessarily or for that reason alone, one arising under those laws, for a suit does not so arise unless it really and substantially involves a dispute or controversy respecting the validity, construction or effect of such a law, upon the determination of which the result depends. This is especially so of a suit involving rights to land acquired under a law of the United States. If it were not, every suit to establish title to land in the central and western States would so arise, as all titles in those States are traceable back to those laws. . . . A controversy in respect of lands has never been regarded as presenting a Federal question merely because one of the parties to it has derived his title under an act of Congress.

Do these cases differ analytically from the case, discussed in *Osborn v. Bank of the United States*, of a contract action brought by a federal

1. The present statute, 17 U.S.C. § 201(d), provides that copyrights "may be transferred in whole or in part by any means of conveyance or by operation of law, and may be bequeathed by will or pass as personal property by the applicable laws of intestate succession."

corporation? [2] Is the principle that for purposes of § 1331 a case arises under federal law only if the plaintiff's cause of action contains *only* federal elements? This rule might well exclude all suits brought by state-created corporations, by a converse application of *Osborn;* but there may be a federal interest, may there not, in protecting the federal rights of state corporations?

(4) As a comparison of *Shulthis* with *Osborn* indicates, the Supreme Court has by and large held that § 1331 does not give the district courts the full federal-question jurisdiction permissible under the identically phrased provision of Article III. See Mishkin, The Federal "Question" in the District Courts, 53 Colum.L.Rev. 157, 160–63 (1953); Hart & Wechsler, The Federal Courts and the Federal System 870–73 (2d ed. 1973). Is this distinction justified? See Mishkin, supra, 53 Colum.L.Rev. at 162–63:

> The potential judicial power of the United States over federal question cases must necessarily be extremely broad. The situations in which a sympathetic forum may be required for the vindication of national rights cannot always be foreseen, and there must be power under the Constitution to provide for those eventualities. Yet some of these situations may fall into patterns abstractly identical with those of many other cases that do not in fact involve any present national interest. To hold that the federal trial courts are actually invested with virtually the full constitutional range of jurisdiction over federal questions might well flood the national courts, thereby deflecting them from their real functions. . . .
>
> [Moreover,] the "arising under" language in Article III, Section 2, provides the foundation for the appellate jurisdiction of the United States Supreme Court over questions of national law, as well as for the exercise of power by the "inferior" federal courts. . . . Any case which ultimately turns on an issue of national law must be constitutionally within the ken of the high Court. . . . [But] to include within the jurisdiction of the lower federal courts all cases which might conceivably turn finally upon an issue of national law would create an impossible situation. . . .

How relevant are these policy arguments to the issue of statutory interpretation? See also id. at 160 & n. 22 (1953), noting some legislative history suggesting, as held in the *Pacific Railroad Removal Cases,* supra p. 147, that the statute was meant to confer "precisely the power which the Constitution confers."

Compare the treatment of statutory language taken from the Constitution in *National Mutual Ins. Co. v. Tidewater Transfer Co.* ("State" for diversity purposes) and in *State Farm Fire & Cas. Co. v. Tashire* (complete diversity), p. 128 supra, p. 249 infra; see also pp. 212–23 infra (admiralty).

2. That case has been explicitly excluded from the jurisdiction by 28 U.S.C. § 1349. See p. 689 infra.

MERRELL DOW PHARMACEUTICALS, INC. v. THOMPSON

478 U.S. 804 (1986).

JUSTICE STEVENS delivered the opinion of the Court.

The question presented is whether the incorporation of a federal standard in a state-law private action, when Congress has intended that there not be a federal private action for violations of that federal standard, makes the action one "arising under the Constitution, laws, or treaties of the United States," 28 U.S.C. § 1331.

I

The Thompson respondents are residents of Canada and the MacTavishes reside in Scotland. They filed virtually identical complaints against petitioner, a corporation, that manufactures and distributes the drug Bendectin. The complaints were filed in the Court of Common Pleas in Hamilton County, Ohio. Each complaint alleged that a child was born with multiple deformities as a result of the mother's ingestion of Bendectin during pregnancy. In five of the six counts, the recovery of substantial damages was requested on common-law theories of negligence, breach of warranty, strict liability, fraud, and gross negligence. In Count IV, respondents alleged that the drug Bendectin was "misbranded" in violation of the Federal Food, Drug, and Cosmetic Act (FDCA), 52 Stat. 1040, as amended, 21 U.S.C. § 301 *et seq.* (1982 ed. and Supp. III), because its labeling did not provide adequate warning that its use was potentially dangerous. Paragraph 26 alleged that the violation of the FDCA "in the promotion" of Bendectin "constitutes a rebuttable presumption of negligence." Paragraph 27 alleged that the "violation of said federal statutes directly and proximately caused the injuries suffered" by the two infants.

Petitioner filed a timely petition for removal from the state court to the Federal District Court alleging that the action was "founded, in part, on an alleged claim arising under the laws of the United States." . . . Respondents filed a motion to remand to the state forum on the ground that the federal court lacked subject-matter jurisdiction. Relying on our decision in Smith v. Kansas City Title & Trust Co., 255 U.S. 180 (1921), the District Court held that Count IV of the complaint alleged a cause of action arising under federal law and denied the motion to remand. . . . The Court of Appeals for the Sixth Circuit reversed. . . .

II . . .

Under our longstanding interpretation of the current statutory scheme, the question whether a claim "arises under" federal law must be determined by reference to the "well-pleaded complaint." *Franchise Tax Board,* [p. ___ supra], 463 U.S., at 9–10. . . . [T]he propriety of the removal in this case thus turns on whether the case falls within the original "federal question" jurisdiction of the federal courts. . . .

The "vast majority" of cases that come within this grant of jurisdiction are covered by Justice Holmes' statement that a " 'suit arises under the law that creates the cause of action.' " Id., at 8–9, quoting American Well Works Co. v. Layne & Bowler Co., 241 U.S. 257, 260 (1916). . . . We have, however, also noted that a case may arise under federal law "where the vindication of a right under state law necessarily turned on some construction of federal law." *Franchise Tax Board,* 463 U.S., at 9.[5] Our actual holding in *Franchise Tax Board* demonstrates that this statement must be read with caution; the central issue presented in that case turned on the meaning of the Employee Retirement Income Security Act of 1974, . . . but we nevertheless concluded that federal jurisdiction was lacking.

This case does not pose a federal question of the first kind; respondents do not allege that federal law creates any of the causes of action that they have asserted. This case thus poses what Justice Frankfurter called the "litigation-provoking problem," Textile Workers v. Lincoln Mills, 353 U.S. 448, 470 (1957) (dissenting opinion)—the presence of a federal issue in a state-created cause of action. . . .

In this case, both parties agree with the Court of Appeals' conclusion that there is no federal cause of action for FDCA violations. For purposes of our decision, we assume that this is a correct interpretation of the FDCA. Thus, as the case comes to us, it is appropriate to assume that, under the settled framework for evaluating whether a federal cause of action lies, some combination of the following factors is present: (1) the plaintiffs are not part of the class for whose special benefit the statute was passed; (2) the indicia of legislative intent reveal no congressional purpose to provide a private cause of action; (3) a federal cause of action would not further the underlying purposes of the legislative scheme; and (4) the respondents' cause of action is a subject traditionally relegated to state law.[7] In short, Congress did not intend a private federal remedy for violations of the statute that it enacted. . . .

The significance of [this] assumption . . . cannot be overstated. For the ultimate import of such a conclusion . . . is that it would flout congressional intent to provide a private federal remedy for the violation of the federal statute. We think it would similarly flout, or at least undermine, congressional intent to conclude that the federal

5. The case most frequently cited for that proposition is Smith v. Kansas City Title & Trust Co., 255 U.S. 180 (1921). In that case the Court upheld federal jurisdiction of a shareholder's bill to enjoin the corporation from purchasing bonds issued by the federal land banks under the authority of the Federal Farm Loan Act on the ground that the federal statute that authorized the issuance of the bonds was unconstitutional. The Court stated:

"The general rule is that where it appears from the bill or statement of the plaintiff that the right to relief depends upon the construction or application of the Constitution or laws of the United States, and that such federal claim is not merely colorable, and rests upon a reasonable foundation, the District Court has jurisdiction under this provision." Id., at 199. . . .

7. See California v. Sierra Club, 451 U.S. 287, 293 (1981) . . . .

courts might nevertheless exercise federal-question jurisdiction and provide remedies for violations of that federal statute solely because the violation of the federal statute is said to be a "rebuttable presumption" or a "proximate cause" under state law, rather than a federal action under federal law.

III

Petitioner advances three arguments to support its position that, even in the face of this congressional preclusion of a federal cause of action for a violation of the federal statute, federal-question jurisdiction may lie for the violation of the federal statute as an element of a state cause of action.

First, petitioner contends that the case represents a straightforward application of the statement in *Franchise Tax Board* that federal-question jurisdiction is appropriate when "it appears that some substantial, disputed question of federal law is a necessary element of one of the well-pleaded state claims." . . . *Franchise Tax Board,* however, did not purport to disturb the long-settled understanding that the mere presence of a federal issue in a state cause of action does not automatically confer federal-question jurisdiction. Indeed, in determining that federal-question jurisdiction was not appropriate in the case before us, we stressed Justice Cardozo's emphasis on principled, pragmatic distinctions: " 'What is needed is something of that common-sense accommodation of judgment to kaleidoscopic situations which characterizes the law in its treatment of causation . . . a selective process which picks the substantial causes out of the web and lays the other ones aside.' " . . .

Far from creating some kind of automatic test, *Franchise Tax Board* thus candidly recognized the need for careful judgments about the exercise of federal judicial power in an area of uncertain jurisdiction. Given the significance of the assumed congressional determination to preclude federal private remedies, the presence of the federal issue as an element of the state tort is not the kind of adjudication for which jurisdiction would serve congressional purposes and the federal system. This conclusion is fully consistent with the very sentence relied on so heavily by petitioner. We simply conclude that the congressional determination that there should be no federal remedy for the violation of this federal statute is tantamount to a congressional conclusion that the presence of a claimed violation of the statute as an element of a state cause of action is insufficiently "substantial" to confer federal-question jurisdiction.[12]

12. Several commentators have suggested that our § 1331 decisions can best be understood as an evaluation of the *nature* of the federal interest at stake. . . . Focusing on the nature of the federal interest . . . suggests that the widely perceived "irreconcilable" conflict between the finding of federal jurisdiction in Smith v. Kansas City Title & Trust Co. . . . and the finding of no jurisdiction in Moore v. Chesapeake & Ohio R. Co., 291 U.S. 205 (1934), . . . is far from clear. For the difference in results can be seen as manifestations of the differences in the nature of the federal issues at stake. In *Smith,* as the Court emphasized, the issue was the constitution-

Second, petitioner contends that there is a powerful federal interest in seeing that the federal statute is given uniform interpretations, and that federal review is the best way of insuring such uniformity. In addition to the significance of the congressional decision to preclude a federal remedy, we do not agree with petitioner's characterization of the federal interest and its implications for federal-question jurisdiction. To the extent that petitioner is arguing that state use and interpretation of the FDCA pose a threat to the order and stability of the FDCA regime, petitioner should be arguing, not that federal courts should be able to review and enforce state FDCA-based causes of action as an aspect of federal-question jurisdiction, but that the FDCA pre-empts state-court jurisdiction over the issue in dispute. Petitioner's concern about the uniformity of interpretation, moreover, is considerably mitigated by the fact that, even if there is no original district court jurisdiction for these kinds of action, this Court retains power to review the decision of a federal issue in a state cause of action.[14]

Finally, petitioner argues that, whatever the general rule, there are special circumstances that justify federal-question jurisdiction in this case. Petitioner emphasizes that it is unclear whether the FDCA applies to sales in Canada and Scotland; there is, therefore, a special reason for having a federal court answer the novel federal question relating to the extraterritorial meaning of the Act. We reject this argument. We do not believe the question whether a particular claim arises under federal law depends on the novelty of the federal issue. Although it is true that federal jurisdiction cannot be based on a frivolous or insubstantial federal question, "the interrelation of federal and state authority and the proper management of the federal judicial system," *Franchise Tax Board,* 463 U.S., at 8, would be ill served by a rule that made the existence of federal-question jurisdiction depend on the district court's case-by-case appraisal of the novelty of the federal question asserted as an element of the state tort. The novelty of an FDCA issue is not sufficient to give it status as a federal cause of action; nor should it be sufficient to give a state-based FDCA claim status as a jurisdiction-triggering federal question.

ality of an important federal statute. See 255 U.S., at 201 ("It is . . . apparent that the controversy concerns the constitutional validity of an act of Congress which is directly drawn in question. The decision depends upon the determination of this issue"). In *Moore,* in contrast, the Court emphasized that the violation of the federal standard as an element of state tort recovery did not fundamentally change the state tort nature of the action. . . .

14. See Moore v. Chesapeake & Ohio R. Co., 291 U.S., at 214–215 ("Questions arising in actions in state courts to recover for injuries sustained by employees in intrastate commerce and relating to the scope or construction of the Federal Safety Appliance Acts are, of course, federal questions which may appropriately be reviewed in this Court. . . . But it does not follow that a suit brought under the state statute which defines liability to employees who are injured while engaged in intrastate commerce, and brings within the purview of the statute a breach of the duty imposed by the federal statute, should be regarded as a suit arising under the laws of the United States and cognizable in the federal court in the absence of diversity of citizenship"). . . .

IV

We conclude that a complaint alleging a violation of a federal statute as an element of a state cause of action, when Congress has determined that there should be no private, federal cause of action for the violation, does not state a claim "arising under the Constitution, laws, or treaties of the United States." 28 U.S.C. § 1331.

The judgment of the Court of Appeals is affirmed. . . .

JUSTICE BRENNAN, with whom JUSTICE WHITE, JUSTICE MARSHALL, and JUSTICE BLACKMUN join, dissenting. . . .

I

While the majority of cases covered by § 1331 may well be described by Justice Holmes' adage that "[a] suit arises under the law that creates the cause of action," . . . it is firmly settled that there may be federal-question jurisdiction even though both the right asserted and the remedy sought by the plaintiff are state created. . . . The rule as to such cases was stated in what Judge Friendly described as "[t]he path-breaking opinion" in Smith v. Kansas City Title & Trust Co., 255 U.S. 180. . . . In *Smith,* a shareholder of the defendant corporation brought suit in the federal court to enjoin the defendant from investing corporate funds in bonds issued under the authority of the Federal Farm Loan Act. The plaintiff alleged that Missouri law imposed a fiduciary duty on the corporation to invest only in bonds that were authorized by a valid law and argued that, because the Farm Loan Act was unconstitutional, the defendant could not purchase bonds issued under its authority. Although the cause of action was wholly state created, the Court held that there was original federal jurisdiction over the case:

> "The general rule is that where it appears from the bill or statement of the plaintiff that the right to relief depends upon the construction or application of the Constitution or laws of the United States, and that such federal claim is not merely colorable, and rests upon a reasonable foundation, the District Court has jurisdiction under [the statute granting federal question jurisdiction]." 255 U.S., at 199.

The continuing vitality of *Smith* is beyond challenge. We have cited it approvingly on numerous occasions, and reaffirmed its holding several times—most recently just three Terms ago by a unanimous Court in Franchise Tax Board v. Construction Laborers Vacation Trust, supra, 463 U.S., at 9. . . . Furthermore, the principle of the *Smith* case has been recognized and endorsed by most commentators as well. . . .[1]

1. Some commentators have argued that the result in *Smith* conflicts with our decision in Moore v. Chesapeake & Ohio R. Co., 291 U.S. 205 (1934). See, e.g., Greene, Hybrid State Law in the Federal Courts, 83 Harv.L.Rev. 289, 323 (1969). In *Moore,* the plaintiff brought an action under Kentucky's Employer Liability Act, which provided that a plaintiff could not be held responsible for contributory negligence or assumption of risk where his injury resulted from the violation of any state or federal statute enacted for the safety of employees. The plaintiff in *Moore* alleged that

There is, to my mind, no question that there is federal jurisdiction over the respondents' fourth cause of action under the rule set forth in *Smith* and reaffirmed in *Franchise Tax Board.* Respondents pleaded that petitioner's labeling of the drug Bendectin constituted "misbranding" in violation of §§ 201 and 502(f)(2) and (j) of the Federal Food, Drug, and Cosmetic Act, . . . and that this violation "directly and proximately caused" their injuries. . . . Respondents asserted in the complaint that this violation established petitioner's negligence *per se* and entitled them to recover damages without more. . . . As pleaded, then, respondents' "right to relief depend[ed] upon the construction or application of the Constitution or laws of the United States," *Smith,* 255 U.S., at 199, . . . and the claim raised by the fourth cause of action is one "arising under" federal law within the meaning of § 1331.

II

The Court apparently does not disagree with any of this—except, of course, for the conclusion. According to the Court, if we assume that Congress did not intend that there be a private federal cause of action under a particular federal law, . . . we must also assume that Congress did not intend that there be federal jurisdiction over a state cause of action that is determined by that federal law. . . .

The Court nowhere explains the basis for this conclusion. Yet it is hardly self-evident. Why should the fact that Congress chose not to create a private federal *remedy* mean that Congress would not want there to be federal *jurisdiction* to adjudicate a state claim that imposes

his injury was due to the defendant's failure to comply with the Federal Safety Appliance Act; therefore, an important issue in the adjudication of the state cause of action was whether the terms of the federal law had been violated. The Court could have dismissed the complaint on the ground that the federal issue would arise only in response to a defense of contributory negligence or assumption of risk, and that therefore there was no jurisdiction under the well-pleaded complaint rule. Instead, the Court held that "a suit brought under the state statute which defines liability to employees who are injured while engaged in intrastate commerce, and brings within the purview of the statute a breach of the duty imposed by the federal statute, should [not] be regarded as a suit arising under the laws of the United States and cognizable in the federal court in the absence of diversity of citizenship." 291 U.S., at 214–215. . . .

In one sense, the Court is correct in asserting that we can reconcile *Smith* and *Moore* on the ground that the "nature" of the federal interest was more significant in *Smith* than in *Moore.* Indeed, as the Court appears to believe, . . . we could reconcile many of the seemingly inconsistent results that have been reached under § 1331 with such a test. But this is so only because a test based upon an ad hoc evaluation of the importance of the federal issue is infinitely malleable: at what point does a federal interest become strong enough to create jurisdiction? . . . Yet it is precisely because the Court believes that federal jurisdiction would be "ill served" by such a case-by-case appraisal that it rejects petitioner's claim that the difficulty and importance of the statutory issue presented by its claim suffices to confer jurisdiction under § 1331. . . . The Court cannot have it both ways.

My own view is in accord with those commentators who view the results in *Smith* and *Moore* as irreconcilable. See, e.g., Redish 67; D. Currie, Federal Jurisdiction in a Nutshell 109 (2d ed. 1981). That fact does not trouble me greatly, however, for I view *Moore* as having been a "sport" at the time it was decided and having long been in a state of innocuous desuetude. . . . [T]o the extent that it is inconsistent with the well-established rule of the *Smith* case, it ought to be overruled.

liability for violating the federal law? Clearly, the decision not to provide a private federal remedy should not affect federal jurisdiction unless the reasons Congress withholds a federal remedy are also reasons for withholding federal jurisdiction. . . .

A . . .

The reasons Congress found it necessary to add this jurisdiction to the district courts are well known. First, Congress recognized "the importance, and even necessity of *uniformity* of decisions throughout the whole United States, upon all subjects within the purview of the constitution." Martin v. Hunter's Lessee, 1 Wheat., at 347–348 . . . . In addition, § 1331 has provided for adjudication in a forum that specializes in federal law and that is therefore more likely to apply that law correctly. . . .

These reasons for having original federal-question jurisdiction explain why cases like this one and *Smith* —i.e., cases where the cause of action is a creature of state law, but an essential element of the claim is federal—"arise under" federal law within the meaning of § 1331. Congress passes laws in order to shape behavior; a federal law expresses Congress' determination that there is a federal interest in having individuals or other entities conform their actions to a particular norm established by that law. Because all laws are imprecise to some degree, disputes inevitably arise over what specifically Congress intended to require or permit. It is the duty of courts to interpret these laws and apply them in such a way that the congressional purpose is realized. As noted above, Congress granted the district courts power to hear cases "arising under" federal law in order to enhance the likelihood that federal laws would be interpreted more correctly and applied more uniformly. In other words, Congress determined that the availability of a federal forum to adjudicate cases involving federal questions would make it more likely that federal laws would shape behavior in the way that Congress intended.

By making federal law an essential element of a state-law claim, the State places the federal law into a context where it will operate to shape behavior: the threat of liability will force individuals to conform their conduct to interpretations of the federal law made by courts adjudicating the state-law claim. It will not matter to an individual found liable whether the officer who arrives at his door to execute judgment is wearing a state or a federal uniform; all he cares about is the fact that a sanction is being imposed—and may be imposed again in the future—because he failed to comply with the federal law. Consequently, the possibility that the federal law will be incorrectly interpreted in the context of adjudicating the state-law claim implicates the concerns that led Congress to grant the district courts power to adjudicate cases involving federal questions in precisely the same way as if it was federal law that "created" the cause of action. It therefore follows that there is federal jurisdiction under § 1331.

B

The only remaining question is whether the assumption that Congress decided not to create a private cause of action alters this analysis in a way that makes it inappropriate to exercise original federal jurisdiction. According to the Court, "the very reasons for the development of the modern implied remedy doctrine" support the conclusion that, where the legislative history of a particular law shows (whether expressly or by inference) that Congress intended that there be no private federal remedy, it must also mean that Congress would not want federal courts to exercise jurisdiction over a state-law claim making violations of that federal law actionable. . . . These reasons are " 'the increased complexity of federal legislation,' " " 'the increased volume of federal litigation,' " and " 'the desirability of a more careful scrutiny of legislative intent.' " . . .

These reasons simply do not justify the Court's holding. Given the relative expertise of the federal courts in interpreting federal law, . . ., the increased complexity of federal legislation argues rather strongly in *favor* of recognizing federal jurisdiction. And, while the increased volume of litigation may appropriately be considered in connection with reasoned arguments that justify limiting the reach of § 1331, I do not believe that the day has yet arrived when this Court may trim a statute solely because it thinks that Congress made it too broad.

This leaves only the third reason: " 'the desirability of a more careful scrutiny of legislative intent.' " . . . I certainly subscribe to the proposition that the Court should consider legislative intent in determining whether or not there is jurisdiction under § 1331. But the Court has not examined the purposes underlying either the FDCA or § 1331. . . . Moreover, such an examination demonstrates . . . that it is the Court's . . . conclusion that is inconsistent with congressional intent. . . . Primary responsibility for overseeing implementation of the Act has been conferred upon a specialized administrative agency, . . . the Food and Drug Administration (FDA). Congress has provided the FDA with a wide-ranging arsenal of weapons to combat violations of the FDCA, including authority to obtain an *ex parte* court order for the seizure of goods subject to the Act, see 21 U.S.C. § 334, authority to initiate proceedings in a federal district court to enjoin continuing violations of the FDCA, see § 332, and authority to request a United States Attorney to bring criminal proceedings against violators, see § 333. . . . Significantly, the FDA has no independent enforcement authority; final enforcement must come from the federal courts, which have exclusive jurisdiction over actions under the FDCA. See §§ 332(a), 333, 334(a)(1). Thus, while the initial interpretive function has been delegated to an expert administrative body whose interpretations are entitled to considerable deference, final responsibility for interpreting the statute in order to carry out the legislative mandate belongs to the federal courts. . . .

Given that Congress structured the FDCA so that all express remedies are provided by the federal courts, it seems rather strange to conclude that it either "flout[s]" or "undermine[s]" congressional intent for the federal courts to adjudicate a private state-law remedy that is based upon violating the FDCA. . . . That is, assuming that a state cause of action based on the FDCA is not pre-empted, it is entirely consistent with the FDCA to find that it "arises under" federal law within the meaning of § 1331. Indeed, it is the Court's conclusion that such a state cause of action must be kept *out* of the federal courts that appears contrary to legislative intent inasmuch as the enforcement provisions of the FDCA quite clearly express a preference for having federal courts interpret the FDCA and provide remedies for its violation. . . .

Notes on State Incorporation of Federal Law and Vice-Versa

(1) As the opinions in *Merrell Dow* suggest, the question whether a suit seeking a state-created remedy for violation of federal law falls within federal-question jurisdiction has long perplexed both the Court and the scholars. For years the leading case was Smith v. Kansas City Title & Trust Co., 255 U.S. 180 (1921), which is discussed by both the majority and the dissent in *Merrell Dow.* The action, you will recall, was filed by a shareholder to enjoin the Trust Company from investing in federal bonds on the ground that the legislation authorizing their issue was unconstitutional. The Court upheld the district court's jurisdiction because "the right to relief depends upon the construction or application of the Constitution or laws of the United States."

Justice Holmes wrote a famous dissent that bears extensive quotation:

> It is evident that the cause of action arises not under any law of the United States but wholly under Missouri law. The defendant is a Missouri corporation and the right claimed is that of a stockholder to prevent the directors from doing an act, that is, making an investment alleged to be contrary to their duty. But the scope of their duty depends upon the charter of their corporation and other laws of Missouri. If those laws had authorized the investment in terms the plaintiff would have had no case, and this seems to me to make manifest what I am unable to deem even debatable, that, as I have said, the cause of action arises wholly under Missouri law. If the Missouri law authorizes or forbids the investment according to the determination of this Court upon a point under the Constitution or acts of Congress, still that point is material only because the Missouri law saw fit to make it so. The whole foundation of the duty is Missouri law, which at its sole will incorporated the other law as it might incorporate a document. The other law or document depends for its relevance and effect not on its own force but upon the law that took it up so I repeat once more the cause of action arises wholly from the law of the state.
>
> But it seems to me that a suit cannot be said to arise under any other law than that which creates the cause of action. It may be

enough that the law relied upon creates a part of the cause of action although not the whole, as held in Osborn v. Bank of the United States, 9 Wheat. [22 U.S.] 738, 819–823, which perhaps, is all that is meant by the less guarded expressions in Cohens v. Virginia, 6 Wheat. [19 U.S.] 264, 379. I am content to assume this to be so, although the *Osborn Case* has been criticized and regretted. But the law must create at least a part of the cause of action by its own force, for it is the suit, not a question in the suit, that must arise under the law of the United States. The mere adoption by a state law of a United States law as a criterion or test, when the law of the United States has no force *proprio vigore*, does not cause a case under the state law to be also a case under the law of the United States, and so it has been decided by this Court again and again. Miller v. Swann, 150 U.S. 132, 136, 137 . . . .

Was *Smith* reconcilable with Moore v. Chesapeake & Ohio Ry., 291 U.S. 205 (1934), as *Merrell Dow* suggests? The plaintiff in *Moore* sought damages for personal injuries pursuant to a state statute providing that violation of the federal Safety Appliance Act made ordinary principles of contributory negligence and assumption of risk inapplicable. The Court held the action did not arise under federal law. Does *Smith* survive *Merrell Dow?*

(2) In Standard Oil Co. v. Johnson, 316 U.S. 481(1942), the company sued for refund of taxes paid for sales of gasoline to Army Post Exchanges, arguing that the sales were exempt under § 10 of the California statute, which stated that the tax did not apply "to any motor vehicle fuel sold to the government of the United States or any department thereof," and that, if the statute were held applicable, it would impose an unconstitutional burden upon instrumentalities of the United States. The state court held the tax applicable and valid. The Supreme Court, without deciding whether the tax would be unconstitutional, held the PX was an essential "arm" of the government and sent the case back:

> [I]n deciding that post exchanges were not "the government of the United States or any department thereof," the court did not rely upon the law of California. On the contrary, it relied upon its determination concerning the relationship between post exchanges and the Government of the United States, a relationship which is controlled by federal law. . . . It was upon a determination of a federal question, therefore, that the Supreme Court of California rested its conclusion that, by § 10, sales to post exchanges were not exempted from the tax. Since this determination of a federal question was by a state court, we are not bound by it. We proceed to consider whether it is correct. . . .

Is there a basis for the distinction drawn in *Merrell Dow* between the jurisdiction of the Supreme Court and that of the district courts in such cases? [1]

1. Cf. Flores v. Beto, 374 F.2d 225, 227 (5th Cir. 1967), refusing to allow habeas corpus on the basis of a state law providing a remedy for the use of illegally obtained evidence before the effective date of the federal exclusionary rule:

Conceivably, the involvement of a federal question because of state reliance upon the United States Constitution and laws would be an adequate ground for the Supreme Court to grant a writ of certiorari. Such question, however, does

(3) Flournoy v. Wiener, 321 U.S. 253 (1944). A Louisiana statute levied a tax on all estates subject to the federal estate tax. In a suit contesting a state tax assessment the state court held for the taxpayer on the ground that the federal statute was unconstitutional. The Court dismissed the appeal on unrelated grounds; Justice Frankfurter, dissenting, thought jurisdiction sustained by *Standard Oil.* Was it?

If a state adopted the Federal Rules of Civil Procedure for its own courts and provided that state courts should follow federal interpretations of the rules, would every procedural issue arising in civil cases in state court present a federal question? [2]

(4) The problem of state incorporation of federal law is discussed in Note, Supreme Court Review of State Interpretations of Federal Law Incorporated by Reference, 66 Harv.L.Rev. 1498 (1953), with particular emphasis on cases dealing with Supreme Court jurisdiction under the Safety Appliance Act. This note distinguishes sharply between cases in which a State has created a damage remedy for violation of a pre-existing federal duty and those in which the state has applied Safety Appliance Standards to railroads not covered by the federal law. In the first situation

> the Supreme Court is merely construing a duty already imposed on the carriers by federal law. It is not regulating conduct in a sphere in which federal law is inoperative, nor is it extending its jurisdiction beyond the scope of such law. . . . The Supreme Court has, in fact, taken review of the FSAA cases, although a thorough analysis of the basis therefor has been lacking. . . .
>
> If a state were to pass a statute making the safety requirements of the FSAA applicable to intrastate trolley cars, the Supreme Court would not be justified in reviewing state interpretations of the incorporated federal law. The federal law would not, of its own force, impose any duty upon mere intrastate carriers, nor would it regulate their conduct in any fashion. Any duty with which they were required to comply would be of state origin, as would the other components of any cause of action provided for its breach. . . . For the Supreme Court to interpret the nature of the FSAA duty in these cases would be to indulge in the rendition of advisory opinions as to federal law, since federal law would in no sense be operative in this sphere. . . .

This distinction is clear enough, isn't it? But are you satisfied with its justification?

not permit a collateral attack on a state conviction. The appropriate statute, 28 U.S.C. § 2241(c)(3), specifically limits the granting of a writ of habeas corpus to a prisoner, "in custody in violation of the Constitution or laws or treaties of the United States."

2. Apart from the *Mottley* problem, was there a federal question in the *Skelly* case (p. 151 supra) at all? See Mishkin, The Federal "Question" in the District Courts, 53 Colum.L.Rev. 157, 183–84 (1953):

> The only significance of national law was that the parties to a local contract had chosen to limit the power of termination by the occurrence of an event authorized by that law. . . . By no stretch can a controversy as to the continued vitality of such a contract be considered to be founded "directly" upon federal law, any more than a wager as to the next incumbent of some government office could be so deemed.

(5) Is there an analytical difference between cases such as *Merrell Dow*, on the one hand, and *T. B. Harms Co. v. Eliscu* or the contract variant of *Osborn v. Bank of the United States*, on the other?

(6) In the foregoing cases an argument could be made that federal law was relevant only because it had been incorporated by state law. The converse argument was suggested in Shoshone Mining Co. v. Rutter, 177 U.S. 505 (1900). A federal statute authorizing the issuance of patents for mining claims on federal land also provided for settlement of disputes between conflicting claimants, prior to issuance of the patent, in "a court of competent jurisdiction." A suit between such claimants, the Court held, did not arise under federal law:

> A suit to enforce a right which takes its origin in the laws of the United States is not necessarily one arising under the Constitution or laws of the United States, within the meaning of the jurisdiction clauses, for if it did every action to establish title to real estate (at least in the newer States) would be such a one. . . .
>
> The adverse suit . . . is "to determine the question of the right of possession." . . . By sections 2319, 2324 and 2332, Revised Statutes, it is expressly provided that this right of possession may be determined by "local customs or rules of miners in the several mining districts, so far as the same are applicable and not inconsistent with the laws of the United States;" or "by the statute of limitations for mining claims of the State or Territory where the same may be situated." So that in a given case the right of possession may not involve any question under the Constitution or laws of the United States, but simply a determination of local rules and customs, or state statutes, or even only a mere matter of fact.
>
> The recognition by Congress of local customs and statutory provisions as at times controlling the right of possession does not incorporate them into the body of Federal law. Section 2 of article I of the Constitution provides that the electors in each State of members of the House of Representatives "shall have the qualifications requisite for electors of the most numerous branch of the state legislature," but this does not make the statutes and constitutional provisions of the various States in reference to the qualifications of electors parts of the Constitution or laws of the United States. . . .

Was the Court right to suggest that decisions refusing to pass upon subsequent transactions in land once obtained from the United States governed a case in which the issue was which party was entitled to obtain the land from the United States to begin with? Do you agree that whether you can vote for Congress is not a federal question? If Congress left it to state law to determine who is a "widow" for purposes of the Federal Employers Liability Act, is the widow unable to sue in federal court? [3]

3. See also Roecker v. United States, 379 F.2d 400, 407–08 (5th Cir. 1967), stating that because the governing federal statute left to state law the question whether a guardian had power to change the beneficiary of his incompetent ward's National Service Life Insurance policy, a challenge to the guardian's designation would not support federal-question jurisdiction.

(7) Should the Court have adhered to Justice Holmes's test, reiterated in his *Smith* dissent, that "a suit arises under the law that creates the cause of action?" Would this mean that there is no jurisdiction in the Safety Appliance Act cases, and no jurisdiction in a modern-day national-bank-contract case, even apart from § 1349? Would it also mean that Congress could provide a federal forum for every kind of state-law controversy by establishing a federal declaratory remedy for the vindication of state-created rights?

In Puerto Rico v. Russell & Co., 288 U.S. 476 (1933), the plaintiff invoked federal-question jurisdiction on the basis of an Act of Congress authorizing the Territory to sue at law to collect taxes imposed by the territorial legislature. The Court held the case did not arise under federal law: "Federal jurisdiction . . . may not be invoked where the right asserted is nonfederal, merely because the plaintiff's right to sue is derived from federal law. . . ."

If the cause of action is not created by federal law giving a right to sue, as in *Russell*, or by federal law creating the duty on whose violation suit is based, as in *Moore*, what element of the cause of action determines the law under which the suit is "created?" Is there, as Hart and Wechsler suggest, a fallacy in "assuming that a cause of action must be created either by state or federal law, . . . in situations in which both systems of law contribute to it?" The Federal Courts and the Federal System 886 (2d ed. 1973).

(8) Professor Cohen argues for a "pragmatic" text to determine which cases arise under federal law, expressing surprise at the "continuing belief that there is, or should be, a single, all-purpose, neutral analytical concept which marks out federal question jurisdiction." Considerations relevant to his suggested test include "the extent of the caseload increase for federal trial courts if jurisdiction is recognized; the extent to which cases of this class will, in practice, turn on issues of state or federal law; the extent of the necessity for an expert federal tribunal to handle issues of federal law that do arise; the extent of the necessity for a sympathetic federal tribunal in cases of this class." He views both *Smith* and *Shoshone* as rightly decided:

> In stockholders' derivative suits presenting substantial federal constitutional objections to federal statutes, taken as a class, the federal constitutional issues are likely to be the most significant in the litigation. . . . Those issues require the same expert and sympathetic federal forum at the trial level as they would if presented in an injunction suit against a federal official. On the other hand, there is little reason to fear that the sustaining of jurisdiction in this class of litigation would add significantly to the workload of an overburdened federal judiciary. By contrast, the practical reasons for returning jurisdiction in *Shoshone Mining Co. v. Rutter* were overwhelming. The congressional directive that controversies between rival claimants for mineral rights be decided by "local customs or rules of miners" meant that most of these lawsuits would turn on a consideration of factual issues and interpretation of local law or custom, not requiring the expertise of a federal trial forum. There was no significant federal

> government interest in the choice between the rival claimants which would require the protective jurisdiction of a federal trial court. Finally, and most important, accepting jurisdiction in *Shoshone* would have added significantly to the business of overburdened federal trial courts in the West.

Cohen, The Broken Compass: The Requirement that a Case Arise "Directly" Under Federal Law, 115 U.Va.L.Rev. 890, 906–07, 916 (1967).

(9) The ALI Study (at 178–79), citing Cohen, concluded that the statute should be left silent on the issues raised by such cases as *Smith, Shoshone Min. Co. v. Rutter*, and *Shulthis v. McDougal*:

> The existing doctrines as to when a case raises a federal question are neither analytical nor entirely logical, but a considerable body of case law has been built up on this subject that is reasonably well understood by courts and litigants and that works well in practice. It has therefore seemed the safer course to follow the traditional language, with only minor change, and thus to make it clear that the subsection preserves that body of law.

Do you agree? But can you draft a satisfactory amendment?

Notes on the Jurisdiction of State Courts in Article III Cases

A. Exclusive Federal Jurisdiction

(1) The constitutional grant of federal judicial power has not been held exclusive; since the federal courts have never been given jurisdiction of all Article III cases, to exclude the state courts would in many cases have left suitors altogether without remedy. Beyond this, however, the courts have in the ordinary case refrained from the more moderate step of interpreting statutory grants of federal jurisdiction as exclusive. The tone was set by Hamilton in the 82d number of The Federalist:

> I mean not, therefore, to contend, that the United States, in the course of legislation upon the objects intrusted to their direction, may not commit the decision of causes arising upon a particular regulation to the Federal courts solely, if such a measure should be deemed expedient; but I hold that the State courts will be divested of no part of their primitive jurisdiction, further than may relate to an appeal; and I am even of opinion, that in every case in which they were not expressly excluded by the future acts of the National Legislature, they will of course take cognizance of the causes to which those acts may give birth. This I infer from the nature of judiciary power, and from the general genius of the system. The judiciary power of every government looks beyond its own local or municipal laws, and in civil cases, lays hold of all subjects of litigation between parties within its jurisdiction, though the causes of dispute are relative to the laws of the most distant parts of the globe. Those of Japan, not less than of New York, may furnish the objects of legal discussion to our courts. When in addition to this we consider the State governments and the National governments, as they truly are, in the light of kindred systems, and as parts of *one whole*, the inference seems to be conclusive, that the State

courts would have a concurrent jurisdiction in all cases arising under the laws of the Union, where it was not expressly prohibited.

For a modern example of the Supreme Court's attitude toward the construction of jurisdictional grants not explicitly exclusive see Charles Dowd Box Co. v. Courtney, 368 U.S. 502 (1962). Section 301 of the Labor-Management Relations Act of 1947, 29 U.S.C. § 185, gives the federal courts jurisdiction over suits for violation of collective-bargaining agreements governed by federal common law, and the Court held in the *Lincoln Mills* case, p. 147 supra, that the governing law was federal. Yet the Court held the state courts had not been ousted of jurisdiction:

> Concurrent jurisdiction has been a common phenomenon in our judicial history, and exclusive federal court jurisdiction over cases arising under federal law has been the exception rather than the rule. This Court's approach . . . [has been] "to affirm the [state court's] jurisdiction, where it is not excluded by express provision, or by incompatibility in its exercise arising from the nature of the particular case." . . . The legislative history makes clear that the basic purpose of § 301(a) was not to limit, but to expand, the availability of forums for the enforcement of contracts made by labor organizations. Moreover, there is explicit evidence that Congress expressly intended not to encroach upon the existing jurisdiction of the state courts.

The Court distinguished Garner v. Teamsters Union, 346 U.S. 485 (1953), in which the grant of authority to the National Labor Relations Board (in § 10 of the same statute) to "prevent any person from engaging in any unfair labor practice (listed in section 8) affecting commerce" had been held to deprive the state courts of jurisdiction over an unfair-labor-practice case: "Congress deliberately chose to leave the enforcement of collective agreements 'to the usual processes of the law,'" while in unfair-labor-practice cases (quoting from *Garner*):

> Congress did not merely lay down a substantive rule of law to be enforced by any tribunal competent to apply law generally to the parties. It went on to confide primary interpretation and application of its rules to a specific and specially constituted tribunal and prescribed a particular procedure for investigation, complaint and notice, and hearing and decision, including judicial relief pending a final administrative order. Congress evidently considered that centralized administration of specially designed procedures was necessary to obtain uniform application of its substantive rules and to avoid these [*sic*] diversities and conflicts likely to result from a variety of local procedures and attitudes toward labor controversies.[1]

(2) The 1789 Judiciary Act expressly excluded state courts from jurisdiction over federal crimes, penalties, forfeitures, and seizures; over suits against consuls and vice-consuls; and, subject to a perplexing and broadly interpreted clause preserving "the right of a common law remedy," see pp. 223–26 infra, over admiralty cases. Agreeing with Hamilton, supra note 1, the Supreme Court held this statute deprived the state courts of power to

1. For implicit limitations on state-court jurisdiction over federal officers see pp. 415–25 infra.

hear an admiralty suit in rem: "The constitutionality of these provisions cannot be seriously questioned. . . ." The Moses Taylor, 71 U.S. (4 Wall.) 411 (1967). What is the source of this congressional power? [2]

(3) Principal subjects of exclusive federal jurisdiction today include criminal, antitrust, and bankruptcy cases (18 U.S.C. § 3231; 15 U.S.C. §§ 15, 26; 28 U.S.C. § 1334), as well as patent and copyright cases under 28 U.S.C. § 1338(a), an earlier version of which was at issue in *T. B. Harms Co. v. Eliscu* (p. 160 supra):

> The district courts shall have original jurisdiction of any civil action arising under any Act of Congress relating to patents, plant variety protection, copyrights and trademarks. Such jurisdiction shall be exclusive of the courts of the states in patent, plant variety protection and copyright cases.

In Pratt v. Paris Gas Light & Coke Co., 168 U.S. 255, 259 (1897), the Court allowed a state court in an action for the price of a patented machine to determine whether the plaintiff's patent was void and whether use of his machine would infringe another patent. The predecessor of § 1338(a), the Court said,

> . . . does not deprive the state courts of the power to determine *questions* arising under the patent laws, but only of assuming jurisdiction of *"cases"* arising under those laws. There is a clear distinction between a case and a question arising under the patent laws. The former arises when the plaintiff in his opening pleading . . . sets up a right under the patent laws as ground for a recovery. Of such the state courts have no jurisdiction. The latter may appear in the plea or answer or in the testimony. The determination of such question is not beyond the competency of the state tribunals.

What is the sense of depriving the state courts of jurisdiction over cases arising under the patent laws, if they are free to determine the validity and infringement of patents in other suits?

(4) Luckett v. Delpark, Inc., 270 U.S. 496, 510–11 (1926). A patentee sued in federal court for an accounting and damages for breach of a patent license, to cancel the license, and to enjoin future infringements. The District Court dismissed for want of jurisdiction, and the Supreme Court affirmed:

2. Compare Tennessee Coal, Iron & Railroad Co. v. George, 233 U.S. 354 (1914), upholding the jurisdiction of a Georgia court to enforce a right of personal-injury recovery created by an Alabama statute despite the statute's provision that actions under it "must be brought in a court of competent jurisdiction within the State of Alabama and not elsewhere":

> The courts of the sister State trying the case would be bound to give full faith and credit to all those substantial provisions of the statute which inhered in the cause of action or which name conditions on which the right to sue depend. But venue is no part of the right; and a State cannot create a transitory cause of action and at the same time destroy the right to sue on that transitory cause of action in any court having jurisdiction. That jurisdiction is to be determined by the law of the court's creation and cannot be defeated by the extraterritorial operation of a statute of another State, even though it created the right of action.

Why should the power of the federal government to confine actions on its causes of action to its own courts be greater than that of the only State with an interest in the transaction?

> A federal district court is held to have jurisdiction of a suit by a patentee for an injunction against infringement and for profits and damages, even though, in anticipation of a defense of a license or authority to use the patent, the complainant includes in his bill averments intended to defeat such a defense. . . . But . . . where a patentee complainant makes his suit one for recovery of royalties under a contract of license or assignment, or for damages for a breach of its covenants, or for a specific performance thereof, or asks the aid of the Court in declaring a forfeiture of the license or in restoring an unclouded title to the patent, he does not give the federal district court jurisdiction of the cause as one arising under the patent laws. Nor may he confer it in such a case by adding to his bill an averment that after the forfeiture shall be declared, or the title to the patent shall be restored, he fears the defendant will infringe and therefore asks an injunction to prevent it. . . . The bill in this case . . . is really not based on threatened infringement but on the contracts. . . .

What is the point of an "exclusive" jurisdiction that the plaintiff can avoid by artful pleading?

(5) Why should state courts ever be permitted to enforce federal law? To put the question the other way, why should federal jurisdiction ever be exclusive?

Are there any cases in which federal interests could not be adequately protected by giving plaintiffs the option of suing in federal or state courts and defendants the option of removal? See the ALI's agreement with the present concurrent jurisdiction over civil suits brought by the United States: "The United States can protect itself by its choice of forum." ALI Study, p. 255. Is this not equally true of federal criminal jurisdiction, now made exclusive by 18 U.S.C. § 3231? [3]

The ALI proposed to retain the exclusive federal jurisdiction in patent, copyright, and certain other cases, but not to extend it, ALI Study 24–25, 182–87, 497:

> The federal judicial system has a well-developed machinery for handling bankruptcy matters, as well as much experience with them. In patent and copyright cases the federal courts again have experience, which the state courts lack, and in these cases there is a federal interest in the monopoly conferred by the patent or copyright that is more important than the wishes of the parties. Similar arguments, though somewhat less forceful, can be made with regard to antitrust cases. . . .

(6) American Well Works Co. v. Layne & Bowler Co., 241 U.S. 257 (1916):

3. See F. Frankfurter & J. Landis, The Business of the Supreme Court 293 (1928):

> Liquor violations, illicit dealings in narcotics, thefts of interstate freight and automobiles, schemes to defraud essentially local in their operation but involving a minor use of the mails, these and like offenses have brought to the federal courts a volume of business which, to no small degree, endangers their capacity to dispose of distinctively federal litigation and to maintain the quality which has heretofore characterized the United States courts. The burden of vindicating the interests behind this body of recent litigation should, on the whole, be assumed by the states.

> This is a suit begun in a state court, removed to the United States Court, and then, on motion to remand by the plaintiff, dismissed by the latter court, on the ground that the cause of action arose under the patent laws of the United States, that the state court had no jurisdiction, and that therefore, that one to which it was removed had none.

Without disputing that this disposition would be proper if the case arose under the patent laws the Supreme Court, in a leading opinion by Mr. Justice Holmes, held that it did not arise under the patent laws. For dismissals of removed cases because federal jurisdiction was exclusive see General Inv. Co. v. Lake Shore & M. S. Ry., 260 U.S. 261, 287–88 (1922); Lambert Run Coal Co. v. Baltimore & O. R. R., 258 U.S. 377, 382 (1922).

This rule was changed by statute in 1986. 28 U.S.C.A. § 1441(e). Why?

B. Removal

(7) From the very beginning the typical pattern has been concurrent federal and state original jurisdiction over cases within Article III, with permission for removal by the defendant. The availability of removal was used by the losing party in Martin v. Hunter's Lessee, 14 U.S. (1 Wheat.) 304 (1816), as an argument that Supreme Court review of state decisions was unnecessary, and Congress's power to authorize removal of Article III cases was upheld in The Mayor v. Cooper, 73 U.S. (6 Wall.) 247 (1868). Was this holding a mistake?

The central removal provisions today are found in 28 U.S.C. §§ 1441–50. Section 1441 is limited to civil actions; it applies to both federal-question and diversity cases, and its scope is discussed at pp. 157–58 supra, p. 246 infra. See the dictum in *Romero v. International T. O. Co.*, infra, p. 203, that § 1441 does not allow removal if federal jurisdiction is based only on the admiralty clause, § 1333, and the discussion of this issue at p. 225. Sections 1442 and 1443 allow removal of criminal as well as civil cases, the former section when a federal officer is sued for an official act, the latter in certain civil-rights cases. See the discussion of these provisions, infra, pp. 424–25, 552–56. Section 1444 allows the United States to remove certain foreclosure actions. Sections 1446–50 prescribe procedures respecting removal; of particular importance are the provisions requiring that a removal petition in a civil action be filed within thirty days after service of process, and in a criminal prosecution before trial.

(8) There are a few important exceptions to the principle that actions within the original federal jurisdiction can be removed. First is the qualification in § 1441(b) that cases in which jurisdiction rests on diversity alone can be removed only if there are no resident defendants, see p. 701 infra. Section 1445 forbids removal of actions under the Federal Employers' Liability Act or under state workers' compensation laws and imposes a minimum jurisdictional amount of $10,000 upon removal of suits against railroads for lost or damaged freight. Pate v. Standard Dredging Corp., 193 F.2d 498 (5th Cir. 1952), disallowed removal of a seaman's personal-injury action because the non-removal provision of § 1445 is a statute "modifying or extending the common-law right or remedy in cases of personal injury to railway employees" and thus made applicable to seamen by the Jones Act, 46 U.S.C. § 688. In Wilkins v. Renault Southwest, Inc., 227 F.Supp. 647

(N.D.Tex.1964), the court held that removal of a minimum-wage action under the Fair Labor Standards Act, 29 U.S.C. § 216, was "expressly" prohibited by that section's provision that such actions "may be *maintained* in any court of competent jurisdiction" and therefore not authorized by § 1441. Contra, Cosme Nieves v. Deshler, 786 F.2d 445 (1st Cir.1986).

(9) Why should removal of cases within original federal jurisdiction ever be forbidden? It is arguable that only the party with reason to fear state-court hostility should be allowed to choose a federal forum, see § 1441(b) and Wechsler, supra p. 157. Somewhat different considerations were suggested by Congress in making workers' compensation cases nonremovable, S.Rep.No.1830, 85th Cong., 2d Sess. (1958):

> In a number of States the workload of the Federal courts has greatly increased because of the removal of workmen's compensation cases from the State courts. . . . Nearly all of the State statutes on workmen's compensation provide summary proceedings for the expeditious and inexpensive settlement of claims by injured workmen against the employer. The procedure provided in such State statutes is not, as a rule, applicable to procedure in Federal courts. When cases are removed to the Federal court, the State statutes, in many instances, are entirely nullified. For instance, some of these State statutes limit the venue to the place where the accident occurred or to the district of the workman's residence. When removed to the Federal court the venue provisions of the State statute cannot be applied. Very often cases removed to the Federal courts require the workman to travel long distances and to bring his witnesses at great expense. This places an undue burden upon the workman and very often the workman settles his claim because he cannot afford the luxury of a trial in federal court. . . .
>
> In the Jones Act, the Fair Labor Standards Act, and the Railway Employers' Liability Act, all of which are in the nature of workmen's compensation cases, the Congress has given the workman the option of filing his case in either the State court or the Federal court. If filed in the State courts the law prohibits removal to the Federal court. This proposed legislation accomplishes this same purpose. . . .

Is it consistent with these purposes to hold, as in Patton v. Cincinnati, N. O. & T. P. Ry., 208 Fed. 29 (E.D.Tenn.1913), that the plaintiff cannot waive the prohibition against removal of an FELA case? [4]

(10) What happens if a claim nonremovable under § 1445 is joined with a claim otherwise removable? Such was the case in *Pate v. Standard Dredging Co.*, supra note 8, in which the injured seaman sought damages not only under the Jones Act but also under the maritime common-law doctrines of unseaworthiness and maintenance and cure. The defendant argued that the entire case was removable under § 1441(c) because there was diversity and the nonstatutory claims were "separate and independent." The court disagreed, holding that the Jones Act and unseaworthiness counts constituted "but a single wrongful invasion of a single primary right" and that the maintenance-and-cure count was not removable be-

4. Contra, Lirette v. N.L. Sperry Sun, Inc., 820 F.2d 116 (5th Cir.1987).

cause it did not satisfy the jurisdictional amount. Does this disposition suggest that the maintenance claim was "separate and independent?" But cf. *Romero v. International T. O. Co.*, infra p. 200; Fitzgerald v. United States Lines, 374 U.S. 16 (1963), holding that trial convenience required submission of claims for maintenance and unseaworthiness to the jury along with a Jones Act count, although a jury was required by statute only for the Jones Act claim. Notice the unsatisfactory nature of any disposition of the general question whether joinder of a "separate" claim makes a Jones Act case removable. On the one hand is the policy against removal of Jones Act cases, on the other the policy of § 1441(c) that the plaintiff should not be allowed to defeat removal of a claim otherwise removable by joining it with a nonremovable claim. Finally, to remove only the claim for maintenance would require two trials arising out of a single accident. See Strother v. Union P. R. R., 220 Fed. 731 (W.D.Mo.1915), holding that by joining a removable claim the plaintiff had waived his right to prevent removal under the FELA. Observe the incompatibility of this solution with the *Patton* case, supra note 9, holding the bar against removal cannot be waived. And is the dilemma adequately solved by affixing the conclusory label of "waiver?"

C. *The Obligation to Provide a Forum*

(11) In the cases thus far discussed in these Notes the issue has been whether a state court *may* entertain an action with the federal judicial power. A few Supreme Court decisions have concerned the further question whether a state court *must* do so. In Mondou v. New York, N. H. & H. R. R., 223 U.S. 1 (1912), a state court had refused to entertain an action under the Federal Employers' Liability Act, which gave the federal courts jurisdiction "concurrent with that of the courts of the several States." The Supreme Court reversed:

> The Superior Courts of the State are courts of general jurisdiction, are empowered to take cognizance of actions to recover for personal injuries and for death, and are accustomed to exercise that jurisdiction, not only in cases where the right of action arose under the laws of that State, but also in cases where it arose in another State, under its laws, and in circumstances in which the laws of Connecticut give no right of recovery, as where the causal negligence was that of a fellow-servant.
>
> The suggestion that the act of Congress is not in harmony with the policy of the State, and therefore that the courts of the State are free to decline jurisdiction, is quite inadmissible, because it presupposes what in legal contemplation does not exist. When Congress . . . adopted that act, it spoke for all the people and all the States, and thereby established a policy for all. . . .
>
> We are not disposed to believe that the exercise of jurisdiction by the state courts will be attended by any appreciable inconvenience or confusion; but, be this as it may, it affords no reason for declining a jurisdiction conferred by law. . . . It never has been supposed that courts are at liberty to decline cognizance of cases of a particular class merely because the rules of law to be applied in their adjudication are unlike those applied in other cases.

> We conclude that rights arising under the act in question may be enforced, as of right, in the courts of the States when their jurisdiction, as prescribed by local laws, is adequate to the occasion.

Accord, McKnett v. St. Louis & S. F. Ry., 292 U.S. 230 (1934):

> While Congress has not attempted to compel states to provide courts for the enforcement of the Federal Employers' Liability Act, . . . the Federal Constitution prohibits state courts of general jurisdiction from refusing to do so solely because the suit is brought under a federal law . . . . A state may not discriminate against rights arising under federal laws.

As suggested in both *Mondou* and *McKnett*, the state court's duty to enforce federal law has not been absolute. In Douglas v. New York, N. H. & H. R. R., 279 U.S. 377 (1929), the Court upheld a state court's refusal to entertain an FELA action on the basis of a statute construed to allow discretionary dismissal of actions by nonresidents against foreign corporations doing business in the State:

> It may very well be that if the Supreme Court of New York were given no discretion, being otherwise competent, it would be subject to a duty. But there is nothing in the Act of Congress that purports to enforce a duty upon such courts as against an otherwise valid excuse.

See also Missouri ex rel. Southern Ry. v. Mayfield, 340 U.S. 1 (1950), reaffirming *Douglas* and explaining for the state courts on remand that forum non conveniens, if applied without discrimination against federal rights, is a "valid excuse."

In Testa v. Katt, 330 U.S. 386 (1947), the Rhode Island Supreme Court threw out a treble-damage action for selling goods above the ceiling price prescribed pursuant to the Emergency Price Control Act, which like the FELA gave federal courts jurisdiction "concurrently with State and Territorial courts," 56 Stat. 34, on the familiar conflict-of-laws ground that the courts of one sovereign do not enforce the penal laws of another. The Supreme Court reversed:

> We cannot accept the basic premise on which the Rhode Island Supreme Court held that it has no more obligation to enforce a valid penal law of the United States than it has to enforce a penal law of another state or a foreign country. Such a broad assumption . . . disregards the purpose and effect of [the Supremacy Clause]. . . . [As in *Mondou*], the fact that Rhode Island has an established policy against enforcement by its courts of statutes of other states and the United States which it deems penal, cannot be accepted as a "valid excuse." . . . For the policy of the federal Act is the prevailing policy in every state. . . .
>
> It is conceded that this same type of claim arising under Rhode Island law would be enforced by that State's courts. . . . Thus the Rhode Island courts have jurisdiction adequate and appropriate under established local law to adjudicate this action. Under these circum-

stances the State courts are not free to refuse enforcement of petitioners' claim.[5]

(12) Granted that a valid federal statute requiring state courts to entertain federal actions is paramount under the Supremacy Clause, where does Congress get power to impose such a requirement? Justice Frankfurter protested (too late?) that "neither Congress nor the British Parliament nor the Vermont Legislature has power to confer jurisdiction upon the New York courts." Brown v. Gerdes, 321 U.S. 178, 188 (1944), (concurring opinion). See Sandalow, Henry v. Mississippi and the Adequate State Ground: Proposals for a Revised Doctrine, 1965 Sup.Ct.Rev. 187, 207 n. 84, finding congressional authority in the Necessary and Proper Clause and suggesting the additional possibility of an inference from "the fact that Article III permits, but does not require, establishment of federal courts inferior to the Supreme Court."

Cf. Garcia v. San Antonio Metropolitan Transit Auth., 469 U.S. 528 (1985), holding that the Fair Labor Standards Act could constitutionally be applied to state employees; Brown v. EPA, 521 F.2d 827 (9th Cir.1975), doubting that Congress could require States to regulate automotive air pollution. Compare General Oil Co. v. Crain, 209 U.S. 211 (1908), infra p. 586, holding sovereign immunity no defense in a state-court suit to enjoin collection of taxes alleged, among other things, unduly to burden interstate commerce. Does this decision suggest that the Commerce Clause impliedly requires the state courts to provide a forum?

(13) Assuming that Congress has the power to require state-court jurisdiction, was the Court right in *Mondou, McKnett,* and *Testa* in holding that Congress had not left the States a choice in the matter? See Sandalow, supra note 12, 1965 Sup.Ct.Rev. at 206–07:

> It is difficult to perceive the federal interest that justifies so substantial an intrusion upon the power of the states to determine the purposes to be served by agencies of state government. . . . In both *Mondou* and *Testa* a federal court was open to the plaintiff, so that a decision sustaining the refusal to adjudicate would in no way have interfered with the vindication of federal rights. . . . Federal policy was substantive, that recovery should be permitted under specified circumstances. State policy, on the other hand, was concerned only with the use to be made of state courts, a matter not touched by the federal policy. . . . In the absence of a declaration by Congress that state courts must enforce rights that Congress has created, there appears to be no substantial reason why the Supreme Court should impose such an obligation.[6]

5. Was the Supreme Court justified in saying, in *Testa v. Katt,* that a state court was under a greater obligation to enforce federal laws than to enforce the laws of other States? Would it be fair to say that it was the purpose of the Full Faith and Credit Clause to make each State's laws supreme in cases in which it alone has an interest? See B. Currie, Selected Essays on the Conflict of Laws, Ch. 5 (1963); Hughes v. Fetter, 341 U.S. 609 (1951), forbidding Wisconsin to dismiss a wrongful-death action simply because it arose under Illinois law.

6. For disagreement with Sandalow on the statutory question see Redish & Muench, Adjudication of Federal Causes of Action in State Court, 75 Mich.L.Rev. 311, 347 (1976): "In giving state courts power to adjudicate federal causes of action, presumably Congress . . . has decided that . . .

Has Professor Sandalow overlooked the significance of 28 U.S.C. § 1445(a), forbidding removal of FELA actions filed in state courts? Or does that section merely evidence congressional intention that if the state courts are willing to exercise jurisdiction the plaintiff should be able to choose his forum?

SECTION 2. THE SCOPE OF A "CASE"

FINLEY v. UNITED STATES

109 S.Ct. 2003 (1989).

JUSTICE SCALIA delivered the opinion of the Court.

On the night of November 11, 1983, a twin-engine plane carrying petitioner's husband and two of her children struck electric transmission lines during its approach to a San Diego, California, airfield. No one survived the resulting crash. Petitioner brought a tort action in state court, claiming that San Diego Gas and Electric Company had negligently positioned and inadequately illuminated the transmission lines, and that the city of San Diego's negligent maintenance of the airport's runway lights had rendered them inoperative the night of the crash. When she later discovered that the Federal Aviation Administration (FAA) was in fact the party responsible for the runway lights, petitioner filed the present action against the United States in the United States District Court for the Southern District of California. The complaint based jurisdiction upon the Federal Tort Claims Act (FTCA), 28 U.S.C. § 1346(b), alleging negligence in the FAA's operation and maintenance of the runway lights and performance of air traffic control functions. Almost a year later, she moved to amend the federal complaint to include claims against the original state-court defendants, as to which no independent basis for federal jurisdiction existed. The District Court granted petitioner's motion and asserted "pendent" jurisdiction under Mine Workers v. Gibbs, 383 U.S. 715 (1966), finding it "clear" that "judicial economy and efficiency" favored trying the actions together, and concluding that they arose "from a common nucleus of operative facts." . . . The District Court certified an interlocutory appeal to the Court of Appeals for the Ninth Circuit under 28 U.S.C. § 1292(b). That court summarily reversed. . . . We granted certiorari . . . to resolve a split among the Circuits on whether the FTCA permits an assertion of pendent jurisdiction over additional parties. . . .

The FTCA provides that "the district courts . . . shall have exclusive jurisdiction of civil actions on claims against the United States" for certain torts of federal employees acting within the scope of their employment. 28 U.S.C. § 1346(b). Petitioner seeks to append her claims against the city and the utility to her FTCA action against the

federal policies . . . are best advanced by distributing the case burden between the state and federal courts" subject to legitimate excuses like forum non conveniens.

United States, even though this would require the District Court to extend its authority to additional parties for whom an independent jurisdictional base—such as diversity of citizenship, 28 U.S.C. § 1332(a)(1)—is lacking.

In 1807 Chief Justice Marshall wrote for the Court that "courts which are created by written law, and whose jurisdiction is defined by written law, cannot transcend that jurisdiction. It is unnecessary to state the reasoning on which this opinion is founded, because it has been repeatedly given by this court; and with the decisions heretofore rendered on this point, no member of the bench has, even for an instant, been dissatisfied." Ex parte Bollman, 4 Cranch 75, 93 (1807). It remains rudimentary law that "[a]s regards all courts of the United States inferior to this tribunal, two things are necessary to create jurisdiction, whether original or appellate. The Constitution must have given to the court the capacity to take it, *and an act of Congress must have supplied it*. . . . To the extent that such action is not taken, the power lies dormant." The Mayor v. Cooper, 6 Wall. 247, 252 (1868). . . .

Despite this principle, in a line of cases by now no less well established we have held, without specific examination of jurisdictional statutes, that federal courts have "pendent" claim jurisdiction—that is, jurisdiction over nonfederal claims between parties litigating other matters properly before the court—to the full extent permitted by the Constitution. Mine Workers v. Gibbs, 383 U.S. 715 (1966); Hurn v. Oursler, 289 U.S. 238 (1933); Siler v. Louisville & Nashville R. Co., 213 U.S. 175 (1909). *Gibbs,* which has come to stand for the principle in question, held that "[p]endent jurisdiction, in the sense of judicial *power,* exists whenever there is a claim 'arising under [the] Constitution, the Laws of the United States, and Treaties made, or which shall be made, under their Authority . . .,' U.S. Const., Art. III, § 2, and the relationship between that claim and the state claim permits the conclusion that the entire action before the court comprises but one constitutional 'case.'" 383 U.S., at 725 (emphasis in original). The requisite relationship exists, *Gibbs* said, when the federal and nonfederal claims "derive from a common nucleus of operative fact" and are such that a plaintiff "would ordinarily be expected to try them in one judicial proceeding." Ibid. Petitioner contends that the same criterion applies here, leading to the result that her state-law claims against San Diego Gas and Electric Company and the city of San Diego may be heard in conjunction with her FTCA action against the United States.

Analytically, petitioner's case is fundamentally different from *Gibbs* in that it brings into question what has become known as pendent-*party* jurisdiction, that is, jurisdiction over parties not named in any claim that is independently cognizable by the federal court. We may assume, without deciding, that the constitutional criterion for pendent-party jurisdiction is analogous to the constitutional criterion for pendent-claim jurisdiction, and that petitioner's state-law claims pass that test. Our cases show, however, that with respect to the addition of parties, as opposed to the addition of only claims, we will not assume that the full constitutional power has been congressionally authorized, and will not read jurisdictional statutes broadly. In Zahn v. International Paper Co., 414 U.S. 291, 301 (1973), we refused to allow a plaintiff pursuing a diversity action worth less than the jurisdictional minimum of $10,000 to append his claim to the jurisdictionally adequate diversity claims of other members of a plaintiff class—even though all of the *claims* would together have amounted to a single "case" under *Gibbs,* see Owen Equipment & Erection Co. v. Kroger, 437 U.S. 365, 372 (1978). We based this holding upon "the statutes defining the jurisdiction of the District Court," 414 U.S., at 292, and did not so much as mention *Gibbs.*

Two years later, the nontransferability of *Gibbs* to pendent-party claims was made explicit. In Aldinger v. Howard, 427 U.S. 1 (1976), the plaintiff brought federal claims under 42 U.S.C. § 1983 against individual defendants, and sought to append to them a related state claim against Spokane County, Washington. (A federal § 1983 claim was unavailable against the county because of this Court's decision in Monroe v. Pape, 365 U.S. 167 (1961).)[3] We specifically disapproved application of the *Gibbs* mode of analysis, finding a "significant legal difference." 427 U.S., at 15. "[T]he addition of a completely new party," we said, "would run counter to the well-established principle that federal courts . . . are courts of limited jurisdiction marked out by Congress." Ibid. "Resolution of a claim of pendent-party jurisdiction . . . calls for careful attention to the relevant statutory language." Id., at 17. We held in *Aldinger* that the jurisdictional statute under which suit was brought, 28 U.S.C. § 1343, which conferred district court jurisdiction over civil actions of certain types "authorized by law to be commenced," did not mean to include as "authorized by law" a state-law claim against a party that had been statutorily insulated from similar federal suit. The county had been "*excluded* from liability in § 1983, and therefore by reference in the grant of jurisdiction under § 1343(3)." . . .

We reaffirmed and further refined our approach to pendent-party jurisdiction in Owen Equipment & Erection Co. v. Kroger, supra, 437 U.S., at 372–375—a case, like *Zahn,* involving the diversity statute, 28 U.S.C. § 1332(a)(1), but focusing on the requirement that the suit be "between . . . citizens of different states," rather than the requirement that it "excee[d] the sum or value of $10,000." We held that the jurisdiction which § 1332(a)(1) confers over a "matter in controversy" between a plaintiff and defendant of diverse citizenship cannot be read to confer pendent jurisdiction over a different, nondiverse defendant, even if the *claim* involving that other defendant meets the *Gibbs* test. "*Gibbs,*" we said, "does not end the inquiry into whether a federal court

3. *Monroe v. Pape* was later overruled by Monell v. New York City Dept. of Social Services, 436 U.S. 658 (1978).

has power to hear the nonfederal claims along with the federal ones. Beyond this constitutional minimum, there must be an examination of the posture in which the nonfederal claim is asserted and of the specific statute that confers jurisdiction over the federal claim," 437 U.S., at 373.

The most significant element of "posture" or of "context," id., at 376, in the present case (as in *Zahn, Aldinger* and *Kroger*) is precisely that the added claims involve added parties over whom no independent basis of jurisdiction exists. While in a narrow class of cases a federal court may assert authority over such a claim "ancillary" to jurisdiction otherwise properly vested—for example, when an additional party has a claim upon contested assets within the court's exclusive control, see, e.g., Krippendorf v. Hyde, 110 U.S. 276 (1884); Freeman v. Howe, 24 How. 450, 460 (1861), or when necessary to give effect to the court's judgment, see, e.g., Local Loan Co. v. Hunt, 292 U.S. 234, 239 (1934); Julian v. Central Trust Co., 193 U.S. 93, 112–114 (1904)—we have never reached such a result solely on the basis that the *Gibbs* test has been met. And little more basis than that can be relied upon by petitioner here. As in *Kroger,* the relationship between petitioner's added claims and the original complaint is one of "mere factual similarity," which is of no consequence since "neither the convenience of the litigants nor considerations of judicial economy can suffice to justify extension of the doctrine of ancillary jurisdiction," 437 U.S., at 376–377. It is true that here, unlike in *Kroger,* see id., at 376, the party seeking to bring the added claims had little choice but to be in federal rather than state court, since the FTCA permits the Federal Government to be sued only there. But that alone is not enough, since we have held that suits against the United States under the Tucker Act, 24 Stat. 505 (which can of course be brought only in federal court, see 28 U.S.C. §§ 1346(a)(2), 1491(a)(1)) cannot include private defendants. United States v. Sherwood, 312 U.S. 584 (1941).

The second factor invoked by *Kroger,* the text of the jurisdictional statute at issue, likewise fails to establish petitioner's case. The FTCA, § 1346(b), confers jurisdiction over "civil actions on claims against the United States." It does not say "civil actions on claims that include requested relief against the United States," nor "civil actions in which there is a claim against the United States"—formulations one might expect if the presence of a claim against the United States constituted merely a minimum jurisdictional requirement, rather than a definition of the permissible scope of FTCA actions. Just as the statutory provision "between . . . citizens of different States" has been held to mean citizens of different States and no one else, see *Kroger,* 437 U.S. 365 (1978), so also here we conclude that "against the United States" means against the United States and no one else. "Due regard for the rightful independence of state governments . . . requires that [federal courts] scrupulously confine their own jurisdiction to the precise limits which the statute has defined." Healy v. Ratta, 292 U.S. 263, 270

(1934). . . . The statute here defines jurisdiction in a manner that does not reach defendants other than the United States.

Petitioner contends, however, that an affirmative grant of pendent-party jurisdiction is suggested by changes made to the jurisdictional grant of the FTCA as part of the comprehensive 1948 revision of the Judicial Code. See Pub.L. 773, 62 Stat. 869. In its earlier form, the FTCA had conferred upon district courts "exclusive jurisdiction to hear, determine, and render judgment *on any claim* against the United States" for specified torts. 28 U.S.C. § 931 (1946 ed.) (emphasis added). In the 1948 revision, this provision was changed to "exclusive jurisdiction of *civil actions on claims* against the United States." 28 U.S.C. § 1346(b) (1952 ed.) (emphasis added). Petitioner argues that this broadened the scope of the statute, permitting the assertion of jurisdiction over any "civil action," so long as that action *includes* a claim against the United States. We disagree.

Under established canons of statutory construction, "it will not be inferred that Congress, in revising and consolidating the laws, intended to change their effect, unless such intention is clearly expressed." Anderson v. Pacific Coast S.S. Co., 225 U.S. 187, 199 (1912) . . . . We have found no suggestion, much less a clear expression, that the minor rewording at issue here imported a substantive change.

The change from "claim against the United States" to "civil actions on claims against the United States" would be a strange way to express the substantive revision asserted by the petitioner—but a perfectly understandable way to achieve another objective. The 1948 recodification came relatively soon after the adoption of the Federal Rules of Civil Procedure, which provide that "[t]here shall be one form of action to be known as 'civil action.'" Fed.Rule Civ.Proc. 2. Consistent with this new terminology, the 1948 revision inserted the expression "civil action" throughout the provisions governing district-court jurisdiction. See H.R.Rep. No. 308, 80th Cong., 1st Sess., App. A114–A125 (1947) (Reviser's Notes).

Reliance upon the 1948 recodification also ignores the fact that the concept of pendent-party jurisdiction was not considered remotely viable until *Gibbs* liberalized the concept of pendent-claim jurisdiction—nearly 20 years later. . . . Indeed, in 1948 even a relatively limited substantive expansion of pendent-*claim* jurisdiction with respect to unfair competition actions provoked considerable discussion, . . . and was described by the chief reviser as one of a dozen "major changes of law" effected by his handiwork, W. Barron, The Judicial Code 1948 Revision, 8 F.R.D. 439, 441–445 (1949). That change, in the already accepted realm of pendent-*claim* jurisdiction, was accomplished by wording that could not be mistaken, referring to "any civil action asserting a claim of unfair competition when joined with a substantial and related claim under the copyright, patent, or trademark laws." § 1338(b), 62 Stat. 931. It is inconceivable that the much more radical change of adopting pendent-party jurisdiction would have been effected by the minor and obscure change of wording at issue here—especially when that revision is more naturally understood as stylistic.

Because the FTCA permits the Government to be sued only in federal court, our holding that parties to related claims cannot necessarily be sued there means that the efficiency and convenience of a consolidated action will sometimes have to be forgone in favor of separate actions in state and federal courts. We acknowledged this potential consideration in *Aldinger,* 427 U.S., at 18, but now conclude that the present statute permits no other result.

. . . .

As we noted at the outset, our cases do not display an entirely consistent approach with respect to the necessity that jurisdiction be explicitly conferred. The *Gibbs* line of cases was a departure from prior practice, and a departure that we have no intent to limit or impair. But *Aldinger* indicated that the *Gibbs* approach would not be extended to the pendent-party field, and we decide today to retain that line. Whatever we say regarding the scope of jurisdiction conferred by a particular statute can of course be changed by Congress. What is of paramount importance is that Congress be able to legislate against a background of clear interpretive rules, so that it may know the effect of the language it adopts. All our cases—*Zahn, Aldinger,* and *Kroger*—have held that a grant of jurisdiction over claims involving particular parties does not itself confer jurisdiction over additional claims by or against different parties. Our decision today reaffirms that interpretive rule; the opposite would sow confusion.

For the foregoing reasons, the judgment of the Court of Appeals is

Affirmed.

JUSTICE BLACKMUN, dissenting.

If Aldinger v. Howard, 427 U.S. 1 (1976), required us to ask whether the Federal Tort Claims Act embraced "an affirmative grant of pendent-party jurisdiction," . . ., I would agree with the majority that no such specific grant of jurisdiction is present. But, in my view, that is not the appropriate question under *Aldinger.* I read the Court's opinion in that case, rather, as requiring us to consider whether Congress has demonstrated an intent to *exempt* "the party as to whom jurisdiction pendent to the principal claim" is asserted from being haled into federal court. . . .

In *Aldinger,* the Court found the requisite intent to exclude municipalities from the relevant jurisdictional statute, because (the Court then thought) municipalities had been affirmatively excluded by Congress from the scope of § 1983. In such a case, the Court barred the use of the pendent-party doctrine, for otherwise the doctrine would permit an end-run around an express congressional limitation of federal power. See id., at 16–17.

In the present case, I find no such substantive limitation. Nor, in my view, is there any other expression of congressional intent to exclude private defendants from federal tort claims litigation. United States v. Sherwood, 312 U.S. 584 (1941), is not to the contrary. There, this Court held that Congress did not intend under the Tucker Act to permit the district courts to adjudicate any cause of action that could not have been brought in the Court of Claims, an Article I court in which no private party could be a defendant. *Sherwood* did not turn solely on a canon of "conservatism which is appropriate in the case of a waiver of sovereign immunity." . . . It turned also upon "the history of the Court of Claims' jurisdiction." Id., at 590–591. There is no equivalent history of adjudication of tort claims against the United States in a tribunal without power to litigate the liability of private tortfeasors; thus, *Sherwood* does not require the result the Court reaches today.

In a case not controlled by any express intent to limit the scope of a constitutional "case," *Aldinger* suggests that the appropriateness of pendent-party jurisdiction might turn on the "alignmen[t] of parties and claims," and that one significant factor is whether "the grant of jurisdiction to [the] federal court is exclusive," 427 U.S., at 18, as is the situation here. Where, as here, Congress' preference for a federal forum for a certain category of claims makes the federal forum the *only* possible one in which the constitutional case may be heard as a whole, the sensible result is to permit the exercise of pendent-party jurisdiction. *Aldinger* imposes no obstacle to that result, and I would not reach out to create one. I therefore dissent.

[A separate dissent by Justice Stevens, joined by Justices Brennan and Marshall, is omitted.]

Notes on Pendent Jurisdiction

(1) The notion that federal-question jurisdiction includes the power to determine state-law issues that are part of the same "case" or "civil action" goes back as far as *Osborn v. Bank of the United States*, supra p. 140, in which Chief Justice Marshall said (and held in the companion case) that if there was a federal "ingredient" in the cause jurisdiction was not ousted by the presence of non-federal issues. It was applied in Siler v. Louisville & Nashville R. R., 213 U.S. 175 (1909), in which a state rate order was attacked on two grounds: that it was unconstitutional, and that it was unauthorized by state statute. Although there was no diverse citizenship, the Court not only upheld federal jurisdiction over the state-law claim but held that the state claim should be decided first in order to avoid unnecessary decision of constitutional questions. It was also applied in Moore v. New York Cotton Exchange, 270 U.S. 593 (1926), an antitrust case in which the Court entertained a non-federal counterclaim arising out of the same transaction as the plaintiff's suit, although the antitrust claim was dismissed for failure to state a claim.

(2) In Hurn v. Oursler, 289 U.S. 238 (1933), the plaintiffs sought to enjoin performance of a play called "The Spider," alleging that "The Spider" infringed their copyright on another play and that its performance constituted unfair competition under state law with both the copyrighted

and uncopyrighted versions of their play. The Supreme Court held there was federal jurisdiction to determine the unfair-competition claim with respect to the copyrighted version of the plaintiffs' play, but not as to the uncopyrighted version: "The bill . . . sets forth facts alleged to be in violation of two distinct rights, namely, the right to the protection of the copyrighted play, and the right to the protection of the uncopyrighted play."

In reading these conclusions, the Court relied principally upon the decisions cited in note 1, supra. Were these decisions authority for the kind of pendent jurisdiction exercised in *Hurn*? In *Moore* the Court spoke only of the Equity Rule making certain counterclaims compulsory; it did not discuss whether there was federal jurisdiction. On the impact of *Osborn* and *Siler* see Hart & Wechsler, The Federal Courts and the Federal System 922 (2d ed. 1973):

> Notice that a federal trial court would often be unable to function as a court at all, in the absence of the jurisdiction over state questions which Marshall asserted in Osborn v. Bank of the United States. At stake there was the ability of such a court, ever, to be sure of being able to decide a whole case.
>
> No such justification, obviously, is available for the ancillary jurisdiction asserted in Siler. The justification there, is it not, is different and two-fold: namely, the policy in favor of avoiding avoidable decisions of federal constitutional questions, plus the policy in favor of having one lawsuit, if possible, instead of two?
>
> Hurn, however, is supported only by the single policy against piecemeal litigation. How strong is this policy? How far does it warrant stretching the constitutional concept of a "case"?

(3) Did the distinction drawn in *Hurn* between the claims respecting the copyrighted and uncopyrighted versions of the plaintiff's play make sense? It was abandoned in United Mine Workers v. Gibbs, 383 U.S. 715 (1966), in which the plaintiff asserted that the defendant's acts in the course of a labor dispute constituted both a secondary boycott under the Labor-Management Relations Act and a tort under state law. In upholding pendent jurisdiction over the state-law claim, Justice Brennan concluded that the approach taken in *Hurn* had been "unnecessarily grudging."

> Pendent jurisdiction, in the sense of judicial *power*, exists whenever there is a claim "arising under [the] Constitution, the Laws of the United States, and Treaties made, or which shall be made, under their Authority . . .," U.S.Const., Art. III, § 2, and the relationship between that claim and the state claim permits the conclusion that the entire action before the court comprises but one constitutional "case." The federal claim must have substance sufficient to confer subject matter jurisdiction on the court. . . . The state and federal claims must derive from a common nucleus of operative fact. But if, considered without regard to their federal or state character, a plaintiff's claims are such that he would ordinarily be expected to try them all in one judicial proceeding, then, assuming substantiality of the federal issues, there is *power* in federal courts to hear the whole.

As Justice Scalia noted in *Finley*, the Court's opinion in *Gibbs* did not explain what statute provided a basis for its decision. Was there one? [1]

After *Gibbs*, what is the function of 28 U.S.C. § 1338(b), which confers jurisdiction of "a claim of unfair competition when joined with a substantial and related claim under the copyright, patent or trade-mark laws"? [2]

(4) The ALI proposed that in any original or removed federal-question case "the court shall have jurisdiction to determine all claims arising under State law that arise out of the same transaction or occurrence or series of transactions or occurrences as the federal claim, defense, or counterclaim, if such a determination is necessary in order to give effective relief on the federal claim or counterclaim or if a substantial question of fact is common" to the federal and state claims. Proposed § 1313(a), ALI Study 28. Is this an improvement on § 1338(b)? On *Hurn v. Oursler*? On *Gibbs*? Does it make sense to equate the scope of pendent jurisdiction with the requirements for compulsory counterclaims under Rule 13? Is it helpful to add the ALI's further qualifications?

Does this suggest that permissive counterclaims cannot be pendent but must be supported by their own jurisdictional grounds? See 3 Moore, Federal Practice 53–57.

(5) Most courts of appeals thought the reasoning of *Gibbs* supported pendent jurisdiction over related claims by additional plaintiffs, or against additional defendants. See, e.g., Leather's Best, Inc. v. S. S. Mormaclynx, 451 F.2d 800 (2d Cir. 1971), an action to recover the value of a shipment of leather that had disappeared after having been unloaded from a ship. Finding that the complaint stated claims within the federal admiralty jurisdiction against the vessel and its owner for breach of the maritime contractual obligation of safe delivery but that the claim for negligence of the bailee from whose land the cargo had been stolen arose under state law, the court in an opinion by then Chief Judge Friendly upheld pendent jurisdiction over the bailee:

> To be sure, the *Gibbs* Court was not confronted with the question whether pendent jurisdiction extended to a state claim against a party not named in the federal claim. But as we have recently observed in Astor-Honor, Inc. v. Grosset & Dunlap, Inc., 441 F.2d 627, 629 (2 Cir. 1971), "Mr. Justice Brennan's language and the common sense considerations underlying it seem broad enough to cover that problem also. See Note, UMW v. Gibbs and Pendent Jurisdiction, 81 Harv.L.Rev. 657, 664 (1968)." In that decision, involving federal claims under the copyright laws and state claims of unfair trade practice and unfair competition, including a defendant not named in the copyright claims, we held that a federal court had power to hear a state claim against a party not named in the federal claim, provided the *Gibbs* test was met,

1. For a sharp criticism of *Gibbs* see Shakman, The New Pendent Jurisdiction of the Federal Courts, 20 Stan.L.Rev. 262 (1967).

2. According to the Reviser this provision was "intended to avoid 'piecemeal' litigation to enforce common-law and statutory copyright, patent, and trade-mark rights by specifically permitting such enforcement in a single civil action in the district court. While this is the rule under Federal decisions, this section would enact it as statutory authority. The problem is discussed at length in Hurn v. Oursler. . . ."

noting that this conclusion was buttressed by our decisions concerning ancillary jurisdiction to entertain compulsory counterclaims under F.R. Civ.P. 13(a), United Artists Corp. v. Masterpiece Productions, Inc., 221 F.2d 213 (2 Cir. 1955), and third-party claims under F.R.Civ.P. 14(a), Dery v. Wyer, 265 F.2d 804 (2 Cir. 1959).

It is true that in those cases, as well as in *Astor-Honor*, the federal claim had arisen in the ordinary civil jurisdiction, whereas the federal claim in this action had been brought under the admiralty jurisdiction. At an earlier date, this difference might have affected our decision here. But the rules of procedure in the admiralty and civil jurisdictions were merged in 1966. . . .

In this case, the same facts are ultimately controlling with respect to both the state and federal claims; the desirability of having both claims tried in the same forum is self-evident.

451 F.2d at 809–11.

The view taken in *The Mormaclynx* was not unanimous. See, e.g., Hymer v. Chai, 407 F.2d 136 (9th Cir. 1969), refusing to allow a wife's claim of loss of consortium (not independently satisfying the jurisdictional amount) to be appended to her husband's federally cognizable claim for injuries based on the same accident, and stating only the conclusion:

> Joinder of claims, not joinder of parties, is the object of the doctrine. It was not designed to permit a party without a federally cognizable claim to invoke federal jurisdiction by joining a different party plaintiff asserting an independent federal claim growing out of the same operative facts.[3]

There were conflicting analogies: the liberal attitude toward ancillary jurisdiction despite incomplete diversity in multiparty cases, pp. 258–60 infra, and the miserly attitude toward ancillary jurisdiction over claims failing to satisfy the jurisdictional amount in multiparty cases, infra pp. 307–08. Which was the closer analogy to a case like *Finley* or *The Mormaclynx*? And what is the bearing of the relevant statutory language? [4]

(6) Does *Gibbs* survive *Finley*? Could Congress give federal courts pendent-party jurisdiction?

3. The Supreme Court, reviewing two later Ninth Circuit decisions, managed to leave the question open by finding other reasons why pendent jurisdiction had properly been refused. Moor v. Alameda County, 411 U.S. 693 (1973) ("unsettled . . . state law and the likelihood of jury confusion" due to "special defenses" available only to the third party); Aldinger v. Howard, 427 U.S. 1 (1976) (refusal of Congress to make local governments liable under 42 U.S.C. § 1983 precluded exercise of jurisdiction over pendent state-law claim against county) (see p. 398 infra). Language in each opinion commented inconclusively on the general question. On the one hand, for example, there was "a significant difference" between *Moor* and *Gibbs* because "the exercise of pendent jurisdiction . . . would require us to bring an entirely new party—a new defendant— into each litigation." On the other hand, "numerous decisions throughout the courts of appeals since *Gibbs* have recognized the existence of judicial power to hear pendent claims involving pendent parties. . . . *Hymer* stands virtually alone . . ., and significantly *Hymer* was largely based on . . . a decision which predated *Gibbs* and the expansion of the concept of pendent jurisdiction beyond the narrow limits set by *Hurn v. Oursler*. . . ." 411 U.S. at 713–14.

4. See generally Currie, Pendent Parties, 45 U.Chi.L.Rev. 753 (1978).

(7) When claims under Federal and state law are joined in a state court, when may the defendant remove? See 28 U.S.C. § 1441(c), enacted in 1948 (to replace a former provision that applied only to diversity cases):

> Whenever a separate and independent claim or cause of action, which would be removable if sued upon alone, is joined with one or more otherwise non-removable claims or causes of action, the entire case may be removed and the district court may determine all issues therein, or, in its discretion, may remand all matters not otherwise within its original jurisdiction.

Is the purpose of this section to prevent frustration of a defendant's right to a federal forum by the joinder of a claim under state law? If so, is it necessary? If the state-law claim is closely enough related to the federal to be pendent under *Gibbs*, presumably the entire case is removable under § 1441(a) because it is within the original jurisdiction of the federal court. If the claims are completely unrelated, there was authority that before 1948 the federal claim alone was removable under the general removal statute, which allowed removal of "any suit of a civil nature" arising under federal law, 28 U.S.C. § 71 (1940). See, e.g., Tillman v. Russo Asiatic Bank, 51 F.2d 1023 (2d Cir. 1931). Was Mr. Lewin correct in concluding, 66 Harv. L.Rev. 423, 426 (1953), that the 1948 revision excluded this possibility by amending the language to permit removal of "any civil action" arising under federal law? Assuming that it makes sense to permit removal of an unrelated federal claim and that § 1441(a) does not allow it, what is the reason—and the constitutional justification—for removing the state-law claim as well?

Before *Gibbs* it could have been argued that there were cases in which federal and state claims were sufficiently related to justify their trial in a single action, but which were not close enough to satisfy the *Hurn* test for pendent jurisdiction. In such cases there might have been a reason to allow removal of the entire case. After *Gibbs* and *American Fire & Cas. Co. v. Finn*, infra p. 260, is a "separate and independent" claim that will support removal under § 1441(c) one that is not pendent under *Gibbs*? [5]

(8) Townsend Corp. v. Davidson, 222 F.Supp. 1 (D.N.J.1963). The complaint charged violations of the Investment Company Act, 15 U.S.C. § 80a–1 et seq., and related breaches of fiduciary duties imposed by state law. Personal jurisdiction over the defendants for the federal claim was obtained by service of process outside the forum State under 15 U.S.C. § 80a–43, authorizing nationwide service of process in Investment Act cases. The court held service of process adequate as to the state-law claims as well on the theory of pendent jurisdiction. "This certainly would seem to be the better view as a matter of judicial economy and convenience of the parties where, as here, the same acts are alleged to be both a violation

5. Judge Posner has questioned whether § 1441(c) applies to federal question cases at all. Its purpose, he argued, was to prevent a plaintiff from frustrating removal by joinder of a nonremovable claim, and joinder of a nonfederal claim in a federal-question case "would not defeat removal." It would be odd, he added, "to attribute to Congress in 1948 an intent to broaden removability by bringing federal-question cases within the scope of the separate-claim removal section" since "the objective in revising [the] section . . . was to narrow it . . . ." Thomas v. Shelton, 740 F.2d 478, 484 (7th Cir.1984).

of the Act and also actionable under state law." The ALI would resolve the conflicting decisions by approving *Townsend*. ALI Study 28, 211–12.

But trial convenience is not the only factor limiting service of process on state-law claims, is it? Is it possible to protect the defendant from the risk that pendent personal jurisdiction may result in a change of the applicable law under *Klaxon Co. v. Stentor Elec. Mfg. Co.*, infra p. 347? Consider the analogy of *Van Dusen v. Barrack*, infra p. 352, which held that after change of venue under 28 U.S.C. § 1404(a) the court should ordinarily apply the law that would have been applied in the courts of the State where the action was originally filed.

Do the same considerations apply to venue? See Ferguson, Pendent Personal Jurisdiction in the Federal Courts, 11 Vill.L.Rev. 56, 73–75 (1965), compiling the decisions and concluding that there was no statutory authority for dispensing with either venue or personal-jurisdiction requirements respecting pendent claims, for the liberal process and venue provisions of the various securities statutes applied only to suits or actions "to enforce any liability or duty created by this subchapter." But see Note, Ancillary Process and Venue in the Federal Courts, 73 Harv.L.Rev. 1164, 1175–76 (1960):

> Any literal statutory barriers to pendent process and venue seem to be eliminated by the analogy of the determination that for purposes of subject-matter jurisdiction the pendent claim is included within one of those "civil actions wherein the matter in controversy arises under [federal law]". (§ 1331).

Should there be pendent venue and personal jurisdiction over third parties impleaded under Fed.R.Civ.P. 14?

(9) Justice Brennan declared in *Gibbs* that there could be pendent jurisdiction only if the federal claim had "substance sufficient to confer subject matter jurisdiction on the court." The dissenters in *Bell v. Hood*, infra p. 409, in which the Court held that a complaint should not be dismissed for want of jurisdiction if it stated a "substantial" though meritless federal claim, thought the effect of that decision would be to permit a federal trial of pendent state claims. Yet the district court in *Bell*, dismissing the federal claim on remand for failure to state a claim, 71 F.Supp. 813, 820–21 (S.D.Cal.1947), dismissed the state-law claims as well as the federal because the latter was "entirely wanting." Observe the statement on this subject in *Gibbs*: "Certainly, if the federal claims are dismissed before trial, even though not insubstantial in a jurisdictional sense, the state claims should be dismissed as well." Why? Because "the dog would be wagged by his tail if plenary trial of an ancillary claim was compelled by a primary claim which could be disposed of on the pleadings?" Hart & Wechsler, The Federal Courts and the Federal System 925 (2d ed. 1973). But suppose the state-law claims can also be disposed of on the pleadings. Can the dismissal of pendent state claims in any of these cases be squared with the common principle that jurisdiction once attached is not ousted by later events? E.g., St. Paul Mercury Indemnity Co. v. Red Cab Co., 303 U.S. 283 (1938) (reduction of damage claim to less than jurisdictional minimum after filing of diversity suit). Can *Gibbs*'s characterization of pendent jurisdiction as discretionary be reconciled with Chief Justice

Marshall's view that a federal court had "no more right to decline the exercise of jurisdiction which is given than to usurp that which is not given. . . ."? Cohens v. Virginia, 19 U.S. (6 Wheat.) 264, 404 (1821). Cf. *Railroad Commission v. Pullman Co.*, infra p. 485.[6]

SECTION 3. MARITIME CASES

ROMERO v. INTERNATIONAL TERMINAL OPERATING CO.

358 U.S. 354 (1959).

[Romero sued his employer, Compania Trasatlantica, and others in a federal district court, claiming damages for personal injuries suffered aboard a vessel. His claims were based on the Jones Act, 46 U.S.C. § 688, and on the federal maritime doctrines of unseaworthiness and of maintenance and cure. The District Court dismissed the complaint for lack of jurisdiction. The Jones Act, that court held, did not apply to foreign seamen in such circumstances. The claims under the maritime common law were dismissed because there was no diversity of citizenship and because such claims did not arise under federal law within 28 U.S.C. § 1331. The Court of Appeals affirmed.]

MR. JUSTICE FRANKFURTER delivered the opinion of the Court.

[The Court first held that a substantial claim had been asserted under the Jones Act and that that claim should not have been dismissed for lack of jurisdiction.] . . .

Jurisdiction under 28 U.S.C. § 1331. Petitioner, a Spanish subject, asserts claims under the general maritime law against Compania Trasatlantica, a Spanish corporation. The jurisdiction of the Federal District Court, sitting as a court of law, was invoked under the provisions of the Judiciary Act of 1875 which granted jurisdiction to the lower federal courts "of all suits of a civil nature at common law or in equity, . . . arising under the Constitution or laws of the United States, . . ." (now 28 U.S.C. § 1331). Whether the Act of 1875 permits maritime claims rooted in federal law to be brought on the law side of the lower federal courts has recently been raised in litigation and has become the subject of conflicting decisions among Courts of Appeals. Jurisdiction has been sustained in the First Circuit, Doucette v. Vincent, 194 F.2d 834, and denied in the Second and Third, Jordine v. Walling, 185 F.2d 662; Paduano v. Yamashita Kisen Kabushiki Kaisha, 221 F.2d 615. . . .

Section 9 of the First Judiciary Act granted the District Courts maritime jurisdiction. This jurisdiction has remained unchanged in substance to the present day. Indeed it was recognition of the need for federal tribunals to exercise admiralty jurisdiction that was one of the

6. See also Carnegie-Mellon Univ. v. Cohill, 484 U.S. 343 (1988), permitting *remand* of a pendent claim to state court after dismissal of the federal claim. Is this conclusion consistent with 28 U.S.C. § 1447(c)?

controlling considerations for the establishment of a system of lower federal courts. . . .

Section 9 not only established federal courts for the administration of maritime law; it recognized that some remedies in matters maritime had been traditionally administered by common-law courts of the original States. This role of the States in the administration of maritime law was preserved in the famous "saving clause"—"saving to suitors, in all cases, the right of a common-law remedy, where the common law is competent to give it." Since the original Judiciary Act also endowed the federal courts with diversity jurisdiction, common-law remedies for maritime causes could be enforced by the then Circuit Courts when the proper diversity of parties afforded access.

Up to the passage of the Judiciary Act of 1875 these jurisdictional bases provided the only claim for jurisdiction in the federal courts in maritime matters. The District Courts, endowed with "exclusive original cognizance of all civil causes of admiralty and maritime jurisdiction," sat to enforce the comprehensive federal interest in the law of the sea which had been a major reason for their creation. This jurisdiction was exercised according to the historic procedure in admiralty, by a judge without a jury. In addition, common-law remedies were, under the saving clause, enforcible in the courts of the States and on the common-law side of the lower federal courts when the diverse citizenship of the parties permitted. Except in diversity cases, maritime litigation brought in state courts could not be removed to the federal courts.

The Judiciary Act of 1875 effected an extensive enlargement of the jurisdiction of the lower federal courts. For the first time their doors were opened to "all suits of a civil nature at common law or in equity, . . . arising under the Constitution or laws of the United States, or treaties made, or which shall be made, under their authority. . . ." From 1875 to 1950 there is not to be found a hint or suggestion to cast doubt on the conviction that the language of that statute was taken straight from Art. III, § 2, cl. 1, extending the judicial power of the United States "to all Cases, in Law and Equity, arising under this Constitution, the Laws of the United States, and Treaties made, or which shall be made, under their Authority." Indeed what little legislative history there is affirmatively indicates that this was the source. Thus the Act of 1875 drew on the scope of this provision of Clause 1, just as the Judiciary Act of 1789 reflected the constitutional authorization of Clause 1 of Section 2, which extended the judicial power "to all Cases of admiralty and maritime Jurisdiction."

These provisions of Article III are two of the nine separately enumerated classes of cases to which "judicial Power" was extended by the Constitution and which thereby authorized grants by Congress of "judicial Power" to the "inferior" federal courts. The vast stream of litigation which has flowed through these courts from the beginning has done so on the assumption that, in dealing with a subject as technical as the jurisdiction of the courts, the Framers, predominantly lawyers, used precise, differentiating and not redundant language. This assumption, reflected in The Federalist Papers, was authoritatively confirmed by Mr. Chief Justice Marshall in American Ins. Co. v. Canter, 1 Pet. [26 U.S.] 511, 544:

> "We are therefore to inquire, whether cases in admiralty, and cases arising under the laws and Constitution of the United States, are identical.
>
> "If we have recourse to that pure fountain from which all the jurisdiction of the Federal Courts is derived, we find language employed which cannot well be misunderstood. The Constitution declares, that 'the judicial power shall extend to all cases in law and equity, arising under this Constitution, the laws of the United States, and treaties made, or which shall be made, under their authority; to all cases affecting ambassadors, or other public ministers, and consuls; to all cases of admiralty and maritime jurisdiction.'
>
> "The Constitution certainly contemplates these as three distinct classes of cases; and if they are distinct, the grant of jurisdiction over one of them does not confer jurisdiction over either of the other two. The discrimination made between them, in the Constitution, is, we think, conclusive against their identity." See also The Sarah, 8 Wheat. [21 U.S.] 391.

This lucid principle of constitutional construction, embodied in one of Marshall's frequently quoted opinions, was never brought into question until 1952. It had been treated as black-letter law in leading treatises. It was part of the realm of legal ideas in which the authors of the Act of 1875 moved. Certainly the accomplished lawyers who drafted the Act of 1875 drew on the language of the constitutional grant on the assumption that they were dealing with a distinct class of cases, that the language incorporated in their enactment precluded "identity" with any other class of cases contained in Article III. Thus the grant of jurisdiction over "suits of a civil nature at common law or in equity . . . arising under the Constitution or laws of the United States . . ." in the Act of 1875, as derived from Article III, could not reasonably be thought of as comprehending an entirely separate and distinct class of cases—"Cases of admiralty and maritime Jurisdiction."

Of course all cases to which "judicial power" extends "arise," in a comprehensive, non-jurisdictional sense of the term, "under this Constitution." It is the Constitution that is the ultimate source of all "judicial Power"—defines grants and implies limits—and so "all Cases of admiralty and maritime Jurisdiction" arise under the Constitution in the sense that they have constitutional sanction. But they are not "Cases, in Law and Equity, arising under this Constitution. . . ."

Neither the aim of the Act of 1875 to provide a forum for the vindication of new federally created rights, nor the pressures which led to its enactment, suggest, even remotely, the inclusion of maritime claims within the scope of that statute. The provision of the Act of

1875 with which we are concerned was designed to give a new content of jurisdiction to the federal courts, not to reaffirm one long-established, smoothly functioning since 1789. We have uncovered no basis for finding the additional design of changing the method by which federal courts had administered admiralty law from the beginning. The federal admiralty courts had been completely adequate to the task of protecting maritime rights rooted in federal law. There is not the slightest indication of any intention, or of any professional or lay demands for a change in the time-sanctioned mode of trying suits in admiralty without a jury, from which it can be inferred that by the new grant of jurisdiction of cases "arising under the Constitution or laws" a drastic innovation was impliedly introduced in admiralty procedure, whereby Congress changed the method by which federal courts had administered admiralty law for almost a century. To draw such an inference is to find that a revolutionary procedural change had undesignedly come to pass. If we are now to attribute such a result to Congress the sole remaining justification for the federal admiralty courts which have played such a vital role in our federal judicial system for 169 years will be to provide a federal forum for the small number of maritime claims which derive from state law, and to afford the ancient remedy of a libel *in rem* in those limited instances when an *in personam* judgment would not suffice to satisfy a claim. . . .

[Moreover,] the infusion of general maritime jurisdiction into the Act of 1875 . . . would have a disruptive effect on the traditional allocation of power over maritime affairs in our federal system.

Thus the historic option of a maritime suitor pursuing a common-law remedy to select his forum, state or federal, would be taken away by an expanded view of § 1331, since saving-clause actions would then be freely removable under § 1441 of Title 28. . . . By making maritime cases removable to the federal courts it would make considerable inroads into the traditionally exercised concurrent jurisdiction of the state courts in admiralty matters—a jurisdiction which it was the unquestioned aim of the saving clause of 1789 to preserve. . . .

To claim that all enforced rights pertaining to matters maritime are rooted in federal law is a destructive oversimplification. . . . It is true that state law must yield to the needs of a uniform federal maritime law when this Court finds inroads on a harmonious system. But this limitation still leaves the States a wide scope. State-created liens are enforced in admiralty. State remedies for wrongful death and state statutes providing for the survival of actions, both historically absent from the relief offered by the admiralty, have been upheld when applied to maritime causes of action. . . . If jurisdiction of maritime claims were allowed to be invoked under § 1331, it would become necessary for courts to decide whether the action "arises under federal law," and this jurisdictional decision would largely depend on whether the governing law is state or federal. Determinations of this nature are among the most difficult and subtle that federal courts are called upon to make. . . . This Court has been able to wait until an actual conflict between state and federal standards has arisen, and only then proceed to resolve the problem of whether the State was free to regulate or federal law must govern. . . .

Typical also of the consequences that are implicit in this proposed modification of maritime jurisdiction, is the restriction of venue that would result from this novel interpretation of § 1331 of the Act of 1875. Litigants of diverse citizenship are now able to invoke the federal law forum for the trial of saving-clause cases. Such litigants are aided in their search for a federal forum by the liberality of the venue provisions applicable to actions based on diversity of citizenship. These provisions allow the action to be brought either "where all plaintiffs or all defendants reside." If saving-clause actions were to be brought within the scope of § 1331, this choice could be no longer made. Plaintiffs would be subject to the rigid requirement that suit must be "brought only in the judicial district where all defendants reside . . ." and this would be so even where there is, in fact, diversity of citizenship. . . .

The considerations of history and policy which investigation has illuminated are powerfully reinforced by the deeply felt and traditional reluctance of this Court to expand the jurisdiction of the federal courts through a broad reading of jurisdictional statutes. A reluctance which must be even more forcefully felt when the expansion is proposed for the first time, eighty-three years after the jurisdiction has been conferred. Mr. Justice Stone, speaking of the Act of 1875, pointed out that "[t]he policy of the statute calls for its strict construction. . . . Due regard for the rightful independence of state governments, which should actuate federal courts, requires that they scrupulously confine their own jurisdiction to the precise limits which the statute has defined." Certainly this wise counsel is deeply persuasive when we are asked to accept a doctrine which would cut into a jurisdiction exercised by the States since Colonial days. . . .

"Pendent" and Diversity Jurisdiction.—Rejection of the proposed new reading of § 1331 does not preclude consideration of petitioner's claims under the general maritime law. These claims cannot, we have seen, be justified under § 1331. However, the District Court may have jurisdiction of them "pendent" to its jurisdiction under the Jones Act. Of course the considerations which call for the exercise of pendent jurisdiction of a state claim related to a pending federal cause of action within the appropriate scope of the doctrine of Hurn v. Oursler, 289 U.S. 238, are not the same when, as here, what is involved are related claims based on the federal maritime law. We perceive no barrier to the exercise of "pendent jurisdiction" in the very limited circumstances before us. Here we merely decide that a district court has jurisdiction to determine whether a cause of action has been stated if that jurisdiction has been invoked by a complaint at law rather than by a libel in admiralty, as long as the complaint also properly alleges a claim under

the Jones Act. We are not called upon to decide whether the District Court may submit to the jury the "pendent" claims under the general maritime law in the event that a cause of action be found to exist. . . .

[Finally, the Court held the Jones Act and the doctrines of unseaworthiness and maintenance inapplicable to a Spanish seaman injured aboard a Spanish ship in Hoboken harbor and sent the case back for further proceedings on negligence counts against American defendants.]

MR. JUSTICE BRENNAN, dissenting in part and concurring in part. . . .

In a long series of decisions tracing from Southern Pacific Co. v. Jensen, 244 U.S. 205, this Court has made it clear that, in a seaman's action to recover damages for a maritime tort from his employer, the substantive law to be applied is federal maritime law made applicable as part of the laws of the United States by the Constitution itself, and that the right of recovery, if any, is a federally created right. . . .

Since petitioner's causes of action for unseaworthiness and for maintenance and cure are created by federal law, his case arises under "the laws . . . of the United States" within the meaning of § 1331, for it is clear that "a suit arises under the law that creates the cause of action." Holmes, J., in American Well Works Co. v. Layne & Bowler Co., 241 U.S. 257, 260. The contention cannot be accepted that since petitioner's rights are judicially defined, The Osceola, 189 U.S. 158, they are not created by "the laws . . . of the United States" within the meaning of § 1331; or, in other words, that only maritime rights created by Act of Congress are created by "the laws . . . of the United States." In another context, that of state law, this Court has recognized that the statutory word "laws" includes court decisions. Erie R. Co. v. Tompkins, 304 U.S. 64. . . .

Any argument that § 1333 is an exclusive grant of jurisdiction would be false to the history of enactments allocating the judicial power of the United States. The fact that, in a diversity case under § 1332, the claimant is free to proceed on the law side of the federal court to enforce rights created by the federal maritime law, Seas Shipping Co. v. Sieracki, 328 U.S. 85, 88–89, clearly runs counter to any theory that the federal courts, because of § 9 of the Judiciary Act of 1789, can adjudicate maritime claims only while sitting in admiralty. There is no compelling reason why § 1333, which does not exclude maritime actions from being brought at law in a federal court under § 1332, should exclude them from being so brought under § 1331. Indeed, I find it a gross anomaly to hold, as the Court holds today, that an action rooted in federal law can be brought on the law side of a federal court only if the diversity jurisdiction, usually a vehicle for the enforcement of state-created rights, can be invoked. . . .

The Court argues, however, that Congress, aware of Chief Justice Marshall's statement that Article III created the admiralty jurisdiction as "distinct" from the "arising under" jurisdiction, American Ins. Co. v. Canter, supra, at page 545, intended that the jurisdictional statutes be mutually exclusive. . . .

The issue before us is not whether all cases "of admiralty and maritime jurisdiction" are *per se* encompassed in the statutory "arising under" jurisdiction. A suit seeking the sort of remedy that the common law is not competent to give could not be fairly contended to lie under § 1331; it would clearly be the sort of suit in which the jurisdictional grant of § 1333 was intended to be exclusive. The issue before us concerns only actions maintainable in some forum "at law" under the Saving Clause. And again, the issue is not even the narrower one whether Saving Clause actions are *per se* cognizable under § 1331. The tests of jurisdiction under § 1331 must still be met, and there is no contention that they are met merely by a showing that an action is one maintainable under the Saving Clause and involving the requisite jurisdictional amount. The plaintiff's right to recovery must still be one rooted in federal substantive law, and it has quite recently been made clear that there are Saving Clause actions that do not meet that test. Wilburn Boat Co. v. Fireman's Fund Ins. Co., 348 U.S. 310. The issue before us is only whether the fact that an action is a Saving Clause action excludes it from § 1331 where it would otherwise be maintainable thereunder.

At issue in American Ins. Co. v. Canter was the power of a territorial court to make a decree selling cargo to satisfy a maritime lien *in rem* existing in favor of its salvors. A state court, even under the Saving Clause, could not pass such a decree at all; it is the enforcement of the classic admiralty remedy, and a matter solely within the competence of the federal admiralty courts. The Hine v. Trevor, 4 Wall. [71 U.S.] 555. In the passage from Marshall's opinion relied upon, the Chief Justice was saying only that the Act of Congress which conferred on certain territorial courts jurisdiction in "cases arising under the laws and constitution of the United States," § 8, 3 Stat. 752, did not by that token alone grant them power to enforce a remedy peculiarly within the competence of admiralty courts. In its broadest permissible interpretation, the dictum only means that the fact that the Constitution creates admiralty *jurisdiction* does not make all admiralty cases arising under the Constitution. But Marshall's opinion does not say that an action seeking remedial relief of a sort which the common law is competent to give, and in which the plaintiff's right to recover is rooted in federal law, ceases to be a suit arising under the laws of the United States merely because it is of a maritime nature. . . .

The fact that the jurisdictional categories are separate and distinct, as Marshall demonstrates, does not mean that a particular action could not come under the heading of more than one of them. Everyone recognizes that this is the case in a maritime matter in which the parties are of diverse citizenship. I see no reason why it should not be true here of Romero's general maritime law claims against his employer. . . .

The Chief Justice joins in this opinion, and Mr. Justice Black and Mr. Justice Douglas join in it except to the extent indicated in their dissents. [Justice Brennan agreed with the Court that American law was inapplicable on the merits; Justices Black and Douglas dissented on this issue.]

Notes on "Laws of the United States"

(1) Why was it necessary to decide whether Romero's claim was one arising under federal law? Did the Court contemplate dismissing the suit for want of jurisdiction?

(2) On remand Romero waived jury trial in his action against other defendants and lost on the merits. 286 F.2d 347 (2d Cir. 1961). In Fitzgerald v. United States Lines, 374 U.S. 16 (1963), the Court held that a seaman's claims for maintenance and cure and for unseaworthiness should be submitted to the jury along with his Jones Act claim, even in the absence of diversity, as a matter of trial convenience. Does this mean the right to a jury will never depend upon whether there is jurisdiction under § 1331 or § 1332?

(3) What has "pendent jurisdiction" to do with *Romero*? See Note, The Supreme Court 1958 Term, 73 Harv.L.Rev. 84, 138–46 (1959).

(4) Does *Romero* mean that cases arising under federal maritime *statutes* cannot be brought under § 1331? For a negative answer see Wethering, Jurisdictional Bases of Maritime Claims Founded on Acts of Congress, 18 U.Miami L.Rev. 163 (1963). Does it matter?

(5) Marine Cooks & Stewards, AFL v. Panama Steamship Co., 265 F.2d 780 (9th Cir. 1959), and Khedivial Line v. Seafarers' International Union, 278 F.2d 49 (2d Cir. 1960), were suits for injunctions against the picketing of vessels on navigable waters, brought in the federal courts under 28 U.S.C. § 1331. *Marine Cooks* was ultimately thrown out on the basis of the Norris-LaGuardia Act, which limits federal injunctions in labor disputes, 362 U.S. 365 (1960). But the Courts of Appeals took different views as to the scope of § 1331 and the meaning of the *Romero* case.

In *Marine Cooks* the court found the suit to be based on federal maritime law because it concerned "interference with maritime traffic on navigable waters and . . . interference with the performance of a maritime contract constituting maritime torts," and acknowledged that *Romero* had excluded saving-clause actions from § 1331:

> The Supreme Court thus held that Congress in utilizing the language of the Constitution in its statutory grants of jurisdiction intended to separate *admiralty and maritime* on the one hand from *law and equity* on the other. Therefore appellee's argument that jurisdiction can be found under § 1331 because it is a savings clause action would be of no avail. But we are convinced that this is not a saving clause

> action. This is an action for an injunction, and admiralty at no time has had jurisdiction of such actions. We emphasize, this is not an action "saved" from the exclusive jurisdiction of admiralty; it is one never cognizable in admiralty. In terms of the Supreme Court distinction made in Romero, it is not a "case of admiralty and maritime jurisdiction" but a suit "of a civil nature . . . in equity" arising because of a breach of federal duty. It cannot be said of this action as it is of "saving clause" actions, that Congress did not intend to give a double jurisdiction as there is no jurisdiction under § 1333.

The Second Circuit in *Khedivial* disagreed:

> Decision on this issue is controlled by Romero v. International Terminal Operating Co., 358 U.S. 354. The rationale of that case, as we read it, is that . . . a tort under the general maritime law is not cognizable by a federal court under 28 U.S.C. § 1331 but only under 28 U.S.C. § 1333; consequently, a plaintiff alleging only a claim for a tort under the general maritime law may have from a federal court such remedies as admiralty can give and no others. . . . It is true that the gap in admiralty jurisdiction here involved may be more important than was that in Romero—jury trial of a personal injury claim on the law side and trial to a judge in admiralty may both result in an award of money damages—whereas here admiralty may award damages only and not an injunction. But we find nothing in Romero to justify reading "under the Constitution, laws or treaties of the United States" in 28 U.S.C. § 1331 to include the general maritime law in cases where admiralty is not competent to give the remedy the plaintiff seeks. . . . We need not consider whether if plaintiff had alleged a substantial and sufficiently related federal claim, the District Court could issue an injunction in aid of plaintiff's claim of maritime tort under the pendent jurisdiction doctrine, see 358 U.S. at pages 380–381; for here no other substantial federal claim was asserted.

(6) As advocated by the ALI Study (p. 181), and for reasons given by Mr. Justice Brennan in *Romero*, the Supreme Court in dismissing an original action for interstate pollution declared that a district court would have jurisdiction under § 1331 because the issue was governed by federal common law. Illinois v. City of Milwaukee, 406 U.S. 91 (1972), infra p. 360.

(7) Proposing to retain the present reference to "laws of the United States" for district-court jurisdiction, the ALI conceded that language had created interpretive difficulties as in *Romero* and in cases under other federal common law. Moreover, the Institute cited cases as holding an interstate compact was not such a "law" under § 1331, e.g., Hinderlider v. La Plata River Co., 304 U.S. 92, 109–10 (1938),[1] and observed that it would

1. Concluding that the Supreme Court had not settled the question, and citing Petty v. Missouri-Tennessee Bridge Comm'n, infra p. 360, which held the interpretation of a compact was a federal question, the Ninth Circuit has held that a compact is a law of the United States within § 1331. League to Save Lake Tahoe v. Tahoe Reg. Plan. Agency, 507 F.2d 517 (1974). The same court has since extended its holding to encompass an ordinance enacted by an agency set up by interstate compact: "Differing interpretations by state courts . . . could impair the effectiveness of the regional plan." [So?] League to Save Lake Tahoe v. B. J. K. Corp., 547 F.2d 1072, 1075 (9th Cir.1976).

be reasonable to hold local laws of the District of Columbia were not either: "There is no justification for permitting a suit arising out of an automobile accident between two Maryland citizens to be heard in the federal court in Maryland simply because they happen to collide in the District of Columbia." ALI Study 179–80. This last exception was enacted in 1970, 28 U.S.C. § 1363: "For the purposes of this chapter [§§ 1331–63], references to the laws of the United States or Acts of Congress do not include laws applicable exclusively to the District of Columbia."

Do you agree that the statute should leave "laws" otherwise undefined?

Notes on the Admiralty Jurisdiction

A. History and Purpose

(1) The law of the sea is a gold mine for legal archaeology. Its age is that of maritime commerce itself. Its history is entwined with that of the Law Merchant, that international, supposedly uniform body of customs administered throughout the civilized world by tribunals independent of the territorial sovereign. Legend has it that the Emperor Antoninus once said in refusing to hear a shipwreck case:

> I am indeed the supreme lord of the land. But custom is the lord of the sea. Let this case be decided by the sea-law of the Rhodians, which our law accepts.

Though discredited by many, the enchanting tradition persists of a maritime code promulgated as early as 300 B.C. on the Island of Rhodes. Customs prevailing during the Middle Ages are said to be reflected in the surviving codifications: The Tablets of Amalfi, the Consolato del Mare (Barcelona), the laws of Oleron and of Wisby, the Ordonnance de la Marine of Louis XIV. Most influential of these upon the English admiralty were the Laws of Oleron—romantically, but (alas) apparently erroneously, attributed to Richard the Lion Hearted (and sometimes to his mother) on his return from the Crusades—, which with those of Wisby are available, prosaically, at 30 Fed.Cas. 1171 et seq. These laws contain, along with distinctive maritime doctrines very much alive today (salvage, general average, maintenance and cure), a great many quaint and specific provisions about shipwrecks, brigands, and the care and feeding of the crew:

> The mariners of Brittany ought to have but one meal a day from the kitchen, because they have beverage going and coming. But those of Normandy are to have two meals a day, because they have only water at the ship's allowance. . . .
>
> If a pilot undertakes the conduct of a vessel, to bring her to St. Malo, or any other port, and fail of his duty therein, so as the vessel miscarry by reason of his ignorance in what he undertook, and the merchants sustain damage thereby, he shall be obliged to make full satisfaction for the same, if he hath wherewithal; and if not, lose his head.

In England, as elsewhere, maritime law was administered by merchants' courts until the middle of the Fourteenth Century. At that point, because of "diplomatic difficulties in which the king found himself involved, from the want of some efficient authority to coerce the marauding and piratical propensities of his subjects," additional powers were given to the Lord High Admiral, commander of the Navy, whose name was probably derived from the Arabic amir-al-baha, ruler of the sea, and whose original duties were administrative and disciplinary.

The Admiral's jurisdiction was of two kinds: "prize" and "instance." Prize was concerned with the disposition of enemy captures; instance embraced ordinary civil and criminal jurisdiction and "droits of the Admiral" (which included rights to flotsam and jetsam—distinguished according to whether the goods had gone down with the ship or been jettisoned). The Admiral's one-time exclusive jurisdiction over crimes at sea was taken away in 1536, for his rule requiring proof by witnesses produced too few convictions. In the civil sphere the Admiral apparently was unable to restrain himself: His encroachments upon the jurisdiction of the merchants' courts provoked Parliament during the reign of Richard II (1389, 1391) to forbid him to "meddle of anything done within the realm" or "within the bodies of counties," but "only of a thing done upon the sea." These limits were imperfectly observed, and Sir Edward Coke waged jealous war against the Admiralty as he did against Chancery by repeated writs of prohibition. See Cradock's Case, 2 Brownl. & G. pt. 2, 37, 123 E.R. 801 (1601); 4th Inst. 134–45. Some writers have suggested that "nothing was to be left to the Admiralty of which the common law could conveniently take cognizance," Roscoe, Admiralty Practice 8–9 (5th ed. 1931), and therefore that admiralty's power was very largely limited to the in rem process unknown to the common law. See Morrison, The Remedial Powers of the Admiralty, 43 Yale L.J. 1, 8–9 (1933). At the time of the Restoration the jurisdiction seems to have been limited essentially to contracts made and to be performed at sea, torts committed there, and suits for seamen's wages.

Vice-admiralty courts in the colonies, some say, were free from the restrictions of Richard II and from Coke's prohibitions; sitting without a jury, they were of great use to the King in dealing with occasionally restive settlers. The one national court under the Articles of Confederation was an admiralty court, designed to hear appeals in prize cases. By the time of the Ratification Debates it seems to have been taken for granted that admiralty ought to be a national subject: "The most bigoted idolizers of State authority," Hamilton wrote, "have not thus far shown a disposition to deny the National Judiciary the cognizance of maritime causes." The Federalist, No. 80.[1]

(2) The Constitution extends federal judicial power to "all cases of admiralty and maritime jurisdiction," and § 9 of the 1789 Judiciary Act (1 Stat. 76) gave the district courts "exclusive original cognizance of all civil causes of admiralty and maritime jurisdiction," including seizures, "saving

1. The history is detailed in 1 W. Holdsworth, A History of English Law 526–73 (4th ed. 1931); Mears, The History of the Admiralty Jurisdiction, 2 AALS Select Essays in Anglo-American Legal History 312 (1908); G. Gilmore & C. Black, Admiralty 1–11 (2d Ed. 1975); Putnam, How the Federal Courts Were Given Admiralty Jurisdiction, 10 Corn.L.Q. 460 (1925). See also the famous (and controverted) account by Mr. Justice Story in DeLovio v. Boit, 7 F.Cas. 418 (C.C.D.Mass.1815), (No. 3,776), and the dissenting opinions cited in note 4, infra.

to suitors, in all cases, the right of a common law remedy, where the common law is competent to give it." The same section exempted "civil causes of admiralty and maritime jurisdiction" from the requirement of trial by jury. The basic provision, now 28 U.S.C. § 1333, is substantially the same except for the 1948 revision changing "common law remedy" to "all other remedies" to which suitors are "otherwise entitled." [2]

(3) Why was admiralty made a federal subject? One reason, somewhat reminiscent of the origins of the English court of Admiralty, is found in The Federalist, No. 80: Maritime causes "so generally depend upon the law of nations, and so commonly affect the rights of foreigners, that they fall within the considerations which are relative to the public peace." What this meant, apparently, was that injustice to foreigners might get us into diplomatic difficulties, and therefore that federal courts should have authority to prevent it. The capture of foreign vessels furnished an especially vivid illustration of these difficulties, and the Supreme Court in its early years decided more than one prize case with important international ramifications. E.g., Glass v. The Sloop Betsey, 3 U.S. (3 Dall.) 6 (1794); see 1 C. Warren, The Supreme Court in United States History 105–18 (Rev. ed. 1926). This jurisdiction has withered away (but see N. Healy & B. Currie, Cases on Admiralty 14 (1965), noting a 1956 revision of the governing statutes and a 1950 Navy manual of instructions for Prize Masters), because, as Professor Stolz has put it, "civilization has matured to the point where ships are sunk rather than stolen." Stolz, footnote 2 supra, 51 Cal.L. Rev. at 669. Professor Stolz concludes that the prize question "probably explains the general acquiescence in the grant of admiralty jurisdiction." Ibid. But if the rights of foreigners were the sole reason for the grant, why wasn't the whole matter taken care of by the jurisdiction over controversies between States or their citizens and foreign states or subjects?

The second commonly encountered reason for the admiralty power is the desirability of a uniform maritime law, although the often-cited remarks of Madison and of Randolph, 3 Elliott's Debates 532, 571 (2d ed. 1900), linked this policy with the impact of maritime litigation upon foreign relations. See Knickerbocker Ice Co. v. Stewart, 253 U.S. 149, 160 (1920); D. Currie, Federalism and the Admiralty: The Devil's Own Mess, 1960 Sup. Ct.Rev. 158, 163 & n. 26. Some commentators have postulated simply a federal interest in the maritime industry: As Professor Black says, the jurisdictional grant "evidences a strong federal interest in the orderly and uniform judicial governance of the concerns of the maritime industry." Admiralty Jurisdiction: Critique and Suggestions, 50 Colum.L.Rev. 259, 262 (1950). See also Stolz, supra, 51 Cal.L.Rev. at 665:

> The original purpose and the sole modern justification for federal admiralty law is the promotion and protection of what may variously

2. Prize jurisdiction is preserved in § 1333(2) and criminal in 18 U.S.C. § 7, which defines the "special maritime and territorial jurisdiction of the United States" to include "the high seas, and other waters [or American-owned vessels] within the admiralty and maritime jurisdiction of the United States and out of the jurisdiction of any particular State" and, for some strange reason, federally licensed vessels on the Great Lakes, as well as certain federal lands and aircraft over the high seas or other non-State waters. See Hoopengarner v. United States, 270 F.2d 465, 470–71 (6th Cir. 1959); Stolz, Pleasure Boating and Admiralty: Erie at Sea, 51 Cal.L.Rev. 661, 667 n. 27 (1963).

be called the business of shipping, the maritime industry, or commerce by water.

B. Waters Within the Jurisdiction

(4) In a series of dissenting opinions during the nineteenth century Justices Woodbury, Daniel, and Campbell, fighting the tide of decisions (sorry about that), maintained that the admiralty jurisdiction was limited, as it had been in England, to the high seas, excluding even salt-water harbors "within the bodies of counties"—even though the old common-law insistence upon jurors from the place the cause arose, which may have been one justification for the English rule, had long since been limited to a few actions respecting land. The dissenters bolstered their historical view with policy arguments about protecting litigants from the "alien" civil law applied in admiralty, securing the right to a jury, and preserving state rights. See, e.g., Waring v. Clarke, 46 U.S. (5 How.) 441 (1847); The Genesee Chief, 53 U.S. (12 How.) 443 (1851); The Magnolia, 61 U.S. (20 How.) 296 (1857) (dissenting opinions).

The majority of the Court never espoused this position. Even in The Thomas Jefferson, 23 U.S. (10 Wheat.) 428 (1825), in denying jurisdiction over a libel for wages earned on a Missouri River voyage, the Court declared that admiralty's authority was coextensive with "the ebb and flow of the tide," and in *Waring v. Clarke*, supra, the majority upheld admiralty jurisdiction over a collision 203 miles up the Mississippi River because the tide, although saltless and without reversing the current, raised the water level there.

In 1845 Congress passed a statute (drafted, it is said by Mr. Justice Story, see Note, From Judicial Grant to Legislative Power: The Admiralty Clause in the Nineteenth Century, 67 Harv.L.Rev. 1214 (1954)) purporting to extend federal jurisdiction to certain cases arising upon the Great Lakes and their connecting waters, 5 Stat. 726, and in response the Court repudiated the tidal limitation in the famous case of *The Genesee Chief*, supra, upholding jurisdiction over a collision on Lake Ontario. The Court was emphatic to deny that Congress, even by invoking the commerce power, could confer jurisdiction beyond that embraced by the admiralty clause of Article III. Compare *National Mut. Ins. Co. v. Tidewater Co.*, supra p. 128. But that clause itself, the Court held, was not limited to tidewaters. *The Thomas Jefferson*, which had adopted the limitation, had been decided "when the commerce on the rivers of the west and on the lakes was in its infancy, and of little importance," and the matter had not received the "deliberate consideration" it deserved in more civilized times. The lakes "are in truth inland seas. Different States border on them on one side, and a foreign nation on the other." They were used for interstate and foreign commerce and had been the scene of naval battles and prize captures. "There is certainly nothing in the ebb and flow of the tide that makes the waters peculiarly suitable for admiralty jurisdiction;" the reason for defining the English jurisdiction as limited to tidal waters was that "there was no navigable stream in the country beyond the ebb and flow of the tide."

There might have been some justification for limiting the new definition to the Great Lakes, which as the opinion pointed out were seas in everything but salinity and the effects of the moon's gravity; but much of the Court's reasoning went further, and the opinion concluded that the reasons for jurisdiction extended to every "public navigable water, on which commerce is carried on between different States or nations." Successive cases upheld jurisdiction over a collision above tidewater in the Alabama River, which is wholly within one State and outside the Act of 1845; an intrastate contract of carriage upon a river navigable in interstate commerce; a Great Lakes case not within the 1845 Act (intended to expand the jurisdiction, the statute could not be read to limit it); [3] and a collision on the Illinois-Michigan Canal, which was artificial, entirely in one State, and state-owned. *The Magnolia*, supra; The Belfast, 74 U.S. (7 Wall.) 624 (1869); The Eagle, 75 U.S. (8 Wall.) 15 (1869); Ex parte Boyer, 109 U.S. 629 (1884). And in Wilburn Boat Co. v. Fireman's Fund Ins. Co., 348 U.S. 310 (1955), while allowing state law to apply because of the nature of the controversy, see p. 369, infra, the Court had no doubt that an insurance policy on a houseboat plying Lake Texoma, an artificial lake between two States, was maritime, although the lake's only outlet to the sea was blocked by a dam.

The current test is often said to be stated by The Daniel Ball, 77 U.S. (10 Wall.) 557, 563 (1871), where the Court was concerned with the scope of federal licensing and inspection laws applicable to the "navigable waters of the United States": These waters include rivers "navigable in fact" (i.e., "susceptible of being used, in their ordinary condition as highways for commerce") "when they form in their ordinary condition by themselves, or by uniting with other waters, a continued highway over which commerce is or may be carried on with other States or foreign countries in the customary modes in which such commerce is conducted by water." A fresh approach, however, was taken in Adams v. Montana Power Co., 528 F.2d 437, 439 (9th Cir. 1975), where the court rejected the equation between commerce power and admiralty jurisdiction. While Congress needed broad authority to enable it to make waters navigable, the court reasoned, admiralty's purpose of "fostering commercial maritime activity" dictated that the jurisdiction extend "only to those waters traversed or susceptible of being traversed by commercial craft." Consequently the jurisdiction did not reach a case arising on a dammed portion of the Missouri River, wholly within a single State, used only by pleasure vessels. Accord, Livingston v. United States, 627 F.2d 165 (8th Cir. 1980).

C. *Contract Cases*

(5) The traditional test of admiralty jurisdiction in this country, limited by the definition of "navigable waters" discussed in note 4, has been that laid down by Mr. Justice Story on circuit in DeLovio v. Boit, 7 F.Cas. 418 (C.C.D.Mass.1815) (No. 3,776), as restated by the Supreme Court:

> While the civil jurisdiction of the admiralty in matters of tort depends upon locality—whether the act was committed upon navigable

3. The 1845 Act, the Court said, was "obsolete and of no effect" except for the right to jury trial, now preserved in 28 U.S.C. § 1873, and apparently granted originally out of caution lest the Seventh Amendment be held applicable if the jurisdiction were upheld under the Commerce Clause. Why wasn't the jury provision held obsolete too? See N. Healy & B. Currie, Cases on Admiralty 28–29 (1965), discussing the decisions respecting the scope of the jury right.

> waters—in matters of contract it depends upon the subject-matter—the nature and character of the contract . . ., as to whether it have reference to maritime service or maritime transactions.

North Pacific S. S. Co. v. Hall Bros. Marine Railway & Shipbuilding Co., 249 U.S. 119 (1919).

As might be expected, application of these tests has created numerous difficulties. Thanks to the groundwork done by Story,[4] it is immaterial that the contract was made on land (as most contracts are) or to be performed there (as is true of marine insurance and even of some contracts for ship repair), so long as it "concerns" the "navigation, business or commerce of the sea." Gilmore and Black list the principal types of maritime contracts:

> [C]ontracts for the carriage of goods and passengers; for the chartering of ships (charter parties); for repairs, supplies, etc., furnished to vessels, and for services such as towage, pilotage, wharfage; for the services of seamen and officers; for recovery of indemnity or premiums on marine insurance policies.

Admiralty 22 (2d Ed. 1975). See also S. Morrison & G. Stumberg, Cases and Materials on Admiralty 48–49, 52–53 (1954), adding stevedoring, lockage, and salvage contracts, general-average, bottomry and respondentia bonds, and indemnity clauses in maritime contracts.

There are some famous omissions from this list that may appear odd. Contracts to build ships are nonmaritime, and this includes contracts to perform work upon an incomplete vessel already in the water: "The structure does not become a ship, in the legal sense, until it is completed and launched"; such contracts are "not nearly enough related to any rights and duties pertaining to commerce and navigation." The Francis McDonald, 254 U.S. 242 (1920); North Pacific S. S. Co. v. Hall Bros. Marine Railway & Shipbuilding Co., 249 U.S. 119, 127 (1919) (dictum). A number of cases have held contracts for the sale of ships outside the jurisdiction, e.g., The Ada, 250 Fed. 194 (2d Cir. 1918); but see The Ciudad De La Habana, 181 F.Supp. 301 (D.Md. 1960), questioning the rule but not passing upon it.

Ship mortgages were outside the jurisdiction until passage of the Ship Mortgage Act in 1920, 46 U.S.C. §§ 911–84. In The Thomas Barlum, 293 U.S. 21 (1934), the Court upheld the constitutionality of the Act as applied to mortgages securing loans obtained largely for nonmaritime purposes:

> The fact that mortgages on ships had not been considered to be maritime contracts was not conclusive as to the constitutional authority of the Congress to alter or supplement the maritime law in this respect, and thus to extend the admiralty jurisdiction, "as experience or changing conditions might require," while keeping within a proper conception of maritime concerns. . . . We cannot fail to regard the encouragement of investment "in shipping and shipping securities"—an objective of the Ship Mortgage Act—as an essential prerogative of the Congress in the exercise of its wide discretion as to the appropriate development of the maritime law of the country. . . . In order to

4. "It was said of the late Justice Story, that if a bucket of water were brought into his court with a corn cob floating in it, he would at once extend the admiralty jurisdiction of the United States over it." Note, 37 Am.L.Rev. 911, 916 (1903).

> create public confidence in such securities, in obligations issued on the faith of ship mortgages, the Congress deemed it necessary, not to hamper their issue or enforcement by compelling inquiries as to the application of loans. . . . New conditions . . . may require that former criteria of jurisdiction be abandoned, as, for example, they were abandoned in discarding the doctrine that the admiralty jurisdiction was limited to tidewaters. *The Genesee Chief*. . . .

The Supreme Court's most recent foray into this particular morass came in Kossick v. United Fruit Co., 365 U.S. 731 (1961), which held maritime a shipowner's contract to assume responsibility for any consequences of improper treatment its ailing crewman might receive in a public hospital:

> The consideration for respondent's alleged promise was petitioner's good faith forbearance to press what he considered—perhaps erroneously—to be the full extent of his maritime right to maintenance and cure. . . . We think that the alleged agreement was sufficiently related to peculiarly maritime concerns as not to put it without more, beyond the pale of admiralty law.

In this pattern of contract jurisdiction, Professor Black has aptly said, "there is about as much 'principle' as there is in a list of irregular verbs." Black, Admiralty Jurisdiction: Critique and Suggestions, 50 Colum.L.Rev. 259, 264 (1950). More recently, describing his earlier view as "somewhat mellowed," Professor Black has adhered to his criticism of the shipbuilding cases and to his insistence that the jurisdiction should be tailored to its purpose by "dealing with the major concerns of the shipping industry—with all of them, and not just with a few of them selected on antiquarian criteria." Yet he concedes the difficulty of drawing the line: "[T]he actual concerns of the shipping industry may reach as far as the last ranch that sends cattle to port, and, even without stretching the matter at all, maritime transactions are inseparably connected with and shade into the non-maritime." G. Gilmore & C. Black, Admiralty 29 (2d Ed. 1975).[5]

5. It has been suggested that "the most relevant determination in deciding whether a contract is within the admiralty jurisdiction is ascertaining its connection with a vessel":

> Once it is shown that the structure involved is in fact a vessel . . . and that the contract sought to be enforced relates to commerce thereon or the navigation thereof, the contract will be deemed maritime. If, however, the structure does not qualify as a vessel, the courts have consistently held that contracts pertaining thereto are not maritime. . . .

Moore & Pelaez, Admiralty Jurisdiction—The Sky's the Limit, 33 J.Air Law 3, 5 (1967). If we accept the argument that a ship under construction is not yet a vessel and that a ship taken out of navigation has ceased to be one, is this generalization accurate? Is it helpful?

The ALI, terming the omission of such matters as shipbuilding contracts "an anomaly of little practical significance . . . since so long as it is understood, as it is, by those who build ships and those for whom they are built, they are able to safeguard their interests," proposed to leave admiralty jurisdiction substantially undefined, ALI Study 34, 228 (1969). After hearings, however, the bill to enact the ALI proposals was reintroduced with new language that would remedy the problem by including within the jurisdiction any claim in contract or tort "arising out of the construction, mortgage, sale, ownership, possession, operation, navigation, chartering, servicing, or scrapping of any vessel of three hundred gross tons or more used or intended to be used on navigable waters, notwithstanding that the damage or injury involved be done or consummated on land." S. 1876, 93d Cong., 1st Sess.,

D. Tort Cases

(6) As an aid in applying the then general rule that admiralty jurisdiction extends to "every species of tort, however occurring, and whether on board a vessel or not, if upon the high seas or the navigable waters," the Supreme Court adopted the hoary choice-of-law principle, see Restatement, Conflict of Laws § 377 (1934), that a tort occurs not where the wrongful act is done but where it takes effect, The Plymouth, 70 U.S. (3 Wall.) 20, 36 (1866), with the absurd and inconvenient result that when a ship collided with a bridge (which was considered land) the shipowner's claim for damages was maritime and the bridge-owner's was not. In 1948, despite warnings of unconstitutionality, see Stolz, footnote 2 supra, 51 Cal.L.Rev. at 690 & n. 111, Congress enacted 46 U.S.C. § 740, which provides that the admiralty jurisdiction "shall extend to and include all cases of damage or injury, to person or property, caused by a vessel on navigable water, notwithstanding that such damage or injury be done or consummated on land." The lower courts have generally upheld the statute, while conceding that Article III limits the admiralty jurisdiction, by noting the obviously close relation of such cases to maritime commerce, the practice of other nations in treating them as maritime, and the Court's decision in Richardson v. Harmon, 222 U.S. 96 (1911), which upheld the statutory admiralty jurisdiction to limit shipowners' liability for torts inflicted on shore. E.g., United States v. Matson Nav. Co., 201 F.2d 610 (9th Cir. 1953); The Gloria O, 98 F.Supp. 71 (E.D.N.Y.1951). In Gutierrez v. Waterman Steamship Corp., 373 U.S. 206 (1963), the Supreme Court upheld jurisdiction under the Extension Act, without discussing its constitutionality, of a suit for injuries to a longshoreman who slipped on beans that had fallen from defective bags onto a pier in Puerto Rico.

Gutierrez expressly decided an important question of the statute's construction, rejecting the argument that damage "caused by a vessel" was limited to such matters as collisions with the ship itself. Gutierrez argued that the damage had been caused by the unseaworthiness of the ship (i.e., of its bean bags) and by its crew's negligence, and the Court agreed:

> There is no distinction in admiralty between torts committed by the ship itself and by the ship's personnel when operating it, any more than there is between torts "committed" by a corporation and by its employees. . . . Various far-fetched hypotheticals are raised such as a suit in admiralty for an ordinary automobile accident involving a ship's officer on ship business in port, or for someone's slipping on beans that continue to leak from these bags in a warehouse in Denver. We think it sufficient for the needs of this occasion to hold that the case is within the maritime jurisdiction under 46 U.S.C. § 740 when, as here, it is alleged that the shipowner commits a tort while or before the ship is being unloaded, and the impact of which is felt ashore at a time and place not remote from the wrongful act.[6]

§ 1316(a)(1) (1973); see the brief explanation at 119 Cong.Rec. 16,679–80 (1973) (Sen. Burdick). Does this mean matters affecting little boats are excluded, or that they are left to the traditional case law?

6. Cf. *Canadian Aviator, Ltd. v. United States* and *American Stevedores, Inc. v. Porello*, infra p. 471 (consent to suit against the Government for "damages caused by a public vessel"). Does *Gutierrez* overrule

In any event the Extension Act applies only when a land injury can be said to have been caused by a ship; and the Supreme Court drew the line in Victory Carriers, Inc. v. Law, 404 U.S. 202 (1971), holding there was no admiralty jurisdiction over an action by a longshoreman injured on the pier by his own truck: Although he was loading a ship at the time, it was not the ship that injured him. *Gutierrez*, the Court said, was different: The injury there had been caused by "an appurtenance of the ship, the defective cargo containers." [7]

In seamen's-injury cases the Supreme Court has given sanction to jurisdiction over injuries on land without regard to the Extension Act. The sailor has long been allowed maintenance and cure for harm incurred off the ship, as in Warren v. United States, 340 U.S. 523 (1951), where he fell from a dance-hall window while on shore leave; [8] this has been reconciled with theory by saying the obligation to care for the seaman while in ship's service is part of his (maritime) contract. In O'Donnell v. Great Lakes Dredge & Dock Co., 318 U.S. 36 (1943), the Court extended this reasoning to the Jones Act, which gives the sailor a right to sue his employer for negligence. The decision was based neither on the Commerce Clause (which even in 1943 might have left an occasional seaman uncovered) nor on the Extension Act (which might cover it, cf. *Gutierrez*, supra, but which was not yet law). After the Extension Act, but without invoking it or quite calling the case one of contract, the Second Circuit explicitly upheld maritime jurisdiction over a suit by a longshoreman injured on the pier by ship's gear, Strika v. Netherlands Ministry of Traffic, 185 F.2d 555 (2d Cir. 1950) ("such a tort, arising as it does out of a maritime 'status' or 'relation,'

Clinton v. Joshua Hendy Corp., 285 F.2d 199 (9th Cir. 1960), which held the statute did not reach a suit for libel written aboard ship by the Chief Mate and causing a seaman, on shore, to be expelled from his union? See also Duluth Superior Excursions, Inc. v. Makela, 623 F.2d 1251 (8th Cir. 1980), upholding Extension Act jurisdiction of a claim based upon the alleged negligence of a cruise organizer in feeding alcoholic beverages to a passenger who drove his car into the plaintiff after leaving the ship. Would *Gutierrez* support jurisdiction of a complaint against a passenger who threw rocks from ship to shore?

7. Moreover, reversing an imaginative lower-court opinion (Marine Stevedoring Corp. v. Oosting, 398 F.2d 900 (4th Cir. 1968)), the Court held federal workers' compensation unavailable to longshoremen injured on the pier even by ship's equipment, since the Extension Act did not modify the compensation law's explicit limitation to injuries "upon . . . navigable waters." Nacirema Operating Co. v. Johnson, 396 U.S. 212 (1969). After *Nacirema* the compensation statute was amended, 86 Stat. 1251 (1972), to include injury or death of a person engaged in "maritime employment" on "any adjoining pier, wharf, dry dock, terminal, building way, marine railway, or other adjoining area customarily used by an employer in loading, unloading, repairing, or building a vessel." See Northeast Marine Terminal Co., Inc. v. Caputo, 432 U.S. 249 (1977).

8. Accord, Koistinen v. American Export Lines, 83 N.Y.S.2d 297 (1948), awarding maintenance and cure to a sailor who had broken his leg in escaping an irate bouncer through the window of a Yugoslavian brothel after an argument over the fee:

> How came he to this parlous pass is neither here nor there.
> If you must know, it was because he had a sailor's flair.
> With seamanship and courage, and at hazard of his skin,
> He saved an able seaman's life to go to sea again.
> In the service of the ship, my lads,
> In the service of the ship.
> Eino he broke his blushin' leg
> In the service of the ship.

B. Currie, Koistinen v. American Export Lines, in C. Harvey, Legal Wit & Whimsy 39 (1988).

is cognizable by the maritime law whether it arises on sea or on land," citing *O'Donnell*). But the Supreme Court's decision in *Victory Carriers, Inc. v. Law*, supra, closing the door to a longshoreman injured on the pier, seems to have put an end to such innovations; for while the opinion did not discuss the contract theory, it made clear that the extension of jurisdiction to land injuries was a task for Congress.

In non-seaman cases not within the Extension Act the courts continue to wrestle with the problem of determining whether an injury has occurred on navigable waters. The leading Supreme Court case had held the place the wrongful act had its initial impact upon the plaintiff decisive: The Admiral Peoples, 295 U.S. 649 (1935). The plaintiff had fallen from a gangplank, which was "a part of the vessel," to the "dock," which was "an extension of land;" the case was maritime because " 'the cause of action originated and the injury had commenced on the ship, the consummation somewhere being inevitable.' " Application of this principle has produced some rather fine distinctions. The Sixth Circuit, having held nonmaritime the case of a seaman who had tripped from the pier into the water (the converse of *The Admiral Peoples*), found distinguishable an action based upon the failure to warn or restrain people from diving into shallow water: A man who trips on the pier suffers a "direct impact" upon land; one who is not prevented from diving does not. Wiper v. Great Lakes Engineering Works, 340 F.2d 727 (6th Cir. 1965); Chapman v. City of Grosse Pointe Farms, 385 F.2d 962, 965 (6th Cir. 1967).[9]

(7) The cases in note 6 dealt with the possible extension of maritime tort jurisdiction beyond navigable waters. Courts and commentators long struggled, without Supreme Court guidance, with the converse possibility that, despite the apparently all-inclusive language quoted from *The Plymouth* at the beginning of note 6, some torts on navigable waters might be excluded from the jurisdiction. The learned Benedict had long before expressed his "celebrated doubt," E. Benedict, The Law of American Admiralty 173 (1850): "If one of several landsmen bathing in the sea should assault or imprison or rob another, it has not been held that admiralty would have jurisdiction."

Benedict was vindicated by the high court in Executive Jet Aviation, Inc. v. City of Cleveland, 409 U.S. 249 (1972), which held that an action for damage to an airplane crashing into Lake Erie on an interstate flight was not within admiralty jurisdiction:

> The mere fact that the alleged wrong "occurs" or "is located" on or over navigable waters—whatever that means in an aviation context—is not of itself sufficient to turn an airplane negligence case into a "maritime tort." It is far more consistent with the history and purpose of admiralty to require also that the wrong bear a significant relationship to traditional maritime activity. . . . The matters with

9. As if this were not enough, in reaching its decision in the tripping case the court had been forced to distinguish an earlier holding, Interlake Steamship Co. v. Nielsen, 338 F.2d 879 (6th Cir. 1964), allowing federal workers' compensation for a shipkeeper who had driven off the pier and cracked his skull on the frozen water: "In the present case it is the locality of the tort that governs . . . rather than the locality where the injuries or death occurred, which . . . determined coverage under the . . . Compensation Act."

which admiralty is basically concerned have no conceivable bearing on the operation of aircraft, whether over land or water. . . .

After it struck the flock of seagulls over the runway, the plane descended and settled in Lake Erie within the territorial waters of Ohio. We can find no significant relationship between such an event befalling a land-based plane flying from one point in the continental United States to another, and traditional maritime activity involving navigation and commerce on navigable waters.

The Fourth Circuit concluded that *Executive Jet* limited admiralty jurisdiction even when boats were involved, holding that a water skier could not sue in admiralty for negligent towing and suggesting that there was no reason for a federal forum in any case involving "pleasure craft": The purpose of the jurisdiction was to promote commercial trade. Crosson v. Vance, 484 F.2d 840 (4th Cir. 1973). The Supreme Court, over four dissents, threw cold water on all this in Foremost Ins. Co. v. Richardson, 457 U.S. 668 (1982), upholding jurisdiction over an action arising out of a collision between two pleasure boats: "Because the 'wrong' here involves the negligent operation of a vessel on navigable waters, we believe that it has a sufficient nexus to traditional maritime activity to sustain admiralty jurisdiction. . . ."[10] See also East River S.S. Corp. v. Transamerica Delaval Inc., 476 U.S. 858 (1986), upholding admiralty jurisdiction over a products-liability claim for damage to vessels on the high seas: Assuming that *Executive Jet's* "maritime nexus" requirement applied on the high seas, it clearly was met here, for these ships were engaged in maritime commerce, a primary concern of admiralty law.[11]

10. See also the entertaining opinion of Judge Godbold in Kelly v. Smith, 485 F.2d 520 (5th Cir. 1973), an action for damages in admiralty by deer poachers who had been shot from shore while attempting to escape the irate landowners' employees in a 15-foot outboard motorboat in the Mississippi River:

> The party most seriously injured was the pilot, the person responsible for the safe navigation of the river. The vehicle involved was a boat, not an automobile or airplane, whose function was transportation across navigable waters, a traditional role of watercraft. . . . Admiralty has traditionally been concerned with furnishing remedies for those injured while traveling navigable waters. . . . Rifle fire directed at a vessel, albeit a small one, on a major commercial artery, and injuring the pilot, presents sufficient danger to maritime commerce for the federal courts of admiralty to assume jurisdiction. . . .

Judge Morgan, in dissent, called the matter "local," found no "overriding federal interest in protecting" poaching, and, noting that the locality test had been "washed to sea," accused the majority of having "run aground on the rocks of admiralty jurisdiction": "Had I been in command, I would have charted our course differently." The majority pointed out, for information only, that in the absence of admiralty jurisdiction a judgment for nearly $70,000 would have been washed out because of the statute of limitations.

For conflicting decisions as to whether pollution damaging fish or shellfish meets the *Executive Jet* test see National Sea Clammers Association v. City of New York, 616 F.2d 1222, 1235 (3d Cir. 1980), reversed on other grounds 453 U.S. 1 (1981) (upholding jurisdiction); Moore v. Hampton Roads Sanitation District Commission, 557 F.2d 1030, 1038–39 (4th Cir. 1976) (contra).

11. In White v. Johns-Manville Corp., 662 F.2d 234 (4th Cir. 1981), the Fourth Circuit applied similar reasoning to uphold admiralty jurisdiction over an action for injuries to workers who had used asbestos in the construction or repair of ships on navigable waters, finding a "'significant relationship to traditional maritime activity' because the installation of the asbestos products has a direct effect on marine navigation and commerce." Other circuits disagreed, and the Fourth Circuit then changed its course, concluding in Oman v. Johns-Manville Corp., 764 F.2d 224 (4th

(8) Even as it cleared the air with regard to the locality test, the Court in *Executive Jet* began to muddy the water with dicta suggesting that some airplane cases might nevertheless be held maritime. These suggestions were confirmed in Offshore Logistics, Inc. v. Tallentire, 477 U.S. 207 (1986), where the Court upheld admiralty jurisdiction over claims for wrongful death arising from the crash of a helicopter carrying workers from an offshore drilling platform to the mainland. To begin with, jurisdiction was "expressly provided" by the Death on the High Seas Act, 46 U.S.C.A. § 761, which authorizes admiralty suits for deaths resulting from "wrongful act, neglect, or default occurring on the high seas, beyond a marine league from the shore of any state," "because the accidental deaths occurred beyond a marine league from shore." Moreover,

> Even without this statutory provision, admiralty jurisdiction is appropriately invoked here under traditional principles because the accident occurred on the high seas and in furtherance of an activity bearing a significant relationship to a traditional maritime activity. . . . Although the decedents were killed while riding in a helicopter and not a more traditional maritime conveyance, that helicopter was engaged in a function traditionally performed by waterborne vessels: the ferrying of passengers from an "island," albeit an artificial one, to the shore.

It shouldn't matter on either theory, should it, whether the airplane has actually fallen into the water? See Notarian v. Trans World Airlines, 244 F.Supp. 874 (W.D. Pa. 1965).

Should it be held, as one court put it in pointing out that the theory had never received "general acceptance," that "the entire ocean of air surrounding the earth is within the admiralty jurisdiction, and that consequently all air flight is within the admiralty and maritime jurisdiction"? Wilson v. Transocean Airlines, 121 F.Supp. 85, 91 n. 23 (N.D.Cal.1954). Isn't the air itself much like the sea in terms of the reasons underlying admiralty jurisdiction? [12]

E. Remedies

(9) Despite contrary English precedents, the Supreme Court has upheld admiralty jurisdiction to determine title to vessels, Ward v. Peck, 59 U.S. (18 How.) 267 (1856), and to partition vessels by sale, Madruga v. Superior Court, 346 U.S. 556 (1954). Yet there has been serious doubt as to the availability of equitable remedies. See Kynoch v. The S. C. Ives, 14 F.Cas. 888 (N.D.Ohio 1856) (No. 7,958):

> Courts of admiralty have no general jurisdiction to administer relief as courts of equity. If a maritime contract is broken, the admiralty, concurrent with the courts of law, can only give damages for

Cir. 1985), that the tort was not maritime after all. See also Woessner v. Johns-Manville Sales Corp., 757 F.2d 634 (5th Cir. 1985): "The traditional concerns of admiralty law do not implicate any interest in uniform resolution of the claims of land-based workers exposed to asbestos while aboard vessels."

12. This suggestion is nothing new; it was hotly debated in the early years of commercial flight, and President Harding went so far as to send a bill to Congress to extend admiralty jurisdiction to all navigable air space. See H.R.Doc. 17, 67th Cong., 1st Sess. (April 19, 1921); Knauth, Aviation and the Admiralty, 6 Air L.Rev. 226 (1935); Crenshaw, Airplanes in the Admiralty Jurisdiction: A Short History, 18 S.C.L.Rev. 572 (1966).

the breach of it; whereas the chancery may compel the party, in some cases, to a specific performance. A court of admiralty has no more power to decree such specific performance, than it has to set aside the contract for fraud, or correct a mistake, or decree the execution of a trust.

Professor Morrison, in his excellent article The Remedial Powers of the Admiralty, 43 Yale L.J. 1, 9–12, 18 (1933), explained the English origins of this difficulty as based in part upon the inability of admiralty to pass upon questions of title (legal or equitable) and more generally upon the virtual exclusion of the admiralty from in personam cases. In this country the courts were troubled by neither of these limitations, and in other contexts (e.g., the waters subject to the jurisdiction, see note 4, supra) they were quite willing to abandon English limitations. The refusal to grant equitable relief was made still more peculiar by the common holding, in contrast again to English precedent, that equitable defenses would be recognized in admiralty, e.g., Rice v. Charles Dreifus Co., 96 F.2d 80 (2d Cir. 1938); and it was always a bit out of place beside the common shibboleth that "Courts of Admiralty, on the matters within their jurisdiction, must be governed by equitable principles. . . ." E.g., Packard v. The Louisa, 18 F.Cas. 958, 962 (C.C.D.Mass.1846) (No. 10,652).

The Supreme Court has made quite clear that there is no constitutional objection to equitable relief in admiralty. See Crowell v. Benson, 285 U.S. 22, 49 (1932), upholding a statutory grant of authority to enjoin a maritime workers'-compensation award; Marine Transit Corp. v. Dreyfus, 284 U.S. 263 (1932), upholding the Arbitration Act's authorization to order specific performance of an arbitration clause in a maritime contract; The Thomas Barlum, 293 U.S. 21 (1934), upholding the statutory power to foreclose ship mortgages. Does this mean the question of "equity jurisdiction" in admiralty is not a jurisdictional matter limited by Article III? See *Marine Transit Corp. v. Dreyfus*, supra: "The general power of the Congress to provide remedies in matters falling within the admiralty jurisdiction of the federal courts, and to regulate their procedure, is indisputable."

Outside the statutory grants of equitable powers the Supreme Court made some inroads upon the old doctrine by holding, in Swift & Co. Packers v. Compania Columbiana, 339 U.S. 684 (1950), that a court whose jurisdiction was based on the admiralty clause had authority, when asked to attach a vessel no longer owned by the respondent, to determine whether the transfer had been fraudulent. Unfortunately the Court took the opportunity to reaffirm the rule that "a court of admiralty will not enforce an independent equitable claim merely because it pertains to maritime property." But, analogizing to cases investigating equitable defenses, the Court described the issue of fraud as "subsidiary to issues wholly within admiralty jurisdiction": "The basis of admiralty's power is to protect its jurisdiction from being thwarted by a fraudulent transfer." To hold that admiralty lacked even this limited equitable power would be "strange indeed" since admiralty "has been so responsive to the practicalities of maritime commerce and so inventive in adapting its jurisdiction to the needs of that commerce." Does *Swift* establish a kind of "pendent jurisdiction" over equitable claims? In Vaughan v. Atkinson, 369 U.S. 527, 530 (1962), the

Court went out of its way to dissociate itself from the restrictive rule in awarding counsel fees in a libel for maintenance and cure: "Equity is no stranger in admiralty; admiralty courts are, indeed, authorized to grant equitable relief," and allowing attorneys' fees was "'a part of the historic equity jurisdiction of the federal courts.'"[13] The First Circuit has taken the final step: "[C]ourts sitting in admiralty may award injunctive relief in accordance with Fed.R.Civ.P. 65 in situations where such relief would be appropriate on land," even if it is not ancillary to a traditional maritime claim. Pino v. Protection Maritime Insurance Co., 599 F.2d 10, 15–16 (1st Cir. 1979).

Professor Morrison's argument is overpowering:

> When a separate maritime jurisdiction was created by the Constitution, it was created for the purpose of dealing effectively with maritime affairs, and should embrace such powers as are necessary adequately to do justice in maritime disputes. Now it is impossible to do justice in such disputes, any more than in non-maritime matters, without occasionally giving equitable relief. Hence, viewed as an original question, the conclusion would seem inevitable that the admiralty should possess such powers, equitable or otherwise, as are reasonably needed to accomplish that aim.

43 Yale L.J. at 18–19.

(10) Professor Morrison's argument is equally dispositive with respect to a second remedial limitation that, strangely, seems to have been first discovered during the present century. In Israel v. Moore & McCormack Co., 295 Fed. 919 (S.D.N.Y.1920), Judge Learned Hand, bowing to recent authority, refused to entertain a libel for recovery of money paid for carrying freight that in fact had been jettisoned; quasi-contractual relief, the earlier decision had said, was based upon "an implied promise to repay the moneys which cannot in good conscience be retained," and this promise was "not a maritime contract." United Transp. Co. v. New York & Baltimore Transp. Line, 185 Fed. 386 (2d Cir. 1911). As Morrison says, this is carrying fiction pretty far; "Certainly adequate power to deal with maritime affairs must include the power in some way to prevent unjust enrichment within that field." As for precedent, the characteristically maritime rights of salvage and of general average are based essentially upon unjust enrichment. 43 Yale L.J. at 26–27.

Archawski v. Hanioti, 350 U.S. 532 (1956), took a giant step toward the abolition of the alleged ban on quasi-contractual relief. The libel was for the return of money paid in advance for passage on a voyage that had been canceled. Instead of suing simply for breach of the contract, the frustrated passenger sought return of the money on the ground that it had been wrongfully applied and fraudulently withheld. Adopting Morrison's rea-

13. See also the optimistic and colorful statement by Judge Brown in allowing an equitable defense, which was permissible even under the old rule:

> The Chancellor is no longer fixed to the woolsack. He may stride the quarter-deck of maritime jurisprudence and, in the role of admiralty judge, dispense, as would his landlocked brother, that which equity and good conscience impels.

Compania Anonima Venezolana v. A. J. Perez Export Co., 303 F.2d 692, 699 (5th Cir. 1962). See also Adm. Rule 59 (now covered by the merged civil rules), purporting to authorize declaratory judgments in admiralty.

soning, the Court denied there was a separate, nonmaritime contract for repayment of the money: "Admiralty has jurisdiction, even where the libel reads like indebitatus assumpsit at common law, provided that the unjust enrichment arose as a result of the breach of a maritime contract."

(11) The talk of "jurisdiction" in *Romero* is indicative of the common tendency to refer to "admiralty courts" as if they were specialized courts dealing only with maritime claims. A glance at § 1333 should eradicate this fallacy, for the admiralty jurisdiction is conferred upon the United States District Courts. See generally B. Currie, The Silver Oar and All That—A Study of the Romero Case, 27 U.Chi.L.Rev. 1 (1959). Until very recently those courts labored under the inconvenience of separate sets of rules for admiralty and for "civil" cases, an inconvenience compounded by the frequent possibility of asserting maritime claims on the "civil side" of the court under § 1332 or (in statutory cases only, after *Romero*) under § 1331. In 1966, however, the Supreme Court adopted a single set of uniform rules applicable alike to cases formerly legal, equitable, or maritime, preserving a few distinctively maritime rules for cases cognizable only under § 1333. Does the merger of civil and admiralty cases remove the last obstacle to affirmative "equitable" relief under § 1333? [14]

F. State–Court Jurisdiction

(12) The statement in § 1333 that federal admiralty jurisdiction is "exclusive" is very largely a delusion, as will appear from this series of episodes in the construction of the clause "saving to suitors" their common-law remedies:

(a). The Moses Taylor, 71 U.S. (4 Wall.) 411 (1867): An in rem proceeding against a vessel, on account of a maritime contract, is not a "remedy afforded by the common law" and therefore not within the power of a state court.

(b). Rounds v. Cloverport Foundry & Mach. Co., 237 U.S. 303 (1915): In an action in personam based upon a maritime contract a state court may attach a vessel for security, because attachment is "essentially a proceeding according to the course of the common law." An in rem proceeding is different: It is one "essentially against the vessel itself as the debtor or offending thing. . . . The decree binds all the world and under it the property itself passes and not merely the title or interest of a personal defendant."

(c). Red Cross Line v. American Fruit Co., 264 U.S. 109 (1924): A state court, pursuant to state statute, may order specific performance of an arbitration clause in a maritime contract. "Common-law" remedies include "all means other than proceedings in admiralty"; they may be both statutory and equitable. Justice McReynolds, dissenting, argued that the saving clause applied only to remedies known to the common-law courts in 1789.

(d). C. J. Hendry Co. v. Moore, 318 U.S. 133 (1943): A state court has jurisdiction over an in rem proceeding to forfeit a fish net used in

14. The 1973 version of S. 1876 would do away with all remedial restrictions by providing that maritime jurisdiction includes actions "for interpleader, declaratory or equitable relief."

violation of state law, because "the common law as received in this country at the time of the adoption of the Constitution gave a remedy *in rem* in cases of forfeiture" even for articles seized on navigable waters. Justice Black dissented, believing the saving clause did not permit state courts, "which cannot reasonably be expected to have knowledge of admiralty law and practice, to give permanent halt to any portion of the maritime trade and commerce of the nation by bringing *in rem* proceedings against ships."

(e). Madruga v. Superior Court, 346 U.S. 556 (1954) (by Justice Black): A state court has jurisdiction to sell a vessel and partition the proceeds among its owners:

> The plaintiffs' quarrel was with their co-owner, not with the ship. Manuel Madruga, not the ship, was made defendant. Thus the state court in this proceeding acts only upon the interests of the parties over which it has jurisdiction *in personam*, and it does not affect the interests of others in the world at large, as it would if this were a proceeding *in rem* to enforce a lien.

Justices Frankfurter and Jackson dissented: "If this is not an action against the thing, . . . then the concepts of a *res* and an *in rem* proceeding have an esoteric meaning which I do not understand."

Is there method in this madness? The upshot seems to be that state courts may entertain anything (apart from certain statutory matters, infra) except a private proceeding against a vessel in rem; but why? The sterile test of 1789 common-law power, employed in *The Moses Taylor* and in *Hendry*, was rejected in *Red Cross* (or is history a minimum and not a maximum of state authority?); the meaningless test of nomenclature suggested in *Madruga* was rejected in *Hendry*. Is the in rem proceeding especially inappropriate for state jurisdiction because, as Justice Black said in his *Hendry* dissent, seizure of a vessel disrupts maritime commerce? But not only *Hendry* is inconsistent with this analysis; what of *Madruga*, in which a ship was to be sold, and, more particularly, of *Rounds*, in which a ship was attached? Moreover, the common practice in an in rem proceeding is to post a bond, releasing the vessel; commerce is not substantially disrupted. See G. Gilmore & C. Black, Admiralty 796 (2d Ed. 1975). Is it determinative, as suggested in *Rounds* and in *Madruga*, that only an in rem decree extinguishes all liens against the vessel, not just those sought to be enforced by the plaintiff, so that the in rem proceeding is likely to be a complex one involving large sums and multiple parties? When the ship is released on bond, liens not in suit survive an in rem proceeding, see Gilmore & Black, supra, at 798–99; should this matter? And, in any event, what excuse is there for *Hendry*? An exceptionally potent state interest?

The Suits in Admiralty Act, 46 U.S.C. §§ 741–42, and the Public Vessels Act, 46 U.S.C. §§ 781–82, provide for exclusive admiralty jurisdiction (and only in personam) of certain suits against the United States respecting government vessels.[15] The Ship Mortgage Act, 46 U.S.C. § 951, also makes federal admiralty jurisdiction exclusive. The Death on the

15. For the interrelationship between these statutes and others waiving sovereign immunity see pp. 471–74 infra.

High Seas Act, 46 U.S.C. § 761, provides for a suit "in admiralty" for wrongful deaths resulting from injuries outside the States. Most lower courts concluded that admiralty jurisdiction under this section was exclusive, although the statute did not say so. Relying on a provision preserving "any *State* statute giving or regulating rights of action or remedies for death," the Supreme Court disagreed: "Because the resolution of DOHSA claims does not normally require the expertise that admiralty courts bring to bear, DOHSA actions are clearly within the competence of state courts to adjudicate." Offshore Logistics, Inc. v. Tallentire, 477 U.S. 207 (1986). Does the reference to "admiralty" in § 761 exclude a diversity action in federal court?

The Limitation of Liability Act, 46 U.S.C. §§ 181–95, permits a shipowner by taking "the appropriate proceedings in any court" to limit liability in many situations to the value of the vessel (or, in the case of personal injury or death, to $60 per ton of its weight). Like the libel in rem, the limitation proceeding affords an opportunity for consolidation of numerous claims—all those that arose during the voyage in question—and the judgment discharges them all. But the Supreme Court has extended the implied exclusivity of the admiralty jurisdiction in limitation cases, see Norwich & N. Y. Transp. Co. v. Wright, 80 U.S. (13 Wall.) 104, 123–24 (1872), beyond the multiple-claimant situation. In Langnes v. Green, 282 U.S. 531 (1931), the Court held that, because only a single claim had been filed, the injured party was entitled to his common-law remedy; the state court was "competent to entertain a claim of the shipowner for limitation of liability and afford him appropriate relief." But, when the case reappeared after remand, the Court explained that the right to limitation, if put in issue, could be determined only in admiralty. Ex parte Green, 286 U.S. 437 (1932). The Court was short on reasons. Are there any good ones?

In 1948 the saving clause was amended to preserve to suitors not "common law" remedies but "all other remedies to which they are otherwise entitled." The purpose of the revision was apparently to codify the *Red Cross* decision allowing equitable and statutory remedies, see 28 U.S.C.A. § 1333, Reviser's Note. What is meant by "other" remedies to which the suitors are "otherwise" entitled? Notice that the new language removes the Court's basis for excluding the States from proceedings in rem. The *Madruga* opinion, supra, assumes that no such sweeping change was meant, and this assumption seems correct. See Black, supra note 5, 50 Colum.L.Rev. at 270–72 (1950).

(13) Justice Frankfurter cited no authority for his statement in *Romero* that saving-clause cases could not be removed into admiralty. Section 1441(a) requires only that the action be a "civil" one and that there be original federal jurisdiction. Section 1333 seems to fulfill the latter requisite; does "civil" mean "not criminal," or "not admiralty?" Why might a Congress generally concerned to give defendants equal access to federal courts have wanted to make the plaintiff's choice irrevocable in maritime cases? Why, if it wanted to do this, did it permit removal when there is also diversity? See Note, Removal to Admiralty, 69 Yale L.J. 442 (1960), arguing that removal would frustrate the saving-clause policy of giving

plaintiffs the option of a jury trial. Is § 1441(b) relevant to the removability of admiralty cases?

(14) Professor Black has paraphrased the saving clause in terms of the Court's decisions:

> (1) The district courts shall have jurisdiction concurrent with the courts of the states (at the election of the plaintiff) in personal actions arising out of maritime occurrences and transactions, where money only is sought. (2) The courts of the states shall have exclusive jurisdiction of all personal actions arising out of maritime occurrences and transactions when any relief other than a money judgment is sought. (3) The district courts shall have exclusive jurisdiction of libels *in rem* enforcing maritime liens.

Black, Admiralty Jurisdiction: Critique and Suggestions, 50 Colum.L.Rev. 259, 266–67 (1950).

Is this summary accurate?

"No one," says Professor Black, "has ever tried to defend the above pattern. . . . It was not consciously planned (one resists the usual allusion to Topsy)." [16] Id. at 267, 270. Professor Black proposed the following:

> The federal district court sitting in admiralty should have exclusive jurisdiction of all those cases involving contractual, commercial, and property adjustment, necessity for which grows out of the conduct of the maritime industry. The state courts, with removal impossible either on diversity or other grounds, should have exclusive jurisdiction of all cases of personal injury, to seamen or others.

The ALI (Study 34, 234–38), would make federal jurisdiction exclusive only in limitation and in rem proceedings, and in actions against the United States, observing that it means to preserve such existing cases as *Madruga* and *Hendry*, supra note 12.

16. Resists it, that is, after the fashion of Byron's Julia, who, "whispering 'I will ne'er consent,'—consented." Invoked by Justice Jackson in his dissent in Everson v. Board of Education, 330 U.S. 1, 19 (1947).

Chapter III

THE DIVERSITY JURISDICTION AND THE APPROPRIATE FEDERAL FORUM

Preliminary Notes on Diversity Jurisdiction

(1) The Judiciary Act of 1789, § 11, 1 Stat. 73, 78, gave the federal trial courts original jurisdiction, concurrent with that of the state courts, of "all suits of a civil nature at common law or in equity, where the matter in dispute exceeds, exclusive of costs, the sum or value of five hundred dollars, and . . . an alien is a party, or the suit is between a citizen of the State where the suit is brought, and a citizen of another State." Section 12 of the same Act permitted the defendant to remove to the federal court a suit "commenced in any state court against an alien, or by a citizen of the state in which the suit is brought against a citizen of another state," when "the matter in dispute exceeds the aforesaid sum or value of five hundred dollars." With modifications of more or less importance these basic provisions have remained in force ever since. The present statutes, 28 U.S.C. §§ 1332, 1441(a) & (b), appear in the Appendix at pp. 683, 701 infra. They should be read carefully.

(2) What is the reason for diversity jurisdiction? Since the decisions in Erie R. R. v. Tompkins, 304 U.S. 64 (1938), and Klaxon Co. v. Stentor Elec. Mfg. Co., 313 U.S. 487 (1941), the jurisdiction cannot serve to create a uniform common law or a uniform doctrine of choice of laws. The Supreme Court has often said diversity jurisdiction exists in order to protect nonresidents from state-court discrimination, or from the fear of it. E.g., Bank of the United States v. Deveaux, 9 U.S. (5 Cr.) 61, 87 (1809); Martin v. Hunter's Lessee, 14 U.S. (1 Wheat.) 304, 347 (1816); Erie R. R. v. Tompkins, supra, 304 U.S. at 74; Guaranty Trust Co. v. York, 326 U.S. 99, 111 (1945). Is this kind of discrimination a significant problem today? Serious attempts to find out are rare; opposing arguments are generally based upon a "plethora of conflicting assertions," Meador, A New Approach to Limiting Diversity Jurisdiction, 46 A.B.A.J. 383, 385, n. 18 (1960), not on proof.[1] If

1. See Summers, Analysis of Factors that Influence Choice of Forum in Diversity Cases, 47 Ia.L.Rev. 933, 937–38 (1962), finding that only 4.3% of responding Wisconsin lawyers even mentioned local bias and that "geographical convenience, avail-

bias is a problem, is federal jurisdiction an effective antidote? If you conclude that bias is a significant problem and that federal jurisdiction ameliorates it, consider whether diversity jurisdiction imposes significant countervailing costs on the federal system.[2]

John P. Frank unabashedly argues for diversity jurisdiction on the ground that federal courts are better than state courts. See, e.g., The Case for Diversity Jurisdiction, 16 Harv.J. on Legis. 403 (1979). Is this argument any more a perversion of constitutional authority than the common use of the commerce and tax powers to combat prostitution or child labor? Cf. Hoke v. United States, 227 U.S. 308 (1913); United States v. Darby, 312 U.S. 100 (1941). See J. S. Wright, The Federal Courts and the Nature and Quality of State Law, 13 Wayne L.Rev. 317, 327–28 (1967), arguing that access to a federal court, "like student-lunch programs and free technical advice from the Department of Agriculture, is a socially beneficent service which the federal government should extend when it is constitutional to do so"; and Judge Friendly's rejoinder that "the marginal utility of this service must rank exceedingly low in any scale of priorities of what the Federal Government should do for citizens of the several states." Federal Jurisdiction: A General View 145–46 (1973).

(3) Tempers have run high over the diversity jurisdiction. Justice Frankfurter found jurisdiction in diversity cases a great curse, see Lumbermen's Mut. Cas. Co. v. Elbert, 348 U.S. 48, 53–60 (1954) (concurring opinion); National Mut. Ins. Co. v. Tidewater Transfer Co., 337 U.S. 582, 650–51 (1949) (dissent); Chief Justice Taft, 8 A.B.A.J. 601, 604 (1922), and Chief Judge Parker, 51 Nw.U.L.Rev. 407 (1956), 18 A.B.A.J. 433, 437–39 (1932), found it a great blessing. In the not-too-distant past the Senate Judiciary Committee twice reported bills to abolish the jurisdiction, See S.Rep. No. 691, 71st Cong., 2d Sess. (1930), and a bill to that effect actually passed the House in 1978, only to perish in the Senate (H.R. 9622, 95th Cong., 2d Sess.).[3]

ability of broader discovery procedures, and the notion that federal juries render higher awards are the most frequently indicated reasons for preferring a federal court"; Note, The Choice Between State and Federal Court in Diversity Cases in Virginia, 51 Va.L.R. 178, 179–84 (1965), reporting that 60% of responding Virginia attorneys assigned bias against out-of-state plaintiffs as a reason for choosing the federal court; Goldman & Marks, Diversity Jurisdiction and Local Bias: A Preliminary Empirical Inquiry, 9 J. Legal Stud. 93 (1980), criticizing the methodology of these two earlier studies, and reporting that 40% of responding Chicago attorneys who had filed diversity suits in 1976 and 53% of responding Chicago attorneys who filed state-court suits in 1976 cited bias against out-of-state plaintiffs as a reason for choosing federal court.

2. See also the argument of Professor Charles Wright (Federal Courts 136–37 (4th ed. 1983)), based upon Chief Justice Taft's idea that "no single element in our governmental system has done so much to secure capital for the legitimate development of enterprises throughout the West and South" as diversity jurisdiction:

> The key question is not whether out-of-state investors will in fact receive fair treatment from state courts, but whether they think they will. If abolition, or significant curtailment, of diversity jurisdiction would give rise to irrational fears by investors, and inhibit their willingness to invest in different parts of the country, then diversity serves a useful purpose and should be retained.

3. Judge Friendly, supra note 2 at 3–4, 139–52, advocated abolition of diversity jurisdiction, except for interpleader and alien cases (see pp. 247–51 infra), in order to reduce what he viewed as the intolerable case load by as much as 25%. See also Professor Shapiro's suggestion, Federal Diversity Jurisdiction: A Survey and a Pro-

(4) The ALI Study concluded that diversity jurisdiction should be modified but retained. The commentary begins with what seems to be a ringing denunciation of diversity: Federal decision of state-law questions without state-court review "is an undesirable interference with state autonomy" and is bad for the federal courts too, for in such cases they lack "the creative function essential to their dignity and prestige." Further, the jurisdiction must be assessed in terms of its present utility; and its original purposes of encouraging freedom of movement and of business activity, and of spreading the good name of the initially weak national government, have long since been fulfilled. But

> ever since 1789 the federal government has pledged to travelers away from their home states the evenhanded justice of its own courts. This pledge is so woven into the fabric of our society that it is taken for granted. It should not lightly be withdrawn. General diversity jurisdiction should be retained unless it can be asserted with confidence that the shortcomings of state court justice which originally gave rise to it no longer exist to any significant degree.

Having thus shifted the burden of proof before suggesting any arguments in favor of diversity, the Reporters proceeded to demolish their case still further: "As to the matter of prejudice, the conventional justification for general diversity jurisdiction, none of the significant prejudices that beset our society today begins or ends when a state line is traversed." But "the bias that was formerly thought to operate against out-of-staters as such seems still to exist to some degree with respect to persons from a more distant part of the country. The diversity jurisdiction thus may give protection from real or imagined prejudice against persons who are indeed out-of-staters although the reason for the prejudice does not lie simply in this fact."

Prejudice, however, ought not to be considered as a separate problem but as "one aspect of the possible shortcomings of state justice." Some state courts suffer from "such infirmities in procedure as to jeopardize the fairness of adjudication;" some state courts are "so congested that justice to litigants, including out-of-staters, is unconscionably delayed;" and "state venue provisions often localize the place of trial in small constituencies," with the result that "justice is likely to be impeded by the provincialism of the local judge and jury, the tendency to favor one of their own against an outsider, and the machinations of the local 'court house gang.'" The Reporters conceded that all these factors might operate to some extent against citizens of the forum state as well as against outsiders. But "the citizen of a state, who may share in its political life, is properly held to responsibility for its institutions, and forced to operate within them, in ways which are inappropriate as to the out-of-stater, who has no such general opportunity to play a role in having the state's system changed." Finally, diversity jurisdiction served to avoid possible friction between States because the loser of a lawsuit, who "very commonly thinks of

posal, 91 Harv.L.Rev. 317, 332, 348–50 (1977), that because "some districts are more burdened than others, . . . sectional prejudices and provincialism are more acute in some areas than in others, and . . . the shortcomings of state court justice are greater in some areas than others," the judges of each district be allowed to determine whether or not to exercise diversity jurisdiction.

himself as a victim of injustice," might "attribute his defeat to bias or incompetence on the part of the deciding authority," and his resentment "may extend to that whole government." This was especially important when one of the parties was not a citizen of the United States. ALI, Study of the Division of Jurisdiction Between State and Federal Courts, 99–108 (1969).

With these principles in mind the ALI proposed a complete set of revised diversity provisions, a number of which are discussed below.

(5) Under the present statutes can a Pennsylvania plaintiff sue a Delaware defendant in a federal court in Delaware? In Pennsylvania? In New Jersey? The current venue statute, 28 U.S.C. § 1391(a), as amended in 1966, allows civil actions based solely on diverse citizenship to be brought "only in the judicial district where all plaintiffs or all defendants reside, or in which the claim arose." Jurisdiction over the person is governed by Rule 4 of the Federal Rules of Civil Procedure, which authorizes service of process on a defendant found or residing in the forum State, and which was amended in 1963 to make clear that service of process on absent nonresidents was permissible if authorized by the law of the forum State. See pp. 742–46 infra.

(6) Can a Delaware defendant remove to the federal court if he is sued by a Pennsylvania plaintiff in a state court in Pennsylvania? In Delaware? In New Jersey? Why should there be a discrepancy between the provisions for original and for removal jurisdiction? The ALI proposed to equalize the situation by forbidding either party to invoke federal jurisdiction in a State of which he was a citizen, because "the in-stater can hardly be heard to ask the federal government to spare him from litigation in the courts of his own state. Any prejudice which he may fear is not of the kind against which the diversity jurisdiction was intended to protect." ALI Study 124. The Institute estimated (id. at 6) that this proposal might cut diversity cases roughly in half. Why didn't the ALI propose a return to the pre-1875 requirement that one of the parties be a citizen of the forum State? Is a New Jersey court likely to be biased in an action between Pennsylvania and Delaware citizens?

Consider, however, the effect of the provisions for removal of state-court actions, § 1441(a), (b), and for transfer of venue in federal actions, § 1404(a), on proposals to forbid invocation of jurisdiction by a party unlikely to suffer from state-court bias. Is it fair to say that in many cases the result of such a limitation would be either simply to delay the process by which the case reaches the court in which it will be tried or to frustrate the policy that actions should be tried in a convenient forum?

SECTION 1. THE DETERMINATION OF CITIZENSHIP

SADAT v. MERTES

615 F.2d 1176 (7th Cir. 1980).

[Claiming to be a "citizen of the United States presently residing" in Egypt, Sadat in 1976 sued Wisconsin and Connecticut citizens for automobile negligence. Responding to a motion to dismiss for want of jurisdiction, Sadat argued that diversity existed on two separate grounds: (1) because his domicile was in Pennsylvania; (2) because he was a citizen of Egypt as well as of the United States. Rejecting both arguments, the district court dismissed, 464 F.Supp. 1311 (E.D.Wis. 1979).]

Per Curiam. . . .

II. The Plaintiff's Travels and Travails

. . . The plaintiff was born in Egypt, received his early schooling there, and apparently served in the Egyptian armed forces as a young man. He left his homeland during the 1950s and studied in Europe and worked in Kuwait before coming to the United States in 1963. While in the United States and prior to the events at issue here, he continued his education at several universities and at various times worked for several corporations. In 1973, he apparently was domiciled in Pittsburgh, Pennsylvania. He owned a home there; his wife worked for the University of Pittsburgh; and his children apparently attended the local schools there.

[In] 1973, [w]ith the permission of the government of Egypt he became a naturalized citizen of the United States. He also received an offer from Kohler International Ltd. to serve as the corporation's Area Manager for the Middle East. The job required the plaintiff, after a brief training period at the corporation's offices in Wisconsin, to relocate to Beirut, Lebanon. The plaintiff accepted the offer. His wife left her position with the university. He sold his house and began to move his family and personal property to Lebanon. On his way to O'Hare International Airport from Kohler's Wisconsin offices, the plaintiff was involved in the automobile accident giving rise to his complaint here. He nevertheless completed his move to Beirut and, once there, notified the U. S. Embassy that Beirut was his permanent overseas residence.

Mr. Sadat and his family stayed in Beirut for about two years. On April 15, 1975, apparently as a result of mutual dissatisfaction complicated by the political unrest in Lebanon, the plaintiff and his employer terminated their association with each other. . . . [Kohler agreed to pay for moving the family "to the United States or other location specified by Mr. Sadat," but hostilities broke out in Lebanon, and the plaintiff took his family to Egypt to avoid danger.]

After the plaintiff's move to Egypt, he stayed in Cairo for several years. According to the plaintiff, Kohler refused to honor its commitment to pay for transportation for him and his family to the location of his choice. He claimed he was financially unable to transport himself or his family back to the United States. He also was unable to obtain employment in Egypt, and, in the interim, he and his family resided in a house in Cairo that his mother purchased for him and he registered with the U. S. Embassy as a permanent resident. Documents submitted by the plaintiff indicate that he was issued Egyptian driver's licenses, paid the real estate taxes on the home, and maintained a checking account in Cairo during this time. In 1978, the plaintiff returned to the States and is now residing in Milwaukee.

III. WAS THE PLAINTIFF A CITIZEN OF ANY OF THE UNITED STATES?

The plaintiff's travels over time have been many, but this court's inquiry must center on his status at the time of the commencement of this action. As the district court noted, that is the time at which the jurisdiction of the court is determined. Smith v. Sperling, 354 U.S. 91, 93 n. 1 (1957). The plaintiff's status of June 7, 1976, therefore determines the capacity in which he brings this suit.

28 U.S.C. § 1332(a)(1) creates the federal courts' jurisdiction over actions between "citizens of different States." For a natural person to fall within the provision he must be both (1) a citizen of the United States and (2) a citizen of a particular state. See Scott v. Sandford, 60 U.S. (19 How.) 393, 405–06 (1857). . . . It is not disputed here that the plaintiff having been naturalized in 1973 is a citizen of the United States. What is contested is whether in 1976 when his complaint was filed he was a citizen of one of the United States. The issue is crucial to the plaintiff's claim of jurisdiction under 28 U.S.C. § 1332(a)(1) because settled precedent establishes that a citizen of the United States who is not also a citizen of one of the United States may not maintain suit under that section. Meyers v. Smith, 460 F.Supp. 621 (D.D.C.1978); . . . Hammerstein v. Lyne, 200 F. 165 (W.D.Mo.1912). Although this doctrine excluding Americans domiciled abroad from the federal courts has been questioned, the plaintiff does not directly attack it here and we see no reason for upsetting settled law now.

State citizenship for the purpose of the state diversity provision is equated with domicile. The standards for determining domicile in this context are found by resort to federal common law. Stifel v. Hopkins, 477 F.2d 1116, 1120 (6th Cir. 1973). . . . To establish a domicile of choice a person generally must be physically present at the location and intend to make that place his home for the time at least. See Restatement (Second) of Conflict of Laws §§ 15, 16, 18 (1971). Applying these standards, the district court found that the plaintiff was domiciled in Egypt in 1976. The plaintiff, however, contends that he should be considered a domiciliary of the State of Pennsylvania. He apparently bases his claim upon his previous domicile there in 1973 and his alleged intention to return there upon leaving Lebanon in 1975. "Unfortunately," the plaintiff's brief opines, "the successive events required [him] to move from Beruit, [sic] Lebanon to Cairo, Egypt and to take up residence there until he was able to return to the United States in 1978."

The plaintiff's deposition testimony makes clear that his move from Pennsylvania to Lebanon in 1973 effected a change in his domicile. He moved his belongings, his family, and his business to Lebanon. Then, in 1975 he moved again to Egypt where he and his family stayed through 1976, the year of the filing of his complaint. The plaintiff's affidavit in opposition to the defendants' motion to dismiss states that he "owns his home in Cairo, Egypt and considers himself a resident of Egypt where he was born and raised [and] that he maintains said home in Cairo, Egypt, which home contains his furniture, books, records and valuables." He also sent his children to school there and secured Egyptian driver's licenses there. This evidence was sufficient to permit the district court to find that the plaintiff was domiciled in Egypt notwithstanding his assertion that he never intended to make Egypt his home.[5] Although the plaintiff disclaimed any intention of settling in Cairo, "[i]ntent is a state of mind which must be evaluated through the circumstantial evidence of a person's manifested conduct," . . . and "statements of intent are entitled to little weight when in conflict with the facts". . . .

But even if the district court's conclusion that the plaintiff intended to make Egypt his home was erroneous, cf. Restatement (Second) of Conflict of Laws § 17, comment *f* (1971), that does not establish that Pennsylvania was the plaintiff's domicile. It only leads to the conclusion that Lebanon was. "A domicil once established continues until it is superseded by a new domicil." Id. at § 19. The plaintiff never returned to Pennsylvania after leaving for Lebanon in 1973 and thus never established the physical presence necessary to reestablish his domicile there. Moreover, his claimed intention to return to that state, assuming *arguendo* that in these circumstances intention alone would be sufficient to establish a new domicile, is refuted by the facts. First, the contract providing for Kohler to pay his moving expenses, contrary to his assertion in his brief, did not specify Pittsburgh as his destination. It gave the plaintiff his choice of destinations and provided that reimbursement would not exceed the cost of relocating the plaintiff to Pittsburgh. Second, the plaintiff's own deposition testimony indicates that his intention to return to Pennsylvania was less than firm. The compulsion which kept the plaintiff in Egypt was a financial one. Arguably, it may have prevented him from forming the intent to make Egypt his home, but it did not establish that his domicile was in one of

5. The plaintiff apparently did vote in the 1976 presidential elections by an absentee ballot sent to him from Pennsylvania. A party's voting practice, however, is only one of the factors considered in determining that person's domicile. No single factor is conclusive. 15 C. Wright, A. Miller, & E. Cooper, Federal Practice and Procedure § 3612 at 717 (1975).

the United States. Because the plaintiff, an American citizen, was domiciled abroad in 1976, he was not a citizen of a state within the meaning of 28 U.S.C. § 1332(a)(1). The jurisdiction of the district court, if it exists, must be found under 28 U.S.C. § 1332(a)(2).

IV. Is the Plaintiff a Citizen or Subject of a Foreign State?

The plaintiff's second argument is that if he is not a citizen of one of the United States, then he is by virtue of his dual American-Egyptian citizenship a citizen of a foreign state and jurisdiction therefore exists under 28 U.S.C. § 1332(a)(2). . . .

28 U.S.C. § 1332(a)(2) vests the district courts with jurisdiction over civil actions between state citizens and citizens of foreign states. This power is sometimes referred to as alienage jurisdiction. Although the basis for alienage jurisdiction is similar to that over controversies between state citizens, it is founded on more concrete concerns than the arguably unfounded fears of bias or prejudice by forums in one of the United States against litigants from another of the United States.

The dominant considerations which prompted the provision for such jurisdiction appear to have been:

> (1) Failure on the part of the individual states to give protection to foreigners under treaties; Farrand, "The Framing of the Constitution" 46 (1913); Nevins, "The American State During and After the Revolution" 644–656 (1924); Friendly, 41 Harvard Law Review 483, 484.
>
> (2) Apprehension of entanglements with other sovereigns that might ensue from failure to treat the legal controversies of aliens on a national level. Hamilton, "The Federalist" No. 80.

Blair Holdings Corp. v. Rubinstein, 133 F.Supp. 496, 500 (S.D.N.Y.1955). Thus, alienage jurisdiction was intended to provide the federal courts with a form of protective jurisdiction over matters implicating international relations where the national interest was paramount. See The Federalist No. 80 (A. Hamilton) ("[T]he peace of the WHOLE ought not to be left at the disposal of a PART. The Union will undoubtedly be answerable to foreign powers for the conduct of its members. And the responsibility for an injury ought ever to be accompanied with the faculty for preventing it.") [7] Recognizing this obvious national interest in such controversies, not even the proponents of the abolition of diversity jurisdiction over suits between citizens of the several United States have advocated elimination of alienage jurisdiction. See, e.g., H. Friendly, Federal Jurisdiction: A General View 149–50 (1973); Rowe,

7. See also American Law Institute, Study of the Division of Jurisdiction Between State and Federal Courts 108 (1969):

> It is important in the relations of this country with other nations that any possible appearance of injustice or tenable ground for resentment be avoided. This objective can best be achieved by giving the foreigner the assurance that he can have his cases tried in a court with the best procedures the federal government can supply and with the dignity and prestige of the United States behind it.

Abolishing Diversity Jurisdiction: Positive Side Effects and Potential for Further Reforms, 92 Harv.L.Rev. 963, 966–68 (1979). . . .

The generally accepted test for determining whether a person is a foreign citizen for purposes of 28 U.S.C. § 1332(a)(2) is whether the country in which citizenship is claimed would so recognize him. This is in accord with the principle of international law that "it is the inherent right of every independent nation to determine for itself, and according to its own constitution and laws, what classes of persons shall be entitled to its citizenship." United States v. Wong Kim Ark, 169 U.S. 649, 668 (1898). See, e.g., Murarka v. Bachrack Bros., 215 F.2d 547, 553 (2d Cir. 1954) (Harlan, J.). . . .

Relying on this principle, the plaintiff maintains that notwithstanding his U.S. naturalization, Egypt still regards him as an Egyptian citizen. The evidence in the record tends to sustain his contention. . . . A letter from the Egyptian Minister of Exterior to the plaintiff states:

> Greetings, we have the honor to inform you that it has been agreed to permit you to be naturalized with United States Citizenship but retaining your Egyptian citizenship. . . .

This evidence is sufficient to establish that, despite his naturalization in the United States, the plaintiff is an Egyptian under that country's laws. Consequently, under the ordinary choice of law rule for determining nationality under 28 U.S.C. § 1332(a)(2) he would be so regarded for the purpose of determining the district court's jurisdiction over the subject matter. Thus, the issue squarely presented to this court is whether a person possessing dual nationality, one of which is United States citizenship, is "a citizen or subject of a foreign state" under 28 U.S.C. § 1332(a)(2). . . .

Whether a person possessing dual nationality should be considered a citizen or subject of a foreign state within the meaning of 28 U.S.C. § 1332(a)(2) is a question of first impression in the courts of appeals. The two district courts other than the district court below which have addressed the question have reached seemingly different conclusions. In Aguirre v. Nagel, 270 F.Supp. 535 (E.D.Mich.1967), the plaintiff, a citizen of the United States and the State of Michigan, sued a Michigan citizen for injuries sustained when she was hit by the defendant's car. The court . . . [found] jurisdiction under 28 U.S.C. § 1332(a)(2) because the plaintiff's parents were citizens of Mexico and Mexico regarded her as a Mexican citizen by virtue of her parentage. The *Aguirre* court's opinion did no more than determine that the cause fell within the literal language of the statute without regard to the policies underlying alienage jurisdiction. As a result it has been questioned by the commentators, see 1 Moore's Federal Practice ¶ 0.75[1.–1] at 709.4–.5 (2d ed. 1979); 13 C. Wright, A. Miller, & E. Cooper, Federal Practice and Procedure § 3621 at 759–60 (1975), and rejected by one other district court in addition to the court below. See Raphael v. Hertzberg, 470 F.Supp. 984 (C.D.Cal.1979). . . .

In rejecting the authority of *Aguirre*, the court in *Raphael* noted several possible objections to permitting naturalized Americans to assert their foreign citizenship:

> To begin with, the holding in *Aguirre* violates the requirement of complete diversity (Strawbridge v. Curtiss, 7 U.S. (3 Cranch) 267 (1806)) since *Aguirre*, like the present case, involved opposing parties who were both American citizens and who resided in the same state. Moreover, where both parties are residents of the state in which the action is brought, there is no reason to expect bias from the state courts. Finally, so long as the party asserting diversity jurisdiction is an American citizen, there is little reason to fear that a foreign government may be affronted by a decision adverse to that citizen, even if the American citizen also purports to be a citizen of that foreign nation. . . .
>
> The rule proposed by the plaintiff would give naturalized citizens nearly unlimited access to the federal courts, access which has been denied to native-born citizens. Such favored treatment is unsupported by the policies underlying 28 U.S.C. § 1332(a)(2). Finally, a new rule that would extend the scope of § 1332 is particularly undesirable in light of the ever-rising level of criticism of the very concept of diversity jurisdiction. . . .

Although the issue facing the courts in *Aguirre* and *Raphael* is the same as the one presented here, the facts in this case are somewhat different. All commentators addressing the issue have noted the anomaly of permitting an American citizen claiming dual citizenship to obtain access to the federal court under 28 U.S.C. § 1332(a)(2) when suing a citizen domiciled in the same state. *See* 1 Moore's Federal Practice ¶ 0.75[1–1] at 709.5 (2d ed. 1979):

> This result is inconsistent with the complete diversity rule of *Strawbridge v. Curtiss*, . . . including the analogous situation of a suit between a citizen of State A and a corporation chartered in State B with its principal place of business in State A. Both state citizenships of the corporation must be considered and diversity is thus found lacking.

. . .[12] In the present case, however, the plaintiff was domiciled abroad when he initiated this action and therefore was not a citizen of any state. Thus, permitting suit under alienage jurisdiction would not run counter to the complete diversity considerations which arguably should have controlled the decisions in *Aguirre* and *Raphael*.[13]

12. The requirement of complete diversity has been held to preclude jurisdiction over actions which otherwise could have been maintained under 28 U.S.C. § 1332(a)(2). See Ed & Fred, Inc. v. Puritan Marine Insurance Underwriters Corp., 506 F.2d 757 (5th Cir. 1975).

13. Moreover, because in this case unlike *Aguirre* and *Raphael* the plaintiff is domiciled abroad, there might be some reason to fear bias if the suit were brought in the state courts. The fear of bias against out-of-state litigants, while a traditional basis for positing jurisdiction, has of recent years been subject to questioning as being too remote and speculative a basis. And, because the plaintiff is an American citizen as well as an Egyptian, the risk of bias in a state forum against the litigant because he is also a foreign national would appear less substantial. The plaintiff's position, therefore, is little different than

The plaintiff seizing upon this factual difference would apparently have this court recognize his dual nationality for purposes of 28 U.S.C. § 1332 in much the same way corporations are regarded as having dual citizenship pursuant to 28 U.S.C. § 1332(c). Because in this case, even applying the corporate citizenship analogy, the complete diversity requirement is satisfied, the plaintiff argues that jurisdiction under 28 U.S.C. § 1332(a)(2) attaches. Such an approach, however, may be both too broad and too narrow and it ignores the paramount purpose of the alienage jurisdiction provision to avoid offense to foreign nations because of the possible appearance of injustice to their citizens. Imagine, for example, a native-born American, born of Japanese parents, domiciled in the State of California, and now engaged in international trade. A dispute could arise in which an Australian customer seeks to sue the American for, say, breach of contract in a federal court in California. The native-born American possibly could claim Japanese citizenship by virtue of his parentage . . . as well as his status as a citizen of California and defeat the jurisdiction of the federal courts because of the absence of complete diversity. Arguably, cases such as this are precisely those in which a federal forum should be afforded the foreign litigant in the interest of preventing international friction.

This hypothetical suggests that the analogy to the dual citizenship of corporations should not be controlling. Instead, the paramount consideration should be whether the purpose of alienage jurisdiction to avoid international discord would be served by recognizing the foreign citizenship of the dual national. Because of the wide variety of situations in which dual nationality can arise, . . . perhaps no single rule can be controlling. Principles establishing the responsibility of nations under international law with respect to actions affecting dual nationals, however, suggest by analogy that ordinarily, as the district court held, only the American nationality of the dual citizen should be recognized under 28 U.S.C. § 1332(a).

Under international law, a country is responsible for official conduct harming aliens, for example, the expropriation of property without compensation. See Restatement (Second) of the Foreign Relations Law of the United States §§ 164–214 (1965). It is often said, however, that a state is not responsible for conduct which would otherwise be regarded as wrongful if the injured person, although a citizen of a foreign state, is also a national of the state taking the questioned action. See id. at § 171, comments b & c. This rule recognizes that in the usual case a foreign country cannot complain about the treatment received by one of its citizens by a country which also regards that person as a national. . . .

Despite the general rule of nonresponsibility under international law for conduct affecting dual nationals, there are recognized excep-

that of any other American national domiciled abroad. Such people, of course, cannot obtain access to the federal courts under the diversity or alienage jurisdiction provisions.

tions. One is the concept of effective or dominant nationality. As qualified by the Restatement, this exception provides that a country (respondent state) will be responsible for wrongful conduct against one of its citizens whose dominant nationality is that of a foreign state, that is,

> (i) his dominant nationality, by reason of residence or other association subject to his control (or the control of a member of his family whose nationality determines his nationality) is that of the other state and (ii) he (or such member of his family) has manifested an intention to be a national of the other state and has taken all reasonably practicable steps to avoid or terminate his status as a national of the respondent state. . . .

Although at the time of the filing of his complaint in 1976 the plaintiff resided in Egypt, his voluntary naturalization in the United States in 1973 indicates that his dominant nationality is not Egyptian. As part of the naturalization process he swore allegiance to the United States and renounced any to foreign states. His actions subsequent to his naturalization evince his resolve to remain a U.S. citizen despite his extended stay abroad. . . . Certainly neither he nor the government of Egypt can complain if he is not afforded a federal forum when the same would be denied a similarly situated native-born American. . . .

The judgment of the district court is Affirmed.

Notes on Determining "Citizenship" in Diversity Cases

(1) *Sadat* states the general principle that for diversity purposes foreign citizenship is determined by nationality and citizenship in an American State by domicile. It also states two qualifications: Only a United States citizen can be a "citizen of a State," [1] and a person with American citizenship cannot also (on the facts of that case) be a "citizen of a foreign state." Do these rules follow from the language or purposes of § 1332?

Why, for example, as the Supreme Court confirmed in Newman–Green, Inc. v. Alfonzo–Larrain, 109 S.Ct. 2218 (1989), is an American domiciled abroad not a "subject" of a foreign state, even if not a "citizen?" See Van Der Schelling v. U. S. News & World Report, Inc., 213 F.Supp. 756, 761 (E.D.Pa.1963), relying on the fact that earlier versions of the statute had used the term "alien" and adding: "It was only by the inclusion of 'subjects' that all aliens, whether they owed allegiance to a sovereign monarch or were citizens of a democracy could sue or be sued in federal courts." Could the statute be amended to include Americans domiciled abroad? Should it be?[2]

1. Notice that what *Sadat* cited for this proposition was the most familiar of all cases involving the meaning of citizenship for diversity purposes: Scott v. Sandford, 60 U.S. (19 How.) 393, 416–17 (1857), where four Justices took the position that a black descended from slaves, even if himself free, was not a citizen of his home State and therefore could not maintain a diversity suit. The Fourteenth Amendment now provides to the contrary.

2. What is a "foreign state" within § 1332 or Article III? See Klausner v. Levy, 83 F.Supp. 599, 600 (E.D.Va.1949), refusing jurisdiction in an action brought by a citizen of Palestine while that was a mandated territory under British supervi-

(2) The general rules enunciated in *Sadat* were modified by a 1988 amendment to § 1332(a)(4): "[A]n alien admitted to the United States for permanent residence shall be deemed a citizen of the State in which such alien is domiciled." Does this provision eliminate jurisdiction of actions between such aliens and other citizens of the same State? If so, is it wise? Does it also *create* jurisdiction between resident and nonresident aliens? If so, is it constitutional? [3]

(3) In Hepburn v. Ellzey, 6 U.S. (2 Cr.) 445 (1805), Chief Justice Marshall for the Court held the District of Columbia was not a "State" within the diversity statute, because it was not a "State" under the Constitution. In 1940 the Congress gave the district courts jurisdiction of cases between "citizens of different states, or citizens of the District of Columbia, the Territory of Hawaii, or Alaska, and any State or Territory." 54 Stat. 143. A majority of the Court in National Mut. Ins. Co. v. Tidewater Transfer Co., 337 U.S. 582 (1949), supra p. 128, adhered to the *Hepburn* dictum that "State" in Article III meant those allegedly quasi-sovereign members of the Union entitled to elect Senators. Don't look now, but the Court nevertheless managed to uphold the statute as applied to an action between citizens of Virginia and of the District of Columbia. If you were drafting a constitutional provision to protect nonresidents from state-court bias, would you leave out citizens of the District of Columbia, of Puerto Rico, or of the United States Territories or Possessions? Does the language of Article III really exclude them?

(4) Domicile, the test of state citizenship for United States citizens,[4] is as *Sadat* indicates a more complicated concept than residence. Domicile is often determinative of other legal questions outside the context of federal jurisdiction, such as taxation, voting, and the choice between conflicting state laws. Scholars have warned against transferring precedents concerning domicile from one field to another without considering the underlying policies, and *Sadat* reflects the common view that domicile for diversity purposes is determined as a matter of federal law. Nevertheless, as *Sadat*

sion. The plaintiff was held not to be a citizen of Great Britain, even though Palestine was "without local autonomy" and its citizens were entitled to British diplomatic protection, because Palestine had power to confer its own citizenship. But Palestine was not a "foreign state," because § 1332 refers only to a state "formally recognized by the executive branch of the government of the United States. . . . As recognition of a sovereignty is a political and not a judicial matter, the courts are conclusively bound by the status accorded a territory by the executive department. . . ." Does this decision comport well with the purposes of the jurisdictional grant? See also Murarka v. Bachrack Bros., Inc., 215 F.2d 547, 552 (2d Cir. 1954) (alternative holding).

3. The original statute purporting to grant jurisdiction whenever "an alien is a party" was narrowed on constitutional grounds in Mossman v. Higginson, 4 U.S. (4 Dall.) 12 (1800). See Verlinden B.V. v. Central Bank of Nigeria, p. 148 supra, construing the Foreign Sovereign Immunities Act's provision for jurisdiction over "any nonjury civil action against a foreign state. . . ." (28 U.S.C. § 1330) to authorize suit by an alien against a foreign government and upholding it on federal-question rather than diversity grounds.

4. This despite the Fourteenth Amendment's declaration that persons born or naturalized in this country are citizens of the United States "and of the State wherein they reside" and an early Supreme Court statement to the same effect respecting diversity jurisdiction, Gassies v. Ballon, 31 U.S. (6 Pet.) 761, 762 (1832). See, e.g., Everhart v. Huntsville Female College, 120 U.S. 223 (1887) (allegation of "residence" insufficient allegation of citizenship); Williamson v. Osenton, 232 U.S. 619, 624–26 (1914).

shows, federal courts commonly refer to the Restatement, Conflict of Laws (1934 and 1971) in ascertaining state citizenship under § 1332, perhaps because it is a convenient and exhaustive compendium.

(5) Thirty-three sections of the first Conflicts Restatement [5] are devoted to determining domicile. In the manner of Procrustes § 11 provides that everyone has a domicile and nobody more than one ("A is a wanderer, without a home; a domicile is assigned him by law." Isn't that nice!) A legitimate child takes its father's domicile at birth, an illegitimate its mother's, § 14.[6]

A married woman, according to §§ 27 and 28 of the first Restatement, took the domicile of her husband, except in cases of separate residence due to a breakdown of the marriage.[7] This rule was followed under § 1332 in Seegers v. Strzempek, 149 F.Supp. 35, 37 (E.D.Mich.1957). But in Mas v. Perry, 489 F.2d 1396 (5th Cir. 1974), the court refused to hold that a Mississippi woman had taken the domicile of her French husband because to do so would render her a citizen of nowhere for diversity purposes. Does the Restatement view survive the Supreme Court's recent pronouncements on sex discrimination under the Equal Protection Clause? Cf. Kirchberg v. Feenstra, 450 U.S. 455 (1981), striking down a state law giving the husband sole control of community property.

(6) Where is the domicile of a person who is housed in New Jersey and works in New York? According to the first Restatement, § 12, domicile is where the home is; and "doing business in a place is not an important element in fixing his home there," § 13, comment f. Why isn't it? On the other hand, "a person may have a home in a place in which he never eats," and "it is conceivable that a person can have a home in a place in which he never sleeps." Ibid. What then is determinative? [8]

(7) Where is the domicile of a law student whose parents live in New York but who attends school in Chicago? Of a soldier who lived with his parents in Maine until he was drafted and stationed in Texas? Of a man who lived in Detroit until he was sent to the federal penitentiary in Leavenworth, Kansas?

5. The Restatement Second is in most respects similar but somewhat less amusing.

6. If the parent's domicile is unknown, the Restatement comes to the rescue: "A, a gipsy, arrives in X with his young son B. Where A comes from is unknown. X may properly be taken to be B's domicil of origin." § 14 illustration 2. "A child abandoned by one parent has the domicil of the other parent," § 33; "if both parents abandon it at the same time, it has the domicil of the father at the time of the abandonment."

7. The Restatement Second, § 21, equivocates on this point.

8. "Where a person has his home in a dwelling-house which is situated upon a dividing line between political divisions of territory, his domicil is within that territorial division in which the preponderant part of his dwelling-house is situated; if there is no preponderance, the domicil is in the territorial division in which the principal entrance to the house is situated." Restatement, § 25. Which is the "preponderant part" of a house? That containing the larger floor area? The greater number of rooms? The kitchen? The bedroom? Suppose the state line runs right across the bed, crosswise? Lengthwise? Is the "principal entrance" always the front door? The Restatement appears to leave these questions unanswered. Do any principles emerge from the Restatement rules that would guide decisions in unanswered cases?

See Lewis v. Splashdam By-Products Corp., 233 F.Supp. 47, 49 (W.D.Va. 1964), sustaining diversity jurisdiction in an action by union leader John L. Lewis against a Virginia corporation: Although the plaintiff had resided in Alexandria, Virginia for thirty years, he alleged that he had "maintained his Illinois residence" and voted only in Illinois during that time. The court held that, like an Illinois congressman, he remained a citizen of Illinois because he had expressed his intention to return: "A change of residence occasioned by the exercise of duties . . . would not result in a new domicile unless . . . accompanied by an intention to abandon the old domicile in Illinois." Accord as to a soldier, Seegers v. Strzempek, 149 F.Supp. 35, 37 (E.D.Mich.1957).

See also the exhaustive opinion of Judge McCree in Stifel v. Hopkins, 477 F.2d 1116 (6th Cir. 1973), holding it error to refuse to ever allow a person in prison in a State away from his former home to establish a new domicile and remanding for findings of fact: "The bare fact that a person has been 'compelled' to relocate within a particular jurisdiction does not ordinarily prevent him from becoming domiciled therein, although courts are justifiably concerned with substantiating declared intentions." The prisoner had alleged that he did not intend to return to his earlier home because the circumstances of his conviction had made him a "target of great public hostility" there; the court added drily that "the fact that he is serving a life sentence, of course, lends a great deal of credibility to his assertion that he will never return to Ohio."

Should it be easier for people in such circumstances to retain old domiciles than to acquire new ones? Would residence be a more satisfactory test of citizenship for diversity cases than domicile? Can you define residence?

(8) The Supreme Court has held that a change of citizenship after suit is filed in federal court does not destroy diversity jurisdiction, because jurisdiction is determined by the facts existing when the complaint is filed. E.g., Mollan v. Torrance, 22 U.S. (9 Wheat.) 537, 539 (1824); accord, Clemmer v. Kummer, 187 F.Supp. 736 (D.Minn.1960). What justification is there for this? Does it follow that a defect in jurisdiction at the time of the complaint cannot be cured by a later change of citizenship? What sense would that make? Compare Mansfield, Coldwater & L. M. Ry. v. Swan, 111 U.S. 379 (1884): To sustain jurisdiction of an action removed from a state court "the difference of citizenship on which the right of removal depends must have existed at the time when the suit was begun, as well as at the time of the removal." Why?

(9) The ALI's Jurisdiction Study was silent as to the definition of citizenship in diversity cases, but it exhibited a certain dissatisfaction with the traditional test of domicile by proposing the following new subsection:

> No individual citizen of the United States who has and for a period of more than two years has had his principal place of business or employment in a State can invoke that [diversity] jurisdiction, either originally or on removal, in any district in that State.

ALI Study 13. The reasons for this subsection are given at pages 130–32:

> Rivers that used to divide now serve to unify. What was originally a natural state boundary has become a magnet to industry and commerce. The result has been the creation of large metropolitan districts none the less unitary in their nature because they transcend state lines. This has produced a category of diversity cases involving commuters that seem to have no proper place in the federal courts. Certainly local prejudice, the classic justification for general jurisdiction is most unlikely. . . . It may be true that state justice has shortcomings that the commuter cannot as a practical matter do anything to correct, but the in-stater who works by his side is not significantly more likely to have an effective voice in the matter.

Would this provision, if enacted, be easy to apply? Is it true that resentment against people who daily enjoy the benefits of New York expenditures without paying full New York taxes is unlikely? Wasn't the ability of a New Yorker to improve New York courts, here so disparaged, an important justification given by the ALI for granting federal jurisdiction only to outsiders? See pp. 229–30 supra.

(10) If you're in a Ray Bradbury mood, you might also consider the significance for diversity purposes of the uninhibited musings of Harold Lasswell, in The Political Science of Science, 50 Am.Pol.Sci.Rev. 961 (1965):

> Apparently we are closer than most of us like to think to the production of species that occupy an intermediate position between man and the lower animals (or even plants) [plants?]. . . . Experimental models of robots have been built who [sic] solve problems of a rather complex order in a given environment. Some of these machines look after themselves to a degree, obtaining and using the raw materials required for energy and repairs. Already it is claimed that the function of reproducing its kind, and of interacting with others, can be in-built. . . . It is not to be overlooked that the problem of human capability can become acute if in the years ahead we escape from our present habitat on the earth, or are visited by other forms of intelligent life. . . .
>
> Given our concern for human dignity when do we wisely extend all or part of the Universal Declaration of Human Rights to these forms?

Mr. Lasswell is a nut, isn't he?

For more details as to the determination of citizenship see Weckstein, Citizenship for Purposes of Diversity Jurisdiction, 26 Sw.L.J. 360 (1972).

Notes on Administrators, Assignments, and Collusion

(1) For many years, when the executor or administrator of a decedent's estate was party to a case, the citizenship of the executor or administrator was determinative. See, e.g., Chappedelaine v. Dechenaux, 8 U.S. (4 Cranch) 306 (1808); Rice v. Houston, 80 U.S. (13 Wall.) 66 (1871).

The opportunity afforded by these decisions for manufacturing or defeating diversity jurisdiction did not escape the bar. In Mecom v. Fitzsimmons Drilling Co., 284 U.S. 183 (1931), an administratrix had filed three successive wrongful-death actions in state court. Each time the defendants had removed on diversity grounds, and each time the plaintiff had had the action dismissed. Finally she resigned and secured the appointment of an administrator from another State, in order, the Supreme Court found, to defeat diversity jurisdiction. In Corabi v. Auto Racing, Inc., 264 F.2d 784 (3d Cir. 1959), an administratrix had asked and been granted leave to resign because "It is the desire of your petitioner that an action be instituted to recover for the death of her son in the District Court of the United States for the Western District of Pennsylvania and herewith tenders her resignation as . . . administratrix in order that Letters of Administration may be granted to a nonresident for the purpose of such action." In both cases the substitution was effective; the Supreme Court in *Mecom* and the Court of Appeals in *Corabi* held the motive of the new appointment immaterial.[1]

(2) Congress has, however, been concerned about efforts to impose upon the jurisdiction. The famous Assignee Clause of § 11 of the 1789 Judiciary Act (p. 759 infra) had flatly required diversity between the plaintiff's assignor and the defendant in an effort "to frustrate one of the obvious means by which a litigant might seek to manufacture a basis of federal jurisdiction," see Hart & Wechsler, The Federal Courts and the Federal System 918 (1953).[2] Moreover, an 1875 statute (18 Stat. 470) required dismissal of any suit in which "the parties . . . have been improperly or collusively made or joined . . . for the purpose of creating" federal jurisdiction. In 1948 these two provisions were amended and combined in the present 28 U.S.C. § 1359, which denies jurisdiction of any case in which "any party, by assignment or otherwise, has been improperly or collusively made or joined to invoke the jurisdiction of the federal courts."

What makes an assignment or other device to join or create parties "improper" or "collusive?" In Black & White Taxicab Co. v. Brown & Yellow Taxicab Co., 276 U.S. 518, 524 (1928), the Court observed that the owners of the plaintiff had dissolved their original corporation and reincorporated in another State "in order to create a diversity of citizenship" but upheld jurisdiction because "the succession and transfer were actual, not feigned or merely colorable"; motive was therefore immaterial. Section 1359 was found to preclude jurisdiction, however, in Kramer v. Caribbean Mills, Inc., 394 U.S. 823 (1969), when a nondiverse creditor assigned his claim to a company diverse to the debtor and was reassigned a 95% interest in the claim:

> If federal jurisdiction could be created by assignments of this kind, which are easy to arrange and involve few disadvantages for the assignor, then a vast quantity of ordinary contract and tort litigation could be channeled into the federal courts at the will of one of the parties. Such "manufacture of Federal jurisdiction" was the very

1. This was in accord with the Supreme Court's statement that the motive for a change of domicile is immaterial; the domicile of the parties at the time of suit determines jurisdiction even if that domicile was acquired in order to create (or presumably to defeat) federal jurisdiction. Williamson v. Osenton, 232 U.S. 619, 624–25 (1914); accord, Rivera v. Chapa, 233 F.Supp. 428 (S.D.Tex.1964).

2. This provision was imprecisely tailored to the need: "While leaving unaffected collusive assignments outside its scope, the section applied indiscriminately to assignments within its scope whether they were collusive or not," ibid.

> thing which Congress intended to prevent when it enacted § 1359 and its predecessors.

The Court added that it had no occasion to re-examine decisions such as *Black & White Taxi*, refusing to look at motive "where the transfer of a claim is absolute, with the transferor retaining no interest in the subject matter."

Is there any answer to *Corabi*'s argument that, if Congress had meant to outlaw every effort to manufacture diversity, there would have been no need for the words "improperly or collusively?"[3]

(3) Dissatisfaction with the rule that the citizenship of the executor or administrator governed, however, was not limited to cases of appointments designed to manufacture or defeat jurisdiction. Taking a flexible view of the precedents, the Fourth Circuit in a long and intricate series of decisions created exceptions for cases in which the appointment of a resident representative was required by state law or in which the executor or administrator was a purely nominal party. In the former instance the court noted that state law could not deprive noncitizens of their right to a federal forum (Miller v. Perry, 456 F.2d 63 (4th Cir.1972)); in the second it argued more generally that jurisdiction should not depend upon the citizenship of an individual who had nothing to win or lose personally in the litigation. Messer v. American Gems, Inc., 612 F.2d 1367 (4th Cir.1980). Following this logic, Congress did away with the old rule entirely by enacting § 1332(c)(2) in 1988:

> [T]he legal representative of the estate of a decedent shall be deemed to be a citizen only of the same State as the decedent, and the legal representative of an infant or incompetent shall be deemed to be a citizen only of the same State as the infant or incompetent.

Is there hope for the world after all?

SECTION 2. "COMPLETE" DIVERSITY AND ANCILLARY JURISDICTION

STRAWBRIDGE v. CURTISS

7 U.S. (3 Cranch) 267 (1806).

This was an appeal from a decree of the Circuit Court, for the district of Massachusetts, which dismissed the complainants' bill in chancery, for want of jurisdiction.

Some of the complainants were alleged to be citizens of the state of Massachusetts. The defendants were also stated to be citizens of the same state, excepting Curtiss, who was averred to be a citizen of the

3. The ALI's proposed § 1307, ALI Study 22–23, 158, would once again separate the assignee problem from the general collusion problem, assimilating the appointment of certain fiduciaries (receivers, trustees, and the like) to the former and barring jurisdiction in the case of assignments when "an object" of the transaction is either "to enable *or to prevent* the invoking of federal jurisdiction. . . ." (emphasis added) Why shouldn't the same be true of *all* improper attempts to defeat jurisdiction?

state of Vermont, and upon whom the *subpoena* was served in that state.

The question of jurisdiction was submitted to the court, without argument, by *P. B. Key*, for the appellants, and *Harper*, for the appellees.

On a subsequent day, MARSHALL, CH. J., delivered the opinion of the court.

The court has considered this case, and is of opinion that the jurisdiction cannot be supported.

The words of the act of congress are, "where an alien is a party; or the suit is between a citizen of a state where the suit is brought, and a citizen of another state." The court understands these expressions to mean, that each distinct interest should be represented by persons, all of whom are entitled to sue, or may be sued, in the federal courts. That is, that where the interest is joint, each of the persons concerned in that interest must be competent to sue, or liable to be sued, in those courts.

But the court does not mean to give an opinion in the case where several parties represent several distinct interests, and some of those parties are, and others are not, competent to sue, or liable to be sued, in the courts of the United States.

Decree affirmed.

Notes on Complete Diversity

(1) The abbreviated and obscure opinion in *Strawbridge v. Curtiss*, reproduced here in full, is the source of the fundamental rule of diversity jurisdiction: Diversity must be "complete." That is, "diversity jurisdiction does not exist unless *each* defendant is a citizen of a different state from *each* plaintiff." Owen Equipment & Erection Co. v. Kroger, 437 U.S. 365, 373 (1978).

Why? Assuming that the defendants in *Strawbridge* were partners sued on a partnership obligation, did the Vermont defendant's common interest with a Massachusetts citizen protect the former from bias in a Massachusetts court? Would a Vermont litigant be protected if the interests were not joint, for example, if he and a Massachusetts party were drivers of two colliding automobiles sued for concurrent negligence? Would even a joint interest between Massachusetts and Vermont defendants protect a lone Massachusetts plaintiff from bias in favor of local people if suit is brought in Vermont? The courts have ignored these questions, requiring complete diversity under § 1332 and its predecessors without regard to forum, see Knoll v. Knoll, 350 F.2d 407 (10th Cir. 1965), and whether the interests are joint or several, see Friend v. Middle Atl. Transp. Co., 153 F.2d 778 (2d Cir. 1946). Indeed at least two courts have invoked *Strawbridge* to deny jurisdiction of actions by aliens against citizens of States and other aliens, even though the opposing alien parties were citizens of different countries. E.g., Field v. Volkswagenwerk AG, 626 F.2d 293 (3rd Cir. 1980); Corporacion Venezolana de Fomento v. Vintero

Sales Corp., 629 F.2d 786 (2d Cir. 1980). Does this result follow from the policies evidently underlying *Strawbridge*?

Notice the somewhat related rule codified in the current removal statute: Absent a federal question, an action is removable "only if none of the parties in interest properly joined and served as defendants is a citizen of the State in which such action is brought." 28 U.S.C. § 1441(b). But see § 1441(c), considered infra pp. 260–67.

(2) Notice the curious provision in § 1332(a)(3) for jurisdiction of actions "between citizens of different States and in which citizens or subjects of a foreign state are additional parties." Does this mean there is jurisdiction of a case involving plaintiffs from France and New York and defendants from France and New Jersey? The specific purpose of the subsection, enacted in 1948, may have been narrower. Earlier decisions were divided as to whether a citizen of one state could sue two defendants, one an alien and the other a citizen of a second State. Although such a case could be said to combine two controversies, each within the statute, some courts refused jurisdiction because the case as a whole was neither a suit between "citizens of different States" nor one "between citizens of a State and citizens or subjects of a foreign state." See, e.g., Roberts v. Pacific & A. Ry., 121 Fed. 785, 787 (9th Cir. 1903), and Ryan v. Ohmer, 233 Fed. 165 (S.D.N.Y.1916), upholding jurisdiction; Tracy v. Morel, 88 Fed. 801 (C.C.D. Neb.1898) (alternative holding), denying jurisdiction; Moore's Commentary on the Judicial Code 154 (1949).

The language of § 1332(a)(3), however, is broad enough to permit jurisdiction, so long as there is complete diversity among state citizens, even though there are citizens of France on both sides of the case. Would it be reasonable to allow jurisdiction in such a case while denying it in *Strawbridge*? If the statute provides for this jurisdiction, is it constitutional? See Friendly, Federal Jurisdiction: A General View 150 n. 42 (1973): "Since the basis for the jurisdiction would be the possible effect on international relations, I would not be inclined to modify [§ 1332(a)(3)] . . . to eliminate jurisdiction in the rare case where the foreign plaintiff and defendant are citizens of the same foreign state."

(3) Newman–Green, Inc. v. Alfonzo–Larrain, 109 S.Ct. 2218 (1989), was an action by an Illinois corporation against a Venezuelan corporation for breach of a licensing agreement and against five guarantors, four of whom were also of Venezuelan nationality. The fifth guarantor was an American domiciled in Venezuela. After the trial court had decided the case on the merits, the court of appeals noticed that there was no jurisdiction under either § 1332(a)(2) or (3) (do you see why?) and ultimately remanded the case to the district court for further proceedings.

Over two dissents, the Supreme Court reversed: Since the nondiverse defendant was not indispensable, the court of appeals could cure the jurisdictional defect by dropping him as a party. "[R]equiring dismissal after years of litigation would impose unnecessary and wasteful burdens." It was true that 28 U.S.C. § 1653 ("[d]efective allegations of jurisdiction may be amended . . . in the trial or appellate courts") "addresses only incorrect statements about jurisdiction that actually exists, and not defects in the jurisdictional facts themselves." But it was "well settled" that Rule

21 of the Federal Rules of Procedure, which permits "parties [to] be dropped or added . . . at any stage of the action," "invests district courts with authority to allow a dispensable nondiverse party to be dropped at any time, even after judgment has been rendered"; and "the policies informing Rule 21 may apply equally to the courts of appeals."

If neither the Rule nor the statute authorized the court of appeals to dismiss the nondiverse party, what did?

TREINIES v. SUNSHINE MINING CO.

308 U.S. 66 (1939).

MR. JUSTICE REED delivered the opinion of the Court.

This writ of certiorari was granted to review the action of the Court of Appeals for the Ninth Circuit in affirming a decree of the District Court of Idaho upon a bill of interpleader filed by the Sunshine Mining Company, a Washington corporation, against Evelyn H. Treinies and other citizens of the State of Washington, claimants to certain stock of the Sunshine Mining Company and the dividends therefrom, and Katherine Mason and T. R. Mason, her husband, and other citizens of the State of Idaho, adverse claimants to the same stock and dividends.

The occasion for the interpleader was the existence of inconsistent judgments as to the ownership of the Sunshine stock. The Superior Court of Spokane County, Washington, in administering the estate of Amelia Pelkes, adjudged that it was the property of John Pelkes, assignor of petitioner, Evelyn H. Treinies; and the District Court of Shoshone County, Idaho, adjudged that the same property belonged to respondent, Katherine Mason. They are the sole disputants. Other parties may be disregarded. On account of conflict between the judgments of the respective courts of sister states and the assertion of the failure to give full faith and credit to both in the interpleader action, we granted certiorari. . . .

Before considering the questions raised by the petition for certiorari, the jurisdiction of the federal court under the Act of January 20, 1936,* must be determined. As this issue affects the jurisdiction of this Court, it is raised on its own motion. By the Act of January 20, 1936, the district courts have jurisdiction of suits in equity, interpleading two or more adverse claimants, instituted by complainants who have property of the requisite value claimed by citizens of different states. The suit may be maintained "although the titles or claims of the conflicting claimants do not have a common origin, or are not identical, but are adverse to and independent of one another." Process may run at least throughout all the states.

As required by the Act this case was begun by the complainant, a corporation of the State of Washington, impleading one group of claimants who are citizens of that same state and another, the adverse group,

* [Now 28 U.S.C.A. §§ 1335, 1397, and 2361—Ed.]

who are citizens of Idaho. Under the Interpleader Act, this identity of citizenship is permissible since diversity only between claimants is required. The Interpleader Act is based upon the clause of § 2, Article III, of the Constitution which extends the judicial power of the United States to controversies "between citizens of different States." Is this grant of jurisdiction broad enough to cover the present situation?

The Judicial Code, § 24, provides for original jurisdiction of suits of a civil nature between citizens of different states in precisely the language of the Constitution. The present wording is practically the same as that of the Act of March 3, 1875, "the circuit courts . . . shall have original cognizance . . . of all suits . . . in which there shall be a controversy between citizens of different States," and that of the original Judiciary Act of September 24, 1789, "the suit is between a citizen of the State where the suit is brought and a citizen of another State." Without ruling as to possible limitations of the constitutional grant, it is held by this Court that the statutory language of the respective judiciary acts forbids suits in the federal courts unless all the parties on one side are of citizenship diverse to those on the other side. For the determination of the validity of the Interpleader Act we need not decide whether the words of the Constitution, "Controversies . . . between Citizens of different States," have a different meaning from that given by judicial construction to similar words in the Judiciary Act. Even though the constitutional language limits the judicial power to controversies wholly between citizens of different states, that requirement is satisfied here.

This is for the reason that there is a real controversy between the adverse claimants. They are brought into the court by the complainant stakeholder who simultaneously deposits the money or property, due and involved in the dispute, into the registry of the court. This was done in this case. The act provides that the "court shall hear and determine the cause and shall discharge the complainant from further liability." Such deposit and discharge effectually demonstrates the applicant's disinterestedness as between the claimants and as to the property in dispute, an essential in interpleaders. The complainant is a proper party for the determination of the controversy between the adverse claimants, citizens of different states. Their controversy could have been settled by litigation between them in the federal courts. Under similar circumstances as to parties, this Court ruled that a removal of separable controversies to the federal court was permissible even though a proper defendant was a citizen of the same state as the plaintiff.[13] We so held as to a stakeholder in Salem Co. v. Manufacturers' Co.[14] There a suit was brought in a state court against the Manufacturers' Company, a Delaware corporation, and against a co-citizen of plaintiff, a Massachusetts corporation, the International Trust Company. The Manufacturers' Company removed and plaintiff

13. Barney v. Latham, 103 U.S 205, 213; cf. Pullman Co. v. Jenkins, 305 U.S. 534, 538.

14. 264 U.S. 182, 189.

sought a remand alleging its co-citizen was a necessary party. The suit was to determine rights to a fund in the co-citizen's hands "and to have the same paid to" the plaintiff. The right of removal was upheld on the ground that the only obligation of the stakeholder was to pay over the money deposited with it. . . .[17]

The Court of Appeals correctly determined that the issue of jurisdiction *vel non* of the Washington court could not be relitigated in this interpleader. As the Idaho District Court was a court of general jurisdiction, its conclusions are unassailable collaterally except for fraud or lack of jurisdiction. The holding by the Idaho court of no jurisdiction in Washington necessarily determined the question raised here as to the Idaho jurisdiction against Miss Treinies' contention. She is bound by that judgment. . . .

MR. JUSTICE BUTLER took no part in the consideration or decision of this case.

Further Notes on Diversity in Multiparty Litigation

(1) John Hancock Mut. Life Ins. Co. v. Kraft, 200 F.2d 952, 953 (2d Cir. 1953):

> This is an action of interpleader brought by a Massachusetts insurance company against the executors and the widow of Irving Korowitz, whose life the plaintiff had insured in four policies payable upon his death to his estate. The defendants are citizens of New York. Immediately after the insured's death his widow notified the insurance company not to pay any policies on her husband's life as she claimed rights in them. . . .
>
> If jurisdiction of the district court depended on 28 U.S.C. § 1335, lack of diversity of citizenship between the adverse claimants would be a fatal objection. But that section did not abolish the equitable remedy of interpleader which has long existed under 28 U.S.C. § 1332, where there is diversity of citizenship between the stakeholder and the claimants. . . .

(2) Did the Supreme Court hold in *Treinies* that the only controversy in an interpleader case was between the claimants? That would mean the *Kraft* case, supra note 1, was wrongly decided, wouldn't it? Or did the Court hold that because there was one controversy between diverse claimants there was ancillary jurisdiction over the non-diverse controversy involving the stakeholder? What justification is there in an interpleader case for ancillary jurisdiction over a controversy not independently within federal jurisdiction? Compare *Finley v. United States*, supra p. 188, discussing pendent jurisdiction in cases arising under federal law.

(3) State Farm Fire & Cas. Co. v. Tashire, 386 U.S. 523, 530–31 (1967) (Fortas, J.):

17. We do not determine whether the ruling here is inconsistent with the conclusion in those cases where jurisdiction was rested on diversity of citizenship between the applicant and co-citizens who are claimants. . . .

> The interpleader statute, 28 U.S.C. § 1335, . . . has been uniformly construed to require only "minimal diversity," that is, diversity of citizenship between two or more claimants, without regard to the circumstance that other rival claimants may be co-citizens. The language of the statute, the legislative purpose broadly to remedy the problems posed by multiple claimants to a single fund, and the consistent judicial interpretation tacitly accepted by Congress, persuade us that the statute requires no more. . . . In *Strawbridge v. Curtiss*, . . . Chief Justice Marshall . . . purported to construe only "The words of the act of Congress," not the Constitution itself. And in a variety of contexts this Court and the lower courts have concluded that Article III poses no obstacle to the legislative extension of federal jurisdiction, founded on diversity, so long as any two adverse parties are not co-citizens. . . .

There were no dissents on this point. See the thorough discussion, in accord with *Tashire*, in Haynes v. Felder, 239 F.2d 868 (5th Cir. 1957).

(4) Building on interpleader as an example of federal jurisdiction based on the inability of state courts to accomplish complete justice, the ALI proposed a new category of diversity cases:

> The district courts shall have original jurisdiction of any civil action in which the several defendants who are necessary for a just adjudication of the plaintiff's claim are not all amenable to process of any one territorial jurisdiction, and one of any two adverse parties is a citizen of a State and the other is a citizen or subject of another territorial jurisdiction.

The proposal must be read in full hideous detail to be appreciated. In six sections covering, with rather brief explanatory notes, eleven pages (ALI Study 67–76), the suggested statute among other things defines a necessary defendant ("complete relief cannot be accorded the plaintiff in his absence" or "an action on the claim would have to be dismissed if he could not be joined") and one not amenable to process (not resident or principally employed, or if a corporation not incorporated or with its "principal office," in the jurisdiction, and not subject to any existing long-arm statute); provides for venue ("where a substantial part of the events or omissions giving rise to the claim occurred or where a substantial part of property which is the subject of the action is situated," and if there is no such district, where "any party resides"), service of process (nationwide, and anywhere else "that process of the United States may reach"), and transfer ("for the convenience of parties and witnesses or otherwise in the interest of justice," on motion of any party or of the court, to "any other district"); permits the court to "make its own determination as to which State rule of decision is applicable"; and authorizes injunctions against related state or federal proceedings. Necessary parties other than defendants may be brought in without regard to citizenship, and there are special provisions permitting removal of state-court actions in which necessary parties cannot be served. The definition of "necessary" in a removal case is not the same as that in an original proceeding: a party is "necessary" in the case of removal "if he claims or may claim an interest relating to the property or transaction that is the subject of the action and is so situated that the disposition of the action in his absence may leave the defendant subject to a substantial risk of incurring double, multiple, or otherwise inconsistent obligations. . . ." In a removal case, moreover, the court may stay proceedings before it "if there is a State court in which an action on the claim may be maintained and to whose process all parties necessary for a just adjudication are answerable or agree to submit," after considering not only trial convenience but also "whether the rules for decision of the action or any substantial part thereof are the laws of the State in whose courts the action would be prosecuted during the pendency of the stay and the reasons why the action was not commenced in that State court originally."

What do you suppose is the extent of the problem that induces the ALI to concoct this monster? Is this an example of the academic imagination running amok?

In response to criticism (e.g., Judge Friendly's gentle observation that since the provisions are "of necessity, exceedingly complicated" and in light of the growth of long-arm statutes, adoption "should await demonstration that . . . there is any real need," Federal Jurisdiction: A General View 150 (1973)), the dispersed-party proposal was omitted from the revised Senate bill. S. 1876, 93d Cong., 1st Sess. (1973); see 119 Cong.Rec. 16,680 (1973) (Senator Burdick).

OWEN EQUIPMENT & ERECTION CO. v. KROGER

437 U.S. 365 (1978).

MR. JUSTICE STEWART delivered the opinion of the Court.

In an action in which federal jurisdiction is based on diversity of citizenship, may the plaintiff assert a claim against a third-party defendant when there is no independent basis for federal jurisdiction over that claim? The Court of Appeals for the Eighth Circuit held in this case that such a claim is within the ancillary jurisdiction of the federal courts. We granted certiorari . . . because this decision conflicts with several recent decisions of other Courts of Appeals.

I

On January 18, 1972, James Kroger was electrocuted when the boom of a steel crane next to which he was walking came too close to a high-tension electric power line. The respondent (his widow, who is the administratrix of his estate) filed a wrongful-death action in the United States District Court for the District of Nebraska against the Omaha Public Power District (OPPD). Her complaint alleged that OPPD's negligent construction, maintenance, and operation of the power line had caused Kroger's death. Federal jurisdiction was based on diversity of citizenship, since the respondent was a citizen of Iowa and OPPD was a Nebraska corporation.

OPPD then filed a third-party complaint pursuant to Fed.Rule Civ. Proc. 14(a) [2] against the petitioner, Owen Equipment and Erection Co. (Owen), alleging that the crane was owned and operated by Owen, and

2. Rule 14(a) provides in relevant part:

that Owen's negligence had been the proximate cause of Kroger's death. OPPD later moved for summary judgment on the respondent's complaint against it. While this motion was pending, the respondent was granted leave to file an amended complaint naming Owen as an additional defendant. Thereafter, the District Court granted OPPD's motion for summary judgment in an unreported opinion. The case thus went to trial between the respondent and the petitioner alone.

The respondent's amended complaint alleged that Owen was "a Nebraska corporation with its principal place of business in Nebraska." Owen's answer admitted that it was "a corporation organized and existing under the laws of the State of Nebraska," and denied every other allegation of the complaint. On the third day of trial, however, it was disclosed that the petitioner's principal place of business was in Iowa, not Nebraska, and that the petitioner and the respondent were thus both citizens of Iowa.[6] The petitioner then moved to dismiss the complaint for lack of jurisdiction. The District Court reserved decision on the motion, and the jury thereafter returned a verdict in favor of the respondent. In an unreported opinion issued after the trial, the District Court denied the petitioner's motion to dismiss the complaint.

The judgment was affirmed on appeal. 558 F.2d 417. The Court of Appeals held that under this Court's decision in Mine Workers v. Gibbs, 383 U.S. 715, the District Court had jurisdictional power, in its discretion, to adjudicate the respondent's claim against the petitioner because that claim arose from the "core of 'operative facts' giving rise to both [respondent's] claim against OPPD and OPPD's claim against Owen." . . . It further held that the District Court had properly exercised its discretion in proceeding to decide the case even after summary judgment had been granted to OPPD, because the petitioner had concealed its Iowa citizenship from the respondent. . . .

II

It is undisputed that there was no independent basis of federal jurisdiction over the respondent's state-law tort action against the petitioner, since both are citizens of Iowa. And although Fed.Rule Civ. Proc. 14(a) permits a plaintiff to assert a claim against a third-party defendant, . . . it does not purport to say whether or not such a claim requires an independent basis of federal jurisdiction. Indeed, it could not determine that question, since it is axiomatic that the Federal Rules of Civil Procedure do not create or withdraw federal jurisdiction.[7]

"At any time after commencement of the action a defending party, as a third-party plaintiff, may cause a summons and complaint to be served upon a person not a party to the action who is or may be liable to him for all or part of the plaintiff's claim against him. . . ."

6. Title 28 U.S.C. § 1332(c) provides that "[f]or the purposes of [diversity jurisdiction] . . ., a corporation shall be deemed a citizen of any State by which it has been incorporated and of the State where it has its principal place of business."

7. Fed.Rule Civ.Proc. 82; see Snyder v. Harris, 394 U.S. 332. . . .

In affirming the District Court's judgment, the Court of Appeals relied upon the doctrine of ancillary jurisdiction, whose contours it believed were defined by this Court's holding in *Mine Workers v. Gibbs*, supra. The *Gibbs* case differed from this one in that it involved pendent jurisdiction, which concerns the resolution of a plaintiff's federal- and state-law claims against a single defendant in one action. By contrast, in this case there was no claim based upon substantive federal law, but rather state-law tort claims against two different defendants. Nonetheless, the Court of Appeals was correct in perceiving that *Gibbs* and this case are two species of the same generic problem: Under what circumstances may a federal court hear and decide a state-law claim arising between citizens of the same State?[8] But we believe that the Court of Appeals failed to understand the scope of the doctrine of the *Gibbs* case.

The plaintiff in *Gibbs* alleged that the defendant union had violated the common law of Tennessee as well as the federal prohibition of secondary boycotts. This Court held that, although the parties were not of diverse citizenship, the District Court properly entertained the state-law claim as pendent to the federal claim. The crucial holding was stated as follows:

> "Pendent jurisdiction, in the sense of judicial *power*, exists whenever there is a claim 'arising under [the] Constitution, the Laws of the United States, and Treaties made, or which shall be made, under their Authority . . .,' U.S.Const., Art. III, § 2, and the relationship between that claim and the state claim permits the conclusion that the entire action before the court comprises but one constitutional 'case.' . . . The state and federal claims must derive from a common nucleus of operative fact. But if, considered without regard to their federal or state character, a plaintiff's claims are such that he would ordinarily be expected to try them all in one judicial proceeding, then, assuming substantiality of the federal issues, there is *power* in federal courts to hear the whole." . . .

It is apparent that *Gibbs* delineated the constitutional limits of federal judicial power. But even if it be assumed that the District Court in the present case had constitutional power to decide the respondent's lawsuit against the petitioner, it does not follow that the decision of the Court of Appeals was correct. Constitutional power is merely the first hurdle that must be overcome in determining that a federal court has jurisdiction over a particular controversy. For the jurisdiction of the federal courts is limited not only by the provisions of Art. III of the Constitution, but also by Acts of Congress. . . .

That statutory law as well as the Constitution may limit a federal court's jurisdiction over nonfederal claims is well illustrated by two recent decisions of this Court, Aldinger v. Howard, 427 U.S. 1, and Zahn v. International Paper Co., 414 U.S. 291. In *Aldinger* the Court held

8. No more than in Aldinger v. Howard, 427 U.S. 1, is it necessary to determine here "whether there are any 'principled' differences between pendent and ancillary jurisdiction; or, if there are, what effect *Gibbs* had on such differences." . . .

that a Federal District Court lacked jurisdiction over a state-law claim against a county, even if that claim was alleged to be pendent to one against county officials under 42 U.S.C. § 1983. In *Zahn* the Court held that in a diversity class action under Fed.Rule Civ.Proc. 23(b)(3), the claim of each member of the plaintiff class must independently satisfy the minimum jurisdictional amount set by 28 U.S.C. § 1332(a), and rejected the argument that jurisdiction existed over those claims that involved $10,000 or less as ancillary to those that involved more. In each case, despite the fact that federal and nonfederal claims arose from a "common nucleus of operative fact," the Court held that the statute conferring jurisdiction over the federal claim did not allow the exercise of jurisdiction over the nonfederal claims.

The *Aldinger* and *Zahn* cases thus make clear that a finding that federal and nonfederal claims arise from a "common nucleus of operative fact," the test of *Gibbs*, does not end the inquiry into whether a federal court has power to hear the nonfederal claims along with the federal ones. Beyond this constitutional minimum, there must be an examination of the posture in which the nonfederal claim is asserted and of the specific statute that confers jurisdiction over the federal claim, in order to determine whether "Congress in [that statute] has . . . expressly or by implication negated" the exercise of jurisdiction over the particular nonfederal claim. . . .

III

The relevant statute in this case, 28 U.S.C. § 1332(a)(1), confers upon federal courts jurisdiction over "civil actions where the matter in controversy exceeds the sum or value of $10,000 . . . and is between . . . citizens of different States." This statute and its predecessors have consistently been held to require complete diversity of citizenship.[13] That is, diversity jurisdiction does not exist unless *each* defendant is a citizen of a different State from *each* plaintiff. . . .[16]

Thus it is clear that the respondent could not originally have brought suit in federal court naming Owen and OPPD as codefendants, since citizens of Iowa would have been on both sides of the litigation. Yet the identical lawsuit resulted when she amended her complaint. Complete diversity was destroyed just as surely as if she had sued Owen initially. In either situation, in the plain language of the statute, the "matter in controversy" could not be "between . . . citizens of different States." . . .

13. E.g., Strawbridge v. Curtiss, 3 Cranch [7 U.S.] 267. . . .

16. Notably, Congress enacted § 1332 as part of the Judicial Code of 1948, 62 Stat. 930, shortly after Rule 14 was amended in 1946. When the Rule was amended, the Advisory Committee noted that "in any case where the plaintiff could not have joined the third party originally because of jurisdictional limitations such as lack of diversity of citizenship, the majority view is that any attempt by the plaintiff to amend his complaint and assert a claim against the impleaded third party would be unavailing." 28 U.S.C. App., p. 7752. The subsequent re-enactment without relevant change of the diversity statute may thus be seen as evidence of congressional approval of that "majority view."

[U]nder the reasoning of the Court of Appeals in this case, a plaintiff could defeat the statutory requirement of complete diversity by the simple expedient of suing only those defendants who were of diverse citizenship and waiting for them to implead nondiverse defendants.[17] If, as the Court of Appeals thought, a "common nucleus of operative fact" were the only requirement for ancillary jurisdiction in a diversity case, there would be no principled reason why the respondent in this case could not have joined her cause of action against Owen in her original complaint as ancillary to her claim against OPPD. Congress' requirement of complete diversity would thus have been evaded completely.

It is true, as the Court of Appeals noted, that the exercise of ancillary jurisdiction over nonfederal claims has often been upheld in situations involving impleader, cross-claims or counterclaims.[18] But in determining whether jurisdiction over a nonfederal claim exists, the context in which the nonfederal claim is asserted is crucial. See Aldinger v. Howard, 427 U.S., at 14. And the claim here arises in a setting quite different from the kinds of nonfederal claims that have been viewed in other cases as falling within the ancillary jurisdiction of the federal courts.

First, the nonfederal claim in this case was simply not ancillary to the federal one in the same sense that, for example, the impleader by a defendant of a third-party defendant always is. A third-party complaint depends at least in part upon the resolution of the primary lawsuit. . . . Its relation to the original complaint is thus not mere factual similarity but logical dependence. Cf. Moore v. New York Cotton Exchange, 270 U.S. 593, 610. The respondent's claim against the petitioner, however, was entirely separate from her original claim against OPPD, since the petitioner's liability to her depended not at all upon whether or not OPPD was also liable. Far from being an ancillary and dependent claim, it was a new and independent one.

17. This is not an unlikely hypothesis, since a defendant in a tort suit such as this one would surely try to limit his liability by impleading any joint tortfeasors for indemnity or contribution. Some commentators have suggested that the possible abuse of third-party practice could be dealt with under 28 U.S.C. § 1359, which forbids collusive attempts to create federal jurisdiction. . . . The dissenting opinion today also expresses this view. . . . But there is nothing necessarily collusive about a plaintiff's selectively suing only those tortfeasors of diverse citizenship, or about the named defendants' desire to implead joint tortfeasors. . . .

18. The ancillary jurisdiction of the federal courts derives originally from cases such as Freeman v. Howe, 24 How. [65 U.S.] 450 which held that when federal jurisdiction "effectively controls the property or fund under dispute, other claimants thereto should be allowed to intervene in order to protect their interests, without regard to jurisdiction." Aldinger v. Howard, 427 U.S., at 11. More recently, it has been said to include cases that involve multiparty practice, such as compulsory counterclaims, e.g., Moore v. New York Cotton Exchange, 270 U.S. 593, impleader, e.g., H. L. Peterson Co. v. Applewhite, 383 F.2d 430, 433 (CA5); Dery v. Wyer, 265 F.2d 804 (CA2); cross-claims, e.g., LASA Per L'Industria Del Marmo Soc. Per Azioni v. Alexander, 414 F.2d 143 (CA6) . . .; or intervention as of right, e.g., Phelps v. Oaks, 117 U.S. 236, 241; Smith Petroleum Service, Inc. v. Monsanto Chemical Co., 420 F.2d 1103, 1113–1115 (CA5).

Second, the nonfederal claim here was asserted by the plaintiff, who voluntarily chose to bring suit upon a state-law claim in a federal court. By contrast, ancillary jurisdiction typically involves claims by a defending party haled into court against his will, or by another person whose rights might be irretrievably lost unless he could assert them in an ongoing action in a federal court. A plaintiff cannot complain if ancillary jurisdiction does not encompass all of his possible claims in a case such as this one, since it is he who has chosen the federal rather than the state forum and must thus accept its limitations. "[T]he efficiency plaintiff seeks so avidly is available without question in the state courts." . . .

It is not unreasonable to assume that, in generally requiring complete diversity, Congress did not intend to confine the jurisdiction of federal courts so inflexibly that they are unable to protect legal rights or effectively to resolve an entire, logically entwined lawsuit. Those practical needs are the basis of the doctrine of ancillary jurisdiction. But neither the convenience of litigants nor considerations of judicial economy can suffice to justify extension of the doctrine of ancillary jurisdiction to a plaintiff's cause of action against a citizen of the same State in a diversity case. Congress has established the basic rule that diversity jurisdiction exists under 28 U.S.C. § 1332 only when there is complete diversity of citizenship. "The policy of the statute calls for its strict construction." . . . To allow the requirement of complete diversity to be circumvented as it was in this case would simply flout the congressional command.

Accordingly, the judgment of the Court of Appeals is reversed. . . .

MR. JUSTICE WHITE, with whom MR. JUSTICE BRENNAN joins, dissenting. . . .

In the present case, Mrs. Kroger's claim against Owen and her claim against OPPD derived from a common nucleus of fact; this is necessarily so because in order for a plaintiff to assert a claim against a third-party defendant, Fed.Rule Civ.Proc. 14(a) requires that it "aris[e] out of the transaction or occurrence that is the subject matter of the plaintiff's claim against the third-party plaintiff. . . ." Furthermore, the substantiality of the claim Mrs. Kroger asserted against OPPD is unquestioned. Accordingly, as far as Art. III of the Constitution is concerned, the District Court had power to entertain Mrs. Kroger's claim against Owen. . . .

The complete-diversity requirement, of course, could be viewed as meaning that in a diversity case, a federal district court may adjudicate only those claims that are between parties of different States. . . . Even the majority, however, refuses to read the complete-diversity requirement so broadly; it recognizes with seeming approval the exercise of ancillary jurisdiction over nonfederal claims in situations involving impleader, cross-claims, and counterclaims. . . . Given the Court's willingness to recognize ancillary jurisdiction in these contexts, despite the requirements of § 1332(a), I see no justification for the Court's refusal to approve the District Court's exercise of ancillary jurisdiction in the present case. . . .

Because in the instant case Mrs. Kroger merely sought to assert a claim against someone already a party to the suit, considerations of judicial economy, convenience, and fairness to the litigants—the factors relied upon in *Gibbs*—support the recognition of ancillary jurisdiction here. Already before the court was the whole question of the cause of Mr. Kroger's death. Mrs. Kroger initially contended that OPPD was responsible; OPPD in turn contended that Owen's negligence had been the proximate cause of Mr. Kroger's death. In spite of the fact that the question of Owen's negligence was already before the District Court, the majority requires Mrs. Kroger to bring a separate action in state court in order to assert that very claim. . . .

The majority, however, brushes aside such considerations of convenience, judicial economy, and fairness because it concludes that recognizing ancillary jurisdiction over a plaintiff's claim against a third-party defendant would permit the plaintiff to circumvent the complete-diversity requirement and thereby "flout the congressional command." Since the plaintiff in such a case does not bring the third-party defendant into the suit, however, there is no occasion for deliberate circumvention of the diversity requirement, absent collusion with the defendant. In the case of such collusion, of which there is absolutely no indication here, the court can dismiss the action under the authority of 28 U.S.C. § 1359.[6] In the absence of such collusion, there is no reason to adopt an absolute rule prohibiting the plaintiff from asserting those claims that he may properly assert against the third-party defendant pursuant to Fed.Rule Civ.Proc. 14(a). The plaintiff in such a situation brings suit against the defendant only with absolutely no assurance that the defendant will decide or be able to implead a particular third-party defendant. . . .

We have previously noted that "[s]ubsequent decisions of this Court indicate that *Strawbridge* is not to be given an expansive reading." State Farm Fire & Cas. Co. v. Tashire, 386 U.S. 523, 531 n. 6 (1967). In light of this teaching, it seems to me appropriate to view § 1332 as requiring complete diversity only between the plaintiff and those parties he actually brings into the suit. Beyond that, I would hold that in a diversity case the District Court has power, both constitutional and statutory, to entertain all claims among the parties arising from the same nucleus of operative fact as the plaintiff's original, jurisdiction-conferring claim against the defendant. . . .

6. Section 1359 states: "A district court shall not have jurisdiction of a civil action in which any party, by assignment or otherwise, has been improperly or collusively made or joined to invoke the jurisdiction of such court."

Notes on Ancillary Jurisdiction

(1) Before *State Farm Fire & Cas. Co. v. Tashire,* p. 249 supra, ancillary jurisdiction was arguably the constitutional basis for the power to determine the claims of a nondiverse stakeholder in interpleader. In non-interpleader cases it has been the basis for statutory as well as constitutional authority over nondiverse claims respecting parties added after the complaint.

The seminal case is Freeman v. Howe, 65 U.S. (24 How.) 450 (1860), in which the Court declared a federal court in which property had been attached could entertain other claims to the same property without an independent jurisdictional basis: Otherwise, since federal control of the property was exclusive, the claimants would be without remedy. Later decisions extended the principle to allow intervention as of right by nondiverse parties who were not indispensable,[1] although the only apparent consequence was to avoid multiple litigation. E.g., Wichita R. & Light Co. v. Public Util. Comm'n, 260 U.S. 48 (1922); Stewart v. Dunham, 115 U.S. 61, 64 (1885).[2] *Stewart* explicitly relied on the principle, see, p. 241 supra, that jurisdiction once attached is not divested by later events: Intervention "did not oust the jurisdiction of the court, already lawfully acquired, as between the original [diverse] parties." This reasoning is not a complete explanation; jurisdiction over the original parties could also have been preserved by refusing to allow intervention.

(2) Numerous lower courts, as the Court noted in *Owen,* have utilized ancillary jurisdiction to entertain nonfederal claims by defendants under Fed.R.Civ.P. 14 against third parties from the same State. E.g., H. L. Peterson Co. v. Applewhite, 383 F.2d 430 (5th Cir. 1967). Similarly, some courts have allowed an impleaded third party to assert a claim against a plaintiff of common citizenship. E.g., Revere Copper & Brass Inc. v. Aetna Cas. & Sur. Co., 426 F.2d 709 (5th Cir. 1970).

Do these decisions survive *Owen*? Are they consistent with *Strawbridge*? Is there the same justification, in statute or in policy, for ancillary jurisdiction in these cases as in interpleader? Is the broad interpretation given the term "civil action" in § 1332 by the intervention and interpleader cases consistent with the narrow interpretation of similar terminology in *Finley v. United States,* p. 188 supra?

Would the result in *Owen* have been the same if the sole defect of the plaintiff's claim against the impleaded party had been lack of the jurisdictional amount?[3]

1. "An intervention needed to cure an otherwise fatal defect of parties can scarcely be regarded as ancillary." Hart & Wechsler, The Federal Courts and the Federal System 1686–87 (3d ed. 1988).

2. "However, if the applicant seeks permissive intervention, independent jurisdictional grounds are required." Developments in the Law—Multiparty Litigation in the Federal Courts, 71 Harv.L.Rev. 874, 906 (1958).

3. The Third Circuit once managed to decide, in the teeth of *Strawbridge,* that a West Virginia administrator suing a Pennsylvania defendant for injuries suffered prior to the decedent's death could join a wrongful-death claim even if it belonged to the decedent's Pennsylvania parents, on the basis of pendent jurisdiction. Borror v. Sharon Steel Co., 327 F.2d 165 (3d Cir. 1964) (alternative holding). This doesn't survive *Owen,* does it?

(3) Should cross-claims between parties on the same side of the original case, or counterclaims to which additional parties are brought in to respond, require independent jurisdictional bases? See H. L. Peterson Co. v. Applewhite, 383 F.2d 430, 433 (5th Cir. 1967), distinguishing between compulsory and permissive counterclaims but affirming that diversity was not required for Rule 14 impleader though that procedure was always permissive. Cf. pp. 306–09 infra, dealing with the jurisdictional amount.

How can it be said, after a decision like *Peterson*, that the Civil Rules do not enlarge the jurisdiction of the district courts in contravention of Rule 82? See 3 Moore, Federal Practice § 14.27 (2d ed. 1974):

> The new Federal Rules provisions for multi-claim, multi-party litigation do not constitute expansions of jurisdiction, but rather, the opportunity for the federal system fully to exercise dormant jurisdiction which pre-existed but which was not developed for lack of procedural devices.

(4) Supreme Tribe of Ben-Hur v. Cauble, 255 U.S. 356, 361, 366–7 (1921), was a bill by an Indiana association to enjoin Indiana citizens from relitigating in state courts questions allegedly decided in a prior federal action. The federal proceeding had been a class action filed by non-Indiana members of the association on behalf of an entire class of members, including the state-court plaintiffs, to enjoin a reorganization and "an unlawful use of trust funds . . . in which all the complainants and other members of Class A of said Supreme Tribe of Ben-Hur had a common but indivisible interest. . . ."

First the Court held the original federal decree binding on the state-court plaintiffs despite the fact that they were of the same citizenship as the association. *Stewart v. Dunham*, supra note 1, "controls this case":

> Diversity of citizenship gave the District Court jurisdiction. Indiana citizens were of the class represented; their rights were duly represented by those before the court. The intervention of the Indiana citizens in the suit would not have defeated the jurisdiction already acquired. *Stewart v. Dunham*, supra. Being thus represented, we think it must necessarily follow that their rights were concluded by the original decree. . . .
>
> The subject-matter included the control and disposition of the funds of a beneficial organization. . . . If the decree is to be effective and conflicting judgments are to be avoided all of the class must be concluded by the decree.

It followed that the current bill to enjoin the state-court action was "ancillary" to the original action and "may be prosecuted from the same court to protect the rights secured to all in the class by the decree rendered."

Does *Ben-Hur* hold that the claims of absent class members are ancillary to those of the named plaintiffs, or that the citizenship of absent members is irrelevant because, like beneficiaries of an estate, see pp. 242–44 supra, they are not parties? Is the former interpretation consistent with *Strawbridge*? And doesn't the holding, on either basis, afford an easy means for the manufacture of diversity jurisdiction?

Would you expect *Ben-Hur* to be applied in class actions under the modern Rule 23(b)(3), in which there is no "common but indivisible interest?"

AMERICAN FIRE & CASUALTY CO. v. FINN

341 U.S. 6 (1951).

MR. JUSTICE REED delivered the opinion of the Court. . . .

Petitioner, the American Fire and Casualty Company, a Florida corporation, and its codefendant, the Indiana Lumbermens Mutual Insurance Company, an Indiana corporation, removed, in accordance with 28 U.S.C. § 1446, a suit brought by respondent Finn in a Texas state court against the two corporations and an individual, Reiss, local agent of both corporations and a resident of Texas. The suit was for a fire loss on Texas property suffered by respondent, a resident of Texas. Respondent tried to have the case remanded before trial but was unsuccessful. After special issues were found by the jury, judgment was entered against petitioner for the amount of insurance claimed and costs, and in favor of the other two defendants. The District Court denied the motion to vacate the judgment and the Court of Appeals affirmed. 181 F.2d 845. The latter court concluded there were causes of action against the foreign insurance companies "separate and independent" from that stated against the resident individual. Since the causes against the companies would have been removable if sued on alone, the entire suit was removable. 28 U.S.C. § 1441(c). That ruling required consideration of the changes concerning removal made by § 1441(c), which superseded 28 U.S.C. (1946 ed.) § 71.

I. . . .

The former provision governing removal, 28 U.S.C. (1946 ed.) § 71, read:

> "And when in any suit mentioned in this section there shall be a controversy which is wholly between citizens of different States, and which can be fully determined as between them, then either one or more of the defendants actually interested in such controversy may remove said suit into the district court of the United States for the proper district."

The new section, 28 U.S.C. § 1441(c), states:

> "(c) Whenever a separate and independent claim or cause of action, which would be removable if sued upon alone, is joined with one or more otherwise nonremovable claims or causes of action, the entire case may be removed and the district court may determine all issues therein, or, in its discretion, may remand all matters not otherwise within its original jurisdiction."

One purpose of Congress in adopting the "separate and independent claim or cause of action" test for removability by § 1441(c) of the 1948 revision in lieu of the provision for removal of 28 U.S.C. (1946 ed.) § 71, was by simplification to avoid the difficulties experienced in determining the meaning of that provision. Another and important purpose was to limit removal from state courts.[2]

In § 71 the removable "controversy" was interpreted as any possible separate suit that a litigant might properly bring in a federal court so long as it was wholly between citizens of different states. So, before the revision, when a suit in a state court had such a separable federally cognizable controversy, the entire suit might be removed to the federal court.[4]

A separable controversy is no longer an adequate ground for removal unless it also constitutes a separate and independent claim or cause of action. Compare Barney v. Latham, 103 U.S. 205, 212, with the revised § 1441. . . .[5] Of course, "separate cause of action" restricts removal more than "separable controversy." In a suit covering multiple parties or issues based on a single claim, there may be only one cause of action and yet be separable controversies.[6] The addition of the word "independent" gives emphasis to congressional intention to require more complete disassociation between the federally cognizable proceedings and those cognizable only in state courts before allowing removal. . . .

Although "controversy" and "cause of action" are treated as synonymous by the courts in situations where the present considerations are absent, here it is obvious different concepts are involved. . . . In a suit turning on the meaning of "cause of action," this Court announced an accepted description. Baltimore S. S. Co. v. Phillips, 274 U.S. 316[10] . . .:

2. 28 U.S.C. § 1441, Reviser's Note. . . .

4. Barney v. Latham, 103 U.S. 205, is a good illustration. This Court held that there were separable controversies in a state court suit against a local corporation and nonresident individuals for an accounting on land sales. One group of sales was by the nonresidents before conveyance to the corporation; the other by the corporation after conveyance.

See also Pullman Co. v. Jenkins, 305 U.S. 534. There a suit was instituted in a California court for damages for a conductor's death caused by a drunken Pullman passenger. The defendants were the passenger (a Californian), the railroad (a Kentucky corporation, allegedly negligent for letting the passenger pass its gates), the Pullman Company (an Illinois corporation), and its porter (a Californian), the latter two allegedly negligent for letting the passenger on the Pullman. Had the porter not been a Californian, the Pullman Company could have removed on the ground of a separable controversy because no facts were alleged as to other defendants' negligence upon which its liability could be predicated. 539. "All persons interested in a separable controversy must be able to remove." Discussed in Moore's Commentary on the U. S. Judicial Code, p. 247.

5. We think the "claim" set out in a petition states the facts upon which the "cause of action" rests. For the purpose of removal, the words cover the same allegations.

Since the *Pullman* case and the *Barney* case do not contain separate and independent causes of action, they would not now be removable under 28 U.S.C. § 1441.

6. See note 4, supra.

10. There a sailor filed a libel in admiralty and recovered for negligence in failing to provide a safe place to work, in failing to use reasonable care to avoid striking libellant, for unseaworthiness, incompetency of officers and failure to instruct plaintiff, an inexperienced sailor, in his duties. Later he sought further damages for the same accident, for negligence of officers and employees in the operation of the vessel. Recovery was denied in the second suit on the ground that it was the same cause of action as the first.

"Upon principle, it is perfectly plain that the respondent suffered but one actionable wrong and was entitled to but one recovery, whether his injury was due to one or the other of several distinct acts of alleged negligence or to a combination of some or all of them. In either view, there would be but a single wrongful invasion of a single primary right of the plaintiff, namely, the right of bodily safety, whether the acts constituting such invasion were one or many, simple or complex. . . ." [A footnote quoted similar language from *Hurn v. Oursler*, p. 194 supra]. . . .

Considering the previous history of "separable controversy," the broad meaning of "cause of action," and the congressional purpose in the revision resulting in 28 U.S.C. § 1441(c), we conclude that where there is a single wrong to plaintiff, for which relief is sought, arising from an interlocked series of transactions, there is no separate and independent claim or cause of action under § 1441(c).

In making this determination we look to the plaintiff's pleading, which controls. Pullman Co. v. Jenkins, 305 U.S. 534, 538.[13] The single wrong for which relief is sought is the failure to pay compensation for the loss on the property. Liability lay among three parties, but it was uncertain which one was responsible. Therefore, all were joined as defendants in one petition. First, facts were stated that made the petitioner, American Fire and Casualty Company, liable. It was alleged that the company, through its agent Reiss, insured the property destroyed for the amount claimed, that Reiss gave plaintiff credit for the premium, controlled her insurance, agreed to keep the property insured at all times. She further alleged that the Company issued the policy but Reiss retained the document in his possession and refused to deliver it after the fire. Then followed a prayer for judgment against the Company.

The next portion of the complaint stated, in the alternative, an obligation by the Indiana Lumbermens Insurance Company to pay the same loss. The policy with Lumbermens was attached as an exhibit, and allegations concerning Reiss similar to those in the first portion were made. A second prayer was added for recovery against Lumbermens.

The last portion of the complaint, alternative to both the preceding, alleged that Reiss, American Fire and Casualty Company and Indiana Lumbermens Insurance Company were jointly and severally liable for the loss. Reiss was said to be plaintiff's insurance broker, responsible for keeping her house insured. Plaintiff alleged Reiss insured her

13. Moore's Commentary on the U. S. Judicial Code, supra, pp. 251–252: "But where the plaintiff joins two or more defendants to recover damages for one injury, and even though he charges them with joint and several liability or only several liability, or charges them with liability in the alternative, there is no joinder of separate and independent causes of action within the meaning of § 1441(c). At most a separable controversy is presented where several or alternative liability is alleged, and is no longer the basis for removal." Compare the opinion in Bentley v. Halliburton Oil Well Cementing Co., 81 F.Supp. 323, with the reversing opinion in 174 F.2d 788.

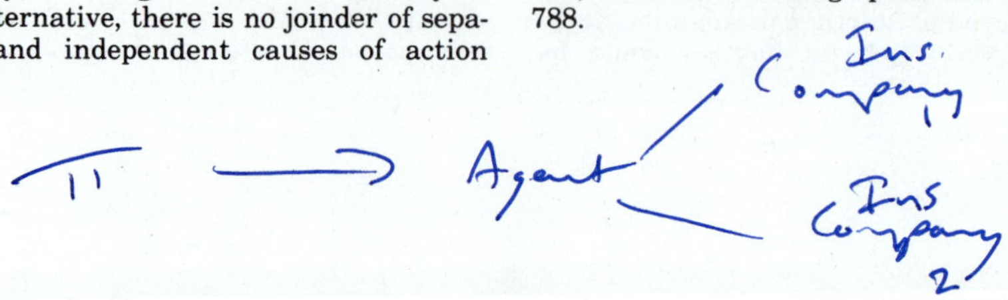

property with Lumbermens and never notified her of any cancellation or expiration. Reiss was alleged to have agreed later to insure her property with American, to have promised after the fire to deliver the policy, to have failed to make the promised delivery. She claimed that Reiss was responsible for "anything that results in the defeat of her recovery on either one of said policies" and that he was "the direct cause of the condition, of said insurance, and the proximate cause of all of plaintiff's troubles and confusion." The pleader then asserted:

> "That such acts and conduct on the part of said Joe Reiss as agent for the said two insurance companies, renders said Joe Reiss, agent, the Joe Reiss Insurance Agency and the American Fire and Casualty Insurance Company of Orlando, Florida, and the Indiana Lumbermens Mutual Insurance Company of Indianapolis, Indiana, jointly and severally liable for the full amount of the damages that plaintiff has suffered by reason of said fire in the amount of Five Thousand Dollars."

The petition concluded with a prayer for joint and several judgment against all three defendants, based on the third set of allegations.

The past history of removal of "separable" controversies, the effort of Congress to create a surer test, and the intention of Congress to restrict the right of removal leads us to the conclusions that separate and independent causes of action are not stated. The facts in each portion of the complaint involve Reiss, the damage comes from a single incident. The allegations in which Reiss is a defendant involve substantially the same facts and transactions as do the allegations in the first portion of the complaint against the foreign insurance companies. It cannot be said that there are separate and independent claims for relief as § 1441(c) requires. Therefore, we conclude there was no right to removal.

II.

There are cases which uphold judgments in the district courts even though there was no right to removal. In those cases the federal trial court would have had original jurisdiction of the controversy had it been brought in the federal court in the posture it had at the time of the actual trial of the cause or of the entry of the judgment. That is, if the litigation had been initiated in the federal court on the issues and between the parties that comprised the case at the time of trial or judgment, the federal court would have had cognizance of the case. This circumstance was relied upon as the foundation of the holdings. The defendant who had removed the action was held to be estopped from protesting that there was no right to removal. Since the federal court could have had jurisdiction originally, the estoppel did not endow it with a jurisdiction it could not possess.

In this case, however, the District Court would not have had original jurisdiction of the suit, as first stated in the complaint, because of the presence on each side of a citizen of Texas. 28 U.S.C. § 1332. The posture of this case even at the time of judgment also barred federal jurisdiction. A Texas citizen was and remained a party defendant. The trial court judgment, after decreeing recovery against American Fire and Casualty Company on the jury's verdict, added, over American's objection,

> "It Is Further Ordered, Adjudged and Decreed that the Plaintiff take nothing as against Defendants, Indiana Lumbermens Mutual Insurance Company and Joe Reiss, individually and doing business as the Joe Reiss Insurance Agency, and that such Defendants go hence without day with their costs."

By this decree the merits of the litigation against Reiss were finally adjudicated. The request of respondent to dismiss Reiss after the judgment was not acted upon by the trial court. . . .

The judgment of the Court of Appeals must be reversed and the cause remanded to the District Court with directions to vacate the judgment entered and, if no further steps are taken by any party to affect its jurisdiction,[18] to remand the case to the District Court of Harris County, Texas. . . .

MR. JUSTICE DOUGLAS, with whom MR. JUSTICE BLACK and MR. JUSTICE MINTON concur, dissenting.

I think petitioner, having asked for and obtained the removal of the case to the Federal District Court, and having lost its case in that court, is now estopped from having it remanded to the state court. . . .

I think it is abusive of the interests of justice when the challenge now made is raised to the dignity of a jurisdictional question. . . . Both Reiss and the other non-resident defendant have been dismissed from the case. The only judgment before the Court is one which satisfies the requirements of original jurisdiction. Petitioner—who invoked federal jurisdiction and as a result suffered the consequences of this judgment—should not now be heard to complain. . . .

Notes on Removal Under § 1441(c)

(1) Why should there be removal when there is a separate and independent claim over which the federal courts could take jurisdiction? Does the statute reflect dissatisfaction with the extended rule of *Strawbridge v. Curtiss*—i.e., a belief that the presence of a non-diverse co-party protects a nonresident from bias only if their interests are closely related? If so, why shouldn't the federal forum be available to a plaintiff in a comparable situation?

(2) Did *Finn* destroy the utility of § 1441(c) in diversity cases? See Developments in the Law—Multiparty Litigation in the Federal Courts, 71 Harv.L.Rev. 874, 896 (1958), opining that after *Finn* "few cases in which

18. Issues not raised in the records or briefs are not passed upon, such as the propriety of the District Court's allowing, after vacation of judgment, a motion to dismiss Reiss, the resident defendant; or the associated problem: whether, if such a dismissal is allowed, a new judgment can be entered on the old verdict without a new trial. . . .

there is proper joinder of defendants in the state court and there is not complete diversity will be removable, since most state procedural codes require that joined claims arise out of the same series of transactions or occurrences."

In Climax Chem. Co. v. C. F. Braun & Co., 370 F.2d 616 (10th Cir. 1966), the Court rejected the "morbid" view taken in the Harvard note, finding a case removable under § 1441(c). The plaintiff sued several defendants for breaches of several contracts relating to the construction of various components of a chemical factory; the court found the contracts separate and independent: "There was more than one primary right, and . . . more than a single wrong was alleged." Moreover, it was immaterial that one defendant had guaranteed the performance of all the others.

(3) May a third party impleaded by a state-court defendant remove under § 1441(c)? The cases conflict. See, e.g., Holloway v. Gamble-Skogmo, Inc., 274 F.Supp. 321, 323 (N.D.Ill.1967): "Several cases have directly held . . . that removal under 28 U.S.C. § 1441(c) is limited to situations where joinder of claims or parties has been by plaintiff only"; Carl Heck Engineers, Inc. v. Lafourche Parish Police Jury, 622 F.2d 133, 136 (5th Cir. 1980): "[T]he language of the statute does not require only those causes of action joined by the original plaintiff to form the basis of removal." What about the purpose of § 1441(c)?

The court in *Holloway* found it "difficult to imagine a third party complaint which is not 'dependent' on the main cause of action, since under even the most liberal state third party practice, a close relation between the third party claim and the case in chief is a minimal requirement." Responded the Fifth Circuit in *Carl Heck*, discussing a typical claim for indemnity in case the original defendant was held liable to the plaintiff: Though the indemnity controversy was "not unrelated to the main claim," it was "sufficiently independent of it that a judgment in an action between those two parties alone can be properly rendered," and such claims "often are brought in a separate suit"; "therefore" the indemnity claim was "separate and independent" under § 1441(c). Was either court faithful to the *Finn* test?

(4) What sense does it make to remove an entire case to the federal court if its parts are "separate and independent?"

Before the 1948 amendment, when claims against joint tortfeasors were sufficiently separable to permit removal, see Pullman Co. v. Jenkins, 305 U.S. 534 (1939), it often made sense in terms of judicial economy to permit the non-diverse claim to be removed as well in order to avoid two trials with substantial duplication of proof. See Barney v. Latham, 103 U.S. 205 (1880). But is there room for pendent jurisdiction of non-diverse claims under the new statute as interpreted in *Finn*? Or is a claim that is "separate and independent" one that is too unrelated to be "pendent?"

Twentieth Century-Fox Film Corp. v. Taylor, 239 F.Supp. 913 (S.D.N.Y. 1965), holds there are claims "independent" enough to be removable under § 1441(c) but related enough to support "pendent" jurisdiction over additional parties. Fox charged Elizabeth Taylor and Richard Burton with breaches of contract and with inducing each other's breaches. Burton, a

British subject, was allowed to remove the entire case under § 1441(c). In *Finn*, said the court,

> the plaintiff suffered a single wrong arising out of the fire, which entitled him to but one recovery. . . . Here . . . there are two separate and distinct employment contracts, one with each defendant, . . . entered into on different dates. . . . Each alleged breach, predicated upon individual acts, gives rise to a separate wrong. . . . The fact that the services were to be rendered by each performer in the production of one film does not coalesce violations of the two separate contracts into a single wrong. . . .
>
> The plaintiff further moves . . . that the Court remand the other four claims, nonremovable in and of themselves, to the State court. . . . Nothing in Article III prohibits Congress from opening the Federal courts to controversies not raising Federal questions, so long as any two adverse parties are of diverse citizenship. Section 1441(c) represents one instance in which Congress has clearly made use of the commodious Article III grant. . . .
>
> As to plaintiff's alternative motion addressed to the Court's discretion, it is abundantly clear that, despite the "separate and independent" quality of the second cause of action, at least the first four claims have some common problems. Items of proof may overlap and the same witnesses may be called to testify with relation to all four claims. . . .

(5) Notice the sub silentio holding in *Taylor* that an alien was entitled to remove under § 1441(c). The language of the prior statute had been held to preclude removal by an alien. King v. Cornell, 106 U.S. 395 (1882).

(6) Is the constitutionality of § 1441(c) in diversity cases assured by the holding in *State Farm Fire & Cas. Co. v. Tashire*, supra p. 249, that the rule of *Strawbridge v. Curtiss* is not constitutionally required? Or are there limits to the definition of a "controversy" within Article III? [4]

(7) The ALI proposed to allow removal of the entire action by a defendant (or, with one exception, by a third party defendant) who "would have been able to remove under subsection (a) of this section [general diversity removal] if sued alone by any party making a claim against him in the State court action." ALI Study 16–17. The commentary made clear that this was designed to permit removal, although diversity was incomplete, even in suits against employer and employee for a single accident, which were not removable even under the "separable controversy" predecessor of § 1441(c), see Pullman Co. v. Jenkins, 305 U.S. 534 (1939), because "when an out-of-stater is joined with a resident defendant in a case involving several liability or liability in the alternative, he is subject to the

4. For a biting criticism of § 1441(c) as presently written see Lewin, The Federal Courts' Hospitable Back Door—Removal of "Separate and Independent" Non-Federal Causes of Action, 66 Harv.L.Rev. 423 (1953). The cases to 1961 are considered in detail in Cohen, Problems in the Removal of a "Separate and Independent Cause of Action," 46 Minn.L.Rev. 1 (1961); the author concludes that § 1441(c) should be repealed because it serves no real need and presents substantial "difficulties of construction and administration." Id. at 41. But see the explication and defense of § 1441(c) in Moore and VanDercreek, Multi-Party, Multi-Claim Removal Problems: The Separate and Independent Claim Under Section 1441(c), 46 Ia.L.Rev. 489 (1961).

risk of local bias to as great a degree as if he were sued alone by an in-state plaintiff." ALI Study 141–47.

(8) After studying the tensions between *Strawbridge* and the liberal joinder provisions of the Federal Rules, and after a glimpse of the charms of the separate-claim-removal response to *Strawbridge*, what do you think of complete diversity?

SECTION 3. CORPORATIONS AND OTHER ASSOCIATIONS

CARDEN v. ARKOMA ASSOCIATES

110 S.Ct. 1015 (1990).

JUSTICE SCALIA delivered the opinion of the Court.

The question presented in this case is whether, in a suit brought by a limited partnership, the citizenship of the limited partners must be taken into account to determine diversity of citizenship among the parties. . . .

Respondent Arkoma Associates (Arkoma), a limited partnership organized under the laws of Arizona, brought suit on a contract dispute in the United States District Court for the Eastern District of Louisiana, relying upon diversity of citizenship for federal jurisdiction. The defendants, C. Tom Carden and Leonard L. Limes, citizens of Louisiana, moved to dismiss, contending that one of Arkoma's limited partners was also a citizen of Louisiana. The District Court denied the motion . . . and awarded Arkoma a money judgment plus interest and attorney's fees; . . . the Fifth Circuit affirmed. . . . With respect to petitioners' jurisdictional challenge, the Court of Appeals found complete diversity, reasoning that Arkoma's citizenship should be determined by reference to the citizenship of the general, but not the limited, partners. . . .

A

We have often had to consider the status of artificial entities created by state law insofar as that bears upon the existence of federal diversity jurisdiction. The precise question posed under the terms of the diversity statute is whether such an entity may be considered a "citizen" of the State under whose laws it was created. . . . Initially, we held that a corporation "is certainly not a citizen," so that to determine the existence of diversity jurisdiction the Court must "look to the character of the individuals who compose [it]." Bank of United States v. Deveaux, 5 Cranch 61, 86, 91–92 (1809). We overruled *Deveaux* 35 years later in Louisville, C. & C. R. Co. v. Letson, 2 How. 497, 558 (1844), which held that a corporation is "capable of being treated as a citizen of [the State which created it], as much as a natural person." Ten years later, we reaffirmed the result of *Letson*, though on the somewhat different theory that "those who use the corporate name, and exercise the faculties conferred by it," should be presumed conclusively to be citizens of the corporation's State of incorporation. Marshall v. Baltimore & Ohio R. Co., 16 How. 314, 329 (1854).

While the rule regarding the treatment of corporations as "citizens" has become firmly established, we have (with an exception to be discussed presently) just as firmly resisted extending that treatment to other entities. For example, in Chapman v. Barney, 129 U.S. 677 (1889), a case involving an unincorporated "joint stock company," we raised the question of jurisdiction on our own motion, and found it to be lacking:

> "On looking into the record we find no satisfactory showing as to the citizenship of the plaintiff. The allegation of the amended petition is, that the United States Express Company is a joint stock company organized under a law of the State of New York, and is a citizen of that State. But the express company cannot be a *citizen* of New York, within the meaning of the statutes regulating jurisdiction, unless it be a corporation. The allegation that the company was *organized* under the laws of New York is not an allegation that it is a corporation. In fact the allegation is, that the company is *not* a corporation, but a joint stock company—that is, a mere partnership." Id., at 682.

Similarly, in Great Southern Fire Proof Hotel Co. v. Jones, 177 U.S. 449 (1900), we held that a "limited partnership association"—although possessing "some of the characteristics of a corporation" and deemed a "citizen" by the law creating it—may not be deemed a "citizen" under the jurisdictional rule established for corporations. Id., at 456. "That rule must not be extended." Id., at 457. As recently as 1965, our unanimous opinion in Steelworkers v. R.H. Bouligny, Inc., 382 U.S. 145, reiterated that "the doctrinal wall of *Chapman v. Barney* . . ." would not be breached.

The one exception to the admirable consistency of our jurisprudence on this matter is Puerto Rico v. Russell & Co., 288 U.S. 476 (1933), which held that the entity known as a *sociedad en comandita*, created under the civil law of Puerto Rico, could be treated as a citizen of Puerto Rico for purposes of determining federal court jurisdiction. The *sociedad*'s juridical personality, we said, "is so complete in contemplation of the law of Puerto Rico that we see no adequate reason for holding that the *sociedad* has a different status for purposes of federal jurisdiction than a corporation organized under that law." . . . [In *Bouligny*] we explained *Russell* as a case resolving the distinctive problem "of fitting an exotic creation of the civil law . . . into a federal scheme which knew it not." . . . There could be no doubt, after *Bouligny,* that at least common-law entities (and likely all entities beyond the Puerto Rican *sociedad en comandita*) would be treated for purposes of the diversity statute pursuant to what *Russell* called "[t]he tradition of the common law," which is "to treat as legal persons only incorporated groups and to assimilate all others to partnerships." . . .

Arkoma claims to have found another exception to our *Chapman* tradition in Navarro Savings Assn. v. Lee, 446 U.S. 458 (1980). That case, however, did not involve the question whether a party that is an artificial entity other than a corporation can be considered a "citizen" of a State, but the quite separate question whether parties that were undoubted "citizens" (viz., natural persons) were the real parties to the controversy. The plaintiffs in *Navarro* were eight individual trustees of a Massachusetts business trust, suing in their own names. The defendant, Navarro Savings Association, disputed the existence of complete diversity, claiming that the trust beneficiaries rather than the trustees were the real parties to the controversy, and that the citizenship of the former and not the latter should therefore control. In the course of rejecting this claim, we did indeed discuss the characteristics of a Massachusetts business trust—not at all, however, for the purpose of determining whether the trust had attributes making it a "citizen," but only for the purpose of establishing that the respondents were "active trustees whose control over the assets held in their names is real and substantial," thereby bringing them under the rule, "more than 150 years" old, which permits such trustees "to sue in their own right, without regard to the citizenship of the trust beneficiaries." . . .

B

As an alternative ground for finding complete diversity, Arkoma asserts that the Fifth Circuit correctly determined its citizenship solely by reference to the citizenship of its general partners, without regard to the citizenship of its limited partners. Only the general partners, it points out, "manage the assets, control the litigation, and bear the risk of liability for the limited partnership's debts," and, more broadly, "have exclusive and complete management and control of the operations of the partnership." . . . This approach of looking to the citizenship of only some of the members of the artificial entity finds even less support in our precedent than looking to the State of organization (for which one could at least point to *Russell*). We have never held that an artificial entity, suing or being sued in its own name, can invoke the diversity jurisdiction of the federal courts based on the citizenship of some but not all of its members. No doubt some members of the joint stock company in *Chapman*, the labor union in *Bouligny*, and the limited partnership association in *Great Southern* exercised greater control over their respective entities than other members. But such considerations have played no part in our decisions.

To support its approach, Arkoma seeks to press *Navarro* into service once again, arguing that just as that case looked to the trustees to determine the citizenship of the business trust, so also here we should look to the general partners, who have the management powers, in determining the citizenship of this partnership. As we have already explained, however, *Navarro* had nothing to do with the citizenship of the "trust," since it was a suit by the trustees in their own names. . . .

In sum, we reject the contention that to determine, for diversity purposes, the citizenship of an artificial entity, the court may consult the citizenship of less than all of the entity's members. We adhere to our oft-repeated rule that diversity jurisdiction in a suit by or against the entity depends on the citizenship of "all the members," *Chapman*, 129 U.S., at 682, "the several persons composing such association," *Great Southern*, 177 U.S., at 456, "each of its members," *Bouligny*, 382 U.S., at 146.

C . . .

Arkoma is undoubtedly correct that limited partnerships are functionally similar to "other types of organizations that have access to federal courts," and is perhaps correct that "[c]onsiderations of basic fairness and substance over form require that limited partnerships receive similar treatment." . . . Similar arguments were made in *Bouligny*. The District Court there had upheld removal because it could divine " 'no common sense reason for treating an unincorporated national labor union differently from a corporation,' " . . ., and we recognized that that contention had "considerable merit" . . . . We concluded, however, that "[w]hether unincorporated labor unions ought to be assimilated to the status of corporations for diversity purposes" . . . is "properly a matter for legislative consideration which cannot adequately or appropriately be dealt with by this Court" . . . . In other words, having entered the field of diversity policy with regard to artificial entities once (and forcefully) in *Letson*, we have left further adjustments to be made by Congress.

Congress has not been idle. In 1958 it revised the rule established in *Letson*, providing that a corporation shall be deemed a citizen not only of its State of incorporation but also "of the State where it has its principal place of business." 28 U.S.C. § 1332(c) (Oct.1989 Supp.). No provision was made for the treatment of artificial entities other than corporations, although the existence of many new, post-*Letson* forms of commercial enterprises, including at least the sort of joint stock company at issue in *Chapman*, the sort of limited partnership association at issue in *Great Southern*, and the sort of Massachusetts business trust at issue in *Navarro*, must have been obvious.

Thus, the course we take today does not so much disregard the policy of accommodating our diversity jurisdiction to the changing realities of commercial organization, as it honors the more important policy of leaving that to the people's elected representatives. Such accommodation is not only performed more legitimately by Congress than by courts, but it is performed more intelligently by legislation than by interpretation of the statutory word "citizen." The fifty States have created, and will continue to create, a wide assortment of artificial entities possessing different powers and characteristics, and composed of various classes of members with varying degrees of interest and control. Which of them is entitled to be considered a "citizen" for diversity purposes, and which of their members' citizenship is to be consulted, are questions more readily resolved by legislative prescription than by legal reasoning, and questions whose complexity is particularly unwelcome at the threshold stage of determining whether a court has jurisdiction. We have long since decided that, having established special treatment for corporations, we will leave the rest to Congress; we adhere to that decision. . . .

Reversed and remanded.

JUSTICE O'CONNOR, with whom JUSTICE BRENNAN, JUSTICE MARSHALL, and JUSTICE BLACKMUN join, dissenting.

The only potentially nondiverse party in this case is a limited partner. All other parties, including the general partners and the limited partnership itself, assuming it is a citizen, are diverse. Thus, the Court has before it a single question—whether the citizenship of a limited partner must be counted for purposes of diversity jurisdiction. . . .

Since the early 19th century, one of the benchmarks for determining whether a particular party among those involved in the litigation must be counted for purposes of diversity jurisdiction has been whether the party has a "real interest" in the suit or, in other words, is a "real party" to the controversy. . . . In Wormley v. Wormley, 8 Wheat. 421 (1823), for example, the Court stated:

> "This Court will not suffer its jurisdiction to be ousted by the mere joinder or non-joinder of formal parties; but will rather proceed without them, and decide upon the merits of the case between the parties, who have the real interests before it, whenever it can be done without prejudice to the rights of others." . . .

[In] Navarro Savings Assn. v. Lee, [446 U.S. 458 (1980),] . . . the Court addressed the question whether the beneficiaries' citizenship must be counted when the trustees [of a business trust] brought suit involving the assets of the trust. . . . Because the trust beneficiaries lacked both control over the conduct of the business and the ability to initiate or control the course of litigation, the Court held that the citizenship of the trust beneficiaries should not be counted. . . .

Application of the parties to the controversy test to the limited partnership yields the conclusion that limited partners should not be considered for purposes of diversity jurisdiction. Like the trust beneficiary in *Navarro*, the limited partner "can neither control the disposition of this action nor intervene in the affairs of the trust except in the most extraordinary situations." . . . See Uniform Limited Partnership Act § 26, 6 U.L.A. 614 (1969) (limited partner "is not a proper party to proceedings by or against a partnership, except where the object is to enforce a limited partner's right against or liability to the partnership"); . . . Arkoma Associates Partnership Agreement, Art. VI, § 6.1 (general partners have "exclusive and complete control of the operations"); id., § 7.1 (limited partners "shall not take any part in the control or management of . . . Partnership"). . . . Without the power to "control . . . the assets" or to initiate or "control the litigation," *Navarro*, supra, 446 U.S., at 465, the limited partner is not a real party to the controversy and, therefore, should not be counted for purposes of diversity jurisdiction. Because the majority of States has adopted the Uniform Limited Partnership Act, this rule would result in uniform treatment of limited partners for purposes of diversity jurisdiction. . . .

The concern perhaps implicit in the Court's holding today is that failure to consider the citizenship of all the members of an unincorporated business association will expand diversity jurisdiction at a time when our federal courts are already seriously overburdened. This concern is more illusory than real in the context of unincorporated business associations. For, despite the Court's holding today, unincorporated associations may gain access to the federal courts by bringing or defending suit as a Rule 23 class action, in which case the citizenship of the members of the class would not be considered. . . .

Notes on Associations as "Citizens"

(1) The opinion in *Carden* traces the development of the Supreme Court's doctrine respecting corporate citizenship for diversity purposes and the sharp and unexplained break with that development in *Chapman v. Barney*. Is there any reason why the Supreme Court should have had less freedom to interpret the jurisdictional statutes in 1889 or in 1990 than it had in earlier times?

(2) Is there a constitutional problem in "deeming" corporations or other associations to be "citizens" for jurisdictional purposes? See the apoplectic argument of McGovney, A Supreme Court Fiction, 56 Harv.L. Rev. 853, 1090, 1225 (1943), that the practice was unconstitutional. Is it material that a corporation has been held not to be a "citizen" within the Privileges and Immunities Clause of Article IV, Blake v. McClung, 172 U.S. 239 (1898)? Compare National Mut. Ins. Co. v. Tidewater Transfer Co., supra p. 128, construing the word "State" in Article III. Is there any force to the constitutional argument if any one of the shareholders is diverse to an adverse party?

(3) The ALI Study, § 1301(b) (2), proposed to recognize a partnership or unincorporated association as a citizen, for the purpose of diversity, of the state where it had its principal place of business. Where is the principal place of business of an international labor union? Should the existence of local unions be taken into account, as the Court suggested in *Bouligny*? How?

(4) Is a local governmental body a "citizen" of a State within § 1332? The Supreme Court long ago took the position that it was, upholding jurisdiction in suits by noncitizens against a county, Cowles v. Mercer County, 74 U.S. (7 Wall.) 118, 121–22 (1869), and against a city, Bullard v. Cisco, 290 U.S. 179, 187 (1933), and permitting removal by a noncitizen sued by a port authority, Port of Seattle v. Oregon & W. R. R., 255 U.S. 56 (1921). But several later Ninth Circuit decisions strikingly held that California counties and school districts were not "citizens": E.g., Miller v.

County of Los Angeles, 341 F.2d 964, 966 (9th Cir. 1965); Lowe v. Manhattan Beach City School Dist., 222 F.2d 258 (9th Cir. 1955). At least as to counties the Supreme Court set this straight in Moor v. Alameda County, 411 U.S. 693 (1973):

> The County in this case contends . . . that unlike the counties of most States, it is not a municipal corporation or an otherwise independent political subdivision, but that it is, under California law, nothing more than an agent or a mere arm of the State itself. . . .
>
> Under California law a county is given "corporate powers" and is designated a "body corporate and politic." In this capacity, a county may sue and be sued, and significantly for purposes of suit, it is deemed to be a "local public entity" in contrast to the State and state agencies. In addition, the county, and from all that appears the county alone, is liable for all judgments against it and is authorized to levy taxes to pay such judgments. A California county may also sell, hold, or otherwise deal in property, and it may contract for the construction and repairs of structures. The counties also are authorized to provide a variety of public services . . . [and] to issue general obligation bonds payable from county taxes. Such bonds create no obligation on the part of the State. . . . These provisions strike us as persuasive indicia of the independent status occupied by California counties relative to the State of California.

Obvious? Not only, as argued by Hart and Wechsler, The Federal Courts and the Federal System 1674 (3d ed. 1988), is this the one situation in which there is plausibility to *Marshall's* presumption that members of a corporation are citizens of its State of incorporation; it is also a case in which the possibility of bias seems entirely real, for the city or county otherwise must be sued in its own courts.

The State itself is not a "citizen" of a State, e.g., Stone v. South Carolina, 117 U.S. 430, 433 (1886): "There is no statute which authorizes the removal of a suit between a State and citizens on the ground of citizenship, for a State cannot in the nature of things be a citizen of any State."

(5) Section 1348 of the Judicial Code provides that national banks, for jurisdictional purposes, "shall . . . be deemed citizens of the States in which they are respectively located." Can this rule be sustained under the diversity clause of the Constitution? Under the federal-question clause? See pp. 140–49 supra. See also Feuchtwanger Corp. v. Lake Hiawatha Fed. Credit Union, 272 F.2d 453 (3d Cir. 1959), holding a federally incorporated credit union a citizen of the state where it operated. Is this decision consistent with § 1349, which destroys jurisdiction based upon federal incorporation? Is it precluded by negative inference from § 1348, which speaks only of national banks, or by *Carden*? Would it be required today by § 1332(c), which makes "a corporation" a citizen of its State of principal business? See Moore & Weckstein, Corporations and Diversity of Citizenship Jurisdiction: A Supreme Court Fiction Revisited, 77 Harv.L.Rev. 1426, 1436–38 (1964).

(6) Notice the proviso to § 1332(c) deeming a liability insurer in a direct action a citizen not only of its States of incorporation and principal business but also of "the State of which the insured is a citizen." This proviso was enacted in 1964 because of a conviction that these cases did not come within the purposes of the diversity grant and in order to reduce the caseload in Louisiana federal courts. S.Rep.No.1308, 88th Cong., 2d Sess. (1964). See Weckstein, The 1964 Diversity Amendment: Congressional Indirect Action Against State "Direct Action" Laws, 1965 Wis.L.Rev. 268, arguing that the pressure on the Louisiana federal courts was not primarily due to direct actions, that the problem should be met by appointing more judges, and that the existence of a resident insured who was not a party did not relieve the need of an out-of-state insurer for a federal forum. Notice also that the proviso, unlike the general diversity provision as construed in *Bouligny*, specifically refers to unincorporated insurers.

In Northbrook Nat. Ins. Co. v. Brewer, 110 S.Ct. 297 (1989), an Illinois insurer sued in federal court to set aside an administrative order awarding workers' compensation to a citizen of Texas. The Fifth Circuit held § 1332(c) barred jurisdiction because the defendant's employer was also a Texas citizen. The Supreme Court, over a single dissent, reversed: "[T]he language of the proviso is unambiguously limited to actions *against* insurers."

(7) Even before the Court held in Navarro Savings Ass'n v. Lee (cited in *Carden*) that the citizenship of beneficiaries of a business trust was irrelevant in a suit by the trustees, some lower courts had reached a similar result with respect to limited partners. E.g., Colonial Realty Corp. v. Bache & Co., 358 F.2d 178 (2d Cir. 1966) (Friendly, J.). See also Judge Hunter's dissenting opinion in Carlsberg Resources Corp. v. Cambria Savings & Loan Ass'n, 554 F.2d 1254 (3d Cir. 1977): *Chapman* and its progeny had held only that unincorporated associations were not to be considered as entities for diversity purposes, not that every member of an association must be treated as a party. "I fail to see . . . how a court knows whose citizenship to count without first determining who the parties are"; and under the applicable law limited partners could not properly be joined. Did Justice Scalia in *Carden* satisfactorily answer this argument? See also Comment, 45 U.Chi.L.Rev. 384, 409 (1978): "The complete diversity requirement attributed to *Strawbridge* is limited to the actual parties to the controversy for good reason: persons only beneficially interested in a lawsuit (be they shareholders, trust beneficiaries, or limited partners) generally will not be known to the court."

KELLY v. UNITED STATES STEEL CORP.

284 F.2d 850 (3d Cir. 1960).

GOODRICH, CIRCUIT JUDGE.

These are appeals from a series of decisions in the United States District Court for the Western District of Pennsylvania in which judgment has been entered for the defendant. The appeals all raise the same question. That question is whether the United States Steel Corporation has its principal place of business in Pennsylvania. If it has, the decision of the court below is correct since all these appellants are Pennsylvania citizens and there is, consequently, no diversity of citizenship on which to base the jurisdiction of a federal court.

The question arises under the 1958 statute, § 1332(c) of Title 28. That section states:

> "(c) For the purposes of this section and section 1441 of this title, a corporation shall be deemed a citizen of any State by which it has been incorporated and of the State where it has its principal place of business."

The new provision is, as appears in its legislative history, an effort to reduce the number of cases coming to federal courts on the ground of diversity of citizenship only.

During the argument in this Court the statement was made that the location of the corporation's principal place of business is a question of fact. To a certain extent this is true because facts about an individual corporation have a great deal to do in determining whether that corporation has its principal place of business in a given state. But what facts are significant and determinative in this matter depends upon the standard by which a court looks at the question and evaluates the facts and decides which facts are important and which facts are relatively unimportant. The conclusion that certain facts are or are not helpful in deciding the question is a question of legal standard, or legal concept, and is one for a court to decide as a question of law.

In some instances the answer will be easy. The simplest case is probably that of a corporation which gets a charter in one state but carries on all its business operations in another state. Obviously, in such a case the connection with the state of charter is nominal and the principal place of business is where the corporate activity is carried on. But from there the question becomes more difficult. A corporation may carry on much of its activity in the state of charter but have another state or perhaps more than one state where a great deal of its business activities take place. In such circumstances one is tempted to try to find some one criterion by which the question can be decided.

The place of the meeting of shareholders will not do. Corporations under modern statutes may have shareholders' meetings in a state other than the state of charter and that place of meeting may be the only corporate act which takes place in that state. The place of meeting of the Board of Directors offers a tempting criterion. This is the more attractive because, subject to the approval of shareholders in some matters, it is the Board of Directors which makes the final decisions regarding corporate activity. One is tempted to say that where those final decisions are made is the principal place of business because the important questions are there decided. But one is on slippery ground in adopting such a test. Subject to the law of charter and the action of shareholders, Boards of Directors may choose their own place to meet at will. One can easily picture a peripatetic board which holds its meetings in some spot where the climate is favorable and recreational opportunities abound. That spot, of course, may change from time to time as the seasons and the board personnel change.

One may also look to the place where physical activity is carried on. We can suppose a mining corporation where the actual digging of iron ore is on the Mesabi Range in Minnesota, the corporation has a New Jersey charter but all the directive activity of the corporation is conducted at its office in Superior, Wisconsin. Should the state of digging be called the principal place of business when all the contracts, sales and plans for expansion or contraction, the bank accounts and all the rest that make up this corporation's business activity take place in Wisconsin? In the absence of a simple single test we are forced to analyze our question further and endeavor to pick out as best we can the factor or combination of factors that seem to point to one place as the "principal" place of business. The concept may get artificial in some cases as indeed it is in the case before us. This great corporation has fourteen divisions of the parent corporation and eleven principal subordinate companies. Its various manufacturing activities are spread over practically all the United States and extend to foreign countries. It has literally dozens of important places of business one of which we must pick out as the principal one because that statute says so.

The appellants urge upon us that the test should be where the "nerve center" of the corporation's business is and they urge that the nerve center is New York. We do not find the figure of speech helpful. Dorland's Medical Dictionary tells us that a nerve center is "any group of cells of gray nerve substance having a common function." We think there will be in the case of United States Steel Corporation, a good many collections of nerve cells serving the common function of making the corporate enterprise go.

We turn, therefore, from a pleasant and alluring figure of speech to a consideration of the facts of the Steel Corporation's life. The appellants in a very well constructed brief list for us the activities of the United States Steel Corporation which to their minds make New York its principal place of business. We make little out of the fact that the federal income tax return is filed in New York. As will be seen from enumeration of other things which take place in that state, New York would be the natural filing place for its tax return. We move then to things more important on the New York side of the question. The Board of Directors regularly meets in New York. It has, however, met in Pittsburgh and as already pointed out the Board can choose its own place of meeting. The Chairman of the Board is in New York, spending one day a week in Pittsburgh. The President divides his time evenly between New York and Pittsburgh. The Executive Committee of the Board meets regularly in New York. So does the Finance Committee. The Secretary of the corporation lives and has his office in New York and the Treasurer, Comptroller and General Counsel have their offices there. The company owns the building at 71 Broadway. From New York is mailed the annual report. Dividends are declared in New York. The Public Relations Department of the corporate enterprise is centered in New York. The Steel Corporation's major banking activities are there. The cash on hand and its government securities are managed and controlled in New York and the corporation's pension funds are invested in New York. To us this adds up to the conclusion that as at present conducted the final decisions through the Board of Directors, the President and top executive officers are made in New York State. If the test of "principal place of business" is where such final decisions are made on corporate policy, including its financing, then the appellants are right in pointing to New York as the principal place of business.

After balancing these important and significant facts with those pointing to Pennsylvania, we reach the conclusion that Pennsylvania and not New York is the principal place of business. It is in Pennsylvania that the Operation Policy Committee sits and conducts its affairs. The Board of Directors has delegated to this committee the duty of conducting the business of the corporation relating to manufacturing, mining, transportation and general operation. It is composed of the Chairman of the Board, the President, the Chairman of the Finance Committee, the General Counsel and the seven Executive Vice Presidents. It makes policy decisions, of course subject to the Board of Directors. It appoints division presidents and corporate officers through the rank of Administrative Vice President. The seven Executive Vice Presidents, one at the head of each of the seven great branches of the corporation, have headquarters and staffs in Pittsburgh. All but one of the seventeen Administrative Vice Presidents and twenty-two out of the twenty-five Vice Presidents are located in Pittsburgh with their staffs. So, too, is the General Solicitor and his staff. In Pennsylvania almost thirty-four per cent of the employees classified as exempt under the Fair Labor Standards Act (29 U.S.C. § 201 et seq.) are located. This is fourteen times as many as there are in New York.

All this points to us the conclusion that business by way of activities is centered in Pennsylvania and we think it is the activities rather than the occasional meeting of policy-making Directors which indicate the principal place of business.

To this center of corporate activity we may add some other facts having to do with physical location of employer's plants and the like. We think these elements are of lesser importance, but added to the items already enumerated pointing to the center of corporate activity, we think they have some significance. For instance, Pennsylvania has 32.13 per cent of employee personnel, twenty-five times as many as New York, and more than twice as many as any other state. More than one-third of the $2,547,594,414 worth of tangible property is in Pennsylvania. In New York there is less than one per cent. Pennsylvania leads in steel productive capacity. This is about thirty-five per cent of the total capacity of the corporation. New York has none. Other items could be added to this list but we have picked those which we think most significant. It is true that Pennsylvania does not have the majority of the productive capacity of this corporation nor the majority of the employees of this corporation. It does have, however, more than any other state. These facts, added to what we have found to be the headquarters of day-to-day corporate activity and management, add up to the irresistible conclusion that the principal place of business of this giant corporation is in Pennsylvania. . . .

The judgments of the district court will be affirmed.

Notes on "Principal Place of Business"

(1) S.Rep.No.1830, 85th Cong. 2d Sess. (1958), recommending § 1332(c):

> [The] fiction of stamping a corporation a citizen of the State of its incorporation has given rise to the evil whereby a local institution, engaged in a local business and in many cases locally owned, is enabled to bring its litigation into the Federal courts simply because it has obtained a corporate charter from another State. . . .
>
> The underlying purpose of diversity of citizenship legislation . . . is to provide a separate form for out-of-State citizens against the prejudices of local courts and local juries. . . . It was never intended to extend to local corporations which, because of a legal fiction, are considered citizens of another State. It is a matter of common knowledge that such incorporations are primarily initiated to obtain some advantage taxwise in the State of incorporation or to obtain the benefits of the more liberal provisions of the foreign State's corporation laws. Such incorporations are not intended for the prime purpose of doing business in the foreign State. It appears neither fair nor proper for such a corporation to avoid trial in the State where it has its principal place of business by resorting to a legal device not available to the individual citizen.
>
> Because of these circumstances, and others, the Judicial Conference of the United States has recommended that the law be amended so that a corporation shall be regarded not only as a citizen of the State of its incorporation but also as a citizen of the State in which it maintains its principal place of business. This will eliminate those corporations doing a local business with a foreign charter but will not eliminate those corporations which do business over a large number of States, such as railroads, insurance companies, and other corporations whose businesses are not localized in one particular State. Even such a corporation, however, would be regarded as a citizen of that one of the States in which was located its principal place of business.
>
> The proposal to rest the test of jurisdiction upon the "principal place of business" of a corporation has ample precedent in the decisions of our courts and in Federal statute such as the provisions of the

Bankruptcy Act (11 U.S.C. 11). There is thus provided sufficient criteria to guide courts in future litigation under this bill.[1]

(2) Anniston Soil Pipe Co. v. Central Foundry Co., 216 F.Supp. 473 (N.D.Ala.1963), aff'd 329 F.2d 313 (5th Cir. 1964), is typical of a large group of cases interpreting § 1332(c). All of the corporation's production was in Alabama, and all top management, including finance and sales headquarters, was in New York. The overwhelming majority of employees were in Alabama. The District Court for the Northern District of Alabama found that the principal place of business was in Alabama and, since the plaintiff was a citizen of Alabama, dismissed for lack of diversity jurisdiction. The Court of Appeals affirmed. This is an example of what has been called the place-of-operations theory of § 1332(c). Accord, Inland Rubber Corp. v. Triple A Tire Serv., Inc., 220 F.Supp. 490 (S.D.N.Y.1963).

(3) A leading case applying the "nerve center" theory rejected by Kelly was Scot Typewriter Co. v. Underwood Corp., 170 F.Supp. 862 (S.D.N.Y. 1959). Underwood's main plant manufacturing typewriters was in Connecticut, but it manufactured other products in New Jersey and in California. Its greatest sales were in California, New York and Connecticut, in that order. The court held that New York was the corporation's "nerve center" and thus its principal place of business, because top management was all there, including the personnel, industrial-relations, public-relations and customer-relations offices. The case was remanded to the state court for lack of diversity jurisdiction. Accord, Sabo v. Standard Oil Co., 295 F.2d 893 (7th Cir. 1961).

(4) A comment in 47 Iowa L.Rev. 1151 (1962) suggests that the place-of-operations theory is preferable if most of the company's production is in one state and its executive offices are in another; but that if there are several places of operation, the nerve-center theory is preferable, especially if the company has substantial central control. See 1 J. Moore, Moore's Federal Practice 717.69–.78 (2d ed. 1964); Bruner v. Marjec, Inc., 250 F.Supp. 426, 427 (W.D.Va.1966), asserting that most courts in fact follow the suggested distinction. Does this thesis reconcile *Scot, Kelly,* and *Anniston*?

(5) Of the standards already mentioned—day-to-day management, place of operations, top management—which is likely to reduce the number of diversity cases most? Is that a proper standard for judging among them? See Moore & Weckstein, footnote 1 supra, at 1441–45, arguing that the principal place of business should be in "the state on which the corporation most impinges, the state in which its greatest impact is felt." This, they say, is likely to be "where the bulk of its litigation arises, where the corporation has most of its dealings with its customers and has its greatest contact with the public in general, where it derives its greatest gross

1. The cited section of the Bankruptcy Act (11 U.S.C. § 11) gave the District Courts jurisdiction to "adjudge persons bankrupt who have had their principal place of business, resided, or had their domicile within their respective territorial jurisdictions for the preceding six months. . . ." Was Congress well advised to suggest that the court follow precedents under this statute in applying § 1332(c)? See also Moore & Weckstein, Corporations and Diversity of Citizenship Jurisdiction: A Supreme Court Fiction Revisited, 77 Harv.L.Rev. 1426, 1439 (1964), finding the bankruptcy precedents inconsistent.

income, and where it is generally considered to be 'at home.'" Specifically, "a mining or manufacturing company would probably have its greatest contact with the public at the sites of its largest operating facility, where most of its employees and equipment are located; a corporation whose primary business is selling would have its greatest contact with the public in the state in which most sales are made." Does the statute really require the courts to find a single principal place of business for United States Steel?

(6) The ALI's proposed § 1301(b)(1) would retain the principal-place-of-business rule, without suggesting any general rule of interpretation. Was this defensible? But the ALI would also bar a corporation from invoking diversity jurisdiction in a controversy arising from the activity of a "local establishment" of the corporation in the forum state, § 1302(b). Was this a sensible proposal?

(7) Do corporations incorporated in foreign countries acquire citizenship in their State of principal business under § 1332(c)? See, e.g., Eisenberg v. Commercial Union Assur. Co., 189 F.Supp. 500 (S.D.N.Y.1960), holding they do not because "the statute differentiates between States of the United States and foreign states by the use of a capital S for the word when applied to a State of the United States." [2] Contra, Jerguson v. Blue Dot Investment, Inc., 659 F.2d 31 (5th Cir. 1981), denying jurisdiction over an action by a Florida citizen against a Panamanian corporation with its sole place of business in Florida:

> Nothing in the statutory formula suggests it was to be limited to domestic corporations. . . . Congress intended to limit the diversity jurisdiction . . . to those out-of-state citizens who should be free of local bias. . . . Applying section 1332(c) to alien corporations effectuates that congressional purpose.

But is bias the only reason for jurisdiction when a citizen of a foreign country is a party? [3]

2. Moreover, the court said, even if alien corporations were included, it would not suffice that New York was the corporation's principal place of United States business, because its overall principal place of business was in England. Jurisdiction was upheld because the corporation was deemed a citizen of its country of incorporation, as held in National Steamship Co. v. Tugman, 106 U.S. 118 (1882). Is this last holding consistent with the court's position that § 1332(c) only applies to American corporations?

3. The ALI, noting that "the 1958 amendment seemingly has no application to alien corporations," would change the law so that "an alien corporation with its principal place of business abroad has no citizenship in any state and that an alien corporation with its principal place of business in a state of the United States is a citizen of that state as well as of the foreign country by which it has been incorporated." Although conceding that an alien individual with his principal place of business in an American State would still be considered only a foreign citizen, the Institute would prefer a different rule for corporations because "otherwise a group of New York businessmen for reasons of their own might, for example, incorporate in Liberia although their principal place of business was in New York, and invoke federal jurisdiction in an action against a citizen of New York." ALI Study 112–13.

MAJEWSKI v. NEW YORK CENTRAL RAILROAD CO.

227 F.Supp. 950 (W.D.Mich.1964).

FOX, DISTRICT JUDGE.

This action was originally brought by the plaintiff in the United States District Court for the Northern District of Illinois, Eastern Division. Jurisdiction was alleged on the grounds that plaintiff, and all of the decedents represented by the plaintiff, were domiciled in and citizens of the State of Michigan, and the defendant, The New York Central Railroad Company, was a resident and citizen of the State of Illinois by virtue of its incorporation under the laws of the State of Illinois. . . .

On July 24, 1962, the District Judge of the Illinois District Court granted defendant New York Central's motion to dismiss for lack of jurisdiction on the grounds that the requisite diversity of citizenship was not present. However, on September 27, 1962, a petition of the plaintiff to reinstate the cause and transfer to the United States District Court for the Western District of Michigan, Southern Division, was granted by the same District Judge.

The first pleading filed by the defendant before this court was a Motion to Dismiss, again on the specific grounds of lack of diversity of citizenship between the parties.

It is undisputed by the parties that plaintiff is a citizen and resident of the State of Michigan. At the time of the filing of this suit, on January 6, 1961, the defendant corporation was a "citizen" of the State of Michigan, as well as the State of Illinois and other states, having incorporated under the laws of several states.

There are ample cases which discuss the question of actions against multiple-state corporations. In Lucas v. New York Central Railroad Company, 88 F.Supp. 536 (D.C.S.D.N.Y.1950), plaintiff, a citizen of Pennsylvania, filed suit in a New York state court against a defendant which was a corporation organized under the laws of New York, Pennsylvania, and four other states. After removal to the United States District Court for the Southern District of New York, defendant sought to have the cause transferred under Title 28 U.S.C. § 1404(a), to a Pennsylvania District Court, where the plaintiff's intestate had been killed in a crossing accident.

In refusing to order the transfer, Judge Kaufman provided an excellent review of the law of the area when he said, 88 F.Supp. at page 537:

> "It is settled that a corporation which is incorporated in several states, is deemed to be a citizen of that state in which it is sued, if incorporated in that state. . . .

"Where the plaintiff sues a corporation in his own state of residence, no diversity exists notwithstanding the fact that the corporation is also incorporated in another state or states.

". . . In any suit in which the defendant is engaged in the courts of Pennsylvania . . . it is deemed to be a citizen of Pennsylvania. In any suit in which the defendant corporation is engaged in the state of New York, it is deemed to be a citizen of New York. Hence, a transfer of this case from New York to Pennsylvania, would result in substituting a Pennsylvania citizen as defendant for a citizen of the state of New York and would oust the federal court of jurisdiction."

Section 1404(a) of Title 28 U.S.C. is the pertinent section for consideration in this case. Section 1404(a) states:

"For the convenience of parties and witnesses, in the interest of justice, a district court may transfer any civil action to any other district or division where it might have been brought." . . .

The simple proposition which flows from this language in the statute is that if a proposed transferee forum would not have jurisdiction because of a lack of requisite diversity, the attempted transfer is void. The cause, however, remains in full force and effect and in the transferor forum, and the valid federal jurisdiction originally obtained is not lost in the attempt to transfer the action. . . .

In the present case, it is clear that the suit could not have been brought in Michigan, since the requirement of diversity of citizenship between the parties could not have been met; defendant New York Central Railroad Company was a Michigan corporation at that time.

As of the commencement of this action in the United States District Court for the Northern District of Illinois, Eastern Division, there was a diversity of citizenship between plaintiff, Bernice Majewski and her decedent plaintiffs, and defendant New York Central Railroad Company, an Illinois corporation. . . .

I find that at the time of the entry of the Order transferring this cause from the Northern District of Illinois, Eastern Division, to the Western District of Michigan, Southern Division, there was no authority in either the transferor or transferee court to effectuate the transfer. . . .

An order has been entered denying defendant Railroad Company's motion to dismiss and returning the cause to the United States District Court for the Northern District of Illinois, Eastern Division, for such further proceedings as may be deemed appropriate by the Illinois Court.

DIESING v. VAUGHN WOOD PRODUCTS, INC.

175 F.Supp. 460 (W.D.Va.1959).

THOMPSON, CHIEF JUDGE. . . .

The plaintiff, a citizen of Nebraska and president of the defendant corporation, a corporation chartered under the laws of Nebraska, obtained a judgment against the defendant in the sum of $102,862 for attorney fees in the Douglas County Court of the state of Nebraska. The defendant's principal and only place of business is in Rocky Mount, Virginia.

The plaintiff instituted this action in this Court on his judgment obtained in the Douglas County Court of Nebraska seeking a judgment in Virginia under the full faith and credit clause of 28 U.S.C. § 1738, and alleged in his complaint that the defendant corporation is a citizen of Virginia under the provisions of 28 U.S.C. § 1332(c), as amended, effective July 29, 1958. . . .

The motion to dismiss for lack of jurisdiction on the ground that the plaintiff and defendant are not citizens of different states requires a construction of the amendment to § 1332, which amendment provides:

> "For the purposes of this section and section 1441 of this title, a corporation shall be deemed a citizen of any State by which it has been incorporated and of the State *where it has its principal place of business.*" (Emphasis supplied.)

The plaintiff and the defendant are citizens of the state of Nebraska. The defendant is not incorporated in any other state. The jurisdictional question to be decided is as follows:

Does the fact that the defendant's principal place of business is in Virginia afford the plaintiff diversity of citizenship when the plaintiff and defendant are citizens of Nebraska?

We are not here dealing with a multi-state incorporated defendant, but we are dealing with a multi-state citizenship defendant. The reasons for recognizing diversity in multi-state incorporated defendants in cases such as Lake Shore & M. S. R. Co. v. Eder, 6 Cir., 1909, 174 F. 944, and Town of Bethel v. Atlantic Coast Line R. Co., 4 Cir., 81 F.2d 60, 69, are not present in this case. In the multi-state incorporations, the corporation is recognized as a corporate entity of each state in which it is so incorporated for all purposes, and it becomes so voluntarily; whereas, under the amendment to 28 U.S.C. § 1332(c), the corporation does not by having its principal place of business in a state other than the state of incorporation become a corporate entity of that state; it merely becomes a citizen of that state for the purpose of diversity of citizenship when jurisdiction in a federal court is invoked.

It is generally known that the amendment to section 1332 was made for the purpose of restricting federal jurisdiction in diversity cases. It is well recognized that it was not the purpose of the amendment to expand federal jurisdiction in such cases. To hold that diversity of citizenship exists between the parties in this case would be to give every citizen of Nebraska, the only place the defendant is incorporated, access to the federal courts in Virginia for the purposes of suits against the defendant; indeed, it would give that right to the citizens of every state, except Virginia, in which the defendant might hereafter become incorporated—a right they have not heretofore enjoyed. It is obvious that to so hold would greatly increase the diversity jurisdiction in federal courts when the recognized purpose of the amendment was to reduce federal jurisdiction in such cases.

In keeping with the declared purpose of the amendment, I conclude that there is no diversity of citizenship in this case, and that the Court is without jurisdiction, and that the motion to dismiss for want of jurisdiction will be granted.

While I have found no appellate decision construing the amendment, I have seen the pamphlet edition of United States District Judge Perry's opinion in the case of Harker v. Kopp, D.C.N.D.Ill.1959, 172 F.Supp. 180, which construes the amendment in a like factual situation. I concur in his reasoning.

An order will be entered dismissing the complaint.

Notes on the Consequence of Multiple Citizenship

(1) Supreme Court opinions prior to the addition of § 1332(c) were less than pellucid as to the effect of multiple incorporation on diversity of citizenship. When the Court first faced the issue, in Ohio & Miss. R. R. v. Wheeler, 66 U.S. (1 Black) 286, 297, 298 (1862), it appeared to say that a suit by a corporation chartered in two States was to be regarded as brought by citizens of both, so that under *Strawbridge v. Curtiss* the corporation was never diverse to citizens of either. But in Railway Co. v. Whitton's Adm'r, 80 U.S. (13 Wall.) 270, 283–84 (1872), the Court seized upon other language in *Wheeler* to uphold jurisdiction of an Illinois plaintiff's suit against an Illinois and Wisconsin corporation because in Wisconsin, where the suit was brought, "the laws of Illinois have no operation. The defendant is a corporation, and as such a citizen of Wisconsin by the laws of that State. It is not *there* a corporation or a citizen of any other State." The apparent rule at this point was that a corporation was to be treated as a citizen of the forum State if incorporated there. But Nashua & Lowell R. R. v. Boston & Lowell R. R., 136 U.S. 356 (1890), permitted a New Hampshire and Massachusetts corporation to sue Massachusetts defendants in Massachusetts federal court, suggesting the polar opposite of the Court's first position: A multistate corporation now seemed diverse to everybody.

Not content to have announced three inconsistent rules without disowning any of them, the Court in St. Louis & S. F. Ry. v. James, 161 U.S. 545, 560–65 (1896), dismissed an action by a Missourian against a Missouri and Arkansas corporation in Arkansas, although both *Whitton* and *Nashua* appeared to support jurisdiction. A corporation, the Court said, could sue and be sued as "a citizen of the State of its original creation"—here Missouri. Arkansas had "adopted" the railroad by requiring it to incorporate locally as a condition of doing business, but the company "was not incorporated as such by the State of Arkansas. The legislation of that State was professedly dealing with the railroad corporations of other States." In order to give the railroad Arkansas citizenship for diversity purposes, "it would be necessary to create it out of natural persons." *Whitton*, the Court explained, was different because there the cause of action had arisen in the forum State and because the report did not show "the character of the legislation by which the Wisconsin company was created." Purporting to follow *James*, the Court in Southern Ry. v. Allison, 190 U.S. 326, 332, (1903), described *James* as having held the "citizenship of a corporation was that of the State originally creating it" and said the place the cause of action arose was not decisive.

In Patch v. Wabash R. R., 207 U.S. 277, 283 (1907), the Court held that an Ohio and Illinois corporation was not a "nonresident" entitled to remove an action brought against it in Illinois. Although the statement that "the defendant exists in Illinois by virtue of the laws of Illinois" suggested a return to the rule of forum citizenship, the Court was at pains to leave matters confused: "What would be the law in case of a suit brought in Illinois upon a cause of action which arose in Ohio is a question that may be left on one side, as also may be the decisions in cases where a corporation originally created in one State afterwards becomes compulsorily a corporation of another State for some purposes in order to extend its powers. . . ." (citing *James* and *Allison*). Finally, in Missouri Pac. Ry. v. Castle, 224 U.S. 541, 546 (1912), a Nebraska plaintiff was allowed to sue in Nebraska federal court a Missouri corporation that had been required to incorporate in Nebraska: "The railway company, if it became a domestic corporation of Nebraska, did so by compulsion of the Nebraska statutes. . . ." Jurisdiction was sustained by *Allison*, which had followed *James* and been cited in *Patch*, and which had approvingly cited a lower-court opinion holding that "a corporation originally created by the State of Illinois although made by the law of Nebraska a domestic corporation of that State, was nevertheless a citizen of Illinois."

Quietly proud, with this the Supreme Court retired from the field for forty-two years. Left to their own devices, the lower courts employed the necessary machete. The Fourth Circuit, vi et armis, pruned away the troublesome *Nashua* decision, blandly saying "it has not influenced the definite course which the courts have followed," and quietly interred the theory that the first incorporation is determinative by noting that it had been suggested in *James* and *Allison* "but not in the latest cases." Town of Bethel v. Atlantic Coast Line R. R., 81 F.2d 60, 69 (1936). The Third Circuit explained *James* as based upon the compulsory nature of the second incorporation and added that it was immaterial where the cause of action arose, whether the ultimate corporation had been formed by consolidation or by purchase, and whether the second charter had been issued to natural persons or to the foreign corporation. But the Fourth Circuit had refused jurisdiction in the charter State of which the opposing party was a citizen, in accord with the forum-citizenship rule of *Whitton*. To Judge Goodrich it made no sense that a New Jersey plaintiff could sue a New York-New Jersey corporation in New York but not in New Jersey, and the Third Circuit held the railroad diverse to everybody in any court. Gavin v. Hudson & M. R. R., 185 F.2d 104 (3d Cir. 1950). The First Circuit disagreed, suggesting that a dual corporation really ought never to be diverse to a citizen of any of its States, but feeling bound by authority to follow the forum rule. Seavey v. Boston & M. R. R., 197 F.2d 485 (1st Cir.1952); Jacobson v. New York, N. H. & H. R. R., 206 F.2d 153 (1st Cir. 1953). In both cases the action had been brought in the State of common citizenship, and jurisdiction was denied.

It was in this state of affairs that the Supreme Court reviewed the First Circuit's decision in *Jacobson*, refusing jurisdiction in Massachusetts of an action by a Massachusetts plaintiff against a Massachusetts and Connecticut corporation. The Court played it close to the vest. Here is its full opinion, 347 U.S. 909:

> The judgment is affirmed. Patch v. Wabash R. Co., 207 U.S. 277; Memphis & Charleston R. Co. v. Alabama, 107 U.S. 581 [which was similar to the *Whitton* case, supra]; Seavey v. Boston & Me. R. Co., 197 F.2d 485.

To some commentators this made everything clear: Except for compulsory incorporations, which were to be disregarded, "if such a corporation was a party to a lawsuit in one of the states in which it was incorporated, it would be considered, for diversity purposes, solely a citizen of that state." C. Wright, Federal Courts 103 (3d Ed. 1976); see also Moore & Weckstein, Corporations and Diversity of Citizenship Jurisdiction: A Supreme Court Fiction Revisited, 77 Harv.L.Rev. 1426, 1429, 1433 (1964). This was indeed what the First Circuit had said in *Seavey*, but the citation of *Patch* and *Memphis* makes it less certain that the Court was embracing everything said in *Seavey*, in view of the suggestions in both the former opinions respecting the place the cause of action arose—a fact noted in the First Circuit's opinion in *Jacobson* as well. One thing the Supreme Court unmistakably did in *Jacobson* was to reject the Third Circuit principle that a dual corporation is always diverse to everybody. Another thing it did was inexcusably to miss a golden opportunity to eliminate the lingering debris. See the continuing doubts expressed by Friedenthal, New Limitations on Federal Jurisdiction, 11 Stan.L.Rev. 213, 232–35 (1959), suggesting that the conflicting decisions may ultimately yield a principle requiring courts to "weigh such factors as whether the incorporation in Z was voluntary, whether Z was the first place of incorporation, and whether the cause of action arose in Z," as well as whether the decision "will increase or decrease diversity jurisdiction."

(2) Does the 1958 amendment deeming a corporation a citizen of "any State in which it has been incorporated" change the law applicable to cases of multiple incorporation? It is clear, isn't it, that there can be no suit in the State of common citizenship? See, e.g., Fitzgerald v. Southern Ry., 176 F.Supp. 445 (S.D.N.Y.1959). But is there jurisdiction in the State where only the corporation is a citizen? In addition to *Majewski* see Hudak v. Port Authority Trans-Hudson Corp., 238 F.Supp. 790 (S.D.N.Y.1965), upholding jurisdiction under the forum rule despite the contrary views of 1 Moore's Federal Practice 723.50–723.58 (2d ed.) and 1 Barron & Holtzoff 142 (Wright ed.). Is there a justification in diversity policy for the forum rule?

(3) Does the law governing multiple incorporations also apply to cases in which a corporation has multiple citizenship because of the 1958 provision deeming it a citizen of "the State where it has its principal place of business?" There is no justification other than historical accident, is there, for treating the principal place of business differently from a second incorporation for this purpose?

(4) Under the principal-place-of-business provision at least six situations can be distinguished. The party opposing the corporation may be a citizen of the State of its incorporation or of the State of its principal business; and the suit may, in either case, be brought in the State of common citizenship, in the State in which only the corporation is a citizen, or in a State in which the corporation is not a citizen. The typical case, like *Kelly v. United States Steel*, supra, is brought in the State of principal business by a citizen of that State; jurisdiction is uniformly denied. E.g., Canton v. Angelina Cas. Co., 279 F.2d 553 (5th Cir. 1960); Jaconski v. McCloskey & Co., 167 F.Supp. 537 (E.D.Pa.1958). This is right enough, isn't it? In the first place, this is exactly the kind of case Congress wanted to exclude from the federal courts; in the second place, the result is consistent with *Jacobson*; in the third place, to uphold jurisdiction in such cases would mean the amendment has completely failed to accomplish its purpose of excluding cases from the federal courts. It seems seldom to occur to litigants to suggest that the amendment created jurisdiction in the charter state between the corporation and a citizen of the forum State; should it have occurred to them?

(5) A number of district courts have held, as in *Diesing*, that there is no jurisdiction in principal-place-of-business cases even when the action is brought in the State where only the corporation is a citizen. E.g., Harker v. Kopp, 172 F.Supp. 180 (N.D.Ill.1959). Should it make a difference if the opposing party is a citizen of the State where the corporation's principal place of business is located, rather than of the State of incorporation as in *Diesing* and *Harker?*

(6) In the few cases involving multistate corporations in States in which they were not chartered it was held prior to 1958 that the corporation was not diverse to a citizen of any incorporating State. E.g., Waller v. New York, N. H. & H. R. R., 127 F.Supp. 863 (S.D.N.Y.1955); Baltimore & O. R. R. v. Thompson, 8 F.R.D. 96, 98 (E.D.Mo.1948). Were these decisions correct? Should they be followed in multi-incorporation cases today? In principal-place-of-business cases?

(7) The American Law Institute proposed to deem a corporation a citizen of "every State and foreign state by which it has been incorporated and of the State or foreign state where it has its principal place of business." The commentary explained that this provision would "destroy diversity between the corporation and a citizen of any one of the specified states." ALI Study, 10, 112. In the light of the history of the effect of multiple corporate citizenship, do you think the proposed statute clearly enough prescribed the intended result?

SMITH v. SPERLING

354 U.S. 91 (1957).

MR. JUSTICE DOUGLAS delivered the opinion of the Court.

This suit was filed in the Federal District Court in California by reason of diversity of citizenship. It is a stockholder's derivative suit. The first cause of action, the only one involved here, is based on alleged fraudulent wastage of assets of Warner Bros. Pictures, Inc. (which we will call Warner Bros.) for the benefit of one Sperling, a son-in-law of a director of Warner Bros., and United States Pictures, Inc. (which we will call United), the son-in-law's corporation. Extended allegations are made concerning various agreements between Warner Bros. and United which, it is charged, are unfair to Warner Bros. Demand on the directors of Warner Bros. to institute this action was not made because, it is averred, such a demand would be futile since, *inter alia*, all or a majority of the board of directors approved the contracts. The plaintiff is a citizen of New York; the defendant directors are citizens of California; and Warner Bros. and United are Delaware corporations.

The complaint joined Warner Bros. as a defendant. It was urged before the District Court, and it is claimed here, that since the cause of action sought to be enforced is one that belongs to the corporation and since the corporation is not "antagonistic" to the stockholder within the meaning of that term as used in Doctor v. Harrington, 196 U.S. 579, 588, Warner Bros. should be realigned as plaintiff. In that event there would be no diversity of citizenship since Delaware corporations would be on both sides of the lawsuit. Strawbridge v. Curtiss, 3 Cranch 267.

The District Court held a hearing on the issue—a hearing that lasted 15 days. It found:

(1) that the contracts in controversy were made in good faith and without fraud; that they were considered by the directors to be in the best interests of Warner Bros. and that, in approving them, they exercised their best business judgment;

(2) that Warner Bros. was not under the domination or control of the Warners on the board; and that the stockholders, officers, or directors were not "antagonistic to the financial interests" of Warner Bros.;

(3) that neither all nor a majority nor any of the directors and officers of Warner Bros. "wrongfully participated" in the acts complained of; that the board was not dominated or controlled by the Warners and Sperling or by any one or more of them;

(4) that if demand had been made on Warner Bros. to institute suit, the management would not have been disqualified "from faithfully doing their duty" as officers and directors but that "such a demand would have been futile."

For these reasons the District Court realigned Warner Bros. as a party plaintiff and dismissed the bill. . . . The Court of Appeals affirmed. . . .

This is a corporate cause of action brought by a stockholder. Whether it is a proper case for assertion by a stockholder of that cause of action is not the question here. Such was the problem involved in Hawes v. Oakland, 104 U.S. 450, upon which so much reliance is placed in supporting the court below. Here we assume that this corporate cause of action may be enforced by the stockholder. We are concerned only with a question of federal diversity jurisdiction.

The gist of the findings of the District Court is that since there was no fraud on the part of the directors in making the contracts but only an exercise of independent business judgment, the management was not antagonistic to the financial interests of the corporation. That is an issue that goes to the merits, not to the question of jurisdiction. There will, of course, be antagonism between the stockholder and the management where the dominant officers and directors are guilty of fraud or misdeeds. But wrongdoing in that sense is not the sole measure of antagonism. There is antagonism whenever the management is aligned against the stockholder and defends a course of conduct which he attacks. The charge normally is cast in terms of fraud, breach of trust, or illegality. See Doctor v. Harrington, supra; Venner v. Great Mutual Casualty Co., 330 U.S. 518, 522, 523. The answer, of course, always denies the charge of wrongdoing. To stop and try the charge of wrongdoing is to delve into the merits. That does not seem to us to be the proper course. It is a time-consuming, wasteful exertion of energy on a preliminary issue in the case. The instant case is a good illustration, for it has been over eight years in the courts on this question of jurisdiction.

Since our decision in Erie R. Co. v. Tompkins, 304 U.S. 64, the law which governs the merits in these derivative actions is local law. . . . The result, then, of the approach followed by the court below is to have more than a preliminary trial on matters going to the merits of the controversy. Obviously federal law would govern the preliminary trial on the issues of wrongdoing, for that matter goes to the question of federal jurisdiction. Yet should the District Court decide those issues in favor of the stockholder, a second trial on the merits will require that the same issues be tried out according to the set of rules supplied by local law.

It seems to us that the proper course is not to try out the issues presented by the charges of wrongdoing but to determine the issue of antagonism on the face of the pleadings and by the nature of the controversy. The bill and answer normally determine whether the management is antagonistic to the stockholder, as Central R. Co. v. Mills, 113 U.S. 249, and Doctor v. Harrington, supra, indicate. The management may refuse or fail to act for any number of reasons. Fraud may be one; the reluctance to take action against a close business associate may be another; honest belief in the wisdom of the course of action which the management has approved may be still another; and so on. As the Court said in Delaware & Hudson Co. v. Albany & S. R. Co., 213 U.S. 435, 451, where the management was deemed to be antagonistic to the stockholder, "The attitude of the directors need not be sinister. It may be sincere." Whenever the management refuses to take action to undo a business transaction or whenever, as in this case, it so solidly approves it that any demand to rescind would be futile, antagonism is evident. The cause of action, to be sure, is that of the corporation. But the corporation has become through its managers hostile and antagonistic to the enforcement of the claim.

Collusion to satisfy the jurisdictional requirements of the District Courts may, of course, always be shown; and it will always defeat jurisdiction. Absent collusion, there is diversity jurisdiction when the real collision of issues, Indianapolis v. Chase National Bank, 314 U.S. 63, 69, or as stated in Helm v. Zarecor, 222 U.S. 32, 36, "the actual controversy," is between citizens of different States. This is a practical not a mechanical determination and is resolved by the pleadings and the nature of the dispute.

Here it is plain that the stockholder and those who manage the corporation are completely and irrevocably opposed on a matter of corporate practice and policy. A trial may demonstrate that the stockholder is wrong and the management right. It may show a dispute that lies in the penumbra of business judgment, unaffected by fraud. But that issue goes to the merits, not to jurisdiction. There is jurisdiction if there is real collision between the stockholder and his corporation. That there is such a collision is evident here.

The judgment must therefore be reversed and the case remanded to the District Court. . . .

MR. JUSTICE FRANKFURTER, whom MR. JUSTICE BURTON, MR. JUSTICE HARLAN, and MR. JUSTICE WHITTAKER join, dissenting.

The Court holds that, collusion aside, whenever a corporation refuses to bring a suit and a derivative suit is brought by a stockholder on its behalf, the corporation is always to be aligned as a defendant for purposes of determining diversity jurisdiction. The Court thus makes the exception the rule, and by confounding the requirements for establishing a substantive cause of action with the requirements of diversity jurisdiction, it overturns a half-century's precedents in this Court. . . .

The initial and leading case dealing with the alignment of parties for jurisdictional purposes in a stockholder's suit is Doctor v. Harrington, 196 U.S. 579. That was a suit by stockholders against two individuals alleged to control the company in question and a third-party corporation. Realigning the corporation as a plaintiff, the Circuit Court held that there was no diversity, and it dismissed the bill for lack of jurisdiction. This Court reversed. After stating that Equity Rule 94 (now Rule 23(b) of the Federal Rules of Civil Procedure) contemplated suits "brought by a stockholder in a corporation founded on rights which may properly be asserted by the corporation," the Court went on to indicate what must have been the basis for aligning the corporation in that case as a defendant:

> "And the decisions of this court establish that such a suit, when between citizens of different States, involves a controversy cognizable in a Circuit Court of the United States. The ultimate interest of the corporation made defendant may be the same as that of the stockhold-

er made plaintiff, but the corporation may be under a control antagonistic to him, and made to act in a way detrimental to his rights. In other words, his interests, and the interests of the corporation, may be made subservient to some illegal purpose. If a controversy hence arise, and the other conditions of jurisdiction exist, it can be litigated in a Federal court." 196 U.S., at page 587. . . .

Mr. Justice Jackson's opinion for the Court [in Koster v. Lumbermens Mutual Co., 330 U.S. 518] throws further light on what is meant by "antagonistic hands" by characterizing "the real party in interest," the corporation, as "disabled from protecting itself." That cannot mean anything else except what the *Venner* case, quoting from Doctor v. Harrington, set forth as the reason for disablement, *viz.*, that the very individuals who have a stranglehold over the corporation are the people against whom suit is sought to be brought and, therefore, in any sense that has any meaning, they are the defendants for that reason. . . .

The Court, purporting to interpret this half-century of precedents, sweeps them away. In so doing, it greatly expands the diversity jurisdiction. "Antagonism" is a difficult standard to meet and is a more unusual situation. Refusal to sue provides automatic entry. Moreover, whenever the corporation and the real defendants are of the same citizenship, there would be no diversity jurisdiction unless antagonism could be shown. No similar restriction on jurisdiction is made because of possible non-diverseness of the stockholder and the corporation defendant because it is generally not too difficult to find a non-diverse [sic] stockholder to institute suit.

The Court professes to do no more than to apply well-settled precedents. But the well-settled precedents that are applied have absolutely "nothing to do with the case." The Court has found support in the line of cases that deal solely with substantive requirements or with the procedural rules for establishing compliance with those requirements. These have nothing to do with the constitutional jurisdiction of the federal courts in diversity suits. . . .

One final matter of general importance should be discussed before applying the general principles adduced to the facts of the present cases. The Court states: "[T]he proper course is not to try out the issues presented by the charges of wrongdoing but to determine the issue of antagonism on the face of the pleadings and by the nature of the controversy." Of course the charges of wrongdoing need not be determined to ascertain the jurisdiction of the federal courts. What must be determined with directors or other persons alleged to control the corporation are joined as defendants is the relation of these people to the corporation. And while in certain cases the issues may be determined from the face of the pleadings, the courts are not so limited. The Court speaks of making "a practical not a mechanical determination," but a more mechanical determination could hardly be imagined. If anything had been regarded as settled until today about federal jurisdiction, it was that "It is our duty, as it is that of the lower federal courts, to 'look beyond the pleadings and arrange the parties according to their sides in the dispute.' Dawson v. Columbia Trust Co., 197 U.S. 178, 180." Indianapolis v. Chase National Bank, 314 U.S. 63, 69. Of course, this may take time and may not always be easy of determination. I had not thought up to now that such considerations should lead us to disregard our constitutional obligation, for, as the District Court in No. 316 stated, "It is more than costly error therefore—it is an unconstitutional invasion of the jurisdiction of the state courts—for a federal court to sustain federal jurisdiction of a civil action between private persons where 'the matter in controversy' exceeds the sum or value of $3,000 . . . but does not arise 'under the Constitution, laws or treaties of the United States,' . . . and diversity of citizenship as to 'the matter in controversy' does not exist. U.S.Const., Art. III; 28 U.S.C. § 1332. . . ." 117 F.Supp., at 808. . . .

I find no justification for overturning the findings and conclusions of the District Court made after extended hearing and analysis and affirmed by the Court of Appeals. I would therefore affirm. . . .

Notes on Shareholders' Derivative Suits

(1) In a companion case to Smith v. Sperling, Swanson v. Traer, 354 U.S. 114 (1957), the Court said:

> For the reasons stated in Smith v. Sperling, supra, we think this case is an instance where the management—for good reasons or for bad—is definitely and distinctly opposed to the institution of this litigation. The management is, therefore, antagonistic to the stockholders as that conception has been used in the cases. It follows that the corporation was properly made a defendant.

(2) Dodge v. Woolsey, 59 U.S. (18 How.) 331 (1856), was a derivative suit by a Connecticut shareholder in an Ohio bank to enjoin the collection of an allegedly unconstitutional Ohio tax on the bank. The Board of Directors of the bank, although considering the tax invalid and intending not to pay it unless required to, refused to sue to enjoin it "in consideration of the many obstacles in the way of testing the law in the courts of the State." The Supreme Court apparently assumed, without mentioning it, that the corporation was properly aligned as a defendant. Would the corporation be realigned as a plaintiff if the *Dodge* case were brought today?

(3) Doctor v. Harrington, 196 U.S. 579 (1905), seems to be the first case where realignment of the corporation to determine diversity was recognized as a possibility. The prior cases, including *Dodge v. Woolsey* above, involved the distinct question whether the shareholder was a proper plaintiff to sue on the corporation's claim—an issue that arises in every shareholder's derivative suit, in state as well as federal courts. These cases developed the rule that was formulated in Hawes v. Oakland, 104 U.S. 450 (1882), requiring the shareholder to show that the board of directors had acted beyond its powers under the corporate charter, or fraudulently, or in opposition to the interests of the corporation, or of the shareholders. The

Court further required that the shareholder-plaintiff have exhausted his remedies within the corporate structure. The Court published Equity Rule 94 to enforce the latter requirement; the successor to that Rule, substantially unchanged, is Rule 23.1, Fed.R.Civ.P., which appears at p. 752 infra. Does *Smith* hold that satisfaction of the pleading requirements of Rule 23.1 is always enough to make a corporation a defendant?

On the other hand, would Justice Frankfurter require the shareholder to *prove* the allegations required by Rule 23.1 in order to prevent realignment? Would he require in addition proof that the shareholder was a proper plaintiff, either under the standards of *Hawes v. Oakland* or under the applicable state law? If so, how does he answer the majority's charge that his rule would require a double trial of the issue of the directors' wrongdoing?

Is there any middle ground that would make the requirement of antagonism more than a formality of pleading and less than a requirement that the plaintiff prove a large part of his case on the merits in order to establish jurisdiction?

(4) § 1332(a) requires that the "matter in controversy" be "between—(1) citizens of different states." What was the "matter in controversy" in *Smith v. Sperling*? Was it the corporation's alleged claim against Sperling? The shareholder's suit to force the corporation to enforce that claim? Or the shareholder's claim against Sperling, which arose when the corporation refused to enforce its claim against Sperling? Who are the plaintiffs and defendants in each of these controversies? Did the Court choose any one of these three interpretations as a general rule? Did Justice Frankfurter choose any one of them? Would it make sense to ignore the corporation's citizenship altogether? Compare the interpleader situation in *Treinies v. Sunshine Mining Co.*, supra p. 247.

(5) Rule 23.1 recognizes the possibility of a derivative suit by a member of an unincorporated association. After *Bouligny*, when is such a suit within the jurisdiction of the federal courts?

(6) The question of realigning parties arises not only in shareholders' derivative suits but in other contexts as well. See, for example, Indianapolis v. Chase National Bank, 314 U.S. 63 (1941). Chase, a New York corporation, was trustee under a mortgage deed securing an issue of bonds by Indianapolis Gas Company, an Indiana corporation. Indianapolis Gas leased its properties to Citizens Gas Company, also an Indiana corporation, in return for a promise to pay the bond interest and additional sums. Citizens Gas then conveyed all its property, including that covered by the lease, to the City of Indianapolis. The City refused to regard itself as bound by the lease, so Chase sued the City, Citizens Gas, and Indianapolis Gas, asking principally that the City be ordered to pay interest on the bonds and that a judgment for interest be entered against the defendants "liable therefor."

The Supreme Court, splitting 5—4, held there was no jurisdiction. "One question permeates this litigation," wrote Justice Frankfurter for the majority: "Is the lease whereby Indianapolis Gas in 1913 conveyed all its gas plant property to Citizens Gas valid and binding upon the City? . . . The rest is window-dressing designed to satisfy the requirements of diversity jurisdiction. Everything else in the case is incidental to this dominating controversy, with respect to which Indianapolis Gas and the City, 'citizens' of the same state, are on opposite sides." Indianapolis Gas was interested in upholding the lease because it assured its shareholders an annual six percent return on their stock, Indianapolis Gas had insufficient assets to pay the defaulted interest, and Chase "did not bring this suit in order to obtain a declaration that, regardless of the validity of the lease, Indianapolis Gas is still ultimately responsible for the interest payments. . . ." For the dissenters, Justice Jackson objected that the Court "forces into the position of co-plaintiff one party which the District Court adjudged entitled to recover over a million dollars, and another which the District Court adjudged solely liable to pay that sum." Chase, said the dissent, had not only alleged a cause of action against the City; it had also alleged one against Indianapolis Gas for the interest.

> If the plaintiff had asserted these demands in two separate actions, no one would doubt that both were within the jurisdiction of the District Court. . . . Jurisdiction of the federal courts is indeed a variable and illusory thing, if the jurisdiction which a District Court admittedly has of two separate causes of action is lost when they are united in one, agreeably to the federal rules of procedure, because the one defendant as a surety seeks to enforce its equitable right to be exonerated by the other, who is alleged to be the principal debtor.

Should this decision be given significance in determining the alignment of parties brought in subsequent to the original complaint, as in impleader under Rule 14? Does *Smith v. Sperling* affect the principles of the *Indianapolis* case?

Would you approve a rule requiring that a party be aligned as plaintiff if the complainant has not sought relief against him?

(7) What do you think of diversity jurisdiction now? See D. Currie, The Federal Courts and the American Law Institute: Part I, 36 U.Chi.L. Rev. 1, 49 (1968): "The security given out-of-state interests by this jurisdiction is not worth the burden of defining and administering it." Surely this snide observation is tongue-in-cheek? Or is it?

SECTION 4. THE JURISDICTIONAL AMOUNT

SNYDER v. HARRIS

394 U.S. 332 (1969).

MR. JUSTICE BLACK delivered the opinion of the Court.

Title 28 U.S.C. § 1332 grants jurisdiction to United States district courts of suits between citizens of different States where "the matter in controversy exceeds the sum or value of $10,000. . . ." * The issue presented by these two cases is whether separate and distinct claims presented by and for various claimants in a class action may be added together to provide the $10,000 jurisdictional amount in controversy.

* [The statutory figure was raised to $50,000 in 1988.—Ed.]

Each of these cases involves a single plaintiff suing on behalf of himself and "all others similarly situated." In No. 109, Mrs. Margaret E. Snyder, a shareholder of Missouri Fidelity Union Trust Life Insurance Company, brought suit against members of the company's board of directors alleging that they had sold their shares of the company's stock for an amount far in excess of its fair market value, that this excess represented payment to these particular directors to obtain complete control of the company, and that under Missouri law the excess should properly be distributed among all the shareholders of the company and not merely to a few of them. The suit was brought in the United States District Court for the Eastern District of Missouri, 268 F.Supp. 701, diversity of citizenship being alleged as the basis for federal jurisdiction. Since petitioner's allegations showed that she sought for herself only $8,740 in damages, respondent moved to dismiss on the grounds that the matter in controversy did not exceed $10,000. Petitioner contended, however, that her claim should be aggregated with those of the other members of her class, approximately 4,000 shareholders of the company stock. If all 4,000 potential claims were aggregated, the amount in controversy would be approximately $1,200,000. The District Court held that the claims could not thus be aggregated to meet the statutory test of jurisdiction and the Court of Appeals for the Eighth Circuit . . . affirmed, 390 F.2d 204 (1967).

In No. 117, Otto R. Coburn, a resident of Kansas, brought suit in the United States District Court for the District of Kansas against the Gas Service Company, a corporation marketing natural gas in Kansas. Jurisdiction was predicated upon diversity of citizenship. The complaint alleged that the Gas Service Company had billed and illegally collected a city franchise tax from Coburn and others living outside city limits. Coburn alleged damages to himself of only $7.81. Styling his complaint as a class action, however, Coburn sought relief on behalf of approximately 18,000 other Gas Service Company customers living outside of cities. The amount by which other members of the class had been overcharged was, and is, unknown, but the complaint alleged that the aggregation of all these claims would in any event exceed $10,000. The District Court overruled the Gas Company's motion to dismiss for failure to satisfy the jurisdictional amount and, on interlocutory appeal, the Court of Appeals for the Tenth Circuit affirmed, holding that because of a 1966 amendment to Rule 23 of the Federal Rules of Civil Procedure relating to class actions, separate and distinct claims brought together in a class action could not be aggregated for the purpose of establishing the jurisdictional amount in diversity cases. 389 F.2d 831. We granted certiorari to resolve the conflict. . . .

The first congressional grant to district courts to take suits between citizens of different States fixed the requirement for the jurisdictional amount in controversy at $500. In 1887 this jurisdictional amount was increased to $2,000; in 1911 to $3,000; and in 1958 to $10,000. The traditional judicial interpretation under all of these statutes has been from the beginning that the separate and distinct claims of two or more plaintiffs cannot be aggregated in order to satisfy the jurisdictional amount requirement. Aggregation has been permitted only (1) in cases in which a single plaintiff seeks to aggregate two or more of his own claims against a single defendant and (2) in cases in which two or more plaintiffs unite to enforce a single title or right in which they have a common and undivided interest. It is contended, however, that the adoption of a 1966 amendment to Rule 23 effectuated a change in this jurisdictional doctrine. Under old Rule 23, class actions were divided into three categories which came to be known as "true," "hybrid," and "spurious." True class actions were those in which the rights of the different class members were common and undivided; in such cases aggregation was permitted. Spurious class actions, on the other hand, were in essence merely a form of permissive joinder in which parties with separate and distinct claims were allowed to litigate those claims in a single suit simply because the different claims involved common questions of law or fact. In such cases aggregation was not permitted: each plaintiff had to show that his individual claim exceeded the jurisdictional amount. The 1966 amendment to Rule 23 replaced the old categories with a functional approach to class actions. The new Rule establishes guidelines for the appropriateness of class actions, makes provision for giving notice to absent members, allows members of the class to remove themselves from the litigation and provides that the judgment will include all members of the class who have not requested exclusion. In No. 117, Gas Service Company, the Court of Appeals for the Tenth Circuit held that these changes in Rule 23 changed the jurisdictional amount doctrine as well. The Court noted that "Because the claims of the individuals constituting the class in the case at bar are neither 'joint' nor 'common' this action under Rule 23 before amendment would not have been classified as a 'true' class action and aggregation of claims would not have been permitted." 389 F.2d 831, 833. The Court of Appeals held, however, that a different result was compelled now that the amendment to Rule 23 abolished the distinctions between true and spurious class actions. The Court held that because aggregation was permitted in some class actions, it must now be permitted in all class actions under the new Rule. We disagree and conclude, as did the Courts of Appeals for the Fifth and Eighth Circuits, that the adoption of amended Rule 23 did not and could not have brought about this change in the scope of the congressionally enacted grant of jurisdiction to the district courts.

The doctrine that separate and distinct claims could not be aggregated was never, and is not now, based upon the categories of old Rule 23 or of any rule of procedure. That doctrine is based rather upon this Court's interpretation of the statutory phrase "matter in controversy." The interpretation of this phrase as precluding aggregation substantially predates the 1938 Federal Rules of Civil Procedure. In 1911 this Court said in Troy Bank v. G. A. Whitehead & Co. that

> "When two or more plaintiffs, having separate and distinct demands, unite for convenience and economy in a single suit, it is

> essential that the demand of each be of the requisite jurisdictional amount; . . ." 222 U.S. 39, 40.

By 1916 this Court was able to say in Pinel v. Pinel, 240 U.S. 594, that it was "settled doctrine" that separate and distinct claims could not be aggregated to meet the required jurisdictional amount. In Clark v. Paul Gray, Inc., 306 U.S. 583 (1939), this doctrine, which had first been declared in cases involving joinder of parties, was applied to class actions under the then recently passed Federal Rules. In that case numerous individuals, partnerships, and corporations joined in bringing a suit challenging the validity of a California statute which exacted fees of $15 on each automobile driven into the State. Raising the jurisdictional amount question *sua sponte*, this Court held that the claims of the various fee payers could not be aggregated "where there are numerous plaintiffs having no joint or common interest or title in the subject matter of the suit." 306 U.S. 583, 588.

Nothing in the amended Rule 23 changes this doctrine. The class action plaintiffs in the two cases before us argue that since the new Rule will include in the judgment all members of the class who do not ask to be out by a certain date, the "matter in controversy" now encompasses all the claims of the entire class. But it is equally true that where two or more plaintiffs join their claims under the joinder provisions of Rule 20, each and every joined plaintiff is bound by the judgment. And it was in joinder cases of this very kind that the doctrine that distinct claims could not be aggregated was originally enunciated. Troy Bank v. G. A. Whitehead & Co., 222 U.S. 39 (1911); Pinel v. Pinel, 240 U.S. 594 (1916). The fact that judgments under class actions formerly classified as spurious may now have the same effect as claims brought under the joinder provisions is certainly no reason to treat them *differently* from joined actions for purposes of aggregation.

Any change in the Rules that did purport to effect a change in the definition of "matter in controversy" would clearly conflict with the command of Rule 82 that "These rules shall not be construed to extend or limit the jurisdiction of the United States district courts. . . ." In Sibbach v. Wilson & Co., this Court held that the rule-making authority was limited by "the inability of a court, by rule, to extend or restrict the jurisdiction conferred by a statute." 312 U.S. 1, 10 (1941). We have consistently interpreted the jurisdictional statute passed by Congress as not conferring jurisdiction where the required amount in controversy can be reached only by aggregating separate and distinct claims. The interpretation of that statute cannot be changed by a change in the Rules. . . .

It is linguistically possible, of course, to interpret the old congressional phrase "matter in controversy" as including all claims that can be joined or brought in a single suit through the class action device. But . . . Congress has . . . consistently amended the amount in controversy section and re-enacted the "matter in controversy" language without change of its jurisdictional effect against a background of judicial interpretation that has consistently interpreted that congressionally enacted phrase as not encompassing the aggregation of separate and distinct claims. . . . There is no compelling reason for this Court to overturn a settled interpretation of an important congressional statute in order to add to the burdens of an already overloaded federal court system. . . .

MR. JUSTICE FORTAS, with whom MR. JUSTICE DOUGLAS joins, dissenting.

The Court today refuses to conform the judge-made formula for computing the amount in controversy in class actions with the 1966 amendment to Rule 23 of the Federal Rules of Civil Procedure. The effect of this refusal is substantially to undermine a generally welcomed and long-needed reform in federal procedure. . . .

The jurisdictional amount statutes require placing a value on the "matter in controversy" in a civil action. Once it is decided under the new Rule that an action may be maintained as a class action, it is the claim of the whole class and not the individual economic stakes of the separate members of the class which is the "matter in controversy." That this is so is perhaps most clearly indicated by the fact that the judgment in a class action properly maintained as such includes all members of the class. Rule 23(c)(3). This effect of the new Rule in broadening the scope of the "controversy" in a class action to include the combined interests of all the members of the class is illustrated by the facts of No. 117. That class action, if allowed to proceed, would, under the Rule, determine not merely whether the gas company wrongfully collected $7.81 in taxes from Mr. Coburn. It would also result in a judgment which, subject to the limits of due process, would determine—authoritatively and not merely as a matter of precedent—the status of the taxes collected from the 18,000 other people allegedly in the class Coburn seeks to represent. That being the case, it is hard to understand why the fact that the alleged claims are, in terms of the old Rule categories, "several" rather than "joint," means that the "matter in controversy" for jurisdictional amount purposes must be regarded as the $7.81 Mr. Coburn claims instead of the thousands of dollars of alleged overcharges of the whole class, the status of all of which would be determined by the judgment. . . .

Permitting aggregation in class action cases does not involve any violation of the principle, expressed in Rule 82 and inherent in the whole procedure for the promulgation and amendment of the Federal Rules, that the courts cannot by rule expand their own jurisdictions. While the Rules cannot change subject-matter jurisdiction, changes in the forms and practices of the federal courts through changes in the Rules frequently and necessarily will affect the occasions on which subject matter jurisdiction is exercised because they will in some cases make a difference in what cases the federal courts will hear and who will be authoritatively bound by the judgment. For example, the development of the law of joinder and ancillary jurisdiction under the

Federal Rules has influenced the "jurisdiction" of the federal courts in this broader sense. Indeed, the promulgation of the old Rule 23 provided a new means for resolving in a single federal litigation, based on the diversity jurisdiction, the claims of all members of a class, even though some in the class were not of diverse citizenship from parties on the other side.[23] Similarly, the creation in a Rule having the effect of a statute of a new type of class action—one meeting the requirements of the new Rule as to suitability for class-wide resolution, although involving "several" interests of the members of the class—has changed the procedural context in which the subject matter jurisdiction statutes, like those referring to jurisdictional amount, are to be applied. Making judicial rules for calculating jurisdictional amount responsive to the new structure of class actions is not an extension of the jurisdiction of the federal courts but a recognition that the procedural framework in which the courts operate has been changed by a provision having the effect of law. . . .

For these reasons, I would measure the value of the "matter in controversy" in a class action found otherwise proper under the amended Rule 23 by the monetary value of the claim of the whole class.

Notes on the Jurisdictional Amount

(1) Ever since the first Judiciary Act, 1 Stat. 73, 78, which imposed a jurisdictional minimum of $500 in diversity cases, access to the federal courts in some classes of cases has been provided only if a more or less substantial money value was at stake. The first general grant of federal-question jurisdiction to the trial courts in 1875 contained a $500 minimum (18 Stat. 470); the requirement in both diversity and federal-question cases was raised to $2000 in 1887 (24 Stat. 552), to $3000 in 1911 (36 Stat. 1087, 1091), to $10,000 in 1958 (72 Stat. 415), and to $50,000 in 1988 (102 Stat. 4646)—reflecting, as was said in 1958, a "marked depreciation" in "the value of the dollar."

The 1958 increase was part of a package whose overall design was to "alleviate the crowded conditions in the district courts" resulting from a 75% increase in civil cases since World War II. See S.Rep.No. 1830, 85th Cong., 2d Sess. (1958), and Statement of Joseph F. Spaniol, printed therein. But the policy behind federal-question and diversity jurisdiction is that a federal forum is necessary to protect nonresidents and litigants with federal rights; why is not the answer to court congestion an increase in the number of judges instead of a compromise of federal policy? This suggestion would have horrified Justice Frankfurter:

> A powerful judiciary implies a relatively small number of judges. Honorific motives of distinction have drawn even to the lower federal bench lawyers of the highest quality and thereby built up a public

23. It has long been established that if the requisite diversity existed between the original parties federal jurisdiction is not ousted merely because later intervenors or members of the class represented by the original parties are citizens of the same State as an adverse party. Stewart v. Dunham, 115 U.S. 61 (1885); Supreme Tribe of Ben-Hur v. Cauble, 255 U.S. 356 (1921). . . .

> confidence comparable to the feelings of Englishmen for their judges. Signs are not wanting that an enlargement of the federal judiciary does not make for maintenance of its great traditions. In 1884 there were only 66 federal judges; they had increased to 115 in 1907; there are about 170 today; the pressure for more is steady. It is idle to ratio the number of judges to changes in the wealth or population of the country. Subtle considerations of psychology and prestige play havoc with the mechanical notion that increase in the business of the federal courts can be met by increasing the number of judges.

Distribution of Judicial Power Between United States and State Courts, 13 Corn.L.Q. 499, 515–16 (1928). The Senate Committee in 1958 observed that the appointment of 51 additional district judges since the War had failed to solve the problem; the total number of district and circuit federal judges in 1980 had reached 582. Annual Report of the Director of the Administrative Office of the United States Courts 19 (1980).

Assuming that the overloading of federal dockets must be attacked by limiting federal jurisdiction, is it clear that the jurisdictional minimum is an appropriate means? See the Senate Committee's 1958 argument that the federal courts should not "fritter away their time in the trial of petty controversies"; ALI Study 173–74: "The jurisdiction is provided for the protection of the parties, and where only a small amount is involved, so it might be argued, the parties will not be greatly harmed if they are denied that protection." [1]

(2) From the beginning there have been categories of cases in which no jurisdictional minimum is required. This is obviously appropriate in areas of exclusive federal jurisdiction, such as federal crimes or bankruptcy, antitrust, patent, and copyright cases, see pp. 181–83 supra. It is less easily explicable in maritime cases for which the state courts have always been allowed to provide common-law remedies, 1 Stat. 73, 77, now 28 U.S.C. § 1333. And a whole series of special enactments have long dispensed with the jurisdictional minimum in particular types of federal-question cases in which the state courts have concurrent jurisdiction, e.g., 28 U.S.C. §§ 1337 (actions under statutes "regulating commerce"), 1338 (trademark cases), 1339 (postal matters), 1343 (civil rights), 1345 (United States as plaintiff), 1352 (bonds authorized by federal law), 1353 (Indian allotments). [2] See also the *$500* minimum in interpleader cases, 28 U.S.C. § 1335, the *$10,000* minimum for *removing* actions against railroads for lost freight, § 1445(b),

1. Professor Meador, in A New Approach to Limiting Diversity Jurisdiction, 46 A.B.A.J. 383, 384 (1960), suggested that as a substitute for the jurisdictional amount Congress should exclude from federal jurisdiction classes of litigation in which state courts are not very likely to be hostile or which are especially burdensome to the federal courts—in particular, personal-injury diversity cases, which he says usually require expensive juries and seldom relate to diversity's arguable purpose of encouraging interstate commercial transactions. Cf. the limitation on direct actions against liability insurers and the restriction against removal of workers' compensation cases, 28 U.S.C. §§ 1332(c), 1445(c).

2. The intricate interpretive problems posed by the various statutes making exceptions to the amount requirement in federal-question cases were explored in detail in earlier editions of this book. For cases interpreting 28 U.S.C. § 1343(3), which are still relevant to the construction of 42 U.S.C. § 1983, see pp. 387–89 infra.

and the *maximum* jurisdictional amount of $10,000 in Tucker Act cases, § 1346(a). What is the point of this last provision?

Until recently, however, there remained substantial categories of federal-question cases in which a jurisdictional minimum was required. Section 1343(3), for example, applied only to persons acting under color of *state* law, and consequently actions against federal officers were often dismissed for want of the necessary amount. E.g., Senate Select Committee v. Nixon, 366 F.Supp. 51 (D.D.C.1973).[3] Responding to incessant criticism, e.g., 1 Recommendations & Reports of the Administrative Conference of the United States 169 (1970), Congress in 1976 finally abolished the amount requirement in actions "brought against the United States, any agency thereof, or any officer or employee thereof in his official capacity." P.L. 94–574, 90 Stat. 2721.

The ALI some time earlier had advocated eliminating the amount requirement altogether in federal-question cases while retaining it in diversity:

> In cases within the diversity jurisdiction, where parties are relying entirely on state law, it is not inappropriate to require the states to provide a forum for cases involving a small amount. Where the right relied on is federal, the national government should bear the burden of providing a forum to parties who wish to be heard in federal court. Congress has the power to require state courts to hear federal question cases, but to exercise that power in such fashion as to force small claims into state courts, while reserving larger claims for federal courts, would smack too much of regarding the state courts as inferior tribunals. . . .

ALI Study 174–75.

Congress has since agreed; the amount requirement was dropped from § 1331 in 1980. Does that mean all those special provisions such as § 1338 (patent and copyright cases) serve no remaining purpose?

(3) In actions for damages a good deal of deference is paid to the plaintiff's statement of his own claim in determining the amount in controversy: "The sum claimed by the plaintiff controls if the claim is apparently made in good faith." St. Paul Mercury Indem. Co. v. Red Cab Co., 303 U.S. 283, 288 (1938). Why? See Wiley v. Sinkler, 179 U.S. 58, 65 (1900):

> What amount of damages the plaintiff shall recover in such an action [for deprivation of the right to vote] is peculiarly appropriate for

3. After 1962 the amount requirement was inapplicable in mandamus cases under 28 U.S.C. § 1361, but, as the *Nixon* case demonstrated, the scope of that provision was narrow. Some courts found refuge in the Administrative Procedure Act, 5 U.S.C. §§ 702, 703, despite its embarrassing requirement that the "judicial review" it provided was to be sought "in a court of competent jurisdiction." See, e.g., Pickus v. United States Board of Parole, 507 F.2d 1107, 1109, & n.5 (D.C.Cir. 1974), collecting the decisions. A final alternative was to bring small claims against federal officers in courts with local jurisdiction over the District of Columbia. See Tatum v. Laird, 444 F.2d 947 (D.C.Cir. 1971), reversed on other grounds, 408 U.S. 1 (1972); D.C. Code, §§ 11–501, 11–921 (1970 Supp.). After the problem was otherwise solved, the Supreme Court finally held the APA was not a grant of jurisdiction. Califano v. Sanders, 430 U.S. 99 (1977).

the determination of a jury, and no opinion of the court upon that subject can justify it in holding that the amount in controversy was insufficient to support the jurisdiction of the Circuit Court.

How is a court to determine whether a claim of damages is made in good faith? See Bell v. Preferred Life Assur. Society, 320 U.S. 238 (1943), holding the then $3000 requirement met in a fraud action based on the plaintiff's investment of $200 toward an insurance policy worth no more than $1000; the plaintiff claimed $200,000, and even though the applicable law required punitive damages to "bear proportion" to the injury, the Court was unwilling to say it was "apparent to a legal certainty from the complaint" that he could recover no more than $3000. But jurisdiction was refused in Arnold v. Troccoli, 344 F.2d 842 (2d Cir. 1965), in which the plaintiff first had sued in a state court for $6000, then dismissed that claim because a federal trial might be faster and filed for $15,000 in the District Court. Anthony v. United Ins. Co., 240 F.Supp. 95 (E.D.S.C.1965), dismissed a fraud action for $1000 actual and $49,000 punitive damages because "under the facts of this case" a jury verdict for more than $10,000 would have to be set aside. Accord, Nelson v. Keefer, 451 F.2d 289 (3d Cir. 1971); contra, Deutsch v. Hewes Street Realty Corp., 359 F.2d 96 (2d Cir. 1966), arguing that "to allow a district court judge to value a plaintiff's claim in a case which involves a demand for unliquidated damages and in which the jurisdictional issue is inextricably bound up with the merits of the controversy is tantamount to depriving the plaintiff of his present statutory right to a jury trial." For discussion of the conclusiveness of the plaintiff's claim see generally Note, Determination of Federal Jurisdictional Amount in Suits on Unliquidated Claims, 64 Mich.L.Rev. 930 (1966), urging that the court determine the legal possibility of a sufficient recovery on the basis of an affidavit specifying the plaintiff's proposed evidence of damages.

The 1973 bill to enact the ALI proposals would have raised the minimum to $15,000 and codified *Nelson v. Keefer*: "When the sufficiency of the amount in controversy is put in issue, the court shall dismiss the action for lack of jurisdiction unless it determines after hearing without jury, upon affidavit or otherwise, that there is a reasonable probability of recovery in excess of . . . $15,000." S. 1876, 93d Cong., 1st Sess. § 1301(a).

Is it consistent with the "legal certainty" test to say, as the Supreme Court said in St. Paul Mercury Indemnity Co. v. Red Cab Co., 303 U.S. 283, 289, 292 (1938), that there is jurisdiction even "if it appears from the face of the complaint that the defendant has a valid defense, if asserted, to all or a portion of the claim"? [4]

4. Do the "good faith" and "legal certainty" tests afford adequate protection against the inflation of claims by plaintiffs seeking to manufacture federal jurisdiction? Section 1332(b), added in 1958, was an attempt to deter such imposition by allowing costs to be taxed against a plaintiff who recovered less than the jurisdictional requirement. The ALI Study (p. 120) found this to have been largely ineffective but nevertheless recommended its retention. An early ALI draft considered the imposition of the adversary's attorney fees, ALI Study 49 (Tent. Draft No. 1, 1963). Should the attorney who files an inflated claim be held in contempt? Should the court dismiss an action if the plaintiff recovers less than the required amount? Apart from the waste such a rule would entail, a small verdict does not prove, does it, that no greater sum was originally in controversy? See St. Paul

(4) In damage cases the plaintiff stands to gain whatever the court may award him, so the amount is necessarily a matter of speculation before trial, unless there are legal limits to the possible award. But in an injunction suit, for example, the amount at stake is an objective fact, often as ascertainable before as after trial, and the good-faith test has not generally been applied; if challenged, the plaintiff must prove the amount is sufficient. See, e.g., Hague v. CIO, 307 U.S. 496 (1939) (Roberts, J., concurring). [5]

In Healy v. Ratta, 292 U.S. 263 (1934), the plaintiff sought to enjoin enforcement of a license tax on his business; the Supreme Court held the amount at stake was neither the value of the business nor the penalty for failure to pay, but the amount of the tax, "since payment of it would avoid the penalty and end the dispute." Cf. McNutt v. General Motors Acceptance Corp., 298 U.S. 178 (1936), holding the amount in controversy in a suit to enjoin enforcement of a regulatory statute was the plaintiff's cost of compliance.

In Glenwood Light & Water Co. v. Mutual Light, Heat & Power Co., 239 U.S. 121, 125 (1915), the Court acknowledged that the defendant could remove his offending poles and wires for $500 but upheld jurisdiction because the equipment allegedly caused more than $3000 damage to the plaintiff, saying the test was "the value of the object to be gained by complaint." Should jurisdiction have been denied if the figures had been reversed, so that only the defendant had more than $3000 at stake? [6] Does

Mercury Indemnity Co. v. Red Cab Co., 303 U.S. 283 (1938), refusing remand of a removed action even though after removal the plaintiff had reduced his claim below the jurisdictional amount, and despite the existence of § 5 of the 1875 Judiciary Act, since omitted, requiring dismissal or remand if "at any time" it appeared the suit "does not really and substantially involve a dispute or controversy within the jurisdiction."

5. But see Hunt v. Washington State Apple Advertising Commission, 432 U.S. 333, 347–8 (1977), where an injunction and a declaration were sought respecting the constitutionality of a state statute regulating labels on apples:

> In actions seeking declaratory or injunctive relief, it is well established that the amount in controversy is measured by the value of the object of the litigation. . . . Here, that object is the right of individual Washington apple growers and dealers to conduct their business affairs in the North Carolina market free from the interference of the challenged statute. The value of that right is measured by the losses that will follow from the statute's enforcement. . . . There is . . . evidence supporting the [District Court's] finding that individual growers and dealers incurred substantial costs in complying with the statute. . . . Both the substantial volume of sales in North Carolina—the record demonstrates that in 1974 alone, such sales were in excess of $2,000,000—and the continuing nature of the statute's interference . . . precludes [sic] our saying "to a legal certainty," on this record, that such losses and expenses will not, over time if they have not done so already, amount to the requisite $10,000 for at least some of the individual growers and dealers.

There were no dissents, and there was no reference to the amount of the alleged losses.

6. See Dobie, Jurisdictional Amount in the United States District Court, 38 Harv. L.Rev. 733 (1925), so arguing; Wright, Federal Courts 192 (4th ed. 1983), saying the Supreme Court has never so held; Mississippi & Missouri Railroad Co. v. Ward, 67 U.S. (2 Black) 485, 492 (1863), upholding jurisdiction of a suit to remove a bridge without regard to the extent of interference with the plaintiff's right of navigation: "The want of a sufficient amount of damage having been sustained to give the Federal Courts jurisdiction, will not defeat the remedy, as the removal of the obstruction is the matter of controversy, and the value of the object must govern"; Wright,

the apparent discrepancy in the value of a single right to the two parties result from a misconception of economics? If the water is worth only $1000 to the plaintiff, cannot the defendant buy it from him for $1000.01? See generally Coase, The Problem of Social Cost, 3 J.Law & Econ. 1 (1960).

(5) Suits respecting continuing liabilities have presented special problems. In Aetna Casualty & Surety Co. v. Flowers, 330 U.S. 464 (1947), a widow sued for death benefits under a state workers'-compensation statute. The maximum amount of allowable compensation exceeded the jurisdictional requirement, but the Court of Appeals ordered dismissal: Because the award would be payable in installments that would terminate on death or remarriage, actual payments might never reach $3000. Reversing, the Supreme Court distinguished cases in which "judgment could be entered only for the installments due at the commencement of the suit"; in such cases future installments could not be considered "even though the judgment would be determinative of liability for future installments as they accrued." In the present case, the Court said, the state statute placed the right to all payments in issue in a single proceeding:

> Future payments are not in any proper sense contingent, although they may be decreased or cut off altogether by the operation of conditions subsequent. . . . And there is no suggestion that by reason of life expectancy or law of averages the maximum amount recoverable can be expected to fall below the jurisdictional minimum. . . . Moreover, the computation of the maximum amount recoverable is not complicated by the necessity of determining the life expectancy of respondent.

Is this reasoning anything more or less than an obvious application of the rule that the plaintiff's claim governs unless recovery of the alleged amount is legally impossible? But if a judgment for past-due installments will by collateral estoppel make liability for future payments contingent only upon survival of the beneficiary, is not the practical effect of the judgment the same as that in *Flowers*? Would the Court have reached a different result if the plaintiff had been 80 years old or engaged to marry?

In *Healy v. Ratta*, supra note 4, the plaintiff argued that the amount in controversy was the capitalized value of an annual tax he sought to enjoin, but the Court held only the current year's tax to be in issue:

> The bill of complaint does not allege, nor can it be assumed, that the appellant will act to compel compliance with the statute by appellee in future years for which no tax is yet payable, or that the appellee will seek to continue his business in Manchester indefinitely in the future, or that the taxing act will be continued on the statute books, unmodified. . . . A different question is presented where the matter in controversy is the validity of a permanent exemption by

supra, at 191, finding this statement "entirely unclear" and referring to Judge Learned Hand's attempt to decipher it in M & M Transportation Co. v. New York, 186 F.2d 157, 158 (2d Cir. 1950); Ronzio v. Denver & Rio Grande Western Railroad Co., 116 F.2d 604, 606 (10th Cir. 1940), upholding jurisdiction when it was stipulated that the water rights in dispute were worth more than $3000 to the defendant but less than $3000 to the plaintiff: "The test for determining the amount in controversy is the pecuniary result to either party which the judgment would directly produce."

contract from an annual property tax, Berryman v. Whitman Coll., 222 U.S. 334, 348 . . ., or the validity of an order of a state commission directing a railroad to construct and maintain an unremunerative spur track. Western & Atlantic R. Co. v. Railroad Commission, 261 U.S. 264, 267. There the value of the matter drawn into controversy, the contract providing permanent immunity from taxation, or the order to maintain a permanent structure for an unlimited time, is more than a limited number of the annual payments demanded.

But both distinguished cases were subject to the same contingencies as was *Healy* itself, weren't they? See the Supreme Court's explanation of its holding in *Western & Atlantic*: "The permanent annual burden on account of interest on such cost, depreciation, maintenance and operating expenses of such side track will exceed $200, and this capitalized at a reasonable rate exceeds $3000."

Compare the refusal in *Healy* to include conjectural future liability with the willingness in *Flowers* to include conjectural future payments. Is the difference entirely justified by the fact that Flowers sought damages and Ratta an injunction? Is *Healy* supported by the fact that in a suit by the tax collector only the current taxes would have been recoverable? Was liability for future years an issue ripe for adjudication?

(6) Some rights do not readily lend themselves to money valuation. As long ago as 1847 the Supreme Court refused jurisdiction of a child-custody case for this reason:

> The words of the act of Congress are plain and unambiguous. They give the right of revision in those cases only where the rights of property are concerned, and where the matter in dispute has a known and certain value, which can be proved and calculated, in the ordinary mode of a business transaction.

Barry v. Mercein, 46 U.S. (5 How.) 103, 120 (1847). But see Cortright v. Resor, 325 F.Supp. 797, 809–10 (E.D.N.Y. 1971), reversed on other grounds, 447 F.2d 245 (2d Cir. 1971):

> The allegation of an amount in controversy in excess of the $10,000 limitation, so far as it applies to grave constitutional deprivations such as deliberate withdrawal of the right to speak by a federal official has taken on an almost formal and incontestable status. It is comparable to such jurisdictional devices developed by the English courts as the incontrovertible Bill of Middlesex or the fictitious writ of trespass, *quare clausum fregit*. . . .
>
> A monetary price can hardly be placed on the rights guaranteed by the First Amendment. To say that these priceless rights so many have fought and died to protect are worth nothing is to insult the basic principles upon which this nation was founded and which still give it its unique vitality. Free speech is almost by definition, worth more than $10,000, so that the allegation of jurisdiction based upon 1331 ought not be subject to denial. The right of free speech is an absolute requisite in our free and democratic society, and its "inherent 'value' must be equal to any amount set for jurisdictional purposes."

What do you think of judges who treat statutory requirements as purely "formal"?

(7) As *Snyder* indicates, special problems of determining the amount in controversy have arisen when more than one claim is joined in a single action.

The commentators have stated flatly that all claims by a single plaintiff against a single defendant may be aggregated, e.g., 1 Moore, Federal Practice 946–50 (2d ed. 1975); Wright, Federal Courts 196 (4th ed. 1983). But several distinct situations may be encompassed within this statement. It is reasonable enough to permit a plaintiff with one claim in excess of $10,000 to litigate with it a related claim for less than the required amount, since the first claim is properly in the federal court anyway. Cf. *United Mine Workers v. Gibbs*, supra p. 195, concerning pendent jurisdiction over non-diverse state-law claims. Many of the decisions cited for the rule fall into this category. E.g., Crawford v. Neal, 144 U.S. 585 (1892) (owner of two judgments sued to set aside fraudulent conveyances each affecting both judgments; aggregation not discussed); Lloyd v. Kull, 329 F.2d 168, 170 (7th Cir. 1964) (two injuries during single operation). Similar considerations of trial convenience suggest that a plaintiff should be allowed to combine two factually related claims of $6,000 each in order to satisfy the amount requirement, but the argument for federal jurisdiction is less compelling than in the first situation because neither claim is independently cognizable. See Edwards v. Bates County, 163 U.S. 269 (1896), upholding jurisdiction over claims based on two bonds of $1000 each and their attached coupons, without discussing aggregation. It would be absurd, wouldn't it, to make jurisdiction depend upon whether an investment is represented by one piece of paper or two?

Finally, the rule stated is broad enough to permit a plaintiff to aggregate wholly unrelated claims, ignoring the apparent basis of the rule in trial convenience and departing from the analogy of state-law claims pendent to a federal cause of action. See, e.g., Davis H. Elliot Co. v. Caribbean Utilities Co., Ltd., 513 F.2d 1176, 1183 (6th Cir. 1975), allowing aggregation of claims for failure to reimburse for expenses as agreed by contract and for misappropriation of a vehicle. Even if the claims are wholly unrelated, however, there is no constitutional problem here; and is the broad rule perhaps justifiable in order to avoid the cumbersome inquiry into the necessary relationship between two claims?

(8) In sharp contrast to the rule allowing aggregation of claims between the same plaintiff and defendant is the general reluctance of the courts, as exemplified by *Snyder v. Harris*, to add together amounts claimed by more than one plaintiff or against more than one defendant. It is commonly said that aggregation of claims respecting different parties will be permitted only if the parties have a "common undivided interest" and a "single title or right" is involved. See Thomson v. Gaskill, 315 U.S. 442 (1942); Wright, Federal Courts 197 (4th ed. 1983). The application of the stated principle is not without difficulties. The Supreme Court has made clear that it is not enough for aggregation that the claims are factually

related or even that they arise out of a single instrument, *Thomson v. Gaskill*, supra, remanding an action by several employees respecting seniority rights under one collective-bargaining agreement because the record was insufficient to show whether the claims were common or several. Cf. Pinel v. Pinel, 240 U.S. 594 (1916), refusing to combine claims by several children mistakenly omitted from a will for an undivided interest in their father's land; Deutsch v. Hewes Street Realty Corp., 359 F.2d 96, 98 n. 1 (2d Cir. 1966), refusing to aggregate a woman's claim for personal injuries with her husband's for loss of her services resulting from the same accident. [7]

Once the Court held that there could be no aggregation among parties permissively joined, could class actions have been distinguished? [8]

Why do you suppose the court is so opposed to aggregation of claims by more than one party? [9]

(9) The reasoning of *Snyder* was carried a step further in Zahn v. International Paper Co., 414 U.S. 291 (1973). A class action was brought by four plaintiffs, each asserting good-faith claims individually exceeding $10,000, for pollution damage to themselves and to others similarly situated. The trial court, relying on *Snyder*, struck the class-action designation on the ground that jurisdiction could not be asserted with respect to any member of the class whose claim did not independently satisfy the amount requirement, a divided Court of Appeals affirmed, and so did the Supreme Court:

> None of the plaintiffs in *Snyder v. Harris* alleged a claim exceeding $10,000, but there is no doubt that the rationale of that case controls this one. . . . *Snyder* invoked the well-established rule that each of

7. For cases allowing aggregation of multiple-party claims see Green County v. Thomas's Executors, 211 U.S. 598 (1909) (action on bonds by joint owners); Sovereign Camp, W.O.W. v. O'Neill, 266 U.S. 292 (1924) (suit to enjoin conspiracy among the defendants to file numerous false claims). Cf. Koster v. Lumbermens Mutual Casualty Co., 330 U.S. 518 (1947), holding that the amount in controversy in a shareholder's derivative suit was not the individual plaintiff's stake in the outcome but "the damage asserted to have been sustained by [his] . . . corporation." Contrast the holding of the Court in the same case that the corporation was properly aligned as a defendant in determining the existence of diversity.

8. Can *Snyder* be evaded by looking to the amount the single defendant stands to lose in a class action? See Committee for G. I. Rights v. Callaway, 518 F.2d 466 (D.C. Cir. 1975) (alternative holding), looking to the cost to the defendant of abandoning the challenged drug-abuse program. Recall the cases in note 4 supra, suggesting it is sufficient if either plaintiff's or defendant's stake satisfies the minimum. What does this approach leave of *Snyder*? Is it significant that in a damage action like *Snyder* the defendant's controversy with each member of the class is less than the required amount, while in an action to enjoin pollution the defendant cannot meet any plaintiff's demand without meeting them all? See Snow v. Ford Motor Co., 561 F.2d 787, 790 (9th Cir. 1977), refusing to look to the defendant's loss in an injunctive case: "The only reason the injunction is worth more than $10,000 to Ford is that it would affect all of Ford's future trailer package sales to thousands of other individual consumers."

9. *Snyder* was applied without comment to permit a district court to entertain a class action for back salary on behalf of all federal judges despite the $10,000 *maximum* jurisdictional amount in the Tucker Act, 28 U.S.C. § 1346(a), in United States v. Will, 449 U.S. 200, 211 n.10 (1980): "The complaints . . . state that the claims of individual members of the classes do not exceed $10,000, an allegation the Government has not disputed." Aggregation takes on a different flavor in this context, doesn't it?

several plaintiffs asserting separate and distinct claims must satisfy the jurisdictional amount requirement if his claim was to survive a motion to dismiss. This rule plainly mandates not only that there may be no aggregation and that the entire case must be dismissed where none of the plaintiffs claims more than $10,000 but also requires that any plaintiff without the jurisdictional amount must be dismissed from the case, even though others allege jurisdictionally sufficient claims.

This follows inescapably from the Court's heavy reliance on Clark v. Paul Gray, Inc. [306 U.S. 583 (1939)], where only one of several plaintiffs had a sufficiently large claim and all other plaintiffs were dismissed from the suit. Moreover, the Court cited with approval the decision in Alvarez v. Pan American Life Ins. Co., 375 F.2d 992 (CA5 1967), cert. denied 389 U.S. 827, which was decided after the 1966 amendments to Rule 23 and which involved a class action with only one member of the class having a claim sufficient to satisfy § 1332. Only that claim was held within the jurisdiction of the District Court.

Justices Brennan, Douglas, and Marshall, dissenting, invoked ancillary or pendent-jurisdiction analogies: the numerous decisions entertaining counterclaims, intervention, or third-party claims not independently satisfying the diversity or amount requirements, pp. 258–59 supra, and the Supreme Court's longstanding holding (*Supreme Tribe of Ben Hur v. Cauble*, supra p. 259) that unnamed class members need not satisfy the requirement of diverse citizenship. Judge Timbers in dissent below added *United Mine Workers v. Gibbs*, supra p. 195, which upheld broad pendent jurisdiction over a nonfederal claim under § 1331. The Supreme Court majority did not deign to distinguish these cases. Were they distinguishable? Was *Snyder*? Cf. *Finley v. United States*, p. 188 supra.

(10) For discussion of the effect of a counterclaim on the jurisdictional amount see Horton v. Liberty Mut. Life Ins. Co., 367 U.S. 348 (1961), apparently allowing the plaintiff in an action to set aside a workers' compensation award for $1,000 to anticipate a counterclaim in excess of the requirement; Shamrock Oil & Gas Corp. v. Sheets, 313 U.S. 100 (1941), supra p. 158, holding that a plaintiff against whom a state-court counterclaim was filed was not a "defendant" entitled to remove to the federal court; Wright, Federal Courts 202 (4th ed. 1983), stating that if the original claim exceeds the jurisdictional amount there is pendent jurisdiction over a counterclaim not involving the required amount if, but only if, the counterclaim is compulsory under Rule 13. But see Note, Federal Jurisdiction and Practice: Requirement of Jurisdictional Amount for Permissive Counterclaims, 16 Okla.L.Rev. 212 (1963), arguing that "much of the language" requiring an independent basis for permissive counterclaims is dictum and that this requirement is inconsistent with decisions allowing a plaintiff to aggregate independent claims; 3 Moore, Federal Practice §§ 13.19–20 (2d ed. 1972), asserting that no independent basis is required for mere setoffs. What sense would there be in this distinction? See also Note, Federal Jurisdictional Amount: Determination of the Matter in Controversy, 73 Harv.L.Rev. 1369, 1376 (1960), declaring that no jurisdiction can exist if neither claim nor counterclaim involves the requisite amount, although their sum exceeds the requirement: "No greater amount can be in contro-

versy than the maximum which may change hands—the amount involved in the larger claim." This is fallacious, isn't it? If the question is the ownership of a fund totaling $60,000, is the impact of a judgment on the parties lessened because half the contested money is already in the plaintiff's hands?

SECTION 5. THE PLACE OF TRIAL AND THE SUPREME COURT'S ORIGINAL JURISDICTION

Notes on the Place of Trial in the Federal Courts

A. Venue and Personal Jurisdiction

(1) It is common understanding that at least three requisites must be satisfied before an action can be entertained by a federal court. First, there must be jurisdiction over the subject matter: The case must be of a type (e.g., federal-question or diversity) cognizable by some federal court. Second, there must be jurisdiction over the person of the defendant, or, if the action is in rem, over the property in suit; third, venue must be proper.

In providing for the place of trial the First Judiciary Act did not explicitly distinguish between venue and personal jurisdiction:

> No person shall be arrested in one district for trial in another, in any civil action before a circuit or district court. And no civil suit shall be brought before either of said courts against an inhabitant of the United States, by any original process in any other district than that whereof he is an inhabitant, or in which he shall be found at the time of serving the writ.

Act of Sept. 24, 1789, c. 20, § 11, 1 Stat. 73, 79.

This section was held to forbid service of process outside the district in which the action had been brought, see Robertson v. Railroad Labor Bd., 268 U.S. 619, 622 (1925). Moreover, the definition of the diversity jurisdiction operated to limit the place of trial, for there was jurisdiction only if the suit was "between a citizen of the State where the suit is brought, and a citizen of another State." Ibid. Cases from state courts were to be removed to the circuit or district court "in the district where the suit is pending," id., § 12.

The 1875 amendments, 18 Stat. 470, authorized general federal-question jurisdiction and removed the restriction of diversity cases to those in which one party was a citizen of the forum State, without altering the provision for place of trial. This meant that suit could be brought in any district where the defendant could be personally served. But in 1887 Congress limited venue to the district in which the defendant was an inhabitant, except that if jurisdiction was founded only on diversity suit could be brought where either the plaintiff or the defendant resided. The principal changes since 1887 affecting the place of trial in federal courts have been the decision that a corporation, by qualifying to do business in the forum State, had waived any venue objection to being sued there, Neirbo Co. v. Bethlehem Shipbuilding Corp., 308 U.S. 165 (1939); the provisions of Rule 4 of the Civil Rules permitting out-of-state service when authorized by state law; and the amendment of November, 1966, establishing venue in diversity and federal-question actions in the district "in which the claim arose."

(2) The basic venue provision today is 28 U.S.C. § 1391:

> (a) A civil action wherein jurisdiction is founded only on diversity of citizenship may, except as otherwise provided by law, be brought only in the judicial district where all plaintiffs or all defendants reside, or in which the claim arose.
>
> (b) A civil action wherein jurisdiction is not founded solely on diversity of citizenship may be brought only in the judicial district where all defendants reside, or in which the claim arose, except as otherwise provided by law.
>
> (c) For purposes of venue under this chapter, a defendant that is a corporation shall be deemed to reside in any judicial district in which it is subject to personal jurisdiction at the time the action is commenced. . . .
>
> (d) An alien may be sued in any district. . . .

Subsections (e) and (f) provide for venue in suits against federal officers and foreign states respectively. [1]

What excuse is there for restricting venue more narrowly when there is a federal question than when there is not? See Hart & Wechsler, The Federal Courts and the Federal System 1715 n. 5 (3d ed. 1988).

Under § 1441 actions filed in state courts are removable, if at all, to the district in which the state action is pending.

(3) According to 1 Moore, Federal Practice 1452–53 (2d ed. 1974), § 1391 applies only to transitory actions; local actions must be brought where the property is located. That this statement accurately reflects the congressional understanding is suggested by § 1392(b): A local action "involving property located in different districts in the same State, may be brought in any of such districts." See also Casey v. Adams, 102 U.S. 66 (1880), construing a statute permitting state-court suits against national banks only where the bank was located: "No one has ever supposed that laws which prescribed generally where one should be sued, included such suits as were local in their character . . . ."

See also Fed.R.Civ.P. 82: ". . . An admiralty or maritime claim within the meaning of Rule 9(h) shall not be treated as a civil action for the

1. Section 1391(e)'s reference to "[a] civil action in which a defendant is an officer or employee of the United States or any agency thereof acting in his official capacity or under color of legal authority" seems on its face to cover actions to recover damages out of the officer's own pocket. The Supreme Court, however, held in Stafford v. Briggs, 444 U.S. 527 (1980), that it did not, relying on the fact that § 1391's broad provisions were part of a 1962 package intended to permit mandamus outside the District of Columbia (see pp. 414–15 infra), quoting committee reports referring to actions "nominally . . . against the officer" but "in essence against the United States," and adding that it was unlikely that Congress meant to impose the burdens of nationwide service of process on individuals who happened to be government officers. Two dissenters pointed to conflicting references to damage actions in the same committee reports and argued that the Government's willingness to represent an officer in a damage suit "relieved" him "of the greatest burden involved in defending himself."

purposes of Title 28, U.S.C., §§ 1391–93." The advisory committee's note explains that this statement preserves existing law, which, according to 7A Moore, Federal Practice 449 (2d ed. 1966), "permitted the venue of a suit in personam [in admiralty] to be laid wherever the defendant could be validly served with process, or in any district where his goods or credits could be attached or garnished. Venue of suits in rem, as formerly, is the district in which the res proceeded against can be arrested."

(4) While diversity jurisdiction is based upon "citizenship," the venue statute speaks of the district in which the parties "reside." Professor Moore says the two concepts are identical, 1 Federal Practice, 1389–90 (2d ed. 1974); the Supreme Court has not spoken, and the cases conflict. Compare Koons v. Kaiser, 91 F.Supp. 511, 517 (S.D.N.Y.1950) (residence "means domicile"), with Townsend v. Bucyrus-Erie Co., 144 F.2d 106 (10th Cir. 1944) ("one may have a residence in a state while his citizenship continues in another"). If residence and citizenship are the same, shouldn't Congress remove the ambiguity by using the same term in both statutes? But should the test for a convenient place of trial be the same as the test of possible prejudice against foreigners?

(5) Under the 1887 venue law a corporation was deemed a "resident" of the State in which it was incorporated. This proved rather restrictive and by no means always convenient; it was alleviated by the *Neirbo* decision, supra note 1, 308 U.S. 165 (1939), which held a corporation had waived its objection to venue by qualifying to do business in the forum State. Section 1391(c), added in 1948, made a corporation a resident of "any judicial district in which it is incorporated or licensed to do business or is doing business." The present formulation, which ties venue to amenability to service of process, was designed to restrict venue in corporate cases: "[A] corporation that confines its activities to Los Angeles (Central California) should not be required to defend in San Francisco (Northern California) unless, of course, venue lies there for other reasons." H.R. Rep. No. 100–889, 100th Cong., 2d Sess. 70 (1988).

(6) Under the *Carden* decision, supra p. 267, an unincorporated association is not a "citizen" for diversity purposes. But Sperry Products, Inc. v. Association of American Railroads, 132 F.2d 408 (2d Cir. 1942), held an association an "inhabitant" of its principal place of business under the patent-venue statute, now 28 U.S.C. § 1400(b). A number of courts applied this holding to the general venue statute, e.g., Brotherhood of Locomotive Firemen v. Graham, 175 F.2d 802 (D.C.Cir. 1948). The Supreme Court, however, over three dissents relying on *Sperry*, held a labor union a "resident" of every district in which it did business, within § 1391. Denver & R. G. W. R. R. v. United States, 387 U.S. 485 (1967). Is either *Denver* or *Sperry* consistent with the reasoning of *Carden?* What should Congress do about associations and venue?

(7) The provision allowing venue in the district "in which the claim arose" was in issue in Leroy v. Great Western United Corp., 443 U.S. 173 (1979). Great Western, with its executive offices in Texas, announced plans to acquire a substantial percentage of stock in Sunshine Mining and Metal Co., whose principal place of business was in Idaho. Informed by Idaho officials that the papers it had submitted did not meet the requirements of

Idaho's Corporate Takeover Act, Great Western filed a federal suit in Texas for a declaration that the Idaho law could not constitutionally be applied. The Supreme Court held venue improper.

Disdaining analogies from the fields of personal jurisdiction and choice of law, the Court held it insufficient that the challenged statute "had its impact on Great Western" in Texas, focusing instead on the place the defendants had acted: "[I]t is action that was taken in Idaho by Idaho residents . . . that provide[d] the basis for Great Western's federal claim." Moreover, while stopping short of holding that no claim ever could arise in more than one district, the opinion added that such a case would be "unusual."

(8) There are a number of special venue provisions for particular types of cases. For example, an interpleader action under 28 U.S.C. § 1335 may be brought in the district where "one or more of the claimants reside," § 1397; a shareholder's derivative suit "in any district where the corporation might have sued the same defendants," § 1401; copyright actions where "the defendant or his agent resides or may be found," § 1400(a); patent-infringement actions where the defendant "resides" or where he has "committed acts of infringement and has a regular and established place of business," § 1400(b). See also Fed.R.Civ.P.Supp.R. F(9) (shipowner's petition to limit liability); Fed.R.Crim.P. 18 (criminal proceedings generally "in a district in which the offense was committed"); 18 U.S.C. §§ 3235–42 (special criminal provisions); 15 U.S.C. §§ 15 (Clayton Act), 77v (Securities Act); 49 U.S.C. § 908(g) (Water Carrier Act); 45 U.S.C. § 56 (FELA); 46 U.S.C. § 688 (Jones Act).

In Stonite Products Co. v. Melvin Lloyd Co., 315 U.S. 561 (1942), two defendants inhabiting different districts in the same State were sued in one of those districts for patent infringement. Venue would have been sustained under the general provision now found in 28 U.S.C. § 1392(a) but not under the special patent provision; the Court held venue improper. Before enactment of the patent section in 1897, the Court said, some courts had allowed patent suits to be brought in any district on the ground that the general venue statute did not apply to cases of exclusive federal jurisdiction. The patent provision, therefore, was a "restrictive measure, limiting a prior, broader venue," and intended "to define the exact jurisdiction of the federal courts in actions to enforce patent rights. . . ." Over the dissent of Justice Harlan the Court adhered to *Stonite* in Fourco Glass Co. v. Transmirra Products Corp., 353 U.S. 222 (1957), holding § 1391(c) inapplicable to a patent case; under § 1400(b) a corporation was a "resident" only of the State of its incorporation. But the defendant had an established place of business in the forum district; why didn't the *Neirbo* waiver doctrine apply?

Despite the *Stonite* and *Fourco* holdings that provisions broadening venue over corporations did not apply to patent cases, the Court held in Brunette Machine Works, Ltd. v. Kockum Industries, Inc., 406 U.S. 706 (1972), that an alien could be sued in any district under 28 U.S.C. § 1391(d) in a patent case:

> It totally misconceives the origin and purpose of § 1391(d) to characterize that statute as an appendage to the general venue stat-

> utes, analogous to the provisions at issue in *Stonite* and *Fourco.* Section 1391(d) is not derived from the general venue statutes that § 1400(b) was intended to replace. Section 1391(d) reflects, rather, the long-standing rule that suits against alien defendants are outside those statutes. Since the general venue statutes did not reach suits against alien defendants, there is no reason to suppose the new substitute in patent cases was intended to do so.

Moreover, said the Court, the Reviser's Notes on the 1948 codification of § 1391(d) had cited two district-court cases holding the patent venue law inapplicable to alien defendants.

In Pure Oil Co. v. Suarez, 384 U.S. 202 (1966), Justice Harlan writing, the Court held § 1391(c) did apply to the venue provision of the Jones Act, 46 U.S.C. § 688, which allows seamen's personal-injury actions in "the district in which the defendant employer resides or in which his principal office is located." The broadened conception of corporate residence in § 1391(c), said the Court, was designed

> to bring venue law in tune with modern concepts of corporate operations. . . . The liberalizing purpose underlying its enactment and the generality of its language support the view that it applies to all venue statutes using residence as a criterion, at least in the absence of contrary restrictive indications in any such statutes.

There was no such indication; the Jones Act's venue provision, in contrast to the patent section in *Stonite* and in *Fourco*, had been intended to liberalize rather than to constrict venue.

Is there any good reason why venue should be different in patent or Jones Act cases than in other cases arising under federal law?

(9) The Securities Exchange Act, 15 U.S.C. § 78aa, allows venue in any district where a violation occurred or where the defendant may be "found"; the National Bank Act, 12 U.S.C. § 94, allows suits against national banks in the district where they are "established." Radzanower v. Touche Ross & Co., 426 U.S. 148 (1976), was the inevitable action against a national bank under the Securities Exchange Act. The Court held the narrow venue provision of the National Bank Act, though earlier enacted, governed, invoking hoary platitudes of statutory construction: "Repeals by implication are not favored," and "a statute dealing with a narrow, precise and specific subject is not submerged by a later-enacted statute covering a more generalized spectrum" absent a clear intention. As Justice Stevens observed in his lone dissent, it was by no means clear which of the two statutes was the more specific, since one dealt with a narrow subject matter and the other with a narrow class of defendants; the latter maxim could cut either way, and to counter the conundrum about implied repeals is the principle that "the more recent of two conflicting statutes shall prevail." How then ought one to resolve such a case?

(10) Statutes allow nationwide service of process in certain kinds of federal-question suits, e.g., 15 U.S.C. § 80a–43 (Investment Company Act), in some in rem proceedings, 28 U.S.C. § 1655, and in interpleader, 28 U.S. § 2361; and 28 U.S.C. § 1693 continues the quaint provision that "Except

as otherwise provided by Act of Congress, no person shall be arrested in one district for trial in another in any civil action in a district court."

In general, however, jurisdiction over the person is covered by Rule 4 of the Federal Rules of Civil Procedure.

The basic provision respecting the territorial limits of service is Rule 4(f), which permits service anywhere within the State where the action is brought, and outside that State if authorized by federal law or by "these rules." The most obvious reference of this last term is to Rule 4(e), which was added in 1963 to make clear that the federal courts could utilize state long-arm statutes conferring jurisdiction over absent nonresidents. [2]

(11) Why should there be independent requirements for venue and for personal jurisdiction? Venue, the Supreme Court has said, is "a limitation designed for the convenience of litigants," Olberding v. Illinois Cent. R. R., 346 U.S. 338, 340 (1953); personal jurisdiction, it has said, requires that the defendant have "certain minimum contacts" with the forum State "such that the maintenance of the suit does not offend 'traditional notions of fair play and substantial justice,' " and an " 'estimate of the inconveniences' which would result" from a trial away from home is relevant to the determination. International Shoe Co. v. Washington, 326 U.S. 310, 316–17 (1945). Should there not be a single test for ascertaining the appropriate location for trying a federal case? Is there any reason why, if the plaintiff's claim is based on federal law, this question should be left even in part to state law?

See ALI Study, pp. 30–31, proposing nationwide service in all federal-question cases but allowing suit only in a district where

> (1) a substantial part of the events or omissions giving rise to the claim occurred, or a substantial part of property that is the subject of the action is situated; or
>
> (2) any defendant resides, if all defendants reside in the same State; or
>
> (3) any defendant may be found, if there is no district within the United States in which the action may otherwise be brought under this subsection. [3]

In a case based upon state law, should the rule be that the federal court is open, if, but only if, the state courts in the same district are open? [4]

B. Forum Non Conveniens and Transfer

(1) The Supreme Court first approved the application of forum non conveniens to a federal-court common-law action in Gulf Oil Corp. v.

2. See also Fed. R.Civ.P.Supp.R. E(3)(a) (maritime process in rem and maritime attachment or garnishment "only within the district.").

3. Does it matter whether the limitation is couched in terms of venue rather than of personal jurisdiction? Under present law a default judgment may be collaterally attacked for lack of personal jurisdiction, but not for improper venue. Should the defendant, at the expense of finality, be permitted to gamble on the propriety of the forum, or should he be required to appear in an inconvenient forum in order to establish his right not to be subjected to suit there?

4. The ALI proposed to adhere to the double standard of both venue and personal jurisdiction in cases based solely on diversity.

Gilbert, 330 U.S. 501 (1947).[1] A Virginia resident sued for a Virginia accident in a federal court in New York, where the defendant was doing business. Although venue and personal jurisdiction existed, the Supreme Court upheld the trial judge's power to dismiss:

> A court may resist imposition upon its jurisdiction even when jurisdiction is authorized by the letter of a general venue statute. These statutes are drawn with a necessary generality and usually give a plaintiff a choice of courts, so that he may be quite sure of some place in which to pursue his remedy. But the open door may admit those who seek not simply justice but perhaps justice blended with some harassment. . . .
>
> Wisely, it has not been attempted to catalogue the circumstances which will justify or require either grant or denial of remedy. . . . An interest to be considered, and the one likely to be most pressed, is the private interest of the litigant. Important considerations are the relative ease of access to sources of proof; availability of compulsory process for attendance of unwilling, and the cost of obtaining attendance of willing, witnesses; possibility of view of premises. . . . There may also be questions as to the enforcibility of a judgment if one is obtained. . . .
>
> Factors of public interest also have place in applying the doctrine. Administrative difficulties follow for courts when litigation is piled up in congested centers instead of being handled at its origin. Jury duty is a burden that ought not to be imposed upon the people of a community which has no relation to the litigation. . . . There is a local interest in having localized controversies decided at home. There is an appropriateness, too, in having the trial of a diversity case in a forum that is at home with the state law that must govern the case. . . .
>
> The only justification for trial in New York advanced here is . . . as follows: "This Court can readily realize that an action of this type, involving as it does a claim for damages in an amount close to $400,000, is one which may stagger the imagination of a local jury which is surely unaccustomed to dealing with amounts of such a nature. . . ." We cannot say the District Court was bound to entertain a provincial fear of the provincialism of a Virginia jury. That leaves the Virginia plaintiff without even a suggested reason for transporting this suit to New York. . . .
>
> [The trial judge] was justified in concluding that this trial is likely to be long and to involve calling many witnesses, and that Lynchburg, some 400 miles from New York, is the source of all proofs for either side, with possible exception of experts. . . . The course of adjudication in New York federal court might be beset with conflict of laws problems all avoided if the case is litigated in Virginia where it arose.

Justice Black dissented, arguing that the federal courts could never refuse jurisdiction, except on traditional equitable principles, of cases

1. For the analogous and long-standing admiralty doctrine of "discretionary jurisdiction" over suits between foreigners see, e.g., Davis v. Leslie, 7 F.Cas. 134 (S.D.N.Y. 1848) (No. 3,639).

Congress had given them power to entertain. Cf. chapter 6 infra. Moreover, Justice Black argued, although the Court's decision was intended to promote trial convenience, it might well do the opposite: "the Court's new rule will thus clutter the very threshold of the federal courts with a preliminary trial of fact concerning the relative convenience of forums."

(2) Forum non conveniens was held inapplicable to civil antitrust actions on the ground that the Clayton Act's venue provision, 15 U.S.C. § 22, was intended to give plaintiffs a broad choice of forum. United States v. National City Lines, 334 U.S. 573 (1948). Similarly, although state courts were permitted to dismiss inconvenient FELA actions, Douglas v. New York, N.H.& H. R. R., 279 U.S. 377 (1929), they could not enjoin them, Baltimore & Ohio R. R. v. Kepner, 314 U.S. 44 (1941); Miles v. Illinois Central R. R., 315 U.S. 698 (1942). Section 1404(a), enacted in 1948, was conceived before *Gilbert* as a reaction to FELA abuses encouraged by *Kepner*. See 28 U.S.C.A., Reviser's Note; B. Currie, Change of Venue and the Conflict of Laws, 22 U.Chi.L.Rev. 405, 416–17, 435 (1955), arguing that *Gilbert* itself would have made such a provision necessary:

> The decision exposed the inadequacy of the general venue statutes; it introduced uncertainty and delay as preferable to oppressive ridigity; and it imposed the disproportionately drastic penalty of dismissal for bad judgment or overreaching by plaintiffs in the selection of the forum.

In the light of the "unmistakable" language of § 1404(a) and of the Reviser's explicit reference the Supreme Court held the transfer provision applicable to FELA and to antitrust cases, respectively, in Ex parte Collett, 337 U.S. 55 (1949), and in United States v. National City Lines, 337 U.S. 78 (1949). See also Continental Grain Co. v. Barge FBL–585, 364 U.S. 19 (1960), and Internatio-Rotterdam, Inc. v. Thomsen, 218 F.2d 514, 515 (4th Cir. 1955), where the Supreme Court without discussion and the court of appeals explicitly applied § 1404(a) in admiralty.

(3) May a *plaintiff* ask for transfer under § 1404(a)? At least one district court has said no, for the plaintiff already had his choice of forum, and "the motivating reason for the enactment of Section 1404(a) was to afford relief to a defendant by placing him on a footing of equality with a plaintiff in the selection of a forum for the trial of the case." Barnhart v. John B. Rogers Producing Co., 86 F.Supp. 595, 599 (N.D.Ohio 1949). Most courts disagree, e.g., Philip Carey Mfg. Co. v. Taylor, 286 F.2d 782, 784 (6th Cir. 1961). See also 1 Moore, Federal Practice, ¶ 0.145[4.–2] (2d ed. 1974), disapproving *Barnhart* because the statutory criterion is "the convenience of all parties" and because in some cases "due to change in conditions and circumstances or for other reasons the plaintiff will have just cause for seeking a transfer"; Pruess v. Udall, 359 F.2d 615, 617–18 (D.C.Cir.1965), in which the plaintiff moved for transfer to a forum that had been opened to him by enlargement of the general venue statute after the suit was brought; Ferens v. John Deere Co., 110 S.Ct. 1274 (1990), where the Supreme Court resolved a difficult question of choice of law following transfer at the plaintiff's request without deciding whether the transfer itself was proper.

May the court order a transfer if neither party requests it? If both parties object? See ALI Study, 18, 20, 32, 149, arguing that "in considering a transfer there may be interests of justice other than the convenience of parties and witnesses" but apparently allowing transfer only on a party's request.

(4) In Hoffman v. Blaski, 363 U.S. 335 (1960), transfer motions had been made by defendants who had waived objection to lack of jurisdiction and venue in the transferee courts. The Court denied transfer because of the plain language of the statute, the necessity for considering "the situation which existed when suit was instituted," and the inadvisability of giving defendants a greater choice of forum than plaintiffs. Justices Frankfurter, Harlan, and Brennan dissented. What policy counsels against transfer to a district in which the defendant has agreed to be sued? [2, 3]

(5) In Van Dusen v. Barrack, 376 U.S. 612 (1964), the plaintiffs were administrators or executors of Pennsylvanians killed in an airplane crash. They objected to transferring their cases from Pennsylvania to Massachusetts, arguing that because they had not qualified to sue in Massachusetts

2. Continental Grain Co. v. Barge FBL–585, 364 U.S. 19 (1960), upheld transfer of an admiralty libel containing two counts, one against the owner of a vessel in personam and the other against the vessel in rem, for a single transaction. The dissenters argued that the transferee district was not one in which the action "might have been brought" because the vessel could not be found there. The Court brushed this aside as a technicality:

> There was admittedly a right on the part of the grain company to subject the owner of the barge, with or without its consent, to a "civil action" in Memphis at the time the New Orleans action was brought. . . . Although the action in New Orleans was technically brought against the barge itself as well as its owner, the obvious fact is that, whatever other advantages may result, this is an alternative way of bringing the owner into court.

The in rem and in personam counts, said the Court, were "inseparable parts of one single 'civil action.' "

Is this decision "as disloyal to Hoffman v. Blaski as it is practical?" 1 Moore, supra, ¶ 0.145 (6.–4). Should the Court have ruled the same way if the only claim had been in rem?

3. The ALI, largely disapproving *Blaski*, proposed to allow transfer in federal-question cases to "any" district, on motion of any party; in cases based solely upon diversity, on motion of any defendant, to "any" district except one in which "one or more plaintiffs and all moving defendants would be barred under section 1302 of this title from invoking federal jurisdiction" [Section 1302 would forbid a party to take a case to federal court in a state in which he is a citizen or he has an established place of business]; and in such actions, on motion of all plaintiffs, to a district where venue and service are proper and no plaintiffs barred by § 1302. A further provision would allow the federal court, if § 1302 would forbid transfer, to stay the action "if it can do so on such terms as will assure the plaintiffs an opportunity to maintain suits upon the claim in an appropriate state court."

The conflict between the policy of hearing cases in the most convenient forum and the desire to reserve diversity jurisdiction to those with reason to fear state prejudice is quite evident here. The Reporters observe that their proposals may cause a diversity plaintiff to end up in the federal court of his own state but find this unobjectionable:

> If the defendant is amenable to process in the plaintiff's state, the plaintiff who prefers a federal forum can choose between suing in his own state court, knowing that the defendant may remove but not being able to count upon it, or suing in the defendant's home federal court, knowing that the defendant may obtain transfer to the plaintiff's federal court but not being able to count upon it.

ALI Study, 18–19, 20–21, 32, 151. Is this game of musical chairs really conducive to the convenience of parties and witnesses, or to the interests of justice?

by obtaining ancillary letters there, the Massachusetts district was not one in which the cases originally "might have been brought." The Court disagreed: "[T]he words 'where it might have been brought' must be construed with reference to the federal laws delimiting the districts in which such an action 'may be brought' and not with reference to laws of the transferee State concerning the capacity of fiduciaries to bring suit." Section 1404(a), the opinion observed, was part of a chapter of the Judicial Code entitled "Venue," and many of its venue provisions used the phrase "may be brought"; "[t]he statutory context is thus persuasive evidence that the 'might-have-been-brought' language . . . refers to the similar wording in the related federal statutes and not directly to the laws of the State of the transferee forum." Moreover, the statute's "remedial purpose—the individualized, case-by-case consideration of convenience and fairness—militates against restricting the number of permissible forums"; and holding state law relevant "would grant personal representatives . . . the power unilaterally to reduce the number of permissible federal forums simply by refraining from qualifying as representatives in States other than the one in which they wished to litigate."

Does *Barrack* mean § 1404(a) authorizes transfer to a district in which there would have been no personal jurisdiction? [4]

(6) In the cases so far considered venue was proper in the original forum. A separate statute, 28 U.S.C. § 1406(a), provides for transfer as an alternative to dismissal when the original venue is improper:

> The district court of a district in which is filed a case laying venue in the wrong division or district shall dismiss, or if it be in the interest of justice, transfer such case to any district or division in which it could have been brought.

In Goldlawr v. Heiman, 369 U.S. 463, 466 (1962), the Court held that transfer under § 1406(a) was permissible even though the transferor court lacked personal jurisdiction as well as venue: The case was a "typical example" of the problem sought to be avoided by § 1406(a), namely, "the injustice which had often resulted to plaintiffs from dismissal of their actions merely because they had made an erroneous guess with regard to the existence of some elusive fact of the kind upon which venue provisions depend." Justices Harlan and Stewart dissented.

It was not clear, however, that either § 1404(a) or § 1406 allowed transfer from a district in which venue was proper but there was no jurisdiction over the defendant.[5] Moreover, the proliferation of provi-

4. For a discussion of the factors relevant to the propriety of a transfer see Kitch, Section 1404(a) of the Judicial Code: In the Interest of Justice or Injustice? 40 Ind.L.J. 99, 131–37 (1965). In general the courts seem to have followed Professor Moore in considering the factors listed in *Gilbert* for determining dismissal as also governing transfer. 1 Moore, Federal Practice ¶ 0.145 [5] (2d ed. 1974). The Supreme Court, however, has expressly held that transfer may be ordered in a case in which dismissal would not have been allowed. Norwood v. Kirkpatrick, 349 U.S. 29 (1955). Is this appropriate? See Kitch, supra, 40 Ind.L.J. at 139, suggesting an ulterior motive: "The suspicion always remains that behind the talk of inconveniences and the interests of justice lies a concern not about plane fares but about juries." Should the legendary prodigality of urban juries be a consideration in determining the place of trial?

5. See, e.g., United States v. Berkowitz, 328 F.2d 358, 361 (3d Cir. 1964), allowing

sions for direct court-of-appeals review of federal administrative action has led to increasing instances in which it is not certain whether jurisdiction lies in a district or in an appellate court. See, e.g., Currie, Judicial Review Under Federal Pollution Laws, 62 Iowa L.Rev. 1221, 1232–54 (1977). In response to such problems, and by analogy to existing provisions authorizing transfers between district courts and the then Court of Claims,[6] Congress in 1982 enacted a new § 1631:

> Whenever a civil action is filed in a court as defined in section 610 of this title or an appeal, including a petition for review of administrative action, is noticed for or filed with such a court and the court finds there is a want of jurisdiction, the court shall, if it is in the interest of justice, transfer such action or appeal to any other such court in which the action or appeal could have been brought at the time it was filed or noticed. . . .

Section 610 defines "courts" to include the courts of appeals, the district courts (including those for the Canal Zone, Guam, and the Virgin Islands), the Court of International Trade, and the new United States Claims Court. It does not, however, include other Article I tribunals such as the Tax Court. Should Congress have included them? Should it have included administrative agencies? State courts? Could it have done so?

(7) 28 U.S.C. § 1407, adopted in 1968 on the recommendation of the Judicial Conference, authorizes transfer of civil cases "involving common questions of fact" to "any district for coordinated or consolidated pretrial proceedings," and retransfer for trial. The decision to transfer is to be made by seven circuit and district judges, all from different circuits, to be designated by the Chief Justice "from time to time." The panel is to initiate transfer proceedings, and presumably to order a transfer, without regard to the wishes of the parties. An order directing transfer is reviewable by extraordinary writ under § 1651, in the Court of Appeals having jurisdiction over the transferee district; all review of orders denying transfer is forbidden.

This proposal grew out of the experience of the federal courts in dealing with the unprecedented deluge of civil antitrust actions in the wake of the 1961 electrical-equipment convictions. Nineteen hundred actions were filed within a short period, and the ad hoc Co-Ordinating Committee for Multiple Litigation, created by the Judicial Conference, was said to have had great success in cutting down the duplication of discovery procedures. See Neal & Goldberg, The Electrical Equipment Antitrust Cases: Novel Judicial Administration, 50 A.B.A.J. 621 (1964). It was surely appropriate, wasn't it, to do something like this in the electrical cases and to suggest making provision for similar situations in the future? But is § 1407 a good solution?

transfer under § 1404(a) because the *Goldlawr* reasoning was equally applicable to that section; Dubin v. United States, 380 F.2d 813, 815–16 (5th Cir. 1967), disagreeing because § 1404(a) applied only "where there are two (or more) forums where a suit could be brought" but upholding transfer under § 1406 "whenever there exists an 'obstacle [to] . . . an expeditious and orderly adjudication' on the merits."

6. Former 28 U.S.C. §§ 1406(c), 1506.

Consider the startling investment of manpower in requiring seven judges to pass upon the question of transfer. Consider how enormously complex a litigation must be in order to justify this massive investment and the delays and costs of not one but two transfers—not to mention the possibility of a third for trial convenience under § 1404(a). Does § 1407 clearly and narrowly restrict itself to these pathological cases? Does it encourage extensive litigation over the desirability of transfers for consolidated pretrial? The prospect is made more foreboding, isn't it, by the provision that all interested parties shall be notified and a hearing held before transfer?

A substantial body of case law has developed under § 1407, and procedural rules governing transfers have been adopted by the Panel. See 28 U.S.C.A. following § 1407.

(8) For other transfer provisions see 46 U.S.C. § 742 (admiralty suits against the United States to "any other district court" upon application of either party, "in the discretion of the court"); Fed.R. Crim.P. 21 (criminal proceeding on defendant's motion "to another district or division" for prejudice or, if the offense was committed in more than one district or division, to another such district or division "in the interest of justice"); Fed.R.Civ.P.Supp.R. F(9) (limitation proceeding "for the convenience of parties and witnesses, in the interest of justice, . . . to any district," or, if venue is improperly laid, to "any district in which it could have been brought"); 28 U.S.C. § 2112 (when "proceedings have been instituted in two or more courts of appeals with respect to the same [administrative] order," mandatory transfer to the court in which the first such proceeding was filed, and discretionary transfer by that court to "any other court of appeals.") Moreover, a number of decisions have upheld the "inherent" power of a court of appeals to transfer any direct administrative-review case, even when venue has been improperly laid. E.g., Georgia-Pacific Corp. v. FPC, 512 F.2d 782 (5th Cir. 1975). Do these decisions mean §§ 1404 and 1406 were unnecessary? Do they mean the courts may ignore the limitations those sections seem to impose upon transfer?

(9) Does § 1404(a) destroy the power of the district judge to dismiss an action on the ground of forum non conveniens? Compare Collins v. American Automobile Insurance Co., 230 F.2d 416 (2d Cir. 1965), holding dismissal improper because transfer was possible, with Piper Aircraft Co. v. Reyno, 454 U.S. 235 (1981), approving dismissal where the appropriate forum was in Scotland.

(10) Section 1404(a) has received "nearly unanimous praise" because of its commendable purpose of conducting trials in appropriate places. See the authorities cited in Kitch, footnote 4 supra, 40 Ind.L.J. at 99 n. 3 (1963). Is it worth it?

Notes on the Original Jurisdiction of the Supreme Court

(1) The jurisdictional provisions thus far considered vest original jurisdiction in the federal district courts; in such cases the Supreme Court

functions, if at all, as an appellate court of last resort. See chapter 7 infra. As we know from *Marbury v. Madison*, however (p. 19 supra), Article III provides that the Supreme Court shall act as a court of first instance in two narrow categories of cases: "In all Cases affecting Ambassadors, other public Ministers and Consuls, and those in which a State shall be Party, the supreme Court shall have original Jurisdiction." This provision was implemented by § 13 of the 1789 Judiciary Act, which with modifications now appears in 28 U.S.C. § 1251:

> (a) The Supreme Court shall have original and exclusive jurisdiction of all controversies between two or more States.
>
> (b) The Supreme Court shall have original but not exclusive jurisdiction of:
>
>> (1) All actions or proceedings to which ambassadors, other public ministers, consuls, or vice consuls of foreign states are parties;
>>
>> (2) All controversies between the United States and a State;
>>
>> (3) All actions or proceedings by a State against the citizens of another State or against aliens.

(2) The most famous decision interpreting these provisions is *Marbury* itself, which held that Congress had no power to enlarge the Constitution's categories of original jurisdiction by giving the Supreme Court power to issue original writs of mandamus in cases to which neither a State nor a diplomat was a party: "If congress remains at liberty to give this court appellate jurisdiction, where the constitution has declared their jurisdiction shall be original; and original jurisdiction where the constitution has declared it shall be appellate; the distribution of jurisdiction, made in the constitution, is form without substance." Was that right? Why do you suppose the Framers provided for original jurisdiction in cases involving States and foreign diplomats? [1]

(3) *Marbury* established that Congress could not add to the original jurisdiction; is it clear, as argued in C. Wright, Federal Courts 764 (4th ed. 1983), that Congress may not subtract from it either? See Chisholm v. Georgia, 2 U.S. (2 Dall.) 419, 432 (1793), upholding original jurisdiction without invoking the statute, over a dissent maintaining that the constitutional grant was not self-executing because legislation was necessary even to determine the number of Justices to be appointed; California v. Arizona, 440 U.S. 59, 66 (1979), construing a statute providing for "exclusive" district-court jurisdiction over certain suits against the United States not to eliminate the Supreme Court's original jurisdiction, in order to avoid the constitutional question: "Congress has broad powers over the jurisdiction

1. Ex parte Bollman, 8 U.S. (4 Cranch) 75, 100–01 (1807), held the Supreme Court could issue a writ of habeas corpus to investigate the validity of a circuit-court order committing the petitioners to custody pending their trial for treason: The proceeding was appellate because it involved "the revision of a decision of an inferior court, by which a citizen has been committed to jail." Stuart v. Laird, 5 U.S. (1 Cranch) 299, 309 (1803), dismissed on the ground of "practice and acquiescence under it" the contention that Supreme Court Justices could not constitutionally sit as circuit judges to try cases to which States and diplomats were not parties. See also p. 606 infra, respecting questions certified to the Supreme Court prior to a trial-court decision.

of the federal courts and over the sovereign immunity of the United States but it is extremely doubtful that they include the power to limit in this manner the original jurisdiction conferred upon this Court by the Constitution."

Does § 1251 grant jurisdiction over all cases that fall within the constitutional provision?

(4) Under the present § 1251 the Supreme Court's original jurisdiction is exclusive only in suits between States; other cases within the constitutional grant may be brought at the plaintiff's option in any other court of competent jurisdiction.[2] This means the Supreme Court under §§ 1254 and 1257 (see pp. 676–77 infra) will have appellate jurisdiction over some cases that Article III places within its original jurisdiction. This situation is the converse of *Marbury*, and Marshall's statement quoted in note 1 suggested that it too would be unconstitutional.

Marshall himself, however, decided otherwise in Cohens v. Virginia, 19 U.S. (6 Wheat.) 264, 392–402 (1821) (alternative holding). If the Court could not exercise appellate jurisdiction when the Constitution gave it original, he observed, it could not set aside an illegal exercise of state-court jurisdiction over a foreign minister: "If this could be maintained, then a clause inserted for the purpose of excluding the jurisdiction of all other Courts than this, in a particular case, would have the effect of excluding the jurisdiction of this Court, in that very case. . . .[3] Does *Cohens* cast doubt on *Marbury*?

(5) Article III provides that the Supreme Court shall have original jurisdiction in "those [Cases] in which a State shall be Party. . . ." Yet the preceding paragraph fails to extend the "judicial Power" to every case to which a State is party, and the context strongly suggests, as the Supreme Court has held, that the original-jurisdiction clause is limited by the definition of judicial power: "This second clause distributes the jurisdiction conferred upon the Supreme Court in the previous one into original and appellate jurisdiction; but does not profess to confer any." Pennsylvania v. Quicksilver Mining Co., 77 U.S. (10 Wall.) 553, 556 (1871).

(6) *Cohens v. Virginia*, supra note 4, not only held that Article III did not preclude the exercise of appellate jurisdiction where it made the Court's power original; it also held that a federal-question case between a State and its own citizens was not within the original jurisdiction at all (19 U.S. (6 Wheat.) at 393–94):

2. See, e.g. 28 U.S.C. § 1351, giving the district courts "jurisdiction, exclusive of the courts of the States, of all civil actions and proceedings against . . . consuls or vice consuls of foreign states. . . ." The predecessor of this provision was upheld in Börs v. Preston, 111 U.S. 252 (1884), over the argument that the Constitution itself made the Supreme Court's jurisdiction exclusive. Cf. p. 179 supra.

3. With respect to *Marbury* the Chief Justice proceeded to consume a portion of crow: "It is a maxim not to be disregarded, that general expressions, in every opinion, are to be taken in connection with the case in which those expressions are used. If they go beyond the case, they may be respected, but ought not to control the judgment in a subsequent suit when the very point is present for decision." Id. at 399.

> When, then, the constitution declares the jurisdiction, in cases where a State shall be a party, to be original, and in all cases arising under the constitution or a law, to be appellate—the conclusion seems irresistible, that its framers designed to include in the first class those cases in which jurisdiction is given, because a State is a party; and to include in the second, those in which jurisdiction is given, because the case arises under the constitution or a law.

In United States v. Texas, 143 U.S. 621, 643–44 (1892), without considering *Cohens*, a divided Court held the United States could sue a State in the Supreme Court, as § 1251(b)(2) now provides, construing the original-jurisdiction provision to "refer to all cases mentioned in the preceding clause in which a State may be made, of right, a party defendant, or in which a State may, of right, be a party plaintiff." Can *Texas* and *Cohens* stand together? [4]

(7) In California v. Southern Pacific Co., 157 U.S. 229, 261–62 (1895), the Court held it could not exercise original jurisdiction of an action by a State against citizens of other States because a citizen of its own was an indispensable party: The provision for jurisdiction "in cases in which the State is plaintiff and citizens of another State defendants" did not extend to "a suit between a State and citizen of another State and of the same State." Why should that be? Why wasn't there pendent jurisdiction? Could Congress overrule this decision? Cf. *Strawbridge v. Curtiss*, p. 244 supra.

(8) Despite Article III's references to "Controversies" and to "Cases" to which a State is party, § 13 of the 1789 Act spoke only of controversies "of a civil nature." In Wisconsin v. Pelican Insurance Co., 127 U.S. 265, 297 (1888), the Court held that one State could not sue the citizen of another in the Supreme Court to enforce a judgment for a penalty: "[T]he jurisdiction conferred by the Constitution upon this court, in cases to which a State is a party, is limited to controversies of a civil nature," and "penal" proceedings were not "civil." [5]

Was this conclusion consistent with the holding in *Cohens v. Virginia*, supra note 4, that criminal cases could be reviewed in the Supreme Court under Article III's provision for "Cases" arising under federal law? Does it mean that, despite § 13's contrasting reference to "suits or proceedings" against ambassadors, an ambassador cannot be prosecuted criminally in the Supreme Court? Does it mean federal criminal cases are not "Controversies to which the United States shall be a Party?" See the Court's explanation in *Pelican* (127 U.S. at 289–90):

> The object of vesting in the courts of the United States jurisdiction of suits by one State against the citizens of another was to . . . avoid the partiality, or suspicion of partiality, which might exist if the plaintiff State were compelled to resort to the courts of the State of which the

4. Three years after *Texas*, Chief Justice Fuller in California v. Southern Pacific Co., 157 U.S. 229, 257–58 (1895), reaffirmed for the Court the absence of original jurisdiction when a State brought a federal-question suit against its own citizens, on the same grounds he had urged in his *Texas* dissent.

5. For more recent views of what constitutes a "penal" proceeding for purposes of the enforcement of foreign law see R. Cramton, D. Currie, & H. Kay, Conflict of Laws—Cases, Questions, Comments 126–29 (4th ed. 1987).

> defendants were citizens. . . . The grant . . . was not intended to confer upon the courts of the United States jurisdiction of a suit or prosecution by the one State, of such a nature that it could not, on the settled principles of public and international law, be entertained by the judiciary of the other State at all.
>
> By the law of England and of the United States, the penal laws of a country . . . must be administered in its own courts only, and cannot be enforced by the courts of another country.

The present § 1251(b)(3) speaks of "all actions or proceedings" by a State against citizens of other States or of foreign States; should *Pelican* be decided differently today? [6]

(9) After *Chisholm v. Georgia*, supra note 3, had held that Article III's provision for controversies "between a State and Citizens of another State" allowed a South Carolina citizen to sue Georgia without consent, the Eleventh Amendment cut back the scope of the jurisdiction: "The Judicial power of the United States shall not be construed to extend to any suit in law or equity, commenced or prosecuted against one of the United States by Citizens of another State, or by Citizens or subjects of any foreign State." For consideration of the scope of this and other immunities affecting the original jurisdiction see chapter 5 infra. Recall also the complicated decisions respecting the standing of States to sue on behalf of their citizens or to enforce sovereign or proprietary interests of their own, pp. 55–56 supra. See further Rhode Island v. Massachusetts, 37 U.S. (12 Pet.) 657 (1838), holding an interstate boundary dispute within the original jurisdiction; Illinois v. City of Milwaukee, 406 U.S. 91 (1972), holding that "[t] he term 'States' as used in 28 U.S.C. § 1251(a)(1) should not be read to include their political subdivisions"; Cherokee Nation v. Georgia, 30 U.S. (5 Pet.) 1 (1831), relying in part on the separate mention of "Indian Tribes" and "foreign Nations" in the Commerce Clause to hold that an Indian tribe was not a "foreign State" within the meaning of Article III.

(10) While Article III speaks only of cases to which a State is a party, it embraces all cases "affecting" ambassadors and other ministers. Accordingly it was argued in United States v. Ortega, 24 U.S. (11 Wheat.) 467 (1826), that the Supreme Court had original jurisdiction of a prosecution of a person for *assaulting* a public minister. The Court said no: "[T]his is not a case affecting a public minister . . . but one in which the minister himself, although he was the person injured by the assault, has no concern, either in the event of the prosecution, or in the costs attending it." Does this result follow from the purposes of the clause? Then how does one explain the discrepancy in wording between public-minister and state cases? [7]

6. Cf. Ohio ex rel. Popovici v. Agler, 280 U.S. 379, 384 (1930), holding that a statutory provision excluding state courts from "all suits and proceedings" against consuls did not apply to divorce cases: " 'Suits against consuls and vice-consuls' must be taken to refer to ordinary civil proceedings and not to include what formerly would have belonged to the ecclesiastical Courts." See also p. 567 infra.

7. See also Ex parte Gruber, 269 U.S. 302 (1925), declining to exercise original jurisdiction in a case brought against the American Consul General at Montreal: Article III's provision respecting "Ambassadors, other public Ministers and Consuls" "refers to diplomatic and consular representatives accredited to the United States by foreign powers, not to those representing this country abroad. . . . The

(11) In Ohio v. Wyandotte Chemicals Corp., 401 U.S. 493 (1971), the State sued foreign corporations in the Supreme Court to abate pollution. Conceding that the case met both constitutional and statutory requirements for the original jurisdiction, the Court nevertheless refused to hear it:

> [A]lthough it may initially have been contemplated that this Court would always exercise its original jurisdiction when properly called upon to do so, it seems evident to us that changes in the American legal system and the development of American society have rendered untenable, as a practical matter, the view that this Court must stand willing to adjudicate all or most legal disputes that may arise between one State and a citizen or citizens of another. . . .

Such disputes had multiplied with increasing social complexity; state long-arm statutes had reduced the need for Supreme Court jurisdiction; the burdens of the Supreme Court's appellate jurisdiction had increased. Moreover, the Court was "ill-equipped for the task of factfinding," and time spent on original cases would "reduce the attention we could give to those matters of federal law and national import as to which we are the primary overseers." *Wyandotte* itself, wrote Justice Harlan, could probably have been brought in a state court, and the complexity of the case also weighed against trying it on the Supreme Court.

Wyandotte was a suit against citizens of other States and of foreign countries, and the Court's original jurisdiction was therefore not exclusive. However, in the face of a concurrence arguing that the issue was different, the Court in Arizona v. New Mexico, 425 U.S. 794 (1976), declined to hear a suit between States that did fall within its exclusive original jurisdiction, concluding that the issues in the case could be adequately litigated in a private action in state court.[8]

Can either *Wyandotte* or *Arizona* be reconciled with Article III or with § 1251? Is it relevant that statutory changes were thought necessary to make the Court's *appellate* jurisdiction discretionary? See pp. 603–05 infra.

(12) Because a nine-judge tribunal with largely appellate functions is "ill-equipped for the task of factfinding," as the Supreme Court said in *Wyandotte*, its practice in original cases is to appoint a master to take evidence and to recommend a decision. See R. Stern, E. Gressman, & S. Shapiro, Supreme Court Practice 494–97 (6th ed. 1986); Mississippi v. Louisiana, 346 U.S. 862 (1953). Neither statute nor court rule explicitly authorizes this procedure. Rule 53(a) of the Federal Rules of Civil Procedure empowers the *district* courts to appoint masters, but Supreme Court Rule 17.2 makes those Rules only a "guide" "when their application is appropriate," and in the district courts "a reference to a master shall be the exception and not the rule," Fed.R.Civ.P. 53(b). Moreover, although Rule 53(e)(2) requires district judges in nonjury cases to "accept the master's finding of fact unless clearly erroneous," the Court has described

provision, no doubt, was inserted in view of the important and sometimes delicate nature of our relations and intercourse with foreign governments."

8. For a more recent discussion and application of the precedents on this question see Maryland v. Louisiana, 451 U.S. 725 (1981).

the recommendations of a Supreme Court master as "advisory only." United States v. Raddatz, 447 U.S. 667, 683 n. 11 (1980). Is the Court's practice respecting masters consistent with Article III and with § 1251? Would it be if the Court followed the clearly-erroneous rule? Cf. *United States v. Raddatz*, supra p. 122.

Chapter IV

THE APPLICABLE LAW

SECTION 1. THE ERIE PROBLEM

ERIE RAILROAD CO. v. TOMPKINS

304 U.S. 64 (1938).

MR. JUSTICE BRANDEIS delivered the opinion of the Court.

The question for decision is whether the oft-challenged doctrine of Swift v. Tyson [1] shall now be disapproved.

Tompkins, a citizen of Pennsylvania, was injured on a dark night by a passing freight train of the Erie Railroad Company while walking along its right of way at Hughestown in that state. He claimed that the accident occurred through negligence in the operation, or maintenance, of the train; that he was rightfully on the premises as licensee because on a commonly used beaten footpath which ran for a short distance alongside the tracks; and that he was struck by something which looked like a door projecting from one of the moving cars. To enforce that claim he brought an action in the federal court for Southern New York, which had jurisdiction because the company is a corporation of that State. It denied liability; and the case was tried by a jury.

The Erie insisted that its duty to Tompkins was no greater than that owed to a trespasser. It contended, among other things, that its duty to Tompkins, and hence its liability, should be determined in accordance with the Pennsylvania law; that under the law of Pennsylvania, as declared by its highest court, persons who use pathways along the railroad right of way—that is a longitudinal pathway as distinguished from a crossing—are to be deemed trespassers; and that the railroad is not liable for injuries to undiscovered trespassers resulting from its negligence, unless it be wanton or wilful. Tompkins denied that any such rule had been established by the decisions of the Pennsylvania courts; and contended that, since there was no statute of the State on the subject, the railroad's duty and liability is to be determined in federal courts as a matter of general law.

1. 16 Pet. [41 U.S.] 1 (1842). . . .

The trial judge refused to rule that the applicable law precluded recovery. The jury brought in a verdict of $30,000; and the judgment entered thereon was affirmed by the Circuit Court of Appeals, which held, 90 F.2d 603, 604, that it was unnecessary to consider whether the law of Pennsylvania was as contended, because the question was one not of local, but of general law, and that "upon questions of general law the federal courts are free, in absence of a local statute, to exercise their independent judgment as to what the law is; and it is well settled that the question of the responsibility of a railroad for injuries caused by its servants is one of general law. . . . Where the public has made open and notorious use of a railroad right of way for a long period of time and without objection, the company owes to persons on such permissive pathway a duty of care in the operation of its trains. . . . It is likewise generally recognized law that a jury may find that negligence exists toward a pedestrian using a permissive path on the railroad right of way if he is hit by some object projecting from the side of the train."

The Erie had contended that application of the Pennsylvania rule was required, among other things, by § 34 of the Federal Judiciary Act of September 24, 1789, c. 20, 28 U.S.C. § 725 [now § 1652], which provides:

> "The laws of the several States, except where the Constitution, treaties, or statutes of the United States otherwise require or provide, shall be regarded as rules of decision in trials at common law, in the courts of the United States, in cases where they apply."

Because of the importance of the question whether the federal court was free to disregard the alleged rule of the Pennsylvania common law, we granted certiorari.

First. Swift v. Tyson, 16 Pet. [41 U.S.] 1, 18, held that federal courts exercising jurisdiction on the ground of diversity of citizenship need not, in matters of general jurisprudence, apply the unwritten law of the State as declared by its highest court; that they are free to exercise an independent judgment as to what the common law of the State is—or should be; and that, as there stated by Mr. Justice Story:

> "the true interpretation of the 34th section limited its application to state laws, strictly local, that is to say, to the positive statutes of the state, and the construction thereof adopted by the local tribunals, and to rights and titles to things having a permanent locality, such as the rights and titles to real estate, and other matters immovable and intraterritorial in their nature and character. It never has been supposed by us, that the section did apply, or was designed to apply, to questions of a more general nature, not at all dependent upon local statutes or local usages of a fixed and permanent operation, as, for example, to the construction of ordinary contracts or other written instruments, and especially to questions of general commercial law, where the state tribunals are called upon to perform the like functions as ourselves, that is, to ascertain upon general reasoning and legal analogies, what is the true exposition of the contract or instrument, or

what is the just rule furnished by the principles of commercial law to govern the case."

The Court in applying the rule of § 34 to equity cases, in Mason v. United States, 260 U.S. 545, 559, said: "The statute, however, is merely declarative of the rule which would exist in the absence of the statute." The federal courts assumed, in the broad field of "general law," the power to declare rules of decision which Congress was confessedly without power to enact as statutes. Doubt was repeatedly expressed as to the correctness of the construction given § 34, and as to the soundness of the rule which it introduced. But it was the more recent research of a competent scholar, who examined the original document, which established that the construction given to it by the Court was erroneous; and that the purpose of the section was merely to make certain that, in all matters except those in which some federal law is controlling, the federal courts exercising jurisdiction in diversity of citizenship cases would apply as their rules of decision the law of the State, unwritten as well as written. [5]

Criticism of the doctrine became widespread after the decision of Black & White Taxicab Co. v. Brown & Yellow Taxicab Co., 276 U.S. 518. There, Brown and Yellow, a Kentucky corporation owned by Kentuckians, and the Louisville & Nashville Railroad, also a Kentucky corporation, wished that the former should have the exclusive privilege of soliciting passenger and baggage transportation at the Bowling Green, Kentucky, railroad station; and that the Black and White, a competing Kentucky corporation, should be prevented from interfering with that privilege. Knowing that such a contract would be void under the common law of Kentucky, it was arranged that the Brown and Yellow reincorporate under the law of Tennessee, and that the contract with the railroad should be executed there. The suit was then brought by the Tennessee corporation in the federal court for western Kentucky to enjoin competition by the Black and White; an injunction issued by the District Court was sustained by the Court of Appeals; and this Court, citing many decisions in which the doctrine of Swift v. Tyson had been applied, affirmed the decree.

Second. Experience in applying the doctrine of Swift v. Tyson had revealed its defects, political and social; and the benefits expected to flow from the rule did not accrue. Persistence of state courts in their own opinions on questions of common law prevented uniformity; and the impossibility of discovering a satisfactory line of demarcation between the province of general law and that of local law developed a new well of uncertainties.

On the other hand, the mischievous results of the doctrine had become apparent. Diversity of citizenship jurisdiction was conferred in order to prevent apprehended discrimination in state courts against those not citizens of the State. Swift v. Tyson introduced grave dis-

5. Charles Warren, New Light on the History of the Federal Judiciary Act of 1789 (1923) 37 Harv.L.Rev. 49, 51–52, 81–88, 108.

crimination by non-citizens against citizens. It made rights enjoyed under the unwritten "general law" vary according to whether enforcement was sought in the state or in the federal court; and the privilege of selecting the court in which the right should be determined was conferred upon the non-citizen.[9] Thus, the doctrine rendered impossible equal protection of the law. In attempting to promote uniformity of law throughout the United States, the doctrine had prevented uniformity in the administration of the law of the State.

The discrimination resulting became in practice far-reaching. This resulted in part from the broad province accorded to the so-called "general law" as to which federal courts exercised an independent judgment. In addition to questions of purely commercial law, "general law" was held to include the obligations under contracts entered into and to be performed within the State; the extent to which a carrier operating within a State may stipulate for exemption from liability for his own negligence or that of his employee; the liability for torts committed within the State upon persons resident or property located there, even where the question of liability depended upon the scope of a property right conferred by the State; and the right to exemplary or punitive damages. Furthermore, state decisions construing local deeds, mineral conveyances, and even devises of real estate were disregarded.

In part the discrimination resulted from the wide range of persons held entitled to avail themselves of the federal rule by resort to the diversity of citizenship jurisdiction. Through this jurisdiction individual citizens willing to remove from their own State and become citizens of another might avail themselves of the federal rule. And, without even change of residence, a corporate citizen of the State could avail itself of the federal rule by re-incorporating under the laws of another State, as was done in the *Taxicab* case.

The injustice and confusion incident to the doctrine of Swift v. Tyson have been repeatedly urged as reasons for abolishing or limiting diversity of citizenship jurisdiction. Other legislative relief has been proposed. If only a question of statutory construction were involved, we should not be prepared to abandon a doctrine so widely applied throughout nearly a century. But the unconstitutionality of the course pursued has now been made clear and compels us to do so.

Third. Except in matters governed by the Federal Constitution or by Acts of Congress, the law to be applied in any case is the law of the State. And whether the law of the State shall be declared by its Legislature in a statute or by its highest court in a decision is not a matter of federal concern. There is no federal general common law. Congress has no power to declare substantive rules of common law applicable in a State whether they be local in their nature or "general," be they commercial law or a part of the law of torts. And no clause in

9. It was even possible for a non-resident plaintiff defeated on a point of law in the highest court of a State nevertheless to win out by taking a nonsuit and renewing the controversy in the federal court. . . .

the Constitution purports to confer such a power upon the federal courts. As stated by Mr. Justice Field when protesting in Baltimore & Ohio R. Co. v. Baugh, 149 U.S. 368, 401, against ignoring the Ohio common law of fellow servant liability: ". . . Supervision over either the legislative or the judicial action of the States is in no case permissible except as to matters by the Constitution specifically authorized or delegated to the United States. Any interference with either, except as thus permitted, is an invasion of the authority of the State, and, to that extent, a denial of its independence."

The fallacy underlying the rule declared in Swift v. Tyson is made clear by Mr. Justice Holmes. [23] The doctrine rests upon the assumption that there is "a transcendental body of law outside of any particular State but obligatory within it unless and until changed by statute," that federal courts have the power to use their judgment as to what the rules of common law are; and that in the federal courts "the parties are entitled to an independent judgment on matters of general law:"

> "but law in the sense in which courts speak of it today does not exist without some definite authority behind it. The common law so far as it is enforced in a State, whether called common law or not, is not the common law generally but the law of that State existing by the authority of that State without regard to what it may have been in England or anywhere else. . . . The authority and only authority is the State, and if that be so, the voice adopted by the State as its own [whether it be of its Legislature or of its Supreme Court] should utter the last word."

Thus the doctrine of Swift v. Tyson is, as Mr. Justice Holmes said, "an unconstitutional assumption of powers by courts of the United States which no lapse of time or respectable array of opinion should make us hesitate to correct." In disapproving that doctrine we do not hold unconstitutional § 34 of the Federal Judiciary Act of 1789 or any other Act of Congress. We merely declare that in applying the doctrine this Court and the lower courts have invaded rights which in our opinion are reserved by the Constitution to the several States.

Fourth. The defendant contended that by the common law of Pennsylvania as declared by its highest court in Falchetti v. Pennsylvania R. Co., 307 Pa. 203, 160 A. 859, the only duty owed to the plaintiff was to refrain from wilful or wanton injury. The plaintiff denied that such is the Pennsylvania law. In support of their respective contentions the parties discussed and cited many decisions of the Supreme Court of the State. The Circuit Court of Appeals ruled that the question of liability is one of general law; and on that ground declined to decide the issue of state law. As we hold this was error, the judgment is reversed and the case remanded to it for further proceedings in conformity with our opinion.

Reversed.

23. Kuhn v. Fairmont Coal Co., 215 U.S. 349, 370–372; Black & White Taxicab Co. v. Brown & Yellow Taxicab Co., 276 U.S. 518, 532–36.

MR. JUSTICE CARDOZO took no part in the consideration or decision of this case; [JUSTICES BUTLER and MCREYNOLDS dissented.]

MR. JUSTICE REED [concurring in part]. . . .

To decide the case now before us and to "disapprove" the doctrine of *Swift v. Tyson* requires only that we say that the words "the laws" include in their meaning the decisions of the local tribunals. As the majority opinion shows, by its reference to Mr. Warren's researches and the first quotation from Mr. Justice Holmes, that this Court is now of the view that "laws" includes "decisions," it is unnecessary to go further and declare that the "course pursued" was "unconstitutional," instead of merely erroneous.

The "unconstitutional" course referred to in the majority opinion is apparently the ruling in *Swift v. Tyson* that the supposed omission of Congress to legislate as to the effect of decisions leaves federal courts free to interpret general law for themselves. I am not at all sure whether, in the absence of federal statutory direction, federal courts would be compelled to follow state decisions. There was sufficient doubt about the matter in 1789 to induce the first Congress to legislate. No former opinions of this Court have passed upon it. Mr. Justice Holmes evidently saw nothing "unconstitutional" which required the overruling of *Swift v. Tyson,* for he said in the very opinion quoted by the majority, "I should leave *Swift v. Tyson* undisturbed, as I indicated in *Kuhn v. Fairmont Coal Co.*, but I would not allow it to spread the assumed dominion into new fields." Black & White Taxicab Co. v. Brown & Yellow Taxicab Co., 276 U.S. 518, 535. If the opinion commits this Court to the position that the Congress is without power to declare what rules of substantive law shall govern the federal courts, that conclusion also seems questionable. The line between procedural and substantive law is hazy but no one doubts federal power over procedure. Wayman v. Southard, 10 Wheat. [23 U.S.] 1. The Judiciary Article and the "necessary and proper" clause of Article One may fully authorize legislation, such as this section of the Judiciary Act.

In this Court, *stare decisis*, in statutory construction, is a useful rule, not an inexorable command. . . . It seems preferable to overturn an established construction of an Act of Congress, rather than, in the circumstances of this case, to interpret the Constitution. . . .

Notes on Erie R. R. v. Tompkins

(1) What was so bad about *Swift v. Tyson*? The problem of fraudulent manufacture of diversity jurisdiction by foreign incorporation has been cured by the 1958 enactment of § 1332(c), under which a corporation is a citizen of its principal place of business. If the trouble with *Swift* was the difficulty of distinguishing between general and local questions, is the *Erie* distinction between substance and procedure much better? See pp. 336–47 infra. *Swift's* "discrimination" between domestic cases and those involving citizens of different States might be defended on the ground that interposition of federal law in the latter case serves to resolve a possible conflict

between the laws of two interested States. The forum-shopping aspect of *Swift*, thought to give the non-citizen an unfair opportunity to choose the more favorable law, could have been remedied by amending the statute to permit removal by a resident defendant. Moreover, to argue that the law should be the same in both federal and state courts does not tell us why state law was chosen; uniformity could equally have been obtained by adopting Professor Crosskey's position that federal common law governed in state courts as well as in federal. See 2 W. Crosskey, Politics and the Constitution chs. 25–26 (1953).

(2) The Court explained its decision as resting partly on the "error" of *Swift v. Tyson* in construing the word "laws" in the Rules of Decision Act, now 28 U.S.C. § 1652. Judge Friendly, however, argued that the Court would have been wrong to overrule *Swift* on this ground. In the first place he agreed with Professor Crosskey, 1 & 2 Politics and the Constitution 626–28, 866–71, that Professor Warren's researches had failed to refute *Swift*. An earlier draft of the Rules of Decision Act would have required the federal courts to apply "the Statute law of the several States in force for the time being and their unwritten and common law now in use"; conceding Warren's argument that the omission of this language was merely stylistic, Crosskey pointed out that the original draft did not support Warren's position that *subsequent* state-court decisions had to be followed. But Judge Friendly's principal argument was that *Swift* had become a part of the statute through the passage of time: "If ever Congress' reenactment of a statute or failure to alter it could fairly be taken as approving a prior judicial interpretation, the unchanged existence of Section 34 for a century after Story's construction was such a case." Friendly, In Praise of Erie—And of the New Federal Common Law, 39 N.Y.U.L.Rev. 383, 389–91 (1964). But can Congress's inaction ever fairly be interpreted as approval?

(3) What, exactly, was held unconstitutional in *Erie*, and why? Surely Congress has power to enact rules for determining the liability of interstate railroads to trespassers, cf. 45 U.S.C. §§ 51–60 (Federal Employers' Liability Act); and how can it violate state rights for the federal courts to determine the law in a field of federal concern? Cf. Textile Workers Union v. Lincoln Mills, 353 U.S. 448 (1957), holding that § 301 of the Taft-Hartley Act, 29 U.S.C. § 185, which gives the federal courts jurisdiction of "suits for violation of contracts between an employer and a labor organization representing employees in an industry affecting commerce," impliedly conferred the power to create federal common law in order to enforce a congressional policy favoring enforcement of collective-bargaining agreements. Does this decision suggest that the real difficulty in *Erie* was the failure of Congress to delegate lawmaking powers to the courts in railroad-accident cases? But can't that gap be filled by Congress's supposed acquiescence in *Swift v. Tyson*?

(4) Even in a case in which Congress lacks power to legislate (Are there such cases any more? Diversity cases?) why isn't the power to declare the law a necessary incident of the function of deciding cases, authorized by the constitutional grant of diversity jurisdiction? Other provisions of Article III, similarly worded, have been given this effect. See e.g., Texas v. New Jersey, 379 U.S. 674, 677 (1965):

> Since the States separately are without constitutional power to provide a rule to settle this interstate controversy and since there is no applicable federal statute, it becomes our responsibility in the exercise of our original jurisdiction to adopt a rule which will settle the question of which State will be allowed to escheat this intangible property.

Perhaps the most jarring contrast to *Erie* in this respect is presented by Southern Pacific Co. v. Jensen, 244 U.S. 205 (1917), in which the Court not only upheld the common-law power of the federal courts on the basis of a jurisdictional grant but inferred a congressional power as well from Article III and held unconstitutional the application of a state workers'-compensation law to the death of a stevedore on a ship in navigable waters:

> Article III, § 2, of the Constitution, extends the judicial power of the United States "To all cases of admiralty and maritime jurisdiction;" and Article I, § 8, confers upon the Congress power "To make all laws which may be necessary and proper for carrying into execution the foregoing powers and all other powers vested by this Constitution in the Government of the United States or in any department or officer thereof." Considering our former opinions, it must now be accepted as settled doctrine that in consequence of these provisions Congress has paramount power to fix and determine the maritime law which shall prevail throughout the country . . . [a]nd further, that in the absence of some controlling statute the general maritime law as accepted by the federal courts constitutes part of our national law applicable to matters within the admiralty and maritime jurisdiction. . . .
>
> The general system of maritime law which was familiar to the lawyers and statesmen of the country when the Constitution was adopted, was most certainly intended and referred to when it was declared in that instrument that the judicial power of the United States shall extend "to all cases of admiralty and maritime jurisdiction." . . . It certainly could not have been intended to place the rules and limits of maritime law under the disposal and regulation of the several States, as that would have defeated the uniformity and consistency at which the Constitution aimed on all subjects of a commercial character affecting the intercourse of the States with each other or with foreign states.[1]

Is the *Jensen* argument for a law uniform throughout the country less persuasive in diversity than in admiralty? See D. Currie, Federalism and the Admiralty, 1960 Sup.Ct.Rev. 158–64, explaining the discrepancy between *Erie* and *Jensen* as based upon "the historical purposes that have been attributed to the two jurisdictional grants":

> A uniform law was apparently one reason for the establishment of the admiralty jurisdiction in 1789, while the diversity jurisdiction is generally regarded as intended only to insure unbiased protection

1. For more recent affirmations of *Jensen* insofar as it upheld the lawmaking powers of the federal courts in maritime cases see Moragne v. States Marine Lines, Inc., 398 U.S. 375 (1970); East River S.S. Corp. v. Transamerica Delaval, Inc., 476 U.S. 858 (1986).

against the provincialism of state courts in the administration of their own laws in cases involving citizens of other states.[2]

(5) Compare with *Erie* the conflict-of-laws principle that a state court violates the Due Process Clause of the Fourteenth Amendment by applying its own law to a case in which it has no interest, Phillips Petroleum Co. v. Shutts, 472 U.S. 797 (1985). On the hypothesis that diversity jurisdiction exists only to protect nonresidents from bias in the administration of state law, is not the position of a federal court in a diversity case comparable to that of a Texas court deciding a Mexican controversy? The Texas court entertains the action in order to provide a convenient forum, the federal court in order to provide an impartial one; in neither case has the forum sovereign any legitimate concern with the substantive law to be applied. In short, is not *Erie* an application of the principle that a disinterested forum may not frustrate the policies of an interested State? See B. Currie, Selected Essays on the Conflict of Laws 443 (1963); Hill, The Erie Doctrine and the Constitution, 53 Nw.U.L.Rev. 427, 440–41 (1958); Weintraub, The Erie Doctrine and State Conflict of Laws Rules, 39 Ind.L.J. 228, 240 (1964).

(6) How is a federal court to ascertain state law? Fortunately, no one seems to have suggested that state law should be treated, as foreign law has often been, as a matter of fact to be proved by witnesses and formal evidence, found by the jury, and subject to correspondingly limited appeal. Cf. B. Currie, supra note 5, ch. 1. Yet it can hardly be a surprise that state law is not always clear. There is, first, the problem of the absent precedent, so aptly put by Judge Friendly:

> Our principal task in this diversity of citizenship case, is to determine what the New York courts would think the California courts would think on an issue about which neither has thought. . . . The court seised of the case is obliged, as best as it can, itself to blaze the trail of the foreign law that it has been directed to follow.

Nolan v. Transocean Air Lines, 276 F.2d 280 (2d Cir. 1960). Some judges have employed the devices of abstention and certification in this situation in order to get a ruling from the state court. See pp. 496–97. Others, less concerned by the possibility of a wrong guess than by the delays of abstention and by the partial or total denial of a federal forum, have muddled through on their own.

Second, what weight should be given the decisions of inferior state courts? Supreme Court decisions requiring adherence even to trial-court rulings "in the absence of more convincing evidence," e.g., Fidelity Union Trust Co. v. Field, 311 U.S. 169, 178 (1940), came in for sharp criticism. See e.g., Clark, State Law in the Federal Courts: The Brooding Omnipresence of Erie v. Tompkins, 55 Yale L.J. 267, 290–95 (1946). *Field* was distinguished in King v. Order of United Commercial Travelers, 333 U.S. 153 (1948), where a federal court was upheld in refusing to follow a state trial court whose decisions were unreported and not regarded as precedent in the State: "It would be incongruous indeed to hold the federal court bound by a decision which would not be binding on any state court." And the Second Circuit later decided that *Field* itself was no longer law: "We do

2. See also Friendly, supra note 2, 39 N.Y.U.L.Rev. at 394–96.

not regard ourselves as bound by the rulings of a state *nisi prius* judge although we treat these with respect." Roginsky v. Richardson-Merrell, Inc., 378 F.2d 832, 851 (2d Cir. 1967).

Roginsky relied not only upon *King* but also upon Bernhardt v. Polygraphic Co., 350 U.S. 198, 204–05, 210–12 (1956), which raised the further question of the respect to be paid ancient state supreme court decisions. Justice Frankfurter argued in dissent that the Court of Appeals might disregard decisions holding arbitration clauses unenforceable, because of the intervening change in general judicial attitudes toward arbitration. The majority disagreed but did not rule out the possibility that federal judges might sometimes anticipate their state brethren:

> Since the federal judge making those findings is from the Vermont bar, we give special weight to his statement of what the Vermont law is. . . . There appears to be no confusion in the Vermont decisions, no developing line of authorities that casts a shadow over the established ones, no dicta, doubts or ambiguities in the opinions of Vermont judges on the question, no legislative development that promises to undermine the judicial rule. [3]

As a general principle, said the court in *Nolan*, the federal judge should ask himself: "What would be the decision of reasonable intelligent lawyers, sitting as judges of the highest New York court, and fully conversant with New York 'jurisprudence'?" Is this an appropriate way to avoid frustrating state policy if the judges in question are not reasonable or intelligent? Is it too burdensome, or too conjectural, to ask the federal court to decide the case as it believes the state's highest court would decide it?

GUARANTY TRUST CO. v. YORK

326 U.S. 99 (1945).

MR. JUSTICE FRANKFURTER delivered the opinion of the Court. . . .

[Guaranty Trust, trustee to enforce the rights of noteholders of Van Sweringen Corp. and itself a substantial creditor of related corporations, cooperated in a plan for the purchase of outstanding notes of Van Sweringen, which could not meet its obligations. York, donee of a noteholder who had rejected the purchase offer, sued in equity in a New York federal court, alleging that Guaranty Trust had failed to protect the interests of the noteholders in assenting to the offer and had failed to disclose its self-interest when sponsoring it. The court of appeals held a New York statute of limitations inapplicable.]

In exercising their jurisdiction on the ground of diversity of citizenship, the federal courts, in the long course of their history, have not differentiated in their regard for State law between actions at law and suits in equity. Although § 34 of the Judiciary Act of 1789 . . .

3. On the question of dicta see *Nolan v. Transocean Air Lines*, supra, looking to the policy of a state statute to decide that a recent "relevant, considered dictum" of the state Supreme Court was not intended to overturn "an unbroken line of decisions of intermediate appellate courts, of thirty years' standing, consistent with that policy."

directed that the "laws of the several States . . . shall be regarded as rules of decision in trials of common law . . .," this was deemed, consistently for over a hundred years, to be merely declaratory of what would in any event have governed the federal courts and therefore was equally applicable to equity suits. See Hawkins v. Barney's Lessee, 5 Pet. [30 U.S.] 457, 464; Mason v. United States, 260 U.S. 545, 559. . . .

Partly because the States in the early days varied greatly in the manner in which equitable relief was afforded and in the extent to which it was available, . . . Congress provided that "the forms and modes of proceeding in suits . . . of equity" would conform to the settled uses of courts of equity. Section 2, 1 Stat. 275, 276. . . . But this enactment gave the federal courts no power that they would not have had in any event when courts were given "cognizance," by the first Judiciary Act, of suits "in equity." . . . In giving federal courts "cognizance" of equity suits in cases of diversity jurisdiction, Congress never gave, nor did the federal courts ever claim, the power to deny substantive rights created by State law or to create substantive rights denied by State law. . . .

Inevitably, therefore, the principle of Erie R. Co. v. Tompkins, an action at law, was promptly applied to a suit in equity. Ruhlin v. New York Life Ins. Co., 304 U.S. 202.

And so this case reduces itself to the narrow question whether, when no recovery could be had in a State court because the action is barred by the statute of limitations, a federal court in equity can take cognizance of the suit because there is diversity of citizenship between the parties. Is the outlawry, according to State law, of a claim created by the States a matter of "substantive rights" to be respected by a federal court of equity when that court's jurisdiction is dependent on the fact that there is a State-created right, or is such statute of "a mere remedial character," . . . which a federal court may disregard?

Matters of "substance" and matters of "procedure" are much talked about in the books as though they defined a great divide cutting across the whole domain of law. But, of course, "substance" and "procedure" are the same key-words to very different problems. Neither "substance" nor "procedure" represents the same invariants. Each implies different variables depending upon the particular problem for which it is used. . . . And the different problems are only distantly related at best, for the terms are in common use in connection with situations turning on such different considerations as those that are relevant to questions pertaining to *ex post facto* legislation, the impairment of the obligations of contract, the enforcement of federal rights in the State courts and the multitudinous phases of the conflict of laws.

Here we are dealing with a right to recover derived not from the United States but from one of the States. When, because the plaintiff happens to be a non-resident, such a right is enforceable in a federal as well as in a State court, the forms and mode of enforcing the right may at times, naturally enough, vary because the two judicial systems are not identic. But since a federal court adjudicating a State-created right solely because of the diversity of citizenship of the parties is for that purpose, in effect, only another court of the State, it cannot afford recovery if the right to recover is made unavailable by the State nor can it substantially affect the enforcement of the right as given by the State.

And so the question is not whether a statute of limitations is deemed a matter of "procedure" in some sense. The question is whether such a statute concerns merely the manner and the means by which a right to recover, as recognized by the State, is enforced, or whether such statutory limitation is a matter of substance in the aspect that alone is relevant to our problem, namely, does it significantly affect the result of a litigation for a federal court to disregard a law of a State that would be controlling in an action upon the same claim by the same parties in a State court?

It is therefore immaterial whether statutes of limitation are characterized either as "substantive" or "procedural" in State court opinions in any use of those terms unrelated to the specific issue before us. *Erie R. Co. v. Tompkins* was not an endeavor to formulate scientific legal terminology. It expressed a policy that touches vitally the proper distribution of judicial power between State and federal courts. In essence, the intent of that decision was to insure that, in all cases where a federal court is exercising jurisdiction solely because of the diversity of citizenship of the parties, the outcome of the litigation in the federal court should be substantially the same, so far as legal rules determine the outcome of a litigation, as it would be if tried in a State court. The nub of the policy that underlies *Erie R. Co. v. Tompkins* is that for the same transaction the accident of a suit by a non-resident litigant in a federal court instead of in a State court a block away should not lead to a substantially different result. And so, putting to one side abstractions regarding "substance" and "procedure," we have held that in diversity cases the federal courts must follow the law of the State as to burden of proof, Cities Service Oil Co. v. Dunlap, 308 U.S. 208, as to conflict of laws, Klaxon Co. v. Stentor Co., 313 U.S. 487, as to contributory negligence, Palmer v. Hoffman, 318 U.S. 109, 117. . . .

Plainly enough, a statute that would completely bar recovery in a suit if brought in a State court bears on a State-created right vitally and not merely formally or negligibly. As to consequences that so intimately affect recovery or non-recovery a federal court in a diversity case should follow State law. . . .

Even before *Erie R. Co. v. Tompkins*, federal courts relied on statutes of limitations of the States in which they sat. In suits at law State limitations statutes were held to be "rules of decision" within § 34 of the Judiciary Act of 1789 and as such applied in "trials at common law." . . . While there was talk of freedom of equity from such State statutes of limitations, the cases generally refused recovery where suit was barred in a like situation in the State courts, even if only by way of analogy. . . .

Diversity jurisdiction is founded on assurance to nonresident litigants of courts free from susceptibility to potential local bias. The Framers of the Constitution, according to Marshall, entertained "apprehension" lest distant suitors be subjected to local bias in State courts, or, at least, viewed with "indulgence the possible fears and apprehensions" of such suitors. Bank of the United States v. Deveaux, 5 Cranch [9 U.S.] 61, 87. And so Congress afforded out-of-State litigants another tribunal, not another body of law. The operation of a double system of conflicting laws in the same State is plainly hostile to the reign of law. Certainly, the fortuitous circumstance of residence out of a State of one of the parties to a litigation ought not to give rise to a discrimination against others equally concerned but locally resident. The source of substantive rights enforced by a federal court under diversity jurisdiction, it cannot be said too often, is the law of the States. Whenever that law is authoritatively declared by a State, whether its voice be the legislature or its highest court, such law ought to govern in litigation founded on that law, whether the forum of application is a State or a federal court and whether the remedies be sought at law or may be had in equity. . . .

The judgment is reversed and the case is remanded for proceedings not inconsistent with this opinion. . . .

[JUSTICES RUTLEDGE and MURPHY dissented; JUSTICES ROBERTS and DOUGLAS did not participate.]

HANNA v. PLUMER

380 U.S. 460 (1965).

MR. CHIEF JUSTICE WARREN delivered the opinion of the Court. . . .

[Petitioner, an Ohio resident, filed suit against the executor of a deceased Massachusetts resident in the United States District Court for the District of Massachusetts, alleging damages in excess of $10,000 for injuries arising out of an automobile accident in South Carolina. A copy of the summons was left with respondent's wife in compliance with Rule 4(d)(1) of the Federal Rules of Civil Procedure, which provides that "service shall be made . . . upon an individual . . . by delivering a copy of the summons and of the complaint to him personally or by leaving copies thereof at his dwelling house . . . with some person of suitable age and discretion then residing therein. . . ." The district court held that the action could not be maintained because Massachusetts law required delivery of the summons to the executor himself, and the court of appeals affirmed.]

We conclude that the adoption of Rule 4(d)(1), designed to control service of process in diversity actions, neither exceeded the congressional mandate embodied in the Rules Enabling Act nor transgressed constitutional bounds, and that the Rule is therefore the standard against which the District Court should have measured the adequacy of the service. Accordingly, we reverse the decision of the Court of Appeals.

The Rules Enabling Act, 28 U.S.C. § 2072 (1958 ed.), provides, in pertinent part:

> "The Supreme Court shall have the power to prescribe, by general rules, the forms of process, writs, pleadings, and motions, and the practice and procedure of the district courts of the United States in civil actions.
>
> "Such rules shall not abridge, enlarge or modify any substantive right and shall preserve the right of trial by jury. . . ."

Under the cases construing the scope of the Enabling Act, Rule 4(d)(1) clearly passes muster. Prescribing the manner in which a defendant is to be notified that a suit has been instituted against him, it relates to the "practice and procedure of the district courts." . . .

> "The test must be whether a rule really regulates procedure,—the judicial process for enforcing rights and duties recognized by substantive law and for justly administering remedy and redress for disregard or infraction of them." Sibbach v. Wilson & Co., 312 U.S. 1, 14.

In Mississippi Pub. Corp. v. Murphree, 326 U.S. 438, this Court upheld Rule 4(f), which permits service of a summons anywhere within the State (and not merely the district) in which a district court sits:

> "We think that Rule 4(f) is in harmony with the Enabling Act. . . . Undoubtedly most alterations of the rules of practice and procedure may and often do affect the rights of litigants. Congress' prohibition of any alteration of substantive rights of litigants was obviously not addressed to such incidental effects as necessarily attend the adoption of the prescribed new rules of procedure upon the rights of litigants who, agreeable to rules of practice and procedure, have been brought before a court authorized to determine their rights. . . ."

Thus were there no conflicting state procedures, Rule 4(d) (1) would clearly control. . . .

Respondent . . . suggests that the *Erie* doctrine acts as a check on the Federal Rules of Civil Procedure, that despite the clear command of Rule 4(d)(1), *Erie* and its progeny demand the application of the Massachusetts rule. Reduced to essentials, the argument is: (1) *Erie*, as refined in *York*, demands that federal courts apply state law whenever application of federal law in its stead will alter the outcome of the case. (2) In this case, a determination that the Massachusetts service requirements obtain will result in immediate victory for respondent. If, on the other hand, it should be held that Rule 4(d)(1) is applicable, the litigation will continue, with possible victory for petitioner. (3) Therefore, *Erie* demands application of the Massachusetts rule. The syllogism possesses an appealing simplicity, but is for several reasons invalid.

In the first place, it is doubtful that, even if there were no Federal Rule making it clear that in-hand service is not required in diversity actions, the *Erie* rule would have obligated the District Court to follow the Massachusetts procedure. "Outcome-determination" analysis was never intended to serve as a talisman. Byrd v. Blue Ridge Cooperative, 356 U.S. 525, 537. Indeed, the message of *York* itself is that choices between state and federal are to be made not by application of any automatic "litmus paper" criterion, but rather by reference to the policies underlying the *Erie* rule. . . .

The *Erie* rule is rooted in part in a realization that it would be unfair for the character or result of a litigation materially to differ because the suit had been brought in a federal court.

> ". . . *Swift v. Tyson* introduced grave discrimination by noncitizens against citizens. . . . Thus, the doctrine rendered impossible equal protection of the law."

The decision was also in part a reaction to the practice of "forum-shopping" which had grown up in response to the rule of *Swift v. Tyson*. . . . That the *York* test was an attempt to effectuate these policies is demonstrated by the fact that the opinion framed the inquiry in terms of "substantial" variations between state and federal litigation. . . . Not only are nonsubstantial, or trivial, variations not likely to raise the sort of equal protection problems which troubed the Court in *Erie*; they are also unlikely to influence the choice of a forum. The "outcome-determination" test therefore cannot be read without reference to the twin aims of the *Erie* rule: discouragement of forum-shopping and avoidance of inequitable administration of the laws.

The difference between the conclusion that the Massachusetts rule is applicable, and the conclusion that it is not, is of course at this point "outcome-determinative" in the sense that if we hold the state rule to apply, respondent prevails, whereas if we hold that Rule 4(d)(1) governs, the litigation will continue. But in this sense *every* procedural variation is "outcome-determinative." . . . Though choice of the federal or state rule will at this point have a marked effect upon the outcome of the litigation, the difference between the two rules would be of scant, if any, relevance to the choice of a forum. Petitioner, in choosing her forum, was not presented with a situation where application of the state rule would wholly bar recovery; rather, adherence to the state rule would have resulted only in altering the way in which process was served. Moreover, it is difficult to argue that permitting service of defendant's wife to take the place of in-hand service of defendant himself alters the mode of enforcement of state-created rights in a fashion sufficiently "substantial" to raise the sort of equal protection problems to which the *Erie* opinion alluded.

There is, however, a more fundamental flaw in respondent's syllogism: the incorrect assumption that the rule of *Erie R. Co. v. Tompkins* constitutes the appropriate test of the validity and therefore the applicability of a Federal Rule of Civil Procedure. The *Erie* rule has never been invoked to void a Federal Rule. It is true that there have been cases where this Court has held applicable a state rule in the face of an argument that the situation was governed by one of the Federal Rules. But the holding of each such case was not that *Erie* commanded displacement of a Federal Rule by an inconsistent state rule, but rather that the scope of the Federal Rule was not as broad as the losing party urged, and therefore, there being no Federal Rule which covered the point in dispute, *Erie* commanded the enforcement of state law.

> "Respondent contends, in the first place, that the charge was correct because of the fact that Rule 8(c) of the Rules of Civil Procedure makes contributory negligence an affirmative defense. We do not agree. Rule 8(c) covers only the manner of pleading. The question of the burden of establishing contributory negligence is a question of local law which federal courts in diversity of citizenship cases . . . must apply." Palmer v. Hoffman, 318 U.S. 109, 117.

(Here, of course, the clash is unavoidable; Rule 4(d)(1) says—implicitly, but with unmistakable clarity—that in-hand service is not required in federal courts.) At the same time, in cases adjudicating the validity of Federal Rules, we have not applied the *York* rule or other refinements of *Erie*, but have to this day continued to decide questions concerning the scope of the Enabling Act and the constitutionality of specific Federal Rules in light of the distinction set forth in *Sibbach*.

Nor has the development of two separate lines of cases been inadvertent. . . . When a situation is covered by one of the Federal Rules, the question facing the court is far cry from the typical, relatively unguided *Erie* choice: the court has been instructed to apply the Federal Rule, and can refuse to do so only if the Advisory Committee, this Court, and Congress erred in their prima facie judgment that the Rule in question transgresses neither the terms of the Enabling Act nor constitutional restrictions.

We are reminded by the *Erie* opinion that neither Congress nor the federal courts can, under the guise of formulating rules of decision for federal courts, fashion rules which are not supported by a grant of federal authority contained in Article I or some other section of the Constitution; in such areas state law must govern because there can be no other law. But the opinion in *Erie*, which involved no Federal Rule and dealt with a question which was "substantive" in every traditional sense (whether the railroad owed a duty of care to Tompkins as a trespasser or a licensee), surely neither said nor implied that measures like Rule 4(d)(1) are unconstitutional. For the constitutional provision for a federal court system (augmented by the Necessary and Proper Clause) carries with it congressional power to make rules governing the practice and pleading in those courts, which in turn includes a power to regulate matters which, though falling within the uncertain area between substance and procedure, are rationally capable of classification as either. . . .

Thus, though a court, in measuring a Federal Rule against the standards contained in the Enabling Act and the Constitution, need not wholly blind itself to the degree to which the Rule makes the character and result of the federal litigation stray from the course it would follow in state courts, *Sibbach v. Wilson & Co.*, supra, at 13–14, it cannot be forgotten that the *Erie* rule, and the guidelines suggested in *York*, were created to serve another purpose altogether. To hold that a Federal Rule of Civil Procedure must cease to function whenever it alters the mode of enforcing state-created rights would be to disembowel either the Constitution's grant of power over federal procedure or Congress' attempt to exercise that power in the Enabling Act. Rule 4(d)(1) is valid and controls the instant case.

Reversed. . . .

MR. JUSTICE HARLAN, concurring. . . .

Erie was something more than an opinion which worried about "forum-shopping and avoidance of inequitable administration of the laws," . . . although to be sure these were important elements of the decision. I have always regarded that decision as one of the modern cornerstones of our federalism, expressing policies that profoundly touch the allocation of judicial power between the state and federal systems. *Erie* recognized that there should not be two conflicting systems of law controlling the primary activity of citizens, for such alternative governing authority must necessarily give rise to a debilitating uncertainty in the planning of everyday affairs.[1] And it recognized that the scheme of our Constitution envisions an allocation of lawmaking functions between state and federal legislative processes which is undercut if the federal judiciary can make substantive law affecting state affairs beyond the bounds of congressional legislative powers in this regard. . . .

To my mind the proper line of approach in determining whether to apply a state or a federal rule, whether "substantive" or "procedural," is to stay close to basic principles by inquiring if the choice of rule would substantially affect those primary decisions respecting human conduct which our constitutional system leaves to state regulation. If so, *Erie* and the Constitution require that the state rule prevail, even in the face of a conflicting federal rule. . . .

So long as a reasonable man could characterize any duly adopted federal rule as "procedural," the Court, unless I misapprehend what is said, would have it apply no matter how seriously it frustrated a State's substantive regulation of the primary conduct and affairs of its citizens. Since the members of the Advisory Committee, the Judicial Conference, and this Court who formulated the Federal Rules are presumably

1. Since the rules involved in the present case are parallel rather than conflicting, this first rationale does not come into play here.

reasonable men, it follows that the integrity of the Federal Rules is absolute. Whereas the unadulterated outcome and forum-shopping tests may err too far toward honoring state rules, I submit that the Court's "arguably procedural, *ergo* constitutional" test moves too fast and far in the other direction. . . .

It remains to apply what has been said to the present case. . . . The evident intent of . . . [the Massachusetts] statute is to permit an executor to distribute the estate which he is administering without fear that further liabilities may be outstanding for which he could be held personally liable. If the Federal District Court in Massachusetts applies Rule 4(d)(1) . . ., it would simply mean that an executor would have to check at his own house or at the federal courthouse as well as the registry of probate before he could distribute the estate with impunity. As this does not seem enough to give rise to any real impingement on the vitality of the state policy which the Massachusetts rule is intended to serve, I concur in the judgment of the Court.

Notes on "Substance" and "Procedure" Under Erie

(1) Was the Court in *Hanna* justified in placing so much emphasis on the existence or absence of a Federal Rule of Civil Procedure? See, in addition to the Enabling Act itself, Fed.R.Civ.P. 1 ("These rules govern the procedure in the United States District Courts in all suits of a civil nature . . ."); 28 U.S.C. § 1652 (state laws as rules of decision "except where the Constitution or treaties of the United States or Acts of Congress otherwise require or provide"); U.S. Constitution, Article VI ("This Constitution, and the Laws of the United States which shall be made in pursuance thereof . . . shall be the supreme Law of the Land"). But before this massive engine of federal supremacy can get under way the Rule must pass two tests: It must be within the authority given the Court by the Enabling Act, and it must be constitutional.

Is the statutory grant of rule-making authority as broad as the power of Congress in diversity cases?[1] "The test," said the Court in Sibbach v. Wilson, 312 U.S. 1, 14 (1941), "must be whether a rule really regulates procedure—the judicial process for enforcing rights and duties recognized by substantive law and for justly administering remedy and redress for disregard or infraction of them."[2] Justice Frankfurter dissented: "A drastic change in public policy on a matter deeply touching the sensibilities of people or even their prejudices as to privacy [such as the physical-examination provision in Rule 35] , ought not to be inferred from a general authorization to formulate rules for the more uniform and effective dispatch of business on the civil side of the federal courts." Professor Ely, in The Irrepressible Myth of Erie, 87 Harv.L.Rev. 693, 718–38 (1974), argues

1. The argument that Congress could not constitutionally delegate rulemaking power to the courts was rejected in Wayman v. Southard, 23 U.S. (10 Wheat.) 1 (1825).

2 See also Provident Tradesmens Bank & Trust Co. v. Patterson, 390 U.S. 102 (1968), upholding Rule 19's provisions respecting what used to be called indispensable parties.

that the *Sibbach* test wholly ignores the statutory requirement that the Rules, even if procedural, not infringe substantive rights; he would strike down (even in a federal-question case?) any Rule that offended "substantive" state policy, i.e., a policy not simply "designed to make the process of litigation a fair and efficient mechanism for the resolution of disputes." Is it clear that the "substantive right" prohibition is not merely a means of emphasizing the limitation to matters of procedure?

(2) Does *Erie*'s perception that the federal diversity court is a disinterested forum mean the Civil Rules are all unconstitutional in diversity cases? Or may a forum with no interest in the merits of a case have a constitutionally sufficient interest in matters affecting the administration of its courts? Cf. Missouri ex rel. Southern Railway Co. v. Mayfield, 340 U.S. 1 (1950), supra p. 186, holding that a state court may dismiss an FELA action on grounds of forum non conveniens; Wells v. Simonds Abrasive Co., 345 U.S. 514 (1953), upholding the right of a state court to dismiss an action based on foreign law in reliance on a forum limitation period shorter than that provided by the State that created the right of action. Does it follow that a federal court could apply a shorter statute of limitation than that of the State in order to keep federal dockets clear for more pressing business? Would any comparable policy support application of a federal statute imposing a limitation period *longer* than that of the State whose law created the right of action? [3]

Was the Court right in *Hanna* in holding constitutional Rule 4(d)(1)'s provision dispensing with the necessity for in-hand service? Would the same reasoning support a statute providing nationwide service of process in diversity cases? Can the Declaratory Judgment Act be constitutionally applied in a diversity case? If the purpose of diversity jurisdiction is simply to protect an out-of-state party from potential state-court bias, is there ever an interest in providing a federal forum when the state courts are closed? What about the Interpleader Act, supra pp. 247–50, whose very reason for existence was the inability of any state court to entertain the whole case?

(3) Recall, further, that *Hanna* does not dispense with the necessity for construing the federal rule. See, e.g., Walker v. Armco Steel Corp., 446 U.S. 740 (1980), requiring a federal court in a diversity case to follow a state rule that a statute of limitations ran until service of process, despite Rule 3's provision that "[a] civil action is commenced by filing a complaint." There was "no indication," said the Court, "that the Rule was intended to toll a state statute of limitations"; it merely "governs the date from which various timing requirements of the federal rules began to run. . . ." See also Arrowsmith v. United Press International, 320 F.2d 219 (2d Cir. 1963), holding that a foreign corporation could not be sued in federal court unless it was subject to personal jurisdiction under state law: Rule 4(d)(3) " 'tells how service of process is to be made upon a corporation

3. Cf. Sun Oil Co. v. Wortman, 486 U.S. 717 (1988), allowing a disinterested *state* court to apply its own longer limitation period because "the procedural rules of its courts are surely matters on which a State is competent to legislate" but distinguishing the *Erie* problem: "*Guaranty Trust* itself rejects the notion that there is an equivalence between what is substantive under the *Erie* doctrine and what is substantive for purposes of conflict of laws."

which is subject to service; but it does not tell when the corporation is so subject.' " Is the degree to which application of a federal rule would frustrate state policy relevant to the question of construction?[4]

(4) The Civil Rules do not answer every procedural question, and neither federal statutes nor rules adopted by the district courts themselves under § 2071 fill all the gaps. What is a court to do when none of these sources provides an answer?

The degree of deference to state "procedural" law under *York's* outcome-determinative rationale reached its zenith in three 1949 decisions. Ragan v. Merchants Transfer & Warehouse Co., 337 U.S. 530 (1949), required the diversity court to follow a state rule that the statute of limitations ran until service of summons on the defendant. Woods v. Interstate Realty Co., 337 U.S. 535 (1949), required dismissal of a diversity action in accordance with a state statute forbidding suits by foreign corporations that had failed to designate an agent to receive service of process. Cohen v. Beneficial Industrial Loan Corp., 337 U.S. 541 (1949), required a federal diversity court to follow a state statute making an unsuccessful plaintiff in a shareholder's derivative suit liable for the expenses of defense and entitling the corporation to require the plaintiff to post security to cover them.[5]

Ragan was reaffirmed in *Walker v. Armco Steel Corp.,* note 3 supra. Would *Woods* and *Cohen* be decided the same way today? [6]

(5) Byrd v. Blue Ridge Rural Electric Cooperative, Inc., 356 U.S. 525 (1958), modified *York's* outcome test by suggesting that the applicability of state procedural rules in federal diversity cases turned on a balance of state and federal interests. State courts had held that the judge rather than the jury should decide whether the plaintiff in a personal-injury action was a "statutory employee" whose sole remedy was workers' compensation; the Supreme Court held the issue should nevertheless be submitted to the jury. "[W]ere 'outcome' the only consideration," wrote Justice Brennan, "a strong case might appear for saying that the federal court should follow the state practice." Yet the state court had enunicated no affirmative reason for keeping the issue from the jury; its decisions "simply reflect a policy

4. Cf. Bernkrant v. Fowler, 55 Cal.2d 588, 12 Cal.Rptr. 266, 360 P.2d 906 (1961), construing a California statute of frauds narrowly to avoid frustrating a countervailing Nevada policy and the parties' expectations.

5. See also Angel v. Bullington, 330 U.S. 183 (1947), holding a federal court could not entertain an action for deficiency judgment after a state court had dismissed the same claim on the basis of a statute held to limit its "jurisdiction" to enter such judgments; Bernhardt v. Polygraphic Co., 350 U.S. 198 (1956), holding the enforceability of an arbitration clause governed by state law because otherwise "the outcome of litigation might depend on the courthouse where suit is brought."

6. Was the Court in *York* justified in dismissing as irrelevant the familiar doctrine that a state court applies its own statute of limitations to an action based on foreign law? Granted that the word "procedure" may have different meanings in various contexts, is it not the premise of *Erie* that the diversity court is in a position substantially identical to that of a state court enforcing foreign law? See Sedler, The Erie Outcome Test as a Guide to Substance and Procedure in the Conflict of Laws, 37 N.Y.U.L.Rev. 813, 821–24, 850 (1962), arguing that *York* was right and that state courts ought to follow it in interstate conflicts cases; Sun Oil Co. v. Wortman, footnote 3 supra, rejecting the analogy.

. . . that administrative determination of 'jurisdictional facts' should not be final but subject to judicial review." On the other side of the ledger,

> [t]he federal system is an independent system for administering justice to litigants who properly invoke its jurisdiction. An essential characteristic of that system is the manner in which, in civil common-law actions, it distributes trial functions between judge and jury and, under the influence—if not the command—of the Seventh Amendment, assigns the decisions of disputed questions of fact to the jury. . . . The policy of uniform enforcement of state-created rights and obligations . . . cannot in every instance exact compliance with a state rule—not bound up with rights and obligations—which disrupts the federal system of allocating functions between judge and jury.

Did *Byrd's* investigation of competing interests better capture the spirit of *Erie* than did *York's* outcome test? Did *Hanna's* emphasis on forum shopping? Did Justice Harlan's concurrence?

(6) Are state procedural rules "rules of decision" whose application § 1652 demands? [7] Have the courts authority to develop common law to fill gaps in the Federal Rules? [8]

KLAXON CO. v. STENTOR ELECTRIC MANUFACTURING CO.

313 U.S. 487 (1941).

MR. JUSTICE REED delivered the opinion of the Court.

The principal question in this case is whether in diversity cases the federal courts must follow conflict of laws rules prevailing in the states in which they sit. . . .

In 1918, respondent, a New York corporation, transferred its entire business to petitioner, a Delaware corporation. Petitioner contracted to use its best efforts to further the manufacture and sale of certain patented devices covered by the agreement, and respondent was to have a share of petitioner's profits. The agreement was executed in New

7. That Congress did not think the Rules of Decision Act embraced all procedural matters was strongly suggested by its contemporaneous enactment of a separate statute providing that "the forms of writs and executions . . . and modes of process" in federal common-law actions conform to those of the States (1 Stat. 93, 94 (1789)). The successor to this conformity provision disappeared with the adoption of the Federal Rules of Civil Procedure in 1938.

8. See Omni Capital International v. Rudolf Wolff & Co., 484 U.S. 97 (1987), declining to adopt a federal rule of nationwide service of process and leaving open the question of power. Cf. Vermont Yankee Nuclear Power Corp. v. Natural Resources Defense Council, 435 U.S. 519 (1978), holding that the Administrative Procedure Act limited any authority of the courts to impose additional procedural rules on administrative agencies; Miner v. Atlass, 363 U.S. 641 (1960), holding that a federal court sitting in admiralty had no inherent power to order discovery and that the omission of discovery from the Supreme Court's then governing admiralty rules meant the subject was not within the district court's rulemaking power now found in § 2071. But the Court based the latter holding on the "particular nature and history" of the discovery problem, refusing to hold that "whenever the General Admiralty Rules deal with part, but not all, of a subject, those practices left unprovided for by the General Rules may not in any circumstances be dealt with by the District Courts" under their general rulemaking power.

York, the assets were transferred there, and petitioner began performance there although later it moved its operations to other states. Respondent was voluntarily dissolved under New York law in 1919. Ten years later it instituted this action in the United States District Court for the District of Delaware, alleging that petitioner had failed to perform its agreement to use its best efforts. Jurisdiction rested on diversity of citizenship. In 1939 respondent recovered a jury verdict of $100,000, upon which judgment was entered. Respondent then moved to correct the judgment by adding interest at the rate of six percent from June 1, 1929, the date the action had been brought. The basis of the motion was the provision in § 480 of the New York Civil Practice Act directing that in contract actions interest be added to the principal sum "whether theretofore liquidated or unliquidated." The District Court granted the motion, taking the view that the rights of the parties were governed by New York law and that under New York law the addition of such interest was mandatory. 30 F.Supp. 425, 431. The Circuit Court of Appeals affirmed, 115 F.2d 268, and we granted certiorari, limited to the question whether § 480 of the New York Civil Practice Act is applicable to an action in the federal court in Delaware. 312 U.S. 674.

The Circuit Court of Appeals was of the view that under New York law the right to interest before verdict under § 480 went to the substance of the obligation, and that proper construction of the contract in suit fixed New York as the place of performance. It then concluded that § 480 was applicable to the case because "it is clear by what we think is undoubtedly the better view of the law that the rules for ascertaining the measure of damages are not a matter of procedure at all, but are matters of substance which should be settled by reference to the law of the appropriate state according to the type of case being tried in the forum. The measure of damages for breach of a contract is determined by the law of the place of performance; Restatement, Conflict of Laws § 413." The court referred also to § 418 of the Restatement, which makes interest part of the damages to be determined by the law of the place of performance. Application of the New York statute apparently followed from the court's independent determination of the "better view" without regard to Delaware law, for no Delaware decision or statute was cited or discussed.

We are of opinion that the prohibition declared in Erie R. Co. v. Tompkins, 304 U.S. 64, against such independent determinations by the federal courts extends to the field of conflict of laws. The conflict of laws rules to be applied by the federal court in Delaware must conform to those prevailing in Delaware's state courts. Otherwise the accident of diversity of citizenship would constantly disturb equal administration of justice in co-ordinate state and federal court sitting side by side. See Erie R. Co. v. Tompkins, supra, 304 U.S. at 74–77. Any other ruling would do violence to the principle of uniformity within a state upon which the *Tompkins* decision is based. Whatever lack of uniformity this may produce between federal courts in different states is attributable to our federal system, which leaves to a state, within the limits permitted by the Constitution, the right to pursue local policies diverging from those of its neighbors. It is not for the federal courts to thwart such local policies by enforcing an independent "general law" of conflict of laws. Subject only to review by this Court on any federal question that may arise, Delaware is free to determine whether a given matter is to be governed by the law of the forum or some other law. . . . This Court's views are not the decisive factor in determining the applicable conflicts rule. . . . And the proper function of the Delaware federal court is to ascertain what the state law is, not what it ought to be. . . .

The judgment is reversed and the case remanded to the Circuit Court of Appeals for decision in conformity with the law of Delaware.

Reversed.

Notes on the Choice Among Conflicting State Laws Under Erie

(1) The problem presented in *Klaxon* can be approached on a number of different levels. First, in regard to forum shopping: Was the Court justified in viewing disuniformity between courts in a single State as more serious than disuniformity between federal courts? See the practical argument of Professor Cavers that "forum-shopping across the courthouse square . . . is a much greater risk than forum shopping across state lines," because the latter requires employment of out-of-state counsel "who might lack the first lawyer's own background knowledge of the controversy and who certainly would share in the fees." ALI Study 158–59 (Tent.Draft No. 1, 1963).

Might it be added that, however unfortunate it may be that the federal courts cannot wipe out disuniformity among the states, the worst thing they could do would be to create a disuniformity of their own?

(2) Professors Hart and Wechsler were sharply critical of *Klaxon*. The greatness of *Erie*, they maintained, was that by destroying the separate federal common law that decision made it easier for people to predict the legal consequences of their actions, and, therefore, to plan their conduct with assurance. Since everyone agreed in *Erie* that Pennsylvania law would govern absent *Swift v. Tyson*, the possibility of a contrary federal law was disruptive. *Klaxon*, in their view, was a step backward from this position; for when there is doubt as to which State's law applies a federal choice-of-law doctrine would promote *Erie's* principle of assuring a predictable uniform result. See Hart & Wechsler, The Federal Courts and the Federal System 634–35 (1953).

Apart from the considerations discussed in note 3, infra, and the question whether the federal courts could be expected to develop a fairly uniform conflicts doctrine, see Cavers, supra note 1, at 165, 183–90, consider 28 U.S.C. § 1441(b), which prohibits removal of a diversity case by a resident defendant. In many cases this would give the plaintiff under the Hart-Wechsler argument an irremediable choice between federal and state conflicts principles, and it was precisely this incomplete availability of removal that made *Swift v. Tyson* such an obstacle to predictability. Note also the difficulty in some cases of predicting at the planning stage whether all parties to a potential suit will be diverse and whether the jurisdictional minimum amount will be satisfied. See Hill, The Erie Doctrine and The Constitution, 53 Nw.U.L.Rev. 427, 561 (1958).

(3) If removal were always available, a federal conflicts doctrine might well enhance predictability. Moreover, it has been argued that *Klaxon* is unfortunate because the federal courts, free from parochial loyalties, are in an ideal position to resolve conflicts between the states. See e.g., Hart, The Relations Between State and Federal Law, 54 Colum.L. Rev. 489, 515 (1954). But is either the active promotion of predictability or the development of choice-of-law rules within the purpose of the diversity grant as defined in *Erie, York*, and succeeding decisions? Does not the notion that the diversity court sits only to provide an unbiased forum suggest, as *Klaxon* in effect held, that (apart from bias, and subject to countervailing policies respecting the adminstration of federal courts) the case should be decided as it would have been if there were no federal courts? [1]

(4) If the basis and effect of *Erie* are that the diversity court is a disinterested forum, should it not, like other disinterested courts, see Restatement, Conflict of Laws § 7 (1934), make its own choice of laws? See Hill, The Erie Doctrine and the Constitution, 53 Nw.U.L.Rev. 427, 545 (1958). In particular, Mr. Hill asks, why should the federal court follow the choice-of-law doctrines of a forum State that itself has no interest in the outcome of the case? Among other things, he observes, this practice may result in applying "procedural" laws of the forum State contrary to the policy of the only interested States.

(5) The discussion of *Klaxon* up to this point has assumed that the conflict of laws is an independent system of rules applied without regard to the content of the substantive law. This assumption was the foundation of the first Conflicts Restatement (1934). Embraced by a number of courts more recently, however, is a quite different theory that denies the independent existence of choice-of-law rules and suggests that the usual *Klaxon* rhetoric is beside the point:

> The applicability of a statute or common-law rule to a case having foreign aspects presents a question of construction or interpretation of the same kind as does the applicability of the same statute or rule to a marginal domestic situation, or a situation existing prior to the enactment of the statute. If this is true, it is clear that a federal court should be bound as firmly to apply the state court's construction of the

1. But see Hill, The Erie Doctrine and the Constitution, 53 Nw.U.L.Rev. 427, 544 (1958): "It is particularly through arbitrary choice of law rules that local bias can effectively be brought to bear against out-of-state litigants; and . . . the state courts were largely free to engage in this practice prior to adoption of the fourteenth amendment"; Baxter, Choice of Law and the Federal System, 16 Stan.L.Rev. 1, 22–42 (1963), arguing that federal choice of law was contemplated in the Rules of Decision Act's reference to state laws "in cases where they apply," and that the Full Faith and Credit Clause should be interpreted "to dictate the initial choice-of-law reference in every case, whether in a state or federal court"; Horowitz, Toward a Federal Common Law of Choice of Law, 14 U.C. L.A.L.Rev. 1191 (1967).

law in its application to cases having foreign aspects as it is bound to apply the state court's construction of the law in its application to marginal domestic situations and pre-existing conditions.

B. Currie, Selected Essays on the Conflict of Laws 434–35 (1963).

It seems clear that the result of this theory would not always be the same as that under *Klaxon.* For while *Klaxon* followed the choice-of-law rule of the forum State, Currie would ask the diversity court to make its own analysis of the laws of each related State, and this might lead to some forum-shopping. There are, moreover, some special problems connected with this approach. First, what is a federal court to do if it interprets a state's policy to be applicable to the case but finds that State would not apply its law because of an old-fashioned choice-of-law rule? [2] Second, what happens if the court concludes that the laws of two States apply? Currie argued that judicial resources were exhausted at this point: "Resolution of a conflict between the interests of coordinate states is a function of a high policital order, which courts are not equipped to perform." B. Currie, The Disinterested Third State, 28 Law & Contemp.Probs. 754, 758 (1963). Accordingly, an interested forum should simply apply its own law, despite the disuniformity this produces; and, not surprisingly, he viewed the task of a disinterested forum confronted by two applicable laws as "a peculiarly difficult one . . . that . . . should not be deliberately thrust on a court except for very good reason." Id. at 790. Fortunately for his theory, he found the disinterested state court a rarity and could respectably urge that in many cases it should dismiss the action on grounds of forum non conveniens. But the diversity court under *Erie* vastly increases the magnitude of this problem, and Currie's none-too-satisfied conclusion that the disinterested court should either apply its own law (assuming it coincides with the law of an interested state) or indulge a frankly legislative choice of the preferable policy, id. at 778–80, is hardly a desirable model for the great mass of diversity cases. One suspects that in his view *Klaxon*—if the laws of two interested states were found to conflict—would be as good a way as any to pass the buck while at the same time minimizing intrastate forum shopping.[3]

(6) Griffin v. McCoach, 313 U.S. 498 (1941), applied *Klaxon* unblinkingly to an interpleader case in a Texas federal court, although some of the parties were non-residents who could not have been sued in a state court in

2 In Lester v. Aetna Life Insurance Co., 433 F.2d 884 (5th Cir. 1970), the Fifth Circuit applied Louisiana law on the basis of an interest analysis, despite Louisiana's adherence to a traditional choice-of-law rule looking to foreign law. Acknowledging that *Klaxon* required it to follow the "conflict of laws rules of the forum state," the court said there was no "conflict of laws" present because only Louisiana policy reached the case. Predictably, the Supreme Court disapproved: "A federal court in a diversity case is not free to engraft onto those state [choice-of-law] rules exceptions or modifications which may commend themselves to the federal court, but which have not commended themselves to the state in which the federal court sits." Day & Zimmermann, Inc. v. Challoner, 423 U.S. 3, 4 (1975).

3. Notice also that Currie's position requires a dissent from the argument, supra note 3, that federal courts are in the best position to formulate impartial choice-of-law principles. In his view federal courts are in the worst position to do so, for they are no more capable than state courts of weighing competing interests, and they lack the state courts' ability to settle the matter by applying their own law.

Texas. Consider also the problem of which state's choice-of-law doctrine to follow if federal service of process is made beyond the limits of state jurisdiction in an impleader case as authorized by Rule 4(f), or if a state-law claim is pendent to a federal claim for which nationwide service is provided. What sense does it make to apply the law of a State in whose courts the action could never have been brought? [4]

(7) Van Dusen v. Barrack, 376 U.S. 612 (1964). Numerous actions arising from a Massachusetts plane crash were filed in federal court in Pennsylvania. The plaintiffs argued that transferring the actions to Massachusetts would not serve the "interest of justice," as required by 28 U.S.C. § 1404(a), because it might diminish their recovery: Massachusetts limited wrongful-death damages to $20,000, and the federal court there was more likely than its Pennsylvania counterpart to apply Massachusetts law. Approving transfer, the Court rejected the premise of the plaintiffs' argument: "[I]n cases such as the present, where the defendants seek transfer, the transferee district court must . . . apply the state law that would have been applied if there had been no change of venue." Though "a superficial reading" of prior statements that federal courts should "apply the laws 'of the states in which they sit' " might suggest the opposite conclusion, the essence of *Erie* was that " 'the accident of a suit by a nonresident litigant in a federal court instead of in a State court a block away, should not lead to a substantially different result' " (quoting *Guaranty Trust Co. v. York*, p. 336 supra). Thus *Erie* forbade "a result in federal court which could not have been achieved in the courts of the State where the action was filed. . . . The legislative history of § 1404(a) certainly does not justify the rather startling conclusion that one might 'get a change of law as a bonus for a change of venue.' "

(8) Ferens v. John Deere Co., 110 S.Ct. 1274 (1990), applied the same reasoning to reach the same result in a case in which it was the *plaintiff* who had requested transfer. Injured in an accident on his farm in Pennsylvania, Ferens filed suit in a Mississippi federal court to take advantage of that state's six-year statute of limitations and then had the case transferred to Pennsylvania, where it was too late to sue. Absent the transfer, wrote Justice Kennedy for the majority, the Mississippi limitation period would have applied; and, as *Van Dusen* had said, the transfer statute was not designed to affect the outcome of the case.

For the four dissenters, Justice Scalia argued that the principles of *Van Dusen* required the opposite result:

> [J]ust as it is unlikely that Congress, in enacting § 1404(a), meant to provide the defendant with a vehicle by which to manipulate in his favor the substantive law to be applied in a diversity case, so too is it unlikely that Congress meant to provide the *plaintiff* with a vehicle by which to appropriate the law of a distant and inconvenient forum in which he does not intend to litigate, and to carry that prize back to the State in which he wishes to try the case.

4. The ALI would allow federal courts to choose their own state law not only in interpleader cases but also in the proposed multiparty jurisdiction, see p. 250 supra, in which, as in interpleader, no state court can handle the entire controversy. ALI Study 73, 87.

Should the choice of law rules of the transferor state also apply when an action is transferred under § 1406 because the original venue was improper?

SECTION 2. THE FEDERAL COMMON LAW

CLEARFIELD TRUST CO. v. UNITED STATES

318 U.S. 363 (1943).

MR. JUSTICE DOUGLAS delivered the opinion of the Court.

On April 28, 1936, a check was drawn on the Treasurer of the United States through the Federal Reserve Bank of Philadelphia to the order of Clair A. Barner in the amount of $24.20 . . . for services rendered by Barner to the Works Progress Administration. . . . Some unknown person obtained it in a mysterious manner . . ., endorsed the check in the name of Barner and transferred it to J. C. Penney Co. in exchange for cash and merchandise. Barner never authorized the endorsement nor participated in the proceeds of the check. J. C. Penney Co. endorsed the check over to the Clearfield Trust Co. which . . . endorsed it as follows: "Pay to the order of Federal Reserve Bank of Philadelphia, Prior Endorsement Guaranteed." [1] Neither the Clearfield Trust Co. nor J. C. Penney Co. had any knowledge or suspicion of the forgery. . . . On or before May 10, 1936, Barner advised the timekeeper and the foreman of the W.P.A. project on which he was employed that he had not received the check. . . . No notice was given the Clearfield Trust Co. or J. C. Penney Co. of the forgery until January 12, 1937. . . . The first notice received by Clearfield Trust Co. that the United States was asking reimbursement was on August 31, 1937.

This suit was instituted in 1939 by the United States against the Clearfield Trust Co., the jurisdiction of the federal District Court being invoked pursuant to the provisions of § 24(1) of the Judicial Code [now 28 U.S.C. § 1345]. The cause of action was based on the express guaranty of prior endorsements made by the Clearfield Trust Co. . . . The District Court held that the rights of the parties were to be determined by the law of Pennsylvania and that since the United States unreasonably delayed in giving notice of the forgery to the Clearfield Trust Co., it was barred from recovery. . . . The Circuit Court of Appeals reversed. . . .

We agree with the Circuit Court of Appeals that the rule of Erie R. Co. v. Tompkins, 304 U.S. 64, does not apply to this action. The rights and duties of the United States on commercial paper which it issues are governed by federal rather than local law. When the United States disburses its funds or pays its debts, it is exercising a constitutional

1. Guarantee of all prior indorsements on presentment for payment of such a check to Federal Reserve banks or member banks depositories is required by Treasury Regulations. . . .

function or power. This check was issued for services performed under the Federal Emergency Relief Act of 1935, 49 Stat. 115. The authority to issue the check had its origin in the Constitution and the statutes of the United States and was in no way dependent on the laws of Pennsylvania or of any other state. Cf. Board of Commissioners v. United States, 308 U.S. 343; Royal Indemnity Co. v. United States, 313 U.S. 289. The duties imposed upon the United States and the rights acquired by it as a result of the issuance find their roots in the same federal sources.[2] Cf. Deitrick v. Greaney, 309 U.S. 190; D'Oench, Duhme & Co. v. Federal Deposit Ins. Corp., 315 U.S. 447. In absence of an applicable Act of Congress it is for the federal courts to fashion the governing rule of law according to their own standards. . . .

In our choice of the applicable federal rule we have occasionally selected state law. See Royal Indemnity Co. v. United States, supra. But reasons which may make state law at times the appropriate federal rule are singularly inappropriate here. The issuance of commercial paper by the United States is on a vast scale and transactions in the paper from issuance to payment will commonly occur in several states. The application of state law, even without the conflict of laws rules of the forum, would subject the rights and duties of the United States to exceptional uncertainty. It would lead to great diversity in results by making identical transactions subject to the vagaries of the laws of the several states. The desirability of a uniform rule is plain. And while the federal law merchant developed for about a century under the regime of Swift v. Tyson, 16 Pet. [41 U.S.] 1, represented general commercial law rather than a choice of a federal rule designed to protect a federal right, it nevertheless stands as a convenient source of reference for fashioning federal rules applicable to these federal questions. . . .

[The Court held the United States not barred because Clearfield had not shown the delay in giving notice had caused it injury.]

BANK OF AMERICA v. PARNELL

352 U.S. 29 (1956).

MR. JUSTICE FRANKFURTER delivered the opinion of the Court.

Petitioner, alleging diversity of citizenship, brought suit in the District Court for the Western District of Pennsylvania alleging that in September and October 1948 two individual defendants, Parnell and Rocco, and two corporate defendants, the First National Bank in Indiana and the Federal Reserve Bank of Cleveland, had converted 73 Home Owners' Loan Corporation bonds which belonged to petitioner. . . .

2. Various Treasury Regulations govern the payment and endorsement of government checks and warrants and the reimbursement of the Treasurer of the United States by Federal Reserve banks and member bank depositories on payment of checks or warrants bearing a forged endorsement. . . . Forgery of the check was an offense against the United States. . . .

At the trial it appeared that these bonds were bearer bonds with payment guaranteed by the United States. They carried interest coupons calling for semi-annual payment. They were due to mature May 1, 1952, but pursuant to their terms, had been called on or about May 1, 1944. On May 2, 1944, the bonds disappeared while petitioner was getting them ready for presentation to the Federal Reserve Bank for payment. In 1948 they were presented to the First National Bank for payment by Parnell on behalf of Rocco. The First National Bank forwarded them to the Federal Reserve Bank of Cleveland. It cashed them and paid the First National Bank, which issued cashier's checks to Parnell. Parnell then turned the proceeds over to Rocco less a fee—there was conflicting testimony as to whether the fee was nominal or substantial.

The principal issue at the trial was whether the respondents took the bonds in good faith, without knowledge or notice of the defect in title. On this issue the trial judge charged: . . . "The two defendants, Parnell and the bank, . . . have the burden of showing that they acted innocently, honestly, and in good faith. . . ." The jury brought in verdicts for petitioner. . . . The Court of Appeals . . . considered our decision in Clearfield Trust Co. v. United States, 318 U.S. 363, controlling and held that federal law placed the burden of proof on petitioner to show notice and lack of good faith on the part of respondents. The court further found that there was no evidence of bad faith by the First National Bank since the bonds were not "overdue" as a matter of federal law when presented to it and therefore directed entry of judgment for it. The court found that there was evidence of bad faith on the part of Parnell but ordered a new trial because of the erroneous instructions. . . .

The Court of Appeals misconceived the nature of this litigation in holding that the *Clearfield Trust* case controlled. . . .

Securities issued by the Government generate immediate interests of the Government. These were dealt with in *Clearfield Trust* and in National Metropolitan Bank v. United States, 323 U.S. 454. But they also radiate interests in transactions between private parties. The present litigation is purely between private parties and does not touch the rights and duties of the United States. The only possible interest of the United States in a situation like the one here, exclusively involving the transfer of Government paper between private persons, is that the floating of securities of the United States might somehow or other be adversely affected by the local rule of a particular State regarding the liability of a converter. This is far too speculative, far too remote a possibility to justify the application of federal law to transactions essentially of local concern.

We do not mean to imply that litigation with respect to Government paper necessarily precludes the presence of a federal interest, to be governed by federal law, in all situations merely because it is a suit between private parties, or that it is beyond the range of federal legislation to deal comprehensively with Government paper. We do not of course foreclose such judicial or legislative action in appropriate situations by concluding that this controversy over burden of proof and good faith represents too essentially a private transaction not to be dealt with by the local law of Pennsylvania where the transactions took place. Federal law of course governs the interpretation of the nature of the rights and obligations created by the Government bonds themselves. A decision with respect to the "overdueness" of the bonds is therefore a matter of federal law, which, in view of our holding, we need not elucidate. . . .

Reversed and remanded.

MR. JUSTICE BLACK and MR. JUSTICE DOUGLAS, dissenting.

We believe that the "federal law merchant," which Clearfield Trust Co. v. United States, 318 U.S. 363, 367, held applicable to transactions in the commercial paper of the United States, should be applicable to all transactions in that paper. . . . Not until today has a distinction been drawn between suits by the United States on that paper and suits by other parties to it. But the Court does not stop there. Because this is "essentially a private transaction," it is to be governed by local law. Yet the nature of the rights and obligations created by commercial paper of the United States Government is said to be controlled by federal law. Thus, federal law is to govern some portion of a dispute between private parties, while that portion of the dispute which is "essentially of local concern" is to be governed by local law. The uncertainties which inhere in such a dichotomy are obvious. . . .

The virtue of a uniform law governing bonds, notes, and other paper issued by the United States is that it provides a certain and definite guide to the rights of all parties rather than subjecting them to the vagaries of the laws of many States. . . . If the rule of the *Clearfield Trust* case is to be abandoned as to some parties, it should be abandoned as to all and we should start afresh on this problem.

BANCO NACIONAL DE CUBA v. SABBATINO

376 U.S. 398 (1964).

MR. JUSTICE HARLAN delivered the opinion of the Court. . . .

[Farr, Whitlock & Co., an American commodity broker, contracted to purchase sugar from a subsidiary of C.A.V., a Cuban corporation owned largely by United States residents. In response to President Eisenhower's reduction of the Cuban sugar quota, and on the day the sugar was being loaded aboard a ship in Cuba, the Cuban Government expropriated all property of certain American-owned companies, including C.A.V. In order to obtain consent for the ship to sail Farr, Whitlock entered into purchase contracts with a Cuban agency, which assigned its rights to Banco Nacional. Banco sued Farr, Whitlock and Sabbatino, receiver of C.A.V., to establish its right to the contract price.

[The federal district court held it was entitled to disregard the expropriation decree because it was retaliatory, discriminatory, and confiscatory, and the court of appeals affirmed. The question, said the Supreme Court, was whether to reverse on the basis of the "act of state" doctrine, which "precludes the courts of this country from inquiring into the validity of the public acts of a recognized foreign sovereign power committed within its own territory."

[Application of the act-of-state doctrine, the Court held, was compelled neither by "international law" nor by the Constitution.]

The act of state doctrine does, however, have "constitutional" underpinnings. It arises out of the basic relationships between branches of government in a system of separation of powers. It concerns the competency of dissimilar institutions to make and implement particular kinds of decisions in the area of international relations. The doctrine as formulated in past decisions expresses the strong sense of the Judicial Branch that its engagement in the task of passing on the validity of foreign acts of state may hinder rather than further this country's pursuit of goals both for itself and for the community of nations as a whole in the international sphere. Many commentators disagree with this view. . . . Whatever considerations are thought to predominate, it is plain that the problems involved are uniquely federal in nature. If federal authority, in this instance this Court, orders the field of judicial competence in this area for the federal courts, and the state courts are left free to formulate their own rules, the purposes behind the doctrine could be as effectively undermined as if there had been no federal pronouncement on the subject. . . .

An issue concerned with a basic choice regarding the competence and function of the Judiciary and the National Executive in ordering our relationships with other members of the international community must be treated exclusively as an aspect of federal law.[23] It seems fair to assume that the Court did not have rules like the act of state doctrine in mind when it decided Erie R. Co. v. Tompkins. Soon thereafter, Professor Philip C. Jessup, now a judge of the International Court of Justice, recognized the potential dangers were *Erie* extended to legal problems affecting international relations.[24] He cautioned that rules of international law should not be left to divergent and perhaps parochial state interpretations. His basic rationale is equally applicable to the act of state doctrine. . . .

We are not without other precedent for a determination that federal law governs; there are enclaves of federal judge-made law which bind the States. A national body of federal-court-built law has

23. At least this is true when the Court limits the scope of judicial inquiry. We need not now consider whether a state court might, in certain circumstances, adhere to a mere restrictive view concerning the scope of examination of foreign acts than that required by this Court.

24. The Doctrine of Erie Railroad v. Tompkins Applied to International Law, 33 Am.J.Int'l L. 740 (1939).

been held to have been contemplated by § 301 of the Labor Management Relations Act, Textile Workers Union of America v. Lincoln Mills, 353 U.S. 448. Principles formulated by federal judicial law have been thought by this Court to be necessary to protect uniquely federal interests, D'Oench, Duhme & Co. v. Federal Deposit Ins. Corp., 315 U.S. 447; Clearfield Trust Co. v. United States, 318 U.S. 363. Of course the federal interest guarded in all these cases is one the ultimate statement of which is derived from a federal statute. Perhaps more directly in point are the bodies of law applied between States over boundaries and in regard to the apportionment of interstate waters.

In Hinderlider v. La Plata River Co., 304 U.S. 92, 110, in an opinion handed down the same day as *Erie* and by the same author, Mr. Justice Brandeis, the Court declared, "For whether the water of an interstate stream must be apportioned between the two States is a question of 'federal common law' upon which neither the statutes nor the decisions of either State can be conclusive." Although the suit was between two private litigants and the relevant States could not be made parties, the Court considered itself free to determine the effect of an interstate compact regulating water apportionment. The decision implies that no State can undermine the federal interest in equitably apportioned interstate waters even if it deals with private parties. This would not mean that, absent a compact, the apportionment scheme could not be changed judicially, or by Congress, but only that apportionment is a matter of federal law. . . . The problems surrounding the act of state doctrine are, albeit for different reasons, as intrinsically federal as are those involved in water apportionment or boundary disputes. The considerations supporting exclusion of state authority here are much like those which led the Court in United States v. California, 332 U.S. 19, to hold that the Federal Government possessed paramount rights in submerged lands though within the three-mile limit of coastal States. We conclude that the scope of the act of state doctrine must be determined according to federal law.[25]

[Because a challenge to the Cuban decree would "be likely to give offense to the expropriating country" and "could seriously interfere with negotiations being carried on by the Executive Branch," the Court held the decree could not be challenged. Justice White, in dissent, did not dispute the conclusion that the issue was one of federal law.] *

25. Various constitutional and statutory provisions indirectly support this determination, see U.S.Const., Art. I, § 8, cls. 3, 10; Art. II, §§ 2, 3; Art. III, § 2; 28 U.S.C. §§ 1251 (a) (2), (b) (1), (b) (3), 1332(a) (2), 1333, 1350–1351, by reflecting a concern for uniformity in this country's dealings with foreign nations and indicating a desire to give matters of international significance to the jurisdiction of federal institutions. . . .

* In response to *Sabbatino* Congress adopted the Hickenlooper Amendment, 78 Stat. 1009, 1013 (1964), 22 U.S.C. § 2370(e)(2), forbidding American courts to invoke the act-of-state doctrine without executive prodding in any case based upon a post-1958 confiscation "in violation of the principles of international law." This amendment, clearly designed to be retroactive, was applied to defeat Cuba's claim on remand in *Sabbatino*, Banco Nacional v. Farr, 383 F.2d 166, 177–178 (2d Cir. 1967), over the objection, cf. *United States v. Klein*, supra, p. 104, that to do so would permit Congress to frustrate the Supreme

Notes on Federal Common Law, Preemption, and Incorporation of State Law

(1) Friendly, In Praise of Erie—and of the New Federal Common Law, 39 N.Y.U.L.Rev. 383, 407, 421 (1964):

> By focusing judicial attention on the nature of the right being enforced, *Erie* caused the principle of a specialized federal common law, binding in all courts because of its source, to develop within a quarter century into a powerful unifying force. . . . The Supreme Court, in the years since *Erie* has been forging a new centripetal tool incalculably useful to our federal system. It has employed a variety of techniques—spontaneous generation as in the cases of government contracts [Priebe & Sons, Inc. v. United States, 332 U.S. 407 (1947)] or interstate controversies [See Hinderlider v. La Plata River & Cherry Creek Ditch Co., 304 U.S. 92, 110 (1938)], implication of a private federal cause of action from a statute providing other sanctions, construing a jurisdictional grant as a command to fashion federal law, and the normal judicial filling of statutory interstices.

(2) What was the source of authority for the creation of federal common law in *Clearfield* and in *Sabbatino*? As those opinions demonstrate, the Supreme Court has not always been very explicit on this question. An obvious possibility in *Clearfield* would have been to hold that the grant of jurisdiction over cases to which the United States is a party, like those in admiralty cases and suits between States, see pp. 333–35 supra, and unlike the diversity grant, gives the courts lawmaking powers. Some lower courts have so indicated, e.g., Tri-State Ins. Co. v. United States, 340 F.2d 542, 544 (8th Cir. 1965); RFC v. United Distillers Corp., 229 F.2d 665, 666 (2d Cir. 1956), but the Supreme Court seems never to have said so. Hamilton was cryptic as to the reasons for this grant of jurisdiction: "Controversies between the nation and its members or citizens, can only be properly referred to the national tribunals. Any other plan would be contrary to reason, to precedent, and to decorum." The Federalist, No. 80. Do you suppose the framers of Article III meant only to protect the Government from bias in the administration of state law, and to leave the definition of its rights to the States in the absence of Congressional action?

In other cases federal statutes have been held to give the courts lawmaking authority. For example, in *Textile Workers v. Lincoln Mills*, supra p. 147, the Supreme Court held that the purposes of the Taft-Hartley Act demanded a federal judge-made law respecting the enforcement of collective-bargaining agreements although the statute spoke only of jurisdiction (accord, Machinists v. Central Airlines, 372 U.S. 682 (1963) (Railway Labor Act)). There is no constitutional objection to a congressional grant of common-law power, is there? Compare the rather rusty doctrines limiting delegation of congressional powers to the executive, Schechter Poultry Corp. v. United States, 295 U.S. 495 (1935), and to the States, Knickerbocker Ice Co. v. Stewart, 253 U.S. 149 (1920). Is it fair to say that the Court in *Clearfield* based its lawmaking authority on statutes and regulations adopt-

Court's mandate. Was there substance to this objection?

ed under the money powers of Congress? Can *Sabbatino* be explained in this fashion? See the attempt in footnote 25 of the opinion to suggest a statutory or constitutional source.

Is *Sabbatino* best understood as an example of what Judge Friendly calls "spontaneous generation?" Though in the two cases he cites for this technique the Court did not specify the basis for its power, both decisions fit easily into the traditional pattern. *Priebe* applied federal common law to determine the validity of a liquidated-damages clause in a government contract authorized by federal statute, in a case to which the United States was a party. *Hinderlider* was a diversity case concerning the division of water in a stream under an interstate compact approved by Congress; the construction of the compact, like that of a federal statute, was a federal question, Petty v. Tennessee-Missouri Bridge Comm., 359 U.S. 275, 278 (1959), and the Court could draw upon the common law it had power to develop in a suit between the States over the same water. Cf. United States v. Standard Oil Co., 332 U.S. 301, 305–311 (1947), holding the Government's right to recover for injuries to a soldier not governed by state law:

> The matter in issue is neither primarily one of state interest nor exclusively for determination by state law within the spirit and purpose of the *Erie* decision. . . . [*Erie*'s] object and effect were . . . to bring federal judicial power under subjection to state authority in matters essentially of local interest and state control. Conversely there was no purpose or effect for broadening state power over matters essentially of federal character. . . .

Does this language authorize the courts to create a federal common law of injuries to trespassers upon interstate railroads, on the basis of the commerce power? Isn't this theory contrary to the Rules of Decision Act? Isn't *Sabbatino*? [1]

The questions posed in this note underline the important point that the *Erie* doctrine is not limited to diversity cases; even in a federal-question case, as well illustrated by bankruptcy proceedings, some issues may be governed by state law: "The federal courts may make substantive law only in effectuation of a policy derived from the Constitution or from a valid act of Congress." Hill, The Erie Doctrine in Bankruptcy, 66 Harv.L.Rev. 1013, 1050 (1953).

(3) Friendly, supra note 1, 39 N.Y.U.L.Rev. at 410:

> *Clearfield* decided not one issue but two. The first, to which most of the opinion was devoted and on which it is undeniably sound, is that the right of the United States to recover for conversion of a Government check is a federal right, so that the courts of the United States may formulate a rule of decision. The second, over which the Supreme

1. In Illinois v. City of Milwaukee, 406 U.S. 91 (1972), an original action in the Supreme Court seeking to enjoin interstate pollution was dismissed on the ground that the case could and should have been filed in a district court under 28 U.S.C. § 1331. Essential to this conclusion was the Court's determination that the case was governed by federal common law. See also City of Milwaukee v. Illinois, 451 U.S. 304 (1981), holding that the earlier decision had been rendered obsolete by the 1972 amendments to the Federal Water Pollution Control Act.

> Court jumped rather quickly and not altogether convincingly, is whether, having this opportunity, the federal courts should adopt a uniform nation-wide rule or should follow state law. . . . The question persists why it is more important that federal fiscal officials rather than Pennsylvanians dealing in commercial paper should have the solace of uniformity. The issue that must be determined in each instance is what heed Congress intended to have paid to state law in an area where no heed need constitutionally be paid—more realistically, in Gray's famous phrase, "to guess what it would have intended on a point not present to its mind, if the point had been present."

Suppose that after the Supreme Court's decision in *Clearfield* the bank sued J.C. Penney, its endorser, to make good its loss. Does *Parnell* mean that in the bank's action the issue of late notice is governed by state law? Would that be tolerable? See Mishkin, The Variousness of "Federal Law:" Competence and Discretion in the Choice of National and State Rules for Decision, 105 U.Pa.L.Rev. 797, 824–32 (1957).

(4) As *Parnell* indicates, issues respecting government contracts are not invariably governed by federal law. In United States v. Yazell, 382 U.S. 341 (1966), the Court's opinion by Justice Fortas began with a dead giveaway of the result: "The question presented is whether, in the circumstances of this case, the Federal Government, in its zealous pursuit of the balance due on a disaster loan made by the Small Business Administration, may obtain judgment against Ethel Mae Yazell of Lampasas, Texas." Less emotively put, the issue was whether Mrs. Yazell, who with her husband had signed a note payable to the United States, could defend on the basis of a Texas law limiting the contractual powers of married women. In large part the opinion rests upon the view that the parties contracted with Texas law in mind, so that the Government was suing to reach assets for which it had not bargained. But the Court also examined the competing interests and concluded that state coverture restrictions, like state homestead exemptions from execution, should be respected in the collection of such debts:

> The impact of the quaint doctrine of coverture upon the federal treasury is . . . of little consequence. Even the Texas law which gave rise to the difficulty was repealed in 1963. The amount in controversy in this extensive litigation, about $4,000, is important only to the Yazell family. . . . Undeniably there is always a federal interest to collect moneys which the Government lends. . . . Both theory and the precedents of this Court teach us solicitude for state interests, particularly in the field of family and family-property arrangments. . . . There is here no need for uniformity. There is no problem in complying with state law; in fact, SBA transactions in each State are specifically and in great detail adapted to state law.

Is *Yazell* to be read as remitting federal contracts to state law wholesale, or is it just a widows-and-orphans case?

(5) Further evidence of the difficulty of predicting when the Supreme Court will resort to federal common law is afforded by decisions concerning torts affecting the Government. Rather early it was established that the United States could sue for trespass although no federal statute said so:

"As an owner of property in almost every state of the Union, they [the United States] have the same right to have it protected by the local laws that other persons have." Cotton v. United States, 52 U.S. (11 How.) 229 (1850). And, still during the era of *Swift v. Tyson*, the Court held the measure of damages for the conversion of oil from federal land was a "local" matter governed by state law. Mason v. United States, 260 U.S. 545 (1923). Moreover, the Federal Tort Claims Act, 28 U.S.C. § 1346(b), enacted in 1946, explicitly makes the tort liability of the United States dependent in the main upon "the law of the place where the act or omission occurred," and as recently as 1963 the Supreme Court squarely held that the liability of a federal officer in tort, if any, had to be based upon state law. Wheeldin v. Wheeler, 373 U.S. 647, 652 (1963). Yet in Howard v. Lyons, 360 U.S. 593, 597 (1959), a diversity case, the Court held that the extent of the privilege accorded federal officers for official statements "allegedly defamatory under state law" was a matter of federal law:

> The authority of a federal officer to act derives from federal sources, and the rule which recognizes a privilege under appropriate circumstances as to statements made in the course of duty is one designed to promote the effective functioning of the Federal Government. No subject could be one of more peculiarly federal concern, and it would deny the very considerations which give the rule of privilege its being to leave determination of its extent to the vagaries of the laws of the several States. Cf. Clearfield Trust Co. v. United States, 318 U.S. 363. We hold that the validity of petitioner's claim of absolute privilege must be judged by federal standards, to be formulated by the courts in the absence of legislative action by Congress.

What sense is there in the distinction between *Howard* and *Wheeldin*? See also Bivens v. Six Unknown Named Agents of Federal Bur. of Narcotics, 403 U.S. 388 (1971), p. 401 infra, upholding a federal right of action for damages for violation of the Fourth Amendment.

(6) Closely related to the question whether a federal statute authorizes the creation of federal common law—indeed often blending imperceptibly with it—are the questions whether a federal statute either preempts or incorporates state law.

It seems mandatory to begin with Hart and Wechsler's famous insight, The Federal Courts and the Federal System 533 (3d ed. 1988):

> Federal law is generally interstitial in its nature. It rarely occupies a legal field completely, totally excluding all participation by the legal systems of the states. . . . It builds upon legal relationships established by the states, altering or supplanting them only so far as necessary for the special purpose. Congress acts, in short, against the background of the total *corpus juris* of the states in much the way that a state legislature acts against the background of the common law, assumed to govern unless changed by legislation. That this is so was partially affirmed in § 34 of the First Judiciary Act, now 28 U.S.C. § 1652 [state laws as rules of decision]. . . .

(7) State law that contradicts federal is outlawed by the Supremacy Clause. Whether there is a contradiction is often not so obvious; even such positive terms as a federal "permit" to trap fish, Kake Village v. Egan, 369

U.S. 60, 63–64 (1962), and a "discharge" of debts in bankruptcy, Kesler v. Department of Public Safety, 369 U.S. 153, 169–74 (1962), have been held to permit considerable state regulation. Although the Court has not always said so, it seems proper to say that the question in such cases is the familiar choice-of-law problem of accommodating conflicting governmental interests: Does the purpose of the federal law require subordination of state policy?

Thus, to give a few examples, in Teamsters v. Oliver, 358 U.S. 283 (1959), the Court forbade application of state antitrust law to a contract resulting from compulsory collective bargaining; in Warren Trading Post v. Arizona State Tax Comm'n, 380 U.S. 685 (1965), it held that the levy of a gross sales tax upon a licensed Indian trader was contrary to the federal licensing statute, whose most nearly relevant provision merely authorized a federal administrator to specify "the prices at which such goods shall be sold to the Indians." On the other hand, the Court allowed the States in *Kesler* to make a bankruptcy discharge no defense to the revocation of driving privileges for failure to satisfy an accident judgment, because of state interests in highway safety; and in *Kake* to conserve salmon by prohibiting fish traps, reading federal permits only to indicate lack of objection to the use of National Forest land and to the obstruction of navigable streams.

Somewhat less obvious in principle, but resting basically upon the same process of construction in the light of state and federal policies, are decisions holding that federal laws preclude application of state laws with parallel rather than with contrary effect. In this category fall, for example, the controversial Pennsylvania v. Nelson, 350 U.S. 497 (1956), which held that state laws against subverting the national government might interfere with enforcement of the substantially identical federal Smith Act; the decision in Mondou v. New York, N. H. & H. R. R., 223 U.S. 1, 55 (1912), that the FELA forbade application of state laws to employees' personal-injury actions against interstate railroads; Sears, Roebuck & Co. v. Stiffel Co. and Compco Corp. v. Day-Brite Lighting, Inc., 376 U.S. 225 and 234 (1964), forbidding a State "to prevent the copying of an article which represents too slight an advance to be patented", and Garner v. Teamsters Union, 346 U.S. 485 (1953), which forbade state injunctions against activities *prohibited* by the Labor-Management Relations Act because the disuniformity and possible conflict caused by parallel state and federal remedies would contravene the federal policy expressed by the statutory vesting of jurisdiction in the National Labor Relations Board.

(8) Sometimes, as in the Tort Claims Act (supra note 5), Congress expressly incorporates state law to determine federal rights. In other cases federal statutes have been held to refer to state law although they were silent on the question. See, for example, De Sylva v. Ballentine, 351 U.S. 570, 580–82 (1956), in which the Court (by Harlan, J.) looked to state law in holding that an illegitimate child came within the statutory provision for renewal of a copyright by the "children" of a deceased author:

> The scope of a federal right is, of course, a federal question but that does not mean that its content is not to be determined by state, rather than federal law. . . . This is especially true where a statute

deals with a familial relationship; there is no federal law of domestic relations, which is primarily a matter of state concern.

See also Holmberg v. Armbrecht, 327 U.S. 392 (1946):

> Congress has usually left the limitation of time for commencing actions under national legislation to judicial implications. As to actions at law, the silence of Congress has been interpreted to mean that it is federal policy to adopt the local law of limitations.

(9) To what extent does the Rules of Decision Act dictate the answer to the cases discussed in these notes?

Notes on Federal and State Laws in Maritime Cases

(1) As pointed out above, p. 334, the Supreme Court has found in the constitutional grant of federal admiralty jurisdiction authority to construct federal decisional law. It has also deduced from this grant and the Necessary and Proper Clause a congressional power to alter and supplement those decisions, see Panama R. R. v. Johnson, 264 U.S. 375 (1924). These federal lawmaking powers, however, have not been held entirely exclusive. The applicability of state law in maritime cases illustrates in rather large microcosm the full range of pre-emption and incorporation problems discussed in the preceding notes. These issues are considered in detail in D. Currie, Federalism and the Admiralty: "The Devil's Own Mess," 1960 Sup.Ct.Rev. 158.

(2) Elementary is the principle that state law cannot subtract from a right given by federal decisional law created under the admiralty power. See, for example, Pope & Talbot, Inc. v. Hawn, 346 U.S. 406 (1953), holding that the federal doctrine of comparative fault, not a state law of contributory negligence, governed in an action for personal injuries sustained aboard a ship in navigable waters. What is not always so obvious, just as in cases based upon federal statutes, is whether or not application of state law would impair a federal right. For example, in Kossick v. United Fruit Co., 365 U.S. 731 (1961), the Court reaffirmed an earlier holding that maritime contracts were not subject to state statutes of frauds, invoking the Supremacy Clause: "It is an established rule of ancient respectability that oral contracts are generally regarded as valid by maritime law." But is it clear that the absence of a writing requirement in admiralty reflects a policy of contractual freedom rather than a felt judicial inability to formulate the details of a statute of frauds? Compare admiralty's willingness before the enactment of a federal statute of limitations for maritime torts (46 U.S.C. App. § 763a) to refer to state law or to related federal statutes for a time limitation to use as a yardstick for applying the maritime doctrine of laches, Czaplicki v. The S.S. Hoegh Silvercloud, 351 U.S. 525, 533–34 (1956); McAllister v. Magnolia Petroleum Co., 357 U.S. 221 (1958).

(3) At one time it might have appeared that the simple principle of federal supremacy in cases of direct conflict was the only limitation placed on state law by the federal admiralty power. Thus Justice White, in an early opinion holding a state rule of municipal tort immunity could not defeat relief under maritime law, Workman v. New York City, 179 U.S. 552, 563 (1900), observed by way of contrast that state statutes "giving a

right to relief" were adopted by the admiralty with "alacrity." It is true that the Rules of Decision Act, now 28 U.S.C. § 1652, originally spoke only of suits at "common law" and was sometimes said not to apply in admiralty, see New England Newspaper Pub. Co. v. United States, 18 F.Supp. 674, 679 (D.Mass.1937), although the principle it embodied had long been applied in equity, see *Guaranty Trust Co. v. York*, supra p. 336, and although the statute itself has been invoked in suits based upon federal statutes, e.g., Moviecolor Ltd. v. Eastman Kodak Co., 288 F.2d 80, 85–86 (2d Cir. 1961). But the statutory grant of admiralty jurisdiction, otherwise "exclusive," has always contained a peculiar clause "saving to suitors, in all cases, the right of a common law remedy where the common law is competent to give it," 1 Stat. 76–77 (1789), amended in 1948 to save to suitors "all other remedies to which they are otherwise entitled," 28 U.S.C. § 1333. To Justice Holmes this clause afforded recourse not only to state courts but to state law as well: If federal jurisdiction carried with it lawmaking powers, so did state jurisdiction. Consequently, before 1917 the Supreme Court never required the application of federal maritime law in an action in a common-law court; and in The Hamilton, 207 U.S. 398 (1907), the Court in a Holmes opinion enforced a state wrongful-death statute in admiralty, just as it would have enforced the law of a foreign country in an appropriate case.

A second theory, propounded by Justice Holmes in his dissent from Southern Pacific Co. v. Jensen, 244 U.S. 205, 220 (1917), suggested at least part of the same result: "The maritime law is not a *corpus juris*—it is a very limited body of customs and ordinances of the sea"—an incomplete system whose gaps could be filled by resort to state law.

(4) These simplistic doctrines have not survived. In the first place an absence of precedent need not indicate an absence of policy, for the general maritime law, like judge-made law in general, is subject to judicial growth. See, e.g., the massive judicial operations performed upon the unseaworthiness doctrine, e.g., Seas Shipping Co. v. Sieracki, 328 U.S. 85 (1946). Moreover, as early as 1903 it was made clear that there were federal interests in maritime cases in addition to those reflecting upon the substantive desirability of particular rules. The Court held in The Roanoke, 189 U.S. 185 (1903), that a State had no power to create liability against a foreign ship for supplies ordered by an independent contractor. In part the decision was based upon antipathy to the policy of the State law; but the Court also stressed the inability of the master "to acquaint himself with the laws of each individual State he must visit," thus suggesting a preemptive effect for the unimplemented Admiralty Clause comparable to that of the Commerce Clause. This preemptive uniformity doctrine became the third prong of Justice McReynolds's notorious opinion holding that a state workers'-compensation law could not constitutionally give relief for the death of a longshoreman whose head had collided with a vessel on navigable waters:

> No [state] . . . legislation is valid if it contravenes the essential purpose expressed by an act of Congress or works material prejudice to the characteristic features of the general maritime law or interferes

with the proper harmony and uniformity of that law in its international and interstate relations.

Southern Pacific Co. v. Jensen, 244 U.S. 205, 216 (1917).

The uniformity doctrine was understandable enough and unimportant enough, in light of the corresponding decisions under the Commerce Clause, except that, for no reason that suggests itself, admiralty preemption was carried to much greater lengths. The Commerce Clause, for one thing, was never held by the Supreme Court to prohibit application of state workers'-compensation laws.[1] Moreover, the Court held, and reaffirmed for an incredulous Congress, that the Constitution even forbade congressional removal of the barrier to state workers' compensation for maritime workers, Knickerbocker Ice Co. v. Stewart, 253 U.S. 149 (1920); Washington v. W. C. Dawson & Co., 264 U.S. 219 (1924), despite contrary analogies under the Commerce Clause, e.g., Clark Distilling Co. v. Western Md. Ry., 242 U.S. 311 (1917). It seems unlikely that *Knickerbocker* and *Dawson* would be adhered to today; see the dictum of Mr. Justice Black for the Court in Wilburn Boat Co. v. Fireman's Fund Ins. Co., 348 U.S. 310, 321 n. 29 (1955), rejecting the suggestion that a state law affecting marine insurance would be invalid even if sanctioned by Congress as "so lacking in merit that it need not be discussed."

Even Justice McReynolds, however, managed to discover "maritime but local" cases in which state law did not conflict with any need for uniformity. See, e.g., Sultan Ry. & Timber Co. v. Department of Labor, 277 U.S. 135 (1928), holding that a State was free to award workers' compensation to an essentially stationary employee of a lumber mill injured while fastening logs together in a navigable river. In such a case, indeed, application of maritime law would create disuniformity by making the outcome depend upon whether the injury occurred on land or in the water. But the Court was rather niggardly in applying the local doctrine. In *Jensen*, where the deceased longshoreman had been employed by a shipowner engaged in interstate operations, the argument for uniformity made sense; but the Court unblinkingly applied the same rule to all longshoremen and seamen, even those seeking compensation from employers whose entire business was localized. E.g., Washington v. W. C. Dawson & Co., 264 U.S. 219 (1924); London Guar. & Acc. Co. v. Industrial Acc. Comm'n, 279 U.S. 109 (1929).

(5) *Jensen* put a definitive end to the earlier unpalatable notion, see note 3, supra, that decisional maritime law and the uniformity doctrine were applicable only in admiralty proceedings in the federal court. The Court hammered this point home, after a momentary lapse in Caldarola v. Eckert, 332 U.S. 155 (1947), in Pope & Talbot, Inc. v. Hawn, 346 U.S. 406, 411 (1953), where it had been argued that state law ought to govern as to contributory negligence because the injured maritime worker had invoked the diversity rather than the admiralty jurisdiction:

> We are asked to use the *Erie-Tompkins* case to bring about the same kind of unfairness it was designed to end. . . . The substantial

1. See Valley S.S. Co. v. Wattawa, 244 U.S. 202 (1917), upholding such a law against Commerce Clause objections where the Admiralty Clause had not been properly invoked.

> rights of an injured person are not to be determined differently whether his case is labelled "law side" or "admiralty side." . . .

Accord, Garrett v. Moore-McCormack Co., 317 U.S. 239 (1942), holding federal decisional law governed in state court the burden of proving fraud in obtaining a release from judicially created liability for a seaman's injury.

(6) Congress tried its best to leave maritime workers' compensation to the States; even after the failure of its two attempts to delegate the entire matter, it provided federal coverage only if recovery "may not validly be provided by State law." 44 Stat. 1426 (1927), 33 U.S.C. § 903. The maritime-but-local doctrine, apparently referred to by the quoted clause, had first been applied five years before, in Grant Smith-Porter Ship Co. v. Rohde, 257 U.S. 469 (1922), and the natural assumption was that Congress had meant to preserve that doctrine in order to leave as much as possible to state law. But the line distinguishing local cases was elusive. Building a ship, for example, was local, *Grant Smith-Porter Ship Co. v. Rohde*, supra; repairing one was not, Messel v. Foundation Co., 274 U.S. 427 (1927). (This particular distinction was lent authority, though not plausibility, by the traditional doctrine that shipbuilding contracts are nonmaritime, see p. 214 supra.) The claimant who made the wrong choice suffered delay and sometimes found recovery barred by time; with tenderer regard for human discomfort than for the statutory scheme, the Court in Davis v. Department of Labor, 317 U.S. 249 (1942), over the biting dissent of Chief Justice Stone, created a "twilight zone" in which, by presuming the constitutionality of state laws and the correctness of federal administrative findings, the courts would uphold either a state or a federal award. Citing *Davis*, later memorandum decisions even managed to uphold awards by what previous Supreme Court decisions clearly indicated was the wrong agency, Baskin v. Industrial Accident Comm'n, 338 U.S. 854 (1949); Bethlehem Steel Co. v. Moore, 335 U.S. 874 (1948).

But it required all the wiles of Justice Brennan to wipe the entire unmanageable edifice from the map by unearthing legislative history to support the extension of the federal remedy to all injuries on navigable waters, whether or not (as in the cases before him, which involved ship construction) state law could constitutionally be applied. The federal compensation act, he said, was designed not only to fill the gap in coverage opened by *Jensen* but also to eliminate the uncertainty of the maritime-but-local doctrine. And the proviso that federal law applied only "if recovery . . . may not validly be provided by State law?"

> By that language Congress reiterated that the Act reached all those cases of injury to employees on navigable waters as to which *Jensen, Knickerbocker* and *Dawson* had rendered questionable the availability of a state compensation remedy. Congress brought under the coverage of the Act all such injuries whether or not a particular one was also within the constitutional reach of a state workmen's compensation law.

Calbeck v. Travelers Insurance Co., 370 U.S. 114, 126–27 (1962). This double-talk prompted dissents by Justices Stewart and Harlan:

> I seriously doubt whether statutory language as clear as that in 33 U.S.C. § 903(a) could ever be ignored in the name of effectuating the

> supposed "Congressional desire." Be that as it may, this particular statutory language does in fact reflect the purpose of Congress, which was only to provide compensation for those whom this Court's decisions had barred from the benefits of state workmen's compensation laws. And at the time of the passage of this federal law the Court had squarely held, as Congress well knew, that state workmen's compensation remedies *were* constitutionally available to workers who, as in the present cases, were engaged in new ship construction on navigable waters.

370 U.S. at 132–33.

Congress confirmed *Calbeck* in 1972, 86 Stat. 1251, by dropping the obsolete limitation; it further extended federal coverage by redefining "navigable waters" to include "any adjoining pier, wharf, dry dock, terminal, building way, marine railway, or other adjoining area customarily used by an employer in loading, unloading, repairing, or building a vessel." For interpretation of the new limits see Northeast Marine Terminal Co. v. Caputo, 432 U.S. 249 (1977), and P. C. Pfeiffer Co. v. Ford, 444 U.S. 69 (1979). Do the judicial and statutory extensions of federal coverage mean that states can no longer provide compensation for local maritime workers? According to 33 U.S.C. § 905, liability under the federal act is "exclusive . . . of all other liability . . . to the employee" or his dependents. Nevertheless the Court allowed a state to compensate a worker within the extended federal coverage of the 1972 amendments, saying that *Davis* and *Calbeck* "did not construe § 905(a) to exclude remedies offered by other jurisdictions." Sun Ship, Inc. v. Pennsylvania, 447 U.S. 715, 723 n. 4 (1980).

(7) In striking down the maritime application of New York's workers'-compensation law in *Jensen,* Justice McReynolds acknowledged that precedent had allowed the States to provide "the right given to recover in death cases." A few years later McReynolds himself held that state wrongful-death statutes could be applied to maritime cases because they were "local"—even though the case before him concerned a longshoreman, to whom state workers' compensation would clearly have been denied in the interest of uniformity by precedents directly in point. Western Fuel Co. v. Garcia, 257 U.S. 233 (1921). In the context of wrongful death, therefore, "local" referred not to the intrastate nature of the particular case but to the conclusion, earlier spelled out by Judge Addison Brown in The City of Norwalk, 55 Fed. 98, 108 (S.D.N.Y.1893), that wrongful-death statutes in general reflected state policy "to protect life" and did not interfere with "needful uniformity" in maritime law. It was rather clear, too, that there was no federal maritime policy opposed to wrongful-death recoveries in general on substantive grounds; when the Supreme Court first held the maritime law gave no such remedy, it was because admiralty left the matter "untouched" and "it is the duty of courts to declare the law, not to make it." The Harrisburg, 119 U.S. 199, 213–14 (1886).

(8) Enactment of the Death on the High Seas Act and the Jones Act in 1920 (now 46 U.S.C. §§ 761, 688) left much wrongful-death business to state law, for the former statute applied only outside the States and the latter only to seamen. The Tungus v. Skovgaard, 358 U.S. 588 (1959) (5–4

decision), held that a death action for unseaworthiness lay only if the State would hold unseaworthiness a "wrongful act" under its death law: " 'If the admiralty adopts the statute as a rule of right to be administered within its own jurisdiction, it must take the right subject to the limitations which have been made a part of its existence.' " This argument is unassailable, isn't it, if as the Court thought state death statutes were applied out of respect for state policy? Concurring in the result, Justice Brennan argued that, as in cases applying state statutes of limitation to federal rights, see p. 364 supra, state death statutes were utilized to further federal rather than state policy—to provide for remedial details, perhaps too specific for a court to fashion comfortably, for the enforcement of a *federal* policy favoring recovery for death caused by unseaworthiness. Isn't it clear that in implementing such a federal policy the Court may pick and choose as it wishes among the provisions of state law? [1]

(9) In Hess v. United States, 361 U.S. 314 (1960), the Court said *The Tungus* allowed application in a maritime case of a state statute imposing liability upon an employer for injury caused by failure to "use every device, care and precaution which it is practicable to use for the protection and safety of life and limb." Justices Harlan and Frankfurter dissented: The state law in *Hess*, unlike that in *The Tungus*, imposed substantive duties beyond those of the maritime law; in such a case Chelentis v. Luckenbach S.S. Co., 247 U.S. 372 (1918), had held state law could not provide recovery for injuries short of death. "Where the duty imposed by a state death act is no greater than that already existing under federal law," as in *The Tungus*, state law could be applied because "there is no real encroachment on federal interests." But "when a State purports, as here, to impose a duty which under federal law a person does not bear, . . . the intrusion into federally regulated interests is no longer minimal."

Was *Hess* wrong, or were the cases denying personal-injury relief under state law?

The *Tungus* problem was made moot, to the displeasure only of scholars who thrive on confusion, by Moragne v. States Marine Lines, 398 U.S. 375 (1970), which held there was a federal maritime right to recover for death resulting from unseaworthiness. What remains of *Hess* after *Moragne*?

(10) *Hess v. United States*, supra note 9, did not establish the demise of the uniformity doctrine in maritime cases. Despite the startling decision in Wilburn Boat Co. v. Fireman's Fund Ins. Co., 348 U.S. 310 (1955), which allowed state law to excuse strict adherence to warranties in a marine insurance policy that the majority of the Court refused to characterize as "maritime but local," the Court reaffirmed the need for uniformity in holding, after *Hess*, that a state statute of frauds was ineffective to defeat relief on a shipowner's contract to assume responsibility for improper

1. Cf. Pearson v. Northeast Airlines, Inc., 309 F.2d 553 (2d Cir. 1962), applying a foreign wrongful-death statute to an action for the death of a resident of the forum State but ignoring the foreign ceiling on damages as contrary to public policy: Because New York had "a legitimate constitutional interest in the application of its own rules of law," it was free to "absorb" the Massachusetts rule into the corpus of New York law without binding itself to respect every facet of the foreign law.

treatment of a crewman in a public hospital. Not only did the Court find a federal policy in favor of upholding oral contracts:

> Considering that sailors of any nationality may join a ship in any port, and that it is the clear duty of the ship to put into the first available port if this be necessary to provide prompt and adequate maintenance and cure to a seaman who falls ill during the voyage, . . . it seems to us that this is such a contract as may well have been made anywhere in the world, and that the validity of it should be judged by one law wherever it was made.

Kossick v. United Fruit Co., 365 U.S. 731 (1961).[2]

(11) To what extent is the rule of *Klaxon Co. v. Stentor Elec. Co.*, supra p. 347, applicable in maritime cases or in others based upon federal law? The question has been little discussed in the cases. When the choice is between federal law and the law of a foreign country, application of state choice-of-law doctrines would be simply silly; the question, as the Supreme Court has made clear, is essentially one of construing the federal statute or rule in the light of foreign interests, and there is no reason to inject disuniformity. See., e.g., Lauritzen v. Larsen, 345 U.S. 571 (1953), determining the foreign applicability of the Jones Act without mentioning *Klaxon*; Siegelman v. Cunard White Star, Ltd., 221 F.2d 189, 192–93 (2d Cir. 1955), expressly rejecting *Klaxon* in deciding between federal and English law respecting the effect of a time limitation for injury claims in a contract of ocean passage. Perhaps, Judge Harlan conceded, *Klaxon* might apply even in admiralty if the claim were based upon a "state-created right," as was then true in wrongful-death cases; even in such a case, however, "it is possible that the federal court would not be bound by the state's choice-of-law rule, unless the rule limited the scope of the right."

The problem of choosing between state laws in maritime cases, left open in *Siegelman*, was vividly presented in Scott v. Eastern Air Lines, 399 F.2d 14 (3d Cir. 1967), an action for wrongful death arising from an airplane crash in navigable waters. A divided court, without giving reasons, held that because the tort claim was maritime (but see *Executive Jet Aviation v. City of Cleveland*, supra p. 218), it was governed by federal choice-of-law principles. Do you agree? See generally D. Currie, The Choice Among State Laws in Maritime Death Cases, 21 Vand.L.Rev. 297 (1968).

TRANSAMERICA MORTGAGE ADVISORS, INC. v. LEWIS

444 U.S. 11 (1979).

MR. JUSTICE STEWART delivered the opinion of the Court.

The Investment Advisers Act of 1940, 15 U.S.C. § 80b–1 et seq., was enacted to deal with abuses that Congress had found to exist in the

2. See also Askew v. American Waterways Operators, Inc., 411 U.S. 325 (1973), upholding a Florida statute providing compensation for shore damage caused by oil spills in navigable waters: *Jensen* and *Knickerbocker* had been "confined to their facts, *viz.* to suits relating to the relationship of vessels, plying the high seas and our navigable waters, to their crews. . . . We decline to move the *Jensen* line of cases shoreward to oust state law from situations involving shoreside injuries by ships on navigable waters."

investment advisers industry. The question in this case is whether that Act creates a private cause of action for damages or other relief in favor of persons aggrieved by those who allegedly have violated it.

The respondent, a shareholder of petitioner Mortgage Trust of America (Trust), brought this suit in a Federal District Court, . . . alleg[ing] that the petitioners in the course of advising or managing the Trust had been guilty of various frauds and breaches of fiduciary duty. . . . The trial court ruled that the Investment Advisers Act confers no private right of action, and accordingly dismissed the complaint. The Court of Appeals reversed . . . .

The Investment Advisers Act nowhere expressly provides for a private cause of action. The only provision of the Act that authorizes any suits to enforce the duties or obligations created by it is § 209, which permits the Securities and Exchange Commission (Commission) to bring suit in a federal district court to enjoin violations of the Act or the rules promulgated under it. The argument is made, however, that the clients of investment advisers were the intended beneficiaries of the Act and that courts should therefore imply a private cause of action in their favor. See Cannon v. University of Chicago, 441 U.S. 677, 689; Cort v. Ash, 422 U.S. 66, 78; J. I. Case v. Borak, 377 U.S. 426, 432.

The question whether a statute creates a cause of action, either expressly or by implication, is basically a matter of statutory construction. Touche Ross & Co. v. Redington, 442 U.S. 560, 568; *Cannon v. University of Chicago,* supra, at 688; see National Railroad Passenger Corp. v. National Association of Railroad Passengers, 414 U.S. 453, 458 (hereinafter *Amtrak*). While some opinions of the Court have placed considerable emphasis upon the desirability of implying private rights of action in order to provide remedies thought to effectuate the purposes of a given statute, e.g., *J. I. Case Co. v. Borak,* supra, what must ultimately be determined is whether Congress intended to create the private remedy asserted, as our recent decisions have made clear. . . .

Accordingly, we begin with the language of the statute itself. . . . It is asserted that the creation of a private right of action can fairly be inferred from the language of two sections of the Act. The first is § 206, which broadly proscribes fraudulent practices by investment advisers, making it unlawful for any investment adviser "to employ any device, scheme, or artifice to defraud . . . [or] to engage in any transaction, practice, or course of business which operates as a fraud or deceit upon any client or prospective client," or to engage in specified transactions with clients without making required disclosures. The second is § 215, which provides that contracts whose formation or performance would violate the Act "shall be void . . . as regards the rights of" the violator and knowing successors in interest.

It is apparent that the two sections were intended to benefit the clients of investment advisers, and, in the case of § 215, the parties to advisory contracts as well. As we have previously recognized, § 206 establishes "federal fiduciary standards" to govern the conduct of investment advisers. . . . Indeed, the Act's legislative history leaves no doubt that Congress intended to impose enforceable fiduciary obligations. . . . But whether Congress intended additionally that these provisions would be enforced through private litigation is a different question. . . .

In the case of § 215, we conclude that the statutory language itself fairly implies a right to specific and limited relief in a federal court. By declaring certain contracts void, § 215 by its terms necessarily contemplates that the issue of voidness under its criteria may be litigated somewhere. At the very least Congress must have assumed that § 215 could be raised defensively in private litigation to preclude the enforcement of an investment advisers contract. But the legal consequences of voidness are typically not so limited. A person with the power to void a contract ordinarily may resort to a court to have the contract rescinded and to obtain restitution of consideration paid. . . . Accordingly, we hold that the Court of Appeals was correct in ruling that the respondent may maintain an action on behalf of the Trust seeking to void the investment advisers contract.

We view quite differently, however, the respondent's claims for damages and other monetary relief under § 206. Unlike § 215, § 206 simply proscribes certain conduct, and does not in terms create or alter any civil liabilities. If monetary liability to a private plaintiff is to be found, it must be read into the Act. Yet it is an elemental canon of statutory construction that where a statute expressly provides a particular remedy or remedies, a court must be chary of reading others into it. . . . See *Amtrak,* supra, 414 U.S., at 458. . . . Congress expressly provided both judicial and administrative means for enforcing compliance with § 206. First, under § 217 willful violations of the Act are criminal offenses, punishable by fine or imprisonment, or both. Second, § 209 authorizes the Commission to bring civil actions in federal courts to enjoin compliance with the Act, including, of course, § 206. Third, the Commission is authorized by § 203 to impose various administrative sanctions on persons who violate the Act, including § 206. In view of these express provisions for enforcing the duties imposed by § 206, it is highly improbable that "Congress absentmindedly forgot to mention an intended private action." Cannon v. University of Chicago, 441 U.S., at 742 (Powell, J., dissenting).

Even settled rules of statutory construction could yield, of course, to persuasive evidence of a contrary legislative intent. . . . But what evidence of intent exists in this case, circumstantial though it be, weighs against the implication of a private right of action for a monetary award in a case such as this. Under each of the securities laws that preceded the Act here in question, and under the Investment Company Act which was enacted as companion legislation, Congress expressly authorized private suits for damages in prescribed circumstances. For example, Congress provided an express damage remedy for misrepresentations contained in an underwriter's registration statement in § 11(a) of the Securities Act of 1933, and for certain materially misleading statements in § 18(a) of the Secruties Exchange Act of 1934. "Obviously, then, when Congress wished to provide a private damage remedy, it knew how to do so and did so expressly." . . . The fact that it enacted no analogous provisions in the legislation here at issue strongly suggests that Congress was simply unwilling to impose any potential monetary liability to a private suitor. . . .

Relying on the factors identified in *Cort v. Ash*, supra, the respondent and the Commission, as *amicus curiae*, argue that our inquiry in this case cannot stop with the intent of Congress, but must consider the utility of a private remedy, and the fact that it may be one not traditionally relegated to state law. We rejected the same contentions last Term in *Touche Ross & Co. v. Redington*, supra, where it was argued that these factors standing alone justified the implication of a private right of action under § 17(a) of the Securities Exchange Act of 1934. We said in that case:

> "It is true that in *Cort v. Ash*, supra, the Court set forth four factors that it considered 'relevant' in determining whether a private remedy is implicit in a statute not expressly providing one. But the Court did not decide that each of these factors is entitled to equal weight. The central inquiry remains whether Congress intended to create, either expressly or by implication, a private cause of action. Indeed, the first three factors discussed in *Cort*—the language and focus of the statute, its legislative history, and its purpose, . . .—are ones traditionally relied upon in determining legislative intent." . . .

The statute in *Touche Ross* by its terms neither granted private rights to the members of any identifiable class, nor proscribed any conduct as unlawful. . . . In those circumstances it was evident to the Court that no private remedy was available. Section 206 of the Act here involved concededly was intended to protect the victims of the fraudulent practices it prohibited. But the mere fact that the statute was designed to protect advisers' clients does not require the implication of a private cause of action for damages on their behalf. Touche Ross & Co. v. Redington, supra, 442 U.S., at 578; Cannon v. University of Chicago, supra, 441 U.S., at 690–93; . . . . The dispositive question remains whether Congress intended to create any such remedy. Having answered that question in the negative, our inquiry is at an end.

For the reasons stated in this opinion, we hold that there exists a limited private remedy under the Investment Advisers Act of 1940 to void an investment advisers contract, but that the Act confers no other private causes of action, legal or equitable. Accordingly, the judgment of the Court of Appeals is affirmed in part and reversed in part, and the case is remanded to that Court for further proceedings consistent with this opinion. . . .

MR. JUSTICE WHITE, with whom MR. JUSTICE BRENNAN, MR. JUSTICE MARSHALL, and MR. JUSTICE STEVENS join, dissenting. . . .

I

This Court has long recognized that private rights of action do not require express statutory authorization. Texas & Pacific R. Co. v. Rigsby, 241 U.S. 33 (1916); Tunstall v. Brotherhood of Locomotive Firemen & Enginemen, 323 U.S. 210 (1944). The preferred approach for determining whether a private right of action should be implied from a federal statute was outlined in Cort v. Ash, 422 U.S. 66, 78 (1975). . . . Four factors were thought relevant; [3] and although subsequent decisions have indicated that the implication of a private right of action "is limited solely to determining whether Congress intended to create the private right of action," . . . these four factors are "the criteria through which this intent could be discerned." Davis v. Passman, 442 U.S. 228, 241 (1979). Proper application of the factors outlined in *Cort* clearly indicates that § 206 of the Act, 15 U.S.C. § 80b–6, creates a private right of action.

II . . .

The Court concedes that the language and legislative history of § 206 leave no doubt that it was "intended to benefit the clients of investment advisers," . . ., as we have previously recognized. . . . Because respondent's claims were brought on behalf of a member of the class the Act was designed to benefit, i.e., the clients of investment advisers, the first prong of the *Cort* test is satisfied in this case.

III

The second inquiry under the *Cort* approach is whether there is evidence of an express or implicit legislative intent to negate the claimed private rights of action. . . .

I find no such intent to foreclose private actions. Indeed, the statutory language evinces an intent to create such actions. In § 215(b) of the Act Congress provided that contracts made in violation of any provision of the Act "shall be void." As the Court recognizes, such a provision clearly contemplates the existence of private rights under the Act. . . .

The Court's conclusion that § 215, but not § 206, creates an implied private right of action ignores the relationship of § 215 to the

3. "First, is the plaintiff 'one of the class for whose especial benefit the statute was enacted,' Texas & Pacific R. Co. v. Rigsby, 241 U.S. 33, 39 (1916) (emphasis supplied)—that is, does the statute create a federal right in favor of the plaintiff? Second, is there any indication of legislative intent, explicit or implicit, either to create such a remedy or to deny one? See, e.g., National Railroad Passenger Corp. v. National Ass'n of Railroad Passengers, 414 U.S. 453, 458, 460 (1974) (*Amtrak*). Third, is it consistent with the underlying purposes of the legislative scheme to imply such a remedy for the plaintiff? See, e.g., *Amtrak,* supra; Securities Investor Protection Corp. v. Barbour, 421 U.S. 412, 423 (1975); Calhoon v. Harvey, 379 U.S. 134 (1964). And finally, is the cause of action one traditionally relegated to state law, in an area basically the concern of the States, so that it would be inappropriate to infer a cause of action based solely on federal law? See Wheeldin v. Wheeler, 373 U.S. 647, 652 (1963); cf. J. I. Case Co. v. Borak, 377 U.S. 426, 434 (1964); Bivens v. Six Unknown Federal Narcotics Agents, 403 U.S. 388, 394–395 (1971); at 400, (Harlan J., concurring in judgment)." Cort v. Ash, 422 U.S. 66, 78 (1975).

substantive provisions of the Act contained in § 206. Like the jurisdictional provisions of a statute, § 215 "creates no cause of action of its own force and effect; it imposes no liabilities." . . . Section 215 merely specifies one consequence of a violation of the substantive prohibitions of § 206. The practical necessity of a private action to enforce this particular consequence of a § 206 violation suggests that Congress contemplated the use of private actions to redress violations of § 206. It also indicates that Congress did not intend the powers given to the SEC to be the exclusive means for enforcement of the Act.[6]

The Court's holding that private litigants are restricted to actions for contract rescission confuses the question whether a cause of action exists with the question of the nature of relief available in such an action. Last Term in Davis v. Passman, 442 U.S., at 239, we recognized that "the question [of] whether a litigant has a 'cause of action' is analytically distinct and prior to the question of what relief, if any, a litigant may be entitled to receive." . . . Thus if a private right of action exists under the Act, the relief available to private litigants may include an award of damages. . . .

IV

The third portion of the *Cort* standard requires consideration of the compatibility of a private right of action with the legislative scheme. . . .

Implication of a private right of action for damages unquestionably would be not only consistent with the legislative goal of preventing fraudulent practices by investment advisers, but also essential to its achievement. While the Act empowers the SEC to take action to seek equitable relief to prevent offending investment advisers from engaging in future violations, in the absence of a private right of action for damages, victimized clients have little hope of obtaining redress for their injuries. . . .

V

The final consideration under the *Cort* analysis is whether the subject matter of the cause of action has been so traditionally relegated to state law as to make it inappropriate to infer a federal cause of action. Regulation of the activities of investment advisers has not been a traditional state concern. During the Senate hearings preceding enactment of the Act, Congress was informed that only six States had

6. The Court concludes that because the Act expressly provides for SEC enforcement proceedings, Congress must not have intended to create private rights of action. This application of the oft-criticized maxim *expressio unius est alterius* ignores our rejection of it in Cort v. Ash, 422 U.S. 66, 82–83, n. 14 (1975), in the absence of specific support in the legislative history for the proposition that express statutory remedies are to be exclusive. Moreover, the Court ignores the fact that the enforcement powers given the SEC under the Investment Advisers Act are virtually identical to those embodied in other securities acts under which implied rights of action have been recognized. Abrahamson v. Fleschner, 568 F.2d 862, 874, n. 19 (CA2 1977).

enacted legislation to regulate investment advisers. . . . Most of the state statutes subsequently enacted have been patterned after the federal legislation. . . .

VI

Each of the *Cort* factors point toward implication of a private cause of action in favor of clients defrauded by investment advisers in violation of the Act. The Act was enacted for the special benefit of clients of investment advisers and there is no indication of any legislative intent to deny such a cause of action, which would be consistent with the legislative scheme governing an area not traditionally relegated to state law. Under these circumstances an implied private right of action for damages should be recognized.

Notes on Implied Rights of Action

(1) *Transamerica* is representative of an important subset of the problem of the *Erie* and *Clearfield* cases: Under what circumstances may a federal court afford a right of action not explicitly provided for by statute?

As early as 1916, in Texas & Pacific Railway Co. v. Rigsby, 241 U.S. 33, the Court had authorized an injured plaintiff to seek damages for the violation of a federal statute; but that was of course before *Erie R. R. v. Tompkins*. The *Rigsby* doctrine was, however, invoked after *Erie* in the famous case of J. I. Case Co. v. Borak, 377 U.S. 426 (1964), which upheld the right of an injured investor to sue for damages resulting from reliance on a misleading proxy statement forbidden by rules adopted under § 14(a) of the Securities Exchange Act, 15 U.S.C. § 78n(a). The statute provided only that the district courts had "exclusive jurisdiction . . . of all suits in equity and actions at law brought to enforce any liability or duty" created by the statute or its regulations. Nevertheless, wrote Justice Clark, "among its chief purposes is 'the protection of investors,' which certainly implies the availability of judicial relief where necessary to achieve that result"; "the possibility of civil damages or injunctive relief serves as a most effective weapon in the enforcement of the proxy requirements"; and it was "the duty of the courts to be alert to provide such remedies as are necessary to make effective the congressional purpose." Similarly, in United States v. Republic Steel Corp., 362 U.S. 482 (1960), the Court allowed the Government to sue to enjoin the creation of an obstruction to navigation under the Rivers and Harbors Act, although for the violation in question the statute provided only for criminal penalties.

(2) *Borak* might have been thought to have adopted the principle of the first Restatement of Torts sustaining actions by injured members of the class protected by a regulatory statute, see p. 51 supra. If it did, however, it was not long to survive. In National Railroad Passenger Corp. v. National Association of Railroad Passengers, 414 U.S. 453 (1974) (*Amtrak*), the Court over only a single dissent refused to allow an injunctive suit by railroad passengers to enforce a statutory limitation on the discontinuance of service, relying in part on legislative history indicating a desire to leave enforcement to the Attorney General. In Cort v. Ash, 422 U.S. 66 (1975),

enunciating the four-part test discussed in *Transamerica*, the Court in a unanimous Brennan opinion held that a stockholder could not obtain damages when his corporation offended a criminal statute limiting political contributions, noting among other things that the protection of shareholders "was at best a secondary concern" of the law.

(3) An extraordinary number of implied-right-of-action cases have been decided since *Cort v. Ash*, and in many of them its test formed the basis of the Court's analysis. In Touche Ross & Co. v. Redington, 442 U.S. 560 (1979), where the Court held that violation of the reporting requirements of the Securities Exchange Act did not give rise to a private damage action, Justice Rehnquist noted that five cases had presented such an issue in a single Term, and in the 1980 Term there were as many more. As in *Transamerica*, the *Cort* factors were played down in *Touche*, where the Court emphasized that its task was "limited solely to determining whether Congress intended to create" a private right of action and that the argument for implication "based on tort principles" was "misplaced." *Borak* was distinguished as relying on a different section of the same statute, but its reasoning was given a severe blow to the head:

> Certainly, the mere fact that § 17(a) was designed to provide protection for brokers' customers does not require the implication of a private damages action in their behalf. . . . To the extent our analysis in today's decision differs from that of the Court in *Borak*, it suffices to say that in a series of cases since *Borak* we have adhered to a stricter standard for the implication of private causes of action, and we follow that stricter standard today. . . . The ultimate question is one of congressional intent, not one of whether this Court thinks that it can improve upon the statutory scheme that Congress enacted into law.

Justice Marshall, invoking *Cort*, dissented alone.

(4) Not only the language but also the results of the post-1975 decisions have been hostile to implicit causes of action. During the 1980 Term, for example, the Court held no private damage action lay for violations of the prevailing-wage provisions of the Davis-Bacon Act (Universities Research Association, Inc. v. Coutu, 450 U.S. 754 (1981)), of the Federal Water Pollution Control Act (Middlesex County Sewerage Authority v. National Sea Clammers Association, 453 U.S. 1 (1981)), or of the navigation-obstruction provision of the Rivers and Harbors act that was involved in the *Republic Steel* case in note 2 above (California v. Sierra Club, 451 U.S. 287 (1981)); it held as well that defendants had no right to contribution from third parties jointly responsible for violations of the antitrust laws (Texas Industries, Inc. v. Radcliff Materials, Inc., 451 U.S. 630 (1981)), or of federal laws outlawing sex discrimination in employment (Northwest Airlines, Inc. v. Transport Workers Union, 451 U.S. 77 (1981)).[1] Perhaps all these results were foreshadowed by the *Touche* and *Transamerica* cases, with their direction away not only from *Borak* but also from the four-part test of *Cort v. Ash*. Yet *Sierra Club* was written by Justice White, who had dissented in *Transamerica* on the ground that *Cort* was being watered down; and the

1. In the two contribution cases the Court stressed that those who violated the statutes were not within the class those statutes were designed to protect.

Sierra opinion once again was based squarely upon the *Cort* factors, with liberal citations to the *Transamerica* dissent.[2]

(5) Thus the language of *Sierra Club,* along with *Transamerica*'s holding that a suit for rescission did lie, makes premature any flat conclusion that implicit rights of action no longer exist. Indeed in the same Term that produced *Touche* the Court managed to hold, in Cannon v. University of Chicago, 441 U.S. 677 (1979), with the concurrence of Justices Stewart and Rehnquist, that a victim of alleged sex discrimination could seek damages from a school that had rejected her. Of substantial importance in reaching this decision were the similarity of the relevant Title IX provision to that of the employment-discrimination provisions enacted in 1964, which had been held by lower courts to create a private remedy, and explicit congressional statements that "[t]he same [enforcement] procedure" would apply under both titles. Significantly, the Court stressed that between the enactment of the two titles "this Court had consistently found implied remedies"; while later cases such as *Cort* had announced a "strict approach" to which "[w]e, of course, adhere," "our evaluation of congressional action in 1972 must take into account its contemporary legal context. . . . [I]t is not only appropriate but also realistic to presume that Congress was thoroughly familiar with these unusually important precedents . . . and that it expected its enactment to be interpreted in conformity with them." Justices Rehnquist and Stewart, authors of *Touche* and *Transamerica,* concurred specially to emphasize this last point: During the *Borak* era Congress had "good reason to think" the courts would infer remedies, but now that the Court had made clear that the task was "basically one of statutory construction," the Court "should be extremely reluctant to imply a cause of action. . . ."

Of particular interest is Justice Powell's dissenting opinion, the strongest statement since *Erie* against the entire practice of implicit causes of action. *Borak,* he concluded, was an "aberrant" decision neither supported by precedent nor followed by later cases; the *Cort* analysis was "an open invitation to federal courts to legislate causes of action not authorized by Congress," "allows the Judicial Branch to assume policymaking authority vested by the Constitution in the Legislative Branch," and "cannot be squared with the doctrine of the separation of powers." "Henceforth," he concluded, "we should not condone the implication of any private action from a federal statute absent the most compelling evidence that Congress in fact intended such an action to exist"; he would be "especially reluctant" to do so when, as in *Cannon,* the statute "expressly provides for an alternative mechanism for enforcing the rights and duties created. . . ."

Why do you suppose the Rules of Decision Act is so seldom mentioned in this line of cases? Did Justice Powell mean to suggest that state-law

2. Critical to Justice White in *Sierra Club* were his conclusion that the Rivers and Harbors Act "was designed to benefit the public at large" rather than "a particular class," and the absence of legislative history one way or another, which made consideration of the other two *Cort* factors unnecessary. Four Justices, including the authors of *Touche* and *Transamerica,* concurred separately on the ground that the Court placed "more emphasis on *Cort v. Ash* . . . than is warranted in light of several more recent 'implied right of action' decisions which limit it."

remedies for the violation of federal statutes were generally to be taken as implicitly preempted?

(6) When the plaintiff seeks not damages but injunctive or declaratory relief against government action, the question whether he has a right to sue is often phrased in terms of standing to sue rather than of an implied cause of action. See pp. 46–52 supra. Is there any reason why this should be so? Aren't the two questions, apart from the Article III requirement that the plaintiff have something to gain by his lawsuit, analytically the same?

Several standing decisions of the *Borak* era spoke essentially in *Borak*'s terms in finding that a member of the class protected by a statute had implicit standing to enforce it. See, e.g., *Hardin v. Kentucky Utilities Co.* and *Association of Data Processing Service Organizations, Inc. v. Camp*, pp. 50–51 supra. What should be the impact of recent decisions receding from *Borak* on these standing cases?

(7) For the analogous problem of nonstatutory damage actions for *constitutional* violations see *Bivens v. Six Unknown Named Agents of Federal Bureau of Narcotics* and accompanying notes, at pp. 401–13 infra.

SECTION 3. REMEDIES AGAINST GOVERNMENT OFFICIALS

MONROE v. PAPE

365 U.S. 167 (1961).

MR. JUSTICE DOUGLAS delivered the opinion of the Court.

This case presents important questions concerning the construction of R.S. § 1979, 42 U.S.C. § 1983, which reads as follows:

> "Every person who, under color of any statute, ordinance, regulation, custom, or usage, of any State or Territory, subjects or causes to be subjected, any citizen of the United States or other person within the jurisdiction thereof to the deprivation of any rights, privileges, or immunities secured by the Constitution and laws, shall be liable to the party injured in an action at law, suit in equity, or other proper proceeding for redress."

The complaint alleges that 13 Chicago police officers broke into petitioners' home in the early morning, routed them from bed, made them stand naked in the living room, and ransacked every room, emptying drawers and ripping mattress covers. It further alleges that Mr. Monroe was then taken to the police station and detained on "open" charges for 10 hours, while he was interrogated about a two-day-old murder, that he was not taken before a magistrate, though one was accessible, that he was not permitted to call his family or attorney, that he was subsequently released without criminal charges being preferred against him. It is alleged that the officers had no search warrant and no arrest warrant and that they acted "under color of the statutes, ordinances, regulations, customs and usages" of Illinois and of the City of Chicago. Federal jurisdiction was asserted under R.S. § 1979, which we have set out above, and 28 U.S.C. § 1343,[1] and 28 U.S.C § 1331.

The City of Chicago moved to dismiss the complaint on the ground that it is not liable under the Civil Rights Acts nor for acts committed in performance of its governmental functions. All defendants moved to dismiss, alleging that the complaint alleged no cause of action under those Acts or under the Federal Constitution. The District Court dismissed the complaint. The Court of Appeals affirmed. . . .

I.

Petitioners claim that the invasion of their home and the subsequent search without a warrant and the arrest and detention of Mr. Monroe without a warrant and without arraignment constituted a deprivation of their "rights, privileges, or immunities secured by the Constitution" within the meaning of R.S. § 1979. . . .

Section 1979 came onto the books as § 1 of the Ku Klux Act of April 20, 1871. 17 Stat. 13. . . . Its purpose is plain from the title of the legislation, "An Act to enforce the Provisions of the Fourteenth Amendment to the Constitution of the United States, and for other Purposes." 17 Stat. 13. Allegation of facts constituting a deprivation under color of state authority of a right guaranteed by the Fourteenth Amendment satisfies to that extent the requirement of R.S. § 1979. See Douglas v. City of Jeannette, 319 U.S. 157, 161–162. So far petitioners are on solid ground. For the guarantee against unreasonable searches and seizures contained in the Fourth Amendment has been made applicable to the States by reason of the Due Process Clause of the Fourteenth Amendment. Wolf v. Colorado, 338 U.S. 25. . . .

II.

There can be no doubt at least since Ex parte Virginia, 100 U.S. 339, 346–347, that Congress has the power to enforce provisions of the Fourteenth Amendment against those who carry a badge of authority of a State and represent it in some capacity, whether they act in accordance with their authority or misuse it. See Home Tel. & Tel. Co. v. City of Los Angeles, 227 U.S. 278, 287–296. The question with which we now deal is the narrower one of whether Congress, in enacting § 1979, meant to give a remedy to parties deprived of constitutional rights, privileges and immunities by an official's abuse of his position. Cf. Williams v. United States, 341 U.S. 97; Screws v. United States, 325

1. This section provides in material part:

"The district courts shall have original jurisdiction of any civil action authorized by law to be commenced by any person: . . .

"(3) To redress the deprivation, under color of any State law, statute, ordinance, regulation, custom or usage, of any right, privilege or immunity secured by the Constitution of the United States or by any Act of Congress providing for equal rights of citizens or of all persons within the jurisdiction of the United States."

U.S. 91; United States v. Classic, 313 U.S. 299. We conclude that it did so intend.

It is argued that "under color of" enumerated state authority excludes acts of an official or policeman who can show no authority under state law, state custom, or state usage to do what he did. In this case it is said that these policemen, in breaking into petitioners' apartment, violated the Constitution and laws of Illinois. It is pointed out that under Illinois law a simple remedy is offered for that violation and that, so far as it appears, the courts of Illinois are available to give petitioners that full redress which the common law affords for violence done to a person; and it is earnestly argued that no "statute, ordinance, regulation, custom or usage" of Illinois bars that redress.

The legislation—in particular the section with which we are now concerned—had several purposes. . . .

First, it might, of course, override certain kinds of state laws. Mr. Sloss of Alabama, in opposition, spoke of that object and emphasized that it was irrelevant because there were no such laws:

> "The first section of this bill prohibits any invidious legislation by States against the rights or privileges of citizens of the United States. The object of this section is not very clear, as it is not pretended by its advocates on this floor that any State has passed any laws endangering the rights or privileges of the colored people."

Second, it provided a remedy where state law was inadequate. That aspect of the legislation was summed up as follows by Senator Sherman of Ohio:

> ". . . it is said the reason is that any offense may be committed upon a negro by a white man, and a negro cannot testify in any case against a white man, so that the only way by which any conviction can be had in Kentucky in those cases is in the United States courts, because the United States courts enforce the United States laws by which negroes may testify."

But the purposes were much broader. The *third* aim was to provide a federal remedy where the state remedy, though adequate in theory, was not available in practice. . . It was not the unavailability of state remedies but the failure of certain States to enforce the laws with an equal hand that furnished the powerful momentum behind this "force bill." . . .

Senator Pratt of Indiana spoke of the discrimination against Union sympathizers and Negroes in the actual enforcement of the laws:

> "Plausibly and sophistically it is said the laws of North Carolina do not discriminate against them; that the provisions in favor of rights and liberties are general; that the courts are open to all; that juries, grand and petit, are commanded to hear and redress without distinction as to color, race, or political sentiment.
>
> "But it is a fact, asserted in the report, that of the hundreds of outrages committed upon loyal people through the agency of this Ku Klux organization not one has been punished. This defect in the

administration of the laws does not extend to other cases. Vigorously enough are the laws enforced against Union people. They only fail in efficiency when a man of known Union sentiments, white or black, invokes their aid. Then Justice closes the door of her temples." . . .

The debates were long and extensive. It is abundantly clear that one reason the legislation was passed was to afford a federal right in federal courts because, by reason of prejudice, passion, neglect, intolerance or otherwise, state laws might not be enforced and the claims of citizens to the enjoyment of rights, privileges, and immunities guaranteed by the Fourteenth Amendment might be denied by the state agencies. . . .

Although the legislation was enacted because of the conditions that existed in the South at that time, it is cast in general language and is as applicable to Illinois as it is to the States whose names were mentioned over and again in the debates. It is no answer that the State has a law which if enforced would give relief. The federal remedy is supplementary to the state remedy, and the latter need not be first sought and refused before the federal one is invoked. Hence the fact that Illinois by its constitution and laws outlaws unreasonable searches and seizures is no barrier to the present suit in the federal court.

We had before us in United States v. Classic, supra, § 20 of the Criminal Code, 18 U.S.C. § 242, which provides a criminal punishment for anyone who "under color of any law, statute, ordinance, regulation, or custom" subjects any inhabitant of a State to the deprivation of "any rights, privileges, or immunities secured or protected by the Constitution or laws of the United States." Section 242 first came into the law as § 2 of the Civil Rights Act, Act of April 9, 1866, 14 Stat. 27. . . . The right involved in the *Classic* case was the right of voters in a primary to have their votes counted. The laws of Louisiana required the defendants "to count the ballots, to record the result of the count, and to certify the result of the election." . . . But according to the indictment they did not perform their duty. In an opinion written by Mr. Justice (later Chief Justice) Stone, in which Mr. Justice Roberts, Mr. Justice Reed, and Mr. Justice Frankfurter joined, the Court ruled, "Misuse of power possessed by virtue of state law and made possible only because the wrongdoer is clothed with the authority of state law, is action taken 'under color of' state law." . . . There was a dissenting opinion; but the ruling as to the meaning of "under color of" state law was not questioned. . . .

Mr. Shellabarger, reporting out the bill which became the Ku Klux Act, said of the provision with which we now deal:

> "The model for it will be found in the second section of the act of April 9, 1866, known as the 'civil rights act.' . . . This section of this bill, on the same state of facts, not only provides a civil remedy for persons whose former condition may have been that of slaves, but also to all people where, under color of State law, they or any of them may be deprived of rights. . . ."

Thus, it is beyond doubt that this phrase should be accorded the same construction in both statutes—in § 1979 and in 18 U.S.C. § 242. . . .

So far, then, the complaint states a cause of action. [The Court went on to hold, for reasons summarized in the case that follows, that the City itself was not a "person" subject to suit under § 1979.] . . .

Accordingly we hold that the motion to dismiss the complaint against the City of Chicago was properly granted. But since the complaint should not have been dismissed against the officials the judgment must be and is reversed. . . .

MR. JUSTICE HARLAN, whom MR. JUSTICE STEWART joins, concurring.

Were this case here as one of first impression, I would find the "under color of any statute" issue very close indeed. However, in *Classic* . . . this Court considered a substantially identical statutory phrase to have a meaning which, unless we now retreat from it, requires that issue to go for the petitioners here. . . . One can agree with the Court's opinion that:

> "It is abundantly clear that one reason the legislation was passed was to afford a federal right in federal courts because, by reason of prejudice, passion, neglect, intolerance or otherwise, state laws might not be enforced and the claims of citizens to the enjoyment of rights, privileges, and immunities guaranteed by the Fourteenth Amendment might be denied by the state agencies . . ."

without being certain that Congress meant to deal with anything other than abuses so recurrent as to amount to "custom, or usage." One can agree with any Brother Frankfurter, in dissent, that Congress had no intention of taking over the whole field of ordinary state torts and crimes, without being certain that the enacting Congress would not have regarded actions by an official, made possible by his position, as far more serious than an ordinary state tort, and therefore as a matter of federal concern. If attention is directed at the rare specific references to isolated abuses of state authority, one finds them neither so clear nor so disproportionately divided between favoring the positions of the majority or the dissent as to make either position seem plainly correct. . . .

The dissent considers that the "under color of" provision of § 1983 distinguishes between unconstitutional actions taken without state authority, which only the State should remedy, and unconstitutional actions authorized by the State, which the Federal Act was to reach. If so, then the controlling difference for the enacting legislature must have been either that the state remedy was more adequate for unauthorized actions than for authorized ones or that there was in some sense, greater harm from unconstitutional actions authorized by the full panoply of state power and approval than from unconstitutional actions not so authorized or acquiesced in by the State. I find less than compelling the evidence that either distinction was important to that Congress. . . .

MR. JUSTICE FRANKFURTER, dissenting. . . .

[R.S. 1979] was patterned on the similar criminal provision of § 2, Act of April 9, 1866. The earlier Act had as its primary object the effective nullification of the Black Codes, those statutes of the Southern legislatures which had so burdened and disqualified the Negro as to make his emancipation appear illusory. The Act had been vetoed by President Johnson, whose veto message describes contemporary understanding of its second section; the section, he wrote,

> "seems to be designed to apply to some existing or future law of a State or Territory which may conflict with the provisions of the bill. . . . It provides for counteracting such forbidden legislation by imposing fine and imprisonment upon the legislators who may pass such conflicting laws, or upon the officers or agents who shall put, or attempt to put, them into execution. It means an official offense, not a common crime committed against law upon the persons or property of the black race. Such an act may deprive the black man of his property, but not of the right to hold property. It means a deprivation of the right itself, either by the State judiciary or the State Legislature."

And Senator Trumbull, then Chairman of the Senate Judiciary Committee, in his remarks urging its passage over the veto, expressed the intendment of the second section as those who voted for it read it:

> "If an offense is committed against a colored person simply because he is colored, in a State where the law affords him the same protection as if he were white, this act neither has nor was intended to have anything to do with his case, because he has adequate remedies in the State courts; but if he is discriminated against under color of State laws because he is colored, then it becomes necessary to interfere for his protection." . . .

The original text of the present § 1979 contained words, left out in the Revised Statutes, which clarified the objective to which the provision was addressed:

> "That any person who, under color of any law, statute, ordinance, regulation, custom, or usage of any State, shall subject, or cause to be subjected, any person within the jurisdiction of the United States to the deprivation of any rights, privileges, or immunities secured by the Constitution of the United States, shall, *any such law, statute, ordinance, regulation, custom, or usage of the State to the contrary notwithstanding*, be liable to the party injured. . . ." . . .

The Court now says, however, that "it was not the unavailability of state remedies but the failure of certain States to enforce the laws with an equal hand that furnished the powerful momentum behind this 'force bill.'" Of course, if the notion of "unavailability" of remedy is limited to mean an absence of statutory, paper right, this is in large part true. Insofar as the Court undertakes to demonstrate—as the bulk of its opinion seems to do—that § 1979 was meant to reach some instances of action not specifically authorized by the avowed, apparent, written law inscribed in the statute books of the States, the argument knocks at an open door. No one would or could, deny this, for by its express terms the statute comprehends deprivations of federal rights under color of any "statute, ordinance, regulation, *custom, or usage*" of a State. (Emphasis added.) The question is, *what* class of cases other than those involving state statute law were meant to be reached. And, with respect to this question, the Court's conclusion is undermined by the very portions of the legislative debates which it cites. For surely the misconduct of individual municipal police officers, subject to the effective oversight of appropriate state administrative and judicial authorities, presents a situation which differs *toto coelo* from one in which "Immunity is given to crime, and the records of the public tribunals are searched in vain for any evidence of effective redress," or in which murder rages while a State makes "no successful effort to bring the guilty to punishment or afford protection or redress" . . . . These statements indicate that Congress—made keenly aware by the post-bellum conditions in the South that States through their authorities could sanction offenses against the individual by settled practice which established state law as truly as written codes—designed § 1979 to reach, as well, official conduct which, because engaged in "permanently and as a rule," or "systematically," came through acceptance by law-administering officers to constitute "custom, or usage" having the cast of law. . . .

The present case comes here from a judgment sustaining a motion to dismiss petitioners' complaint. That complaint, insofar as it describes the police intrusion, makes no allegation that that intrusion was authorized by state law other than the conclusory and unspecific claim that "During all times herein mentioned the individual defendants and each of them were acting under color of the statutes, ordinances, regulations, customs and usages of the State of Illinois, of the County of Cook and of the defendant City of Chicago." In the face of Illinois decisions holding such intrusions unlawful and in the absence of more precise factual averments to support its conclusion, such a complaint fails to state a claim under § 1979.

However, the complaint does allege, as to the ten-hour detention of Mr. Monroe, that "it was, and it is now, the custom or usage of the Police Department of the City of Chicago to arrest and confine individuals in the police stations and jail cells of the said department for long periods of time on 'open' charges." . . . Such averments do present facts which, admitted as true for purposes of a motion to dismiss, seem to sustain petitioners' claim that Mr. Monroe's detention—as contrasted with the night-time intrusion into the Monroe apartment—was "under color" of state authority. . . .

Notes on 42 U.S.C. § 1983

(1) Enacted in 1871, § 1983 and its companion jurisdictional provision (28 U.S.C. § 1343(3)) were for many years largely ignored. Justice Powell noted in *Maine v. Thiboutot*, n. 2 infra, that "[o]ne writer found only 21

cases decided under § 1983 in the first 50 years of its history" and that "[a]nother lamented, as late as 1952, that the statute could not be given its intended broad effect without a 'judicial and constitutional upheaval of the first magnitude.'" *Monroe* marks the rebirth of these provisions; they have provided a principal jurisdictional and remedial basis for the Supreme Court's recent revolution in Fourteenth Amendment law.[1]

(2) When originally enacted, these provisions provided a remedy only for violations of "the Constitution of the United States." The present reference to "the Constitution and laws" dates from the general codification of 1874, in which the jurisdictional and remedial provisions were put into separate titles. The new section providing for circuit court jurisdiction (predecessor of the current 28 U.S.C. § 1343(3)) spoke more narrowly of rights secured by the Constitution or "by any Act of Congress providing for equal rights of citizens of the United States."

Chapman v. Houston Welfare Rights Organization, 441 U.S. 600 (1979), predictably held that § 1343(3) did not give the district courts jurisdiction over a complaint alleging that a state welfare regulation conflicted with the Social Security Act. That statute, the Court concluded, was not one "providing for equal rights," because it was not phrased in terms of equality. Moreover, although state law that conflicts with federal statute offends the Supremacy Clause, "the additional language which describes a limited category of Acts of Congress—those 'providing for equal rights of citizens'—plainly negates the notion that jurisdiction over *all* statutory claims had already been conferred by the preceding reference to constitutional claims."

Maine v. Thiboutot, 448 U.S. 1 (1980), presented the same question in the context of § 1983, the remedial provision. This section does not contain the limiting language relied on in *Chapman;* it provides a remedy for violations of "the Constitution and laws." In dissent, Justice Powell argued that the difference in phrasing was inadvertent, and that "laws" in § 1983 meant laws "providing for equal rights" as in § 1343(3)—buttressing this conclusion with evidence that the codification was not meant to change existing law.[2] The majority was unimpressed. Section 1983 covered violations of the Social Security Act even though § 1343(3) did not provide jurisdiction; "the legislative history does not demonstrate that the plain language was not intended."

1. Section 1983 cases arise under federal law, so 28 U.S.C. § 1331 provides jurisdiction over them. Until 1980, however, § 1331 contained a $10,000 minimum amount-in-controversy requirement; the great advantage of § 1343(3) was that it did not. With the abolition of § 1331's amount requirement, the scope of § 1343(3) lost its independent significance; but cases construing that section are still important for the light they cast on the cause of action conferred by § 1983. For a comprehensive study of § 1983 see Note, Developments in the Law: Section 1983 and Federalism, 90 Harv.L.Rev. 1133 (1977). Additional issues arising in § 1983 cases are discussed in chapters 5 and 6, infra.

2. After the committee had employed an expert "'to strike out . . . modifications of the existing law' 'wherever the meaning of the law had been changed,'" the bill was introduced "with the solemn assurance that [it] 'embodies the law as it is.'" "The addition of 'and laws' did not change the meaning" of the provision, Justice Powell added, "because Congress assumed that that phrase referred only to federal equal rights legislation . . ., which conferred rights also secured by the recently adopted Fourteenth Amendment."

Does the word "laws" in § 1983 include federal regulations? Federal common law? Acts of Congress applying only to the District of Columbia? Is it limited to *federal* laws?

(3) The practical effect of *Thiboutot* was significantly limited not long after its decision by Middlesex County Sewerage Authority v. National Sea Clammers Association, 453 U.S. 1 (1981). In an action seeking damages for harm caused by waste discharges allegedly violating the Federal Water Pollution Control Act and the Marine Protection, Research, and Sanctuaries Act, the Court in an opinion by Justice Powell (who had dissented in *Thiboutot*) held not only that no action lay under those statutes themselves or under federal common law, but also that the plaintiffs could not prevail under § 1983:

> [W]hen "a state official is alleged to have violated a federal statute which provides its own comprehensive enforcement scheme, the requirements of that enforcement procedure may not be bypassed by bringing suit directly under § 1983." As discussed above, the FWPCA and MPRSA do provide quite comprehensive enforcement mechanisms. It is hard to believe that Congress intended to preserve the § 1983 right of action when it created so many specific statutory remedies including . . . two citizen-suit provisions. . . . We therefore conclude that the existence of these express remedies demonstrates not only that Congress intended to foreclose implied private actions but also that it intended to supplant any remedy that otherwise would be available under § 1983.

Justices Stevens and Blackmun dissented.[3]

(4) On its face § 1983's reference to "the Constitution" looks as all-embracing as its reference to "laws," but for many years the Court declined to give it a broad interpretation. Carter v. Greenhow, 114 U.S. 317, 322 (1885), held no cause of action stated under § 1983's predecessor by a complaint based upon the refusal of a collector to accept bond coupons in satisfaction of taxes: The right to pay in coupons was derived not from the Constitution but from contract; the right "secured" by the Contract Clause of the Constitution was the "right to have a judicial determination, declaring the nullity of the attempt to impair" the contractual obligation, and that right had not been impaired. Holt v. Indiana Manufacturing Co., 176 U.S. 68, 72 (1900), dismissed for want of jurisdiction a complaint that state taxes upon federally granted patent rights violated the patent laws and the due-process and equal-protection clauses: "Assuming that" the predecessor to § 1343(3) was "still in force," it applied "to civil rights only" and was therefore inapplicable. Reminiscent of the *Holt* reasoning was that of Justice Stone in Hague v. CIO, 307 U.S. 496 (1939), upholding jurisdiction

3. Both statutes contained saving clauses; that in the FWPCA provided that "[n]othing in this section shall restrict any right which any person . . . may have under any statute or common law to seek enforcement of any effluent standard or limitation or to seek any other relief. . . ." 33 U.S.C. § 1365(e). The Court was unimpressed: The saving clause "relate[d] only to the effect of the accompanying citizen-suit provision" in the same "section" and did not "limit the effect of the overall remedial scheme[ ]" of the Act; in any event it preserved only remedies "under *other* statutes," not for violation of the FWPCA itself, "even if the *remedy* asserted is based on the separate right-of-action created in § 1983."

under what is now § 1343(3) of what he conceived to be a claim of free speech and assembly under the Due Process Clause but refusing to read the statute to mean what it said lest it swallow up the jurisdictional-amount requirement of the later-enacted general federal-question section in constitutional cases:

> There are many rights and immunities secured by the Constitution, of which freedom of speech and assembly are conspicuous examples, which are not capable of money valuation, and in many instances, like the present, no suit in equity could be maintained for their protection if proof of the jurisdictional amount were prerequisite. . . . By treating § 24(14) [now §1343(3)] as conferring federal jurisdiction of suits brought under the Act of 1871 in which the right asserted is inherently incapable of pecuniary valuation, we harmonize the two parallel provisions of the Judicial Code, construe neither as superfluous, and give to each a scope in conformity with its history and manifest purpose. . . . Whenever the right or immunity is one of personal liberty, not dependent for its existence upon the infringement of property rights, there is jurisdiction in the district court . . . without proof that the amount in controversy exceeds $3,000.[4] . . .

Both Stone's test and the *Holt* distinction were wiped out by a unanimous Supreme Court in Lynch v. Household Finance Corp., 405 U.S. 538 (1972). The complaint was a $525 attack on the constitutionality of a state garnishment law essentially on grounds of procedural due process. Jurisdiction was upheld:

> Neither the words of § 1343(3) nor the legislative history . . . distinguishes between personal and property rights. . . . The supposed conflict between §§ 1343(3) and 1331 simply does not exist. Section 1343 (3) applies only to alleged infringements of rights under "color of . . . State law," whereas § 1331 contains no such requirement. Thus, for example, in suits against federal officials for alleged deprivations of constitutional rights, it is necessary to satisfy the amount-in-controversy requirement. . . . But the more fundamental point . . . is that any such contraction of § 1343(3) jurisdiction is not supported by the legislative history of § 1331. The 1875 Act giving the federal courts power to hear suits arising under . . . the Constitution was, like the Act of 1871, an expansion of national authority. . . . There is . . . no indication whatsoever that Congress . . . intended to narrow the scope of a provision passed four years earlier as part of major civil rights legislation. . . .

4. Stone spoke for only three Justices; the two others who addressed the issue classified the complaint as charging a violation of the Privileges and Immunities Clause, which some observers took to suggest that they thought the statute applied *only* to privileges and immunities.

Note the ambiguity of Stone's opinion, as illustrated by the later case of Douglas v. City of Jeannette, 319 U.S. 157, 161–62 (1943), sustaining jurisdiction of an action challenging a license tax on solicitation on First Amendment grounds: Although freedoms of religion and expression seem clearly "personal" rather than "proprietary," the rights at stake could have been purchased by paying the license fee, which the cases had long held established the amount in controversy. See p. 303 supra.

> A final, compelling reason for rejecting a "personal liberties" limitation upon § 1343(3) is the virtual impossibility of applying it. The federal courts have been particularly bedeviled by "mixed" cases in which both personal and property rights are implicated, and the line between them has been difficult to draw with any consistency. . . . The right to enjoy property without unlawful deprivation, no less than the right to speak or the right to travel, is in truth a "personal" right, whether the "property" in question be a welfare check, a home, or a savings account. In fact, a fundamental interdependence exists between the personal right to liberty and the personal right in property. . . . Mrs. Lynch . . . alleged that because of the garnishment she was unable to pay her rent on time and encountered difficulty maintaining her family on a minimally adequate diet. If these allegations are true, Mrs. Lynch's personal liberty could be profoundly affected by garnishment of her savings.[5]

Does *Lynch* mean that a complaint like that in *Carter v. Greenhow*, supra, would state a § 1983 claim today?

(5) Not every violation of "the Constitution and laws" can be remedied under § 1983, but only those committed "under color of any statute, ordinance, custom, or usage, of any State or Territory or the District of Columbia." One thing that is clear from this language is that not every private violation of federal rights is actionable under that section. "Color of" law requires at a minimum that an individual purport to "act with the knowledge of and pursuant to" some law or custom. On the other hand, " 'to act "under color" of law does not require that the accused be an officer of the State. It is enough that he is a willful participant in joint activity with the State or its agents.' " Adickes v. S.H. Kress & Co., 398 U.S. 144 (1970) (holding that a restaurant owner could be found liable under § 1983 for racial discrimination in concert with the police). Is it enough that a private actor argues that state law legitimizes his conduct, or must he be attempting to enforce the law? Cf. *City of Greenwood v. Peacock,* p. 555 infra, construing similar language in the removal provision of 28 U.S.C. § 1443(2).[6]

(6) Not only does the "under color of" law provision limit the applicability of § 1983 in respect of private conduct; the law under color of which the defendant acts must be that of a "State or Territory or the District of Columbia." Thus federal officers may not be held under § 1983, Wheeldin v. Wheeler, 373 U.S. 647, 650 & n. 2 (1963), unless they act in concert with state authorities acting pursuant to state law, Dombrowski v. Eastland, 387 U.S. 82 (1967). Moreover, before the statute was amended in 1979 to include the District of Columbia, the District was held to be neither a "State" nor a "Territory" for § 1983 purposes, District of Columbia v. Carter, 409 U.S. 418 (1973). The Commonwealth of Puerto Rico, on the other hand, has been held a "State" for purposes of the jurisdictional

5. For a gentle criticism of this decision see H. Friendly, Federal Jurisdiction: A General View 91–92 (1973).

6. *Adickes* also declared that "a 'custom or usage, of [a] State' for purposes of § 1983 must have the force of law by virtue of the persistent practices of state officials"; it was not enough to show "a practice that respects longstanding social habits, generally observed by the people in a locality."

provision of § 1343(3), which does not even include § 1983's explicit reference to "Territor[ies]." Examining Board of Engineers, Architects and Surveyors v. Flores de Otero, 426 U.S. 572 (1976); cf. *National Mutual Insurance Co. v. Tidewater Transfer Co.*, supra p. 128; see Currie, The Supreme Court and Federal Jurisdiction: 1975 Term, 1976 Sup.Ct.Rev. 183, 202–05. Was there any sense in this distinction?

(7) Justice Frankfurter's attempt in *Monroe* to limit the "color of" law provision to actions actually authorized by state law did not come out of the blue; an analogous argument had once apparently been embraced by the Court in interpreting the Fourteenth Amendment itself. In Barney v. City of New York, 193 U.S. 430 (1904), the plaintiff sought to enjoin the construction of a railway tunnel without prior compensation for its impact on adjacent land, invoking both due process and state law. The Fourteenth Amendment, said the Court,

> prohibits deprivation by a State, and here the bill alleged that what was done was without authority. . . . [T]he bill on its face proceeded on the theory that the construction . . . was not only not authorized, but was forbidden by the legislation, and hence was not action by the State of New York within the intent and meaning of the Fourteenth Amendment, and the Circuit Court was right in dismissing it for want of jurisdiction.

Although the *Barney* thesis was rejected as early as 1913 in Home Telephone & Telegraph Co. v. City of Los Angeles, 227 U.S. 278, which was cited in *Monroe* (see also United States v. Raines, 362 U.S. 17 (1960)), Justice Frankfurter continued to invoke it as late as 1944. Snowden v. Hughes, 321 U.S. 1, 17 (concurring opinion): "I am unable to grasp the principle on which the State can here be said to deny the plaintiff the equal protection of the laws of the State when the foundation of his claim is that the Board had disobeyed the authentic command of the State." Is there any answer to this argument?

Did the Court's rejection of *Barney* compel the rejection of Frankfurter's narrow reading of § 1983? Is it so clear that "under color of" law means whenever law is invoked as a defense, rather than only when the state has actually attempted to authorize the challenged action? Would it have been far-fetched for Congress to think there was greater need for federal forum when state law has been followed than when it has been flouted? How useful is the legislative history cited by both sides in *Monroe*? Then how does one decide what the statute means? [7]

MONELL v. DEPARTMENT OF SOCIAL SERVICES

436 U.S. 658 (1978).

MR. JUSTICE BRENNAN delivered the opinion of the Court.

7. See also Lugar v. Edmondson Oil Co., 457 U.S. 922, 935 (1982), concluding that "[i]f the challenged conduct . . . constitute[d] state action . . ., then that conduct was also action under color of state law and will support a suit under § 1983": "The history of the Act is replete with statements indicating that Congress thought it was creating a remedy as broad as the protection that the Fourteenth Amendment affords."

Petitioners, a class of female employees of the Department of Social Services and of the Board of Education of the city of New York, commenced this action under 42 U.S.C. § 1983 in July 1971. The gravamen of the complaint was that the Board and the Department had as a matter of official policy compelled pregnant employees to take unpaid leaves of absence before such leaves were required for medical reasons. Cf. Cleveland Board of Education v. LaFleur, 414 U.S. 632 (1974). The suit sought injunctive relief and backpay for periods of unlawful forced leave. Named as defendants in the action were the Department and its Commissioner, the Board and its Chancellor, and the city of New York and its Mayor. In each case, the individual defendants were sued solely in their official capacities.

On cross-motions for summary judgment, . . . plaintiffs' prayers for backpay were denied because any such damages would come ultimately from the City of New York and, therefore, to hold otherwise would be to "circumven[t]" the immunity conferred on municipalities by Monroe v. Pape, 365 U.S. 167 (1961). . . .

I

In *Monroe v. Pape*, we held that "Congress did not undertake to bring municipal corporations within the ambit of [§ 1983]." . . . The sole basis for this conclusion was an inference drawn from Congress' rejection of the "Sherman amendment" to the bill which became the Civil Rights Act of 1871, 17 Stat. 13, the precursor of § 1983. The Amendment would have held a municipal corporation liable for damage done to the person or property of its inhabitants by *private* persons "riotously and tumultuously assembled." . . . Although the Sherman amendment did not seek to amend § 1 of the Act, which is now § 1983, and although the nature of the obligation created by that amendment was vastly different from that created by § 1, the Court nonetheless concluded in *Monroe* that Congress must have meant to exclude municipal corporations from the coverage of § 1 because " 'the House [in voting against the Sherman amendment] had solemnly decided that in their judgment Congress had no constitutional power to impose any *obligation* upon county and town organizations, the mere instrumentality for the administration of state law,' " . . . quoting . . . Rep. Poland. This statement, we thought, showed that Congress doubted its "constitutional power . . . to impose *civil liability* on municipalities," . . . and that such doubt would have extended to any type of civil liability.

A fresh analysis of the debate on the Civil Rights Act of 1871, and particularly of the case law which each side mustered in its support, shows, however, that *Monroe* incorrectly equated the "obligation" of which Representative Poland spoke with "civil liability." . . .

House opponents of the Sherman amendment—whose views are particularly important since only the House voted down the amendment—. . . argued that the local units of government upon which the amendment fastened liability were not obligated to keep the peace at state law and further that the Federal Government could not constitutionally require local governments to create police forces, whether this requirement was levied directly, or indirectly by imposing damages for breach of the peace on municipalities. The most complete statement of this position is that of Representative Blair:

> "The proposition known as the Sherman amendment . . . claims the power in the General Government to go into the States of this Union and lay such obligations as it may please upon the municipalities, which are the creations of the States alone. . . .
>
> "Now, only the other day, the Supreme Court . . . decided [in Collector v. Day, 11 Wall. [78 U.S.] 113 (1871)] that there is no power in the Government of the United States, under its authority to tax, to tax the salary of a State officer. . . . It was held also in the case of Prigg v. Pennsylvania, 16 Pet. [41 U.S.] 539 (1842) that it is not within the power of the Congress of the United States to lay duties upon a State officer; that we cannot command a State officer to do any duty whatever, as such; and I ask . . . the difference between that and commanding a municipality, which is equally the creature of the State, to perform a duty." . . .

Blair's exegesis of the reigning constitutional theory of his day . . . was clearly supported by precedent—albeit precedent that has not survived, see Ex parte Virginia, 100 U.S. 339, 347–348 (1880); Graves v. New York ex rel. O'Keefe, 306 U.S. 466, 486 (1939)—and no other constitutional formula was advanced by participants in the House debates. . . .

Thus, there was ample support for Blair's view that the Sherman amendment, by putting municipalities to the Hobson's choice of keeping the peace or paying civil damages, attempted to impose obligations on municipalities by indirection that could not be imposed directly, thereby threatening to "destroy the government of the States." . . .

If municipal liability under § 1 of the Civil Rights Act of 1871 created a similar Hobson's choice, we might conclude, as *Monroe* did, that Congress could not have intended municipalities to be among the "persons" to which that section applied. But this is not the case.

First, opponents expressly distinguished between imposing an obligation to keep the peace and merely imposing civil liability for damages on a municipality that was obligated by state law to keep the peace, but which had not in violation of the Fourteenth Amendment. . .:

> "I presume . . . that where a State had imposed a duty [to keep the peace] upon [a] municipality . . . an action would be allowed to be maintained against them in the courts of the United States under the ordinary restrictions as to jurisdiction. But the enforcing a liability, existing by their own contract, or by a State law, in the courts, is a very widely different thing from devolving a new duty or liability upon them by the national Government, which has no power either to create or destroy them, and no power or control over them whatever." [citing Rep. Poland] . . .

Second, the doctrine of dual sovereignty apparently put no limit on the power of federal courts to enforce the Constitution against municipalities that violated it. . . . [T]he same Court which rendered *Day* also vigorously enforced the Contract Clause against municipalities—an enforcement effort which included various forms of "positive" relief, such as ordering that taxes be levied and collected to discharge federal-court judgments, once a constitutional infraction was found. . . . Since § 1 of the Civil Rights Act simply conferred jurisdiction on the federal courts to enforce § 1 of the Fourteenth Amendment—a situation precisely analogous to the grant of diversity jurisdiction under which the Contract Clause was enforced against municipalities—there is no reason to suppose that opponents of the Sherman amendment would have found any constitutional barrier to § 1 suits against municipalities. . . .

From the foregoing discussion, it is readily apparent that nothing said in debate on the Sherman amendment would have prevented holding a municipality liable under § 1 of the Civil Rights Act for its own violations of the Fourteenth Amendment. The question remains, however, whether the general language describing those to be liable under § 1—"any person"—covers more than natural persons. An examination of the debate on § 1 and application of appropriate rules of construction show unequivocally that § 1 was intended to cover legal as well as natural persons. . . .

In both Houses, statements of the supporters of § 1 corroborated that Congress, in enacting § 1, intended to give a broad remedy for violations of federally protected civil rights. Moreover, since municipalities through their official acts could, equally with natural persons, create the harms intended to be remedied by § 1, and, further, since Congress intended § 1 to be broadly construed, there is no reason to suppose that municipal corporations would have been excluded from the sweep of § 1. . . . One need not rely on this inference alone, however, for the debates show that Members of Congress understood "persons" to include municipal corporations.

Representative Bingham, for example, in discussing § 1 of the bill, explained that he had drafted § 1 of the Fourteenth Amendment with the case of Barron v. Mayor of Baltimore, 7 Pet. [32 U.S.] 243 (1833), especially in mind. "In [that] case the city had taken private property for public use, without compensation . . ., and there was no redress for the wrong. . . ." . . . Bingham's further remarks clearly indicate his view that such takings by cities, as had occurred in *Barron*, would be redressable under § 1 of the bill. . . . Given this purpose, it beggars reason to suppose that Congress would have exempted municipalities from suit, insisting instead that compensation for a taking come from an officer in his individual capacity rather than from the government unit that had the benefit of the property taken.

In addition, by 1871, it was well understood that corporations should be treated as natural persons for virtually all purposes of constitutional and statutory analysis. This had not always been so. When this Court first considered the question of the status of corporations, Mr. Chief Justice Marshall, writing for the Court, denied that corporations "as such" were persons as that term was used in Art. III and the Judiciary Act of 1789. See Bank of the United States v. Deveaux, 5 Cranch [9 U.S.] 61, 86 (1809). By 1844, however, the *Deveaux* doctrine was unhesitatingly abandoned:

> "[A] corporation created by and doing business in a particular state, is to be deemed *to all intents and purposes as a person*, although an artificial person, . . . capable of being treated as a citizen of that state, as much as a natural person." Louisville R. Co. v. Letson, 2 How. [43 U.S.] 497, 558 (1844) (emphasis added), discussed in Globe 752.

And only two years before the debates on the Civil Rights Act, in Cowles v. Mercer County, 7 Wall. [74 U.S.] 118, 121 (1869), the *Letson* principle was automatically and without discussion extended to municipal corporations. Under this doctrine, municipal corporations were routinely sued in the federal courts and this fact was well known to Members of Congress.

That the "usual" meaning of the word "person" would extend to municipal corporations is also evidenced by an Act of Congress which had been passed only months before the Civil Rights Act was passed. This Act provided that

> "in all acts hereafter passed . . . the word 'person' may extend and be applied to bodies politic and corporate . . . unless the context shows that such words were intended to be used in a more limited sense." Act of Feb. 25, 1871, § 2, 16 Stat. 431.

Municipal corporations in 1871 were included within the phrase "bodies politic and corporate" and, accordingly, the "plain meaning" of § 1 is that local government bodies were to be included within the ambit of the persons who could be sued under § 1 of the Civil Rights Act. . . .[54]

II . . .

On the other hand, the language of § 1983, read against the background of the same legislative history, compels the conclusion that Congress did not intend municipalities to be held liable unless action pursuant to official municipal policy of some nature caused a constitutional tort. In particular, we conclude that a municipality cannot be held liable *solely* because it employs a tortfeasor—or, in other words, a

54. There is certainly no constitutional impediment to municipal liability. "The Tenth Amendment's reservation of nondelegated powers to the States is not implicated by a federal-court judgment enforcing the express prohibitions of unlawful state conduct enacted by the Fourteenth Amendment." Milliken v. Bradley, 433 U.S. 267, 291 (1977); see Ex parte Virginia, 100 U.S., at 347–348. . . . Nor is there any basis for concluding that the Eleventh Amendment is a bar to municipal liability. See e.g., . . . Lincoln County v. Luning, 133 U.S. 529, 530 (1890). Our holding today is, of course, limited to local government units which are not considered part of the State for Eleventh Amendment purposes.

municipality cannot be held liable under § 1983 on a *respondeat superior* theory.

We begin with the language of § 1983 as originally passed:

> "*[A]ny person who*, under color of any law, statute, ordinance, regulation, custom, or usage of any State, *shall subject or cause to be subjected*, any person . . . to the deprivation of any rights, privileges, or immunities secured by the Constitution of the United States, shall, any such law, statute, ordinance, regulation, custom, or usage of the State to the contrary notwithstanding, be liable to the party injured in any action at law, suit in equity, or other proper proceeding for redress. . . ." . . .

The italicized language plainly imposes liability on a government that, under color of some official policy, "causes" an employee to violate another's constitutional rights. At the same time, that language cannot be easily read to impose liability vicariously on governing bodies solely on the basis of the existence of an employer-employee relationship with a tortfeasor. Indeed, the fact that Congress did specifically provide that A's tort became B's liability if B "caused" A to subject another to a tort suggests that Congress did not intend § 1983 liability to attach where such causation was absent.[57] . . .

Equally important, creation of a federal law of *respondeat superior* would have raised all the constitutional problems associated with the obligation to keep the peace, an obligation Congress chose not to impose because it thought imposition of such an obligation unconstitutional. To this day, there is disagreement about the basis for imposing liability on an employer for the torts of an employee when the sole nexus between the employer and the tort is the fact of the employer-employee relationship. . . . Nonetheless, two justifications tend to stand out. First is the common-sense notion that no matter how blameless an employer appears to be in an individual case, accidents might nonetheless be reduced if employers had to bear the cost of accidents. . . . Second is the argument that the cost of accidents should be spread to the community as a whole on an insurance theory. . . .

The first justification is of the same sort that was offered for statutes like the Sherman amendment: "The obligation to make compensation for injury resulting from riot is, by arbitrary enactment of statutes, affirmatory law, and the reason of passing the statute is to secure a more perfect police regulation." Globe 777 (Sen. Frelinghuysen). This justification was obviously insufficient to sustain the amendment against perceived constitutional difficulties and there is no reason

57. Congress' treatment of the Sherman amendment gives a clue to whether it would have desired to impose *respondeat superior* liability. . . . Strictly speaking, of course, the fact that Congress refused to impose vicarious liability for the wrongs of a few private citizens does not conclusively establish that it would similarly have refused to impose vicarious liability for the torts of a municipality's employees. Nonetheless, when Congress' rejection of the only form of vicarious liability presented to it is combined with the absence of any language in § 1983 which can easily be construed to create *respondeat superior* liability, the inference that Congress did not intend to impose such liability is quite strong.

to suppose that a more general liability imposed for a similar reason would have been thought less constitutionally objectionable. The second justification was similarly put forward as a justification for the Sherman amendment: "we do not look upon [the Sherman amendment] as a punishment. . . . It is a mutual insurance." Id., at 792 (Rep. Butler). Again, this justification was insufficient to sustain the amendment.

We conclude, therefore, that a local government may not be sued under § 1983 for an injury inflicted solely by its employees or agents. Instead, it is when execution of a government's policy or custom, whether made by its lawmakers or by those whose edicts or acts may fairly be said to represent official policy, inflicts the injury that the government as an entity is responsible under § 1983. Since this case unquestionably involves official policy as the moving force of the constitutional violation found by the District Court, . . . we must reverse the judgment below. . . .

MR. JUSTICE REHNQUIST, with whom THE CHIEF JUSTICE joins, dissenting. . . .

[T]he Dictionary Act . . . expressly provided that corporations need not be included within the scope of the word "person" where the context suggests a more limited reach. Not a word in the legislative history of the Act gives any indication of the contexts in which Congress felt it appropriate to include a corporation as a person. . . .

There are other factors, however, which suggest that the Congress which enacted § 1983 may well have intended the word "person" "to be used in a more limited sense," as *Monroe* concluded. It is true that this Court had held that both commercial corporations . . . and municipal corporations . . . were "citizens" of a State within the meaning of the jurisdictional provisions of Art. III. Congress, however, also knew that this label did not apply in all contexts, since this Court in Paul v. Virginia, 8 Wall. [75 U.S.] 168 (1869), had held commercial corporations not to be "citizens" within the meaning of the Privileges and Immunities Clause, U.S.Const., Art. IV, § 2. . . . Indeed, it may be presumed that Congress intended that a corporation should enjoy the same status under the Ku Klux Klan Act as it did under the Fourteenth Amendment, since it had been assured that § 1 "was so very simple and really reënact[ed] the Constitution." Cong.Globe, 42d Cong., 1st Sess., 569 (1871) (remarks of Sen. Edmunds). At the time § 1983 was enacted the only federal case to consider the status of corporations under the Fourteenth Amendment had concluded, with impeccable logic, that a corporation was neither a "citizen" nor a "person." Insurance Co. v. New Orleans, 13 Fed.Cas. 67 (No. 7,052) (CC La. 1870). . . .

The meaning of § 1 of the Act of 1871 has been subjected in this case to a more searching and careful analysis than it was in *Monroe*, and it may well be that on the basis of this closer analysis of the legislative debates a conclusion contrary to the *Monroe* holding could have been reached when that case was decided 17 years ago. But the rejection of the Sherman amendment remains instructive in that here alone did the legislative debates squarely focus on the liability of municipal corporations, and that liability was rejected. Any inference which might be drawn from the Dictionary Act or from general expressions of benevolence in the debate on § 1 that the word "person" was intended to include municipal corporations falls far short of showing "beyond doubt" that this Court in *Monroe* "misapprehended the meaning of the controlling provision." Errors such as the Court may have fallen into in *Monroe* do not end the inquiry as to *stare decisis*; they merely begin it. I would adhere to the holding of *Monroe* as to the liability of a municipal corporation under § 1983. . . .

Further Notes on § 1983

(1) Justice Brennan in *Monell* effectively exposes the weakness of the arguments made against municipal liability under § 1983 in *Monroe v. Pape.* Does he do as well in defending his own dictum excluding *vicarious* municipal liability? Is there any municipal liability that is not vicarious?

(2) How does one determine what constitutes "official policy" for which a city is liable under § 1983? In *Monell* the city did not deny that the challenged practice had once represented "citywide policy," and without explanation the Court said it "unquestionably" did.[1] Oklahoma City v. Tuttle, 471 U.S. 808 (1985), made the obvious point that a single violent act by a policeman did not constitute official policy and added that it could not be the basis for inferring a policy of inadequate police training either. Pembaur v. Cincinnati, 475 U.S. 469 (1986), over three dissents, found the city liable for an unreasonable search ordered by an assistant prosecutor, on the ground that "policy" could be made on an ad hoc basis by an officer with policymaking authority under state law.[2] Does any of this help? Can you?

(3) The *Monell* distinction is subjected to heavy criticism in Kramer & Sykes, Municipal Liability Under § 1983: A Legal and Economic Analysis, 1987 Sup.Ct.Rev. 249. Arguing that the lack of detail in § 1983 leaves the Court free to determine the extent of municipal liability as a matter of federal common law, they find that a blanket denial of responsibility for acts not representing official policy provides too little deterrence of unlawful action and an inefficient allocation of risk in cases in which the individual officer is judgment-proof. Their solution: either the ordinary rule of respondeat superior or—in their view perhaps even better—municipal liability for failure to take reasonable steps to prevent wrongdoing by individual officers. Do you see why?

(4) In Fitzpatrick v. Bitzer, 427 U.S. 445 (1976), the Court relied on *Monroe v. Pape* to hold that a *state* could not be sued under § 1983: If a

1. See also Pembaur v. Cincinnati, 475 U.S. 469, 481 (1986), explaining that *Monell* had involved "a written rule."

2. See also St. Louis v. Praprotnik, 485 U.S. 112 (1988), concluding that under the applicable state law a supervisor who had transferred the plaintiff to a less attractive job had no authority to make policy; Schnapper, Civil Rights Litigation After *Monell,* 79 Colum.L.Rev. 213 (1979).

city was not a person for purposes of this provision, neither was a state. *Monell* destroyed the original basis for this conclusion, but the Court adhered to it anyway in Will v. Michigan Dept. of State Police, 109 S.Ct. 2304 (1989). Ordinarily, said Justice White, the word "person" was construed not to include the sovereign. Moreover, if Congress meant to "alter the 'usual constitutional balance between the States and the Federal Government,'" it must make its intention clear. The Court had already held that § 1983 was not plain enough to remove the state's normal immunity from suit in federal court (see p. 466 infra), and it would be odd to conclude that a statute designed principally to provide a federal forum for the vindication of federal rights made states suable only in state court. Moreover, the plaintiff could not "circumvent congressional intent" by the "mere pleading device" of bringing the suit against a state officer in his official capacity, for such an action was "no different from a suit against the State itself." Four Justices dissented for the reasons given in holding a municipality suable in *Monell.*

(5) In Aldinger v. Howard, 427 U.S. 1 (1976), the plaintiff in a § 1983 action against county officials before *Monell* attempted to join a state-law claim against the county itself on the basis of pendent jurisdiction. The Court said no: *Monroe* had held that a local government was not a "person" under § 1983, and pendent jurisdiction should not be allowed "to circumvent this exclusion." Was this a fair reading of *Monroe*? Three dissenters thought not: The House had refused to adopt the Sherman Amendment not out of "hostility to federal judicial forums entertaining claims arising under state law" but because it thought "'Congress had no constitutional power to impose any obligation upon county and town organizations. . . .'"

Does *Aldinger* mean that a state-law claim against a county on the basis of vicarious liability cannot be joined to a § 1983 claim in federal court after *Monell*? Does *Finley v. United States,* p. 188 supra?

(6) Section 1983 is a very sparely written provision. It contains no statute of limitations; it does not say whether it allows an action for wrongful death; it does not mention traditional tort defenses such as consent or official immunity; it does not specify a measure of damages. 42 U.S.C. § 1988 seems to speak to the problem of filling gaps in § 1983 and in related civil-rights statutes:

> The jurisdiction in civil and criminal matters conferred on the district courts by the provisions of this Title, and of Title "Civil Rights," and of Title "Crimes," for the protection of all persons in the United States in their civil rights, and for their vindication, shall be exercised and enforced in conformity with the laws of the United States, so far as such laws are suitable to carry the same into effect; but in all cases where they are not adapted to the object, or are deficient in the provisions necessary to furnish suitable remedies and punish offenses against law, the common law, as modified and changed by the constitution and statutes of the state where in the court having jurisdiction of such civil or criminal cause is held, so far as the same is not inconsistent with the Constitution and laws of the United States, shall be extended to and govern the said courts in the trial and disposition of

> the cause, and, if it is of a criminal nature, in the infliction of punishment on the party found guilty. . . .

In a series of cases culminating in Owens v. Okure, 488 U.S. 235 (1989), the Supreme Court relied on § 1988 to reinforce its conclusion that state statutes of limitations were applicable to actions under § 1983. See also p. 364 supra. For reasons of certainty and simplicity, *Owens* concluded as a matter of federal law that the appropriate statute was that generally governing actions for personal injury. Board of Regents v. Tomanio, 446 U.S. 478 (1980), and Hardin v. Straub, 109 S.Ct. 1998 (1989), held that state law determined whether the limitation period should be tolled because of obstacles to the bringing of suit: Neither tolling (as in *Hardin*) nor the refusal to toll (as in *Tomanio*) was "inconsistent with the Constitution and laws of the United States" within the meaning of § 1988.

(7) Sullivan v. Little Hunting Park, Inc., 396 U.S. 229 (1969), was an action for private racial discrimination under 42 U.S.C. § 1982, which is even less informative than § 1983: It guarantees to every citizen "the same right . . . as is enjoyed by white citizens . . . to inherit, purchase, lease, sell, hold, and convey real and personal property," without mentioning any remedies whatever. Relying on cases analogous to *J. I. Case Co. v. Borak*, supra p. 376, the Court first declared that "[t]he existence of a statutory right implies the existence of all necessary and appropriate remedies." It then invoked § 1988 as authority that "[c]ompensatory damages for deprivation of a federal right are governed by federal standards" and added that under that section "both federal and state rules on damages may be utilized, whichever better serves the policies expressed in the federal statutes." Three dissenters protested, in an opinion by Justice Harlan, emphasizing that the case had come from a state court:

> Section 1988 . . . is concerned with the remedial powers of *federal district courts* and it provides that the federal courts shall look to state law to find appropriate remedies when the applicable federal civil rights law is "deficient. . . ." But the majority turns this provision on its head by suggesting (1) that § 1988 creates a federal remedy, apart from state law, when the remedial provisions of a civil rights statute, like § 1982, are "deficient;" and (2) that § 1988 itself somehow imposes this federal remedy on the States.

Was this an accurate reading of the majority opinion?

(8) In Robertson v. Wegmann, 436 U.S. 584 (1978), the plaintiff in a § 1983 action died while the case was pending. Section 1983 is silent as to the survival of actions, and the relevant state law afforded no relief since the complainant had left no close relatives. The trial court, despite § 1988, refused to dismiss the case, finding the limited state survival provision "inconsistent with the . . . laws of the United States" within the meaning of § 1988 because inadequate to protect § 1983 rights, and creating a broader "federal common law of survival in civil rights actions in favor of the personal representative of the deceased." The Fifth Circuit affirmed, but the Supreme Court, in an opinion by Justice Marshall, reversed:

> The goal of compensating those injured by a deprivation of rights provides no basis for requiring compensation of one who is merely

> suing as the executor of the deceased's estate. And, given that most Louisiana actions survive the plaintiff's death, the fact that a particular action might abate surely would not adversely affect § 1983's role in preventing official illegality, at least in situations in which there is no claim that the illegality caused the plaintiff's death. . . . A different situation might well be presented . . . if state law "did not provide for survival of any tort actions,". . . or if it significantly restricted the types of actions that survive. . . . We intimate no view, moreover, about whether abatement based on state law could be allowed in a situation in which deprivation of federal rights caused death.

Three dissenters, in an opinion by Justice Blackmun, argued that the state law did indeed impair § 1983's purposes. They also raised a more fundamental objection.

> Section 1988 requires the utilization of federal law ("shall be exercised and enforced in conformity with the laws of the United States"). It authorizes resort to state statute only if the federal laws "are not adapted to the object" . . . or are "deficient in the provisions necessary to furnish suitable remedies. . . ." . . . [That] survivorship . . . is not specifically covered by the federal statute . . . does not mean that "the laws of the United States" are not "suitable" or are "not adapted to the object" or are "deficient in the provisions necessary."

Sullivan had said the court might choose either federal or state damage rules under § 1988, though the statute was silent as to damages; federal common law had been the basis of the Court's decisions on official immunity (see pp. 474–84 infra) and the measure of damages in § 1983 cases; in cases outside the civil-rights context the Court had developed interstitial federal common law despite the command of 28 U.S.C. § 1652 that state law provides the rule of decision "except where the Constitution or treaties of the United States or Acts of Congress otherwise require or provide." The majority's response: The courts below had rejected the dissent's argument that federal law was not "deficient," and "respondent here [the plaintiff] agrees with them." [3]

Do you see any reason why § 1988 should be taken to impose a *greater* restriction on the lawmaking powers of federal courts than the Rules of Decision Act does? Take another look at their respective provisions.

Does *Robertson* really hold that state law determines survival in § 1983 cases? If so, does such a case arise under federal law? [4]

3. The Court expressly declined to decide whether § 1988's reference to "the common law" meant state law or "the kind of general common law that was an established part of our federal jurisprudence by the time of § 1988's passage". "It makes no difference for our purposes which interpretation is the correct one, because Louisiana has a survivorship statute that, under the terms of § 1988, plainly governs this case." Was that so plain?

4. See 436 U.S. at 588: "Regardless of the source of the law applied in a particular case, however, it is clear that the ultimate rule adopted under § 1988 'is a federal rule responsive to the need whenever a federal right is impaired.'" Does § 1343(3) still make a difference?

(9) Professor Theodore Eisenberg has argued that § 1988 was never meant to apply to § 1983 cases at all. It was initially enacted as part of a statute (now 28 U.S.C. § 1443, discussed at pp. 552–56 infra) providing for removal of certain proceedings brought under state law; only its separation from the removal provision in the general statutory revision of 1874 created the appearance of its broader applicability; and the revision was not meant to alter the law. Thus in his view the otherwise insuperable difficulties of construing § 1988 disappear: "Federal law is deficient within the meaning of section 1988 only when a substantive state rule, civil or criminal, is the source of the action. . . . [S]tate laws are inconsistent with federal law only if they violate it." [5] Persuasive? Eisenberg, State Law in Federal Civil Rights Cases: The Proper Scope of Section 1988, 128 U.Pa.L.Rev. 499, 531–32 (1980).

BIVENS v. SIX UNKNOWN NAMED AGENTS OF FEDERAL BUREAU OF NARCOTICS

403 U.S. 388 (1971).

MR. JUSTICE BRENNAN delivered the opinion of the Court.

The Fourth Amendment provides that:

> "The right of the people to be secure in their persons, houses, papers, and effects, against unreasonable searches and seizures, shall not be violated. . . ."

In Bell v. Hood, 327 U.S. 678 (1946), we reserved the question whether violation of that command by a federal agent acting under color of his authority gives rise to a cause of action for damages consequent upon his unconstitutional conduct. Today we hold that it does.

This case has its origin in an arrest and search carried out on the morning of November 26, 1965. Petitioner's complaint alleged that on that day respondents, agents of the Federal Bureau of Narcotics acting under claim of federal authority, entered his apartment and arrested him for alleged narcotics violations. The agents manacled petitioner in front of his wife and children, and threatened to arrest the entire family. They searched the apartment from stem to stern. Thereafter, petitioner was taken to the federal courthouse in Brooklyn, where he was interrogated, booked, and subjected to a visual strip search.

On July 7, 1967, petitioner brought suit in Federal District Court. In addition to the allegations above, his complaint asserted that the arrest and search were effected without a warrant, and that unreasona-

5. Eisenberg quotes the sponsor of the original bill:

> [The third section of the bill] provides further that no person whose equal civil rights are denied him in the State courts shall be tried by those courts for any offense, but that he shall have a right to remove his cause into the courts of the United States, and be there tried if it be for an offense against the laws of the United States, according to those laws, and if it be for an offense which is not provided for by the laws of the United States, then according to the common law as modified by the statutes and constitution of the State where the offense is committed, so far as they are not inconsistent with the Constitution and laws of the United States.

ble force was employed in making the arrest; fairly read, it alleges as well that the arrest was made without probable cause. Petitioner claimed to have suffered great humiliation, embarrassment, and mental suffering as a result of the agents' unlawful conduct, and sought $15,000 damages from each of them. The District Court, on respondents' motion, dismissed the complaint on the ground, *inter alia*, that it failed to state a cause of action. 276 F.Supp. 12 (EDNY 1967). The Court of Appeals, one judge concurring specially, affirmed on that basis. 409 F.2d 718 (CA2 1969). . . . We reverse.

I

Respondents do not argue that petitioner should be entirely without remedy for an unconstitutional invasion of his rights by federal agents. In respondents' view, however, the rights that petitioner asserts—primarily rights of privacy—are creations of state and not of federal law. Accordingly, they argue, petitioner may obtain money damages to redress invasion of these rights only by an action in tort, under state law, in the state courts. In this scheme the Fourth Amendment would serve merely to limit the extent to which the agents could defend the state law tort suit by asserting that their actions were a valid exercise of federal power: if the agents were shown to have violated the Fourth Amendment, such a defense would be lost to them and they would stand before the state law merely as private individuals. Candidly admitting that it is the policy of the Department of Justice to remove all such suits from the state to the federal courts for decision, respondents nevertheless urge that we uphold dismissal of petitioner's complaint in federal court, and remit him to filing an action in the state courts in order that the case may properly be removed to the federal court for decision on the basis of state law.

We think that respondents' thesis rests upon an unduly restrictive view of the Fourth Amendment's protection against unreasonable searches and seizures by federal agents, a view that has consistently been rejected by this Court. . . .

[T]he Fourth Amendment operates as a limitation upon the exercise of federal power regardless of whether the State in whose jurisdiction that power is exercised would prohibit or penalize the identical act if engaged in by a private citizen. It guarantees to citizens of the United States the absolute right to be free from unreasonable searches and seizures carried out by virtue of federal authority. And "where federally protected rights have been invaded, it has been the rule from the beginning that courts will be alert to adjust their remedies so as to grant the necessary relief." Bell v. Hood, 327 U.S., at 684 . . . .

That damages may be obtained for injuries consequent upon a violation of the Fourth Amendment by federal officials should hardly seem a surprising proposition. Historically, damages have been regarded as the ordinary remedy for an invasion of personal interests in liberty. See Nixon v. Condon, 286 U.S. 73 (1932) . . . . Of course, the Fourth Amendment does not in so many words provide for its enforcement by an award of money damages for the consequences of its violation. But "it is . . . well settled that where legal rights have been invaded, and a federal statute provides for a general right to sue for such invasion, federal courts may use any available remedy to make good the wrong done." Bell v. Hood, 327 U.S., at 684 (footnote omitted.) The present case involves no special factors counselling hesitation in the absence of affirmative action by Congress. We are not dealing with a question of "federal fiscal policy," as in United States v. Standard Oil Co., 332 U.S. 301, 311 (1947). In that case we refused to infer from the Government-soldier relationship that the United States could recover damages from one who negligently injured a soldier and thereby caused the Government to pay his medical expenses and lose his services during the course of his hospitalization. Noting that Congress was normally quite solicitous where the federal purse was involved, we pointed out that "the United States [was] the party plaintiff to the suit. And the United States has power at any time to create the liability." . . . Nor are we asked in this case to impose liability upon a congressional employee for actions contrary to no constitutional prohibition, but merely said to be in excess of the authority delegated to him by the Congress. Wheeldin v. Wheeler, 373 U.S. 647 (1963). Finally, we cannot accept respondents' formulation of the question as whether the availability of money damages is necessary to enforce the Fourth Amendment. For we have here no explicit congressional declaration that persons injured by a federal officer's violation of the Fourth Amendment may not recover money damages from the agents, but must instead be remitted to another remedy, equally effective in the view of Congress. The question is merely whether petitioner, if he can demonstrate an injury consequent upon the violation by federal agents of his Fourth Amendment rights, is entitled to redress his injury through a particular remedial mechanism normally available in the federal courts. Cf. J. I. Case Co. v. Borak, 377 U.S. 426, 433 (1964). . . . "The very essence of civil liberty certainly consists in the right of every individual to claim the protection of the laws, whenever he receives an injury." Marbury v. Madison, 1 Cranch [5 U.S.] 137, 163 (1803). Having concluded that petitioner's complaint states a cause of action under the Fourth Amendment, . . . we hold that petitioner is entitled to recover money damages for any injuries he has suffered as a result of the agents' violation of the Amendment. . . .

The judgment of the Court of Appeals is reversed and the case is remanded for further proceedings consistent with this opinion. . . .

MR. JUSTICE HARLAN, concurring in the judgment. . . .

For the reasons set forth below, I am of the opinion that federal courts do have the power to award damages for violation of "constitutionally protected interests" and I agree with the Court that a traditional judicial remedy such as damages is appropriate to the vindication of the personal interests protected by the Fourth Amendment. . . .

II

The contention that the federal courts are powerless to accord a litigant damages for a claimed invasion of his federal constitutional rights until Congress explicitly authorizes the remedy cannot rest on the notion that the decision to grant compensatory relief involves a resolution of policy considerations not susceptible of judicial discernment. Thus, in suits for damages based on violations of federal statutes lacking any express authorization of a damage remedy, this Court has authorized such relief where, in its view, damages are necessary to effectuate the congressional policy underpinning the substantive provisions of the statute. J. I. Case Co. v. Borak, 377 U.S. 426 (1964). . . .[4]

I do not think that the fact that the interest is protected by the Constitution rather than statute or common law justifies the assertion that federal courts are powerless to grant damages in the absence of explicit congressional action authorizing the remedy. Initially, I note that it would be at least anomalous to conclude that the federal judiciary—while competent to choose among the range of traditional judicial remedies to implement statutory and common-law policies, and even to generate substantive rules governing primary behavior in furtherance of broadly formulated policies articulated by statute or Constitution, see Textile Workers Union v. Lincoln Mills, 353 U.S. 448 (1957); United States v. Standard Oil Co., 332 U.S. 301, 304–311 (1947); Clearfield Trust Co. v. United States, 318 U.S. 363 (1943)—is powerless to accord a damages remedy to vindicate social policies which, by virtue of their inclusion in the Constitution, are aimed predominantly at restraining the Government as an instrument of the popular will.

More importantly, the presumed availability of federal equitable relief against threatened invasions of constitutional interests appears entirely to negate the contention that the status of an interest as constitutionally protected divests federal courts of the power to grant damages absent express congressional authorization. Congress provided specially for the exercise of equitable remedial powers by federal courts, see Act of May 8, 1792, § 2, 1 Stat. 276; C. Wright, Law of Federal Courts 257 (2d ed. 1970), in part because of the limited availability of equitable remedies in state courts in the early days of the

4. The *Borak* case is an especially clear example of the exercise of federal judicial power to accord damages as an appropriate remedy in the absence of any express statutory authorization of a federal cause of action. There we "implied"—from what can only be characterized as an "exclusively procedural provision" affording access to a federal forum . . .—a private cause of action for damages for violation of § 14(a) of the Securities Exchange Act of 1934, 48 Stat. 895, 15 U.S.C. § 78n(a). We did so in an area where federal regulation has been singularly comprehensive and elaborate administrative enforcement machinery had been provided. The exercise of judicial power involved in *Borak* simply cannot be justified in terms of statutory construction, see Hill, Constitutional Remedies, 69 Col.L.Rev. 1109, 1120–1121 (1969); nor did the *Borak* Court purport to do so. . . . The notion of "implying" a remedy, therefore, as applied to cases like *Borak*, can only refer to a process whereby the federal judiciary exercises a choice among *traditionally available* judicial remedies according to reasons related to the substantive social policy embodied in an act of positive law. . . .

Republic. See Guaranty Trust Co. v. York, 326 U.S. 99, 104–105 (1945). And this Court's decisions make clear that, at least absent congressional restrictions, the scope of equitable remedial discretion is to be determined according to the distinctive historical traditions of equity as an institution, Holmberg v. Armbrecht, 327 U.S. 392, 395–396 (1946); Sprague v. Ticonic National Bank, 307 U.S. 161, 165–166 (1939). . . .

[I]f a general grant of jurisdiction to the federal courts by Congress is thought adequate to empower a federal court to grant equitable relief for all areas of subject-matter jurisdiction enumerated therein, see 28 U.S.C. § 1331(a), then it seems to me that the same statute is sufficient to empower a federal court to grant a traditional remedy at law. Of course, the special historical traditions governing the federal equity system, see Sprague v. Ticonic National Bank, 307 U.S. 161 (1939), might still bear on the comparative appropriateness of granting equitable relief as opposed to money damages. That possibility, however, relates, not to whether the federal courts have the power to afford one type of remedy as opposed to the other, but rather to the criteria which should govern the exercise of our power. . . .

III . . .

The question then, is, as I see it, whether compensatory relief is "necessary" or "appropriate" to the vindication of the interest asserted. . . . In resolving that question, it seems to me that the range of policy considerations we may take into account is at least as broad as the range of a legislature would consider with respect to an express statutory authorization of a traditional remedy. In this regard I agree with the Court that the appropriateness of according Bivens compensatory relief does not turn simply on the deterrent effect liability will have on federal official conduct. Damages as a traditional form of compensation for invasion of a legally protected interest may be entirely appropriate even if no substantial deterrent effects on future official lawlessness might be thought to result. Bivens, after all, has invoked judicial processes claiming entitlement to compensation for injuries resulting from allegedly lawless official behavior, if those injuries are properly compensable in money damages. I do not think a court of law—vested with the power to accord a remedy—should deny him his relief simply because he cannot show that future lawless conduct will thereby be deterred.

And I think it is clear that Bivens advances a claim of the sort that, if proved, would be properly compensable in damages. The personal interests protected by the Fourth Amendment are those we attempt to capture by the notion of "privacy"; while the Court today properly points out that the type of harm which officials can inflict when they invade protected zones of an individual's life are different from the types of harm private citizens inflict on one another, the experience of judges in dealing with private trespass and false imprisonment claims supports the conclusion that courts of law are capable of making the types of judgment concerning causation and magnitude of injury necessary to accord meaningful compensation for invasion of Fourth Amendment rights.[9]

On the other hand, the limitations on state remedies for violation of common-law rights by private citizens argue in favor of a federal damages remedy. The injuries inflicted by officials acting under color of law, while no less compensable in damages than those inflicted by private parties, are substantially different in kind. . . . It seems to me entirely proper that these injuries be compensable according to uniform rules of federal law, especially in light of the very large element of federal law which must in any event control the scope of official defenses to liability. See Wheeldin v. Wheeler, 373 U.S. 647, 652 (1963); . . . Howard v. Lyons, 360 U.S. 593 (1959). Certainly, there is very little to be gained from the standpoint of federalism by preserving different rules of liability for federal officers dependent on the State where the injury occurs. Cf. United States v. Standard Oil Co., 332 U.S. 301, 305–311 (1947).

Putting aside the desirability of leaving the problem of federal official liability to the vagaries of common-law actions, it is apparent that some form of damages is the only possible remedy for someone in Bivens' alleged position. It will be a rare case indeed in which an individual in Bivens' position will be able to obviate the harm by securing injunctive relief from any court. However desirable a direct remedy against the Government might be as a substitute for individual official liability, the sovereign still remains immune to suit. Finally, assuming Bivens' innocence of the crime charged, the "exclusionary rule" is simply irrelevant. For people in Bivens' shoes, it is damages or nothing.

The only substantial policy consideration advanced against recognition of a federal cause of action for violation of Fourth Amendment rights by federal officials is the incremental expenditure of judicial resources that will be necessitated by this class of litigation. There is, however, something ultimately self-defeating about this argument. For if, as the Government contends, damages will rarely be realized by plaintiffs in these cases because of jury hostility, the limited resources of the official concerned, etc., then I am not ready to assume that there will be a significant increase in the expenditure of judicial resources on these claims. Few responsible lawyers and plaintiffs are likely to choose the course of litigation if the statistical chances of success are truly *de minimis*. And I simply cannot agree with my Brother Black that the possibility of "frivolous" claims—if defined simply as claims with no legal merit—warrants closing the courthouse doors to people in Bivens' situation. There are other ways, short of that, of coping with frivolous lawsuits.

9. The same, of course, may not be true with respect to other types of constitutionally protected interests, and therefore the appropriateness of money damages may well vary with the nature of the personal interest asserted. . . .

On the other hand, if—as I believe is the case with respect, at least, to the most flagrant abuses of official power—damages to some degree will be available when the option of litigation is chosen, then the question appears to be how Fourth Amendment interests rank on a scale of social values compared with, for example, the interests of stockholders defrauded by misleading proxies. See, J. I. Case Co. v. Borak, supra. Judicial resources, I am well aware, are increasingly scarce these days. Nonetheless, when we automatically close the courthouse door solely on this basis, we implicitly express a value judgment on the comparative importance of classes of legally protected interests. And current limitations upon the effective functioning of the courts arising from budgetary inadequacies should not be permitted to stand in the way of the recognition of otherwise sound constitutional principles. . . .

For these reasons, I concur in the judgment of the Court.

MR. CHIEF JUSTICE BURGER, dissenting.

I dissent from today's holding which judicially creates a damage remedy not provided for by the Constitution and not enacted by Congress. We would more surely preserve the important values of the doctrine of separation of powers—and perhaps get a better result—by recommending a solution to the Congress as the branch of government in which the Constitution has vested the legislative power. Legislation is the business of the Congress, and it has the facilities and competence for that task—as we do not. . . .

The problems of both error and deliberate misconduct by law enforcement officials call for a workable remedy. Private damage actions against individual police officers concededly have not adequately met this requirement, and it would be fallacious to assume today's work of the Court in creating a remedy will really accomplish its stated objective. There is some validity to the claims that juries will not return verdicts against individual officers except in those unusual cases where the violation has been flagrant or where the error has been complete, as in the arrest of the wrong person or the search of the wrong house. There is surely serious doubt, for example, that a drug peddler caught packing his wares will be able to arouse much sympathy in a jury on the ground that the police officer did not announce his identity and purpose fully or because he failed to utter a "few more words." . . . In any event an actual recovery depends on finding nonexempt assets of the police officer from which a judgment can be satisfied.

I conclude, therefore, that an entirely different remedy is necessary but it is one that in my view is as much beyond judicial power as the step the Court takes today. Congress should develop an administrative or quasi-judicial remedy against the government itself to afford compensation and restitution for persons whose Fourth Amendment rights have been violated. . . .

MR. JUSTICE BLACK, dissenting.

In my opinion for the Court in Bell v. Hood, 327 U.S. 678 (1946), we did as the Court states, reserve the question whether an unreasonable search made by a federal officer in violation of the Fourth Amendment gives the subject of the search a federal cause of action for damages against the officers making the search. There can be no doubt that Congress could create a federal cause of action for damages for an unreasonable search in violation of the Fourth Amendment. Although Congress has created such a federal cause of action against *state* officials acting under color of state law,* it has never created such a cause of action against federal officials. If it wanted to do so, Congress could, of course, create a remedy against federal officials who violate the Fourth Amendment in the performance of their duties. But the point of this case and the fatal weakness in the Court's judgment is that neither Congress nor the State of New York has enacted legislation creating such a right of action. For us to do so is, in my judgment, an exercise of power that the Constitution does not give us.

Even if we had the legislative power to create a remedy, there are many reasons why we should decline to create a cause of action where none has existed since the formation of our Government. The courts of the United States as well as those of the States are choked with lawsuits. The number of cases on the docket of this Court have reached an unprecedented volume in recent years. A majority of these cases are brought by citizens with substantial complaints—persons who are physically or economically injured by torts or frauds or governmental infringement of their rights; persons who have been unjustly deprived of their liberty or their property; and persons who have not yet received the equal opportunity in education, employment, and pursuit of happiness that was the dream of our forefathers. Unfortunately, there have also been a growing number of frivolous lawsuits, particularly actions for damages against law enforcement officers whose conduct has been judicially sanctioned by state trial and appellate courts and in many instances even by this Court. My fellow Justices on this Court and our brethren throughout the federal judiciary know only too well the time-consuming task of conscientiously poring over hundreds of thousands of pages of factual allegations of misconduct by police, judicial, and corrections officials. Of course, there are instances of legitimate grievances, but legislators might well desire to devote judicial resources to other problems of a more serious nature.

We sit at the top of a judicial system accused by some of nearing the point of collapse. Many criminal defendants do not receive speedy trials and neither society nor the accused are assured of justice when inordinate delays occur. Citizens must wait years to litigate their private civil suits. Substantial changes in correctional and parole

* . . . Rev.Stat. § 1979, 42 U.S.C. § 1983.

systems demand the attention of the lawmakers and the judiciary. If I were a legislator I might well find these and other needs so pressing as to make me believe that the resources of lawyers and judges should be devoted to them rather than to civil damage actions against officers who generally strive to perform within constitutional bounds. There is also a real danger that such suits might deter officials from the *proper* and honest performance of their duties.

All of these considerations make imperative careful study and weighing of the arguments both for and against the creation of such a remedy under the Fourth Amendment. I would have great difficulty for myself in resolving the competing policies, goals, and priorities in the use of resources, if I thought it were my job to resolve those questions. But that is not my task. The task of evaluating the pros and cons of creating judicial remedies for particular wrongs is a matter for Congress and the legislatures of the States. Congress has not provided that any federal court can entertain a suit against a federal officer for violations of Fourth Amendment rights occurring in the performance of his duties. A strong inference can be drawn from creation of such actions against state officials that Congress does not desire to permit such suits against federal officials. Should the time come when Congress desires such lawsuits, it has before it a model of valid legislation, 42 U.S.C. § 1983, to create a damage remedy against federal officers. Cases could be cited to support the legal proposition which I assert, but it seems to me to be a matter of common understanding that the business of the judiciary is to interpret the laws and not to make them.

I dissent.

MR. JUSTICE BLACKMUN, dissenting.

I, too, dissent. I do so largely for the reasons expressed in Chief Judge Lumbard's thoughtful and scholarly opinion for the Court of Appeals. But I also feel that the judicial legislation, which the Court by its opinion today concededly is effectuating, opens the door for another avalanche of new federal cases. . . .

Notes on Other Remedies Against Government Officals

(1) In Bell v. Hood, 327 U.S. 678 (1946), as in *Bivens*, the plaintiff sought damages under federal law for a federal officer's alleged invasion of his Fourth Amendment rights. The district court dismissed for want of jurisdiction; the Supreme Court, assuming that no federal law provided for damages in such a case, nevertheless reversed in an opinion by Justice Black:

> [I]t is well settled that the failure to state a proper cause of action calls for a judgment on the merits and not for a dismissal for want of jurisdiction. . . . [A] suit may sometimes be dismissed for want of jurisdiction where the alleged claim under the Constitution or federal statutes clearly appears to be immaterial and made solely for the

> purpose of obtaining jurisdiction or where such a claim is wholly insubstantial and frivolous. . . . Respondents' contention does not show that petitioners' cause is insubstantial or frivolous, and the complaint does in fact raise serious questions, both of law and fact, which the District Court can decide only after it has assumed jurisdiction over the controversy.

Cf. *Zucht v. King*, infra p. 580, holding the Supreme Court's jurisdiction over state-court judgments limited by the requirement that the federal question be "substantial."

On remand the district court in *Bell v. Hood* took jurisdiction and dismissed for failure to state a claim on which relief could be granted. 71 F.Supp. 813, 820–21 (S.D.Cal.1947). Was this disposition inconsistent with the Supreme Court's decision? Does it make any difference whether a case is dismissed for want of jurisdiction or for failure to state a claim?

(2) Is there any answer to Justice Harlan's argument in *Bivens* that the case was indistinguishable both from those allowing equitable relief against constitutional violations and from those allowing damages for violations of federal statutes? See pp. 46–52 and 370–79 supra. If not, what is the impact on *Bivens* of the numerous Supreme Court decisions since 1975 refusing to allow damages in statutory cases in the absence of explicit language in the statute?

(3) In light of the Rules of Decision Act (28 U.S.C. § 1652) as construed in *Erie R. R. v. Tompkins*, p. 327, supra, what business have the federal courts creating common-law remedies either in *Bivens* or in either of the categories of cases relied on by Justice Harlan? [1] Or isn't that what the Court was doing?

Can Congress abolish the *Bivens* remedy? Can it abolish the defensive remedy for unconstitutional action recognized by *Marbury v. Madison*? Is there a reasoned basis for distinguishing these two questions? Is *General Oil Co. v. Crain*, infra p. 586, relevant here?

(4) Davis v. Passman, 442 U.S. 228 (1979). Congressman Passman fired Shirley Davis from his staff on the ground "that it was essential that the understudy to my Administrative Assistant be a man." She sued in federal court, seeking damages on the basis of the "equal-protection component" of the Fifth Amendment's Due Process Clause. The Fifth Circuit affirmed a dismissal on the ground that no law afforded her a right of action for damages; the Supreme Court, in an opinion by Justice Brennan, reversed.

The court below, concluding that the *Bivens* remedy was "not wholly of constitutional dimensions" but was "implied as a matter of federal common law . . . subject . . . to the power of Congress to alter or withdraw," had applied the tests laid down for determining the right to seek damages for *statutory* violations in Cort v. Ash, 422 U.S. 66 (1975), p. 374 supra. The Supreme Court said the *Cort* tests were inapplicable:

1. From the beginning, procedural matters in equity cases were governed not by state law, as at common law, but by "the principles, rules and usages which belong to courts of equity" (1 Stat. 275, 276 (1792)). This provision disappeared with the adoption of the Federal Rules of Civil Procedure in 1938.

> Statutory rights and obligations are established by Congress, and it is entirely appropriate for Congress, in creating these rights and obligations, to determine in addition who may enforce them and in what manner. For example, statutory rights and obligations are often embedded in complex regulatory schemes, so that if they are not enforced through private causes of action, they may nevertheless be enforced through alternative mechanisms, such as criminal prosecutions. . . . In each case, however, the question is the nature of the legislative intent informing a specific statute, and *Cort* set out the criteria through which this intent could be discerned.
>
> The Constitution, on the other hand, does not "partake of the prolixity of a legal code." . . . One of "its important objects" . . . is the designation of rights. And in "its great outlines" . . . the judiciary is clearly discernible as the primary means through which these rights may be enforced. . . . [U]nless such rights are to become merely precatory, the class of those litigants who allege that their own constitutional rights have been violated, and who at the same time have no effective means other than the judiciary to enforce these rights, must be able to invoke the existing jurisdiction of the courts. . . . For Davis, as for Bivens, "it is damages or nothing." [2]

Moreover, an equitable remedy for federal denials of equal protection had been recognized in the school-segregation case of Bolling v. Sharpe, 347 U.S. 497 (1954); and Congress by omitting congressional employees from the Title VII remedies for discrimination in federal employment (42 U.S.C. § 2000e–16a) had given no indication that it meant "to foreclose alternative remedies available to those not covered by the statute." [3]

(5) Carlson v. Green, 446 U.S. 14 (1980). The plaintiff sued for failure of federal prison authorities to render competent medical assistance to her son, who had died of an asthma attack suffered in prison. The Court, in another opinion by Justice Brennan, held that *Bivens* applied to Eighth Amendment claims of cruel and unusual punishment and that the prisoner's claim survived his death as a matter of federal law. *Bivens* and *Davis* had established, the Court said, "that the victims of a constitutional violation by a federal agent have a right to recover damages . . . despite the absence of any federal statute" unless one of two conditions was met:

> The first is when defendants demonstrate "special factors counselling hesitation in the absence of affirmative action by Congress." . . . The second is when defendants show that Congress has provided an alternative remedy which it explicitly declared to be a *substitute* for recovery directly under the Constitution and viewed as equally effective.

2. Passman was no longer in Congress when the case was decided.

3. Four dissenters invoked separation-of-powers concerns to argue against implication of a damage remedy or viewed the question of immunity under the Speech or Debate Clause as a threshold issue; three of them added that Congress by taking "pains to exempt itself from . . . Title VII" had "indicated an intention to reserve to its Members the right to select, employ, promote, and discharge staff personnel without judicial interference." For consideration of the immunity issue see p. 481 infra.

Neither factor, Justice Brennan continued, was present. Though the Federal Tort Claims Act had been amended in 1974 to allow the United States itself to be sued in a case like *Carlson* (28 U.S.C. § 2680(h)), that statute was "not a sufficient protector of the citizens' constitutional rights" for several reasons. It did not allow punitive damages or a jury trial; it made liability dependent upon state law; and Government liability was a less effective deterrent than liability of the officer himself. Moreover, the Senate Report at the time the Tort Claims Act was amended had expressly stated that "innocent individuals who are subjected to raids will have a cause of action against the individual Federal agents *and* the Federal Government." S.Rep. No. 93–588 (1973), p. 3.[4] Finally, despite the holding in *Robertson v. Wegmann*, p. 399 supra, that state law governed the survival of a statutory damage claim against state officers under § 1983, "only a uniform federal rule of survivorship will suffice to redress the constitutional deprivation here alleged and to protect against repetition of such conduct." [5]

(6) *Monroe v. Pape*, you remember (see p. 391 supra), held that a city was not a "person" suable under 42 U.S.C. § 1983 for depriving the plaintiff of federal rights under color of state law. Several lower courts applied *Bivens* to circumvent this limitation: Section 1331 provided jurisdiction over constitutional claims against state governments, and a damage remedy could be inferred from the constitutional provision allegedly violated. E.g., Hostrop v. Board of Junior College, 523 F.2d 569, 576–77 (7th Cir. 1975); Skehan v. Board of Trustees, 501 F.2d 31, 41–44 (3d Cir. 1974), vacated on other grounds, 421 U.S. 983 (1975).

Kostka v. Hogg, 560 F.2d 37 (1st Cir. 1977), held to the contrary. *Bivens*, the First Circuit reasoned, had not held that a damage remedy was "constitutionally necessary" (later cases having recognized various official-immunity defenses, pp. 474–84 infra); in contrast to *Bivens*, the plaintiffs in *Kostka* had an alternative remedy "measured by constitutional standards" against the offending officer under § 1983, and the refusal of Congress to extend § 1983 itself to actions against municipalities was "akin to an explicit Congressional determination that political subdivisions are not to be held liable in damages for violations of constitutional rights." Although *Monroe* itself had been based on the perceptions of the Reconstruction Congress as to limits on federal power, the Court's later refusal to

4. Justice Rehnquist wrote a long dissent attacking *Bivens* itself as an invasion of legislative authority contrary to the *Erie* principle and the Rules of Decision Act but conceding (fatally?) that "federal courts have historically had broad authority to fashion equitable remedies," and arguing that Congress had precluded common-law damages by providing relief under the Tort Claims Act. Justices Powell and Stewart, concurring in the judgment, criticized the Brennan opinion for formulating the issue in terms of an explicit Congressional "substitute" for the common law remedy but agreed that *Carlson* satisfied the *Davis* requirement that there be "no [other] effective means of redress" because, for the Court's reasons, the Tort Claims Act "simply is not an adequate remedy." Chief Justice Burger's dissent took the position that it was.

5. What sense is there in this distinction? See 446 U.S. at 24 & n. 11: In *Robertson* "the plaintiff's death was not caused by the acts of the defendant upon which the suit was based" [so?]; and *Robertson* was based on 42 U.S.C. § 1988, which refers expressly to state law to fill gaps in § 1983 cases. Doesn't the Rules of Decision Act (28 U.S.C. § 1652) impose the same requirement in *Bivens* cases?

entertain pendent jurisdiction of a state-law claim against a county in a § 1983 case (*Aldinger v. Howard*, p. 398 supra) had been based upon an "affirmative policy against federal court imposition of liability on political subdivisions, which policy the Court found in" § 1983.

Cities are now § 1983 "persons" (see pp. 390–97 supra); should *Bivens* be applied to hold them "vicariously" liable for unauthorized acts despite the *Monell* dictum that they cannot be held for such acts under § 1983? [6]

(7) Damages is not the only remedy against federal officers that has caused difficulties for litigants and for the courts; mandamus against federal officers has had a long and checkered history.

The tale begins, as so many do, with *Marbury v. Madison*, which construed § 13 of the 1789 Judiciary Act to empower the Supreme Court to issue mandamus to federal officers as an original matter, but also held it unconstitutional (see pp. 21–22 supra). The next step, predictably, was an attempt to obtain mandamus from a federal circuit court. The plaintiff sought an order directing the register of a federal land-office to grant him lands to which he claimed to be entitled, but the Court rebuffed him too:

> Independent of the particular objections which this case presents, from its involving a question of freehold, we are of opinion, that the power of the circuit courts to issue the writ of mandamus, is confined exclusively to those cases in which [as specified in § 14 of the 1789 Judiciary Act, now 28 U.S.C. § 1651] it may be necessary to the exercise of their jurisdiction. Had the 11th section of the judiciary act covered the whole ground of the constitution, there would be much reason for exercising this power, in many cases wherein some ministerial act is necessary to the completion of an individual right arising under laws of the United States, and the 14th section of the same act would sanction the issuing of the writ for such a purpose. But although the judicial power of the United States extends to cases arising under the laws of the United States, the legislature have not thought proper to delegate the exercise of that power to its circuit courts, except in certain specified cases.

McIntire v. Wood, 11 U.S. (7 Cranch) 504 (1813).

A funny thing happened to this decision when the same claimant tried again, this time alleging diversity of citizenship. The plaintiff argued that the deficiency in *McIntire* had been remedied, since § 11 flatly granted jurisdiction over "all suits of a civil nature at common law or in equity" satisfying the diversity and amount requirements, and that, as one of the quoted sentences from *McIntire* suggested, § 14 therefore authorized the

6. For a review of the cases and a negative answer in a procedural-due-process case see Cale v. City of Covington, 586 F.2d 311 (4th Cir. 1978), arguing among other things that a judicially created remedy "would seem to be a violation of the fifth clause of the Fourteenth Amendment which has expressly entrusted to Congress the 'power to enforce, by appropriate legislation, the provisions of this article.'"

issuance of the writ as "necessary for the exercise of [its] . . . jurisdiction[ ]." The Court threw him out again:

> [W]e think it perfectly clear, from an examination of the decision alluded to, that it was wholly uninfluenced by any considerations drawn from the want of personal attributes of the parties. . . . The 14th section . . . could only have been intended to vest the power now contended for, in cases where the jurisdiction already exists, and not where it is to be courted or acquired, by means of the writ proposed to be sued out.

Why § 11 itself did not grant the requisite authority the opinion did not say. McClung v. Silliman, 19 U.S. (6 Wheat.) 598 (1821).

Similarly, after the gap that had defeated mandamus in *McIntire* had apparently been filled by the enactment of the general federal-question provision in 1875, that statute too was construed not to authorize an independent action for mandamus. See Knapp v. Lake Shore & Michigan Southern Railway Co., 197 U.S. 536, 541 (1905).

Quite difficult to reconcile with whatever unspoken philosophy may have underlain the *McClung* opinion was the Court's decision in Kendall v. United States ex rel. Stokes, 37 U.S. (12 Pet.) 524 (1838), upholding the power of federal courts in the District of Columbia to issue mandamus to federal officers without regard to the strictures of § 14. Maryland common law, which provided for mandamus, had been adopted in the District by statute; the act creating the District's courts gave them jurisdiction over "all cases, in law and equity, between parties, both or either of which shall be resident or be found within the district" and over all cases within the jurisdiction of the general Circuit Courts; at the time this statute was passed (1801) the Circuit Courts had jurisdiction over federal-question "cases in law or equity" under the short-lived Midnight Judges Act (p. 113 supra). Whatever policy forbade mandamus in the other Circuit Courts would appear equally infringed by this decision, and words almost identical to those that had been held elsewhere to exclude mandamus were here held to embrace it. Chief Justice Taney's dissent based on precedent was easy, and two others joined him.

The situation brought about by *McClung* and *Kendall* was allowed to persist for over 100 years: People entitled to mandamus against a federal officer had to sue in the District of Columbia to get it. In 1962 Congress finally enacted 28 U.S.C. § 1361 to provide the same relief in a more convenient forum:

> The district courts shall have original jurisdiction of any action in the nature of mandamus to compel an officer or employee of the United States or any agency thereof to perform a duty owed to the plaintiff.

At the same time the present § 1391(e) was added to broaden venue in certain actions against federal officers (see p. 310 supra). See generally Byse & Fiocca, Section 1361 of the Mandamus and Venue Act of 1962 and "Nonstatutory" Judicial Review of Federal Administrative Action, 81 Harv. L.Rev. 308, 310–18 (1967) (but beware of the authors' erroneous description of *McIntire*).

Before § 1361 it was important to distinguish mandamus from other suits against federal officers because only the District of Columbia courts could hear the former; between 1962 and 1976 it was important because only mandamus cases could be heard without regard to the amount in controversy. See, e.g., McGaw v. Farrow, 472 F.2d 952 (4th Cir. 1973). Is it important now that the amount requirement has been abolished in all federal-question cases?

TARBLE'S CASE

80 U.S. (13 Wall.) 397 (1872).

[Tarble's father, alleging that his minor son had joined the army without parental consent in violation of federal law, obtained a writ of habeas corpus from a court commissioner of Dane County, Wisconsin, directing the army officer in whose custody Tarble was to produce him. The officer appeared and challenged the court's jurisdiction, but the commissioner after hearing the merits ordered Tarble released, and the Wisconsin Supreme Court affirmed.]

MR. JUSTICE FIELD, after stating the case, delivered the opinion of the court, as follows:

The important question is presented by this case, whether a State court commissioner has jurisdiction, upon *habeas corpus*, to inquire into the validity of the enlistment of soldiers into the military service of the United States, and to discharge them from such service when, in his judgment, their enlistment has not been made in conformity with the laws of the United States. The question presented may be more generally stated thus: Whether any judicial officer of a State has jurisdiction to issue a writ of *habeas corpus*, or to continue proceedings under the writ when issued, for the discharge of a person held under the authority, or claim and color of the authority, of the United States, by an officer of that government. For it is evident, if such jurisdiction may be exercised by any judicial officer of a State, it may be exercised by the court commissioner within the county for which he is appointed; and if it may be exercised with reference to soldiers detained in the military service of the United States, whose enlistment is alleged to have been illegally made, it may be exercised with reference to persons employed in any other department of the public service when their illegal detention is asserted. It may be exercised in all cases where parties are held under the authority of the United States, whenever the invalidity of the exercise of that authority is affirmed. The jurisdiction, if it exist at all, can only be limited in its application by the legislative power of the State. It may even reach to parties imprisoned under sentence of the National courts, after regular indictment, trial, and conviction, for offences against the laws of the United States. As we read the opinion of the Supreme Court of Wisconsin in this case, this is the claim of authority asserted by that tribunal for itself and for the judicial officers of that State. It does, indeed, disclaim any right of either to interfere with parties in custody, under judicial sentence, when the National court pronouncing sentence had jurisdiction to try and punish the offenders, but it asserts, at the same time, for itself and for each of those officers, the right to determine, upon *habeas corpus*, in all cases, whether that court ever had such jurisdiction. In the case of Booth, which subsequently came before this court, it not only sustained the action of one of its justices in discharging a prisoner held in custody by a marshal of the United States, under a warrant of commitment for an offence against the laws of the United States, issued by a commissioner of the United States; but it discharged the same prisoner when subsequently confined under sentence of the District Court of the United States for the same offence, after indictment, trial, and conviction, on the ground that, in its judgment, the act of Congress creating the offence was unconstitutional; and in order that its decision in that respect should be final and conclusive, directed its clerk to refuse obedience to the writ of error issued by this court, under the act of Congress, to bring up the decision for review.

It is evident, as said by this court when the case of Booth was finally brought before it, if the power asserted by that State court existed, no offence against the laws of the United States could be punished by their own tribunals, without the permission and according to the judgment of the courts of the State in which the parties happen to be imprisoned; that if that power existed in that State court, it belonged equally to every other State court in the Union where a prisoner was within its territorial limits; and, as the different State courts could not always agree, it would often happen that an act, which was admitted to be an offence and justly punishable in one State, would be regarded as innocent, and even praiseworthy in another, and no one could suppose that a government, which had hitherto lasted for seventy years, "enforcing its laws by its own tribunals, and preserving the union of the States, could have lasted a single year, or fulfilled the trusts committed to it, if offences against its laws could not have been punished without the consent of the State in which the culprit was found."

The decision of this court in the two cases which grew out of the arrest of Booth, that of Ableman v. Booth, and that of The United States v. Booth,* disposes alike of the claim of jurisdiction by a State court, or by a State judge, to interfere with the authority of the United States, whether that authority be exercised by a Federal officer or be exercised by a Federal tribunal. In the first of these cases Booth had been arrested and committed to the custody of a marshal of the United States by a commissioner appointed by the District Court of the United States, upon a charge of having aided and abetted the escape of a fugitive slave. Whilst thus in custody a justice of the Supreme Court of Wisconsin issued a writ of *habeas corpus* directed to the marshal, requiring him to produce the body of Booth with the cause of his imprisonment. The marshal made a return, stating that he held the

* 21 Howard [62 U.S.], 506.

prisoner upon the warrant of the commissioner, a copy of which he annexed to and returned with the writ. To this return Booth demurred as insufficient in law to justify his detention, and, upon the hearing which followed, the justice held his detention illegal, and ordered his discharge. The marshal thereupon applied for and obtained a *certiorari*, and had the proceedings removed to the Supreme Court of the State, where, after argument, the order of the justice discharging the prisoner from custody was affirmed. The decision proceeded upon the ground that the act of Congress respecting fugitive slaves was unconstitutional and void.

In the second case, Booth had been indicted for the offence with which he was charged before the commissioner, and from which the State judge had discharged him, and had been tried and convicted in the District Court of the United States for the District of Wisconsin, and been sentenced to pay a fine of $1000, and to be imprisoned for one month. Whilst in imprisonment, in execution of this sentence, application was made by Booth to the Supreme Court of the State, for a writ of *habeas corpus*, alleging in his application that his imprisonment was illegal, by reason of the unconstitutionality of the fugitive slave law, and that the District Court had no jurisdiction to try or punish him for the matter charged against him. The court granted the application, and issued the writ, to which the sheriff, to whom the prisoner had been committed by the marshal, returned that he held the prisoner by virtue of the proceedings and sentence of the District Court, a copy of which was annexed to his return. Upon demurrer to this return, the court adjudged the imprisonment of Booth to be illegal, and ordered him to be discharged from custody, and he was accordingly set at liberty.

For a review in this court of the judgments in both of these cases, writs of error were prosecuted. . . . And in answer to this assumption of judicial power by the judges and by the Supreme Court of Wisconsin thus made, the Chief Justice said as follows: If they "possess the jurisdiction they claim, they must derive it either from the United States or the State. It certainly has not been conferred on them by the United States; and it is equally clear it was not in the power of the State to confer it, even if it had attempted to do so; for no State can authorize one of its judges or courts to exercise judicial power, by *habeas corpus* or otherwise, within the jurisdiction of another and independent government. And although the State of Wisconsin is sovereign within its territorial limits to a certain extent, yet that sovereignty is limited and restricted by the Constitution of the United States. And the powers of the General government and of the State, although both exist and are exercised within the same territorial limits, are yet separate and distinct sovereignties, acting separately and independently of each other, within their respective spheres. And the sphere of action appropriated to the United States, is as far beyond the reach of the judicial process issued by a State judge or a State court, as if the line of division was traced by landmarks and monuments visible to the eye. And the State of Wisconsin had no more power to authorize these proceedings of its judges and courts, than it would have had if the prisoner had been confined in Michigan, or in any other State of the Union, for an offence against the laws of the State in which he was imprisoned."

It is in the consideration of this distinct and independent character of the government of the United States, from that of the government of the several States, that the solution of the question presented in this case, and in similar cases, must be found. There are within the territorial limits of each State two governments, restricted in their spheres of action, but independent of each other, and supreme within their respective spheres. Each has its separate departments; each has its distinct laws, and each has its own tribunals for their enforcement. Neither government can intrude within the jurisdiction, or authorize any interference therein by its judicial officers with the action of the other. The two governments in each State stand in their respective spheres of action in the same independent relation to each other, except in one particular, that they would if their authority embraced distinct territories. That particular consists in the supremacy of the authority of the United States when any conflict arises between the two governments. The Constitution and the laws passed in pursuance of it, are declared by the Constitution itself to be the supreme law of the land, and the judges of every State are bound thereby, "anything in the constitution or laws of any State to the contrary notwithstanding." Whenever, therefore, any conflict arises between the enactments of the two sovereignties, or in the enforcement of their asserted authorities, those of the National government must have supremacy until the validity of the different enactments and authorities can be finally determined by the tribunals of the United States. . . .

Such being the distinct and independent character of the two governments, within their respective spheres of action, it follows that neither can intrude with its judicial process into the domain of the other, except so far as such intrusion may be necessary on the part of the National government to preserve its rightful supremacy in cases of conflict of authority. In their laws, and mode of enforcement, neither is responsible to the other. How their respective laws shall be enacted; how they shall be carried into execution; and in what tribunals, or by what officers; and how much discretion, or whether any at all shall be vested in their officers, are matters subject to their own control, and in the regulation of which neither can interfere with the other.

Now, among the powers assigned to the National government, is the power "to raise and support armies," and the power "to provide for the government and regulation of the land and naval forces." The execution of these powers falls within the line of its duties; and its control over the subject is plenary and exclusive. It can determine, without question from any State authority, how the armies shall be raised, whether by voluntary enlistment or forced draft, the age at which the soldier shall be received, and the period for which he shall be taken, the compensation he shall be allowed, and the service to which he shall be assigned. And it can provide the rules for the government and regulation of the forces after they are raised, define what shall constitute military offences, and prescribe their punishment. No interference with the execution of this power of the National government in the formation, organization, and government of its armies by any State officials could be permitted without greatly impairing the efficiency, if it did not utterly destroy, this branch of the public service. Probably in every county and city in the several States there are one or more officers authorized by law to issue writs of *habeas corpus* on behalf of persons alleged to be illegally restrained of their liberty; and if soldiers could be taken from the army of the United States, and the validity of their enlistment inquired into by any one of these officers, such proceeding could be taken by all of them, and no movement could be made by the National troops without their commanders being subjected to constant annoyance and embarrassment from this source. The experience of the late rebellion has shown us that, in times of great popular excitement, there may be found in every State large numbers ready and anxious to embarrass the operations of the government, and easily persuaded to believe every step taken for the enforcement of its authority illegal and void. Power to issue writs of *habeas corpus* for the discharge of soldiers in the military service, in the hands of parties thus disposed, might be used, and often would be used, to the great detriment of the public service. In many exigencies the measures of the National government might in this way be entirely bereft of their efficacy and value. An appeal in such cases to this court, to correct the erroneous action of these officers, would afford no adequate remedy. Proceedings on *habeas corpus* are summary, and the delay incident to bringing the decision of a State officer, through the highest tribunal of the State, to this court for review, would necessarily occupy years, and in the meantime, where the soldier was discharged, the mischief would be accomplished. It is manifest that the powers of the National government could not be exercised with energy and efficiency at all times, if its acts could be interfered with and controlled for any period by officers or tribunals of another sovereignty.

It is true similar embarrassment might sometimes be occasioned, though in a less degree, by the exercise of the authority to issue the writ possessed by judicial officers of the United States, but the ability to provide a speedy remedy for any inconvenience following from this source would always exist with the National legislature.

State judges and State courts, authorized by laws of their States to issue writs of *habeas corpus*, have undoubtedly a right to issue the writ in any case where a party is alleged to be illegally confined within their limits, unless it appear upon his application that he is confined under the authority, or claim and color of the authority, of the United States, by an officer of that government. If such fact appear upon the application the writ should be refused. If it do not appear, the judge or court issuing the writ has a right to inquire into the cause of imprisonment, and ascertain by what authority the person is held within the limits of the State; and it is the duty of the marshal, or other officer having the custody of the prisoner, to give, by a proper return, information in this respect. His return should be sufficient, in its detail of facts, to show distinctly that the imprisonment is under the authority, or claim and color of the authority, of the United States, and to exclude the suspicion of imposition or oppression on his part. And the process or orders, under which the prisoner is held, should be produced with the return and submitted to inspection, in order that the court or judge issuing the writ may see that the prisoner is held by the officer, in good faith, under the authority, or claim and color of the authority, of the United States, and not under the mere pretence of having such authority.

This right to inquire by process of *habeas corpus*, and the duty of the officer to make a return, "grows necessarily," says Mr. Chief Justice Taney, "out of the complex character of our government and the existence of two distinct and separate sovereignties within the same territorial space, each of them restricted in its power, and each within its sphere of action, prescribed by the Constitution of the United States, independent of the other. But, after the return is made, and the State judge or court judicially apprised that the party is in custody under the authority of the United States, they can proceed no further. They then know that the prisoner is within the dominion and jurisdiction of another government, and that neither the writ of *habeas corpus* nor any other process issued under State authority can pass over the line of division between the two sovereignties. He is then within the dominion and exclusive jurisdiction of the United States. If he has committed an offence against their laws, their tribunals alone can punish him. If he is wrongfully imprisoned, their judicial tribunals can release him and afford him redress."

Some attempt has been made in adjudications, to which our attention has been called, to limit the decision of this court in Ableman v. Booth, and The United States v. Booth, to cases where a prisoner is held in custody under undisputed lawful authority of the United States, as distinguished from his imprisonment under claim and color of such authority. But it is evident that the decision does not admit of any such limitation. It would have been unnecessary to enforce, by any extended reasoning, such as the Chief Justice uses, the position that when it appeared to the judge or officer issuing the writ, that the prisoner was held under undisputed lawful authority, he should proceed no further. . . .

This limitation upon the power of State tribunals and State officers furnishes no just ground to apprehend that the liberty of the citizen will thereby be endangered. The [federal] . . . . courts and judicial officers are clothed with the power to issue the writ of *habeas corpus* in all cases, where a party is illegally restrained of his liberty by an officer of the United States, whether such illegality consist in the character of the process, the authority of the officer, or the invalidity of the law under which he is held. And there is no just reason to believe that they will exhibit any hesitation to exert their power, when it is properly invoked. . . .

It follows, from the views we have expressed, that the court commissioner of Dane County was without jurisdiction to issue the writ of *habes corpus* for the discharge of the prisoner in this case. . . .

Judgment reversed.

THE CHIEF JUSTICE, dissenting:

I cannot concur in the opinion just read. I have no doubt of the right of a State court to inquire into the jurisdiction of a Federal court upon *habeas corpus*, and to discharge when satisfied that the petitioner for the writ is restrained of liberty by the sentence of a court without jurisdiction. If it errs in deciding the question of jurisdiction, the error must be corrected in the mode prescribed by the 25th section of the Judiciary Act; not by denial of the right to make inquiry.

I have still less doubt, if possible, that a writ of *habeas corpus* may issue from a State court to inquire into the validity of imprisonment or detention, without the sentence of any court whatever, by an officer of the United States. The State court may err; and if it does, the error may be corrected here. The mode has been prescribed and should be followed.

To deny the right of State courts to issue the writ, or, what amounts to the same thing, to concede the right to issue and to deny the right to adjudicate, is to deny the right to protect the citizen by *habeas corpus* against arbitrary imprisonment in a large class of cases; and, I am thoroughly persuaded, was never within the contemplation of the Convention which framed, or the people who adopted, the Constitution. That instrument expressly declres that "the privilege of the writ of *habeas corpus* shall not be suspended, unless when, in case of rebellion or invasion, the public safety may require it."

Notes on the Jurisdiction of State Courts Over Federal Officers

(1) It is easy enough to understand the policy concerns that argue against state jurisdiction in cases like *Tarble* and the *Booth* cases there discussed; in both instances the Court was confronted by a concerted effort by Wisconsin to nullify federal law. But what was the *legal* basis for holding the state court without power?

(2) Did *Tarble* and *Booth* hold that the statute empowering federal courts to grant habeas corpus on behalf of persons in federal custody gave them exclusive jurisdiction to do so? Did the Court hold that the relevant provisions of Article III defining the federal judicial power implicitly prevented state courts from hearing these cases? Neither constitutional nor statutory grants of federal jurisdiction, you will recall, are generally

held exclusive of state courts in the absence of explicit language to that effect, see pp. 179–80 supra, and the provisions for federal habeas corpus made no mention of exclusivity.

(3) Was the Court suggesting in *Tarble* that the Supremacy Clause required the state court to accept every federal bureaucrat's assertion that he was acting within his authority, without asking whether he was acting in accord with federal law? Was it suggesting that that clause forbade state courts to examine the constitutionality of federal statutes, which it had been assumed they could do at least since *Martin v. Hunter's Lessee* (infra p. 578)? See Arnold, The Power of State Courts to Enjoin Federal Officers, 73 Yale L.J. 1385, 1402 (1964):

> The supremacy clause demands, not that *any* federal law be automatically enforced by state judges, until invalidated by a federal court, as *Tarble's Case* suggests, but that state judges apply federal laws "made in Pursuance" of the Constitution. . . . It follows that state courts are not only permitted but obligated, to examine the validity of federal authority asserted in cases before them.

(4) Some of the language of *Tarble* is reminiscent of Marshall's familiar epigram that "the power to tax involves the power to destroy," McCulloch v. Maryland, 17 U.S. (4 Wheat.) 316, 431 (1819). Was the Court suggesting, by analogy to *McCulloch*, that state-court jurisdiction in *Tarble* was implicitly precluded either by Article I's grant of congressional power to raise armies or by the federal statute providing for enlistment? Wouldn't it be relevant, in considering whether an immunity is implicit in the Constitution, that Congress could protect the federal interest by enacting a statute excluding state-court jurisdiction?

(5) Federal habeas corpus had been extended to prisoners in state custody in 1867, five years before *Tarble* was decided. When Justice Field declared that "[n]either [federal nor state government can intrude within the jurisdiction, or authorize any interference therein by its judicial officers with the action of the other," did he mean that the 1867 act was unconstitutional? See pp. 578–80 infra.

(6) In *Booth*, quoted in *Tarble*, the Court had said the question was not whether federal law forbade state jurisdiction but whether it authorized it:

> There can be no such thing as judicial authority, unless it is conferred by a Government or sovereignty. . . . It certainly has not been conferred . . . by the United States; and . . . Wisconsin had no more power to authorize these proceedings . . . than it would have had if the prisoner had been confined in Michigan . . . for an offense against [its] . . . laws. . . .

Was this passage based on natural law? Was the Court reversing the state Supreme Court on its interpretation of the state constitution? What business has the Supreme Court telling a state what the limits of its powers are, except insofar as they are limited by federal law?

(7) How persuasive a precedent was *Booth* for *Tarble*? Did Booth hold anything more than that a state court was bound to respect a federal

judgment? Was there anything surprising about that?[1] But is there anything to suggest that a state court should be required to give *more* credit to a federal judgment than a federal court would? Cf. Kovacs v. Brewer, 356 U.S. 604 (1958). And the federal courts have always had power to reexamine on habeas corpus at least the question whether the court convicting the petitioner had jurisdiction. See pp. 610–11 infra.

(8) McClung v. Silliman, 19 U.S. (6 Wheat.) 598 (1821), not only held that a federal circuit court lacked power to issue mandamus in a diversity case to compel a federal land-office registrar to utter a deed (see pp. 413–14 supra); it also held a state court could not do so either. "[N]o one will seriously contend," wrote Justice Johnson, that this authority was "among the reserved powers of the States, because not communicated by law to the Courts of the United States." A federal officer's conduct

> can only be controlled by the power that created him; since, whatever doubts have from time to time been suggested, as to the supremacy of the United States, in its legislative, judicial, or executive powers, no one has ever contested its supreme right to dispose of its own property in its own way. And when we find it withholding from its own Courts, the exercise of this controlling power over its ministerial officers, . . . the inference clearly is, that all violations of private right, resulting from the acts of such officers, should be the subject of actions for damages, or to recover the specific property . . . in Courts of competent jurisdiction.

Was it a fair inference, in light of the reasons the Court had given for the want of federal authority, that Congress meant to exclude the state courts as well? Does the reasoning of *McClung* lend support to *Tarble*?

Despite Northern Pacific Railway Co. v. North Dakota ex rel. Langer, 250 U.S. 135, 152 (1919), which reversed on the merits a state-court mandamus against a federal officer with the dictum that the power of the state to restrain him from exceeding his statutory authority was "undoubted," the lower courts have continued to follow *McClung*, e.g., Ex parte Shockley, 17 F.2d 133 (N.D.Ohio 1926), and a perceptive observer has declared "there is no good reason to predict that *McClung* will not govern whenever a plaintiff makes the mistake of labeling his papers 'mandamus'." Arnold, supra note 3, 73 Yale L.J. at 1392 (1964).[2]

(9) Did you get the impression from *Tarble* and *McClung* that federal officers may never be sued in state courts? The jurisdiction of a state court to replevy cargo illegally seized by a federal customs official was upheld four years before *McClung*, in Slocum v. Mayberry, 15 U.S. (2 Wheat.) 1, 12 (1817): "The act of congress neither expressly, nor by implication, forbids the state courts to take cognizance of suits instituted for property in possession of an officer of the United States not detained under some law of

1. What law requires state courts to give full faith and credit to a federal judgment? Both the Full Faith and Credit Clause of Article IV and its implementing statute (28 U.S.C § 1738) are silent on the subject.

2. Can it be argued that the enactment of 28 U.S.C. § 1361, by authorizing federal courts to issue mandamus to federal officers, removed the basis for the *McClung* holding? Is *Tarble* good authority for continuing to follow *McClung* anyway?

Is it constitutional for Congress to close *both* federal and state courts to claims arising under federal law? See pp. 98–111 supra.

the United States." Teal v. Felton, 53 U.S. (12 How.) 284 (1851), upheld state court jurisdiction of a trover action against a federal postmaster for damages arising from his refusal to deliver a newspaper, on the same reasoning. And United States ex rel. Drury v. Lewis, 200 U.S. 1 (1906), upheld the jurisdiction of a state court over the criminal prosecution of a soldier for a killing in the course of his federal duties: It was for the state court to determine whether the soldier had a substantive defense. How are we to reconcile these decisions with *Tarble* and *McClung*?

(10) Can a state court *enjoin* a federal officer? The Supreme Court seems never to have addressed the question, and the occasional lower-court opinions are in conflict. In Pennsylvania Turnpike Commission v. McGinnes, 179 F.Supp. 578 (E.D.Pa.1959), the plaintiff asked a state court to enjoin a federal tax official from refunding an overpayment to a taxpayer, on the ground that the funds used to pay the tax had been obtained from the plaintiff by fraud. The defendant removed under 28 U.S.C. § 1442(a)(1), and the federal court dismissed: Removal was proper only if the state court had jurisdiction (see p. 183 supra), and the state court had none. In part this holding was based on sovereign-immunity principles that at the time would have barred an original federal action too, see pp. 447–55 infra. But the court principally relied on *Tarble* and *McClung*:

> If a state court does not have jurisdiction to require a Federal officer to perform an act which Federal law requires him to perform (to repay a taxpayer overpayment of taxes) . . ., it would appear rather anomalous to recognize jurisdiction in that same State court to compel a Federal officer to perform an act which Federal law does not require him to perform (to pay a tax refund to a creditor of a taxpayer).

For the view that state courts may enjoin federal officers see McNally v. Jackson, 7 F.2d 373 (E.D.La.1925).

(11) Congress has dealt with the question of state-court jurisdiction over federal officers only obliquely, by authorizing removal. First employed for the protection of federal officers in 1815, 3 Stat. 195, 198, in a temporary statute applying only to customs collection, removal was frequently provided for in "special situations deemed to present special needs," Hart & Wechsler, The Federal Courts and the Federal System 1057 (3d ed. 1988), and in 1948 the Revisers made removal available in any civil or criminal case brought against a federal officer acting "under color of such office." 28 U.S.C. § 1442(a). The removal scheme was upheld in Tennessee v. Davis, 100 U.S. 257 (1880), in which a federal revenue agent was prosecuted for murder and defended on the ground of self-defense in suppressing a moonshine operation: The federal Government could not function if it could not protect its officers from harassing suits; the case was one arising under the federal statutes under which the agent held his office, for those statutes impliedly protected him against prosecution for actions in the line of duty.

Willingham v. Morgan, 395 U.S. 402 (1969), established that removal was at least as broad as the substantive immunity it was designed to implement: The "color of law" requirement was satisfied by a showing that the relationship between the parties "derived solely from . . . official duties" of the defendants.

In Bradford v. Harding, 284 F.2d 307 (2d Cir. 1960), a state-court action for false arrest and imprisonment was filed against 54 defendants, all but one of whom were federal officers. Some of the federal officers sought removal; others did not. Removal was allowed. Although the general removal provision, § 1441(a), has been held to require all defendants to join in the removal petition, Fletcher v. Hamlet, 116 U.S. 408 (1886) (diversity); Chicago, R. I. & P. Ry. v. Martin, 178 U.S. 245 (1900), § 1442 "rests upon far stronger considerations of policy" and "vindicates . . . the interests of government itself" as well as those of individuals:

> When an action of the sort specified in § 1442 is brought against a federal officer and others, even the most literal reading would permit the federal officer alone to remove. . . . For "by them" means "by any of the following persons" and the defendants who are not federal officers are not such persons. Moreover, the policy of the section would be frustrated if a plaintiff or a prosecutor, by joining non-federal defendants with no desire to remove, could retain the suit in a tribunal that might administer not only the laws of the State, but equally Federal law, in such a manner as to paralyze the operations of the government. . . .
>
> These considerations of policy also require a construction in favor of removal where, as here, some persons entitled to join in the removal petition did not. The "general government" must be able to assure each of its officers that a federal forum will be available if he wishes it, whether others sued with him wish it or not. This would scarcely be doubted if removal were sought here by the District Judge or the United States Attorney and a solitary grand juror declined to join. . . .

Why isn't this policy argument equally persuasive in a case of incomplete diversity of citizenship? Does *Bradford* mean the entire action was removed, or only that part of it against the petitioning federal officers? [3]

Does the availability of removal provide sufficient safeguard for federal interests that state courts should be permitted to take jurisdiction over federal officers in mandamus and habeas corpus cases? Or are the policies protected by the rule against state court jurisdiction too important to be entrusted to individual federal officers who may choose not to remove?

3. See Murphy v. Kodz, 351 F.2d 163 (9th Cir. 1965), allowing removal of claims against both federal and nonfederal defendants arising from an airplane collision. Does this conclusion survive the decision against pendent-party jurisdiction in *Finley v. United States*, p. 188 supra?

SECTION 4. FEDERAL LAW IN STATE COURTS

DICE v. AKRON, CANTON & YOUNGSTOWN RAILROAD CO.

342 U.S. 359 (1952).

Opinion of the Court by MR. JUSTICE BLACK. . . .

Petitioner, a railroad fireman, was seriously injured when an engine in which he was riding jumped the track. Alleging that his injuries were due to respondent's negligence, he brought this action for damages under the Federal Employers' Liability Act, 35 Stat. 65, 45 U.S.C. § 51 et seq., in an Ohio court of common pleas. Respondent's defenses were (1) a denial of negligence and (2) a written document signed by petitioner purporting to release respondent in full for $924.63. Petitioner admitted that he had signed several receipts for payments made him in connection with his injuries but denied that he had made a full and complete settlement of all his claims. He alleged that the purported release was void because he had signed it relying on respondent's deliberately false statement that the document was nothing more than a mere receipt for back wages.

After both parties had introduced considerable evidence the jury found in favor of petitioner and awarded him a $25,000 verdict. The trial judge later entered judgment notwithstanding the verdict. In doing so he reappraised the evidence as to fraud, found that petitioner had been "guilty of supine negligence" in failing to read the release, and accordingly held that the facts did not "sustain either in law or equity the allegations of fraud by clear, unequivocal and convincing evidence." [1] This judgment notwithstanding the verdict was reversed by the Court of Appeals of Summit County, Ohio, on the ground that under federal law, which controlled, the jury's verdict must stand because there was ample evidence to support its finding of fraud. The Ohio Supreme Court, one judge dissenting, reversed the Court of Appeals' judgment and sustained the trial court's action, holding that: (1) Ohio, not federal, law governed; (2) under that law petitioner, a man of ordinary intelligence who could read, was bound by the release even though he had been induced to sign it by the deliberately false statement that it was only a receipt for back wages; and (3) under controlling Ohio law factual issues as to fraud in the execution of this release were properly decided by the judge rather than by the jury. 155 Ohio St. 185, 98 N.E.2d 301. We granted certiorari because the decision of the Supreme Court of Ohio appeared to deviate from previous decisions

1. The trial judge had charged the jury that petitioner's claim of fraud must be sustained "by clear and convincing evidence," but since the verdict was for petitioner, he does not here challenge this charge as imposing too heavy a burden under controlling federal law.

of this Court that federal law governs cases arising under the Federal Employers' Liability Act. 342 U.S. 811.

First. . . . Validity of releases under the Federal Employers' Liability Act raises a federal question to be determined by federal rather than state law. . . . Manifestly the federal rights affording relief to injured railroad employees under a federally declared standard could be defeated if states were permitted to have the final say as to what defenses could and could not be properly interposed to suits under the Act. Moreover, only if federal law controls can the federal Act be given that uniform application throughout the country essential to effectuate its purposes. . . .

Second. . . . The correct federal rule is that . . . a release of rights under the Act is void when the employee is induced to sign it by the deliberately false and material statements of the railroad's authorized representatives made to deceive the employee as to the contents of the release. The trial court's charge to the jury correctly stated this rule of law.

Third. Ohio provides and has here accorded petitioner the usual jury trial of factual issues relating to negligence. But Ohio treats factual questions of fraudulent releases differently. It permits the judge trying a negligence case to resolve all factual questions of fraud "other than fraud in the factum." The factual issue of fraud is thus split into fragments, some to be determined by the judge, others by the jury.

It is contended that since a state may consistently with the Federal Constitution provide for trial of cases under the Act by a nonunanimous verdict, Minneapolis & St. Louis R. Co. v. Bombolis, 241 U.S. 211, Ohio may lawfully eliminate trial by jury as to one phase of fraud while allowing jury trial as to all other issues raised. The *Bombolis* case might be more in point had Ohio abolished trial by jury in all negligence cases including those arising under the federal Act. But Ohio has not done this. It has provided jury trials for cases arising under the federal Act but seeks to single out one phase of the question of fraudulent releases for determination by a judge rather than by a jury. Compare Testa v. Katt, 330 U.S. 386.

We have previously held that "The right to trial by jury is 'a basic and fundamental feature of our system of federal jurisprudence' " and that it is "part and parcel of the remedy afforded railroad workers under the Employers' Liability Act." Bailey v. Central Vermont R. Co., 319 U.S. 350, 354. We also recognized in that case that to deprive railroad workers of the benefit of a jury trial where there is evidence to support negligence "is to take away a goodly portion of the relief which Congress has afforded them." It follows that the right to trial by jury is too substantial a part of the rights accorded by the Act to permit it to be classified as a mere "local rule of procedure" for denial in the manner that Ohio has here used. Brown v. Western R. Co., 338 U.S. 294.

The trial judge and the Ohio Supreme Court erred in holding that petitioner's rights were to be determined by Ohio law and in taking away petitioner's verdict when the issues of fraud had been submitted to the jury on conflicting evidence and determined in petitioner's favor. . . .

Reversed and remanded. . . .

MR. JUSTICE FRANKFURTER, whom MR. JUSTICE REED, MR. JUSTICE JACKSON and MR. JUSTICE BURTON join, concurring for reversal but dissenting from the Court's opinion. . . .

It has been settled ever since the Second Employers' Liability Cases [Mondou v. New York, N. H. & H. R. Co.], 223 U.S. 1, that no State which gives its courts jurisdiction over common law actions for negligence may deny access to its courts for a negligence action founded on the Federal Employers' Liability Act. Nor may a State discriminate disadvantageously against actions for negligence under the Federal Act as compared with local causes of action in negligence. McKnett v. St. Louis & S. F. R. Co., 292 U.S. 230, 234; Missouri ex rel. Southern R. Co. v. Mayfield, 340 U.S. 1, 4. Conversely, however, simply because there is concurrent jurisdiction in Federal and State courts over actions under the Employers' Liability Act, a State is under no duty to treat actions arising under that Act differently from the way it adjudicates local actions for negligence, so far as the mechanics of litigation, the forms in which law is administered, are concerned. This surely covers the distribution of functions as between judge and jury in the determination of the issues in a negligence case.

In 1916 the Court decided without dissent that States in entertaining actions under the Federal Employers' Liability Act need not provide a jury system other than that established for local negligence actions. States are not compelled to provide the jury required of Federal courts by the Seventh Amendment. Minneapolis & St. L. R. Co. v. Bombolis, 241 U.S. 211. . . .

Ohio and her sister States with a similar division of functions between law and equity are not trying to evade their duty under the Federal Employers' Liability Act; nor are they trying to make it more difficult for railroad workers to recover, than for those suing under local law. The States merely exercise a preference in adhering to historic ways of dealing with a claim of fraud; they prefer the traditional way of making unavailable through equity an otherwise valid defense. The state judges and local lawyers who must administer the Federal Employers' Liability Act in State courts are trained in the ways of local practice; it multiplies the difficulties and confuses the administration of justice to require, on purely theoretical grounds, a hybrid of State and Federal practice in the State courts as to a single class of cases. Nothing in the Employers' Liability Act or in the judicial enforcement of the Act for over forty years forces such judicial hybridization upon the States. The fact that Congress authorized actions under the Federal Employers' Liability Act to be brought in State as well as in Federal courts seems a strange basis for the inference that Congress overrode State procedural arrangements controlling all other negligence suits in a State, by imposing upon State courts to which plaintiffs choose to go the rules prevailing in the Federal courts regarding juries. Such an inference is admissible, so it seems to me, only on the theory that Congress included as part of the right created by the Employers' Liability Act an assumed likelihood that trying all issues to juries is more favorable to plaintiffs. At least, if a plaintiff's right to have all issues decided by a jury rather that the court is "part and parcel of the remedy afforded railroad workers under the Employers Liability Act," the *Bombolis* case should be overruled explicitly instead of left as a derelict bound to occasion collisions on the waters of the law. . . .

The judgment of the Ohio Supreme Court must be reversed for it applied the State rule as to validity of releases. . . . Moreover, we cannot say with confidence that the Ohio trial judge applied the Federal standard correctly. . . . We would return the case for further proceedings on the sole question of fraud in the release.

Notes on State-Court Enforcement of Federal Law

(1) The important questions whether state courts may enforce federal law and whether they must do so have been considered at pp. 179–88 supra. In brief: The normal presumption is that federal jurisdiction is not exclusive, and the FELA was amended in 1910 to make state jurisdiction clear. The Supreme Court has held that both the FELA and the war-time price legislation required state courts to provide a forum under certain conditions, despite the arguably "penal" nature of the latter statute, but in FELA cases the Court has permitted the States to invoke the doctrine of forum non conveniens, provided they do so without "discriminating against" federal causes of action. See Missouri ex rel. Southern Ry. v. Mayfield, 340 U.S. 1 (1950).

Does this mean that a state court is free to close its doors to an FELA claim on the basis of an expired local statute of limitations? Time limitations, like rules respecting the convenient forum, may reflect to some extent policies affecting the efficient administration of the state courts; cf. Wells v. Simonds Abrasive Co., 345 U.S. 514 (1953), permitting a court of one State to apply a local statute of limitation to defeat a cause of action created by another State, despite the policy of the Full Faith and Credit Clause favoring enforcement of foreign rights. Notice, moreover, that the case supposed is not simply the converse of *Guaranty Trust Co. v. York*, supra p. 336, for that case held that a disinterested federal court could not enlarge the relevant limitation period, not that such a court could not protect its docket by applying its own *shorter* limitation period. Nevertheless the Supreme Court has long held that a state court cannot dismiss an action based on the FELA before the expiration of the federal limitation period. Engel v. Davenport, 271 U.S. 33 (1926) (Jones Act, which incorporates FELA in seamen's actions); McAllister v. Magnolia Petroleum Co., 357 U.S. 221

(1958) (unseaworthiness claim joined to Jones Act count); see Burnett v. New York Central R. R., 380 U.S. 424 (1965), holding the FELA limitation tolled as a matter of federal law during pendency of a state-court action later dismissed for improper venue. Should these holdings be extended to all federal limitation statutes, or do they reflect some peculiarly plaintiff-oriented policy of the FELA? Notice further that in the case of a state limitation period *longer* than that of the FELA the state is not, as is a federal diversity court, disinterested; the holding that the state court cannot entertain an action in that case, Atlantic Coast Line R. R. v. Burnette, 239 U.S. 199 (1915), must be explained in relation to the general preemption of additional state remedies for railroad plaintiffs, see p. 363, supra, rather than by a lack of state concern.

(2) If a state court does entertain an action based on federal law, as in *Dice*, is the applicability of state procedural laws governed by the same considerations that determine the use of federal procedure in diversity cases? See Central Vermont Ry. v. White, 238 U.S. 507 (1915) (burden of proof respecting contributory negligence is federal question); Brady v. Southern Ry., 320 U.S. 476 (1943) (sufficiency of evidence to sustain verdict, also federal question). Indeed the bulk of the Supreme Court's decisions reversing state courts in FELA cases have been concerned with the sufficiency of the evidence. Is there any doubt that to permit state law to govern these issues would threaten substantial federal policies? See also Garrett v. Moore-McCormack Co., 317 U.S. 239 (1942), holding federal law governs the burden of proof respecting fraud in the inducement of a release from liability to a seaman under both the Jones Act and the general maritime law.

Is it correct to say that the question in a case like *Dice* is the extent to which state interests in the efficient administration of state courts should be allowed to impinge upon federal policy? Two differences between this situation and that of *Erie* suggest themselves: First, in any direct conflict federal law must prevail in either case under the Supremacy Clause; second, the states are not without interests in the merits of the litigation as are diversity courts under *Erie*.

(3) Is it possible to reconcile *Dice* with the decisions holding federal law governs the division of function between judge and jury in diversity cases? *Byrd v. Blue Ridge Rural Coop.*, supra p. 346, is not hard to distinguish if one accepts the Court's conclusions that while the FELA expressed a policy in favor of broad jury discretion the South Carolina workers' compensation law expressed no anti-jury policy. But if the Court was right in its earlier holding that the housekeeping interest of the federal courts in dividing the functions of jury and judge overrides a strongly pro-plaintiff state policy of upholding jury verdicts, *Herron v. Southern Pac. Co.*, 283 U.S. 91 (1931), why was it necessary to ignore a similar state housekeeping interest in *Dice*?

(4) Is it possible to reconcile *Dice* and the decisions in note 2, supra, with *Bombolis* and its companion cases, cited in *Dice*, allowing a state court to empanel a jury of seven or to accept a less-than-unanimous verdict in an FELA case? The Seventh Amendment, discussed at

length in *Bombolis*, was surely a red herring, for the issue in all these cases is the policy of the federal statute. Is trial to a judge more likely to frustrate federal policy than trial to a seven-man jury or to a jury that need not be unanimous? If a state abolished civil juries altogether, would it be permitted to try FELA cases to the judge? Would it be permitted to refuse to entertain FELA actions on the ground of inconvenience if federal law forbade a judge trial?

(5) See also Brown v. Western Ry., 338 U.S. 294 (1949), in which a state court had dismissed, with prejudice to any further state proceeding, an FELA complaint found insufficient to state a claim under a local rule construing allegations "most strongly against the pleader." Reversing, the Supreme Court said that "strict local rules of pleading cannot be used to impose unnecessary burdens upon rights of recovery authorized by federal laws" and that it was the duty of the Court "to construe the allegations of this complaint ourselves in order to determine whether petitioner has been denied a right of trial granted him by Congress." The state court, wrote Justice Black, "has decided as a matter of law that no inference of railroad negligence could be drawn from the facts alleged," which included negligently leaving clinkers beside the tracks; but "these allegations are sufficient," the Court concluded, "to permit introduction of evidence from which a jury might infer that petitioner's injuries were due to the railroad's negligence." Justices Frankfurter and Jackson dissented, comparing the issue to that raised by application of the federal procedure rules in a diversity case. How would this issue be resolved in a diversity case after *Hanna v. Plumer*, supra p. 339? How would it have been resolved in 1949?

If all that was involved in *Brown* was the proper form of words to use in a pleading, should the state rule be allowed to apply, in the interest of simplifying the state courts' job, because the matter is within the control of the plaintiff's lawyer and has no effect on primary conduct? Or is there an applicable federal policy of protecting plaintiffs against dismissals based upn the inexactness of their attorneys' language? Is the decision better explained as passing not upon the technicalities of pleading but upon the minimum proof required in an FELA action? See Hill, Substance and Procedure in State FELA Actions—The Converse of the Erie Problem? 17 Ohio St.L.J. 384 (1956); Note, State Enforcement of Federally Created Rights, 73 Harv.L.Rev. 1551 (1960).[1]

(6) It is important to observe the intimate connection between the question of state procedure in federal actions in state courts, discussed in these notes, and the question of the adequacy of state procedural

1. See also Norfolk & Western Railway Co. v. Liepelt, 444 U.S. 490 (1980), requiring a state trial judge in an FELA case to instruct the jury, in accord with federal practice, that a damage award would not be subject to federal income tax. "[Q]uestions concerning the measure of damages in an FELA action," said the Court, "are federal in character"; and the purpose of the federal rule was to prevent " 'the jury from inflating the award and thus overcompensating the plaintiff on the basis of an erroneous assumption that the judgment will be taxable.' " The dissent found no federal interest implicated: "This issue truly can be characterized as one of the 'ordinary incidents of state procedure.' "

grounds asserted to defeat federal defenses or replies raised in suits based upon state law. The adequate-state-ground cases appear at pp. 573–87 infra. Is there any reason why the extent of deference to federal policy by state courts should be any greater or less when federal law is asserted as a shield rather than as a sword?

Chapter V

SOVEREIGN IMMUNITY AND RELATED PROBLEMS

SECTION 1. THE ELEVENTH AMENDMENT AND SOVEREIGN IMMUNITY

HANS v. LOUISIANA

134 U.S. 1 (1890).

[Louisiana had issued bonds in 1874, but an 1879 amendment to the state constitution stopped the payment of interest on them. Hans, a Louisiana citizen holding bonds, sued the State in federal court, alleging that the amendment impaired the obligation of contract in violation of Article I, § 10.]

MR. JUSTICE BRADLEY . . . delivered the opinion of the court.

The question is presented, whether a State can be sued in a Circuit Court of the United States by one of its own citizens upon a suggestion that the case is one that arises under the Constitution or laws of the United States.

The ground taken is, that under the Constitution, as well as under the act of Congress passed to carry it into effect, a case is within the jurisdiction of the federal courts, without regard to the character of the parties, if it arises under the Constitution or laws of the United States, or, which is the same thing, if it necessarily involves a question under said Constitution or laws. The language relied on is that clause of the 3d article of the Constitution, which declares that "the judicial power of the United States shall extend to all cases in law and equity arising under this Constitution, the laws of the United States, and treaties made, or which shall be made, under their authority;" and the corresponding clause of the act conferring jurisdiction upon the Circuit Court, which, as found in the act of March 3, 1875, 18 Stat. 470, c. 137, § 1, is as follows, to wit: "That the Circuit Courts of the United States shall have original cognizance, concurrent with the courts of the several states, of all suits of a civil nature at common law or in equity,

. . . arising under the Constitution or laws of the United States, or treaties made, or which shall be made, under their authority." It is said that these jurisdictional clauses make no exception arising from the character of the parties, and, therefore, that a State can claim no exemption from suit, if the case is really one arising under the Constitution, laws or treaties of the United States. . . .

That a State cannot be sued by a citizen of another State, or of a foreign state, on the mere ground that the case is one arising under the Constitution or laws of the United States, is clearly established by the decisions of this court in several recent cases. Louisiana v. Jumel, 107 U.S. 711; Hagood v. Southern, 117 U.S. 52; In re Ayers, 123 U.S. 443. Those were cases arising under the Constitution of the United States, upon laws complained of as impairing the obligation of contracts, one of which was the constitutional amendment of Louisiana complained of in the present case. Relief was sought against state officers who professed to act in obedience to those laws. This court held that the suits were virtually against the States themselves and were consequently violative of the Eleventh Amendment of the Constitution, and could not be maintained. It was not denied that they presented cases arising under the Constitution; but, notwithstanding that, they were held to be prohibited by the amendment referred to.

In the present case the plaintiff in error contends that he, being a citizen of Louisiana, is not embarrassed by the obstacle of the Eleventh Amendment, inasmuch as that amendment only prohibits suits against a State which are brought by the citizens of another State, or by citizens or subjects of a foreign State. It is true, the amendment does so read: and if there were no other reason or ground for abating his suit, it might be maintainable; and then we should have this anomalous result, that in cases arising under the Constitution or laws of the United States, a State may be sued in the federal courts by its own citizens, though it cannot be sued for a like cause of action by the citizens of other States, or of a foreign state; and may be thus sued in the federal courts, although not allowing itself to be sued in its own courts. If this is the necessary consequence of the language of the Constitution and the law, the result is no less startling and unexpected than was the original decision of this court, that under the language of the Constitution and of the judiciary act of 1789, a State was liable to be sued by a citizen of another State, or of a foreign country. That decision was made in the case of Chisholm v. Georgia, 2 Dall. [2 U.S.] 419, and created such a shock of surprise throughout the country that, at the first meeting of Congress thereafter, the Eleventh Amendment to the Constitution was almost unanimously proposed, and was in due course adopted by the legislatures of the States. This amendment, expressing the will of the ultimate sovereignty of the whole country, superior to all legislatures and all courts, actually reversed the decision of the Supreme Court. It did not in terms prohibit suits by individuals against the States, but declared that the Constitution should not be construed to import any power to authorize the bringing of such suits.

The language of the amendment is that "the judicial power of the United States shall *not be construed to extend* to any suit in law or equity, commenced or prosecuted against one of the United States by citizens of another State or by citizens or subjects of any foreign state." The Supreme Court had construed the judicial power as extending to such a suit, and its decision was thus overruled. . . .

This view of the force and meaning of the amendment is important. It shows that, on this question of the suability of the States by individuals, the highest authority of this country was in accord rather with the minority than with the majority of the court in the decision of the case of *Chisholm v. Georgia*; and this fact lends additional interest to the able opinion of Mr. Justice Iredell on that occasion. The other justices were more swayed by a close observance of the letter of the Constitution, without regard to former experience and usage; and because the letter said that the judicial power shall extend to controversies "between a State and citizens of another State;" and "between a State and foreign states, citizens or subjects," they felt constrained to see in this language a power to enable the individual citizens of one State, or of a foreign state, to sue another State of the Union in the federal courts. Justice Iredell, on the contrary, contended that it was not the intention to create new and unheard of remedies, by subjecting sovereign States to actions at the suit of individuals, (which he conclusively showed was never done before,) but only, by proper legislation, to invest the federal courts with jurisdiction to hear and determine controversies and cases, between the parties designated, that were properly susceptible of litigation in courts.

Looking back from our present standpoint at the decision in *Chisholm v. Georgia*, we do not greatly wonder at the effect which it had upon the country. Any such power as that of authorizing the federal judiciary to entertain suits by individuals against the States, had been expressly disclaimed, and even resented, by the great defenders of the Constitution whilst it was on its trial before the American people. As some of their utterances are directly pertinent to the question now under consideration, we deem it proper to quote them.

The eighty-first number of the Federalist, written by Hamilton, has the following profound remarks:

"It has been suggested that an assignment of the public securities of one State to the citizens of another, would enable them to prosecute that State in the federal courts for the amount of those securities; a suggestion which the following considerations prove to be without foundation:

"It is inherent in the nature of sovereignty not to be amenable to the suit of an individual *without its consent.* This is the general sense and the general practice of mankind; and the exemption, as one of the attributes of sovereignty, is now enjoyed by the government of every State in the Union. Unless, therefore, there is a surrender of this immunity in the plan of the convention, it will remain with the States, and the danger intimated must be merely ideal. The circumstances which are necessary to produce an alienation of state sovereignty were discussed in considering the article of taxation, and need not be repeated here. A recurrence to the principles there established will satisfy us, that there is no color to pretend that the state governments would, by the adoption of that plan, be divested of the privilege of paying their own debts in their own way, free from every constraint but that which flows from the obligations of good faith. The contracts between a nation and individuals are only binding on the conscience of the sovereign, and have no pretension to a compulsive force. They confer no right of action independent of the sovereign will. To what purpose would it be to authorize suits against States for the debts they owe? How could recoveries be enforced? It is evident that it could not be done without waging war against the contracting State; and to ascribe to the federal courts by mere implication, and in destruction of a preexisting right of the state governments, a power which would involve such a consequence, would be altogether forced and unwarrantable."

The obnoxious clause to which Hamilton's argument was directed, and which was the ground of the objections which he so forcibly met, was that which declared that "the judicial power shall extend to all . . . controversies between a State and citizens of another State, . . . and between a State and foreign states, citizens or subjects." It was argued by the opponents of the Constitution that this clause would authorize jurisdiction to be given to the federal courts to entertain suits against a State brought by the citizens of another State, or of a foreign state. Adhering to the mere letter, it might be so; and so, in fact, the Supreme Court held in *Chisholm v. Georgia*; but looking at the subject as Hamilton did, and as Mr. Justice Iredell did, in the light of history and experience and the established order of things, the views of the latter were clearly right,—as the people of the United States in their sovereign capacity subsequently decided.

But Hamilton was not alone in protesting against the construction put upon the Constitution by its opponents. In the Virginia convention the same objections were raised by George Mason and Patrick Henry, and were met by Madison and Marshall as follows. Madison said: "Its jurisdiction [the federal jurisdiction] in controversies between a State and citizens of another State is much objected to, and perhaps without reason. It is not in the power of individuals to call any State into court. The only operation it can have is that, if a State should wish to bring a suit against a citizen, it must be brought before the federal court. This will give satisfaction to individuals, as it will prevent citizens on whom a State may have a claim being dissatisfied with the state courts. . . . It appears to me that this [clause] can have no operation but this—to give a citizen a right to be heard in the federal courts; and if a State should condescend to be a party, this court may take cognizance of it." 3 Elliot Debates, 2d ed. 533. Marshall, in answer to the same objection, said: "With respect to disputes between a State and the citizens of another State, its jurisdiction has been decried with unusual vehemence. I hope that no gentleman will think that a State will be called at the bar of the federal court. . . . It is not rational to suppose that the sovereign power should be dragged before a court. The intent is to enable States to recover claims of individuals residing in other States. . . . But, say they, there will be partiality in it if a State cannot be defendant—if an individual cannot proceed to obtain judgment against a State, though he may be sued by a State. It is necessary to be so, and cannot be avoided. I see a difficulty in making a State defendant which does not prevent its being plaintiff." Id. 555.

It seems to us that these views of those great advocates and defenders of the Constitution were most sensible and just; and they apply equally to the present case as to that then under discussion. The letter is appealed to now, as it was then, as a ground for sustaining a suit brought by an individual against a State. The reason against it is as strong in this case as it was in that. It is an attempt to strain the Constitution and the law to a construction never imagined or dreamed of. Can we suppose that, when the Eleventh Amendment was adopted, it was understood to be left open for citizens of a State to sue their own state in the federal courts, whilst the idea of suits by citizens of other states, or of foreign states, was indignantly repelled? Suppose that Congress, when proposing the Eleventh Amendment, had appended to it a proviso that nothing therein contained should prevent a State from being sued by its own citizens in cases arising under the Constitution or laws of the United States: can we imagine that it would have been adopted by the States? The supposition that it would is almost an absurdity on its face.

The truth is, that the cognizance of suits and actions unknown to the law, and forbidden by the law, was not contemplated by the Constitution when establishing the judicial power of the United States. Some things, undoubtedly, were made justiciable which were not known as such at the common law; such, for example, as controversies between States as to boundary lines, and other questions admitting of judicial solution. And yet the case of Penn v. Lord Baltimore, 1 Ves. Sen. 444, shows that some of these unusual subjects of litigation were not unknown to the courts even in colonial times; and several cases of the same general character arose under the Articles of Confederation, and were brought before the tribunal provided for that purpose in those articles. 131 U.S. App. 1. The establishment of this new branch of jurisdiction seemed to be necessary from the extinguishment of diplomatic relations between the States. Of other controversies between a State and another State or its citizens, which, on the settled principles of public law, are not subjects of judicial cognizance, this court has often declined to take jurisdiction. See Wisconsin v. Pelican Ins. Co., 127 U.S. 265, 288, 289, and cases there cited.

The suability of a State without its consent was a thing unknown to the law. This has been so often laid down and acknowledged by courts and jurists that it is hardly necessary to be formally asserted. It was fully shown by an exhaustive examination of the old law by Mr. Justice Iredell in his opinion in *Chisholm v. Georgia*; and it has been conceded in every case since, where the question has, in any way, been presented, even in the cases which have gone farthest in sustaining suits against the officers or agents of States. Osborn v. Bank of United States, 9 Wheat. [22 U.S.] 738; Davis v. Gray, 16 Wall. [83 U.S.] 203; Board of Liquidation v. McComb, 92 U.S. 531; United States v. Lee, 106 U.S. 196; Poindexter v. Greenhow, 109 U.S. 63; Virginia Coupon Cases, 114 U.S. 269. In all these cases the effort was to show, and the court held, that the suits were not against the State or the United States, but against the individuals; conceding that if they had been against either the State or the United States, they could not be maintained. . . .

But besides the presumption that no anomalous and unheard-of proceedings or suits were intended to be raised up by the Constitution—anomalous and unheard of when the Constitution was adopted—an additional reason why the jurisdiction claimed for the Circuit Court does not exist, is the language of the act of Congress by which its jurisdiction is conferred. The words are these: "The circuit courts of the United States shall have original cognizance, concurrent with the courts of the several States, of all suits of a civil nature at common law or in equity, . . . arising under the Constitution or laws of the United States, or treaties," etc.—"Concurrent with the courts of the several States." Does not this qualification show that Congress, in legislating to carry the Constitution into effect, did not intend to invest its courts with any new and strange jurisdictions? The state courts have no power to entertain suits by individuals against a State without its consent. Then how does the Circuit Court, having only concurrent jurisdiction, acquire any such power? It is true that the same qualification existed in the judiciary act of 1789, which was before the court in *Chisholm v. Georgia*, and the majority of the court did not think that it was sufficient to limit the jurisdiction of the Circuit Court. Justice Iredell thought differently. In view of the manner in which that decision was received by the country, the adoption of the Eleventh Amendment, the light of history and the reason of the thing, we think we are at liberty to prefer Justice Iredell's views in this regard.

Some reliance is placed by the plaintiff upon the observations of Chief Justice Marshall, in Cohens v. Virginia, 6 Wheat. [19 U.S.] 264, 410. The Chief Justice was there considering the power of review exercisable by this court over the judgments of a state court, wherein it might be necessary to make the State itself a defendant in error. He showed that this power was absolutely necessary in order to enable the judiciary of the United States to take cognizance of all cases arising under the Constitution and laws of the United States. He also showed that making a State a defendant in error was entirely different from suing a State in an original action in prosecution of a demand against it, and was not within the meaning of the Eleventh Amendment; that the prosecution of a writ of error against a State was not the prosecution of a suit in the sense of that amendment, which had reference to the prosecution, by suit, of claims against a State. "Where," said the Chief Justice, "a State obtains a judgment against an individual, and the court rendering such judgment overrules a defence set up under the Constitution or laws of the United States, the transfer of this record into the Supreme Court for the sole purpose of inquiring whether the judgment violates the Constitution of the United States, can, with no propriety, we think, be denominated a suit commenced or prosecuted against the State whose judgment is so far reëxamined. Nothing is demanded from the State. No claim against it of any description is asserted or prosecuted. The party is not to be restored to the possession of any thing. . . . He only asserts the constitutional right to have his defence examined by that tribunal whose province it is to construe the Constitution and laws of the Union. . . ."

After thus showing by incontestable argument that a writ of error to a judgment recovered by a State, in which the State is necessarily the defendant in error, is not a suit commenced or prosecuted against a State in the sense of the amendment, he added, that if the court were mistaken in this, its error did not affect that case, because the writ of error therein was not prosecuted by "a citizen of another State" or "of any foreign state," and so was not affected by the amendment; but was governed by the general grant of judicial power, as extending "to all cases arising under the Constitution or laws of the United States, without respect to parties." p. 412.

It must be conceded that the last observation of the Chief Justice does favor the argument of the plaintiff. But the observation was unnecessary to the decision, and in that sense *extra judicial*, and though made by one who seldom used words without due reflection, ought not to outweigh the important considerations referred to which lead to a different conclusion. With regard to the question then before the court, it may be observed, that writs of error to judgments in favor of the crown, or of the State, had been known to the law from time immemorial; and had never been considered as exceptions to the rule, that an action does not lie against the sovereign.

To avoid misapprehension it may be proper to add that, although the obligations of a State rest for their performance upon its honor and good faith, and cannot be made the subjects of judicial cognizance unless the State consents to be sued, or comes itself into court; yet where property or rights are enjoyed under a grant or contract made by a State, they cannot wantonly be invaded. Whilst the State cannot be compelled by suit to perform its contracts, any attempt on its part to violate property or rights acquired under its contracts, may be judicially resisted; and any law impairing the obligation of contracts under which such property or rights are held is void and powerless to affect their enjoyment. . . .

The judgment of the Circuit Court is Affirmed.

MR. JUSTICE HARLAN concurring.

I concur with the court in holding that a suit directly against a State by one of its own citizens is not one to which the judicial power of the United States extends, unless the State itself consents to be sued. Upon this ground alone I assent to the judgment. But I cannot give my assent to many things said in the opinion. The comments made upon the decision in *Chisholm v. Georgia* do not meet my approval. They are not necessary to the determination of the present case. Besides I am of opinion that the decision in that case was based upon a sound interpretation of the Constitution as that instrument then was.

Notes on the Eleventh Amendment and Related Immunities

(1) Chisholm v. Georgia, 2 U.S. (2 Dall.) 419 (1793). South Carolina citizens sued the State of Georgia in the Supreme Court on a contract claim. The Court upheld its jurisdiction, holding that the controversy was one "between a State and Citizens of another State" within Article III. Each Justice wrote an opinion. Cushing and Blair relied essentially on the unqualified words of Article III, adding that the parallel provision respecting "Controversies between two or more States" made clear that a State could be defendant as well as plaintiff. Wilson added that governments were suable in other countries, that on "general principles of right and equality" a State should not be permitted to avoid its obligations, and that suability was implicit in the clause forbidding States to impair contracts, which otherwise would be a dead letter. Jay added that the old-world notion of state sovereignty underlying immunity was incompatible with the concept of popular sovereignty expressed in the preamble. Iredell dissented without reaching the constitutional question, reading into the statutory provision for issuance of writs "agreeable to the principles and usages of law" the common-law principle that the sovereign was not subject to suit without his consent. Wilson disputed Iredell's history, arguing that in fact the King of England had been regularly sued through the mechanism of the petition of right. Iredell responded by quoting Blackstone that the petition was "a matter of grace" and not of "compulsion," but Wilson replied: "[T]he difference is only in the form, not in the thing." [1]

No one in *Chisholm* referred to the impressive statements of the Framers, quoted in *Hans*, denying that States could be sued. Numerous opponents of the Constitution had argued to the contrary; so had Edmund Randolph, later counsel for Chisholm, who praised the Constitution *because* it made States suable: "[W]hatever the law of nations may say, . . . any doubt respecting the construction that a state may be plaintiff, and not defendant, is taken away by the words *where a state shall be a party*. . . ." 3 J. Elliot, The Debates in the Several State Conventions on the Adoption of the Federal Constitution 573 (2d Ed. 1836). For further

1. Professor Jaffe, writing much later, agreed: "[W]hen it was necessary to sue the Crown eo nomine consent apparently was given as of course." L. Jaffe, Judicial Control of Administrative Action 197 (Student ed. 1965).

discussion of *Chisholm* see Currie, The Constitution in the Supreme Court: The First Hundred Years 14–20 (1985).

(2) The *Chisholm* decision, according to Professor Warren, "fell upon the country with a profound shock."

One newspaper asserted that the *Chisholm* decision could lead to "the overthrow of the State Governments, to the consolidation of the Union for the purpose of arbitrary power, to the downfall of liberty and the subversion of the rights of the people"; but the "real source" of the opposition to *Chisholm*, according to Warren, was the "very concrete fear" of raids on the state treasuries: "In the crucial condition of the finances of most of the States at that time, only disaster was to be expected if suits could be successfully maintained by holders of State issues of paper and other credits, or by Loyalist refugees to recover property confiscated or sequestered by the States; and that this was no theoretical danger was shown by the immediate institution of such suits against the States in South Carolina, Georgia, Virginia and Massachusetts." The Georgia House of Representatives was so excited that it passed a bill providing that anyone attempting to execute process in the *Chisholm* case should be declared "guilty of felony and shall suffer death, without benefit of clergy, by being hanged." 1 C. Warren, The Supreme Court in United States History 96–100 (2d ed. 1926).

Others have disputed Warren's emphasis on the protection of state treasuries, arguing that by 1794 the States were basically solvent and Congress was controlled by Federalists believing in the sanctity of obligations.[2] But everyone seems to agree that the Eleventh Amendment was a direct and immediate response to *Chisholm.*

(3) Was the decision that Hans could not sue his own State of Louisiana based upon (a) an expansive reading of the Eleventh Amendment itself; (b) a restrictive interpretation of Article III; or (c) the common law of sovereign immunity? Are you sure you know why it matters? Was *Hans* either more or less justifiable than the decision in McCulloch v. Maryland, 17 U.S. (4 Wheat.) 316 (1819), that federal instrumentalities were implicitly immunized from state taxation?

(4) Similarly, despite the narrow words of the Eleventh Amendment, the Court has held that a State may not be sued in federal court without its consent in admiralty, Ex parte New York, 256 U.S. 490, 498 (1921); or by a corporation created by federal law, Smith v. Reeves, 178 U.S. 436 (1900); or by a foreign country, Monaco v. Mississippi, 292 U.S. 313 (1934). On the other hand, as the Court observed in *Monaco*, a State may be sued by another State, Rhode Island v. Massachusetts, 37 U.S. (12 Pet.) 657, 720 (1838), or by the United States, United States v. Texas, 143 U.S. 621, 644–45 (1892):

> The establishment of a permanent tribunal with adequate authority to determine controversies between the States . . . was essential to the peace of the Union. . . . With respect to such controversies, the States by the adoption of the Constitution . . . waived their exemp-

2. See, e.g., C. Jacobs, The Eleventh Amendment and Sovereign Immunity 67–74 (1972).

> tion from judicial power. . . . Upon a similar basis rests the jurisdiction of this Court of a suit by the United States against a State, albeit without the consent of the latter. While that jurisdiction is not conferred by the Constitution in express words, it is inherent in the constitutional plan. . . . Without such a provision, as this Court said in United States v. Texas, supra, "the permanence of the Union might be endangered."

Accord, United States v. Mississippi, 380 U.S. 128 (1965).

The considerations discussed in *United States v. Texas,* the Court said in *Monaco,* do not apply to a suit by a foreign state, which "lies outside the structure of the Union" and which cannot be said to have waived its immunity from suit. Moreover, "It cannot be supposed that it was the intention that a controversy growing out of the action of a State, which involves a matter of national concern and which is said to affect injuriously the interests of a foreign State, or a dispute arising from conflicting claims of a State of the Union and a foreign State as to territorial boundaries, should be taken out of the sphere of international negotiations and adjustment through a resort by the foreign State to a suit under the provisions of § 2 of Article III." Finally, the Court added in dictum, "The foreign State enjoys a similar sovereign immunity and without her consent may not be sued by a State of the Union."

What scope does this statement leave for the provision in Article III for jurisdiction over controversies "between a State . . . and foreign states"?

Can the United States sue a foreign state in federal court?

(5) "There is no express provision that the United States may not be sued in the absence of consent. . . . But by reason of the established doctrine of the immunity of the sovereign from suit except upon consent, the provision of Clause one of § 2 of Article III does not authorize the maintenance of suits against the United States." Monaco v. Mississippi, supra note 4, 292 U.S. at 321. The doctrine of federal immunity "developed largely in dicta" before the statutory grant of federal-question jurisdiction in 1875, see Hart & Wechsler, The Federal Courts and the Federal System 1109 (3d ed. 1988). Chief Justice Jay, for example, in his opinion upholding jurisdiction over a State in Chisholm v. Georgia, supra note 1, 2 U.S. (2 Dall.), at 478, suggested that the United States might not be subject to private suit:

> In all cases of actions against states or individual citizens, the national courts are supported in all their legal and constitutional proceedings and judgments, by the arm of the executive power of the United States; but in cases of actions against the United States, there is no power which the courts can call to their aid. From this distinction, important conclusions are deducible, and they place the case of a state, and the case of the United States, in very different points of view.

(6) In Kansas v. United States, 204 U.S. 331 (1907) (alternative holding), the Court held the United States immune from suit by a State: "It does not follow that because a State may be sued by the United States without its consent, therefore the United States may be sued by a State

without its consent. Public policy forbids that conclusion." What public policy is that? Why is not the allowance of such suits "inherent in the constitutional plan" and necessary to protect the permanence of the Union? Is it not just as true when the State is plaintiff as when it is defendant that unless a court is open the dispute can only be resolved by "a trial of physical strength"? See *United States v. Texas*, supra note 4.

(7) In Bank of the United States v. Planters' Bank, 22 U.S. (9 Wheat.) 904 (1824), the National Bank sued the Planters' Bank on promissory notes. The defendant argued that the Eleventh Amendment barred the action, because the State of Georgia was one of its shareholders. The Court, in an opinion by Chief Justice Marshall, disagreed on three grounds. First, the suit was against the corporation, and therefore was "no more a suit against the state of Georgia, than against any other individual corporator." [3] Second, "when a government becomes a partner in any trading company, it divests itself, so far as concerns the transactions of that company, of its sovereign character, and takes that of a private citizen." Finally, "[t]he State of Georgia, by giving the bank the capacity to sue and be sued, voluntarily strips itself of its sovereign character, so far as respects the transactions of the bank, and waives all the privileges of that character." [4] No reasons were offered for any of these conclusions.

The suggestion that the Eleventh Amendment is inapplicable to government "trading," reminiscent of the familiar distinction between "governmental" and "proprietary" activities for purposes of municipal tort liability, has had a checkered career. Justice Johnson protested in *Planters' Bank* itself: "If it be said, that the amendment . . . has regard only to suits instituted against states in their sovereign capacity, I would ask, in what other capacity can a state appear, or even exist?"

Merchant ships owned by the United States were as immune as warships from court process until the Shipping Act of 1916, see infra p. 471. The immunity of a foreign sovereign under international law was held applicable to a commercial vessel owned by the Italian government in Berizzi Brothers Co. v. The Pesaro, 271 U.S. 562 (1926).[5] In Ex parte New York, 256 U.S. 490 (1921), without considering whether the activity was governmental or proprietary, the Supreme Court upheld the State's immunity to admiralty libels in rem arising out of the operation of tugboats on the Erie Canal. Yet the proprietary nature of the activities played a role in determining the scope of the State's related implicit immunities from federal taxation and regulation during their heyday,[6] and it cropped up not

3. As Justice Johnson pointed out in dissent, this was a bit tricky to square with Marshall's decision in *Bank of the United States v. Deveaux*, supra p. 267, that a corporation was not a citizen for diversity purposes. Cf. the question whether a suit against a state *officer* is barred by the Amendment, pp. 444–55 infra.

4. The question of state waiver of immunity is further considered at pp. 455–60 infra.

5. This rule was changed by statute in 1976. See pp. 454–55 infra.

6. See South Carolina v. United States, 199 U.S. 437 (1905), upholding a tax on a state liquor business; National League of Cities v. Usery, 426 U.S. 833, 854 n. 18 (1976), distinguishing United States v. California, 297 U.S. 175 (1936), which had upheld federal regulation of a state-owned railroad. *National League of Cities* was overruled in Garcia v. San Antonio Metropolitan Transit Auth., 469 U.S. 528 (1985).

so long ago as a factor in ascertaining whether a State had waived its immunity from suit, see pp. 455–60 infra. Does the language or purpose of the Eleventh Amendment suggest any distinction between governmental and proprietary activities?

(8) Both a county, Chicot County v. Sherwood, 148 U.S. 529 (1893), and a city, Workman v. City of New York, 179 U.S. 552 (1900), have been held subject to suit in the federal courts without their consent. Cf. the problem of determining whether a municipal corporation is a "citizen" in a diversity case, supra pp. 272–73.[7] On the other hand, local officials are considered to be acting for the State for Fourteenth Amendment purposes, e.g., Griffin v. Prince Edward County School Board, 377 U.S. 218 (1964), and the Court held in National League of Cities v. Usery, 426 U.S. 833 (1976), that the minimum wages of local as well as state employees were immune from federal prescription under the Fair Labor Standards Act. Is there any basis for these distinctions?

EX PARTE YOUNG

209 U.S. 123 (1908).

[Minnesota citizens brought shareholders' derivative suits in federal court to enjoin the enforcement of a Minnesota statute establishing maximum railroad rates allegedly confiscatory in violation of the Fourteenth Amendment. Disregarding a preliminary injunction, the Attorney General of Minnesota instituted state-court proceedings to enforce the statute, and he was cited for contempt. After issuing a show-cause order on the Attorney General's petition for habeas corpus and certiorari, the Supreme Court upheld the citation in an opinion by Justice Peckham. The original suit, said the Court, was one arising under the Constitution, and the statute was invalid. The "most material" objection to jurisdiction was that the suit was "in effect, one against the State of Minnesota."] . . .

Osborn v. United States Bank (1824) 9 Wheat. [22 U.S.] 738, 846, 857, . . . held that the [Eleventh] Amendment applied only to those suits in which the state was a party on the record. In the subsequent case of Governor of Georgia v. Madrazo (1828), 1 Pet. [26 U.S.] 110, 122, 123, that holding was somewhat enlarged, and Chief Justice Marshall, delivering the opinion of the court, while citing Osborn v. United States Bank, supra, said that where the claim was made, as in the case then before the court, against the Governor of Georgia as governor, and the demand was made upon him, not personally, but officially (for moneys in the treasury of the State and for slaves in possession of the state government), the State might be considered as the party on the record (page 123), and therefore the suit could not be maintained.

Davis v. Gray, 16 Wall. [83 U.S.] 203, 220, reiterates the rule of Osborn v. United States Bank, so far as concerns the right to enjoin a

7. However, to the extent that state law is determinative of liability under *Erie R. R. v. Tompkins*, supra p. 327, the federal courts have recognized the immunity of local governments under state law. E.g., Broward County v. Wickman, 195 F.2d 614 (5th Cir. 1952).

state officer from executing a state law in conflict with the Constitution or a statute of the United States, when such execution will violate the rights of the complainant. . . .

Hagood v. Southern, 117 U.S. 52, 67, decided that the bill was in substance a bill for the specific performance of a contract between the complainants and the State of South Carolina, and, although the State was not in name made a party defendant, yet being the actual party to the alleged contract the performance of which was sought and the only party by whom it could be performed, the State was, in effect, a party to the suit, and it could not be maintained for that reason. The things required to be done by the actual defendants were the very things which when done would constitute a performance of the alleged contract by the State. . . .

The various authorities we have referred to furnish ample justification for the assertion that individuals, who, as officers of the State, are clothed with some duty in regard to the enforcement of the laws of the State, and who threaten and are about to commence proceedings, either of a civil or criminal nature, to enforce against parties affected an unconstitutional act, violating the Federal Constitution, may be enjoined by a Federal court of equity from such action. . . .

It is also argued that the only proceeding which the Attorney General could take to enforce the statute, so far as his office is concerned, was one by mandamus, which would be commenced by the state in its sovereign and governmental character, and that the right to bring such action is a necessary attribute of a sovereign government. It is contended that the complainants do not complain and they care nothing about any action which Mr. Young might take or bring as an ordinary individual, but that he was complained of as an officer, to whose discretion is confided the use of the name of the State of Minnesota so far as litigation is concerned, and that when or how he shall use it is a matter resting in his discretion and cannot be controlled by any court.

The answer to all this is the same as made in every case where an official claims to be acting under the authority of the State. The act to be enforced is alleged to be unconstitutional, and if it be so, the use of the name of the State to enforce an unconstitutional act to the injury of complainants is a proceeding without the authority of and one which does not affect the State in its sovereign or governmental capacity. It is simply an illegal act upon the part of a state official in attempting, by the use of the name of the State, to enforce a legislative enactment which is void because unconstitutional. If the act which the state Attorney General seeks to enforce be a violation of the Federal Constitution, the officer, in proceeding under such enactment comes into conflict with the superior authority of that Constitution, and he is in that case stripped of his official or representative character and is subjected in his person to the consequences of his individual conduct.

The State has no power to impart to him any immunity from responsibility to the supreme authority of the United States. . . .

It is further objected (and the objection really forms part of the contention that the State cannot be sued) that a court of equity has no jurisdiction to enjoin criminal proceedings, by indictment or otherwise, under the state law. This, as a general rule, is true. But there are exceptions. When such indictment or proceeding is brought to enforce an alleged unconstitutional statute, which is the subject matter of inquiry in a suit already pending in a Federal court, the latter court, having first obtained jurisdiction over the subject matter, has the right in both civil and criminal cases, to hold and maintain such jurisdiction, to the exclusion of all other courts, until its duty is fully performed. Prout v. Starr, 188 U.S. 537, 542–544. But the Federal court cannot, of course, interfere in a case where the proceedings were already pending in a state court. Taylor v. Taintor, 16 Wall. [83 U.S.] 366–370; Harkrader v. Wadley, 172 U.S. 148. . . .

It is further objected that there is a plain and adequate remedy at law open to the complainants, and that a court of equity, therefore, has no jurisdiction in such case. It has been suggested that the proper way to test the constitutionality of the act is to disobey it, at least once, after which the company might obey the act pending subsequent proceedings to test its validity. But in the event of a single violation the prosecutor might not avail himself of the opportunity to make the test, as obedience to the law was thereafter continued, and he might think it unnecessary to start an inquiry. If, however, he should do so while the company was thereafter obeying the law, several years might elapse before there was a final determination of the question, and if it should be determined that the law was invalid, the property of the company would have been taken during that time without due process of law, and there would be no possibility of its recovery.

Another obstacle to making the test on the part of the company might be to find an agent or employe who would disobey the law, with a possible fine and imprisonment staring him in the face if the act should be held valid. Take the passenger rate act, for instance: A sale of a single ticket above the price mentioned in that act might subject the ticket agent to a charge of felony, and upon conviction to a fine of $5,000 and imprisonment for five years. It is true the company might pay the fine, but the imprisonment the agent would have to suffer personally. It would not be wonderful if, under such circumstances, there would not be a crowd of agents offering to disobey the law. The wonder would be that a single agent should be found ready to take the risk.

If, however, one should be found and the prosecutor should elect to proceed against him, the defense that the act was invalid, because the rates established by it were too low, would require a long and difficult examination of quite complicated facts upon which the validity of the act depended. Such investigation it would be almost impossible to make before a jury, as such body could not intelligently pass upon the matter. Questions of the cost of transportation of passengers and freight, the net earnings of the road, the separation of the cost and earnings, within the State from those arising beyond its boundaries, all depending upon the testimony of experts and the examination of figures relating to these subjects, as well, possibly as the expenses attending the building and proper cost of the road, would necessarily form the chief matter of inquiry, and intelligent answers could only be given after a careful and prolonged examination of the whole evidence, and the making of calculations based thereon. All material evidence having been taken upon these issues, it has been held that it ought to be referred to the most competent and reliable master to make all needed computations and to find therefrom the necessary facts upon which a judgment might be rendered that might be reviewed by this court. . . . From all these considerations it is plain that this is not a proper suit for investigation by a jury. Suits for penalties, or indictment or other criminal proceedings for a violation of the act, would therefore furnish no reasonable or adequate opportunity for the presentation of a defense founded upon the assertion that the rates were too low and therefore the act invalid. . . .

[The Court found support for its holding in habeas corpus decisions,] in some of which cases persons in the custody of state officers for alleged crimes against the State have been taken from that custody and discharged by a Federal court or judge, because the imprisonment was adjudged to be in violation of the Federal Constitution. The right to so discharge has not been doubted by this court, and it has never been supposed there was any suit against the State by reason of serving the writ upon one of the officers of the State in whose custody the person was found. . . .

The rule to show cause is discharged and the petition for writs of *habeas corpus* and certiorari is dismissed. . . .

[JUSTICE HARLAN, dissenting, argued that the Court's decision would "practically obliterate the Eleventh Amendment" and "enable the subordinate Federal courts to supervise and control the official action of the States as if they were 'dependencies' or provinces. . . . Too little consequence has been attached to the fact that the courts of the States are under an obligation equally strong with that resting upon the courts of the Union to respect and enforce the provisions of the Federal Constitution. . . . If they fail to do so, the party complaining has a clear remedy for the protection of his rights; for, he can come by writ of error, in an orderly, judicial way, from the highest court of the State to this tribunal for redress. . . ."]

EDELMAN v. JORDAN

415 U.S. 651 (1974).

[Jordan filed a class action in federal court, alleging that Illinois officials had been dilatory in processing applications under the joint federal-state programs for Aid to the Aged, Blind and Disabled (AABD) and had refused to make payments retroactive to the initial date of eligibility, all in violation of federal regulations under the Social Security Act and of the Equal Protection Clause. The district court declared the state practices contrary to federal regulations, issued a permanent injunction requiring future compliance, and ordered the defendants to pay all past benefits wrongfully withheld. The Seventh Circuit affirmed over an argument based on "the Eleventh Amendment," Jordan v. Weaver, 472 F.2d 985 (1973).]

MR. JUSTICE REHNQUIST delivered the opinion of the Court. . . .

Because we believe the Court of Appeals erred in its disposition of the Eleventh Amendment claim, we reverse that portion of the Court of Appeals decision which affirmed the District Court's order that retroactive benefits be paid by the Illinois state officials. . . .

While the Amendment by its terms does not bar suits against a State by its own citizens, this Court has consistently held that an unconsenting State is immune from suits brought in federal courts by her own citizens as well as by citizens of another State. Hans v. Louisiana, 134 U.S. 1 (1890). . . . It is also well established that even though a State is not named a party to the action, the suit may nonetheless be barred by the Eleventh Amendment. In Ford Motor Co. v. Department of Treasury, 323 U.S. 459 (1945), the Court said:

> "[W]hen the action is in essence one for the recovery of money from the state, the state is the real, substantial party in interest and is entitled to invoke its sovereign immunity from suit even though individual officials are nominal defendants." Id., at 464.

Thus the rule has evolved that a suit by private parties seeking to impose a liability which must be paid from public funds in the state treasury is barred by the Eleventh Amendment. Great Northern Life Insurance Co. v. Read, supra; Kennecott Copper Corp. v. State Tax Comm'n, 327 U.S. 573 (1946).

The Court of Appeals in this case, while recognizing that the *Hans* line of cases permitted the State to raise the Eleventh Amendment as a defense to suit by its own citizens, nevertheless concluded that the Amendment did not bar the award of retroactive payments of the statutory benefits found to have been wrongfully withheld. The Court of Appeals held that the above cited cases, when read in light of the Court's landmark decision in Ex parte Young, 209 U.S. 123 (1908), do not preclude the grant of such a monetary award in the nature of equitable restitution.

Petitioner concedes that Ex parte Young, supra, is no bar to that part of the District Court's judgment that prospectively enjoined petitioner's predecessors from failing to process applications within the time limits established by the federal regulations. Petitioner argues, however, that Ex parte Young does not extend so far as to permit a suit which seeks the award of an accrued monetary liability which must be met from the general revenues of a State, absent consent or waiver by the State of its Eleventh Amendment immunity, and that therefore the award of retroactive benefits by the District Court was improper.

Ex parte Young was a watershed case in which this Court held that the Eleventh Amendment did not bar an action in the federal courts seeking to enjoin the Attorney General of Minnesota from enforcing a statute claimed to violate the Fourteenth Amendment of the United States Constitution. This holding has permitted the Civil War Amendments to the constitution to serve as a sword, rather than merely as a shield, for those whom they were designed to protect. But the relief awarded in Ex parte Young was prospective only; the Attorney General of Minnesota was enjoined to conform his future conduct of that office to the requirement of the Fourteenth Amendment. Such relief is analogous to that awarded by the District Court in the prospective portion of its order under review in this case.

But the retroactive portion of the District Court's order here, which requires the payment of a very substantial amount of money which that court held should have been paid, but was not, stands on quite a different footing. These funds will obviously not be paid out of the pocket of petitioner Edelman. Addressing himself to a similar situation in Rothstein v. Wyman, 467 F.2d 226 (CA2 1972), . . . 411 U.S. 921 (1973), Judge McGowan observed for the court:

> . . . "It is one thing to tell the Commissioner of Social Services that he must comply with the federal standards for the future if the state is to have the benefit of federal funds in the programs he administers. It is quite another thing to order the Commissioner to use state funds to make reparation for the past. The latter would appear to us to fall afoul of the Eleventh Amendment if that basic constitutional provision is to be conceived of as having any present force." . . .

We agree with Judge McGowan's observations. The funds to satisfy the award in this case must inevitably come from the general revenues of the State of Illinois, and thus the award resembles far more closely the monetary award against the State itself, Ford Motor Co. v. Department of Treasury, supra, than it does the prospective injunctive relief awarded in Ex parte Young.

The Court of Appeals, in upholding the award in this case, held that it was permissible because it was in the form of "equitable restitution" instead of damages, and therefore capable of being tailored in such a way as to minimize disruptions of the state program of categorical assistance. But we must judge the award actually made in this case, and not one which might have been differently tailored in a different case, and we must judge it in the context of the important constitutional principle embodied in the Eleventh Amendment.

We do not read Ex parte Young or subsequent holdings of this Court to indicate that any form of relief may be awarded against a state officer, no matter how closely it may in practice resemble a money judgment payable out of the state treasury, so long as the relief may be labeled "equitable" in nature. The Court's opinion in Ex parte Young hewed to no such line. Its citation of Hagood v. Southern, 117 U.S. 52 (1886), and In re Ayers, 123 U.S. 443 (1887), which were both actions against state officers for specific performance of a contract to which the State was a party, demonstrate that equitable relief may be barred by the Eleventh Amendment.

As in most areas of the law, the difference between the type of relief barred by the Eleventh Amendment and that permitted under Ex parte Young will not in many instances be that between day and night. The injunction issued in Ex parte Young was not totally without effect on the State's revenues, since the state law which the Attorney General was enjoined from enforcing provided substantial monetary penalties against railroads which did not conform to its provisions. Later cases from this Court have authorized equitable relief which has probably had greater impact on state treasuries than did that awarded in Ex parte Young. In Graham v. Richardson, 403 U.S. 365 (1971), Arizona and Pennsylvania welfare officials were prohibited from denying welfare benefits to otherwise qualified recipients who were aliens. In Goldberg v. Kelly, 397 U.S. 254 (1970), New York City welfare officials were enjoined from following New York State procedures which authorized the termination of benefits paid to welfare recipients without prior hearing.[12] But the fiscal consequences to state treasuries in these cases were the necessary result of compliance with decrees which by their terms were prospective in nature. State officials, in order to shape their official conduct to the mandate of the Court's decrees, would more likely have to spend money from the state treasury than if they had been left free to pursue their previous course of conduct. Such an ancillary effect on the state treasury is a permissible and often an inevitable consequence of the principle announced in Ex parte Young, supra.

But that portion of the District Court's decree which petitioners challenge on Eleventh Amendment grounds goes much further than any of the cases cited. It requires payment of state funds, not as a necessary consequence of compliance in the future with a substantive federal question determination, but as a form of compensation to those whose applications were processed on the slower time schedule at a time when petitioners were under no court-imposed obligation to conform to a different standard. While the Court of Appeals described this retroactive award of monetary relief as a form of "equitable restitution," it is in practical effect indistinguishable in many aspects from an award of damages against the State. It will to a virtual certainty be paid from state funds, and not from the pocket of the individual state official who was the defendant in the action. It is measured in terms of

12. The Court of Appeals considered the Court's decision in Griffin v. School Board, 377 U.S. 218 (1964), to be of like import. But as may be seen from *Griffin's* citation of Lincoln County v. Luning, 133 U.S. 529 (1890), a county does not occupy the same position as a State for purposes of the Eleventh Amendment. . . .

a monetary loss resulting from a past breach of a legal duty on the part of the defendant state officials.

Were we to uphold this portion of the District Court's decree, we would be obligated to overrule the Court's holding in Ford Motor Co. v. Department of Treasury, supra. There a taxpayer, who had, under protest, paid taxes to the State of Indiana, sought a refund of those taxes from the Indiana state officials who were charged with their collection. The taxpayer claimed that the tax had been imposed in violation of the United States Constitution. The term "equitable restitution" would seem even more applicable to the relief sought in that case, since the taxpayer had at one time had the money, and paid it over to the State pursuant to an allegedly unconstitutional tax exaction. Yet this Court had no hesitation in holding that the taxpayer's action was a suit against the State, and barred by the Eleventh Amendment. We reach a similar conclusion with respect to the retroactive portion of the relief awarded by the District Court in this case. . . .

The judgment of the Court of Appeals is therefore reversed and the cause remanded for further proceedings consistent with this opinion. . . .

MR. JUSTICE BRENNAN, dissenting. . . . In my view Illinois may not assert sovereign immunity for the reason I expressed in dissent in Employees v. Department of Public Health and Welfare, 411 U.S. 279, 298 (1973): the States surrendered that immunity in Hamilton's words "in the plan of the Convention," that formed the Union, at least insofar as the States granted Congress specifically enumerated powers. . . .

MR. JUSTICE DOUGLAS, dissenting. . . . As the complaint in the instant case alleges violations by officials of Illinois of the Equal Protection Clause of the Fourteenth Amendment, it seems that the case is governed by Ex parte Young so far as injunctive relief is concerned. The main thrust of the argument is that the instant case asks for relief which if granted would affect the treasury of the State.

Most welfare decisions by federal courts have a financial impact on the States. Under the existing federal-state cooperative system, a state desiring to participate, submits a "state plan" to HEW for approval; once HEW approves the plan the State is locked into the cooperative scheme until it withdraws. . . . Rosado v. Wyman, 397 U.S. 397, held that under this state-federal cooperative program a State could not reduce its standard of need in conflict with the federal standard. It is true that *Rosado* did not involve retroactive payments as are involved here. But the distinction is not relevant or material because the result in every welfare case coming here is to increase or reduce the financial responsibility of the participating State. . . . Whether the decree is prospective only or requires payments for the weeks or months wrongfully skipped over by the state officials, the nature of the impact on the state treasury is precisely the same. . . .

[JUSTICES MARSHALL and BLACKMUN dissented on the ground that Illinois had waived its immunity by participating in the federal welfare program.]

Notes on Immunity in Suits Against Government Officers

(1) The Eleventh Amendment and other governmental-immunity doctrines would have been meaningless in injunction cases, wouldn't they, if the Court had adhered to Chief Justice Marshall's statement in Osborn v. Bank of the United States, 22 U.S. (9 Wheat.) 738, 857 (1824), that suit was forbidden only if the State was "a party of record?" Despite the tortuous fictions of the Court in *Ex parte Young*, wasn't Justice Harlan right in saying the decree had the same effect as if the State had been named defendant? On the other hand, can the Constitution be adequately enforced against the States if state officers cannot be sued for violating it? Justice Harlan had made this point himself in dissenting from the holding that a State could not be sued by its own citizens under the Contract Clause, Louisiana v. Jumel, 107 U.S. 711 (1883), yet he was the one who objected in *Ex parte Young* that permitting state officers to be sued eviscerated the Eleventh Amendment. Can he have been right on both points?

(2) If the unconstitutionality of the authorizing statute in *Ex parte Young* "stripped" the Attorney General of his official character so that the suit was not against the State, how could his enforcement of the statute violate the Fourteenth Amendment, which limits only state action? [1]

(3) Does the distinction between *Young* and *Edelman* make any sense? As Justice Rehnquist's citation of the *Ford Motor Co.* decision suggests, the line *Edelman* attempted to draw did not come out of the blue; both before and after *Young* there were a number of decisions declining relief against government officers on the ground that in practical effect the suit was against the government itself.

The leading case was In re Ayers, 123 U.S. 443 (1887), in which the plaintiffs sought to enjoin the institution of suits against holders of coupons that the State had contracted to receive in payment of taxes. The ground of attack was that the statutes authorizing suit impaired the obligation of contract, but the Court held the suit barred by the Eleventh Amendment. Earlier cases allowing suit against state officers were distinguished because the acts there challenged "considered apart from the official authority alleged as its justification, and as the personal act of the individual defendant, constituted a violation of right for which the plaintiff was entitled to a remedy at law against the wrongdoer in his individual character." But the essence of the suit in *Ayers*, said the Court, was to enforce specific performance by enjoining suits in breach of contract; and "the defendants, as individuals, not being parties to that contract, are not capable in law of committing a breach of it."

1. For the fate of the argument that unauthorized action by state officials is not "state" action for Fourteenth Amendment purposes see p. 390 supra.

What does this sort of reasoning have to do with the policies of the Eleventh Amendment? Is it a product of the difficulties discussed in note 2? [2] Does it help to explain the result in *Edelman*?

(4) Milliken v. Bradley, 433 U.S. 267 (1977). Finding that both local and state officers were responsible for school segregation, the district court ordered them to share the cost of instituting remedial reading programs and in-service training for teachers and administrators. The Supreme Court unanimously affirmed:

> The decree to share the future costs of educational components in this case fits squarely within the prospective-compliance exception reaffirmed by *Edelman*. . . . The decree requires state officials, held responsible for unconstitutional conduct, in findings which are not challenged, to eliminate a *de jure* segregated school system. . . . The educational components, which the District Court ordered into effect *prospectively*, are plainly designed to wipe out continuing conditions of inequality produced by the inherently unequal dual code school system long maintained by Detroit. . . . In contrast to *Edelman*, there was no money award here in favor of respondent Bradley or any member of his class. This case simply does not involve individual citizens' conducting a raid on the state treasury for an accrued monetary liability.

But wasn't the relief sought in *Edelman* equally "prospective" in the sense that it was to be afforded in the future?

(5) In Hutto v. Finney, 437 U.S. 678 (1978), over two dissents, the Court upheld an order of attorneys' fees to be paid from the state treasury in an injunctive action otherwise appropriately filed against a state officer. "Once issued, an injunction" with prospective effect "may be enforced"; a fine for disobedience of the injunction would be "ancillary to the federal court's power to impose injunctive relief," even if framed so as to "compensate[ ] the party who won the injunction for the effects of . . . noncompliance", and "the award of attorney's fees for bad faith served the same purpose as a remedial fine imposed for civil contempt." Thus it fell within the "ancillary" doctrine announced in *Edelman*: "like other enforcement powers, it is integral to the court's grant of prospective relief." Was this decision consistent with the precedents on which *Edelman* relied? [3]

(6) In Pennhurst State School & Hospital v. Halderman, 465 U.S. 89 (1984), the plaintiffs sued state officials in federal court, alleging that conditions in a public institution for the mentally retarded offended both

2. See Currie, Sovereign Immunity and Suits Against Government Officers, 1984 Sup.Ct.Rev. 149, 154: "The fact that a suit may not be against the state is no excuse for holding liable a person who has committed no wrong."

3. See also Quern v. Jordan, 440 U.S. 332 (1979), holding that state officials in the *Edelman v. Jordan* controversy could be required to notify the plaintiff class "that there is a state administrative procedure available if they desire to have the state determine whether or not they may be eligible for past benefits": "[W]hether or not the class member will receive retroactive benefits rests entirely with the State"; Green v. Mansour, 474 U.S. 64 (1985), holding that relief similar to that in *Quern* could be granted only when ancillary to a grant of prospective relief; Papasan v. Allain, 478 U.S. 265 (1986), holding that state officials could not be ordered to remedy past breaches of trust but could be enjoined from administering assets in violation of the Equal Protection Clause in the future.

federal and state law. As the case reached the Supreme Court on this occasion, the court of appeals had approved an injunction on state-law grounds without addressing the remaining arguments based on federal law. A bare majority concluded that relief was barred by sovereign immunity.

Ex parte Young, wrote Justice Powell for the majority, had been based on the necessity of "permit[ting] the federal courts to vindicate federal rights"; there was no such necessity "when a plaintiff alleges that a state official has violated state law." As Justice Stevens observed in dissent, this was a glaring departure from precedent, for the Court had entertained state-law claims against state officers both before and after *Ex parte Young.* Indeed it had long been the Court's explicit rule that pendent state-law claims in actions against state officers should be decided first in order to avoid unnecessary constitutional questions. Siler v. Louisville & N.R.R., p. 194 supra. Apart from precedent, was the *theory* of *Ex parte Young* limited to federal claims? See Currie, supra note 3, 1984 Sup.Ct.Rev. at 164–67.[4]

Not long after *Pennhurst,* the Court built upon its reasoning to suggest a new justification for the distinction between *Young* and *Edelman:*

> Remedies designed to end a continuing violation of federal law are necessary to vindicate the federal interest in assuring the supremacy of that law. . . . But compensatory or deterrence interests are insufficient to overcome the dictates of the Eleventh Amendment.

Green v. Mansour, 474 U.S. 64, 68 (1985). Is that a satisfactory explanation?

(7) Until 1976 the question of immunity in suits against *federal* officers was handled very much along the lines of the state officer cases.[5] In that year, however, Congress amended § 702 of the Administrative Procedure Act to abolish the immunity of the United States in most nonmonetary actions:

> An action in a court of the United States seeking relief other than money damages and stating a claim that an agency or an officer or employee thereof acted or failed to act in an official capacity or under color of legal authority shall not be dismissed nor relief therein denied on the ground that it is against the United States or that the United States is an indispensable party. The United States may be named as a defendant in any such action, and a judgment or decree may be entered against the United States, provided, that any mandatory or

4. A footnote evidently added in response to Justice Stevens's dissent suggested that the Court might not be excluding all state-law claims against state officers after all, expressly leaving open the question whether they could be sued on the ground that they had acted "without any statutory authority." Justice Stevens thought that was precisely what the plaintiffs were asserting in *Pennhurst;* the majority responded that the defendants had not acted "beyond their delegated authority."

5. Recall the dictum in *Chisholm v. Georgia,* quoted at p. 442 supra, that the case for federal immunity was the stronger because there was nobody to enforce a decree against a federal executive. But see Scalia, Sovereign Immunity and Nonstatutory Review of Federal Administrative Action: Some Conclusions from the Public-Lands Cases, 68 Mich.L.Rev. 867, 886 (1970), arguing that "exemption from the compulsory process of another sovereign . . . is certainly much more deserving of protection against formalistic evasion than is the exemption of the state's executive or legislative branches from the compulsory process of its own judiciary."

> injunctive decree shall specify the Federal officer or officers (by name or title), and their successors in office, personally responsible for compliance. Nothing herein (1) affects other limitations on judicial review or the power or duty of the court to dismiss any action or deny relief on any other appropriate legal or equitable ground; or (2) confers authority to grant relief if any other statute that grants consent to suit expressly or impliedly forbids the relief which is sought.

Does this amendment give rise to interpretive problems? See H.R.Rep. No. 94–1656, in 1976 U.S.Code Cong. & Admin. News at 6553, stating that the amendment does not permit actions for specific performance of government contracts, since the damage remedy (28 U.S.C. §§ 1346(a), 1471) is impliedly exclusive; Bowen v. Massachusetts, 487 U.S. 879 (1988), holding over three dissents that an action to require the Secretary of Health and Human Services to reimburse a State for Medicaid expenditures was not a forbidden claim for "money damages." [6]

Pre-1976 decisions on federal-officer immunity remain important, despite the amendment, to the extent they laid down principles applicable also to state officers.

(8) See Professor Jaffe's summary of the decisions in Suits Against Governments and Officers: Sovereign Immunity, 77 Harv.L.Rev. 1, 28–29, 39 (1963):

> Every suit involving the legality of governmental action, whether brought in name against the state or against an officer by name, is either a suit against the state, or not, as you choose. . . . It is thus in my opinion false to ask as an abstract analytic question whether such and such a proceeding is *really* a suit against the state. The question is to be answered, as it has over the centuries for the most part been answered, in terms of our legal tradition. This tradition does not always give us the answer. But it does tell us that the sensitive areas—the areas where consent to suit is likely to be required—are those involving the enforcement of contracts, treasury liability for tort, and the adjudication of interests in property which has come unsullied by tort into the bosom of the government.

Have subsequent developments blunted the force of these observations?

Notes on Suits Against Consenting Governments

(1) Justices Marshall and Blackmun, you may recall, dissented in *Edelman v. Jordan* on the ground that the State had waived its immunity from suit. Despite the apparently ironclad language of the Eleventh Amendment, the Supreme Court held over a century ago that one State could consent to be sued by a citizen of another: "The immunity from suit belonging to a State, which is respected and protected by the Constitution

6. Justice Stevens quoted from an earlier court of appeals opinion by Judge Bork:

"Damages are given to the plaintiff to *substitute* for a suffered loss, whereas specific remedies 'are not substitute remedies at all, but attempt to give the plaintiff the very thing to which he was entitled.' . . . [The plaintiff] is seeking funds to which a statute allegedly entitles it, rather than money in compensation for the losses, whatever they may be, that [it] will suffer or has suffered by virtue of the withholding of those funds."

within the limits of the judicial power of the United States, is a personal privilege which it may waive at pleasure." Clark v. Barnard, 108 U.S. 436, 447 (1883). Was this holding a mistake?

(2) The Court has often held that the interpretation of a state statute waiving immunity is a question of state law, e.g., Ford Motor Co. v. Department of Treasury, 323 U.S. 459 (1945), and that the State is free to consent to suit in its own courts while retaining its immunity from federal jurisdiction, subject to the condition that the state-court judgment is reviewable in the Supreme Court if it involves a federal question. Smith v. Reeves, 178 U.S. 436, 445 (1900). What is the source of this condition? [1]

Moreover, the Court has on several occasions resolved ambiguities in state consent statutes against a waiver of federal-court immunity. See, e.g., Kennecott Copper Corp. v. State Tax Comm'n, 327 U.S. 573, 577 (1946), disallowing federal suit despite a state statute permitting an action to recover illegally exacted taxes "in any court of competent jurisdiction" because "clear declaration of a State's consent to suit against itself in the federal court on fiscal claims is required."

Yet in Petty v. Tennessee-Missouri Bridge Commission, 359 U.S. 275 (1959), the Court found that two States had consented to be sued in federal court for wrongful death by entering into a compact creating an interstate agency with power "to sue and be sued in its own name." Construction of the compact was a federal question; Congress in consenting to the agreement had provided that nothing in it should "affect, impair, or diminish any right, power, or jurisdiction of the United States," and the compact had been "made in an era when the immunity of corporations performing governmental functions was not in favor in the federal field."

(3) The Supreme Court has held that the immunity of the United States from suit in the federal courts cannot be waived by its officer's appearance and failure to object, e.g., Case v. Terrell, 78 U.S. (11 Wall.) 199 (1871), and even that a judgment against the United States can be attacked collaterally on the basis of immunity despite failure to assert the defense during the original proceeding, United States v. United States Fidelity & Guaranty Co., 309 U.S. 506 (1940). Are these results compelled by the shibboleth that a jurisdictional defect can be noticed at any time? But cf. *McCormick v. Sullivant*, supra p. ___, refusing to permit collateral attack upon a judgment allegedly void for want of diverse citizenship or other jurisdictional basis. Doesn't *Clark v. Barnard* (supra note 1) suggest that sovereign immunity should be analogized for this purpose to venue or to jurisdiction over the person, which reflect policies protective of the defendant and which therefore can be lost by failure to object? [2]

1. Compare Markham v. Newport News, 292 F.2d 711 (4th Cir. 1961), holding it unconstitutional for a state to waive *municipal* immunity from tort liability (as a substantive matter) in the state but not in the federal courts. Is there merit to this distinction?

2. Cf. Richardson v. Fajardo Sugar Co., 241 U.S. 44 (1916); Flota Maritima Browning v. M/V Ciudad De La Habana, 335 F.2d 619, 624–25 (4th Cir. 1964), holding that the then Territory of Puerto Rico and the Republic of Cuba, respectively, had lost their immunity by defending on the merits without objecting. What sense is there in these distinctions?

On the other hand, the Court has allowed a defendant sued by the United States to set off against the Government's recovery amounts due him from the United States, e.g., United States v. Ringgold, 33 U.S. (8 Pet.) 150 (1834). See also United States v. Buchanan, 49 U.S. (8 How.) 83, 105 (1850), declaring that in a suit by the United States a setoff is allowed even as to matters distinct from the Government's cause of action, but that "any wrongs or torts done, and any unliquidated damages claimed, have never been permitted as a set-off"; United States v. Shaw, 309 U.S. 495 (1940), holding that the United States by suing in a state court did not become subject to an affirmative judgment on a crossclaim: "Against the background of complete immunity we find no Congressional action modifying the immunity rule in favor of cross-actions beyond the amount necessary as a set-off." [3] What sense is there in these distinctions?

(4) Such was the state of precedents regarding waiver of immunity when the Court decided Parden v. Terminal Railway, 377 U.S. 184 (1964), an action by Alabama citizens against the State of Alabama for personal-injury damages under the Federal Employers' Liability Act. In contrast to the earlier waiver cases, the State had raised the immunity defense in *Parden* by a timely special appearance; no relevant state statute spoke of capacity to be sued, much less in federal court; and the State's highest court had consistently held the state constitution forbade both the legislature and other state officers to consent to suits against the State, e.g., State Tax Commission v. Commercial Realty Co., 236 Ala. 358, 361, 182 So. 31, 35 (1938). Yet the Supreme Court over four dissents (White, Douglas, Harlan, and Stewart) held flatly that "Alabama has consented to the present suit."

First, wrote Justice Brennan, Congress had intended that State-owned railroads should be subject to federal-court suits: The statute made "every" interstate railroad liable in damages to injured employees; the Safety Appliance Act, similarly worded, had been held in a suit by the United States (where there was no problem of sovereign immunity) to impose substantive liability on State railroads. Therefore, "to read a 'sovereign immunity exception' into the Act would result . . . in a right without a remedy. . . . We are unwilling to conclude that Congress intended so pointless and frustrating a result."

Next, Congress was held to have power to make consent to suit a condition of engaging in interstate commerce, and the State had accepted the condition:

> By empowering Congress to regulate commerce, . . . the States necessarily surrendered any portion of their sovereignty that would stand in the way of such regulation. Since imposition of the FELA

3. See also The Siren, 74 U.S. (7 Wall.) 152 (1869), in which the Court held the United States by filing a libel against a ship it had captured as a prize subjected the proceeds of the suit to a claim for collision damages caused by Government employees in charge of the prize; The Thekla, 266 U.S. 328 (1924), in which the Court declared that the United States by seeking relief in a maritime collision case had subjected itself to a cross-libel for damages suffered by the other vessel: "The libel in such a case is like a bill for an account, which imports an offer to pay the balance if it should turn out against the party bringing the bill." *The Thekla* was distinguished in *Shaw* as resting upon "a relationship characteristic of claims for collision in admiralty but entirely absent in claims and cross-claims in settlement of estates."

> right of action upon interstate railroads is within the congressional regulatory power, it must follow that application of the Act to such a railroad cannot be precluded by sovereign immunity. . . .
>
> It remains the law that a State may not be sued by an individual without its consent. Our conclusion is simply that Alabama, when it began operation of an interstate railroad approximately 20 years after enactment of the FELA, necessarily consented to such suit as was authorized by that Act. By adopting and ratifying the Commerce Clause, the States empowered Congress to create such a right of action against interstate railroads; by enacting the FELA in the exercise of this power, Congress conditioned the right to operate a railroad in interstate commerce upon amenability to suit in federal court as provided by the Act; by thereafter operating a railroad in interstate commerce, Alabama must be taken to have accepted that condition and thus to have consented to suit.

The dissenters in *Parden* conceded Congress's power to condition a State's engaging in railroading on a waiver of immunity but found no evidence that the FELA was meant to impose such a condition.

(5) Is it so clear that the constitutional argument in *Parden* was without weight? How can *Parden* be reconciled with the established principle, see Terral v. Burke Construction Co., 257 U.S. 529, 532–33 (1922), that a State cannot require a foreign corporation to surrender its right to litigate in the federal courts as a condition of doing intrastate business in the State?

> The Federal Constitution confers upon citizens of one State the right to resort to federal courts in another . . . [;] state action, whether legislative or executive, necessarily calculated to curtail the free exercise of the right thus secured is void because the sovereign power of a State in excluding foreign corporations, as in the exercise of all others of its sovereign powers, is subject to the limitations of the supreme fundamental law.

See generally French, Unconstitutional Conditions: An Analysis, 50 Geo. L.J. 234, 247–48 (1961).

(6) Later decisions soon began to nibble away at *Parden.* In Employees of Department of Public Health and Welfare v. Department of Public Health and Welfare, 411 U.S. 279 (1973), the Court held that Congress by extending the Fair Labor Standards Act to state hospitals and schools had not conditioned their continued operation on consent to suit under the wage and hour provisions of that statute. "It is not easy," wrote Justice Douglas, "to infer that Congress in legislating pursuant to the Commerce Clause . . . desired silently to deprive the States of an immunity they have long enjoyed under another part of the Constitution." *Parden,* he concluded, was distinguishable. "*Parden* involved the railroad business which Alabama operated 'for profit' "; "[s]tate mental hospitals, state cancer hospitals, and training schools for delinquent girls . . . are not proprietary." Moreover, denying individuals the power to sue the State would not leave them a right without a remedy (as it would have done in *Parden*), for the statute gave the Secretary of Labor authority to obtain restitution on behalf of the employees. Finally, the Fair Labor Standards

Act provided for double damages, and "we are reluctant to believe that Congress in pursuit of a harmonious federalism desired to treat the States so harshly."

Justices Marshall and Stewart, concurring in the result, concluded that by authorizing actions against "[a]ny employer" and defining "employer" to include a State Congress had intended to subject States to suit, but that it could not constitutionally do so. For *Hans v. Louisiana* had held that Article III did not extend to suits against States without their consent, and Missouri had not consented to be sued. While Alabama (in *Parden*) had begun operation of its railroad " 'approximately 20 years after enactment of the FELA,' "

> [h]ere the State was fully engaged in the operation of the affected hospitals and schools at the time of the 1966 amendments. To suggest that the State had the choice of either ceasing operation of these vital public services or "consenting" to federal suit suffices, I believe, to demonstrate that the State had no true choice at all and thereby that the State did not voluntarily consent to the exercise of federal jurisdiction in this case.

Justice Brennan wrote a blistering dissent. The case against immunity was *more* compelling than in *Parden*, he argued, because "the FELA contains no provision expressly including employees of public railroads"; the Court had rejected any governmental-proprietary distinction in upholding the substantive provisions of the statute; the Secretary was too overburdened to make public enforcement an adequate remedy; and the double-damages provision, as the Court had earlier held, was " 'not penal in nature but constitutes compensation for . . . damages too obscure and difficult of proof. . . .' " More fundamentally, he contended that *Parden* made the issue of waiver irrelevant: "*Parden* held that a federal court determination of such suits cannot be precluded by the doctrine of sovereign immunity because the States surrendered their sovereignty to that extent when they granted Congress the power to regulate commerce." Thus Congress was free to make a State suable by its own citizens on a statutory claim without its consent: *Hans* was based not on a narrow interpretation of Article III but on "the ancient nonconstitutional doctrine of sovereign immunity."

(7) *Edelman v. Jordan* carried the retreat from *Parden* one step further in holding that Illinois had not consented to suit by participating in a federal welfare program. It was not necessary, said Justice Rehnquist, to decide whether *Edelman* was more like *Employees* than it was like *Parden*, for "the threshold fact" that had justified the inquiry into consent in those cases was "wholly absent":

> Both *Parden* and *Employees* involved a congressional enactment which by its terms authorized suit by designated plaintiffs against a general class of defendants which literally included States or state instrumentalities. . . . The only language in the Social Security Act which purports to provide a federal sanction against a State which does not comply with federal requirements . . . is found in 42 U.S.C. § 1384, which provides for termination of future allocations of federal

> funds. . . . This provision by its terms does not authorize suit against anyone. . . .

Nor did the ubiquitous § 1983 fill the bill: "[I]t has not heretofore been suggested that § 1983 was intended to create a waiver of the State's Eleventh Amendment immunity merely because an action could be brought under that section against state officers, rather than against the State itself." The peroration was enough to put *Parden* itself under a cloud:

> Constructive consent is not a doctrine commonly associated with the surrender of constitutional rights, and we see no place for it here. In deciding whether a State has waived its constitutional protection under the Eleventh Amendment, we will find waiver only where stated "by the most express language or by such overwhelming implications from the text as will leave no room for any other reasonable construction."

(8) *Parden* was formally buried in Welch v. Texas Department of Highways, 483 U.S. 468 (1987), which held that a State could not be sued under the Jones Act for negligent operation of a dock, even though that statute expressly incorporated the FELA provisions that had been held to justify a finding of waiver in *Parden*. *Employees* and subsequent decisions, wrote Justice Powell for four members of the Court, had undermined *Parden*'s view of "congressional intent to negate Eleventh Amendment immunity"; Justice Scalia agreed with them that *Parden* must be overruled. Is it now fair to say that a State will not be found to have consented to suit unless it has actually consented? Are you sorry?

(9) The Eleventh Amendment limits only *federal* jurisdiction; the majority in *Employees* expressly reserved the question whether Missouri could be sued under the Fair Labor Standards Act in its own courts. Justice Marshall argued that Congress had effectively removed any state-court immunity:

> Section 16(b)'s authorization for employee suits to be brought "in any court of competent jurisdiction" includes state as well as federal courts. . . . As I have already noted, Congress has the power to lift the State's common-law immunity from suit insofar as that immunity conflicts with the regulatory authority conferred upon it by the Commerce Clause. . . . While constitutional limitations upon the federal judicial power bar a federal court action by these employees to enforce their rights, the courts of the State nevertheless have an independent constitutional obligation to entertain employee actions to enforce those rights. See Testa v. Katt, 330 U.S. 386 (1947). See also General Oil Co. v. Crain, 209 U.S. 211 (1908). . . .

Is the reasoning of *Hans v. Louisiana* relevant to this question?

FITZPATRICK v. BITZER

427 U.S. 445 (1976).

MR. JUSTICE REHNQUIST delivered the opinion of the Court.

In the 1972 Amendments to Title VII of the Civil Rights Act of 1964, Congress, acting under § 5 of the Fourteenth Amendment, authorized federal courts to award money damages in favor of a private individual against a state government found to have subjected that person to employment discrimination on the basis of "race, color, religion, sex, or national origin." The principal question presented by these cases is whether, as against the shield of sovereign immunity afforded the State by the Eleventh Amendment, Edelman v. Jordan, 415 U.S. 651 (1974), Congress has the power to authorize federal courts to enter such an award against the State as a means of enforcing the substantive guarantees of the Fourteenth Amendment. The Court of Appeals for the Second Circuit held that the effect of our decision in *Edelman* was to foreclose Congress' power. . . . We reverse.

I

Petitioners in No. 75–251 sued in the United States District Court for the District of Connecticut on behalf of all present and retired male employees of the State of Connecticut. Their amended complaint asserted, inter alia, that certain provisions in the State's statutory retirement benefit plan discriminated against them because of their sex, and therefore contravened Title VII of the 1964 Act, 78 Stat. 253, as amended, 42 U.S.C. § 2000e et seq. (1970 ed. and Supp. IV). Title VII, which originally did not include state and local governments, had in the interim been amended to bring the States within its purview.[2]

The District Court held that the Connecticut State Employees Retirement Act violated Title VII's prohibition against sex-based employment discrimination. 390 F.Supp. 278, 285–288 (D.C.1974). It entered prospective injunctive relief in petitioners' favor against respondent state officials.[4] Petitioners also sought an award of retroactive retirement benefits as compensation for losses caused by the State's discrimination,[5] as well as "a reasonable attorney's fee as part of the costs."[6] But the District Court held that both would constitute recovery of money damages from the State's treasury, and were therefore precluded by the Eleventh Amendment and by this Court's decision in *Edelman v. Jordan*, supra. . . .

2. As relevant here, the definition of "person" in § 701(a) of the 1964 Act, 78 Stat. 253, 42 U.S.C. § 2000e(a), was amended by § 2(1) of the Equal Employment Opportunity Act of 1972 (hereinafter the 1972 Amendments), 86 Stat. 103, 42 U.S.C. § 2000e(a) (1970 ed., Supp. IV), to include "governments, governmental agencies, [and] political subdivisions." . . .

4. . . . [R]espondent Bitzer is the Chairman of the State Employees' Retirement Commission, and the other respondents are the Treasurer and the Comptroller of the State of Connecticut. . . .

5. Section 706(g) of the 1964 Act, 78 Stat. 261, as amended, 86 Stat. 107, 42 U.S.C. § 2000e–5(g) (1970 ed., Supp. IV), provides in part:

"If the court finds that the respondent has intentionally engaged in or is intentionally engaging in an unlawful employment practice charged in the complaint, the court may enjoin the respondent from engaging in such unlawful employment practice, and order such affirmative action as may be appropriate, which may include, but is not limited to, reinstatement of hiring of employees, with or without back pay (payable by the employer, employment agency or labor organization, as the case may be, responsible for the unlawful employment practice), or any other equitable relief as the court deems appropriate. Back pay liability shall not accrue from a date more than two years prior to the filing of a charge with the Commission."

6. See § 706(k) of the 1964 Act, 78 Stat. 261. 42 U.S.C. § 2000e–5(k).

The Court of Appeals . . . found that under the 1972 Amendments to Title VII, "Congress intended to authorize a private suit for backpay by state employees against the state." . . . Notwithstanding this statutory authority, the Court of Appeals affirmed the District Court and held that under *Edelman* a "private federal action for retroactive damages" is not a "constitutionally permissible method of enforcing Fourteenth Amendment rights." . . . It reversed the District Court and remanded as to attorneys' fees, however, reasoning that such an award would have only an "ancillary effect" on the state treasury of the kind permitted under *Edelman*. . . .

II

In *Edelman* this Court held that monetary relief awarded by the District Court to welfare plaintiffs, by reason of wrongful denial of benefits which had occurred previous to the entry of the District Court's determination of their wrongfulness, violated the Eleventh Amendment. Such an award was found to be indistinguishable from a monetary award against the State itself which had been prohibited in Ford Motor Co. v. Department of Treasury, 323 U.S. 459, 464 (1945). It was therefore controlled by that case rather than by Ex parte Young, 209 U.S. 123 (1908), which permitted suits against state officials to obtain prospective relief against violations of the Fourteenth Amendment.

Edelman went on to hold that the plaintiffs in that case could not avail themselves of the doctrine of waiver expounded in cases such as Parden v. Terminal R. Co., 377 U.S. 184 (1964), and Employees v. Missouri Public Health Dept., 411 U.S. 279 (1973), because the necessary predicate for that doctrine was congressional intent to abrogate the immunity conferred by the Eleventh Amendment. We concluded that none of the statutes relied upon by plaintiffs in *Edelman* contained any authorization by Congress to join a State as defendant. The Civil Rights Act of 1871, 42 U.S.C. § 1983, had been held in Monroe v. Pape, 365 U.S. 167, 187–191 (1961), to exclude cities and other municipal corporations from its ambit; that being the case, it could not have been intended to include States as parties defendant. The provisions of the Social Security Act relied upon by plaintiffs were held by their terms not to "authorize suit against anyone," . . . and they, too, were incapable of supplying the predicate for a claim of waiver on the part of the State.

All parties in the instant litigation agree with the Court of Appeals that the suit for retroactive benefits by the petitioners is in fact indistinguishable from that sought to be maintained in *Edelman*, since what is sought here is a damages award payable to a private party from the state treasury.

Our analysis begins where *Edelman* ended, for in this Title VII case the "threshold fact of congressional authorization" . . . to sue the State as employer is clearly present. This is, of course, the prerequisite found present in *Parden* and wanting in *Employees*. We are aware of the factual differences between the type of state activity involved in *Parden* and that involved in the present case, but we do not think that difference is material for our purposes. The congressional authorization involved in *Parden* was based on the power of Congress under the Commerce Clause; here, however, the Eleventh Amendment defense is asserted in the context of legislation passed pursuant to Congress' authority under § 5 of the Fourteenth Amendment.

As ratified by the States after the Civil War, that Amendment quite clearly contemplates limitations on their authority. In relevant part, it provides:

> "Section 1. . . . No State shall make or enforce any law which shall abridge the privileges or immunities of citizens of the United States; nor shall any State deprive any person of life, liberty, or property, without due process of law; nor deny to any person within its jurisdiction the equal protection of the laws. . . .
>
> "Section 5. The Congress shall have power to enforce by appropriate legislation, the provisions of this article."

The substantive provisions are by express terms directed at the States. Impressed upon them by those provisions are duties with respect to their treatment of private individuals. Standing behind the imperatives is Congress' power to "enforce" them "by appropriate legislation."

The impact of the Fourteenth Amendment upon the relationship between the Federal Government and the States, and the reach of congressional power under § 5, were examined at length by this Court in Ex parte State of Virginia, 100 U.S. 339 (1880). A state judge had been arrested and indicted under a federal criminal statute prohibiting the exclusion on the basis of race of any citizen from service as a juror in a state court. The judge claimed that the statute was beyond Congress' power to enact under either the Thirteenth or the Fourteenth Amendment. The Court first observed that these Amendments "were intended to be, what they really are, limitations of the power of the States and enlargements of the power of Congress." . . . It then addressed the relationship between the language of § 5 and the substantive provisions of the Fourteenth Amendment:

> "The prohibitions of the Fourteenth Amendment are directed to the States, and they are to a degree restrictions of State power. It is these which Congress is empowered to enforce, and to enforce against State action, however put forth, whether that action be executive, legislative, or judicial. Such enforcement is no invasion of State sovereignty. No law can be, which the people of the States have, by the Constitution of the United States, empowered Congress to enact. . . . It is said the selection of jurors for her courts and the administration of her laws belong to each State; that they are her rights. This is true in the general. But in exercising her rights, a State cannot disregard the limitations which the Federal Constitution has applied to her power. Her rights do not reach to that extent. Nor can she deny to the general government the right to exercise all its granted powers, though

they may interfere with the full enjoyment of rights she would have if those powers had not been thus granted. Indeed, every addition of power to the general government involves a corresponding diminution of the governmental powers of the States. It is carved out of them. . . ."

Ex parte State of Virginia's early recognition of this shift in the federal-state balance has been carried forward by more recent decisions of this Court. See, e.g., South Carolina v. Katzenbach, 383 U.S. 301 (1966); Mitchum v. Foster, 407 U.S. 225, 238–239 (1972).

There can be no doubt that this line of cases has sanctioned intrusions by Congress, acting under the Civil War Amendments, into the judicial, executive, and legislative spheres of autonomy previously reserved to the States. The legislation considered in each case was grounded on the expansion of Congress' powers—with the corresponding diminution of state sovereignty—found to be intended by the Framers and made part of the Constitution upon the States' ratification of those Amendments, a phenomenon aptly described as a "carv[ing] out" in *Ex parte State of Virginia*. . . .

It is true that none of these previous cases presented the question of the relationship between the Eleventh Amendment and the enforcement power granted to Congress under § 5 of the Fourteenth Amendment. But we think that the Eleventh Amendment, and the principle of state sovereignty which it embodies, see Hans v. Louisiana, 134 U.S. 1 (1890), are necessarily limited by the enforcement provisions of § 5 of the Fourteenth Amendment. In that section Congress is expressly granted authority to enforce "by appropriate legislation" the substantive provisions of the Fourteenth Amendment, which themselves embody significant limitations on state authority. When Congress acts pursuant to § 5, not only is it exercising legislative authority that is plenary within the terms of the constitutional grant, it is exercising that authority under one section of a constitutional Amendment whose other sections by their own terms embody limitations on state authority. We think that Congress may, in determining what is "appropriate legislation" for the purpose of enforcing the provisions of the Fourteenth Amendment, provide for private suits against States or state officials which are constitutionally impermissible in other contexts. See Edelman v. Jordan, 415 U.S. 651 (1974); Ford Motor Co. v. Department of Treasury, 323 U.S. 459 (1945).

III

In No. 75–283, the state officials contest the Court of Appeals' conclusion that an award of attorneys' fees in this case would under *Edelman* have only an "ancillary effect" on the state treasury and could therefore be permitted as falling outside the Eleventh Amendment under the doctrine of Ex parte Young, 209 U.S. 123 (1908). . . . We need not address this question, since, given the express congressional authority for such an award in a case brought under Title VII, it follows necessarily from our holding in No. 75–251 that Congress' exercise of power in this respect is also not barred by the Eleventh Amendment. We therefore affirm the Court of Appeals' judgment in No. 75–283 on this basis. . . .

MR. JUSTICE BRENNAN, concurring in the judgment.

This suit was brought by present and retired employees of the State of Connecticut against the State Treasurer, the State Comptroller, and the Chairman of the State Employees' Retirement Commission. In that circumstance, Connecticut may not invoke the Eleventh Amendment, since that Amendment bars only federal-court suits against States by citizens of other States. Rather, the question is whether Connecticut may avail itself of the nonconstitutional but ancient doctrine of sovereign immunity as a bar to a claim for damages under Title VII. In my view Connecticut may not assert sovereign immunity for the reason I expressed in dissent in Employees v. Missouri Public Health Dept., 411 U.S. 279, 298 (1973): The States surrendered that immunity, in Hamilton's words, "in the plan of the Convention" that formed the Union, at least insofar as the States granted Congress specifically enumerated powers. . . .

[JUSTICE STEVENS concurred in the judgment on the ground that the money sought "will not be paid directly from the state treasury, but rather from two separate and independent pension funds."]

Notes on Congressional Power to Subject States to Suit

(1) The Fourteenth Amendment was adopted after the Eighth as well as the Eleventh; does that mean Congress can authorize cruel and unusual punishments to enforce the Equal Protection Clause?

(2) Congress in 1976 amended 42 U.S.C. § 1988 to provide that in actions under various statutes, including § 1983, "the court may . . . allow the prevailing party . . . a reasonable attorney's fee as part of the costs." States are not mentioned in either § 1983 or § 1988, but the Senate Report was explicit: "[I]t is intended that the attorneys' fees, like other items of costs, will be collected either directly from the official, in his official capacity, from funds of his agency or under his control, or from the State or local government (whether or not the agency or government is a named party.)" S.Rep. No. 1011, 94th Cong., 2d Sess. 5 (1976). The Supreme Court has consequently held this section authorizes fee awards to be paid out of state treasuries in § 1983 cases and has upheld it as an exercise of the power to implement the Fourteenth Amendment, citing *Fitzpatrick v. Bitzer*. Hutto v. Finney, 437 U.S. 678 (1978). Four dissenters protested: "[I]n this sensitive area of conflicting interests of constitutional dimension, we should not permit items of legislative history to substitute for explicit statutory language."

(3) Section 1983 itself, however, has been held not to abrogate a State's immunity to suit even though it was enacted in part on the basis of the Fourteenth Amendment. This conclusion was implicit in *Edelman*'s decision that Congress had not intended to make states suable under § 1983, and it was reaffirmed in *Bitzer* on the ground that States, like cities under

Monroe v. Pape, were not "persons" within the meaning of that provision. After *Monell* had removed the basis of this argument, Justice Brennan argued in a concurring opinion in *Hutto* that § 1983 should be construed to override immunity after all. The majority did not respond directly, but in Alabama v. Pugh, 438 U.S. 781 (1978), it held that immunity barred a § 1983 action based on the Fourteenth Amendment, and a dictum in *Quern v. Jordan* made the matter clear: Whether or not a State was a "person" under § 1983, that section was not explicit enough to abrogate the State's immunity from suit in federal court. See also Will v. Michigan Dept. of State Police, 109 S.Ct. 2304, 2309 (1989), noted at p. 398 supra, reaffirming this conclusion in dictum; Atascadero State Hospital v. Scanlon, 473 U.S. 234 (1985), finding that "a general authorization for suit in federal court" against recipients of federal aid did not authorize suits against States under the Rehabilitation Act:

> Congress may abrogate the States' constitutionally secured immunity from suit in federal court only by making its intention unmistakably clear in the language of the statute. The fundamental nature of the interests implicated by the Eleventh Amendment dictates this conclusion.

(4) *Fitzpatrick v. Bitzer* seemed to suggest that there was something special about the Fourteenth Amendment:

> Congress may, in determining what is "appropriate legislation" for the purpose of enforcing the provisions of the Fourteenth Amendment, provide for private suits against States or state officials which are constitutionally impermissible in other contexts.

Nevertheless it was not long before the courts of appeals began to uphold congressional power to override state immunities under other constitutional provisions as well. E.g., Jennings v. Illinois Office of Education, 589 F.2d 935 (7th Cir.1979), holding that a provision explicitly authorizing suits against States to enforce a federal statute giving returning veterans a right of reemployment was a valid exercise of the war powers.

This position had been vigorously advocated by several commentators. See, e.g., Field, the Eleventh Amendment and Other Sovereign Immunity Doctrines, 126 U.Pa.L.Rev. 515 and 1203 (1978). Even Alexander Hamilton, Professor Field argued, had said only that Article III itself would not abrogate the States' immunity, not that it would "impose sovereign immunity as a constitutional requirement"; and Hamilton had been contradicted by numerous contemporaries, including two members of the committee that had drafted the relevant language.

Should the question be not whether the Constitution "imposes" immunity but whether it empowers Congress to make States suable? And isn't it pretty well established that Congress cannot give the courts jurisdiction over cases that are not within Article III?

Then how does one explain *Fitzpatrick v. Bitzer?*

(5) In Pennsylvania v. Union Gas Co., 109 S.Ct. 2273 (1989), the Supreme Court adopted the position taken by the Seventh Circuit in *Jennings*—not with a bang but with a whimper. By a 5–4 vote the Court concluded that the Commerce Clause empowered Congress to open federal

courts to suits against States under the Superfund statute (CERCLA) for reimbursement of costs incurred in cleaning up hazardous substances. Speaking for four Justices, Justice Brennan invoked the reasoning of the recently discredited *Parden* decision (p. 457 supra) and argued that the arguments in *Bitzer* applied equally to the commerce power: "Like the Fourteenth Amendment, the Commerce Clause with one hand gives power to Congress while, with the other, it takes power away from the States." Justice White, who thought Congress had not attempted to abrogate immunity in Superfund suits, agreed that it had power to do so, but he did not say why: "I agree with the conclusion reached by Justice Brennan . . ., although I do not agree with much of his reasoning." Justice Scalia's dissent was joined by Chief Justice Rehnquist and by Justices O'Connor and Kennedy. You already know what they said, don't you?

Is there any point to an immunity that Congress can remove at will?

(6) The Foreign Sovereign Immunities Act of 1976, 90 Stat. 2891, added to Title 28 a new § 1330, giving the district courts jurisdiction, without regard to the amount in controversy, of "any nonjury civil action against a foreign state . . . as to any claim for relief in personam with respect to which the foreign state is not entitled to immunity either under sections 1605–1607 of this title or under any applicable international agreement." A new § 1441(d) authorizes the foreign state to remove such actions brought in state courts. A new § 1604 states a general statutory principle of foreign-state immunity from suit in federal and state courts. The principal exceptions are for actions "based upon a commercial activity" or a "tortious act or omission" (with exceptions reminiscent of those of the Federal Tort Claims Act, see pp. 469–71 infra), with sufficient connection to the United States (§ 1605(a)(2), (5)). Whether an activity is "commercial," according to § 1603(d), is to be determined "by reference to the nature of the course of conduct or particular transaction or act, rather than by reference to its purpose." This means, according to the House Report, that contracts to buy military supplies or to repair an embassy are "commercial" since contracting is an activity "customarily carried on for profit," though waging war and negotiating treaties sometimes are not.

The Act, the House Report says, means to adopt the "restrictive" international-law position, followed abroad, that immunity extends only to "public" acts, not to "commercial or private" ones. H.R.Rep.No. 1487 94th Cong., 2d Sess (1976).

Is this statute constitutional? Ignoring the dictum in *Monaco v. Mississippi,* supra p. 442, which followed a long discussion that seemed to base Mississippi's immunity from Monaco's suit upon Article III, the House Report traces immunity to The Schooner Exchange v. McFadden, 11 U.S. (7 Cranch) 116 (1812), which had construed the statutory grant of admiralty jurisdiction to respect international usage. *The Pesaro,* supra p. 443 was based upon *The Exchange.* Does *Pennsylvania v. Union Gas Co.* remove any question as to the constitutionality of the Act?

(7) In Santa Clara Pueblo v. Martinez, 436 U.S. 49 (1978), the Supreme Court reaffirmed that Indian tribes enjoy a common-law sovereign immunity from suit, subject to abrogation by Congress.

Notes on Statutes Consenting to Suits Against the United States

(1) The Supreme Court has consistently upheld the jurisdiction of the federal courts over suits against the United States that Congress has authorized. In Williams v. United States, 289 U.S. 553 (1933), however, the Court declared that the clause of Article III conferring jurisdiction of "Controversies to which the United States shall be a Party" included only those in which the Government was plaintiff; without considering whether suits in the Court of Claims to recover on government debts were "Cases . . . arising under . . . the Laws of the United States," the Court held that jurisdiction of such claims was based not on Article III but on Congress's power, in Article I, to "pay the Debts" of the United States. This conclusion was relied upon by Justice Jackson in his opinion for three Justices in National Mutual Insurance Co. v. Tidewater Transfer Co., 337 U.S. 582 (1949), but it was contrary to earlier authority, Minnesota v. Hitchcock, 185 U.S. 373, 382–83 (1902), and it has since been explicitly rejected by at least three members of the Court. See Glidden Co. v. Zdanok, 370 U.S. 530, 584 (1962) (opinion of Harlan, J.).

(2) Before the establishment of the Court of Claims in 1855, virtually all claims against the United States were disposed of by private legislation in Congress, for there was no general statute consenting to suits against the Government. The present situation is an agglomeration of piecemeal legislation, replete with overlaps and gaps in coverage and representing no coherent principle.

Because of "the burden on Congress of private bills, the delays and inequities of the private bill procedure, and the resulting impairment of government credit," see Hart & Wechsler, The Federal Courts and the Federal System 103 (3d ed. 1988), Congress in 1855, 10 Stat. 612, created the Court of Claims with jurisdiction to pass upon money claims against the United States "founded upon any law of Congress, or upon any regulation of an executive department, or upon any contract, express or implied, with the Government of the United States." Under the original statute the Court of Claims' decisions were merely advisory to Congress, and even after an 1863 amendment granting the court power to render judgment the Supreme Court refused to accept an appeal from the Court of Claims because its decisions were subject to revision by the Secretary of the Treasury. Gordon v. United States, 69 U.S. (2 Wall.) 561 (1865). The objectionable provision was repealed in 1866, and thereafter the Supreme Court accepted jurisdiction to review judicial decisions of the Court of Claims. United States v. Jones, 119 U.S. 477 (1886).

The present jurisdiction of the United States Claims Court, which replaced the Court of Claims in 1982, is defined in 28 U.S.C. §§ 1491–1506. The central provision, as expanded by the Tucker Act (March 3, 1887, 24 Stat. 505), is § 1491(a)(1):

> The United States Claims Court shall have jurisdiction to render judgment upon any claim against the United States founded either upon the Constitution, or any Act of Congress, or any regulation of an executive department, or upon any express or implied contract with

> the United States, or for liquidated or unliquidated damages in cases not sounding in tort. . . .[1]

Although predecessor provisions similarly phrased were held to apply only to claims for money, United States v. Jones, 131 U.S. 1 (1889), § 1491(a)(2) and (3) now empower the court in any case to issue "incidental" orders such as those "directing restoration to office or position," and in certain contract cases "to grant declaratory judgments and such equitable and extraordinary relief as it deems proper" in order to "afford complete relief."

Under 28 U.S.C. § 1346(a), the District Courts have concurrent jurisdiction of all § 1491(a) claims not exceeding $10,000 and of all actions to recover taxes or penalties unlawfully collected, except that § 1491(a)(3) declares the equitable and declaratory jurisdiction of the Claims Court to be "exclusive."

(3) The Federal Tort Claims Act, 60 Stat. 812, 842 (1946), gives the district courts exclusive jurisdiction of suits against the United States

> for money damages . . . for injury or loss of property, or personal injury or death caused by the negligent or wrongful act or omission of any employee of the Government while acting within the scope of his office or employment, under circumstances where the United States, if a private person, would be liable to the claimant in accordance with the law of the place where the act or omission occurred.

The several sections of this Act are scattered throughout Title 28. The basic jurisdictional grant, quoted above, is now § 1346(b); procedural provisions are found in §§ 1402(b), 2401, 2402, and 2671–79; and important exceptions to the general grant appear in § 2680.

Numerous interesting questions have arisen in construing the Tort Claims Act. First, § 1346(b) provides relief only for harm caused by "negligent or wrongful act or omission." In Laird v. Nelms, 406 U.S. 797 (1972), over two dissents arguing the statute "was intended to include the entire range of conduct classified as tortious under state law," the Court held it did not embrace strict liability even where state law would have imposed it.

Second, early decisions suggested that the provision for liability "under circumstances where . . . a private person would be liable" might exclude liability for activities that only governments engaged in (e.g., Feres v. United States, 340 U.S. 135 (1950), emphasizing in denying relief to servicemen on duty that there were no private armies). This reasoning was abandoned in Indian Towing Co. v. United States, 350 U.S. 61 (1955), which held the Government suable for the negligent operation of a lighthouse, taking a broader view of what the statute meant by the "circumstances": "[I]t is hornbook tort law that one who undertakes to warn the public of

1. Among the more important specific Claims Court provisions are § 1505, giving jurisdiction over certain Indian claims; § 1495, allowing the Court to award damages to "any person unjustly convicted of an offense against the United States and imprisoned"; and § 1492, "Congressional reference cases," which continues the power of the court to advise Congress. Congressional-reference cases are non-judicial and hence not reviewable by the Supreme Court, In re Sanborn, 148 U.S. 222 (1893), but the power of the Claims Court to entertain them is clear, since the court was established under Article I. See Ex parte Bakelite Corp., 279 U.S. 438 (1929); 28 U.S.C. § 171, p. 671 infra.

danger and thereby induces reliance must perform his 'good Samaritan' task in a careful manner." [2]

Third, the applicable law under § 1346(b) is that of "the place where the act or omission" in question "occurred." The ambiguity of this innocuous clause was exposed in Richards v. United States, 369 U.S. 1 (1962), where suit was brought for harm caused in one State by negligence in another. Relying on the "precise language" of the statute, the Court first held that the reference was to the place of negligence, not to that of injury. Then, because this interpretation departed from "[t]he general conflict-of-laws rule . . . to apply the law of the place of injury" and because Congress had intended to equate governmental with private liability, the Court held that "the law of the place where the act or omission occurred" referred to "the whole law" of that State, and not to its "internal law" alone. In other words, the statute adopted the choice-of-law rules of the State of the negligence, and the case should be decided as the courts of that State would decide an analogous private suit. Was this a case of two wrongs making a right?

(4) The most significant and most ambiguous exception to the Tort Claims Act is that for damage caused by government employees in performing or failing to perform a "discretionary function or duty," § 2680(a).

The seminal case construing this provision was Dalehite v. United States, 346 U.S. 15 (1953), in which the United States was permitted to escape liability for the massive damage caused by its negligent manufacture and handling of ammonium-nitrate fertilizer that exploded while being loaded for export at Texas City, Texas. The district court held that the United States had failed to exercise due care in investigating the hazards of a chemical with known explosive qualities; in packaging the nitrate at high temperatures; in coating the bags with flammable material; and in failing to label the bags as containing explosives. All these acts or omissions, the Supreme Court held, fell within the "discretionary function" exemption.

The paradigm case for liability under the Tort Claims Act, wrote Justice Reed, was a traffic accident.

> It was not contemplated that the Government should be subject to liability arising from acts of a governmental nature or function. . . . Where there is room for policy judgment and decision there is discretion. It necessarily follows that acts of subordinates in carrying out the operations of government in accordance with official directions cannot be actionable.

It was not seriously disputed, he continued, that "the Cabinet-level decision to institute the fertilizer export program was a discretionary act"; the plan for executing the program "clearly required the exercise of expert judgment"; and each of the acts alleged to be negligent was done in accordance with specifications in the plan. Three Justices dissented:

2. See also United States v. Muniz, 374 U.S. 150 (1963), allowing suit by inmates of federal prisons; Rayonier, Inc. v. United States, 352 U.S. 315 (1957), holding the Government suable for negligence in fighting a fire. *Muniz* has since been limited on the unrelated ground that another statute provided the prisoner's exclusive remedy. United States v. Demko, 385 U.S. 149 (1966).

> Of course, it is not a tort for government to govern. . . . [But t]he common sense of this matter is that a policy adopted in the exercise of an immune discretion was carried out carelessly by those in charge of detail.

Later cases have somewhat softened the grudging approach taken in *Dalehite.* In holding the United States could not be held liable for negligent failure to inspect an airliner that later caught fire, the Court declared that the purpose of the discretionary exception was "to prevent judicial 'second-guessing' of legislative and administrative decisions grounded in social, economic, and political policy through the medium of an action in tort" and emphasized that the agency and its employees were "specifically empowered to make policy judgments" in determining which planes to inspect. United States v. Varig Airlines, 467 U.S. 797 (1984). In concluding that the Government could be held liable for negligence in approving the release of a defective batch of polio vaccine, the Court specifically rejected the argument "that the exception precludes liability for any and all acts arising out of the regulatory programs of federal agencies" and reaffirmed the test laid down in *Varig*: The exception applied "only to conduct that involves the permissible exercise of policy judgment," and the agency had no discretion to ignore the duties imposed on it by federal law. Berkovitz v. United States, 486 U.S. 531 (1988).[3]

(5) The history of Government consent to suit in maritime cases is detailed in Canadian Aviator, Ltd. v. United States, 324 U.S. 215 (1945). All tort suits were excluded from the jurisdiction of the Court of Claims, and private bills proved inadequate to deal with collision claims arising from the operation of the large government-owned merchant fleet during World War I. Consequently the Shipping Act of 1916 subjected vessels owned by the federal Shipping Board to "all laws, regulations, and liabilities governing merchant vessels" as if they were privately owned, 39 Stat. 728, 46 U.S.C. § 801 et seq. In The Lake Monroe, 250 U.S. 246 (1919), the Supreme Court held that the Shipping Act permitted seizure of Shipping Board merchant vessels in admiralty proceedings in rem. Fearing that the arrest of Government ships might interfere with national defense, Congress enacted the Suits in Admiralty Act, 41 Stat. 525 (1920), 46 U.S.C. § 741 et seq., which exempts from seizure all vessels and cargoes owned, possessed, or operated by or for the United States or its wholly owned corporations and which originally authorized, in place of the in rem procedure, a "libel in personam" against the United States or its corporation "in cases where if such vessel were privately owned or operated, or if such cargo were privately owned and possessed, a proceeding in admiralty could be maintained . . ., provided that such vessel is employed as a merchant vessel or is a tugboat operated by such corporation." Not all government ships were included in the grant of jurisdiction; a battleship, for example, was plainly

3. See also Bearce v. United States, 614 F.2d 556, 560–61 (7th Cir. 1980), holding the decision not to place a warning light on a breakwater was "discretionary" in reliance on Indian Towing Co. v. United States, 350 U.S. 61 (1955), where the Court had upheld liability for negligent lighthouse operation: " '*The Coast Guard need not undertake the lighthouse service.* But once it exercised its discretion to operate a light on Chandeleur Island and engendered reliance on the guidance afforded by the light, it was obligated to use due care to make certain that the light was kept in good working order. . . .' (Emphasis added.)"

neither a "merchant vessel" nor a "tugboat." Therefore in 1925 Congress adopted the Public Vessels Act, 43 Stat. 1112, 46 U.S.C. § 781 et seq., which authorizes a libel in personam in admiralty against the United States "for damages caused by a public vessel of the United States, and for compensation for towage and salvage services, including contract salvage, rendered to a public vessel. . . ." [4]

Although the Government argued that suits for "damages caused by a public vessel" in the Public Vessels Act applied only to collisions with government ships, the Supreme Court upheld claims for the negligence of a patrol-boat crew in guiding another vessel into collision with a submerged wreck, Canadian Aviator, Ltd. v. United States, 324 U.S. 215 (1945), and for personal injuries and wrongful death resulting from non-collision negligence aboard a public vessel, American Stevedores, Inc. v. Porello, 330 U.S. 446 (1947) (over the dissent of Justice Frankfurter). Cf. *Gutierrez v. Waterman S. S. Corp.*, supra p. 216 (construing the Admiralty Extension Act, 46 U.S.C. § 740). Moreover, a 1960 amendment added the italicized words in the following quotation of the Suits in Admiralty Act, which seem to eliminate any requirement that actions under that statute relate to a ship at all:

> In cases where if such vessel were privately owned or operated, or if such cargo were privately owned or possessed, *or if a private person or property were involved*, a proceeding in admiralty could have been maintained, any appropriate non-jury proceeding in personam may be brought against the United States.

Most courts have held the amended provision embraces suits unrelated to Government vessels. E.g., Bearce v. United States, 614 F.2d 556 (7th Cir. 1980) (Coast Guard's failure to install light on breakwater). Contra, McCormick v. United States, 645 F.2d 299 (5th Cir. 1981) (obstruction in navigable waters), listing the cases.[5]

4. It was not always obvious whether a government vessel was a "merchant vessel" within the Suits in Admiralty Act or a "public vessel' within the 1925 statute. See, e.g., Calmar Steamship Corp. v. United States, 345 U.S. 446 (1953), holding a privately owned ship under voyage charter to the United States to transport military supplies to be a "merchant vessel." In 1960 Congress appeared to abolish the distinction, omitting from Section 2 of the Suits in Admiralty Act the requirement that the ship be operated as a merchant vessel. 74 Stat. 912, 46 U.S.C. § 742. But in United States v. United Continental Tuna Corp., 425 U.S. 164 (1976), the Supreme Court over a single dissent, concerned that the obvious reading of the amendment would render nugatory the limitations on recovery in the still extant Public Vessels Act, held on the basis of legislative history that the amendment's sole purpose was to eliminate uncertainties as to the proper forum between the Tucker Act on the one hand and the two maritime statutes on the other.

5. *McCormick* relied on a committee report declaring the term "cargo" had been omitted in order to overrule a decision that merchandise was not cargo " 'during the interval it was being trucked across the pier from a lighter to a Government vessel's tackle' " and paraphrased the Supreme Court's explanation of the amendment in the *Continental Tuna* case, footnote 4 supra: "Congress' sole concern was the conflict in jurisdiction between the district court and the Court of Claims in that category of cases that might fall within the scope of the admiralty acts . . . on the one hand, or the Tucker Act, on the other."

In *Bearce*, while holding the Suits in Admiralty Act did cover a claim not involving a Government vessel, the Seventh Circuit held the claim implicitly subject to the discretionary-act exception to the Tort

(6) Although suits for maritime claims not sounding in tort were already permitted under the Tucker Act in the Court of Claims (see note 2 supra), the Supreme Court from the beginning allowed maritime contracts to be sued on in the district courts under the Suits in Admiralty Act. See Johnson v. United States Shipping Board Emergency Fleet Corp., 280 U.S. 320, 324 (1930) (bills of lading); Calmar Steamship Corp. v. United States, 345 U.S. 446 (1953) (charter party).[6]

Neither the Suits in Admiralty Act nor the Public Vessels Act contains an express provision making its remedy exclusive. It was obvious enough that the former's statute of limitations was intended to govern all admiralty proceedings that could have been brought under its provisions, Fleet Corp. v. Rosenberg Bros. & Co., 276 U.S. 202, 214 (1928), and that the United States had not consented to be sued on such claims in the state courts, Johnson v. U.S. Shipping Board Emergency Fleet Corp., 280 U.S. 320, 327 (1930). Moreover, the later-enacted Tort Claims Act, 28 U.S.C. § 2680(d), is expressly inapplicable to claims cognizable under either the Suits in Admiralty Act or the Public Vessels Act. It was less clear that the Suits in Admiralty Act was designed to destroy the jurisdiction of maritime non-tort cases previously given to the District Courts and to the Court of Claims by the Tucker Act. But so the Court held, without dissent, in *Johnson v. Fleet Corp.*, supra, in order to establish uniformity in all government maritime cases as to "venue, service of process, rules of decision and procedure, rate of interest, and periods of limitation. . . .": "The remedies given by the Act are exclusive in all cases where a libel might be filed under it." 280 U.S. at 326–27.

(7) Nevertheless, in Johansen v. United States, 343 U.S. 427 (1952), and Patterson v. United States, 359 U.S. 495 (1959), the Court held the sole remedy for personal injuries to government-employed seamen aboard United States vessels was an application for workers' compensation under the Federal Employees Compensation Act, 5 U.S.C. § 751, though the exclusivity provision of that statute contained an explicit exception for "a master or a member of the crew of any vessel" (5 U.S.C. § 757(b)). The exception, the Court said, was designed not to permit alternative remedies but to leave the question open; and neither the Public Vessels Act nor the Suits in Admiralty Act afforded a remedy to government employees. The purpose of the former, the Court concluded, was to put aside the " 'sovereign armor . . .,' " but that had already been done in the earlier Compensation Act, and "there is no reason to have two systems of redress." Similarly, in

Claims Act: The amendment was intended only "to eliminate jurisdictional difficulties," not "to extend the waiver of sovereign immunity." 614 F.2d at 559, citing contrary cases.

6. In this respect the Public Vessels Act may be narrower. See Calmar Steamship Corp. v. United States, supra, 345 U.S. at 456 n. 8 (dictum): "It is not to be assumed that all claims sounding in contract can form the basis of a suit under the Public Vessels Act. The Act expressly authorizes towage and salvage claims. We intimate no opinion as to other claims, and do not suggest that all or any of the causes of action in this very suit would or would not qualify under the Public Vessels Act." However, in Thomason v. United States, 184 F.2d 105 (9th Cir. 1950), the court held that wage claims were claims for "damages caused by a public vessel": "The phrase includes damages arising from those acts for which a private ship is held legally responsible as a juristic person under the customary legal terminology of the admiralty law."

Amell v. United States, 384 U.S. 158 (1966), where federally employed seamen sued under the Tucker Act for lost wages, the Court over two dissents managed to hold, despite the decisions summarized in note 6, that the Suits in Admiralty Act (whose short limitation period had expired) did not provide their exclusive remedy: "[W]ith respect to these wage claims, Congress thought of these petitioners more as government employees who happened to be seamen than as seamen who by chance worked for the Government." Does this mean the claims were not within the Suits in Admiralty Act, or that its remedy was not exclusive? Can the various decisions in this note and in note 6 be reconciled?

(8) The 1960 amendments to the Suits in Admiralty Act have somewhat reduced the danger of choosing the wrong remedy against the United States. Moreover, the consequence of a wrong choice is now seldom dismissal, for Congress has provided for transfer of suits between the Claims Court and the District Courts, 28 U.S.C. § 1631, and no statute is needed to permit a District Court to retain suits erroneously filed under one statute when it has jurisdiction under another. See Aho v. Jacobsen, 359 U.S. 25 (1959) (suit erroneously filed under § 1331 ordered retried in admiralty, § 1333). But litigation over the boundaries between the Tucker Act, the Tort Claims Act, and the Suits in Admiralty Act continues because of their different venue and limitation provisions and the specific exceptions of the Tort Claims Act.

What excuse is there for retaining these distinctions? Should not Congress abolish the Claims Court and give the district courts, in a single statute, jurisdiction over all claims against the United States, subject to such exceptions of those now contained in the Tort Claims Act as are supported by sound policy? What should those exceptions be? Is there any justification for § 2680(b), (h), or (k)?

SECTION 2. OFFICIAL AND CONGRESSIONAL IMMUNITIES

HARLOW v. FITZGERALD

457 U.S. 800 (1982).

JUSTICE POWELL delivered the opinion of the Court.

The issue in this case is the scope of the immunity available to the senior aides and advisers of the President of the United States in a suit for damages based upon their official acts.

I

In this suit for civil damages petitioners Bryce Harlow and Alexander Butterfield are alleged to have participated in a conspiracy to violate the constitutional and statutory rights of the respondent A. Ernest Fitzgerald. Respondent avers that petitioners entered the conspiracy in their capacities as senior White House aides to former President Richard M. Nixon. . . .

[The District Court, denying a motion for summary judgment, upheld the legal sufficiency of Fitzgerald's *Bivens* claim and ruled that the defendants were not absolutely immune from suit. The Court of Appeals dismissed an appeal, and the Supreme Court granted certiorari.]

II . . .

[O]ur decisions consistently have held that government officials are entitled to some form of immunity from suits for damages. As recognized at common law, public officers require this protection to shield them from undue interference with their duties and from potentially disabling threats of liability.

Our decisions have recognized immunity defenses of two kinds. For officials whose special functions or constitutional status requires complete protection from suit, we have recognized the defense of "absolute immunity." The absolute immunity of legislators, in their legislative functions, see, e.g., Eastland v. United States Servicemen's Fund, 421 U.S. 491 (1975), and of judges, in their judicial functions, see, e.g., Stump v. Sparkman, 435 U.S. 349 (1978), now is well settled. Our decisions also have extended absolute immunity to certain officials of the Executive Branch. These include prosecutors and similar officials, see Butz v. Economou, 438 U.S. 478, 508–512 (1978), executive officers engaged in adjudicative functions, *id.,* at 513–517, and the President of the United States, see Nixon v. Fitzgerald, [457 U.S. 731, decided the same day as *Harlow*].

For executive officials in general, however, our cases make plain that qualified immunity represents the norm. In Scheuer v. Rhodes, 416 U.S. 232 (1974), we acknowledged that high officials require greater protection than those with less complex discretionary responsibilities. Nonetheless, we held that a governor and his aides could receive the requisite protection from qualified or good-faith immunity. . . . In *Butz v. Economou,* supra, we extended the approach of *Scheuer* to high federal officials of the Executive Branch. . . . [W]e explained that the recognition of a qualified immunity defense for high executives reflected an attempt to balance competing values: not only the importance of a damages remedy to protect the rights of citizens, . . ., but also "the need to protect officials who are required to exercise their discretion and the related public interest in encouraging the vigorous exercise of official authority." . . . Without discounting the adverse consequences of denying high officials an absolute immunity from private lawsuits alleging constitutional violations—consequences found sufficient in Spalding v. Vilas, 161 U.S. 483 (1896), and Barr v. Matteo, 360 U.S. 564 (1959), to warrant extension to such officials of absolute immunity from suits at common law—we emphasized our expectation that insubstantial suits need not proceed to trial:

> ". . . [D]amages suits concerning constitutional violations . . . can be terminated on a properly supported motion for summary judgment based on the defense of immunity. . . . In responding to such a

motion, plaintiffs may not play dog in the manger; and firm application of the Federal Rules of Civil Procedure will ensure that federal officials are not harassed by frivolous lawsuits." . . .

Butz continued to acknowledge that the special functions of some officials might require absolute immunity. But the Court held that "federal officials who seek absolute exemption from personal liability for unconstitutional conduct must bear the burden of showing that public policy requires an exemption of that scope." . . .

III

A

Petitioners argue that they are entitled to a blanket protection of absolute immunity as an incident of their offices as Presidential aides. In deciding this claim we do not write on an empty page. In *Butz v. Economou,* supra, the Secretary of Agriculture—a Cabinet official directly accountable to the President—asserted a defense of absolute official immunity from suit for civil damages. We rejected his claim. In so doing we did not question the power or the importance of the Secretary's office. Nor did we doubt the importance to the President of loyal and efficient subordinates in executing his duties of office. Yet we found these factors, alone, to be insufficient to justify absolute immunity. "[T]he greater power of [high] officials," we reasoned, "affords a greater potential for a regime of lawless conduct." . . . Damages actions against high officials were therefore "an important means of vindicating constitutional guarantees." . . . Moreover, we concluded that it would be "untenable to draw a distinction for purposes of immunity law between suits brought against state officials under [42 U.S.C.] § 1983 and suits brought directly under the Constitution against federal officials." . . .

Having decided in *Butz* that Members of the Cabinet ordinarily enjoy only qualified immunity from suit, we conclude today that it would be equally untenable to hold absolute immunity an incident of the office of every Presidential subordinate based in the White House. Members of the Cabinet are direct subordinates of the President, frequently with greater responsibilities, both to the President and to the Nation, than White House staff. The considerations that supported our decision in *Butz* apply with equal force to this case. . . .

B

In disputing the controlling authority of *Butz,* petitioners rely on the principles developed in Gravel v. United States, 408 U.S. 606 (1972). In *Gravel* we endorsed the view that "it is literally impossible . . . for Members of Congress to perform their legislative tasks without the help of aides and assistants" and that "the day-to-day work of such aides is so critical to the Members' performance that they must be treated as the latter's alter egos. . . ." . . . Having done so, we held the Speech and Debate Clause derivatively applicable to the "legislative acts" of a Senator's aide that would have been privileged if performed by the Senator himself. . . .

Petitioners contend that the rationale of *Gravel* mandates a similar "derivative" immunity for the chief aides of the President of the United States. Emphasizing that the President must delegate a large measure of authority to execute the duties of his office, they argue that recognition of derivative absolute immunity is made essential by all the considerations that support absolute immunity for the President himself.

Petitioners' argument is not without force. Ultimately, however, it sweeps too far. If the President's aides are derivatively immune because they are essential to the functioning of the Presidency, so should the Members of the Cabinet—Presidential subordinates some of whose essential roles are acknowledged by the Constitution itself—be absolutely immune. Yet we implicitly rejected such derivative immunity in *Butz.* Moreover, in general our cases have followed a "functional" approach to immunity law. We have recognized that the judicial, prosecutorial, and legislative functions require absolute immunity. But this protection has extended no further than its justification would warrant. In *Gravel,* for example, we emphasized that Senators and their aides were absolutely immune only when performing "acts legislative in nature," and not when taking other acts even "in their official capacity." . . . Our cases involving judges [15] and prosecutors [16] have followed a similar line. The undifferentiated extension of absolute "derivative" immunity to the President's aides therefore could not be reconciled with the "functional" approach that has characterized the immunity decisions of this Court, indeed including *Gravel* itself.[17]

C

Petitioners also assert an entitlement to immunity based on the "special functions" of White House aides. This form of argument accords with the analytical approach of our cases. For aides entrusted with discretionary authority in such sensitive areas as national security or foreign policy, absolute immunity might well be justified to protect the unhesitating performance of functions vital to the national interest. But a "special functions" rationale does not warrant a blanket recognition of absolute immunity for all Presidential aides in the performance

15. See, e.g., Supreme Court of Virginia v. Consumers Union of United States, 446 U.S. 719, 731–737 (1980). . . .

16. In Imbler v. Pachtman, 424 U.S. 409, 430–431 (1976), this Court reserved the question whether absolute immunity would extend to "those aspects of the prosecutor's responsibility that cast him in the role of an administrator or investigative officer." Since that time the Courts of Appeals generally have ruled that prosecutors do not enjoy absolute immunity for acts taken in those capacities. . . .

17. Our decision today in *Nixon v. Fitzgerald* . . . in no way abrogates this general rule. As we explained in that opinion, the recognition of absolute immunity for all of a President's acts in office derives in principal part from factors unique to his constitutional responsibilities and station. Suits against other officials—including Presidential aides—generally do not invoke separation-of-powers considerations to the same extent as suits against the President himself.

of all their duties. . . . In order to establish entitlement to absolute immunity a Presidential aide first must show that the responsibilities of his office embraced a function so sensitive as to require a total shield from liability. He then must demonstrate that he was discharging the protected function when performing the act for which liability is asserted.

Applying these standards to the claims advanced by petitioners Harlow and Butterfield, we cannot conclude on the record before us that either has shown that "public policy requires [for any of the functions of his office] an exemption of [absolute] scope." . . . Nor, assuming that petitioners did have functions for which absolute immunity would be warranted, could we now conclude that the acts charged in this lawsuit—if taken at all—would lie within the protected area. . . .

IV

Even if they cannot establish that their official functions require absolute immunity, petitioners assert that public policy at least . . . requires an adjustment of the "good faith" standard [for qualified immunity] established by our decisions. . . .

The subjective element of the good-faith defense frequently has proved incompatible with our admonition in *Butz* that insubstantial claims should not proceed to trial. Rule 56 of the Federal Rules of Civil Procedure provides that disputed questions of fact ordinarily may not be decided on motions for summary judgment. And an official's subjective good faith has been considered to be a question of fact that some courts have regarded as inherently requiring resolution by a jury.

In the context of *Butz'* attempted balancing of competing values, it now is clear that substantial costs attend the litigation of the subjective good faith of government officials. Not only are there the general costs of subjecting officials to the risks of trial—distraction of officials from their governmental duties, inhibition of discretionary action, and deterrence of able people from public service. . . . Judicial inquiry into subjective motivation . . . may entail broad-ranging discovery and the deposing of numerous persons, including an official's professional colleagues. Inquiries of this kind can be peculiarly disruptive of effective government.

[W]e conclude today that bare allegations of malice should not suffice to subject government officials either to the costs of trial or to the burdens of broad-reaching discovery. We therefore hold that government officials performing discretionary functions, generally are shielded from liability for civil damages insofar as their conduct does not violate clearly established statutory or constitutional rights of which a reasonable person would have known. . . .

The judgment of the Court of Appeals is vacated, and the case is remanded for further action consistent with this opinion. . . .

JUSTICE REHNQUIST, concurring.

At such time as a majority of the Court is willing to reexamine our holding in *Butz v. Economou,* . . . I shall join in that undertaking with alacrity. But until that time comes, I agree that the Court's opinion in this case properly disposes of the issues presented, and I therefore join it.

CHIEF JUSTICE BURGER, dissenting.

The Court today decides in *Nixon v. Fitzgerald* . . . what has been taken for granted for 190 years, that it is implicit in the Constitution that a President of the United States has absolute immunity from civil suits arising out of official acts as Chief Executive. I agree fully that absolute immunity for official acts of the President is, like executive privilege, "fundamental to the operation of Government and inextricably rooted in the separation of powers under the Constitution." United States v. Nixon, 418 U.S. 683, 708 (1974).

In this case the Court decides that senior aides of the President do not have derivative immunity from the President. I am at a loss, however, to reconcile this conclusion with our holding in *Gravel v. United States*. . . .

Butz v. Economou . . . does not dictate that senior Presidential aides be given only qualified immunity. *Butz* held only that a Cabinet officer exercising discretion was not entitled to absolute immunity; we need not abandon that holding. A senior Presidential aide works more intimately with the President on a daily basis than does a Cabinet officer, directly implementing Presidential decisions literally from hour to hour. . . .

Notes on Congressional and Official Immunities

(1) Members of Congress enjoy two explicit constitutional immunities under Art. I, § 6. First, they are "privileged from Arrest during their Attendance" in Congress and while coming and going, except in cases of "Treason, Felony and Breach of the Peace." This privilege has been given a narrow construction, exempting members only from arrest in civil cases: A Congressman or Senator may be civilly sued or called as a witness, and "the constitutional freedom of arrest does not exempt Members of Congress from the operation of the ordinary criminal laws, even though imprisonment may prevent or interfere with the performance of their duties. . . ." Gravel v. United States, 408 U.S. 606 (1972) (dictum); Williamson v. United States, 207 U.S. 425 (1908).

The more significant immunity provided by Art. I, § 6 is the provision that for "any Speech or Debate in either House" a member "shall not be questioned in any other Place." The purposes of this clause were expounded by Justice Harlan in United States v. Johnson, 383 U.S. 169, 178, 181 (1966):

> Behind these simple phrases lies a history of conflict between the Commons and the Tudor and Stuart monarchs during which successive

> monarchs utilized the criminal and civil law to suppress and intimidate critical legislators. Since the Glorious Revolution in Britain, and throughout United States history, the privilege has been recognized as an important protection of the independence and integrity of the legislature.

A short time later the Court added that it was the purpose of the clause to protect legislators "not only from the consequences of litigation's results but also from the burden of defending themselves." Dombrowski v. Eastland, 387 U.S. 82, 84–85 (1967).

The scope of the Speech or Debate Clause has been the subject of a handful of Supreme Court decisions, all but one of them relatively recent. The first was Kilbourn v. Thompson, 103 U.S. 168, 200–05 (1881), an action for damages for false imprisonment against members of Congress who had participated in the adoption of a resolution directing an illegal arrest and against the sergeant-at-arms who had carried out the order. Judgment for the Congressmen was affirmed, the Court holding the privilege not limited to words spoken in debate:

> The reason of the rule is as forcible in its application to written reports presented in that body by its committees, to resolutions offered, which, though in writing, must be reproduced in speech, and to the act of voting, whether it is done vocally or by passing between the tellers. In short, to things generally done in a session of the House by one of its members in relation to the business before it.

Judgment for the sergeant-at-arms, however, was reversed and the case remanded for further proceedings, the Court merely quoting with approval from an English decision: "If the Speaker by authority of the House order an illegal act, though that authority shall exempt him from question, his order shall no more justify the person who executed it than King Charles's warrant for levying ship-money could justify his revenue officer."

Kilbourn 's distinction between members and their agents was followed in Powell v. McCormack, 395 U.S. 486 (1969), where the Court held that employees of the House of Representatives could be sued for a declaration that the House had no right to exclude a duly elected member for misconduct: "Freedom of legislative activity and the purposes of the Speech or Debate Clause are fully protected if legislators are relieved of the burden of defending themselves." As *Harlow* reveals, the Court abandoned this position in United States v. Gravel, 408 U.S. 606 (1972): Because the help of employees was essential to the performance of legislative functions, congressional aides enjoyed the same immunity as members.

At the same time, *Gravel* elaborated on *Kilbourn*'s definition of what constituted "Speech or Debate" for purposes of this immunity. The question was whether the Senator's aide was subject to a grand-jury subpoena in connection with the acquisition and disposition of the notorious Pentagon Papers, which allegedly revealed sensitive information respecting the Vietnam War. "The heart of the Clause," wrote Justice White, was "speech or debate in either House"; other matters were included only if they were "an integral part of the deliberative and communicative processes" with respect to legislation or to "other matters which the Constitution places within the jurisdiction of either House." Accordingly, the majority concluded, neither the Senator nor his aide could be questioned as to the reading of the Papers in subcommittee. However, the privilege did not prevent asking either about the Senator's arrangements for their private publication, which was "in no way essential to the deliberations of the Senate." Nor was there any protection against "questions relevant to tracing the source of obviously highly classified documents that came into the Senator's possession . . ., as long as no legislative act is implicated by the questions." Dissenting Justices objected that both informing the public and gathering information for hearings were essential legislative functions protected by the clause.[1]

In Eastland v. United States Servicemen's Fund, 421 U.S. 491 (1975), the court of appeals on the basis of these precedents had held that neither a Senator nor his staff was protected by the Clause in connection with the actual issuance and service of a committee subpoena. The Supreme Court reversed, holding service of the subpoena a part of the legislative process. The interesting question was not noticed: Without discussion or precedent, the immunity was applied to a suit for injunction. Was this result justifiable?[2]

(2) In striking contrast to Members of Congress, Presidents enjoy no explicit constitutional or statutory immunity from suit; yet Mississippi v. Johnson, 71 U.S. (4 Wall.) 475 (1867), held that federal courts lacked power to enjoin the President from enforcing an unconstitutional statute, because neither the Congress nor the President "can be restrained in its action by the judicial department; though the acts of both, when performed, are, in proper cases, subject to its cognizance." Leaving open whether a President could be ordered to perform a "purely ministerial act under a positive law," the Court said that the enforcement of the Reconstruction Acts was not ministerial but "executive" and that it made no difference that the complaint sought to restrain rather than to require enforcement. Then the Court discussed at some length the difficulties of enforcing its decree:

> Suppose the bill filed and the injunction prayed for allowed. If the President refused obedience, it is needless to observe that the court is without power to enforce its process. If, on the other hand, the President complies with the order of the court and refuses to execute the acts of Congress, is it not clear that a collision may occur between the executive and legislative departments of the government? May not the House of Representatives impeach the President for such

1. See also United States v. Johnson, 383 U.S. 169 (1966), holding that a Congressman could not be prosecuted for taking a bribe to make a speech in the House because the court would have to inquire into his motive for speaking but holding he was not immune from charges of attempting improperly to influence the Department of Justice because such activity was "in no wise related to the due functioning of the legislative process."

2. See also Davis v. Passman, 544 F.2d 865, 880–81 (5th Cir. 1977), holding, over one dissent, that the Speech and Debate Clause did not bar a damage action against a Congressman for sex discrimination in dismissal of a member of his staff:

> The Constitution establishes an immunity for aberrations in a representative's legislative activities, but . . . [w]hen members of Congress dismiss employees they are neither legislating nor formulating legislation.

On rehearing en banc this decision was set aside on other grounds; the Supreme Court reversed and remanded for consideration of the immunity issue. See pp. 410–11 supra.

refusal? And in that case could this court interfere, in behalf of the President, thus endangered by compliance with its mandate, and restrain by injunction the Senate of the United States from sitting as a court of impeachment?

The Court nowhere identified the source of the President's immunity; and both before and after *Johnson* the Court upheld judicial power, under appropriate jurisdictional provisions, to grant relief against Cabinet officers that would have comparable consequences. E.g., Marbury v. Madison, 5 U.S. (1 Cranch) 137 (1803) (mandamus to Secretary of State); Youngstown Sheet & Tube Co. v. Sawyer, 343 U.S. 579 (1952) (enjoining Secretary of Commerce from seizing steel mills in accordance with Presidential instructions). The District of Columbia Circuit in Nixon v. Sirica, 487 F.2d 700, 708–12 (D.C.Cir. 1973), upholding judicial authority to order the President to produce Watergate tapes, distinguished *Johnson* as holding only that the courts could not "coerce a discretionary act" of the President and went on to pronounce *Johnson* dead: "There is not the slightest hint in any of the *Youngstown* opinions that the case would have been viewed differently if President Truman . . . had been the named party." The Supreme Court, upholding a later federal-court order directing the President to produce documentary evidence, did not advert to any argument of total Presidential immunity from judicial process. United States v. Nixon, 418 U.S. 683 (1974).[3]

In Nixon v. Fitzgerald, 457 U.S. 731 (1982), the Court over four dissents held an ex-President absolutely immune from damages on account of the allegedly unlawful dismissal of a subordinate during his Presidency, finding such immunity "a functionally mandated incident of the President's unique office, rooted in the constitutional tradition of the separation of powers and supported by our history." Professing to leave open the question whether Congress could create damage actions against the President, Justice Powell insisted the Court was deciding only the "constitutional issue" of immunity in the absence of legislation. If the immunity is based on the Constitution, isn't it clear Congress cannot remove it? But cf. *Fitzpatrick v. Bitzer*, p. 460 supra.

May a President be indicted and tried for crime during his term?[4] May he be subpoenaed to testify in person in a state court?

(3) To the extent that actions against federal officers are based upon federal common law (see pp. 401–12 supra), the federal courts are of course

3. The much discussed question of executive privilege is a separate and narrower doctrine: Assuming an officer is not immune to process altogether, it is an argument for withholding particular evidence. See *Nixon v. Sirica*, supra, 487 F.2d at 712–21; *United States v. Nixon*, supra, 418 U.S. at 703–13.

4. See the argument of President Nixon's Justice Department in response to Vice President Agnew's effort to enjoin his threatened indictment: Immunity from prosecution while in office should be implied only for a President, for only in his case, as recognized by the special constitutional provision for his replacement in case of disability, would the operation of the criminal process substantially impair the functioning of an entire branch of government; and only in his case would prosecution be inconsistent with the constitutional grant of the powers of prosecution and pardon. Memorandum for the United States Concerning the Vice President's Claim for Constitutional Immunity at 15–20, In re Proceedings of the Grand Jury Impaneled, Dec. 5, 1972, No. Civ. 73–965 (D.Md.1973).

as free to create immunities for policy reasons as they were to create the right of action itself. If, on the other hand, the right of action for illegal searches discovered in the *Bivens* case was created by the Fourth Amendment itself, what right has the Court to cut it down?

(4) Only Justice Douglas dissented when the Court held in Tenney v. Brandhove, 341 U.S. 367 (1951), that state legislators were immune from damages under 42 U.S.C. § 1983 for actions that "may fairly be deemed within [the legislative] . . . province," even if they acted in bad faith. Was this question the same as that presented by such cases as *Harlow*? Recall that § 1983 flatly provides that "every person" depriving another of federal rights under color of state law "shall be liable to the party injured in an action at law, suit in equity, or other proper proceeding for redress." Said the Court in *Tenney*: § 1983 was not intended to override the traditional freedom of legislators from "civil liability for acts within the sphere of legislative activity."

The opinion in *Harlow* traces the subsequent course of official immunity. Do you find the distinctions drawn among various types of officers persuasive?

(5) In Pulliam v. Allen, 466 U.S. 522 (1984), the Court held not only that a state judge could be sued for an injunction under § 1983 but that he could be made personally liable for the plaintiff's legal fees under § 1988: Tradition allowed such specific relief against a judge as mandamus and prohibition, and the House Report showed " 'that Congress intended to permit attorney's fees awards in cases in which prospective relief was properly awarded against defendants who would be immune from damages awards.' " Four dissenters argued that judges could not be sued for injunctions at all. Was either of these positions correct?

(6) In Owen v. City of Independence, 445 U.S. 622 (1980), the Court refused to extend the good-faith damage immunity of local executive officers to the city itself: The official's immunity was based upon tradition, and "there is no tradition of immunity for municipal corporations"; municipal immunity would impair the remedial and deterrent purposes of § 1983; the policies underlying immunity were inapplicable, because "it is fairer to allocate any resulting financial loss to . . . the taxpayers" than to the victim, and because "it is questionable whether the hazard of municipal loss will deter a public officer from the conscientious exercise of his duties." Justice Powell's dissent, joined by three other Justices, argued that municipal immunity was required by "basic fairness," by the traditional absence of municipal liability for "governmental" torts, and because "[i]f officials must look over their shoulders at strict municipal liability for unknowable constitutional deprivations, the resulting degree of governmental paralysis will be little different from that caused by fear of personal liability." [5]

(7) With the above cases on immunity of state officers from damages compare the ringing dictum as to the criminal liability of state judges in O'Shea v. Littleton, 414 U.S. 488 (1974), based in turn on a dictum in Ex

5. See also Kramer & Sykes, Municipal Liability Under § 1983: A Legal and Economic Analysis, 1987 Sup.Ct.Rev. 249, 300: "[T]he danger of self-protective behavior [by municipalities] certainly weakens the case for the imposition of liability . . . ."

parte Virginia, 100 U.S. 339 (1879), where the judge had been acting "ministerially" in compiling jury lists:

> Whatever may be the case with respect to civil liability . . ., we have never held that the performance of the duties of judicial, legislative, or executive officers, requires or contemplates the immunization of otherwise criminal deprivations of constitutional rights. . . . On the contrary, . . . official immunity does not reach "so far as to immunize criminal conduct proscribed by an Act of Congress. . . ."

See also United States v. Gillock, 445 U.S. 360 (1980), reaching the same result in a prosecution of a state legislator for taking bribes to introduce legislation; Kattan, Knocking on *Wood*: Some Thoughts on the Immunities of State Officials to Civil Rights Damage Actions, 30 Vand.L.Rev. 941, 962 (1977): "The likelihood of vexatious suits or harassment in this context is minimal because the decision to prosecute is committed to the discretion of a federal prosecutor."

(8) Do you think the Court's decisions on official immunity adequately reflect the differing statutory and constitutional provisions applicable to members of Congress, to other federal officers, and to state officers?

Chapter VI

ABSTENTION AND SUCH

SECTION 1. PULLMAN ABSTENTION AND CERTIFICATION

RAILROAD COMMISSION v. PULLMAN CO.

312 U.S. 496 (1941).

MR. JUSTICE FRANKFURTER delivered the opinion of the Court.

In those sections of Texas where the local passenger traffic is slight, trains carry but one sleeping car. These trains, unlike trains having two or more sleepers, are without a Pullman conductor; the sleeper is in charge of a porter who is subject to the train conductor's control. As is well known, porters on Pullmans are colored and conductors are white. Addressing itself to this situation, the Texas Railroad Commission after due hearing ordered that "no sleeping car shall be operated on any line of railroad in the State of Texas . . . unless such cars are continuously in the charge of an employee . . . having the rank and position of Pullman conductor." Thereupon, the Pullman Company and the railroads affected brought this action in a federal district court to enjoin the Commission's order. Pullman porters were permitted to intervene as complainants, and Pullman conductors entered the litigation in support of the order. Three judges having been convened, . . . [see p. 568], the court enjoined enforcement of the order. From this decree, the case came here directly. [see 28 U.S.C. § 1253] . . .

The Pullman Company and the railroads assailed the order as unauthorized by Texas law as well as violative of the Equal Protection, the Due Process and the Commerce Clauses of the Constitution. The intervening porters adopted these objections but mainly objected to the order as a discrimination against Negroes in violation of the Fourteenth Amendment.

The complaint of the Pullman porters undoubtedly tendered a substantial constitutional issue. It is more than substantial. It touches a sensitive area of social policy upon which the federal courts ought not to enter unless no alternative to its adjudication is open. Such constitutional adjudication plainly can be avoided if a definitive ruling on the state issue would terminate the controversy. It is therefore our duty to turn to a consideration of questions under Texas law.

The Commission found justification for its order in a Texas statute which we quote in the margin.[1] It is common ground that if the order is within the Commission's authority its subject matter must be included in the Commission's power to prevent "unjust discrimination . . . and to prevent any and all other abuses" in the conduct of railroads. Whether arrangements pertaining to the staffs of Pullman cars are covered by the Texas concept of "discrimination" is far from clear. What practices of the railroads may be deemed to be "abuses" subject to the Commission's correction is equally doubtful. Reading the Texas statutes and the Texas decisions as outsiders without special competence in Texas law, we would have little confidence in our independent judgment regarding the application of that law to the present situation. The lower court did deny that the Texas statutes sustained the Commission's assertion of power. And this represents the view of an able and experienced circuit judge of the circuit which includes Texas and of two capable district judges trained in Texas law. Had we or they no choice in the matter but to decide what is the law of the state, we should hesitate long before rejecting their forecast of Texas law. But no matter how seasoned the judgment of the district court may be, it cannot escape being a forecast rather than a determination. The last word on the meaning of Article 6445 of the Texas Civil Statutes, and therefore the last word on the statutory authority of the Railroad Commission in this case, belongs neither to us nor to the district court but to the supreme court of Texas. In this situation a federal court of equity is asked to decide an issue by making a tentative answer which may be displaced tomorrow by a state adjudication. Glenn v. Field Packing Co., 290 U.S. 177; Lee v. Bickell, 292 U.S. 415. The reign of law is hardly promoted if an unnecessary ruling of a federal court is thus supplanted by a controlling decision of a state court. The resources of equity are equal to an adjustment that will avoid the waste of a tentative decision as well as the friction of a premature constitutional adjudication.

1. Vernon's Anno.Texas Civil Statutes, Article 6445: "Power and authority are hereby conferred upon the Railroad Commission of Texas over all railroads, and suburban, belt and terminal railroads, and over all public wharves, docks, piers, elevators, warehouses, sheds, tracks and other property used in connection therewith in this State, and over all persons, associations and corporations, private or municipal, owning or operating such railroad, wharf, dock, pier, elevator, warehouse, shed, track or other property to fix, and it is hereby made the duty of the said Commission to adopt all necessary rates, charges and regulations, to govern and regulate such railroads, persons, associations and corporations, and to correct abuses and prevent unjust discrimination in the rates, charges and tolls of such railroads, persons, associations and corporations, and to fix division of rates, charges and regulations between railroads and other utilities and common carriers where a division is proper and correct, and to prevent any and all other abuses in the conduct of their business and to do and perform such other duties and details in connection therewith as may be provided by law."

An appeal to the chancellor, as we had occasion to recall only the other day, is an appeal to the "exercise of the sound discretion, which guides the determination of courts of equity." Beal v. Missouri Pacific R. Co., 312 U.S. 45. The history of equity jurisdiction is the history of regard for public consequences in employing the extraordinary remedy of the injunction. There have been as many and as variegated applications of this supple principle as the situations that have brought it into play. See, for modern instances, Beasley v. Texas & Pacific Ry. Co., 191 U.S. 492; Harrisonville v. Dickey Clay Co., 289 U.S. 334; United States v. Dern, 289 U.S. 352. Few public interests have a higher claim upon the discretion of a federal chancellor than the avoidance of a needless friction with state policies, whether the policy relates to the enforcement of the criminal law, Fenner v. Boykin, 271 U.S. 240; Spielman Motor Co. v. Dodge, 295 U.S. 89; or the administration of a specialized scheme for liquidating embarrassed business enterprises, Pennsylvania v. Williams, 294 U.S. 176; or the final authority of a state court to interpret doubtful regulatory laws of the state, Gilchrist v. Interborough Co., 279 U.S. 159; cf. Hawks v. Hamill, 288 U.S. 52, 61. These cases reflect a doctrine of abstention appropriate to our federal system whereby the federal courts, "exercising a wise discretion," restrain their authority because of "scrupulous regard for the rightful independence of the state governments" and for the smooth working of the federal judiciary. See Cavanaugh v. Looney, 248 U.S. 453, 457; Di Giovanni v. Camden Ins. Assn., 296 U.S. 64, 73. This use of equitable powers is a contribution of the courts in furthering the harmonious relation between state and federal authority without the need of rigorous congressional restriction of those powers. . . .

Regard for these important considerations of policy in the administration of federal equity jurisdiction is decisive here. If there was no warrant in state law for the Commission's assumption of authority there is an end of the litigation; the constitutional issue does not arise. The law of Texas appears to furnish easy and ample means for determining the Commission's authority. Article 6453 of the Texas Civil Statutes gives a review of such an order in the state courts. Or, if there are difficulties in the way of this procedure of which we have not been apprised, the issue of state law may be settled by appropriate action on the part of the State to enforce obedience to the order. Beal v. Missouri Pacific R. R. Co., supra; Article 6476, Texas Civil Statutes. In the absence of any showing that these obvious methods for securing a definitive ruling in the state courts cannot be pursued with full protection of the constitutional claim, the district court should exercise its wise discretion by staying its hands. Compare Thompson v. Magnolia Co., 309 U.S. 478.

We therefore remand the cause to the district court, with directions to retain the bill pending a determination of proceedings, to be brought with reasonable promptness, in the state court in conformity with this opinion. Compare Atlas Ins. Co. v. Southern, Inc., 306 U.S. 563, 573, and cases cited.

Reversed. . . .

ENGLAND v. LOUISIANA STATE BOARD OF MEDICAL EXAMINERS

375 U.S. 411 (1964).

MR. JUSTICE BRENNAN delivered the opinion of the Court.

Appellants are graduates of schools of chiropractic who seek to practice in Louisiana without complying with the educational requirements of the Louisiana Medical Practice Act, Title 37, La.Rev.Stat. §§ 1261–1290. They brought this action against respondent Louisiana State Board of Medical Examiners in the Federal District Court for the Eastern District of Louisiana, seeking an injunction and a declaration that, as applied to them, the Act violated the Fourteenth Amendment. A statutory three-judge court invoked, *sua sponte*, the doctrine of abstention, on the ground that "The state court might effectively end this controversy by a determination that chiropractors are not governed by the statute," and entered an order "staying further proceedings in this Court until the courts of the State of Louisiana shall have been afforded an opportunity to determine the issues here presented, and retaining jurisdiction to take such steps as may be necessary for the just disposition of the litigation should anything prevent a prompt state court determination." 180 F.Supp. 121, 124.

Appellants thereupon brought proceedings in the Louisiana courts. They did not restrict those proceedings to the question whether the Medical Practice Act applied to chiropractors. They unreservedly submitted for decision, and briefed and argued, their contention that the Act, if applicable to chiropractors, violated the Fourteenth Amendment. The state proceedings terminated with a decision by the Louisiana Supreme Court declining to review an intermediate appellate court's holding both that the Medical Practice Act applied to chiropractors and that, as so applied, it did not violate the Fourteenth Amendment. 126 So.2d 51.

Appellants then returned to the District Court, where they were met with a motion by appellees to dismiss the federal action. This motion was granted, on the ground that "since the courts of Louisiana have passed on all issues raised, including the claims of deprivation under the Federal Constitution, this court, having no power to review these proceedings, must dismiss the complaint. The proper remedy was by appeal to the Supreme Court of the United States." . . . Appellants appealed directly to this Court under 28 U.S.C. § 1253, and we noted probable jurisdiction. 372 U.S. 904. We reverse and remand to the District Court for decision on the merits of appellants' Fourteenth Amendment claims.

There are fundamental objections to any conclusion that a litigant who has properly invoked the jurisdiction of a Federal District Court to consider federal constitutional claims can be compelled, without his consent and through no fault of his own, to accept instead a state court's determination of those claims.[5] Such a result would be at war with the unqualified terms in which Congress, pursuant to constitutional authorization, has conferred specific categories of jurisdiction upon the federal courts, and with the principle that "When a Federal court is properly appealed to in a case over which it has by law jurisdiction, it is its duty to take such jurisdiction. . . . The right of a party plaintiff to choose a Federal court where there is a choice cannot be properly denied." Wilcox v. Consolidated Gas Co., 212 U.S. 19, 40. Nor does anything in the abstention doctrine require or support such a result. Abstention is a judge-fashioned vehicle for according appropriate deference to the "respective competence of the state and federal court systems." Louisiana P. & L. Co. v. Thibodaux, 360 U.S. 25, 29. Its recognition of the role of state courts as the final expositors of state law implies no disregard for the primacy of the federal judiciary in deciding questions of federal law. Accordingly, we have on several occasions explicitly recognized that abstention "does not, of course, involve the abdication of federal jurisdiction, but only the postponement of its exercise." Harrison v. NAACP, 360 U.S. 167, 177; accord, Louisiana P. & L. Co. v. Thibodaux, supra, 360 U.S., at 29.

It is true that, after a post-abstention determination and rejection of his federal claims by the state courts, a litigant could seek direct review in this Court. NAACP v. Button, 371 U.S. 415; Lassiter v. Northhampton County Board of Elections, 360 U.S. 45. But such review, even when available by appeal rather than only by discretionary writ of certiorari, is an inadequate substitute for the initial District Court determination—often by three judges, 28 U.S.C. § 2281—to which the litigant is entitled in the federal courts. This is true as to issues of law; it is especially true as to issues of fact. Limiting the litigant to review here would deny him the benefit of a federal trial court's role in constructing a record and making fact findings. How the facts are found will often dictate the decision of federal claims. . . . Thus in cases where, but for the application of the abstention doctrine, the primary fact determination would have been by the District Court, a litigant may not be unwillingly deprived of that determination. . . . We made this clear only last Term in NAACP v. Button, supra, 371 U.S., at 427, when we said that "a party has the right to return to the District Court, after obtaining the authoritative state court construction for which the court abstained, for a final determination of his claim."

5. At least this is true in a case, like the instant one, not involving the possibility of unwarranted disruption of a state administrative process. Compare Burford v. Sun Oil Co., 319 U.S. 315; Alabama Public Service Comm'n v. Southern R. Co., 341 U.S. 341.

We also made clear in *Button*, however, that a party may elect to forgo that right. Our holding in that case was that a judgment of the Virginia Supreme Court of Appeals upon federal issues submitted to the state tribunals by parties remitted there under the abstention doctrine was "final" for purposes of our review under 28 U.S.C. § 1257. . . . We saw no inconsistency with the abstention doctrine in allowing a litigant to decide, once the federal court has abstained and compelled him to proceed in the state courts in any event, to abandon his original choice of a federal forum and submit his entire case to the state courts . . . If a party freely and without reservation submits his federal claims for decision by the state courts, litigates them there, and has them decided there, then—whether or not he seeks direct review of the state decision in this Court—he has elected to forgo his right to return to the District Court.

This rule requires clarification of our decision in Government Employees v. Windsor, 353 U.S. 364. . . . The plaintiffs in *Windsor* had submitted to the state courts only the question whether the state statute they challenged applied to them, and had not "advanced" or "presented" to those courts their contentions against the statute's constitutionality. We held that "the bare adjudication by the Alabama Supreme Court that the [appellant] union is subject to this Act does not suffice, since that court was not asked to interpret the statute in light of the constitutional objections presented to the District Court. If appellants' freedom-of-expression and equal-protection arguments had been presented to the state court, it might have construed the statute in a different manner." . . . On oral argument in the instant case, we were advised that appellants' submission of their federal claims to the state courts had been motivated primarily by a belief that *Windsor* required this. The District Court likewise thought that under *Windsor* a party is required to litigate his federal question in the state courts and "dare not restrict his state court case to local law issues." . . . Others have read *Windsor* the same way. It should not be so read. The case does not mean that a party must litigate his federal claims in the state courts, but only that he must inform those courts what his federal claims are, so that the state statute may be construed "in light of" those claims. . . . Thus mere compliance with *Windsor* will not support a conclusion, much less create a presumption, that a litigant has freely and without reservation litigated his federal claims in the state courts and so elected not to return to the District Court. . . .

On the record in the instant case, the rule we announce today would call for affirmance of the District Court's judgment. But we are unwilling to apply the rule against these appellants. As we have noted, their primary reason for litigating their federal claims in the state courts was assertedly a view that *Windsor* required them to do so. That view was mistaken, and will not avail other litigants who rely upon it after today's decision. But we cannot say, in the face of the support given the view by respectable authorities, including the court below, that appellants were unreasonable in holding it or acting upon it. We therefore hold that the District Court should not have dismissed their action. The judgment is reversed, and the case is remanded for further proceedings consistent with this opinion. . . .

Notes on Abstention and Certification to Clarify State Law

(1) Should the Supreme Court have held abstention precluded by 28 U.S.C. §§ 1331 and 1332, which grant the district courts jurisdiction of "all civil actions" arising under federal law or between citizens of different States and involving the requisite amount? See Chief Justice Marshall's famous statement in Cohens v. Virginia, 19 U.S. (6 Wheat.) 264, 404 (1821): "It is most true that this Court will not take jurisdiction if it should not but it is equally true that it must take jurisdiction if it should. . . . We have no more right to decline the exercise of jurisdiction which is given, than to usurp that which is not given. . . ."[1]

Can *Pullman* be justified on the ground that, as the Court later said, abstention does not involve "the abdication of federal jurisdiction, but only the postponement of its exercise"? Harrison v. NAACP, 360 U.S. 167, 177 (1959). By the traditional principle denying equitable relief when there is an adequate legal remedy? Justice Frankfurter's opinion in Alabama Public Service Commission v. Southern Ry., 341 U.S. 341 (1951), suggests otherwise:

> An "adequate remedy at law," as a bar to equitable relief in the federal courts, refers to a remedy on the law side of federal courts. . . . It was never a doctrine of equity that a federal court should exercise its judicial discretion to dismiss a suit merely because a State court could entertain it. This is so because discretion based solely on the availability of a remedy in the State courts would for all practical purposes repeal the Act of 1875.

Was it not the very basis for the grant of federal jurisdiction that state-court remedies were inadequate to protect federal rights?

1. Compare with Justice Frankfurter's opinion for abstention in *Pullman* the opinion of the same Justice protesting the Court's dismissal of a suit challenging a state administrative order in Alabama Public Service Commission v. Southern Ry., 341 U.S. 341 (1951):

> The Court has consistently held to the view that it cannot overrule the determination of Congress as to whether federal courts should be allowed jurisdiction. . . . We are concerned with a jurisdictional issue which has been continuously before Congress and with which it has dealt by explicit and detailed legislation. . . . It required that the case be heard by three judges, that a speedy appeal be available, and that the State courts could have exclusive jurisdiction if they would stay the administrative order. It withdrew jurisdiction to enjoin enforcement of State statutes and orders in the two fields where the greatest dissatisfaction with federal jurisdiction existed—rate orders and taxation—so long as a State remedy was available. But Congress did not take away the power of the district court to decide a case like the one before us. Instead, it recognized by the wording of § 17 of the Mann-Elkins Act and later legislation that it had given a right to resort to the federal courts and that such power was obligatory jurisdiction, not to be denied because as a matter of policy it might be more desirable to raise such constitutional claims in a State court. . . .

With this view of the obligatory nature of district-court jurisdiction, how could Justice Frankfurter write for abstention in *Pullman*?

If you think the statute precludes abstention for the purpose of instituting a state-court inquiry, do you think it also forbids a federal court to continue an action pending the outcome of a related state-court suit that is already pending? See pp. 556–67 infra. Can you distinguish Gulf Oil Corp. v. Gilbert, p. 314 supra, which upheld, without statutory authority, a dismissal of a diversity action on grounds of forum non conveniens? Can you distinguish the cases requiring exhaustion of administrative remedies (supra pp. 62–63), or of state-court remedies when federal habeas corpus is sought before conviction (pp. 639–40 infra)? See Shapiro, Jurisdiction and Discretion, 60 N.Y.U.L.Rev. 543 (1985):

> Suggestions of an overriding obligation [to exercise jurisdiction granted by statute] are far too grudging in their recognition of judicial discretion in matters of jurisdiction. . . . [T]he existence of this discretion is far more pervasive than is generally realized, and . . . it has ancient and honorable roots at common law as well as in equity.

Cf. *Hans v. Louisiana* and *Tenney v. Brandhove,* pp. 433, 483 supra, finding states and state legislators immune from suit despite the unqualified words of Article III and of 42 U.S.C. § 1983, respectively.

(2) The ALI reporters were not happy with *England.* Terming the procedure prescribed by the Court "exotic," they pointed out that "shuttling of a case from one court to another . . . is time-consuming and costly. . . . Decision on the merits in the *England* case came after nine years of litigation in a variety of courts. . . . 384 U.S. 885 (1966). The *Leiter Minerals* litigation was dismissed as moot, . . . 381 U.S. 413 (1965), more than eleven years after commencement of the action and eight years after abstention was ordered." ALI Study 48–50, 282–87. See also Note, 73 Harv.L.Rev. 1358 (1960), for discussion of the rather tortuous paths followed by some abstention cases prior to *England.*

The Reporters found no perfect solution to the problem:

> To litigate these cases entirely through the federal courts strains state-federal relations, may make necessary the premature decision of federal constitutional questions, and requires the federal court to pass on questions of state law in circumstances under which an erroneous decision may seriously interfere with state substantive policies. To litigate such cases entirely through the state courts, with review in the United States Supreme Court, deprives plaintiff of federal fact-finding, and of federal protection during the pendency of the state action. To shuttle the cases back and forth from state to federal court, as present doctrines permit, "operates to require piecemeal adjudication in many courts . . . thereby delaying ultimate adjudication on the merits for an undue length of time."

Faced with this aggravated dilemma, the Reporters proposed to eliminate in most cases the return to federal court contemplated by *England.* If there was real need for a federal forum the entire case would be tried in federal court: Abstention could be ordered only if "the parties' claims of federal right, if any, including any issues of fact material thereto, can be adequately protected by review of the State court decision by the Supreme Court of the United States." On the other hand, if the federal court abstained, it should retain jurisdiction only in order to grant "interim relief" if state law could not prevent irreparable harm during litigation, and in order to proceed to judgment "if the State proceeding proves ineffective in reaching a prompt and final disposition on the merits." Except in these extraordinary circumstances, after abstention the entire dispute would be resolved in the state court, with review of the state-court decision by the Supreme Court of the United States, "to the extent provided by section 1257 of this title."

Some years ago the Florida legislature authorized the state Supreme Court to answer doubtful questions of state law certified by federal courts in which the questions arose. In a situation meeting the criteria for abstention under *Pullman,* the United States Supreme Court gave this procedure its blessing, and other states hastened to follow Florida's example. Clay v. Sun Insurance Office, 363 U.S. 207 (1960) (Frankfurter, J.). Does certification avoid the disadvantages of abstention under *Pullman* and *England?*[2]

(3) So long as Justice Frankfurter was on the Court, *Pullman* was regularly invoked to justify abstention in cases in which state-court resolution of ambiguous state law might avoid decision of a substantial constitutional question. E.g., Harrison v. NAACP, 360 U.S. 167 (1959); Leiter Minerals, Inc. v. United States, 352 U.S. 220 (1957), ordering abstention in a suit brought by the United States. After his retirement, however, the doctrine was perceived to have gone into something of a decline. In each of the seven cases presenting the issue between 1963 and 1967 the Court managed to avoid abstention. *Pullman* was distinguished on a variety of grounds: that state law was not unclear (McNeese v. Board of Education, 373 U.S. 668 (1963); Davis v. Mann, 377 U.S. 678 (1964)); that a single state decision could not eliminate the chilling effect of a vague or overbroad statute affecting speech (Baggett v. Bullitt, 377 U.S. 360 (1964); Dombrow-

2. See the dissenting opinion of Justice Douglas in *Clay,* giving "renewed protest to our practice of making litigants travel a long, expensive road in order to obtain justice." Not all States have been receptive to the prospect of helping to decide cases in the federal courts. After abstention in United Services Life Ins. Co. v. Delaney, 328 F.2d 483 (5th Cir.1964), a declaratory-judgment suit was filed in a Texas court to determine a disputed issue of Texas law. Dismissal was affirmed:

> If the state court is to entertain a suit for declaratory relief, it must have the power and jurisdiction to settle the controversy by entry of a final judgment. . . . Here, in effect, the same suit is pending in both the state and federal courts by reason of a directive which contemplates that the final judgment will be rendered by a federal court. The Circuit Court's reservation of jurisdiction to render final judgment renders these proceedings advisory in nature. . . . The rendition of advisory opinions by courts is unauthorized by our constitution. . . .

After this the federal Court of Appeals decided the case on the merits, 358 F.2d 714 (1966). Later, however, faced with a case in which it thought abstention appropriate and with Texas's refusal to entertain declaratory proceedings in aid of retained federal jurisdiction, the Fifth Circuit ordered the federal proceeding dismissed outright. Romero v. Coldwell, 455 F.2d 1163 (5th Cir.1972). The Supreme Court approved in Harris County Comm'rs v. Moore, 420 U.S. 77, 88–89 & n. 14 (1975), ordering dismissal "without prejudice so that any remaining federal claim may be raised in a federal forum after the state courts have been given the opportunity to address the state law questions," citing *England.* Is it clear that res judicata will not be a bar if the state court decides the federal questions, or if state law bars litigation of issues that might have been raised and were not? Take another look at 28 U.S.C. § 1738. And if the state's judgment on the federal issues is not to be binding, does dismissal of the first federal suit satisfy the Texas court's objections in *Delaney?*

ski v. Pfister, 380 U.S. 479 (1965)); that a challenge to the validity of a statute as applied did not pose a severe threat to state policy (Hostetter v. Idlewild Bon Voyage Liquor Corp., 377 U.S. 324 (1964)); that there had already been too much delay (Griffin v. County School Board, 377 U.S. 218 (1964); *Hostetter v. Idelwild Bon Voyage Liquor Corp.*, supra); and that "the importance and immediacy" of an attack on a state poll tax demanded prompt federal action since an election was impending and since the case concerned "fundamental civil rights of a broad class of citizens" (Harman v. Forssenius, 380 U.S. 528 (1965)). See generally Note, Federal Question Abstention: Justice Frankfurter's Doctrine in an Activist Era, 80 Harv.L. Rev. 604 (1967).

(4) More recent cases, however, demonstrate that the Court may still abstain when state-court resolution of unclear state law might avoid a substantial federal constitutional question. In Reetz v. Bozanich, 397 U.S. 82 (1970), state and federal grounds were asserted against an Alaska law limiting fishing rights on a grandfather-clause basis; the trial court found no ambiguity in state constitutional provisions reserving fishing rights to the people and forbidding exclusive fishing privileges, and it said the plaintiffs would suffer grave injury if their rights were not vindicated in time for the coming season. It was Justice Douglas who wrote in reversing the refusal to abstain:

> The provisions of the Alaska Constitution at issue have never been interpreted by an Alaska court. . . . The constitutional provision relates to fish resources, an asset unique in its abundance in Alaska. The statute and regulations relate to that same unique resource, the management of which is a matter of great state concern.[3]

But there are still limits to abstention in constitutional cases. In Pike v. Bruce Church, Inc., 397 U.S. 137 (1970), for example, delay in deciding whether a state statute respecting the packing of cantaloupes could constitutionally be applied to a 30-mile interstate shipment to a packing house would have resulted in loss of a $700,000 crop. Despite *Reetz*, abstention was held unnecessary "in view of the emergency situation presented, and the fact that only a narrow and specific application of the Act was challenged." Cf. *Hostetter v. Idlewild Bon Voyage Liquor Corp.*, supra note 3.[4]

3. See also Askew v. Hargrave, 401 U.S. 476 (1971); Manard v. Miller, 405 U.S. 982 (1972); Lake Carriers' Ass'n v. MacMullan, 406 U.S. 498 (1972); Boehning v. Indiana State Employees Association, Inc., 423 U.S. 6 (1975), approving abstention in a § 1983 case involving discharge of a public employee.

Does the *Pennhurst* decision (p. 453 supra) impair the basis of *Pullman* abstention by depriving the federal court of jurisdiction over pendent state-law claims against state officers? Cf. Muskegon Theatres, Inc. v. City of Muskegon, 507 F.2d 199, 204 (6th Cir.1974) (decided before *Pennhurst*), sending the parties to state court on an issue not raised by the complaint: Plaintiffs "cannot be allowed to frustrate the policies underlying the doctrine of abstention" by the "simple expedient" of failure to make claims under state law.

4. See also Catrone v. Massachusetts State Racing Commission, 535 F.2d 669 (1st Cir. 1976), directing abstention in an action challenging the exclusion of the plaintiff from a racetrack but authorizing a preliminary injunction to prevent irreparable harm while state courts resolved the disputed state-law issue; Wells, Preliminary Injunctions and Abstention: Some Problems in Federalism, 63 Corn.L.R. 65 (1977), approving *Catrone* as an intermediate course between the extremes of simply abstaining, as in *Reetz v. Bozanich*, and of

Moreover, in Wisconsin v. Constantineau, 400 U.S. 433, 438–39 (1971), the Court refused to approve abstention in the face of a dissent arguing that "for all we know, the state courts would find this statute invalid under the State Constitution" and lamenting that nobody had discussed the issue.[5] See also Harris County Commissioners Court v. Moore, 420 U.S. 77, 84–85 n. 8 (1975); Examining Board v. Flores de Otero, 426 U.S. 572, 598 (1976), explaining that to abstain on the ground that interpretation of a state equal-protection clause might have avoided a federal constitutional question "would convert abstention from an exception into a general rule." See Herald Co. v. McNeal, 553 F.2d 1125, 1130 n. 8 (8th Cir. 1977) (dictum): "Abstention is not required where the state constitutional provision is the mirror of the federal one. Wisconsin v. Constantineau. . . ." But aren't the policies favoring abstention equally applicable when the ambiguous provision is a "mirror" of the federal?[6]

(5) One of the reasons given for abstaining in *Pullman* was the danger of making a wrong guess in resolving an uncertain question of state law. In *Pullman* and most of the decisions following it, however, an additional factor was the desire to avoid a substantial constitutional question; and in Meredith v. Winter Haven, 320 U.S. 228 (1943), the Court held the court of appeals had erred in ordering a trial judge to abstain in a diversity case simply because the state law was unclear. *Pullman*, wrote Chief Justice Stone, was an "exceptional" case in which abstention was based upon "the salutary policy of refraining from the unnecessary decision of constitutional questions"; "Congress having adopted the policy of opening the federal courts to suitors in all diversity cases involving the jurisdictional amount, we can discern in its action no recognition of a policy which would exclude cases from the jurisdiction merely because they involve state law or because the law is uncertain or difficult to determine."[7]

(6) Nevertheless, in extraordinary situations the Court has approved abstention to clarify ambiguous state law in nonconstitutional cases as well, as exemplified by Kaiser Steel Corp. v. W. S. Ranch Co., 391 U.S. 593 (1968), where an action for trespass had been brought against a coal-mine

refusing to abstain, as in *Pike v. Bruce Church*.

5. The Court in *Constantineau* expressly held it immaterial that nobody had requested abstention. See also Ohio Bureau of Employment Services v. Hodory, 431 U.S. 471, 480 n. 11 (1977): "*Pullman* abstention, where deference to the state process may result in elimination or material alteration of the constitutional issue, surely does not require that this Court defer to the wishes of the parties concerning adjudication." Yet in the same breath the Court held the State could waive the *Younger* doctrine's limitation on enjoining state-court proceedings, see p. 539 infra. Does this distinction withstand scrutiny?

6. Should a court abstain where state law is unclear and the only federal question to be avoided is possible conflict with a federal statute under the Supremacy Clause? An affirmative answer was given without much discussion in Druker v. Sullivan, 458 F.2d 1272 (1st Cir. 1972). Propper v. Clark, 337 U.S. 472, 490 (1949), seems contrary: "Where a case involves a nonconstitutional federal issue . . ., the necessity for deciding which depends upon the decision of an underlying issue of state law, the practice in federal courts has been, where necessary, to decide both issues." Cf. *Swift & Co. v. Wickham*, infra p. 570.

7. See also Thermtron Products, Inc. v. Hermansdorfer, 423 U.S. 336, 344 (1976): "[A]n otherwise properly removed action may no more be remanded because the district court considers itself too busy to try it than an action properly filed in the federal court in the first instance may be dismissed or referred to state courts for such reason."

operator that had entered the plaintiff's land to secure water to which it was entitled. The plaintiff argued that if state law were construed to grant the power of eminent domain it would offend the state Constitution, which allowed private property to be taken only for "public use." The Supreme Court unanimously ordered abstention: The crucial issue of the meaning of "public use" was both "a truly novel one" and "one of vital concern in the arid State of New Mexico, where water is one of the most valuable natural resources." Justice Brennan, joined by Justices Douglas and Marshall, concurred specially to stress that he viewed the State's vital concern with water as bringing the case within the "narrowly limited 'special circumstances' " required to justify abstention.

See also Louisiana Power & Light Co. v. City of Thibodaux, 360 U.S. 25 (1959), approving abstention to clarify ambiguous state law in a city's suit to expropriate a private electric company because of the "special and peculiar nature" of eminent domain proceedings, which were "intimately involved with sovereign prerogative"; County of Allegheny v. Frank Mashuda Co., 360 U.S. 185 (1959), disapproving dismissal of a similar case in which, as a concurring opinion in *Thibodaux* pointed out, "the controlling state law [was] clear." Note also that *Thibodaux* extended the "equitable" *Pullman* doctrine to an action at law. Was that justifiable?

(7) Dissenting in *Thibodaux,* Justice Brennan argued that the decision effectively overruled *Winter Haven*, so that abstention would be permissible "in even the routine diversity negligence and contract actions." For a time the Fifth Circuit agreed with him, relying on *Thibodaux* in ordering a district court to abstain from determining whether a pilot was a "passenger" within the meaning of life-insurance policies because the relevant Texas law was "obscure." United Services Life Insurance Co. v. Delaney, 328 F.2d 483 (5th Cir. 1964). Even after receding from this position in Howell v. Union Producing Co., 392 F.2d 95 (5th Cir. 1968), the Fifth Circuit has continued to certify ambiguous state-law questions to Florida courts in routine diversity cases, e.g., Martinez v. Rodriguez, 394 F.2d 156 (5th Cir. 1968). Professing to distinguish *Winter Haven,* the Supreme Court approved this procedure in Lehman Brothers v. Schein, 416 U.S. 386 (1974), stressing that the governing law was that of Florida and that the action had been brought in New York: "When federal judges in New York attempt to predict uncertain Florida law, they act . . . as 'outsiders' lacking the common exposure to local law which comes from sitting in the jurisdiction." Resort to certification to clarify state law, the Court declared, "rests in the sound discretion of the federal court."

(8) For an effort to codify the *Pullman* doctrine see the ALI Study at 49–50, 292–98; for the argument that the relevant factors are too complex to be reduced to any statutory formula see Friendly, Federal Jurisdiction: A General View 95 (1973); for the argument that the costs of abstention are too high to justify its benefits see Field, Abstention in Constitutional Cases: The Scope of the Pullman Doctrine, 122 U.Pa.L.Rev. 1071 (1974).

Is abstention harder to reconcile with the reasons for federal jurisdiction in a diversity case than in a federal-question case? After resolution of the state-law issue in a case like *Thibodaux* or *Delaney*, what remains for the federal court to decide? See Liebenthal, A Dialogue on England: The

England Case, Its Effect on the Abstention Doctrine, and Some Suggested Solutions, 18 Case W.Res.L.Rev. 157, 158 n. 2, 183–95 (1966).

SECTION 2. STATE ADMINISTRATIVE AGENCIES AND TAXES

BURFORD v. SUN OIL CO.

319 U.S. 315 (1943).

MR. JUSTICE BLACK delivered the opinion of the Court.

In this proceeding brought in a federal district court, the Sun Oil Co. attacked the validity of an order of the Texas Railroad Commission granting the petitioner Burford a permit to drill four wells on a small plot of land in the East Texas oil field. Jurisdiction of the federal court was invoked because of the diversity of citizenship of the parties, and because of the Companies' contention that the order denied them due process of law. . . . While many other questions are argued, we find it necessary to decide only one: Assuming that the federal district court had jurisdiction, should it, as a matter of sound equitable discretion, have declined to exercise that jurisdiction here?

The order under consideration is part of the general regulatory system devised for the conservation of oil and gas in Texas, an aspect of "as thorny a problem as has challenged the ingenuity and wisdom of legislatures." . . . The East Texas field, in which the Burford tract is located, is one of the largest in the United States. It is approximately forty miles long and between five and nine miles wide, and over 26,000 wells have been drilled in it. Oil exists in the pores and crevices of rocks and sand and moves through these channels. A large area of this sort is called a pool or reservoir and the East Texas field is a giant pool. The chief forces causing oil to move are gas and water, and it is essential that the pressures be maintained at a level which will force the oil through wells to the surface. As the gas pressure is dissipated, it becomes necessary to put the well "on the pump" at great expense; and the sooner the gas from a field is exhausted, the more oil is irretrievably lost. Since the oil moves through the entire field, one operator can not only draw the oil from under his own surface area, but can also, if he is advantageously located, drain oil from the most distant parts of the reservoir. The practice of attempting to drain oil from under the surface holdings of others leads to offset wells and other wasteful practices; and this problem is increased by the fact that the surface rights are split up into many small tracts. There are approximately nine hundred operators in the East Texas field alone.

For these, and many other reasons based on geologic realities, each oil and gas field must be regulated as a unit for conservation purposes. . . . While there is no question of the constitutional power of the State to take appropriate action to protect the industry and protect the public interest, . . . the State's attempts to control the flow of oil and at the same time protect the interest of the many operators have from time to time been entangled in geological-legal problems of novel nature. . . .

To prevent "past, present, and imminent evils" in the production of natural gas, a statute was enacted "for the protection of public and private interests against such evils by prohibiting waste and compelling ratable production." The primary task of attempting adjustment of these diverse interests is delegated to the Railroad Commission which Texas has vested with "broad discretion" in administering the law.

The Commission, in cooperation with other oil producing states, has accepted State oil production quotas and has undertaken to translate the amount to be produced for the State as a whole into a specific amount for each field and for each well. These judgments are made with due regard for the factors of full utilization of the oil supply, market demand, and protection of the individual operators, as well as protection of the public interest. As an essential aspect of the control program, the State also regulates the spacing of wells. The legislature has disavowed a purpose of requiring that "the separately owned properties in any pool [should] be unitized under one management, control or ownership" and the Commission must thus work out the difficult spacing problem with due regard for whatever rights Texas recognizes in the separate owners to a share of the common reservoir. At the same time it must restrain waste, whether by excessive production or by the unwise dissipation of the gas and other geologic factors that cause the oil to flow.

Since 1919 the Commission has attempted to solve this problem by its Rule 37. The rule provides for certain minimum spacing between wells, but also allows exceptions where necessary "to prevent waste or to prevent the confiscation of property." The prevention of confiscation is based on the premises that, insofar as these privileges are compatible with the prevention of waste and the achievement of conservation, each surface owner should be permitted to withdraw the oil under his surface area, and that no one else can fairly be permitted to drain his oil away. Hence the Commission may protect his interest either by adjusting his amount of production upward, or by permitting him to drill additional wells. "By this method each person will be entitled to recover a quantity of oil and gas substantially equivalent in amount to the recoverable oil and gas under his land."

Additional wells may be required to prevent waste as has been noticed, where geologic circumstances require immediate drilling: "The term 'waste', as used in oil and gas Rule 37, undoubtedly means the ultimate loss of oil. If a substantial amount of oil will be saved by the drilling of a well that otherwise would ultimately be lost, the permit to drill such well may be justified under one of the exceptions provided in Rule 37 to prevent waste." . . .

The delusive simplicity with which these principles of exception to Rule 37 can be stated should not obscure the actual nonlegal complexities involved in their application. While the surface holder may, subject to qualifications noted, be entitled under current Texas law to the oil under his land, there can be no absolute certainty as to how much oil actually is present, . . . and since the waste and confiscation problems are as a matter of physical necessity so closely interrelated, decision of one of the questions necessarily involves recognition of the other. The sheer quantity of exception cases makes their disposition of great public importance. It is estimated that over two-thirds of the wells in the East Texas field exist as exceptions to the rule, and since each exception may provoke a conflict among the interested parties, the volume of litigation arising from the administration of the rule is considerable. The instant case arises from just such an exception. It is not peculiar that the state should be represented here by its Attorney General, for cases like this, involving "confiscation", are not mere isolated disputes between private parties. Aside from the general principles which may evolve from these proceedings, the physical facts are such that an additional permit may affect pressure on a well miles away. . . .

With full knowledge of the importance of the decisions of the Railroad Commission both to the State and to the oil operators, the Texas legislature has established a system of thorough judicial review by its own State courts. The Commission orders may be appealed to a State district court in Travis County, and are reviewed by a branch of the Court of Civil Appeals and by the State Supreme Court. While the constitutional power of the Commission to enforce Rule 37 or to make exceptions to it is seldom seriously challenged, . . . the validity of particular orders from the standpoint of statutory interpretation may present a serious problem, and a substantial number of such cases have been disposed of by the Texas courts which alone have the power to give definite answers to the questions of State law posed in these proceedings.

In describing the relation of the Texas court to the Commission no useful purpose will be served by attempting to label the court's position as legislative, Prentis v. Atlantic Coast Line Co., 211 U.S. 210, . . . or judicial, Bacon v. Rutland Railroad Co., 232 U.S. 134—suffice it to say that the Texas courts are working partners with the Railroad Commission in the business of creating a regulatory system for the oil industry. The Commission is charged with principal responsibility for fact finding and for policy making and the courts expressly disclaim the administrative responsibility, . . . but on the other hand, the orders of the Commission are tested for "reasonableness" by trial de novo before the court, . . . and the Court may on occasion make a careful analysis of all the facts of the case in reversing a Commission order. . . . The court has fully as much power as the Commission to determine particular cases, since after trial de novo it can either restrain the leaseholder from proceeding to drill, or, if the case is appropriate, can restrain the Commission from interfering with the leaseholder. The court may even formulate new standards for the Commission's administrative practice and suggest that the Commission adopt them. Thus, in the Shell Oil case . . . the Court took the responsibility of "laying down some standard to guide the Commission in the exercise of its discretion" in Rule 37 cases; and in Brown v. Humble Oil Co., . . . the Court explicitly suggested a revision in Rule 37.

To prevent the confusion of multiple review of the same general issues, the legislature provided for concentration of all direct review of the Commission's orders in the State district courts of Travis County. The Texas courts have authoritatively declared the purpose of this restriction. . . . To permit various state courts to pass upon the Commission's rules and orders, "would lead to intolerable confusion. If all district courts of this state had jurisdiction of such matters, different courts of equal dignity might reach different and conflicting conclusions as to the same rule. Manifestly, the jurisdictional provision under discussion was incorporated in the act for the express purpose of avoiding such confusion." . . . Concentration of judicial supervision of Railroad Commission orders permits the state courts, like the Railroad Commission itself, to acquire a specialized knowledge which is useful in shaping the policy of regulation of the ever-changing demands in this field. At the present time, less than ten per cent of these cases come before the federal district court.

The very "confusion" which the Texas legislature and Supreme Court feared might result from review by many state courts of the Railroad Commission's orders has resulted from the exercise of federal equity jurisdiction. As a practical matter, the federal courts can make small contribution to the well organized system of regulation and review which the Texas statutes provide. Texas courts can give fully as great relief, including temporary restraining orders, as the federal courts. Delay, misunderstanding of local law, and needless federal conflict with the State policy, are the inevitable product of this double system of review. The most striking example of misunderstanding has come where the federal court has flatly disagreed with the position later taken by a State court as to State law. . . . In those cases, the federal court attributed a given meaning to the state statute which went to the heart of the control program. The Court of Civil Appeals disagreed, but before ultimate review could be had either in Texas or here, the legislature amended its statutes so that the cases became moot. Had the Texas Civil Appeals decision come first, it would have been unnecessary to make the changes which were made in an effort to stay within the limit thought by the Governor of Texas to have been set by the tone of the federal court's opinion. The Texas legislature later changed the law back to its original state, as clear an example of waste motion as can be imagined. The federal court has been called upon constantly to determine whether the Railroad Commission has acted within the scope of statutory authority, while the important constitutional issues have, as the federal court has repeatedly said, been fairly well settled from the beginning. . . .

As has been noted the federal court cases have dealt primarily with the interpretation of state law, some of it state law fairly remote from oil and gas problems. The instant case raised a number of problems of no general significance on which a federal court can only try to ascertain state law. For example, we are asked to determine whether a previous Travis county district court decision makes this case res adjudicata and whether another case pending in Travis county deprived the Commission of jurisdiction to consider Burford's application. The existence of these problems throughout the oil regulatory field creates a further possibility of serious delay which can injure the conservation program, for under our decision in Railroad Commission v. Pullman Co., 312 U.S. 496, it may be necessary to stay federal action pending authoritative determination of the difficult state questions. . . . It is now argued that . . . the courts, whether federal or state, are required to review the Commission's order not for constitutional validity, but for compliance with a standard of "reasonableness" under the state statute which, it is said, is different from the constitutional standard of due process. . . .

These questions of regulation of the industry by the State administrative agency, whether involving gas or oil prorationing programs or Rule 37 cases, so clearly involves [sic] basic problems of Texas policy that equitable discretion should be exercised to give the Texas courts the first opportunity to consider them. "Few public interests have a higher claim upon the discretion of a federal chancellor than the avoidance of needless friction with state policies. . . . These cases reflect a doctrine of abstention appropriate to our federal system whereby the federal courts, 'exercising a wise discretion', restrain their authority because of 'scrupulous regard for the rightful independence of the state governments' and for the smooth working of the federal judiciary. . . . This use of equitable powers is a contribution of the courts in furthering the harmonious relation between state and federal authority without the need of rigorous congressional restriction of those powers." Railroad Commission v. Pullman Co., supra, 312 U.S. 500, 501.

The state provides a unified method for the formation of policy and determination of cases by the Commission and by the state courts. The judicial review of the Commission's decisions in the state courts is expeditious and adequate. Conflicts in the interpretation of state law, dangerous to the success of state policies, are almost certain to result from the intervention of the lower federal courts. On the other hand, if the state procedure is followed from the Commission to the State Supreme Court, ultimate review of the federal questions is fully preserved here. . . . Under such circumstances, a sound respect for the independence of state action requires the federal equity court to stay its hand.

The decision of the Circuit Court of Appeals is reversed and the judgment of the District Court dismissing the complaint is affirmed for the reasons here stated. . . .

MR. JUSTICE FRANKFURTER, dissenting.

To deny a suitor access to a federal district court under the circumstances of this case is to disregard a duty enjoined by Congress and made manifest by the whole history of the jurisdiction of the United States courts based upon diversity of citizenship between parties. . . .

Aside from the Johnson Act of May 14, 1934 [see 28 U.S.C. § 1342],[1] the only limitations upon the exercise of diversity jurisdiction . . . are, broadly speaking, those illustrated by Railroad Comm. v. Rowan & Nichols Oil Co., 310 U.S. 573, as amended in 311 U.S. 614, 615, Railroad Comm. v. Pullman Co., 312 U.S. 496, and City of Chicago v. Fieldcrest Dairies, 316 U.S. 168. In Rowan & Nichols the claim based upon state law was derived from a statute requiring proration on a "reasonable basis", and it was not clear from the decisions of the state courts whether such courts might exercise an independent judgment as to what was "reasonable". . . .

It is true that Texas law governing review of Commission orders under Rule 37 has not always been clear and certain, and that there may be parts of the statute and some of the Railroad Commission's Rules, with which we are not now concerned, which, like other legal materials, are not as clear as they might be. But, in a series of recent decisions, the Supreme Court of Texas has not only given precision to the concepts of "waste" and "confiscation of property" employed in Rule 37, it has also defined with clarity the scope of judicial review of Commission action. . . .

[Moreover, said Justice Frankfurter, the State had not attempted to preclude the exercise of federal jurisdiction, for the provision permitting suit "in a court of competent jurisdiction in Travis County, Texas," in a comparable context, had been construed in Reagan v. Farmers' Loan & Trust Co., 154 U.S. 362 (1894), to allow federal suit.]

And so, the case really reduces itself to this: in the actual application of the standards governing judicial review of Commission orders allowing exceptions under Rule 37—standards which today have been authoritatively and precisely defined—a different result may be obtained if suit is brought in the federal rather than the state courts. . . . It is the essence of diversity jurisdiction that federal judges and juries should pass on asserted claims because the result might be different if they were decided by a state court. There may be excellent reasons why Congress should abolish diversity jurisdiction. But, with all deference, it is not a defensible ground for having this Court by indirection abrogate diversity jurisdiction. . . .

1. . . . Since the order under review in this case did not in any way affect rates chargeable by any public utility, the Johnson Act is inapplicable.

Notes on Federal Courts and State Administrative Agencies

(1) To what extent may a federal court, on the basis of diverse citizenship, grant relief in the first instance that state law says only its administrative agency may give? Because of the Supremacy Clause, state law cannot of its own force limit federal jurisdiction.[1] If the relief sought is not judicial, there is no "civil action" within § 1332: No one would be likely to ask a federal court to formulate regulations, for example, and the setting of railroad rates has been held legislative in the related context of exhausting administrative remedies, see *Prentis v. Atlantic Coast Line*, infra note 4.[2] But suppose a State has set up a quasi-judicial procedure for workers' compensation, for restraining violations of regulatory laws, or for variances or review of permit denials in zoning or pollution cases. See Tool & Die Makers Lodge No. 78 v. General Electric Co., 170 F.Supp. 945, 950 (E.D.Wis. 1959), allowing removal of a labor-contract dispute that had been filed before the Wisconsin Employment Relations Board:

> The question of whether a proceeding may be regarded as an action in a State court within the meaning of the statute is determined by reference to the procedures and functions of the State tribunal rather than the name by which the tribunal is designated. . . . State laws . . . which depart from traditional and customary usages and procedures, . . . cannot operate to defeat the right of a litigant otherwise entitled to have his cause heard in Federal court.

Should a federal court in such a case defer to a state's interest in providing an exclusive uniform, expeditious, and expert administration of the law? Does *Burford* lend support to the denial of jurisdiction in such cases?

In cases confronting federal courts with issues within the special knowledge of *federal* administrative agencies, the Supreme Court has developed a doctrine of "primary jurisdiction," somewhat analogous to abstention, under which the technical question is referred to the agency for decision. E.g., United States v. Western Pacific Railroad Co., 352 U.S. 59 (1956).[3] Can this doctrine be employed in connection with state agencies?

1. See Chicago & N.W. Railway Co. v. Whitton's Administrator, 80 U.S. (13 Wall.) 270, 286 (1872), upholding diversity jurisdiction over a wrongful-death action under a state statute purporting to require the action to be brought in a state court; Markham v. City of Newport News, 292 F.2d 711, 718 (4th Cir. 1961), holding a state may not limit state-law actions for municipal torts to state courts even after *Erie Railroad Co. v. Tompkins*, supra p. 327.

2. The Supreme Court has also held that a proceeding to reduce a tax assessment could not be removed from a county "court" whose functions were said to be "as purely administrative as are those of the county assessors in making the original assessment," Upshur County v. Rich, 135 U.S. 467, 477 (1890). Cf. *Federal Radio Commission v. General Electric Co.*, supra p. 16, as to "administrative" duties that fall outside Article III.

3. Primary jurisdiction shares with the requirement that administrative remedies be exhausted the purpose of obtaining the views of an agency on matters within its competence. But exhaustion is a prerequisite to judicial review of agency action, while primary jurisdiction is invoked in actions not challenging agency action at all. See 352 U.S. at 63–65. *Western Pacific* itself was an action to collect unpaid freight charges; the issue of the meaning of the applicable tariff was referred to the ICC.

(2) For a variety of reasons, litigants seem seldom to ask federal courts to take action that States have entrusted to administrative agencies. In contrast, federal courts are often asked to *review* state administrative action. As Justice Frankfurter pointed out in his dissent in *Burford,* the Johnson Act of 1934, 28 U.S.C. § 1342, severely limits the authority of federal courts to enjoin or restrain state administrative orders "affecting rates chargeable by a public utility" when the state courts afford "a plain, speedy and efficient remedy." [4] *Burford* is the best known case in which the Supreme Court went beyond the Johnson Act to refuse to hear a challenge to a state administrative order not involving public utility rates on the basis of "equitable discretion."

Equitable discretion was invoked once again in Alabama Public Service Commission v. Southern Railway Co., 341 U.S. 341 (1951), where the railroad attacked as confiscatory a Commission order refusing to allow discontinuance of two passenger trains between Tuscumbia, Alabama, and Chattanooga, Tennessee, "a distance of approximately 145 miles mainly within Alabama." Conceding that the case did not require "construction of a state statute so ill-defined that a federal court should hold the case pending a definitive construction of that statute in the state courts," the Court ordered the suit dismissed:

> A federal court has been asked to intervene in resolving the essentially local problem of balancing the loss to the railroad from continued operation of trains Nos. 7 and 8 with the public need for that service in Tuscambia, Decatur, Huntsville, Scottsboro, and the other Alabama communities directly affected. . . . Statutory appeal from an order of the Commission is an integral part of the regulatory process under the Alabama Code. Appeals, concentrated in one circuit court, are "supervisory in character." . . . As adequate state court review of an administrative order based upon predominantly local factors is available to appellee, intervention of a federal court is not necessary for the protection of federal rights.

Justice Frankfurter, joined by Justice Jackson, concurred in the order of dismissal on the ground that the constitutional claim was insubstantial but protested that the Court's reasoning was "in plain disregard of congressional legislation." Not only was there concededly "no State statute to construe"; even *Burford* was no authority for the Court's argument, but only an example of the principle that the court may "decline to consider a case which involves a specialized aspect of a complicated system of local law outside the normal competence of a federal court," while "the claim that is made here is within the easy grasp of federal judges."

4. Cf. 28 U.S.C. § 1341, discussed at pp. 506–13 below, which imposes similar limits on federal interference with state taxes. The Johnson Act bars a federal remedy only if federal jurisdiction "is based solely on diversity of citizenship or repugnance . . . to the Federal Constitution," the order "does not interfere with interstate commerce," and the order was made "after reasonable notice and hearing." The first of these requirements has been held to permit a federal court to enjoin a rate order preempted by federal statute, International Brotherhood of Electrical Workers v. Public Service Commission, 614 F.2d 206, 209–11 (9th Cir.1980). What is the justification for these exceptions?

After *Burford* and *Alabama*, how can a federal court review a school board's order refusing to desegregate a public school, or an administrator's denial of welfare benefits?

See also New Orleans Public Service, Inc. v. Council of City of New Orleans, 109 S.Ct. 2506 (1989), holding *Burford* inapplicable although the suit challenged an order setting rates for the sale of electric power. Since the "primary claim" that the order on its face was preempted by federal law could be determined with "no inquiry beyond the four corners of the Council's rate order," said Justice Scalia, its resolution "would not unduly intrude into the processes of state government or undermine the State's ability to maintain desired uniformity." Although analysis of a further claim "requires an inquiry into industry practice, wholesale rates, and power availability" and thus "demands some level of industry-specific expertise," the issue related to "wholesale electricity," which "is not bought and sold within a predominantly local market"; thus federal resolution of the claim "does *not* demand significant familiarity with, and will not disrupt state resolution of, distinctively local facts or policies." Does *Alabama* survive this decision?[5]

(3) The Court in both *Burford* and *Alabama* ordered the complaint dismissed, not held pending state-court adjudication, and Justice Brennan in *England* expressly excepted cases like *Burford* and *Alabama* from his principle that a litigant may return after the state decision and obtain a federal determination of his federal claim. Why? Is it appropriate to say that *Burford* and *Alabama* "are not . . . abstention cases at all"? Liebenthal, p. 496 supra, 18 Case W.Res.L.Rev. 157, 159 (1966). Is it helpful?

(4) The question in *Burford* and *Alabama* was whether federal courts would review state administrative action at all. In Patsy v. Board of Regents, 457 U.S. 496 (1982), where the plaintiff alleged that a state university had denied her employment opportunities on grounds of race and sex, the question was the timing of review that nobody doubted the federal court could ultimately afford.

In a number of early decisions the Supreme Court had refused to entertain challenges to state administrative action before the administrative process was over. It was to be presumed, the Court said, that administrators would act within constitutional limits; it would be "time enough to consider what may be done to prevent it when they attempt to go beyond." McChord v. Louisville & N. R.R., 183 U.S. 483, 495–96 (1902). The cost of participating in an administrative proceeding, the Court added in Petroleum Exploration, Inc. v. Public Service Commission, 304 U.S. 209, 220–21 (1938), was "not the sort of irreparable injury against which equity protects." Awaiting completion of the state administrative process serves all the policies that underlie the requirement that a litigant exhaust

5. Citing *Burford* and *Kaiser Steel Corp. v. W.S. Ranch Co.*, p. 495 supra, the ALI proposed to extend § 1342 to actions challenging state orders affecting "the conservation, production, or use of minerals, water, or other like resource of the State," because of "the strong state interest in these natural resources, the complex regulatory systems commonly provided for them by the states, and the perplexities, both geological and economic, that controversies as to such resources present." What would the amendment do to *Alabama?*

federal administrative remedies before going to court, p. 62 supra. Indeed the Court once declared that the exhaustion rule was "of especial force when resort is had to the federal courts to restrain the action of state officers" because of the additional factor of federalism. Natural Gas Pipeline Co. v. Slattery, 302 U.S. 300 (1937).[6]

Despite these precedents, the Court over two dissents held in *Patsy* that the rule requiring exhaustion of administrative remedies was inapplicable to actions brought under 42 U.S.C. § 1983: The very basis of that provision was that state agencies could not be trusted to provide adequate remedies for the infringement of federal rights.[7] Does this distinguish § 1983 cases from any others within federal jurisdiction? Is *Patsy* consistent with the numerous decisions (see p. 494 supra) approving *Pullman* abstention in § 1983 cases? Do you really think Congress meant to allow a state employee to get a federal court order against his immediate superior without asking the department head to correct the problem?

FAIR ASSESSMENT IN REAL ESTATE ASS'N, INC. v. McNARY

454 U.S. 100 (1981).

JUSTICE REHNQUIST delivered the opinion of the Court.

In this action we are required to reconcile two somewhat intermittent and conflicting lines of authority as to whether a damages action may be brought under 42 U.S.C. § 1983 to redress the allegedly unconstitutional administration of a state tax system. The United States District Court for the Eastern District of Missouri held that such suits were barred by both 28 U.S.C. § 1341 (the Tax Injunction Act) and the principle of comity, and the Court of Appeals for the Eighth Circuit affirmed by an equally divided court sitting en banc. We granted certiorari to resolve a conflict among the Courts of Appeals, and we now affirm. . . .

This Court, even before the enactment of § 1983, recognized the important and sensitive nature of state tax systems and the need for federal-court restraint when deciding cases that affect such systems.

6. Prentis v. Atlantic Coast Line Co., 211 U.S. 210 (1908), carried this principle one step further. When the State allowed its courts in reviewing rate orders to "substitute such order as in its opinion the commission should have made," the appeal was a part of the rulemaking process and must be exhausted before attacking the order in federal court: "Litigation cannot arise until the moment of legislation is past." The Court made clear in Bacon v. Rutland R.R., 232 U.S. 134 (1914), however, that once the administrative process was completed there was no need to pursue truly judicial remedies in state court. Do you see why? See Friendly, Federal Jurisdiction: A General View 101 (1973): "[I]f the federal claims have been raised in a state court and decided against plaintiff on the merits, such a judgment would be res judicata and bar a subsequent federal suit on the same issue." See also Oklahoma Natural Gas Co. v. Russell, 261 U.S. 290 (1923), holding that exhaustion even of "legislative" review of the *Prentis* variety was unnecessary when the state court refused to stay the challenged order during pendency of the proceeding: "The plaintiffs will have no adequate remedy for what they may have lost before the Court shall have acted."

7. The Court also argued that a "judicially imposed exhaustion requirement would be inconsistent with" 42 U.S.C. § 1997e, which enacted a narrow exhaustion rule respecting claims by state prisoners. What is to be said for this argument?

As Justice Field wrote for the Court shortly before the enactment of § 1983:

> "It is upon taxation that the several States chiefly rely to obtain the means to carry on their respective governments, and it is of the utmost importance to all of them that the modes adopted to enforce the taxes levied should be interfered with as little as possible. Any delay in the proceedings of the officers, upon whom the duty is devolved of collecting the taxes, may derange the operations of government, and thereby cause serious detriment to the public." Dows v. Chicago, 78 U.S. (11 Wall.) 108, 110 (1871).

After this Court conclusively decided [in *Ex parte Young*] that federal courts *may* enjoin state officers from enforcing an unconstitutional state law, . . . Congress also recognized that the autonomy and fiscal stability of the States survive best when state tax systems are not subject to scrutiny in federal courts. Thus, in 1937 Congress provided:

> "The district courts shall not enjoin, suspend or restrain the assessment, levy or collection of any tax under State law where a plain, speedy and efficient remedy may be had in the courts of such State." 28 U.S.C. § 1341. . . .

Contrasted with this statute and line of cases . . . is the doctrine originating in Monroe v. Pape [365 U.S. 167 (1961),] that comity does not apply where § 1983 is involved, and that a litigant challenging the constitutionality of any state action may proceed directly to federal court. With this divergence of views in mind, we turn now to the facts of this case, a § 1983 challenge to the administration of state tax laws which implicates both lines of authority. We hold that at least as to such actions, which is all we need decide here, the principle of comity controls. . . .

Petitioner Fair Assessment in Real Estate is a non-profit corporation formed by taxpayers in St. Louis County ("County") to promote equitable enforcement of property tax laws in Missouri. Petitioners J. David and Lynn F. Cassilly own real property with recent improvements in the County. Petitioners filed suit under § 1983 alleging that respondents, the County's Tax Assessors, Supervisors, and Director of Revenue, and three members of the Missouri State Tax Commission, had deprived them of equal protection and due process of law by unequal taxation of real property. . . .

The Cassillys sought actual damages in the amount of overassessments from 1975 to 1979, and punitive damages of $75,000.00 from each respondent. Petitioner Fair Assessment sought actual damages in the amount of expenses incurred in efforts to obtain equitable property assessments for its members. . . . Because we decide today that the principle of comity bars federal courts from granting damages relief in such cases, we do not decide whether the Act, standing alone, would require such a result.[4] . . .

4. . . . We need not decide in this case whether the comity spoken of would also bar a claim under § 1983 which requires no scrutiny whatever of state tax assess-

Prior to enactment of § 1341, virtually all federal cases challenging state taxation sought equitable relief. Consequently, federal court restraint in state tax matters was based upon the traditional doctrine that courts of equity will stay their hand when remedies at law are plain, adequate, and complete. . . . Even with this basis in equity law, these cases recognized that the doctrine of equitable restraint was of "notable application," . . . and carried "peculiar force," . . . in suits challenging the constitutionality of state tax laws. Such restraint was particularly appropriate because of the delicate balance between the federal authority and state governments, and the concomitant respect that should be accorded state tax laws in federal court. . . . Neither the legislative history of the Act nor that of its precursor, 28 U.S.C. § 1342, suggests that Congress intended that federal court deference in state tax matters be limited to the actions enumerated in those sections. . . . Thus, the principle of comity which predated the Act was not restricted by its passage. . . .

The post-Act vitality of the comity principle is perhaps best demonstrated by our decision in Great Lakes Dredge & Dock Co. v. Huffman, [319 U.S. 293 (1943)]. Several Louisiana taxpayers brought an action in federal district court seeking a declaratory judgment that the state tax law as applied to them was unconstitutional and void. Although § 1341 was raised as a possible bar to the suit, as it has been raised in this case, "we [found] it unnecessary to inquire whether the words of the statute may be so construed as to prohibit a declaration by federal courts concerning the invalidity of a state tax law." . . . Instead, "we [were] of the opinion that those considerations which have led federal courts of equity to refuse to enjoin the collection of state taxes, save in exceptional cases, require[d] a like restraint in the use of the declaratory judgment procedure." . . . The focus was not on the specific form of relief requested, but on the fact that "in every practical respect [it] operate[d] to suspend collection of the state taxes until the litigation [was] ended." . . . As will be seen below, the relief sought in this case would have a similarly disruptive effect. . . .

In arguments primarily addressed to the applicability of the Act, petitioners contend that damages actions are inherently less disruptive of state tax systems than injunctions or declaratory judgments, and therefore should not be barred by prior decisions of this Court. Petitioners emphasize that their § 1983 claim seeks recovery from individual state officers, not from state coffers, and that the doctrine of qualified immunity will protect such officers' good faith actions and will thus avoid chilling their administration of the Missouri tax scheme.

We disagree. Petitioners will not recover damages under § 1983 unless a district court first determines that respondents' administration of the County tax system violated petitioners' constitutional rights. In

ment practices, such as a facial attack on tax laws colorably claimed to be discriminatory as to race.

effect, the district court must first enter a declaratory judgment like that barred in *Great Lakes*. We are convinced that such a determination would be fully as intrusive as the equitable actions that are barred by principles of comity. Moreover, the intrusiveness of such § 1983 actions would be exacerbated by the nonexhaustion doctrine of *Monroe v. Pape*, supra. Taxpayers such as petitioners would be able to invoke federal judgments without first permitting the State to rectify any alleged impropriety.

In addition to the intrusiveness of the judgment, the very maintenance of the suit itself would intrude on the enforcement of the state scheme. As the District Court in this case stated:

> "To allow such suits would cause disruption of the states' revenue collection systems equal to that caused by anticipatory relief. State tax collection officials could be summoned into federal court to defend their assessments against claims for refunds as well as prayers for punitive damages, merely on the assertion that the tax collected was willfully and maliciously discriminatory against a certain type of property. Allowance of such claims would result in this Court being a source of appellate review of all state property tax classifications."
>
> . . .

This intrusion, although undoubtedly present in every § 1983 claim, is particularly highlighted by the facts of this case. Defendants are not one or two isolated administrators, but virtually every key tax official in St. Louis County. They include the County executive, the Director of Revenue, the Tax Assessor, and three supervising members of the State Tax Commission. In addition, the actions challenged in the complaint—unequal assessment of new and old property and retaliatory assessment of property belonging to those who successfully appeal to the Board of Equalization—may well be the result of policies or practicalities beyond the control of any individual officer. For example, failure annually to reassess old property may well result from a practical allocation of limited resources. In addition, according to respondents' attorney at oral argument, Missouri law requires that all property, including property which belongs to those who successfully appeal to the Board of Equalization, be assessed at 33⅓% of market value. Thus, a judicial determination of official liability for the acts complained of, even though necessarily based upon a finding of bad faith, would have an undeniable chilling effect upon the actions of all County officers governed by the same practicalities or required to implement the same policies. There is little doubt that such officials, faced with the prospect of personal liability to numerous taxpayers, not to mention the assessment of attorney's fees under 42 U.S.C. § 1988, would promptly cease the conduct found to have infringed petitioners' constitutional rights, whether or not those officials were acting in good faith. In short, petitioners action would "in every practical sense operate to suspend collection of the state taxes . . .," *Great Lakes*, . . . a form of federal court interference previously rejected by this Court on principles of federalism. . . .

Therefore, despite the ready access to federal courts provided by *Monroe* and its progeny, we hold that taxpayers are barred by the principle of comity from asserting § 1983 actions against the validity of state tax systems in federal courts. Such taxpayers must seek protection of their federal rights by state remedies, provided of course that those remedies are plain, adequate, and complete,[8] and may ultimately seek review of the state decisions in this Court. . . .

The adequacy of available Missouri remedies is not at issue in this case. The District Court expressly found "that [petitioners] have means to rectify what they consider an unjust situation through the state's own processes," . . . and petitioners do not contest this finding. In addition, the Missouri Supreme Court has expressly held that plaintiffs such as petitioners may assert a § 1983 claim in state court. . . .

Affirmed.

JUSTICE BRENNAN, with whom JUSTICE MARSHALL, JUSTICE STEVENS, and JUSTICE O'CONNOR join, concurring in the judgment.

I agree that the judgment of the district court dismissing petitioners' complaint should be affirmed. But I arrive at that conclusion by a different route for I cannot agree that this case, and the jurisdiction of the federal courts over an action for damages brought pursuant to express congressional authority, is to be governed by applying a "principle of comity" grounded solely on this Court's notion of an appropriate division of responsibility between the federal and state judicial systems. Subject only to constitutional constraints, it is exclusively Congress' responsibility to determine the jurisdiction of the federal courts. Federal courts have historically acted within their assigned jurisdiction in accordance with established principles respecting the prudent exercise of equitable power. But this practice lends no credence to the authority which the Court asserts today to renounce jurisdiction over an entire class of damages actions brought pursuant to 42 U.S.C. § 1983. . . .

Dismissal of the suit [in *Great Lakes*] was permissible only because the claim for declaratory relief was designed to gain "an adjudication of rights in anticipation of their threatened infringement." Such a suit, precisely like one for an injunction, would "in every practical respect operate to suspend collection of the state taxes until the litigation ended." . . . No similar concern is raised by the present case.

[Nevertheless Justice Brennan concluded that the action should be dismissed for failure to exhaust administrative remedies: Although exhaustion was not generally required in § 1983 cases (see *Patsy v. Board of Regents*, p. 505 supra), exhaustion in tax cases was consonant with the purpose of § 1341 to assure "that federal courts exercise at

8. We discern no significant difference, for purposes of the principles recognized in this case, between remedies which are "plain, adequate, and complete," as that phrase has been used in articulating the doctrine of equitable restraint, and those which are "plain, speedy, and efficient," within the meaning of the Tax Injunction Act. . . .

least the same restraint in dealing with questions of state tax administration as the courts of the State."]

Notes on Federal Court Remedies for Unlawful Taxes

(1) In California v. Grace Brethren Church, 457 U.S. 393, 408 (1982), the Court over two dissents held that a federal declaratory judgment respecting the validity of a state tax—which as *McNary* reports had been forbidden on comity grounds in *Great Lakes Dredge & Dock Co. v. Huffman*—was also precluded by § 1341 itself:

> [B]ecause there is little practical difference between injunctive and declaratory relief, we would be hard pressed to conclude that Congress intended to prohibit taxpayers from seeking one form of anticipatory relief . . . while permitting them to seek another, thereby defeating the principal purpose of the Tax Injunction Act: "to limit drastically federal district court jurisdiction to interfere with so important a local concern as the collection of taxes." [1]

Was *McNary* right in concluding that a damage award also had an effect on state tax collection similar to that of an injunction? Does that mean a damage action is one to "enjoin, suspend or restrain" state taxes under § 1341? What about an action seeking a refund of taxes illegally collected? See United Gas Pipe Line Co. v. Whitman, 595 F.2d 323 (5th Cir.1979), holding a refund action barred by § 1341.[2]

(2) Is it clear after *McNary* that § 1341 itself applies to cases brought under § 1983? Would that conclusion be consistent with the decision in *Patsy v. Board of Regents,* p. 505 supra, that the policy of § 1983 forbids application of the normal rule requiring exhaustion of administrative remedies? Can *McNary* itself be squared with *Patsy?* Can Justice Brennan's concurring opinion in *McNary?*

(3) In Wells v. Malloy, 510 F.2d 74 (2d Cir. 1975), the plaintiff failed to pay a tax on the purchase and use of a vehicle, and as a result the State took away his driver's license. Alleging inability to pay and invoking the Equal Protection Clause, he sued to get the license back. The court held § 1341 not a bar because the plaintiff was not seeking to restrain the "assessment, levy or collection" of the tax:

> [D]oubtless the state believed that the sanction of revocation of a driver's license, like the older method of imprisonment for debt, might cause some money to be produced from somewhere, despite a taxpay-

1. Cf. *Samuels v. Mackell,* p. 539 infra, applying the judicial rule limiting injunctive interference with pending state proceedings to a suit for declaratory judgment; *Kennedy v. Mendoza–Martinez,* infra p. 570, holding a requirement that three judges be convened before enjoining enforcement of a state statute inapplicable to a declaratory judgment.

2. The Ninth Circuit has held that the statute does not bar a suit by the State for a declaration that its tax is consistent with federal law:

> Section 1341 was designed to eliminate interference by federal courts in state internal economy and taxation matters. . . . This policy would not be served by applying the statute to bar a state itself from invoking the jurisdiction of the federal courts.

Arizona v. Atchison, Topeka & Santa Fe Railroad Co., 656 F.2d 398 (9th Cir. 1981). Does this decision survive *McNary*?

er's protest that he has none. "Collection," of course, could be read broadly to include anything that a state has determined to be a likely method to securing payment . . . . [H]owever, . . . [t]he context and the legislative history . . . lead us to conclude that, in speaking of "collection," Congress was referring to methods similar to assessment and levy, *e.g.*, distress or execution, . . . that would produce money or other property directly, rather than indirectly through a more general use of coercive power.

(4) Is it clear what constitutes a "tax under State law"? See Robinson Protective Alarm Co. v. City of Philadelphia, 581 F.2d 371 (3d Cir. 1978), which held § 1341 applicable to an exaction of 5% of gross earnings attributable to the "privilege" of running signal wires under city streets. In another context the state Supreme Court had held this change was "neither a tax nor a license fee" but an "an annual rental" for "the use of space . . . ." The Third Circuit found this decision irrelevant: Federal law determined what a "tax" was for purposes of § 1341, and the ordinance in question was "a revenue raising measure collected annually in a manner similar to other gross receipts levies." See also Schneider Transport, Inc. v. Cattanach, 657 F.2d 128, 132 (7th Cir. 1981), holding § 1341 barred a suit to enjoin enforcement of truck-registration fees because they were "imposed for revenue-raising purposes," and contrasting "permit fees, whose purpose is to identify authorized vehicles for regulatory purposes. . . ." [3]

What about a tax imposed by Puerto Rico or by the District of Columbia?

(5) What constitutes a "plain, speedy, and efficient" state remedy within the meaning of § 1341? In Rosewell v. LaSalle National Bank, 450 U.S. 503 (1981), the plaintiff argued that a suit for refund of taxes paid under protest was not "plain, speedy or efficient" because there was no provision for interest if the suit was successful, and the average time between payment and receipt of a refund was two years.

The Court held a federal suit barred by § 1341. Even before that section became law, the Court had "found adequate two state refund remedies that apparently did not pay interest," although the issue had not been expressly addressed. The House and Senate Reports on the Act had suggested that refund actions would suffice to bar federal intervention, and it was "only common sense to presume that Congress was also aware that some of these same States did not pay interest on their refunds." Moreover, § 1341 had been enacted in order to restrict the authority that federal courts had exercised under preexisting law; a state remedy need not be "adequate" under general equitable principles in order to be "plain, speedy and efficient" under § 1341. Under the precedents a remedy was not "plain" if its availability was uncertain, not "efficient" if it "would require a multiplicity of suits," and not "speedy" if it took too long in comparison with "the usual time for

3. Cf. Massachusetts v. United States, 435 U.S. 444 (1978), upholding a federal registration tax on airplanes used by state police, despite constitutional limits on federal power to tax States, essentially on the ground the fee was a user charge for services rendered.

similar litigation." Two years was a typical delay for cases even in federal courts, and the unavilability of interest was immaterial.

Justice Stevens, joined by Stewart, Marshall, and Powell, dissented vehemently. "Plain, speedy and efficient" was another way of requiring that the state remedy be adequate; the statute was designed to limit preexisting federal authority by deferring to equitable as well as legal state remedies, not to permit irreparable harm. "[I]f a county may collect 3 to 10 times the amount of tax that a citizen owes and use the excess for two years without paying any interest, the value of that which is ultimately returned is not complete or adequate compensation for the value of what was unjustly taken."

(6) In Coon v. Teasdale, 567 F.2d 820, 822 (8th Cir. 1977), the plaintiffs argued that the state remedy was not "plain, speedy, and efficient" because "Missouri courts have upheld the constitutionality of these statutes in earlier cases and therefore plaintiffs' state court challenge would be futile." The court disagreed: "[T]he mere allegation of unlikelihood of success in the state court does not render the state remedy inadequate for purposes of 28 U.S.C. § 1341." Cf. *Hicks v. Miranda*, infra p. 539 (*Younger* doctrine); *Schlesinger v. Councilman*, infra p. 536 (exhaustion of military remedies); *Layton v. Carson*, infra p. 641 (habeas corpus). After *Rosewell*, is a state remedy "plain, speedy, and efficient" if it fails to allow class actions?

(7) The district court in *Rosewell*, while holding § 1341 barred relief on the merits, issued an injunction to preserve the status quo pending appeal. Was that consistent with the statute? Cf. *Baines v. City of Danville*, p. 507 supra (anti-injunction provision of § 2283).

(8) In Department of Employment v. United States, 385 U.S. 355 (1966), the Supreme Court held, "in accord with an unbroken line of [lower court] authority and convincing evidence of legislative purpose," that § 1341 does not apply to suits brought by the United States. Cf. *Leiter Minerals, Inc. v. United States*, supra p. 493 (abstention) and infra p. 527 (§ 2283).

(9) Closely analogous to § 1341 is 26 U.S.C. § 7421(a), which forbids injunctions "restraining the assessment or collection of any [federal] tax." In Miller v. Standard Nut Margarine Co., 284 U.S. 498, 509 (1932), the Court held this statute merely codified the equity principle that tax collection would not be enjoined absent "special and extraordinary circumstances sufficient to bring the case within some acknowledged head of equity jurisdiction." Retreating from this disemboweling view in Enochs v. Williams Packing & Nav. Co., 370 U.S. 1, 7 (1962), the Court added in dictum that the statute still did not mean what it said: An injunction could issue "if it is clear that under no circumstances could the Government ultimately prevail." In Commissioner v. Shapiro, 424 U.S. 614, 627 (1976), where the record was inadequate to show whether or not the Government had a chance of success, the Court affirmed an order reversing the denial of an injunction and remanding for examination of "the facts on which the Government bases its claim": "[I]t is obvious that the Court [in *Enochs*] . . . intended some disclosure by the Government."

This conclusion was buttressed by the Court's fear that otherwise the statute might offend due process by depriving the taxpayer of his property without a timely hearing, citing Fuentes v. Shevin, 407 U.S. 67 (1972). The constitutional concern of the Court in *Shapiro* has led one observant commentator to the conclusion that a state procedure providing for challenging taxes only by suit for refund, which the *Great Lakes* case in note 1 found adequate to preclude federal jurisdiction, offends due process because it fails to provide a prompt post-deprivation hearing. Comment, Procedural Due Process in Tax Collection: An Opportunity for a Prompt Postdeprivation Hearing, 44 U.Chi.L.Rev. 594 (1977). Does *Rosewell* hold the contrary? Does the *Enochs* dictum apply to § 1341?

See also Federal Energy Adm'n v. Algonquin SNG, Inc., 426 U.S. 548 (1976), holding that § 7421 applies only to taxes under the Internal Revenue Code, of which it is a part; 28 U.S.C. § 2201, prohibiting declaratory judgments "involving federal taxes."

SECTION 3. INJUNCTIONS AGAINST SUIT

MITCHUM v. FOSTER

407 U.S. 225 (1972).

MR. JUSTICE STEWART delivered the opinion of the Court.

The federal anti-injunction statute provides that a federal court "may not grant an injunction to stay proceedings in a State court except as expressly authorized by Act of Congress, or where necessary in aid of its jurisdiction, or to protect or effectuate its judgments."[1] An Act of Congress, 42 U.S.C. § 1983, expressly authorizes a "suit in equity" to redress "the deprivation," under color of state law, "of any rights, privileges, or immunities secured by the Constitution. . . ."[2] The question before us is whether this "Act of Congress" comes within the "expressly authorized" exception of the anti-injunction statute so as to permit a federal court in a § 1983 suit to grant an injunction to stay a proceeding pending in a state court. This question, which has divided the federal courts, has lurked in the background of many of our recent cases, but we have not until today explicitly decided it.

I

The prosecuting attorney of Bay County, Florida, brought a proceeding in a Florida court to close down the appellant's bookstore as a public nuisance under the claimed authority of Florida law. The state court entered a preliminary order prohibiting continued operation of the bookstore. After further inconclusive proceedings in the state

1. 28 U.S.C. § 2283.

2. The statute provides in full: "Every person who, under color of any statute, ordinance, regulation, custom, or usage, of any State or Territory, subjects, or causes to be subjected, any citizen of the United States or other person within the jurisdiction thereof to the deprivation of any rights, privileges, or immunities secured by the Constitution and laws, shall be liable to the party injured in an action at law, suit in equity, or other proper proceeding for redress."

courts, the appellant filed a complaint in the United States District Court for the Northern District of Florida, alleging that the actions of the state judicial and law enforcement officials were depriving him of rights protected by the First and Fourteenth Amendments. Relying upon 42 U.S.C. § 1983, he asked for injunctive and declaratory relief against the state court proceedings, on the ground that Florida laws were being unconstitutionally applied by the state court so as to cause him great and irreparable harm. . . .

II

In denying injunctive relief, the District Court relied on this Court's decision in Atlantic Coast Line R. Co. v. Brotherhood of Locomotive Engineers, 398 U.S. 281. The *Atlantic Coast Line* case did not deal with the "expressly authorized" exception of the anti-injunction statute, but the Court's opinion in that case does bring into sharp focus the critical importance of the question now before us. For in that case we expressly rejected the view that the anti-injunction statute merely states a flexible doctrine of comity, and made clear that the statute imposes an absolute ban upon the issuance of a federal injunction against a pending state court proceeding, in the absence of one of the recognized exceptions. . . .

It follows, in the present context, that if 42 U.S.C. § 1983 is not within the "expressly authorized" exception of the anti-injunction statute, then a federal equity court is wholly without power to grant any relief in a § 1983 suit seeking to stay a state court proceeding . . ., whether civil or criminal, and regardless of how extraordinary the particular circumstances may be.

Last Term, in Younger v. Harris, 401 U.S. 37 and its companion cases, the Court dealt at length with the subject of federal judicial intervention in pending state criminal prosecutions. In *Younger* a three-judge federal district court in a § 1983 action had enjoined a criminal prosecution pending in a California court. In asking us to reverse that judgment, the appellant argued that the injunction was in violation of the federal anti-injunction statute. . . . But the Court carefully eschewed any reliance on the statute in reversing the judgment, basing its decision instead upon what the Court called "Our Federalism"—upon "the national policy forbidding federal courts to stay or enjoin pending state court proceedings except under special circumstances." . . . At the same time . . . the Court clearly left room for federal injunctive intervention in a pending state court prosecution in certain exceptional circumstances—where irreparable injury is "both great and immediate". . . .

While the Court in *Younger* and its companion cases expressly disavowed deciding the question now before us—whether § 1983 comes within the "expressly authorized" exception of the anti-injunction statute, 401 U.S., at 54, it is evident that our decisions in those cases cannot be disregarded in deciding this question. In the first place, if § 1983 is not within the statutory exception, then the anti-injunction statute would have absolutely barred the injunction issued in *Younger*, as the appellant in that case argued, and there would have been no occasion whatever for the Court to decide that case upon the "policy" ground of "Our Federalism." Secondly, if § 1983 is not within the "expressly authorized" exception of the anti-injunction statute, then we must overrule *Younger* and its companion cases insofar as they recognized the permissibility of injunctive relief against pending criminal prosecutions in certain limited and exceptional circumstances. For, under the doctrine of *Atlantic Coast Line*, the anti-injunction statute would, in a § 1983 case, then be an "absolute prohibition" against federal equity intervention in a pending state criminal *or* civil proceeding—under any circumstances whatever. . . .

III

The anti-injunction statute goes back almost to the beginnings of our history as a Nation. In 1793 Congress enacted a law providing that no "writ of injunction be granted [by any federal court] to stay proceedings in any court of a state. . . ." Act of March 2, 1793; 1 Stat. 335. The precise origins of the legislation are shrouded in obscurity, but the consistent understanding has been that its basic purpose is to prevent "needless friction between state and federal courts." Oklahoma Packing Co. v. Gas Co., 309 U.S. 4, 9. The law remained unchanged until 1875, when it was amended to permit a federal court to stay state court proceedings that interfered with the administration of a federal bankruptcy proceeding.[11] The present wording of the legislation was adopted with the enactment of Title 28 of the United States Code in 1948.

Despite the seemingly uncompromising language of the anti-injunction statute prior to 1948, the Court soon recognized that exceptions must be made to its blanket prohibition if the import and purpose of other Acts of Congress were to be given their intended scope. So it was that, in addition to the bankruptcy law exception that Congress explicitly recognized in 1875, the Court through the years found that federal courts were empowered to enjoin state court proceedings, despite the anti-injunction statute, in carrying out the will of Congress under at least six other federal laws. These covered a broad spectrum of congressional action: (1) legislation providing for removal of litigation from state to federal courts,[12] (2) legislation limiting the liability of shipowners,[13] (3) legislation providing for federal interpleader ac-

11. As so amended, the statute provided that state court proceedings could be enjoined "where such injunction may be authorized by any law relating to proceedings in bankruptcy." Rev.Stat. § 720 (1874).

12. See French v. Hay, 22 Wall. [89 U.S.] 250; Kline v. Burke Construction Co., 260 U.S. 226. The federal removal provisions, both civil and criminal, 28 U.S.C. §§ 1441–1450, provide that once a copy of the removal petition is filed with the clerk of the state court, the "State court shall proceed no further unless and until the case is remanded." 28 U.S.C. § 1446(e).

13. See Providence & N. Y. S. S. Co. v. Hill Mfg. Co., 109 U.S. 578. The Act of 1851, 9 Stat. 635, as amended, provides that once a shipowner has deposited with the court an amount equal to the value of his interest in the ship, "all claims and proceedings against the owner with respect to the matter in question shall cease." 46 U.S.C. § 185.

tions,[14] (4) legislation conferring federal jurisdiction over farm mortgages,[15] (5) legislation governing federal habeas corpus proceedings,[16] and (6) legislation providing for control of prices.[17]

In addition to the exceptions to the anti-injunction statute found to be embodied in these various Act of Congress, the Court recognized other "implied" exceptions to the blanket prohibition of the anti-injunction statute. One was an "in rem" exception, allowing a federal court to enjoin a state court proceeding in order to protect its jurisdiction of a res over which it had first acquired jurisdiction.[18] Another was a "relitigation" exception, permitting a federal court to enjoin relitigation in a state court of issues already decided in federal litigation.[19] Still a third exception, more recently developed, permits a federal injunction of state court proceedings when the plaintiff in the federal court is the United States itself, or a federal agency asserting "superior federal interests."[20]

In Toucey v. N. Y. Life Ins. Co., 314 U.S. 118, the Court in 1941 issued an opinion casting considerable doubt upon the approach to the anti-injunction statute reflected in its previous decisions. The Court's opinion expressly disavowed the "relitigation" exception to the statute, and emphasized generally the importance of recognizing the statute's basic directive "of 'hands off' by the federal courts in the use of the injunction to stay litigation in a state court." . . . The congressional response to *Toucey* was the enactment in 1948 of the anti-injunction statute in its present form in 28 U.S.C. § 2283, which, as the Reviser's Note makes evident, served not only to overrule the specific holding of

14. See Treinies v. Sunshine Mining Co., 308 U.S. 66. The Interpleader Act of 1926, 44 Stat. 416, as currently written provides that in "any civil action of interpleader . . . a district court may . . . enter its order restraining [all claimants] . . . from instituting or prosecuting any proceeding in any State or United States court affecting the property, instrument or obligation involved in the interpleader action." 28 U.S.C. § 2361.

15. See Kalb v. Feuerstein, 308 U.S. 433. The Frazier-Lemke Farm-Mortgage Act, as amended in 1935, 49 Stat. 944, provides that in situations to which it is applicable a federal court shall "stay all judicial or official proceedings in any court." 11 U.S.C. § 203(s)(2) (1940 ed.).

16. See Ex parte Royall, 117 U.S. 241, 248–249. The Federal Habeas Corpus Act provides that a federal court before which a habeas corpus proceeding is pending may "stay any proceeding against the person detained in any State Court . . . for any matter involved in the habeas corpus proceeding." 28 U.S.C. § 2251.

17. Section 205(a) of the Emergency Price Control Act of 1942, 56 Stat. 33, provided that the Price Administrator could request a federal district court to enjoin acts that violated or threatened to violate the Act. In Porter v. Dicken, 328 U.S. 252, we held that this authority was broad enough to justify an injunction to restrain state court proceedings. Id., at 255. The Emergency Price Control Act was thus considered a congressionally authorized exception to the anti-injunction statute. Ibid.; see also Bowles v. Willingham, 321 U.S. 503. Section 205(a) expired in 1947, Act of July 25, 1946, 60 Stat. 664.

18. See, e.g., Toucey v. New York Life Ins. Co., 314 U.S. at 135–136; Freeman v. Howe, 24 How. [65 U.S.] 450; Kline v. Burke Construction Co., 260 U.S. 226.

19. See, e.g., Toucey, supra, at 137–141; Dial v. Reynolds, 96 U.S. 340; Supreme Tribe of Ben-Hur v. Cauble, 255 U.S. 356. See generally 1A J. Moore, Federal Practice 2302–2311 (1965).

20. Leiter Minerals Inc. v. United States, 352 U.S. 220; N. L. R. B. v. Nash-Finch Co., 404 U.S. 138.

Toucey, but to restore "the basic law as generally understood and interpreted prior to the *Toucey* decision."

We proceed, then, upon the understanding that in determining whether § 1983 comes within the "expressly authorized" exception of the anti-injunction statute, the criteria to be applied are those reflected in the Court's decisions prior to *Toucey.* A review of those decisions makes reasonably clear what the relevant criteria are. In the first place, it is evident that, in order to qualify under the "expressly authorized" exception of the anti-injunction statute, a federal law need not contain an express reference to that statute. As the Court has said, "no prescribed formula is required; an authorization need not expressly refer to § 2283." Amalgamated Clothing Workers v. Richman Bros. Co., 348 U.S. 511, 516. Indeed, none of the previously recognized statutory exceptions contains any such reference. Secondly, a federal law need not expressly authorize an injunction of a state court proceeding in order to qualify as an exception. Three of the six previously recognized statutory exceptions contain no such authorization.[25] Thirdly, it is clear that, in order to qualify as an "expressly authorized" exception to the anti-injunction statute, an Act of Congress must have created a specific and uniquely federal right or remedy, enforceable in a federal court of equity, that could be frustrated if the federal court were not empowered to enjoin a state court proceeding. This is not to say that in order to come within the exception an Act of Congress must, on its face and in every one of its provisions, be totally incompatible with the prohibition of the anti-injunction statute. The test, rather, is whether an Act of Congress, clearly creating a federal right or remedy enforceable in a federal court of equity, could be given its intended scope only by the stay of a state court proceeding. . . .

With these criteria in view, we turn to consideration of 42 U.S.C. § 1983.

IV

Section 1983 was originally § 1 of the Civil Rights Act of 1871. 17 Stat. 13. It was "modeled" on § 2 of the Civil Rights Act of 1866, 14 Stat. 27, and was enacted for the express purpose of "enforc[ing] the Provisions of the Fourteenth Amendment." 17 Stat. 13. The predecessor of § 1983 was thus an important part of the basic alteration in our federal system wrought in the Reconstruction era through federal legislation and constitutional amendment. As a result of the new structure of law that emerged in the post-Civil War era—and especially of the Fourteenth Amendment, which was its centerpiece, the role of

25. See nn. 12, 13, and 17 supra. The federal courts have found that other Acts of Congress that do not refer to § 2283 or to injunctions against state court proceedings nonetheless come within the "expressly authorized" language of the anti-injunction statute. See, e.g., Walling v. Black Diamond Coal Mining Co., 59 F.Supp. 348, 351 (W.D.Ky.) (the Fair Labor Standards Act); Okin v. SEC, 161 F.2d 978, 980 (C.A.2) (the Public Utility Holding Company Act); Dilworth v. Reiner, 343 F.2d 226, 230 (C.A.5) (the 1964 Civil Rights Act); Studebaker Corp. v. Gittlin, 360 F.2d 692 (C.A.2) (the Securities and Exchange Act).

the Federal Government as a guarantor of basic federal rights against state power was clearly established. Monroe v. Pape, 365 U.S. 167; . . . H. Flack, The Adoption of the Fourteenth Amendment (1908); J. TenBroek, The Anti-Slavery Origins of the Fourteenth Amendment (1951). Section 1983 opened the federal courts to private citizens, offering a uniquely federal remedy against incursions under the claimed authority of state law upon rights secured by the Constitution and laws of the Nation.

It is clear from the legislative debates surrounding passage of § 1983's predecessor that the Act was intended to enforce the provisions of the Fourteenth Amendment "against state action, . . . whether that action be executive, legislative or *judicial.*" Ex parte Virginia, 100 U.S. 339, 346 (emphasis supplied). Proponents of the legislation noted that state courts were being used to harass and injure individuals, either because the state courts were powerless to stop deprivations or were in league with those who were bent upon abrogation of federally protected rights.

As Representative Lowe stated, the "records of the [state] tribunals are searched in vain for evidence of effective redress [of federally secured rights]. . . . What less than this [the Civil Rights Act of 1871] will afford an adequate remedy? The Federal Government cannot serve a writ of mandamus upon State Executives or upon State courts to compel them to protect the rights, privileges and immunities of citizens . . . . The case has risen . . . when the Federal Government must resort to its own agencies to carry its own authority into execution. Hence this bill throws open the doors of the United States courts to those whose rights under the Constitution are denied or impaired." Cong.Globe, 42d Cong., 1st Sess., 374–376 (1871). This view was echoed by Senator Osborn: "If the State courts had proven themselves competent to suppress the local disorders, or to maintain law and order, we should not have been called upon to legislate. . . . We are driven by existing facts to provide for the several states in the South what they have been unable to fully provide for themselves; i.e., the full and complete administration of justice in the courts. And the courts with reference to which we legislate must be the United States courts." Id., at 653. . . .

Those who opposed the Act of 1871 clearly recognized that the proponents were extending federal power in an attempt to remedy the state courts' failure to secure federal rights. The debate was not about whether the predecessor of § 1983 extended to actions of state courts, but whether this innovation was necessary or desirable.

This legislative history makes evident that Congress clearly conceived that it was altering the relationship between the States and the Nation with respect to the protection of federally created rights; it was concerned that state instrumentalities could not protect those rights; it realized that state officers might, in fact, be antipathetic to the vindication of those rights; and it believed that these failings extended to the state courts.

V

Section 1983 was thus a product of a vast transformation from the concepts of federalism that had prevailed in the late 18th century when the anti-injunction statute was enacted. The very purpose of § 1983 was to interpose the federal courts between the States and the people, as guardians of the people's federal rights—to protect the people from unconstitutional action under color of state law, "whether that action be executive, legislative or judicial." Ex parte Virginia, 100 U.S. at 346.

In carrying out that purpose, Congress plainly authorized the federal courts to issue injunctions in § 1983 actions, by expressly authorizing a "suit in equity" as one of the means of redress. And this Court long ago recognized that federal injunctive relief against a state court proceeding can in some circumstances be essential to prevent great, immediate, and irreparable loss of a person's constitutional rights. Ex parte Young, 209 U.S. 123. . . . For these reasons we conclude that, under the criteria established in our previous decisions construing the anti-injunction statute, § 1983 is an Act of Congress that falls within the "expressly authorized" exception of that law.

In so concluding, we do not question or qualify in any way the principles of equity, comity, and federalism that must restrain a federal court when asked to enjoin a state court proceeding. These principles, in the context of state criminal prosecutions, were canvassed at length last Term in Younger v. Harris, 401 U.S. 37, and its companion cases. They are principles that have been emphasized by this Court many times in the past. . . . Today we decide only that the District Court in this case was in error in holding that, because of the anti-injunction statute, it was absolutely without power in this § 1983 action to enjoin a proceeding pending in a state court under any circumstances whatsoever.

The judgment is reversed and the case is remanded to the District Court for further proceedings consistent with this opinion. . . .

[There were no dissents; Justices Powell and Rehnquist did not participate. The concurring opinion of the Chief Justice, joined by two others, did not discuss § 2283.]

Notes on the Statute Limiting Injunctions Against State–Court Suits

(1) As *Mitchum* indicates, the accepted wisdom is that the restriction now found in § 2283 dates back to an absolute prohibition enacted in 1793: "[N]or shall a writ of injunction be granted to stay proceedings in any court of a state. . . ." 1 Stat. 333. Recent scholarship has suggested, however, that the traditional understanding is mistaken. The quoted language appears between semicolons in a section dealing with the power of a single

Supreme Court Justice, and it was fifty-five years before it was taken to limit the power of the trial courts; the original meaning was obscured when the various clauses of this section were separated in the general 1874 "codification not intended to effect any substantive changes in the existing statutory law. . . ." Mayton, Ersatz Federalism Under the Anti-Injunction Statute, 78 Colum.L.Rev. 330, 346 (1978).

(2) What is so objectionable about federal injunctions against state-court proceedings? "The use of injunctions to stay actions at law," says Pomeroy, "was almost coeval with the establishment of chancery jurisdiction." 5 Equity Jurisprudence § 2058 (4th ed. 1919). The Supreme Court has held it proper for one federal court to restrain a litigant from proceeding in another federal court, Steelman v. All Continent Corp. 301 U.S. 278 (1937), and for a court of one State to enjoin a litigant from suing in another State, Cole v. Cunningham, 133 U.S. 107, 121 (1890). Nevertheless such injunctions have not always been swallowed painlessly;[1] and Justice Frankfurter explained in Toucey v. New York Life Ins. Co., 314 U.S. 118 (1941), that the anti-injunction statute "expresses the desire of Congress to avoid friction between the federal government and the states resulting from the intrusion of federal authority into the orderly functioning of a state's judicial process."

(3) As *Mitchum* reveals, the essentially absolute language of the statute as it stood before 1948 was given considerably less than absolute effect. Justice Frankfurter attempted in the *Toucey* case, supra note 2, to demonstrate that most of the exceptions were based upon later statutes expressly or impliedly modifying the injunction ban. Admitting he could not explain on this ground the "firmly established" principle allowing injunctions against state proceedings "seeking to interfere with property in the custody of the [federal] court" in actions in rem, Frankfurter refused to recognize a second exception respecting relitigation of matters concluded by a federal judgment and attempted to set the Court back on the straight and narrow: "[T]he fact that one exception as found its way into [the statute] . . . is no justification for making another. . . . Loose language and a sporadic, ill-considered decision cannot be held to have imbedded in our law a doctrine which so patently violates the expressed prohibition of Congress."

It seems pretty clear that Frankfurter's efforts in *Toucey* represented a major break with past practice. See, e.g., Sovereign Camp Woodmen of the World v. O'Neill, 266 U.S. 292 (1924), in which the Court authorized an injunction against the maintenance of multiple and harassing state-court suits even in the absence of a prior federal judgment, saying that the statute "does not deprive a district court of the jurisdiction otherwise conferred by the federal statutes, but merely goes to the question of equity

1. For instance, in James v. Grand Trunk W. R. R., 14 Ill.2d 356, 152 N.E.2d 858 (1958), a Michigan court had enjoined a Michigan resident from suing in Illinois for a Michigan accident, on the ground that Michigan was a more appropriate forum. The Illinois court not only refused to respect the Michigan injunction but piquedly enjoined the defendant from enforcing his Michigan decree: "This court need not, and will not, countenance having its right to try cases, of which it has proper jurisdiction, determined by the courts of other States, through their injunctive process." Objected Justice Schaefer in dissent: "Just as the first injunction sired the second, so the second might sire a third. The ultimate end is not foreseeable. The place to stop this unseemly kind of judicial disorder is where it begins."

in the particular bill. . ."; Durfee & Sloss, Federal Injunction Against Proceedings in State Courts: The Life History of a Statute, 30 Mich.L.Rev. 1145, 1169 (1932), arguing that "except for the prohibition, in some cases, of injunction before judgment, the statute has long been dead"; Mayton, supra note 1, 78 Colum.L.Rev. at 347–49.

(4) The present § 2283 was enacted in the revision of 1948. As recited in *Mitchum* at p. 514 supra, it contains three exceptions, whose purposes were stated in the Reviser's Notes as follows:

> An exception as to Acts of Congress relating to bankruptcy was omitted and the general exception substituted to cover all exceptions.
>
> The phrase "in aid of its jurisdiction" was added to conform to section 1651 of this title and to make clear the recognized power of the Federal courts to stay proceedings in State cases removed to the district courts.
>
> The exceptions specifically include the words "to protect or effectuate its judgments" for lack of which the Supreme Court held that the Federal courts are without power to enjoin relitigation of cases and controversies fully adjudicated by such courts. (See Toucey v. New York Life Ins. Co. . . . A vigorous dissenting opinion . . . notes that at the time of the 1911 revision of the Judicial Code, the power of the courts of the United States to protect their judgments was unquestioned and that the revisers of that code noted no change and Congress intended no change.)
>
> Therefore the revised section restores the basic law as generally understood and interpreted prior to the Toucey decision. . . .

(5) What is the meaning of the exception in § 2283 permitting an injunction when "expressly authorized by Act of Congress?" The Interpleader Act seems express enough, authorizing an injunction "against prosecuting any suit or proceeding in any State court," "notwithstanding any provision of the Judicial Code to the contrary." But the bankruptcy exception, which rather plainly the Reviser meant to preserve, is less "express:" "A suit which is founded upon a claim from which a discharge would be a release, and which is pending against a person at the time of the filing of a petition by or against him, shall be stayed until an adjudication or the dismissal of the petition. . . ." 11 U.S.C. § 29. A suit can be "stayed" by the court in which it is pending as well as by another court's injunction, see P. Beiersdorf & Co. v. McGohey, 187 F.2d 14 (2d Cir. 1951), and the bankruptcy provision does not mention state courts. The Limitation Act, which had been held before the revision to authorize anti-suit injunctions, is still less explicit, mentioning neither injunction, stay, nor state court: "All claims and proceedings against the owner or owners shall cease." Yet it seems doubtful, doesn't it, in the light of the Reviser's declaration that the new section was intended to "cover all exceptions" and to "restore the basic law as generally understood" before *Toucey*, that the Limitation Act exception was eliminated? And if the authorization of the Limitation Act is sufficiently "express" to allow an anti-suit injunction, is not that of every statute providing for federal jurisdiction "exclusive of the courts of the states?" E.g., 28 U.S.C. § 1338(a) (patent and copyright cases). In Amalgamated Clothing Wkrs. v. Richman Bros. Co., 348 U.S. 511 (1955),

the Court found no express authorization to enjoin a state court from interfering with picketing argued to be within the exclusive jurisdiction of the NLRB, but the Taft-Hartley Act is quite silent as to exclusivity; pre-emption of court remedies has been judicially inferred. Finally, in considering the meaning of "expressly authorized," observe that the Reviser specifically placed the established exception for removal cases under the provision for injunctions in aid of federal jurisdiction. Does this suggest that 28 U.S.C. § 1446(e), directing that upon removal "the State court shall proceed no further," is not "express" enough to fit within the first exception? It is hardly less explicit, is it, than the Limitation Act?

Did the precedents sustain the result in *Mitchum*? In every instance but one cited by the Court, Congress had made clear at least its determination that proceedings in other courts ought not to proceed. The exception was the price control cases, decided before the adoption of the present § 2283. The Court had no occasion to hold the statute an "express" authorization; it sufficed that the price-control act impliedly amended the pre-existing prohibition. For the argument against *Mitchum* see Baines v. Danville, 337 F.2d 579 (4th Cir. 1964): Section 1983

> creates a federal cause of action, but with no suggestion, explicit or implicit, that appropriate relief shall include an injunction which another Act of Congress forbids. . . . If every grant of general equity jurisdiction created an exception to the anti-injunction statute, the statute would be meaningless.[2]

(6) Vendo Co. v. Lektro-Vend Corp., 433 U.S. 623, 631–41 (1977), was a federal action attacking covenants not to compete under the Sherman Act. While this suit was pending a state court entered a damage judgment against the federal plaintiff for breach of those covenants. The federal court enjoined collection of the state judgment, holding that it was "expressly authorized" to do so by the Clayton Act, 15 U.S.C. § 26, which provides:

> Any person . . . shall be entitled to sue for and have injunctive relief, in any court of the United States having jurisdiction over the parties, against threatened loss or damage by violation of the antitrust laws . . . when and under the same conditions and principles as injunctive relief against threatened conduct that will cause loss or damage is granted by courts of equity, under the rules governing such proceedings.

The Supreme Court reversed. Said Justice Rehnquist, joined by only two others:

2. See also Stockslager v. Carroll Elec. Coop. Corp., 528 F.2d 949 (8th Cir. 1976), relying on *Mitchum* to hold that the Environmental Policy Act, 42 U.S.C. § 4332, "expressly authorized" a suit injunction by requiring the preparation of an environmental-impact statement in connection with major federal actions affecting the environment: The statute "need not . . . expressly authorize injunction of state court proceedings [sic]. The question is whether the statute creates a federal right or remedy enforceable in a federal court of equity which can only be effectuated by injunction of the state court proceedings." See McMillan, Abstention—The Judiciary's Self-Inflicted Wound, 56 N.C.L.Rev. 527, 529 (1978), arguing that the courts have "treated [§ 2283] . . . like a skunk at a picnic; they have observed it only from afar."

On its face, the language merely authorizes private injunctive relief for antitrust violations. Not only does the statute not mention § 2283 or the enjoining of state court proceedings, but the granting of injunctive relief under § 16 is by the terms of that section limited to "the same conditions and principles" employed by courts of equity, and by "the rules governing such proceedings. . . ." . . . When § 16 was enacted in 1914 the bar of the Anti-Injunction Act had long constrained the equitable power of federal courts to issue injunctions. Thus, on its face, § 16 is far from an express exception to the Anti-Injunction Act, and may be fairly read as virtually incorporating the prohibitions of the Anti-Injunction Act with restrictive language not found, for example, in 42 U.S.C. § 1983. . . .

The private action for damages conferred by the Clayton Act is a "uniquely federal right or remedy," in that actions based upon it may be brought only in the federal courts. . . . It thus meets the first part of the test laid down in the quoted language from *Mitchum.*

But that authorization for private actions does not meet the second part of the *Mitchum* test; it is not an "Act of Congress [which] could be given its intended scope only by the stay of a state court proceeding. . . ." Crucial to our determination in *Mitchum* that 42 U.S.C. § 1983 fulfilled this requirement—but wholly lacking here—was our recognition that one of the clear congressional concerns underlying the enactment of § 1983 was the possibility that state courts, as well as other branches of state government, might be used as instruments to deny citizens their rights under the federal constitution. . . . The relevant legislative history of § 16 simply suggests that in enacting § 16 Congress was interested in extending the right to enjoin antitrust violations to private citizens.

Four Justices dissented: The Clayton Act authorizes an injunction against "a violation of the antitrust laws;" prior decisions not disputed by the Court had held that "the prosecution of litigation in a state court may itself constitute a form of violation" of these laws; and this was such a case. The two remaining Justices (Blackmun and Burger) agreed with the dissenters in principle but, because there was no "pattern of baseless, repetitive claims" in the case before them, concluded the injunction was improper because "it cannot be said on this record that Vendo was using the state-court proceeding as an anticompetitive device in and of itself."

(7) When may a federal court enjoin a state proceeding under the exception in § 2283 for orders "necessary in aid of its jurisdiction?" The Reviser made clear that this exception was intended to allow injunctions in cases removed from state courts. But what is so "necessary" about such an injunction? If the state court refuses to desist from trying the case, its judgment can be set aside on direct review by the Supreme Court; and if the state court is determined to ignore a removal petition, what is to assure it will heed an injunction?

Section 10(j) and (*l*) of the Labor-Management Relations Act, 29 U.S.C. § 160(j), (*l*), authorize the National Labor Relations Board to request, and the district court to grant, "such injunctive relief or temporary restraining order as it deems just and proper," when an unfair labor practice has been charged. In Capital Service, Inc. v. NLRB, 347 U.S. 501 (1954), an employer responded to a secondary boycott by obtaining a state-court injunction and filing unfair-labor-practice charges with the Board. The Board, acting under § 10(*l*), persuaded a district court to enjoin the boycott and, because the LMRA pre-empts state-court jurisdiction over unfair labor practices, Garner v. Teamsters Union, 346 U.S. 485 (1953), to enjoin enforcement of the state-court injunction as well.

The Supreme Court affirmed in an opinion by Justice Douglas, finding it "unnecessary to consider whether, apart from the specific exception contained in § 2283, the District Court was justified in enjoining this intrusion on an exclusive federal jurisdiction:"

> In order to make the § 10(*l*) power effective the Board must have authority to take all steps necessary to preserve its case. If the state court decree were to stand, the Federal District Court would be limited in the action it might take. If the Federal District Court were to have unfettered power to decide for or against the union, and to write such decree as it deemed necessary in order to effectuate the policies of the Act, it must be freed of all restraints from the other tribunal. To exercise its jurisdiction freely and fully it must first remove the state decree. When it did so, it acted "where necessary in aid of its jurisdiction."

However, in Amalgamated Clothing Wkrs. v. Richman Bros. Co., 348 U.S. 511 (1955), when a union sought to enjoin a state-court suit against picketing argued to be within the exclusive jurisdiction of the NLRB, *Capital Service* was readily distinguished: When the Board was not the plaintiff, there was no statute authorizing any action in the district court at all; "such non-existent jurisdiction therefore cannot be aided." It was not enough that, as argued by the dissent, the injunction against suit might be as necessary as that in *Capital Service* because time is often of the essence in labor disputes; the injunction must also be ancillary to an independently existing jurisdiction of the federal court.[3]

(8) Does the exception for injunctions necessary in aid of jurisdiction preserve the pre-1948 cases allowing injunctions against concurrent state proceedings when federal jurisdiction is in rem? Hyde Constr. Co. v. Koehring Co., 388 F.2d 501, 508 (10th Cir. 1968), said it did. In such a case the injunction is not only ancillary, as required by *Richman*, and not simply necessary to protect the parties' rights; it is necessary if jurisdiction over the underlying suit is to be preserved, because if the state court obtains the res the federal court loses jurisdiction. As the Supreme Court said in Atlantic Coast Line R.R. v. Brotherhood of Locomotive Engineers, 398 U.S. 281 (1970), the "aid of jurisdiction" provision implies "that some federal injunctive relief may be necessary to prevent a state court from so interfering with a federal court's consideration or disposition of a case as to seriously impair the federal court's flexibility and authority to decide that case."

3. Cf. *McIntire v. Wood*, supra p. 413, *LaBuy v. Howes Leather Co.*, infra p. 597, and *United States v. Morgan*, infra p. 653, construing the similar requirement of the All Writs Act, 28 U.S.C. § 1651, in a variety of contexts.

Does this reasoning suggest that a federal court may enjoin concurrent state *in personam* proceedings as well in order to avoid multiple litigation of the same controversy? If the state action proceeds first to judgment, the federal court will not technically lose jurisdiction, but it will be bound by res judicata and its proceedings effectively set at naught. Nevertheless, the Court in *Atlantic Coast Line* held that no injunction could be issued when the state court had concurrent jurisdiction in personam, citing Kline v. Burke Constr. Co., 260 U.S. 226 (1922), which had reached the same conclusion before the 1948 revision on the ground that a second in personam suit on the same cause "does not tend to impair or defeat the jurisdiction of the court in which a prior action . . . is pending." Is it likely Congress meant to overturn so firmly established a rule while professing to restore the law as it stood prior to *Toucey*? But is the interference with federal jurisdiction in a removed case, or in *Capital Service*, anything more than the potential res judicata effect held insufficient in *Atlantic Coast Line*?

Would an injunction against a state-court suit for patent infringement be necessary in aid of federal jurisdiction?

(9) The exception allowing a federal court to enjoin state proceedings "to protect or effectuate its judgments" (is this exception modified by "necessary," or does that word relate only to the exception for injunctions in aid of jurisdiction?) was expressly designed to overturn the result in *Toucey* and to permit injunctions against relitigation of matters already settled by a federal court. It has been so applied. E.g., Jackson v. Carter Oil Co., 179 F.2d 524 (10th Cir. 1950). But why should there be an injunction in such a case? Res judicata is a defense in the state court, and the state court's refusal to give appropriate effect to a federal judgment raises a federal question reviewable by the Supreme Court. Dupasseur v. Rochereau, 88 U.S. (21 Wall.) 130 (1875). See the reasons given by a Colorado court in affirming an injunction against relitigation in Iowa of claims determined by a Colorado judgment:

> We have no doubt but that Mr. Burns could have pleaded in the Iowa action the former litigation in this state, and the result thereof, as a complete defense, . . . but why compel him to go over 500 miles to a foreign jurisdiction from that from which both parties reside where the original cause of action, if any, accrued, from where the property over which the original contention arose was situate, and from where all the witnesses reside, in order to present these facts to a foreign tribunal? . . . Besides, if O'Haire is allowed to continue his Iowa suit, and is defeated, under this same rule he could, if aided by persons with means, bring another action in some other state wherever perchance he might secure personal service. . . .

O'Haire v. Burns, 45 Colo. 432, 441, 101 P. 755, 757–58 (1909). Consider also the argument that "the enjoining court, having previously adjudicated the case on the merits, would seem in most cases to be in a better position to determine the extent and nature of duplication," Comment, Anti-suit Injunctions Between State and Federal Courts, 32 U.Chi.L.Rev. 471, 474 n. 17 (1965), and the observation in that comment of the vexatious possibilities suggested by the filing of suits in five different Delaware courts after a federal judgment in one of the *Toucey* cases.

Can it be argued that this third exception to § 2283 authorizes injunctions to protect future federal judgments as well as existing ones and therefore permits federal courts to enjoin simultaneous state-court litigation of matters pending in federal courts? This view was rejected in *Baines v. Danville*, supra note 5: "There is no prior federal judgment to protect or effectuate." Does the exception apply to interlocutory judgments?

(10) Both *Mitchum* and *Atlantic Coast Line*, supra note 8, reaffirm Justice Frankfurter's statement for the Court in the *Richman* case, supra note 7, that as the words of the statute suggest the three exceptions stated in § 2283 exhaust the possibilities under present law for federal injunctions against state-court proceedings:

> Congress made clear beyond cavil that the prohibition is not to be whittled away by judicial improvisation. . . . Legislative policy is here expressed in a clear-cut prohibition qualified only by specifically defined exceptions.

Is this an appropriate view of a statute designed to permit more injunctions against state suits than the prior law, which had been held amenable to judicially created exceptions? Is it an appropriate view of any statute?

Indeed the Court has not adhered to the strict view it has professed. In Leiter Minerals, Inc. v. United States, 352 U.S. 220 (1957), the Supreme Court held § 2283 inapplicable to suits brought by the United States. The Court noted that the Norris-LaGuardia Act, which without express qualification as to plaintiffs imposes severe limits on federal-court labor injunctions, had been construed the same way in United States v. United Mine Workers, 330 U.S. 258 (1947), partly because of the "old and well-known rule" that "statutes which in general terms divest pre-existing rights or privileges will not be applied to the sovereign without express words to that effect." Can this be squared with the Court's acceptance of direct appeals from three-judge district courts in suits brought by the United States? Department of Employment v. United States, 385 U.S. 355 (1966); United States v. Mississippi, 380 U.S. 128 (1965). With the holding in *Leiter* itself that the trial court should abstain from decision pending a state-court interpretation of disputed state law? See p. 493 supra. Does it surprise you that the Court's opinion permitting an injunction in *Leiter* was written by Justice Frankfurter, author of the restrictive philosophy of *Richman*?

Although the Court of Appeals in *Baines v. Danville*, supra note 5, held the Civil Rights Act of 1871 did not expressly authorize an injunction against state-court proceedings, it upheld the district court's authority to preserve the status quo while determining whether permanent relief was barred, observing that § 2283

> is not a jurisdictional statute. It is a limitation upon the exercise by a District Court of its equity jurisdiction. . . . Since the statute was fathered by the principles of comity, it has been held that the statute should be read in the light of those principles and, though absolute in its terms, is inapplicable in extraordinary cases in which an injunction against state court proceedings is the only means of avoiding grave and

> irreparable injury. In our view, the congressional command ought to be ignored only in the face of the most compelling reasons, but we have certainly been told by the Supreme Court that in those circumstances it may be disregarded, for its parentage discloses that it was not intended to be as absolute as it sounds. [337 F.2d at 593].

Was this statement justified by *Leiter*, the case on which the court of appeals principally relied?

(11) When do state-court proceedings begin and end for purposes of § 2283? In Lynch v. Household Finance Corp., 405 U.S. 538, 553–55 (1972), a federal action was brought for declaratory and injunctive relief against invocation of a Connecticut statute allowing garnishment of bank accounts without notice prior to the institution of suit by a creditor. At the time the federal action was filed the creditor had garnished the plaintiff's account and then had filed an action on the debt. The Court held § 2283 no bar:

> In [Hill v. Martin, 296 U.S. 393 (1935)], we said that the "proceeding" that a federal court is forbidden to enjoin "includes all steps taken or which may be taken *in the state court or by its officers* from the *institution* to the close of the final process." . . . In this case, the garnishment occurred before the appellee corporation had served the appellant with process.
>
> More important, the state court and its officers are insulated from control over the garnishment. Connecticut appears to be one of the few States authorizing an attorney for an alleged creditor to garnish or attach property without any participation by a judge or clerk of the court.

Two Justices did not participate, and three dissented:

> In Connecticut, garnishment or attachment is one method of beginning a lawsuit. . . . Its purpose, as the majority notes, is to secure property that will thus be made available for the satisfaction of a judgment. . . . [The majority's] approach . . . was, I thought, laid to rest in *Hill v. Martin*, . . . where the Court construed "proceedings in any court of a State" . . . as embracing . . . "not only . . . an execution issued on a judgment, but . . . any proceeding supplemental or ancillary taken with a view to making the suit or judgment effective."

See also *Atlantic Coast Line*, note 8 supra, 398 U.S. at 287: "It is settled that the prohibition of § 2283 cannot be evaded by addressing the order to the parties or prohibiting utilization of the results of a completed state proceeding."

YOUNGER v. HARRIS

401 U.S. 37 (1971).

MR. JUSTICE BLACK delivered the opinion of the Court.

Appellee, John Harris, Jr., was indicted in a California state court, charged with violation of the California Penal Code §§ 11400 and 11401, known as the California Criminal Syndicalism Act. . . . He then filed a complaint in the Federal District Court, asking that court to enjoin the appellant, Younger, the District Attorney of Los Angeles County, from prosecuting him, and alleging that the prosecution and even the presence of the Act inhibited him in the exercise of his rights of free speech and press, rights guaranteed him by the First and Fourteenth Amendments. . . . A three-judge Federal District Court, convened pursuant to 28 U.S.C. § 2284, held that it had jurisdiction and power to restrain the District Attorney from prosecuting, held that the State's Criminal Syndicalism Act was void for vagueness and overbreadth in violation of the First and Fourteenth Amendments, and accordingly restrained the District Attorney from "further prosecution of the currently pending action against plaintiff Harris for alleged violation of the Act." 281 F.Supp. 507, 517 (1968). . . . [It is argued] that issuance of the injunction was a violation of a longstanding judicial policy and of 28 U.S.C. § 2283, which provides:

> "A court of the United States may not grant an injunction to stay proceedings in a State court except as expressly authorized by Act of Congress, or where necessary in aid of its jurisdiction, or to protect or effectuate its judgments."

. . . The judgment of the District Court, enjoining appellant Younger from prosecuting under these California statutes, must be reversed as a violation of the national policy forbidding federal courts to stay or enjoin pending state court proceedings except under special circumstances. We express no view about the circumstances under which federal courts may act when there is no prosecution pending in state courts at the time the federal proceeding is begun. . . .

Since the beginning of this country's history Congress has, subject to few exceptions, manifested a desire to permit state courts to try state cases free from interference by federal courts. In 1793 an Act unconditionally provided: "[N]or shall a writ of injunction be granted to stay proceedings in any court of a state. . . ." 1 Stat. 335, c. 22, § 5. A comparison of the 1793 Act with 28 U.S.C. § 2283, its present-day successor, graphically illustrates how few and minor have been the exceptions granted from the flat, prohibitory language of the old Act. During all this lapse of years from 1793 to 1970 the statutory exceptions to the 1793 congressional enactment have been only three: (1) "except as expressly authorized by Act of Congress"; (2) "where necessary in aid of its jurisdiction;" and (3) "to protect or effectuate its judgments." In addition, a judicial exception to the longstanding policy evidenced by the statute has been made where a person about to be prosecuted in a state court can show that he will, if the proceeding in the state court is not enjoined, suffer irreparable damages. See Ex parte Young, 209 U.S. 123 (1908).

The precise reasons for this longstanding public policy against federal court interference with state court proceedings have never been specifically identified but the primary sources of the policy are plain. One is the basic doctrine of equity jurisprudence that courts of equity should not act, and particularly should not act to restrain a criminal prosecution, when the moving party has an adequate remedy at law and will not suffer irreparable injury if denied equitable relief. The doctrine may originally have grown out of circumstances peculiar to the English judicial system and not applicable in this country, but its fundamental purpose of restraining equity jurisdiction within narrow limits is equally important under our Constitution, in order to prevent erosion of the role of the jury and avoid a duplication of legal proceedings and legal sanctions where a single suit would be adequate to protect the rights asserted. This underlying reason for restraining courts of equity from interfering with criminal prosecutions is reinforced by an even more vital consideration, the notion of "comity," that is, a proper respect for state functions, a recognition of the fact that the entire country is made up of a Union of separate state governments, and a continuance of the belief that the National Government will fare best if the States and their institutions are left free to perform their separate functions in their separate ways. This, perhaps for lack of a better and clearer way to describe it, is referred to by many as "Our Federalism" . . . . What the concept does represent is a system in which there is sensitivity to the legitimate interests of both State and National Governments, and in which the National Government, anxious though it may be to vindicate and protect federal rights and federal interests, always endeavors to do so in ways that will not unduly interfere with the legitimate activities of the States. . . .

This brief discussion should be enough to suggest some of the reasons why it has been perfectly natural for our cases to repeat time and time again that the normal thing to do when federal courts are asked to enjoin pending proceedings in state courts is not to issue such injunctions. In Fenner v. Boykin, 271 U.S. 240 (1926), suit had been brought in the Federal District Court seeking to enjoin state prosecutions under a recently enacted state law that allegedly interfered with the free flow of interstate commerce. The Court, in a unanimous opinion made clear that such a suit, even with respect to state criminal proceedings not yet formally instituted, could be proper only under very special circumstances:

> "Ex parte Young, 209 U.S. 123, and following cases have established the doctrine that, when absolutely necessary for protection of constitutional rights, courts of the United States have power to enjoin state officers from instituting criminal actions. But this may not be done, except under extraordinary circumstances, where the danger of irreparable loss is both great and immediate. Ordinarily, there should be no interference with such officers; primarily, they are charged with the duty of prosecuting offenders against the laws of the state, and must decide when and how this is to be done. The accused should first set up and rely upon his defense in the state courts, even though this involves a challenge of the validity of some statute, unless it plainly appears that this course would not afford adequate protection." Id., at 243–244.

These principles, made clear in the *Fenner* case, have been repeatedly followed and reaffirmed in other cases involving threatened prosecutions. . . .

In all of these cases the Court stressed the importance of showing irreparable injury, the traditional prerequisite to obtaining an injunction. In addition, however, the Court also made clear that in view of the fundamental policy against federal interference with state criminal prosecutions, even irreparable injury is insufficient unless it is "both great and immediate." *Fenner*, supra. Certain types of injury, in particular, the cost, anxiety, and inconvenience of having to defend against a single criminal prosecution, could not by themselves be considered "irreparable" in the special legal sense of that term. Instead, the threat to the plaintiff's federally protected rights must be one that cannot be eliminated by his defense against a single criminal prosecution. . . .

This is where the law stood when the Court decided Dombrowski v. Pfister, 380 U.S. 479 (1965), and held that an injunction against the enforcement of certain state criminal statutes could properly issue under the circumstances presented in that case. In *Dombrowski*, unlike many of the earlier cases denying injunctions, the complaint made substantial allegations that:

> "the threats to enforce the statutes against appellants are not made with any expectation of securing valid convictions, but rather are part of a plan to employ arrests, seizures, and threats of prosecution under color of the statutes to harass appellants and discourage them and their supporters from asserting and attempting to vindicate the constitutional rights of Negro citizens of Louisiana". . . .

These circumstances, as viewed by the Court sufficiently establish the kind of irreparable injury, above and beyond that associated with the defense of a single prosecution brought in good faith, that had always been considered sufficient to justify federal intervention. . . .

> "But the allegations in this complaint depict a situation in which defense of the State's criminal prosecution will not assure adequate vindication of constitutional rights. They suggest that a substantial loss of or impairment of freedoms of expression will occur if appellants must await the state court's disposition and ultimate review in this Court of any adverse determination. These allegations, if true, clearly show irreparable injury." . . .

It is against the background of these principles that we must judge the propriety of an injunction under the circumstances of the present case. Here a proceeding was already pending in the state court, affording Harris an opportunity to raise his constitutional claims. There is no suggestion that this single prosecution against Harris is brought in bad faith or is only one of a series of repeated prosecutions to which he will be subjected. In other words, the injury that Harris faces is solely "that incidental to every criminal proceeding brought lawfully and in good faith," . . . and therefore under the settled doctrine we have already described he is not entitled to equitable relief "even if such statutes are unconstitutional." . . .

The District Court, however, thought that the *Dombrowski* decision substantially broadened the availability of injunctions against state criminal prosecutions and that under that decision the federal courts may give equitable relief, without regard to any showing of bad faith or harassment, whenever a state statute is found "on its face" to be vague or overly broad, in violation of the First Amendment. We recognize that there are some statements in the *Dombrowski* opinion that would seem to support this argument. But, as we have already seen, such statements were unnecessary to the decision of that case, because the Court found that the plaintiffs had alleged a basis for equitable relief under the long-established standards. In addition, we do not regard the reasons adduced to support this position as sufficient to justify such a substantial departure from the established doctrines regarding the availability of injunctive relief. It is undoubtedly true, as the Court stated in *Dombrowski*, that "[a] criminal prosecution under a statute regulating expression usually involves imponderables and contingencies that themselves may inhibit the full exercise of First Amendment freedoms." 380 U.S., at 486. But this sort of "chilling effect," as the Court called it, should not by itself justify federal intervention. In the first place, the chilling effect cannot be satisfactorily eliminated by federal injunctive relief. In *Dombrowski* itself the Court stated that the injunction to be issued there could be lifted if the State obtained an "acceptable limiting construction" from the state courts. The Court then made clear that once this was done, prosecutions could then be brought for conduct occurring before the narrowing construction was made, and proper convictions could stand so long as the defendants were not deprived of fair warning. 380 U.S., at 491 n. 7. The kind of relief granted in *Dombrowski* thus does not effectively eliminate uncertainty as to the coverage of the state statute and leaves most citizens with virtually the same doubts as before regarding the danger that their conduct might eventually be subjected to criminal sanctions. . . .

Moreover, the existence of a "chilling effect," even in the area of First Amendment rights, has never been considered a sufficient basis, in and of itself, for prohibiting state action. Where a statute does not directly abridge free speech, but—while regulating a subject within the State's power—tends to have the incidental effect of inhibiting First Amendment rights, it is well settled that the statute can be upheld if the effect on speech is minor in relation to the need for control of the conduct and the lack of alternative means for doing so. . . . Just as the incidental "chilling effect" of such statutes does not automatically render them unconstitutional, so the chilling effect that admittedly can result from the very existence of certain laws on the statute books does not in itself justify prohibiting the State from carrying out the important and necessary task of enforcing these laws against socially harmful conduct that the State believes in good faith to be punishable under its laws and the Constitution.

Beyond all this is another, more basic consideration. Procedures for testing the constitutionality of a statute "on its face" in the manner apparently contemplated by *Dombrowski*, and for then enjoining all action to enforce the statute until the State can obtain court approval for a modified version, are fundamentally at odds with the function of the federal courts in our constitutional plan. . . . Ever since the Constitutional Convention rejected a proposal for having members of the Supreme Court render advice concerning pending legislation it has been clear that, even when suits of this kind involve a "case or controversy" sufficient to satisfy the requirements of Article III of the Constitution, the task of analyzing a proposed statute, pinpointing its deficiencies, and requiring correction of these deficiencies before the statute is put into effect, is rarely if ever an appropriate task for the judiciary. . . .

For these reasons, fundamental not only to our federal system but also to the basic functions of the Judicial Branch of the National Government under our Constitution, we hold that the *Dombrowski* decision should not be regarded as having upset the settled doctrines that have always confined very narrowly the availability of injunctive relief against state criminal prosecutions. We do not think that opinion stands for the proposition that a federal court can properly enjoin enforcement of a statute solely on the basis of a showing that the statute "on its face" abridges First Amendment rights. There may, of course, be extraordinary circumstances in which the necessary irreparable injury can be shown even in the absence of the usual prerequisites of bad faith and harassment. For example, as long ago as the *Buck* case [Watson v. Buck, 313 U.S. 387 (1941)], . . . we indicated:

> "It is of course conceivable that a statute might be flagrantly and patently violative of express constitutional prohibitions in every clause, sentence and paragraph, and in whatever manner and against whomever an effort might be made to apply it." 313 U.S., at 402.

Other unusual situations calling for federal intervention might also arise, but there is no point in our attempting now to specify what they might be. It is sufficient for purposes of the present case to hold, as we do, that the possible unconstitutionality of a statute "on its face" does not in itself justify an injunction against good-faith attempts to enforce it, and that appellee Harris has failed to make any showing of bad faith, harassment, or any other unusual circumstance that would call for equitable relief. Because our holding rests on the absence of the factors necessary under equitable principles to justify federal intervention, we have no occasion to consider whether 28 U.S.C. § 2283, which prohibits an injunction against state court proceedings "except as expressly authorized by Act of Congress" would in and of itself be controlling under the circumstances of this case.

The judgment of the District Court is reversed, and the case is remanded for further proceedings not inconsistent with this opinion.

Reversed.

[JUSTICE DOUGLAS dissented; JUSTICES STEWART and HARLAN joined in one separate concurrence, and JUSTICES BRENNAN and MARSHALL in another.]

Notes on Nonstatutory Limits on Enjoining Proceedings

(1) How does one reconcile *Younger* with § 1983, or with the purposes of that statute as announced in *Mitchum v. Foster*? Was *Younger* supported by the decisions (p. 494 supra) allowing *Pullman* abstention in § 1983 cases? Is it consistent with the holding in *Patsy v. Board of Regents,* p. 505 supra, that state administrative remedies need not be exhausted in § 1983 cases? Does the limitation on removal in § 1441(a), in conjunction with *Louisville & N.R.R. v. Mottley,* p. 149 supra, lend support to *Younger*?

The Court invoked precedent. But the cases relied on, for reasons that should be obvious, all involved injunctions against state prosecutions that were not pending but only threatened; and in that context (see pp. 540–51 infra) they were exceptions. See Wechsler, Federal Courts, State Criminal Law and the First Amendment, 49 N.Y.U.L.Rev. 740 (1974) ("[P]rior to *Younger* the Supreme Court consistently encouraged the use of lower federal court declaratory and injunctive relief against unconstitutional state criminal laws"); Laycock, Federal Interference with State Prosecutions: The Cases *Dombrowski* Forgot, 46 U.Chi.L.Rev. 636 (1979). Perhaps most nearly in point was a series of cases beginning with Stefanelli v. Minard, 342 U.S. 117 (1951), where the Court refused for want of a "clear and imminent" irreparable injury to allow an injunction against use of the fruits of an allegedly unconstitutional search in a pending state-court prosecution: "If we were to sanction this intervention, . . . every question of procedural due process of law—with its far-flung and undefined range—would invite a flanking movement against the system of State courts by resort to the federal forum." Did *Stefanelli* support *Younger*? [1]

(2) Samuels v. Mackell, 401 U.S. 66 (1971), a companion case, held *Younger* equally applicable to a claim for declaratory judgment with respect to pending state criminal proceedings, relying on *Great Lakes Dredge & Dock Co. v. Huffman*, supra p. 508 which had equated declaratory judgments with injunctions respecting the validity of state taxes:

> Ordinarily a declaratory judgment will result in precisely the same interference with and disruption of state proceedings that the long-standing policy limiting injunctions was designed to avoid. . . . In

1. Why didn't § 2283 bar the injunction in *Stefanelli*? See Pugach v. Dollinger, 365 U.S. 458, 462 (1961) (Douglas, J., dissenting), arguing in a similar case that § 2283 was inapplicable because "*the thrust of the relief is only to enjoin the use of wire-tap evidence, not to enjoin the action itself.*"

In Perez v. Ledesma, 401 U.S. 82 (1971), *Younger* was held applicable to a federal-court order that fell short of enjoining the state criminal proceeding but ordered material that had been seized returned to the criminal defendants; the effect of this order suppressing evidence was to "effectively stifle" the prosecution.

the first place, the Declaratory Judgment Act provides that after a declaratory judgment is issued the district court may enforce it by granting "further necessary or proper relief," . . . and therefore a declaratory judgment issued while state proceedings are pending might serve as the basis for a subsequent injunction against those proceedings to "protect or effectuate" the declaratory judgment, 28 U.S.C. § 2283, and thus result in a clearly improper interference with the state proceedings. Secondly, even if the declaratory judgment is not used as a basis for actually issuing an injunction, the declaratory relief alone has virtually the same practical impact as a formal injunction would. As we said in the *Wycoff* case . . .:

> "Is the declaration contemplated here to be *res judicata,* so that the [state court] cannot hear evidence and decide any matter for itself? If so, the federal court has virtually lifted the case out of the State [court] before it could be heard. If not, the federal judgment serves no useful purpose as a final determination of rights." . . .

For obvious reasons, no reference was made to *Kennedy v. Mendoza-Martinez,* infra p. 570 which had refused to equate declaratory judgments with injunctions for three-judge court purposes because the two remedies had such different effects upon state enforcement. There were no dissents in either *Samuels* or *Mendoza.*

Should *Younger* be extended to limit federal *damage* actions, as Justice White suggested in Deakins v. Monaghan, 484 U.S. 193 (1988) (concurring opinion)? Cf. *Fair Assessment in Real Estate Ass'n v. McNary,* p. 506 supra.

(3) The Supreme Court in Huffman v. Pursue, Ltd., 420 U.S. 592, 604–605 (1975), held over three dissents that *Younger* forbade an injunction against a civil action to close a dirty-movie house as a nuisance:

> The State is a party . . ., and the proceeding is both in aid of and closely related to criminal statutes which prohibit the dissemination of obscene materials. Thus, an offense to the State's interest in the nuisance litigation is likely to be every bit as great as it would be were this a criminal proceeding. . . . [T]he . . . injunction . . . has disrupted [the] . . . State's efforts to protect the very interests which underlie its criminal laws and to obtain compliance with precisely the standards which are embodied in its criminal laws. . . . We need make no general pronouncements upon the applicability of *Younger* to all civil litigation.

The plaintiff had argued that civil proceedings were distinguishable because the criminal defendant could return to the district court under habeas corpus after his conviction (*Brown v. Allen,* p. 620, infra), while in a civil case § 1738, as the Court later confirmed, would give the state judgment res judicata effect (see Allen v. McCurry, 449 U.S. 90 (1980)). The Court demurred: *Younger* had not been based upon the availability of habeas corpus.

Juidice v. Vail, 430 U.S. 327 (1977), held that *Younger* barred federal interference with a state-court proceeding for civil contempt growing out of a private bill-collection case:

> The contempt power lies at the core of the administration of a State's judicial system. . . . Whether disobedience of a court-sanctioned subpoena, and the resulting process leading to a finding of contempt of court, is labeled civil, quasi-criminal, or criminal in nature, we think the salient fact is that federal court interference with the State's contempt process is "an offense to the State's interest . . . likely to be every bit as great as it would be were this a criminal proceeding."

Trainor v. Hernandez, 431 U.S. 434 (1977), applied *Younger* to preclude interference with an action by the State to recover welfare payments obtained by fraud:

> [T]he State was a party to the suit in its role of administering its public assistance programs. Both the suit and the accompanying writ of garnishment were brought to vindicate important state policies such as safeguarding the integrity of those programs.

Pennzoil Co. v. Texaco, Inc., 481 U.S. 1 (1987), held that *Younger* forbade an injunction against execution of a state-court judgment for tortious interference with contractual relations:

> There is little difference between the State's interest in forcing persons to transfer property in response to a court's judgment and in forcing persons to respond to the court's process on pain of contempt. Both *Juidice* and this case involve challenges to the processes by which the State compels compliance with the judgments of its courts.

There were anguished dissents in all three cases. Are there any state judicial proceedings to which *Younger* does *not* apply?[2]

(4) What constitutes bad-faith enforcement so as to bring a case within the exception to the anti-injunction policy recognized in *Younger*? Some guidance was given in Cameron v. Johnson, 390 U.S. 611 (1968), where civil-rights demonstrators were being prosecuted in state courts under a Mississippi statute declaring it unlawful to picket or demonstrate "in such a manner as to obstruct or interfere with free ingress or egress to and from any public premises . . . or . . . with free use of public streets . . . adjacent or contiguous thereto." The Supreme Court affirmed the denial of an injunction, holding in an opinion by Justice Brennan that the record did not establish bad-faith enforcement. It was argued that bad faith was shown by the fact that the evidence would not be sufficient to sustain a conviction, but the Court disagreed: "The question for the District Court was not the guilt or innocence of the persons charged; the question was whether the statute was enforced against them with no expectation of convictions but only to discourage exercise of protected rights. . . . Ap-

2. See also Schlesinger v. Councilman, 420 U.S. 738 (1975), relying on *Younger* as well as the doctrine of exhaustion of administrative remedies in holding that a federal court should not enjoin a pending court-martial; Ohio Civil Rights Commission v. Dayton Christian Schools, 477 U.S. 619 (1986), holding that *Younger* precluded a federal court from enjoining on freedom of religion grounds an administrative antidiscrimination proceeding brought by the State; New Orleans Public Service, Inc. v. Council of City of New Orleans, 109 S.Ct. 2506 (1989), holding *Younger* inapplicable to administrative proceedings that were not " 'judicial in nature.' " Is the *Dayton* decision consistent with *Patsy v. Board of Regents*, p. 505 supra, which held that administrative remedies need not be exhausted in § 1983 actions?

pellants say that the picketing was nonobstructive, but the State claims quite the contrary, and the record is not totally devoid of support for the State's claim." Nor had an improper policy of "selective enforcement" been shown: "There was no evidence of conduct . . . at any other place which would have brought the statute into play, let alone evidence that the authorities allowed such conduct without enforcing the statute." Justices Fortas and Douglas dissented:

> *Dombrowski* means precious little, I submit, if the presumption supporting state action is not overcome by facts such as those before us now. . . . There is no evidence that access to the courthouse was actually obstructed. . . . The arrests and their sequence demonstrate that the State was not here engaged in policing access to the courthouse or even freedom of the sidewalks, but in a deliberate plan to put an end to the voting-rights demonstration.[3]

In cases of bad faith should the Court insist on a showing that an adequate injunction could not be obtained from a state court? It didn't in *Dombrowski.* Is the point that when the criminal defense is inadequate there must be a second proceeding anyway, and that might as well be federal? Why, if we are concerned about avoiding unnecessary federal-state friction?

(5) *Younger* devoted quite a little space to demonstrating that Dombrowski v. Pfister, 380 U.S. 479 (1965), did not require a second exception from the anti-injunction policy when a statute affecting expression was attacked as overbroad. In *Dombrowski* the plaintiffs had sought to enjoin prosecutions for alleged violations of a state law respecting subversive activities. Bad faith and overbreadth were both explicitly discussed in connection with the separate argument that the federal court should abstain under the *Pullman* principle, p. 485 supra, for a clarification of state law. The passage holding the anti-injunction policy overridden was in part as follows:

> A criminal prosecution under a statute regulating expression usually involves imponderables and contingencies that themselves may inhibit the full exercise of First Amendment freedoms. . . . When the statutes also have an overbroad sweep, as is here alleged, the hazard of loss or substantial impairment of those precious rights may be critical. . . . The assumption that defense of a criminal prosecution will generally assure ample vindication of constitutional rights is unfounded in such cases. . . . For "[t]he threat of sanctions may deter . . . almost as potently as the actual application of sanctions. . . ." [Therefore,] we have consistently allowed attacks on

3. See also Zwickler v. Boll, 391 U.S. 353 (1968), affirming the denial of an injunction on the authority of *Cameron* in the face of a dissent asserting that the district court had not held a hearing on the plaintiff's allegations of discriminatory enforcement; Grandco Corp. v. Rochford, 536 F.2d 197, 204 (7th Cir. 1976), holding that a course of "well over 100" prosecutions for operating a theater without a license did not demonstrate bad faith:

> In *Dombrowski* . . ., harassment and bad faith were inferred from evidence of multiple *unsuccessful* prosecutions. In the case at bar, prosecutions against the manager of plaintiff Wabash Books' enterprise have generally resulted in convictions. Continued prosecution under the ordinance for repeated violations indicates only good faith enforcement of a judicially approved provision against judicially disapproved conduct.

> overly broad statutes with no requirement that the person making the attack demonstrate that his own conduct could not be regulated by a statute drawn with the requisite narrow specificity, Thornhill v. Alabama, 310 U.S. 88, 97–98 . . ., because of the ". . . danger of tolerating, in the area of First Amendment freedoms, the existence of a penal statute susceptible of sweeping and improper application." . . . If the rule were otherwise, the contours of regulation would have to be hammered out case by case—tested only by those hardy enough to risk criminal prosecution. . . .

Did Justice Black successfully deal with this passage in *Younger*?

(6) Trainor v. Hernandez, note 3 supra, dealt rather slightingly with the argument that a due-process challenge to a state attachment statute came within *Younger*'s dicta allowing injunctions when the state statute is "patently" unconstitutional. The trial court had held several sections of the statute "on their face patently violative of the due process clause . . .;" dissenting Justices agreed that, because the statute allowed the court clerk to issue an attachment upon conclusory allegations and provided for no prompt subsequent hearing, it was "constitutionally indistinguishable" from one struck down two years before. Said the Court:

> It is urged that this case comes within the exception that we said in *Younger* might exist where a state statute is "flagrantly and patently violative of express constitutional prohibitions in every clause, sentence and paragraph, and in whatever manner and against whomever an effort might be made to apply it." . . . Even if such a finding was made below, which we doubt . . ., it would not have been warranted in light of our cases. Compare North Georgia Finishing Inc. v. Di-Chem Inc., 419 U.S. 601 (1975), with Mitchell v. W. T. Grant Co., 416 U.S. 600 (1974).

North Georgia Finishing was the case relied on by the dissenters. Justice Stevens protested that the Court, apparently focusing on the "every clause" language of *Younger*, "seems to be saying" that the exception was "unavailable whenever a statute has a legitimate title, or a legitimate severability clause, or some other equally innocuous provision. . . . In effect, this treatment . . . eliminates one of the exceptions from the doctrine."

Is there any basis in the philosophy of *Younger* for this alleged exception?

(7) What other circumstances can justify a federal injunction against pending state criminal proceedings under the general tests stated in *Younger*: that the "danger of irreparable loss must be great and immediate" and that the threat "must be one that cannot be eliminated by . . . defense against a single criminal prosecution?"

Gibson v. Berryhill, 411 U.S. 564, 577 (1973), assuming without deciding that *Younger* applied when the state proceedings were not criminal, allowed an injunction against a license-revocation proceeding:

> *Younger v. Harris* contemplates the outright dismissal of the federal suit, and the presentation of all claims, both state and federal, to the state courts. Such a course naturally presupposes the opportunity to raise and have timely decided by a competent state tribunal the federal

> issues involved. Here the predicate for a *Younger v. Harris* dismissal was lacking, for the appellees alleged, and the District Court concluded, that the State Board of Optometry was incompetent by reason of bias to adjudicate the issues pending before it.

The prospect of de novo state-court review did not alter the Court's conclusion: The adverse publicity attending the initial revocation " 'would cause irreparable damage' . . . for which no adequate remedy is afforded by state law." See also Gerstein v. Pugh, 420 U.S. 103, 108 n. 9 (1975), allowing an injunction requiring a preliminary hearing for pretrial incarceration because the issue "could not be raised in defense of the criminal prosecution" and because the injunction "could not prejudice the conduct of trial on the merits"; Hicks v. Miranda, 422 U.S. 332 (1975) (5–4), holding it not enough to avoid *Younger* that a state appellate court had already upheld the challenged statute: Courts "sometimes change their minds," and in any event the decision was that of an intermediate court. Does *Younger* allow an injunction against a pending second prosecution for a single offense? Cf. *Fain v. Duff*, p. 641 infra; *Abney v. United States*, p. 593 infra.

Is the test for enjoining pending state criminal proceedings under *Younger* the same as that for aborting them by pre-trial habeas corpus? See pp. 640–41 infra. Shouldn't it be?[4]

(8) Ohio Bureau of Employment Serv. v. Hodory, 431 U.S. 471, 480 (1977):

> In the present case, Ohio either believes that the District Court was correct in [refusing to invoke *Younger*] . . . or, faced with the prospect of lengthy administrative appeals followed by equally protracted state judicial proceedings, now has concluded to submit the constitutional issue to this Court for immediate resolution. In either event, under these circumstances *Younger* principles of equity and comity do not require this Court to refuse Ohio the immediate adjudication it seeks.

But cf. the holding in the same case, p. 495 supra, that a request by the State was not necessary for abstention to resolve ambiguous state law.

(9) Donovan v. City of Dallas, 377 U.S. 408 (1964). After losing a state-court action to restrain the proposed expansion of an airport, some of the same plaintiffs filed suit in federal court seeking similar relief. The state court enjoined them from proceeding, and the Supreme Court reversed:

> Early in the history of our country a general rule was established that state and federal courts would not interfere with or try to restrain

4. State law in the *Pennzoil* case, note 3 supra, required the defendant to post a thirteen billion dollar bond to obtain a stay of judgment pending appeal; the Court said the state courts were competent to determine the constitutionality of this requirement.

See also McLucas v. DeChamplain, 421 U.S. 21 (1975), refusing to interfere with a pending court-martial although the result was that the plaintiff would remain in jail:

> [I]f such harm were deemed sufficient to warrant equitable interference into pending court-martial proceedings, any constitutional ruling at the court-martial presumably would be subject to immediate relitigation in federal district courts, resulting in disruption to the court-martial and circumvention of the military appellate system provided by Congress.

> each other's proceedings. . . . An exception has been made in cases where a court has custody of property, that is, proceedings *in rem* or *quasi in rem.* In such cases this Court has said that the state or federal court having custody of such property has exclusive jurisdiction to proceed. Princess Lida v. Thompson, 305 U.S. 456, 465–68. . . . While Congress has seen fit to authorize courts of the United States to restrain state-court proceedings in some special circumstances, it has in no way relaxed the old and well-established judicially declared rule that state courts are completely without power to restrain federal-court proceedings in *in personam* actions like the one here. . . .
>
> Petitioners being properly in the federal court had a right granted by Congress to have the court decide the issues they presented. . . . The Texas courts were without power to take away this federal right. . . .

Justice Harlan, joined by Clark and Stewart, dissented, arguing that precedent allowed state courts to enjoin "vexatious, duplicative litigation" and that the statutory grant of federal jurisdiction did not answer the question:

> [T]he statutory boundaries of federal jurisdiction are hardly to be regarded as a license to conduct litigation in the federal courts for the purpose of harassment. The exception which the Court recognizes for *in rem* actions demonstrates that no such view of federal jurisdiction is tenable; for in those cases, too, the federal courts have statutory jurisdiction to proceed.

For further criticism of the opinion see Arnold, State Power to Enjoin Federal Court Proceedings, 51 Va.L.Rev. 59 (1965), agreeing with the result on the narrower ground that a federal injunction would have sufficed to prevent multiple litigation: "[T]he state-federal injunction was properly denied because there was an adequate federal remedy."

STEFFEL v. THOMPSON

415 U.S. 452 (1974).

MR. JUSTICE BRENNAN delivered the opinion of the Court.

When a state criminal proceeding under a disputed state criminal statute is pending against a federal plaintiff at the time his federal complaint is filed, Younger v. Harris, 401 U.S. 37 (1971), and Samuels v. Mackell, 401 U.S. 66 (1971), held, respectively, that, unless bad faith enforcement or other special circumstances are demonstrated, principles of equity, comity, and federalism preclude issuance of a federal injunction restraining enforcement of the criminal statute and, in all but unusual circumstances, a declaratory judgment upon the constitutionality of the statute. This case presents the important question reserved in Samuels v. Mackell, 401 U.S., at 73–74, whether declaratory relief is precluded when a state prosecution has been threatened, but is not pending, and a showing of bad faith enforcement or other special circumstances has not been made.

Petitioner, and others, filed a complaint in the District Court for the Northern District of Georgia, invoking the Civil Rights Act, 42 U.S.C. § 1983, and its jurisdictional implementation. 28 U.S.C. § 1343. The complaint requested a declaratory judgment pursuant to 28 U.S.C. §§ 2201–2202, that Ga.Code Ann. § 26–1503 [a criminal trespass statute] was being applied in violation of petitioner's First and Fourteenth Amendment rights, and an injunction restraining respondents—the Solicitor of the Civil and Criminal Court of DeKalb County, the Chief of the DeKalb County Police, the owner of the North DeKalb Shopping Center, and the manager of that shopping center—from enforcing the statute so as to interfere with petitioner's constitutionally protected activities.

The parties stipulated to the relevant facts: On October 8, 1970, while petitioner and other individuals were distributing handbills protesting American involvement in Viet Nam on an exterior sidewalk of the North DeKalb Shopping Center, shopping center employees asked them to stop handbilling and leave. They declined to do so, and police officers were summoned. The officers told them that they would be arrested if they did not stop handbilling. The group then left to avoid arrest. Two days later petitioner and a companion returned to the shopping center and again began handbilling. The manager of the center called the police, and petitioner and his companion were once again told that failure to stop their handbilling would result in their arrests. Petitioner left to avoid arrest. His companion stayed, however, continued handbilling, and was arrested and subsequently arraigned on a charge of criminal trespass in violation of § 26–1503. Petitioner alleged in his complaint that, although he desired to return to the shopping center to distribute handbills, he had not done so because of his concern that he too would be arrested for violation of § 26–1503; the parties stipulated that, if petitioner returned and refused upon request to stop handbilling, a warrant would be sworn out and he might be arrested and charged with a violation of the Georgia statute.[4]

After hearing, the District Court denied all relief and dismissed the action . . . . Petitioner appealed only from the denial of declaratory relief. The Court of Appeals for the Fifth Circuit . . . . affirmed . . . . The court recognized that [*Younger* and *Samuels*] were expressly limited to situations where state prosecutions were pending when the federal action commenced, but was of the view that Younger v. Harris "made it clear beyond peradventure that irreparable injury must be measured by bad faith harassment and such test must be applied to a request for injunctive relief against *threatened* state court criminal prosecution" . . .; and, furthermore, since the opinion in Samuels v. Mackell reasoned that declaratory relief would normally disrupt the state criminal justice system in the manner of injunctive relief, it followed that "the same test of bad faith harassment is

4. At the District Court hearing, counsel for the police officers indicated that arrests in fact would be made if warrants sworn out by shopping center personnel were facially proper. . . .

prerequisite . . . for declaratory relief in a threatened prosecution." . . .

We granted certiorari . . . and now reverse.

I

At the threshold we must consider whether petitioner presents an "actual controversy," a requirement imposed by Art. III of the Constitution and the express terms of the Federal Declaratory Judgment Act, 28 U.S.C. § 2201. . . .

[P]etitioner has alleged threats of prosecution that cannot be characterized as "imaginary or speculative." . . . He has been twice warned to stop handbilling that he claims is constitutionally protected and has been told by the police that, if he again handbills at the shopping center and disobeys a warning to stop, he will likely be prosecuted. The prosecution of petitioner's handbilling companion is ample demonstration that petitioner's concern with arrest has not been "chimerical," Poe v. Ullman, 367 U.S. 497, 508 (1961). In these circumstances, it is not necessary that petitioner first expose himself to actual arrest or prosecution to be entitled to challenge a statute that he claims deters the exercise of his constitutional rights. . . .

II

We now turn to the question of whether the District Court and the Court of Appeals correctly found petitioner's request for declaratory relief inappropriate.

Sensitive to principles of equity, comity, and federalism, we recognized in Younger v. Harris, supra, that federal courts should ordinarily refrain from enjoining ongoing state criminal prosecutions. We were cognizant that a pending state proceeding, in all but unusual cases, would provide the federal plaintiff with the necessary vehicle for vindicating his constitutional rights, and, in that circumstance, the restraining of an ongoing prosecution would entail an unseemly failure to give effect to the principle that state courts have the solemn responsibility, equally with the federal courts "to guard, enforce, and protect every right granted or secured by the Constitution of the United States. . . ." . . . In Samuels v. Mackell, supra, the Court also found that the same principles ordinarily would be flouted by issuance of a federal declaratory judgment when a state proceeding was pending, since the intrusive effect of declaratory relief "will result in precisely the same interference with and disruption of state proceedings that the long-standing policy limiting injunctions was designed to avoid." . . .

Neither *Younger* nor *Samuels*, however, decided the question whether federal intervention might be permissible in the absence of a pending state prosecution.

[Express reservations in those opinions] anticipated the Court's recognition that the relevant principles of equity, comity, and federalism "have little force in the absence of a pending state proceeding."

Lake Carriers' Assn. v. MacMullan, 406 U.S. 498, 509 (1972). When no state criminal proceeding is pending at the time the federal complaint is filed, federal intervention does not result in duplicative legal proceedings or disruption of the state criminal justice system; nor can federal intervention, in that circumstance, be interpreted as reflecting negatively upon the state courts' ability to enforce constitutional principles. In addition, while a pending state prosecution provides the federal plaintiff with a concrete opportunity to vindicate his constitutional rights, a refusal on the part of the federal courts to intervene when no state proceeding is pending may place the hapless plaintiff between the Scylla of intentionally flouting state law and the Charybdis of foregoing what he believes to be constitutionally protected activity in order to avoid becoming enmeshed in a criminal proceeding. Cf. Dombrowski v. Pfister, 380 U.S. 479, 490 (1965).

When no state proceeding is pending and thus considerations of equity, comity, and federalism have little vitality, the propriety of granting federal declaratory relief may properly be considered independently of a request for injunctive relief. Here, the Court of Appeals held that because injunctive relief would not be appropriate since petitioner failed to demonstrate irreparable injury—a traditional prerequisite to injunctive relief, e.g., Dombrowski v. Pfister, supra—, it followed that declaratory relief was also inappropriate. Even if the Court of Appeals correctly viewed injunctive relief as inappropriate—a question we need not reach today since petitioner has abandoned his request for that remedy, . . .[12] the court erred in treating the requests for injunctive and declaratory relief as a single issue. . . .

First, as Congress recognized in 1934, a declaratory judgment will have a less intrusive effect on the administration of state criminal laws. As was observed in Perez v. Ledesma, 401 U.S., at 124–126 (footnote omitted): ". . . If a declaration of partial unconstitutionality is affirmed by this Court, the implication is that this Court will overturn particular applications of the statute, but that if the statute is narrowly construed by the state courts it will not be incapable of constitutional applications. Accordingly, the declaration does not necessarily bar prosecutions under the statute, as a broad injunction would. Thus, where the highest court of a State has had an opportunity to give a statute regulating expression a narrowing or clarifying construction but has failed to do so, and later a federal court declares the statute unconstitutionally vague or overbroad, it may well be open to a state prosecutor, after the federal court decision, to bring a prosecution under the statute if he reasonably believes that the defendant's conduct

12. We note that, in those cases where injunctive relief has been sought to restrain an imminent, but not yet pending, prosecution *for past conduct*, sufficient injury has not been found to warrant injunctive relief, see Beal v. Missouri P. R. Corp., 312 U.S. 45 (1941); Spielman Motor Sales Co., Inc. v. Dodge, 295 U.S. 89 (1935); Fenner v. Boykin, 271 U.S. 240 (1926). There is some question, however, whether a showing of irreparable injury might be made in a case where, although no prosecution is pending or impending, an individual demonstrates that he will be required to *forego* constitutionally protected activity in order to avoid arrest. . . .

is not constitutionally protected and that the state courts may give the statute a construction so as to yield a constitutionally valid conviction. Even where a declaration of unconstitutionality is not reviewed by this Court, the declaration may still be able to cut down the deterrent effect of an unconstitutional state statute. The persuasive force of the court's opinion and judgment may lead state prosecutors, courts, and legislators to reconsider their respective responsibilities toward the statute. Enforcement policies or judicial construction may be changed, or the legislature may repeal the statute and start anew. Finally, the federal court judgment may have some *res judicata* effect, though this point is not free from difficulty and the governing rules remain to be developed with a view to the proper workings of a federal system. What is clear, however, is that even though a declaratory judgment has 'the force and effect of a final judgment,' 28 U.S.C. § 2201, it is a much milder form of relief than an injunction. Though it may be persuasive, it is not ultimately coercive; noncompliance with it may be inappropriate, but is not contempt." . . .[19]

Second, engrafting upon the Declaratory Judgment Act a requirement that all of the traditional equitable prerequisites to the issuance of an injunction be satisfied before the issuance of a declaratory judgment is considered would defy Congress' intent to make declaratory relief available in cases where an injunction would be inappropriate.* . . . Thus, the Court of Appeals was in error when it ruled that a failure to demonstrate irreparable injury—a traditional prerequisite to injunctive relief, having no equivalent in the law of declaratory judgments, . . .—precluded the granting of declaratory relief.

The only occasions where this Court has disregarded these "different considerations" and found that a preclusion of injunctive relief inevitably led to a denial of declaratory relief have been cases in which principles of federalism militated altogether against federal intervention into a class of adjudications. See Great Lakes Co. v. Huffman, 319 U.S. 293 (1943) (federal policy against interfering with the enforcement of state tax laws); Samuels v. Mackell, supra. In the instant case, principles of federalism not only do not preclude federal intervention, they compel it. Requiring the federal courts totally to step aside when no state criminal prosecution is pending against the federal plaintiff

19. The pending prosecution of petitioner's handbilling companion does not affect petitioner's action for declaratory relief. . . .

* [Footnote 18 by the Court, here transposed]

18. As Professor Borchard, a principal proponent and author of the Federal Declaratory Judgment Act, said in a written statement introduced at the hearings on the Act:

"It often happens that courts are unwilling to grant injunctions to restrain the enforcement of penal statutes or ordinances, and relegate the plaintiff to his option, either to violate the statute and take his chances in testing constitutionality on a criminal prosecution, or else to forego, in the fear of prosecution, the exercise of his claimed rights. Into this dilemma no civilized legal system operating under a constitution should force any person. The court, in effect, by refusing an injunction informs the prospective victim that the only way to determine whether the suspect is a mushroom or a toadstool, is to eat it. . . ." . . .

would turn federalism on its head. When federal claims are premised on 42 U.S.C. § 1983 and 28 U.S.C. § 1343(3)—as they are here—we have not required exhaustion of state judicial or administrative remedies, recognizing the paramount role Congress has assigned to the federal courts to protect constitutional rights. . . .

We therefore hold that, regardless of whether injunctive relief may be appropriate, federal declaratory relief is not precluded when no state prosecution is pending and a federal plaintiff demonstrates a genuine threat of enforcement of a disputed state criminal statute, whether an attack is made on the constitutionality of the statute on its face or as applied. The judgment of the Court of Appeals is reversed, and the case is remanded for further proceedings consistent with this opinion. . . .

MR. JUSTICE WHITE, concurring.

I offer the following few words in light of Mr. Justice Rehnquist's concurrence. . . . I would anticipate that a final declaratory judgment entered by a federal court holding particular conduct of the federal plaintiff to be immune on federal constitutional grounds from prosecution under state law should be accorded *res judicata* effect in any later prosecution of that very conduct. There would also, I think, be additional circumstances in which the federal judgment should be considered as more than a mere precedent bearing on the issue before the state court.

Neither can I at this sitting agree that the federal court, having rendered a declaratory judgment in favor of the plaintiff, could not enjoin a later state prosecution for conduct that the federal court has declared immune. The Declaratory Judgments Act itself provides that a "declaration shall have the force and effect of a final judgment or decree." 28 U.S.C. § 2201; eminent authority anticipated declaratory judgments would be *res judicata.* Borchard, Declaratory Judgments 10–11 (2d ed. 1941); and there is every reason for not reducing declaratory judgments to mere advisory opinions. . . . The statute provides for "[f] urther necessary or proper relief . . . against any adverse party whose rights have been determined by such judgment," 28 U.S.C. § 2202, and it would not seem improper to enjoin local prosecutors who refuse to observe adverse federal judgments.

Finally, I would think that a federal suit challenging a state criminal statute on federal constitutional grounds could be sufficiently far along so that ordinary considerations of economy would warrant refusal to dismiss the federal case solely because a state prosecution has subsequently been filed and the federal question may be litigated there.

MR. JUSTICE REHNQUIST with whom THE CHIEF JUSTICE joins, concurring. . . .

The Court quite properly leaves for another day whether the granting of a declaratory judgment by a federal court will have any subsequent *res judicata* effect or will perhaps support the issuance of a later federal injunction. But since possible resolutions of those issues would substantially undercut the principles of federalism reaffirmed in *Younger v. Harris*, . . . and preserved by the decision today, I feel it appropriate to add a few remarks.

First, the legislative history of the Declaratory Judgments Act and the Court's opinion in this case both recognize that the declaratory judgment procedure is an alternative to pursuit of the arguably illegal activity. There is nothing in the Act's history to suggest that Congress intended to provide persons wishing to violate state laws with a federal shield behind which they could carry on their contemplated conduct. Thus I do not believe that a federal plaintiff in a declaratory judgment action can avoid, by the mere filing of a complaint, the principles so firmly expressed in *Samuels*, supra. The plaintiff who continues to violate a state statute after the filing of his federal complaint does so both at the risk of state prosecution and at the risk of dismissal of his federal lawsuit. For any arrest prior to resolution of the federal action would constitute a pending prosecution and bar declaratory relief under the principles of *Samuels*.

Second, I do not believe that today's decision can properly be raised to support the issuance of a federal injunction based upon a favorable declaratory judgment. The Court's description of declaratory relief as "a milder alternative to the injunction remedy," having a "less instrusive effect on the administration of state criminal laws" than an injunction, indicates to me critical distinctions which make declaratory relief appropriate where injunctive relief would not be. It would all but totally obscure these important distinctions if a successful application for declaratory relief came to be regarded, not as the conclusion of a lawsuit, but as a giant step towards obtaining an injunction against a subsequent criminal prosecution. . . .

A declaratory judgment is simply a statement of rights, not a binding order supplemented by continuing sanctions. State authorities may choose to be guided by the judgment of a lower federal court, but they are not compelled to follow the decision by threat of contempt or other penalties. If the federal plaintiff pursues the conduct for which he was previously threatened with arrest and is in fact arrested, he may not return the controversy to federal court, although he may of course raise the federal declaratory judgment in the state court for whatever value it may prove to have.[3] . . .

Third, attempts to circumvent *Younger* by claiming that enforcement of a statute declared unconstitutional by a federal court is *per se* evidence of bad faith should not find support in the Court's decision in

3. The Court's opinion notes that the possible *res judicata* effect of a federal declaratory judgment in a subsequent state court prosecution is a question "not free from difficulty." . . . I express no opinion on that issue here. However, I do note that the federal decision would not be accorded the *stare decisis* effect in state court that it would have in a subsequent proceeding within the same federal jurisdiction. Although the state court would not be compelled to follow the federal holding, the opinion might of course be viewed as highly persuasive.

this case. As the Court notes, quoting my Brother Brennan's opinion in Perez v. Ledesma, 401 U.S. 82, 124–126:

> "The persuasive force of the [federal] court's opinion *may* lead state prosecutors, courts, and legislators to reconsider their respective responsibilities toward the statute. Enforcement policies or judicial construction *may* be changed, or the legislature *may* repeal the statute and start anew." (Emphasis added.)

This language clearly recognizes that continued belief in the constitutionality of the statute by state prosecutorial officials would not commonly be indicative of bad faith and that such allegations, in the absence of highly unusual circumstances, would not justify a federal court's departure from the general principles of restraint discussed in *Younger*. . . .

Notes on Interference With Threatened Proceedings

(1) *Dombrowski v. Pfister*, supra p. 537 reaffirmed the long-standing doctrine that § 2283 and its predecessors, despite their apparently flat reference to "proceedings in a State court," "do not preclude injunctions against the institution of state court proceedings, but only bar stays of suits already instituted," citing *Ex parte Young*. Why this should be may perhaps emerge from the discussion below.

(2) In *Ex parte Young*, supra p. 444, in which no prosecution was pending when federal suit was filed, an injunction respecting the unconstitutionality of a state law was affirmed on the express ground that a criminal defense would not provide an adequate means of testing the statute: To obtain such a test it would be necessary to disobey the law, and among other things the penalties for losing the defense would be severe. This holding was reaffirmed in Terrace v. Thompson, 263 U.S. 197, 216 (1923), which allowed an injunction against threatened enforcement of a law forbidding the lease of land to aliens: The plaintiffs, who had not violated the law, were "not obliged to take the risk of prosecution, fines and imprisonment and loss of property in order to secure an adjudication of their rights." The Supreme Court has entertained numerous similar pre-enforcement attacks, whether injunctive or declaratory, without adverting to any problem. See, e.g., *Pierce v. Society of Sisters*, supra p. 63; Village of Euclid v. Ambler, 272 U.S. 365 (1926); West Virginia State Board of Education v. Barnette, 319 U.S. 624 (1943). Indeed the typical *Pullman* abstention case is an action to enjoin enforcement of some state law; and Congress recognized the legitimacy of such suits, at least in some cases, by passing a statute requiring them to be heard by a three-judge district court. See pp. 568–72 infra.

(3) *Younger* cited six decisions as holding that injunctions against merely threatened proceedings must be justified by special circumstances but nowhere suggested that the need to disobey the law in order to test it would fail to qualify as a special circumstance. In holding improper an injunction against enforcement of full-crew law in Beal v. Missouri Pacific Railroad Corp., 312 U.S. 45, 51 (1941), the Court suggested a narrow reading of *Ex parte Young* that might seriously impair pre-enforcement

review: It was not asserted in *Beal* that the statutory penalties were "so great as to prevent recourse to the courts for the adjudication of respondent's rights under it," citing *Young*. But the case does not hold that only in such a case may there be an injunction, for it was clear that the railroad had already violated the statute; the Attorney General had promised to file a single test suit "without seeking to inflict financial penalties or loss on respondent prior to a final determination of the suit in the state courts," and the Court held that because of "certain concessions" further consideration of the issue of multiplicity of suits had been waived.

Williams v. Miller, 317 U.S. 599 (1942), was more troublesome. A landowner and two prospective employees, wishing to build a house for sale, attacked a statute requiring such work to be done by a licensed contractor. Though the plaintiffs had not yet violated the statute, the Supreme Court affirmed a dismissal on the authority of *Beal* and two other decisions in a memorandum opinion without further explanation: "The bill does not allege facts which would warrant the granting of equitable relief by a federal court to restrain enforcement of the state statute." Was this a conscious decision to overrule *Terrace v. Thompson*? A failure to perceive, in the hurry to get rid of an unwanted appeal, significant distinctions between the cases? Or a narrow holding as to the adequacy of the complaint as drafted?

The other decisions relied on in *Younger* were easily distinguishable from *Steffel*.[1]

(4) Doran v. Salem Inn, Inc., 422 U.S. 922 (1975), held that, while under *Steffel* a declaratory judgment was the preferred remedy, a preliminary injunction could be issued against a threatened state prosecution: Since a declaration cannot issue until the case is over, the injunction may be required to avoid the need to act at one's peril.

Wooley v. Maynard, 430 U.S. 705, 712 (1977), went further, authorizing permanent injunctive relief against future prosecutions for ob-

1. For reasons similar to those in *Beal*, there was no need to risk additional penalties in order to determine the legality of conduct in Spielman Motor Sales Co. v. Dodge, 295 U.S. 89, 96 (1935), or in Fenner v. Boykin, 271 U.S. 240 (1926), as indicated by the lower court, 3 F.2d 674, 676 (N.D. Ga.1925). The essential reason for denial of relief in Watson v. Buck, 313 U.S. 387, 399 (1941), was that the case was not ripe: "The most that can possibly be gathered . . . is that though no suits had been threatened . . . the state officials stood ready to perform their duties . . . should they acquire knowledge of violations." In Douglas v. City of Jeannette, 319 U.S. 157, 164–65 (1943), "the ordinance sought to be enjoined was that same day declared unconstitutional in Murdock v. Pennsylvania, . . . and nothing in the *Douglas* record suggested that the threat of its enforcement endured a decision of the Supreme Court striking it down." Amsterdam, Criminal Prosecutions Affecting Federally Guaranteed Civil Rights: Federal Removal and Habeas Corpus Jurisdiction to Abort State Court Trial, 113 U.Pa.L.Rev. 793, 904–05 n. 476 (1965). For a detailed examination of these precedents and the conclusion that cases refusing to enjoin threatened proceedings were highly exceptional see Wechsler, Federal Courts, State Criminal Law and the First Amendment, 49 N.Y. U.L.Rev. 740 (1974); Laycock, Federal Interference with State Prosecutions: The Cases Dombrowski Forgot, 46 U.Chi.L.Rev. 636 (1979). See also O'Shea v. Littleton, 414 U.S. 488 (1974) (alternative holding), refusing after *Younger* to enjoin allegedly discriminatory sentencing and bail practices by state-court judges in hypothetical future prosecutions: "Apparently the order would contemplate interruption of state proceedings to adjudicate assertions of noncompliance. . . ."

scuring the state motto on New Hampshire license plates. While acknowledging that ordinarily a declaratory judgment would provide adequate relief, the Court said:

> [T]hree successive prosecutions were undertaken against Mr. Maynard in the span of five weeks. This is quite different from a claim for federal equitable relief when a prosecution is threatened for the first time. The threat of repeated prosecutions in the future against both him and his wife, and the effect of such a continuing threat on their ability to perform the ordinary tasks of daily life which require an automobile, is sufficient to justify injunctive relief.

Three dissenters argued that enforcement of the challenged law before a federal court declared it invalid was no proof that the federal declaration would be ignored.[2]

(5) If a person is prosecuted in state court for a course of conduct he wishes to continue, can he obtain a federal injunction against additional prosecutions in the future? Cline v. Frink Dairy Co., 274 U.S. 445 (1927), in such circumstances allowed an injunction against future but not against pending prosecution. Roe v. Wade, 410 U.S. 113, 125–27 (1973), however, denied relief as to both pending and future prosecutions to a doctor against whom a state abortion case was pending although he attempted to "distinguish his status as a present state defendant from his status as a 'potential future defendant' . . .," saying only "[w]e see no merit in that distinction." See Laycock, Federal Interference with State Prosecutions: The Need for Prospective Relief, 1977 Sup.Ct.Rev. 193, 204–07, arguing that the Court "has failed to realize that, even if a pending prosecution is an adequate remedy for a completed violation, it is often no remedy at all for a contemplated future violation."

Do you agree? Wouldn't a decision in the criminal proceeding on the ground that the statute was unconstitutional have given the doctor in *Roe* pretty good assurance that he could not be prosecuted again? Professor Laycock has reservations even after the state court reaches its decision: The collateral-estoppel effect of a criminal judgment on an issue of law may be doubtful, especially if the decision is that of a trial court, which the State may be unable to appeal, and the stare decisis effect of even a high-court decision is subject to the risk of overruling. Id. at 215–16. His more fundamental concern is for the necessity of interlocutory relief to protect people in the position of the doctor in *Roe*:

> If Hallford's constitutional claims had been vindicated, he would ultimately have been acquitted, and the prosecutions would have furnished a remedy with respect to the two completed abortions. But meanwhile, what was he to do with subsequent patients? As to them, he faced precisely the dilemma described in *Steffel*: he could perform the abortions, risking further indictments and consecutive sentences if

2. General Atomic Co. v. Felter, 434 U.S. 12, 17 (1977), held a state court without power to enjoin the institution of future federal suits although the injunction did not affect federal suits that were already pending between the same parties: "[T]he rights conferred by Congress to bring in personam actions in federal courts are not subject to abridgment by state-court injunctions, regardless of whether the federal litigation is pending or prospective." Does *Steffel* cast doubt on this decision?

his constitutional claims were rejected, or he could await the outcome of the pending litigation, forever forfeiting his asserted rights with respect to patients who reached term and delivered or sought abortion during the pendency of the litigation.

Is the answer that the burden of this dilemma, unlike that in *Steffel*, is limited to the period during which the state suit is being litigated? We might so conclude if it were not for *Doran v. Salem Inn*, note 4 above, which held that *Steffel* authorized an interlocutory injunction against threatened prosecutions to prevent irreparable harm during the pendency of a suit for declaratory federal relief. As Laycock observes, the inconsistency was highlighted in *Doran* itself, where the Court gave one plaintiff preliminary relief and denied it to another facing an identical dilemma simply because the second plaintiff was a party to a state-court prosecution: "How the delay that would irreparably injure Salem Inn would not injure M & L or how the state criminal court could alleviate such injury was not explained."

Can the distinction be sustained by looking to the other side of the *Younger* balance, since only as to the second plaintiff would a federal order have disrupted an ongoing proceeding?

(6) Hicks v. Miranda, 422 U.S. 332, 349, 357 (1975), held that *Younger* applied "in full force" when a state prosecution was filed after the federal complaint but "before any proceedings of substance on the merits" in the federal court. There were four dissents: "The Court's new rule . . . is an open invitation to state officials to institute state proceedings in order to defeat federal jurisdiction." *Ex parte Young* had stated the rule otherwise: "Where one commences a criminal proceeding who is already a party to a suit then pending in a court of equity, if the criminal proceedings are brought to enforce the same right that is in issue before that court, the latter may enjoin such criminal proceedings." 209 U.S. at 162. See also Laycock, supra note 5, 1977 Sup.Ct.Rev. at 225: "The settled equity rule had been that legal remedies which first became available after the equity suit was filed were irrelevant."

(7) Huffman v. Pursue, Ltd., 420 U.S. 592, 611 n. 22 (1975), applied *Younger* to preclude an injunction against the execution of a state-court decree ordering the closing of a movie house, without deciding whether or not the time for appealing the state decree had expired: "[A]ppellee may not avoid the standards of *Younger* by simply failing to comply with the procedures of perfecting its appeal within the Ohio judicial system." Would you agree that *Younger* reflects the policy that federal courts ought not to interfere with state criminal processes when state courts provide an adequate opportunity to resolve federal claims? That a litigant's failure to appeal does not render the State's process inadequate? That *Younger's* policy to channel defenses to state prosecutions into state courts should not be defeated by a litigant's contrary desire? That *Huffman* was right?

(8) Wooley v. Maynard, 430 U.S. 705, 711 (1977), refused to extend *Huffman* to forbid an injunction against future prosecutions on behalf of parties who had failed to appeal past convictions under the same statute: "[T]he suit is in no way 'designed to annul the results of a state trial' since the relief sought is wholly prospective. . . ." Is this decision an obvious

corollary of the distinction between *Younger* and *Steffel*? But while the earlier prosecutions were pending they furnished a remedy that *Roe* and *Doran*, supra note 5, found adequate even as to future prosecutions; wasn't *Huffman's* policy of sanctions for failure to employ adequate state remedies equally applicable? See Laycock, supra note 5.

(9) Rizzo v. Goode, 423 U.S. 362 (1976), was a § 1983 injunctive action against Philadelphia's mayor and police commissioner for failure to remedy alleged violations by policemen of minority civil rights. The Court doubted both the existence of a case or controversy and that the defendants had been responsible for depriving the plaintiffs of any constitutional rights. The opinion went on as follows:

> [T]he principles of federalism which play such an important part in governing the relationship between federal courts and state governments, though initially expounded and perhaps entitled to their greatest weight in cases where it was sought to enjoin a criminal prosecution in progress . . ., likewise have applicability where injunctive relief is sought not against the judicial branch of the state government, but against those in charge of an executive agency of state or local governments. . . .

What are we to make of this? Did the Court mean to repeal § 1983's express provision for equitable relief? To overrule *Ex parte Young, Steffel v. Thompson*, and a hundred years of injunctions against state officers? To apply *Younger* to cases in which, like *Steffel*, there is no suggestion of the adequate state remedy that is the essence of *Younger*? Should we assume the Court did not mean what it said but was just casting about for a way to rid itself of an unusual and undesirable case? See Weinberg, The New Judicial Federalism, 29 Stan.L.Rev. 1191, 1222 n. 187 (1977), viewing *Rizzo* as part of a disturbing contraction by the Supreme Court of federal jurisdiction in general and of federal-court authority over state officers in particular.

Notes on Alternatives to Enjoining State-Court Proceedings

(1) *Cameron v. Johnson*, supra p. 536, was a prosecution of civil-rights workers in Mississippi during the 1960's for obstructing access to a courthouse. Similar prosecutions were common in those days, and there was a widespread belief, as documented by Professor Amsterdam, both that many of the charges were brought simply to harass innocent people attempting to exercise their constitutional rights and that the ordinary processes of state trial and federal review were inadequate to prevent such abuse. See Amsterdam, Criminal Prosecutions Affecting Federally Guaranteed Civil Rights: Federal Removal and Habeas Corpus Jurisdiction to Abort State Court Trial, 113 U.Pa.L.Rev. 793 (1965). *Cameron* held the *Younger* doctrine barred an injunction against state prosecution even when there were plausible allegations of bad faith. As Amsterdam's title suggests, litigants sought to invoke two alternative remedies to prevent their state trials: habeas corpus and removal.

(2) The principal obstacle to habeas before trial is the requirement that the petitioner first exhaust his state-court remedies, see pp. 639–43 infra. This requirement is statutory, however, only as to persons already convicted, 28 U.S.C. § 2254; accordingly the courts are relatively free to tailor the remedy to the need. Indeed the statutory exception to the exhaustion requirement for persons already convicted suggests a flexible standard for other habeas cases: Exhaustion is not required if circumstances render state processes "ineffective to protect the rights of the prisoner." If Mr. Amsterdam's allegations concerning the repressive effect of Mississippi justice were substantiated, the availability of habeas under this standard ought to have been fully established. But in Brown v. Rayfield, 320 F.2d 96 (1963), despite allegations of state-court inadequacy similar to those made by Amsterdam, the Fifth Circuit upheld the denial of habeas corpus before appeal to civil-rights pickets who had been summarily convicted for parading without a license. Mr. Amsterdam concluded that it would be improper to base the availability of pre-trial habeas on a determination that the state courts were likely to treat the petitioner unfairly in a particular case; he would allow anticipatory habeas in all cases "raising claims under the substantive guarantees of federal civil rights" because of the importance of these rights and the general likelihood that they would not be adequately protected in state courts. 113 U.Pa.L.Rev. 882–908.

Would you expect the Court that decided *Younger* and *Cameron* to agree?

(3) The second effort to get around the limitations on enjoining state–court prosecutions focused on 28 U.S.C. § 1443, a removal statute enacted during Reconstruction and then largely forgotten:

> Any of the following civil actions or criminal prosecutions, commenced in a State court may be removed by the defendant to the district court of the United States for the district and division embracing the place wherein it is pending:
>
> (1) Against any person who is denied or cannot enforce in the courts of such State a right under any law providing for the equal civil rights of citizens of the United States, or of all persons within the jurisdiction thereof;
>
> (2) For any act under color of authority derived from any law providing for equal rights, or for refusing to do any act on the ground that it would be inconsistent with such law.

Mr. Amsterdam argued for a broad construction of § 1443, and the Fifth Circuit briefly resuscitated the statute; but the Supreme Court essentially put it back to sleep in the companion cases of Georgia v. Rachel and City of Greenwood v. Peacock, 384 U.S. 780 and 808 (1966). At least four ambiguities in § 1443 were resolved in these decisions; they are discussed in the notes that follow.

(4) Both paragraphs of § 1443 allow removal only on the basis of a "law providing for (. . .) equal (. . .) rights." The Court said in *Rachel*:

> On the basis of the historical material that is available, we conclude that the phrase "any law providing for . . . equal civil

rights" must be construed to mean any law providing for specific civil rights stated in terms of racial equality. Thus, the defendants' broad contentions under the First Amendment and the Due Process Clause of the Fourteenth Amendment cannot support a valid claim for removal under § 1443, because the guarantees of those clauses are phrased in terms of general application available to all persons or citizens, rather than in the specific language of racial equality that § 1443 demands. . . .

In Chestnut v. New York, 370 F.2d 1, 3 (2d Cir. 1966), the court held an equal-protection challenge to property qualifications for grand jurors did not support removal under § 1443, quoting from *Rachel*: "[T]he phrase 'any law providing for . . . equal civil rights' must be construed to mean any law providing for specific civil rights state in terms of racial equality. . . ." Is the Equal Protection Clause such a law or isn't it? See also Bass v. Mississippi, 381 F.2d 692, 697 (5th Cir. 1967), refusing removal of a case in which a state statute excluded women from jury duty; Johnson v. Mississippi, 488 F.2d 284 (5th Cir. 1974), affirmed on other grounds, 421 U.S. 213 (1975), holding 18 U.S.C. § 245 not a law "providing for" equal civil rights: "While a variety of acts which interfere with the exercise of civil rights are made criminal by § 245, that statute confers no rights whatsoever."

(5) Section 1443(1)'s provision for removal by a person "who is denied or cannot enforce [his equal rights] in the courts of such State" is unclear: Is removal authorized whenever an equal right is denied, or only when it is denied in a state court?

In two early cases the Court not only adopted the latter interpretation but established a quite restrictive test for determining whether it could be predicted in advance of trial that a state court would fail to protect the defendant's equal rights. The first was Strauder v. West Virginia, 100 U.S. 303 (1880), which allowed removal because a state statute excluded blacks from jury service; the second was Virginia v. Rives, 100 U.S. 313 (1880), which refused removal despite allegations that the State in violation of its own statute excluded blacks from the jury. *Rives* explained the distinction:

> When a statute of the State denies his right, or interposes a bar to his enforcing it, in the judicial tribunals, the presumption is fair that they will be controlled by it in their decisions; and in such a case a defendant may affirm on oath what is necessary for a removal. . . . But when a subordinate officer of the State, in violation of State law, undertakes to deprive an accused party of a right which the statute law accords to him, as in the case at bar, it can hardly be said that he is denied, or cannot enforce, "in the judicial tribunals of the State" the rights which belong to him. In such a case it ought to be presumed the court will redress the wrong. . . .

Rachel and *Peacock* reaffirmed and expanded upon this distinction. *Rachel* involved trespass prosecutions for refusing to leave restaurants at the request of the owners; the defendants argued their expulsions had been racially motivated in violation of the Civil Rights Act of 1964, which provided that "no person shall . . . punish or attempt to punish any person for exercising or attempting to exercise" the right of nondiscriminatory access to public accommodations. 42 U.S.C. § 2000a–2. The Court allowed removal:

> [T]he precise terms of § 203(c) . . . prohibit any "attempt to punish" persons for exercising rights of equality conferred upon by them by the Act. The explicit terms of that section compel the conclusion that "nonforcible attempts to gain admittance to or remain in establishments covered by the Act, are immunized from prosecution. . . ." . . . Hence, if as alleged in the present removal petition, the defendants were asked to leave solely for racial reasons, then the mere pendency of the prosecutions enables the federal court to make the clear prediction that the defendants will be "denied or cannot enforce in the courts of [the] State" the right to be free of any "attempt to punish" them for protected activity. It is no answer in these circumstances that the defendants might eventually prevail in the state court. The burden of having to defend the prosecutions is itself the denial of a right explicitly conferred by the Civil Rights Act of 1964. . . .

In *Peacock*, however, removal was denied. Prosecuted for various offenses such as obstructing the streets, the defendants argued that they were being punished because of their efforts to register black voters. Invoking the Equal Protection Clause as well as a statute protecting the equal right to vote, they alleged in detail why they could not expect a fair trial in a state court:

> Under § 1443(1), the defendants alleged that they had been denied and could not enforce in the courts of the State rights under laws providing for equal civil rights, in that the courts and law enforcement officers of the State were prejudiced against them because of their race or their association with Negroes, and because of the commitment of the courts and officers to the State's declared policy of racial segregation. The defendants also alleged that the trial would take place in a segregated courtroom, that Negro witnesses and attorneys would be addressed by their first names, that Negroes would be excluded from the juries, and that the judges and prosecutors who would participate in the trial had gained office at elections in which Negro voters were excluded.

Said the Court:

> The present case differs from *Rachel* in two significant respects. First, no federal law confers an absolute right on private citizens—on civil rights advocates, on Negroes, or on anybody else—to obstruct a public street, to contribute to the delinquency of a minor, to drive an automobile without a license, or to bite a policeman. Second, no federal law confers immunity from state prosecution on such charges.
>
> To sustain removal of these prosecutions to a federal court upon the allegations of the petitions in this case would therefore mark a complete departure from the terms of the removal statute, which allow removal only when a person is "denied or cannot enforce" a specified federal right "in the courts of [the] State," and a complete departure as well from the consistent line of this Court's decisions from Strauder v. West Virginia, 100 U.S. 303 (1880), to Kentucky v. Powers, 201 U.S. 1 (1906). Those cases all stand for at least one basic proposition: It is

> *not* enough to support removal under § 1443(1) to allege or show that the defendant's federal equal civil rights have been illegally and corruptly denied by state administrative officials in advance of trial, that the charges against the defendant are false, or that the defendant is unable to obtain a fair trial in a particular state court. The motives of the officers bringing the charges may be corrupt, but that does not show that the state trial court will find the defendant guilty if he is innocent, or that in any other manner the defendant will be "denied or cannot enforce in the courts" of the State any right under a federal law providing for equal civil rights. The civil rights removal statute does not require and does not permit the judges of the federal courts to put their brethren of the state judiciary on trial. Under § 1443(1), the vindication of the defendant's federal rights is left to the state courts except in the rare situations where it can be clearly predicted by reason of the operation of a pervasive and explicit state or federal law that those rights will inevitably be denied by the very act of bringing the defendant to trial in the state court. . . .

There were four dissents.

Is the fact that a state statute is facially unconstitutional a better indicator of probable failure in state court than the allegations in *Peacock*?

Does *Rachel's* emphasis on the statutory right not to be prosecuted at all suggest that removal is allowable whenever the prosecution is in bad faith? See Perkins v. Mississippi, 455 F.2d 7 (5th Cir. 1972) (Brown, C.J., dissenting), arguing that the bad-faith exception to the analogous *Younger* doctrine was based on the fact that "the very pendency of the prosecution entails the deprivation of a Federal right—the right to pursue in a lawful manner the freedom guaranteed by the Constitution without being required as a precondition to defend against an illegitimate criminal charge." Is this consistent with *Peacock's* statement that the "corrupt" "motives" of the prosecutor are irrelevant under § 1443?[1]

(6) The *Peacock* defendants also invoked § 1443(2), which authorizes removal of a prosecution "[f]or any act under color of authority derived from any law providing for equal rights," arguing that they had acted "under color of" the Equal Protection Clause and other provisions that allegedly protected their conduct. Relying on a predecessor provision that had allowed removal of actions against "any officer . . . or other person, for any arrest or imprisonment" etc. under the Freedmen's Bureau Act and the 1948 Revisers' disavowal of any substantive change when the "officer" language was dropped, the Court held the "under color" provision was "available only to federal officers and to persons assisting such officers in the performance of their official duties":

> The language of the original Civil Rights Act—"arrest or imprisonment, trespasses, or wrongs"—is pre-eminently the language of enforcement. The words themselves denote the very sorts of activity for

1. See also Johnson v. Mississippi, 421 U.S. 213 (1975) (alternative holding), where the plaintiffs alleged they were being prosecuted in order to penalize protected conduct and the Court held it was not enough to claim that there was "no basis in fact" for the charges.

which federal officers, seeking to enforce the broad guarantees of the 1866 Act, were likely to be prosecuted in the state courts. . . .[2]

(7) Finally, said the Court in *Peacock*,

> the second phrase of 28 U.S.C. § 1443(2), "for refusing to do any act on the ground that it would be inconsistent with such law," has no relevance to this case. It is clear that removal under that language is available only to state officers. The phrase was added by the House of Representatives as an amendment to the Senate bill during the debates on the Civil Rights Act of 1866. In reporting the House bill, Representative Wilson, the chairman of the House Judiciary Committee and the floor manager of the bill, said, "I will state that this amendment is intended to enable State officers, who shall refuse to enforce State laws discriminating in reference to [the rights created by § 1 of the bill] on account of race or color, to remove their cases to the United States courts when prosecuted for refusing to enforce those laws." Cong. Globe, 39th Cong., 1st Sess., 1367.

(8) After *Rachel* and *Peacock*, what does § 1443 do that could not be done under the *Younger* exceptions and the general provision in § 1442 for removal of suits against federal officers? Is an amendment in order, or has the need disappeared? If additional relief against state-court proceedings should be provided, should it be by injunction, habeas corpus, or removal?[3]

SECTION 4. PENDING ACTIONS AND OTHER PROBLEMS

COLORADO RIVER WATER CONSERVATION DISTRICT v. UNITED STATES

424 U.S. 800 (1976).

MR. JUSTICE BRENNAN delivered the opinion of the Court.

The McCarran Amendment, 66 Stat. 560, 43 U.S.C. § 666, provides that "consent is hereby given to join the United States as a defendant

2. See also New York v. Galamison, 342 F.2d 255 (2d Cir. 1965), which Amsterdam, supra note 1, describes as holding that color of authority "is not made out unless federal civil rights law *directs* the state defendant to act as distinguished from guaranteeing him freedom to act if he chooses."

3. See the ALI Study (pp. 203–06), proposing to deal with the *Peacock* problem by amending the anti-injunction statute:

> An injunction is a far more delicate remedy than removal, since an injunction will issue only after a judicial determination of irreparable harm, while removal automatically brings the state proceedings to a halt until the case is remanded. It is of less importance that a properly restricted formula be devised if injunction, rather than removal, is contemplated, since the formula in the case of injunction will be applied initially by a federal judge, and is not mechanically applicable as it would be with removal. . . . There are certainly circumstances in which an injunction can issue without requiring the federal courts to prejudge their brethren of the state judiciary.

See also Bator, The State Courts and Federal Constitutional Litigation, 22 Wm. & Mary L.Rev. 605, 616–17 (1981), terming injunction the "most elegant and economical" route: "Unlike federal–defense removal, it does not necessarily draw into the federal court surrounding issues of state law and policy."

in any suit (1) for the adjudication of rights to the use of water of a river system or other source, or (2) for the administration of such rights, where it appears that the United States is the owner of or is in the process of acquiring water rights by appropriation under State law, by purchase, by exchange, or otherwise, and the United States is a necessary party to such suit." The questions presented by this case concern the effect of the McCarran Amendment upon the jurisdiction of the federal district courts under 28 U.S.C. § 1345 over suits for determination of water rights brought by the United States as trustee for certain Indian tribes and as owner of various non-Indian Government claims.

I

It is probable that no problem of the Southwest section of the Nation is more critical than that of scarcity of water. As southwestern populations have grown, conflicting claims to this scarce resource have increased. To meet these claims, several Southwestern States have established elaborate procedures for allocation of water and adjudication of conflicting claims to that resource. . . .

Under the Colorado Act, the State is divided into seven Water Divisions, each Division encompassing one or more entire drainage basins for the larger rivers in Colorado. Adjudication of water claims within each Division occurs on a continuous basis. Each month, Water Referees in each Division rule on applications for water rights filed within the preceding five months or refer those applications to the Water Judge of their Division. Every six months, the Water Judge passes on referred applications and contested decisions by Referees. A State Engineer and engineers for each Division are responsible for the administration and distribution of the waters of the State according to the determinations in each Division.

Colorado applies the doctrine of prior appropriation in establishing rights to the use of water. Under that doctrine, one acquires a right to water by diverting it from its natural source and applying it to some beneficial use. Continued beneficial use of the water is required in order to maintain the right. In periods of shortage, priority among confirmed rights is determined according to the date of initial diversion.

The reserved rights of the United States extend to Indian reservations, Winters v. United States, 207 U.S. 564 (1908), and other federal lands, such as national parks and forests, Arizona v. California, 373 U.S. 546 (1963). The reserved rights claimed by the United States in this case affect waters within Colorado Water Division No. 7. On November 14, 1972, the Government instituted this suit in the United States District Court for the District of Colorado, invoking the court's jurisdiction under 28 U.S.C. § 1345. The District Court is located in Denver, some 300 miles from Division 7. The suit, against some 1,000 water users, sought declaration of the Government's rights to waters in certain rivers and their tributaries located in Division 7. In the suit, the government asserted reserved rights on its own behalf and on behalf of certain Indian tribes, as well as rights based on state law. It sought appointment of a water master to administer any waters decreed to the United States.

Prior to institution of this suit, the Government had pursued adjudication of non-Indian reserved rights and other water claims based on state law in Water Divisions 4, 5, and 6, and the Government continues to participate fully in those Divisions.

Shortly after the federal suit was commenced, one of the defendants in that suit filed an application in the state court for Division 7, seeking an order directing service of process on the United States in order to make it a party to proceedings in Division 7 for the purpose of adjudicating all of the Government's claims, both state and federal. On January 3, 1973, the United States was served pursuant to authority of the McCarran Amendment. Several defendants and intervenors in the federal proceeding then filed a motion in the District Court to dismiss on the ground that under the Amendment, the court was without jurisdiction to determine federal water rights. Without deciding the jurisdictional question, the District Court, on June 21, 1973, granted the motion in an unreported oral opinion stating that the doctrine of abstention required deference to the proceedings in Division 7. On appeal, the Court of Appeals for the Tenth Circuit reversed, United States v. Akin, 504 F.2d 115 (1974). . . . We reverse.

II

We first consider the question of district-court jurisdiction under 28 U.S.C. § 1345. That section provides that the district courts shall have original jurisdiction over all civil actions brought by the Federal Government "[e]xcept as otherwise provided by Act of Congress." It is thus necessary to examine whether the McCarran Amendment is such an Act of Congress excepting jurisdiction under § 1345.

The McCarran Amendment does not by its terms, at least, indicate any repeal of jurisdiction under § 1345. . . . Further, the Senate report on the Amendment states: "The purpose of the proposed legislation, as amended, is to permit the joinder of the United States as a party defendant in any suit for the adjudication of rights to the use of water. . . ." Nothing in this statement of purpose indicates an intent correlatively to diminish federal-district-court jurisdiction. . . .

Accordingly, we hold that the McCarran Amendment in no way diminished federal-district-court jurisdiction under § 1345 and that the District Court had jurisdiction to hear this case.

III

We turn next to the question whether this suit nevertheless was properly dismissed in view of the concurrent state proceedings in Division 7.

A

First, we consider whether the McCarran Amendment provided consent to determine federal reserved rights held on behalf of Indians in state court. This is a question not previously squarely addressed by this Court, and given the claims for Indian water rights in this case, dismissal clearly would have been inappropriate if the state court had no jurisdiction to decide those claims. We conclude that the state court had jurisdiction over Indian water rights under the Amendment. . . .

B

Next, we consider whether the District Court's dismissal was appropriate under the doctrine of abstention. We hold that the dismissal cannot be supported under that doctrine in any of its forms. . . .

(a) Abstention is appropriate "in cases presenting a federal constitutional issue which might be mooted or presented in a different posture by a state court determination of pertinent state law." . . . See, e.g., . . . Railroad Comm'n of Texas v. Pullman Co., 312 U.S. 496 (1941). This case, however, presents no federal constitutional issue for decision.

(b) Abstention is also appropriate where there have been presented difficult questions of state law bearing on policy problems of substantial public import whose importance transcends the result in the case then at bar. Louisiana Power & Light Co. v. City of Thibodaux, 360 U.S. 25 (1959), for example, involved such a question. In particular, the concern there was with the scope of the eminent domain power of municipalities under state law. See also Kaiser Steel Corp. v. W. S. Ranch Co., 391 U.S. 593 (1968). . . . In some cases . . . [i]t is enough that exercise of federal review of the question in a case and in similar cases would be disruptive of state efforts to establish a coherent policy with respect to a matter of substantial public concern. . . . Burford v. Sun Oil Co., 319 U.S. 315 (1943). . . .

The present case clearly does not fall within this second category of abstention. While state claims are involved in the case, the state law to be applied appears to be settled. No questions bearing on state policy are presented for decision. Nor will decision of the state claims impair efforts to implement state policy as in *Burford*. To be sure, the federal claims that are involved in the case go to the establishment of water rights which may conflict with similar rights based on state law. But the mere potential for conflict in the results of adjudications, does not, without more, warrant staying exercise of federal jurisdiction. See Meredith v. Winter Haven, 320 U.S. 228 (1943). . . . The potential conflict here, involving state claims and federal claims, would not be such as to impair impermissibly the State's effort to effect its policy respecting the allocation of state waters. Nor would exercise of federal jurisdiction here interrupt any such efforts by restraining the exercise of authority vested in state officers. . . .

(c) Finally, abstention is appropriate where, absent bad faith, harassment, or a patently invalid state statute, federal jurisdiction has been invoked for the purpose of restraining state criminal proceedings, Younger v. Harris, 401 U.S. 37 (1971); . . . state nuisance proceedings antecedent to a criminal prosecution, which are directed at obtaining the closure of places exhibiting obscene films, Huffman v. Pursue, Ltd., 420 U.S. 592 (1975); or collection of state taxes, Great Lakes Dredge & Dock Co. v. Huffman, 319 U.S. 293 (1943). Like the previous two categories, this category also does not include this case. We deal here neither with a criminal proceeding, nor such a nuisance proceeding, nor a tax collection. We also do not deal with an attempt to restrain such actions or to seek a declaratory judgment as to the validity of a state criminal law under which criminal proceedings are pending in a state court.

C

Although this case falls within none of the abstention categories, there are principles unrelated to considerations of proper constitutional adjudication and regard for federal-state relations which govern in situations involving the contemporaneous exercise of concurrent jurisdictions, either by federal courts or by state and federal courts. These principles rest on considerations of "[w]ise judicial administration, giving regard to conservation of judicial resources and comprehensive disposition of litigation." Kerotest Mfg. Co. v. C–O–Two Fire Equipment Co., 342 U.S. 180, 183 (1952). . . . Generally, as between state and federal courts, the rule is that "the pendency of an action in the state court is no bar to proceedings concerning the same matter in the Federal court having jurisdiction. . . ." . . . As between federal district courts, however, though no precise rule has evolved, the general principle is to avoid duplicative litigation. See Kerotest Mfg. Co. v. C–O–Two Fire Equipment Co. supra; . . . Landis v. North American Co., 299 U.S. 248, 254 (1936). This difference in general approach between state-federal concurrent jurisdiction and wholly federal concurrent jurisdiction stems from the virtually unflagging obligation of the federal courts to exercise the jurisdiction given them. . . . Given this obligation, and the absence of weightier considerations of constitutional adjudication and state-federal relations, the circumstances permitting the dismissal of a federal suit due to the presence of a concurrent state proceeding for reasons of wise judicial administration are considerably more limited than the circumstances appropriate for abstention. The former circumstances, though exceptional, do nevertheless exist.

It has been held, for example, that the court first assuming jurisdiction over property may exercise that jurisdiction to the exclusion of other courts. Donovan v. City of Dallas, [377 U.S. 408, 412 (1964)]. . . . This has been true even where the Government was a claimant in existing state proceedings and then sought to invoke district-court jurisdiction under the jurisdictional provision antecedent to 28 U.S.C. § 1345. . . . In assessing the appropriateness of dismissal in the event of an exercise of concurrent jurisdiction, a federal court may also consider such factors as the inconvenience of the federal forum, cf. Gulf Oil Corp. v. Gilbert, 330 U.S. 501 (1947); the desirability of avoiding piecemeal litigation, cf. Brillhart v. Excess Ins. Co., 316 U.S. 491, 495 (1942); and the order in which jurisdiction was obtained by the concurrent forums, Pacific Live Stock Co. v. Oregon Water Bd., 241 U.S. 440, 447 (1916). No one factor is necessarily determinative; a carefully considered judgment taking into account both the obligation to exercise jurisdiction and the combination of factors counselling against that exercise is required. . . . Only the clearest of justifications will warrant dismissal.

Turning to the present case, a number of factors clearly counsel against concurrent federal proceedings. The most important of these is the McCarran Amendment itself. The clear federal policy evinced by that legislation is the avoidance of piecemeal adjudication of water rights in a river system. This policy is akin to that underlying the rule requiring that jurisdiction be yielded to the court first acquiring control of property, for the concern in such instances is with avoiding the generation of additional litigation through permitting inconsistent dispositions of property. This concern is heightened with respect to water rights, the relationships among which are highly interdependent. Indeed, we have recognized that actions seeking the allocation of water essentially involve the disposition of property and are best conducted in unified proceedings. . . . The consent to jurisdiction given by the McCarran Amendment bespeaks a policy that recognizes the availability of comprehensive state systems for adjudication of water rights as the means for achieving these goals.

As has already been observed, the Colorado Water Rights Determination and Administration Act established such a system for the adjudication and management of rights to the use of the State's waters. As the Government concedes and as this Court recognized in *Eagle County* and *Water Div. 5*, the Act established a single continuous proceeding for water rights adjudication which antedated the suit in District Court. . . . That proceeding "reaches all claims, perhaps month by month but inclusively in the totality." . . . Additionally, the responsibility of managing the State's waters, to the end that they be allocated in accordance with adjudicated water rights, is given to the State Engineer.

Beyond the congressional policy expressed by the McCarran Amendment and consistent with furtherance of that policy, we also find significant (a) the apparent absence of any proceedings in the District Court, other than the filing of the complaint, prior to the motion to dismiss, (b) the extensive involvement of state water rights occasioned by this suit naming 1,000 defendants, (c) the 300-mile distance between the District Court in Denver and the court in Division 7, and (d) the existing participation by the Government in Division 4, 5, and 6 proceedings. We emphasize, however, that we do not overlook the heavy obligation to exercise jurisdiction. We need not decide, for example, whether, despite the McCarran Amendment, dismissal would be warranted if more extensive proceedings had occurred in the District Court prior to dismissal, if the involvement of state water rights were less extensive than it is here, or if the state proceeding were in some respect inadequate to resolve the federal claims. But the opposing factors here, particularly the policy underlying the McCarran Amendment, justify the District Court's dismissal in this particular case.

The judgment of the Court of Appeals is reversed and the judgment of the District Court dismissing the complaint is affirmed. . . .

MR. JUSTICE STEWART, with whom MR. JUSTICE BLACKMUN and MR. JUSTICE STEVENS concur, dissenting. . . .

The Court's principal reason for deciding to close the doors of the federal courthouse to the United States in this case seems to stem from the view that its decision will avoid piecemeal adjudication of water rights.[6] To the extent that this view is based on the special considerations governing *in rem* proceedings, it is without precedential basis, [since the federal suit was not in rem] . . . . To the extent that the Court's view is based on the realistic practicalities of this case, it is simply wrong, because the relegation of the Government to the state courts will not avoid piecemeal litigation.

The Colorado courts are currently engaged in two types of proceedings under the State's water-rights law. First, they are processing new claims to water based on recent appropriations. Second, they are integrating these new awards of water rights with all past decisions awarding such rights into one all-inclusive tabulation for each water source. The claims of the United States that are involved in this case have not been adjudicated in the past. . . . The state court will, therefore, have to conduct separate proceedings to determine these claims. And only after the state court adjudicates the claims will they be incorporated into the water source tabulations. If this suit were allowed to proceed in federal court the same procedures would be

6. The Court lists four other policy reasons for the "appropriateness" of the District Court's dismissal of this lawsuit. All of those reasons are insubstantial. First, the fact that no significant proceedings had yet taken place in the federal court at the time of the dismissal means no more than that the federal court was prompt in granting the defendants' motion to dismiss. At that time, of course, no proceedings involving the Government's claims had taken place in the state court either. Second, the geographic distance of the federal court from the rivers in question is hardly a significant factor in this age of rapid and easy transportation. Since the basic issues here involve the determination of the amount of water the Government intended to reserve rather than the amount it actually appropriated on a given date, there is little likelihood that live testimony by water district residents would be necessary. In any event, the Federal District Court in Colorado is authorized to sit at Durango, the headquarters of Water Division 7, 28 U.S.C. § 85. Third, the Government's willingness to participate in some of the state proceedings certainly does not mean that it had no right to bring this action, unless the Court has today unearthed a new kind of waiver. Finally, the fact that there were many defendants in the federal suit is hardly relevant. It only indicates that the federal court had all the necessary parties before it in order to issue a decree finally settling the Government's claims. . . .

followed, and the federal court decree would be incorporated into the state tabulation, as other federal court decrees have been incorporated in the past. . . . Whether the virtually identical separate proceedings take place in a federal court or a state court, the adjudication of the claims will be neither more nor less "piecemeal." . . .

As the Court says, it is the virtual "unflagging obligation" of a federal court to exercise the jurisdiction that has been conferred upon it. Obedience to that obligation is particularly "appropriate" in this case, for at least two reasons.

First, the issues involved are issues of federal law. A federal court is more likely than a state court to be familiar with federal water law and to have had experience in interpreting the relevant federal statutes, regulations, and Indian treaties. Moreover, if tried in a federal court, these issues of federal law will be reviewable in a federal appellate court, whereas federal judicial review of the state courts' resolution of issues of federal law will be possible only on review by this Court in the exercise of its certiorari jurisdiction.

Second, some of the federal claims in this lawsuit relate to water reserved for Indian reservations. It is not necessary to determine that there is no state-court jurisdiction of these claims to support the proposition that a federal court is a more appropriate forum than a state court for determination of questions of life-and-death importance to Indians. This Court has long recognized that " '[t]he policy of leaving Indians free from state jurisdiction and control is deeply rooted in the Nation's history.' " . . .

I would affirm the judgment of the Court of Appeals. . . .

Notes on Pending Actions, Estates, and Domestic Relations

(1) It is possible to view *Colorado River* as expanding the Court's willingness to allow federal courts to refuse to hear cases within their jurisdiction:

> The Court used to say that when a statute gave jurisdiction a court could not refuse to exercise it. . . . The abstention doctrine is basically in conflict with this principle; so is forum non conveniens. The former doctrine, however, generally preserves the right to return to federal court, and the latter to sue in federal court elsewhere. . . . [M]ost of the time the Court at least has been fairly careful to confine the cases in which jurisdiction will not be exercised within fairly narrow and specific categories.

Currie, The Supreme Court and Federal Jurisdiction: 1975 Term, 1976 Sup. Ct.Rev. 183, 214–15.

Yet *Colorado River* invoked a line of authority we have not yet considered, in which federal courts had sometimes held that the mere pendency of related state-court litigation justified the refusal to accept a case over which there was federal jurisdiction.

In Stanton v. Embrey, 93 U.S. 548, 554 (1877), the Supreme Court without discussion upheld the refusal of a trial judge to dismiss a damage action in such circumstances: "The pendency of a prior suit in another jurisdiction is not a bar . . ., even though the two suits are for the same cause of action." But in P. Beiersdorf & Co. v. McGohey, 187 F.2d 14 (2d Cir. 1951), a federal trial court was upheld in refusing to proceed with an action for trademark infringement until completion of a previously filed state-court suit for a declaration that the mark had not been infringed. Accord, Amdur v. Lizars, 372 F.2d 103 (4th Cir. 1967) (derivative suit). Judge Clark, dissenting in *Beiersdorf*, appeared to suggest that a stay was forbidden by the statute giving the federal court jurisdiction; Justice Douglas attacked *Beiersdorf* and a related case as "decisions which baldly deny a suitor the remedy granted by Congress because it is not convenient to the district judge to decide the case." England v. Louisiana State Bd. of Medical Examiners, 375 U.S. 411, 430 n. 2 (1964) (dissenting opinion).

(2) At least three Supreme Court decisions before *Colorado River* lent support, more directly than did the strict abstention cases, to the stay in *Beiersdorf*. In Langnes v. Green, 282 U.S. 531 (1931), a personal-injury claim had been filed against a shipowner in a state court; he petitioned a federal court to limit his liability under 46 U.S.C. § 185. Though reaffirming that the state court could not determine the right to limit liability and that the federal court had jurisdiction, the Supreme Court held it was error to exercise it. There was no probability that additional claimants would appear and thus no necessity for a "concourse" of claims in one court. Therefore,

> to retain the cause would be to preserve the right of the ship owner, but to destroy the right of the suitor in the state court to a common law remedy [now 28 U.S.C. § 1333]; to remit the cause to the state court would be to preserve the rights of both parties. . . . The district court . . . should have . . . permit[ted] the cause to proceed in the state court, retaining, as a matter of precaution, the petition for a limitation of liability to be dealt with in the possible but . . . the unlikely event that the right of petitioner to a limited liability might be brought into question in the state court. . . .

In Brillhart v. Excess Ins. Co., 316 U.S. 491 (1942), the federal trial court had dismissed a declaratory-judgment suit because of related litigation pending in state court, and the court of appeals had reversed. The Supreme Court sent the case back for determination whether the controversy would be adequately settled by the state-court proceedings:

> Although the District Court had jurisdiction of the suit under the Federal Declaratory Judgments Act, it was under no compulsion to exercise that jurisdiction. The petitioner's motion to dismiss the bill was addressed to the discretion of the court. . . . Ordinarily it would be uneconomical as well as vexatious for a federal court to proceed in a declaratory judgment suit where another suit is pending in a state court presenting the same issues, not governed by federal law, between the same parties. . . . Where a District Court is presented with a claim such as was made here, it should ascertain whether the questions in controversy between the parties to the federal

suit, and which are not foreclosed under the applicable substantive law, can better be settled in the proceeding pending in the state court.

Brillhart was reaffirmed in dictum in Provident Tradesmens Bank v. Patterson, 390 U.S. 102, 126 (1968). To what extent is *Brillhart* dependent upon the peculiarly "discretionary" nature of declaratory relief? Compare *Louisiana Power & Light Co. v. Thibodaux*, supra 496, extending to actions at "law" the originally "equitable" doctrine of abstention for clarification of state law. Why does the *Brillhart* opinion contain the qualification "issues, not governed by federal law?" Compare the dissent of Judge Clark in *Beiersdorf*, supra, distinguishing an earlier case allowing a stay because it had involved "not a federal speciality, but stockholders' suits in the diversity jurisdiction." Is the suggestion that the more appropriate forum is the one whose law is being applied? But the law governing maritime personal injuries such as that in *Langnes v. Green*, supra, was federal. See Robins Dry Dock & Repair Co. v. Dahl, 266 U.S. 449 (1925). And what about the policy underlying the grant of diversity jurisdiction?

Finally, in Scott v. Germano, 381 U.S. 407 (1965), the Court without dissent directed a district court to stay implementation of its order invalidating a state legislative apportionment, because the state Supreme Court, in a suit filed *after* the federal one, had also held the statute unconstitutional. Without even saying whether or not the same parties were involved in the state-court suit, the Supreme Court declared it desirable for state courts rather than federal to do this kind of housecleaning. See also Landis v. North American Co., 299 U.S. 248, 254 (1936) (dictum), declaring a judge may in a proper case postpone decision pending the outcome of another case filed by different parties in another federal court raising the same legal issue: "The power to stay proceedings is incidental to the power inherent in every court to control the disposition of the causes on its docket with economy of time and effort. . . ." Does the fact that the parties are different make a stay more or less appropriate? Does it matter that both courts in *Landis* were federal?

Should both federal and state courts be required to suspend their own proceedings pending conclusion of a related action previously filed in another court? If a race to the courthouse is no less unseemly than a race to judgment, at least it avoids multiple litigation. However, it is entirely possible that the first forum chosen will not be the most appropriate one. For example, in *Langnes v. Green*, supra, the governing consideration was the right to sue at common law; should the result have been otherwise if the federal proceeding had been the first in time? And see Kerotest Mfg. Co. v. C–O–Two Fire Equip. Co., 342 U.S. 180 (1952), in which the Supreme Court decided that only the later-filed of two federal-court actions between the parties should proceed; the prior action could not have settled the entire controversy because an interested party could not have been served.

In connection with any solution to the problem of duplicative proceedings consider not only the transfer provision of 28 U.S.C. § 1404(a), General Tire & Rubber Co. v. Watkins, 373 F.2d 361 (4th Cir. 1967), but also Judge Clark's objection in *Beiersdorf* to conducting "a trial to decide if there shall be a trial." See generally Note, Stays of Federal Proceedings in Deference to Pending State Court Suits, 60 Colum.L.Rev. 684 (1960). On the related question of enjoining duplicative state-court actions see pp. 525–26 supra.

(3) In light of such decisions as those discussed in notes 1 and 2, an interesting Comment (Federal Court Stays and Dismissals in Deference to Parallel State Court Proceedings: The Impact of *Colorado River*, 44 U.Chi. L.Rev. 641, 653–58, 661, 664 (1977)), took the position that *Colorado River* actually narrowed the category of dismissals or stays in deference to pending state proceedings:

> A plurality of the circuits have adopted a broad discretionary standard and have upheld stays in deference to state proceedings in a variety of circumstances. . . . In Judge Hand's view, [for example, in Mottolese v. Kaufman, 176 F.2d 301, 303 (2d Cir. 1949),] the mere fact of duplication supplied . . . [a positive] reason [for a stay], for "equity has always interfered to prevent multiplicity of suits." . . . The Fifth Circuit . . . [, in PPG Industries, Inc. v. Continental Oil Co., 478 F.2d 674 (1973),] [p]ointing out that injunctive relief, like declaratory relief [in the *Brillhart* case, supra], is discretionary, . . . concluded that the considerations favoring stays where the federal action is declaratory similarly justify a discretionary power to stay injunctive actions in deference to parallel state proceedings. . . .
>
> [In *Colorado River*, however,] [t]he Court stated that . . . the power to dismiss in deference to the parallel [state] proceeding is limited by the "virtually unflagging obligation of the federal courts to exercise the jurisdiction given them." The circumstances that justify dismissal in deference to a state proceeding must, therefore, be "exceptional" . . . . The Court concluded that while concerns of judicial efficiency alone might justify stays to avoid duplicative litigation in two federal courts, the obligation to exercise federal jurisdiction outweighs such concerns when the parallel suit is pending in a state court. The circuits that follow the pragmatic view . . . had . . . applied essentially the same criteria in reviewing stays in deference to state court proceedings [and] . . . to . . . federal. . . .

In applying *Colorado River's* "exceptional circumstances" requirement, however, the Comment would allow stays in a great many cases, largely on the basis of the policy of the removal statutes. When the state-court plaintiff files a repetitive federal suit, the fact that only defendants may remove "arguably expresses a policy determination that it is not unfair to make the plaintiff abide by his initial choice of forum." When the state-court defendant files a reactive federal suit (as for declaratory judgment), and the state action is removable, "the avoidance of duplicative litigation justifies . . . forcing the state defendant to use the more efficient and convenient method of removal." If the state action is not removable, the defendant's reactive federal suit should fail when the unavailability of removal reflects "the judgment that the state forum is adequate," as with federal defenses, or with local defendants in diversity cases. 44 U.Chi.L. Rev. at 666–68.

Do you think such a broad stay power is consistent with the Court's stress on "exceptional circumstances"?

Do you think *Brillhart* would qualify for stay or dismissal under the *Colorado River* standard? Do you think the Court really meant the circumstances must be "exceptional"? Do you think they were "exceptional" in *Colorado River?*[1]

(4) Even when jurisdictional requirements are otherwise met, the Supreme Court has taken the position that federal courts cannot take jurisdiction to grant a divorce or to award alimony, Barber v. Barber, 62 U.S. (21 How.) 582, 584 (1859) (dictum), to probate a will, or to administer an estate, Markham v. Allen, 326 U.S. 490, 494 (1946) (dictum). Cf. Hernstadt v. Hernstadt, 373 F.2d 316 (2d Cir. 1967) (child custody and visitation rights) (alternative holding). Why can't they?

The entire subject of federal jurisdiction in matrimonial affairs was canvassed by Judge Weinstein's scholarly opinion in Spindel v. Spindel, 283 F.Supp. 797 (E.D.N.Y.1968), which upheld diversity jurisdiction to declare invalid a Mexican divorce and for damages for fraudulent inducement to marriage and for fraudulently obtaining a divorce. The power to grant divorces, the court said, was not beyond the judicial power of Article III if other jurisdictional requisites were met; the Supreme Court had reviewed divorce cases coming from federal courts in the Territories, De La Rama v. De La Rama, 201 U.S. 303 (1906). The dicta excluding divorce cases from statutory diversity jurisdiction, and the holding that state courts could entertain divorce suits against vice-consuls in the face of exclusive federal jurisdiction (§ 1351) over "actions . . . against consuls," Ohio ex rel. Popovici v. Agler, 280 U.S. 379 (1930), were explained as based on the historical argument that divorce suits were neither legal nor equitable, as required by §§ 1332 and 1351, which codified antecedents specifically limited to law and equity, but ecclesiastical. While casting minor aspersions on the Supreme Court's view of history, Judge Weinstein held these historical reasons inapplicable to the traditionally equitable and legal actions that were before him in *Spindel.*

Compare the discussion in *Markham v. Allen,* supra:

> It is true that a federal court has no jurisdiction to probate a will or administer an estate, the reason being that the equity jurisdiction conferred by the Judiciary Act . . ., which is that of the English Court of Chancery in 1789, did not extend to probate matters. . . . But it has been established by a long series of decisions of this Court that federal courts of equity have jurisdiction to entertain suits "in favor of creditors, legatees and heirs" and other claimants against a decedent's estate "to establish their claims" so long as the federal court does not interfere with the probate proceedings or assume general jurisdiction of the probate or control of the property in the custody of the state court. . . . The effect of the judgment [in the present action to determine the right of the Alien Property Custodian to share

1. See also Moses H. Cone Memorial Hospital v. Mercury Constr. Corp., 460 U.S. 1 (1983) (Brennan, J.), holding it error to stay a federal suit seeking an order requiring arbitration, although the state proceeding had been filed first: Nothing significant had yet been done in state court; the stay would not prevent piecemeal litigation; federal law governed; it was not clear that the state court would grant adequate relief; and the stay "frustrated the statutory policy [of the United States Arbitration Act] of rapid and unobstructed enforcement of arbitration agreements."

in a decedent's estate] was to leave undisturbed the orderly administration of decedent's estate in the state probate court and to decree petitioner's right in the property to be distributed after its administration. This, as our authorities demonstrate, is not an exercise of probate jurisdiction or an interference with property in the possession or custody of a state court.

See also Hess v. Reynolds, 113 U.S. 73, 77 (1885), allowing removal of an action on a claim against an estate in the face of a state statute purporting to make the jurisdiction of the state probate court exclusive: The statutory federal right to have such a question tried in a federal court "cannot be defeated by State statutes enacted for the more convenient settlement of estates of decedents." [2]

For an interesting introductory discussion of federal jurisdiction in such matters as decedents' estates and family status see Vestal & Foster, Implied Limitations on the Diversity Jurisdiction of Federal Courts, 41 Minn.L.Rev. 1 (1956).

Notes on Three-Judge District Courts

(1) Most cases in federal district courts are heard and determined by a single judge. For many years, however, Congress has provided for a special three-judge panel in certain categories of cases thought to require special safeguards against arbitrary action, with direct review in the Supreme Court. Three judges were first required in certain ICC and Sherman Act cases; these provisions (formerly 28 U.S.C. § 2325 and 15 U.S.C. § 28) were repealed by P.L. 93–584, 88 Stat. 1917 (1975), and P.L. 93–528, 88 Stat. 1706 (1974), respectively. Three judges are required in condemnation suits involving the TVA, 16 U.S.C. § 831X, and in certain actions under the 1964 Civil Rights and 1965 Voting Rights Acts, 42 U.S.C. §§ 1971(g), 1973(a), 1973(c), 1973h(c), 2000a–5(b), 2003–6(b). Of most significance, however, were the former 28 U.S.C. §§ 2281 and 2282, which required three judges in suits to enjoin enforcement of state or federal statutes, or state administrative orders, on constitutional grounds.

Section 2281 was a direct response to *Ex parte Young*, supra, 444, and other decisions upholding the power of federal courts to enjoin the enforce-

2. Recent developments in the domestic and probate fields include three thoughtful opinions by Judge Posner. In Lloyd v. Loeffler, 694 F.2d 489 (7th Cir.1982), the court upheld its jurisdiction to award compensatory damages for the abduction of a child in violation of a state custody decree, emphasizing that in the state that had issued the decree the tort suit "would be litigated as an independent civil action and not as an appendix to the custody proceeding. . . . There is thus no issue of judicial economy here." Cf. Hamilton v. Nielsen, 678 F.2d 709, 710 (7th Cir.1982), allowing federal suit to surcharge executors for alleged mismanagement: "the fact that such cases when brought in state courts in Illinois are brought in its courts of general jurisdiction . . . means that retention of federal diversity jurisdiction over such cases will not interfere with a state policy of channeling all probate-related matters to specialized courts"; Dragan v. Miller, 679 F.2d 712 (7th Cir.1982), declining jurisdiction over a suit to set aside a will because, inter alia, Illinois made such a suit part of the probate proceeding. An award of punitive damages, Judge Posner added in *Lloyd,* was more doubtful: Like an injunction, such an award would "implicitly answer the question who should have custody . . . today." And that question, the court suggested, was one at the heart of the domestic-relations exception. Do these distinctions hold water?

ment of state laws. "There are 150 cases of this kind now," said Senator Overman, "where one federal judge has tied the hands of the state officer. . . . I am opposed to allowing one little federal judge to stand up against the governor and the legislature and the attorney general of the State and say, 'This act is unconstitutional.'" 45 Cong.Rec. 7256 (1910). Overman would have liked to forbid all federal injunctions against enforcing state laws, ibid., but Congress was in a milder mood. In providing for trial by three judges and for direct appeal to the Supreme Court, Congress assuaged state feelings by enhancing the dignity of the tribunal, reduced the risk of honest or deliberate error, and cut down the adverse effect of a wrong initial decision by accelerating Supreme Court correction. Under the original statute the special court was required only if an interlocutory injunction was sought; permanent injunctions were later included. Section 2282, adopted in 1937, extended the three-judge requirement to suits attacking an "Act of Congress," as part of a package designed to protect federal programs from "the evils of conflicting decisions by inferior courts on constitutional questions and . . . the alleged abuse of the power of injunction by some of the Federal courts." S.Rep.No.711, 75th Cong., 1st Sess. 3 (1937). See generally D. Currie, The Three-Judge District Court in Constitutional Litigation, 32 U.Chi.L.Rev. 1 (1964).

(2) The three-judge provisions imposed substantial burdens both on the district courts and on the Supreme Court, leading to an explicit policy of narrow construction:

> [T]he requirement of three judges, of whom one must be a Justice of this Court or a circuit judge, entails a serious drain upon the federal judicial system particularly in regions where, despite modern facilities, distance still plays an important part in the effective administration of justice. And all but the few great metropolitan areas are such regions. Moreover, inasmuch as this procedure also brings direct review of a district court to this Court, any loose construction of the requirements of [§ 2281] . . . would defeat the purpose of Congress, as expressed by the Jurisdictional Act of February 13, 1925, to keep within narrow confines our appellate docket. . . . The history of [the section] . . ., the narrowness of its original scope, the piecemeal explicit amendments which were made to it . . ., the close construction given the section in obedience to Congressional policy . . ., combine to reveal [§ 2281] . . . not as a measure of broad social policy to be construed with great liberality, but as an enactment technical in the strict sense of the term and to be applied as such.

Phillips v. United States, 312 U.S. 246, 250–51 (1941).

As docket pressures grew and fears of arbitrary district-court action declined, there was increasing clamor for repeal of the three-judge provisions. The American Law Institute advocated abolition of the requirement in suits attacking federal statutes: "For the courts of one sovereign to strike down the legislation of another sovereign is a sufficiently grave matter to require a court of the greatest dignity. This consideration is absent when it is a federal statute that is challenged in the federal court." ALI Study 325. The Judicial Conference, the Chief Justice, and Judge Friendly argued for complete repeal. See Friendly, Federal Jurisdiction: A

General View 33 (1973), and authorities cited. In P.L. 94–381 (Aug. 12, 1976) Congress went nearly all the way, limiting the three-judge requirement in constitutional litigation to reapportionment cases:

> § 2284(a) A district court of three judges shall be convened when otherwise required by Act of Congress, or when an action is filed challenging the constitutionality of the apportionment of congressional districts or the apportionment of any statewide legislative body. . . .

Sections 2281 and 2282 were repealed. See S.Rep.No.94–204 (1975), p. 9: "These [reapportionment] issues are of such importance that they ought to be heard by a three-judge court and, in any event, they have never constituted a large number of cases."

(3) There was extensive litigation to determine when three judges were required under the earlier law, and the 1976 revision eliminated some of the problems. Prior law required, for example, that the attack be upon a "statute," "Act of Congress," or state administrative order; while a challenge to the validity of a statute *as applied* sufficed, Department of Employment v. United States, 385 U.S. 355 (1966), a challenge to "a wrong done by officers under the statute" did not, Ex parte Bransford, 310 U.S. 354, 359 (1940); cf. Phillips v. United States, supra note 2. The distinction was vague. The new law does not require that a statute or order be attacked; is there likely to be a problem in determining whether an action really challenges the "apportionment of [a] . . . statewide legislative body"? [1]

(4) Prior law also required three judges only when there was a request for an "injunction." Kennedy v. Mendoza-Martinez, 372 U.S. 144 (1963), held (contrast *Samuels v. Mackell*, supra p. 534) that declaratory judgments were not included because they left the Government "free to continue to apply the statute" pending appellate review. More realistically, the new law does not make the necessity for three judges turn on the type of relief requested.

(5) Section 2284 requires three judges in apportionment cases only when the "constitutionality" of an apportionment is challenged. Swift & Co. v. Wickham, 382 U.S. 111 (1965), held the similarly worded former provision of § 2281 did not apply when a state statute was challenged on Supremacy Clause grounds because it conflicted with a federal statute. Congress had passed the three-judge law, wrote Justice Harlan, in response to federal "injunctions against the enforcement of progressive state regulatory legislation, usually on substantive due process grounds. . . . In contrast, a case involving an alleged incompatibility between state and federal statutes . . . involves more confining legal analysis and can hardly be thought to raise the worrisome possibilities that economic or political predilections will find their way into a judgment." Moreover,

1. Cf. Consumers Union v. Supreme Court of Virginia, 446 U.S. 719 (1980) (judges enjoy legislative immunity when making general rules); Board of Regents v. New Left Education Project, 404 U.S. 541 (1972), holding three judges not required under the prior § 2281 because the regulation attacked had been adopted by a board with authority over fewer than all the institutions of higher learning in Texas; Stainback v. Mo Hock Ke Lok Po, 336 U.S. 368, 377–78 (1949), holding § 2281 did not apply to suits challenging territorial laws; Calero-Toledo v. Pearson Yacht Leasing Co., 416 U.S. 663 (1974) (contra as to the Commonwealth of Puerto Rico).

"[s]ince all federal actions to enjoin a state enactment rest ultimately on the Supremacy Clause, the words 'upon the ground of the constitutionality of such statute' would appear to be superfluous unless they are read to exclude some types of such injunctive suits." Is this last statement correct? See also Louisville & Nashville R.R. Co. v. Garrett, 231 U.S. 298, 303–04 (1914), stating that three judges were not required under the prior law when a state statute was attacked on *state* constitutional grounds. Why should that be?[2]

(6) The *Swift* case cited in note 5 also reaffirmed the holding of Ex parte Poresky, 290 U.S. 30 (1933), that three judges were not required if the constitutional ground was "insubstantial." This was not to say a single judge was free to *deny* injunctions because the statute only provided that he should not grant them; for the Court very early held, as § 2284 now makes clear, that a lone judge may not "enter judgment on the merits." Ex parte Metropolitan Water Co., 220 U.S. 539, 545 (1911). But the absence of a substantial federal question is often a jurisdictional defect, see p. 409 supra, and, said the Court in *Poresky*, "the provision requiring the presence of a court of three judges necessarily assumes that the District Court has jurisdiction." Why "necessarily?" Is there any sense in permitting a single judge to dismiss for lack of jurisdiction but not for failure to state a claim? Would three judges have been required in *Poresky* if the parties had been of diverse citizenship? Is *Poresky* law under the current § 2284?

Can a single judge dismiss because the plaintiff has an adequate legal remedy? Because an injunction is forbidden by § 1341 or § 2283 or by *Younger v. Harris*? For failure to join an indispensable party? Can a single judge abstain? Before the 1976 amendments the Court said no:

> When an application for a statutory three-judge court is addressed to a district court, the court's inquiry is appropriately limited to determining whether the constitutional question raised is substantial, whether the complaint at least formally alleges a basis for equitable relief, and whether the case presented otherwise comes within the requirements of the three-judge statute. Those criteria were assuredly met here, and the applicable jurisdictional statute therefore made it impermissible for a single judge to decide the merits of the case, either by granting or by withholding relief.

Idlewild Bon Voyage Liquor Corp. v. Epstein, 370 U.S. 713 (1962).

(7) Bailey v. Patterson, 369 U.S. 31 (1962), presented the converse of *Poresky*: An attack on state segregation laws that were obviously *unconstitutional*. Invoking *Poresky*, the Court held three judges not required under the statute as it then stood: "The statute comes into play only when an injunction is sought 'upon the ground of the constitutionality' of a statute. There is no such ground when the constitutional issue presented is essentially fictitious." Is that persuasive? Does *Bailey* survive the 1976 amendments, which forbid a single judge to "enter judgment on the merits"?

2. What happens if an apportionment is challenged both on federal constitutional and on state constitutional or federal statutory grounds? See Hagans v. Lavine, 415 U.S. 528, 543 (1974), allowing a single judge under prior law to decide a Supremacy Clause claim before referring the constitutional claim to a three-judge court. Does the new § 2284 alter this practice?

(8) In *Mendoza-Martinez*, supra note 4, neither party had asked for three judges, yet the Supreme Court felt compelled to raise the issue on its own. Was this really necessary? Section 2284 at the time required the trial judge to set the three-judge machinery in motion "on the filing of the application" for injunction in an action required to be heard by three judges. Cf. *Mansfield, Coldwater & L. M. Ry. v. Swan*, supra p. 153. See Paul v. United States, 368 U.S. 965 (1962), where Justices Black and Douglas dissented from the Court's order, on direct appeal from a three-judge decision striking down a state statute, requesting the parties to brief the question whether three judges were required. Was the Court as wrong to raise the issue in *Paul* as it was in *Mendoza*, where a single judge had sat? See 28 U.S.C. § 1253. Does the present § 2284 affect this holding of *Mendoza*?

Chapter VII

APPELLATE AND COLLATERAL REVIEW IN THE FEDERAL COURTS

SECTION 1. DIRECT APPELLATE REVIEW

HENRY v. MISSISSIPPI

379 U.S. 443 (1965).

MR. JUSTICE BRENNAN delivered the opinion of the Court.

Petitioner was convicted of disturbing the peace, by indecent proposals to and offensive contact with an 18-year-old hitchhiker to whom he is said to have given a ride in his car. The trial judge charged the jury that "you cannot find the defendant guilty on the unsupported and uncorroborated testimony of the complainant alone." The petitioner's federal claim derives from the admission of a police officer's testimony, introduced to corroborate the hitchhiker's testimony. The Mississippi Supreme Court held that the officer's testimony was improperly admitted as the fruit of "an unlawful search and was in violation of § 23, Miss.Constitution 1890." 154 So.2d 289, 294. The tainted evidence tended to substantiate the hitchhiker's testimony by showing its accuracy in a detail which could have been seen only by one inside the car. In particular, it showed that the right-hand ash tray of the car in which the incident took place was full of Dentyne chewing gum wrappers, and that the cigarette lighter did not function. The police officer testified that after petitioner's arrest he had returned to the petitioner's home and obtained the permission of petitioner's wife to look in petitioner's car. The wife provided the officer with the keys, with which the officer opened the car. He testified that he tried the lighter and it would not work, and also that the ashtray "was filled with red Dentyne chewing gum wrappers."

The Mississippi Supreme Court first filed an opinion which reversed petitioner's conviction and remanded for a new trial. The court held that the wife's consent to the search of the car did not waive petitioner's constitutional rights, and noted that the "[t] estimony of the State's witness . . . is, in effect, uncorroborated without the evidence disclosed by the inspection of defendant's automobile." 154 So.2d, at 296 (advance sheet). Acting in the belief that petitioner had been represented by nonresident counsel unfamiliar with local procedure, the court reversed despite petitioner's failure to comply with the Mississippi requirement that an objection to illegal evidence be made at the time it is introduced. The court noted that petitioner had moved for a directed verdict at the close of the State's case, assigning as one ground the use of illegally obtained evidence; it did not mention petitioner's renewal of his motion at the close of all evidence.

After the first opinion was handed down, the State filed a Suggestion of Error, pointing out that petitioner was in fact represented at his trial by competent local counsel, as well as by out-of-state lawyers. Thereupon the Mississippi Supreme Court withdrew its first opinion and filed a new opinion in support of a judgment affirming petitioner's conviction. The new opinion is identical with the first save for the result, the statement that petitioner had local counsel, and the discussion of the effect of failure for whatever reason to make timely objection to the evidence. "In such circumstances, even if honest mistakes of counsel in respect to policy or strategy or otherwise occur, they are binding upon the client as a part of the hazards of courtroom battle." 154 So.2d, at 296 (bound volume). Moreover, the court reasoned, petitioner's cross-examination of the State's witness before the initial motion for directed verdict, and introduction of other evidence of the car's interior appearance afterward, "cured" the original error and estopped petitioner from complaining of the tainted evidence. We granted certiorari, 376 U.S. 904. We vacate the judgment of conviction and remand for a hearing on the question whether the petitioner is to be deemed to have knowingly waived decision of his federal claim when timely objection was not made to the admission of the illegally seized evidence.

It is, of course, a familiar principle that this Court will decline to review state court judgments which rest on independent and adequate state grounds, even where those judgments also decide federal questions. The principle applies not only in cases involving state substantive grounds, Murdock v. City of Memphis, 20 Wall. [87 U.S.] 590, but also in cases involving state procedural grounds. Compare Herb v. Pitcairn, 324 U.S. 117, 125–126, with Davis v. Wechsler, 263 U.S. 22. But it is important to distinguish between state substantive grounds and state procedural grounds. Where the ground involved is substantive, the determination of the federal question cannot affect the disposition if the state court decision on the state law question is allowed to stand. Under the view taken in *Murdock* of the statutes conferring appellate jurisdiction on this Court, we have no power to revise judgments on questions of state law. Thus, the adequate nonfederal ground doctrine is necessary to avoid advisory opinions.

These justifications have no application where the state ground is purely procedural. A procedural default which is held to bar challenge to a conviction in state courts, even on federal constitutional grounds, prevents implementation of the federal right. Accordingly, we have consistently held that the question of when and how defaults in compliance with state procedural rules can preclude our consideration of a federal question is itself a federal question. Cf. Lovell v. City of Griffin, 303 U.S. 444, 450. As Mr. Justice Holmes said:

> "When as here there is a plan assertion of federal rights in the lower court, local rules as to how far it shall be reviewed on appeal do not necessarily prevail. . . . Whether the right was denied or not given due recognition by the [state court] . . . is a question as to which the plaintiffs are entitled to invoke our judgment." Love v. Griffith, 266 U.S. 32, 33–34.

Only last Term, we reaffirmed this principle, holding that a state appellate court's refusal, on the ground of mootness, to consider a federal claim, did not preclude our independent determination of the question of mootness; that is itself a question of federal law which this Court must ultimately decide. Liner v. Jafco, Inc., 375 U.S. 301. These cases settle the proposition that a litigant's procedural defaults in state proceedings do not prevent vindication of his federal rights unless the State's insistence on compliance with its procedural rule serves a legitimate state interest. In every case we must inquire whether the enforcement of a procedural forfeiture serves such a state interest. If it does not, the state procedural rule ought not be permitted to bar vindication of important federal rights.[3]

The Mississippi rule requiring contemporaneous objection to the introduction of illegal evidence clearly does serve a legitimate state interest. By immediately apprising the trial judge of the objection, counsel gives the court the opportunity to conduct the trial without using the tainted evidence. If the objection is well taken the fruits of the illegal search may be excluded from jury consideration, and a reversal and new trial avoided. But on the record before us it appears that this purpose of the contemporaneous-objection rule may have been substantially served by petitioner's motion at the close of the State's evidence asking for a directed verdict because of the erroneous admission of the officer's testimony. For at this stage the trial judge could have called for elaboration of the search and seizure argument and, if persuaded, could have stricken the tainted testimony or have taken other appropriate corrective action. For example, if there was sufficient competent evidence without this testimony to go to the jury, the motion for a directed verdict might have been denied, and the case submitted to the jury with a properly worded appropriate cautionary

3. This will not lead inevitably to a plethora of attacks on the application of state procedural rules; where the state rule is a reasonable one and clearly announced to defendant and counsel, application of the waiver doctrine will yield the same result as that of the adequate nonfederal ground doctrine in the vast majority of cases.

instruction. In these circumstances, the delay until the close of the State's case in presenting the objection cannot be said to have frustrated the State's interest in avoiding delay and waste of time in the disposition of the case. If this is so, and enforcement of the rule here would serve no substantial state interest, then settled principles would preclude treating the state ground as adequate; giving effect to the contemporaneous-objection rule for its own sake "would be to force resort to an arid ritual of meaningless form." Staub v. City of Baxley, 355 U.S. 313, 320; see also Wright v. Georgia, 373 U.S. 284, 289–291.[5]

We have no reason, however, to decide that question now or to express any view on the merits of petitioner's substantial constitutional claim. For even assuming that the making of the objection on the motion for a directed verdict satisfied the state interest served by the contemporaneous-objection rule, the record suggests a possibility that petitioner's counsel deliberately bypassed the opportunity to make timely objection in the state court, and thus that the petitioner should be deemed to have forfeited his state court remedies. Although the Mississippi Supreme Court characterized the failure to object as an "honest mistake," 154 So.2d, at 296 (bound volume), the State, in the brief in support of its Suggestion of Error in the Supreme Court of Mississippi asserted its willingness to agree that its Suggestion of Error "should not be sustained if either of the three counsel [for petitioner] participating in this trial would respond hereto with an affidavit that he did not know that at some point in a trial in criminal court in Mississippi that an objection to such testimony must have been made." The second opinion of the Mississippi Supreme Court does not refer to the State's proposal and thus it appears that the Court did not believe that the issue was properly presented for decision. Another indication of possible waiver appears in an affidavit attached to the State's brief in this Court; there, the respondent asserted that one of petitioner's lawyers stood up as if to object to the officer's tainted testimony, and was pulled down by co-counsel. Again, this furnishes an insufficient basis for decision of the waiver question at this time. But, together with the proposal in the Suggestion of Error, it is enough to justify an evidentiary hearing to determine whether petitioner "after consultation with competent counsel or otherwise, understandingly and knowingly forewent the privilege of seeking to vindicate his federal claims in the state courts, whether for strategic, tactical, or any other reasons that can fairly be described as the deliberate bypassing of state procedures. . . ." Fay v. Noia, 372 U.S. 391, 439.

The evidence suggests reasons for a strategic move. Both the complaining witness and the police officer testified that the cigarette lighter in the car did not work. After denial of its motion for a directed

5. We do not rely on the principle that our review is not precluded when the state court has failed to exercise discretion to disregard the procedural default. See Williams v. Georgia, 349 U.S. 375. We read the second Mississippi Supreme Court opinion as holding that there is no such discretion where it appears that petitioner was represented by competent local counsel familiar with local procedure.

verdict the defense called a mechanic who had repaired the cigarette lighter. The defense might have planned to allow the complaining witness and the officer to testify that the cigarette lighter did not work, and then, if the motion for directed verdict were not granted, to discredit both witnesses by showing that it did work, thereby persuading the jury to acquit. Or, by delaying objection to the evidence, the defense might have hoped to invite error and lay the foundation for a subsequent reversal. If either reason motivated the action of petitioner's counsel, and their plans backfired, counsel's deliberate choice of the strategy would amount to a waiver binding on petitioner and would preclude him from a decision on the merits of his federal claim either in the state courts or here. Although trial strategy adopted by counsel without prior consultation with an accused will not, where the circumstances are exceptional, preclude the accused from asserting constitutional claims, see Whitus v. Balkcom, 333 F.2d 496 (C.A. 5th Cir. 1964), we think that the deliberate bypassing by counsel of the contemporaneous-objection rule as a part of trial strategy would have that effect in this case.

Only evidence extrinsic to the record before us can establish the fact of waiver, and the State should have an opportunity to establish that fact. . . . Therefore, the judgment is vacated and the case is remanded to the Mississippi Supreme Court for further proceedings not inconsistent with this opinion. . . .

[Justice Black, dissenting, argued that the Court should reach the merits because there was neither evidence of waiver nor an adequate state ground. In the past, he said, the Mississippi Supreme Court had held that "errors affecting fundamental rights are exceptions to the rule that questions not raised in the trial court cannot cannot be raised for the first time on appeal."

["Yet this Court now apparently holds that the state court may, if it chooses to do so, depart from its prior cases and apply a new, stricter rule against this defendant and thereby prevent this Court from reviewing the case to see that his federal constitutional rights were safeguarded. . . . I think such a procedural device for shutting off our review of questions involving constitutional rights is too dangerous to be tolerated. . . ."

[Justice Harlan, joined by Justices Clark and Stewart, dissented because the Court's opinion "portends a severe dilution, if not complete abolition, of the concept of 'adequacy' as pertaining to state procedural grounds." The Mississippi rule served a substantial interest, he argued, because an objection buried in a long motion for directed verdict did not present the same opportunity for reaching the correct decision as an objection at the same time the evidence was offered. Yet, he said, the Court's opinion implies "that under 'settled principles,' the contemporaneous-objection rule relied upon in this case could be declared inadequate."]

Notes on Supreme Court Review of State-Court Decisions

A. Reviewing Federal Questions

(1) The position that the States are the ultimate judges of the meaning of the Constitution was asserted in the Kentucky and Virginia Resolutions, 4 Elliot's Debates 528–540; in South Carolina's Ordinance of Nullification, 1 S.C.Stat. 329 (1832); and more recently by Mississippi's Governor Ross Barnett. But the Supreme Court had passed upon the validity of a state law as early as 1796, in Ware v. Hylton, 3 U.S. (3 Dall.) 199; and the Civil War, if not the Supreme Court's decisions, resolved this question in favor of a federal power of decision. Is this regrettable?

> If the national government is to have vitality, it is often said, the states may not be left with the last word in delineating federal and state powers. See e.g., Holmes, Collected Legal Papers 295–96 (1920); Jackson, The Struggle for Judicial Supremacy 15, 17 (1941). Quite the same view of human nature supports the argument that if the states are not to be reduced to administrative departments, the federal government may not have final say; as Spencer Roane wrote, "there is a Charybdis to be avoided, as well as a Scylla; . . . a centripetal, as well as a centrifugal principle, exists in the government." Hunter v. Martin, 4 Munf. (18 Va.) 1, 26 (1815). See 1 Warren, The Supreme Court in United States History 448 (2d ed. 1926). But the last word must reside somewhere; the federal courts, independent of most federal as well as state political pressures, are the most impartial repository of the power to arbitrate between the states and the nation.

D. Currie, The Three-Judge District Court in Constitutional Litigation, 32 U.Chi.L.Rev. 1, 4–5 (1964). But Spencer Roane was dead right, wasn't he?

(2) It was a narrower question that came before the Court in the famous case of Martin v. Hunter's Lessee, 14 U.S. (1 Wheat.) 304 (1816). This was a dispute over Virginia land once owned by a British subject and allegedly confiscated by Virginia. The defendant argued that Virginia had not escheated the land until after the treaties of 1783 and 1794, which confirmed British titles and forbade future confiscations. The Virginia Court of Appeals held for the plaintiff, and the United States Supreme Court reversed, finding that the Virginia statutes had not dispensed with the common-law requirement of an "inquest of office" and therefore that there had been no escheat prior to the treaties confirming the British title. Fairfax's Devisee v. Hunter's Lessee, 11 U.S. (7 Cranch) 603 (1813). On remand the Virginia court refused to obey the mandate, holding that § 25 of the Judiciary Act (see p. 764 infra), which gave the Supreme Court jurisdiction over state-court judgments, was unconstitutional.

The Supreme Court reversed again. Since federal questions were certain to come up as defenses in state courts, said Justice Story, the only way the federal judicial power could reach *all* cases arising under federal law, as the Constitution prescribed, was for federal courts to assert appellate jurisdiction over cases in the state courts. (The Virginia court had anticipated this ploy, pointing out that it would give the Supreme Court power to review cases from English and French courts as well.) Removal was no answer; it too, said Story, was an exercise of appellate jurisdiction (contrary both to common sense and to Marshall's statement in *Marbury v. Madison*, supra p. 21, that appellate jurisdiction "revises and corrects the proceedings in a cause already instituted"). There was nothing novel about the Supreme Court's jurisdiction over state-court decisions, he continued, because a similar provision had been made regarding prize cases under the Confederation. Friends and enemies alike of the new Constitution had declared that the power existed;[1] it had been written into the statutes in 1789 by men who had helped to draft the Constitution itself; it had been exercised on many occasions and had never before been questioned.

It had been argued that "no great public mischief" would result from denying Supreme Court jurisdiction, because state-court judges, oath-bound to support the Constitution, "must be presumed to be men of learning and integrity." Of course they must, said the Court "very cheerfully," but "the constitution has presumed (whether rightly or wrongly we do not inquire) that state attachments, state prejudices, state jealousies, and state interests, might sometimes obstruct, or control, or be supposed to obstruct or control, the regular administration of justice."[2] Moreover, "judges of equal learning and integrity, in different states, might differently interpret a statute, or a treaty of the United States, or even the constitution itself." If there were no court to resolve these conflicts, matters would be "truly deplorable." Original federal-court jurisdiction was no answer to these problems, for equality demanded that defendants as well as plaintiffs have access to a federal forum. Removal was not only appellate but inadequate too: "In respect to criminal prosecutions, the difficulty seems admitted to be insurmountable" (why?), and in civil cases, "if state courts should deny the constitutionality of the authority to remove suits from their cognizance, in what manner could they be compelled to relinquish the jurisdiction?"

Finally, although it did not believe the question properly before it, the Court added that the earlier appeal had been within its statutory jurisdiction: Despite the final clause of § 25 limiting review to questions immediately affecting the construction of a treaty or federal law, it was impossible to decide whether a title was protected by the treaty without investigating the title itself, and if § 25 were construed to forbid this it would be "wholly inadequate for the purposes which it professes to have in view" and might be "evaded at pleasure."

For detailed accounts of the background to this litigation see 1 C. Warren, The Supreme Court in United States History, 442–50 (Rev. ed.

1. Indeed it was assumed by both sides in the Convention argument over the creation of lower federal courts (see p. 108 supra) that the Supreme Court could review state courts; the issue was whether additional protection for federal rights was needed. See, e.g., 1 M. Farrand, Records of the Federal Convention of 1787 124 (Rutledge), "arguing that the State Tribunals might and ought to be left in all cases to decide in the first instance, the right of appeal to the supreme national tribunal being sufficient to secure the national rights & uniformity of judgments. . . ."

2. The renowned States-Righter John C. Calhoun likewise acknowledged the importance of Supreme Court review, though from the opposite perspective: "If the appellate power from the State courts to the U. States court provided for by the 25th Sec. did not exist, the practical consequence would be, that each government would have a negative on the other. . . ." Quoted in G. Gunther, Cases & Materials on Constitutional Law 38 n. 8 (11th ed. 1985).

1926); 2 W. Crosskey, Politics and the Constitution in the History of the United States 785–817 (1953).

(3) The spirit of the Virginia and Kentucky Resolutions will not down. In crisis after crisis, from *McCulloch v. Maryland* to *Baker v. Carr*, every important decision invalidating a state law has brought forth a rash of irresponsible proposals to limit the Court's jurisdiction, to alter its procedures or composition, or to subject its decisions to review by an unwieldy tribunal composed of judges from the courts of each of the fifty states. South Carolina once prescribed criminal penalties for appealing state court decisions to the Supreme Court. Others sought to deprive the Court of its jurisdiction over state judgments, to require the concurrence of five of the then seven Justices to hold a state law invalid, or to give appellate jurisdiction to the Senate whenever the validity of a state law was questioned.

D. Currie, The Three-Judge District Court in Constitutional Litigation, 32 U.Chi.L.Rev. 1, 5 & n. 27 (1964). What is "irresponsible" about these proposals?

See generally Warren, Legislative and Judicial Attacks on the Supreme Court of the United States—A History of the Twenty-Fifth Section of the Judiciary Act, 47 Am.L.Rev. 1, 161 at 163–164 (1913).

(4) Until 1867 § 25 provided for review only if the *validity* of a treaty or of a federal or state statute or "authority," or the *construction* of a federal treaty, statute, or commission, or of the Constitution was drawn in question, and only if the federal claim had been denied. The 1867 revision allowed review without respect to questions of validity or construction, "where any title, right, privilege, or immunity is claimed under the constitution, or any treaty or statute of, or commission held, or authority exercised under the United States," but, as before, only if the state court had decided against the federal claim. In 1914, following the decision in Ives v. South Buffalo Ry., 201 N.Y. 271, 94 N.E. 431 (1911), holding a state's workers'-compensation law contrary to both federal and state constitutions, Congress gave the Supreme Court jurisdiction over cases in which the federal right had been upheld. Act of Dec. 23, 1914, c. 2, 38 Stat. 790. Why?

The provisions for review of state-court decisions were extended to Puerto Rico in 1961, and to the District of Columbia in 1970. 28 U.S.C. §§ 1258, 1257(b). Under the present statute, 28 U.S.C. § 1257, can every kind of federal question resolved by state courts be taken to the Supreme Court? [3]

B. *Questions of State Law*

(5) In 1867 Congress, which was not exactly in a States'-rights mood (see pp. 102–03 supra), repealed the clause of § 25 limiting Supreme Court review of state-court decisions to errors immediately respecting the questions giving jurisdiction to review. It is "highly probable," according to

3. See also Zucht v. King, 260 U.S. 174 (1922), holding that the Supreme Court had no jurisdiction to review a state-court judgment unless the federal question was "substantial." Cf. *Bell v. Hood*, supra p. 409, applying the same principle in determining district court jurisdiction.

Professor Warren, that by this repeal Congress meant to provide that "every question passed on by the State Court should be open for reconsideration in the Supreme Court." 2 The Supreme Court in United States History 682 (rev. ed. 1926). But the Supreme Court rejected this argument in the almost-as-famous-as-*Martin* case of Murdock v. Memphis, 87 U.S. (20 Wall.) 590 (1875), making clear that as a rule only federal questions may be decided.

Murdock's ancestors had conveyed land to the city some years before, with an equitable reversion in case the property was not appropriated for a naval depot. The city had conveyed without strings to the United States, which had built a depot but then ceded the land back to Memphis. Murdock claimed under the federal cession statute as well as the general law of trusts; the state court held against him on both grounds; and the Supreme Court, affirming on the federal issue, refused to look further.

Much of Justice Miller's tedious opinion is devoted to arguments based upon the language of § 25 as it then stood, providing for review of state-court judgments "in the same manner, and under the same regulations, and the writ shall have the same effect, as if the judgment were that of a federal court." Murdock urged that this meant the scope of review was the same as in writs of error to lower federal courts, which brought up the entire case. The Court disagreed: That the writ shall have the same "effect" meant that the case should be transferred to the Supreme Court; "manner" and "regulations" referred to technical procedures. The scope of review could not be the same in any event, because chancery cases from federal courts were reviewed by appeal and those from state courts by writ of error; only on appeal, and not on writ of error, were the facts tried de novo.

The repeal of the restrictive clause, the Court thought, might have been favored for "varying reasons," among them that the statutory limitation had been declaratory of a constitutional one; Mr. Justice Miller refused to construe such an ambiguous omission as intended to reverse a long-standing policy "vital" to the "independence of the State courts." The reasons for giving the Supreme Court jurisdiction, as the Court had said in *Martin*, were to preserve uniformity in the interpretation of federal law and to protect the federal rights of the litigant. Neither of these purposes required the investigation of non-federal issues. For these reasons, and in order to avoid what it saw as a flood of Supreme Court litigation on local questions brought in on the coattails of frivolous federal issues, the Court held the statute did not authorize review of non-federal matters, not reaching the question whether a broader review would be constitutional. Three dissenters argued that if jurisdiction existed it extended to the whole case; one of these, finding no federal issue, would have dismissed the writ.

Consider the effect a contrary holding in *Murdock* would have had upon the lawmaking powers of the States. Consider also the sporadic nature of that effect if the Supreme Court had power to determine state law only in the fortuitous event that there was a federal question in the case. The consequence would have been, wouldn't it, that no one would have been in a position to supervise the development of state law? Is this one reason why the Supreme Court, unlike the district courts, lacks pendent jurisdiction over ancillary questions of local law?

C. *The Adequate State Ground*

(6) In *Murdock v. Memphis* the court said that if the state-court decision was supported by an adequate, independent non-federal ground the federal question should be decided and the judgment affirmed. *Henry v. Mississippi* states the current view that the presence of an adequate and independent state ground deprives the Supreme Court of jurisdiction to decide even the federal question. In Jankovich v. Indiana Toll Road Commission, 379 U.S. 487 (1965), for example, the state court had held that an airport-zoning ordinance violated both the federal and state constitutions; the Supreme Court threw out the entire case for want of jurisdiction.

The reasons for the current rule are concisely stated in Herb v. Pitcairn, 324 U.S. 117, 125–26 (1945):

> Our only power over state judgments is to correct them to the extent that they incorrectly adjudge federal rights. And our power is to correct wrong judgments, not to revise opinions. We are not permitted to render an advisory opinion, and if the same judgment would be rendered by the state court after we corrected its views of federal laws, our review could amount to nothing more than an advisory opinion.[1]

(7) When it is not clear whether a state-court decision rests on state or federal law or on both, should the Supreme Court accept jurisdiction because it cannot be certain that a reversal on federal grounds would be merely advisory?[2] Should it dismiss the case because the party seeking review has not met his burden of establishing jurisdiction, cf. Memphis Natural Gas Co. v. Beeler, 315 U.S. 649, 651 (1942), or because the Court should "choose the interpretation which does not face us with a constitutional question," Black v. Cutter Laboratories, 351 U.S. 292, 299 (1956)? In *Herb v. Pitcairn*, supra note 6, the Court seemed to disapprove both these extremes:

> We cannot perform our duty to refrain from interfering in state law questions and also to review federal ones without making a determination whether the one or the other controls the judgment.

324 U.S. at 127.

1. See Sandalow, Henry v. Mississippi and the Adequate State Ground: Proposals for a Revised Doctrine, 1965 Sup.Ct.Rev. 187, 201–02, arguing that the adequate-state-ground rule is not of constitutional dimension:

> Cases may arise in which a statement by the Court on the federal issues presented would serve a useful purpose. . . . [T]he frequency with which state courts, in interpreting state constitutions, rely on federal decisions construing a similar provision in the federal constitution suggests that the Court ought not to be blind to the leadership that it in fact exerts in this area. . . . The independence of state courts would not be sacrificed since the judgment would be undisturbed. Moreover, the record before the Court will normally be fully adequate to illumine the issues and the Court will frequently have the benefit of adversary proceedings, thus removing the primary objections to "advisory opinions."

2. See Cicenia v. Lagay, 357 U.S. 504, 507, n. 2 (1958).

In accordance with this reasoning, in Minnesota v. National Tea Co., 309 U.S. 551 (1940), the judgment was vacated for clarification; in *Herb* the Supreme Court held the case while the parties asked the state courts for an explanation.

Acknowledging that earlier decisions had not "developed a satisfying and consistent approach" for determining whether a state court had intended to rest its decision on an independent state ground, the Supreme Court announced a new test in Michigan v. Long, 463 U.S. 1032 (1983). The state Supreme Court had held that a search offended both "the Fourth Amendment of the United States Constitution and art. 1, § 11 of the Michigan Constitution." Noting that only federal cases had been cited for this conclusion, the Court reached the merits: "[W]hen . . . a state court decision fairly appears to rest primarily on federal law, or to be interwoven with the federal law, and when the adequacy and independence of any possible state ground is not clear from the face of the opinion, we will accept as the most reasonable explanation that the state court decided the case the way it did because it believed that federal law required it to do so." Justice Stevens dissented.

(8) In order to preclude review of a federal question, as the Court said in *Henry*, the state ground must be both "adequate" and "independent." What is meant by the second requirement was illustrated in Delaware v. Prouse, 440 U.S. 648 (1979), in which the court reviewed a decision holding that a search violated the federal constitution, although the state court had also held its own constitution offended:

> As we understand the opinion below, Art. I, § 6, of the Delaware Constitution will automatically be interpreted at least as broadly as the Fourth Amendment; that is, every police practice authoritatively determined to be contrary to the Fourth and Fourteenth Amendments will, without further analysis, be held to be contrary to Art. I, § 6. . . . This is one of those cases where "at the very least, the [state] court felt compelled by what it understood to be federal constitutional considerations to construe . . . its own law in the manner it did." . . . If the state court misapprehended federal law, "[i]t should be freed to decide . . . these suits according to its own local law."

(9) One aspect of the requirement that the state ground be "adequate" is that it be "sufficient, in itself, to maintain the judgment," Eustis v. Bolles, 150 U.S. 361, 369–70 (1893). Would the Supreme Court have had jurisdiction in the *Jankovich* case, supra note 6, if Indiana had held the ordinance violated *neither* the federal nor the state constitution?

(10) The adequacy of a state ground, however, has other dimensions as well. To begin with, a state-law ground that is unconstitutional obviously cannot be "adequate" to preclude Supreme Court review. In Brinkerhoff-Faris Trust & Savings Co. v. Hill, 281 U.S. 673 (1930), for example, the state court had denied relief "for failure to resort to an administrative remedy that earlier decisions held the state administrative body lacked the power to award and that it was then too late to pursue," Hart & Wechsler, The Federal Courts and the Federal System 605 (3d ed. 1988); the Supreme Court held the state decision a denial of due process.

(11) Moreover, despite *Murdock v. Memphis*, supra note 5, as early as *Martin v. Hunter's Lessee* the Court asserted an authority to investigate the legitimacy of the state ground that went beyond the question whether the state law in itself was unconstitutional. For in *Martin*, note 2 supra, despite the statutory provision restricting review to issues that "immediately respect[ed]" the treaty's construction, the Court reversed Virginia's decision as to the date of escheat under state law, saying that if § 25 did not give the Court power to do this the section would be "wholly inadequate for the purposes which it professes to have in view, and may be evaded at pleasure."

See also Ward v. Love County, 253 U.S. 17 (1920), in which a state court had refused relief to Indians claiming federal immunity from taxation, on the ground that they had paid the tax voluntarily. Without denying that state law governed the question, the Court held that the "decision that the taxes were paid voluntarily was without any fair or substantial support," justifying its intervention as follows:

> The right to the exemption was a federal right, and was specifically set up and claimed as such in the petition. Whether the right was denied, or not given due recognition, by the Supreme Court is a question as to which the claimants were entitled to invoke our judgment, and this they have done in the appropriate way. It therefore is within our province to inquire not only whether the right was denied in express terms, but also whether it was denied in substance and effect, as by putting forward non-federal grounds of decision that were without any fair or substantial support. . . . Of course, if non-federal grounds, plainly untenable, may be thus put forward successfully, our power to review easily may be avoided. . . . With this qualification, it is true that a judgment of a state court, which is put on independent non-federal grounds broad enough to sustain it, cannot be reviewed by us. But the qualification is a material one and cannot be disregarded without neglecting or renouncing a jurisdiction conferred by law and designed to protect and maintain the supremacy of the Constitution and the laws made in pursuance thereof.[3]

3. In Indiana ex rel. Anderson v. Brand, 303 U.S. 95 (1938), a teacher argued that a law repealing an earlier tenure provision impaired the obligation of her contract in violation of Article I, § 10. The state court held that the original Tenure Law had not created a contract but had merely stated a rule relating to "the exercise of their powers by the school authorities"; examining the state law precedents, the Supreme Court reversed. Conceding that whether Indiana had bound itself by contract was a question "primarily of state law" on which the Court must "accord respectful consideration and great weight to the views of the State's highest court," the Supreme Court held that "in order that the constitutional mandate may not become a dead letter, we are bound to decide for ourselves whether a contract was made, what are its terms and conditons, and whether the State has, by later legislation, impaired its obligation."

Is this just another application of the principle of *Ward v. Love County*, or is it a special rule for contract-clause cases? Chief Justice Marshall's argument that the contract clause created its own law of contract was rejected by the Court in Ogden v. Saunders, 25 U.S. (12 Wheat.) 213 (1827), which held the purpose and effect of that clause were simply to prevent retroactive legislation destroying state-created rights. Nevertheless, in United States Mortgage Co. v. Matthews, 293 U.S. 232 (1934), in which the state court had held there was a contract and that it had been impaired, the Supreme Court reversed, holding there had

(12) Is there a basis for Justice Brennan's distinction in *Henry* between "substantive" and "procedural" state grounds? Professor Sandalow says no: Whether the state ground is substantive or procedural, if it is permitted to stand the Court's decision of the federal question cannot affect the result; and a substantive state ground, as well as a procedural one, can obstruct the enforcement of a federal right. Sandalow, Henry v. Mississippi and the Adequate State Ground: Proposals for a Revised Doctrine, 1965 Sup.Ct.Rev. 187, 197–98. Is the distinction between substance and procedure a clearer one here than in other areas of the law, such as the applicability of state law in diversity cases? [4]

(13) In light of Article VI's provision that state judges are "bound" by federal law "any Thing in the Constitution or Laws of any State to the Contrary notwithstanding," why is it that state procedural rules are ever permitted to preclude the assertion of federal rights?

Analogies may be helpful. Just as the Supremacy Clause requires state courts to apply applicable federal law, the Full Faith and Credit Clause requires a state court entertaining an action based entirely on foreign facts to apply the law of a State with an interest in the outcome; and *Erie Railroad Co. v. Tompkins*, p. 327 supra, held the Constitution required federal courts in diversity cases to apply state law. Yet both a state court enforcing foreign law and a federal court in diversity may often follow their own procedures. See, e.g., Wells v. Simonds Abrasive Co., 345 U.S. 514 (1953) (short local limitation statute); *Hanna v. Plumer*, p. 339 supra (Federal Rules of Civil Procedure). One explanation sometimes given is that a forum that is disinterested as to the merits of a case may nevertheless have a legitimate interest in the administration of its courts. See B. Currie, Selected Essays on the Conflict of Laws 360 (1963); *Byrd v. Blue Ridge Rural Electric Cooperative, Inc.*, p. 346 supra ("there is a strong federal policy against allowing state rules to disrupt the judge-jury relationship in the federal courts").

Do these analogies suggest that the Supremacy Clause should also be interpreted to allow state courts to preclude the assertion of federal rights by invoking procedural rules that serve legitimate interests in the administration of justice? In other words, isn't the test Justice Brennan laid down in *Henry* in accord with the Court's treatment of analogous cases? But did Justice Brennan apply his test properly to the facts of *Henry*? [5]

been no obligation. Does this follow from *Brand?*

See also Ford v. Ford, 371 U.S. 187 (1962). A South Carolina court had held itself bound by a Virginia judgment under the Full Faith and Credit Clause. The Supreme Court reversed, holding that the judgment was not conclusive as a matter of Virginia law.

4. The Supreme Court has often refused to decide federal questions that were not properly raised or preserved in the state courts below. Sometimes, as in Herndon v. Georgia, 295 U.S. 441 (1935), the Court's refusal has been based upon the language of § 1257 ("this court is without jurisdiction for the reason that no federal question was seasonably raised in the court below or passed upon by that court"); sometimes upon a "waiver" of federal rights, as in Parker v. Illinois, 333 U.S. 571 (1948); and sometimes upon the principle that the decision below is supported by an adequate state ground, as in Edelman v. California, 344 U.S. 357 (1953).

5. Cf. Fed.R.Crim.P. 41(e), which requires a motion in the federal courts to suppress illegally seized evidence to be made "before trial or hearing unless opportunity therefor did not exist or the defendant was not aware of the grounds for the motion" but allows the court "in its discre-

Yet there is a final analogy that is closer still: cases such as *Dice v. Akron, Canton & Youngstown Railroad Co.*, supra p. 426, which required a state court to follow federal practice as to the scope of issues triable by jury in a case under the Federal Employers' Liability Act. Don't these decisions establish that a legitimate state interest will not always suffice to allow a State to follow its own procedures in enforcing federal law? And isn't the adequate-state-ground problem just a subcategory of the problem presented in *Dice*? Did Professor Sandalow (supra note 12, at 228) get to the heart of the matter when he wrote that the Court "must assure . . . that state law, though evenly applied, does not unduly burden federal rights?"

(14) The Supremacy Clause clearly requires the state courts, absent an adequate procedural ground, to entertain defenses based on federal law. Does it also require state courts to entertain actions by plaintiffs seeking relief under federal law? Or is a state law denying jurisdiction an adequate state ground?

In General Oil Co. v. Crain, 209 U.S. 211 (1908), a state court dismissed a suit to enjoin the enforcement of an allegedly unconstitutional tax on the ground of sovereign immunity. The Supreme Court upheld its jurisdiction and decided the merits:

> If a suit against state officers is precluded in the national courts by the Eleventh Amendment to the Constitution and may be forbidden by a state to its courts, . . . it must be evident that an easy way is open to prevent the enforcement of many provisions of the Constitution. . . . It being then the right of a party to be protected against a law which violates a constitutional right, . . . it is manifest that a decision which denies such protection gives effect to the law, and the decision is reviewable by this court.

See also Ward v. Love County, 253 U.S. 17, 24 (1920), reversing a state court that had refused to order the refund of illegally collected taxes:

> As the payment was not voluntary, but made under compulsion, no statutory authority was essential to enable or require the county to refund the money. . . . To say that the county could collect these unlawful taxes by coercive means and not incur any obligation to pay them back is nothing short of saying that it could take or appropriate the property of these Indian allottees arbitrarily and without due process of law. Of course this would be in contravention of the Fourteenth Amendment. . . .[6]

tion" to entertain the motion "at the trial or hearing"; Rule 12(h) of the federal civil rules, which with a few exceptions provides that a party "waives all defenses and objections" he does not present in his answer or pre-trial motion; 28 U.S.C. §§ 2101, 2107, see FTC v. Minneapolis-Honeywell Regulator Co., 344 U.S. 206 (1952), imposing time limits on seeking review in federal courts. Are all these provisions invalid? Or are the state courts subject to more stringent federal procedural requirements than the federal courts themselves?

6. Cf. Testa v. Katt, 330 U.S. 386 (1947), supra p. 186, requiring a state court to hear a suit under federal price-control legislation; Young v. Ragen, 337 U.S. 235 (1949), suggesting, see Sandalow, supra note 12, 1965 Sup.Ct.Rev. at 210–15, that States may be required to provide post-conviction remedies for federal rights; Hughes v. Fetter, 341 U.S. 609 (1951), holding the Full Faith and Credit Clause required Wisconsin to entertain an action based on Illinois law; Douglas v. New York, New Haven & Hartford Railroad Co.,

If the federal courts are open, as they were in *Crain* under *Ex parte Young*, p. 444 supra, does the denial of a state forum for a plaintiff with a federal claim have as detrimental an effect on federal rights as the refusal of a state court to entertain a federal defense? See Georgia Rail Road & Banking Co. v. Musgrove, 335 U.S. 900 (1949), dismissing an appeal in a case evidently identical to *Crain* as based on an adequate state ground.

(15) What policies support the *Henry* Court's doctrine of "waiver" or "forfeiture" by deliberate failure to raise federal questions in accord with state procedure, and how does one fit it into § 1257? To what extent does this doctrine undermine the Court's position respecting the adequate state ground? [7]

COX BROADCASTING CORP. v. COHN

420 U.S. 469 (1975).

MR. JUSTICE WHITE delivered the opinion of the Court.

The issue before us in this case is whether, consistently with the First and Fourteenth Amendments, a State may extend a cause of action for damages for invasion of privacy caused by the publication of the name of a deceased rape victim which was publicly revealed in connection with the prosecution of the crime. . . .

In the course of the proceedings that day, appellant Wassell, a reporter covering the incident for his employer, learned the name of the victim from an examination of the indictments which were made available for his inspection in the courtroom. . . . Later that day, Wassell broadcast over the facilities of station WSB–TV, a television station owned by appellant Cox Broadcasting Corporation, a news report concerning the court proceedings. The report named the victim of the crime and was repeated the following day.

In May 1972, appellee brought an action for money damages against appellants. . . . The trial court, rejecting appellants' constitutional claims and holding that the Georgia statute gave a civil remedy to those injured by its violation, granted summary judgment to appellee as to liability, with the determination of damages to await trial by jury.

On appeal, the Georgia Supreme Court, in its initial opinion, held that the trial court had erred in construing [the statute] to extend a civil cause of action for invasion of privacy and thus found it unnecessa-

279 U.S. 377 (1929), permitting a state court to decline jurisdiction, on grounds of forum non conveniens, of an FELA claim it would otherwise have been required to hear.

7. On remand the Supreme Court of Mississippi, after further proceedings before a trial judge, held Henry had knowingly waived his right to object to introduction of the evidence, Henry v. State, 198 So.2d 213 (Miss.1967). After further proceedings a federal district court took more evidence and granted habeas corpus, finding there had been no waiver or deliberate bypass: The failure to object earlier had been "deliberate" only in the sense that Henry's attorneys had thought they had no right to object at that stage for their intended purpose of obtaining a directed verdict; the State had offered nothing more than "innuendo" to sustain its burden of showing waiver. Henry v. Williams, 299 F.Supp. 36 (D.Miss.1969).

ry to consider the constitutionality of the statute. . . . The court went on to rule, however, that the complaint stated a cause of action "for the invasion of appellee's right of privacy, or for the tort of public disclosure"—a "common law tort exist[ing] in this jurisdiction without the help of the statute that the trial judge in this case relied on." . . . The court explained, however, that liability did not follow as a matter of law and that summary judgment was improper; whether the public disclosure of the name actually invaded appellee's "zone of privacy," and if so, to what extent, were issues to be determined by the trier of fact. . . .

Upon motion for rehearing . . . the court felt compelled to determine the constitutionality of the statute and sustained it as a "legitimate limitation on the right of freedom of expression contained in the First Amendment." . . .

Since 1789, Congress has granted this Court appellate jurisdiction with respect to state litigation only after the highest state court in which judgment could be had has rendered a "final judgment or decree." . . . 28 U.S.C. § 1257 retains this limitation on our power to review cases coming from state courts. The Court has noted that "[c]onsiderations of English usage as well as those of judicial policy" would justify an interpretation of the final judgment rule to preclude review "where anything further remains to be determined by a State court, no matter how dissociated from the only federal issue that has finally been adjudicated by the highest court of the State." Radio Station WOW, Inc. v. Johnson, 326 U.S. 120, 124 (1945). But the Court there observed that the rule had not been administered in such a mechanical fashion and that there were circumstances in which there has been "a departure from this requirement of finality for federal appellate jurisdiction." Ibid.

These circumstances were said to be "very few," ibid.; but as the cases have unfolded, the Court has recurringly encountered situations in which the highest court of a State has finally determined the federal issue present in a particular case, but in which there are further proceedings in the lower state courts to come. There are now at least four categories of such cases in which the Court has treated the decision on the federal issue as a final judgment for the purposes of 28 U.S.C. § 1257 and has taken jurisdiction without awaiting the completion of the additional proceedings anticipated in the lower state courts. . . .

In the first category are those cases in which there are further proceedings—even entire trials—yet to occur in the state courts but where for one reason or another the federal issue is conclusive or the outcome of further proceedings preordained. In these circumstances, because the case is for all practical purposes concluded, the judgment of the state court on the federal issue is deemed final. In Mills v. Alabama, 384 U.S. 214 (1966), for example, a demurrer to a criminal complaint was sustained on federal constitutional grounds by a state trial court. The State Supreme Court reversed, remanding for jury trial. This Court took jurisdiction on the reasoning that the appellant had no defense other than his federal claim and could not prevail at trial on the facts or any nonfederal ground. To dismiss the appeal "would not only be an inexcusable delay of the benefits Congress intended to grant by providing for appeal to this Court, but it would also result in a completely unnecessary waste of time and energy in judicial systems already troubled by delays due to congested dockets." . . .

Second, there are cases such as *Radio Station WOW*, supra, . . . in which the federal issue, finally decided by the highest court in the State, will survive and require decision regardless of the outcome of future state-court proceedings. In *Radio Station WOW*, the Nebraska Supreme Court directed the transfer of the properties of a federally licensed radio station and ordered an accounting, rejecting the claim that the transfer order would interfere with the federal license. The federal issue was held reviewable here despite the pending accounting on the "presupposition . . . that the federal questions that could come here have been adjudicated by the State court, and that the accounting which remains to be taken could not remotely give rise to a federal question . . . that may later come here. . . ." . . . Nothing that could happen in the course of the accounting, short of settlement of the case, would foreclose or make unnecessary decision on the federal question. . . .

In the third category are those situations where the federal claim has been finally decided, with further proceedings on the merits in the state courts to come, but in which later review of the federal issue cannot be had, whatever the ultimate outcome of the case. Thus, in these cases, if the party seeking interim review ultimately prevails on the merits, the federal issue will be mooted; if he were to lose on the merits, however, the governing state law would not permit him again to present his federal claims for review. The Court has taken jurisdiction in these circumstances prior to completion of the case in the state courts. California v. Stewart, 384 U.S. 436 (1966) (decided with Miranda v. Arizona), epitomizes this category. There the state court reversed a conviction on federal constitutional grounds and remanded for a new trial. Although the State might have prevailed at trial, we granted its petition for certiorari and affirmed, explaining that the state judgment was "final" since an acquittal of the defendant at trial would preclude, under state law, an appeal by the State. . . .

Lastly, there are those situations where the federal issue has been finally decided in the state courts with further proceedings pending in which the party seeking review here might prevail on the merits on nonfederal grounds, thus rendering unnecessary review of the federal issue by this Court, and where reversal of the state court on the federal issue would be preclusive of any further litigation on the relevant cause of action rather than merely controlling the nature and character of, or determining the admissibility of evidence in, the state proceedings still to come. In these circumstances, if a refusal immediately to review the state court decision might seriously erode federal policy, the Court has entertained and decided the federal issue, which itself has been finally determined by the state courts for purposes of the state litigation.

In Local No. 438 v. Curry, 371 U.S. 542 (1963), the state courts temporarily enjoined labor-union picketing over claims that the National Labor Relations Board had exclusive jurisdiction of the controversy. The Court took jurisdiction for two independent reasons. First, the power of the state court to proceed in the face of the preemption claim was deemed an issue separable from the merits and ripe for review in this Court, particularly "when postponing review would seriously erode the national labor policy requiring the subject matter of respondent's cause to be heard by the . . . Board, not by the state courts." . . . Second, the Court was convinced that in any event the union had no defense to the entry of a permanent injunction other than the preemption claim that had already been ruled on in the state courts. Hence the case was for all practical purposes concluded in the state tribunals.

In Mercantile National Bank v. Langdeau, 371 U.S. 555 (1963), the two national banks were sued, along with others, in the courts of Travis County, Texas. . . . The banks as a preliminary matter asserted that a special federal venue statute immunized them from suit in Travis County and that they could properly be sued only in another county. Although trial was still to be had and the banks might well prevail on the merits, the Court, relying on *Curry*, entertained the issue as a "separate and independent matter, anterior to the merits and not enmeshed in the factual and legal issues comprising the plaintiff's cause of action." . . . Moreover, it would serve the policy of the federal statute "to determine now in which state court appellants may be tried rather than to subject them . . . to long and complex litigation which may all be for naught if consideration of the preliminary question of venue is postponed until the conclusion of the proceedings." . . .

Miami Herald Publishing Company v. Tornillo, 418 U.S. 241 (1974), is the latest case in this category. There a candidate for public office sued a newspaper for refusing, allegedly contrary to a state statute, to carry his reply to the paper's editorial critical of his qualifications. The trial court held the act unconstitutional, denying both injunctive relief and damages. The State Supreme Court reversed, sustaining the statute against the challenge based upon the First and Fourteenth Amendments and remanding the case for a trial and appropriate relief, including damages. The newspaper brought the case here. We sustained our jurisdiction, relying on the principles elaborated in the *North Dakota* case and observing:

> "Whichever way we were to decide on the merits, it would be intolerable to leave unanswered, under these circumstances, an important question of freedom of the press under the First Amendment; an

uneasy and unsettled constitutional posture of § 104.38 could only further harm the operation of a free press. . . ."

In light of the prior cases, we conclude that we have jurisdiction to review the judgment of the Georgia Supreme Court rejecting the challenge under the First and Fourteenth Amendments to the state law authorizing damage suits against the press for publishing the name of a rape victim whose identity is revealed in the course of a public prosecution. The Georgia Supreme Court's judgment is plainly final on the federal issue and is not subject to further review in the state courts. Appellants will be liable for damages if the elements of the State cause of action are proved. They may prevail at trial on nonfederal grounds, it is true, but if the Georgia court erroneously upheld the statute, there should be no trial at all. Moreover, even if appellants prevailed at trial and made unnecessary further consideration of the constitutional question, there would remain in effect the unreviewed decision of the State Supreme Court that a civil action for publishing the name of a rape victim disclosed in a public judicial proceeding may go forward despite the First and Fourteenth Amendments. Delaying final decision of the First Amendment claim until after trial will "leave unanswered . . . an important question of freedom of the press under the First Amendment," "an uneasy and unsettled constitutional posture [that] could only further harm the operation of a free press." *Tornillo,* supra. On the other hand, if we now hold that the First and Fourteenth Amendments bar civil liability for broadcasting the victim's name, this litigation ends. Given these factors—that the litigation could be terminated by our decision on the merits and that a failure to decide the question now will leave the press in Georgia operating in the shadow of the civil and criminal sanctions of a rule of law and a statute the constitutionality of which is in serious doubt—we find that reaching the merits is consistent with the pragmatic approach that we have followed in the past in determining finality. . . .

[JUSTICE REHNQUIST dissented. Accepting the first three categories of "exceptions" cited by the majority, he objected to the fourth as "virtually formless," argued that it required the Court to evaluate the merits in order to determine its jurisdiction, and accused the majority of reaching out unnecessarily to decide constitutional questions. The need for immediate review, he added, was far less in the case before him than it had been in *Tornillo,* which had involved "protecting the press in its role of providing uninhibited political discourse," or in *Curry* and *Langdeau,* which had understandably held that "the proper forum" should be determined as soon as practicable. Finally, he insisted, the uncertainty of the Court's test would encourage a litigant to seek immediate review of interlocutory decisions "as a matter of assuring that his federal contentions are not lost for want of timely filing. The inevitable result will be totally unnecessary additions to our docket and serious interruptions of the state adjudicatory process."]

Notes on the Final-Judgment Rule and its Exceptions

(1) Since the beginning, Congress has been wary of permitting interlocutory appeals. Not only does § 1257, as *Cox* tells us, limit Supreme Court review of state courts to "final judgments or decrees"; § 1291 similarly provides as a general rule that the courts of appeals may review only "final decisions" of the district courts. The relevant policies are discussed in Note, Appealability in the Federal Courts, 75 Harv.L.Rev. 351, 351–52 (1961):

> The basic rationale of the finality rule is conservation of judicial resources. Constant interruption of trial would follow from a general practice of interlocutory appeals and would consume trial court time, forestall the ultimate resolution of the case, and facilitate the harassment of one party by his opponent. Since substantial time elapses before appellate determination, it would be necessary for the trial court to spend extra hours refamiliarizing itself with the case and perhaps to select a new jury and begin anew. A single appeal consolidating all alleged errors also minimizes the appellate court burden by eliminating more than one set of records, briefs, and arguments in an individual case. And if the prejudiced party is the ultimate victor, if parties settle, or if the trial court later corrects its own error, appellate review will prove unnecessary. The requirement of finality also helps to ensure the correct disposition of the merits. After the proceedings below are complete, the appellate court is in position to assess the wisdom of particular interlocutory orders with heightened perspective; the lower court is apt to consider its orders with greater care, for errors not requiring reversal will never be corrected and those that warrant reversal will compel a complete retrial. Finally, to allow an appeal from every order to which an objection is lodged might reduce respect for the authority of the trial judge.
>
> But there are frequent situations in which prompt review is urgent. Reversal of some interlocutory orders will terminate litigation or preclude subsequent retrial, thereby eliminating needless proceedings in the lower court. Fairness demands swift appeal in cases where delayed review will be of little or no avail. Certain types of frequently recurring orders, such as discovery orders, seldom require reversal and hence may never be reviewed; the absence of appellate guidance may result in inconsistent treatment by the lower courts. Finally there must be some means for immediately restraining a district judge in the rare case where his conduct exceeds all bounds of judicial propriety.

Working out an appropriate accommodation of these competing goals has proved no easy task.

(2) Neither in the context of Supreme Court review of "final judgments" of state courts nor in that of court-of-appeals review of "final decisions" of district courts has the Court adhered to the appealing position of Catlin v. United States, 324 U.S. 229, 233 (1945), that a "final" decision is one that "ends the litigation on the merits and leaves nothing for the court to do but execute the judgment." *Cox* neatly summarizes the principal

cases watering down the finality requirement with respect to state judgments. The most important line of cases doing so in the context of federal decisions derives from Cohen v. Beneficial Industrial Loan Corp., 337 U.S. 541 (1949).

The district court in *Cohen* refused to apply a state statute requiring the plaintiff in a shareholder's derivative action to post security for costs, and the defendant took an immediate appeal. The Supreme Court held the order refusing to require security "final":

> This decision appears to fall in that small class which finally determine claims of right separable from, and collateral to, rights asserted in the action, too important to be denied review and too independent of the cause itself to require that appellate consideration be deferred until the whole case is adjudicated.

If no appeal were allowed until conclusion of the proceeding, the Court emphasized, it would be "too late effectively to review the present order, and the rights conferred by the statute, if applicable, [would] have been lost. . . ."

The Court paraphrased the *Cohen* test in Coopers & Lybrand v. Livesay, 437 U.S. 463, 468 (1978): "[T]he order must conclusively determine the disputed question, resolve an important issue completely separate from the merits of the action, and be effectively unreviewable on appeal from a final judgment." Much ink has been spilled in attempting to apply this standard.

(3) Abney v. United States, 431 U.S. 651 (1977), unanimously held the denial of a motion to dismiss an indictment on double-jeopardy grounds "final" under the *Cohen* doctrine:

> [S]uch orders constitute a complete, formal and, in the trial court, a final rejection of a criminal defendant's double jeopardy claim. . . . Moreover, the very nature of a double jeopardy claim is that it is collateral to, and separable from the principal issue at . . . trial, i.e., whether or not the accused is guilty. . . . [H]e is contesting the very authority of the Government to hale him into court to face trial . . . . Finally, . . . if appellate review of double jeopardy claims were postponed until after conviction and sentence, . . . even if the accused has his conviction ultimately reversed on double jeopardy grounds, he has still been forced to endure a trial that the Double Jeopardy Clause was designed to prohibit.[2]

2. The Court has employed the same reasoning to permit immediate review of a refusal to dismiss on grounds of legislative or official immunity, Helstoski v. Meanor, 442 U.S. 500 (1979); Mitchell v. Forsyth, 472 U.S. 511 (1985). On the other hand, when the motion to dismiss was based upon the immunity of an extradited suspect from unrelated service of process or a contractual forum-selection clause, immediate review was denied: "An entitlement to avoid suit is different in kind from an entitlement to be sued only in a particular forum." Van Cauwenberghe v. Biard, 486 U.S. 517 (1988); Lauro Lines v. Chasser, 109 S.Ct. 1976 (1989). The Court also denied immediate review of denials of motions to dismiss in United States v. MacDonald, 435 U.S. 850 (1978) (where the motion alleged failure to afford a speedy trial), and in United States v. Hollywood Motor Car Co., 458 U.S. 263 (1982) (where the defendant asserted vindictive prosecution). Cf. Flynt v. Ohio, 451 U.S. 619 (1981), declining despite the analogy of *Younger v. Harris*, p. 528 supra, to review a *state court's* refusal to dismiss a prosecution allegedly brought in bad faith.

(4) In Eisen v. Carlisle & Jacquelin, 370 F.2d 119 (2d Cir. 1966), the trial judge, without dismissing the plaintiff's individual claim, held he could not maintain a class action. An appeal was allowed:

> No lawyer of competence is going to undertake this complex and costly case to recover $70 for Mr. Eisen. . . . Where the effect of a district court's order . . . is the death knell of the action, review should be allowed.

In Coopers & Lybrand v. Livesay, 437 U.S. 463 (1978), the Supreme Court held that refusal to certify a class was not a final order under the *Cohen* doctrine because it could be revised below, was reviewable later, and was enmeshed with the merits. No separate "death knell" doctrine was permissible: the "incremental benefit" of immediate appeal "is outweighed by the impact of such an individualized jurisdictional inquiry on the . . . overall capacity to administer justice."

(5) When, if ever, is an abstention order "final"? In Idlewild Bon Voyage Liquor Corp. v. Epstein, 370 U.S. 713 (1962), the district court had invoked *Pullman* abstention "in order to give the state courts an opportunity to pass upon the constitutional [!] issues presented," and had "retained jurisdiction of the cause." Said the Supreme Court: "The Court of Appeals properly rejected the argument that the order of the District Court 'was not final and hence unappealable under 28 U.S.C. §§ 1291, 1292,' pointing out that '[a]ppellant was effectively out of court.' " In Moses H. Cone Memorial Hospital v. Mercury Constr. Corp., 460 U.S. 1 (1983) (Brennan, J.), the Court over three dissents held "final" an order staying federal proceedings pending the outcome of a related state suit. Even more clearly than in *Idlewild*, said the Court, the stay "meant that there would be no further litigation in the federal forum." In addition, the *Cohen* doctrine was applicable although the district judge might theoretically reconsider his decision: "The reasoning of *Coopers & Lybrand* does not reach all pretrial orders that are formally subject to revision, but only those as to which some revision might reasonably be expected in the ordinary course of litigation." Is an abstention order any more final than an order staying proceedings pending arbitration, which the Court once held not to be final? Schoenamsgruber v. Hamburg American Line, 294 U.S. 454, 456 (1935).

(6) Is the test of a "final decision" under § 1291 the same as that of a "final judgment" under § 1257? Should it be? [3]

(7) Congress too has made exceptions to the final-judgment rule. Section 1292(a) permits appeals from interlocutory decrees of federal (not state) courts respecting injunctions. The reason for this, the Court has surmised, was to avoid irreparable harm. Baltimore Contractors, Inc. v. Bodinger, 348 U.S. 176, 181 (1955). Until recently, however, on historical grounds that do not bear repeating, the Court in interpreting this provision

3. Orders remanding cases removed from state courts, except in civil-rights cases removed under § 1443, are expressly made unreviewable "on appeal or otherwise" by 28 U.S.C. § 1447(d). Yet the Supreme Court, over three unanswerable dissents, has allowed review of an order remanding a case on the ground that the federal docket was too crowded, holding that the prohibition of § 1447(d) applies only if the trial judge purports to remand for the reasons authorizing remand in § 1447(e), namely, that the action was removed "improvidently and without jurisdiction." Thermtron Products, Inc. v. Hermansdorfer, 423 U.S. 336 (1976).

drew some rather fine distinctions quite unrelated to the degree of necessity for immediate review. For example, the decision to postpone trial of a damage action pending resolution of an equitable counterclaim was treated as an injunction subject to immediate appeal; an identical ruling in a case in which the equitable claim had been filed first was not. Ettelson v. Metropolitan Life Ins. Co., 317 U.S. 188 (1942); City of Morgantown v. Royal Ins. Co., 337 U.S. 254 (1949). Pointing out that an order "that relates only to the conduct or progress of litigation before th[e] court is not ordinarily considered an injunction" for purposes of appeal, the Court cheerfully overruled *Ettelson* in Gulfstream Aerospace Corp. v. Mayacamas Corp., 485 U.S. 271 (1988): "[O]rders granting or denying stays of 'legal' proceedings on 'equitable' grounds are not automatically appealable under § 1292(a)."

A different problem of interpreting § 1292(a) was presented in Switzerland Cheese Ass'n v. Horne's Market, Inc., 385 U.S. 23 (1966), where the Court held unreviewable the denial of a motion for summary judgment respecting a permanent injunction. In a similar case the Second Circuit had just held that the statute applied only to rulings on interlocutory injunctions, not to interlocutory rulings respecting permanent injunctions. Chappell & Co. v. Frankel, 367 F.2d 197 (1966). Motions respecting interlocutory injunctions, the court reasoned, could be reviewed without delving into the merits of the case and thus duplicating review of the ultimate judgment, because the question in such cases was simply whether or not to preserve the status quo pending trial. Moreover, the irreparable harm Congress feared from the erroneous grant or denial of interlocutory relief was less likely to result from denial of a "garden variety" motion for summary judgment in a suit seeking only a permanent injunction. Justice Harlan, concurring in the *Switzerland Cheese* case, agreed with the Second Circuit's analysis. The majority, however, refused to hold that § 1292(a) was always inapplicable to motions respecting permanent injunctions, saying instead that the denial of summary judgment was not "interlocutory"(?) because it related only to "pretrial procedures": "The denial of a motion for a summary judgment because of unresolved issues of fact does not settle or even tentatively decide anything about the merits of the claim. It is strictly a pretrial order that decides only one thing—that the case should go to trial." [4]

(8) Section 1292(b), enacted in 1958, permits interlocutory appeal on the certificate of the trial judge, if the court of appeals agrees to review.

4. In Gardner v. Westinghouse Broadcasting Co., 437 U.S. 478 (1978), the Court held that an order denying class certification in an injunctive case was not the denial of an injunction appealable under § 1291(a) though its effect was "to refuse a substantial portion of the injunctive relief requested:" The order " 'in no way touch[ed] on the merits . . . but only relate[d] to pretrial procedures . . . .' " In Carson v. American Brands, Inc., 450 U.S. 79, 87 (1981), the Court allowed § 1292(a) review of an interlocutory refusal to enter a proposed consent decree in a suit for injunction, arguing that a later appeal might be ineffective: "[A] party . . . might be legally justified in withdrawing its consent to the agreement once trial is held and final judgment entered . . . ."

Consider also Steinberg v. American Bantam Car Co., 173 F.2d 179 (3rd Cir. 1949), holding a temporary restraining order not an "injunction" within § 1292(a). Does this decision endanger the policy of the statute? See Note, Appealability in the Federal Courts, 75 Harv.L.Rev. 351, 368–69 (1961).

The judge is to make this certificate only if the challenged order "involves a controlling question of law as to which there is substantial ground for difference of opinion" and if immediate appeal "may materially advance the ultimate termination of the litigation." See Note, Appealability in the Federal Courts, 75 Harv.L.Rev. 351, 379 (1961):

> The legislative history of § 1292(b) makes clear that the statute was intended to apply only when an immediate appeal may avoid "protracted and expensive litigation;" an order seemingly presents a controlling question of law if resolution of the question would be a basis for reversal of the final judgment; and the extent of difference of opinion refers to the likelihood that the judge has erred.[5]

What happens if the trial judge refuses to certify a question appropriate for interlocutory review? See Note, Interlocutory Appeals in the Federal Courts Under 28 U.S.C. § 1292(b), 88 Harv.L.Rev. 607, 616–17 (1975), reporting with approval that the courts of appeals had remained "unanimous in refusing to grant mandamus . . . to reverse the trial court's decision on certification:" "[M]andamus . . . requires the substitution of the court of appeals' opinion for that of the trial court in precisely those situations where Congress said the trial court's decision is best informed."

(9) Appealability is also affected by Rule 54(b) of the Federal Rules of Civil Procedure:

> When more than one claim for relief is presented in an action, whether as a claim, counterclaim, cross-claim, or third-party claim, or when multiple parties are involved, the court may direct the entry of a final judgment as to one or more but fewer than all of the claims or parties only upon an express determination that there is no just reason for delay and upon an express direction for the entry of judgment.

Before this rule was adopted the Supreme Court had held that no appeal could be taken from an order finally disposing of one claim if other claims involving the same or additional parties remained for decision. Collins v. Miller, 252 U.S. 364, 370 (1920). This appeared awkward in the light of the Federal Rules, which greatly expanded the opportunities for joining multiple claims in one action, and the original draft of Rule 54(b) provided that an order disposing of a separate claim in such a case "shall terminate the action with respect to the claim so disposed of." The Supreme Court held such orders final and appealable, Reeves v. Beardall, 316 U.S. 283 (1942). Unfortunately it was not always obvious whether or not the order disposed of a separate claim, and the litigant who waited until the end of the trial to appeal such an order sometimes found he had forfeited his right by not appealing at once. Dickinson v. Petroleum Conversion Corp., 338 U.S. 507 (1950). Consequently the Rule was

5. The criteria for § 1292(b) certification are further explored in light of the decisions in Note, Interlocutory Appeals in the Federal Courts Under 28 U.S.C. § 1292(b), 88 Harv.L.Rev. 607 (1975), noting that some courts have limited certification to "exceptional cases," e.g., Milbert v. Bison Laboratories, Inc., 260 F.2d 431, 433 (3d Cir. 1958), and arguing that legislative history shows the statute was meant solely to avoid "unnecessary trial court proceedings," not—as is sometimes the goal of interlocutory review—to avert irreparable harm or to determine "issues not normally open on final appeal." See also Rule 5 of the Federal Rules of Appellate Procedure.

amended to make the order final only when so certified by the trial judge. In Sears, Roebuck & Co. v. Mackey, 351 U.S. 427 (1956), the Court rejected the contention that Rule 54(b) was invalid because it allowed the District Judge to make "final" judgments that were interlocutory under § 1291 as construed by the Supreme Court: The Rule "scrupulously recognizes the statutory requirement of a 'final decision' under § 1291. . . . It merely administers that requirement in a practical manner in multiple claims actions and does so by rule instead of by judicial decision." [6]

The courts of appeals have on numerous occasions refused to review certified orders on the ground that the certification was an abuse of discretion. E.g., Flynn & Emrich Co. v. Greenwood, 242 F.2d 737, 741 (4th Cir. 1957).

(10) Finally, there is 28 U.S.C. § 1651(a), the "All Writs" Statute:

> The Supreme Court and all courts established by Act of Congress may issue all writs necessary or appropriate in aid of their respective jurisdictions and agreeable to the usages and principles of law.[7]

What is meant by the requirement that the issuance of the writ be "in aid of" the appellate court's jurisdiction? See La Buy v. Howes Leather Co., 352 U.S. 249, 255 (1957): "Since the Court of Appeals could at some stage of the antitrust proceedings entertain appeals in these cases, it has power in proper circumstances, as here, to issue writs of mandamus reaching them;" and the dissent, id. at 264:

> The focal question . . . is whether the action of the District Court tends to frustrate or impede the ultimate exercise by the Court of Appeals of its appellate jurisdiction granted in some other provision of the law. The answer is clearly in the affirmative where, for example, the order of the District Court transfers a cause to a District Court of another circuit for decision. . . . "The effect of the order is that the district judge has declined to proceed with the determination of a case which could eventually come to this court by appeal from a 'final decision.' " . . . In contrast, a District Court order denying a transfer would not come under the umbrella of power under the All Writs Act, since retention of the cause by the District Court can hardly thwart or tend to defeat the power of the Court of Appeals to review that order after final decision of the case.[8]

6. *Sears* and its companion case, Cold Metal Process Co. v. United Engineering & Foundry Co., 351 U.S. 445 (1956), also had something to say about determining whether or not a judgment could be said to dispose of a "claim." Although those decisions seemed to reject the earlier position that the judgment was not final unless it resolved all issues arising out of the same transaction or occurrence (while common facts were relevant to both dismissed and pending claims, "they certainly *can* be decided independently of each other"), there are later court-of-appeals decisions based upon the old rule, e.g., Seaboard Machinery Corp. of Delaware v. Seaboard Machinery Corp. of New Jersey, 267 F.2d 178 (2d Cir. 1959).

7. The original Judiciary Act, § 13, 1 Stat. 80, 81 (1789), had limited the Supreme Court's use of mandamus and prohibition as appellate tools to cases in the lower federal courts, but the Court has upheld its power under the present section to issue writs to state courts as well. Deen v. Hickman, 358 U.S. 57 (1958).

8. Compare the decisions interpreting the same language in the same statute with respect to the writ of error coram nobis, infra p. 653, and to original writs of mandamus, supra pp. 413–14, and similar

That the writ is found to be in aid of jurisdiction by no means assures its issuance. Mandamus and prohibition, it is commonly said, are not to be used if a statutory appeal is provided; nor are they to be used wholesale to undermine the policy against piecemeal appeals. Roche v. Evaporated Milk Ass'n, 319 U.S. 21 (1943). In that case, said the Court, the availability of an extraordinary writ was a matter of discretion rather than of power, but the court of appeals was reversed for using mandamus to test a motion to strike a criminal defendant's pleas in abatement:

> The traditional use of the writ in aid of appellate jurisdiction both at common law and in the federal courts has been to confine an inferior court to a lawful exercise of its prescribed jurisdiction or to compel it to exercise its authority when it is its duty to do so. . . . Even in such cases appellate courts are reluctant to interfere with the decision of a lower court on jurisdictional questions which it was competent to decide and which are reviewable in the regular course of appeal.

However, the Supreme Court has upheld mandamus in the courts of appeals to review the denial of a civil jury trial, Beacon Theatres, Inc. v. Westover, 359 U.S. 500 (1959), and to order a trial judge not to refer a case to a master, La Buy v. Howes Leather Co., 352 U.S. 249 (1957), finding a general practice in the Northern District of Illinois of referring too many cases to masters. See Will v. United States, 389 U.S. 90 (1967), holding mandamus could not be used to correct a trial judge who had ordered a bill of particulars on pain of dismissal: There was insufficient proof of a continuous practice as in *La Buy*; the judge at most had erred on a matter within his jurisdiction; and a narrow construction of the mandamus power in that case was buttressed by the policy of limiting government appeals in criminal cases. Cf. Bankers Life & Cas. Co. v. Holland, 346 U.S. 379, 382–83 (1953), refusing to allow mandamus to test an order transferring a case to another district under § 1406(a) because the order, even if erroneous, involved "no abuse of judicial power." Finally, in Schlagenhauf v. Holder, 379 U.S. 104, 109–12 (1964), the Court held mandamus available when it was argued that Rule 35 could not validly be construed to authorize an order for a defendant's medical examination, because the allegation was of "usurpation of power." Moreover, said the Court, although the writ would not usually lie, absent a "clear abuse of discretion," to determine whether there had been good cause for the examination, here that issue too should have been determined because the question of power was already before the court, "so as to avoid piecemeal litigation and to settle new and important problems." This was not to be construed, the Court insisted, as opening the door: "The writ of mandamus is not to be used when 'the most that could be claimed is that the district courts have erred in ruling on matters within their jurisdiction.'" Justice Harlan dissented from the use of the writ to test "good cause."

language in the anti-injunction statute, 28 U.S.C. § 2283, supra pp. 524–26. Note also the *La Buy* dissent's argument that the same words in § 1651 confer greater mandamus power on the Supreme Court than on the Courts of Appeals because they were not meant to alter the meaning of divergent provisions of prior law, 352 U.S. at 265–66, citing sections 13 and 14 of the 1789 Act, p. 761 infra.

All this was neatly summed up in General Motors Corp. v. Lord, 488 F.2d 1096 (8th Cir. 1973), citing *Roche, La Buy,* and *Schlagenhauf* and relying heavily on Note, Supervisory and Advisory Mandamus Under the All Writs Act, 86 Harv.L.Rev. 595 (1973):

> Extraordinary circumstances may be presented where the district court's order was made without jurisdiction . . ., where the order under attack is characteristic of an erroneous practice likely to reoccur . . ., [or] where the order under attack exemplifies a novel and important question in need of guidelines for the future resolution of similar cases.[9]

(11) Section 1254(1) allows the Supreme Court to review, on certiorari, "any civil or criminal case" in the courts of appeals "before or after rendition of judgment." Why? Notice that this provision not only permits review of interlocutory orders (the standard practice is indicated, however, by Brotherhood of Locomotive Firemen v. Bangor & Aroostook R. R., 389 U.S. 327 (1967) ("because the Court of Appeals remanded the case, it is not ripe for review by this Court")); it has also been used by bypass the courts of appeals entirely. E.g., Youngstown Sheet & Tube Co. v. Sawyer, 343 U.S. 579 (1952) (over the dissent of Justice Frankfurter); United States v. Nixon, 418 U.S. 683 (1974). See Sup.Ct.R. 11, declaring that this practice will be indulged "only upon a showing that the case is of such imperative public importance as to justify deviation from normal appellate practice and to require immediate settlement in this Court"; Aaron v. Cooper, 357 U.S. 566 (1958), refusing certiorari before

9. Special problems under the All Writs Act have arisen in administering the provision, now in 28 U.S.C. § 2284, requiring the convening of a three-judge district court in certain cases, see pp. 568–72 supra. As noted at p. 603 infra, § 1253 provides for Supreme Court review of certain actions of a three-judge court, but the Supreme Court in Stratton v. St. Louis Southwestern Railway Co., 282 U.S. 10 (1930), held that neither § 1253 nor § 1291 authorized an appeal when a single judge had taken action that only three judges were permitted to take. The proper remedy "where a court of three judges should have been convened, and was not," the Court said in *Stratton,* was mandamus from the Supreme Court ordering the convening of a three-judge panel.

Faithful to the implications of this ruling, the Second Circuit in Idlewild Bon Voyage Liquor Corp. v. Epstein, 370 U.S. 713 (1962), upon finding that a single judge had no power to abstain in a case otherwise requiring three judges, held it had no jurisdiction to correct his error. This result was obviously wasteful, and the Supreme Court disagreed:

> In the *Stratton* case it was held that a court of appeals was precluded from reviewing on the merits of a case which should have originally been determined by a court of three judges. *Stratton* does not stand for the broad proposition that a court of appeals is powerless ever to give any guidance when a single judge has erroneously invaded the province of a three-judge court. The Court of Appeals clearly stated its opinion that a court of three judges ought to have been convened to consider this litigation. That view was correct and should have been followed upon the petitioner's renewed motion that such a statutory court be impaneled.

Both the *Idlewild* statement itself and later memorandum dispositions invoking it left something to be desired in terms of clarity, see D. Currie, Appellate Review of the Decision Whether or not to Empanel a Three-Judge Federal Court, 37 U.Chi.L. Rev. 159 (1969). Yet in Gonzalez v. Automatic Employees Credit Union, 419 U.S. 90, 100 n. 19 (1974) (dictum), the Court said flatly that the court of appeals has jurisdiction whenever a request for three judges is denied: under § 1291 if there is a final order, by mandamus or § 1292(b) certification if there is not. How can mandamus in such a case be "necessary in aid of [the] . . . jurisdiction" of the *court of appeals*?

judgment in the Little Rock school-segregation case; Lurk v. United States, 366 U.S. 712, 713–14 (1961).[11]

(12) Can the Supreme Court review a state-court decision if the appellant or petitioner has failed to ask the state court for a rehearing en banc? Gorman v. Washington University, 316 U.S. 98 (1942), held that a judgment rendered by a panel consisting of four of the seven judges of the Missouri Supreme Court was not that of the "highest court of a State in which a decision may be had." The Missouri constitution provided that cases involving federal questions "shall be transferred" to the whole court on the application of the losing party, and the Supreme Court declared it the purpose of the highest-state-court requirement that "no decision of a state court should be brought here for review either by appeal or certiorari until the possibilities afforded by state procedure for its review by all state tribunals have been exhausted."

But in Local 174, Teamsters Union v. Lucas Flour Co., 369 U.S. 95 (1962), the Supreme Court accepted jurisdiction to review the judgment of a panel of the Supreme Court of Washington despite the petitioner's failure to seek a rehearing en banc. *Gorman* was distinguished:

> The Constitution of the State of Missouri expressly conferred the *right* to an *en banc* rehearing by the Supreme Court of Missouri in any case originally decided by a division of the court in which a federal question was involved. . . . By contrast, a rehearing *en banc* before the Supreme Court of Washington is not granted as a matter of right.

Is this distinction tenable in light of the Court's consistent holding that an applicant must seek even discretionary review from the State's highest court before the Supreme Court will review the judgment of a lower state court? See, e.g., Parker v. Illinois, 333 U.S. 571 (1948).

That the highest-state-court requirement embodies an element of forfeiture as well as one of exhausting presently available remedies is shown by Gotthilf v. Sills, 375 U.S. 79 (1963). Certiorari was there dismissed because the petitioner had failed to ask an intermediate state court to certify a disputed question for further review. Three dissenters would have excused the failure on the ground of surprise.

Further Notes on Appellate Review

(1) In addition to their jurisdiction over district-court judgments, the courts of appeals have authority to review many orders made by federal administrative agencies. The provisions for review in administrative cases, not having been gathered into Title 28 (see the fragmentary list in § 2342), are scattered throughout the United States Code. Notice that review of agency regulations, as contrasted with quasi-judicial orders, is often (though not always, see Clean Air Act, § 307(b), 42 U.S.C. § 7607(b)) in the district court, e.g., *Abbott Laboratories v. Gardner*, supra p. 57. Why? See

11. For a thorough survey and criticism of the Court's practice under this provision see Lindgren & Marshall, The Supreme Court's Extraordinary Power to Grant Certiorari Before Judgment in the Court of Appeals, 1986 Sup.Ct.Rev. 259, suggesting that the Rule does not accurately reflect the law: "[T]he writ is more often granted to consolidate a case with another case pending before the Court." Id. at 297.

generally Currie & Goodman, Judicial Review of Federal Administrative Action: Quest for the Optimum Forum, 75 Colum.L.Rev. 1 (1975).

(2) The United States Court of Appeals for the Federal Circuit, established in 1982, is a specialized Article III tribunal. Under 28 U.S.C. § 1295 it has exclusive jurisdiction not only of appeals from decisions of the United States Claims Court, the Court of International Trade, and the Board of Patent Appeals, but also of appeals from District Court decisions in certain cases. The central provisions respecting District Court decisions are as follows:

> (a) The United States Court of Appeals for the Federal Circuit shall have exclusive jurisdiction—
>
> > (1) of an appeal from a final decision of a district court of the United States . . ., if the jurisdiction of that court was based, in whole or in part, on section 1338 of this title, except that a case involving a claim arising under any Act of Congress relating to copyrights, exclusive rights in mask works, or trademarks and no other claims under section 1338(a) shall be governed by sections 1291, 1292, and 1294 of this title;
> >
> > (2) of an appeal from a final decision of a district court . . ., if the jurisdiction of that court was based, in whole or in part, on section 1346 of this title, except that jurisdiction of an appeal in a case brought in a district court under section 1346(a)(1), 1346(b), 1346(e), or 1346(f) of this title or under section 1346(a)(2) when the claim is founded upon an Act of Congress or a regulation of an executive department providing for internal revenue shall be governed by sections 1291, 1292, and 1294 of this title. . . .

What do you think of this provision? Its central purpose was to promote uniformity in the law governing patents and government contracts. Is this purpose well served by making appellate jurisdiction dependent on the basis for jurisdiction in the trial court? Is it easy to determine whether a case falls under § 1338(a) or § 1346(a)(2)? What happens if a government-contract claim is joined with a claim under the Federal Tort Claims Act, § 1346(b)? See United States v. Hohri, 482 U.S. 64 (1987). What happens if the Federal Circuit transfers a case on the ground that it does not arise under the patent law, and the transferee court thinks it does? See Christianson v. Colt Industries Operating Corp., 486 U.S. 800 (1988). What happens if the Federal Circuit concludes that the District Court had *no* jurisdiction? Cf. the tortured course of decision under 28 U.S.C. § 1253, which provides for a direct appeal to the Supreme Court in cases *required* to be heard by three judges, p. 599 supra. See generally Van Drasek v. Lehman, 762 F.2d 1065 (D.C.Cir.1985): "The burden of wading through this jurisdictional quagmire outweighs, we think, the limited utility of providing uniform adjudication. . . ."

(3) In the interest of efficient disposition of business the courts of appeals normally sit in panels of three judges, though in all circuits there are more than three active circuit judges. This practice has been known to result in conflicting decisions within a single circuit, to the obvious discomfiture of district judges and of litigants. Accordingly the Supreme Court in 1941 upheld the power of the courts of appeals to hear exceptional cases en

banc, Textile Mills Securities Corp. v. Commissioner, 314 U.S. 326, and Congress responded with § 46(c) of the 1948 Judicial Code, which after amendments reads as follows:

> Cases and controversies shall be heard and determined by a court or panel of not more than three judges, . . . unless a hearing or rehearing before the court in banc is ordered by a majority of the circuit judges of the circuit who are in regular active service. A court in banc shall consist of all circuit judges in regular active service. . . .

The Supreme Court undertook a full review of this provision in Western Pac. R. R. Corp. v. Western Pac. R. R. Co., 345 U.S. 247 (1953), holding that litigants must be free to suggest the en banc procedure but have no right to insist that all active judges pass upon their request. "Because § 46(c) is a grant of power, and nothing more, each Court of Appeals is vested with a wide latitude of discretion to decide for itself just how that power shall be exercised." But in the case before the Court the original panel and the full court of appeals had each denied its authority to pass upon the litigant's request, and the decision was remanded with the admonition that "the court should determine and clearly set forth the particular procedure it will follow" and give either the panel or the full court authority to pass upon the request.[1]

Appellate Rule 35(a) prescribes a standard for en banc hearings:

> Such a hearing or rehearing is not favored and ordinarily will not be ordered except (1) when consideration by the full court is necessary to secure or maintain uniformity of its decisions, or (2) when the proceeding involves a question of exceptional importance.[2]

1. In Shenker v. Baltimore & Ohio Railroad Co., 374 U.S. 1 (1963), four of six participating judges had voted to grant a rehearing, but a rule of the court of appeals required a majority of all eight active judges. This rule, said the Supreme Court, "is clearly within the scope of the court's discretion as we spoke of it in *Western Pacific.*"

Rule 35 of the Appellate Rules, see Appendix A infra, prescribes the en banc procedure. See also the Third Circuit procedure, twice lauded by the Supreme Court and described in 14 F.R.D. 91 (1954), among whose important features, as suggested by Justice Frankfurter in a concurring opinion in *Western Pacific*, was the circulation of all draft opinions to judges not on the original panel. Notice that en banc hearings need not be rehearings; on occasion a case is heard en banc initially, and in the Third Circuit, at least, en banc rehearings after argument were more common before than after decision by the panel. See 14 F.R.D. at 92–94.

2. See Note, En Banc Review in Federal Circuit Courts: A Reassessment, 72 Mich. L.Rev. 1637 (1974), doubting that the costly en banc procedure was of particular utility either in resolving important questions or in achieving uniformity, and quoting Judge Mansfield (Eisen v. Carlisle & Jacquelin, 479 F.2d 1005, 1021 (2d Cir. 1973) (concurring opinion)): "If . . . recent history . . . is any indication, . . . an *en banc* hearing will result in opinions expressing diverse views. . . ." The Note suggested eliminating the burden of considering litigant requests for en banc hearings, allowing the original panel to foreclose en banc consideration, requiring a two-thirds vote and a statement of reasons for the extraordinary procedure, and limiting its use to "those rare conflicts that involve the integrity of the judicial process," such as cases having "dramatic political repercussions, and perhaps cases involving professional discipline." See also the *Eisen* case, supra, refusing to hear a case en banc because of the likelihood that certiorari would be granted, a decision that "reversed the 'exceptional importance' rationale by citing the importance of a case as a ground for denying a rehearing en banc." 72 Mich.L.Rev. at 1652.

What happens when a panel of the court of appeals has reversed the trial court's judgment and the court en banc is equally divided? Does the panel's decision stand because no majority has set it aside, or is the district court affirmed? See Farrand Optical Co. v. United States, 317 F.2d 875, 886 (2d Cir. 1963), taking the latter view; Drake Bakeries Inc. v. American Bakery Workers, 294 F.2d 399, 400 (2d Cir. 1961), where Judges Lumbard and Friendly, alone among six judges, had taken the opposite position. Is the issue one the Supreme Court should leave to the discretion of the courts of appeals under the *Western Pacific* case?

(4) Under the 1789 Judiciary Act, recourse to the Supreme Court was principally by writ of error or by appeal, and in both situations review was a matter of right. Increasing pressures on the Court's docket, however, have induced Congress to give the Supreme Court increasing discretion to refuse review; and the usual vehicle for this discretion is the writ of certiorari.

Certiorari was first provided for in the Evarts Act of 1891, 26 Stat. 826, which created the circuit courts of appeals and made their decisions in diversity, admiralty, criminal, patent, and revenue cases final, subject to Supreme Court review by certiorari or on questions certified by the circuit courts of appeals. Certiorari was extended to cases coming from state courts in 1914, when for the first time the Court was given jurisdiction over state-court decisions upholding federal rights, 38 Stat. 790. The scope of obligatory Supreme Court review regarding both state and federal decisions was considerably reduced by the Act of September 6, 1916, c. 448, § 2, 39 Stat. 726, and by the "Judges' Bill," Act of February 13, 1925, 43 Stat. 936, which was drafted by the Justices in order to bring their workload under control. Review by appeal, which was intended to be obligatory, remained in a few classes of cases—most notably when a state court had upheld a state statute or struck down a federal on constitutional challenge and when, conversely, a federal court of appeals had struck down a state statute.

Mandatory appeals placed an onerous burden on a Court that had plenty to do without them. After years of virtually unanimous pressure, Congress finally did away with nearly all of them in 1988, retaining only the provision in 28 U.S.C. § 1253 for direct appeals from decisions of three-judge district courts—principally in suits challenging state legislative apportionments.[3]

3. § 1253 applies only to "an order granting or denying . . . an interlocutory or permanent injunction" in a case "required . . . to be heard and determined by a district court of three judges." The Court has held these conditions satisfied only when three judges both were actually required, Phillips v. United States, 312 U.S. 246 (1941), and in fact were convened, Stratton v. St. Louis Southwestern Railway Co., 282 U.S. 10 (1930). For the proper remedy when a single judge has taken action requiring three judges see p. 599 supra.

In Gonzalez v. Automatic Employees Credit Union, 419 U.S. 90 (1974), the Supreme Court refused to review a three-judge court's dismissal for lack of standing in a case otherwise requiring three judges, on the ground that a single judge would have had power to make the same disposition. MTM, Inc. v. Baxley, 420 U.S. 799 (1975), went further, refusing to review a three-judge court's dismissal on the basis of the anti-injunction policy of *Younger v. Harris*, p. 528 supra. Without saying a single judge could enter such an order (cf. *Idlewild Bon Voyage Liquor Corp. v. Ep-*

(5) Criteria said to influence the decision whether or not to grant a writ of certiorari are laid out in Supreme Court Rule 10:

CONSIDERATIONS GOVERNING REVIEW ON WRIT OF CERTIORARI

1. A review on writ of certiorari is not a matter of right, but of judicial discretion. A petition for a writ of certiorari will be granted only when there are special and important reasons therefor. The following, while neither controlling nor fully measuring the Court's discretion, indicate the character of reasons that will be considered:

(a) When a United States court of appeals has rendered a decision in conflict with the decision of another United States court of appeals on the same matter; or has decided a federal question in a way in conflict with a state court of last resort; or has so far departed from the accepted and usual course of judicial proceedings, or sanctioned such a departure by a lower court, as to call for an exercise of this Court's power of supervision.

(b) When a state court of last resort has decided a federal question in a way that conflicts with the decision of another state court of last resort or of a United States court of appeals.

(c) When a state court or a United States court of appeals has decided an important question of federal law which has not been, but should be, settled by this Court, or has decided a federal question in a way that conflicts with applicable decisions of this Court. . . .

See the thorough discussion of certiorari practice in R. Stern, E. Gressman & S. Shapiro, Supreme Court Practice 254–300 (6th ed. 1986); the suggested revision of the rule in Hart & Wechsler, The Federal Courts and the Federal System 1628 (2d ed. 1973); and the statement of Chief Justice Vinson, 69 Sup.Ct. v., that "The Supreme Court must continue to decide only those cases which present questions whose resolution will have immediate importance far beyond the particular facts and parties involved." Do you agree that the Court should allow a grievous error to stand, in a case involving serious detriment to the losing party, whenever the issue is not of general importance? Notice the tension between the certiorari standard and the familiar doctrine that the function of the Court is to decide cases, not to determine the law.

On the Court as well as off there have been vigorous disputes over certiorari policy, as illustrated by Justice Frankfurter's famous protest against what he saw as the Court's propensity to take FELA cases (30 in a decade, he said in Wilkerson v. McCarthy, 336 U.S. 53 (1949) (concurring opinion)) "merely to review facts already canvassed by two and sometimes three courts."[4] Not only, in his view, did acceptance of such cases waste

stein, p. 599 supra), the Court ruled that a direct appeal lay only when the lower court passed upon the merits. What is there in § 1253 to support this conclusion?

4. Justice Frankfurter was not alone in this view. See, e.g., Michalic v. Cleveland Tankers, Inc., 364 U.S. 325 (1960) (dissenting opinion of Justice Harlan, joined by Justices Whittaker and Stewart).

Among the disputed FELA cases was that of the engineer Boyd Ringhiser, who lost a leg when a gondola car in which he was relieving himself was bumped during switching operations:

the Court's time on trivial matters; it also encouraged lawyers to burden the Court with frivolous petitions in the hope that lightning might strike.[5] See Professor Hart's caustic criticism of FELA practice (Foreword: Time Chart of the Justices, 73 Harv.L.Rev. 84, 96–98 (1959)) and Judge Arnold's reply (Professor Hart's Theology, 73 Harv.L.Rev. 1298, 1300–04 (1960)): "In the FELA cases the Court is setting standards which directly or indirectly affect the lives of millions. . . ."[6]

An understanding of the criteria for granting certiorari should make clear that the Court means exactly what it says in its frequent pronouncements that the denial of certiorari implies no approval of the decision below. See, e.g., Maryland v. Baltimore Radio Show, Inc., 338 U.S. 912, 917–920 (1950) (opinion of Frankfurter, J.); Stern, Gressman & Shapiro, supra, at 269–73.

Required reading for anyone considering petitioning for certiorari is Prettyman, Petitioning the United States Supreme Court—A Primer for Hopeful Neophytes, 51 Va.L.Rev. 582 (1965).

And now Boyd rides the F. E. L. & A.,
The C. & O. will maybe have to pay.
The jury said he'd never have to beg,
Gave him forty thousand dollars for his poor lost leg.
But the railroad lawyers did a double take:
"Why should *we* pay damages, for heaven's sake?
The statute says we can't be charged a cent
If the plaintiff doesn't prove that we were negligent."
C. & O. files a little motion,
C. & O. nasty as can be;
C. & O. makes a big commotion
And the judge he gives defendant judgment N.O.V.
The Brotherhood came to poor Boyd's support,
Appealed the ruling to the *Su*-preme Court.
Railroads generally have to pay
When the Big Court rides the F. E. L. & A. . . .
Now Felix wanted to dismiss the cert.;
There was nothing novel in the case but dirt.
But don't give up until you've heard the end,
For the *Su*-preme Court's the gandy-dancer's friend. . . .
Su-preme Court rendered its decision,
Su-preme Court, reason sharp and clean;
Su-preme Court said railroads should envision
That a hogger'd use a rattler for a durned latrine.

Ringhiser v. Chesapeake & O. Ry., 354 U.S. 901 (1957), as paraphrased in B. Currie, Casey Jones Redivivus (unpublished).

5. In *Ferguson* and a number of other cases Justice Frankfurter carried his objection to reviewing factual matters so far as to refuse to vote on the merits even after certiorari had been granted. Other Justices found it impossible to reconcile this practice with the Court's familiar "rule of four," under which four votes are sufficient to secure review. See Ferguson v. Moore-McCormack Lines, 352 U.S. 521, 559 (1957) (Harlan, J.); Sentilles v. Inter-Caribbean Shipping Corp., 361 U.S. 107, 111 (1959) (Stewart, J.). See also Bickel, The Least Dangerous Branch 142 (1962), questioning the rule itself: "There are times when avoidance should rest on merits of its own, and it is not clear why a majority of the Court should lack the power to make this judgment."

6. See also Ratchford v. Gay Lib, 434 U.S. 1080, 1081 (1978) (Rehnquist, J., dissenting), protesting the Court's denial of certiorari in a case posing the constitutionality of a state university's refusal to recognize an organization concerned with the status of homosexuals: "[T]he existence of . . . discretion does not imply that it should be used as a sort of judicial storm cellar to which we may flee to escape from controversial or sensitive cases."

(6) Ever since 1802 the Supreme Court has had jurisdiction in some instances to answer questions certified to it by other federal courts. Section 1254 currently authorizes the courts of appeals to certify "any question of law" to the Supreme Court in "any civil or criminal case" (is that all-inclusive?) in which instructions are desired. The Supreme Court "may give binding instructions" or may "require the entire record to be sent up for decision of the entire matter in controversy." No similar provision was made respecting the Court of Claims when the certification procedure applied to that court, because of the fear that to decide the whole case before decision by the trial court might be unconstitutional in view of the limited original jurisdiction of the Supreme Court. See Wheeler Lumber Bridge & Supply Co. v. United States, 281 U.S. 572, 576–77 (1930) (dictum); Stern, Gressman & Shapiro, Supreme Court Practice 43 (6th ed. 1986), suggesting the same difficulty in the case of questions certified by courts of appeals in cases coming directly from federal administrative agencies. But why doesn't this objection, if valid at all, equally preclude the decision of a single issue? Cf. United States v. Barnett, 376 U.S. 681 (1964), where the Court without comment answered a question certified by a court of appeals in a proceeding in that court to punish disobedience of its own orders.

Although the words of the statute seem permissive, it is often said that the Supreme Court has no discretion to refuse to answer certified questions, see R. Robertson & F. Kirkham, Jurisdiction of the Supreme Court of the United States 254 (Wolfson & Kurland ed. 1951); Moore & Vestal, Present and Potential Role of Certification in Federal Appellate Procedure, 35 Va. L.Rev. 1, 3, 42 (1949). The Court has, however, developed rules limiting the types of questions that may be submitted. The statute itself requires that the question be one of "law"; the Court has imposed the further requirement that the question not be abstract or overly general, see NLRB v. White Swan Co., 313 U.S. 23 (1941); S.Ct. Rule 24.1. Other decisions strongly suggest that the Court does not feel its jurisdiction over certified questions obligatory at all: Busby v. Electric Utilities Union, 323 U.S. 72 (1944), where the Court said it would not answer questions of District of Columbia law without the views of local judges, and Wisniewski v. United States, 353 U.S. 901 (1957), holding that "doubt about the respect to be accorded to a previous decision of a different panel [of the same court of appeals] should not be the occasion for invoking so exceptional a jurisdiction of this Court as that on certification. It is primarily the task of a Court of Appeals to reconcile its internal difficulties." The Court took occasion in *Wisniewski* to discourage certification generally:

> It is also the task of a Court of Appeals to decide all properly presented cases coming before it, except in the rare instances, as for example the pendency of another case before this Court raising the same issue, when certification may be advisable in the proper administration and expedition of judicial business.[7]

7. See also Taylor v. Atlantic Maritime Co., 181 F.2d 84, 85 (2d Cir. 1950): "We have not for many years certified questions except in cases where the point was involved in another appeal, already pending in that court. . . . We can see no reason for imposing an appeal upon the Supreme Court, which it does not choose to take of its own motion, except in cases when no petition for certiorari is available to the aggrieved party."

Is certification a good idea? Its history and scope are detailed in Robertson & Kirkham, supra, at 244–97, and in Moore & Vestal, supra, 35 Va.L.Rev. 1 (1949). Noting the Supreme Court's apparently hostile statements about certification, the Revisers in 1948 considered dropping the provision from the Judicial Code but were dissuaded by a committee composed of Chief Justice Stone and Justices Frankfurter and Douglas. See Moore & Vestal, supra, 35 Va.L.Rev. at 3, 7–8, 21, 42–43, arguing for discretionary Supreme Court jurisdiction over certified questions in order to aid the lower courts in reaching correct decisions on doubtful though not necessarily important issues: "By eliminating the necessity for a petition for certiorari and by requiring only a minimum amount of printing, [certification] saves the litigants both expense and time. Moreover, the courts of appeals relieve the Supreme Court of much work by eliminating from consideration all questions except those clearly in doubt." [8]

(7) During the 1988 Term the Supreme Court disposed of 4806 cases, only 254 of them "on the merits;" this designation excludes appeals dismissed. These figures include an enormous number of in forma pauperis (Miscellaneous Docket) cases (2626), nearly all frivolous (1.1% reviewed on merits), most of them filed by prisoners. See Note, The Supreme Court, 1988 Term, 103 Harv.L.Rev. at 398 (1989). The great discrepancy between cases filed and cases decided even on the Appellate Docket, however, has led to some concern that the Court is no longer in a position to assure uniformity in the interpretation of federal law, much less to correct errors in lower-court decisions. See Federal Judicial Center, Report of the Study Group on the Caseload of the Supreme Court (Dec. 1972), suggesting, among other things, that a new National Court of Appeals be established to resolve minor conflicts between circuits and to sift certiorari petitions for the Supreme Court. Denial of review by the NCA would be final; the Supreme Court would select cases from those the NCA had certified. Is it wise to give another court a veto over the Supreme Court's docket? Is the reading of petitions a worthy use of Circuit Judges' time? What kind of proof would you want that such a drastic measure is needed? [9]

The Commission on Revision of the Federal Court Appellate System in 1975 (Structure and Internal Procedures: Recommendations for Change) recommended the creation of a new National Court of Appeals with authority to make nationally binding the decisions on matters of federal law, subject to review in the Supreme Court by certiorari. The Supreme Court could refer any pending case to the National Court, and a court of appeals could transfer any case "in which an immediate decision by the National Court of Appeals is in the public interest" if the case involved an

8. Perhaps because of the Supreme Court's lack of enthusiasm, certification is not very common; Moore & Vestal, supra, 35 Va.L.Rev. at 26, report that only twenty cases were decided on certificate in the ten years 1937–46. But the certified questions have included some important ones, e.g., United States v. Barnett, 376 U.S. 681 (1964) (right to jury trial for contempt of court, where the court of appeals was equally divided, and where there was no lower-court judgment to affirm).

9. The national Court of Appeals proposal aroused a storm of controversy. See, for example, the strongly negative views of Justice Brennan in The National Court of Appeals: Another Dissent, 40 U.Chi.L.Rev. 473 (1973). Citations to additional commentary can be found in id. at 475 n. 2.

issue on which federal decisions conflict, a "recurring factual situation," or the interpretation of a rule previously announced by that court.[10]

SECTION 2. HABEAS CORPUS AND POST-CONVICTION RELIEF

WAINWRIGHT v. SYKES

433 U.S. 72 (1977).

MR. JUSTICE REHNQUIST delivered the opinion of the Court.

We granted certiorari to consider the availability of federal habeas to review a state convict's claim that testimony was admitted at his trial in violation of his *Miranda* rights, a claim which the Florida courts have previously refused to consider on the merits because of noncompliance with a state contemporaneous objection rule. Petitioner Wainwright, on behalf of the State of Florida, here challenges a decision of the Court of Appeals for the Fifth Circuit ordering a hearing in state court on the merits of respondent's contention.

Respondent Sykes was convicted of third-degree murder after a jury trial in the Circuit Court of DeSoto County. He testified at trial that on the evening of January 8, 1972, he commanded his wife to summon the police because he had just shot Willie Gilbert. Other evidence indicated that when the police arrived at respondent's trailer home, they found Gilbert dead of a shotgun wound, lying a few feet from the front porch. Shortly after their arrival, respondent came from across the road and volunteered that he had shot Gilbert, and a few minutes later respondent's wife approached the police and told them the same thing. Sykes was immediately arrested and taken to the police station.

Once there, it is conceded that he was read his *Miranda* rights, and that he declined to seek the aid of counsel and indicated a desire to talk. He then made a statement, which was admitted into evidence at trial through the testimony of the two officers who heard it, to the

10. See G. Casper & R. Posner, The Workload of the Supreme Court 92, 117–18 (1976), a statistical analysis finding no compelling evidence that the increase in workload either "has interfered significantly with the ability of the Court to discharge its various responsibilities or that the Court is denying review in cases where Supreme Court review would serve an important function." Concluding that there was thus no need for "radical changes" such as proposed by the Study Group and the Commission, Casper and Posner suggested that "more modest reforms" might have salutary effect:

> the abolition of the remaining obligatory jurisdiction of the Supreme Court [which was basically accomplished in 1988] and of direct appeals to the Court from federal district courts, the creation of supreme courts of patent and tax appeals, the greater pooling of law clerks for screening applications for review, reduction in the number of concurring and dissenting opinions, denial or curtailment of oral argument in some cases, greater use of short per curiam opinions to decide unanimous cases, and the promulgation of detailed guidelines regarding the criteria for the grant and denial of review.

effect that he had shot Gilbert from the front porch of his trailer home. There were several references during the trial to respondent's consumption of alcohol during the preceding day and to his apparent state of intoxication, facts which were acknowledged by the officers who arrived at the scene. At no time during the trial, however, was the admissibility of any of respondent's statements challenged by his counsel on the ground that respondent had not understood the *Miranda* warnings. Nor did the trial judge question their admissibility on his own motion or hold a fact-finding hearing bearing on that issue.

Respondent appealed his conviction, but apparently did not challenge the admissibility of the inculpatory statements. He later filed in the trial court a motion to vacate the conviction and, in the State District Court of Appeals and Supreme Court, petitions for habeas corpus. These filings, apparently for the first time, challenged the statements made to police on grounds of involuntariness. In all of these efforts respondent was unsuccessful.

Having failed in the Florida courts, respondent initiated the present action under 28 U.S.C. § 2254, asserting the inadmissibility of his statements by reason of his lack of understanding of the *Miranda* warnings. The United States District Court for the Middle District of Florida ruled . . . that respondent had not lost his right to assert such a claim by failing to object at trial or on direct appeal, since only "exceptional circumstances" of "strategic decisions at trial" can create such a bar to raising federal constitutional claims in a federal habeas action. . . . The United States Court of Appeals for the Fifth Circuit . . . directed its attention to the effect on respondent's right of Florida Rule of Criminal Procedure 3.190(i), which it described as "a contemporaneous objection rule" applying to motions to suppress a defendant's inculpatory statements. It focused on this Court's decisions in Henry v. Mississippi, 379 U.S. 443 (1965); Davis v. United States, 411 U.S. 233 (1973), and Fay v. Noia, 372 U.S. 391 (1963), and concluded that the failure to comply with the rule requiring objection at the trial would only bar review of the suppression claim where the right to object was deliberately by-passed for reasons relating to trial tactics. . . . Concluding that "[t]he failure to object in this case cannot be dismissed as a trial tactic, and thus a deliberate by-pass," the court affirmed. . . .

The simple legal question before the Court calls for a construction of the language of 28 U.S.C. § 2254(a), which provides that the federal courts shall entertain an application for a writ of habeas corpus "in behalf of a person in custody pursuant to the judgment of the state court only on the ground that he is in custody in violation of the Constitution or laws or treaties of the United States." But, to put it mildly, we do not write on a clean slate in construing this statutory provision.[6] Its earliest counterpart, applicable only to prisoners de-

6. For divergent discussions of the historic role of federal habeas corpus, compare: Hart, Foreword: The Time Chart of the Justices, 73 Harv.L.Rev. 84 (1959); Reitz, Federal Habeas Corpus: Impact of an Abortive State Proceeding, 74 Harv.L. Rev. 1315 (1961); Brennan, Federal Habeas Corpus and State Prisoners: An

tained by federal authority, is found in the Judiciary Act of 1789. Construing that statute for the Court in Ex parte Watkins, 28 U.S. (3 Pet.) 193, 202 (1830), Chief Justice Marshall said:

> "An imprisonment under a judgment cannot be unlawful, unless that judgment be an absolute nullity; and it is not a nullity if the Court has general jurisdiction of the subject, although it should be erroneous."
>
> . . .

In 1867, Congress expanded the statutory language so as to make the writ available to one held in state as well as federal custody. . . . Where the habeas petitioner challenges a final judgment of conviction rendered by a state court, this Court has been called upon to decide no fewer than four different questions, all to a degree interrelated with one another: (1) What types of federal claims may a federal habeas court properly consider; (2) Where a federal claim is cognizable by a federal habeas court, to what extent must that court defer to a resolution of the claim in prior state proceedings; (3) To what extent must the petitioner who seeks federal habeas exhaust state remedies before resorting to the federal court; (4) In what instances will an adequate and independent state ground bar consideration of otherwise cognizable federal issues on federal habeas review?

Each of these four issues has spawned its share of litigation. With respect to the first, the rule laid down in *Ex parte Watkins*, supra, was gradually changed by judicial decisions expanding the availability of habeas relief beyond attacks focused narrowly on the jurisdiction of the sentencing court. See Ex parte Wells, 59 U.S. (18 How.) 307 (1855); Ex parte Lange, 85 U.S. (18 Wall.) 163 (1873). Ex parte Siebold, 100 U.S. 371 (1879), authorized use of the writ to challenge a conviction under a federal statute where the statute was claimed to violate the United States Constitution. Frank v. Mangum, 237 U.S. 309 (1915) and Moore v. Dempsey, 261 U.S. 86, 543 (1923), though in large part inconsistent with one another, together broadened the concept of jurisdiction to allow review of a claim of "mob domination" of what was in all other respects a trial in a court of competent jurisdiction.

In Johnson v. Zerbst, 304 U.S. 458, 463 (1938), an indigent federal prisoner's claim that he was denied the right to counsel at his trial was held to state a contention going to the "power and authority" of the trial court, which might be reviewed on habeas. Finally, in Waley v. Johnston, 316 U.S. 101 (1942), the Court openly discarded the concept of jurisdiction—by then more a fiction than anything else—as a touchstone of the availability of federal habeas review, and acknowledged that such review is available for claims of "disregard of the constitutional rights of the accused, and where the writ is the only effective

Exercise in Federalism, 7 Utah L.Rev. 423 (1961); Bator, Finality in Criminal Law and Federal Habeas Corpus for State Prisoners, 76 Harv.L.Rev. 441, 468 (1963); Oaks, Legal History in the High Court—Habeas Corpus, 64 Mich.L.Rev. 451 (1966); Friendly, Is Innocence Irrelevant? Collateral Attack on Criminal Judgments, 38 U.Chi.L.Rev. 142, 170–171 (1970); and Note, Developments in the Law—Federal Habeas Corpus, 83 Harv.L.Rev. 1038 (1970).

means of preserving his rights." Id., at 104–105. In Brown v. Allen, 344 U.S. 443 (1953), it was made explicit that a state prisoner's challenge to the trial court's resolution of dispositive federal issues is always fair game on federal habeas. Only last Term in Stone v. Powell, 428 U.S. 465 (1976), the Court removed from the purview of a federal habeas court challenges resting on the Fourth Amendment, where there has been a full and fair opportunity to raise them in the state court.

The degree of deference to be given to a state court's resolution of a federal law issue was elaborately canvassed in the Court's opinions in *Brown v. Allen*, supra. Speaking for the Court, Mr. Justice Reed stated that such "state adjudication carries the weight that federal practice gives to the conclusion of a court of last resort of another jurisdiction on federal constitutional issues. It is not *res judicata*." 344 U.S., at 458. The duty of the federal habeas court to hold a factfinding hearing in specific situations, notwithstanding the prior resolution of the issues in state court, was thoroughly explored in this Court's later decision in Townsend v. Sain, 372 U.S. 293 (1963). Congress addressed this aspect of federal habeas in 1966 when it amended § 2254 to deal with the problem treated in *Townsend*.

The exhaustion of state remedies requirement was first articulated by this Court in the case of Ex parte Royall, 117 U.S. 241 (1886). There, a state defendant sought habeas in advance of trial on a claim that he had been indicted under an unconstitutional statute. The writ was dismissed by the District Court, and this Court affirmed, stating that while there was power in the federal courts to entertain such petitions, as a matter of comity they should usually stay their hand pending consideration of the issue in the normal course of the state trial. This rule has been followed in subsequent cases . . . and has been incorporated into the language of § 2254. . . .

There is no need to consider here in greater detail these first three areas of controversy attendant to federal habeas review of state convictions. Only the fourth area—the adequacy of state grounds to bar federal habeas review—is presented in this case. The foregoing discussion of the other three is pertinent here only as it illustrates this Court's historic willingness to overturn or modify its earlier views of the scope of the writ, even where the statutory language authorizing judicial action has remained unchanged.

As to the role of adequate and independent state grounds, it is a well-established principle of federalism that a state decision resting on an adequate foundation of state substantive law is immune from review in the federal courts. Fox Film Corp. v. Muller, 296 U.S. 207 (1935); Murdock v. Memphis, 87 U.S. (20 Wall.) 590 (1875). The application of this principle in the context of a federal habeas proceeding has therefore excluded from consideration any questions of state *substantive* law, and thus effectively barred federal habeas review where questions of that sort are either the only ones raised by a petitioner or are in themselves dispositive of his case. The area of controversy which has developed has concerned the reviewability of federal claims which the state court has declined to pass on because not presented in the manner prescribed by its *procedural* rules. The adequacy of such an independent state procedural ground to prevent federal habeas review of the underlying federal issue has been treated very differently than where the state law ground is substantive. The pertinent decisions marking the Court's somewhat tortuous efforts to deal with this problem are: Ex parte Spencer, 228 U.S. 652 (1913); Daniels v. Allen, 344 U.S. 443 (1953); *Fay v. Noia*, supra; Davis v. United States, 411 U.S. 233 (1973); and Francis v. Henderson, 425 U.S. 536 (1976).

In *Daniels*, supra, petitioners' lawyer had failed to mail the appeal papers to the state supreme court on the last day provided by law for filing, and hand delivered them one day after that date. Citing the state rule requiring timely filing, the Supreme Court of North Carolina refused to hear the appeal. This Court, relying in part on its earlier decision in *Ex parte Spencer*, supra, held that federal habeas was not available to review a constitutional claim which could not have been reviewed on direct appeal here because it rested on an independent and adequate state procedural ground.

In *Fay v. Noia*, supra, respondent Noia sought federal habeas to review a claim that his state court conviction had resulted from the introduction of a coerced confession in violation of the Fifth Amendment to the United States Constitution. While the convictions of his two codefendants were reversed on that ground in collateral proceedings following their appeals, Noia did not appeal and the New York courts ruled that his subsequent *coram nobis* action was barred on account of that failure. This Court held that petitioner was nonetheless entitled to raise the claim in federal habeas, and thereby overruled its decision 10 years earlier in *Daniels v. Allen*, supra:

> "[T]he doctrine under which state procedural defaults are held to constitute an adequate and independent state law ground barring direct Supreme Court review is not to be extended to limit the power granted the federal courts under the federal habeas statute."

As a matter of comity but not of federal power, the Court acknowledged "a limited discretion in the federal judge to deny relief . . . to an applicant who had deliberately by-passed the orderly procedure of the state courts and in so doing has forfeited his state remedies." In so stating, the Court made clear that the waiver must be knowing and actual—"an intentional relinquishment or abandonment of a known right or privilege," quoting *Johnson v. Zerbst*, supra. Noting petitioner's "grisly choice" between acceptance of his life sentence and pursuit of an appeal which might culminate in a sentence of death, the Court concluded that there had been no deliberate bypass of the right to have the federal issues reviewed through a state appeal.

A decade later we decided Davis v. United States, 411 U.S. 233 (1973), in which a federal prisoner's application under § 2255 sought for the first time to challenge the makeup of the grand jury which indicted him. The Government contended that he was barred by the requirement of Fed.Rule Crim.Proc. 12(b)(2) providing that such challenges must be raised "by motion before trial." The rule further provides that failure to so object constitutes a waiver of the objection, but that "the Court for cause shown may grant relief from the waiver." We noted that the rule "promulgated by this Court and, pursuant to 18 U.S.C. § 3771, 'adopted' by Congress, governs by its terms the manner in which the claims of defects in the institution of criminal proceedings may be waived," and held that this standard contained in the rule, rather than the *Fay v. Noia* concept of waiver, should pertain in federal habeas as on direct review. Referring to previous constructions of Rule 12(b)(2), we concluded that review of the claim should be barred on habeas, as on direct appeal, absent a showing of cause for the noncompliance and some showing of actual prejudice resulting from the alleged constitutional violation.

Last Term, in Francis v. Henderson, 425 U.S. 536 (1976), the rule of *Davis* was applied to the parallel case of a state procedural requirement that challenges to grand jury composition be raised before trial. The Court noted that there was power in the federal courts to entertain an application in such a case, but rested its holding on "considerations of comity and concerns for the orderly administration of criminal justice . . .". While there was no counterpart provision of the state rule which allowed an exception upon some showing of cause, the Court concluded that the standard derived from the federal rule should nonetheless be applied in that context since "[t]here is no reason to . . . give greater preclusive effect to procedural defaults by federal defendants than to similar defaults by state defendants." As applied to the federal petitions of state convicts, the *Davis* cause and prejudicial standard was thus incorporated directly into the body of law governing the availability of federal habeas corpus review.

To the extent that the dicta of *Fay v. Noia* may be thought to have laid down an all-inclusive rule rendering state timely objection rules ineffective to bar review of underlying federal claims in federal habeas proceedings—absent a "knowing waiver" or a "deliberate bypass" of the right to so object—its effect was limited by *Francis*, which applied a different rule and barred a habeas challenge to the makeup of a grand jury. Petitioner Wainwright in this case urges that we further confine its effect by applying the principle enunciated in *Francis* to a claimed error in the admission of a defendant's confession. . . .

Respondent . . . urges that a defendant has a right under Jackson v. Denno, 378 U.S. 368 (1964), to a hearing as to the voluntariness of a confession, even though the defendant does not object to its admission. But we do not read *Jackson* as creating any such requirement. . . . We therefore conclude that Florida procedure did, consistently with the United States Constitution, require that petitioner's confession be challenged at trial or not at all, and thus his failure to timely object to its admission amounted to an independent and adequate state procedural ground which would have prevented direct review here. See Henry v. Mississippi, 379 U.S. 443 (1965). We thus come to the crux of this case. Shall the rule of *Francis v. Henderson*, supra, barring federal habeas review absent a showing of "cause" and "prejudice" attendant to a state procedural waiver, be applied to a waived objection to the admission of a confession at trial? We answer that question in the affirmative.

As earlier noted in the opinion, since *Brown v. Allen*, supra, it has been the rule that the federal habeas petitioner who claims he is detained pursuant to a final judgment of a state court in violation of the U.S. Constitution is entitled to have the federal habeas court make its own independent determination of his federal claim, without being bound by the determination on the merits of that claim reached in the state proceedings. This rule of *Brown v. Allen* is in no way changed by our holding today. Rather, we deal only with contentions of federal law which were *not* resolved on the merits in the state proceeding due to the petitioner's failure to raise them there as required by state procedure. We leave open for resolution in future decisions the precise definition of the "cause" and "prejudice" standard, and note here only that it is narrower than the standard set forth in dicta in *Fay v. Noia*, supra, which would make federal habeas review generally available to state convicts absent a knowing and deliberate waiver of the federal constitutional contention. It is the sweeping language of *Fay v. Noia*, supra, going far beyond the facts of the case eliciting it, which we today reject.[12]

The reasons for our rejection of it are several. The contemporaneous objection rule itself is by no means peculiar to Florida, and deserves greater respect than *Fay* gives it, both for the fact that it is employed by a coordinate jurisdiction within the federal system and for the many interests which it serves in its own right. A contemporaneous objection enables the record to be made with respect to the constitutional claim when the recollections of witnesses are freshest, not years later in a federal habeas proceeding. It enables the judge who observed the demeanor of those witnesses to make the factual determinations necessary for properly deciding the federal constitutional question. While the 1966 amendment to § 2254 requires deference to be given to such determinations made by state courts, the determinations themselves are less apt to be made in the first instance if there is no contemporaneous objection to the admission of the evidence on federal constitutional grounds.

A contemporaneous objection rule may lead to the exclusion of the evidence objected to, thereby making a major contribution to finality in criminal litigation. Without the evidence claimed to be vulnerable on federal constitutional grounds, the jury may acquit the defendant, and

12. We have no occasion today to consider the *Fay* rule as applied to the facts there confronting the Court. . . .

that will be the end of the case; or it may nonetheless convict the defendant, and he will have one less federal constitutional claim to assert in his federal habeas petition. If the state trial judge admits the evidence in question after a full hearing, the federal habeas court pursuant to the 1966 amendment to § 2254 will gain significant guidance from the state ruling in this regard. Subtler considerations as well militate in favor of honoring a state contemporaneous objection rule. An objection on the spot may force the prosecution to take a hard look at its hole card, and even if the prosecutor thinks that the state trial judge will admit the evidence he must contemplate the possibility of reversal by the state appellate courts or the ultimate issuance of a writ of federal habeas corpus based on the impropriety of the state court's rejection of the federal constitutional claim.

We think that the rule of *Fay v. Noia*, broadly stated, may encourage "sand bagging" on the part of defense lawyers, who may take their chances on a verdict of not guilty in a state trial court and intend to raise their constitutional claims in a federal habeas court if their initial gamble does not pay off. The refusal of federal habeas courts to honor contemporaneous objection rules may also make state courts themselves less stringent in their enforcement. Under the rule of *Fay v. Noia*, supra, state appellate courts know that a federal constitutional issue raised for the first time in the proceeding before them may well be decided in any event by a federal habeas tribunal. Thus their choice is between addressing the issue notwithstanding the petitioner's failure to timely object, or else face the prospect that the federal habeas court will decide the question without the benefit of their views.

The failure of the federal habeas courts generally to require compliance with a contemporaneous objection rule tends to detract from the perception of the trial of a criminal case in state court as a decisive and portentous event. A defendant has been accused of a serious crime, and this is the time and place set for him to be tried by a jury of his peers and found either guilty or not guilty by that jury. To the greatest extent possible all issues which bear on this charge should be determined in this proceeding: the accused is in the court room, the jury is in the box, the judge is on the bench, and the witnesses, having been subpoenaed and duly sworn, await their turns to testify. Society's resources have been concentrated at that time and place in order to decide, within the limits of human fallibility, the question of guilt or innocence of one of its citizens. Any procedural rule which encourages the result that those proceedings be as free of error as possible is thoroughly desirable, and the contemporaneous objection rule surely falls within this classification. . . .

The "cause" and "prejudice" exception of the *Francis* rule will afford an adequate guarantee, we think, that the rule will not prevent a federal habeas court from adjudicating for the first time the federal constitutional claim of a defendant who in the absence of such an adjudication will be the victim of a miscarriage of justice. Whatever precise content may be given those terms by later cases, we feel confident in holding without further elaboration that they do not exist here. Respondent has advanced no explanation whatever for his failure to object at trial, and, as the proceeding unfolded, the trial judge is certainly not to be faulted for failing to question the admission of the confession himself. The other evidence of guilt presented at trial, moreover, was substantial to a degree that would negate any possibility of actual prejudice resulting to the respondent from the admission of his inculpatory statement.

We accordingly conclude that the judgment of the Court of Appeals for the Fifth Circuit must be reversed, and the cause remanded to the United States District Court for the Middle District of Florida with instructions to dismiss respondent's petition for a writ of habeas corpus. . . .

MR. JUSTICE BRENNAN, with whom MR. JUSTICE MARSHALL joins, dissenting. . . .

If it could be assumed that a procedural default more often than not is the product of a defendant's conscious refusal to abide by the duly constituted, legitimate processes of the state courts, then I might agree that a regime of collateral review weighted in favor of a State's procedural rules would be warranted. *Fay*, however, recognized that such rarely is the case; and therein lies *Fay's* basic unwillingness to embrace a view of habeas jurisdiction that results in "an airtight system of [procedural] forfeitures." . . .

In the ordinary case, litigants simply have no incentive to slight the state tribunal, since constitutional adjudication on the state and federal levels are not mutually exclusive. Under the regime of collateral review recognized since the days of *Brown v. Allen*, and enforced by the *Fay* bypass test, no rational lawyer would risk the "sandbagging" feared by the Court. . . .

The Court makes no effort to identify a tactical motive for the failure of Sykes' attorney to challenge the admissibility or reliability of a highly inculpatory statement. . . . Indeed, there is no basis for inferring that Sykes or his state trial lawyer were even aware of the existence of his claim under the Fifth Amendment; for this is not a case where the trial judge expressly drew the attention of the defense to a possible constitutional contention or procedural requirement, compare Murch v. Mottram, 409 U.S. 41 (1972); or where the defense signals its knowledge of a constitutional claim by abandoning a challenge previously raised, e.g., Sanders v. United States, 373 U.S. 1, 18 (1963). Rather, any realistic reading of the record demonstrates that we are faced here with a simple lawyer's error. . . .

If the standard adopted today is later construed to require that the simple mistakes of attorneys are to be treated as binding forfeitures, it would serve to subordinate the fundamental rights contained in our constitutional charter to inadvertent defaults of rules promulgated by state agencies, and would essentially leave it to the States, through the enactment of procedure and the certification of the competence of local attorneys, to determine whether a habeas applicant will be permitted the access to the federal forum that is guaranteed him by Congress. . . .

But federal review is not the full measure of Sykes' interest, for there is another of even greater immediacy: assuring that his constitutional claims can be addressed to *some* court. For the obvious consequence of barring Sykes from the federal courthouse is to insulate Florida's alleged constitutional violation from any and all judicial review because of a lawyer's mistake. From the standpoint of the habeas petitioner, it is a harsh rule indeed that denies him "any review at all where the state has granted none," Brown v. Allen, supra, 344 U.S. at 552 (Black, J., dissenting)—particularly when he would have enjoyed both state and federal consideration had his attorney not erred. . . .

A regime of federal habeas corpus jurisdiction that permits the reopening of state procedural defaults does not invalidate any state procedural rule as such; Florida's courts remain entirely free to enforce their own rules as they choose, and to deny any and all state rights and remedies to a defendant who fails to comply with applicable state procedure. The relevant inquiry is whether more is required—specifically, whether the fulfillment of important interests of the State necessitates that federal courts be called upon to impose additional sanctions for inadvertent noncompliance with state procedural requirements such as the contemporary objection rule involved here.

Florida, of course, can point to a variety of legitimate interests in seeking allegiance to its reasonable procedural requirements, the contemporary objection rule included. . . . The strict enforcement of procedural defaults may be seen as a means of deterring any tendency on the part of the defense to slight the state forum, to deny state judges their due opportunity for playing a meaningful role in the evolving task of constitutional adjudication, or to mock the needed finality of criminal trials. All of these interests are referred to by the Court in various forms.[11] . . .

Punishing a lawyer's unintentional errors by closing the federal courthouse door to his client is both a senseless and misdirected method of deterring the slighting of state rules. It is senseless because unplanned and unintentional action of any kind generally is not subject to deterrence; and, to the extent that it is hoped that a threatened sanction addressed to the defense will induce greater care and caution

11. In my view, the strongest plausible argument for strict enforcement of a contemporary objection rule is one that the Court barely relies on at all: the possibility that the failure of timely objection to the admissibility of evidence may foreclose the making of a fresh record and thereby prejudice the prosecution in later litigation involving that evidence. There may be force to this contention, but it rests on the premise that the State in fact has suffered actual prejudice because of a procedural lapse. Florida demonstrates no such injury here. . . .

on the part of trial lawyers, thereby forestalling negligent conduct or error, the potential loss of all valuable state remedies would be sufficient to this end. And it is a misdirected sanction because even if the penalization of incompetence or carelessness will encourage more thorough legal training and trial preparation, the habeas applicant, as opposed to his lawyer, hardly is the proper recipient of such a penalty. . . . This is especially true when so many indigent defendants are without any realistic choice in selecting who ultimately represents them at trial. . . .

In short, I believe that the demands of our criminal justice system warrant visiting the mistakes of a trial attorney on the head of a habeas corpus applicant only when we are convinced that the lawyer actually exercised his expertise and judgment in his client's service, and with his client's knowing and intelligent participation where possible. This, of course, is the precise system of habeas review established by *Fay v. Noia*. . . .

Notes on Habeas Corpus

A. The Issues Cognizable

(1) The demise of the traditional theory that habeas for state convicts lay only to examine the trial court's jurisdiction is adequately traced in the *Sykes* opinion. This movement reached its high point in Fay v. Noia, 372 U.S. 391 (1963), a confession case in which the Court appeared to say that all constitutional questions were within the scope of habeas corpus for state prisoners: The statute provides "a federal forum for state prisoners having constitutional defenses"; "federal court jurisdiction is conferred by the allegation of an unconstitutional restraint."

(2) In Kaufman v. United States, 394 U.S. 217 (1969), over vehement dissents by Justices Black and Harlan, the Court held that the introduction of evidence obtained by unreasonable search or seizure could be challenged under 28 U.S.C. § 2255, the modern equivalent of habeas corpus for federal prisoners. This conclusion was substantially qualified in Stone v. Powell, 428 U.S. 465 (1976). "The primary justification for the exclusionary rule," wrote Justice Powell for the majority, "is the deterrence of police conduct that violates Fourth Amendment rights." Because the rule precluded resort to reliable evidence, its application inevitably "deflects the truthfinding process and often frees the guilty." Past decisions had balanced this cost against the need for additional deterrence in limiting standing to those whose rights had been violated by the search, in permitting introduction of illegally seized evidence for impeachment purposes and before a grand jury, and in refusing to apply the rule to cases decided before its announcement. The costs were even greater when the error was corrected on collateral review, with its adverse impact on finality. When a state court had "provided an opportunity for full and fair litigation of a Fourth Amendment claim," any additional deterrence afforded by reopening the question collaterally would be "small in relation to the costs," and federal habeas corpus would not lie.

Insisting that a person imprisoned on the basis of illegally obtained evidence was "in custody in violation of the Constitution" within the meaning of 28 U.S.C. § 2254(a), Justice Brennan in dissent expressed the fear that the Court's balancing analysis laid the "groundwork . . . for a drastic withdrawal of federal habeas jurisdiction, . . . at least for claims—for example, of double jeopardy, entrapment, self-incrimination, *Miranda* violations, and use of invalid identification procedures—that this Court later decides are not 'guilt-related.' " The majority responded that its decision was "*not* concerned with the scope of the habeas corpus statute as authority for litigating constitutional claims generally":

> Our decision does not mean that the federal court lacks jurisdiction over such a claim, but only that the application of the [exclusionary] rule is limited to cases in which there has been such a showing [no opportunity for full and fair litigation] and a Fourth Amendment violation.

(3) *Stone v. Powell*'s test of an opportunity for full and fair litigation resembles the position taken in *Waley v. Johnston*, noted in *Sykes*, that habeas lay only when the State had failed to provide adequate machinery for processing federal claims.[1] Yet any suspicion that *Stone* portended an across-the-board return to the *Waley* test was quashed in Jackson v. Virginia, 443 U.S. 307, 323 (1979), where the Court refused to hold habeas precluded by a full and fair state determination of the claim that there was insufficient evidence to support a finding of guilt beyond a reasonable doubt: "The question whether a defendant has been convicted upon inadequate evidence is central to the basic question of guilt or innocence."

(4) Moreover, Justice Brennan's fear that *Stone* foreshadowed a "withdrawal of federal habeas jurisdiction" for all claims that were not "guilt-related" proved unfounded when the Court held the full-and-fair standard inapplicable to a claim of racial discrimination in the selection of the grand jury in Rose v. Mitchell, 443 U.S. 545, 560–64 (1979). Justice Powell, author of *Stone v. Powell*, argued in a separate concurrence that a comparison of "costs and benefits" showed "habeas corpus should not be available for . . . claims . . . that have nothing to do with the fairness of the claimant's conviction." The majority, in an opinion by Justice Blackmun, began by suggesting that any balancing of costs and benefits was improper: The Court in *Stone* "stressed that its decision to limit review was '*not* concerned with the scope of the habeas corpus statute as authority for litigating constitutional claims generally' . . . [but] was confining its ruling to cases involving the judicially created exclusionary rule. . . ." In the next breath, however, the Court performed a cost-benefit comparison of its own to distinguish *Stone* on the merits. On the one hand there was greater need for a federal forum than in the case of an illegal search, for in a grand-jury case it was "the trial court itself" that was accused of unconstitutional selection; it was doubtful that this same court would give a claim of its own transgression "the type of full and fair hearing deemed essential to the holding of *Stone*." On the other hand, federal interference would be less disruptive of state interests than in *Stone*: While "[e]vidence

1. The issue in *Waley*, a coerced guilty plea, depended upon facts outside the record, "not open to consideration and review or appeal."

suppressed under the Fourth Amendment may not be used . . . in any new trial," a finding of grand-jury discrimination leaves the State "free to use at a second trial any and all evidence it employed at the first proceeding." Thus "[a] prisoner who is guilty in fact is less likely to go free . . . than in cases involving the exclusionary rule." [2]

(5) Is there any answer to Justice Brennan's argument in *Stone* from the language of § 2254?

B. Prior Adjudication

(6) In Brown v. Allen, 344 U.S. 443, 500, 544 (1953), discussed in *Sykes,* the confession and grand-jury issues had been adversely decided by the state courts. Why was relitigation not precluded by res judicata, as 28 U.S.C. § 1738 seems to require? "The District Court must take due account of the proceedings that are challenged by the application for a writ," said Justice Frankfurter for the Court. "But the prior State determination of a claim under the United States Constitution cannot foreclose consideration of such a claim, else the State court would have the final say which the Congress, by the Act of 1867, provided it should not have."[4] Justice Jackson disagreed: "Call it res judicata or what one will, courts ought not to be obliged to allow a convict to litigate again and again exactly the same question on the same evidence."

As a policy matter, can relitigation of decided questions be defended on the ground that, because of the severity of criminal sanctions and the importance of observing constitutional limitations, it is never too late to correct injustice? On the ground (see Hart, Foreword, The Supreme Court: 1958 Term, 73 Harv.L.Rev. 84, 106–07 (1959)) that "a state prisoner ought

2. The Court added that the ban on discrimination was "the direct command of the Fourteenth Amendment," while the exclusionary rule was " 'a judicially created remedy rather than a personal constitutional right' "; that "the constitutional interests" in the grand-jury case were "more compelling" than in *Stone* because "discrimination on account of race in the administration of justice strikes at the core concerns of the Fourteenth Amendment and at fundamental values of our society and our legal system"; and that, unlike the use of illegally obtained evidence, "[t]he claim that the court has discriminated on the basis of race in a given case brings the integrity of the judicial system into direct question."

See also Greene v. Massey, 546 F.2d 51, 53 n. 6 (5th Cir. 1977), refusing to apply *Stone v. Powell* to a double-jeopardy claim that had been fully litigated in state court, quoting from note 37 of the *Stone* opinion and adding that double jeopardy is a "specifically proclaimed 'personal constitutional right.' "

4. Is it clear that Brown was "restrained of his . . . liberty in violation of the constitution," as the statute requires? See Hart & Wechsler, The Federal Courts and the Federal System 1427 (2d ed. 1973): "There is a sense . . . in which a prisoner can be deemed to be legally detained if he is held pursuant to the judgment or decision of a competent tribunal or authority, even though the decision to detain rested on an error as to law or fact." Neither Frankfurter in *Brown* nor Brennan in *Noia* interpreted the statute to require release of everyone unconstitutionally *convicted*: Notice the former's treatment of questions of historical fact and the latter's discussion of deliberate bypass; and see *Daniels v. Allen,* infra note 9.

Can *Brown v. Allen's* rejection of res judicata be justified by the provision of the 1867 Act that any state-court "proceeding" involving the subject of a federal habeas petition was "null and void?" By the 1948 provision that federal relief should not be granted "unless . . . the applicant has exhausted the remedies available in the courts of the State?" Is the result supported today by §§ 2254(b) and (d)?

to have an opportunity for a hearing on a federal constitutional claim in a federal constitutional court?" [5]

(7) It was not only pure questions of law that *Brown v. Allen* permitted to be re-examined on habeas corpus after a state-court decision. In addition, "the interpretation of the legal significance of . . . facts," for example whether questioning for fourteen hours rendered a confession "involuntary," was also a question for the habeas court to resolve de novo. But state determinations of "primary fact," such as whether or not the defendant had been beaten, could be accepted absent "unusual circumstances" unless there was a "vital flaw" in the state fact-finding process. Why the difference?

As to "primary" facts *Brown* was "supersede[d]" by the 5–4 decision in Townsend v. Sain, 372 U.S. 293 (1963), which concerned a claim that a confession had been involuntarily extracted by the use of "truth serum": Because detention that violates the "fundamental liberties of the person" is "intolerable," the habeas court always "has the power to receive evidence and try the facts anew" if the petition "alleges facts which, if proven, would entitle him to relief" and "must hold an evidentiary hearing if the habeas applicant did not receive a full and fair evidentiary hearing in a state court," i.e.,

> If (1) the merits of the factual dispute were not resolved in the state hearing; (2) the state factual determination is not fairly supported by the record as a whole; (3) the fact-finding procedure employed by the state court was not adequate to afford a full and fair hearing; (4) there is a substantial allegation of newly discovered evidence; (5) the material facts were not adequately developed at the state-court hearing; or (6) for any reason it appears that the state trier of fact did not afford the habeas applicant a full and fair fact hearing.[6]

How does the 1966 amendment to § 2254(d), infra p. 724, affect *Townsend*?

(8) Is *Stone v. Powell* best understood as affording deference to state-court decisions, rather than as limiting the issues cognizable on habeas corpus?

The Court nowhere explained in *Stone* what it meant by the "opportunity for full and fair litigation" that would preclude federal review, apart from a footnote reference: "Cf. *Townsend v. Sain.*"

The lower courts have grappled extensively with the problem. At one extreme is United States ex rel. Petillo v. New Jersey, 418 F.Supp. 686, 689

5. For a negative answer see Bator, Finality in Criminal Law and Federal Habeas Corpus for State Prisoners, 76 Harv.L.Rev. 441, 474–77, 500–501 (1963).

6. Townsend was held entitled to a hearing because it was unclear whether the trial judge had applied the proper constitutional standard for admitting confessions. Moreover, the drug was not identified at trial as "truth serum," and this disclosure "was indispensable to a fair, rounded, development of the material facts." See Wright & Sofaer, Federal Habeas Corpus for State Prisoners: The Allocation of Fact-Finding Responsibility, 75 Yale L.J. 895 (1966), arguing among other things that by findings "fairly supported by the record as a whole" the Court should be taken to have referred to the clearly-erroneous rule, and that at times the district courts ought to pass the fact-finding job back to the state courts by holding the absence of a "full and fair hearing" to violate the Due Process Clause.

(D.N.J.1976), reversed on other grounds 562 F.2d 903 (3rd Cir. 1977), where state law was said to give no right to a hearing on allegations that an affidavit of probable cause was perjured:

> New Jersey thus effectively denies the subject of the search the right to suppress the fruits of warrants procured by perjury by denying him a hearing on the veracity of the underlying affidavit—no matter how compelling his preliminary showing of perjury may be.

On the other hand, despite *Townsend's* requirement of a decision "on the merits," several courts have relied on *Stone's* reference to an "opportunity" for full and fair litigation to hold that the petitioner cannot avoid *Stone* by unexcused failure to raise the issue properly before the state courts. As the Fifth Circuit said in Caver v. Alabama, 577 F.2d 1188, 1192–93 (5th Cir. 1978):

> If police officers who are conducting a search or making an arrest are aware that the state criminal justice system provides an opportunity for full and fair litigation of fourth amendment suppression claims, the policy underlying the exclusionary rule will be served. That a defendant later at trial might choose not to assert his fourth amendment claim could not remove the system's deterrence to police misconduct.

For the contrary argument see Goldberg, J., dissenting in O'Berry v. Wainwright, 546 F.2d 1204, 1221 (5th Cir. 1977). Does *Wainwright v. Sykes* moot this controversy?

Moreover, notwithstanding *Townsend*'s second criterion ("the state factual determination is not fairly supported by the record as a whole"), the courts have exhibited a marked reluctance to investigate the correctness of the state court's decision. E.g., Tisnado v. United States, 547 F.2d 452, 455 n. 2 (9th Cir. 1976) ("whether the state court correctly applied the law of search and seizure is apparently totally irrelevant as long as state procedures were 'fair' "); Swicegood v. Alabama, 577 F.2d 1322, 1324 (5th Cir. 1978) ("[i]f the term 'fair hearing' means that the state courts must correctly apply federal constitutional law, *Stone* becomes a nullity"). But see Gamble v. Oklahoma, 583 F.2d 1161, 1165 (10th Cir. 1978), concluding that *Stone* "contemplates recognition and at least colorable application of the correct Fourth Amendment constitutional standards" and reviewing the search issue because "the very standard" the Supreme Court had rejected in another case "formed the basis of the state court decisions."

A refusal to overturn state decisions that are fairly debatable is surely necessary if *Stone* is to have any meaning. But do you think the *Stone* Court would have viewed the power to set aside wholly arbitrary state decisions as unnecessary to the purposes of the exclusionary rule? See generally Halpern, Federal Habeas Corpus and the *Mapp* Exclusionary Rule After *Stone v. Powell*, 82 Colum.L.Rev. 1 (1982).

C. Procedural Defaults

(9) *Wainwright v. Sykes* accurately recites the history of the effect upon federal habeas corpus of a failure to litigate the issue during the state proceedings. Daniels v. Allen, 344 U.S. 443 (1953), in holding the failure to take a timely appeal barred federal habeas, invoked the statutory requirement (28 U.S.C. § 2254) that the applicant exhaust available states reme-

dies; other language in the opinion suggested waiver and, as *Sykes* tells us, the presence of an adequate state ground. The contrast to *Brown v. Allen*, decided in the same opinion, was striking: As Justice Black observed in dissent, Brown was given a second review and Daniels no review at all. Yet the two decisions together had the advantage of equating the jurisdiction of the district courts in habeas corpus with the Supreme Court's jurisdiction on direct review and thus of unloading on the District Courts the increasing burden of reviewing state criminal convictions.

(10) Fay v. Noia, 372 U.S. 391, 429–33 (1963), drastically departed from prior practice as illustrated by *Daniels*. "Waiver," as *Sykes* tells us, was redefined to require a "deliberate bypass" of state remedies, not to mean inadvertent forfeiture. The exhaustion requirement, the Court ruled, did not imply forfeiture: It "is limited in its application to failure to exhaust state remedies still open to the habeas applicant at the time he files his application in federal court." See p. 642 infra. Most interesting was the Court's conclusion that the existence of a state procedural ground adequate to preclude direct review would not bar habeas corpus:

> The adequate state-ground rule is a function of the limitations of appellate review. Most of the opinion in the *Murdock* Case is devoted to demonstrating the Court's lack of jurisdiction on direct review to decide questions of state law in cases also raising federal questions. It followed from this holding that if the state question was dispositive of the case, the Court could not decide the federal question. The federal question was moot; nothing turned on its resolution. And so we have held that the adequate state-ground rule is a consequence of the Court's obligation to refrain from rendering advisory opinions or passing upon moot questions.
>
> But while our appellate function is concerned only with the judgments or decrees of state courts, the habeas corpus jurisdiction of the lower federal courts is not so confined. The jurisdictional prerequisite is not the judgment of a state court but detention *simpliciter*. . . . Habeas lies to enforce the right of personal liberty; when that right is denied and a person confined, the federal court has the power to release him. . . .
>
> To be sure, this may not be the entire answer to the contention that the adequate state-ground principle should apply to the federal courts on habeas corpus as well as to the Supreme Court on direct review of state judgments. The *Murdock* decision may be supported not only by the factor of mootness, but in addition by certain characteristics of the federal system. . . . For the federal courts to refuse to give effect in habeas proceedings to state procedural defaults might conceivably have some effect upon the States' regulation of their criminal procedures. But the problem is crucially different from that posed in *Murdock* of the federal courts' deciding questions of substantive state law. In Noia's case the only relevant substantive law is federal—the Fourteenth Amendment. State law appears only in the procedural framework for adjudicating the substantive federal question. The paramount interest is federal. . . .

Justice Harlan, joined by Justices Clark and Stewart, dissented:

> [T]he federal courts have no *power*, statutory or constitutional, to release the respondent Noia from state detention. This is because his custody by New York does not violate any federal right, since it is pursuant to a conviction whose validity rests upon an adequate and independent state ground which the federal courts are required to respect. . . .

Whether federal review was direct or collateral, he argued, to decide the federal question alone would be to render an advisory opinion forbidden by Article III; to overrule the state court's interpretation of the state procedural law would invade powers reserved to the State. To "ignore" the state ground and order the defendant released would "decide the state law question *sub silentio*" because "if the petitioner is detained pursuant to the judgment, and his detention is to be terminated, that must mean that the state ground is not adequate to support the only purpose for which the judgment was rendered;" and the effect would be to destroy the state rule.

> Of course, as the majority states, a judgment is not a "jurisdictional prerequisite" to a habeas corpus application . . . but that is wholly irrelevant. The point is that if the applicant is detained *pursuant* to a judgment, termination of the detention necessarily nullifies the judgment.

Was *Noia* right about the adequate state ground? Didn't both the majority and the dissent overlook the Supreme Court's power, on direct review or on habeas, to hold the state rule invalid as imposing an unreasonable burden on the enforcement of federal rights? Wasn't Justice Brennan wrong in his assessment of the impact of habeas corpus on state procedural policy in a case like Noia's? But would you dissent from an opinion releasing Noia on the ground that, in contrast to "the preservation of personal liberty and assurance against its wrongful deprivation, considerations of economy of judicial time and procedures, important as they undoubtedly are, become comparatively insignificant?" Rutledge, J., dissenting, in Sunal v. Large, 332 U.S. 174, 189 (1947).

Is the deliberate-bypass doctrine consistent with this position? And in what sense was Noia's failure to appeal not "deliberate?"

(11) Was *Sykes* based on the adequate state ground doctrine? The Court said it was in Harris v. Reed, 109 S.Ct. 1038 (1989), although in neither case did the Justices bother to refute Justice Brennan's argument in *Noia.* What then is the basis of *Sykes's* qualification excusing noncompliance with the state rule for "cause" and "prejudice"?

Mere attorney error, the Court has held, does not constitute "cause" for this purpose, although incompetence of counsel in the constitutional sense would; ordinarily the petitioner must show "that some objective factor external to the defense impeded counsel's efforts to comply with the state's procedural rule." Murray v. Carrier, 477 U.S. 478 (1986). Later decisions have found cause when the "constitutional claim is so novel that its legal basis is not reasonably available to counsel," Reed v. Ross, 468 U.S. 1 (1984), and when the State had concealed the evidence on which the constitutional claim was based, Amadeo v. Zant, 486 U.S. 214 (1988). Does the "grisly choice" faced by the petitioner in *Fay v. Noia* qualify as "cause"? See generally Meltzer, State Court Forfeitures of Federal Rights, 99 Harv.L.Rev. 1128 (1986).

(12) The due process revolution of the Warren years created the risk that a great many prisoners would have to be retried—in many cases long after the relevant evidence had disappeared—on the basis of procedures that had been thought constitutional at the time of the original trial. To reduce this risk, the Court in a series of decisions beginning with Linkletter v. Walker, 381 U.S. 618 (1965), limited the retroactive application of many of its new rules. This practice was severely criticized, and two decades later it was modified along lines suggested by Justice Harlan in a concurring opinion in Mackey v. United States, 401 U.S. 667 (1971).

Griffith v. Kentucky, 479 U.S. 314 (1987), abandoned the nonretroactivity approach for all cases pending on direct review at the time a new rule was announced, stressing the desirability "of treating similarly situated defendants the same." Teague v. Lane, 109 S.Ct. 1060 (1989), over two dissents, reformulated the remaining principle in terms of the criteria governing the availability of habeas corpus. "Application of constitutional rules not in existence at the time a conviction became final," wrote Justice O'Connor, "seriously undermines the principle of finality which is essential to the operation of our criminal justice system." Consequently, new rules should not be applied in such cases unless they "place[d] 'certain kinds of primary, private conduct beyond the power of the criminal law-making authority to proscribe'" or embodied "procedures . . . central to an accurate determination of innocence or guilt." A holding extending to the petit jury the fair cross section requirement initially applied to grand juries, she continued, would be a "new rule" for this purpose because it "was not *dictated* by precedent at the time the defendant's conviction became final," and it fell within neither exception: Its application "would not accord constitutional protection to any primary activity" or seriously improve "the likelihood of obtaining an accurate conviction." It followed, the majority concluded, that habeas corpus could not be used as a vehicle to enunciate the new rule.

Notes on Post-Conviction Relief for Federal Prisoners

(1) Before the enactment of 28 U.S.C. § 2255 in 1948, habeas corpus had of course been available to persons convicted of federal crimes. But habeas had to be sought in the district where the prisoner was confined. Consequently "the few District Courts in whose territorial jurisdiction major federal penal institutions are located were required to handle an inordinate number of habeas corpus actions far from the scene of the facts, the homes of the witnesses and the records of the sentencing court solely because of the fortuitous concentration of federal prisoners within the district." United States v. Hayman, 342 U.S. 205 (1952). Section 2255 provided that no habeas application should be entertained on behalf of a federal prisoner unless he had first applied for relief to the court that had sentenced him; and if that court denied relief, habeas was still unavailable unless the remedy in the sentencing court was "inadequate or ineffective to test the legality of his detention." In *United States v. Hayman*, supra, the

Court of Appeals held this statute an unconstitutional suspension of habeas corpus. The Supreme Court reversed, holding that no constitutional issue was presented, because there was nothing to show that the statutory procedure was inadequate, and because habeas would be available if it were. The "sole purpose" of § 2255, the Court noted, "was to minimize the difficulties encountered in habeas corpus hearings by affording the same rights in another and more convenient forum."

(2) What kinds of issues may be raised by a federal prisoner under § 2255? The statute itself seems to give two inconsistent answers. Its first paragraph authorizes a motion "upon the ground that the sentence was imposed in violation of the Constitution or laws of the United States, or that the court was without jurisdiction to impose such sentence, or that the sentence was in excess of the maximum authorized by law, or is otherwise subject to collateral attack." Yet the third paragraph provides for granting the motion on a finding "that the judgment was rendered without jurisdiction, or that the sentence imposed was not authorized by law or otherwise open to collateral attack, or that there has been such a denial or infringement of the constitutional rights of the prisoner as to render the judgment vulnerable to collateral attack." This obscure language has figured less prominently in determining the scope of § 2255 than has the legislative history indicating, as stated in *United States v. Hayman*, supra note 1, that the new motion was to provide the same rights as habeas corpus in a better forum.

First, although the first paragraph of § 2255 speaks only of attacks upon the "sentence," which the third paragraph appears to distinguish from attacks upon the conviction ("judgment") (cf. Fed.R.Crim.P. 35, p. 653 infra), the *Hayman* case itself, without discussion, permitted a § 2255 attack on the validity of the conviction itself (for inadequate counsel). "Sentence" in the first paragraph cannot be read narrowly, can it, if the use of "judgment" in the third is to have any meaning, or if the remedy is to be as broad as habeas corpus?

(3) Second, long after both *Hayman* and *Brown v. Allen*, lower courts continued to hold not all constitutional objections to a conviction could be raised under § 2255, relying variously upon the traditional scope of post-conviction relief, the language of the statute, and a consideration of competing policies. Then in Kaufman v. United States, 394 U.S. 217 (1969), with no attempt to fit its decision within the language of the statute, the Court held § 2255 reached claims of unreasonable search or seizure. This led Justice Harlan, who had there dissented, to say the court might inquire under § 2255 into "any constitutional defect in any criminal trial, where the petitioner remains 'in custody' because of the judgment in that trial, unless the error committed was knowingly and deliberately waived or constitutes mere harmless error." Mackey v. United States, 401 U.S. 667, 685–86 (1971) (concurring opinion).

Stone v. Powell explicitly disapproved *Kaufman*, leaving open the question whether the result could be justified on the basis of the Court's supervisory power over lower federal courts. Is the scope of collateral review the same today for federal as for state prisoners? Should it be? See *Kaufman*, 394 U.S. at 226:

> [W]e are told that the federal prisoner, having already had his day in federal court, stands in a different position. . . . The opportunity to assert federal rights in a federal forum is clearly not the sole justification for federal post-conviction relief, otherwise there would be no need to make such relief available to federal prisoners at all. The provision of federal collateral remedies rests more fundamentally upon a recognition that adequate protection of constitutional rights relating to the criminal trial process requires the continuing availability of a mechanism for relief. This is no less true for federal prisoners than it is for state prisoners.

(4) Third, in pre-*Kaufman* cases raising non-constitutional issues the lower courts were quite chary of granting collateral relief. The Supreme Court turned to this problem in Davis v. United States, 417 U.S. 333 (1974). Having failed to report for an Army physical examination, the petitioner was classified delinquent, ordered to report for induction, and convicted for disobeying the induction order. He argued that the regulation authorizing induction orders for delinquency was without statutory support. The Court held the case fell within § 2255: The statute made no exception for nonconstitutional claims, as its first paragraph authorized a motion by one "claiming the right to be released upon the ground that the sentence was imposed in violation of the Constitution *or laws* of the United States"; legislative history showed, as held in the *Hayman* case, supra note 1, that "the grounds for relief under § 2255 are equivalent to those encompassed by § 2254" [sic], the general federal habeas corpus statute, under which relief is available on the ground that " 'a person is in custody . . . in violation of the Constitution *or laws* or treaties of the United States.' " Justice Rehnquist alone dissented: The first paragraph of § 2255 spoke of attacks only on "sentences," not on judgments, and was "concerned only with motions for relief, not with the Court's power to grant relief"; paragraph three allowed relief against a judgment as contrasted with a sentence only on jurisdictional or constitutional grounds.

The Court in *Davis* took pains to make clear that it did not wish to press its literal reading of the first paragraph too far: The decision was "not to say . . . that every asserted error of law" could be raised under § 2255. Specifically approved was Hill v. United States, 368 U.S. 424, 428–29 (1962), which had refused to entertain a contention that the petitioner had not been asked whether he wanted to make a statement in his own behalf before sentencing, as required by Rule 32(a) of the Federal Rules of Criminal Procedure:

> The failure of a trial court to ask a defendant represented by an attorney whether he has anything to say before sentence is imposed is not of itself an error of the character or magnitude cognizable under a writ of habeas corpus. It is an error which is neither jurisdictional nor constitutional. It is not a fundamental defect which inherently results in a complete miscarriage of justice, nor an omission inconsistent with the rudimentary demands of fair procedure. It does not present "exceptional circumstances where the need for the remedy afforded by the writ of *habeas corpus* is apparent."

These tests were satisfied, the Court said, in *Davis:* If his claim was well-taken, "then Davis' conviction and punishment are for an act that the law does not make criminal."

(5) Is the effect of a prior decision of post-conviction claims the same for a federal as for a state prisoner? See Kaufman v. United States, 394 U.S. 217, 227 n. 8 (1969):

> Where a trial or appellate court has determined the federal prisoner's claim, discretion may in a proper case be exercised against the grant of a § 2255 hearing. Section 2255 provides for hearing "Unless the motion and the files and records of the case conclusively show that the prisoner is entitled to no relief . . . ." In Sanders v. United States, 373 U.S. 1 (1963), we announced standards governing the determination whether a hearing should be ordered in the case of a successive motion under § 2255. Similarly, where the trial or appellate court has had a "say" on a federal prisoner's claim, it may be open to the § 2255 court to determine that on the basis of the motion, files, and records, "the prisoner is entitled to no relief."

Sanders v. United States, cited in *Kaufman*, had reaffirmed in the context of a federal prisoner that "[c]onventional notions of finality of litigation have no place where life or liberty is at stake and infringement of constitutional rights is alleged":

> Controlling weight may be given to denial of a prior application for federal habeas corpus or § 2255 relief only if (1) the same ground presented in the subsequent application was determined adversely to the applicant on the prior application, (2) the prior determination was on the merits, and (3) the ends of justice would not be served by reaching the merits of the subsequent application.
>
> (1) By "ground," we mean simply a sufficient legal basis for granting the relief sought by the applicant. For example, the contention that an involuntary confession was admitted in evidence against him is a distinct ground for federal collateral relief. But a claim of involuntary confession predicated on alleged psychological coercion does not raise a different "ground" than does one predicated on alleged physical coercion. . . .
>
> (2) The prior denial must have rested on an adjudication of the merits of the ground presented in the subsequent application. . . . This means that if factual issues were raised in the prior application, and it was not denied on the basis that the files and records conclusively resolved these issues, an evidentiary hearing was held. . . .
>
> (3) Even if the same ground was rejected on the merits on a prior application, it is open to the applicant to show that the ends of justice would be served by permitting the redetermination of the ground. If factual issues are involved, the applicant is entitled to a new hearing upon showing that the evidentiary hearing on the prior application was not full and fair; we canvassed the criteria of a full and fair evidentiary hearing recently in Townsend v. Sain, supra, and that discussion need not be repeated here. If purely

> legal questions are involved, the applicant may be entitled to a new hearing upon showing an intervening change in the law or some other justification for having failed to raise a crucial point or argument in the prior application. . . .

Sanders's first motion, said the Court, had been denied not on the merits but because of its pleading deficiency; the record could not "conclusively show" that he was entitled to no relief, because the facts underlying the narcotics claim were outside the record.

(6) There were suggestions in both *Kaufman* and *Sanders* that the deliberate-bypass rule of *Fay v. Noia* would be applied to federal prisoners seeking relief under § 2255. *Kaufman* went so far as to say "there is no reason . . . to give greater preclusive effect to procedural defaults by federal defendants than to similar defaults by state defendants."

Davis v. United States, 411 U.S. 233, 236 (1973), suggested there might be a difference between state and federal prisoners in this regard, holding with no finding of deliberate bypass that a federal prisoner was barred from § 2255 relief because of his failure to object to the composition of his grand jury by motion before trial under Rule 12(b)(2) of the Federal Rules of Criminal Procedure. *Francis* and *Sykes*, however, have since applied the *Davis* standards to state prisoners; and United States v. Frady, 456 U.S. 152 (1982), applied them in a § 2255 action to Criminal Rule 30, which contains no explicit exception to the requirement of a timely challenge to jury instructions.

(7) To what extent does the provision in Art. I, § 9 that "The Privilege of the Writ of Habeas Corpus shall not be suspended, unless . . . the public safety may require it," make the issues in these Notes constitutional ones? See Swain v. Pressley, 430 U.S. 372, 384–85 (1977) (Chief Justice Burger, joined by Justices Blackmun and Rehnquist, concurring). The Court upheld a statute providing an analog to § 2255 in the Superior Court of the District of Columbia for those convicted of violations of the District Code, invoking *United States v. Hayman*, supra note 1, and *Palmore v. United States*, supra p. 118. The Chief Justice argued that there was no reason to consider the Suspension Clause at all:

> The sweep of the Suspension Clause must be measured by reference to the intention of the Framers and their understanding of what the writ of habeas corpus meant at the time the Constitution was drafted. . . . The writ in 1789 was not considered "a means by which one court . . . exercises post-conviction review over the judgment of another. . . ."

Notes on Post-Conviction Review for Military Prisoners

(1) Despite the statutory provision, 10 U.S.C. § 876, that military criminal proceedings shall be "final and conclusive" and "binding upon all departments, courts, agencies, and officers of the United States," it is clear that a person in custody pursuant to court-martial can challenge, on habeas corpus, the jurisdiction of the military court. See, e.g., Gusik v. Schilder, 340 U.S. 128, 132–33 (1950), rejecting on this ground the contention that the finality provision rendered the statute an unconstitutional suspension

of habeas corpus; Reid v. Covert, 354 U.S. 1 (1957) (no jurisdiction to try servicemen's wives); McElroy v. Guagliardo, 361 U.S. 281 (1960) (civilian employees abroad); S.Rep. No. 486, p. 32, and H.R.Rep. No. 491, p. 35, 81st Cong., 1st Sess. (1950), recognizing the habeas exception when the finality provision was recodified. In *Covert* and *Guagliardo* the issues were of constitutional dimension, but it seems reasonably clear, as Justice Douglas stated in his dissent in *Burns v. Wilson*, infra note 3, that nonconstitutional issues of pure "jurisdiction" may also be considered, as was true before the finality provision was enacted, McClaughry v. Deming, 186 U.S. 49, 65, 66, 68 (1902). See e.g., Jackson v. Taylor, 353 U.S. 569 (1957).

(2) Beyond this, however, lies fog. Long after Johnson v. Zerbst, 304 U.S. 458 (1938), had stretched, and Waley v. Johnston, 316 U.S. 101 (1942), had abandoned for civil prisoners the shibboleth that habeas was limited to questions of jurisdiction, the Supreme Court kept saying that jurisdiction was the only question open on military habeas. E.g., Humphrey v. Smith, 336 U.S. 695 (1949); Hiatt v. Brown, 339 U.S. 103 (1950). However, in Whelchel v. McDonald, 340 U.S. 122, 124 (1950), the Court, while adhering to the verbal formula of "jurisdiction," proceeded to expand it much in the fashion of *Johnson v. Zerbst*:

> We think it plain from the law governing court-martial procedure that there must be afforded a defendant at some point of time an opportunity to tender the issue of insanity. It is only a denial of that opportunity which goes to the question of jurisdiction. That opportunity was afforded here. Any error that may be committed in evaluating the evidence tendered is beyond the reach of review by the civil courts.

(3) The most influential Supreme Court decision, unfortunately, has been one in which there was no majority opinion: Burns v. Wilson, 346 U.S. 137 (1953). Court-martialed prisoners raised a number of constitutional objections ranging from denial of the right to effective counsel of their choice to coerced confessions, suppression of evidence, perjured testimony, and an "atmosphere . . . conducive to mob violence." The District Court refused to inquire into anything beyond jurisdiction; the Court of Appeals rejected each claim on the merits; the Supreme Court affirmed. Only Justice Minton contended that the District Court was correct in limiting the inquiry to jurisdiction; as Justice Frankfurter noted in his dissent, decisions so holding were obsolete because they rested on no peculiarities of the military system but reflected a view of habeas generally that antedated *Johnson v. Zerbst*. Chief Justice Vinson, joined by three others, nevertheless took pains to say that military prisoners were less equal than others:

> The statute which vests federal courts with jurisdiction over applications for habeas corpus from persons confined by the military courts is the same statute which vests them with jurisdiction over the applications of persons confined by the civil courts. But in military habeas corpus the inquiry, the scope of matters open for review, has always been more narrow than in civil cases. Hiatt v. Brown, 339 U.S. 103 (1950). . . .
>
> Military law, like state law, is a jurisprudence which exists separate and apart from the law which governs in our federal judicial establishment. This Court has played no role in its development; we

> have exerted no supervisory power over the courts which enforce it; the rights of men in the armed forces must perforce be conditioned to meet certain overriding demands of discipline and duty, and the civil courts are not the agencies which must determine the precise balance to be struck in this adjustment. The Framers expressly entrusted that task to Congress.

The petitioners' claims, the Chief Justice concluded, were of the sort cognizable on habeas: "Had the military courts manifestly refused to consider those claims, the District Court was empowered to review them *de novo.*" But in military cases, "even more than in state habeas corpus cases," the federal court must "take account of the prior proceedings"; while the finality provision does not completely oust habeas jurisdiction, it does mean that "when a military decision has dealt fully and fairly with an allegation . . ., it is not open to a federal civil court to grant the writ simply to reevaluate the evidence. . . . It is the limited function of the civil courts to determine whether the military have given fair consideration to each of these claims." Because the military courts had given exhaustive consideration to each claim, the opinion concluded that no further inquiry was proper. Whether the military decision was supported by the evidence the opinion did not ask.

Justice Jackson concurred in the result without even the smallest opinion.

Justice Frankfurter argued (see also his dissent from denial of a rehearing, 346 U.S. 844) that it was not enough to find "that the military sentence has been reviewed by the military hierarchy, although in a debatable situation we should no doubt attach more weight to the conclusions reached on controversial facts by military appellate courts than to those reached by the highest court of a State." Justices Douglas and Black, in an opinion by the former, also dissented:

> If the military agency has fairly and conscientiously applied the standards of due process formulated by this Court, I would agree that a rehash of the same facts by a federal court would not advance the cause of justice. But where the military reviewing agency has not done that, a court should entertain the petition for habeas corpus. In the first place, the military tribunals in question are federal agencies subject to no other judicial supervision except what is afforded by the federal courts. In the second place, the rules of due process which they apply are constitutional rules which we, not they, formulate.
>
> The *undisputed* facts in this case make a prima facie case that our rule on coerced confessions expressed in Watts v. Indiana, 338 U.S. 49, was violated here. No court has considered the question whether repetitious questioning over a period of 5 days while the accused was held incommunicado without benefit of counsel violated the Fifth Amendment.

(4) A common view in the lower courts has been that the law is what Chief Justice Vinson said it was in *Burns.* See, for example, Kehrli v. Sprinkle, 524 F.2d 328 (10th Cir. 1975). But there has been an increasing willingness to allow relitigation of issues already decided by military courts. For example, Shaw v. United States, 357 F.2d 949, 953–54 (Ct.Cls.

1966), declaring that "denial of significant constitutional rights" invalidates military convictions and allows an award of back pay, distinguished an earlier decision that had followed the "full and fair" rule:

> In that case the constitutional issues (involving alleged illegal searches and seizures, police interrogation, criticism of the accused's counsel during the trial, and claimed interference with the right to appeal) all turned on an evaluation of the particular facts; this court was unwilling to reassess those circumstances for itself, once the military had done so with care. Whether or not this rule of deference to the military findings has been modified or refined by Townsend v. Sain . . . and Sanders v. United States . . . we think that such abstinence is not to be practiced where the serviceman presents pure issues of constitutional law, unentangled with an appraisal of a special set of facts. That type of unmixed legal question this court has always decided for itself. . . . We must face the claim that, on the Navy's own factual findings, plaintiff could not constitutionally be held to have committed any crime.[1]

(5) Two later Supreme Court decisions not involving habeas corpus cast additional reflections on the question. In United States v. Augenblick, 393 U.S. 348 (1969), like *Shaw* a back-pay case filed under 28 U.S.C. § 1491, the Court without reasons held that the issues raised—the necessity for corroboration of accomplice testimony and the defendant's right to examine witness statements—could not be examined because they were not of constitutional dimension. Schlesinger v. Councilman, 420 U.S. 738 (1975), held that 10 U.S.C. § 876, note 1 supra, did not bar a suit to enjoin a pending court-martial on the ground that the alleged offense was not service-connected. While the provision giving finality to "all action taken pursuant to . . . [court-martial] proceedings" affects pre-conviction as well as post-conviction relief, it merely codifies the doctrine of res judicata, which does not forbid challenges on grounds of "lack of jurisdiction or some other equally fundamental defect." Whether an issue may be raised collaterally "may turn on the nature of the alleged defect, and the gravity of the harm from which relief is sought." That the same principles applied to back-pay suits the Court in dictum expressly affirmed.

(6) The decisions in note 4 concerned issues that had been litigated in the military proceedings. In Suttles v. Davis, 215 F.2d 760, 763 (10th Cir. 1954), the court refused to consider the adequacy of trial counsel because the issue should have been raised, but was not, in those proceedings: "Civil courts may review only claims of infringement of constitutional rights which the military courts refused to give fair consideration. *Burns v. Wilson*. . . . Obviously, it cannot be said that they have refused to fairly consider claims not asserted."

But see Williams v. Heritage, 323 F.2d 731 (5th Cir.1963), rejecting the doctrine of forfeiture altogether for military habeas: *Fay v. Noia* "governs in principle." How does *Sykes* affect this question?

1. See also Calley v. Calloway, 519 F.2d 184 (5th Cir. 1975).

See also Gusik v. Schilder, 340 U.S. 128, 131–32 (1950), requiring exhaustion of military remedies available at the time of the habeas application or thereafter.

(7) Is the scope of habeas for military prisoners, as a majority of Justices said in *Burns v. Wilson*, really narrower than for civil prisoners? Should it be? What is the relevance of 28 U.S.C. § 1259, enacted in 1983, which for the first time empowers the Supreme Court to review decisions of the Court of Military Appeals?

(8) Compare the question of habeas corpus for persons held pursuant to conviction by an Indian tribal court. The 1968 Civil Rights Act, 25 U.S.C. § 1303, provides that "The privilege of the writ of habeas corpus shall be available to any person, in a court of the United States, to test the legality of his detention by order of an Indian tribe." What is the constitutional basis for this grant of power? What issues are open for decision? What weight should be given to the tribal court's decision of those issues, or to the petitioner's failure to raise the issues in accord with tribal procedure?

PREISER v. RODRIGUEZ

411 U.S. 475 (1973).

MR. JUSTICE STEWART delivered the opinion of the Court.

The respondents in this case were state prisoners who were deprived of good conduct time credits by the New York State Department of Correctional Services as a result of disciplinary proceedings. They then brought actions in a federal district court, pursuant to the Civil Rights Act, 42 U.S.C. § 1983. Alleging that the Department had acted unconstitutionally in depriving them of the credits, they sought injunctive relief to compel restoration of the credits, which in each case would result in their immediate release from confinement in prison. The question before us is whether state prisoners seeking such redress may obtain equitable relief under the Civil Rights Act, even though the federal habeas corpus statute, 28 U.S.C. § 2254, clearly provides a specific federal remedy.

The question is of considerable practical importance. For if a remedy under the Civil Rights Act is available, a plaintiff need not first seek redress in a state forum. Monroe v. Pape, 365 U.S. 167, 183 (1961) . . . . If, on the other hand, habeas corpus is the exclusive federal remedy in these circumstances, then a plaintiff cannot seek the intervention of a federal court until he has first sought and been denied relief in the state courts, if a state remedy is available and adequate. 28 U.S.C. § 2254(b). . . .

Rodriguez was charged in two separate disciplinary action reports with possession of contraband material in his cell. The deputy warden determined that as punishment, 120 days of Rodriguez's earned good conduct time credits should be cancelled, and that Rodriguez should be placed in segregation, where he remained for more than 40 days. . . . Rodriguez then filed in the District Court a complaint pursuant to § 1983, combined with a petition for a writ of habeas corpus. He asserted that he was not really being punished for possession of the contraband material, but for refusal to disclose how he had obtained it, and that he had received no notice or hearing on the charges for which he had ostensibly been punished. Thus he contended that he had been deprived of his good conduct time credits without due process of law. . . .

[The District Court upheld Rodriguez's claim; the Court of Appeals reversed, saying the action was actually one for habeas: " 'Release from penal custody is not an available remedy under the Civil Rights Act.' " On rehearing en banc, however, a divided Court of Appeals held the § 1983 claim sustainable on the authority of Wilwording v. Swenson, 404 U.S. 249 (1971), which the present opinion characterized as "holding that complaints of state prisoners relating to the conditions of their confinement were cognizable either in federal habeas corpus or under the Civil Rights Act, and that as civil rights actions they were not subject to any requirement of exhaustion of state remedies."]

The relevant habeas corpus statutes are 28 U.S.C. §§ 2241 and 2254. Section 2241(c)(3) provides that "[t]he writ of habeas corpus shall not extend to a prisoner unless . . . [h]e is in custody in violation of the Constitution or laws or treaties of the United States. . . ." Section 2254 provides in pertinent part: . . .

> "(b) An application for a writ of habeas corpus in behalf of a person in custody pursuant to the judgment of a State court shall not be granted unless it appears that the applicant has exhausted the remedies available in the courts of the State, or that there is either an absence of available State corrective process or the existence of circumstances rendering such process ineffective to protect the rights of the prisoner. . . ." . . .

It is clear not only from the language of § 2241(c)(3) and § 2254(a), but also from the common-law history of the writ, that the essence of habeas corpus is an attack by a person in custody upon the legality of that custody, and that the traditional function of the writ is to secure release from illegal custody. . . .

In the case before us, the respondents' suits in the District Court fell squarely within this traditional scope of habeas corpus. They alleged that the deprivation of their good conduct time credits was causing or would cause them to be in illegal physical confinement, i.e., that once their conditional release date had passed, any further detention of them in prison was unlawful; and they sought restoration of those good time credits, which, by the time the District Court ruled on their petitions, meant their immediate release from physical custody. . . .

It is beyond doubt, then, that the respondents could have sought and obtained fully effective relief through federal habeas corpus proceedings.

Although conceding that they could have proceeded by way of habeas corpus, the respondents argue that the Court of Appeals was correct in holding that they were nonetheless entitled to bring their suits under § 1983 so as to avoid the necessity of first seeking relief in a state forum. Pointing to the broad language of § 1983, they argue that since their complaints plainly came within the literal terms of that statute, there is no justifiable reason to exclude them from the broad remedial protection provided by that law. According to the respondents, state prisoners seeking relief under the Civil Rights Act should be treated no differently from any other civil rights plaintiffs, when the language of the Act clearly covers their causes of action.

The broad language of § 1983, however, is not conclusive of the issue before us. . . . The respondents' counsel acknowledged at oral argument that a state prisoner challenging his underlying conviction and sentence on federal constitutional grounds in a federal court is limited to habeas corpus. It was conceded that he cannot bring a § 1983 action, even though the literal terms of § 1983 might seem to cover such a challenge, because Congress has passed a more specific act to cover that situation, and, in doing so, has provided that a state prisoner challenging his conviction must first seek relief in a state forum, if a state remedy is available. It is clear to us that the result must be the same in the case of a state prisoner's challenge to the fact or duration of his confinement, based, as here, upon the alleged unconstitutionality of state administrative action. Such a challenge is just as close to the core of habeas corpus as an attack on the prisoner's conviction, for it goes directly to the constitutionality of his physical confinement itself and seeks either immediate release from that confinement or the shortening of its duration.

In amending the habeas corpus laws in 1948, Congress clearly required exhaustion of adequate state remedies as a condition precedent to the invocation of federal judicial relief under those laws. It would wholly frustrate explicit congressional intent to hold that the respondents in the present case could evade this requirement by the simple expedient of putting a different label on their pleadings. In short, Congress has determined that habeas corpus is the appropriate remedy for state prisoners attacking the validity of the fact or length of their confinement, and that specific determination must override the general terms of § 1983. . . .

In the respondents' view, the whole purpose of the exhaustion requirement, now codified in § 2254(b), is to give state *courts* the first chance at remedying *their own* mistakes, and thereby to avoid "the unseemly spectacle of federal district courts trying the regularity of proceedings had in *courts* of coordinate jurisdiction." . . . This policy, the respondents contend, does not apply when the challenge is not to the action of a state court, but, as here, to the action of a state administrative body. . . .

The respondents, we think, view the reasons for the exhaustion requirement of § 2254(b) far too narrowly. The rule of exhaustion in federal habeas corpus actions is rooted in considerations of federal-state comity. That principle was defined in Younger v. Harris, 401 U.S. 37, 44 (1971), as "a proper respect for state functions," and it has as much relevance in areas of particular state administrative concern as it does where state judicial action is being attacked. . . .

Requiring exhaustion in situations like that before us means, of course, that a prisoner's state remedy must be adequate and available, as indeed § 2254(b) provides. The respondents in this case concede that New York provided them with an adequate remedy for the restoration of their good time credits, through § 79–c of the New York Civil Rights Act, McKinney's Consol. Laws, c. 6, which explicitly provides for injunctive relief to a state prisoner "for improper treatment where such treatment constitutes a violation of his constitutional rights."

But while conceding the availability in the New York courts of an opportunity for equitable relief, the respondents contend that confining state prisoners to federal habeas corpus, after first exhausting state remedies, could deprive those prisoners of any damage remedy to which they might be entitled for their mistreatment, since damages are not available in federal habeas corpus proceedings, and New York provides no damage remedy at all for state prisoners. . . .

The answer to this contention is that the respondents here sought no damages, but only equitable relief—restoration of their good time credits—and our holding today is limited to that situation. If a state prisoner is seeking damages, he is attacking something other than the fact or length of his confinement, and he is seeking something other than immediate or more speedy release—the traditional purpose of habeas corpus. In the case of a damage claim, habeas corpus is *not* an appropriate or available federal remedy. Accordingly, as the State itself concedes, a damage action by a state prisoner could be brought under the Civil Rights Act in federal court without any requirement of prior exhaustion of state remedies. . . .

The respondents place a great deal of reliance on our recent decisions upholding the right of state prisoners to bring federal civil rights actions to challenge the conditions of their confinement. Cooper v. Pate, 378 U.S. 546 (1964); Houghton v. Shafer, 392 U.S. 639 (1968); Wilwording v. Swenson, 404 U.S. 249 (1971); Haines v. Kerner, 404 U.S. 519 (1972). But none of the state prisoners in those cases was challenging the fact or duration of his physical confinement itself, and none was seeking immediate or more speedy release from that confinement—the heart of habeas corpus. In *Cooper*, the prisoner alleged that, solely because of his religious beliefs, he had been denied permission to purchase certain religious publications and had been denied other privileges enjoyed by his fellow prisoners. In *Houghton*, the prisoner's contention was that prison authorities had violated the Constitution by confiscating legal materials which he had acquired for pursuing his appeal, but which, in violation of prison rules, had been found in the possession of another prisoner. In *Wilwording*, the prisoners' complaints related solely to their living conditions and disciplinary measures while confined in maximum security. And in *Haines*, the prisoner claimed that prison officials had acted unconstitutionally by placing him in solitary confinement as a disciplinary measure, and he sought damages for claimed physical injuries sustained while so segregated. It is clear, then, that in all those cases, the prisoners' claims related solely to the States' alleged unconstitutional treatment of them while in confinement. None sought, as did the respondents here, to challenge the very fact or duration of the confinement itself. Those cases, therefore, merely establish that a § 1983 action is a proper remedy for a state prisoner who is making a constitutional challenge to the conditions of his prison life, but not to the fact or length of his custody. Upon that understanding, we reaffirm those holdings. . . .

This is not to say that habeas corpus may not also be available to challenge such prison conditions. See Johnson v. Avery, 393 U.S. 483 (1969); Wilwording v. Swenson, supra. . . .

But we need not in this case explore the appropriate limits of habeas corpus as an alternative remedy to a proper action under § 1983. That question is not before us. What is involved here is the extent to which § 1983 is a permissible alternative to the traditional remedy of habeas corpus. Upon that question, we hold today that when a state prisoner is challenging the very fact or duration of his physical imprisonment, and the relief he seeks is a determination that he is entitled to immediate or more speedy release from that imprisonment, his sole federal remedy is a writ of habeas corpus. Accordingly, we reverse the judgment before us. . . .

MR. JUSTICE BRENNAN, with whom MR. JUSTICE DOUGLAS and MR. JUSTICE MARSHALL join, dissenting.

The question presented by this case is one that I, like the Court of Appeals, had thought already resolved by our decision last Term in Wilwording v. Swenson. . . .

II

Putting momentarily to one side the grave analytic shortcomings of the Court's approach, it seems clear that the scheme's unmanageability is sufficient reason to condemn it. . . .

For in many instances a prisoner's claims will be under simultaneous consideration in two distinct forums, even though the identical legal and factual questions are involved in both proceedings. Thus, if a prisoner's punishment for some alleged misconduct is both a term in solitary and the deprivation of good time credits, and if he believes that the punishment was imposed pursuant to unconstitutional disciplinary procedures, he can now litigate the legality of those procedures simultaneously in state court (where he seeks restoration of good time credits) and in federal court (where he seeks damages or an injunction against continued segregation). Moreover, if the federal court is the first to reach decision, and if that court concludes that the procedures are, in fact, unlawful, then the entire state proceeding must be immediately aborted, even though the state court may have devoted substantial time and effort to its consideration of the case. By the same token, if traditional principles of res judicata are applicable to suits under § 1983, . . . the prior conclusion of the state court suit would effectively set at naught the entire federal court proceeding. This is plainly a curious prescription for improving relations between state and federal courts. . . .

III . . .

The undisputable concern of all our decisions concerning the [exhaustion] doctrine has been the relationship "between the *judicial tribunals* of the Union and of the states . . . . We have grounded the doctrine squarely on the view that "it would be unseemly in our dual system of government for a federal district court to upset a *state court conviction* without an opportunity to the state courts to correct a constitutional violation." Fay v. Noia, 372 U.S. 391, 419–420 (1963) (emphasis added). . . .

With these considerations in mind, it becomes clear that the Court's decision does not serve the fundamental purposes behind the exhaustion doctrine. For although respondents were confined pursuant to the judgment of a state judicial tribunal, their claims do not relate to their convictions or sentences, but only to the administrative action of prison officials who subjected them to allegedly unconstitutional treatment, including the deprivation of good time credits. This is not a case, in other words, where federal intervention would interrupt a state proceeding or jeopardize the orderly administration of state judicial business. Nor is it a case where an action in federal court might imperil the relationship between state and federal courts. . . .

To be sure, respondents do call into question the constitutional validity of action by state officials, and friction between those officials and the federal court is by no means an inconceivable result. But standing alone, that possibility is simply not enough to warrant application of an exhaustion requirement. First, while we spoke in Younger v. Harris, 401 U.S. 37, 44 (1971), of the need for federal courts to maintain a "proper respect for state functions," neither that statement nor our holding there supports the instant application of the exhaustion doctrine. Our concern in Younger v. Harris was the "longstanding public policy against federal court interference with *state court proceedings,*" . . . by means of a federal injunction against the continuation of those proceedings. . . .

Second, the situation that exists in the case before us—an attack on state administrative rather than judicial action—is the stereotypical situation in which relief under § 1983 is authorized. See, e.g., McNeese v. Board of Education, 373 U.S. 668, (attack on school districting scheme); Damico v. California, 389 U.S. 416 (1967) (attack on welfare requirements); Monroe v. Pape, 365 U.S. 167, 183 (1961) (attack on police conduct). In each of these cases the exercise of federal jurisdiction was potentially offensive to the State and its officials. In each of these cases the attack was directed at an important state function in an area in which the State has wide powers of regulation. Yet in each of these cases we explicitly held that exhaustion of state remedies was not required. . . .

Third, if the Court is correct in assuming that the exhaustion requirement must be applied whenever federal jurisdiction might be a source of substantial friction with the State, then I simply do not understand why the Court stops where it does in rolling back the district courts' jurisdiction under § 1983. . . . It seems highly doubtful to me that a constitutional attack on prison conditions is any less disruptive of federal-state relations than an attack on prison conditions joined with a plea for restoration of good time credits. . . . Since I share the Court's view that exhaustion of state judicial remedies is not required in any suit properly brought in federal court under § 1983, and since I am convinced that respondents have properly invoked the jurisdictional grant of § 1983, I would affirm the judgment of the Court of Appeals.

Notes on the Exhaustion Requirement in Habeas Corpus

(1) The 1867 statute extending federal habeas to persons in state custody made no mention of any requirement that state-court remedies be first exhausted; it flatly gave federal courts jurisdiction to issue the writ on behalf of persons "restrained of . . . liberty in violation of the constitution, or of any treaty or law of the United States," 14 Stat. 385. Yet the Supreme Court lost little time in finding such a requirement implicit, Ex parte Royall, 117 U.S. 241 (1886).

The petitioner argued that Virginia bond legislation under which he was to be tried was unconstitutional; habeas jurisdiction was upheld because the statutory provision (now in modified form found in 28 U.S.C. § 2251) nullifying further state-court proceedings after filing of the federal petition demonstrated that Congress had contemplated habeas before trial. However, the court below was held justified in denying the writ in its discretion

> in the light of the relations existing, under our system of government, between the judicial tribunals of the Union and of the States, and in recognition of the fact that the public good requires that those relations be not disturbed by unnecessary conflict between courts equally bound to guard and protect rights secured by the Constitution.

The state court had power to consider the federal defense; it was not alleged that the petitioner was

> unable to give security for his appearance in the State court, or that reasonable bail is denied him, or that his trial will be unnecessarily delayed. . . . The Circuit Court was not at liberty, under the circumstances disclosed, to presume that the decision of the State court would be otherwise than is required by the fundamental law of the land. . . .

One observer has attacked the exhaustion requirement of *Royall* as a "flat contravention of the statutory command" that a federal judge "forthwith" issue the writ, determine the facts, and discharge the petitioner if he is held in violation of federal law. Amsterdam, Criminal Prosecutions Affecting Federally Guaranteed Civil Rights: Federal Removal and Habeas Corpus Jurisdiction to Abort State Court Trial, 113 U.Pa.L.Rev. 793, 901 (1965). Yet analogous instances of judicial refusal to exercise a jurisdiction apparently given by statute appear throughout this book. Cf. *Myers v. Bethlehem Shipbuilding Corp.*, supra p. 62 (exhaustion of administrative remedies); *Texas & Pacific R. R. v. Abilene Cotton Oil Co.,* supra p. 68 (primary administrative jurisdiction); *Railroad Commission v. Pullman Co.*, supra p. 485 (abstention for state-court resolution of ambiguous state-law issue); *Younger v. Harris*, supra p. 528 (reluctance to enjoin pending state-court criminal proceedings).

(2) Exhaustion was invoked in *Royall* to avoid disruption of a pending state criminal proceeding; despite *Preiser's* flat statement that "exhaustion" was foreign to § 1983 cases, similar considerations have sharply limited the use of § 1983 injunctions in such cases. See *Younger v. Harris*, supra p. 528. Such decisions as Ex parte Hawk, 321 U.S. 114 (1944), extended the exhaustion principle to petitions attacking convictions that had already been obtained, holding that if the State provided an independent post-conviction remedy, that too had to be exhausted before seeking federal habeas corpus. Interestingly, it was only this aspect of the exhaustion requirement, not the original *Royall* limitation on pre-trial habeas, that was finally codified in § 2254(b) in 1948:

> An application for a writ of habeas corpus in behalf of a person in custody pursuant to the judgment of a State court shall not be granted unless it appears that the applicant has exhausted the remedies available in the courts of the State. . . .

Why is it that plaintiffs are not similarly sent off to institute state-court actions before suing under § 1983?

(3) Although it is often said that the 1948 enactment of § 2254(b) was meant to codify the *Hawk* doctrine of exhaustion in attacks upon state convictions, the section is not phrased so narrowly: It requires exhaustion when a petition is filed by "a person in custody pursuant to the judgment of a State court." Thus literally it covers cases such as *Preiser* and *Wilwording*, although there is no challenge to the conviction or sentence and thus no interference with past state-court proceedings. Why might Congress have thought it mattered, when the validity of the judgment was not at issue, whether or not the petitioner was in custody under a court judgment?

(4) Braden v. 30th Judicial Circuit Court, 410 U.S. 484 (1973). Braden filed for habeas corpus in an effort to compel the State to afford him a speedy trial on a pending criminal charge. Writing for the three dissenters, Justice Rehnquist pointed out that the failure to try the petitioner promptly could be raised as a defense when ultimately he was brought to trial and invoked *Ex parte Royall*: "Absent extraordinary circumstances, federal habeas corpus should not be used to adjudicate the merits of an affirmative defense to a state criminal charge prior to a judgment of

conviction by a state court." Justice Brennan, for a majority holding state remedies exhausted, conceded both points but distinguished *Royall*:

> Petitioner does not, however, seek at this time to litigate a federal defense to a criminal charge, but only to demand enforcement of the Commonwealth's affirmative constitutional obligation to bring him promptly to trial. . . . He has exhausted all available state court remedies for consideration of that constitutional claim. . . . He has already presented his federal constitutional claim of a *present* denial of a speedy trial to the courts of Kentucky. The state courts rejected the claim, apparently on the grounds that since he had once escaped from custody the Commonwealth should not be obligated to incur the risk of another escape by returning him for trial. . . . Moreover, petitioner made no effort to abort a state proceeding or to disrupt the orderly functioning of state judicial processes. He comes to federal court not in an effort to forestall a state prosecution, but to enforce the Commonwealth's obligation to provide him with a state court forum.[1]

(5) Fain v. Duff, 488 F.2d 218 (5th Cir. 1973). In custody in a juvenile home on account of rape, Fain was indicted by the adult authorities for the same act and sought habeas on the ground of double jeopardy. There was no need, the court said, to exhaust state-court remedies by waiting until after conviction to seek habeas corpus. In the first place, he had already exhausted his state-court remedies on the double-jeopardy question: The trial judge had dismissed the indictment on double-jeopardy grounds and the state Supreme Court had reversed. Moreover, the right against double jeopardy "consists of more than having the second conviction set aside. It consists of being protected from having to undergo the rigors and dangers of a second—illegal—trial. Double jeopardy is not a mere defense to a criminal charge; it is a right to be free from a second *prosecution*, not merely a second *punishment* for the same offense. . . ." Cf. *Abney v. United States*, p. 593 supra.

(6) What makes a state remedy "ineffective" in a post-conviction case so that exhaustion is not required? A long line of Fifth Circuit cases has held that exhaustion is not required under § 2254 if "the state's highest court has recently rendered an adverse decision in an identical case, and if there is no reason to believe that the state court will change its position." E.g., Layton v. Carson, 479 F.2d 1275, 1276 (5th Cir. 1973). See also United States ex rel. Goodman v. Kehl, 456 F.2d 863 (2d Cir. 1972), holding the exhaustion requirement can require a petitioner to spend the weekend in jail while waiting for the state appellate court to meet on his appeal; Rose v. Lundy, 455 U.S. 509 (1982), holding, largely in order to avoid "piecemeal litigation," that a petition containing both exhausted and unexhausted claims must be dismissed, "leaving the prisoner the choice of returning to state court to exhaust his claims or of amending or resubmitting the habeas petition to present only exhausted claims to the district court." Justice Blackmun, concurring on other grounds, saw this requirement as "a trap for the uneducated" increasing both caseload and delay and added that the

1. Brown v. Estelle, 530 F.2d 1280 (5th Cir. 1976), holds *Braden* inapplicable and pre-trial habeas unavailable on the speedy-trial issue when the petitioner seeks dismissal rather than trial.

option of "resubmitting" the exhausted claims alone seemed to deprive the Court's rule of its force. Four Justices in the majority suggested that a later petition presenting subsequently exhausted claims might be dismissed as an abuse of the writ; Justices Brennan and Marshall, who otherwise joined the opinion, disagreed.[2]

(7) Where state remedies must be exhausted, a further question arises as to when a petitioner has done enough to exhaust them. At one time it was argued that § 2254 rendered federal habeas altogether unavailable if the state courts permitted repeated applications on the same issue. The Court rejected this view in Brown v. Allen, 344 U.S. 443, 447 (1953): "It is not necessary . . . for the prisoner to ask the state for collateral relief, based on the same evidence and issues already decided by direct review. . . ." See also Fay v. Noia, 372 U.S. 391 (1963) (dictum), declaring it unnecessary to seek certiorari from the Supreme Court before filing for habeas.

(8) In Fay v. Noia, 372 U.S. 391, 434–5 (1963), it was argued that, because the petitioner had failed to "exhaust" his right to appeal his conviction, he was barred from federal habeas by § 2254. The Court disagreed:

> [T]he . . . contention that 28 U.S.C. § 2254 embodies a doctrine of forfeitures and cuts off relief when there has been a failure to exhaust state remedies no longer available at the time habeas is sought . . . is refuted by the language of the statute and by its history. It was enacted to codify the judicially evolved rule of exhaustion, particularly as formulated in Ex parte Hawk, 321 U.S. 114. . . . Nothing in the *Hawk* opinion points to past exhaustion. . . . We hold that § 2254 is limited in its application to failure to exhaust state remedies still open to the habeas applicant at time he files his application in federal court. . . .

Professor Hart, in Foreword: The Supreme Court, 1958 Term, 73 Harv. L.Rev. 84, 108–21 (1959), confirms this view of the history of § 2254. But cf. McGee v. United States, 402 U.S. 479, 489 (1971), holding a criminal defendant barred from challenging the refusal to classify him as a conscientious objector because of his failure to exhaust administrative remedies that were no longer available. Since the claim "depended on the application of expertise . . . in resolving underlying issues of fact," McGee's failure to exhaust "implicates decisively the purposes served by the exhaustion requirement, especially the purpose of ensuring that the Selective Service System have full opportunity to 'make a factual record' and 'apply its expertise'. . . ."

2. What happens if a state remedy becomes available only after a habeas petition is filed in federal court? Lower courts have required such remedies to be exhausted. See, e.g., Spencer v. Wainwright, 403 F.2d 778, 781 n. 2 (5th Cir. 1968). The Supreme Court, relying on state-prisoner decisions antedating the 1948 codification in § 2254, has made clear that the same principle applies to court-martialed military prisoners as to whom the exhaustion rule is not explicit in the statute. *Gusik v. Schilder*, supra p. 629. However, the Fifth Circuit has sensibly refused to require exhaustion of a state-court remedy that became available only after hearing and judgment on the habeas petition in the district court. Simpson v. Rice, 396 F.2d 499 (1968). The Supreme Court affirmed on the merits without discussing exhaustion, sub nom. North Carolina v. Pearce, 395 U.S. 711 (1969).

Why isn't this reasoning applicable to exhaustion in habeas cases? What is the point of deferring to state courts if there are no teeth to enforce the requirement?

(9) United States ex rel. Trantino v. Hatrack, 563 F.2d 86, 96 (3rd Cir. 1977), held the state Attorney General could not waive the exhaustion requirement of § 2254:

> Exhaustion . . . serves an interest *not* of state prosecutors but of state courts. . . . [T]he state court interest in having "an initial 'opportunity to pass upon and correct'" alleged violations of its prisoners' federal rights is simply not an interest that state prosecutors have been empowered to yield.

Cf. *Ohio Bur. of Employment Services v. Hodory*, pp. 495, 539 supra (state counsel may waive *Younger* doctrine but not *Pullman* abstention); *Ford Motor Co. v. Department of Treasury*, p. 456 supra (state law determines whether Attorney General may waive sovereign immunity from suit in federal court).

JONES v. CUNNINGHAM

371 U.S. 236 (1963).

MR. JUSTICE BLACK delivered the opinion of the Court.

A United States District Court has jurisdiction under 28 U.S.C. § 2241, to grant a writ of habeas corpus "to a prisoner . . . in custody in violation of the Constitution . . . of the United States." The question in this case is whether a state prisoner who has been placed on parole is "in custody" within the meaning of this section so that a Federal District Court has jurisdiction to hear and determine his charge that his state sentence was imposed in violation of the United States Constitution.

In 1953 petitioner was convicted in a Virginia state court of an offense requiring confinement in the state penitentiary, and as this was his third such offense he was sentenced to serve 10 years in the state penitentiary. In 1961 he filed this petition for habeas corpus in the United States District Court for the Eastern District of Virginia, alleging that his third-offender sentence was based in part upon a 1946 larceny conviction which was invalid because his federal constitutional right to counsel had been denied at the 1946 trial. The District Court dismissed the petition but the Court of Appeals for the Fourth Circuit granted a certificate of probable cause and leave to appeal in *forma pauperis*. Shortly before the case came on for oral argument before the Court of Appeals petitioner was paroled by the Virginia Parole Board. The parole order placed petitioner in the "custody and control" of the Parole Board and directed him to live with his aunt and uncle in Lafayette, Georgia. It provided that his parole was subject to revocation or modification at any time by the Parole Board and that petitioner could be arrested and returned to prison for cause. Among other restrictions and conditions, petitioner was required to obtain the permission of his parole officer to leave the community, to change residence, or to own or operate a motor vehicle. He was further required to make monthly reports to his parole officer, to permit the officer to visit his home or place of employment at any time, and to follow the officer's instructions and advice. When petitioner was placed on parole, the Superintendent of the Virginia State Penitentiary, who was the only respondent in the case, asked the Court of Appeals to dismiss the case as moot since petitioner was no longer in his custody. Petitioner opposed the motion to dismiss but, in view of his parole to the custody of the Virginia Parole Board, moved to add its members as respondents. The Court of Appeals dismissed, holding that the case was moot as to the superintendent because he no longer had custody or control over petitioner "at large on parole." It refused to permit the petitioner to add the Parole Board members as respondents, because they did not have "physical custody" of the person of petitioner and were therefore not proper parties. 294 F.2d 608. We granted certiorari to decide whether a parolee is "in custody" within the meaning of 28 U.S.C. § 2241 and is therefore entitled to invoke the habeas corpus jurisdiction of the United States District Court. 369 U.S. 809.

The habeas corpus jurisdictional statute implements the constitutional command that the writ of habeas corpus be made available. While limiting its availability to those "in custody," the statute does not attempt to mark the boundaries of "custody" nor in any way other than by use of that word attempt to limit the situations in which the writ can be used. To determine whether habeas corpus could be used to test the legality of a given restraint on liberty, this Court has generally looked to common-law usages and the history of habeas corpus both in England and in this country.

In England, as in the United States, the chief use of habeas corpus has been to seek the release of persons held in actual, physical custody in prison or jail. Yet English courts have long recognized the writ as a proper remedy even though the restraint is something less than close physical confinement. For example the King's Bench as early as 1722 held that habeas corpus was appropriate to question whether a woman alleged to be the applicant's wife was being constrained by her guardians to stay away from her husband against her will. The test used was simply whether she was "at her liberty to go where she please[d]." So also, habeas corpus was used in 1763 to require the production in court of an indentured 18-year-old girl who had been assigned by her master to another man "for bad purposes." Although the report indicates no restraint on the girl other than the covenants of the indenture, the King's Bench ordered that she "be discharged from all restraint, and be at liberty to go where she will." And more than a century ago an English court permitted a parent to use habeas corpus to obtain his children from the other parent, even though the children were "not under imprisonment, restraint, or duress of any kind." These examples show clearly that English courts have not treated the Habeas Corpus Act of 1679, 31 Car. II, c. 2—the forerunner of all habeas corpus acts—as permitting relief only to those in jail or like physical confinement.

Similarly, in the United States the use of habeas corpus has not been restricted to situations in which the applicant is in actual, physical custody. This Court itself has repeatedly held that habeas corpus is available to an alien seeking entry into the United States, although in those cases each alien was free to go anywhere else in the world. "[H]is movements," this Court said, "are restrained by authority of the United States, and he may by habeas corpus test the validity of his exclusion." Habeas corpus has also been consistently regarded by lower federal courts as the appropriate procedural vehicle for questioning the legality of an induction or enlistment into the military service.[11] The restraint, of course, is clear in such cases, but it is far indeed from the kind of "present physical custody" thought by the Court of Appeals to be required. Again, in the state courts, as in England, habeas corpus has been widely used by parents disputing over which is the fit and proper person to have custody of their child, one of which we had before us only a few weeks ago. History, usage, and precedent can leave no doubt that, besides physical imprisonment, there are other restraints on a man's liberty, restraints not shared by the public generally, which have been thought sufficient in the English-speaking world to support the issuance of habeas corpus.

Respondent strongly urges upon us that however numerous the situations in which habeas corpus will lie prior decisions of this Court conclusively determine that the liberty of a person released on parole is not so restrained as to permit the parolee to attack his conviction in habeas corpus proceedings. In some of those cases, upon which the Court of Appeals in this case also relied, the petitioner had been completely and unconditionally released from custody; such cases are obviously not controlling here where petitioner has not been unconditionally released. Other cases relied upon by respondent held merely that the dispute between the petitioner and the named respondent in each case had become moot because that particular respondent no longer held the petitioner in his custody. So here, as in the cases last mentioned, when the petitioner was placed on parole, his cause against the Superintendent of the Virginia State Penitentiary became moot because the superintendent's custody had come to an end, as much as if he had resigned his position with the State. But it does not follow that this petitioner is wholly without remedy. His motion to add the members of the Virginia Parole Board as parties respondent squarely raises the question, not presented in our earlier cases, of whether the Parole Board now holds the petitioner in its "custody" within the meaning of 28 U.S.C. § 2241 so that he can by habeas corpus require the Parole Board to point to and defend the law by which it justifies any restraint on his liberty.

11. E.g., Ex parte Fabiani, 105 F.Supp. 139 (E.D.Pa.1952); United States ex rel. Steinberg v. Graham, 57 F.Supp. 938 (E.D. Ark.1944).

The Virginia statute provides that a paroled prisoner shall be released "into the custody of the Parole Board," and the parole order itself places petitioner "under the custody and control of the Virginia Parole Board." And in fact, as well as in theory, the custody and control of the Parole Board involves significant restraints on petitioner's liberty because of his conviction and sentence, which are in addition to those imposed by the State upon the public generally. Petitioner is confined by the parole order to a particular community, house, and job at the sufferance of his parole officer. He cannot drive a car without permission. He must periodically report to his parole officer, permit the officer to visit his home and job at any time, and follow the officer's advice. He is admonished to keep good company and good hours, work regularly, keep away from undesirable places and live a clean, honest, and temperate life. Petitioner must not only faithfully obey these restrictions and conditions but he must live in constant fear that a single deviation, however slight, might be enough to result in his being returned to prison to serve out the very sentence he claims was imposed upon him in violation of the United States Constitution. He can be rearrested at any time the Board or parole officer believes he has violated a term or condition of his parole, and he might be thrown back in jail to finish serving the allegedly invalid sentence with few, if any, of the procedural safeguards that normally must be and are provided to those charged with crime. It is not relevant that conditions and restrictions such as these may be desirable and important parts of the rehabilitative process; what matters is that they significantly restrain petitioner's liberty to do those things which in this country free men are entitled to do. Such restraints are enough to invoke the help of the Great Writ. Of course, that writ always could and still can reach behind prison walls and iron bars. But it can do more. It is not now and never has been a static, narrow, formalistic remedy; its scope has grown to achieve its grand purpose—the protection of individuals against erosion of their right to be free from wrongful restraints upon their liberty. While petitioner's parole releases him from immediate physical imprisonment, it imposes conditions which significantly confine and restrain his freedom; this is enough to keep him in the "custody" of the members of the Virginia Parole Board within the meaning of the habeas corpus statute; if he can prove his allegations this custody is in violation of the Constitution, and it was therefore error for the Court of Appeals to dismiss his case as moot instead of permitting him to add the Parole Board members as respondents. . . .

The case is reversed and remanded to the Court of Appeals with directions to grant petitioner's motion to add the members of the Parole Board as respondents and proceed to a decision on the merits of petitioner's case.

Reversed.

PEYTON v. ROWE

391 U.S. 54 (1968).

MR. CHIEF JUSTICE WARREN delivered the opinion of the Court.

This case concerns the scope of 28 U.S.C. § 2241(c)(3), which specifies that the United States District Courts may issue writs of habeas corpus on behalf of prisoners who are "in custody in violation of the Constitution . . . of the United States." The question presented is whether a district court may entertain a petition for a writ of habeas corpus from a prisoner incarcerated under consecutive sentences who claims that a sentence that he is scheduled to serve in the future is invalid because of a deprivation of rights guaranteed by the Constitution. The Court considered this issue in McNally v. Hill, 293 U.S. 131 (1934), and held that the habeas corpus statute does not authorize attacks upon future consecutive sentences. . . .

Respondents Robert Rowe and Clyde Thacker are serving prison terms in the Virginia State Penitentiary. In June 1963 Rowe was sentenced to 30 years' imprisonment after a jury found him guilty of rape. Subsequently, he pleaded guilty to an indictment charging him with felonious abduction with intent to defile arising from the same events which had led to the rape conviction. He was sentenced to a 20-year term on this conviction to run consecutively to the 30-year sentence. After exhausting state remedies, Rowe petitioned for a writ of habeas corpus in the United States District Court for the Western District of Virginia. He did not attack the rape conviction, but alleged that the conviction for felonious abduction was constitutionally defective because he had been subjected to double jeopardy, because his plea of guilty had been involuntary, because the indictment had failed to state an offense and because he had been inadequately represented by trial counsel. Without reaching the merits of Rowe's claims, the District Court denied relief. Applying *McNally*, the court found Rowe was then detained under the 30-year sentence for rape. Since he did not claim that sentence was invalid, it was held that he was not then "in custody" under an unconstitutionally imposed sentence within the meaning of § 2241. The court concluded that it could not entertain Rowe's challenge to the conviction for felonious abduction until he was confined under the sentence imposed for that conviction. That time would not arrive until 1993. [Thacker's case was similar.] . . .

The Court of Appeals for the Fourth Circuit reversed. . . . 383 F.2d 709 (1967). . . . Chief Judge Haynsworth reasoned that this Court would no longer follow *McNally*, which in his view represented a "doctrinaire approach" based on an "old jurisdictional concept" which had been "thoroughly rejected by the Supreme Court in recent cases."[6]

6. The decision of the Court of Appeals in the present case was preceded by two cases in which it held that § 2241(c)(3) permits attack upon a future consecutive sentence which affects or may affect a prisoner's current parole eligibility. Williams v. Peyton, 372 F.2d 216 (C.A.4th Cir. 1967); Martin v. Virginia, 349 F.2d 781 (C.A.4th

Id., at 714. We are in complete agreement with this conclusion and the considerations underlying it. . . .

A federal jury had found McNally guilty of three counts of an indictment charging offenses under the Motor Vehicle Theft Act. . . .[15] He had been sentenced to two years on the first count and four years each on the second and third counts, the sentences on the first and second counts to run concurrently and the sentence on the third consecutively. In his application in a district court for a writ of habeas corpus, McNally claimed that the indictment failed to state an offense as to the third count. He did not attack the convictions under the first and second counts. When he filed his petition he was serving under the second count. The lower courts denied relief on the merits. But this Court affirmed on a jurisdictional ground, holding that because McNally had not begun to serve the sentence on the third count—and therefore was not "in custody" under that sentence—his petition for relief was premature:

> "[W]ithout restraint which is unlawful, the writ may not be used. A sentence which the prisoner has not begun to serve cannot be the cause of restraint which the statute makes the subject of inquiry." 293 U.S., at 138.

The effect of this disposition was ameliorated somewhat by the Court's suggestion that McNally might seek relief by another route. . . . Moreover, McNally's challenge was directed at the face of the indictment. Therefore, postponement of adjudication of his claims probably would not result in the loss of crucial evidence. But the harshness of a rule which may delay determination of federal claims for decades becomes obvious when applied to the cases of Rowe and Thacker. . . .

Both Rowe and Thacker allege that they were so inadequately represented at trial that they were denied the assistance of counsel in violation of the Sixth and Fourteenth Amendments. Petitioner concedes that, but for *McNally*, respondents' allegations would entitle them to plenary hearings in the District Courts. . . . Yet, under the current schedules of confinement, it is argued, neither Rowe nor Thacker may obtain adjudication of his claims until after 1990. By that time, dimmed memories or the death of witnesses are bound to render it difficult or impossible to secure crucial testimony on disputed issues of fact. Of course prejudice to meritorious claims resulting from the kind

Cir. 1965). In *McNally*, the Court rejected the prisoner's argument that he was entitled to habeas corpus relief because he would be eligible for parole if the challenged sentence were invalidated. McNally v. Hill, 293 U.S., at 134, 140. In *Williams* and *Martin*, the Court of Appeals concluded that this Court's decision in Jones v. Cunningham, 371 U.S. 236 (1963), represented a departure from this narrow reading of the habeas corpus statute.

15. Because McNally was imprisoned by federal authorities, his application for habeas corpus relief could have rested on the clause of Rev.Stat. § 753 (1875) which authorized federal courts to entertain petitions from prisoners in the custody of the United States. However, the Court's interpretation of the custody requirement in *McNally* was equally applicable to state prisoners claiming their incarceration violated the Constitution. E.g., Darr v. Burford, 339 U.S. 200, 203 (1950).

of delay which *McNally* imposes is not limited to situations involving ineffective assistance of counsel. To name but a few examples, factual determinations are ofen dispositive on claims of coerced confession, e.g., Reck v. Pate, 367 U.S. 433 (1961); Leyra v. Denno, 347 U.S. 556 (1954), lack of competency to stand trial, e.g., Pate v. Robinson, 383 U.S. 375 (1966), and denial of a fair trial, e.g., Sheppard v. Maxwell, 384 U.S. 333 (1966). Postponement of the adjudication of such issues for years can harm both the prisoner and the State and lessens the probability that final disposition of the case will do substantial justice. As the Court of Appeals observed:

> "Years hence, the prisoner, at least, may be expected to give testimonial support to the allegations of his petition, but if they are false in fact, the Commonwealth of Virginia may be unable to refute them because of the unavailability of records and of the testimony of the responsible officials and participants in the trial. The greater the lapse of time, the more unlikely it becomes that the state could reprosecute if retrials are held to be necessary. It is to the great interest of the Commonwealth and to the prisoner to have these matters determined as soon as possible when there is the greatest likelihood the truth of the matter may be established." [17] 383 F.2d, at 715.

Clearly, to the extent that the rule of *McNally* postpones plenary consideration of issues by the district courts, it undermines the character of the writ of habeas corpus as the instrument for resolving fact issues not adequately developed in the original proceedings. . . .

McNally is also at odds with the purpose of the writ of habeas corpus in another respect. As noted above, a principal aim of the writ is to provide for swift judicial review of alleged unlawful restraints on liberty. Calendar congestion, considerations of federalism, see, e.g., Fay v. Noia, 372 U.S., at 415–420; Ex parte Royall, 117 U.S. 241 (1886), and the exigencies of appellate review account for largely unavoidable delays in the processing of criminal cases. But the prematurity rule of *McNally* in many instances extends without practical justification the time a prisoner entitled to release must remain in confinement. Rowe and Thacker eventually may establish that the convictions they challenge were obtained in violation of the Constitution. If they do, each day they are incarcerated under those convictions while their cases are

17. This consideration has led at least two States which previously followed the prematurity doctrine to reject it in recent years. See Commonwealth ex rel. Stevens v. Myers, 419 Pa. 1, 213 A.2d 613 (1965); Ore.Rev.Stat. § 138.510 (1963). See also Landreth v. Gladden, 213 Ore. 205, 324 P.2d 475 (1958). California does not follow the *McNally* rule. In re Chapman, 43 Cal. 2d 385, 273 P.2d 817 (1954). Finally, while this case was under consideration in this Court, Virginia repudiated the prematurity doctrine by statute. See Va.S. No. 44, 1968 Sess., amending Va.Code Ann. § 8–596 (effective June 28, 1968). A commitee of the American Bar Association which is inquiring into post-conviction remedies has recommended abandonment of the prematurity doctrine which it calls "one of the most frustrating elements of present post-conviction practice." Advisory Committee on Sentencing and Review, A.B.A. Project on Minimum Standards for Criminal Justice, Standards Relating to Post-Conviction Remedies 43 (Tent.Draft 1967).

in the courts will be time that they might properly have enjoyed as free men. . . .

The foregoing analysis demonstrates that *McNally* is inconsistent with the purposes underlying the federal writ of habeas corpus. Moreover, in arriving at its decision, the Court in *McNally* relied in part upon an unnecessarily narrow interpretation of the habeas corpus statute. . . . In common understanding "custody" comprehends respondents' status for the entire duration of their imprisonment. Practically speaking, Rowe is in custody for 50 years, or for the aggregate of his 30- and 20-year sentences. For purposes of parole eligibility, under Virginia law he is incarcerated for 50 years. Va.Code Ann. § 53–251 (1967); see n. 3, supra. Nothing on the face of § 2241 militates against an interpretation which views Rowe and Thacker as being "in custody" under the aggregate of the consecutive sentences imposed on them. Under that interpretation, they are "in custody in violation of the Constitution" if any consecutive sentence they are scheduled to serve was imposed as the result of a deprivation of constitutional rights. . . .

We find unpersuasive the arguments made in *McNally* to support the narrower interpretation of the custody requirement. No prior decision of the Court was cited as clear authority for the prematurity doctrine. . . .

Notes on "Custody" and Other Issues in Habeas Corpus

(1) Hensley v. Municipal Court, 411 U.S. 345 (1973). Convicted and sentenced by a state court, the petitioner was released on his own recognizance while pursuing state-court remedies and was still at large when he petitioned for federal habeas. The Supreme Court held that he was nevertheless in "custody" within the meaning of the statute:

> First, he is subject to restraints "not shared by the public generally," Jones v. Cunningham, . . . that is, the obligation to appear "at all times and places as ordered" by "[a] ny court or magistrate of competent jurisdiction." . . . He cannot come and go as he pleases. His freedom of movement rests in the hands of state judicial officers, who may demand his presence at any time and without a moment's notice. Disobedience is itself a criminal offense. The restraint on his liberty is surely no less severe than the conditions imposed on the unattached reserve officer whom we held to be "in custody" in Strait v. Laird, [406 U.S. 341 (1972)].
>
> Second, petitioner remains at large only by the grace of a stay entered first by the state trial court and then extended by two Justices of this Court. The State has emphatically indicated its determination to put him behind bars, and the State has taken every possible step to secure that result. . . . The need to keep the stay in force is itself an unusual and substantial impairment of his liberty.
>
> Moreover, our conclusion that the petitioner is presently in custody does not interfere with any significant interest of the State. Indeed,

> even if we were to accept the State's argument that petitioner is not in custody, that result would do no more than postpone this habeas corpus action until petitioner had begun service of his sentence. . . . Plainly, we would badly serve the purposes and the history of the writ to hold that under these circumstances the petitioner's failure to spend even 10 minutes in jail is enough to deprive the District Court of power to hear his constitutional claim.

Three dissenters protested: The only restraint on the petitioner was "that at the time of the expiration of the stay . . . petitioner would have had to surrender himself to the custody of the sheriff. . . . Petitioner was under no greater restriction than one who had been subpoenaed to testify in court as a witness." [1]

(2) An issue receiving increasing attention in recent years is the extent to which habeas can be used to test the legality of conditions of custody by one concededly not entitled to complete freedom. The early case of In re Bonner, 151 U.S. 242 (1894), held that habeas would lie when the petitioner had been locked up in the wrong jail; and in Creek v. Stone, 379 F.2d 106, 109 (D.C.Cir. 1967), habeas was used to test the right of a prisoner to be held in an institution with psychiatric facilities: The writ is available "not only to an applicant who claims he is entitled to be freed of all restraints, but also to an applicant who protests his confinement in a certain place, or under certain conditions. . . ." Sensible enough?

In Wilwording v. Swenson, 404 U.S. 249 (1971), a habeas petition alleged a number of illegal conditions of confinement:

> that each petitioner is in a maximum security section; that the facilities are inadequate in many ways and lack conveniences for hygiene, recreational, educational and religious practices . . ., physical mistreatment by prison employees and . . . that their conditions of confinement are more stringent and restrictive than is necessary for the maintenance of prison discipline and security.

439 F.2d 1331, 1332 n. 2 (8th Cir. 1971). Reversing a decision that the petitioners had failed to exhaust available state remedies, the Supreme Court held that in any event exhaustion was unnecessary because the action was also cognizable under 42 U.S.C. § 1983. Of most immediate interest, however, is the almost parenthetical remark of the Court, in the course of holding it unnecessary to meet the exhaustion requirements of habeas, that the claims were indeed "cognizable in federal habeas corpus."

How far should this principle be carried? Is habeas an appropriate remedy when a prisoner has been beaten by a guard, because the "conditions of confinement" were improper during the beating?

1. The courts have so far resisted the attempt to equate with "custody" the imposition of money fines, e.g., Edmunds v. Won Bae Chang, 509 F.2d 39 (9th Cir. 1975); Russell v. City of Pierre, 530 F.2d 791 (8th Cir. 1976), or the civil disabilities of criminal conviction (inability to practice certain professions or possess firearms, liability to recidivist penalties), Harvey v. South Dakota, 526 F.2d 840 (8th Cir. 1975). Justice Douglas, dissenting from the denial of certiorari in Jones v. United States, 419 U.S. 907 (1974), argued that to deny collateral review to persons who had been merely fined "raises a substantial federal question of a denial of equal protection [sic]." Does it?

(3) Carafas v. LaVallee, 391 U.S. 234 (1968). A habeas corpus applicant had been released from state custody after his case had been decided by the district court. An earlier 5–4 Supreme Court decision had held such a case "moot," Parker v. Ellis, 362 U.S. 574. In *Carafas* the Court unanimously adopted the views of the *Parker* dissent: The continuing effects of the conviction prevented mootness; § 2241 required custody only at the time the application is filed; jurisdiction once attached was not divested by later events, cf. p. 241 supra; and § 2243, allowing the court to "dispose of the matter as law and justice require," did not limit relief to discharge from custody. The *Carafas* rule was held applicable to a federal prisoner under § 2255 in Castle v. United States, 399 F.2d 642 (5th Cir. 1968).

(4) What is the effect of *Peyton v. Rowe* upon the old doctrine that a prisoner serving two or more concurrent sentences cannot attack only one of them? Two courts have allowed an attack on the longer of two concurrent sentences, because its invalidation would result in discharge when the shorter expired and because *Rowe* demanded immediate resolution of such an actual though future controversy. Lydy v. Beto, 399 F.2d 59 (5th Cir. 1968); Rhodus v. Patterson, 404 F.2d 890 (10th Cir. 1968). The Tenth Circuit has gone even further, allowing an attack on one of two coterminous concurrent sentences because its invalidity might in the future affect the likelihood of parole and result in a lessened sentence in the event of a later conviction. Sciberras v. United States, 404 F.2d 247 (1968).

(5) In Braden v. 30th Judicial Circuit Court, 410 U.S. 484 (1973), a prisoner serving an Alabama sentence he did not challenge filed federal habeas to compel Kentucky to bring him speedily to trial on a quite independent charge. A detainer had been filed to assure that he was turned over to Kentucky when he was through with Alabama. Over three dissents that focused principally on the exhaustion doctrine (see p. 640 supra), the Court in an opinion by Justice Brennan held the action was not premature, relying on *Peyton v. Rowe*, and went on to resolve a troublesome question of venue. The petitioner was in an Alabama prison, but he was attacking the inaction of Kentucky officials with respect to a Kentucky offense. Where should the petition be filed? Section 2241 authorizes judges to issue the writ "within their respective jurisdictions," and Ahrens v. Clark, 335 U.S. 188 (1948), in holding the District of Columbia courts could not entertain a petition attacking custody in New York, had construed the quoted words to require custody within the district where the writ was sought: "The presence within the territorial jurisdiction of the District Court of the person detained is [a] prerequisite to filing a petition for writ of habeas corpus."

Finding Kentucky the more convenient forum, the majority disagreed with *Ahrens*:

> The writ of habeas corpus does not act upon the prisoner who seeks relief, but upon the person who holds him in what is alleged to be unlawful custody. . . . Read literally, the language of § 2241(a) requires nothing more than that the court issuing the writ have jurisdiction over the custodian. So long as the custodian can be reached by service of process, the court can issue a writ "within its

jurisdiction" . . . even if the prisoner himself is confined outside the court's territorial jurisdiction. . . .

We cannot assume that Congress intended to require the Commonwealth of Kentucky to defend its action in a distant State and to preclude the resolution of the dispute by a federal judge familiar with the laws and practices of Kentucky.

(6) When a prisoner is sentenced to consecutive terms, one state and the other federal (in either order you like), is his proper remedy habeas corpus or a motion under § 2255? See Maleng v. Cook, 109 S.Ct. 1923 (1989), upholding jurisdiction over a habeas petition filed by a federal prisoner attacking a detainer based on a state sentence to be served in the future; Desmond v. United States Board of Parole, 397 F.2d 386 (1st Cir. 1968), allowing a § 2255 motion in the converse case.

(7) A complete study of federal post-conviction relief would have to include Fed.R.Crim.P. 35, which until very recently provided that "the court may correct an illegal sentence at any time." If read broadly this Rule might have eliminated the necessity for construing § 2255. However, in Hill v. United States, 368 U.S. 424, 430 (1962), the Court held that a defendant could not argue in a Rule 35 motion that he had been denied the right given by Rule 32(a) to speak in his own behalf before sentencing: "The narrow function of Rule 35 is to permit correction at any time of an illegal *sentence*, not to reexamine errors occurring at the trial or other proceedings prior to the imposition of sentence. The sentence in this case was not illegal. The punishment meted out was not in excess of that prescribed by the relevant statutes, multiple terms were not imposed for the same offense, nor were the terms of the sentence itself legally or constitutionally invalid in any other respect." There were four dissents: "I would have thought that a sentence imposed in an illegal manner—whether the amount or form of the punishment meted out constitutes an additional violation of law or not—would be recognized as an 'illegal sentence' under any normal reading of the English language." The dissenters conceded, however, that "This does not of course mean that Rule 35 permits attack upon a sentence based upon mere trial errors. Rule 35 applies to any 'illegal sentence' not to any illegal conviction, and thus by its terms the Rule protects only those rights which a defendant retains even if the judgment of guilt against him is proper." 368 U.S. at 431–32 and n. 2. Is there any good reason why collateral attack should be more available to correct an excessive sentence than to vacate an improper conviction?

(8) United States v. Morgan, 346 U.S. 502 (1954). Having completed a sentence for federal crime, petitioner was convicted of a state crime and given a longer term as a second offender because of his federal conviction. He then attacked the federal conviction for lack of counsel. Relief under § 2255 was unavailable, because the petitioner was no longer in federal custody. Nor was Rule 35 of any assistance, since "sentences subject to correction under that rule are those that the judgment of conviction did not authorize." 346 U.S. at 506. Yet the Court held the District Court had power to grant relief "in the nature of a writ of error coram nobis" under 28 U.S.C. § 1651: "The Supreme Court and all courts established by Act of Congress may issue all writs necessary or appropriate in aid of their

respective jurisdictions and agreeable to the usages and principles of law." Because this motion was "a step in the criminal case and not, like habeas corpus where relief is sought in a separate case and record, the beginning of a separate civil proceeding," Rule 60(b) of the Civil Rules, which abolishes coram nobis in civil cases, was inapplicable; and § 2255 was not exclusive because it was not intended "to impinge upon prisoners' rights of collateral attack," quoting United States v. Hayman, 342 U.S. 205, 219 (1952). There were four dissents, arguing that § 2255 was exclusive; that coram nobis in any event lay only to correct errors of fact unknown at the time of judgment; that the writ was not "in aid of jurisdiction," as required by § 1651, because the District Court lost jurisdiction when petitioner completed his federal sentence; and that petitioner had forfeited any remedy by inexcusable delay in filing his petition.

(9) Isn't it about time this whole area was cleared up? How?

Appendix A

CURRENT STATUTES AND RULES

CONSTITUTION OF THE UNITED STATES OF AMERICA—1787

ARTICLE I

Section 1. All legislative powers herein granted shall be vested in a Congress of the United States, which shall consist of a Senate and House of Representatives. . . .

Section 8. The Congress shall have Power to lay and collect Taxes, Duties, Imposts and Excises, to pay the Debts and provide for the common Defence and general Welfare of the United States; but all Duties, Imposts and Excises shall be uniform throughout the United States;

To borrow Money on the credit of the United States;

To regulate Commerce with foreign Nations, and among the several States, and with the Indian Tribes;

To establish a uniform Rule of Naturalization, and uniform Laws on the subject of Bankruptcies throughout the United States;

To coin Money, regulate the Value thereof, and of foreign Coin, and fix the Standard of Weights and Measures;

To provide for the Punishment of counterfeiting the Securities and current Coin of the United States;

To establish Post Offices and post Roads;

To promote the Progress of Science and useful Arts, by securing for limited Times to Authors and Inventors the exclusive Right to their respective Writings and Discoveries;

To constitute Tribunals inferior to the supreme Court;

To define and punish Piracies and Felonies committed on the high Seas, and Offences against the Law of Nations;

To declare War, grant Letters of Marque and Reprisal, and make Rules concerning Captures on Land and Water;

To raise and support Armies, but no Appropriation of Money to that Use shall be for a longer Term than two Years;

To provide and maintain a Navy;

To make Rules for the Government and Regulation of the land and naval Forces;

To provide for calling forth the Militia to execute the Laws of the Union, suppress Insurrections and repel Invasions;

To provide for organizing, arming, and disciplining, the Militia, and for governing such Part of them as may be employed in the Service of the United States, reserving to the States respectively, the Appointment of the Officers, and the Authority of training the Militia according to the discipline prescribed by Congress;

To exercise exclusive Legislation in all Cases whatsoever, over such District (not exceeding ten Miles square) as may, by Cession of particular States, and the Acceptance of Congress, become the Seat of the Government of the United States, and to exercise like Authority over all Places purchased by the Consent of the Legislature of the State in which the Same shall be, for the Erection of Forts, Magazines, Arsenals, dock-Yards, and other needful Buildings;—And

To make all Laws which shall be necessary and proper for carrying into Execution the foregoing Powers, and all other Powers vested by this Constitution in the Government of the United States, or in any Department or Officer thereof.

Section 9. . . .

The Privilege of the Writ of Habeas Corpus shall not be suspended, unless when in Cases of Rebellion or Invasion the public Safety may require it. . . .

Section 10. No State shall enter into any Treaty, Alliance, or Confederation; grant Letters of Marque and Reprisal; coin Money; emit Bills of Credit; make any Thing but gold and silver Coin a Tender in Payment of Debts; pass any Bill of Attainder, ex post facto Law, or Law impairing the Obligation of Contracts, or grant any Title of Nobility. . . .

ARTICLE II

Section 1. The executive Power shall be vested in a President of the United States of America. . . .

Section 2. The President shall be Commander in Chief of the Army and Navy of the United States, and of the Militia of the several States, when called into the actual Service of the United States; he may require the Opinion, in writing, of the principal Officer in each of the executive Departments, upon any Subject relating to the Duties of their respective Offices, and he shall have Power to grant Reprieves and Pardons for Offences against the United States, except in Cases of Impeachment.

He shall have Power, by and with the Advice and Consent of the Senate, to make Treaties, provided two thirds of the Senators present concur; and he shall nominate, and by and with the Advice and

Consent of the Senate, shall appoint Ambassadors, other public Ministers and Consuls, Judges of the supreme Court, and all other Officers of the United States, whose Appointments are not herein otherwise provided for, and which shall be established by Law: but the Congress may by Law vest the Appointment of such inferior Officers, as they think proper, in the President alone, in the Courts of Law, or in the Heads of Departments.

The President shall have Power to fill up all Vacancies that may happen during the Recess of the Senate, by granting Commissions which shall expire at the End of their next Session. . . .

Section 4. The President, Vice President and all civil Officers of the United States, shall be removed from Office on Impeachment for, and Conviction of, Treason, Bribery, or other high Crimes and Misdemeanors.

ARTICLE III

Section 1. The judicial Power of the United States, shall be vested in one supreme Court, and in such inferior Courts as the Congress may from time to time ordain and establish. The Judges, both of the supreme and inferior Courts, shall hold their Offices during good Behaviour, and shall, at stated Times, receive for their Services, a Compensation, which shall not be diminished during their Continuance in Office.

Section 2. The judicial Power shall extend to all Cases, in Law and Equity, arising under this Constitution, the Laws of the United States, and Treaties made, or which shall be made, under their Authority;—to all Cases affecting Ambassadors, other public Ministers and Consuls;—to all Cases of admiralty, and maritime Jurisdiction;—to Controversies to which the United States shall be a Party;—to Controversies between two or more States; between a State and Citizens of another State;—between Citizens of different States,—between Citizens of the same State claiming Lands under Grants of different States, and between a State, or the Citizens thereof, and foreign States, Citizens or Subjects.

In all Cases affecting Ambassadors, other public Ministers and Consuls, and those in which a State shall be Party, the supreme Court shall have original Jurisdiction. In all the other Cases before mentioned, the supreme Court shall have appellate Jurisdiction, both as to Law and Fact, with such Exceptions, and under such Regulations as the Congress shall make.

The Trial of all Crimes, except in Cases of Impeachment, shall be by Jury; and such Trial shall be held in the State where the said Crimes shall have been committed; but when not committed within any State, the Trial shall be at such Place or Places as the Congress may by Law have directed.

Section 3. Treason against the United States, shall consist only in levying War against them, or in adhering to their Enemies, giving them Aid and Comfort. No Person shall be convicted of Treason unless on the Testimony of two Witnesses to the same overt Act, or on Confession in open Court.

The Congress shall have Power to declare the Punishment of Treason, but no Attainder of Treason shall work Corruption of Blood, or Forfeiture except during the Life of the Person attainted.

ARTICLE IV

Section 1. Full Faith and Credit shall be given in each State to the public Acts, Records, and judicial Proceedings of every other State. And the Congress may by general Laws prescribe the Manner in which such Acts, Records and Proceedings shall be proved, and the Effect thereof.

Section 2. The Citizens of each State shall be entitled to all Privileges and Immunities of Citizens in the several States. . . .

Section 3. . . .

The Congress shall have Power to dispose of and make all needful Rules and Regulations respecting the Territory or other Property belonging to the United States; and nothing in this Constitution shall be so construed as to Prejudice any Claims of the United States, or of any particular State.

Section 4. The United States shall guarantee to every State in this Union a Republican Form of Government, and shall protect each of them against Invasion; and on Application of the Legislature, or of the Executive (when the Legislature cannot be convened) against domestic Violence. . . .

ARTICLE VI

This Constitution, and the laws of the United States which shall be made in Pursuance thereof; and all Treaties made, or which shall be made, under the Authority of the United States, shall be the supreme Law of the Land; and the Judges in every State shall be bound thereby, any Thing in the Constitution or Laws of any State to the Contrary notwithstanding.

The Senators and Representatives before mentioned, and the Members of the several State Legislatures, and all executive and judicial Officers, both of the United States and of the several States, shall be bound by Oath or Affirmation, to support this Constitution; but no religious Test shall ever be required as a Qualification to any Office or public Trust under the United States.

ARTICLES IN ADDITION TO, AND AMENDMENT OF THE CONSTITUTION

ARTICLE [I]

Congress shall make no law respecting an establishment of religion, or prohibiting the free exercise thereof; or abridging the freedom of speech, or of the press; or the right of the people peaceably to assemble, and to petition the Government for a redress of grievances. . . .

ARTICLE [IV]

The right of the people to be secure in their persons, houses, papers, and effects, against unreasonable searches and seizures, shall not be violated, and no warrants shall issue, but upon probable cause, supported by oath or affirmation, and particularly describing the place to be searched, and the persons or things to be seized.

ARTICLE [V]

No person shall be held to answer for a capital, or otherwise infamous crime, unless on a presentment or indictment of a Grand Jury, except in cases arising in the land or naval forces, or in the militia, when in actual service in time of war or public danger; nor shall any person be subject for the same offence to be twice put in jeopardy of life or limb; nor shall be compelled in any criminal case to be a witness against himself, nor be deprived of life, liberty, or property, without due process of law; nor shall private property be taken for public use, without just compensation. . . .

ARTICLE [VII]

In Suits at common law, where the value in controversy shall exceed twenty dollars, the right of trial by jury shall be preserved, and no fact tried by a jury, shall be otherwise reexamined in any Court of the United States, than according to the rules of the common law. . . .

ARTICLE [X]

The powers not delegated to the United States by the Constitution, nor prohibited by it to the States, are reserved to the States respectively, or to the people.

ARTICLE [XI]

The Judicial power of the United States shall not be construed to extend to any suit in law or equity, commenced or prosecuted against one of the United States by Citizens of another State, or by Citizens or Subjects of any Foreign State. . . .

ARTICLE [XIV]

Section 1. All persons born or naturalized in the United States, and subject to the jurisdiction thereof, are citizens of the United States and of the State wherein they reside. No State shall make or enforce any law which shall abridge the privileges or immunities of citizens of the United States; nor shall any State deprive any person of life, liberty, or property, without due process of law; nor deny to any person within its jurisdiction the equal protection of the laws. . . .

Section 5. The Congress shall have power to enforce, by appropriate legislation, the provisions of this article.

ARTICLE [XV]

Section 1. The right of citizens of the United States to vote shall not be denied or abridged by the United States or by any State on account of race, color, or previous condition of servitude.

Section 2. The Congress shall have power to enforce this article by appropriate legislation. . . .

UNITED STATES CODE

As Amended to December 31, 1989

TITLE 5.—GOVERNMENT ORGANIZATION AND EMPLOYEES

Chapter 5.—Administrative Procedure

§ 701. Application; definitions.

(a) This chapter applies, according to the provisions thereof, except to the extent that—

(1) statutes preclude judicial review; or

(2) agency action is committed to agency discretion by law.

(b) For the purpose of this chapter—

(1) "agency" means each authority of the Government of the United States, whether or not it is within or subject to review by another agency, but does not include—

(A) the Congress;

(B) the courts of the United States;

(C) the governments of the territories or possessions of the United States;

(D) the government of the District of Columbia;

(E) agencies composed of representatives of the parties or of representatives of organizations of the parties to the disputes determined by them;

(F) courts martial and military commissions;

(G) military authority exercised in the field in time of war or in occupied territory; or

(H) functions conferred by sections 1738, 1739, 1743, and 1744 of title 12; chapter 2 of title 41; or sections 1622, 1884, 1891–1902, and former section 1641(b)(2), of title 50, appendix; and

(2) "person", "rule", "order", "license", "sanction", "relief", and "agency action" have the meanings given them by section 551 of this title.

§ 702. Right of review.

A person suffering legal wrong because of agency action, or adversely affected or aggrieved by agency action within the meaning of a relevant statute, is entitled to judicial review thereof. An action in a court of the United States seeking relief other than money damages and stating a claim that an agency or an officer or employee thereof acted or failed to act in an official capacity or under color of legal authority shall not be dismissed nor relief therein be denied on the ground that it is against the United States or that the United States is an indispensable party. The United States may be named as a defendant in any such action, and a judgment or decree may be entered against the United States: *Provided*, That any mandatory or injunctive decree shall specify the Federal officer or officers (by name or title), and their successors in office, personally responsible for compliance. Nothing herein (1) affects other limitations on judicial review or the power or duty of the court to dismiss any action or deny relief on any other appropriate legal or equitable ground; or (2) confers authority to grant relief if any other statute that grants consent to suit expressly or impliedly forbids the relief which is sought.

§ 703. Form and venue of proceeding.

The form of proceeding for judicial review is the special statutory review proceeding relevant to the subject matter in a court specified by statute or, in the absence or inadequacy thereof, any applicable form of legal action, including actions for declaratory judgments or writs of prohibitory or mandatory injunction or habeas corpus, in a court of competent jurisdiction. If no special statutory review proceeding is applicable, the action for judicial review may be brought against the United States, the agency by its official title, or the appropriate officer. Except to the extent that prior, adequate, and exclusive opportunity for judicial review is provided by law, agency action is subject to judicial review in civil or criminal proceedings for judicial enforcement.

§ 704. Actions reviewable.

Agency action made reviewable by statute and final agency action for which there is no other adequate remedy in a court are subject to judicial review. A preliminary, procedural, or intermediate agency action or ruling not directly reviewable is subject to review on the review of the final agency action. Except as otherwise expressly required by statute, agency action otherwise final is final for the purposes of this section whether or not there has been presented or determined an application for a declaratory order, for any form of reconsideration, or, unless the agency otherwise requires by rule and provides that the action meanwhile is inoperative, for an appeal to superior agency authority.

§ 706. Scope of review.

To the extent necessary to decision and when presented, the reviewing court shall decide all relevant questions of law, interpret constitutional and statutory provisions, and determine the meaning or applicability of the terms of an agency action. The reviewing court shall—

(1) compel agency action unlawfully withheld or unreasonably delayed; and

(2) hold unlawful and set aside agency action, findings, and conclusions found to be—

(A) arbitrary, capricious, an abuse of discretion, or otherwise not in accordance with law;

(B) contrary to constitutional right, power, privilege, or immunity;

(C) in excess of statutory jurisdiction, authority, or limitations, or short of statutory right;

(D) without observance of procedure required by law;

(E) unsupported by substantial evidence in a case subject to sections 556 and 557 of this title or otherwise reviewed on the record of an agency hearing provided by statute; or

(F) unwarranted by the facts to the extent that the facts are subject to trial de novo by the reviewing court.

In making the foregoing determinations, the court shall review the whole record or those parts of it cited by a party, and due account shall be taken of the rule of prejudicial error.

TITLE 15.—COMMERCE AND TRADE

Chapter 1.—Monopolies and Combinations in Restraint of Trade

§ 29. Appeals.

(a) **Court of Appeals; review by Supreme Court.** Except as otherwise expressly provided by this section, in every civil action brought in any district court of the United States under the Act entitled "An Act to protect trade and commerce against unlawful restraints and monopolies", approved July 2, 1890, or any other Acts having like purpose that have been or hereafter may be enacted, in which the United States is the complainant and equitable relief is sought, any appeal from a final judgment entered in any such action shall be taken to the court of appeals pursuant to sections 1291 and 2107 of Title 28. Any appeal from an interlocutory order entered in any such action shall be taken to the court of appeals pursuant to sections 1292(a)(1) and 2107 of Title 28 but not otherwise. Any judgment entered by the court of appeals in any such action shall be subject to review by the Supreme Court upon a writ of certiorari as provided in section 1254(1) of Title 28.

(b) **Direct appeals to Supreme Court.** An appeal from a final judgment pursuant to subsection (a) of this section shall lie directly to the Supreme Court if, upon application of a party filed within fifteen days of the filing of a notice of appeal, the district judge who adjudicated the case enters an order stating that immediate consideration of the appeal by the Supreme Court is of general public importance in the administration of justice. Such order shall be filed within thirty days after the filing of a notice of appeal. When such an order is filed, the appeal and any cross appeal shall be docketed in the time and manner prescribed by the rules of the Supreme Court. The Supreme Court shall thereupon either (1) dispose of the appeal and any cross appeal in the same manner as any other direct appeal authorized by law, or (2) in its discretion, deny the direct appeal and remand the case to the court of appeals, which shall then have jurisdiction to hear and determine the same as if the appeal and any cross appeal therein had been docketed in the court of appeals in the first instance pursuant to subsection (a) of this section.

TITLE 18.—CRIMES AND CRIMINAL PROCEDURE

Chapter 211.—Jurisdiction and Venue

§ 3231. District Courts.

The District Courts of the United States shall have original jurisdiction, exclusive of the courts of the States, of all offenses against the laws of the United States.

Nothing in this title shall be held to take away or impair the jurisdiction of the courts of the several States under the laws thereof.

Chapter 235.—Appeal

§ 3731. Appeal by United States.

In a criminal case an appeal by the United States shall lie to a court of appeals from a decision, judgment, or order of a district court dismissing an indictment or information or granting a new trial after verdict or judgment, as to any one or more counts, except that no appeal shall lie where the double jeopardy clause of the United States Constitution prohibits further prosecution.

An appeal by the United States shall lie to a court of appeals from a decision or order of a district court suppressing or excluding evidence or requiring the return of seized property in a criminal proceeding, not made after the defendant has been put in jeopardy and before the verdict or finding on an indictment or information, if the United States attorney certifies to the district court that the appeal is not taken for purpose of delay and that the evidence is a substantial proof of a fact material in the proceeding. . . .

The appeal in all such cases shall be taken within thirty days after the decision, judgment or order has been rendered and shall be diligently prosecuted.

The provisions of this section shall be liberally construed to effectuate its purposes.

§ 3742. Review of a sentence

(a) Appeal by a defendant.—A defendant may file a notice of appeal in the district court for review of an otherwise final sentence if the sentence—

(1) was imposed in violation of law;

(2) was imposed as a result of an incorrect application of the sentencing guidelines; or

(3) is greater than the sentence specified in the applicable guideline range to the extent that the sentence includes a greater fine or term of imprisonment, probation, or supervised release than the maximum established in the guideline range, or includes a more limiting condition of probation or supervised release under section 3563(b)(6) or (b)(11) than the maximum established in the guideline range; or

(4) was imposed for an offense for which there is no sentencing guideline and is plainly unreasonable.

(b) Appeal by the Government.—The Government may, with the personal approval of the Attorney General or the Solicitor General, file a notice of appeal in the district court for review of an otherwise final sentence if the sentence—

(1) was imposed in violation of law;

(2) was imposed as a result of an incorrect application of the sentencing guidelines;

(3) is less than the sentence specified in the applicable guideline range to the extent that the sentence includes a lesser fine or term of imprisonment, probation, or supervised release than the minimum established in the guideline range, or includes a less limiting condition of probation or supervised release under section 3563(b)(6) or (b)(11) than the minimum established in the guideline range; or

(4) was imposed for an offense for which there is no sentencing guideline and is plainly unreasonable. . . .

TITLE 26.—INTERNAL REVENUE CODE

Chapter 63.—Assessment

§ 6213. Restrictions applicable to deficiencies; petition to Tax Court.

(a) Time for filing petition and restriction on assessment.

Within 90 days, or 150 days if the notice is addressed to a person outside the United States, after the notice of deficiency authorized in section 6212 is mailed (not counting Saturday, Sunday, or a legal holiday in the District of Columbia as the last day), the taxpayer may file a petition with the Tax Court for a redetermination of the deficiency. Except as otherwise provided in section 6851 or section 6861 no assessment of a deficiency in respect of any tax imposed by subtitle A, or B, chapter 41, 42, 43, 44, or 45 and no levy or proceeding in court for its collection shall be made, begun, or prosecuted until such notice has been mailed to the taxpayer, nor until the expiration of such 90-day or 150-day period, as the case may be, nor, if a petition has been filed with the Tax Court, until the decision of the Tax Court has become final. Notwithstanding the provisions of section 7421(a) the making of such assessment or the beginning of such proceeding or levy during the time such prohibition is in force may be enjoined by a proceeding in the proper court.

Chapter 76.—Judicial Proceedings

SUBCHAPTER B.—PROCEEDINGS BY TAXPAYERS AND THIRD PARTIES

§ 7421. Prohibition of suits to restrain assessment or collection.

(a) Tax.

Except as provided in sections 6212(a) and (c), 6213(a), 6672(b), 6694(c), and 7426(a) and (b)(1), no suit for the purpose of restraining the assessment or collection of any tax shall be maintained in any court by any person, whether or not such person is the person against whom such tax was assessed.

SUBCHAPTER C.—THE TAX COURT

§ 7441. Status.

There is hereby established, under article I of the Constitution of the United States, a court of record to be known as the United States Tax Court. The members of the Tax Court shall be the chief judge and the judges of the Tax Court.

§ 7442. Jurisdiction.

The Tax Court and its divisions shall have such jurisdiction as is conferred on them by this title, by chapters 1, 2, 3, and 4 of the Internal Revenue Code of 1939, by title II and title III of the Revenue Act of 1926 (44 Stat. 10–87), or by laws enacted subsequent to February 26, 1926.

§ 7443. Membership.

(a) Number.

The Tax Court shall be composed of 19 members.

(b) Appointment.—

Judges of the Tax Court shall be appointed by the President, by and with the advice and consent of the Senate, solely on the grounds of fitness to perform the duties of the office.

(c) Salary.—

(1) Each judge shall receive salary at the same rate and in the same installments as judges of the district courts of the United States. . . .

(e) Term of office.—

The term of office of any judge of the Tax Court shall expire 15 years after he takes office.

(f) Removal from office.

Judges of the Tax Court may be removed by the President, after notice and opportunity for public hearing, for inefficiency, neglect of duty, or malfeasance in office, but for no other cause.

§ 7447. Retirement. . . .

(h) Retirement for disability.—

(1) Any judge who becomes permanently disabled from performing his duties shall certify to the President his disability in writing. If the chief judge retires for disability, his retirement shall not take effect until concurred in by the President. If any other judge retires for disability, he shall furnish to the President a certificate of disability signed by the chief judge.

(2) Whenever any judge who becomes permanently disabled from performing his duties does not retire and the President finds that such judge is unable to discharge efficiently all the duties of his office by reason of permanent mental or physical disability and that the appointment of an additional judge is necessary for the efficient dispatch of business, the President shall declare such judge to be retired.

§ 7453. Rules of practice, procedure, and evidence.

Except in the case of proceedings conducted under section 7463, the proceedings of the Tax Court and its divisions shall be conducted in accordance with such rules of practice and procedure (other than rules of evidence) as the Tax Court may prescribe and in accordance with the rules of evidence applicable in trials without a jury in the United States District Court of the District of Columbia.

§ 7458. Hearings.

Notice and opportunity to be heard upon any proceeding instituted before the Tax Court shall be given to the taxpayer and the Secretary. If an opportunity to be heard upon the proceeding is given before a division of the Tax Court, neither the taxpayer nor the Secretary shall be entitled to notice and opportunity to be heard before the Tax Court upon review, except upon a specific order of the chief judge. Hearings before the Tax Court and its divisions shall be open to the public, and the testimony, and, if the Tax Court so requires, the argument, shall be stenographically reported. The Tax Court is authorized to contract (by renewal of contract or otherwise) for the reporting of such hearings, and in such contract to fix the terms and conditions under which transcripts will be supplied by the contractor to the Tax Court and to other persons and agencies.

SUBCHAPTER D.—COURT REVIEW OF TAX COURT DECISIONS

§ 7482. Courts of review.

(a) Jurisdiction.

The United States Courts of Appeals shall have exclusive jurisdiction to review the decisions of the Tax Court, except as provided in section 1254 of Title 28 of the United States Code, in the same manner and to the same extent as decisions of the district courts in civil actions tried without a jury; and the judgment of any such court shall be final, except that it shall be subject to review by the Supreme Court of the United States upon certiorari, in the manner provided in section 1254 of Title 28 of the United States Code.

(b) Venue.

(1) In general.

Except as provided in paragraphs (2) and (3), such decisions may be reviewed by the United States court of appeals for the circuit in which is located

(A) in the case of a petitioner seeking redetermination of tax liability other than a corporation, the legal residence of the petitioner,

(B) in the case of a corporation seeking redetermination of tax liability, the principal place of business or principal office or agency of the corporation, or, if it has no principal place of business or principal office or agency in any judicial circuit, then the office to which was made the return of the tax in respect of which the liability arises,

(C) in the case of a person seeking a declaratory decision under section 7476, the principal place of business or principal office or agency of the employer,

(D) in the case of a person seeking a declaratory judgment under section 7477, the legal residence of such person if such person is not a corporation, or the principal place of business or principal office or agency of such person if such person is a corporation, or

(E) in the case of an organization seeking a declaratory decision under section 7428, the principal office or agency of the organization.

If for any reason no subparagraph of the preceding sentence applies, then such decisions may be reviewed by the Court of Appeals for the District of Columbia. For the purposes of this paragraph, the legal residence, principal place of business, or principal office or agency referred to herein shall be determined as of the time the petition seeking redetermination of tax liability was filed with the Tax Court or as of the time the petition seeking a declaratory decision under section 7428, 7476 or 7477 was filed with the Tax Court.

(2) By agreement.

Notwithstanding the provisions of paragraph (1), such decisions may be reviewed by any United States Court of Appeals which may be designated by the Secretary or his delegate and the taxpayer by stipulation in writing.

(3) Declaratory judgment actions relating to status of certain governmental obligations.

In the case of any decision of the Tax Court in a proceeding under section 7478, such decision may only be reviewed by the Court of Appeals for the District of Columbia.

(c) Powers.

(1) To affirm, modify, or reverse.

Upon such review, such courts shall have power to affirm or, if the decision of the Tax Court is not in accordance with law, to modify or to reverse the decision of the Tax Court, with or without remanding the case for a rehearing, as justice may require.

TITLE 28.—JUDICIARY AND JUDICIAL PROCEDURE

PART I.—ORGANIZATION OF COURTS

Chapter 6.—Bankruptcy Judges . . .

§ 151. Designation of bankruptcy courts.

In each judicial district, the bankruptcy judges in regular active service shall constitute a unit of the district court to be known as the bankruptcy court for that district. Each bankruptcy judge, as a judicial officer of the district court, may exercise the authority conferred under this chapter with respect to any action, suit, or proceeding and may preside alone and hold a regular or special session of the court, except as otherwise provided by law or by rule or order of the district court.

§ 152. Appointment of bankruptcy judges.

(a)(1) The United States court of appeals for the circuit shall appoint bankruptcy judges for the judicial districts established in paragraph (2) in such numbers as are established in such paragraph. Such appointments shall be made after considering the recommendations of the Judicial Conference submitted pursuant to subsection (b). Each bankruptcy judge shall be appointed for a term of fourteen years, subject to the provisions of subsection (e). Bankruptcy judges shall serve as judicial officers of the United States district court established under Article III of the Constitution. . . .

(e) A bankruptcy judge may be removed during the term for which such bankruptcy judge is appointed, only for incompetence, misconduct, neglect of duty, or physical or mental disability and only by the judicial council of the circuit in which the judge's official duty station is located. Removal may not occur unless a majority of all of the judges of such council concur in the order of removal. Before any order of removal may be entered, a full specification of charges shall be furnished to such bankruptcy judge who shall be accorded an opportunity to be heard on such charges.

§ 153. Salaries; character of service.

(a) Each bankruptcy judge shall serve on a full-time basis and shall receive as full compensation for his services a salary at an annual rate that is equal to 92 percent of the salary of a judge of the district court of the United States as determined pursuant to section 135, to be paid at such times as the Judicial Conference of the United States determines. . . .

§ 157. Procedures.

(a) Each district court may provide that any or all cases under title 11 and any or all proceedings arising under title 11 or arising in or related to a case under title 11 shall be referred to the bankruptcy judges for the district.

(b)(1) Bankruptcy judges may hear and determine all cases under title 11 and all core proceedings arising under title 11, or arising in a case under title 11, referred under subsection (a) of this section, and may enter appropriate orders and judgments, subject to review under section 158 of this title.

(2) Core proceedings include, but are not limited to—

(A) matters concerning the administration of the estate;

(B) allowance or disallowance of claims against the estate or exemptions from property of the estate, and estimation of claims or interest for the purposes of confirming a plan under chapter 11, 12 or 13 of title 11 but not the liquidation or estimation of contingent or unliquidated personal injury tort or wrongful death claims against the estate for purposes of distribution in a case under title 11;

(C) counterclaims by the estate against persons filing claims against the estate;

(D) orders in respect to obtaining credit;

(E) orders to turn over property of the estate;

(F) proceedings to determine, avoid, or recover preferences;

(G) motions to terminate, annul or modify the automatic stay;

(H) proceedings to determine, avoid, or recover fraudulent conveyances;

(I) determinations as to the dischargeability of particular debts;

(J) objections to discharges;

(K) determinations of the validity, extent, or priority of liens;

(L) confirmations of plans;

(M) orders approving the use or lease of property, including the use of cash collateral;

(N) orders approving the sale of property other than property resulting from claims brought by the estate against persons who have not filed claims against the estate; and

(O) other proceedings affecting the liquidation of the assets of the estate or the adjustment of the debtor-creditor or the equity security holder relationship, except personal injury tort or wrongful death claims.

(3) The bankruptcy judge shall determine, on the judge's own motion or on timely motion of a party, whether a proceeding is a core proceeding under this subsection or is a proceeding that is otherwise related to a case under title 11. A determination that a proceeding is not a core proceeding shall not be made solely on the basis that its resolution may be affected by State law.

(4) Non-core proceedings under section 157(b)(2)(B) of title 28, United States Code, shall not be subject to the mandatory abstention provisions of section 1334(c)(2).

(5) The district court shall order that personal injury tort and wrongful death claims shall be tried in the district court in which the bankruptcy case is pending, or in the district court in the district in which the claim arose, as determined by the district court in which the bankruptcy case is pending.

(c)(1) A bankruptcy judge may hear a proceeding that is not a core proceeding but that is otherwise related to a case under title 11. In such proceeding, the bankruptcy judge shall submit proposed findings of fact and conclusions of law to the district court, and any final order or judgment shall be entered by the district judge after considering the bankruptcy judge's proposed findings and conclusions and after reviewing de novo those matters to which any party has timely and specifically objected.

(2) Notwithstanding the provisions of paragraph (1) of this subsection, the district court, with the consent of all the parties to the proceeding, may refer a proceeding related to a case under title 11 to a bankruptcy judge to hear and determine and to enter appropriate orders and judgments, subject to review under section 158 of this title.

(d) The district court may withdraw, in whole or in part, any case or proceeding referred under this section, on its own motion or on timely motion of any party, for cause shown. The district court shall, on timely motion of a party, so withdraw a proceeding if the court determines that resolution of the proceeding requires consideration of both title 11 and other laws of the United States regulating organizations or activities affecting interstate commerce.

§ 158. Appeals.

(a) The district courts of the United States shall have jurisdiction to hear appeals from final judgments, orders, and decrees, and, with leave of the court, from interlocutory orders and decrees, of bankruptcy judges entered in cases and proceedings referred to the bankruptcy judges under section 157 of this title. An appeal under this subsection shall be taken only to the district court for the judicial district in which the bankruptcy judge is serving.

(b)(1) The judicial council of a circuit may establish a bankruptcy appellate panel, comprised of bankruptcy judges from districts within the circuit, to hear and determine, upon the consent of all the parties, appeals under subsection (a) of this section.

(2) No appeal may be referred to a panel under this subsection unless the district judges for the district, by majority vote, authorize such referral of appeals originating within the district.

(3) A panel established under this section shall consist of three bankruptcy judges, provided a bankruptcy judge may not hear an appeal originating within a district for which the judge is appointed or designated under section 152 of this title.

(c) An appeal under subsections (a) and (b) of this section shall be taken in the same manner as appeals in civil proceedings generally are taken to the courts of appeals from the district courts and in the time provided by Rule 8002 of the Bankruptcy Rules.

(d) The courts of appeals shall have jurisdiction of appeals from all final decisions, judgments, orders, and decrees entered under subsections (a) and (b) of this section. . . .

Chapter 7.—United States Claims Court

§ 171. Appointment and number of judges; character of court; designation of chief judge.

(a) The President shall appoint, by and with the advice and consent of the Senate, sixteen judges who shall constitute a court of record known as the United States Claims Court. The court is declared to be a court established under article I of the Constitution of the United States. . . .

§ 172. Tenure and salaries of judges.

(a) Each judge of the United States Claims Court shall be appointed for a term of fifteen years.

(b) Each judge shall receive a salary at an annual rate determined under section 225 of the Federal Salary Act of 1967 (2 U.S.C. 351–361), as adjusted by section 461 of this title.

§ 176. Removal from office.

(a) Removal of a judge of the United States Claims Court during the term for which he is appointed shall be only for incompetency, misconduct, neglect of duty, engaging in the practice of law, or physical or mental disability. Removal shall be by the United States Court of Appeals for the Federal Circuit, but removal may not occur unless a majority of all the judges of such court of appeals concur in the order of removal.

(b) Before any order of removal may be entered, a full specification of the charges shall be furnished to the judge involved, and such judge shall be accorded an opportunity to be heard on the charges. . . .

Chapter 11.—Court of International Trade

§ 251. Appointment and number of judges; offices.

(a) The President shall appoint, by and with the advice and consent of the Senate, nine judges who shall constitute a court of record to be known as the United States Court of International Trade. Not more than five of such judges shall be from the same political party. The court is a court established under article III of the Constitution of the United States.

(b) The President shall designate one of the judges of the Court of International Trade who is less than seventy years of age to serve as chief judge. The chief judge shall continue to serve as chief judge until he reaches the age of seventy years and another judge is designated as chief judge by the President. After the designation of another judge to serve as chief judge, the former chief judge may continue to serve as a judge of the court.

(c) The offices of the Court of International Trade shall be located in New York, New York.

Chapter 21.—General Provisions Applicable to Courts and Judges

§ 451. Definitions.

As used in this title:

The term "court of the United States" includes the Supreme Court of the United States, courts of appeals, district courts constituted by chapter 5 of this title, including the Court of International Trade and any court created by Act of Congress the judges of which are entitled to hold office during good behavior, and bankruptcy courts, the judges of which are entitled to hold office for a term of 14 years.

The terms "district court" and "district court of the United States" mean the courts constituted by chapter 5 of this title. . . .

Chapter 43.—United States Magistrates

§ 631. Appointment and tenure.

(a) The judges of each United States district court and the district court of the Virgin Islands shall appoint United States magistrates in such numbers and to serve at such locations within the judicial district as the conference may determine under this chapter. . . .

(b) No individual may be appointed or reappointed to serve as a magistrate under this chapter unless:

(1) He has been for at least five years a member in good standing of the bar of the highest court of a State, the District of Columbia, the Commonwealth of Puerto Rico, or the Virgin Islands . . . ,

except that an individual who does not meet the bar membership requirements of this paragraph may be appointed and serve as a part-time magistrate if the appointing court or courts and the conference find that no qualified individual who is a member of the bar is available to serve at a specific location;

(2) He is determined by the appointing district court or courts to be competent to perform the duties of the office; . . .

(4) He is not related by blood or marriage to a judge of the appointing court or courts at the time of his initial appointment; and

(5) He is selected pursuant to standards and procedures promulgated by the Judicial Conference of the United States. . . .

(d) Except as otherwise provided in sections 375 and 636(h) of this title, no individual may serve under this chapter after having attained the age of seventy years: *Provided, however,* That upon majority vote of all the judges of the appointing court or courts, . . . a magistrate who has attained the age of seventy years may continue to serve and may be reappointed under this chapter.

(e) The appointment of any individual as a full-time magistrate shall be for a term of eight years, and the appointment of any individual as a part-time magistrate shall be for a term of four years . . . .

(i) Removal of a magistrate during the term for which he is appointed shall be only for incompetency, misconduct, neglect of duty, or physical or mental disability, but a magistrate's office shall be terminated if the conference determines that the services performed by his office are no longer needed. Removal shall be by the judges of the district court for the judicial district in which the magistrate serves; where there is more than one judge of a district court, removal shall not occur unless a majority of all the judges of such court concur in the order of removal . . . .

§ 636. Jurisdiction, powers, and temporary assignment.

(a) Each United States magistrate serving under this chapter shall have within the territorial jurisdiction prescribed by his appointment—

(1) all powers and duties conferred or imposed upon United States commissioners by law or by the Rules of Criminal Procedure for the United States District Courts;

(2) the power to administer oaths and affirmations, issue orders pursuant to section 3142 of title 18 concerning release or detention of persons pending trial, and take acknowledgements, affidavits, and depositions; and

(3) the power to conduct trials under section 3401, title 18, United States Code, in conformity with and subject to the limitations of that section, and

(4) the power to enter a sentence for a misdemeanor or infraction with the consent of the parties.

(b)(1) Notwithstanding any provision of law to the contrary—

(A) a judge may designate a magistrate to hear and determine any pretrial matter pending before the court, except a motion for injunctive relief, for judgment on the pleadings, for summary judgment, to dismiss or quash an indictment or information made by the defendant, to suppress evidence in a criminal case, to dismiss or to permit maintenance of a class action, to dismiss for failure to state a claim upon which relief can be granted, and to involuntarily dismiss an action. A judge of the court may reconsider any pretrial matter under this subparagraph (A) where it has been shown that the magistrate's order is clearly erroneous or contrary to law.

(B) a judge may also designate a magistrate to conduct hearings, including evidentiary hearings, and to submit to a judge of the court proposed findings of fact and recommendations for the disposition, by a judge of the court, of any motion excepted in subparagraph (A), of applications for posttrial relief made by individuals convicted of criminal offenses and of prisoner petitions challenging conditions of confinement.

(C) the magistrate shall file his proposed findings and recommendations under subparagraph (B) with the court and a copy shall forthwith be mailed to all parties.

Within ten days after being served with a copy, any party may serve and file written objections to such proposed findings and recommendations as provided by rules of court. A judge of the court shall make a de novo determination of those portions of the report or specified proposed findings or recommendations to which objection is made. A judge of the court may accept, reject, or modify, in whole or in part, the findings or recommendations made by the magistrate. The judge may also receive further evidence or recommit the matter to the magistrate with instructions.

(2) A judge may designate a magistrate to serve as a special master pursuant to the applicable provisions of this title and the Federal Rules of Civil Procedure for the United States district courts. A judge may designate a magistrate to serve as a special master in any civil case, upon consent of the parties, without regard to the provisions of rule 53(b) of the Federal Rules of Civil Procedure for the United States district courts.

(3) A magistrate may be assigned such additional duties as are not inconsistent with the Constitution and laws of the United States.

(4) Each district court shall establish rules pursuant to which the magistrates shall discharge their duties.

(c) Notwithstanding any provision of law to the contrary—

(1) Upon the consent of the parties, a full-time United States magistrate or a part-time United States magistrate who serves as a full-time judicial officer may conduct any or all proceedings in a jury or nonjury civil matter and order the entry of judgment in the case, when specially designated to exercise such jurisdiction by the district court or courts he serves. Upon the consent of the parties, pursuant to their specific written request, any other part-time magistrate may exercise such jurisdiction, if such magistrate meets the bar membership requirements set forth in section 631(b)(1) and the chief judge of the district court certifies that a full-time magistrate is not reasonably available in accordance with guidelines established by the judicial council of the circuit. When there is more than one judge of a district court, designation under this paragraph shall be by the concurrence of a majority of all the judges of such district court, and when there is no such concurrence, then by the chief judge.

(2) If a magistrate is designated to exercise civil jurisdiction under paragraph (1) of this subsection, the clerk of court shall, at the time the action is filed, notify the parties of their right to consent to the exercise of such jurisdiction. The decision of the parties shall be communicated to the clerk of court. Thereafter, neither the district judge nor the magistrate shall attempt to persuade or induce any party to consent to reference of any civil matter to a magistrate. Rules of court for the reference of civil matters to magistrates shall include procedures to protect the voluntariness of the parties' consent.

(3) Upon entry of judgment in any case referred under paragraph (1) of this subsection, an aggrieved party may appeal directly to the appropriate United States court of appeals from the judgment of the magistrate in the same manner as an appeal from any other judgment of a district court. In this circumstance, the consent of the parties allows a magistrate designated to exercise civil jurisdiction under paragraph (1) of this subsection to direct the entry of a judgment of the district court in accordance with the Federal Rules of Civil Procedure. Nothing in this paragraph shall be construed as a limitation of any party's right to seek review by the Supreme Court of the United States.

(4) Notwithstanding the provisions of paragraph (3) of this subsection, at the time of reference to a magistrate, the parties may further consent to appeal on the record to a judge of the district court in the same manner as on an appeal from a judgment of the district court to a court of appeals. Wherever possible the local rules of the district court and the rules promulgated by the conference shall endeavor to make such appeal expeditious and inexpensive. The district court may affirm, reverse, modify, or remand the magistrate's judgment.

(5) Cases in the district courts under paragraph (4) of this subsection may be reviewed by the appropriate United States court of appeals upon petition for leave to appeal by a party stating specific objections to the judgment. Nothing in this paragraph shall be construed to be a limitation on any party's right to seek review by the Supreme Court of the United States.

(6) The court may, for good cause shown on its own motion, or under extraordinary circumstances shown by any party, vacate a reference of a civil matter to a magistrate under this subsection.

. . .

PART IV.—JURISDICTION AND VENUE

Chapter 81.—Supreme Court

§ 1251. Original jurisdiction.

(a) The Supreme Court shall have original and exclusive jurisdiction of all controversies between two or more States;

(b) The Supreme Court shall have original but not exclusive jurisdiction of:

(1) All actions or proceedings to which ambassadors, other public ministers, consuls, or vice consuls of foreign states are parties;

(2) All controversies between the United States and a State;

(3) All actions or proceedings by a State against the citizens of another State or against aliens.

§ 1253. Direct appeals from decisions of three-judge courts.

Except as otherwise provided by law, any party may appeal to the Supreme Court from an order granting or denying, after notice and hearing, an interlocutory or permanent injunction in any civil action, suit or proceeding required by any Act of Congress to be heard and determined by a district court of three judges.

§ 1254. Courts of appeals; certiorari; appeal; certified questions.

Cases in the courts of appeals may be reviewed by the Supreme Court by the following methods:

(1) By writ of certiorari granted upon the petition of any party to any civil or criminal case, before or after rendition of judgment or decree;

(2) By certification at any time by a court of appeals of any question of law in any civil or criminal case as to which instructions are desired, and upon such certification the Supreme Court may give binding instructions or require the entire record to be sent up for decision of the entire matter in controversy.

§ 1257. State courts; appeal; certiorari.

(a) Final judgments or decrees rendered by the highest court of a State in which a decision could be had, may be reviewed by the

Supreme Court by writ of certiorari, where the validity of a treaty or statute of the United States is drawn in question or where the validity of a State statute is drawn in question on the ground of its being repugnant to the Constitution, treaties or laws of the United States, or where any title, right, privilege or immunity is specially set up or claimed under the Constitution, treaties or statutes of, or commission held or authority exercised under, the United States.

(b) For the purposes of this section, the term "highest court of a State" includes the District of Columbia Court of Appeals.

§ 1258. Supreme Court of Puerto Rico; appeal; certiorari.

Final judgments or decrees rendered by the Supreme Court of the Commonwealth of Puerto Rico may be reviewed by the Supreme Court by writ of certiorari, where the validity of a treaty or statute of the United States is drawn in question or where the validity of a statute of the Commonwealth of Puerto Rico is drawn in question on the ground of its being repugnant to the Constitution, treaties, or laws of the United States, or where any title, right, privilege, or immunity is specially set up or claimed under the Constitution, treaties, or statutes of, or commission held or authority exercised under, the United States.

§ 1259. Court of Military Appeals; certiorari.

Decisions of the United States Court of Military Appeals may be reviewed by the Supreme Court by writ of certiorari in the following cases:

(1) Cases reviewed by the Court of Military Appeals under section 867(b)(1) of title 10.

(2) Cases certified to the Court of Military Appeals by the Judge Advocate General under section 867(b)(2) of title 10.

(3) Cases in which the Court of Military Appeals granted a petition for review under section 867(b)(3) of title 10.

(4) Cases, other than those described in paragraphs (1), (2), and (3) of this subsection, in which the Court of Military Appeals granted relief.

Chapter 83.—Courts of Appeals

§ 1291. Final decisions of district courts.

The courts of appeals (other than the United States Court of Appeals for the Federal Circuit) shall have jurisdiction of appeals from all final decisions of the district courts of the United States, the United States District Court for the District of the Canal Zone, the District Court of Guam, and the District Court of the Virgin Islands, except where a direct review may be had in the Supreme Court. The jurisdiction of the United States Court of Appeals for the Federal Circuit shall be limited to the jurisdiction described in sections 1292(c) and (d) and 1295 of this title.

Reviser's Note:

In addition to the jurisdiction conferred by this chapter, the courts of appeals also have appellate jurisdiction in proceedings under Title 11, Bankruptcy, and jurisdiction to review:

(1) Orders of the Secretary of the Treasury denying an application for, suspending, revoking, or annulling a basic permit under chapter 8 of title 27;

(2) Orders of the Interstate Commerce Commission, the Federal Communications Commission, the Civil Aeronautics Board, the Board of Governors of the Federal Reserve System, and the Federal Trade Commission, based on violations of the antitrust laws or unfair or deceptive acts, methods, or practices in commerce;

(3) Orders of the Secretary of the Army under sections 504, 505 and 516 of title 33, U.S.C., 1940 ed., Navigation and Navigable Waters;

(4) Orders of the Civil Aeronautics Board under chapter 9 of title 49, except orders as to foreign air carriers which are subject to the President's approval;

(5) Orders under chapter 1 of title 7, refusing to designate boards of trade as contract markets or suspending or revoking such designations, or excluding persons from trading in contract markets;

(6) Orders of the Federal Power Commission under chapter 12 of title 16;

(7) Orders of the Federal Security Administrator under section 371(e) of title 21, in a case of actual controversy as to the validity of any such order, by any person adversely affected thereby;

(8) Orders of the Federal Power Commission under chapter 15B of title 15;

(9) Final orders of the National Labor Relations Board;

(10) Cease and desist orders under section 193 of title 7;

(11) Orders of the Securities and Exchange Commission;

(12) Orders to cease and desist from violating section 1599 of title 7;

(13) Wage orders of the Administrator of the Wage and Hour Division of the Department of Labor under section 208 of title 29;

(14) Orders under sections 81r and 1641 of title 19, U.S.C., 1940 ed., Customs Duties.

The courts of appeals also have jurisdiction to enforce:

(1) Orders of the Interstate Commerce Commission, the Federal Communications Commission, the Civil Aeronautics Board, the Board of Governors of the Federal Reserve System, and the Federal Trade Commission, based on violations of the antitrust laws or unfair or deceptive acts, methods, or practices in commerce;

(2) Final orders of the National Labor Relations Board;

(3) Orders to cease and desist from violating section 1599 of title 7.

The Court of Appeals for the District of Columbia also has jurisdiction to review orders of the Post Office Department under section 576 of title 39 relating to discriminations in sending second-class publications by freight; Maritime Commission orders denying transfer to foreign registry of vessels under subsidy contract; sugar allotment orders; decisions of the Federal Communications Commission granting or refusing applications for construction permits for radio stations, or for radio station licenses, or for renewal or modification of radio station licenses, or suspending any radio operator's license.

§ 1292. Interlocutory decisions.

(a) Except as provided in subsections (c) and (d) of this section, the courts of appeals shall have jurisdiction of appeals from:

(1) Interlocutory orders of the district courts of the United States, the United States District Court for the District of the Canal Zone, the District Court of Guam, and the District Court of the Virgin Islands, or of the judges thereof, granting, continuing, modifying, refusing or dissolving injunctions, or refusing to dissolve or modify injunctions, except where a direct review may be had in the Supreme Court.

(2) Interlocutory orders appointing receivers, or refusing orders to wind up receiverships or to take steps to accomplish the purposes thereof, such as directing sales or other disposals of property;

(3) Interlocutory decrees of such district courts or the judges thereof determining the rights and liabilities of the parties to admiralty cases in which appeals from final decrees are allowed.

(b) When a district judge, in making in a civil action an order not otherwise appealable under this section, shall be of the opinion that such order involves a controlling question of law as to which there is substantial ground for difference of opinion and that an immediate appeal from the order may materially advance the ultimate termination of the litigation, he shall so state in writing in such order. The Court of Appeals may thereupon, in its discretion, permit an appeal to be taken from such order, if application is made to it within ten days after the entry of the order: *Provided, however,* That application for an appeal hereunder shall not stay proceedings in the district court unless the district judge or the Court of Appeals or a judge thereof shall so order.

(c) The United States Court of Appeals for the Federal Circuit shall have exclusive jurisdiction—

(1) of an appeal from an interlocutory order or decree described in subsection (a) of this section in any case over which the court would have jurisdiction of an appeal under section 1295 of this title; and

(2) of an appeal from a judgment in a civil action for patent infringement which would otherwise be appealable to the United States Court of Appeals for the Federal Circuit and is final except for an accounting.

(d)(1) When the chief judge of the Court of International Trade issues an order under the provisions of section 256(b) of this title, or when any judge of the Court of International Trade, in issuing any other interlocutory order, includes in the order a statement that a controlling question of law is involved with respect to which there is a substantial ground for difference of opinion and that an immediate appeal from that order may materially advance the ultimate termination of the litigation, the United States Court of Appeals for the Federal Circuit may, in its discretion, permit an appeal to be taken from such order, if application is made to that Court within ten days after the entry of such order.

(2) When any judge of the United States Claims Court, in issuing an interlocutory order, includes in the order a statement that a controlling question of law is involved with respect to which there is a substantial ground for difference of opinion and that an immediate appeal from that order may materially advance the ultimate termination of the litigation, the United States Court of Appeals for the Federal Circuit may, in its discretion, permit an appeal to be taken from such order, if application is made to that Court within ten days after the entry of such order.

(3) Neither the application for nor the granting of an appeal under this subsection shall stay proceedings in the Court of International Trade or in the Claims Court, as the case may be, unless a stay is ordered by a judge of the Court of International Trade or of the Claims Court or by the United States Court of Appeals for the Federal Circuit or a judge of that court.

§ 1294. Circuits in which decisions reviewable.

Except as provided in sections 1292(c), 1292(d), and 1295 of this title, appeals from reviewable decisions of the district, bankruptcy, and territorial courts shall be taken to the courts of appeals as follows:

(1) From a district court of the United States to the court of appeals for the circuit embracing the district;

(2) From the United States District Court for the District of the Canal Zone, to the Court of Appeals for the Fifth Circuit;

(3) From the District Court of the Virgin Islands, to the Court of Appeals for the Third Circuit;

(4) From the District Court of Guam, to the Court of Appeals for the Ninth Circuit.

§ 1295. Jurisdiction of the United States Court of Appeals for the Federal Circuit.

(a) The United States Court of Appeals for the Federal Circuit shall have exclusive jurisdiction—

(1) of an appeal from a final decision of a district court of the United States, the United States District Court for the District of the Canal Zone, the District Court of Guam, the District Court of the Virgin Islands, or the District Court for the Northern Mariana Islands, if the jurisdiction of that court was based, in whole or in part, on section 1338 of this title, except that a case involving a claim arising under any Act of Congress relating to copyrights or trademarks and no other claims under section 1338(a) shall be governed by sections 1291, 1292, and 1294 of this title;

(2) of an appeal from a final decision of a district court of the United States, the United States District Court for the District of the Canal Zone, the District Court of Guam, the District Court of the Virgin Islands, or the District Court for the Northern Mariana Islands, if the jurisdiction of that court was based, in whole or in part, on section 1346 of this title, except that jurisdiction of an appeal in a case brought in a district court under section 1346(a)(1), 1346(b), 1346(e), or 1346(f) of this title or under section 1346(a)(2) when the claim is founded upon an Act of Congress or a regulation of an executive department providing for internal revenue shall be governed by sections 1291, 1292, and 1294 of this title;

(3) of an appeal from a final decision of the United States Claims Court;

(4) of an appeal from a decision of—

(A) the Board of Appeals or the Board of Patent Interferences of the Patent and Trademark Office with respect to patent applications and interferences, at the instance of an applicant for a patent or any party to a patent interference, and any such appeal shall waive the right of such applicant or party to proceed under section 145 or 146 of title 35;

(B) the Commissioner of Patents and Trademarks or the Trademark Trial and Appeal Board with respect to applications for registration of marks and other proceedings as provided in section 21 of the Trademark Act of 1946 (15 U.S.C. 1071); or

(C) a district court to which a case was directed pursuant to section 145 or 146 of title 35;

(5) of an appeal from a final decision of the United States Court of International Trade;

(6) to review the final determinations of the United States International Trade Commission relating to unfair practices in import trade, made under section 337 of the Tariff Act of 1930 (19 U.S.C. 1337);

(7) to review, by appeal on questions of law only, findings of the Secretary of Commerce under headnote 6 to schedule 8, part 4, of the Tariff Schedules of the United States (relating to importation of instruments or apparatus);

(8) of an appeal under section 71 of the Plant Variety Protection Act (7 U.S.C. 2461);

(9) of an appeal from a final order or final decision of the Merit Systems Protection Board, pursuant to sections 7703(b)(1) and 7703(d) of title 5; and

(10) of an appeal from a final decision of an agency board of contract appeals pursuant to section 8(g)(1) of the Contract Disputes Act of 1978 (41 U.S.C. 607(g)(1)).

(b) The head of any executive department or agency may, with the approval of the Attorney General, refer to the Court of Appeals for the Federal Circuit for judicial review any final decision rendered by a board of contract appeals pursuant to the terms of any contract with the United States awarded by that department or agency which the head of such department or agency has concluded is not entitled to finality pursuant to the review standards specified in section 10(b) of the Contract Disputes Act of 1978 (41 U.S.C. 609(b)). The head of each executive department or agency shall make any referral under this section within one hundred and twenty days after the receipt of a copy of the final appeal decision.

(c) The Court of Appeals for the Federal Circuit shall review the matter referred in accordance with the standards specified in section 10(b) of the Contract Disputes Act of 1978. The court shall proceed with judicial review on the administrative record made before the board of contract appeals on matters so referred as in other cases pending in such court, shall determine the issue of finality of the appeal decision, and shall, if appropriate, render judgment thereon, or remand the matter to any administrative or executive body or official with such direction as it may deem proper and just.

Chapter 85.—District Courts; Jurisdiction

§ 1330. Actions against foreign states.

(a) The district courts shall have original jurisdiction without regard to amount in controversy of any nonjury civil action against a foreign state as defined in section 1603(a) of this title as to any claim for relief in personam with respect to which the foreign state is not entitled to immunity either under sections 1605–1607 of this title or under any applicable international agreement.

(b) Personal jurisdiction over a foreign state shall exist as to every claim for relief over which the district courts have jurisdiction under subsection (a) where service has been made under section 1608 of this title.

(c) For purposes of subsection (b), an appearance by a foreign state does not confer personal jurisdiction with respect to any claim for relief not arising out of any transaction or occurrence enumerated in sections 1605–1607 of this title.

§ 1331. Federal question.

The district courts shall have original jurisdiction of all civil actions arising under the Constitution, laws, or treaties of the United States.

§ 1332. Diversity of citizenship; amount in controversy; costs.

(a) The district courts shall have original jurisdiction of all civil actions where the matter in controversy exceeds the sum or value of $50,000, exclusive of interest and costs, and is between—

(1) citizens of different States;

(2) citizens of a State and citizens or subjects of a foreign state;

(3) citizens of different States and in which citizens or subjects of a foreign state are additional parties; and

(4) a foreign state, defined in section 1603(a) of this title, as plaintiff and citizens of a State or of different States. For the purposes of this section, section 1335, and section 1441, an alien admitted to the United States for permanent residence shall be deemed a citizen of the State in which such alien is domiciled.

(b) Except when express provision therefor is otherwise made in a statute of the United States, where the plaintiff who files the case originally in the Federal courts is finally adjudged to be entitled to recover less than the sum or value of $50,000, computed without regard to any setoff or counterclaim to which the defendant may be adjudged to be entitled, and exclusive of interest and costs, the district court may deny costs to the plaintiff and, in addition, may impose costs on the plaintiff.

(c) For the purposes of this section and section 1441 of this title—

(1) a corporation shall be deemed to be a citizen of any State by which it has been incorporated and of the State where it has its principal place of business, except that in any direct action against the insurer of a policy or contract of liability insurance, whether incorporated or unincorporated, to which action the insured is not joined as a party-defendant, such insurer shall be deemed a citizen of the State of which the insured is a citizen, as well as of any State by which the insurer has been incorporated and of the State where it has its principal place of business; and

(2) the legal representative of the estate of a decedent shall be deemed to be a citizen only of the same State as the decedent, and the legal representative of an infant or incompetent shall be deemed to be a citizen only of the same State as the infant or incompetent.

(d) The word "States", as used in this section, includes the Territories, the District of Columbia, and the Commonwealth of Puerto Rico.

§ 1333. Admiralty, maritime and prize cases.

The district courts shall have original jurisdiction, exclusive of the courts of the States, of:

(1) Any civil case of admiralty or maritime jurisdiction, saving to suitors in all cases all other remedies to which they are otherwise entitled.

(2) Any prize brought into the United States and all proceedings for the condemnation of property taken as prize.

§ 1334. Bankruptcy cases and proceedings.

(a) Except as provided in subsection (b) of this section, the district courts shall have original and exclusive jurisdiction of all cases under title 11.

(b) Notwithstanding any Act of Congress that confers exclusive jurisdiction on a court or courts other than the district courts, the district courts shall have original but not exclusive jurisdiction of all civil proceedings arising under title 11, or arising in or related to cases under title 11.

(c)(1) Nothing in this section prevents a district court in the interest of justice, or in the interest of comity with State courts or respect for State law, from abstaining from hearing a particular proceeding arising under title 11 or arising in or related to a case under title 11.

(2) Upon timely motion of a party in a proceeding based upon a State law claim or State law cause of action, related to a case under title 11 but not arising under title 11 or arising in a case under title 11, with respect to which an action could not have been commenced in a court of the United States absent jurisdiction under this section, the district court shall abstain from hearing such proceeding if an action is commenced, and can be timely adjudicated, in a State forum of appropriate jurisdiction. Any decision to abstain made under this subsection is not reviewable by appeal or otherwise. This subsection shall not be construed to limit the applicability of the stay provided for by section 362 of title 11, United States Code, as such section applies to an action affecting the property of the estate in bankruptcy.

(d) The district court in which a case under title 11 is commenced or is pending shall have exclusive jurisdiction of all of the property, wherever located, of the debtor as of the commencement of such case, and of property of the estate.

§ 1335. Interpleader.

(a) The district courts shall have original jurisdiction of any civil action of interpleader or in the nature of interpleader filed by any person, firm, or corporation, association, or society having in his or its custody or possession money or property of the value of $500 or more, or having issued a note, bond, certificate, policy of insurance, or other instrument of value or amount of $500 or more, or providing for the delivery or payment or the loan of money or property of such amount or value, or being under any obligation written or unwritten to the amount of $500 or more, if

(1) Two or more adverse claimants, of diverse citizenship as defined in section 1332 of this title, are claiming or may claim to be entitled to such money or property, or to any one or more of the benefits arising by virtue of any note, bond, certificate, policy or other instrument, or arising by virtue of any such obligation; and if (2) the plaintiff has deposited such money or property or has paid the amount of or the loan or other value of such instrument or the amount due under such obligation into the registry of the court, there to abide the judgment of the court, or has given bond payable to the clerk of the court in such amount and with such surety as the court or judge may deem proper, conditioned upon the compliance by the plaintiff with the future order or judgment of the court with respect to the subject matter of the controversy.

(b) Such an action may be entertained although the titles or claims of the conflicting claimants do not have a common origin, or are not identical, but are adverse to and independent of one another.

§ 1336. Interstate Commerce Commission's orders.

(a) Except as otherwise provided by Act of Congress, the district courts shall have jurisdiction of any civil action to enforce, enjoin, in whole or in part, any order of the Interstate Commerce Commission, and to enjoin or suspend, in whole or in part, any order of the Interstate Commerce Commission for the payment of money or the collection of fines, penalties, and forfeitures.

(b) When a district court or the United States Claims Court refers a question or issue to the Interstate Commerce Commission for determination, the court which referred the question or issue shall have exclusive jurisdiction of a civil action to enforce, enjoin, set aside, annul, or suspend, in whole or in part, any order of the Interstate Commerce Commission arising out of such referral.

(c) Any action brought under subsection (b) of this section shall be filed within 90 days from the date that the order of the Interstate Commerce Commission becomes final.

§ 1337. Commerce and antitrust regulations; amount in controversy, costs.

(a) The district courts shall have original jurisdiction of any civil action or proceeding arising under any Act of Congress regulating commerce or protecting trade and commerce against restraints and monopolies: *Provided, however,* That the district courts shall have original jurisdiction of an action brought under section 20(11) of part I of the Interstate Commerce Act (49 U.S.C. 20(11)) or section 219 of part II of such Act (49 U.S.C. 319), only if the matter in controversy for each receipt or bill of lading exceeds $10,000, exclusive of interest and costs.

(b) Except when express provision therefor is otherwise made in a statute of the United States, where a plaintiff who files the case under section 20(11) of part I of the Interstate Commerce Act (49 U.S.C. 20(11)) or section 219 of part II of such Act (49 U.S.C. 319), originally in the Federal courts is finally adjudged to be entitled to recover less than the sum or value of $10,000, computed without regard to any setoff or counterclaim to which the defendant may be adjudged to be entitled, and exclusive of any interest and costs, the district court may deny costs to the plaintiff and, in addition, may impose costs on the plaintiff.

(c) The district courts shall not have jurisdiction under this section of any matter within the exclusive jurisdiction of the Court of International Trade under chapter 95 of this title.

§ 1338. Patents, plant variety protection, copyrights, trade-marks, and unfair competition.

(a) The district courts shall have original jurisdiction of any civil action arising under any Act of Congress relating to patents, plant variety protection, copyrights and trade-marks. Such jurisdiction shall be exclusive of the courts of the states in patent, plant variety protection, and copyright cases.

(b) The district courts shall have original jurisdiction of any civil action asserting a claim of unfair competition when joined with a substantial and related claim under the copyright, patent, plant variety protection, or trade-mark laws.

§ 1339. Postal matters.

The district courts shall have original jurisdiction of any civil action arising under any Act of Congress relating to the postal service.

§ 1340. Internal revenue; customs duties.

The district courts shall have original jurisdiction of any civil action arising under any Act of Congress providing for internal revenue, or revenue from imports or tonnage except matters within the jurisdiction of the Court of International Trade.

§ 1341. Taxes by States.

The district courts shall not enjoin, suspend or restrain the assessment, levy or collection of any tax under State law where a plain, speedy and efficient remedy may be had in the courts of such State.

§ 1342. Rate orders of State agencies.

The district courts shall not enjoin, suspend or restrain the operation of, or compliance with, any order affecting rates chargeable by a public utility and made by a State administrative agency or a rate-making body of a State political subdivision, where:

(1) Jurisdiction is based solely on diversity of citizenship or repugnance of the order to the Federal Constitution; and,

(2) The order does not interfere with interstate commerce; and,

(3) The order has been made after reasonable notice and hearing; and

(4) A plain, speedy and efficient remedy may be had in the courts of such State.

§ 1343. Civil rights and elective franchise.

(a) The district courts shall have original jurisdiction of any civil action authorized by law to be commenced by any person:

(1) To recover damages for injury to his person or property, or because of the deprivation of any right or privilege of a citizen of the United States, by any act done in furtherance of any conspiracy mentioned in section 1985 of Title 42;

(2) To recover damages from any person who fails to prevent or to aid in preventing any wrongs mentioned in section 1985 of Title 42 which he had knowledge were about to occur and power to prevent;

(3) To redress the deprivation, under color of any State law, statute, ordinance, regulation, custom or usage, of any right, privilege or immunity secured by the Constitution of the United States or by any Act of Congress providing for equal rights of citizens or of all persons within the jurisdiction of the United States;

(4) To recover damages or to secure equitable or other relief under any Act of Congress providing for the protection of civil rights, including the right to vote.

(b) For purposes of this section—

(1) the District of Columbia shall be considered to be a State; and

(2) any Act of Congress applicable exclusively to the District of Columbia shall be considered to be a statute of the District of Columbia.

§ 1344. Election disputes.

The district courts shall have original jurisdiction of any civil action to recover possession of any office, except that of elector of President or Vice President, United States Senator, Representative in or delegate to Congress, or member of a state legislature, authorized by law to be commenced, wherein it appears that the sole question touching the title to office arises out of denial of the right to vote, to any citizen offering to vote, on account of race, color or previous condition of servitude.

The jurisdiction under this section shall extend only so far as to determine the rights of the parties to office by reason of the denial of the right, guaranteed by the Constitution of the United States and secured by any law, to enforce the right of citizens of the United States to vote in all the States.

§ 1345. United States as plaintiff.

Except as otherwise provided by Act of Congress, the district courts shall have original jurisdiction of all civil actions, suits or proceedings commenced by the United States, or by any agency or officer thereof expressly authorized to sue by Act of Congress.

§ 1346. United States as defendant.

(a) The district courts shall have original jurisdiction, concurrent with the United States Claims Court, of:

(1) Any civil action against the United States for the recovery of any internal-revenue tax alleged to have been erroneously or illegally assessed or collected, or any penalty claimed to have been collected without authority or any sum alleged to have been excessive or in any manner wrongfully collected under the internal-revenue laws;

(2) Any other civil action or claim against the United States, not exceeding $10,000 in amount, founded either upon the Constitution, or any Act of Congress, or any regulation of an executive department, or upon any express or implied contract with the United States, or for liquidated or unliquidated damages in cases not sounding in tort, except that the district courts shall not have jurisdiction of any civil action or claim against the United States founded upon any express or implied contract with the United States or for liquidated or unliquidated damages in cases not sounding in tort which are subject to sections 8(g)(1) and 10(a)(1) of the Contract Disputes Act of 1978. . . .

(b) Subject to the provisions of chapter 171 of this title, the district courts, together with the United States District Court for the District of the Canal Zone and the District Court of the Virgin Islands, shall have exclusive jurisdiction of civil actions on claims against the United States, for money damages, accruing on and after January 1, 1945, for injury or loss of property, or personal injury or death caused by the negligent or wrongful act or omission of any employee of the Government while acting within the scope of his office or employment, under circumstances where the United States, if a private person, would be liable to the claimant in accordance with the law of the place where the act or omission occurred.

(c) The jurisdiction conferred by this section includes jurisdiction of any set-off, counterclaim, or other claim or demand whatever on the part of the United States against any plaintiff commencing an action under this section.

(d) The district courts shall not have jurisdiction under this section of any civil action or claim for a pension.

(e) The district courts shall have original jurisdiction of any civil action against the United States provided in section 7426 or section 7428 (in the case of the United States district court for the District of Columbia) or section 7429 of the Internal Revenue Code of 1954.

(f) The district courts shall have exclusive original jurisdiction of civil actions under section 2409a to quiet title to an estate or interest in real property in which an interest is claimed by the United States.

§ 1347. Partition action where United States is joint tenant.

The district courts shall have original jurisdiction of any civil action commenced by any tenant in common or joint tenant for the partition of lands where the United States is one of the tenants in common or joint tenants.

§ 1348. Banking association as party.

The district courts shall have original jurisdiction of any civil action commenced by the United States, or by direction of any officer thereof, against any national banking association, any civil action to wind up the affairs of any such association, and any action by a banking association established in the district for which the court is held, under chapter 2 of Title 12, to enjoin the Comptroller of the Currency, or any receiver acting under his direction, as provided by such chapter.

All national banking associations shall, for the purposes of all other actions by or against them, be deemed citizens of the States in which they are respectively located.

§ 1349. Corporation organized under federal law as party.

The district courts shall not have jurisdiction of any civil action by or against any corporation upon the ground that it was incorporated by or under an Act of Congress, unless the United States is the owner of more than one-half of its capital stock.

§ 1350. Alien's action for tort.

The district courts shall have original jurisdiction of any civil action by an alien for a tort only, committed in violation of the law of nations or a treaty of the United States.

§ 1351. Consuls, vice consuls, and members of a diplomatic mission as defendant.

The district courts shall have original jurisdiction, exclusive of the courts of the States, of all civil actions and proceedings against—

(1) consuls or vice consuls of foreign states; or

(2) members of a mission or members of their families (as such terms are defined in section 2 of the Diplomatic Relations Act).

§ 1352. Bonds executed under federal law.

The district courts shall have original jurisdiction, concurrent with State courts, of any action on a bond executed under any law of the United States, except matters within the jurisdiction of the Court of International Trade under section 1582 of this title.

§ 1353. Indian allotments.

The district courts shall have original jurisdiction of any civil action involving the right of any person, in whole or in part of Indian blood or descent, to any allotment of land under any Act of Congress or treaty.

The judgment in favor of any claimant to an allotment of land shall have the same effect, when properly certified to the Secretary of the Interior, as if such allotment had been allowed and approved by him; but this provision shall not apply to any lands held on or before December 21, 1911, by either of the Five Civilized Tribes, the Osage Nation of Indians, nor to any of the lands within the Quapaw Indian Agency.

§ 1354. Land grants from different states.

The district courts shall have original jurisdiction of actions between citizens of the same state claiming lands under grants from different states.

§ 1355. Fine, penalty or forfeiture.

The district courts shall have original jurisdiction, exclusive of the courts of the States, of any action or proceeding for the recovery or enforcement of any fine, penalty, or forfeiture, pecuniary or otherwise, incurred under any Act of Congress, except matters within the jurisdiction of the Court of International Trade under section 1582 of this title.

§ 1356. Seizures not within admiralty and maritime jurisdiction.

The district courts shall have original jurisdiction, exclusive of the courts of the States, of any seizure under any law of the United States on land or upon waters not within admiralty and maritime jurisdiction, except matters within the jurisdiction of the Court of International Trade under section 1582 of this title.

§ 1357. Injuries under Federal laws.

The district courts shall have original jurisdiction of any civil action commenced by any person to recover damages for any injury to his person or property on account of any act done by him, under any Act of Congress, for the protection or collection of any of the revenues, or to enforce the right of citizens of the United States to vote in any State.

§ 1358. Eminent domain.

The district courts shall have original jurisdiction of all proceedings to condemn real estate for the use of the United States or its departments or agencies.

§ 1359. Parties collusively joined or made.

A district court shall not have jurisdiction of a civil action in which any party, by assignment or otherwise, has been improperly or collusively made or joined to invoke the jurisdiction of such court.

§ 1360. State civil jurisdiction in actions to which Indians are parties.

(a) Each of the States or Territories listed in the following table shall have jurisdiction over civil causes of action between Indians or to which Indians are parties which arise in the area of Indian country listed opposite the name of the State or Territory to the same extent that such State or Territory has jurisdiction over other civil causes of action, and those civil laws of such State or Territory that are of general application to private persons or private property shall have the same force and effect within such Indian country as they have elsewhere within the State or Territory:

State or Territory of	*Indian country affected*
Alaska	All Indian country within the State.
California	All Indian country within the State.
Minnesota	All Indian country within the State, except the Red Lake Reservation.
Nebraska	All Indian country within the State.
Oregon	All Indian country within the State, except the Warm Springs Reservation.
Wisconsin	All Indian country within the State.

(b) Nothing in this section shall authorize the alienation, encumbrance, or taxation of any real or personal property, including water rights, belonging to any Indian or any Indian tribe, band, or community that is held in trust by the United States or is subject to a restriction against alienation imposed by the United States; or shall authorize regulation of the use of such property in a manner inconsistent with any Federal treaty, agreement, or statute or with any regulation made pursuant thereto; or shall confer jurisdiction upon the State to adjudicate, in probate proceedings or otherwise, the ownership or right to possession of such property or any interest therein.

(c) Any tribal ordinance or custom heretofore or hereafter adopted by an Indian tribe, band, or community in the exercise of any authority which it may possess shall, if not inconsistent with any applicable civil law of the State, be given full force and effect in the determination of civil causes of action pursuant to this section.

§ 1361. Action to compel an officer of the United States to perform his duty.

The district courts shall have original jurisdiction of any action in the nature of mandamus to compel an officer or employee of the United States or any agency thereof to perform a duty owed to the plaintiff.

§ 1362. Indian Tribes.

The district courts shall have original jurisdiction of all civil actions, brought by any Indian tribe or band with a governing body duly recognized by the Secretary of the Interior, wherein the matter in controversy arises under the Constitution, laws, or treaties of the United States.

§ 1363. Jurors' employment rights.

The district courts shall have original jurisdiction of any civil action brought for the protection of jurors' employment under section 1875 of this title.

§ 1364. Direct actions against insurers of members of diplomatic missions and their families.

(a) The district courts shall have original and exclusive jurisdiction, without regard to the amount in controversy, of any civil action commenced by any person against an insurer who by contract has insured an individual, who is a member of a mission (as defined in the Vienna Convention on Diplomatic Relations) or a member of the family of such a member of a mission, or an individual described in section 19 of the Convention on Privileges and Immunities of the United Nations of February 13, 1946, against liability for personal injury, death, or damage to property.

(b) Any direct action brought against an insurer under subsection (a) shall be tried without a jury, but shall not be subject to the defense that the insured is immune from suit, that the insured is an indispensable party, or in the absence of fraud or collusion, that the insured has violated a term of the contract, unless the contract was cancelled before the claim arose.

§ 1365. Senate actions.

(a) The United States District Court for the District of Columbia shall have original jurisdiction, without regard to the amount in controversy, over any civil action brought by the Senate or any authorized committee or subcommittee of the Senate to enforce, to secure a declaratory judgment concerning the validity of, or to prevent a threatened refusal or failure to comply with, any subpena or order issued by the Senate or committee or subcommittee of the Senate to any entity acting or purporting to act under color or authority of State law or to any natural person to secure the production of documents or other materials of any kind or the answering of any deposition or interrogatory or to secure testimony or any combination thereof. This section shall not apply to an action to enforce, to secure a declaratory judgment concerning the validity of, or to prevent a threatened refusal to comply with, any subpena or order issued to an officer or employee of the Federal Government acting within his official capacity.

(b) Upon application by the Senate or any authorized committee or subcommittee of the Senate, the district court shall issue an order to an entity or person refusing, or failing to comply with, or threatening to refuse or not to comply with, a subpena or order of the Senate or committee or subcommittee of the Senate requiring such entity or person to comply forthwith. Any refusal or failure to obey a lawful order of the district court issued pursuant to this section may be held by such court to be a contempt thereof. A contempt proceeding shall be commenced by an order to show cause before the court why the entity or person refusing or failing to obey the court order should not be held in contempt of court. Such contempt proceeding shall be tried by the court and shall be summary in manner. The purpose of sanctions imposed as a result of such contempt proceeding shall be to compel obedience to the order of the court. Process in any such action or contempt proceeding may be served in any judicial district wherein the entity or party refusing, or failing to comply, or threatening to refuse or not to comply, resides, transacts business, or may be found, and subpenas for witnesses who are required to attend such proceeding may run into any other district. Nothing in this section shall confer upon such court jurisdiction to affect by injunction or otherwise the issuance or effect of any subpena or order of the Senate or any committee or subcommittee of the Senate or to review, modify, suspend, terminate, or set aside any such subpena or order. An action, contempt proceeding, or sanction brought or imposed pursuant to this section shall not abate upon adjournment sine die by the Senate at the end of a Congress if the Senate or the committee or subcommittee of the Senate which issued the subpena or order certifies to the court that it maintains its interest in securing the documents, answers, or testimony during such adjournment.

(c) In any civil action or contempt proceeding brought pursuant to this section, the court shall assign the action or proceeding for hearing at the earliest practicable date and cause the action or proceeding in every way to be expedited. Any appeal or petition for review from any order or judgment in such action or proceeding shall be expedited in the same manner.

(d) The Senate or any committee or subcommittee of the Senate commencing and prosecuting a civil action or contempt proceeding under this section may be represented in such action by such attorneys as the Senate may designate.

(e) A civil action commenced or prosecuted under this section, may not be authorized pursuant to the Standing Order of the Senate "authorizing suits by Senate Committees" (S. Jour. 572, May 28, 1928).

(f) For the purposes of this section the term "committee" includes standing, select, or special committees of the Senate established by law or resolution.

§ 1366. Construction of references to laws of the United States or Acts of Congress.

For the purposes of this chapter, references to laws of the United States or Acts of Congress do not include laws applicable exclusively to the District of Columbia.

Chapter 87.—District Courts; Venue

§ 1391. Venue generally.

(a) A civil action wherein jurisdiction is founded only on diversity of citizenship may, except as otherwise provided by law, be brought only in the judicial district where all plaintiffs or all defendants reside, or in which the claim arose.

(b) A civil action wherein jurisdiction is not founded solely on diversity of citizenship may be brought only in the judicial district where all defendants reside, or in which the claim arose, except as otherwise provided by law.

(c) For purposes of venue under this chapter, a defendant that is a corporation shall be deemed to reside in any judicial district in which it is subject to personal jurisdiction at the time the action is commenced. In a State which has more than one judicial district and in which a defendant that is a corporation is subject to personal jurisdiction at the time an action is commenced, such corporation shall be deemed to reside in any district in that State within which its contacts would be sufficient to subject it to personal jurisdiction if that district were a separate State, and, if there is no such district, the corporation shall be deemed to reside in the district within which it has the most significant contacts.

(d) An alien may be sued in any district.

(e) A civil action in which each defendant is an officer or employee of the United States or any agency thereof acting in his official capacity or under color of legal authority, or an agency of the United States, may, except as otherwise provided by law, be brought in any judicial district in which: (1) a defendant in the action resides, or (2) the cause of action arose, or (3) any real property involved in the action is situated, or (4) the plaintiff resides if no real property is involved in the action. Additional persons may be joined as parties to any such action in accordance with the Federal Rules of Civil Procedure and with such other venue requirements as would be applicable if the United States or one of its officers, employees, or agencies were not a party.

The summons and complaint in such an action shall be served as provided by the Federal Rules of Civil Procedure except that the delivery of the summons and complaint to the officer or agency as required by the rules may be made by certified mail beyond the territorial limits of the district in which the action is brought.

(f) A civil action against a foreign state as defined in section 1603(a) of this title may be brought—

(1) in any judicial district in which a substantial part of the events or omissions giving rise to the claim occurred, or a substantial part of property that is the subject of the action is situated;

(2) in any judicial district in which the vessel or cargo of a foreign state is situated, if the claim is asserted under section 1605(b) of this title;

(3) in any judicial district in which the agency or instrumentality is licensed to do business or is doing business, if the action is brought against an agency or instrumentality of a foreign state as defined in section 1603(b) of this title; or

(4) in the United States District Court for the District of Columbia if the action is brought against a foreign state or political subdivision thereof.

§ 1392. Defendants or property in different districts in same State.

(a) Any civil action, not of a local nature, against defendants residing in different districts in the same State, may be brought in any of such districts.

(b) Any civil action, of a local nature, involving property located in different districts in the same State, may be brought in any of such districts.

§ 1393. Divisions; single defendant; defendants in different divisions.

(a) Except as otherwise provided, any civil action not of a local nature, against a single defendant in a district containing more than one division must be brought in the division where he resides.

(b) Any such action, against defendants residing in different divisions of the same district or different districts in the same State, may be brought in any of such divisions.

§ 1394. Banking association's action against Comptroller of Currency.

Any civil action by a national banking association to enjoin the Comptroller of the Currency, under the provisions of any Act of Congress relating to such associations, may be prosecuted in the judicial district where such association is located.

§ 1395. Fine, penalty or forfeiture.

(a) A civil proceeding for the recovery of a pecuniary fine, penalty or forfeiture may be prosecuted in the district where it accrues or the defendant is found.

(b) A civil proceeding for the forfeiture of property may be prosecuted in any district where such property is found.

(c) A civil proceeding for the forfeiture of property seized outside any judicial district may be prosecuted in any district into which the property is brought.

(d) A proceeding in admiralty for the enforcement of fines, penalties and forfeitures against a vessel may be brought in any district in which the vessel is arrested.

(e) Any proceeding for the forfeiture of a vessel or cargo entering a port of entry closed by the President in pursuance of law, or of goods and chattels coming from a State or section declared by proclamation of the President to be in insurrection, or of any vessel or vehicle conveying persons or property to or from such State or section or belonging in whole or in part to a resident thereof, may be prosecuted in any district into which the property is taken and in which the proceeding is instituted.

§ 1396. Internal revenue taxes.

Any civil action for the collection of internal revenue taxes may be brought in the district where the liability for such tax accrues, in the district of the taxpayer's residence, or in the district where the return was filed.

§ 1397. Interpleader.

Any civil action of interpleader or in the nature of interpleader under section 1335 of this title may be brought in the judicial district in which one or more of the claimants reside.

§ 1398. Interstate Commerce Commission's orders.

(a) Except as otherwise provided by law, a civil action brought under section 1336(a) of this title shall be brought only in a judicial district in which any of the parties bringing the action resides or has its principal office.

(b) A civil action to enforce, enjoin, set aside, annul, or suspend, in whole or in part, an order of the Interstate Commerce Commission made pursuant to the referral of a question or issue by a district court or by the United States Claims Court, shall be brought only in the court which referred the question or issue.

§ 1399. Partition action involving United States.

Any civil action by any tenant in common or joint tenant for the partition of lands, where the United States is one of the tenants in common or joint tenants, may be brought only in the judicial district where such lands are located or, if located in different districts in the same State, in any of such districts.

§ 1400. Patents and copyrights.

(a) Civil actions, suits, or proceedings arising under any Act of Congress relating to copyrights may be instituted in the district in which the defendant or his agent resides or may be found.

(b) Any civil action for patent infringement may be brought in the judicial district where the defendant resides, or where the defendant has committed acts of infringement and has a regular and established place of business.

§ 1401. Stockholder's derivative action.

Any civil action by a stockholder on behalf of his corporation may be prosecuted in any judicial district where the corporation might have sued the same defendants.

§ 1402. United States as defendant.

(a) Any civil action in a district court against the United States under subsection (a) of section 1346 of this title may be prosecuted only:

(1) Except as provided in paragraph (2), in the judicial district where the plaintiff resides;

(2) In the case of a civil action by a corporation under paragraph (1) of subsection (a) of section 1346, in the judicial district in which is located the principal place of business or principal office or agency of the corporation; or if it has no principal place of business or principal office or agency in any judicial district (A) in the judicial district in which is located the office to which was made the return of the tax in respect of which the claim is made, or (B) if no return was made, in the judicial district in which lies the District of Columbia. Notwithstanding the foregoing provisions of this paragraph a district court, for the convenience of the parties and witnesses, in the interest of justice, may transfer any such action to any other district or division.

(b) Any civil action on a tort claim against the United States under subsection (b) of section 1346 of this title may be prosecuted only in the judicial district where the plaintiff resides or wherein the act or omission complained of occurred.

(c) Any civil action against the United States under subsection (e) of section 1346 of this title may be prosecuted only in the judicial district where the property is situated at the time of levy, or if no levy is made, in the judicial district in which the event occurred which gave rise to the cause of action.

(d) Any civil action under section 2409a to quiet title to an estate or interest in real property in which an interest is claimed by the United States shall be brought in the district court of the district where the property is located or, if located in different districts, in any of such districts.

§ 1403. Eminent domain.

Proceedings to condemn real estate for the use of the United States or its departments or agencies shall be brought in the district court of the district where the land is located or, if located in different districts in the same State, in any of such districts.

§ 1404. Change of venue.

(a) For the convenience of parties and witnesses, in the interest of justice, a district court may transfer any civil action to any other district or division where it might have been brought.

(b) Upon motion, consent or stipulation of all parties, any action, suit or proceeding of a civil nature or any motion or hearing thereof, may be transferred, in the discretion of the court, from the division in which pending to any other division in the same district. Transfer of proceedings in rem brought by or on behalf of the United States may be transferred under this section without the consent of the United States where all other parties request transfer.

(c) A district court may order any civil action to be tried at any place within the division in which it is pending.

(d) As used in this section, "district court" includes the United States District Court for the District of the Canal Zone; and "district" includes the territorial jurisdiction of that court.

§ 1405. Creation or alteration of district or division.

Actions or proceedings pending at the time of the creation of a new district or division or transfer of a county or territory from one division or district to another may be tried in the district or division as it existed at the institution of the action or proceeding, or in the district or division so created or to which the county or territory is so transferred as the parties shall agree or the court direct.

§ 1406. Cure or waiver of defects.

(a) The district court of a district in which is filed a case laying venue in the wrong division or district shall dismiss, or if it be in the interest of justice, transfer such case to any district or division in which it could have been brought.

(b) Nothing in this chapter shall impair the jurisdiction of a district court of any matter involving a party who does not interpose timely and sufficient objection to the venue.

(c) As used in this section, "district court" includes the United States District Court for the District of the Canal Zone; and "district" includes the territorial jurisdiction of that court.

§ 1407. Multidistrict litigation.

(a) When civil actions involving one or more common questions of fact are pending in different districts, such actions may be transferred to any district for coordinated or consolidated pretrial proceedings. Such transfers shall be made by the judicial panel on multidistrict litigation authorized by this section upon its determination that transfers for such proceedings will be for the convenience of parties and witnesses and will promote the just and efficient conduct of such actions. Each action so transferred shall be remanded by the panel at or before the conclusion of such pretrial proceedings to the district from which it was transferred unless it shall have been previously terminated: *Provided, however,* That the panel may separate any claim, cross-claim, counter-claim, or third-party claim and remand any of such claims before the remainder of the action is remanded.

(b) Such coordinated or consolidated pretrial proceedings shall be conducted by a judge or judges to whom such actions are assigned by the judicial panel on multidistrict litigation. For this purpose, upon request of the panel, a circuit judge or a district judge may be designated and assigned temporarily for service in the transferee district by the Chief Justice of the United States or the chief judge of the circuit, as may be required, in accordance with the provisions of chapter 13 of this title. With the consent of the transferee district court, such actions may be assigned by the panel to a judge or judges of such district. The judge or judges to whom such actions are assigned, the members of the judicial panel on multidistrict litigation, and other circuit and district judges designated when needed by the panel may exercise the powers of a district judge in any district for the purpose of conducting pretrial depositions in such coordinated or consolidated pretrial proceedings.

(c) Proceedings for the transfer of an action under this section may be initiated by—

(i) the judicial panel on multidistrict litigation upon its own initiative, or

(ii) motion filed with the panel by a party in any action in which transfer for coordinated or consolidated pretrial proceedings under this section may be appropriate. A copy of such motion shall be filed in the district court in which the moving party's action is pending.

The panel shall give notice to the parties in all actions in which transfers for coordinated or consolidated pretrial proceedings are contemplated, and such notice shall specify the time and place of any hearing to determine whether such transfer shall be made. Orders of the panel to set a hearing and other orders of the panel issued prior to the order either directing or denying transfer shall be filed in the office of the clerk of the district court in which a transfer hearing is to be or has been held. The panel's order of transfer shall be based upon a record of such hearing at which material evidence may be offered by any party to an action pending in any district that would be affected by the proceedings under this section, and shall be supported by findings of fact and conclusions of law based upon such record. Orders of transfer and such other orders as the panel may make thereafter shall be filed in the office of the clerk of the district court of the transferee district and shall be effective when thus filed. The clerk of the transferee district court shall forthwith transmit a certified copy of the panel's order to transfer to the clerk of the district court from which the action is being transferred. An order denying transfer shall be filed in each district wherein there is a case pending in which the motion for transfer has been made.

(d) The judicial panel on multidistrict litigation shall consist of seven circuit and district judges designated from time to time by the Chief Justice of the United States, no two of whom shall be from the same circuit. The concurrence of four members shall be necessary to any action by the panel.

(e) No proceedings for review of any order of the panel may be permitted except by extraordinary writ pursuant to the provisions of title 28, section 1651, United States Code. Petitions for an extraordinary writ to review an order of the panel to set a transfer hearing and other orders of the panel issued prior to the order either directing or denying transfer shall be filed only in the court of appeals having jurisdiction over the district in which a hearing is to be or has been held. Petitions for an extraordinary writ to review an order to transfer or orders subsequent to transfer shall be filed only in the court of appeals having jurisdiction over the transferee district. There shall be no appeal or review of an order of the panel denying a motion to transfer for consolidated or coordinated proceedings.

(f) The panel may prescribe rules for the conduct of its business not inconsistent with Acts of Congress and the Federal Rules of Civil Procedure.

(g) Nothing in this section shall apply to any action in which the United States is a complainant arising under the antitrust laws. "Antitrust laws" as used herein include those acts referred to in the Act of October 15, 1914, as amended (38 Stat. 730; 15 U.S.C. 12), and also include the Act of June 19, 1936 (49 Stat. 1526; 15 U.S.C. 13, 13a, and 13b) and the Act of September 26, 1914, as added March 21, 1938 (52 Stat. 116, 117; 15 U.S.C. 56); but shall not include section 4A of the Act of October 15, 1914, as added July 7, 1955 (69 Stat. 282; 15 U.S.C. 15a).

(h) Notwithstanding the provisions of section 1404 or subsection (f) of this section, the judicial panel on multidistrict litigation may consolidate and transfer with or without the consent of the parties, for both pretrial purposes and for trial, any action brought under section 4C of the Clayton Act.

§ 1408. Venue of cases under title 11.

Except as provided in section 1410 of this title, a case under title 11 may be commenced in the district court for the district—

(1) in which the domicile, residence, principal place of business in the United States, or principal assets in the United States, of the person or entity that is the subject of such case have been located for the one hundred and eighty days immediately preceding such commencement, or for a longer portion of such one-hundred-and-eighty-day period than the domicile, residence, or principal place of business, in the United States, or principal assets in the United States, of such person were located in any other district; or

(2) in which there is pending a case under title 11 concerning such person's affiliate, general partner, or partnership.

§ 1409. Venue of proceedings arising under title 11 or arising in or related to cases under title 11.

(a) Except as otherwise provided in subsections (b) and (d), a proceeding arising under title 11 or arising in or related to a case under title 11 may be commenced in the district court in which such case is pending.

(b) Except as provided in subsection (d) of this section, a trustee in a case under title 11 may commence a proceeding arising in or related to such case to recover a money judgment of or property worth less than $1,000 or a consumer debt of less than $5,000 only in the district court for the district in which the defendant resides.

(c) Except as provided in subsection (b) of this section, a trustee in a case under title 11 may commence a proceeding arising in or related to such case as statutory successor to the debtor or creditors under section 541 or 544(b) of title 11 in the district court for the district where the State or Federal court sits in which, under applicable nonbankruptcy venue provisions, the debtor or creditors, as the case may be, may have commenced an action on which such proceeding is based if the case under title 11 had not been commenced.

(d) A trustee may commence a proceeding arising under title 11 or arising in or related to a case under title 11 based on a claim arising after the commencement of such case from the operation of the business of the debtor only in the district court for the district where a State or Federal court sits in which, under applicable nonbankruptcy venue provisions, an action on such claim may have been brought.

(e) A proceeding arising under title 11 or arising in or related to a case under title 11, based on a claim arising after the commencement of such case from the operation of the business of the debtor, may be commenced against the representative of the estate in such case in the district court for the district where the State or Federal court sits in which the party commencing such proceeding may, under applicable nonbankruptcy venue provisions, have brought an action on such claim, or in the district court in which such case is pending.

§ 1412. Change of venue.

A district court may transfer a case or proceeding under title 11 to a district court for another district, in the interest of justice or for the convenience of the parties.

Chapter 89.—District Courts; Removal of Cases from State Courts

§ 1441. Actions removable generally.

(a) Except as otherwise expressly provided by Act of Congress, any civil action brought in a State court of which the district courts of the United States have original jurisdiction, may be removed by the defendant or the defendants, to the district court of the United States for the district and division embracing the place where such action is pending. For purposes of removal under this chapter, the citizenship of defendants sued under fictitious names shall be disregarded.

(b) Any civil action of which the district courts have original jurisdiction founded on a claim or right arising under the Constitution, treaties or laws of the United States shall be removable without regard to the citizenship or residence of the parties. Any other such actions shall be removable only if none of the parties in interest properly joined and served as defendants is a citizen of the State in which such action is brought.

(c) Whenever a separate and independent claim or cause of action, which would be removable if sued upon alone, is joined with one or more otherwise non-removable claims or causes of action, the entire case may be removed and the district court may determine all issues therein, or, in its discretion, may remand all matters not otherwise within its original jurisdiction.

(d) Any civil action brought in a State court against a foreign state as defined in section 1603(a) of this title may be removed by the foreign state to the district court of the United States for the district and division embracing the place where such action is pending. Upon removal the action shall be tried by the court without jury. Where removal is based upon this subsection, the time limitations of section 1446(b) of this chapter may be enlarged at any time for cause shown.

(e) The court to which such civil action is removed is not precluded from hearing and determining any claim in such civil action because the State court from which such civil action is removed did not have jurisdiction over that claim.

§ 1442. Federal officers sued or prosecuted.

(a) A civil action or criminal prosecution commenced in a State court against any of the following persons may be removed by them to the district court of the United States for the district and division embracing the place wherein it is pending:

(1) Any officer of the United States or any agency thereof, or person acting under him, for any act under color of such office or on account of any right, title or authority claimed under any Act of Congress for the apprehension or punishment of criminals or the collection of the revenue.

(2) A property holder whose title is derived from any such officer, where such action or prosecution affects the validity of any law of the United States.

(3) Any officer of the courts of the United States, for any act under color of office or in the performance of his duties;

(4) Any officer of either House of Congress, for any act in the discharge of his official duty under an order of such House.

(b) A personal action commenced in any State court by an alien against any citizen of a State who is, or at the time the alleged action accrued was, a civil officer of the United States and is a nonresident of such State, wherein jurisdiction is obtained by the State court by personal service of process, may be removed by the defendant to the district court of the United States for the district and division in which the defendant was served with process.

§ 1442a. Members of armed forces sued or prosecuted.

A civil or criminal prosecution in a court of a State of the United States against a member of the armed forces of the United States on account of an act done under color of his office or status, or in respect to which he claims any right, title, or authority under a law of the United States respecting the armed forces thereof, or under the law of war, may at any time before the trial or final hearing thereof be removed for trial into the district court of the United States for the district where it is pending in the manner prescribed by law, and it shall thereupon be entered on the docket of the district court, which shall proceed as if the cause had been originally commenced therein and shall have full power to hear and determine the cause.

§ 1443. Civil rights cases.

Any of the following civil actions or criminal prosecutions, commenced in a State court may be removed by the defendant to the district court of the United States for the district and division embracing the place wherein it is pending:

(1) Against any person who is denied or cannot enforce in the courts of such State a right under any law providing for the equal civil rights of citizens of the United States, or of all persons within the jurisdiction thereof;

(2) For any act under color of authority derived from any law providing for equal rights, or for refusing to do any act on the ground that it would be inconsistent with such law.

§ 1444. Foreclosure action against United States.

Any action brought under section 2410 of this title against the United States in any State court may be removed by the United States to the district court of the United States for the district and division in which the action is pending.

§ 1445. Nonremovable actions.

(a) A civil action in any State court against a railroad or its receivers or trustees, arising under sections 51–60 of Title 45, may not be removed to any district court of the United States.

(b) A civil action in any State court against a common carrier or its receivers or trustees to recover damages for delay, loss, or injury of shipments, arising under section 11707 of Title 49, may not be removed to any district court of the United States unless the matter in controversy exceeds $10,000 exclusive of interest and costs.

(c) A civil action in any State court arising under the workmen's compensation laws of the State may not be removed to any district court of the United States.

§ 1446. Procedure for removal.

(a) A defendant or defendants desiring to remove any civil action or criminal prosecution from a State court shall file in the district court of the United States for the district and division within which such action is pending a verified petition containing a short and plain statement of the facts which entitle him or them to removal together with a copy of all process, pleadings and orders served upon him or them in such action.

(b) The petition for removal of a civil action or proceeding shall be filed within thirty days after the receipt of the defendant, through service or otherwise, of a copy of the initial pleading setting forth the claim for relief upon which such action or proceeding is based, or within thirty days after the service of summons upon the defendant if such initial pleadings has then been filed in court and is not required to be served on the defendant, whichever period is shorter.

If the case stated by the initial pleading is not removable, a petition for removal may be filed within thirty days after receipt by the defendant, through service or otherwise, of a copy of an amended pleading, motion, order or other paper from which it may first be ascertained that the case is one which is or has become removable.

(c)(1) A petition for removal of a criminal prosecution shall be filed not later than thirty days after the arraignment in the State court, or at any time before trial, whichever is earlier, except that for good cause shown the United States district court may enter an order granting the petitioner leave to file the petition at a later time.

(2) A petition for removal of a criminal prosecution shall include all grounds for such removal. A failure to state grounds which exist at the time of the filing of the petition shall constitute a waiver of such grounds, and a second petition may be filed only on grounds not existing at the time of the original petition. For good cause shown, the United States district court may grant relief from the limitations of this paragraph.

(3) The filing of a petition for removal of a criminal prosecution shall not prevent the State court in which such prosecution is pending from proceeding further, except that a judgment of conviction shall not be entered unless the petition is first denied.

(4) The United States district court to which such petition is directed shall examine the petition promptly. If it clearly appears on the face of the petition and any exhibits annexed thereto that the petition for removal should not be granted, the court shall make an order for its summary dismissal.

(5) If the United States district court does not order the summary dismissal of such petition, it shall order an evidentiary hearing to be held promptly and after such hearing shall make such disposition of the petition as justice shall require. If the United States district court determines that such petition shall be granted, it shall so notify the State court in which prosecution is pending, which shall proceed no further.

(d) Promptly after the filing of such petition for the removal of a civil action and bond the defendant or defendants shall give written notice thereof to all adverse parties and shall file a copy of the petition with the clerk of such State court, which shall effect the removal and the State court shall proceed no further unless and until the case is remanded.

(e) If the defendant or defendants are in actual custody on process issued by the State court, the district court shall issue its writ of habeas corpus, and the marshal shall thereupon take such defendant or defendants into his custody and deliver a copy of the writ to the clerk of such State court.

§ 1447. Procedure after removal generally.

(a) In any case removed from a State court, the district court may issue all necessary orders and process to bring before it all proper parties whether served by process issued by the State court or otherwise.

(b) It may require the petitioner to file with its clerk copies of all records and proceedings in such State court or may cause the same to be brought before it by writ of certiorari issued to such State court.

(c) If at any time before final judgment it appears that the case was removed improvidently and without jurisdiction, the district court shall remand the case, and may order the payment of just costs. A certified copy of the order of remand shall be mailed by its clerk to the clerk of the State court. The State court may thereupon proceed with such case.

(d) An order remanding a case to the State court from which it was removed is not reviewable on appeal or otherwise, except that an order remanding a case to the State court from which it was removed pursuant to section 1443 of this title shall be reviewable by appeal or otherwise.

§ 1448. Process after removal.

In all cases removed from any State court to any district court of the United States in which any one or more of the defendants has not been served with process or in which the service has not been perfected prior to removal, or in which process served proves to be defective, such process or service may be completed or new process issued in the same manner as in cases originally filed in such district court.

This section shall not deprive any defendant upon whom process is served after removal of his right to move to remand the case.

§ 1449. State court record supplied.

Where a party is entitled to copies of the records and proceedings in any suit or prosecution in a State court, to be used in any district court of the United States, and the clerk of such State court, upon demand, and the payment or tender of the legal fees, fails to deliver certified copies, the district court may, on affidavit reciting such facts, direct such record to be supplied by affidavit or otherwise. Thereupon such proceedings, trial, and judgment may be had in such district court, and all such process awarded, as if certified copies had been filed in the district court.

§ 1450. Attachment or sequestration; securities.

Whenever any action is removed from a State court to a district court of the United States, any attachment or sequestration of the goods or estate of the defendant in such action in the State court shall hold the goods or estate to answer the final judgment or decree in the same manner as they would have been held to answer final judgment or decree had it been rendered by the State court.

All bonds, undertakings, or security given by either party in such action prior to its removal shall remain valid and effectual notwithstanding such removal.

All injunctions, orders, and other proceedings had in such action prior to its removal shall remain in full force and effect until dissolved or modified by the district court.

§ 1451. Definitions.

For purposes of this chapter—

(1) The term "State court" includes the Superior Court of the District of Columbia.

(2) The term "State" includes the District of Columbia.

§ 1452. Removal of claims related to bankruptcy cases.

(a) A party may remove any claim or cause of action in a civil action other than a proceeding before the United States Tax Court or a civil action by a governmental unit to enforce such governmental unit's police or regulatory power, to the district court for the district where such civil action is pending, if such district court has jurisdiction of such claim or cause of action under section 1334 of this title.

(b) The court to which such claim or cause of action is removed may remand such claim or cause of action on any equitable ground. An order entered under this subsection remanding a claim or cause of action, or a decision to not remand, is not reviewable by appeal or otherwise.

Chapter 91.—United States Claims Court

§ 1491. Claims against United States generally; actions involving Tennessee Valley Authority.

(a)(1) The United States Claims Court shall have jurisdiction to render judgment upon any claim against the United States founded either upon the Constitution, or any Act of Congress or any regulation of an executive department, or upon any express or implied contract with the United States, or for liquidated or unliquidated damages in cases not sounding in tort. For the purpose of this paragraph, an express or implied contract with the Army and Air Force Exchange Service, Navy Exchanges, Marine Corps Exchanges, Coast Guard Exchanges, or Exchange Councils of the National Aeronautics and Space Administration shall be considered an express or implied contract with the United States.

(2) To provide an entire remedy and to complete the relief afforded by the judgment, the court may, as an incident of and collateral to any such judgment, issue orders directing restoration to office or position, placement in appropriate duty or retirement status, and correction of applicable records, and such orders may be issued to any appropriate official of the United States. In any case within its jurisdiction, the court shall have the power to remand appropriate matters to any administrative or executive body or official with such direction as it may deem proper and just. The Claims Court shall have jurisdiction to render judgments upon any claim by or against, or dispute with, a contractor arising under section 10(a) of the Contract Disputes Act of 1978.

(3) To afford complete relief on any contract claim brought before the contract is awarded, the court shall have exclusive jurisdiction to grant declaratory judgments and such equitable and extraordinary relief as it deems proper, including but not limited to injunctive relief. In exercising this jurisdiction, the court shall give due regard to the interests of national defense and national security.

(b) Nothing herein shall be construed to give the United States Claims Court jurisdiction of any civil action within the exclusive jurisdiction of the Court of International Trade, or of any action against, or founded on actions of, the Tennessee Valley Authority, or to amend or modify the provisions of the Tennessee Valley Authority Act of 1933, as amended, with respect to suits by or against the Authority.

§ 1492. Congressional reference cases.

Any bill, except a bill for a pension, may be referred by either House of Congress to the chief judge of the United Claims Court for a report in conformity with section 2509 of this title.

Chapter 95.—Court of International Trade

§ 1581. Civil actions against the United States and agencies and officers thereof.

(a) The Court of International Trade shall have exclusive jurisdiction of any civil action commenced to contest the denial of a protest, in whole or in part, under section 515 of the Tariff Act of 1930.

(b) The Court of International Trade shall have exclusive jurisdiction of any civil action commenced under section 516 of the Tariff Act of 1930.

(c) The Court of International Trade shall have exclusive jurisdiction of any civil action commenced under section 516A of the Tariff Act of 1930.

(d) The Court of International Trade shall have exclusive jurisdiction of any civil action commenced to review—

(1) any final determination of the Secretary of Labor under section 223 of the Trade Act of 1974 with respect to the eligibility of workers for adjustment assistance under such Act;

(2) any final determination of the Secretary of Commerce under section 251 of the Trade Act of 1974 with respect to the eligibility of a firm for adjustment assistance under such Act; and

(3) any final determination of the Secretary of Commerce under section 271 of the Trade Act of 1974 with respect to the eligibility of a community for adjustment assistance under such Act.

(e) The Court of International Trade shall have exclusive jurisdiction of any civil action commenced to review any final determination of the Secretary of the Treasury under section 305(b)(1) of the Trade Agreements Act of 1979.

(f) The Court of International Trade shall have exclusive jurisdiction of any civil action involving an application for an order directing the administering authority or the International Trade Commission to make confidential information available under section 777(c)(2) of the Tariff Act of 1930.

(g) The Court of International Trade shall have exclusive jurisdiction of any civil action commenced to review—

(1) any decision of the Secretary of the Treasury to deny or revoke a customhouse broker's license under section 641(a) of the Tariff Act of 1930; and

(2) any order of the Secretary of the Treasury to revoke or suspend a customhouse broker's license under section 641(b) of the Tariff Act of 1930.

(h) The Court of International Trade shall have exclusive jurisdiction of any civil action commenced to review, prior to the importation of the goods involved, a ruling issued by the Secretary of the Treasury, or a refusal to issue or change such a ruling, relating to classification, valuation, rate of duty, marking, restricted merchandise, entry requirements, drawbacks, vessel repairs, or similar matters, but only if the party commencing the civil action demonstrates to the court that he would be irreparably harmed unless given an opportunity to obtain judicial review prior to such importation.

(i) In addition to the jurisdiction conferred upon the Court of International Trade by subsections (a)–(h) of this section and subject to the exception set forth in subsection (j) of this section, the Court of International Trade shall have exclusive jurisdiction of any civil action commenced against the United States, its agencies, or its officers, that arises out of any law of the United States providing for—

(1) revenue from imports or tonnage;

(2) tariffs, duties, fees, or other taxes on the importation of merchandise for reasons other than the raising of revenue;

(3) embargoes or other quantitative restrictions on the importation of merchandise for reasons other than the protection of the public health or safety; or

(4) administration and enforcement with respect to the matters referred to in paragraphs (1)–(3) of this subsection and subsections (a)–(h) of this section.

(j) The Court of International Trade shall not have jurisdiction of any civil action arising under section 305 of the Tariff Act of 1930.

§ 1582. Civil actions commenced by the United States.

The Court of International Trade shall have exclusive jurisdiction of any civil action which arises out of an import transaction and which is commenced by the United States—

(1) to recover a civil penalty under section 592, 704(i)(2), or 734(i)(2) of the Tariff Act of 1930;

(2) to recover upon a bond relating to the importation of merchandise required by the laws of the United States or by the Secretary of the Treasury; or

(3) to recover customs duties.

§ 1583. Counterclaims, cross-claims, and third-party actions.

In any civil action in the Court of International Trade, the court shall have exclusive jurisdiction to render judgment upon any counterclaim, cross-claim, or third-party action of any party, if (1) such claim or action involves the imported merchandise that is the subject matter of such civil action, or (2) such claim or action is to recover upon a bond or customs duties relating to such merchandise.

§ 1585. Powers in law and equity.

The Court of International Trade shall possess all the powers in law and equity of, or as conferred by statute upon, a district court of the United States.

Chapter 97.—Jurisdictional Immunities of Foreign States

§ 1602. Findings and declaration of purpose.

The Congress finds that the determination by United States courts of the claims of foreign states to immunity from the jurisdiction of such courts would serve the interests of justice and would protect the rights of both foreign states and litigants in United States courts. Under international law, states are not immune from the jurisdiction of foreign courts insofar as their commercial activities are concerned, and their commercial property may be levied upon for the satisfaction of judgments rendered against them in connection with their commercial activities. Claims of foreign states to immunity should henceforth be decided by courts of the United States and of the States in conformity with the principles set forth in this chapter.

§ 1603. Definitions.

For purposes of this chapter—

(a) A "foreign state", except as used in section 1608 of this title, includes a political subdivision of a foreign state or an agency or instrumentality of a foreign state as defined in subsection (b).

(b) An "agency or instrumentality of a foreign state" means any entity—

(1) which is a separate legal person, corporate or otherwise, and

(2) which is an organ of a foreign state or political subdivision thereof, or a majority of whose shares or other ownership interest is owned by a foreign state or political subdivision thereof, and

(3) which is neither a citizen of a State of the United States as defined in section 1332(c) and (d) of this title, nor created under the laws of any third country.

(c) The "United States" includes all territory and waters, continental or insular, subject to the jurisdiction of the United States.

(d) A "commercial activity" means either a regular course of commercial conduct or a particular commercial transaction or act. The commercial character of an activity shall be determined by reference to the nature of the course of conduct or particular transaction or act, rather than by reference to its purpose.

(e) A "commercial activity carried on in the United States by a foreign state" means commercial activity carried on by such state and having substantial contact with the United States.

§ 1604. Immunity of a foreign state from jurisdiction.

Subject to existing international agreements to which the United States is a party at the time of enactment of this Act a foreign state shall be immune from the jurisdiction of the courts of the United States and of the States except as provided in sections 1605 to 1607 of this chapter.

§ 1605. General exceptions to the jurisdictional immunity of a foreign state.

(a) A foreign state shall not be immune from the jurisdiction of courts of the United States or of the States in any case—

(1) in which the foreign state has waived its immunity either explicitly or by implication, notwithstanding any withdrawal of the waiver which the foreign state may purport to effect except in accordance with the terms of the waiver;

(2) in which the action is based upon a commercial activity carried on in the United States by the foreign state; or upon an act performed in the United States in connection with a commercial activity of the foreign state elsewhere; or upon an act outside the

territory of the United States in connection with a commercial activity of the foreign state elsewhere and that act causes a direct effect in the United States;

(3) in which rights in property taken in violation of international law are in issue and that property or any property exchanged for such property is present in the United States in connection with a commercial activity carried on in the United States by the foreign state; or that property or any property exchanged for such property is owned or operated by an agency or instrumentality of the foreign state and that agency or instrumentality is engaged in a commercial activity in the United States;

(4) In which rights in property in the United States acquired by succession or gift or rights in immovable property situated in the United States are in issue; or

(5) not otherwise encompassed in paragraph (2) above, in which money damages are sought against a foreign state for personal injury or death, or damage to or loss of property, occurring in the United States and caused by the tortious act or omission of that foreign state or of any official or employee of that foreign state while acting within the scope of his office or employment; except this paragraph shall not apply to—

(A) any claim based upon the exercise or performance or the failure to exercise or perform a discretionary function regardless of whether the discretion be abused, or

(B) any claim arising out of malicious prosecution, abuse of process, libel, slander, misrepresentation, deceit, or interference with contract rights; or

(6) in which the action is brought, either to enforce an agreement made by the foreign State with or for the benefit of a private party to submit to arbitration all or any differences which have arisen or which may arise between the parties with respect to a defined legal relationship, whether contractual or not, concerning a subject matter capable of settlement by arbitration under the laws of the United States, or to confirm an award made pursuant to such an agreement to arbitrate, if (A) the arbitration takes place or is intended to take place in the United States, (B) the agreement or award is or may be governed by a treaty or other international agreement in force for the United States calling for the recognition and enforcement of arbitral awards, (C) the underlying claim, save for the agreement to arbitrate, could have been brought in a United States court under this section or section 1607, or (D) paragraph (1) of this subsection is otherwise applicable.

(b) A foreign state shall not be immune from the jurisdiction of the courts of the United States in any case in which a suit in admiralty is brought to enforce a maritime lien against a vessel or cargo of the foreign state, which maritime lien is based upon a commercial activity of the foreign state . . . .

(d) A foreign state shall not be immune from the jurisdiction of the courts of the United States in any action brought to foreclose a preferred mortgage, as defined in the Ship Mortgage Act, 1920 (46 U.S.C. 911 and following). Such action shall be brought, heard, and determined in accordance with the provisions of that Act and in accordance with the principles of law and rules of practice of suits in rem, whenever it appears that had the vessel been privately owned and possessed a suit in rem might have been maintained.

§ 1606. Extent of liability.

As to any claim for relief with respect to which a foreign state is not entitled to immunity under section 1605 or 1607 of this chapter, the foreign state shall be liable in the same manner and to the same extent as a private individual under like circumstances; but a foreign state except for an agency or instrumentality thereof shall not be liable for punitive damages; if, however, in any case wherein death was caused, the law of the place where the action or omission occurred provides, or has been construed to provide, for damages only punitive in nature, the foreign state shall be liable for actual or compensatory damages measured by the pecuniary injuries resulting from such death which were incurred by the persons for whose benefit the action was brought.

§ 1607. Counterclaims.

In any action brought by a foreign state, or in which a foreign state intervenes, in a court of the United States or of a State, the foreign state shall not be accorded immunity with respect to any counterclaim—

(a) for which a foreign state would not be entitled to immunity under section 1605 of this chapter had such claim been brought in a separate action against the foreign state; or

(b) arising out of the transaction or occurrence that is the subject matter of the claim of the foreign state; or

(c) to the extent that the counterclaim does not seek relief exceeding in amount or differing in kind from that sought by the foreign state.

Chapter 99.—General Provisions

§ 1631. Transfer to cure want of jurisdiction.

Whenever a civil action is filed in a court as defined in section 610 of this title or an appeal, including a petition for review of administrative action, is noticed for or filed with such a court and that court finds that there is a want of jurisdiction, the court shall, if it is in the interest of justice, transfer such action or appeal to any other such court in which the action or appeal could have been brought at the time it was filed or noticed, and the action or appeal shall proceed as if it had been filed in or noticed for the court to which it is transferred on the date upon which it was actually filed in or noticed for the court from which it is transferred.

PART V.—PROCEDURE

Chapter 111.—General Procedures

§ 1651. Writs.

(a) The Supreme Court and all courts established by Act of Congress may issue all writs necessary or appropriate in aid of their respective jurisdictions and agreeable to the usages and principles of law.

(b) An alternative writ or rule nisi may be issued by a justice or judge of a court which has jurisdiction.

§ 1652. State laws as rules of decision.

The laws of the several states, except where the Constitution or treaties of the United States or Acts of Congress otherwise require or provide, shall be regarded as rules of decision in civil actions in the courts of the United States, in cases where they apply.

§ 1653. Amendment of pleadings to show jurisdiction.

Defective allegations of jurisdiction may be amended, upon terms, in the trial or appellate courts.

Chapter 115.—Evidence; Documentary

§ 1738. State and Territorial statutes and judicial proceedings; full faith and credit.

The Acts of the legislature of any State, Territory, or Possession of the United States, or copies thereof, shall be authenticated by affixing the seal of such State, Territory or Possession thereto.

The records and judicial proceedings of any court of any such State, Territory or Possession, or copies thereof, shall be proved or admitted in other courts within the United States and its Territories and Possessions by the attestation of the clerk and seal of the court annexed, if a seal exists, together with a certificate of a judge of the court that the said attestation is in proper form.

Such Acts, records and judicial proceedings or copies thereof, so authenticated, shall have the same full faith and credit in every court within the United States and its Territories and Possessions as they have by law or usage in the courts of such State, Territory or Possession from which they are taken.

§ 1738A. Full faith and credit given to child custody determinations.

(a) The appropriate authorities of every State shall enforce according to its terms, and shall not modify except as provided in subsection (f) of this section, any child custody determination made consistently with the provisions of this section by a court of another State.

(b) As used in this section, the term—

(1) "child" means a person under the age of eighteen;

(2) "contestant" means a person, including a parent, who claims a right to custody or visitation of a child;

(3) "custody determination" means a judgment, decree, or other order of a court providing for the custody or visitation of a child, and includes permanent and temporary orders, and initial orders and modifications;

(4) "home State" means the State in which, immediately preceding the time involved, the child lived with his parents, a parent, or a person acting as parent, for at least six consecutive months, and in the case of a child less than six months old, the State in which the child lived from birth with any of such persons. Periods of temporary absence of any of such persons are counted as part of the six-month or other period;

(5) "modification" and "modify" refer to a custody determination which modifies, replaces, supersedes, or otherwise is made subsequent to, a prior custody determination concerning the same child, whether made by the same court or not;

(6) "person acting as a parent" means a person, other than a parent, who has physical custody of a child and who has either been awarded custody by a court or claims a right to custody;

(7) "physical custody" means actual possession and control of a child; and

(8) "State" means a State of the United States, the District of Columbia, the Commonwealth of Puerto Rico, or a territory or possession of the United States.

(c) A child custody determination made by a court of a State is consistent with the provisions of this section only if—

(1) such court has jurisdiction under the law of such State; and

(2) one of the following conditions is met:

(A) such State (i) is the home State of the child on the date of the commencement of the proceeding, or (ii) had been the child's home State within six months before the date of the commencement of the proceeding and the child is absent from such State because of his removal or retention by a contestant or for other reasons, and a contestant continues to live in such State;

(B)(i) it appears that no other State would have jurisdiction under subparagraph (A), and (ii) it is in the best interest of the child that a court of such State assume jurisdiction because (I) the child and his parents, or the child and at least one contestant, have a significant connection with such State other than mere physical presence in such State, and (II) there is available in such State substantial evidence concerning the child's present or future care, protection, training, and personal relationships;

(C) the child is physically present in such State and (i) the child has been abandoned, or (ii) it is necessary in an emergency to protect the child because he has been subjected to or threatened with mistreatment or abuse;

(D)(i) it appears that no other State would have jurisdiction under subparagraph (A), (B), (C), or (E), or another State has declined to exercise jurisdiction on the ground that the State whose jurisdiction is in issue is the more appropriate forum to determine the custody of the child, and (ii) it is in the best interest of the child that such court assume jurisdiction; or

(E) the court has continuing jurisdiction pursuant to subsection (d) of this section.

(d) The jurisdiction of a court of a State which has made a child custody determination consistently with the provisions of this section continues as long as the requirement of subsection (c)(1) of this section continues to be met and such State remains the residence of the child or of any contestant.

(e) Before a child custody determination is made, reasonable notice and opportunity to be heard shall be given to the contestants, any parent whose parental rights have not been previously terminated and any person who has physical custody of a child.

(f) A court of a State may modify a determination of the custody of the same child made by a court of another State, if—

(1) it has jurisdiction to make such a child custody determination; and

(2) the court of the other State no longer has jurisdiction, or it has declined to exercise such jurisdiction to modify such determination.

(g) A court of a State shall not exercise jurisdiction in any proceeding for a custody determination commenced during the pendency of a proceeding in a court of another State where such court of that other State is exercising jurisdiction consistently with the provisions of this section to make a custody determination.

Chapter 125.—Pending Actions and Judgments

§ 1963. Registration of judgments of the district courts and the Court of International Trade.

A judgment in an action for the recovery of money or property entered in any district court or in the Court of International Trade may be registered by filing a certified copy of such judgment in any other district or, with respect to the Court of International Trade, in any judicial district, when the judgment has become final by appeal or expiration of the time for appeal or when ordered by the court that entered the judgment for good cause shown. A judgment so registered shall have the same effect as a judgment of the district court of the district where registered and may be enforced in like manner.

A certified copy of the satisfaction of any judgment in whole or in part may be registered in like manner in any district in which the judgment is a lien.

Chapter 131.—Rules of Courts

§ 2071. Rule-making power generally.

(a) The Supreme Court and all courts established by Act of Congress may from time to time prescribe rules for the conduct of their business. Such rules shall be consistent with Acts of Congress and rules of practice and procedure prescribed under section 2072 of this title.

(b) Any rule prescribed by a court, other than the Supreme Court, under subsection (a) shall be prescribed only after giving appropriate public notice and an opportunity for comment. Such rule shall take effect upon the date specified by the prescribing court and shall have such effect on pending proceedings as the prescribing court may order.

(c)(1) A rule of a district court prescribed under subsection (a) shall remain in effect unless modified or abrogated by the judicial council of the relevant circuit.

(2) Any other rule prescribed by a court other than the Supreme Court under subsection (a) shall remain in effect unless modified or abrogated by the Judicial Conference.

(d) Copies of rules prescribed under subsection (a) by a district court shall be furnished to the judicial council, and copies of all rules prescribed by a court other than the Supreme Court under subsection (a) shall be furnished to the director of the Administrative Office of the United States Courts and made available to the public.

(e) If the prescribing court determines that there is an immediate need for a rule, such court may proceed under this section without public notice and opportunity for comment, but such court shall promptly thereafter afford such notice and opportunity for comment.

(f) No rule may be prescribed by a district court other than under this section.

§ 2072. Rules of procedure and evidence; power to prescribe.

(a) The Supreme Court shall have the power to prescribe general rules of practice and procedure and rules of evidence for cases in the United States district courts (including proceedings before magistrates thereof) and courts of appeals.

(b) Such rules shall not abridge, enlarge or modify any substantive right. All laws in conflict with such rules shall be of no further force or effect after such rules have taken effect.

§ 2074. Rules of procedure and evidence; submission to Congress; effective date.

(a) The Supreme Court shall transmit to the Congress not later than May 1 of the year in which a rule prescribed under section 2072 is to become effective a copy of the proposed rule. Such rule shall take effect no earlier than December 1 of the year in which such rule is so transmitted unless otherwise provided by law. The Supreme Court may fix the extent such rule shall apply to proceedings then pending, except that the Supreme Court shall not require the application of such rule to further proceedings then pending to the extent that, in the opinion of the court in which such proceedings are pending, the application of such rule in such proceedings would not be feasible or would work injustice, in which event the former rule applies.

(b) Any such rule creating, abolishing, or modifying an evidentiary privilege shall have no force or effect unless approved by Act of Congress.

§ 2075. Bankruptcy rules.

The Supreme Court shall have the power to prescribe by general rules, the forms of process, writs, pleadings, and motions, and the practice and procedure in cases under Title 11.

Such rules shall not abridge, enlarge, or modify any substantive right.

Such rules shall not take effect until they have been reported to Congress by the Chief Justice at or after the beginning of a regular session thereof but not later than the first day of May and until the expiration of ninety days after they have been thus reported.

Chapter 133.—Review—Miscellaneous Provisions

§ 2101. Supreme Court; time for appeal or certiorari; docketing; stay.

(a) A direct appeal to the Supreme Court from any decision under section 1253 of this title, holding unconstitutional in whole or in part, any Act of Congress, shall be taken within thirty days after the entry of the interlocutory or final order, judgment or decree. The record shall be made up and the case docketed within sixty days from the time such appeal is taken under rules prescribed by the Supreme Court.

(b) Any other direct appeal to the Supreme Court which is authorized by law, from a decision of a district court in any civil action, suit or proceeding, shall be taken within thirty days from the judgment, order or decree, appealed from, if interlocutory, and within sixty days if final.

(c) Any other appeal or any writ of certiorari intended to bring any judgment or decree in a civil action, suit or proceeding before the Supreme Court for review shall be taken or applied for within ninety days after the entry of such judgment or decree. A justice of the

Supreme Court, for good cause shown, may extend the time for applying for a writ of certiorari for a period not exceeding sixty days.

(d) The time for appeal or application for a writ of certiorari to review the judgment of a State court in a criminal case shall be as prescribed by rules of the Supreme Court.

(e) An application to the Supreme Court for a writ of certiorari to review a case before judgment has been rendered in the court of appeals may be made at any time before judgment.

(f) In any case in which the final judgment or decree of any court is subject to review by the Supreme Court on writ of certiorari, the execution and enforcement of such judgment or decree may be stayed for a reasonable time to enable the party aggrieved to obtain a writ of certiorari from the Supreme Court. The stay may be granted by a judge of the court rendering the judgment or decree or by a justice of the Supreme Court, and may be conditioned on the giving of security, approved by such judge or justice, that if the aggrieved party fails to make application for such writ within the period allotted therefor, or fails to obtain an order granting his application, or fails to make his plea good in the Supreme Court, he shall answer for all damages and costs which the other party may sustain by reason of the stay.

(g) The time for application for a writ of certiorari to review a decision of the United States Court of Military Appeals shall be as prescribed by rules of the Supreme Court.

§ 2106. Determination.

The Supreme Court or any other court of appellate jurisdiction may affirm, modify, vacate, set aside or reverse any judgment, decree, or order of a court lawfully brought before it for review, and may remand the cause and direct the entry of such appropriate judgment, decree, or order, or require such further proceedings to be had as may be just under the circumstances.

§ 2107. Time for appeal to court of appeals.

Except as otherwise provided in this section, no appeal shall bring any judgment, order or decree in an action, suit or proceeding of a civil nature before a court of appeals for review unless notice of appeal is filed, within thirty days after the entry of such judgment, order or decree.

In any such action, suit or proceeding in which the United States or an officer or agency thereof is a party, the time as to all parties shall be sixty days from such entry.

In any action, suit or proceeding in admiralty, the notice of appeal shall be filed within ninety days after the entry of the order, judgment or decree appealed from, if it is a final decision, and within fifteen days after its entry if it is an interlocutory decree.

The district court or the bankruptcy court may extend the time for appeal not exceeding thirty days from the expiration of the original time herein prescribed, upon a showing of excusable neglect based on failure of a party to learn of the entry of the judgment, order or decree.

§ 2108. Proof of amount in controversy.

Where the power of any court of appeals to review a case depends upon the amount or value in controversy, such amount or value, if not otherwise satisfactorily disclosed upon the record, may be shown and ascertained by the oath of a party to the case or by other competent evidence.

§ 2111. Harmless error.

On the hearing of any appeal or writ of certiorari in any case, the court shall give judgment after an examination of the record without regard to errors or defects which do not affect the substantial rights of the parties.

PART VI.—PARTICULAR PROCEEDINGS

Chapter 151.—Declaratory Judgments

§ 2201. Creation of remedy.

(a) In a case of actual controversy within its jurisdiction, except with respect to Federal taxes other than actions brought under section 7428 of the Internal Revenue Code of 1986, or a proceeding under section 505 or 1146 of title 11, or in any civil action involving an antidumping or countervailing duty proceeding regarding a class or kind of Canadian merchandise, as determined by the administering authority, any court of the United States, upon the filing of an appropriate pleading, may declare the rights and other legal relations of any interested party seeking such declaration, whether or not further relief is or could be sought. Any such declaration shall have the force and effect of a final judgment or decree and shall be reviewable as such.

. . .

§ 2202. Further relief.

Further necessary or proper relief based on a declaratory judgment or decree may be granted, after reasonable notice and hearing, against any adverse party whose rights have been determined by such judgment.

Chapter 153.—Habeas Corpus

§ 2241. Power to grant writ.

(a) Writs of habeas corpus may be granted by the Supreme Court, any justice thereof, the district courts and any circuit judge within their respective jurisdictions. The order of a circuit judge shall be entered in the records of the district court of the district wherein the restraint complained of is had.

(b) The Supreme Court, any justice thereof, and any circuit judge may decline to entertain an application for a writ of habeas corpus and may transfer the application for hearing and determination to the district court having jurisdiction to entertain it.

(c) The writ of habeas corpus shall not extend to a prisoner unless—

(1) He is in custody under or by color of the authority of the United States or is committed for trial before some court thereof; or

(2) He is in custody for an act done or omitted in pursuance of an Act of Congress, or an order, process, judgment or decree of a court or judge of the United States; or

(3) He is in custody in violation of the Constitution or laws or treaties of the United States; or

(4) He, being a citizen of a foreign state and domiciled therein is in custody for an act done or omitted under any alleged right, title, authority, privilege, protection, or exemption claimed under the commission, order or sanction of any foreign state, or under color thereof, the validity and effect of which depend upon the law of nations; or

(5) It is necessary to bring him into court to testify or for trial.

(d) Where an application for a writ of habeas corpus is made by a person in custody under the judgment and sentence of a State court of a State which contains two or more Federal judicial districts, the application may be filed in the district wherein such person is in custody or in the district court for the district within which the State court was held which convicted and sentenced him and each of such district courts shall have concurrent jurisdiction to entertain the application. The district court for the district wherein such application is filed in the exercise of its discretion and in furtherance of justice may transfer the appliction to the other district court for hearing and determination.

§ 2242. Application.

Application for a writ of habeas corpus shall be in writing signed and verified by the person for whose relief it is intended or by someone acting in his behalf.

It shall allege the facts concerning the applicant's commitment or detention, the name of the person who has custody over him and by virtue of what claim or authority, if known.

It may be amended or supplemented as provided in the rules of procedure applicable to civil actions.

If addressed to the Supreme Court, a justice thereof or a circuit judge it shall state the reasons for not making application to the district court of the district in which the applicant is held.

§ 2243. Issuance of writ; return; hearing; decision.

A court, justice or judge entertaining an application for a writ of habeas corpus shall forthwith award the writ or issue an order directing the respondent to show cause why the writ should not be granted, unless it appears from the application that the applicant or person detained is not entitled thereto.

The writ, or order to show cause shall be directed to the person having custody of the person detained. It shall be returned within three days unless for good cause additional time, not exceeding twenty days, is allowed.

The person to whom the writ or order is directed shall make a return certifying the true cause of the detention.

When the writ or order is returned a day shall be set for hearing, not more than five days after the return unless for good cause additional time is allowed.

Unless the application for the writ and the return present only issues of law the person to whom the writ is directed shall be required to produce at the hearing the body of the person detained.

The applicant or the person detained may, under oath, deny any of the facts set forth in the return or allege any other material facts.

The return and all suggestions made against it may be amended, by leave of court, before or after being filed.

The court shall summarily hear and determine the facts, and dispose of the matter as law and justice require.

§ 2244. Finality of determination.

(a) No circuit or district judge shall be required to entertain an application for a writ of habeas corpus to inquire into the detention of a person pursuant to a judgment of a court of the United States if it appears that the legality of such detention has been determined by a judge or court of the United States on a prior application for a writ of habeas corpus and the petition presents no new ground not theretofore presented and determined, and the judge or court is satisfied that the ends of justice will not be served by such inquiry.

(b) When after an evidentiary hearing on the merits of a material factual issue, or after a hearing on the merits of an issue of law, a person in custody pursuant to the judgment of a State court has been denied by a court of the United States or a justice or judge of the United States release from custody or other remedy on an application for a writ of habeas corpus, a subsequent application for a writ of habeas corpus in behalf of such person need not be entertained by a court of the United States or a justice or judge of the United States unless the application alleges and is predicated on a factual or other ground not adjudicated on the hearing of the earlier application for the writ, and unless the court, justice, or judge is satisfied that the applicant has not on the earlier application deliberately withheld the newly asserted ground or otherwise abused the writ.

(c) In a habeas corpus proceeding brought in behalf of a person in custody pursuant to the judgment of a State court, a prior judgment of the Supreme Court of the United States on an appeal or review by a writ of certiorari at the instance of the prisoner of the decision of such State court, shall be conclusive as to all issues of fact or law with respect to an asserted denial of a Federal right which constitutes ground for discharge in a habeas corpus proceeding, actually adjudicated by the Supreme Court therein, unless the applicant for the writ of habeas corpus shall plead and the court shall find the existence of a material and controlling fact which did not appear in the record of the proceeding in the Supreme Court and the court shall further find that the applicant for the writ of habeas corpus could not have caused such fact to appear in such record by the exercise of reasonable diligence.

§ 2245. Certificate of trial judge admissible in evidence.

On the hearing of an application for a writ of habeas corpus to inquire into the legality of the detention of a person pursuant to a judgment the certificate of the judge who presided at the trial resulting in the judgment, setting forth the facts occurring at the trial, shall be admissible in evidence. Copies of the certificate shall be filed with the court in which the application is pending and in the court in which the trial took place.

§ 2246. Evidence; depositions; affidavits.

On application for a writ of habeas corpus, evidence may be taken orally or by deposition, or, in the discretion of the judge, by affidavit. If affidavits are admitted any party shall have the right to propound written interrogatories to the affiants, or to file answering affidavits.

§ 2247. Documentary evidence.

On application for a writ of habeas corpus documentary evidence, transcripts of proceedings upon arraignment, plea and sentence and a transcript of the oral testimony introduced on any previous similar application by or in behalf of the same petitioner, shall be admissible in evidence.

§ 2248. Return or answer; conclusiveness.

The allegations of a return to the writ of habeas corpus or of an answer to an order to show cause in a habeas corpus proceeding, if not traversed, shall be accepted as true except to the extent that the judge finds from the evidence that they are not true.

§ 2249. Certified copies of indictment, plea and judgment; duty of respondent.

On application for a writ of habeas corpus to inquire into the detention of any person pursuant to a judgment of a court of the United States, the respondent shall promptly file with the court certified copies of the indictment, plea of petitioner and the judgment, or such of them as may be material to the questions raised, if the petitioner fails to attach them to his petition, and same shall be attached to the return to the writ, or to the answer to the order to show cause.

§ 2250. Indigent petitioner entitled to documents without cost.

If on any application for a writ of habeas corpus an order has been made permitting the petitioner to prosecute the application in forma pauperis, the clerk of any court of the United States shall furnish to the petitioner without cost certified copies of such documents or parts of the record on file in his office as may be required by order of the judge before whom the application is pending.

§ 2251. Stay of State court proceedings.

A justice or judge of the United States before whom a habeas corpus proceeding is pending, may, before final judgment or after final judgment of discharge, or pending appeal, stay any proceeding against the person detained in any State court or by or under the authority of any State for any matter involved in the habeas corpus proceeding.

After the granting of such a stay, any such proceeding in any State court or by or under the authority of any state shall be void. If no stay is granted, any such proceeding shall be as valid as if no habeas corpus proceedings or appeal were pending.

§ 2252. Notice.

Prior to the hearing of a habeas corpus proceeding in behalf of a person in custody of State officers or by virtue of State laws notice shall be served on the attorney general or other appropriate officer of such State as the justice or judge at the time of issuing the writ shall direct.

§ 2253. Appeal.

In a habeas corpus proceeding before a circuit or district judge, the final order shall be subject to review, on appeal, by the court of appeals for the circuit where the proceeding is had.

There shall be no right of appeal from such an order in a proceeding to test the validity of a warrant to remove, to another district or place for commitment or trial, a person charged with a criminal offense against the United States, or to test the validity of his detention pending removal proceedings.

An appeal may not be taken to the court of appeals from the final order in a habeas corpus proceeding where the detention complained of arises out of process issued by a State court, unless the justice or judge who rendered the order or a circuit justice or judge issues a certificate of probable cause.

§ 2254. State custody; remedies in Federal courts.

(a) The Supreme Court, a Justice thereof, a circuit judge, or a district court shall entertain an application for a writ of habeas corpus in behalf of a person in custody pursuant to the judgment of a State court only on the ground that he is in custody in violation of the Constitution or laws or treaties of the United States.

(b) An application for a writ of habeas corpus in behalf of a person in custody pursuant to the judgment of a State court shall not be granted unless it appears that the applicant has exhausted the remedies available in the courts of the State, or that there is either an absence of available State corrective process or the existence of circumstances rendering such process ineffective to protect the rights of the prisoner.

(c) An applicant shall not be deemed to have exhausted the remedies available in the courts of the State, within the meaning of this section, if he has the right under the law of the State to raise, by any available procedure, the question presented.

(d) In any proceeding instituted in a Federal court by an application for a writ of habeas corpus by a person in custody pursuant to the judgment of a State court, a determination after a hearing on the merits of a factual issue, made by a State court of competent jurisdiction in a proceeding to which the applicant for the writ and the State or an officer or agent thereof were parties, evidenced by a written finding, written opinion, or other reliable and adequate written indicia, shall be presumed to be correct, unless the applicant shall establish or it shall otherwise appear, or the respondent shall admit—

(1) that the merits of the factual dispute were not resolved in the State court hearing;

(2) that the factfinding procedure employed by the State court was not adequate to afford a full and fair hearing;

(3) that the material facts were not adequately developed at the State court hearing;

(4) that the State court lacked jurisdiction of the subject matter or over the person of the applicant in the State court proceeding;

(5) that the applicant was an indigent and the State court, in deprivation of his constitutional right, failed to appoint counsel to represent him in the State court proceeding;

(6) that the applicant did not receive a full, fair, and adequate hearing in the State court proceeding; or

(7) that the applicant was otherwise denied due process of law in the State court proceeding;

(8) or unless that part of the record of the State court proceeding in which the determination of such factual issue was made, pertinent to a determination of the sufficiency of the evidence to support such factual determination, is produced as provided for hereinafter, and the Federal court on a consideration of such part of the record as a whole concludes that such factual determination is not fairly supported by the record:

And in an evidentiary hearing in the proceeding in the Federal court, when due proof of such factual determination has been made, unless the existence of one or more of the circumstances respectively set forth in paragraphs numbered (1) to (7), inclusive, is shown by the applicant, otherwise appears, or is admitted by the respondent, or unless the court concludes pursuant to the provisions of paragraph numbered (8) that the record in the State court proceeding, considered as a whole, does not fairly support such factual determination, the burden shall rest upon the applicant to establish by convincing evidence that the factual determination by the State court was erroneous.

(e) If the applicant challenges the sufficiency of the evidence adduced in such State court proceeding to support the State court's determination of a factual issue made therein, the applicant, if able, shall produce that part of the record pertinent to a determination of the sufficiency of the evidence to support such determination. If the applicant, because of indigency or other reason is unable to produce such part of the record, then the State shall produce such part of the record and the Federal court shall direct the State to do so by order directed to an appropriate State official. If the State cannot provide such pertinent part of the record, then the court shall determine under the existing facts and circumstances what weight shall be given to the State court's factual determination.

(f) A copy of the official records of the State court, duly certified by the clerk of such court to be a true and correct copy of a finding, judicial opinion, or other reliable written indicia showing such a factual determination by the State court shall be admissible in the Federal court proceeding.

§ 2255. Federal custody; remedies on motion attacking sentence.

A prisoner in custody under sentence of a court established by Act of Congress claiming the right to be released upon the ground that the sentence was imposed in violation of the Constitution or laws of the United States, or that the court was without jurisdiction to impose such sentence, or that the sentence was in excess of the maximum authorized by law, or is otherwise subject to collateral attack, may move the court which imposed the sentence to vacate, set aside or correct the sentence.

A motion for such relief may be made at any time.

Unless the motion and the files and records of the case conclusively show that the prisoner is entitled to no relief, the court shall cause notice thereof to be served upon the United States attorney, grant a prompt hearing thereon, determine the issues and make findings of fact and conclusions of law with respect thereto. If the court finds that the judgment was rendered without jurisdiction, or that the sentence imposed was not authorized by law or otherwise open to collateral attack, or that there has been such a denial or infringement of the constitutional rights of the prisoner as to render the judgment vulnerable to collateral attack, the court shall vacate and set the judgment aside and shall discharge the prisoner or resentence him or grant a new trial or correct the sentence as may appear appropriate.

A court may entertain and determine such motion without requiring the production of the prisoner at the hearing.

The sentencing court shall not be required to entertain a second or successive motion for similar relief on behalf of the same prisoner.

An appeal may be taken to the court of appeals from the order entered on the motion as from a final judgment on application for a writ of habeas corpus.

An application for a writ of habeas corpus in behalf of a prisoner who is authorized to apply for relief by motion pursuant to this section, shall not be entertained if it appears that the applicant has failed to apply for relief, by motion, to the court which sentenced him, or that such court has denied him relief, unless it also appears that the remedy by motion is inadequate or ineffective to test the legality of his detention.

Chapter 155.—Injunctions; Three-Judge Courts

§ 2283. Stay of State court proceedings.

A court of the United States may not grant an injunction to stay proceedings in a State court except as expressly authorized by Act of Congress, or where necessary in aid of its jurisdiction, or to protect or effectuate its judgments.

§ 2284. Three-judge court; when required; composition; procedure

(a) A district court of three judges shall be convened when otherwise required by Act of Congress, or when an action is filed challenging the constitutionality of the apportionment of congressional districts or the apportionment of any statewide legislative body.

(b) In any action required to be heard and determined by a district court of three judges under subsection (a) of this section, the composition and procedure of the court shall be as follows:

(1) Upon the filing of a request for three judges, the judge to whom the request is presented shall, unless he determines that three judges are not required, immediately notify the chief judge of the circuit, who shall designate two other judges, at least one of whom shall be a circuit judge. The judges so designated, and the judge to whom the request was presented, shall serve as members of the court to hear and determine the action or proceeding.

(2) If the action is against a State, or officer or agency thereof, at least five days' notice of hearing of the action shall be given by registered or certified mail to the Governor and attorney general of the State. The hearing shall be given precedence and held at the earliest practicable day.

(3) A single judge may conduct all proceedings except the trial, and enter all orders permitted by the rules of civil procedure except as provided in this subsection. He may grant a temporary restraining order on a specific finding, based on evidence submitted, that specified

irreparable damage will result if the order is not granted, which order, unless previously revoked by the district judge, shall remain in force only until the hearing and determination by the district court of three judges of an application for a preliminary injunction. A single judge shall not appoint a master, or order a reference, or hear and determine any application for a preliminary or permanent injunction or motion to vacate such an injunction, or enter judgment on the merits. Any action of a single judge may be reviewed by the full court at any time before final judgment.

Chapter 158.—Orders of Federal Agencies; Review

§ 2342. Jurisdiction of court of appeals.

The court of appeals other than the United States Court of Appeals for the Federal Circuit has exclusive jurisdiction to enjoin, set aside, suspend (in whole or in part), or to determine the validity of—

(1) all final orders of the Federal Communications Commission made reviewable by section 402(a) of title 47;

(2) all final orders of the Secretary of Agriculture made under chapters 9 and 20A of title 7, except orders issued under sections 210(e), 217a, and 499g(a) of title 7;

(3) all rules, regulations, or final orders of—

(A) the Secretary of Transportation issued pursuant to section 2, 9, 37, 41, or 43 of the Shipping Act, 1916 (46 U.S.C. App. 802, 803, 808, 835, 839, and 841a); and

(B) the Federal Maritime Commission issued pursuant to—

(i) section 23, 25, or 43 of the Shipping Act, 1916 (46 U.S.C.App. 822, 824, or 841a);

(ii) section 19 of the Merchant Marine Act, 1920 (46 U.S.C.App. 876);

(iii) section 2, 3, 4, or 5 of the Intercoastal Shipping Act, 1933 (46 U.S.C.App. 844, 845, 845a, or 845b);

(iv) section 14 or 17 of the Shipping Act of 1984 (46 U.S.C.App. 1713 or 1716); or

(v) section 2(d) or 3(d) of the Act of November 6, 1966 (46 U.S.C.App. 817d(d) or 817e(d);

(4) all final orders of the Atomic Energy Commission made reviewable by section 2239 of title 42;

(5) all rules, regulations, or final orders of the Interstate Commerce Commission made reviewable by section 2321 of this title and all final orders of such Commission made reviewable under section 11901(j)(2) of Title 49, United States Code; and

(6) All final orders under section 812 of the Fair Housing Act.

Jurisdiction is invoked by filing a petition as provided by section 2344 of this title.

§ 2343. Venue.

The venue of a proceeding under this chapter is in the judicial circuit in which the petitioner resides or has its principal office, or in the United States Court of Appeals for the District of Columbia Circuit.

§ 2347. Petitions to review; proceedings.

(a) Unless determined on a motion to dismiss, petitions to review orders reviewable under this chapter are heard in the court of appeals on the record of the pleadings, evidence adduced, and proceedings before the agency, when the agency has held a hearing whether or not required to do so by law.

(b) When the agency has not held a hearing before taking the action of which review is sought by the petition, the court of appeals shall determine whether a hearing is required by law. After that determination, the court shall—

(1) remand the proceedings to the agency to hold a hearing, when a hearing is required by law;

(2) pass on the issues presented, when a hearing is not required by law and it appears from the pleadings and affidavits filed by the parties that no genuine issue of material facts is presented; or

(3) transfer the proceedings to a district court for the district in which the petitioner resides or has its principal office for a hearing and determination as if the proceedings were originally initiated in the district court, when a hearing is not required by law and a genuine issue of material fact is presented. The procedure in these cases in the district court is governed by the Federal Rules of Civil Procedure.

(c) If a party to a proceeding to review applies to the court of appeals in which the proceeding is pending for leave to adduce additional evidence and shows to the satisfaction of the court that—

(1) the additional evidence is material; and

(2) there were reasonable grounds for failure to adduce the evidence before the agency;

the court may order the additional evidence and any counterevidence the opposite party desires to offer to be taken by the agency. The agency may modify its findings of fact, or make new findings, by reason of the additional evidence so taken, and may modify or set aside its order, and shall file in the court the additional evidence, the modified findings or new findings, and the modified order or the order setting aside the original order.

§ 2403. Intervention by United States or a State; constitutional question.

(a) In any action, suit or proceeding in a court of the United States to which the United States or any agency, officer or employee thereof is not a party, wherein the constitutionality of any Act of Congress affecting the public interest is drawn in question, the court shall certify such fact to the Attorney General, and shall permit the United States to intervene for presentation of evidence, if evidence is otherwise admissible in the case, and for argument on the question of constitutionality. The United States shall, subject to the applicable provisions of law, have all the rights of a party and be subject to all liabilities of a party as to court costs to the extent necessary for a proper presentation of the facts and law relating to the question of constitutionality.

(b) In any action, suit, or proceeding in a court of the United States to which a State or any agency, officer, or employee thereof is not a party, wherein the constitutionality of any statute of that State affecting the public interest is drawn in question, the court shall certify such fact to the attorney general of the State, and shall permit the State to intervene for presentation of evidence, if evidence is otherwise admissible in the case, and for argument on the question of constitutionality. The State shall, subject to the applicable provisions of law, have all the rights of a party and be subject to all liabilities of a party as to court costs to the extent necessary for a proper presentation of the facts and law relating to the question of constitutionality.

Chapter 159.—Interpleader

§ 2361. Process and procedure.

In any civil action of interpleader or in the nature of interpleader under section 1335 of this title, a district court may issue its process for all claimants and enter its order restraining them from instituting or prosecuting any proceeding in any State or United States court affecting the property, instrument or obligation involved in the interpleader action until further order of the court. Such process and order shall be returnable at such time as the court or judge thereof directs, and shall be addressed to and served by the United States marshals for the respective districts where the claimants reside or may be found.

Such district court shall hear and determine the case, and may discharge the plaintiff from further liability, make the injunction permanent, and make all appropriate orders to enforce its judgment.

Chapter 161.—United States As Party Generally

§ 2409. Partition actions involving United States.

Any civil action by any tenant in common or joint tenant owning an undivided interest in lands, where the United States is one of such tenants in common or joint tenants, against the United States alone or against the United States and any other of such owners, shall proceed, and be determined, in the same manner as would a similar action between private persons.

Whenever in such action the court orders a sale of the property or any part thereof the Attorney General may bid for the same in behalf of the United States. If the United States is the purchaser, the amount of the purchase money shall be paid from the Treasury upon a warant drawn by the Secretary of the Treasury on the requisition of the Attorney General.

§ 2409a. Real property quiet title actions.

(a) The United States may be named as a party defendant in a civil action under this section to adjudicate a disputed title to real property in which the United States claims an interest, other than a security interest or water rights. This section does not apply to trust or restricted Indian lands, nor does it apply to or affect actions which may be or could have been brought under sections 1346, 1347, 1491, or 2410 of this title, sections 7424, 7425, or 7426 of the Internal Revenue Code of 1954, as amended (26 U.S.C. 7424, 7425, and 7426), or section 208 of the Act of July 10, 1952 (43 U.S.C. 666). . . .

(n) Nothing in this section shall be construed to permit suits against the United States based upon adverse possession.

§ 2410. Actions affecting property on which United States has lien.

(a) Under the conditions prescribed in this section and section 1444 of this title for the protection of the United States, the United States may be named a party in any civil action or suit in any district court, or in any State court having jurisdiction of the subject matter—

(1) to quiet title to,

(2) to foreclose a mortgage or other lien upon,

(3) to partition,

(4) to condemn, or

(5) of interpleader or in the nature of interpleader with respect to,

real or personal property on which the United States has or claims a mortgage or other lien. . . .

Chapter 165.—United States Claims Court Procedure

§ 2509. Congressional reference cases.

(a) Whenever a bill, except a bill for a pension, is referred by either House of Congress to the chief judge of the United States Claims Court pursuant to section 1492 of this title, the chief judge shall designate a judge as hearing officer for the case and a panel of three judges of the court to serve as a reviewing body. One member of the review panel shall be designated as presiding officer of the panel.

(b) Proceedings in a congressional reference case shall be under rules and regulations prescribed for the purpose by the chief judge who is hereby authorized and directed to require the application of the pertinent rules of practice of the Claims Court insofar as feasible. Each hearing officer and each review panel shall have authority to do and perform any acts which may be necessary or proper for the efficient performance of their duties, including the power of subpena and the power to administer oaths and affirmations. None of the rules, rulings, findings, or conclusions authorized by this section shall be subject to judicial review.

(c) The hearing officer to whom a congressional reference case is assigned by the chief judge shall proceed in accordance with the applicable rules to determine the facts, including facts relating to delay or laches, facts bearing upon the question whether the bar of any statute of limitation should be removed, or facts claimed to excuse the claimant for not having resorted to any established legal remedy. He shall append to his findings of fact conclusions sufficient to inform Congress whether the demand is a legal or equitable claim or a gratuity, and the amount, if any, legally or equitably due from the United States to the claimant.

(d) The findings and conclusions of the hearing officer shall be submitted by him, together with the record in the case, to the review panel for review by it pursuant to such rules as may be provided for the purpose, which shall include provision for submitting the report of the hearing officer to the parties for consideration, exception, and argument before the panel. The panel, by majority vote, shall adopt or modify the findings or the conclusions of the hearing officer.

(e) The panel shall submit its report to the chief judge for transmission to the appropriate House of Congress.

(f) Any act or failure to act or other conduct by a party, a witness, or an attorney which would call for the imposition of sanctions under the rules of practice of the Claims Court shall be noted by the panel or the hearing officer at the time of occurrence thereof and upon failure of the delinquent or offending party, witness, or attorney to make prompt compliance with the order of the panel or the trial commissioner a full statement of the circumstances shall be incorporated in the report of the panel.

(g) The Claims Court is hereby authorized and directed, under such regulations as it may prescribe, to provide the facilities and services of the office of the clerk of the court for the filing, processing, hearing and dispatch of congressional reference cases and to include within its annual appropriations the costs thereof and other costs of administration, including (but without limitation to the items herein listed) the salaries and traveling expenses of the judges serving as hearing officers and panel members, mailing and service of process, necessary physical facilities, equipment, and supplies, and personnel (including secretaries and law clerks).

Chapter 171.—Tort Claims Procedure

§ 2680. Exceptions.

The provisions of this chapter and section 1346(b) of this title shall not apply to—

(a) Any claim based upon an act or omission of an employee of the Government, exercising due care, in the execution of a statute or regulation, whether or not such statute or regulation be valid, or based upon the exercise or performance or the failure to exercise or perform a discretionary function or duty on the part of a federal agency or an employee of the Government, whether or not the discretion involved be abused.

(b) Any claim arising out of the loss, miscarriage, or negligent transmission of letters or postal matter.

(c) Any claim arising in respect of the assessment or collection of any tax or customs duty, or the detention of any goods or merchandise by any officer of customs or excise or any other law-enforcement officer.

(d) Any claim for which a remedy is provided by sections 741–752, 781–790 of Title 46, relating to claims or suits in admiralty against the United States.

(e) Any claim arising out of an act or omission of any employee of the Government in administering the provisions of sections 1–31 of Title 50, Appendix.

(f) Any claim for damages caused by the imposition or establishment of a quarantine by the United States.

(g) [Repealed]

(h) Any claim arising out of assault, battery, false imprisonment, false arrest, malicious prosecution, abuse of process, libel, slander, misrepresentation, deceit, or interference with contract rights: *Provided,* That, with regard to acts or omissions of investigative or law enforcement officers of the United States Government, the provisions of this chapter and section 1346(b) of this title shall apply to any claim arising, on or after the date of the enactment of this proviso, out of assault, battery, false imprisonment, false arrest, abuse of process, or malicious prosecution. For the purpose of this subsection, "investigative or law enforcement officer" means any officer of the United States who is empowered by law to execute searches, to seize evidence, or to make arrests for violations of Federal law.

(i) Any claim for damages caused by the fiscal operations of the Treasury or by the regulation of the monetary system.

(j) Any claim arising out of the combatant activities of the military or naval forces, or the Coast Guard, during time of war.

(k) Any claim arising in a foreign country.

(l) Any claim arising from the activities of the Tennessee Valley Authority.

(m) Any claim arising from the activities of the Panama Canal Company.

(n) Any claim arising from the activities of a Federal land bank, a Federal intermediate credit bank, or a bank for co-operatives.

TITLE 29.—LABOR

NORRIS–LaGUARDIA ACT

§ 101. Issuance of restraining orders and injunctions; limitation; public policy.

No court of the United States, as defined in this chapter, shall have jurisdiction to issue any restraining order or temporary or permanent injunction in a case involving or growing out of a labor dispute, except in a strict conformity with the provisions of this chapter; nor shall any such restraining order or temporary or permanent injunction be issued contrary to the public policy declared in this chapter.

§ 102. Public policy in labor matters declared.

In the interpretation of this chapter and in determining the jurisdiction and authority of the courts of the United States, as such jurisdiction and authority are defined and limited in this chapter, the public policy of the United States is declared as follows:

Whereas under prevailing economic conditions, developed with the aid of governmental authority for owners of property to organize in the corporate and other forms of ownership association, the individual unorganized worker is commonly helpless to exercise actual liberty of contract and to protect his freedom of labor, and thereby to obtain acceptable terms and conditions of employment, wherefore, though he should be free to decline to associate with his fellows, it is necessary that he have full freedom of association, self-organization, and designation of representatives of his own choosing, to negotiate the terms and conditions of his employment, and that he shall be free from the interference, restraint, or coercion of employers of labor, or their agents, in the designation of such representatives or in self-organization or in other concerted activities for the purpose of collective bagaining or other mutual aid or protection; therefore, the following definitions of and limitations upon the jurisdiction and authority of the courts of the United States are enacted.

§ 104. Enumeration of specific acts not subject to restraining orders or injunctions.

No court of the United States shall have jurisdiction to issue any restraining order or temporary or permanent injunction in any case involving or growing out of any labor dispute to prohibit any person or persons participating or interested in such dispute (as these terms are herein defined) from doing whether singly or in concert, any of the following acts:

(a) Ceasing or refusing to perform any work or to remain in any relation of employment;

(b) Becoming or remaining a member of any labor organization or of any employer organization regardless of any such undertaking or promise as is described in section 103 of this title;

(c) Paying or giving to, or withholding from, any person participating or interested in such labor dispute any strike or unemployment benefits or insurance, or other moneys or things of value;

(d) By all lawful means aiding any person participating or interested in any labor dispute who is being proceeded against in or is prosecuting, any action or suit in any court of the United States or of any State;

(e) Giving publicity to the existence of, or the facts involved in, any labor dispute, whether by advertising, speaking, patrolling, or by any other method not involving fraud or violence;

(f) Assembling peaceably to act or to organize to act in promotion of their interests in a labor dispute;

(g) Advising or notifying any person of an intention to do any of the acts heretofore specified;

(h) Agreeing with other persons to do or not to do any of the acts heretofore specified; and

(i) Advising, urging, or otherwise causing or inducing without fraud or violence the acts heretofore specified, regardless of any such undertaking or promise as is described in section 103 of this title.

TAFT–HARTLEY ACT, § 301

§ 185. Suits by and against labor organizations.

(a) Venue, amount, and citizenship.

Suits for violation of contracts between an employer and a labor organization representing employees in an industry affecting commerce as defined in this chapter, or between any such labor organizations, may be brought in any district court of the United States having jurisdiction of the parties, without respect to the amount in controversy or without regard to the citizenship of the parties.

(b) . . . Entity for purposes of suit . . .

Any labor organization which represents employees in an industry affecting commerce . . . may sue or be sued as an entity and in behalf of the employees whom it represents in the courts of the United States. . . .

TITLE 33.—NAVIGATION AND NAVIGABLE WATERS

Chapter 18.—Longshore and Harbor Workers' Compensation

§ 902. Definitions.

When used in this chapter—. . .

(3) The term "employee" means any person engaged in maritime employment, including any longshoreman or other person engaged in longshoring operations, and any harborworker includ-

ing a ship repairman, shipbuilder, and ship-breaker, but such term does not include—. . .

(G) a master or member of a crew of any vessel . . . .

§ 903. Coverage.

(a) Except as otherwise provided in this section, compensation shall be payable under this chapter in respect of disability or death of an employee, but only if the disability or death results from an injury occurring upon the navigable waters of the United States (including any adjoining pier, wharf, dry dock, terminal, building way, marine railway, or other adjoining area customarily used by an employer in loading, unloading, repairing, dismantling, or building a vessel).

(b) No compensation shall be payable in respect of the disability or death of an officer or employee of the United States, or any agency thereof, or of any State or foreign government, or any subdivision thereof.

(c) No compensation shall be payable if the injury was occasioned solely by the intoxication of the employee or by the willful intention of the employee to injure or kill himself or another. . . .

§ 905. Exclusiveness of liability.

(a) The liability of an employer prescribed in section 904 of this title shall be exclusive and in place of all other liability of such employer to the employee, his legal representative, husband or wife, parents, dependents, next of kin, and anyone otherwise entitled to recover damages from such employer at law or in admiralty on account of such injury or death, except that if an employer fails to secure payment of compensation as required by this chapter, an injured employee, or his legal representative in case death results from the injury, may elect to claim compensation under the chapter, or to maintain an action at law or in admiralty for damages on account of such injury or death. In such action the defendant may not plead as a defense that the injury was caused by the negligence of a fellow servant, or that the employee assumed the risk of his employment, or that the injury was due to the contributory negligence of the employee. . . .

(b) In the event of injury to a person covered under this chapter caused by the negligence of a vessel, then such person, or anyone otherwise entitled to recover damages by reason thereof, may bring an action against such vessel as a third party in accordance with the provisions of section 933 of this title, and the employer shall not be liable to the vessel for such damages directly or indirectly and any agreements or warranties to the contrary shall be void. If such person was employed by the vessel to provide stevedoring services, no such action shall be permitted if the injury was caused by the negligence of persons engaged in providing stevedoring services to the vessel. If such person was employed by the vessel to provide shipbuilding, repairing or breaking services and such person's employer was the owner, owner pro hac vice, agent, operator, or charterer of the vessel, no such action shall be permitted . . . against the injured person's employer . . . . The liability of the vessel under this subsection shall not be based upon the warranty of seaworthiness or a breach thereof at the time the injury occurred. The remedy provided in this subsection shall be exclusive of all other remedies against the vessel except remedies available under this chapter.

TITLE 42.—THE PUBLIC HEALTH AND WELFARE

§ 1983. Civil action for deprivation of rights.

Every person who, under color of any statute, ordinance, regulation, custom, or usage, of any State or Territory or the District of Columbia, subjects, or causes to be subjected, any citizen of the United States or other person within the jurisdiction thereof to the deprivation of any rights, privileges, or immunities secured by the Constitution and laws, shall be liable to the party injured in an action at law, suit in equity, or other proper proceeding for redress. For the purposes of this section, any Act of Congress applicable exclusively to the District of Columbia shall be considered to be a statute of the District of Columbia. (R.S. § 1979.)

§ 1988. Proceedings in vindication of civil rights; attorney's fees.

The jurisdiction in civil and criminal matters conferred on the district courts by the provisions of this Title, and of Title "CIVIL RIGHTS," and of Title "CRIMES," for the protection of all persons in the United States in their civil rights, and for their vindication, shall be exercised and enforced in conformity with the laws of the United States, so far as such laws are suitable to carry the same into effect; but in all cases where they are not adapted to the object, or are deficient in the provisions necessary to furnish suitable remedies and punish offenses against law, the common law, as modified and changed by the constitution and statutes of the State wherein the court having jurisdiction of such civil or criminal cause is held, so far as the same is not inconsistent with the Constitution and laws of the United States, shall be extended to and govern the said courts in the trial and disposition of the cause, and, if it is of a criminal nature, in the infliction of punishment on the party found guilty. In any action or proceeding to enforce a provision of sections 1981, 1982, 1983, 1985, and 1986 of this title, title IX of Public Law 92–318 [20 U.S.C. 1681 et seq.], or title VI of the Civil Rights Act of 1964 [42 U.S.C. 2000d et seq.], the court, in its discretion, may allow the prevailing party, other than the United States, a reasonable attorney's fee as part of the costs. (R.S. § 722.)

TITLE 46.—SHIPPING

JONES ACT

§ 688. Recovery for injury to or death of seaman.

Any seaman who shall suffer personal injury in the course of his employment may, at his election, maintain an action for damages at law, with the right of trial by jury, and in such action all statutes of the United States modifying or extending the common-law right or remedy in cases of personal injury to railway employees shall apply; and in case of the death of any seaman as a result of any such personal injury the personal representative of such seaman may maintain an action for damages at law with the right of trial by jury, and in such action all statutes of the United States conferring or regulating the right of action for death in the case of railway employees shall be applicable. Jurisdiction in such actions shall be under the court of the district in which the defendant employer resides or in which his principal office is located.

EXTENSION OF JURISDICTION

§ 740. Extension of admiralty and maritime jurisdiction; libel in rem or in personam; exclusive remedy; waiting period.

The admiralty and maritime jurisdiction of the United States shall extend to and include all cases of damage or injury, to person or property, caused by a vessel on navigable water, notwithstanding that such damage or injury be done or consummated on land. . . .

SUITS IN ADMIRALTY ACT

§ 741. Exemption of United States vessels and cargoes from arrest or seizure.

No vessel owned by the United States or by any corporation in which the United States or its representatives shall own the entire outstanding capital stock or in the possession of the United States or of such corporation or operated by or for the United States or such corporation, and no cargo owned or possessed by the United States or by such corporation, shall, in view of the provision herein made for a libel in personam, be subject to arrest or seizure by judicial process in the United States or its possessions: *Provided*, That this chapter shall not apply to the Panama Railroad Company.

§ 742. Libel in personam.

In cases where if such vessel were privately owned or operated, or if such cargo were privately owned or possessed, or if a private person or property were involved, a proceeding in admiralty could be maintained, any appropriate nonjury proceeding in personam may be brought against the United States or against any corporation mentioned in section 741 of this title. Such suits shall be brought in the district court of the United States for the district in which the parties so suing, or any of them, reside or have their principal place of business in the United States, or in which the vessel or cargo charged with liability is found. The libelant shall forthwith serve a copy of his libel on the United States attorney for such district and mail a copy thereof by registered mail to the Attorney General of the United States, and shall file a sworn return of such service and mailing. Such service and mailing shall constitute valid service on the United States and such corporation. In case the United States or such corporation shall file a libel in rem or in personam in any district, a cross libel in personam may be filed or a set-off claimed against the United States or such corporation with the same force and effect as if the libel had been filed by a private party. Upon application of either party the cause may, in the discretion of the court, be transfered to any other district court of the United States.

§ 745. Causes of action for which suits may be brought; limitations; exceptions; actions which may not be revived; interest on claims.

Suits as authorized by this chapter may be brought only within two years after the cause of action arises: *Provided*, That where a remedy is provided by this chapter it shall hereafter be exclusive of any other action by reason of the same subject matter against the agent or employee of the United States or of any incorporated or unincorporated agency thereof whose act or omission gave rise to the claim: *Provided further*, That the limitations contained in this section for the commencement of suits shall not bar any suit against the United States brought hereunder within one year after December 13, 1950 if such suit is based upon a cause of action whereon a prior suit in admiralty or an action at law was timely commenced and was or may hereafter be dismissed solely because improperly brought against any person, partnership, association, or corporation engaged by the United States to manage and conduct the business of a vessel owned or bareboat chartered by the United States or against the master of any such vessel: *And provided further*, That after June 30, 1932, no interest shall be allowed on any claim prior to the time when suit on such claim is brought as authorized by section 742 of this title unless upon a contract expressly stipulating for the payment of interest.

DEATH ON THE HIGH SEAS ACT

§ 761. Right of action; where and by whom brought.

Whenever the death of a person shall be caused by wrongful act, neglect, or default occurring on the high seas beyond a marine league from the shore of any State, or the District of Columbia, or the Territories or dependencies of the United States, the personal representative of the decedent may maintain a suit for damages in the district courts of the United States, in admiralty, for the exclusive benefit of the decedent's wife, husband, parent, child, or dependent relative against the vessel, person, or corporation which would have been liable if death had not ensued.

PUBLIC VESSELS ACT

§ 781. Libel in admiralty against or impleader of United States.

A libel in personam in admiralty may be brought against the United States, or a petition impleading the United States, for damages caused by a public vessel of the United States, and for compensation for towage and salvage services, including contract salvage, rendered to a public vessel of the United States: *Provided*, That the cause of action arose after the 6th day of April, 1920.

§ 782. Venue of suit; application of provisions of chapter 20.

Such suit shall be brought in the district court of the United States for the district in which the vessel or cargo charged with creating the liability is found within the United States, or if such vessel or cargo be outside the territorial waters of the United States, then in the district court of the United States for the district in which the parties so suing, or any of them, reside or have an office for the transaction of business in the United States; or in case none of such parties reside or have an office for the transaction of business in the United States, and such vessel or cargo be outside the territorial waters of the United States, then in any district court of the United States. Such suits shall be subject to and proceed in accordance with the provisions of chapter 20 of this title [Suits in Admiralty Act] or any amendment thereof, insofar as the same are not inconsistent herewith, except that no interest shall be allowed on any claim up to the time of the rendition of judgment unless upon a contract expressly stipulating for the payment of interest.

SUPREME COURT RULES (1990)

Rule 10. Considerations governing review on writ of certiorari.

1. A review on writ of certiorari is not a matter of right, but of judicial discretion. A writ of certiorari will be granted only when there are special and important reasons therefor. The following, while neither controlling nor fully measuring the Court's discretion, indicate the character of reasons that will be considered:

(a) When a United States court of appeals has rendered a decision in conflict with the decision of another United States court of appeals on the same matter; or has decided a federal question in a way in conflict with a state court of last resort; or has so far departed from the accepted and usual course of judicial proceedings, or sanctioned such a departure by a lower court, as to call for an exercise of this Court's power of supervision.

(b) When a state court of last resort has decided a federal question in a way in conflict with the decision of another state court of last resort or of a United States court of appeals.

(c) When a state court or a United States court of appeals has decided an important question of federal law which has not been, but should be, settled by this Court, or has decided a federal question in a way that conflicts with applicable decisions of this Court.

2. The same general considerations outlined above will control in respect to a petition for a writ of certiorari to review a judgment of the United States Court of Military Appeals.

Rule 11. Certiorari to a United States Court of Appeals before judgment.

A petition for writ of certiorari to review a case pending in a United States court of appeals, before judgment is given in such court, will be granted only upon a showing that the case is of such imperative public importance as to justify deviation from normal appellate practice and to require immediate settlement in this Court. 28 U.S.C. § 2101(e).

Rule 17. Procedure in an original action.

1. This Rule applies only to actions within the Court's original jurisdiction under Article III of the Constitution of the United States. . . .

2. The form of pleadings and motions prescribed by the Federal Rules of Civil Procedure should be followed in an original action to be filed in this Court. In other respects those Rules, when their application is appropriate, may be taken as a guide to procedure in an original action in this Court.

3. The initial pleading in any original action shall be prefaced by a motion for leave to file . . . . A brief in support of the motion for leave to file . . . may also be filed with the motion and pleading. . . .

Rule 19. Procedure on a certified question.

1. A United States court of appeals may certify to this Court a question or proposition of law concerning which it desires instruction for the proper decision of a case. The certificate submitted shall contain a statement of the nature of the case and the facts on which such question or proposition of law arises. Only questions or propositions of law may be certified, and they must be distinct and definite.

2. When a question is certified by a United States court of appeals, this Court, on application or on its own motion, may consider and decide the entire matter in controversy. See 28 U.S.C. § 1254(2).

Rule 20. Procedure on a petition for an extraordinary writ.

1. The issuance by the Court of an extraordinary writ authorized by 28 U.S.C. § 1651(a) is not a matter of right, but of discretion sparingly exercised. To justify the granting of any writ under that provision, it must be shown that the writ will be in aid of the Court's appellate jurisdiction, that there are present exceptional circumstances warranting the exercise of the Court's discretionary powers, and that adequate relief cannot be obtained in any other form or from any other court. . . .

FEDERAL RULES OF APPELLATE PROCEDURE (1980)

Rule 5. Appeals by Permission Under 28 U.S.C. § 1292(b)

(a) Petition for Permission to Appeal. An appeal from an interlocutory order containing the statement prescribed by 28 U.S.C. § 1292(b) may be sought by filing a petition for permission to appeal with the clerk of the court of appeals within 10 days after the entry of such order in the district court with proof of service on all other parties to the action in the district court. An order may be amended to include the prescribed statement at any time, and permission to appeal may be sought within 10 days after entry of the order as amended.

(b) Content of Petition; Answer. The petition shall contain a statement of the facts necessary to an understanding of the controlling question of law determined by the order of the district court; a statement of the question itself; and a statement of the reasons why a substantial basis exists for a difference of opinion on the question and why an immediate appeal may materially advance the termination of the litigation. The petition shall include or have annexed thereto a copy of the order from which appeal is sought and of any findings of fact, conclusions of law and opinion relating thereto. Within 7 days after service of the petition an adverse party may file an answer in opposition. The application and answer shall be submitted without oral argument unless otherwise ordered.

(c) Form of Papers; Number of Copies. All papers may be typewritten. Three copies shall be filed with the original, but the court may require that additional copies be furnished.

(d) Grant of Permission; Cost Bond; Filing of Record. Within 10 days after the entry of an order granting permission to appeal the appellant shall (1) pay to the clerk of the district court the fees established by statute and the docket fee prescribed by the Judicial Conference of the United States and (2) file a bond for costs if required pursuant to Rule 7. The clerk of the district court shall notify the clerk of the court of appeals of the payment of the fees. Upon receipt of such notice the clerk of the court of appeals shall enter the appeal upon the docket. The record shall be transmitted and filed in accordance with Rules 11 and 12(b). A notice of appeal need not be filed.

Rule 35. Determination of Causes by the Court in Banc.

(a) When Hearing or Rehearing in Banc Will be Ordered. A majority of the circuit judges who are in regular active service may order that an appeal or other proceeding be heard or reheard by the court of appeals in banc. Such a hearing or rehearing is not favored and ordinarily will not be ordered except (1) when consideration by the full court is necessary to secure or maintain uniformity of its decisions, or (2) when the proceeding involves a question of exceptional importance.

(b) Suggestion of a Party for Hearing or Rehearing in Banc. A party may suggest the appropriateness of a hearing or rehearing in

banc. No response shall be filed unless the court shall so order. The clerk shall transmit any such suggestion to the members of the panel and the judges of the court who are in regular active service but a vote need not be taken to determine whether the cause shall be heard or reheard in banc unless a judge in regular active service or a judge who was a member of the panel that rendered a decision sought to be reheard requests a vote on such a suggestion made by a party.

(c) Time for Suggestion of a Party for Hearing or Rehearing in Banc; Suggestion Does Not Stay Mandate. If a party desires to suggest that an appeal be heard initially in banc, the suggestion must be made by the date on which the appellee's brief is filed. A suggestion for a hearing in banc must be made within the time prescribed by Rule 40 for filing a petition for rehearing, whether the suggestion is made in such petition or otherwise. The pendency of such a suggestion whether or not included in a petition for rehearing shall not affect the finality of the judgment of the court of appeals or stay the issuance of the mandate.

FEDERAL RULES OF CIVIL PROCEDURE

As Amended to July 1, 1989.

Rule 4. Process.

(a) SUMMONS: ISSUANCE. Upon the filing of the complaint the clerk shall forthwith issue a summons and deliver the summons to the plaintiff or the plaintiff's attorney, who shall be responsible for prompt service of the summons and a copy of the complaint. Upon request of the plaintiff separate or additional summons shall issue against any defendants.

(b) SAME: FORM. The summons shall be signed by the clerk, be under the seal of the court, contain the name of the court and the names of the parties, be directed to the defendant, state the name and address of the plaintiff's attorney, if any, otherwise the plaintiff's address, and the time within which these rules require the defendant to appear and defend, and shall notify him that in case of his failure to do so judgment by default will be rendered against him for the relief demanded in the complaint. When, under Rule 4(e), service is made pursuant to a statute or rule of court of a state, the summons, or notice, or order in lieu of summons shall correspond as nearly as may be to that required by the statute or rule.

(c) SERVICE.

(1) Process, other than a subpoena or a summons and complaint, shall be served by a United States marshal or deputy United States marshal, or by a person specially appointed for that purpose.

(2)(A) A summons and complaint shall, except as provided in subparagraphs (B) and (C) of this paragraph, be served by any person who is not a party and is not less than 18 years of age.

(B) A summons and complaint shall, at the request of the party seeking service or such party's attorney, be served by a United States marshal or deputy United States marshal, or by a person specially appointed by the court for that purpose, only—

(i) on behalf of a party authorized to proceed in forma pauperis pursuant to Title 28, U.S.C. § 1915, or of a seaman authorized to proceed under Title 28, U.S.C. § 1916,

(ii) on behalf of the United States or an officer or agency of the United States, or

(iii) pursuant to an order issued by the court stating that a United States marshal or deputy United States marshal, or a person specially appointed for that purpose, is required to serve the summons and complaint in order that service be properly effected in that particular action.

(C) A summons and complaint may be served upon a defendant of any class referred to in paragraph (1) or (3) of subdivision (d) of this rule—

(i) pursuant to the law of the State in which the district court is held for the service of summons or other like process upon such defendant in an action brought in the courts of general jurisdiction of that State, or

(ii) by mailing a copy of the summons and of the complaint (by first-class mail, postage prepaid) to the person to be served, together with two copies of a notice and acknowledgment conforming substantially to form 18–A and a return envelope, postage prepaid, addressed to the sender. If no acknowledgment of service under this subdivision of this rule is received by the sender within 20 days after the date of mailing, service of such summons and complaint shall be made under subparagraph (A) or (B) of this paragraph in the manner prescribed by subdivision (d)(1) or (d)(3).

(D) Unless good cause is shown for not doing so the court shall order the payment of the costs of personal service by the person served if such person does not complete and return within 20 days after mailing, the notice and acknowledgment of receipt of summons.

(E) The notice and acknowledgment of receipt of summons and complaint shall be executed under oath or affirmation.

(3) The court shall freely make special appointments to serve summonses and complaints under paragraph (2)(B) of this subdivision of this rule and all other process under paragraph (1) of this subdivision of this rule.

(d) SUMMONS AND COMPLAINT: PERSON TO BE SERVED. The summons and complaint shall be served together. The plaintiff shall furnish the person making service with such copies as are necessary. Service shall be made as follows:

(1) Upon an individual other than an infant or an incompetent person, by delivering a copy of the summons and of the complaint to him personally or by leaving copies thereof at his dwelling house or usual place of abode with some person of suitable age and discretion then residing therein or by delivering a copy of the summons and of the complaint to an agent authorized by appointment or by law to receive service of process.

(2) Upon an infant or an incompetent person, by serving the summons and complaint in the manner prescribed by the law of the state in which the service is made for the service of summons or other like process upon any such defendant in an action brought in the courts of general jurisdiction of that state.

(3) Upon a domestic or foreign corporation or upon a partnership or other unincorporated association which is subject to suit under a common name, by delivering a copy of the summons and of the complaint to an officer, a managing or general agent, or to any other agent authorized by appointment or by law to receive service of process and, if the agent is one authorized by statute to receive service and the statute so requires, by also mailing a copy to the defendant.

(4) Upon the United States, by delivering a copy of the summons and of the complaint to the United States attorney for the district in which the action is brought or to an assistant United States attorney or clerical employee designated by the United States attorney in a writing filed with the clerk of the court and by sending a copy of the summons and of the complaint by registered or certified mail to the Attorney General of the United States at Washington, District of Columbia, and in any action attacking the validity of an order of an officer or agency of the United States not made a party, by also sending a copy of the summons and of the complaint by registered or certified mail to such officer or agency.

(5) Upon an officer or agency of the United States, by serving the United States and by delivering a copy of the summons and of the complaint to such officer or agency. If the agency is a corporation the copy shall be delivered as provided in paragraph (3) of this subdivision of this rule.

(6) Upon a state or municipal corporation or other governmental organization thereof subject to suit, by delivering a copy of the summons and of the complaint to the chief executive officer thereof or by serving the summons and complaint in the manner prescribed by the law of that state for the service of summons or other like process upon any such defendant.

(e) SAME: SERVICE UPON PARTY NOT INHABITANT OF OR FOUND WITHIN STATE. Whenever a statute of the United States or an order of court thereunder provides for service of a summons, or of a notice, or of an order in lieu of summons upon a party not an inhabitant of or found within the state in which the district court is held, service may be made under the circumstances and in the manner prescribed by the statute or order, or, if there is no provision therein prescribing the manner of service, in a manner stated in this rule. Whenever a statute or rule of court of the state in which the district court is held provides (1) for service of a summons, or of a notice, or of an order in lieu of summons upon a party not an inhabitant of or found within the state, or (2) for service upon or notice to such a party to appear and respond or defend in an action by reason of the attachment or garnishment or similar seizure of the party's property located within the state, service may in either case be made under the circumstances and in the manner prescribed in the statute or rule.

(f) TERRITORIAL LIMITS OF EFFECTIVE SERVICE. All process other than a subpoena may be served anywhere within the territorial limits of the state in which the district court is held, and, when authorized by a statute of the United States or by these rules, beyond the territorial limits of that state. In addition, persons who are brought in as parties pursuant to Rule 14, or as additional parties to a pending action or a counterclaim or cross-claim therein pursuant to Rule 19, may be served in the manner stated in paragraphs (1)–(6) of subdivision (d) of this rule at all places outside the state but within the United States that are not more than 100 miles from the place in which the action is commenced, or to which it is assigned or transferred for trial; and persons required to respond to an order of commitment for civil contempt may be served at the same places. A subpoena may be served within the territorial limits provided in Rule 45.

(g) RETURN. The person serving the process shall make proof of service thereof to the court promptly and in any event within the time during which the person served must respond to the process. If service is made by a person other than a United States marshal or his deputy, he shall make affidavit thereof. . . . Failure to make proof of service does not affect the validity of the service.

(h) AMENDMENT. At any time in its discretion and upon such terms as it deems just, the court may allow any process or proof of service thereof to be amended, unless it clearly appears that material prejudice would result to the substantial rights of the party against whom the process issued.

(i) ALTERNATIVE PROVISIONS FOR SERVICE IN A FOREIGN COUNTRY.

(1) Manner. When the federal or state law referred to in subdivision (e) of this rule authorizes service upon a party not an inhabitant of or found within the state in which the district court is held, and service is to be effected upon the party in a foreign country, it is also sufficient if service of the summons and complaint is made: (A) in the manner prescribed by the law of the

foreign country for service in that country in an action in any of its courts of general jurisdiction; or (B) as directed by the foreign authority in response to a letter rogatory, when service in either case is reasonably calculated to give actual notice; or (C) upon an individual, by delivery to him personally, and upon a corporation or partnership or association, by delivery to an officer, a managing or general agent; or (D) by any form of mail, requiring a signed receipt, to be addressed and dispatched by the clerk of the court to the party to be served; or (E) as directed by order of the court. Service under (C) or (E) above may be made by any person who is not a party and is not less than 18 years of age or who is designated by order of the district court or by the foreign court. On request, the clerk shall deliver the summons to the plaintiff for transmission to the person or the foreign court or officer who will make the service.

(2) Return. Proof of service may be made as prescribed by subdivision (g) of this rule, or by the law of the foreign country, or by order of the court. When service is made pursuant to subparagraph (1)(D) of this subdivision, proof of service shall include a receipt signed by the addressee or other evidence of delivery to the addressee satisfactory to the court. . . .

Rule 13. Counterclaim and Cross-Claim.

(a) COMPULSORY COUNTERCLAIMS. A pleading shall state as a counterclaim any claim which at the time of serving the pleading the pleader has against any opposing party, if it arises out of the transaction or occurrence that is the subject matter of the opposing party's claim and does not require for its adjudication the presence of third parties of whom the court cannot acquire jurisdiction. But the pleader need not state the claim if (1) at the time the action was commenced the claim was the subject of another pending action, or (2) the opposing party brought suit upon his claim by attachment or other process by which the court did not acquire jurisdiction to render a personal judgment on that claim, and the pleader is not stating any counterclaim under this Rule 13.

(b) PERMISSIVE COUNTERCLAIMS. A pleading may state as a counterclaim any claim against an opposing party not arising out of the transaction or occurrence that is the subject matter of the opposing party's claim.

(c) COUNTERCLAIM EXCEEDING OPPOSING CLAIM. A counterclaim may or may not diminish or defeat the recovery sought by the opposing party. It may claim relief exceeding in amount or different in kind from that sought in the pleading of the opposing party.

(d) COUNTERCLAIM AGAINST THE UNITED STATES. These rules shall not be construed to enlarge beyond the limits now fixed by law the right to assert counterclaims or to claim credits against the United States or an officer or agency thereof.

(e) COUNTERCLAIM MATURING OR ACQUIRED AFTER PLEADING. A claim which either matured or was acquired by the pleader after serving his pleading may, with the permission of the court, be presented as a counterclaim by supplemental pleading.

(f) OMITTED COUNTERCLAIM. When a pleader fails to set up a counterclaim through oversight, inadvertence, or excusable neglect, or when justice requires, he may by leave of court set up the counterclaim by amendment.

(g) CROSS–CLAIM AGAINST CO–PARTY. A pleading may state as a cross-claim any claim by one party against a co-party arising out of the transaction or occurrence that is the subject matter either of the original action or of a counterclaim therein or relating to any property that is the subject matter of the original action. Such cross-claim may include a claim that the party against whom it is asserted is or may be liable to the cross-claimant for all or part of a claim asserted in the action against the cross-claimant.

(h) JOINDER OF ADDITIONAL PARTIES. Persons other than those made parties to the original action may be made parties to a counterclaim or cross-claim in accordance with the provisions of Rules 19 and 20.

(i) SEPARATE TRIALS; SEPARATE JUDGMENTS. If the court orders separate trials as provided in Rule 42(b), judgment on a counterclaim or cross-claim may be rendered in accordance with the terms of Rule 54(b) when the court has jurisdiction so to do, even if the claims of the opposing party have been dismissed or otherwise disposed of.

Rule 14. Third-Party Practice.

(a) WHEN DEFENDANT MAY BRING IN THIRD PARTY. At any time after commencement of the action a defending party, as a third-party plaintiff, may cause a summons and complaint to be served upon a person not a party to the action who is or may be liable to him for all or part of the plaintiff's claim against him. The third-party plaintiff need not obtain leave to make the service if he files the third-party complaint not later than 10 days after he serves his original answer. Otherwise he must obtain leave on motion upon notice to all parties to the action. The person served with the summons and third-party complaint, hereinafter called the third-party defendant, shall make his defenses to the third-party plaintiff's claim as provided in Rule 12 and his counterclaims against the third-party plaintiff and cross-claims against other third-party defendants as provided in Rule 13. The third-party defendant may assert against the plaintiff any defenses which the third-party plaintiff has to the plaintiff's claim. The third-party defendant may also assert any claim against the plaintiff arising out of the transaction or occurrence that is the subject matter of the plaintiff's claim against the third-party plaintiff. The plaintiff may assert any claim against the third-party defendant arising out of the transaction or occurrence that is the subject matter of the plaintiff's claim against the third-party plaintiff, and the third-party defendant thereupon shall assert any defenses as provided in Rule 12 and any counterclaims and cross-claims as provided in Rule 13. Any party may move to strike the third-party claim, or for its severance or separate trial. A third-party defendant may proceed under this rule against any person not a party to the action who is or may be liable to the third-party defendant for all or part of the claim made in the action against the third-party defendant. The third-party complaint, if within the admiralty and maritime jurisdiction, may be in rem against a vessel, cargo, or other property subject to admiralty or maritime process in rem, in which case references in this rule to the summons include the warrant of arrest, and references to the third-party plaintiff or defendant include, where appropriate, the claimant of the property arrested.

(b) WHEN PLAINTIFF MAY BRING IN THIRD PARTY. When a counterclaim is asserted against a plaintiff, the plaintiff may cause a third party to be brought in under circumstances which under this rule would entitle a defendant to do so.

(c) ADMIRALTY AND MARITIME CLAIMS. When a plaintiff asserts an admiralty or maritime claim within the meaning of Rule 9(h), the defendant or claimant, as a third-party plaintiff, may bring in a third-party defendant who may be wholly or partly liable, either to the plaintiff or to the third-party plaintiff, by way of remedy over, contribution, or otherwise on account of the same transaction, occurrence, or series of transactions or occurrences. In such a case the third-party plaintiff may also demand judgment against the third-party defendant in favor of the plaintiff, in which event the third-party defendant shall make any defenses to the claim of the plaintiff as well as to that of the third-party plaintiff in the manner provided in Rule 12 and the action shall proceed as if the plaintiff had commenced it against the third-party defendant as well as the third-party plaintiff.

Rule 17. Parties Plaintiff and Defendant; Capacity.

(a) REAL PARTY IN INTEREST. Every action shall be prosecuted in the name of the real party in interest. An executor, administrator, guardian, bailee, trustee of an express trust, a party with whom or in whose name a contract has been made for the benefit of another, or a party authorized by statute may sue in that person's own name without joining with him the party for whose benefit the action is brought; and when a statute of the United States so provides, an action for the use or benefit of another shall be brought in the name of the United States. No action shall be dismissed on the ground that it is not prosecuted in the name of the real party in interest until a reasonable time has been allowed after objection for ratification of commencement of the action by, or joinder or substitution of, the real party in interest; and such ratification, joinder, or substitution shall have the same effect as if the action had been commenced in the name of the real party in interest.

(b) CAPACITY TO SUE OR BE SUED. The capacity of an individual, other than one acting in a representative capacity, to sue or be sued shall be determined by the law of the individual's domicile. The capacity of a corporation to sue or be sued shall be determined by the law under which it was organized. In all other cases capacity to sue or be sued shall be determined by the law of the state in which the district court is held, except (1) that a partnership or other unincorporated association, which has no such capacity by the law of such state, may sue or be sued in its common name for the purpose of enforcing for or against it a substantive right existing under the Constitution or laws of the United States, and (2) that the capacity of a receiver appointed by a court of the United States to sue or be sued in a court of the United States is governed by Title 28, U.S.C., §§ 754 and 959(a).

(c) INFANTS OR INCOMPETENT PERSONS. Whenever an infant or incompetent person has a representative, such as a general guardian, committee, conservator, or other like fiduciary, the representative may sue or defend on behalf of the infant or incompetent person. An infant or incompetent person who does not have a duly appointed representative may sue by his next friend or by a guardian *ad litem*. The court shall appoint a guardian *ad litem* for an infant or incompetent person not otherwise represented in an action or shall make such other order as it deems proper for the protection of the infant or incompetent person.

Rule 18. Joinder of Claims and Remedies.

(a) JOINDER OF CLAIMS. A party asserting a claim to relief as an original claim, counterclaim, cross-claim, or third-party claim, may join, either as independent or as alternate claims, as many claims, legal, equitable, or maritime, as the party has against an opposing party.

(b) JOINDER OF REMEDIES; FRAUDULENT CONVEYANCES. Whenever a claim is one heretofore cognizable only after another claim has been prosecuted to a conclusion, the two claims may be joined in a single action; but the court shall grant relief in that action only in accordance with the relative substantive rights of the parties. In particular, a plaintiff may state a claim for money and a claim to have set aside a conveyance fraudulent as to that plaintiff, without first having obtained a judgment establishing the claim for money.

Rule 22. Interpleader.

(1) Persons having claims against the plaintiff may be joined as defendants and required to interplead when their claims are such that the plaintiff is or may be exposed to double or multiple liability. It is not ground for objection to the joinder that the claims of the several claimants or the titles on which their claims depend do not have a common origin or are not identical but are adverse to and independent of one another, or that the plaintiff avers that the plaintiff is not liable in whole or in part to any or all of the claimants. A defendant exposed

to similar liability may obtain such interpleader by way of cross-claim or counterclaim. The provisions of this rule supplement and do not in any way limit the joinder of parties permitted in Rule 20.

(2) The remedy herein provided is in addition to and in no way supersedes or limits the remedy provided by Title 28, U.S.C., §§ 1335, 1397, and 2361. Actions under those provisions shall be conducted in accordance with these rules.

Rule 23. Class Actions.

(a) PREREQUISITES TO CLASS ACTION. One or more members of a class may sue or be sued as representative parties on behalf of all only if (1) the class is so numerous that joinder of all members is impracticable, (2) there are questions of law or fact common to the class, (3) the claims or defenses of the representative parties are typical of the claims or defenses of the class, and (4) the representative parties will fairly and adequately protect the interests of the class.

(b) CLASS ACTIONS MAINTAINABLE. An action may be maintained as a class action if the prerequisites of subdivision (a) are satisfied, and in addition:

(1) the prosecution of separate actions by or against individual members of the class would create a risk of

(A) inconsistent or varying adjudications with respect to individual members of the class which would establish incompatible standards of conduct for the party opposing the class, or

(B) adjudications with respect to individual members of the class which would as a practical matter be dispositive of the interests of the other members not parties to the adjudications or substantially impair or impede their ability to protect their interests; or

(2) the party opposing the class has acted or refused to act on grounds generally applicable to the class, thereby making appropriate final injunctive relief or corresponding declaratory relief with respect to the class as a whole; or

(3) the court finds that the questions of law or fact common to the members of the class predominate over any questions affecting only individual members, and that a class action is superior to other available methods for the fair and efficient adjudication of the controversy. The matters pertinent to the findings include: (A) the interest of members of the class in individually controlling the prosecution or defense of separate actions; (B) the extent and nature of any litigation concerning the controversy already commenced by or against members of the class; (C) the desirability or undesirability of concentrating the litigation of the claims in the particular forum; (D) the difficulties likely to be encountered in the management of a class action.

(c) DETERMINATION BY ORDER WHETHER CLASS ACTION TO BE MAINTAINED; NOTICE; JUDGMENT; ACTIONS CONDUCTED PARTIALLY AS CLASS ACTIONS.

(1) As soon as practicable after the commencement of an action brought as a class action, the court shall determine by order whether it is to be so maintained. An order under this subdivision may be conditional, and may be altered or amended before the decision on the merits.

(2) In any class action maintained under subdivision (b) (3), the court shall direct to the members of the class the best notice practicable under the circumstances including individual notice to all members who can be identified through reasonable effort. The notice shall advise each member that (A) the court will exclude the member from the class if the member so requests by a specified date; (B) the judgment, whether favorable or not, will include all members who do not request exclusion; and (C) any member who does not request exclusion may, if the member desires, enter an appearance through counsel.

(3) The judgment in an action maintained as a class action under subdivision (b) (1) or (b) (2), whether or not favorable to the class, shall include and describe those whom the court finds to be members of the class. The judgment in an action maintained as a class action under subdivision (b) (3), whether or not favorable to the class, shall include and specify or describe those to whom the notice provided in subdivision (c) (2) was directed, and who have not requested exclusion, and whom the court finds to be members of the class.

(4) When appropriate (A) an action may be brought or maintained as a class action with respect to particular issues, or (B) a class may be divided into subclasses and each subclass treated as a class, and the provisions of this rule shall then be construed and applied accordingly.

(d) ORDERS IN CONDUCT OF ACTIONS. In the conduct of actions to which this rule applies, the court may make appropriate orders: (1) determining the course of proceedings or prescribing measures to prevent undue repetition or complication in the presentation of evidence or argument; (2) requiring, for the protection of the members of the class or otherwise for the fair conduct of the action, that notice be given in such manner as the court may direct to some or all of the members of any step in the action, or of the proposed extent of the judgment, or of the opportunity of members to signify whether they considered the representation fair and adequate, to intervene and present claims or defenses, or otherwise to come into the action; (3) imposing conditions on the representative parties or on intervenors; (4) requiring that the pleadings be amended to eliminate therefrom allegations as to representation of absent persons, and that the action proceed accordingly; (5) dealing with similar procedural matters. The orders may be combined with an order under Rule 16, and may be altered or amended as may be desirable from time to time.

(e) DISMISSAL OR COMPROMISE. A class action shall not be dismissed or compromised without the approval of the court, and notice of the proposed dismissal or compromise shall be given to all members of the class in such manner as the court directs.

Rule 23.1. Derivative Actions by Shareholders.

In a derivative action brought by one or more shareholders or members to enforce a right of a corporation or of an unincorporated association, the corporation or association having failed to enforce a right which may properly be asserted by it, the complaint shall be verified and shall allege (1) that the plaintiff was a shareholder or member at the time of the transaction of which the plaintiff complains or that the plaintiff's share or membership thereafter devolved on him by operation of law, and (2) that the action is not a collusive one to confer jurisdiction on a court of the United States which it would not otherwise have. The complaint shall also allege with particularity the efforts, if any, made by the plaintiff to obtain the action the plaintiff desires from the directors or comparable authority and, if necessary, from the shareholders or members, and the reasons for the plaintiff's failure to obtain the action or for not making the effort. The derivative action may not be maintained if it appears that the plaintiff does not fairly and adequately represent the interests of the shareholders or members similarly situated in enforcing the right of the corporation or association. The action shall not be dismissed or compromised without the approval of the court, and notice of the proposed dismissal or compromise shall be given to shareholders or members in such manner as the court directs.

Rule 23.2. Actions Relating to Unincorporated Associations.

An action brought by or against the members of an unincorporated association as a class by naming certain members as representative parties may be maintained only if it appears that the representative parties will fairly and adequately protect the interests of the association and its members. In the conduct of the action the court may make appropriate orders corresponding with those described in Rule 23(d), and the procedure for dismissal or compromise of the action shall correspond with that provided in Rule 23(e).

Rule 24. Intervention.

(a) INTERVENTION OF RIGHT. Upon timely application anyone shall be permitted to intervene in an action: (1) when a statute of the United States confers an unconditional right to intervene; or (2) when the applicant claims an interest relating to the property or transaction which is the subject of the action and the applicant is so situated that the disposition of the action may as a practical matter impair or impede the applicant's ability to protect that interest, unless the applicant's interest is adequately represented by existing parties.

(b) PERMISSIVE INTERVENTION. Upon timely application anyone may be permitted to intervene in an action: (1) when a statute of the United States confers a conditional right to intervene; or (2) when an applicant's claim or defense and the main action have a question of law or fact in common. When a party to an action relies for ground of claim or defense upon any statute or executive order administered by a federal or state governmental officer or agency or upon any regulation, order, requirement, or agreement issued or made pursuant to the statute or executive order, the officer or agency upon timely application may be permitted to intervene in the action. In exercising its discretion the court shall consider whether the intervention will unduly delay or prejudice the adjudication of the rights of the original parties.

(c) PROCEDURE. A person desiring to intervene shall serve a motion to intervene upon the parties as provided in Rule 5. The motion shall state the grounds therefor and shall be accompanied by a pleading setting forth the claim or defense for which intervention is sought. The same procedure shall be followed when a statute of the United States gives a right to intervene. When the constitutionality of an act of Congress affecting the public interest is drawn in question in any action to which the United States or an officer, agency, or employee thereof is not a party, the court shall notify the Attorney General of the United States as provided in Title 28, U.S.C., § 2403.

Rule 43. Taking of Testimony.

(a) FORM. In all trials the testimony of witnesses shall be taken orally in open court, unless otherwise provided by an Act of Congress or by these rules, the Federal Rules of Evidence, or other rules adopted by the Supreme Court. . . .

Rule 54. Judgments; Costs . . .

(b) JUDGMENT UPON MULTIPLE CLAIMS OR INVOLVING MULTIPLE PARTIES. When more than one claim for relief is presented in an action, whether as a claim, counterclaim, cross-claim, or third-party claim, or when multiple parties are involved, the court may direct the entry of a final judgment as to one or more but fewer than all of the claims or parties only upon an express determination that there is no just reason for delay and upon an express direction for the entry of judgment. In the absence of such determination and direction, any order or other form of decision, however designated, which adjudicates fewer than all the claims or the rights and liabilities of fewer than all the parties shall not terminate the action as to any of the claims or parties, and the order or other form of decision is subject to revision at any time before the entry of judgment adjudicating all the claims and the rights and liabilities of all the parties. . . .

Rule 82. Jurisdiction and Venue Unaffected.

These rules shall not be construed to extend or limit the jurisdiction of the United States district courts or the venue of actions therein. An admiralty or maritime claim within the meaning of Rule 9(h) shall not be treated as a civil action for the purposes of Title 28, U.S.C., §§ 1391–93.

FEDERAL RULES OF CRIMINAL PROCEDURE

Rule 35. Correction or Reduction of Sentence.*

(a) Correction of a Sentence on Remand. The court shall correct a sentence that is determined on appeal under 18 U.S.C. 3742 to have been imposed in violation of law, to have been imposed as a result of an incorrect application of the sentencing guidelines, or to be unreasonable, upon remand of the case to the court—

(1) for imposition of a sentence in accord with the findings of the court of appeals; or

(2) for further sentencing proceedings if, after such proceedings, the court determines that the original sentence was incorrect.

(b) Correction of Sentence for Changed Circumstances. The court, on motion of the Government, may within one year after the imposition of a sentence, lower a sentence to reflect a defendant's subsequent, substantial assistance in the investigation or prosecution of another person who has committed an offense in accordance with the guidelines and policy statements issued by the Sentencing Commission pursuant to section 994 of title 28, United States Code. The court's authority to lower a sentence under this subdivision includes the authority to lower such sentence to a level below that established by statute as a minimum sentence.

* For crimes committed before November 1, 1987, the applicable rule is as follows:

Rule 35. Correction or Reduction of Sentence.

(a) Correction of Sentence. The court may correct an illegal sentence at any time and may correct a sentence imposed in an illegal manner within the time provided herein for the reduction of sentence.

(b) Reduction of Sentence. A motion to reduce a sentence may be made, or the court may reduce a sentence without motion, within 120 days after the sentence is imposed or probation is revoked, or within 120 days after receipt by the court of a mandate issued upon affirmance of the judgment or dismissal of the appeal, or within 120 days after entry of any order or judgment of the Supreme Court denying review of, or having the effect of upholding, a judgment of conviction or probation revocation. The court shall determine the motion within a reasonable time. Changing a sentence from a sentence of incarceration to a grant of probation shall constitute a permissible reduction of sentence under this subdivision.

APPENDIX B

THE JUDICIARY ACT OF 1789

(1 Stat. 73)

An Act to establish the Judicial Courts of the United States.

Section 1. *Be it enacted by the Senate and House of Representatives of the United States of America in Congress assembled,* That the supreme court of the United States shall consist of a chief justice and five associate justices, any four of whom shall be a quorum, and shall hold annually at the seat of government two sessions, the one commencing the first Monday of February, and the other the first Monday of August. That the associate justices shall have precedence according to the date of their commissions, or when the commissions of two or more of them bear date on the same day, according to their respective ages.

Sec. 2. *And be it further enacted,* That the United States shall be, and they hereby are divided into thirteen districts, to be limited and called as follows, to wit: one to consist of that part of the State of Massachusetts which lies easterly of the State of New Hampshire, and to be called Maine District; one to consist of the State of New Hampshire, and to be called New Hampshire District; one to consist of the remaining part of the State of Massachusetts, and to be called Massachusetts District; one to consist of the State of Connecticut, and to be called Connecticut District; one to consist of the State of New York, and to be called New York District; one to consist of the State of New Jersey, and to be called New Jersey District; one to consist of the State of Pennsylvania, and to be called Pennsylvania District; one to consist of the State of Delaware, and to be called Delaware District; one to consist of the State of Maryland, and to be called Maryland District; one to consist of the State of Virginia, except that part called the District of Kentucky, and to be called Virginia District; one to consist of the remaining part of the State of Virginia, and to be called Kentucky District; one to consist of the State of South Carolina, and to be called South Carolina District; and one to consist of the State of Georgia, and to be called Georgia District.

Sec. 3. *And be it further enacted*, That there be a court called a District Court, in each of the aforementioned districts, to consist of one judge, who shall reside in the district for which he is appointed, and shall be called a District Judge, and shall hold annually four sessions, the first of which to commence as follows, to wit: in the districts of New York and of New Jersey on the first, in the district of Pennsylvania on the second, in the district of Connecticut on the third, and in the district of Delaware on the fourth, Tuesdays of November next; in the districts of Massachusetts, of Maine, and of Maryland, on the first, in the district of Georgia on the second, and in the districts of New Hampshire, of Virginia, and of Kentucky, on the third Tuesdays of December next; and the other three sessions progressively in the respective districts on the like Tuesdays of every third calendar month afterwards, and in the district of South Carolina, on the third Monday in March and September, the first Monday in July, and the second Monday in December of each and every year, commencing in December next; and that the District Judge shall have power to hold special courts at his discretion. That the stated District Court shall be held at the places following, to wit: in the district of Maine, at Portland and Pownalsborough alternately, beginning at the first; in the district of New Hampshire, at Exeter and Portsmouth alternately, beginning at the first; in the district of Massachusetts, at Boston and Salem alternately, beginning at the first; in the district of Connecticut, alternately at Hartford and New Haven, beginning at the first; in the district of New York, at New York; in the district of New Jersey, alternately at New Brunswick and Burlington, beginning at the first; in the district of Pennsylvania, at Philadelphia and York Town alternately, beginning at the first; in the district of Delaware, alternately at Newcastle and Dover, beginning at the first; in the district of Maryland, alternately at Baltimore and Easton, beginning at the first; in the district of Virginia, alternately at Richmond and Williamsburgh, beginning at the first; in the district of Kentucky, at Harrodsburgh; in the district of South Carolina, at Charleston; and in the district of Georgia, alternately at Savannah and Augusta, beginning at the first; and that the special courts shall be held at the same place in each district as the stated courts, or in districts that have two, at either of them, in the discretion of the judge, or at such other place in the district, as the nature of the business and his discretion shall direct. And that in the districts that have but one place for holding the District Court, the records thereof shall be kept at that place; and in districts that have two, at that place in each district which the judge shall appoint.

Sec. 4. *And be it further enacted*, That the before mentioned districts, except those of Maine and Kentucky, shall be divided into three circuits, and be called the eastern, the middle, and the southern circuit. That the eastern circuit shall consist of the districts of New Hampshire, Massachusetts, Connecticut and New York; that the middle circuit shall consist of the districts of New Jersey, Pennsylvania, Delaware, Maryland and Virginia; and that the southern circuit shall consist of the districts of South Carolina and Georgia, and that there shall be held annually in each district of said circuits, two courts, which shall be called Circuit Courts, and shall consist of any two justices of the Supreme Court, and the district judge of such districts, any two of whom shall constitute a quorum: *Provided,* That no district judge shall give a vote in any case of appeal or error from his own decision; but may assign the reasons of such his decision.

Sec. 5. *And be it further enacted,* That the first session of the said circuit court in the several districts shall commence at the times following, to wit: in New Jersey on the second, in New York on the fourth, in Pennsylvania on the eleventh, in Connecticut on the twenty-second, and in Delaware on the twenty-seventh, days of April next; in Massachusetts on the third, in Maryland on the seventh, in South Carolina on the twelfth, in New Hampshire on the twentieth, in Virginia on the twenty-second, and in Georgia on the twenty-eighth, days of May next, and the subsequent sessions in the respective districts on the like days of every sixth calendar month afterwards, except in South Carolina, where the session of the said court shall commence on the first, and in Georgia where it shall commence on the seventeenth day of October, and except when any of those days shall happen on a Sunday, and then the session shall commence on the next day following. And the sessions of the said circuit court shall be held in the district of New Hampshire, at Portsmouth and Exeter alternately, beginning at the first; in the district of Massachusetts, at Boston; in the district of Connecticut, alternately at Hartford and New Haven, beginning at the last; in the district of New York, alternately at New York and Albany, beginning at the first; in the district of New Jersey, at Trenton; in the district of Pennsylvania, alternately at Philadelphia and Yorktown, beginning at the first; in the district of Delaware, alternately at New Castle and Dover, beginning at the first; in the district of Maryland, alternately at Annapolis and Easton, beginning at the first; in the district of Virginia, alternately at Charlottesville and Williamsburgh, beginning at the first; in the district of South Carolina, alternately at Columbia and Charleston, beginning at the first; and in the district of Georgia, alternately at Savannah and Augusta, beginning at the first. And the circuit courts shall have power to hold special sessions for the trial of criminal causes at any other time at their discretion, or at the discretion of the Supreme Court.

Sec. 6. *And be it further enacted,* That the Supreme Court may, by any one or more of its justices being present, be adjourned from day to day until a quorum be convened; and that a circuit court may also be adjourned from day to day by any one of its judges, or if none are present, by the marshal of the district until a quorum be convened; and that a district court, in case of the inability of the judge to attend at the commencement of a session, may by virtue of a written order from the said judge, directed to the marshal of the district, be adjourned by the said marshal to such day, antecedent to the next stated session of the said court, as in the said order shall be appointed; and in case of the death of the said judge, and his vacancy not being supplied, all process, pleadings and proceedings of what nature soever, pending before the said court, shall be continued of course until the next stated session after the appointment and acceptance of the office by his successor.

Sec. 7. *And be it [further enacted*, That the Supreme Court, and the district courts shall have power to appoint clerks for their respective courts, and that the clerk for each district court shall be clerk also of the circuit court in such district, and each of the said clerks shall, before he enters upon the execution of his office, take the following oath or affirmation, to wit: "I, A. B., being appointed clerk of ______, do solemnly swear, or affirm, that I will truly and faithfully enter and record all the orders, decrees, judgments and proceedings of the said court, and that I will faithfully and impartially discharge and perform all the duties of my said office, according to the best of my abilities and understanding. So help me God." Which words, so help me God, shall be omitted in all cases where an affirmation is admitted instead of an oath. And the said clerks shall also severally give bond, with sufficient sureties, (to be approved of by the Supreme and district courts respectively) to the United States, in the sum of two thousand dollars, faithfully to discharge the duties of his office, and seasonably to record the decrees, judgments and determinations of the court of which he is clerk.

Sec. 8. *And be it further enacted*, That the justices of the Supreme Court, and the district judges, before they proceed to execute the duties of their respective offices, shall take the following oath or affirmation, to wit: "I, A. B., do solemnly swear or affirm, that I will administer justice without respect to persons, and do equal right to the poor and to the rich, and that I will faithfully and impartially discharge and perform all the duties incumbent on me as ______ according to the best of my abilities and understanding, agreeably to the constitution and laws of the United States. So help me God."

Sec. 9. *And be it further enacted*, That the district courts shall have, exclusively of the courts of the several States, cognizance of all crimes and offences that shall be cognizable under the authority of the United States, committed within their respective districts, or upon the high seas; where no other punishment than whipping, not exceeding thirty stripes, a fine not exceeding one hundred dollars, or a term of imprisonment not exceeding six months, is to be inflicted; and shall also have exclusive original cognizance of all civil causes of admiralty and maritime jurisdiction, including all seizures under laws of impost, navigation or trade of the United States, where the seizures are made, on waters which are navigable from the sea by vessels of ten or more tons burthen, within their respective districts as well as upon the high seas; saving to suitors, in all cases, the right of a common law remedy, where the common law is competent to give it; and shall also have exclusive original cognizance of all seizures on land, or other waters than as aforesaid, made, and of all suits for penalties and forfeitures incurred, under the laws of the United States. And shall also have cognizance, concurrent with the courts of the several States, or the circuit courts, as the case may be, of all causes where an alien sues for a tort only in violation of the law of nations or a treaty of the United States. And shall also have cognizance, concurrent as last mentioned, of all suits at common law where the United States sue, and the matter in dispute amounts, exclusive of costs, to the sum or value of one hundred dollars. And shall also have jurisdiction exclusively of the courts of the several States, of all suits against consuls or vice-consuls, except for offences above the description aforesaid. And the trial of issues in fact, in the district courts, in all causes except civil causes of admiralty and maritime jurisdiction, shall be by jury.

Sec. 10. *And be it further enacted,* That the district court in Kentucky district shall, besides the jurisdiction aforesaid, have jurisdiction of all other causes, except of appeals and writs of error, hereinafter made cognizable in a circuit court, and shall proceed therein in the same manner as a circuit court, and writs of error and appeals shall lie from decisions therein to the Supreme Court in the same causes, as from a circuit court to the Supreme Court, and under the same regulations. And the district court in Maine district shall, besides the jurisdiction hereinbefore granted, have jurisdiction of all causes, except of appeals and writs of error herein after made cognizable in a circuit court, and shall proceed therein in the same manner as a circuit court: And writs of error shall lie from decisions therein to the circuit court in the district of Massachusetts in the same manner as from other district courts to their respective circuit courts.

Sec. 11. *And be it further enacted,* That the circuit courts shall have original cognizance, concurrent with the courts of the several States, of all suits of a civil nature at common law or in equity, where the matter in dispute exceeds, exclusive of costs, the sum or value of five hundred dollars, and the United States are plaintiffs, or petitioners; or an alien is a party, or the suit is between a citizen of the State where the suit is brought, and a citizen of another State. And shall have exclusive cognizance of all crimes and offences cognizable under the authority of the United States, except where this act otherwise provides, or the laws of the United States shall otherwise direct, and concurrent jurisdiction with the district courts of the crimes and offences cognizable therein. But no person shall be arrested in one district for trial in another, in any civil action before a circuit or district court. And no civil suit shall be brought before either of said courts against an inhabitant of the United States, by any original process in any other district than that whereof he is an inhabitant, or in which he shall be found at the time of serving the writ, nor shall any district or circuit court have cognizance of any suit to recover the contents of any promissory note or other chose in action in favour of an assignee, unless a suit might have been prosecuted in such court to recover the said contents if no assignment had been made, except in cases of foreign bills of exchange. And the circuit courts shall also have appellate jurisdiction from the district courts under the regulations and restrictions herein after provided.

Sec. 12. *And be it further enacted,* That if a suit be commenced in any state court against an alien, or by a citizen of the state in which the suit is brought against a citizen of another state, and the matter in dispute exceeds the aforesaid sum or value of five hundred dollars, exclusive of costs, to be made to appear to the satisfaction of the court; and the defendant shall, at the time of entering his appearance in such state court, file a petition for the removal of the cause for trial into the next circuit court, to be held in the district where the suit is pending, or if in the district of Maine to the district court next to be holden therein, or if in Kentucky district to the district court next to be holden therein, and offer good and sufficient surety for his entering in such court, on the first day of its session, copies of said process against him, and also for his there appearing and entering special bail in the cause, if special bail was originally requisite therein, it shall then be the duty of the state court to accept the surety, and proceed no further in the cause, and any bail that may have been originally taken shall be discharged, and the said copies being entered as aforesaid, in such court of the United States, the cause shall there proceed in the same manner as if it had been brought there by original process. And any attachment of the goods or estate of the defendant by the original process, shall hold the goods or estate so attached, to answer the final judgment in the same manner as by the laws of such state they would have been holden to answer final judgment had it been rendered by the court in which the suit commenced. And if in any action commenced in a state court, the title of land be concerned, and the parties are citizens of the same state, and the matter in dispute exceeds the sum or value of five hundred dollars, exclusive of costs, the sum or value being made to appear to the satisfaction of the court, either party, before the trial, shall state to the court and make affidavit if they require it, that he claims and shall rely upon a right or title to the land, under a grant from a state other than that in which the suit is pending, and produce the original grant or an exemplification of it, except where the loss of public records shall put it out of his power, and shall move that the adverse party inform the court, whether he claims a right or title to the land under a grant from the state in which the suit is pending; the said adverse [party] shall give such information, or otherwise not be allowed to plead such grant, or give it in evidence upon the trial, and if he informs that he does claim under such grant, the party claiming under the grant first mentioned may then, on motion, remove the cause for trial to the next circuit court to be holden in such district, or if in the district of Maine, to the court next to be holden therein; or if in Kentucky district, to the district court next to be holden therein; but if he is the defendant, shall do it under the same regulations as in the beforementioned case of the removal of a cause into such court by an alien; and neither party removing the cause, shall be allowed to plead or give evidence of any other title than that by him stated as aforesaid, as the ground of his claim; and the trial of issues in fact in the circuit courts shall, in all suits, except those of equity, and of admiralty, and maritime jurisdiction, be by jury.

Sec. 13. *And be it further enacted*, That the Supreme Court shall have exclusive jurisdiction of all controversies of a civil nature, where a state is a party, except between a state and its citizens; and except also between a state and citizens of other states, or aliens, in which latter case it shall have original but not exclusive jurisdiction. And shall have exclusively all such jurisdiction of suits or proceedings against ambassadors, or other public ministers, or their domestics, or domestic servants, as a court of law can have or exercise consistently with the law of nations; and original, but not exclusive jurisdiction of all suits brought by ambassadors, or other public ministers, or in which a consul, or vice consul, shall be a party. And the trial of issues in fact in the Supreme Court, in all actions at law against citizens of the United States, shall be by jury. The Supreme Court shall also have appellate jurisdiction from the circuit courts and courts of the several states, in the cases herein after specially provided for; and shall have power to issue writs of prohibition to the district courts, when proceeding as courts of admiralty and maritime jurisdiction, and writs of *mandamus*, in cases warranted by the principles and usages of law, to any courts appointed, or persons holding office, under the authority of the United States.

Sec. 14. *And be it further enacted*, That all the before-mentioned courts of the United States, shall have power to issue writs of *scire facias*, *habeas corpus*, and all other writs not specially provided for by statute, which may be necessary for the exercise of their respective jurisdictions, and agreeable to the principles and usages of law. And that either of the justices of the supreme court, as well as judges of the district courts, shall have power to grant writs of *habeas corpus* for the purpose of an inquiry into the cause of commitment.—*Provided*, That writs of *habeas corpus* shall in no case extend to prisoners in gaol, unless where they are in custody, under or by colour of the authority of the United States, or are committed for trial before some court of the same, or are necessary to be brought into court to testify.

Sec. 15. *And be it further enacted*, That all the said courts of the United States, shall have power in the trial of actions at law, on motion and due notice thereof being given, to require the parties to produce books or writings in their possession or power, which contain evidence pertinent to the issue, in cases and under circumstances where they might be compelled to produce the same by the ordinary rules of proceeding in chancery; and if a plaintiff shall fail to comply with such order, to produce books or writings, it shall be lawful for the courts respectively, on motion, to give the like judgment for the defendant as in cases of nonsuit; and if a defendant shall fail to comply with such order, to produce books or writings, it shall be lawful for the courts respectively on motion as aforesaid, to give judgment against him or her by default.

Sec. 16. *And be it further enacted,* That suits in equity shall not be sustained in either of the courts of the United States, in any case where plain, adequate and complete remedy may be had at law.

Sec. 17. *And be it further enacted,* That all the said courts of the United States shall have power to grant new trials, in cases where there has been a trial by jury for reasons for which new trials have usually been granted in the courts of law; and shall have power to impose and administer all necessary oaths or affirmations, and to punish by fine or imprisonment, at the discretion of said courts, all contempts of authority in any cause or hearing before the same; and to make and establish all necessary rules for the orderly conducting business in the said courts, provided such rules are not repugnant to the laws of the United States.

Sec. 18. *And be it further enacted,* That when in a circuit court, judgment upon a verdict in a civil action shall be entered, execution may on motion of either party, at the discretion of the court, and on such conditions for the security of the adverse party as they may judge proper, be stayed forty-two days from the time of entering judgment, to give time to file in the clerk's office of said court, a petition for a new trial. And if such petition be there filed within said term of forty-two days, with a certificate thereon from either of the judges of such court, that he allows the same to be filed, which certificate he may make or refuse at his discretion, execution shall of course be further stayed to the next session of said court. And if a new trial be granted, the former judgment shall be thereby rendered void.

Sec. 19. *And be it further enacted,* That it shall be the duty of circuit courts, in causes in equity and of admiralty and maritime jurisdiction, to cause the facts on which they found their sentence or decree, fully to appear upon the record either from the pleadings and decree itself, or a state of the case agreed by the parties, or their counsel, or if they disagree by a stating of the case by the court.

Sec. 20. *And be it further enacted,* That where in a circuit court, a plaintiff in an action, originally brought there, or a petitioner in equity, other than the United States, recovers less than the sum or value of five hundred dollars, or a libellant, upon his own appeal, less than the sum or value of three hundred dollars, he shall not be allowed, but at the discretion of the court, may be adjudged to pay costs.

Sec. 21. *And be it further enacted,* That from final decrees in a district court in causes of admiralty and maritime jurisdiction, where the matter in dispute exceeds the sum or value of three hundred dollars, exclusive of costs, an appeal shall be allowed to the next circuit court, to be held in such district. *Provided nevertheless,* That all such appeals from final decrees as aforesaid, from the district court of Maine, shall be made to the circuit court, next to be holden after each appeal in the district of Massachusetts.

Sec. 22. *And be it further enacted,* That final decrees and judgments in civil actions in a district court, where the matter in dispute exceeds the sum or value of fifty dollars, exclusive of costs, may be reexamined, and reversed or affirmed in a circuit court, holden in the same district, upon a writ of error, whereto shall be annexed and returned therewith at the day and place therein mentioned, and authenticated transcript of the record, and assignment of errors, and prayer for reversal, with a citation to the adverse party, signed by the judge of such district court, or a justice of the Supreme Court, the adverse party having at least twenty days' notice. And upon a like process, may final judgments and decrees in civil actions, and suits in equity in a circuit court, brought there by original process, or removed there from courts of the several States, or removed there by appeal from a district court where the matter in dispute exceeds the sum or value of two thousand dollars, exclusive of costs, be re-examined and reversed or affirmed in the Supreme Court, the citation being in such case signed by a judge of such circuit court, or justice of the Supreme Court, and the adverse party having at least thirty days' notice. But there shall be no reversal in either court on such writ of error for error in ruling any plea in abatement, other than a plea to the jurisdiction of the court, or such plea to a petition or bill in equity, as is in the nature of a demurrer, or for any error in fact. And writs of error shall not be brought but within five years after rendering or passing the judgment or decree complained of, or in case the person entitled to such writ of error be an infant, *feme covert, non compos mentis,* or imprisoned, then within five years as aforesaid, exclusive of the time of such disability. And every justice or judge signing a citation on any writ of error as aforesaid, shall take good and sufficient security, that the plaintiff in error shall prosecute his writ to effect, and answer all damages and costs if he fail to make his plea good.

Sec. 23. *And be it further enacted,* That a writ of error as aforesaid shall be a supersedeas and stay execution in cases only where the writ of error is served, by a copy thereof being lodged for the adverse party in the clerk's office where the record remains, within ten days, Sundays exclusive, after rendering the judgment or passing the decree complained of. Until the expiration of which term of ten days, executions shall not issue in any case where a writ of error may be a supersedeas; and whereupon such writ of error the Supreme or a circuit court shall affirm a judgment or decree, they shall adjudge or decree to the respondent in error just damages for his delay, and single or double costs at their discretion.

Sec. 24. *And be it further enacted,* That when a judgment or decree shall be reversed in a circuit court, such court shall proceed to render such judgment or pass such decree as the district court should have rendered or passed; and the Supreme Court shall do the same on reversals therein, except where the reversal is in favour of the plaintiff, or petitioner in the original suit, and the damages to be assessed, or matter to be decreed, are uncertain, in which case they shall remand the cause for a final decision. And the Supreme Court shall not issue execution in causes that are removed before them by writs of error, but shall send a special mandate to the circuit court to award execution thereupon.

Sec. 25. *And be it further enacted,* That a final judgment or decree in any suit, in the highest court of law or equity of a State in which a decision in the suit could be had, where is drawn in question the validity of a treaty or statute of, or an authority exercised under the United States, and the decision is against their validity; or where is drawn in question the validity of a statute of, or an authority exercised under any State, on the ground of their being repugnant to the constitution, treaties or laws of the United States, and the decision is in favour of such their validity, or where is drawn in question the construction of any clause of the constitution or of a treaty, or statute of, or commission held under the United States, and the decision is against the title, right, privilege or exemption specially set up or claimed by either party, under such clause of the said Constitution, treaty, statute or commission, may be re-examined and reversed or affirmed in the Supreme Court of the United States upon a writ of error, the citation being signed by the chief justice, or judge or chancellor of the court rendering or passing the judgment or decree complained of, or by a justice of the Supreme Court of the United States, in the same manner and under the same regulations, and the writ shall have the same effect, as if the judgment or decree complained of had been rendered or passed in a circuit court, and the proceeding upon the reversal shall also be the same, except that the Supreme Court, instead of remanding the cause for a final decision as before provided, may at their discretion, if the cause shall have been once remanded before, proceed to a final decision of the same, and award execution. But no other error shall be assigned or regarded as a ground of reversal in any such case as aforesaid, than such as appears on the face of the record, and immediately respects the before mentioned questions of validity or construction of the said constitution, treaties, statutes, commissions, or authorities in dispute.

Sec. 26. *And be it further enacted,* That in all causes brought before either of the courts of the United States to recover the forfeiture annexed to any articles of agreement, covenant, bond, or other speciality, where the forfeiture, breach or non-performance shall appear, by the default or confession of the defendant, or upon demurrer, the court before whom the action is, shall render judgment therein for the plaintiff to recover so much as is due according to equity. And when the sum for which judgment should be rendered is uncertain, the same shall, if either of the parties request it, be assessed by a jury.

Sec. 27. *And be it further enacted,* That a marshal shall be appointed in and for each district for the term of four years, but shall be removable from office at pleasure, whose duty it shall be to attend the district and circuit courts when sitting therein, and also the

Supreme Court in the district in which that court shall sit. And to execute throughout the district, all lawful precepts directed to him, and issued under the authority of the United States, and he shall have power to command all necessary assistance in the execution of his duty, and to appoint as there shall be occasion, one or more deputies, who shall be removable from office by the judge of the district court, or the circuit court sitting within the district, at the pleasure of either; and before he enters on the duties of his office, he shall become bound for the faithful performance of the same, by himself and by his deputies before the judge of the district court to the United States, jointly and severally, with two good and sufficient sureties, inhabitants and freeholders of such district, to be approved by the district judge, in the sum of twenty thousand dollars, and shall take before said judge, as shall also his deputies, before they enter on the duties of their appointment, the following oath of office: "I, A. B., do solemnly swear or affirm, that I will faithfully execute all lawful precepts directed to the marshal of the district of ______ under the authority of the United States, and true returns make, and in all things well and truly, and without malice or partiality, perform the duties of the office of marshal (or marshal's deputy, as the case may be) of the district of ______, during my continuance in said office, and take only my lawful fees. So help me God."

Sec. 28. *And be it further enacted*, That in all causes wherein the marshal or his deputy shall be a party, the writs and precepts therein shall be directed to such disinterested person as the court, or any justice or judge thereof may appoint, and the person so appointed, is hereby authorized to execute and return the same. And in case of the death of any marshal, his deputy or deputies shall continue in office, unless otherwise specially removed; and shall execute the same in the name of the deceased, until another marshal shall be appointed and sworn: and the defaults or misfeasances in office of such deputy or deputies in the mean time, as well as before, shall be adjudged a breach of the condition of the bond given, as before directed, by the marshal who appointed them; and the executor or administrator of the deceased marshal shall have like remedy for the defaults and misfeasances in office of such deputy or deputies during such interval, as they would be entitled to if the marshal had continued in life and in the exercise of his said office, until his successor was appointed, and sworn or affirmed: And every marshal or his deputy when removed from office, or when the term for which the marshal is appointed shall expire, shall have power notwithstanding to execute all such precepts as may be in their hands respectively at the time of such removal or expiration of office; and the marshal shall be held answerable for the delivery to his successor of all prisoners which may be in his custody at the time of his removal, or when the term for which he is appointed shall expire, and for that purpose may retain such prisoners in his custody until his successor shall be appointed and qualified as the law directs.

Sec. 29. *And be it further enacted,* That in cases punishable with death, the trial shall be had in the county where the offence was committed, or where that cannot be done without great inconvenience, twelve petit jurors at least shall be summoned from thence. And jurors in all cases to serve in the courts of the United States shall be designated by lot or otherwise in each State respectively according to the mode of forming juries therein now practised, so far as the laws of the same shall render such designation practicable by the courts or marshals of the United States; and the jurors shall have the same qualifications as are requisite for jurors by the laws of the State of which they are citizens, to serve in the highest courts of law of such State, and shall be returned as there shall be occasion for them, from such parts of the district from time to time as the court shall direct, so as shall be most favourable to an impartial trial, and so as not to incur an unnecessary expense, or unduly to burthen the citizens of any part of the district with such services. And writs of *venire facias* when directed by the court shall issue from the clerk's office, and shall be served and returned by the marshal in his proper person, or by his deputy, or in case the marshal or his deputy is not an indifferent person, or is interested in the event of the cause, by such fit person as the court shall specially appoint for that purpose, to whom they shall administer an oath or affirmation that he will truly and impartially serve and return such writ. And when from challenges or otherwise there shall not be a jury to determine any civil or criminal cause, the marshal or his deputy shall, by order of the court where such defect of jurors shall happen, return jurymen *de talibus circumstantibus* sufficient to complete the panel; and when the marshal or his deputy are disqualified as aforesaid, jurors may be returned by such disinterested person as the court shall appoint.

Sec. 30. *And be it further enacted,* That the mode of proof by oral testimony and examination of witnesses in open court shall be the same in all the courts of the United States, as well in the trial of causes in equity and of admiralty and maritime jurisdiction, as of actions at common law. And when the testimony of any person shall be necessary in any civil cause depending in any district in any court of the United States, who shall live at a greater distance from the place of trial than one hundred miles, or is bound on a voyage to sea, or is about to go out of the United States, or out of such district, and to a greater distance from the place of trial than as aforesaid, before the time of trial, or is ancient or very infirm, the deposition of such person may be taken *de bene esse* before any justice or judge of any of the courts of the United States, or before any chancellor, justice or judge of a supreme or superior court, mayor or chief magistrate of a city, or judge of a county court or court of common pleas of any of the United States, not being of counsel or attorney to either of the parties, or interested in the event of the cause, provided that a notification from the magistrate before whom the deposition is to be taken to the adverse party, to be present at the taking of the same, and to put interrogatories, if he think fit, be first made out and served on the adverse party or his attorney as either may be nearest, if either is within one hundred miles of the place of such caption, allowing time for their attendance after notified, not less than at the rate of one day, Sundays exclusive, for every twenty miles travel. And in causes of admiralty and maritime jurisdiction, or other cases of seizure when a libel shall be filed, in which an adverse party is not named, and depositions of persons circumstanced as aforesaid shall be taken before a claim be put in, the like notification as aforesaid shall be given to the person having the agency or possession of the property libelled at the time of the capture or seizure of the same, if known to the libellant. And every person deposing as aforesaid shall be carefully examined and cautioned, and sworn or affirmed to testify the whole truth, and shall subscribe the testimony by him or her given after the same shall be reduced to writing, which shall be done only by the magistrate taking the deposition, or by the deponent in his presence. And the depositions so taken shall be retained by such magistrate until he deliver the same with his own hand into the court for which they are taken, or shall, together with a certificate of the reasons as aforesaid of their being taken, and of the notice if any given to the adverse party, be by him the said magistrate sealed up and directed to such court, and remain under his seal until opened in court. And any person may be compelled to appear and depose as aforesaid in the same manner as to appear and testify in court. And in the trial of any cause of admiralty or maritime jurisdiction in a district court, the decree in which may be appealed from, if either party shall suggest to and satisfy the court that probably it will not be in his power to produce the witnesses there testifying before the circuit court should an appeal be had, and shall move that their testimony be taken down in writing, it shall be so done by the clerk of the court. And if an appeal be had, such testimony may be used on the trial of the same, if it shall appear to the satisfaction of the court which shall try the appeal, that the witnesses are then dead or gone out of the United States, or to a greater distance than as aforesaid from the place where the court is sitting, or that by reason of age, sickness, bodily infirmity or imprisonment, they are unable to travel and appear at court, but not otherwise. And unless the same shall be made to appear on the trial of any cause, with respect to witnesses whose depositions may have been taken therein, such depositions shall not be admitted or used in the cause. *Provided*, That nothing herein shall be construed to prevent any court of the United States from granting a *dedimus potestatem* to take depositions according to common usage, when it may be necessary to prevent a failure or delay of justice, which power they shall severally possess, nor to extend to depositions taken in *perpetuam rei memoriam*, which if they relate to matters that may be cognizable in any court of the United States, a circuit court on application thereto made as a court of equity, may, according to the usages in chancery direct to be taken.

Sec. 31. *And be it further enacted*, That where any suit shall be depending in any court of the United States, and either of the parties shall die before final judgment, the executor or administrator of such deceased party who was plaintiff, petitioner, or defendant, in case the cause of action doth by law survive, shall have full power to prosecute or defend any such suit or action until final judgment; and the defendant or defendants are hereby obliged to answer thereto accordingly; and the court before whom such cause may be depending, is hereby empowered and directed to hear and determine the same, and to render judgment for or against the executor or administrator, as the case may require. And if such executor or administrator having been duly served with a *scire facias* from the office of the clerk of the court where such suit is depending, twenty days beforehand, shall neglect or refuse to become a party to the suit, the court may render judgment against the estate of the deceased party, in the same manner as if the executor or administrator had voluntarily made himself a party to the suit. And the executor or administrator who shall become a party as aforesaid, shall, upon motion to the court where the suit is depending, be entitled to a continuance of the same until the next term of the said court. And if there be two or more plaintiffs or defendants, and one or more of them shall die, if the cause of action shall survive to the surviving plaintiff or plaintiffs, or against the surviving defendant or defendants, the writ or action shall not be thereby abated; but such death being suggested upon the record, the action shall proceed at the suit of the surviving plaintiff or plaintiffs against the surviving defendant or defendants.

Sec. 32. *And be it further enacted*, That no summons, writ, declaration, return, process, judgment, or other proceedings in civil causes in any of the courts of the United States, shall be abated, arrested, quashed or reversed, for any defect or want of form, but the said courts respectively shall proceed and give judgment according as the right of the cause and matter in law shall appear unto them, without regarding any imperfections, defects, or want of form in such writ, declaration, or other pleading, return, process, judgment, or course of proceeding whatsoever, except those only in cases of demurrer, which the party demurring shall specially set down and express together with his demurrer as the cause thereof. And the said courts respectively shall and may, by virtue of this act, from time to time, amend all and every such imperfections, defects and wants of form, other than those only which the party demurring shall express as aforesaid, and may at any time permit either of the parties to amend any defect in the process or pleadings, upon such conditions as the said courts respectively shall in their discretion, and by their rules prescribe.

Sec. 33. *And be it further enacted*, That for any crime or offence against the United States, the offender may, by any justice or judge of the United States, or by any justice of the peace, or other magistrate of any of the United States where he may be found agreeably to the usual mode of process against offenders in such state, and at the expense of the United States, be arrested, and imprisoned or bailed, as the case may be, for trial before such court of the United States as by this act has cognizance of the offence. And copies of the process shall be returned as speedily as may be into the clerk's office of such court, together with the recognizances of the witnesses for their appearance to testify in the case; which recognizances the magistrate before whom the examination shall be, may require on pain of imprisonment. And if such commitment of the offender, or the witnesses shall be in a district other than that in which the offence is to be tried, it shall be the duty of the judge of that district where the delinquent is imprisoned, seasonably to issue, and of the marshal of the same district to execute, a warrant for the removal of the offender, and the witnesses, or either of them, as the case may be, to the district in which the trial is to be had. And upon all arrests in criminal cases, bail shall be admitted, except where the punishment may be death, in which cases it shall not be admitted but by the supreme or a circuit court, or by a justice of the supreme court, or a judge of a district court, who shall exercise their discretion therein, regarding the nature and circumstances of the offence, and of the evidence, and the usages of law. And if a person committed by a justice of the supreme or a judge of a district court for an offence not punishable with death, shall afterwards procure bail, and there be no judge of the United States in the district to take the same, it may be taken by any judge of the supreme or superior court of law of such state.

Sec. 34. *And be it further enacted,* That the laws of the several states, except where the constitution, treaties or statutes of the United States shall otherwise require or provide, shall be regarded as rules of decision in trials at common law in the courts of the United States in cases where they apply.

Sec. 35. *And be it further enacted,* That in all the courts of the United States, the parties may plead and manage their own causes personally or by the assistance of such counsel or attorneys at law as by rules of the said courts respectively shall be permitted to manage and conduct causes therein. And there shall be appointed in each district a meet person learned in the law to act as attorney for the United States in such district, who shall be sworn or affirmed to the faithful execution of his office, whose duty it shall be to prosecute in such district all delinquents for crimes and offences, cognizable under the authority of the United States, and all civil actions in which the United States shall be concerned, except before the supreme court in the district in which that court shall be holden. And he shall receive as a compensation for his services such fees as shall be taxed therefor in the respective courts before which the suits or prosecutions shall be. And there shall also be appointed a meet person, learned in the law, to act as attorney-general for the United States, who shall be sworn of affirmed to a faithful execution of his office; whose duty it shall be to prosecute and conduct all suits in the Supreme Court in which the United States shall be concerned, and to give his advice and opinion upon questions of law when required by the President of the United States, or when requested by the heads of any of the departments, touching any matters that may concern their departments, and shall receive such compensation for his services as shall by law be provided.

Approved September 24, 1789.

Index

References are to Pages

References are to Pages

References are to Pages

References are to Pages

References are to Pages

References are to Pages

†